American Government
Politics and Political Culture

Fourth Edition

William Lyons
John M. Scheb II
University of Tennessee-Knoxville

Australia · Canada · Mexico · Singapore · Spain · United Kingdom · United States

American Government Politics and Political Culture

William Lyons
John M. Scheb II

Executive Editors:
Michele Baird, Maureen Staudt &
Michael Stranz

Project Development Manager:
Linda de Stefano

Marketing Coordinators:
Lindsay Annett and Sara Mercurio

Production/Manufacturing Supervisor:
Donna M. Brown

Pre-Media Services Supervisor:
Dan Plofchan

Rights & Permissions Specialist
Kalina Hintz and Bahman Narag

Cover Image
Getty Images*

The Adaptable Courseware Pro
consists of products and additio
existing Thomson products that
produced from camera-ready co
Peer review, class testing, and
accuracy are primarily the respo
of the author(s).

American Government / William
Lyons/John M. Scheb
ISBN 1-592-60237-1

International Divisions List

Asia (Including India):
Thomson Learning
(a division of Thomson Asia Pte Ltd)
5 Shenton Way #01-01
UIC Building
Singapore 068808
Tel: (65) 6410-1200
Fax: (65) 6410-1208

Australia/New Zealand:
Thomson Learning Australia
102 Dodds Street
Southbank, Victoria 3006
Australia

Latin America:
Thomson Learning
Seneca 53
Colonia Polano
11560 Mexico, D.F., Mexico
Tel (525) 281-2906
Fax (525) 281-2656

Canada:
Thomson Nelson
1120 Birchmount Road
Toronto, Ontario
Canada M1K 5G4
Tel (416) 752-9100
Fax (416) 752-8102

UK/Europe/Middle East/Africa:
Thomson Learning
High Holborn House
50-51 Bedford Row
London, WC1R 4LS
United Kingdom
Tel 44 (020) 7067-2500
Fax 44 (020) 7067-2600

Spain (Includes Portugal):
Thomson Paraninfo
Calle Magallanes 25
28015 Madrid
España
Tel 34 (0)91 446-3350
Fax 34 (0)91 445-621

Contents

Appendix

Preface

This textbook is designed to be a comprehensive introduction to American government and politics. In writing this book, we are drawing on a combined fifty years of experience in teaching introductory courses in American politics. In teaching these classes over the years, we have found that students need a firm grounding in the historical development of our constitutional framework, political system, governing institutions, and policy-making process. They also need some exposure to what political scientists have contributed to our understanding of political behavior. Most of all, students need to see how politics and government are connected to their lives—not merely how public policy decisions affect them but also how their participation in American culture shapes the nature of our politics.

Unifying Theme—Political Culture

What distinguishes our text is its emphasis on American political culture—the political values, expectations, and beliefs of the masses of American citizens. We continually refer to the way political culture shapes our institutions, our political campaigns, and the way that questions of policy are framed and addressed. Moreover, many of this book's special features are designed to amplify the political culture theme. In particular, the "What Americans Think About" features throughout the book provide an explicit link between political culture and the topic being discussed in the chapter. The features labeled "Popular Culture and American Politics" explore links between American political culture and popular culture—movies, TV, books, and music, for example.

Chapters

Chapter 1 introduces the concept of political culture and discusses other basic concepts, including democracy and ideology. Chapter 2 examines the constitutional system, with emphasis on the idea of the "living Constitution." Chapter 3 focuses on federalism, highlighting both its historical development and contemporary complexity. Chapter 3 also includes an overview of state and local government.

Chapter 4 discusses civil liberties, and Chapter 5 covers civil rights. Some texts combine civil rights and civil liberties in one chapter. We think that these issues are far too important and much too interesting to students of American politics to attempt to cover both in one chapter. Although some texts treat civil liberties and civil rights as "outputs" and thus place them in the section of the book dealing with public policy, we see civil liberties and civil rights as part of the foundations of the political system. Moreover, in our teaching, we have found that students enjoy the civil rights and civil liberties material as much, if not more than, any other part of the introductory American politics course. Putting these chapters up front is designed to help get students "turned on" to the subject.

Chapter 6 includes an examination of public opinion—what it is, why it's important, and how it's measured. The next chapter examines political participation, including both voting and less conventional modes of participation. Chapters 8, 9, and 10 deal with the intermediary institutions: political parties, interest groups, and the mass media. This portion of the book deals with politics in its most conventional sense—the struggle among individuals and groups to achieve influence over their government—and concludes with a close look at campaigns and elections; it takes the student from the initial formation of political opinion through its expression to its organization and ultimately to the choice of the president and Congress.

The next section of the book, Chapters 11–15, examines the major institutions of the national government, beginning with Congress because the Framers of the Constitution began with Congress, then proceeding through examinations of the presidency and the judiciary and concluding with a look at the federal bureaucracy—a virtual fourth branch of government. Each chapter stresses the constitutional foundations and historical development of the institution as well as its place in contemporary political culture.

Finally, the last three chapters look at public policy and the policy-making process. Chapter 16 provides an overview of policy making and a survey of major domestic policy issues. Chapter 17 focuses on fiscal policy and the budgetary process. Chapter 18 concludes this section—and this book—with a look at foreign policy and national defense. In all three of the policy chapters, the emphasis is on political culture—what the American people expect from their government.

Currency

Although we place considerable emphasis on history, our experience has shown the desirability of using current examples to facilitate student understanding. We have therefore incorporated substantial material dealing with events that took place during George W. Bush's first term as president, especially the terrorist attacks of 9-11-2001, the ensuing war on terrorism, the wars in Afghanistan and Iraq, and the 2004 presidential election. Throughout we discuss numerous current political issues, from same-sex marriage to foreign trade.

Accessibility

Our goal in teaching an introductory course in U.S. government is to make American politics more accessible to students. Accordingly, we have endeavored to make our book accessible too. Although we have not tried to minimize the complexity of the issues, we have adopted a straightforward, conversational style of prose, using words that any college student should be able to understand. Political science or legal terminology, when used, is clearly defined. Key concepts in the chapters are presented in boldface type to guide students in studying. These terms are also defined in a comprehensive glossary at the back of this book.

Ideological Balance

In writing this book, we have tried to be fair and balanced in describing political actors, institutions, issues, and events. Some degree of ideological bias inevitably comes into play in writing a book of this kind. It is practically impossible to describe and explain American government and politics without some degree of ideological coloration. Nevertheless, that is our goal. Our objective is to define, describe, and explain American politics, but certainly not to indoctrinate students into anyone's idea of "political correctness," either on the right or on the left.

Special Features

This text incorporates a variety of special features:

What Americans Think About...   This feature provides a recent snapshot of American public opinion in relation to the topic of the chapter. For example, Chapter 2 features a poll of what Americans think of the U.S. Constitution, how well it has worked over the years, and whether it should be fundamentally reconsidered. In constructing these features, which provide insights into American political culture, we have drawn on a number of established sources of survey data, including the Gallup poll and the University of Michigan's National Election Studies.

Comparative Perspective.   The United States is not the world's only democracy, and democracy is not the only type of political system. Therefore, each chapter includes a look at another country and another perspective on politics. These examples reflect a wide variety of political cultures.

Profiles & Perspectives.   American politics is as much about people as it is about institutions. These individuals make their contributions in a variety of ways—leading others in protest or perhaps bringing a fresh perspective to a government position. Throughout the text, these people are highlighted through a discussion of their backgrounds, their points of view, and their special contributions to American politics.

Case in Point.   Some of the toughest issues in American politics are resolved in court. Of course, no introduction to American government would be complete without strong chapters dealing with civil rights, civil liberties, and the federal courts. We go beyond this standard treatment by incorporating throughout this book summaries and excerpts from leading Supreme Court decisions. For example, Chapter 2 contains a feature on *Marbury v. Madison*, without question the most important decision ever rendered by the Supreme Court.

Controversy.   In many ways, the study of politics is the study of controversy and its resolution, if indeed any resolution is forthcoming. Various controversies in American politics are highlighted, including whether we should have term limits for members of Congress, whether the Supreme Court was right to have intervened in the 2000 election, and whether the First Amendment should protect flag burning as a vehicle of political speech.

Popular Culture and American Politics.   In this feature, we examine links between the popular culture and political life. Many of the themes of American political culture—for example, distrust of government—are reflected in the movies, books, music, and television programming that Americans so eagerly consume. In addition to the nearly twenty such features prepared by the authors, the publisher has enlisted another scholar, Chapman Rackaway of Fort Hays State University, to prepare another forty similar features, which are included throughout the book.

> I believe that one of the most vital themes you will pick up in this textbook is that while political participation is vital to our democracy, younger Americans do so in the most minimal way possible. In the areas of voting, running for office, and communicating with elected officials, people younger than thirty lag behind other age groups in their political participation. A functioning democracy needs everyone to participate, though, and so it's important to increase the participation of younger citizens. To solve the problem, we have to understand why, and I have a theory—my theory is that younger people don't see the relevance of politics to their daily lives. If you saw politics on your TV screen, in your iPod, or in your daily life more directly, you may be inspired to action. That's why you'll see a lot of short pieces spread throughout this book on things that are relevant both to your life and politics. Popular culture can be an effective way to bring people into political action.

Michael Moore's *Fahrenheit 9/11* can be as much an inspiration to political action as can party identification, for instance. A twenty-year-old Eminem fan might abstain from political activity until someone in his or her community tries to ban sales of the rapper's albums. So throughout this book you will see pieces I've written about movies, TV shows, music, and other opportunities where young people get the chance to put a more human face on politics. I hope it shows you that politics is very relevant to your day-to-day life, and I hope it inspires you to a more active role in your government.

—Chapman Rackaway

Ancillaries

Atomic Dog is pleased to offer a robust suite of supplemental materials for instructors using its textbooks. These ancillaries include a Test Bank, PowerPoint® Slides, Instructors' Manual, and Lecture Animations.

The Test Bank for this book includes multiple-choice questions in a wide range of difficulty levels for each chapter. The Test Bank offers not only the correct answer for each question, but also a rationale or explanation for the correct answer and a reference—the location in the chapter where materials addressing the question content can be found.

A full set of PowerPoint® Slides is available for this text. This is designed to provide instructors with comprehensive visual aids for each chapter in the book. These slides include outlines of each chapter, highlighting important terms, concepts, and discussion points.

The Instructor's Manual for this book offers suggested syllabi for 10 and 14 week terms; lecture outlines and notes; in-class and take-home assignments; recommendations for multi-media resources such as films and websites; and long and short essay questions and their answers, appropriate for use on tests.

Lecture Animations allow instructors to use the animations from our online editions in their own PowerPoint slideshows. These include all of the animated figures from each chapter of the text in an easy-to-use format as well as animated figures from other Atomic Dog Publishing American government textbooks.

Online and in Print

American Government: Politics and Political Culture, Fourth Edition, is available online as well as in print. The online chapters demonstrate how the interactive media components of the text enhance presentation and understanding. For example,

- Animated illustrations, tables, and boxes help clarify concepts.
- Clickable glossary terms provide immediate definitions of key concepts.
- The search function allows you to quickly locate discussions of specific topics throughout the text.
- *QuickCheck* interactive questions and chapter quizzes test your knowledge of various topics and provide immediate feedback.
- Highlighting capabilities allow you to emphasize main ideas. You can also add personal notes in the margin.

You may choose to use just the online version of the text, or both the online and the print versions together. This gives you the flexibility to choose which combination of resources works best for you. To assist those who use the online and print versions together, the primary heads and subheads in each chapter are numbered the same. For example, the first primary head in Chapter 1 is labeled 1-1, the second primary head in this chapter is labeled 1-2, and so on. The subheads build from the designation of their corresponding primary head: 1-1a, 1-1b, etc. This numbering system is designed to make moving between the online and print versions as seamless as possible.

Finally, next to a number of figures, boxes, and tables in the print version of the text, you will see icons similar to the ones on the right. These icons indicate that these figures, boxes, or tables in the online version of the text are interactive in a way that applies, illustrates, or reinforces the concept.

Acknowledgments

Naturally, the completion of a book of this kind requires the assistance of numerous individuals. We were fortunate in being surrounded with people who were ready, willing, and able to help. At the outset, we must acknowledge the important contribution of Lilliard E. Richardson, Jr., a former colleague at the University of Tennessee who is now on the faculty at the University of Missouri–Columbia. Professor Richardson was a coauthor of the initial edition of this book, published in 1995 by West Publishing Company. We want to express our sincere gratitude to Professor Richardson for not only his contribution to that edition but also his support of the current project.

We wish also to recognize the important contributions of Professor Chapman Rackaway of Fort Hays State University, who wrote numerous pop culture features for this edition and offered excellent suggestions as to how the book could be improved.

We also want to thank the many academicians who reviewed our text, adopted the book for their courses, or provided informal feedback to us:

L. Gerald Adams
Central Missouri State University

Lyle K. Alberts
University of Northern Iowa

Sheldon Appleton
Oakland University

Steven Amberg
University of Texas–San Antonio

Thomas J. Baldino
Wilkes University

Ron Beeson
University of Central Oklahoma

James J. Best
Kent State University

Robert Brown
University of Mississippi

Richard Buckner
Santa Fe Community College

David S. Calihan
Longwood College

Alan Cigler
University of Kansas

Gloria Cox
University of North Texas

Robert Delorne
California State University–Long Beach

John Domino
Sam Houston State University

Lois L. Duke
Clemson University

Richard Foster
Idaho State University

Wolf D. Fuhrig
MacMurray College

William Giles
Mississippi State University

Laurence Giventer
California State University–Stanislaus

Gerald Gryski
Auburn University

Justin Halpern
Northeastern State University

Mary A. Harada
Northern Essex Community College

John Hitt
University of North Texas

Michael J. Horan
University of Wyoming

Asad Husain
Northeastern Illinois University

Robert Jacobs
Central Washington University

Willoughby Jarrell
Kennesaw State College

Evan M. Jones
St. Cloud State University

Carol Kamper
Rochester Community College

John Kay
Santa Barbara City College

Thomas Keating
Arizona State University

William Kelly
Auburn University

Michael L. Kurtz
Southeastern Louisiana University

Michael LeMay
University of California–San Bernardino

Will McLauchlan
Purdue University

Dennis Meier
Lansing Community College

Michael Milakovich
University of Miami

Jerry Peterson
Kellogg Community College

Laura A. Reese
Eastern Michigan University

Eleanor Schwab
South Dakota State University

Alan Siegel
Franklin Institute of Boston

Valerie Simms
Northeastern Illinois University

Sandra Vergari
Michigan State University

Benjamin Walter
Vanderbildt University

Laura Winski-Mattei
Hamilton College

We hope that our current efforts will live up to their expectations.

Thanks are also due to the staff at Atomic Dog Publishing who worked with us throughout this project, especially our editor, Kendra Leonard.

Finally, we want to express our appreciation to our families for their continuing support, encouragement, and patience. We hope that this book is useful to students and teachers of American politics and that it makes teaching and learning this subject more enjoyable for all concerned. Naturally, we take full responsibility for any errors of commission or omission in this book.

William Lyons
John M. Scheb II

About the Authors

William Lyons earned his Ph.D. from the University of Oklahoma in 1974. Since 1975, he has been a member of the political science faculty at the University of Tennessee, Knoxville. Professor Lyons has extensive experience in public opinion polling and has worked as a consultant to numerous public agencies, private companies, and political candidates. He has also served as an expert witness in cases involving voting rights, employment discrimination, and city annexation. Professor Lyons' principal teaching and research areas are state and local government, public opinion, urban politics, political behavior, political communications, and research methodology. He has published numerous articles in professional journals, including *American Journal of Political Science, American Politics Quarterly, Journal of Politics, Social Science Quarterly, State and Local Government Review, Journal of Marketing Research,* and *Public Administration Review.* He is also the coauthor, with John M. Scheb II and Billy Stair, of *Government and Politics in Tennessee* (University of Tennessee Press 2002). Professor Lyons has also served as Director of Economic Development for the City of Knoxville, chairman of the board of Knoxville's Community Development Corporation, and political analyst for WBIR-TV, Knoxville.

John M. Scheb II received his Ph.D. from the University of Florida in 1982. Since then, he has been a member of the political science faculty at the University of Tennessee, Knoxville. Professor Scheb's primary interest is public law, which includes constitutional law, administrative law, and criminal law and procedure. His secondary interest is public opinion. Professor Scheb has been involved in numerous survey research projects for government agencies, political candidates, and private businesses. He is the coauthor, with his father, Judge John M. Scheb, of *Criminal Law and Procedure,* 5th edition (Wadsworth 2005) and, with Otis H. Stephens, Jr., of *American Constitutional Law,* 3rd edition (Wadsworth 2003). He is also the coauthor, with William Lyons and Billy Stair, of *Government and Politics in Tennessee* (University of Tennessee Press 2002). Professor Scheb's research has been published in a number of professional journals, including *Journal of Politics, American Politics Quarterly, Social Science Quarterly, Political Behavior, Law and Policy, Tennessee Law Review, Judicature,* and *State and Local Government Review.* Professor Scheb is the chair of the legal studies program at the University of Tennessee.

About Popular Culture and American Politics Contributor Chapman Rackaway: *Chapman Rackaway* is Assistant Professor of Political Science at Fort Hays State University, where he runs the Political Management program. Students interested in a career in campaign politics can train to run for office, lobby, or consult in the program. Professor Rackaway is active in the American Democracy Project, which encourages college-aged students to become more active in politics and their communities. Professor Rackaway's background is in political consulting, having managed and provided media services for campaigns. Professor Rackaway received his Ph.D. from the University of Missouri, and has published research in the *Journal of Politics.*

The Political Culture of American Democracy

1

majority rule	popular culture	separation of powers
masses	presidential systems	social contract
moderates	prime minister	socialism
multiculturalism	private enterprise	socialist economy
natural law	private property	societal culture
natural rights	public benefits	societal institutions
parliament	public interest	sovereignty
parliamentary systems	public regardedness	state of nature
participatory democracy	regulatory state	statutes
political culture	representative institutions	universal suffrage
political socialization	rule of law	welfare state
politics	secular humanism	

1-1 Politics, Government, and Political Culture

When asked about politics, most Americans immediately think of the process of running for public office. The word *politics* brings to mind an image of a candidate making a speech, meeting with supporters, or staging a media event. But politics involves much more than the activities associated with elections and campaigns. **Politics** is the process by which societies govern themselves. In every society, conflicts arise that must be resolved. Politics is the process through which people resolve their conflicts peacefully. In its most successful form, politics lifts society out of chaos and violence.[1] Thus, politics is fundamentally about getting along.

1-1a Government

The term **government** refers to the institutions that have the authority to make rules that are binding on society. Government is necessary to avoid what the English political philosopher Thomas Hobbes (1588–1679) called "the war of every man against every man." Without government, wrote Hobbes, there is "continual fear and danger of violent death and the life of man [is] solitary, poor, nasty, brutish, and short."[2] The world has witnessed many examples of what happens when governments disappear—in Lebanon, Bosnia, Somalia, and many other places. People are brutalized. They lose their jobs, their homes, and their possessions. Cities are plundered and devastated. Entire peoples are even subjected to genocide.

Another way of defining government is to say that it consists of those institutions that hold a monopoly on the legitimate use of force in society. Government is legitimate when it is generally perceived as having the right to rule its population. Even if a government is universally regarded among its people as legitimate, it must, on occasion, use force to back up its rules and policies. Even if force is rarely used, the threat of it is always there. By using force, a government can exist without being perceived as legitimate. In such a situation, citizens may not recognize the government's laws and policies. However, no government wishes, or can afford for long, to rule where it is not accorded **legitimacy** by the people it governs.

Although the fundamental purpose of government is to maintain order, peace, and security, governments do much more than that. Governments play a role in managing their economies, providing for the public welfare, fostering the growth of knowledge, and maintaining a healthy environment. They also provide **public benefits,** such as projects and programs that benefit society as a whole—roads, dams, water and sewer systems, schools, and parks, for example. Ideally, governments provide public benefits in which all citizens have an equal interest, but in reality governments often redistribute burdens and benefits among different groups in society. Even when governments do not redistribute burdens and benefits, they set the rules by which these elements are distributed. The importance of the distributive aspect of government decision making has led some political scientists to define politics as "who gets what, when, [and] how."[3]

> **politics** The process by which societies are governed and conflicts are resolved.

> **government** The institutions in a society that have authority to make rules that are binding on that society.

> **legitimacy** Acknowledgment by a society that government has the right to rule.

> **public benefits** Projects and programs that benefit society as a whole, such as schools, roads, dams, water and sewer systems, airports, and parks.

Because people need rules to live by, every society needs a government. The key questions are these: What type of government will a society have? What role will government play? What functions will it perform? What values will it promote? Which groups will it favor? How much power will leaders have, and how will they use their power? The answers to these questions cannot be ascertained in a cultural vacuum. The role and scope of government reflect a people's view of human nature and of individual capability and responsibility. Few societies are in complete agreement on these questions. Over time, however, societies develop answers to these questions. As a consensus emerges, these answers form a nation's political culture.

1-1b The Importance of Political Culture

In this text, politics and government are presented as they reflect the political culture of the United States. **Political culture** consists of the values that most members of a society hold about what politics ought to address and how these matters should be addressed. Political culture gives people a sense of what government ought to deal with, what is appropriate, and what is not appropriate for public consideration. This basic understanding affects the way people look at government—what they expect government to do and how they expect it to be done. Political culture also embraces people's emotional reactions to the "symbols, institutions, and rules that constitute the fundamental political order. . . ."[4] Political culture is thus a broad term referring to shared values, expectations, and feelings having to do with politics and government.

> **political culture** Values generally held in a society about what government should do and what issues should be addressed in the political arena.

A political culture is "integrated" if most people react favorably to their political system and a reasonable degree of agreement on basic values exists. An integrated political culture is necessary to maintain a healthy political system, whereas a "fragmented" political culture makes the task of governance very difficult and threatens the long-term survival of political institutions. Of course, any society has some degree of fragmentation. Always, some groups of people do not consider themselves to be part of the political community. Often, these people refuse to recognize the legitimacy of the existing government.

The importance of political culture was made abundantly clear when world attention focused on Afghanistan following the terrorist attack on the World Trade Center and the Pentagon on September 11, 2001. The ruling Taliban wielded its political power based on an extreme interpretation of the Koran—the sacred scriptures of Islam. For some time the Taliban had supported and received support from the al Qaeda terrorist network, headed by Osama bin Laden. By harboring bin Laden and al Qaeda, the terrorist organization he heads, the Taliban converted Afghanistan into a base for training terrorists who would strike at the United States and its allies. The Taliban ruled Afghanistan with an iron hand, ruthlessly suppressing dissent and enforcing its harsh version of Islam. Women were not permitted to hold jobs or leave their homes without covering themselves from head to toe. Girls were not permitted to attend school. The Taliban shocked the world when it destroyed ancient Buddhist monuments and required Hindus to wear identifying labels. Although religious tolerance and the separation of church and state are fundamental components of American political culture, the Taliban rejected these values.

Although the Taliban's fusion of religion and government is unthinkable in a Western-style democracy, to many Afghans and others in the Islamic world, that mixture seemed perfectly natural. Human beings in Afghanistan and the United States did not come to hold these different beliefs in a vacuum. From childhood onward, people in each society are bombarded with a variety of messages and images that set the boundaries for what they come to regard as possible and desirable. Of course, at the same time, each person develops a sense of what is impossible or undesirable. Many of the limits of and possibilities for politics are determined by the limits and possibilities that the broader societal culture sets for all behavior.

It is important to recognize that political cultures evolve. Usually, cultural change comes about slowly, but sometimes it can be rapid and dramatic. Consider the political culture of Japan. Seventy years ago Japanese political culture supported a ruthless dictatorship

Building Democracy in Iraq?
Given Iraq's intense ethnic, political, and religious conflicts, many observers question whether America and its allies can foster a democratic political system in that beleaguered country.

AP/WIDE WORLD PHOTOS

that attempted to subjugate much of Asia and the Pacific. As the result of its defeat in World War II, Japan's political culture was reshaped dramatically, largely by American influence. Today, Japan's government is a Western-style democracy. Japan no longer threatens its neighbors and is a close ally of the United States. With few exceptions, the Japanese people today hold democratic values. Of course, the overwhelming majority of Japanese citizens alive today were born after the Second World War and have lived their entire lives under a democratic regime. Much the same can be said of Germany. In the 1930s, most Germans supported Adolph Hitler and the totalitarian state his Nazi Party created. Today, Germany is among the strongest of the world's democracies. Like Japan, Germany's former bellicose tendencies have been replaced by, if anything, a tendency to embrace pacifism. Both Japan and Germany illustrate rapid and profound change in political culture. Of course, in both instances, such change was the result of losing a cataclysmic world war and being subjected to the cultural influence of the victors—America and its allies.

In justifying the invasion of Iraq, President George W. Bush talked not only about the need to remove a threat to American security, but of his desire to reshape the political culture of the Middle East. The president's stated objective was to create a free, democratic, and peaceful Iraq that would serve as a model for other societies in the region. In November 2003, President Bush asserted, "Iraqi democracy will succeed—and that success will send forth the news, from Damascus to Teheran—that freedom can be the future of every nation. The establishment of a free Iraq at the heart of the Middle East will be a watershed event in the global democratic revolution."[5] A year later the prospects for achieving a free, democratic, and peaceful Iraq seemed remote. Assassinations, kidnappings, car bombings, and other forms of terrorism were common, threatening to undermine America's efforts to nurture democratic institutions and even plunge Iraq into sectarian civil war.

Hopes for democracy were buoyed by the holding of elections in January 2005, but the new Iraqi government operated under constant threat of attack. Some observers suggested that the ethnic and religious differences among the Iraqi people were such that it was not reasonable to suppose that a stable democracy could ever be established there. Many feared that after American forces were removed the country would degenerate into anarchy and civil war. In the heat of the 2004 presidential campaign, some of President Bush's critics suggested that it would have been better to leave Saddam Hussein in power. In their view, Hussein was not an imminent threat to American security and at least provided stability in the region, albeit through brutal repression. Whether one agrees or disagrees with President Bush's decision to invade Iraq, it is clear that toppling Saddam Hussein's dictatorship was the easy part. The far more difficult project is the reestablishment of order and security, the rebuilding of the country, the creation of new political institutions, and, ultimately, the reshaping of the political culture.

Political Culture and the Larger Societal Culture   Political culture is embedded within the larger **societal culture,** which includes all socially transmitted patterns of behavior as well as all the beliefs, customs, and institutions within the society. Culture embraces the arts, music, literature, science, philosophy, and religion and includes the ways that we entertain ourselves—sports, movies, magazines, and television. Culture includes the ways we communicate with one another, the words and images we use, and the media that transmit those words and images. In short, culture embraces all the products of work, thought, and experience that are characteristic of a particular people.

> **societal culture**   All socially transmitted patterns of behavior as well as all the beliefs, customs, and institutions within the society.

Just as political culture sets the stage for what government considers as viable options, the broader societal culture provides individuals with options for personal activities. Cultures simplify the lives of individuals by limiting choices. Without this simplification, individuals would be overwhelmed by the options available to them. As cultures change, they often give individuals more freedom, but at a cost. In nineteenth century America, for instance, churches, schools, and families communicated a clear set of standards regarding appropriate sexual behavior. An individual could "choose" to be promiscuous, but few felt that they could really opt for that choice. Society, through the church and other powerful institutions, clearly disapproved. After the sexual revolution of the 1960s and 1970s, individuals found themselves receiving complex and contradictory cultural messages about sexuality. Behavior that was clearly frowned on in the past was becoming acceptable. The wide array of options presented to Americans fostered confusion and frustration among people of both sexes. The culture changed, but with this cultural change came conflict.

Changing sexual attitudes and behaviors is just one of many ways in which American society is dramatically different than when the country was founded more than two hundred years ago. Indeed, the daily life of the average American living today would be incomprehensible to the average American of the late eighteenth century. As the society has evolved, so has the political culture. Most fundamentally, contemporary Americans expect so much more from their government than did citizens in the early days of the Republic. Yet, despite this and other profound changes in political culture, certain cultural tendencies unite Americans across the centuries. We might think of these cultural continuities as forming the "American personality."

To see how the broader societal culture affects political life, consider some differences between the United States and Sweden. In Swedish culture, two characteristics are particularly important. Swedes, who have been described as "painfully shy," value "safety, consensus, and security, and the absence of all things uncomfortable or unpleasant." In individual behavior, Swedes seek "not too little, not too much, but just the right amount."[6] These attitudes are very different from the values emphasized in American culture. Americans, by contrast, value independence and individualism and do not shy away from competition and conflict. These cultural differences help explain why Swedes are much more supportive than Americans of the idea that government should play a major role in regulating economic life, promoting social welfare, and reducing inequality.

Culture and Authority   As another example of the interaction of culture and politics, consider the matter of authority. Essentially, **authority** is the right to tell others what to do. Some cultures are more supportive of authority than others. Many people have wondered how the Germans could have gone along with the atrocities committed by the Nazis during World War II. Noting that German culture stresses obedience to authority, an obedience that is ingrained from childhood, some have speculated that the Germans' cultural definition of authority spilled over into their political culture; that is, patterns of behavior from the culture at large became patterns of behavior in politics. What happened in Nazi Germany probably could not happen in the United States, although no one can be certain

> **authority**   The right to enforce laws or issue commands.

of it. Clearly, though, the political culture of modern America is significantly different from that of Nazi Germany.[7] Americans are distrustful of authority and are not accustomed to blind obedience.

> **popular culture** The elements of culture consumed by masses of people. They include movies, music, novels, and television programs.

Popular Culture: A Reflection of the American Experience

The American experience is chronicled and analyzed by historians, sociologists, political scientists, and even novelists. It is also depicted in **popular culture** (or "pop" culture), a term often used to denote the elements of culture that masses of people find enjoyable or entertaining. In this book, we use the term *popular culture* to include movies, books, plays, and, of course, television programs. Sometimes popular culture deals explicitly with political themes. An obvious example is the highly successful television series *The West Wing*, which depicts life inside the White House in a very compelling way, drawing heavily on real political events and issues and offering a heavy dose of political commentary.

Hollywood has a long history of making feature films of this genre, from the 1939 classic *Mr. Smith Goes to Washington* to the 1997 comedy *Wag the Dog*. While films, plays, and television series dealing with political themes reflect many different perspectives on politics, they all help to shape (or sometimes reinforce) political attitudes and opinions. *Mr. Smith Goes to Washington* inspired moviegoers with its depiction of a courageous young senator battling forces of corruption on Capitol Hill. By presenting a narrative in which an embattled president employs a media specialist to boost his approval rating by creating an illusion of war, *Wag the Dog* appealed to (and probably reinforced) popular cynicism about politics and mass media.

Films like *Wag the Dog* and television series such as *The West Wing* are not standard fare. The great mass of American pop culture is ostensibly nonpolitical, offering entertainment with heavy doses of comedy, sexual innuendo, and violence. Yet even mainstream entertainment can be quite revealing of the attitudes and beliefs that underlie American politics. Consider the standard Hollywood "cop" movie in which the hero is usually something of a rebel or a renegade. Excellent examples include the Clint Eastwood *Dirty Harry* movies of the 1960s and 1970s and the Bruce Willis *Die Hard* series of the 1990s. In these films the hero is a cop who doesn't play by the rules. He is constantly struggling, not only against the bad guys but also against "the system." The authorities are often portrayed as stupid, venal, or selfish bureaucrats or politicians. Of course, in the end, the rebellious hero saves the day and vanquishes the villains. These movies resonate with Americans precisely because they reflect a distrust of authority, a disdain for bureaucracy, and a hostility to politicians that are deeply embedded in the American personality.

Sometimes a movie or TV program itself becomes the object of political controversy. That was certainly the case in 2004 when Mel Gibson's film *The Passion of the Christ* was criticized on the ground that it might inspire anti-Semitism. Michael Moore's documentary *Fahrenheit 9/11*, which painted an extremely negative portrait of the Bush Administration, proved to be even more controversial as it became part of the national political conversation leading up to the 2004 presidential election.

Political controversy over pop culture is nothing new. It occurred in 1992, when then–Vice President Dan Quayle attacked the TV show *Murphy Brown* for eroding "traditional family values" by favorably portraying a career woman's decision to have a child out of wedlock. The fact that the vice president of the United States would single out a TV program suggests that our leaders are aware of the tremendous importance of popular culture and its relevance to politics.

In the 1990s, a controversy developed over certain forms of rap music, especially "gangsta" rap. Some people objected to what they considered to be bad language; others charged that rap lyrics were derogatory toward women. Still others complained that rap music seemed to promote violence. Some went so far as to demand that this music be curtailed, if not by government, then by the music industry itself.

This issue was revisited in slightly different terms during the 2000 presidential election campaign. Both candidates scolded Hollywood for its targeting of R-rated movie ads to children as well as for the violence and sexual content in many productions. Although the defenders of marketing adult material to children are few and far between, some were troubled by potential censorship issues and stressed the idea of artistic freedom, which is a powerful value in American culture. This popular culture debate forced Americans to think about two competing values: the desire for a "good society" and the commitment to free expression. Pop culture is often the vehicle through which conflicting cultural values are explored. Much of the anger felt by the terrorists who launched their attack on September 11, 2001, was grounded in opposition to the spread of American popular culture throughout the world.

1-2 The Meaning of Democracy

Belief in democracy is one of the fundamental elements of American political culture. Many Americans mistakenly consider their political system to be thoroughly democratic. *Democracy* is a broad term encompassing a variety of related ideas and practices. And some facets of the American political system would be considered undemocratic by many people around the world. Nevertheless, the study of American politics logically begins with an examination of the idea of democracy.

The term **democracy** is derived from the Greek word *demos,* meaning "the people," and *kratia,* meaning "rule" or "authority." Literally, then, democracy means "rule by the people." The Greek philosopher Aristotle (384–322 B.C.) defined democracy as the rule of the many, as opposed to **aristocracy,** which means the rule of the few.[8] More familiar to Americans is Abraham Lincoln's definition of democracy as "government of the people, by the people, and for the people."[9]

In the real world, even under the most favorable conditions, democracy only approximates the ideal of "government by the people." In every human association, power inevitably is wielded by the few over the many.[10] Every society can be divided into two basic groups: those who lead and those who follow. Political scientists refer to leaders— whether of government, business, science, education, the mass media, or the arts—as **elites.** Although every society has its elites, societies vary greatly in the way their elites are

> **democracy**   Literally, "rule by the people." As defined by Aristotle, the term refers to the rule of the many, as distinct from the rule of the few.

> **aristocracy**   A hereditary ruling class; government by such a class of rulers.

> **elites**   Those persons in a society who possess a disproportionate amount of wealth, power, or status. In a political system, elites are those persons who possess the authority to make decisions affecting the masses.

Statue of Abraham Lincoln inside the Lincoln Memorial, Washington, D.C.
In his famous Gettysburg Address, President Abraham Lincoln defined democracy as "government of the people, by the people, and for the people."
Photo courtesy of the author.

masses   The great numbers of people in a society.

authoritarian regime   A political system in which power is concentrated in one or very few elites, which are not accountable to the masses except in the rare instances of revolutions.

dictatorship   An extreme form of authoritarianism whereby power is concentrated in the hands of one individual.

coup d'état   The overthrow of rulers by those who become the rulers.

structured, the way power is distributed among them, and the relationship the elites have to the **masses.**

In an **authoritarian regime,** power is concentrated in one elite or a few elites, which are not accountable to the masses except in the rare instances of revolutions. In the most extreme case, a **dictatorship,** power is concentrated in the hands of one individual. Adolf Hitler's Germany and Joseph Stalin's Soviet Union are good historical examples of dictatorships. In both cases, no one dared challenge or even question the dictator. Iraq under Saddam Hussein provides a familiar recent example of a dictatorship. Usually, though, power in an authoritarian regime is wielded by one ruling family, a dominant political party, or a group of religious leaders.

In a democracy, on the other hand, power is distributed among multiple elites in society. Moreover, elites in government are accountable to the masses through free and fair competitive elections. In a democracy, governmental power changes hands from time to time, if not at regular intervals, between rival political parties. This change comes about peaceably, through the electoral process. In an authoritarian system, changes in political leadership require some extraordinary event, such as the death of the dictator, a **coup d'état,** or a revolution.

The closest approximation to the ideal of pure democracy was the *polis,* or city-state, of Athens from approximately the mid-fifth to the mid-fourth century B.C. All citizens were members of the assembly, which held monthly meetings to enact laws, dispense justice, set foreign policy, and manage the city-state's finances. After free and open debate, decisions were made by majority vote. As with modern government, the policies established by the assembly had to be carried out by administrators. These officials were selected in two ways: The assembly elected administrators for posts that required special knowledge or skills, and positions that required only ordinary ability were filled by administrators selected annually by lottery from among the citizenry. This procedure ensured that Athenian government was truly conducted by its citizens. Ironically, citizenship in the Athenian *polis* was limited to adult male property holders whose families had lived in Athens for several generations. Women, children, slaves, and newcomers to Athens were excluded, so participation in Athenian democracy was confined to a small minority of the population. Although contemporary Americans might question whether such a system was truly a democracy, the culture of ancient Greece found slavery acceptable and did not think that women should participate in the political process.

1-2a The Intellectual Foundations of Modern Democracy

After the decline of ancient Athens, the idea of democracy lay dormant until it was resurrected in Europe during the late seventeenth century, when intellectuals began to question the legitimacy of monarchs and aristocrats, whose authority was based solely on heredity. The most influential political thinker in the late seventeenth and early eighteenth centuries was England's John Locke, whose principal work, *Two Treatises of Government,* laid the foundation for modern democratic theory. Locke, along with other writers, provided the intellectual roots for the American version of democracy. The elites who have played a major role in the political development of the United States have been heavily influenced by Lockean ideas. Indeed, these ideas have permeated American political culture. Although most Americans are probably not familiar with John Locke or his writings, they tend to view his ideas as "self-evident truths," to use the language of the Declaration of Independence.

natural law   Laws whose existence does not depend on recognition by government.

state of nature   A condition of society, postulated by both John Locke and Thomas Hobbes, in which there is no government.

One of Locke's principal motivations in writing the *Two Treatises* was to justify the Glorious Revolution of 1688, in which the English Parliament asserted its power over the monarchy. Locke started with the premise that humans are rational beings who are capable of acting in their own self-interest and discovering the **natural law** ordained by the Creator for the conduct of human affairs. Locke postulated a **state of nature,** a condition of society in which no government exists. According to Locke, "[t]o understand political power aright, and derive it from its original, we must consider what estate all men are naturally in, and that is a state of perfect freedom. . . ." In Locke's view, that estate was also a "state . . . of equality, wherein all the power and jurisdiction is reciprocal, no one having more than another."[11] Although Locke's hypothetical state of nature is characterized by perfect freedom and total equality, it is also fraught with danger. Because this state has no authority, people are insecure. Nothing can stop the strong and cunning from exploiting the weak and vulnerable. In Locke's view, government exists by virtue of a **social contract** among rational individuals who prefer to be ruled by others than to live in the chaos and insecurity of the state of nature. **Sovereignty,** or the right to rule, is thus vested ultimately in the people, not in the rulers.

Locke's ideas were built on those of another English philosopher, Thomas Hobbes. Hobbes, who also wrote in the seventeenth century, envisioned a state of nature that was much worse than Locke's. Writing in *Leviathan* (1651), Hobbes described life in the state of nature as "nasty, brutish, and short." He thought that people were so anxious for security that they would give up all their freedom by surrendering all power to a king. This king would have absolute power because government's only obligation to the people is to keep them safe. In Hobbes's view, no middle ground exists between **anarchy,** the total absence of government, and an all-powerful king. People are not capable of governing themselves.

Locke's state of nature, like Hobbes', was a state of total lawlessness. But Locke had a different view of human nature. In Locke's view, people are capable of surrendering authority to government on a limited basis, retaining certain rights while allowing the government certain powers. This idea, that of **limited government,** is the basis of the U.S. Constitution. The idea is a powerful one, but one that demands a great deal from human beings. It requires them to make rational determinations about what is in their best interests and what is the appropriate role for government. The concept of limited government requires that people pay attention to what their government is doing and speak out when they believe that government has acted improperly. At the same time, it requires that people obey the government when it acts within its legitimate sphere of authority. In short, limited government requires that the individual become a **citizen.**

When government fails to protect the individual's **natural rights** to life, liberty, and property, argued Locke, people have the right to demand that their government be replaced. This radical idea was the justification for the Glorious Revolution of 1688 (and for the more violent and bloody revolutions that would follow in America and France). Although Locke was critical of absolute monarchy, he was careful not to call for the abolition of the monarchy. Rather, Locke called for the supremacy of Parliament (the English legislature). Of course, the Parliament of John Locke's day represented wealthy landowners, not the English masses. Yet, as Lockean assumptions, which were quite radical in their time, came to be accepted, it seemed natural that monarchies should be replaced by legislative assemblies and that assemblies should become more representative of the people they ruled.

Rousseau and the French Revolution   After Locke, the preeminent democratic thinker of the Enlightenment was the Frenchman Jean-Jacques Rousseau (1712–1778). Rousseau began with similar assumptions, postulating a state of nature and a social contract. But Rousseau advocated a more direct, **participatory democracy** than Locke believed to be possible or desirable. Rousseau believed that representative institutions could only distort the general will of the people, which he regarded as infallible. Rousseau stressed the importance of sentiment and emotion, which led him to glorify national unity at the expense of individual rights. In France, Rousseau's extreme version of popular sovereignty came up against ideas of absolute monarchy—with explosive consequences. But the French Revolution of 1789, largely based on Rousseau's ideas, failed to establish a successful democracy. Rather, it brought about a "reign of terror" in which no one was safe from the guillotine. The French Revolution eventually degenerated into a militaristic dictatorship that wreaked havoc on Europe. Given the awful experience of the French Revolution, the appeal of Rousseauian ideas of democracy has diminished considerably, at least insofar as they might be applied to mass societies.

Lockean, rather than Rousseauian, thinking became part of the intellectual tradition of the United States. Perhaps the reason is that, unlike France, whose revolution shook the foundations of French society with incredible violence, the United States of America came into being without a tremendous upheaval in society. Although the British colonial rulers were defeated and expelled, the basic structures of society were not shaken.

social contract   A hypothetical agreement among rational individuals in a society who choose to be ruled by others in order to escape the chaos and insecurity of anarchy.

sovereignty   The legitimate right to rule a society.

anarchy   The absence of government; referred to as the "state of nature" by political theorists.

limited government   A government that is limited to certain powers and responsibilities and is prohibited from transgressing the rights of citizens.

citizen   A person who is a member of a given political community.

natural rights   Rights ordained by God or by nature, which cannot be infringed by government. In classical liberal thought, these rights include the right to life, liberty, and property.

participatory democracy   A system of government in which ordinary citizens are directly involved in the day-to-day decisions of government.

1-2b　Democratic Regimes

In the nineteenth and twentieth centuries, as the essential democratic idea caught on, theories of democracy proliferated. Today, one can find a variety of theories of democracy. As democratic theories vary, so do their practical applications. Societies differ in wealth, geography, history, language, and the number of religious and racial groups. Consequently, no two democratic regimes look exactly alike, and some seem to work much better than others. Despite these differences, one can distill the essential features that make a political system democratic.

First, a democracy must have one or more **representative institutions** empowered to make decisions for the society. Authoritarian regimes, seeking to gain legitimacy by posing as democracies, sometimes have "representative" assemblies that have no real policy-making power or influence over the government. Second, in a democracy, members of the representative assemblies must be elected in **free, fair, and open elections.** Here, too, authoritarian systems trying to display the trappings of democracy often hold elections that are neither free nor fair nor open. One good indicator that a political system is truly democratic is that power changes hands from time to time. Whatever its superficial appearance, any system in which power is exercised by the same party or group over a long period is unlikely to qualify as a democracy.

Universal Suffrage　　Democracy is predicated on the essential worth and dignity of all human beings. Consequently, each person has the right to pursue his or her own interests and seek to control his or her own destiny. Although the participation of all citizens in the day-to-day governance of their country is a practical impossibility, all citizens—at least all adults—ought to have the right to participate in elections. Indeed, voting is generally considered to be the elemental act of political participation in a representative democracy.

Universal suffrage means that all adult citizens have the right to vote. In many democratic countries, protracted and sometimes bloody struggles were necessary to achieve universal suffrage. The thought simply did not occur to John Locke and the classical liberals of the Enlightenment that women ought to have the right to vote; indeed, the franchise was not extended to all women in the United States until 1920. At the time of the American Revolution, the overwhelming majority of people of African descent living in this country were slaves. A bloody civil war, several constitutional amendments, a series of important acts of Congress, and numerous judicial decisions would be required over a period of more than a century before African Americans could enjoy the right to vote. Does the lack of universal suffrage in the United States over most of its history mean that America was not a democracy? Arguably so, but as you shall see in Chapter 2, "The Development of American Constitutional Democracy," the Founders of the American republic were not all that enthusiastic about democracy. Yet two centuries of social, economic, political, and legal change have brought about the democratization of the United States.

Democracy and Human Rights　　Whether one considers Lockean liberalism or other formulations of democratic theory, the two core values of democracy are clearly **freedom** and **equality:** All citizens are entitled to certain basic rights, and all citizens must be treated equally by the state. Given their philosophical underpinnings, democracies tend to be much more supportive of human rights than do authoritarian regimes. Yet nothing in the structure of representative democracy *per se* requires the system to respect or foster human rights.

Representative democracy, which is based on the principle of **majority rule,** is subject to two basic problems: the **majority/individual problem** and the **majority/minority problem.** In a system based squarely on majority rule, no guarantee exists that the majority will not run roughshod over the rights of the individual. Nor does any assurance exist that the majority will respect and tolerate an ethnic, racial, or religious minority group.

One approach to dealing with the majority/individual and majority/minority problems is to specify in law the rights of individuals and minorities and to establish legal constraints on the power of the majority to infringe those rights. But how is this process to be

---

representative institutions
Governmental institutions whose members are chosen so as to reflect the interests of their constituencies.

free, fair, and open elections
Elections in which all citizens have a right to vote, but are not required to do so, and the results of the voting are reported accurately.

universal suffrage　A condition under which all adult citizens have the right to vote.

freedom　One of the core values of democracy—the idea that citizens should be free from unwarranted governmental control.

equality　One of the core values of democracy—the idea that people should be equal before the law and equal before their government.

majority rule　A basic tenet of democracy which holds that laws are subject to majority approval.

majority/individual problem
The possibility that government based squarely on majority rule will diminish the rights of individuals.

majority/minority problem
The possibility that government based squarely on majority rule will oppress members of minority groups.

accomplished if the majority can change the law? What can ensure that democracy will not degenerate into tyranny of the majority? The answer of the Founders of the American Republic was to enact a constitution, a fundamental law superior to the will of transient majorities and changeable only through extraordinary means requiring a firm national consensus. Thus, in describing the American form of government, the term **constitutional democracy** is more appropriate than the term *representative democracy*. Of course, the United States is not the only democratic country to have adopted a written constitution to protect the rights of citizens and limit the power of popular majorities. Yet in no country is the written constitution taken as seriously in the day-to-day operations of government as it is in the United States. It is one of the features that makes the American system of government unique and interesting.

Parliamentary and Presidential Systems   Two basic types of democratic systems of government exist: **parliamentary systems** and **presidential systems.** The prototypical parliamentary system is the British government, whereas the government of the United States is the most widely copied presidential system. Both systems have been highly influential on other countries that have undergone democratization. But, as we have pointed out, no two systems of government are exactly alike, and many democratic systems combine features of both the presidential and parliamentary models.

The fundamental institution of government in a democratic system is the **legislature**—the body that makes the laws, or **statutes,** the society must live by. The **executive agencies** of government enforce and implement these laws. Parliamentary systems are based on the idea of **legislative supremacy**—a powerful legislature, or **parliament,** to which other agencies of the government are subordinated. The executive power in a parliamentary system

Comparative Perspective

The British Parliamentary System

As countries make the transition to democracy, they look to successful democratic countries for models of how to build democratic institutions. In this respect, both the United States and Great Britain have been widely imitated. Both are successful democracies, yet their systems of government have important differences. The fundamental difference is that Great Britain employs a parliamentary democracy.

The British Parliament consists of the House of Commons and the House of Lords. The House of Lords is a holdover from the days when the aristocracy had real power; its role is now largely symbolic. The real power of government now resides in the House of Commons, a democratically elected body composed of 635 members. The House of Commons elects the prime minister, who is the executive head of the British government. By modern tradition, the prime minister is a member of the House of Commons and is the leader of the political party that holds the majority (or plurality) of seats in the Commons. The prime minister chooses his or her cabinet from the members of the House of Commons or House of Lords. Unlike in the American system, a member of the legislature does not have to give up his or her seat to become a member of the cabinet. Parliamentary elections are held at least every five years, but the prime minister may call for an election at any time, as long as no more than one election is held per year. Thus, in Britain, as in all parliamentary systems, the legislative and the executive are not separate branches of government, as they are in the United States.

Political scientists have long debated whether the parliamentary model is better than the model used in the United States. Many argue that the system is more efficient and better mirrors what the public wants. As you will see in Chapter 2, "The Development of American Constitutional Democracy," the Framers of the U.S. Constitution had their reasons for rejecting a parliamentary system. Fundamentally, because of their extreme distrust of power, they believed that political authority needed to be dispersed across separate branches of government.

---

constitutional democracy   A governmental system in which a fundamental law is superior to the will of transient majorities and changeable only through extraordinary means requiring a firm national consensus. Characteristic of the U.S. system of governance.

parliamentary systems   Governmental systems in which the legislature is supreme and the executive exists only for the purpose of implementing the legislature's enactments.

presidential system   A governmental system in which a clear division of powers exists between the legislative and executive branches of government.

legislature   A governmental institution that makes laws for the society.

statutes   General laws enacted by a legislature.

executive agencies   Institutions of government responsible for implementing the laws passed by the legislature.

legislative supremacy   A characteristic of parliamentary systems of government in which other agencies of government are subordinate to the legislature.

parliament   Any legislative body in a parliamentary system of government. The legislative body in England.

Figure 1-1
The Presidential System and the Parliamentary System
The Presidential system in the United States is composed of three equal but separate branches: executive (president), legislative (Congress), and judicial (the courts).

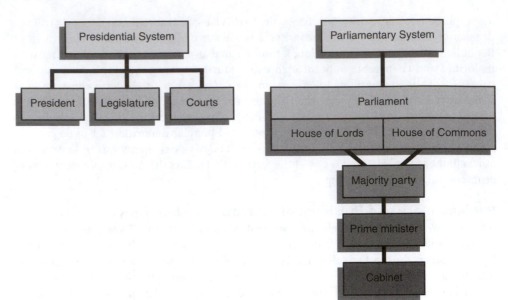

is vested in a **prime minister** and a **cabinet,** all of whom are members of the parliament. The political party holding the majority of seats in the parliament "puts together a government," meaning that it selects the prime minister and cabinet from the leadership of the party.

In contrast, under a presidential system, the executive is a separate and distinct branch of government. The chief executive, or president, is chosen independently in a national election. One cannot simultaneously be a member of the president's cabinet and hold a seat in the legislature. The essential characteristic of the presidential system, then, is the **separation of powers** between the legislative and executive agencies of the government. Under a parliamentary system, executive and legislative power tend to be fused (see Figure 1-1).

Courts of Law   **Courts of law** are extremely important democratic institutions, in that they serve to maintain democratic procedures and protect the rights of individuals and minority groups. In parliamentary systems, courts tend to be subordinated to the legislative and executive powers, whereas in presidential systems they tend to be separate branches of government. Certainly, that is the case in the United States, where the judiciary is a distinct and coordinate branch in a tripartite system of government. The formidable character of the American judiciary is enhanced by the power of **judicial review**—the authority to strike down legislative and executive decisions that are found to be inconsistent with the U.S. Constitution. In few other democratic countries do the legal systems have the power and prominence of the American courts of law. This fact was certainly highlighted by the Supreme Court's December 2000 decision in the case of *Bush v. Gore,*[12] a decision that effectively decided the outcome of the 2000 presidential election in favor of Republican candidate George W. Bush.

1-2c Democracy and Capitalism

Politics and economics are not totally separate spheres of activity. What happens in the political system can have enormous consequences for the economy and vice versa. Both politics and economics deal with the distribution of power in society. To a great extent, economic power translates into political power. The United States has, for the most part, a **capitalist economy**—it is based on the principles of **private property** and **private enterprise** (see Table 1-1). Political theorists have debated at length about the relationship between

prime minister   The executive head in a parliamentary system who is selected directly from the legislative body.

cabinet   Advisers to the chief executive, who is responsible for implementing legislative acts. In a parliamentary system, the cabinet is chosen from the parliament.

separation of powers   A system of government in which the three functions of government—legislative, executive, and judicial—are dispersed among three equal and separate branches.

courts of law   Governmental institutions established for the purpose of resolving disputes and interpreting the law.

judicial review   The authority of a court of law to strike down legislative and executive decisions if they are found to be unconstitutional.

Socialist	Capitalist
Government-controlled industry	Private enterprise
Collective property	Private property
Less stratified economic classes	Stratification of economic classes
Free or low-cost access to education, health care, transportation; extensive government-run social services	Competitive for-profit educational, health care, and transportation companies
State-provided minimum housing	Open market housing
Government intervention in economy	Self-regulating market economy

TABLE 1-1

Socialist Economies Versus Capitalist Economies

INTERACTIVE TABLE

democracy and capitalism. Some argue that private property and free enterprise are desirable, if not strictly necessary, conditions for democracy, in that they help to limit the power of the state. Others believe that the economic inequalities inherent in capitalism are inconsistent with the egalitarian ideals of democracy. Some democratic theorists believe that people must be more or less equal economically if they are to be equal politically. These theorists prefer a **socialist economy,** where government controls major industries and works to eradicate differences in wealth. In many democracies, **socialism** is an accepted alternative to be considered within the democratic institutions of that country. These countries, such as France, Italy, and Sweden, have viable socialist parties, some of which have captured the government at various times. However, socialism has rarely been considered acceptable within the political culture of the United States, which is unabashedly capitalistic.

The world's most successful democracies do seem to be found among the advanced, industrialized nations, most of which are essentially capitalist. Included in this category are Great Britain, of course, as well as Canada, France, Germany, Italy, Japan, and a number of others. As one scholar notes, capitalism and democracy "are historically tied together because in the forms in which they have arisen, . . . both are manifestations of constitutional liberalism."[13] The fledgling democracies of Eastern Europe have by and large adopted capitalist economies; it remains to be seen how well they will succeed.

The case of China has been unique. In the 1980s, China began a significant movement toward capitalism, which led to demands for political reform. Following the massacre of student protesters at Tiananmen Square in Beijing in June 1989, the government crushed the attempt to develop democratic political institutions. During the 1990s, China continued its movement toward capitalism, but did so under authoritarian means. The question remains of whether pressures for democratic reform will inevitably follow as the Chinese economy becomes more fully capitalist and the standard of living continues to rise.

Without resolving the theoretical debate over the relationship between capitalism and democracy, we can say that democracies tend to function best when a large middle class exists. A society in which a small minority of the population is very rich and the rest of the people are very poor is not a good candidate for a successful democracy. A tremendous disparity in wealth intensifies social conflict and makes consensus and compromise virtually impossible. This concept helps to explain why achieving democracy has been so difficult among the world's least developed nations.

1-2d Political Culture and Democracy

A democratic form of government cannot simply be created out of thin air nor imposed on a country by a dominant foreign power (although it has been tried from time to time). Not only must economic conditions be favorable, as just discussed, but the country must also have an integrated political culture that is hospitable to democratic values and

capitalist economy Economic system characterized by private property, private enterprise, and limited governmental control.

private property Claims by individuals and corporations involving the right to use and control real estate and other forms of property.

private enterprise An element of capitalist economy that is closely linked to the doctrine of *laissez-faire.*

socialist economy An economic system in which government controls major industries and works to eradicate differences in wealth.

socialism An ideology stressing government control of the means of production for the purpose of equalizing the wealth in society.

Popular Culture and American Politics
Goodbye Lenin

By Chapman Rackaway

Political ideologies are central parts of any political culture. In the United States, we follow a general ideology of capitalist democracy. From the end of World War II until 1990, East Germany was its own nation following a Communist ideology. In less than a year, though, communism collapsed. Your ideology makes up a big part of not only your political outlook, but your life. If everything you believed in changed, seemingly overnight, how would you deal with the changes? Would you concede and try to adapt, or would you fight against it? Imagine your mother fell into an eight-month coma, and while she was unconscious, the American system of capitalist democracy fell apart. Knowing the shock of such a dramatic change could kill her when she woke up, how far would you go to protect her from the truth that her ideology and way of life was gone?

In the movie *Goodbye Lenin,* that deception is the main part of the story. Alex, an East German teenager, sees his mother fall into a coma while protesting against the rapidly collapsing Communist government. Alex's mother had been a stalwart of the Communist party, a proud supporter of Marxist ideology, and the surprise of seeing her apathetic son become involved in a protest overcomes her. For nearly a year, Alex's mother remains unconscious while the world she knew almost completely disappears. When she awakes, doctors tell Alex that any great shock could give her a fatal heart attack, so he goes to extraordinary lengths to convince his bedridden mother that the Berlin Wall still stands and Marx's words still guide their government. Alex travels far and wide to find the low-quality food that was formerly sold in state-owned food stores, he keeps the shades closed to shield his mother's eyes from advertising that hung outside her window, and he collects videotapes of old television news footage to keep up the illusion that communism still governs their lives.

The German movie is funny, but also a lesson in how important ideology is to people. Communism was such a central part of Alex's mother's life that she would not have been able to deal with the huge changes that the collapse of that ideology brought. Ideology changes from generation to generation, and even though your parents may look at politics differently, those outlooks are incredibly important to the people we are.

---

institutions. A nation accustomed to authoritarianism would have difficulty adjusting to the cultural requirements of democracy.

Democracy requires, at a minimum, a tolerance of different groups and ideologies, an abiding faith that conflicts can be resolved through reasoned discussion and compromise, and the willingness to abide by decisions that one does not like and to support one's government even when it is dominated by the political opposition. Most fundamentally, democracy requires a degree of trust between its leaders and its masses.

This element of democratic political culture is, of course, challenged when a nation fears for its safety. Following the September 11, 2001, terrorist attacks, there were reports of hate crimes against Muslims and Arabs, although at levels far below what some had predicted. President George W. Bush called for tolerance of persons of the Islamic faith, and leaders throughout the country echoed this call. The overwhelming majority of Americans were able to make a distinction between Islam and terrorism. Most Americans did not define the "war on terrorism" that followed the terrorist attacks on the United States as a war against Islam, although Osama bin Laden and his followers sought to characterize the conflict in such terms. The public response to President Bush's actions and messages after the terrorist attack indicated a high level of public trust in the president. Unfortunately for President Bush, public trust in his leadership waned considerably after the controversial decision in early 2003 to invade Iraq and topple Saddam Hussein.

1-3 The Contours of American Political Culture

American political culture is not only fundamentally democratic and antiauthoritarian but also varied and complex. It varies across regions of the country and among groups in society. Moreover, American political culture is constantly evolving, reflecting the demographic, economic, and technological changes in society. Despite the tremendous diversity that now characterizes this country, the broad outlines of American political culture remain clearly discernible.

To a great extent, contemporary American political culture still reflects the values of the European people who settled this country hundreds of years ago. Settlers did not come with a blank cultural slate; they brought with them elements of the cultures of their native lands. Educated people brought with them the knowledge of political philosophy. Many regarded America as a grand experiment in political science—a place where the best ideas from the history of political thought could be put into practice. Most people who came to this country in its early days were not, of course, highly educated. Yet they brought with them something as important as knowledge of political theory: a thirst for freedom and a desire for a better way of life.

American political culture is also a product of the land itself. Geographically, America was very different from Europe. The challenge of confronting the wilderness and the frontier made different demands on the political system than had been the case in relatively civilized Europe. Much of what is special about American culture is related to its frontier history. On the frontier, settlers did not have the luxury of a social support system, but had to face challenges themselves. Thus, the individual came to be, and still remains, at the core of "American values." Thus, the dominant characteristic of American political culture is **individualism**.[14]

To many people, individualism means self-reliance, or what has been called "rugged individualism." To a great extent, rugged individualism is a thing of the past, a vestige of the frontier. All of us are dependent now on each other and on government to an extent that many of us do not realize. But Americans still value individualism. We admire the entrepreneur, the inventor, and the artist. For the most part, Americans understand that individualism also means the right to express an alternative point of view or pursue an unconventional lifestyle, even one that most people find offensive. To a great extent, the rugged individualism of the American frontier has been replaced by the "expressive individualism" of an increasingly diverse, rapidly changing society.

> **individualism** A concept used to refer to the American idea of self-reliance, especially as it applies to economic and social activities.

1-3a Regional Variations in American Political Culture

Individualism is inextricably intertwined with Americans' faith in democracy. Indeed, individualism colors the way in which American democracy operates and the kinds of policies it produces. But individualism does not have a monopoly on the political culture. Individualism exists in constant tension with Americans' attachments to traditional values and their desire to foster a good society. One can find various mixtures of these competing cultural values in different regions of the country, reflecting the predispositions to government and politics of the groups that settled there.

In the 1960s, the political scientist Daniel Elazar helped to popularize the concept of political culture as a way of understanding American politics. According to Elazar, the European settlers brought with them two competing perspectives on what politics in America should be about. The first perspective views government's role as that of protecting a marketplace of individuals and groups as they pursue their economic self-interest. The second perspective is that government should protect and nurture that which individuals and groups have in common.[15] In this view, the role of government is to nurture society in general rather than nurture the potential for individuals to achieve success.

Popular Culture and American Politics
High Noon

© John Springer Collection / CORBIS

In the classic film *High Noon* (1952), Marshal Kane (Gary Cooper) prepares to face a gang of outlaws alone.

American popular culture reflects and reinforces the value of individualism by celebrating the heroic individual. In *High Noon* (1952), Will Kane, played by Gary Cooper, is the marshal in a small, isolated Western town. Kane learns that a killer he had sent to prison has just been released and is seeking revenge on the marshal and the town. As the killer approaches with his outlaw gang, Kane has a choice: He can run from the confrontation, or he can put together a force to defend the town. After wavering, and even leaving once, Kane decides to stand and fight. His choice is all the more difficult because he has just gotten married and is at the end of his term in office.

But when Kane asks for help, nobody will join him. Those who had supported him over the years turn away. Even his deputy, ambitious for the marshal's job, refuses. Kane must walk alone into the corral at high noon. Every step on his lonely trek to face the enemy reminds us that he must do his duty not only for himself but also for his town and that he will confront the four evil men by himself. One by one, Kane guns down the outlaws. The townsfolk then come out of hiding to cheer him. But Kane contemptuously throws down his badge and rides away with his bride.

High Noon celebrates the individual's abilities and the responsibility to do one's duty. At the same time, its negative view of the broader society is merciless. When the sun was high in the sky on that day, the town needed Will Kane, but its people weren't there for him. Will Kane didn't really need the town, but he was there to save it. The message of the film is that if greatness is among us, it will be found in certain special individuals who are fated to act alone.

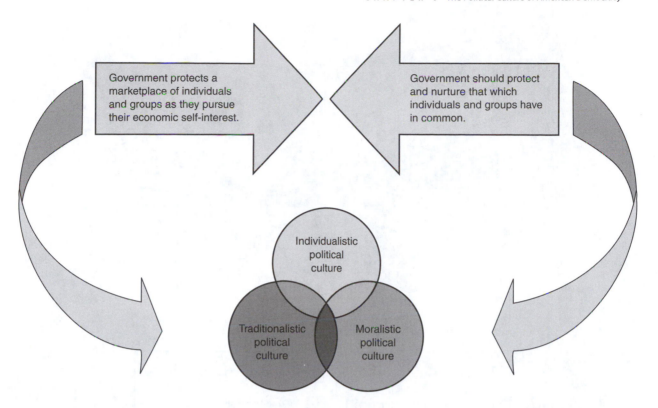

Figure 1-2
Daniel Elazar's Model of American Political Culture

In Elazar's model, two competing cultural forces blend to form a three-layer tapestry of American culture.

Elazar sought to explain the variation in political cultures among the American states as blends of these two competing cultural currents (see Figure 1-2). He described the fabric of American political culture as a tapestry of three subcultures, each of which found a different way to combine protecting the individual with fostering the needs of society.[16]

In the *individualistic political culture*, government exists mainly to keep order in the marketplace. The role of government is quite limited; it need not concern itself with fostering the "good society." Individual responsibility for one's actions is stressed. This culture would not support the government's becoming involved in how a person uses his or her land. Nor would it support laws making it criminal for people to do irresponsible things that affect only themselves—the so-called victimless crimes.

The government in a *moralistic political culture* stresses the public good over the rights of the individual and enters people's lives in a variety of ways to ensure that the "general welfare" is advanced and the "good society" achieved. One might expect states in which this culture is dominant to tax and spend more and to provide more social services. One might also expect more restrictions on individual conduct that is deemed contrary to the public welfare.

In a *traditionalistic political culture*, government becomes somewhat involved in defining the "good society." Rather than expect government to ensure a certain level of public welfare, however, this culture would support government involvement to protect traditional values. For instance, this type of government would be likely to try to legislate against homosexuality, which violates traditional restrictions on sexual conduct. On the other hand, the government might not adopt strong measures to counter race or sex discrimination because the inequalities that these types of discrimination perpetuate are part of the traditional social order.

The map shown in Figure 1-3 provides a rough approximation of Elazar's mapping of the various political cultures across the United States, as he perceived them in the 1960s. Note that the regions vary considerably. The South, where church attendance is the highest, is predominantly traditionalistic. The individualistic culture is strongest in parts of the

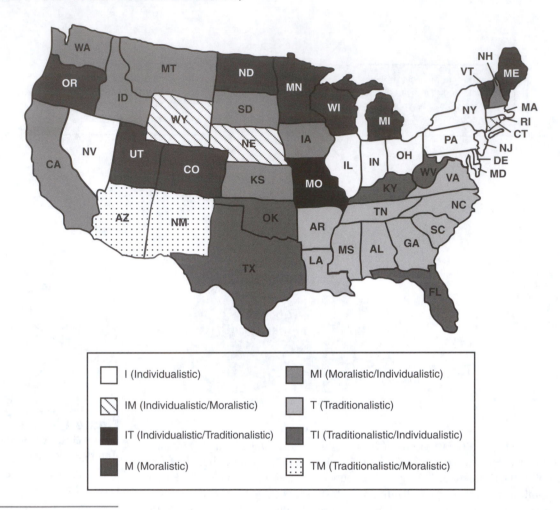

I (Individualistic)   MI (Moralistic/Individualistic)

IM (Individualistic/Moralistic)   T (Traditionalistic)

IT (Individualistic/Traditionalistic)   TI (Traditionalistic/Individualistic)

M (Moralistic)   TM (Traditionalistic/Moralistic)

Figure 1-3
**Dominant Political Culture
by State**

Source: Adapted from Daniel J. Elazar,
American Federalism: A View from the States
(New York: Thomas Crowell, 1966), p. 108.

Northeast and Midwest, where diverse immigrant groups have intermingled, and in parts of the West, where the frontier ideal is still popular. The moralistic culture is centered in the Upper Midwest, where state governments have maintained active roles, especially in spending on education. Yet these are all variations around the basic American political culture. American regions are still more alike than different when compared to other countries. The differences that do exist may well be attributed to what the settlers brought with them. For instance, the moralistic culture of Minnesota and Wisconsin may be an extension of the cultures found in Scandinavia, especially Sweden, where the individual takes much of his or her identity from the society.

1-3b The American Political Consensus

Although individualism and support for democratic institutions are the fundamental characteristics of American political culture, a number of other important values also comprise what is called "the American national character," "the American political consensus," or "the American way of life." Chief among these values are commitments to individual freedom, equality of opportunity, and the rule of law. These commitments are far from complete, not universally shared, and are sometimes overtaken by competing values and sentiments.

The Commitment to Individual Freedom   In the abstract, *liberty* is the right of the individual to be free from undue interference or restraint by government. Liberty presupposes that individuals are capable of rationally determining what is in their best interests. Americans are lovers of freedom. The word resonates through our culture. American literature, music, cinema, theater, and poetry all celebrate the idea of human freedom. But what do Americans mean by "freedom"?

Certainly, most Americans support the idea of free expression that is enshrined in the First Amendment to the Constitution. Americans believe in the right to speak one's mind, especially to offer criticism of the government. But in the mid-twentieth century, the American people supported a variety of restrictions on those who embraced communism and other radical political ideas. The public seemed unwilling to support freedom of expression when it involved "un-American" ideas. The question of free expression now has more to do with the issues of pornography and violence than with radical political ideas. Some people feel that pornography is degrading to women and actually perpetuates sex discrimination. Many believe that graphic depictions of violence in television shows, movies, and video games contribute to the epidemic of violence in society. Although no one claims to support pornography and violence, the public seems to have strong appetites for both. Those who produce and profit from such fare claim the protection of the First Amendment. But history suggests that when the American public feels seriously threatened, the constitutional guarantee of freedom of expression will give way.

Faith and Freedom   One of the principal reasons that people left Europe to come to the New World was to escape religious persecution. Recognizing the centrality of religion in the life of the American people, the framers of the Bill of Rights included in the First Amendment a guarantee of the free exercise of religion and a prohibition against government establishing one religion as the official creed of the United States. Religion remains important in the lives of Americans. Americans are more likely to express a belief in God and to attend church than are citizens of the democracies of Western Europe. Polls reveal that a strong majority of people in this country think that believing in God is an important part of what it means to be a "true American." As Yale law professor Stephen Carter notes, "deep religiosity has always been a facet of the American character."[17]

This country was settled primarily by Protestants, although Roman Catholics and Jews have always had a significant presence in the United States. The proportions of Jews and Catholics in the population increased significantly as a result of the great waves of immigration from Southern and Eastern Europe in the late nineteenth and early twentieth centuries. These new immigrants were not always greeted with hospitality. The Ku Klux Klan and other nativist groups fanned the flames of intolerance. Jews, in particular, have often been the victims of discrimination and even persecution. The Constitution guarantees people the right to exercise their religion freely, although it does not (and cannot) guarantee social acceptance. Now, however, anti-Semitism and anti-Romanism have largely subsided in this country. The contemporary conflict over religion has a very different character.

The conflict over religion now has more to do with whether, and to what extent, government acknowledges, accommodates, and supports religious beliefs and practices. No one doubts that the framers of the Bill of Rights meant to prohibit the establishment of a national religion. But does the Constitution also require a strict separation of religion and government? Is government required to be neutral and detached on matters of religious belief?

The Pledge of Allegiance calls America "one nation under God." The Declaration of Independence invokes the "firm protection of divine Providence." Our currency bears the slogan "In God We Trust." Congress begins its sessions with a prayer. Even the Supreme Court begins its public sessions with the statement "God save the United States and this honorable Court." Christmas is a national holiday. Our most popular patriotic song is "God Bless America." Only the strongest advocates of the separation of church and state would object to public affirmations of America's religious heritage. But what about organized prayer and Bible reading in the public schools? Or religious invocations at public school graduation exercises? Though supported by large majorities in the communities where they took place, these practices have been challenged and declared unconstitutional by the courts (see Case in Point 1-1). In one controversial decision in the mid-1980s, the Supreme Court even held that it was unconstitutional for a state to require its public school students to observe a moment of silence for the purpose of prayer or meditation.[18] More recently, the Court has struck down the practices of offering invocations at high school graduation exercises and high school football games.[19]

Case in Point 1-1

Does Government Have the Power to Force American Citizens to Embrace a National Symbol?

***West Virginia v. Barnette* (1943) and *Texas v. Johnson* (1989)**

In 1942, Walter Barnette and two other members of the Jehovah's Witnesses, all of whom had children in the public schools, filed a lawsuit to prohibit school officials from requiring their children to participate in a daily flag salute ceremony. According to their religious beliefs, the flag salute constituted worship of a "graven image" in violation of Scripture. Dividing 6-3, the Supreme Court declared the compulsory flag salute unconstitutional. Writing for the Court, Justice Robert H. Jackson observed that "if there is any fixed star in our constitutional constellation, it is that no official, high or petty, can prescribe what shall be orthodox in politics, nationalism, religion, or other matters of opinion or force citizens to confess by word or act their faith therein."

In 1984, Gregory Lee Johnson burned an American flag on a Dallas street outside the building where the Republican Party was holding its national convention. Although he claimed that his action was a legitimate protest against American foreign policies, Johnson was convicted of desecrating a flag in violation of Texas law. The Texas Court of Criminal Appeals reversed the conviction, holding that the law under which Johnson was convicted was unconstitutional. The Supreme Court, in a controversial 5-4 decision, agreed. Writing for the Court, Justice William Brennan observed that "we do not consecrate the flag by punishing its desecration, for in doing so we dilute the freedom that this cherished emblem represents."

Capitol police arrest a protestor for burning the American flag on the step of the Capitol, October 1989.

AP Photo / FILE / Charles Tasnadi

Atheists and agnostics, as well as Unitarians and members of other religious minorities, have figured prominently in challenges to school prayer. Needless to say, these people have not always endeared themselves to the general public. But the idea of separation of church and state has advocates among all the nation's religions—people who believe that religious liberty is best ensured if government stays out of it. On the other side of the issue are religious people, often fundamentalist Protestants, who sincerely believe that America is turning its back on its religious heritage. In particular, they argue that the public schools have fallen under the influence of **secular humanism**, "an educational philosophy characterized by an emphasis on moral relativism and the celebration of self."[20] These critics of the contemporary educational system believe that America always has been, is now, and should forever be a religious nation. In their view, the government's acknowledgment of this statement is both necessary and proper. Many religious people believe that by contributing to the erosion of religious faith, government undermines traditional values and institutions and hastens the nation's demise.

Many of the religious people who support school prayer and oppose secular humanism live in rural areas or small towns where communities are religiously homogeneous. But the United States is increasingly diverse religiously, especially in urban areas. People from India, Africa, the Middle East, and China, whose religious orientations are more likely to be Hindu, Islamic, or Buddhist, are not likely to agree that this is a "Christian nation" or that students in the public schools would be better off reading the Bible than modern social studies textbooks. As this country becomes even more diverse, it will be more difficult to maintain a societal consensus in support of public affirmations of religion.

Freedom, Autonomy, and Privacy America has a strong tradition of personal and familial privacy. Americans have always reacted negatively to attempts by government to interfere in people's private lives, whether through eavesdropping or legislation. The courts have recognized that people have a right of privacy under the Constitution.[21] The growing consensus now is that government should not interfere in people's sexual relationships. The old laws forbidding adultery, fornication, and contraception have largely been done away with through judicial decisions, legislative action, or simple nonenforcement. The Supreme Court has even said that the constitutional right of privacy is broad enough to include the right of a woman to have an abortion.[22] And although many people are troubled by the number of abortions performed in this country, and a vocal minority intensely opposes legalized abortion, public opinion is generally supportive of a "woman's right to choose."

Today, one of the most heated public issues is that of gay rights. Historically, gay men and lesbians generally remained "in the closet." But in the 1960s and 1970s, many began to "come out" and admit their sexual orientation. Many did so at the risk of alienating friends and losing their jobs. In the 1980s, gays organized and began to push for social acceptance, political power, and legal protection against discrimination. Today, people are rarely prosecuted for engaging in private homosexual conduct, at least outside the military services. Again, most people do not believe that government should intervene in people's private lives. Expressing this cultural theme, the Supreme Court in 2003 struck down a Texas law that criminalized private, consensual homosexual conduct. Writing for the Supreme Court in *Lawrence v. Texas*, Justice Anthony Kennedy observed:

> Liberty protects the person from unwarranted government intrusions into a dwelling or other private places. In our tradition the State is not omnipresent in the home. And there are other spheres of our lives and existence, outside the home, where the State should not be a dominant presence. Freedom extends beyond spatial bounds. Liberty presumes an autonomy of self that includes freedom of thought, belief, expression, and certain intimate conduct.[23]

Economic Liberty: Support for the Free Enterprise System The area of American social life in which our individualism has manifested itself most clearly is the economy. America has a capitalist economy built on deep-seated cultural commitments to the values of private property and free enterprise. As Table 1-2 shows, the overwhelming majority of Americans credit the free enterprise system for making the United States a great

▶ **secular humanism**
A philosophy that elevates human interests, desires, and values over religious beliefs and precepts.

TABLE 1-2					
Things That Made America Great	**Reason**	**Percentage Saying "Major Reason"**	**Percentage Saying "Minor Reason"**	**Percentage Saying "Not a Reason"**	**Percentage Saying "Don't Know"**
	The U.S. Constitution	85	10	4	1
	Free elections	84	11	3	2
	Free enterprise system	81	11	4	4
	Abundant natural resources	78	15	4	3
	Cultural diversity	71	20	6	3
	Freedom of the press	69	22	7	2
	Character of the American people	69	21	8	2
	God's will	65	15	16	4
	Geographic isolation	53	26	17	4
	Two-party system	49	32	13	6
	Judeo-Christian beliefs	41	28	20	11
	Separation of church & state	41	33	23	3
	Good luck	25	30	43	2

Source: National telephone survey of 1,546 adults conducted by Princeton Survey Research Associates, April 6 to May 6, 1999.

laissez-faire The principle that there should be minimal governmental interference with the free enterprise system.

regulatory state A characterization used to describe the increasing role of government in the economic affairs of American citizens subsequent to the industrial revolution.

welfare state A characterization used to describe the increasing role of government in creating programs to ensure social welfare.

country. Until the late nineteenth century, American government followed the doctrine of *laissez-faire,* or minimal interference with the free enterprise system. As the Industrial Revolution progressed, however, public support for government intervention began to grow. Increasingly, people began to look to government to regulate the excesses of the market economy and ensure a minimal standard of living. Changing attitudes led to the establishment of the modern **regulatory state** and the **welfare state,** terms that highlight the modern relationship of government to the economy. Although American political culture has come to accept, and even demand, a role for government in managing the economy, there is clearly a limit to which the public will support government efforts to redistribute wealth to the less fortunate.

Equality in American Political Culture Another core value of democracy is equality. Americans believe in equality. After all, the Declaration of Independence declares that "all men are created equal." But what type of equality do Americans believe in? The Constitution guarantees "equal protection of the laws," that is, equality before the law. Historically, however, African Americans, women, and various minority groups have been denied legal equality. To a great extent, these legal inequalities have been eradicated, although social and economic inequalities clearly remain.

When polled, the overwhelming majority of Americans agree that people should be treated equally without regard to their race, sex, or religion. Of course, not everyone lives up to this ideal. People in this country, as elsewhere in the world, still harbor prejudices that affect their attitudes and behavior toward people who are "different." Prejudice in the form of racism, sexism, and religious bigotry is one cause of economic inequality, although it is certainly not the only cause.

American political culture does not offer much support for the idea that it is government's responsibility to eliminate social and economic inequalities. On the contrary, most people believe that trying to get ahead on one's own is an important part of what

Percentage Saying Characteristic is "Essential or Very Important"		TABLE 1-3
Ambition	90	**Getting Ahead in Life**
Having a good education	88	
Natural ability	87	
Knowing the right people	43	
Having well-educated parents	41	
Coming from a wealthy family	18	
Having political connections	18	
Being born a man or woman	17	
A person's race	15	
A person's religion	15	
A person's political beliefs	11	

Source: International social survey program (National Opinion Research Center, February/April 1992).

it means to be a true American (see Table 1-3). Most Americans believe that they will do well in society if they are ambitious, educated, and hard working. About half as many Americans believe that success can be achieved through having connections, and fewer still think that success is based on race, sex, or religion. The belief that a person can get ahead through his or her abilities, hard work, and ambition is a key element of American political culture. This way of thinking is so fundamental to most Americans that many do not realize that it is not shared by people in other societies. Thus, to most Americans, the marriage of democracy and capitalism seems perfectly natural. To substantial numbers of people living in other democratic countries, however, including Great Britain, Sweden, and even Canada, democracy and capitalism seem incompatible. In their view, it is government's job to reduce the inequalities that result from the operation of the marketplace.

The Rule of Law and the Problem of Violence   Americans are committed to the **rule of law** as a core democratic value. This commitment is most clearly expressed in the U.S. Constitution and the judicial institutions that interpret and enforce its principles. The American legal system is highly developed and tremendously complex. If citizens feel that they have been wronged by others, they have opportunities to seek justice through the courts, which operate according to rational and clear procedures. Likewise, criminal behavior is clearly defined by government, with specific rules limiting government officials as they arrest and prosecute those suspected of having committed a crime. In many ways, this society's commitment to the rule of law is reflected in its very large number of attorneys. The United States has more attorneys per capita than any other nation on earth.

> **rule of law**   The idea that the power of government is based on legal principles rather than on the personal wishes of the rulers.

Despite America's apparent commitment to the rule of law, Americans have a persistent tendency to settle disputes outside the legal system. Alongside the highly developed legal system exists a parallel criminal world that follows different rules. These rules are akin to those of the frontier—complete with violent outlaws and vigilante justice. By the end of the twentieth century, America was awash in images of violence and bloodshed. Guns were readily available to young people, and, despite declines at the end of the century, the murder rate in American cities remained far higher than in any other advanced nation. Moreover, major incidents of students murdering their classmates in Colorado, Kentucky, Oregon, Mississippi, Arkansas, and Michigan became imprinted on the nation's conscience.

How could this lawlessness persist in a nation committed to the rule of law? Or, to put it another way, how can a nation remain committed to the rule of law when so many operate

*Profiles &
Perspectives*

**Alexis de Tocqueville
(1805–1859)**

© Bettman / CORBIS

Some of the best commentary on American political culture was offered more than 150 years ago by the French aristocrat Alexis de Tocqueville, who toured the United States for nine months in 1831. Tocqueville filled fourteen notebooks with his observations of American public life. In 1835 he published *Democracy in America*, a two-volume work that remains one of the classics of American political science. *Democracy in America* describes an emerging democracy where the "aristocratic principle" has been all but buried. Tocqueville placed considerable emphasis on the "habits of the heart" that he believed were nurturing the emerging American democracy. He stressed the importance of the family and Christianity in developing tolerance and shaping a sense of obligation to obey the law and work for the common good. But Tocqueville also identified forces that he believed could threaten the success of American democracy. One of the these was majoritarianism, which, if unchecked, could threaten the rights of minorities and individuals. But Tocqueville also recognized the danger of unbridled individualism, which carried the potential to undermine morality, institutions, and culture itself. Tocqueville wrote: "The democratic principle . . . has gained so much strength by time, by events, and by legislation, as to have become not only predominant but all-powerful. There is no family or corporate authority, and it is rare to find even the influence of individual character enjoying any durability."

For more information on de Tocqueville including articles and books, go to http://www.tocqueville.org/.

outside the law? Is this violence an indelible part of our national character? Does it suggest a breakdown of social norms and institutions? Is it a function of the easy availability of guns? Is it being encouraged by our mass media and popular culture? Obviously, the answers to these questions are not mutually exclusive.

Some have attributed America's seeming obsession with violence to the influence of the frontier culture on the American character.[24] Since the frontier days, Americans have widely believed that firearms should be easily available. But as crime and violence reached epidemic proportions in the 1980s, many people began to question the wisdom of allowing guns to be produced, sold, possessed, and used without significant restrictions. In the 1990s, a sharp, and often angry, debate developed between the advocates of gun control and the proponents of the "right to keep and bear arms." This debate continued into the first decade of the twenty-first century and will likely go on for years to come.

Many believe that the violence on television and in recorded music stimulates violent behavior, especially among young people. In the 1990s, a loud outcry occurred over rap songs such as "Cop Killer." A number of groups, including police officers, began to urge major record companies to refuse to market material that seems to encourage or glorify murder. This mode of expression often glorified violence against women as well as members of opposition gangs and the police. By the turn of the century, the appeal crossed over to mainstream audiences. Many people, especially inner-city youth, were drawn to rap as a compelling expression of the grim realities of the urban experience. But others maintained that its violent lyrics legitimized and glamorized violence.

The debate remained: Were the media merely reflecting the national mood, or were they in fact contributing to it? Although this question was not easily answered, politicians were feeling the heat. Some members of Congress threatened to consider regulating the content of network television. A large segment of American society wanted government to rein in some elements of the popular culture. The rule of law seemed preferable to the law of the jungle. Nevertheless, characterizing Americans as being of one mind on these issues would be a mistake. Although some people thought that government ought to assume responsibility for community safety, others remained skeptical of enforcing community values that would limit the rights of individuals. Of course, this disagreement was not new. Americans have always disagreed about the appropriate role of government. As you have seen, much of this disagreement is traceable to the differing cultural backgrounds of the people who came to this country and their experiences in settling it.

1-3c Institutions and American Political Culture

An **institution** is an established pattern of behavior that transcends and outlives the individuals who occupy it. Government agencies, corporations, churches, universities, and professional sports teams certainly all qualify as institutions, but so do some social arrangements that may not be so obvious. You can divide American institutions into three broad categories: **governmental institutions,** the existence of which may be traced to the federal and state constitutions; **intermediary institutions,** which are quasipublic institutions, such as political parties, that mediate between government and the people; and **societal institutions,** which exist primarily by custom and are not primarily political in character. The family is a good example of a societal institution.

Governmental Institutions   Much of this book is devoted to describing the workings of governmental institutions in the United States: the Congress, the presidency, the Supreme Court and other courts of law, and the many bureaucratic agencies that exist at all levels of government. At the beginning of the twenty-first century, serious concern exists over whether governmental institutions that were designed in the eighteenth century can manage the complex problems of the postindustrial age and meet the demands of an increasingly diverse society. The American people appear to be losing faith in their institutions. Long-term trends in public opinion show that Americans now have less confidence in their institutions and less faith in their leaders than they did thirty years ago. Since the early 1970s, due in part to the failure in Vietnam and the Watergate scandal, popular trust and confidence in government have been in decline. Given this declining public trust and the increasingly difficult problems to be managed, one must ask whether American institutions can continue to govern without serious modification. The question is far from academic—and the answer has implications for the quality of life of future generations of Americans.

Intermediary Institutions   Governmental bodies are not the only institutions of importance in the United States or in any democracy. Political scientists consider political parties, interest groups, and the mass media to be nearly as important as government in the political system. Because these entities provide linkages between the governing elites and the masses, they are sometimes referred to as *intermediary* institutions. These institutions help connect people to the political process by providing channels for political participation or at least a means of following what government is doing. Few people are elected or appointed to high public office, but millions of people can join interest groups or get involved in political parties. And nearly everyone in society has access to television, radio, and newspapers.

Societal Institutions   Basic societal institutions—such as the family, school, and church, although not primarily political entities—play an important role in **political socialization,** the transmission of political values and beliefs. Accordingly, as primary agents of political culture, these institutions may provide considerable support for a particular political system. Over the past several decades, some commentators have expressed concern about the apparent erosion of these institutions: the breakdown of the family, the decline of organized religion, and the crisis in the public schools. This concern is partially motivated by the important role these institutions have played historically in holding the nation together, maintaining social order and stability, and transmitting values that foster political and economic progress.

Some commentators believe that the tremendous social and economic change that America has experienced over the past century has undermined the societal institutions that have nurtured our democratic political culture. These commentators, who may be referred to as **communitarians,** believe that unbridled individualism is corrosive to a democratic political system. They fear that American citizens are losing their sense of community and their commitment to the **public interest.** Communitarians worry that Americans are increasingly unwilling to make the kinds of sacrifices that are sometimes necessary to ensure the long-term survival of the political system. In his widely read book *Habits of the Heart,* sociologist Robert Bellah argues that Americans "have committed what to the republican founders of our nation was the cardinal sin: We have put our own good, as individuals, as

---

institution   An established pattern of behavior that transcends and outlives the individuals who occupy it.

governmental institutions   Specific offices of government that have the authority to make rules that are binding on society.

intermediary institutions   Institutions, such as political parties and interest groups, that mediate between government and the people.

societal institutions   Institutions that exist primarily by custom and are not primarily political in character.

political socialization   The transmission of political values and beliefs; the process by which people learn about their political world.

communitarians   Those who believe that unbridled individualism is corrosive to a democratic political system. Their concern is that American citizens are losing their sense of community and their sense of the public interest.

public interest   A common interest shared by all members of the society.

groups, as a nation, ahead of the common good."[25] In a similar vein, sociologist Robert Put-nam argues that the relationships that traditionally bound Americans into a civil society have badly decayed, leading to a deficit in "social capital."[26]

> **public regardedness**   A willingness to acknowledge public interests that are superior to one's immediate self-interest and, moreover, a willingness to sacrifice one's interests for the common good.

Although this textbook is not intended as a manual in good citizenship, one must recognize the importance of citizenship in maintaining a strong political system. Part of citizenship is **public regardedness,** a willingness to acknowledge public interests that are superior to one's immediate self-interest and, moreover, a willingness to sacrifice one's interests for the common good. Although democracy may rest ultimately on a foundation of individualism (certainly, Lockean liberalism rests on this premise), it, like all political systems, must maintain a reasonable degree of integration, lest the system degenerate into ungovernable chaos. Thus, providing the shared values and symbols that help to hold a nation together is the vital function of political culture.

> **multiculturalism**   The belief that different cultures can and should coexist in the same society.

Unfortunately, two powerful forces work against the maintenance of an integrated political culture in this country. One is our highly successful capitalist economy, which is "a relentless engine of change, a revolutionary inflamer of appetites."[27] The other is the ever increasing ethnic, racial, and religious diversity of our society. And the goal of maintaining an integrated political culture seems hard to reconcile with the current drive toward **multiculturalism,** the belief that different cultures can and should coexist in the same society. The nation's old motto "E pluribus unum," meaning "Out of many, one," has fallen into disfavor in some quarters. The traditional idea that America should be a melting pot for people of different cultures is increasingly being rejected in favor of the belief that immigrants should strive to maintain their distinct cultural identity. Yet, when polled, most Americans still come down on the side of the melting pot. Native Americans are the only exception to this trend. By a margin of 2-1, Native Americans believe in maintaining their own distinctive culture. Asian Americans are the most likely to favor the concept of the melting pot, which may help to explain their rapid economic advancement in this society.

The historian Arthur M. Schlesinger puts the issue succinctly: "The question America confronts as a pluralistic society is how to vindicate cherished cultures and traditions without breaking the bonds of cohesion—common ideals, common political institutions, common language, common culture, common fate—that hold the republic together."[28]

1-3d The Evolving American Political Culture

American political culture is constantly changing. Of course, by their very nature, cultures change slowly. Values persist, and culture persists. Yet American political culture has been evolving in a number of ways. First, although regionalism is still an important force in American politics, American political culture has become somewhat nationalized. The South, the part of the country with the most distinctive political culture, has become much more like the rest of the country. Two major reasons underlie the nationalization of American political culture. First, the media in the United States are national. No matter where people live, they likely watch the same television programs, read the same news magazines, and watch the same news. Second, the national government has clearly become dominant over the states, and the federal courts have long since ruled that states may not restrict the rights of minorities in order to maintain the region's traditions.

Other changes in American political culture reflect shifts in the larger societal culture. American society has become much more open than it once was. Fewer constraints are placed on personal expression. One can see this readily in the popular culture—movies, music, television, novels, plays, and the like. For example, the difference between television programs in the early part of the twenty-first century and those from the late 1950s and early 1960s is tremendous, especially in the portrayal of sexuality and family life. *Ozzie and Harriet* has given way to *The Osbournes.*

In addition to wider boundaries for personal expression, Americans are now much more tolerant of a variety of lifestyles. Some states and cities now have laws prohibiting discrimination on the basis of sexual orientation. Many American political jurisdictions now allow live-in partners to receive health benefits formerly reserved for spouses. In some cities, such as New York, gay and lesbian couples can be considered partners for purposes of receiving benefits. In Vermont, gay and lesbian couples can enter into civil unions that legally resemble marriages. Other states are on the verge of legalizing gay marriage through the courts. Such policies would have been inconceivable as recently as a decade ago.

A Cultural War? American political culture has followed and reflected the changes in the broader societal culture. Many Americans have criticized these changes and sought to use politics to put a brake on cultural change. The presidential candidate Pat Buchanan, addressing the Republican convention in the summer of 1992, spoke of a cultural war in the nation. Buchanan was referring to legalized abortion, gay rights, and other trends that he thought threatened the moral foundations of the country. In many ways, Buchanan wanted to frame the election as a contest between the defenders of traditional American culture and those who would attack it. Although Buchanan's speech undoubtedly struck a chord in society, it also alienated many who saw his attack as intolerant. The political culture of the early 1990s set the parameters for this public debate, which could not have occurred twenty years earlier; at that time, the culture itself had not yet rendered many of these topics suitable for open discussion.

In 2000, the Republican candidate George W. Bush sensed that America wanted no part of a cultural war, and he used the Republican national convention to offer a portrait of a diverse, softer, kinder Republican party—far from the judgmental, overbearing picture painted by Buchanan eight years earlier. Bush's sense of the electorate proved to be correct and helped him win a narrow victory in the presidential election. Seeking reelection in 2004, President Bush said little about these cultural themes, stressing instead the war on terrorism. Although Americans may not want to engage in overt cultural warfare, many are troubled by the current pace and direction of cultural change.[29] And there is little doubt that an upsurge in "cultural conservatism" helped to secure President Bush's reelection in 2004. Voters motivated primarily by concern for "moral values" voted nearly eight to one in favor of George W. Bush in 2004.[30]

1-3e Ideology

When people talk of a cultural war in the United States, they typically frame the conflict in terms of two opposing ideologies—liberalism and conservatism. The concept of **ideology** is related to political culture, but is conceptually distinct. Ideology refers to a coherent system of beliefs and values that lead people to form opinions on social, economic, and political questions. American ideologies are typically defined in terms of the **liberal-conservative continuum** (see Figure 1-4). People at the center of the spectrum are **moderates;** those to the right of center are **conservatives;** and those to the left are known as **liberals.** The left-right formulation can be traced to the seating patterns of delegates to the national assembly after the French Revolution: Liberals sat on the left, conservatives on the right.

To put it simply, conservatives believe in maintaining traditional values and institutions, whereas liberals favor reform and progress. Conservatives, on the other hand, are generally pessimistic about the desirability and possibility of social progress. They prefer order and stability to progressive experimentation. For liberals, progress is defined in terms of the core values of democracy—namely, freedom and equality. Thus, liberals have sought to use the power of government to promote economic equality and social justice. Conser-

ideology A coherent system of political beliefs and values, such as conservatism or liberalism; those ideas, or system of ideas, that are in conflict in society.

liberal-conservative continuum The standard approach to describing the range of political ideologies in the United States.

moderates Those persons who are in the middle of the liberal-conservative continuum; that is, neither liberal nor conservative. Also known as "centrists."

conservatives Those persons on the right of the liberal-conservative continuum. Generally speaking, conservatives believe in maintaining traditional values and institutions.

liberals Those persons on the left of the liberal-conservative continuum. Generally speaking, liberals favor progress and reform and question traditional modes of thought and behavior.

Figure 1-4
The Liberal-Conservative Spectrum

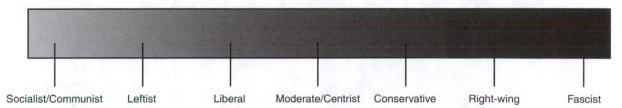

| Socialist/Communist | Leftist | Liberal | Moderate/Centrist | Conservative | Right-wing | Fascist |

vatives have argued against government interference in the free enterprise system but have looked to government as a means of preserving the social order.

Obviously, liberals have a more favorable view of human nature than do conservatives. Liberals want to loosen social controls so as to unleash the creative energies of the individual. The conservative, not having much faith in human nature, would argue that constraints should be maintained on the appetites and passions of individuals. Accordingly, conservatives tend to favor traditional institutions, such as the family and the church, as a means of maintaining these constraints. Liberals are more likely to see institutions such as the church and the family as sources of unnecessary repression. These basic philosophical differences have led to debates over civil rights, feminism, gay rights, prayer in public schools, welfare programs, and many other issues of public policy. Ideology also tends to be a major factor in voting behavior, especially in recent presidential elections. For example, in 2004, 85 percent of self-identified liberals voted for the Democratic candidate, Senator John Kerry, whereas 84 percent of conservatives voted to reelect President Bush.[31]

1-4 Conclusion: Politics and the American Future

Because of the inherent dynamism of capitalism, the ever-increasing diversity of American society, and the constantly accelerating pace of life in the information age, politics in America is complex and dynamic. The student of American government may at times feel overwhelmed by the myriad perspectives, theories, and ideologies of American politics, let alone the tremendous volume of factual information being generated on the subject. No one, from presidents to pundits, can legitimately claim to understand all there is to comprehend about American politics and government. Nevertheless, in a democratic society such as ours, citizens must make the effort.

The dynamics of American politics take place in an evolving political culture that sets the limits for political discourse and action. This culture, with its roots in the American frontier and its commitment to free-market capitalism, has changed greatly as the broader societal culture has been transformed. At the beginning of the twenty-first century, the American political system faces a number of serious challenges. Perhaps the most fundamental of these is the governance of a society that is becoming increasingly diverse. How can such a society maintain the integrated political culture necessary to sustain democratic institutions? Can American democracy survive an attack by outsiders who characterize their grievances in terms of a religious war without a lessening of religious tolerance in this country? In the decades to come, American democracy must find a way to ensure that diversity is a source of strength rather than a threat to the viability of the system.

Questions for Thought and Discussion

1. Why do Americans tend to hold negative views of politics and politicians?
2. Is it possible to conceive of a political system in a modern mass society in which all citizens who desire could participate equally in the making of public decisions?
3. How much do political cultures change? What are the factors that cause them to change?
4. Why is individualism the dominant characteristic of American political culture? How is the nature of American individualism changing?
5. How have the liberal and conservative ideologies changed since the United States was founded? Do any underlying continuities exist in these opposing ideologies?

Practice Quiz

Note: You can find the correct answers to these questions by taking the quiz and then submitting your answers in the Online Edition. The program will automatically score your submission. If you miss a question, the program will provide the correct answer, a rationale for the answer, and the section number in the chapter where the topic is discussed.

1. _____ political culture stresses the need for government to become involved in defining and achieving the "good society."
   a. An individualistic
   b. A moralistic
   c. A traditionalistic
   d. An authoritarian

2. In providing public benefits, government _____.
   a. almost always provides goods that benefit each citizen equally
   b. provides only those goods that benefit elites
   c. often redistributes burdens and benefits among different groups in society
   d. must consider regional variations

3. A nation's _____ culture includes all socially transmitted patterns of behavior as well as all the beliefs, customs, and institutions within the society.
   a. institutional
   b. political
   c. governmental
   d. societal

4. _____ is the right to tell others what to do.
   a. Power
   b. Authority
   c. Legitimacy
   d. Sovereignty

5. John Locke's principal work, _____, laid the foundation for modern democratic theory.
   a. *Two Treatises of Government*
   b. *The Social Contract*
   c. *Leviathan*
   d. *The Republic*

6. A system based solely on _____ provides no guarantee that the majority will not run roughshod over the rights of the individual.
   a. a constitution
   b. minority rights
   c. majority rule
   d. a social contract

7. There are two basic types of democratic governmental systems: _____.
   a. parliamentary and legislative
   b. legislative and judicial
   c. pluralistic and elite
   d. parliamentary and presidential

8. The United States government is an example of _____ system.
   a. a presidential
   b. an authoritarian
   c. a parliamentary
   d. an institutional

9. The dominant characteristic of American political culture is _____.
   a. communitarianism
   b. traditionalism
   c. individualism
   d. nihilism

10. The term _____ refers to the transmission of political values and beliefs.
    a. political symbolism
    b. political socialization
    c. public interest
    d. political ideology

For Further Reading

Almond, Gabriel A., and Sidney Verba, eds. *The Civic Culture Revisited* (Thousand Oaks, CA: Sage Publications, 1989).

Bellah, Robert, et al. *Habits of the Heart: Individualism and Commitment in American Life* (Berkeley: University of California Press, 1985).

Bryce, James. *The American Commonwealth* (New York: Macmillan, 1934).

Carter, Stephen L. *The Culture of Disbelief: How American Law and Politics Trivialize Religious Devotion* (New York: Basic Books, 1993).

Derber, Charles. *The Wilding of America: How Greed and Violence Are Eroding Our National Character* (New York: St. Martin's Press, 1996).

Devine, Donald. *The Political Culture of the United States* (Boston: Little, Brown, 1972).

Elazar, Daniel J. *American Federalism: A View from the States,* 3d ed. (New York: Harper and Row, 1984).

Hartz, Louis. *The Liberal Tradition in America* (New York: Harcourt Brace Jovanovich, 1955).

Putnam, Robert D. *Bowling Alone: The Collapse and Revival of American Community* (New York: Simon & Schuster, 2001).

Rosenbaum, Walter A. *Political Culture* (New York: Praeger, 1975).

Schlesinger, Arthur M., Jr. *The Disuniting of America* (New York: W. W. Norton, 1992).

Stewart, William S. *Understanding Politics: The Cultures of Societies and the Structures of Governments* (Novato, CA: Chandler and Sharp, 1988).

Tocqueville, Alexis de. *Democracy in America* (New York: Knopf, 1991) (First published in 1835).

White, John. *The Values Divide: American Politics and Culture in Transition* (Washington, D.C.: CQ Press, 2003).

Wills, Garry. *Under God* (New York: Simon and Schuster, 1990).

Wray, J. Harry. *Sense and Non-Sense: American Culture and Politics* (Upper Saddle River, NJ: Prentice-Hall, 2001).

Endnotes

1. See, generally, Bernard Crick, *In Defense of Politics,* 4th ed. (Chicago: University of Chicago Press, 1993).

2. Thomas Hobbes, *Leviathan* (New York: Macmillan, 1947), p. 82.

3. Harold D. Lasswell, *Politics: Who Gets What, When, How* (New York: McGraw-Hill, 1936).

4. Walter A. Rosenbaum, *Political Culture* (New York: Praeger, 1975), p. 4.

5. Remarks by President George W. Bush at the Twentieth Anniversary of the National Endowment for Democracy, United States Chamber of Commerce, Washington, D.C., November 6, 2003.

6. Don Belt, "Sweden: In Search of a New Model," *National Geographic,* August 1993, pp. 2–35.

7. Gabriel Almond and Sidney Verba, *The Civic Culture* (Princeton, NJ: Princeton University Press, 1963), p. X.

8. *The Politics of Aristotle,* ed. and trans. by Ernest Barker (New York: Oxford University Press, 1958); see, generally, "Oligarchy and Democracy," pp. 110–37.

9. Abraham Lincoln, Gettysburg Address, November 19, 1863.

10. The classic formulation of the so-called iron law of oligarchy can be found in Roberto Michels' *Political Parties: A Study of the Oligarchical Tendencies of Modern Democracies* (New York: Free Press, 1962).

11. John Locke, *Second Treatise of Civil Government* (Everyman's Library, 1924), ch. 1, sec. 4, p. 118.

12. *Bush v. Gore,* 531 U.S. 98 (2000).

13. Charles Lindblom, *Politics and Markets* (New York: Basic Books, 1977), p. 162.

14. See J. Harry Wray, *Sense and Non-Sense: American Culture and Politics* (Upper Saddle River, NJ: Prentice-Hall, 2001), in particular Chapter 3, "Making it Alone."

15. Daniel J. Elazar, *American Federalism: A View from the States* (New York: Thomas Crowell, 1966), pp. 85–86.

16. Ibid., pp. 90–95.

17. Stephen L. Carter, *The Culture of Disbelief: How American Law and Politics Trivialize Religious Devotion* (New York: Basic Books, 1993), p. 4.

18. *Wallace v. Jaffree,* 472 U.S. 38 (1985).

19. *Lee v. Weisman,* 505 U.S. 577 (1992); *Santa Fe Independent School District v. Doe,* 530 U.S. 290 (2000).

20. Carter, *The Culture of Disbelief,* p. 171.

21. See, for example, *Griswold v. Connecticut,* 381 U.S. 479 (1965).

22. *Roe v. Wade,* 410 U.S. 113 (1973).

23. *Lawrence v. Texas,* 539 U.S. 558, 578 (2003).

24. Joe B. Frantz, "The Frontier Tradition: An Invitation to Violence." In *The History of Violence in America: A Report to the National Commission on the Causes and Prevention of Violence* (New York: Bantam Books, 1969), pp. 157–64.

25. Robert Bellah, et al., *Habits of the Heart* (Berkeley: University of California Press, 1985), p. 285.

26. Robert D. Putnam, *Bowling Alone: The Collapse and Revival of American Community* (New York: Simon & Schuster, 2001).

27. George Will, *The Pursuit of Virtue and Other Tory Notions* (New York: Simon & Schuster, 1982), p. 36.

28. Arthur M. Schlesinger, Jr., *The Disuniting of America,* rev. ed. (New York: Norton, 1998), p. 138.

29. For an excellent analysis of America's ongoing cultural transformation and its implications for politics, see John White, *The Values Divide: American Politics and Culture in Transition* (Washington, D.C.: CQ Press, 2003).

30. Katherine Q. Seelye, "Moral Values Cited as a Defining Issue of the Election," *New York Times,* November 4, 2004, p. 4.

31. Marjorie Connelly, "How Americans Voted: A Political Portrait," *New York Times Week in Review,* November 7, 2004, p. 4.

The Development of American Constitutional Democracy

2

representative
government
republic
Second Continental
Congress

Shays' Rebellion
sovereign immunity
Stamp Act
states' rights
tyranny of the majority

unicameral legislature
unitary system
veto
Virginia Plan
writ of mandamus

2-1 The Constitution and American Political Culture

As Chapter 1, "The Political Culture of American Democracy," points out, the American political consensus embraces a commitment to individual freedom, democratic institutions, equality of opportunity, and the rule of law. All these values are enshrined in the U.S. Constitution—some in its original conception and others added as it has evolved over two hundred years. Through twenty-seven formal amendments and many more changes in interpretation, the U.S. Constitution is this country's evolving political covenant. It sets forth the general parameters of government and defines the citizens' relationship to that government. The Constitution represents the most basic expression of our shared political culture.

The U.S. Constitution is extremely resilient. It has withstood the Civil War, two world wars, the Cold War, the Great Depression, numerous recessions, as well as massive social upheavals. The Constitution is now being tested by the war on terrorism. When planes commandeered by terrorists crashed into the twin towers of the World Trade Center on September 11, 2001, life in the United States changed dramatically and probably forever. Americans are now coming to terms with the fact that government at all levels will be waging war on terrorism for many years. Americans will be inconvenienced, and in some instances will have their freedom reduced, by new security measures imposed by government. Yet with all the discussion of warfare and domestic security threats, no one has suggested that the existing constitutional order was fundamentally inadequate to meet the challenge of terrorism. Americans are convinced of the viability and adaptability of their constitutional system.

The American people believe in their Constitution, even though relatively few have even read it. They believe that the Constitution has worked well over the years, although they acknowledge that the political system has changed dramatically since the time the Constitution was adopted. Indeed, support for the Constitution itself, and for the system of government it created, is an essential element of American political culture.

Probably no idea is more basic to what it means to be an American than the view that government is limited and that individuals have rights that the government may not transgress. The **Bill of Rights** (Amendments I through X of the Constitution) reflects the ideals of early America more than its reality. However, these ideals have gained such force that they have done much to guide the evolution of our culture. And with the changing culture has come a changed sense of what the Constitution means. This idea of change within the framework of guiding principles is probably the most fundamental aspect of American constitutional democracy. Many constitutional disputes are framed in terms of whether the Constitution should be understood according to the Founders' original intentions or whether the meaning of the document should be adapted to the needs of the present day.

Nearly all Americans understand the need for the Constitution to be amended from time to time, and most believe that the meaning of the Constitution should evolve to reflect changing social and economic conditions. But Americans are understandably opposed to any attempt to change the Constitution wholesale. Indeed, they are even wary of holding a new constitutional convention to try to improve on the document. But they are comfortable with some gradual change in what the Constitution means. As long as the meaning of the Constitution changes to reflect an evolving societal consensus, its legitimacy is not seriously threatened.

The Constitution begins with the phrase "We the people...." This phrase is somewhat ironic in that the Constitution itself was written by aristocrats. But over the years, the Con-

▶ **Bill of Rights** The first ten amendments to the Constitution, enumerating rights that are protected from government infringement.

What Americans Think About

The U.S. Constitution

The following survey data indicate that Americans hold their Constitution in high regard. Most think it would be a bad idea to have another national convention to reconsider and revise the Constitution. Yet the overwhelming majority believes that the political system we have today is not what the Framers of the Constitution designed. Indeed, nearly half believe that the political system has changed dramatically since the Constitution was adopted. And, of course, they are right.

"How well do you think the Constitution has worked over the two hundred years since it was adopted? Generally speaking, has it worked very well, rather well, so-so, or poorly?"

Very well	38%
Rather well	40%
So-so	16%
Poorly	5%
Not sure	1%

"Do you think the meaning of the Constitution should evolve over time, or should it mean what the people who wrote it two hundred years ago intended for it to mean?"

Evolve over time	60%
Intentions of those who wrote it	37%
Not sure	4%

"Generally speaking, do you think that the political system we have now is pretty much what was planned by the people who wrote the Constitution, or do you think that the system has changed? If so, has it changed somewhat or changed dramatically?"

Same as planned	8%
Changed somewhat	41%
Changed dramatically	48%
Not sure	3%

"Some people think that we should have another national convention to reconsider and revise the Constitution. Generally speaking, do you think that this is a good idea or a bad idea?"

Good idea	38%
Bad idea	57%
Not sure	5%

Source: National telephone survey of 603 adults, conducted January 15–16, 1994, by the Social Science Research Institute at the University of Tennessee, Knoxville. The margin of error is ±4 percentage points at the 95 percent confidence level.

stitution has come to be accepted by the American people and, in many ways, to embody their values and aspirations. Frequently, the most oppressed and least powerful people in our society have turned to the Constitution as their weapon for change. Somewhat ironically, the document that is the legal foundation of American government is also the basis for protecting individuals from their government. Such is the legacy of the "living Constitution."

2-2 Establishment of the American Colonies

To comprehend the contemporary constitutional system, you must understand how it has evolved from its inception. Although the origin of the American constitutional system might reasonably be seen as the Declaration of Independence in 1776 or the adoption of the Constitution in 1787, those documents emerged from the political culture that had developed in the American colonies. Accordingly, our examination must begin with the colonial background of the nation.

Colonies were established in the New World primarily for economic reasons. Governments in Europe saw the colonies as sources of raw materials for industry and as consumer markets for finished products. Ambitious Europeans, frustrated by rigid class structures and guild systems, viewed the colonies as places of economic opportunity. Yet economics and the desire for a better standard of living were not the only motives that led Europeans to make the long, hazardous journey across the Atlantic Ocean. Just as important was the desire for religious and political freedom.

The Protestant Reformation of the fifteenth and sixteenth centuries gave rise to a new religious diversity in Europe, but also led to a plague of religious warfare and persecution. Lutherans and Calvinists of many varieties came into conflict with the Roman Catholic Church, the new Church of England, and each other. Increasingly, members of persecuted minorities sought refuge in the New World. For example, the Puritans established their colony at Plymouth to create a safe haven for their religion, a strict variety of Protestantism based on the teachings of John Calvin. In *Democracy in America,* written some two hundred years later, Alexis de Tocqueville credited the Puritans with providing the moral foundation of American democracy. Certainly, the Puritan values of hard work, self-reliance, and personal responsibility were instrumental in creating a society in which self-government could succeed. For many years, these values remained at the core of American political culture. Whether they still do is open to question.

By the 1770s, 2.5 million inhabitants were spread over thirteen American colonies from New Hampshire in the north to Georgia in the south. Although 60 percent of the colonists were of English origin, many other ethnic groups were present, including the Dutch, Welsh, Scots, and Germans. In the southern colonies, 28 percent of the population were slaves forcibly brought to America from Africa. Compared to European countries of the eighteenth century, America was quite ethnically diverse. Thus, the heterogeneity of the United States, which is still a source of both pride and conflict, is rooted in the early settlement of the country.

Although most colonists were dissatisfied with the established order in Europe, they were certainly not anarchists. From the beginning, they understood the need for government. Before the Puritans' ship arrived at Plymouth, forty-one of the male passengers signed the **Mayflower Compact,** the first written agreement for self-government in America. Insofar as the compact authorized the adoption of laws for the common good and committed all members of the colony to obey those laws, it foreshadowed the adoption of the U.S. Constitution 167 years later. Samuel Eliot Morison has written that the Mayflower Compact "is justly regarded as a key document in American history. It proves the determination of a small group of English emigrants to live under a rule of law, based on consent of the people, and to set up their own civil government."[1]

2-2a Government in the Colonies

The powers exercised by the colonial governments were generally limited by written charters, predecessors to the state constitutions that would be written after the American Revolution. The idea that government must be based on a written charter is thus deeply rooted in American political culture. Except for Pennsylvania, the colonies had **bicameral legislatures** (two-house legislatures). In most colonies, the upper house of the legislature was appointed by the governor and consisted largely of aristocrats. The lower house was elected by "the people," that is, by white male adult property owners. All colonial governors had broad powers, including the absolute right to **veto,** or reject, legislation and the authority to appoint all judges. The colonial courts followed the **common law,** which was the traditional law of England. Because the courts were bound by an elaborate body of law that had developed over the centuries, and were not making new law, they were by far the least important institutions of government during the colonial era.

2-3 The American Revolution

One can argue that the American Revolution was made virtually inevitable by the British defeat of France and Spain in the Seven Years War (also known as the French and Indian

---

Mayflower Compact The first written agreement for self-government in America, adopted in 1620 by Puritans coming to America on the Mayflower.

bicameral legislatures Two-house legislative bodies. Both houses in a bicameral legislature must agree in order to pass legislation.

veto The power of the chief executive to nullify acts of the legislature.

common law The body of judge-made law inherited from England; also refers to the legal tradition that accepts judicial decisions as the source of law.

War), which lasted from 1756 to 1763. The British victory removed the threats to the American colonies from France in the north and Spain in Florida and the west. As the historian Paul Kennedy has observed: "Freed from foreign threats which hitherto had induced loyalty to Westminster, American colonists could now insist upon a merely nominal link with Britain, and, if denied that by an imperial government with different ideas, engage in rebellion."[2] Thus, the seeds of independence were sown. No longer helpless outposts subject to the constant threat of attack, the colonies could begin to exist as a country.

The British, as a result of their victory, acquired the extensive lands of the Ohio and Mississippi river valleys. To the restless American colonists, these lands beckoned for settlement. The British, however, worried about the difficulties and costs they would incur in trying to protect settlers from conflicts with the Native Americans who occupied the lands over the mountains. Consequently, Parliament prohibited the colonists from purchasing land west of the Appalachians. To enforce this policy, the British sent an army of ten thousand troops to the colonies. Many colonists were outraged by what they considered to be a wholly inappropriate use of military power during peacetime.

2-3a Causes of the Revolution

Maintaining a large standing army in America was very expensive, and Britain was still struggling to repay the massive debt it had incurred in the Seven Years War. Taxes in Britain were considerably higher than in the colonies—indeed, more than twenty-five times higher for the average taxpayer. Not surprisingly, the British looked for a way to make the colonies pay more of the cost of their own defense. This idea seemed only fair to the British, who were still resentful that the colonies, which had been the principal beneficiaries of the British victory in the Seven Years War, had contributed little to the war effort.

In March 1765, Parliament passed the **Stamp Act,** which required the colonists to purchase stamps to be placed on envelopes, newspapers, wills, playing cards, college degrees, marriage licenses, and land titles, among other things. Violators were subject to trial without jury. The act was conceived by George Grenville, First Lord of the Treasury under King George III. Grenville believed the Stamp Act was necessary both to raise revenue for the defense of the colonies and to reassert British control over the insubordinate colonists.

In America, reaction to the Stamp Act came fast and furious. Americans have never been fond of taxes, but the colonists were particularly angry that Parliament would impose a tax on British subjects who were not represented in the House of Commons. In Boston, the self-styled Sons of Liberty hung in effigy the agents and supporters of the king. They also looted the home of Andrew Oliver, the king's agent for stamp distribution in Massachusetts. Oliver resigned from office and was never replaced. In October 1765, delegates from all thirteen colonies met in New York. This "Stamp Act Congress" demanded repeal of the despised legislation and called for a boycott of British goods. Faced with declining exports to the colonies, Parliament gave in to the colonists' demands.

In 1766, Parliament enacted the Townshend duties, another revenue-raising measure that imposed taxes on a variety of imports to the colonies. The colonists protested, and the duties were repealed except for the tax on tea. In 1773, Parliament passed the Tea Act, which granted the East India Company the exclusive right to sell tea to American distributors. This monopoly, which eliminated American importers from the tea trade, prompted the **Boston Tea Party,** in which some 150 colonists disguised as Native Americans dumped tea from British ships into Boston harbor. Parliament responded quickly to this act of lawlessness by passing the Coercive Acts, which were dubbed the "Intolerable Acts" by the Massachusetts colonists. These acts closed the port of Boston until reparations were made to the East India Company, restricted public assemblies, increased the powers of the governor, and, most onerous of all, required colonists to quarter British soldiers in their homes.

The Intolerable Acts helped to galvanize public opinion against Great Britain throughout the colonies. Responding to this new climate, disgruntled delegates from twelve colonies convened in Philadelphia in September 1774. Calling itself the **First Continental Congress,** the assembly called for a boycott of English goods. Some of the more radical delegates urged revolution, although more moderate sentiments prevailed. Yet forces were in motion that would propel the colonies into a violent uprising against the British.

Stamp Act Act of British Parliament that required American colonists to purchase stamps to be placed on envelopes, newspapers, wills, playing cards, college degrees, marriage licenses, land titles, and other documents.

Boston Tea Party An act of protest against the British tax on imported tea. It occurred in 1773, when about 150 American colonists disguised as Native Americans boarded three ships and dumped the tea they were carrying into Boston harbor.

First Continental Congress Meeting of delegates in Philadelphia in 1774 to protest British treatment of the colonies.

Popular Culture and American Politics

The Patriot

By Chapman Rackaway

Although this textbook focuses on the economic and philosophical foundations of the American Revolution, the movie *The Patriot* tries to show a more personal motive for fighting in the American War for Independence. In *The Patriot,* family is the guiding force that leads one man to change his mind and join the fighting.

Mel Gibson plays Benjamin Martin, a French and Indian War hero whose character is based on a number of different historical figures from the Revolutionary era, such as Andrew Pickens, Francis Marion, and Thomas Sumter. Sickened by his own brutality in the French and Indian War, Martin returns home to South Carolina, hoping to put that ugly moment in his own life behind him, and becomes staunchly antiwar. Martin wants nothing more than to continue farming, maintaining a peaceful life surrounded by his family.

The movie accurately traces the growing post–French and Indian War dissent among American colonists toward England. The costs of the war (and foreign colonization) were very high for Britain, and those costs were passed on to the American colonists. The result, as described in this chapter, was rising anger that eventually led to war. Many young men who lived at the time were similar to the portrayal of Martin's son Gabriel, who willingly and enthusiastically goes out to fight. Captured by the British Army and sentenced to hanging, Gabriel is saved by his brother Thomas, but Gabriel and his father, Benjamin, watch Thomas die in the attempt.

The tragedy galvanizes Benjamin Martin's resolve to return to the battlefield to avenge his son and improve the future lives of his other children at home. Using guerilla tactics common during the Revolution, Martin and his colleagues fight back the Redcoats. Shot in South Carolina, the fictionalized movie manages to put a reasonable and accurate human face on the conflict—both between nations and in the hearts of the people who fought the war.

2-3b Contrasting Political Cultures

One underlying cause of the antagonism between the colonies and Great Britain was their contrasting political cultures. By the eighteenth century, Britain was moving slowly but steadily in the direction of political democracy. The age of absolute monarchy had passed. As a result of the Glorious Revolution of 1688, Parliament was no longer under the thumb of the monarch. Yet, because of property qualifications for voting, less than 20 percent of the adult male population of Britain was entitled to vote in parliamentary elections. Parliament therefore still retained much of an upper-class bias.

In contrast, the American colonies were considerably more democratic. Voting in elections for colonial assemblies was limited to white men of property, of course, but property qualifications were much less stringent than in Britain. Consequently, more than half the adult male population was entitled to vote. The colonial assemblies reflected this enfranchisement. Among the members of the lower houses of the colonial legislatures were the owners of small farms, shopkeepers, and artisans as well as lawyers, physicians, and planters. Consequently, the assemblies came to reflect the more democratic sensibilities of the colonies. This more democratic political culture certainly reflected the more egalitarian nature of American society, a society in which traditional European ideas about social class and hierarchy were being rapidly discarded.[3]

In 1775, the voyage from Bristol, England, to Boston took at least a month. Because of their remoteness, the American colonists lost their sense of attachment to Great Britain and developed an independent sense of political identity. And because the colonies were spread out along the Atlantic seaboard, the colonists developed a strong sense of localism. Most Americans in the 1770s believed that their affairs were better governed by their local and state assemblies than by Parliament in faraway London. Colonists, especially those who had been born in the New World, began to think of themselves as Georgians, Marylanders, and New Yorkers rather than as English subjects.

2-3c American Independence

With so many of the colonists no longer identifying with Britain, a violent break became almost inevitable. The Revolutionary War began in April 1775 when a band of sixty Minutemen armed with muskets confronted six companies of the British army in the village of Lexington, Massachusetts. The British were on their way to Concord, Massachusetts, to seize a cache of weapons that the rebellious colonists had been stockpiling. No one knows which side fired "the shot heard round the world." When the badly outnumbered colonists retreated, eight of their compatriots lay dead on the village green. Although the fighting began in Lexington, John Adams was quite correct in observing that "[t]he Revolution was affected before the war commenced. The Revolution was in the minds and hearts of the people."[4]

If the colonies were to act as a nation, they needed a way to govern themselves, even if initially only for the purposes of waging war. A transitional government was needed before a fighting force could be organized and funded. Convening in May 1775, the **Second Continental Congress** decided to raise an army to oppose the British. It also opened channels of communication to European powers in an effort to obtain military support. Despite a rising tide of revolutionary sentiment in the colonies, the Continental Congress declined to declare independence from Britain. Over the next year, a great debate took place between radicals who wanted full independence and moderates who believed that reconciliation with Britain was still possible.

One of the most influential and colorful radicals was Thomas Paine, a recent arrival from England. His pamphlet *Common Sense,* published in January 1776, helped to stir the revolutionary cauldron. In the first three months after it was published, *Common Sense* sold more than one hundred twenty thousand copies, making it by far the best-selling book of 1776. Paine's pamphlet portrayed the struggle of the American colonies against George III as part of a larger democratic struggle against corrupt and decadent monarchies. But the colonists were most impressed by Paine's eminently practical argument that it was silly to think that "a continent could be perpetually governed by an island."

By the spring of 1776, it was apparent to most Americans that independence from Britain was both necessary and desirable. On July 2, the Second Continental Congress adopted a resolution of independence. Two days later, it approved the **Declaration of Independence.** Authored by Thomas Jefferson, the Declaration outlined the colonies' grievances against King George and asserted the right of revolution. The ideas expressed in the Declaration were by no means original to Jefferson or to the American colonies. They were articulated a century earlier in John Locke's *Two Treatises of Government.* When the Declaration of Independence refers to "life, liberty and the pursuit of happiness" as being the "inalienable rights" of individuals, it echoes Locke's formulation of the natural rights of "life, liberty and property." Although the Declaration asserted American independence, it did so by drawing on ideas that had already taken hold in Britain. Thus, in a sense, the Declaration of Independence was an affirmation of the links between the British and American political cultures. Despite the considerable cultural differences that led to the Revolution, the essential ideas of the Declaration of Independence came from Britain.

2-4 The "Disunited" States of America

Several weeks before the Declaration of Independence was adopted, Richard Henry Lee, of Virginia, proposed to the Continental Congress that a "plan of confederation" be prepared for the colonies. The plan was drafted by a committee and adopted by the Continental Congress in November 1777. By its own terms, the **Articles of Confederation** had to be ratified by all thirteen states. Persuading all thirteen states to go along took four years, but on March 1, 1781, the Maryland legislature finally ratified the document. Thus, on March 2, 1781, the old Continental Congress became the "United States of America in Congress Assembled."

Second Continental Congress Colonial body that drafted the Declaration of Independence and served as the government until the Articles of Confederation were ratified in 1781.

Declaration of Independence Document adopted July 4, 1776, that proclaimed and justified the independence of the American colonies from Great Britain.

Articles of Confederation The colonists' first attempt at a charter for the national government. Although the Articles were adopted by Congress in 1777, they were not ratified until 1781. In 1788, they were superseded by the U.S. Constitution.

When Lord Cornwallis, the British commanding general, surrendered to General George Washington at Yorktown in October 1781, Americans were generally optimistic about their new nation and the "league of friendship" they had established among their respective states. The British and many Europeans, however, were doubtful that the United States would succeed. They had ample reason for their skepticism.

2-4a Government under the Articles of Confederation

The "Articles of Confederation and Perpetual Union" were written with the idea of maintaining the thirteen separate states as sovereign entities. During the Revolution, all thirteen states established new constitutions and political institutions. In keeping with the prevailing philosophical sentiments of the Revolution, the constitutions made the legislatures the most powerful institutions of the newly constituted state governments. In most states, governors and judges were appointed by the legislature. By the mid-1770s, all thirteen states had well-established political systems, which they intended to protect against encroachments by the national government.

The national government created by the Articles of Confederation was intentionally minimalist in character. Congress, the sole institution of the national government, was provided with little meaningful power. Congress was a **unicameral legislature** (one-house legislature) where each state had one vote. A supermajority of nine states was required to adopt any significant measure, making it impossible for Congress to act decisively.

Congress' greatest deficiency under the Articles was that it lacked the power to tax. It was reduced to requesting funds from the states, which were less than magnanimous. During the first two years under the Articles, Congress received less than $1.5 million of the more than $10 million it requested from the states. This arrangement became especially problematic as Congress tried to fund the Continental Army, which remained at war with the British until the Peace of Paris was signed in 1783. After the peace, Congress struggled to repay the massive war debt it had incurred; the states, for the most part, treated the national debt as somebody else's problem.

The Articles of Confederation did not give Congress any power to regulate foreign and interstate commerce. Commercial regulations varied widely among the states, which sought to protect their interests by instituting **protective tariffs** and fees. A tariff is a charge imposed on a product being brought into a country or, in this case, a state. In addition to raising money, the purpose of a tariff is to protect domestic producers by increasing the price of imported goods. Of course, when one state instituted a tariff, other states retaliated with tariffs of their own. These impositions frustrated the emergence of a national economy and depressed economic growth. Although Congress could coin money, states were not prohibited from issuing their own currency, which further inhibited interstate economic activity.

Under the Articles, there was no president to provide leadership and speak for the new nation with a unified voice. This omission was deliberate, of course, because many Americans feared a restoration of the monarchy. But as a consequence, states began to develop their own foreign policies; some even entered into negotiations with other countries.

Nor did the Articles of Confederation provide for a national court system to settle disputes between states or parties residing in different states. The lack of predictable enforcement of contracts between parties in different states also inhibited interstate economic activity. The fact that no one could look to any overarching authority to settle disputes or provide leadership contributed to the sense of disunity. Finally, by their own terms, the Articles could not be amended except by unanimous consent of the states. Any state could veto a proposed change in the confederation. As a result, under the Articles of Confederation, the national government was ineffectual. Meanwhile, much to the delight of the European colonial powers, the "Perpetual Union" was disintegrating. It soon became clear that the Articles could loosely guide a collection of states, but were incapable of providing government for a nation.

The Annapolis Convention Among those who were extremely dissatisfied with the Articles of Confederation were James Madison of Virginia and Alexander Hamilton of New

---

> **unicameral legislature** A one-house legislative body.

> **protective tariffs** Charges imposed on a product being brought into a state; the purpose is to protect those in the state who want to produce and sell that product.

York. Together they engineered a conference, which was held in Annapolis, Maryland, in 1786. Officially called for the purpose of discussing issues of commerce, the Annapolis convention was actually a forum for expressing dissatisfaction with the Articles of Confederation. Although only five states sent delegations to Annapolis, the convention adopted a resolution calling for a convention to revise the Articles. Shortly after the close of the Annapolis Convention, the idea of a new constitution gained considerable support from an event in Massachusetts: **Shays' Rebellion.**

Shays' Rebellion   In the wake of the American Revolution, most owners of small farms were saddled with high debts. By the mid-1780s, a rash of foreclosures occurred. In some states, legislatures provided relief by passing laws prohibiting foreclosures. In other states, judges permitted debtors to reschedule their debts. In Massachusetts, however, no such relief was provided. Debtors were routinely thrown into jail, and farms were seized for debt. In the fall of 1786, an angry mob of some 1,500 farmers, armed with muskets and pitchforks, marched on a courthouse in western Massachusetts. The rebellion was led by Daniel Shays, a veteran of the Revolutionary War. Shays' Rebellion, as it came to be called, was finally put down in early 1787 by the state militia. Congress provided no assistance. Shays and his cohorts were eventually pardoned by the governor of Massachusetts.

Shays' Rebellion galvanized dissatisfaction with the Articles of Confederation. A consensus developed, at least among the nation's elites, that the national government needed to be strengthened. In particular, bankers and other creditors believed that the national government needed the power to protect contracts and other property rights, both from popular uprisings and from state legislative and judicial action. Responding to these concerns, Congress finally adopted a resolution calling for a convention to be held at Philadelphia for the express purpose of "revising" the Articles of Confederation.

> ▶ **Shays' Rebellion**   An uprising in western Massachusetts in 1786. The rebellion helped demonstrate the weaknesses of the Articles of Confederation and served as a catalyst in the call for the Constitutional Convention.

2-5 The Constitutional Convention

Fifty-five men from twelve states assembled in Philadelphia during the hot summer of 1787 to see whether they could make the national government work. The Rhode Island legislature refused to send a delegation, fearing that the convention would greatly strengthen the national government and thereby threaten the sovereignty of the states. While ostensibly gathering to update the Articles, the convention soon validated those concerns by moving far beyond a mere revision of this discredited document.

2-5a The Delegates

When the state legislatures named their delegates to the **Constitutional Convention,** Thomas Jefferson was serving as the American minister to France. After reading the names of the delegates in a Paris newspaper, Jefferson remarked that the convention would be "an assembly of demi-gods."[5] To be sure, the fifty-five delegates were an impressive lot. Twenty-one of them had fought in the Revolution; eight had signed the Declaration of Independence; seven had served as state governors. Among the delegates were six planters, three physicians, eight businessmen, and thirty-three lawyers. They were highly educated, wealthy, and quite influential in their respective states. The delegates were, quite simply, a representative sample of the young nation's elite. In James Madison's words, they were "the best contribution of talents the states could make for the occasion."[6]

> ▶ **Constitutional Convention** Meeting in Philadelphia during the summer of 1787; called originally for the purpose of revising the Articles of Confederation but ultimately framed a new constitution. A meeting of delegates for the purpose of creating or changing a constitution.

The Motives of the Delegates   In 1913, historian Charles A. Beard argued that the primary motive of the delegates to the Constitutional Convention was a desire to protect their own upper-class economic interests. According to Beard, the Constitution was "an economic document drawn with superb skill by men whose property interests were immediately at stake."[7] Beard pointed out that most of the signers of the Constitution were merchants, lenders, wealthy landowners, or speculators. In other words, they were people who stood to benefit from a strong national government that would protect contracts and foster economic growth. Several scholars have since challenged, if not refuted, Beard's thesis. Forrest McDonald, for example, after studying the delegates, asserts that only a minority were motivated primarily by personal economic concerns or the interests of the upper class.[8] Historian John Garraty has written that "[t]o call men like Washington, Franklin and Madison self-seeking would be utterly absurd."[9] The author of a recent book that is sympathetic to the Beard interpretation acknowledges that "[m]ost general discussions of the issue today argue that the Constitution came about because of a consensus to improve the general well-being of the country, not as a result of a conflict over economic interests.[10]

Philosophical Influences on the Delegates   The discussions leading to the creation of the Constitution were based much more on philosophy than on the crass economic interests of the delegates and the social class from which they were drawn. The eighteenth century was, after all, the Enlightenment and the Age of Reason, and the delegates prided themselves on being enlightened and reasonable men. As an educated lot, the delegates were generally familiar with the writings of Adam Smith, Jean-Jacques Rousseau, James Harrington, David Hume, and other philosophers. Without question, the greatest influence on the delegates was exerted by the English philosopher John Locke, whose major work, *Two Treatises of Government* (1690), was published almost a century before the Constitutional Convention.

Although Locke's ideas provided the philosophical underpinnings of the Constitution, as well as of the Declaration of Independence a decade earlier, the ideas of a Frenchman, Baron de Montesquieu, had the greatest impact on the delegates' thinking about the structure of the national government. Montesquieu's *Spirit of the Laws,* published in 1748, argued that the essential functions of government—legislative, executive, and judicial—must be separated into different branches of government. A failure to do so would, in Montesquieu's view, lead inevitably to tyranny. The success of parliamentary systems in such modern European democracies as France, Germany, Sweden, and Italy raises serious doubts about Montesquieu's insights. Yet to the Framers of the Constitution, Montesquieu's idea of separation of powers was gospel.

Another Source of Influence: The English Constitutional Tradition   You must understand that the delegates to the Constitutional Convention were not beginning with a clean slate. Although they intended to scrap the Articles of Confederation, they were not out to do something original. Rather, they meant to perfect, or at least significantly improve, the idea of constitutionalism that had its roots in the Old Testament covenant between God and the Israelites. This idea of a covenant found historical expression in the **Magna Carta** of 1215, in which England's King John consented to limitations on the power of the monarchy. This idea was extended by the **English Bill of Rights** (1689), which guaranteed the supremacy of Parliament over the monarchy. In America, the idea of constitutionalism appeared first in the Mayflower Compact of 1620 and later in the state constitutions adopted after the American Revolution.

Political Considerations Facing the Delegates   In addition to being men of wealth and learning, the Framers of the Constitution were, above all, practical politicians who understood the need for compromise. They were distinctly aware that they represented well-established states with varying interests and that the product of their labors would ultimately have to be approved by conventions in their states. Their political sensitivity, skill, and sophistication have been praised by numerous commentators, including political scientist John P. Roche, who has written that "the Philadelphia Convention was not a College of Cardinals or a council of Platonic Guardians . . . ; it was a *nationalist* reform caucus which had to operate with great delicacy and skill in a political cosmos full of enemies to achieve the one definitive goal—popular approbation."[11] As Roche suggests, uppermost in the minds of the delegates was the need for the popular acceptance of the new constitution. That is why the Constitution of 1787, unlike the Articles of Confederation, begins with the majestic phrase "We the People of the United States. . . ."

▶ **Magna Carta** The "Great Charter" of 1215 in which King John guaranteed the rights of English subjects.

▶ **English Bill of Rights** Document adopted in 1689 after the Glorious Revolution; supplemented the Magna Carta by guaranteeing the supremacy of Parliament over royal authority and further strengthening the rights of English subjects.

2-5b Consensus on Basic Principles

When the convention began in May 1787, the delegates made a number of significant procedural decisions. First, they selected George Washington to preside over the convention. Washington, easily the best known and most admired American of his day, lent prestige and credibility to the proceedings, and his association with the convention probably assisted subsequent ratification efforts.

After selecting Washington to preside, the delegates decided to conduct their business in secret. The doors and windows were kept closed despite the heat and humidity of the worst summer to afflict Philadelphia in many years. By modern procedural standards, the delegates' decision to hold secret sessions seems rather undemocratic. Certainly, a secret constitutional convention today would arouse a firestorm of controversy. Ironically, the delegates thought secrecy was necessary to encourage free and open debate on the difficult issues before the convention. Secrecy probably contributed to the convention's success by enabling delegates to compromise, something that can be difficult for people who have taken a position publicly and feel compelled to maintain it. Fortunately, James Madison, who was an assiduous note taker, recorded the proceedings of the convention for posterity. The notes were made public only after Madison's death in 1836.

The delegates argued over many ideas at the convention, but were in agreement on basic principles. They believed in popular sovereignty—the Lockean idea expressed in the Declaration of Independence that power is vested ultimately in the people, not in the government. Accordingly, the delegates believed in **representative government,** or the idea that most policy decisions ought to emanate from legislatures that represent the people, even if indirectly (see Figure 2-1).

Yet the delegates rejected the concept of **direct democracy,** in which the masses would be involved in government on a regular basis. In fact, many delegates equated the term *democracy* with mob rule. They sought to build a **republic,** not a democracy. When they looked to ancient models, their inspiration was the Roman republic, not the Athenian democracy.

The delegates also believed in limited government. Government exists to ensure the social contract and to accomplish what people cannot do by acting alone. The new national government would be designed to accomplish what the several states could not do on their own—namely, provide for the national defense, settle disputes between states, and create a legal climate in which interstate commerce could flourish. The new national government was not to be a leviathan—a mammoth government that dominates its people and values order above all. This type of government is not limited at all and has no implied contractual arrangement with the governed other than to protect them. This form of government had been advocated by Thomas Hobbes, whose book *Leviathan* was a blueprint for government in the turbulent environment of seventeenth-century Europe.[12]

> **representative government**
> A political system in which most policy decisions emanate from legislatures that represent the people, even if indirectly.

> **direct democracy**   A political system in which all citizens participate in the making of significant public policy decisions rather than elect representatives to make these decisions.

> **republic**   A form of government in which power is exercised by representative institutions that are limited by the rule of law.

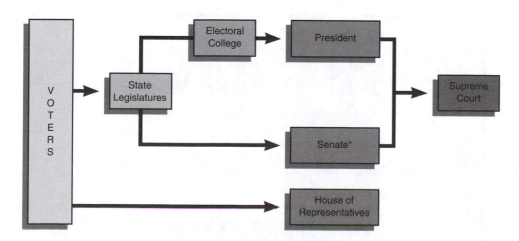

Figure 2-1
The Use of Indirect Elections in the Constitution

The delegates rejected the concept of direct democracy, in which the masses would be involved in government on a regular basis, choosing instead a method of indirect elections except for the House of Representatives.

*The Seventeenth Amendment, which provided for direct election of senators by the people, eliminated the state legislatures' role in choosing senators in 1913.

Finally, the delegates believed in the rule of law. Ideally, in their view, government should be a government of laws, not of men. No one in power should be above the law, and the legislature itself should be bound to respect the principles and limitations contained in the Constitution, the "supreme law of the land." They viewed the law as principally a means of protecting individual rights to life, liberty, and property.

Federalism   The delegates were committed to two basic organizing principles for the new political system (see Figure 2-2). The first was **federalism,** the distribution of power between the national government and the states. As noted in section 2-4a, "Government under the Articles of Confederation," the states had well-established governments by the mid-1770s. Most delegates simply could not conceive that the state governments would be abolished in favor of a **unitary system,** in which all political power would rest in the central government.

The decision to retain the states as units of government was much more than a concession to political necessity. The delegates, who represented their respective states at the convention, believed in federalism as a means of dispersing power. After a revolutionary war fought against distant colonial rulers, the Founders believed that government should be closer to the governed. Moreover, given the dramatically different political cultures of the states, a distant national government could never hope to command the loyalty and support of a diverse people. Finally, the delegates recognized the practical problems of trying to administer a country spread out along a thousand-mile seaboard. The states were much better equipped for this task.

Separation of Powers   The second basic organizing principle for the new government was the separation of powers. The delegates had no interest in creating a parliamentary system. They believed that parliaments could be manipulated by monarchs or captured by impassioned but short-lived majorities. Accordingly, parliaments provided insufficient security for liberty and property. The delegates believed that only by allocating the three basic functions of government (legislative, executive, and judicial) into three separate branches could power be appropriately dispersed. In James Madison's words, "[T]he accumulation of all powers, legislative, executive, and judiciary, in the same hands . . . may justly be pronounced the very definition of tyranny."[13]

As you have read, the separation of powers was not an original idea. Not only were Madison and the other delegates well aware of Montesquieu's arguments for separation of powers, but the new state constitutions adopted during or after the Revolutionary War were based on that principle. Yet the Framers were also aware that in most states the legislatures dominated the executive and judicial branches. At Madison's urging, the delegates

> **federalism**   The constitutional distribution of sovereignty between the national government and the states.

> **unitary system**   A system of government in which sovereignty is vested exclusively in one central government.

Figure 2-2
Organizing Principles of American Government

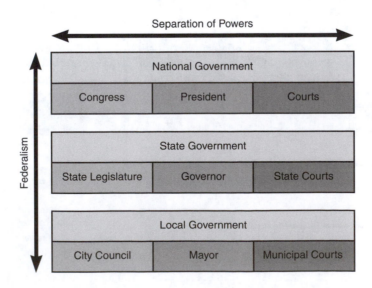

Profiles & Perspectives

James Madison (1751–1836)

© Bettmann / CORBIS

The "Father of the American Constitution" was born in 1751 in Port Conway, Virginia, and died eighty-five years later at his home in Montpelier, Virginia. At age eighteen, he enrolled at Princeton University, where he completed the four-year course of study in two years. In 1776, Madison was elected to Virginia's revolutionary convention, where he was a principal architect of the state's guarantee of religious freedom. Although Madison never had a formal religious affiliation, in later life he expressed an affinity for Unitarianism. In 1780, he was made a delegate to the Continental Congress. As the principal author of the Virginia Plan, Madison emerged as the leading thinker behind the Constitution of 1787. His copious notes of the Constitutional Convention were published shortly after his death. To promote the ratification of the Constitution, Madison wrote twenty-nine of the eighty-five *Federalist Papers,* which have become classics in American political thought.

In *The Federalist* No. 51, one of his greatest essays, Madison wrote about the system of checks and balances in the Constitution:

> [T]he great security against a gradual concentration of the several powers [of the government] in the same department, consists in giving to those who administer each department, the necessary constitutional means, and personal motives, to resist encroachments of the others. The provision for defense must in this, as in all other cases, be made commensurate to the danger of attack. Ambition must be made to counteract ambition. The interest of the man must be connected with the constitutional rights of the place. It may be a reflection on human nature, that such devices should be necessary to control the abuses of government. But what is government itself, but the greatest of all reflections on human nature?

Madison served in the U.S. House of Representatives from 1789 to 1797, where his principal accomplishment was drafting the proposed constitutional amendments that would become the Bill of Rights. In 1794, Madison married Dolley Payne Todd, a well-known socialite sixteen years his junior. From 1801 to 1809, Madison served as secretary of state in the administration of President Thomas Jefferson. Madison succeeded Jefferson as president, serving two terms in office (1809–1817). After leaving the presidency, Madison returned to his beloved home at Montpelier, where he remained for the rest of his life. He spent his final years writing articles arguing for the preservation of the Union.

For more information on Madison, check out these links:

http://www.jmu.edu/madison/center/index.htm

http://www.whitehouse.gov/history/presidents/jm4.html

---

agreed that a system of **checks and balances** would be necessary if separate branches of government were to be maintained. As Madison would later argue in *The Federalist* No. 51, "[A]mbition must be made to counteract ambition. . . ."

2-5c Conflict and Compromise in Philadelphia

Although the delegates agreed on basic assumptions, goals, and organizing principles, they differed sharply over many other matters. By far the greatest sources of disagreement were the conflict between the small and large states over representation in Congress and the cleavage between northern and southern states over slavery. But a number of other issues were also divisive. Should we have one president or a multiple executive? How should the president be chosen? Should we have a national system of courts or merely a national supreme court to review decisions of the existing state tribunals? What powers should the national government have over interstate and foreign commerce? Some of these disagreements were so serious that several delegates packed their bags and left Philadelphia, and for a time it appeared that the convention might fail altogether.

Representation in Congress   As noted in section 2-4a, "Government under the Articles of Confederation," under the Articles of Confederation all states were equally represented in a unicameral Congress. Representatives of the larger states preferred that representation be proportional to state population. The **Virginia Plan,** conceived by James Madison and presented to the convention by Governor Edmund Randolph of Virginia, called for a bicameral Congress in which representation in both houses would be based on state population. Delegates from the smaller states, fearing that their states would be dom-

checks and balances Fundamental principle underlying the American constitutional system whereby institutions of government can check one another in order to prevent one branch from becoming too powerful.

Virginia Plan   Governmental plan conceived by James Madison and presented to the Constitutional Convention by Virginia governor Edmund Randolph, which called for a bicameral Congress, in which representation in both houses would be based on state population.

	Virginia Plan	Issue	New Jersey Plan	End compromise
T A B L E 2-1 **Key Features of the Virginia Plan, the New Jersey Plan, and the Constitution** INTERACTIVE TABLE	Bicameral	Structure of Congress	Unicameral	Bicameral
	Both chambers to be based on state population	Representation in Congress	Each state to have equal representation	Each state equally represented in the Senate; representation in the House of Representatives based on state population.
	Single executive to be selected by Congress	Structure of executive	Multiple executive to be selected by Congress	Single executive selected by the Electoral College.
	Removal by Congress	Removal of executive	Removal by majority of state legislatures	Removal by Congress through bicameral impeachment procedure.
	National court system; judges appointed for life by Congress	The courts	No national court system	National court system; judges appointed for life by president with consent of the Senate.

New Jersey Plan Plan proposed at the Constitutional Convention to counter the Virginia Plan. The New Jersey Plan called for preserving Congress as it was under the Articles of Confederation.

inated by the large states under such an arrangement, countered with the **New Jersey Plan,** which called for preserving Congress as it was under the Articles. Supporters of the New Jersey Plan, including William Paterson and David Brearley, of New Jersey; John Dickinson and Gunning Bedford, of Delaware; Luther Martin, of Maryland; and Elbridge Gerry, of Massachusetts, argued that a constitution based on the Virginia Plan would never be ratified. After a few days of intense debate described by Alexander Hamilton as a "struggle for power, not for liberty," Roger Sherman, of Connecticut, proposed a compromise. Congress would be composed of two houses: a House of Representatives, in which representation would be based on a state's population, and a Senate, in which all states would be equally represented (see Table 2-1).

Slavery   Although not fully apparent in 1787, the most fundamental conflict underlying the convention was the division between North and South over the slavery question. The conflict involved more than human rights; it was also a clash of different economies and political cultures. The South had a thriving plantation economy based on slave labor, which generated considerable wealth for the plantation owners. The political culture of the South tended toward the aristocratic and traditional. By contrast, the North was on the verge of an industrial revolution. Northern agriculture was based on family farms. The political culture was more democratic and, from the southern point of view, considerably more moralistic. Southern delegates at the Constitutional Convention feared that the new national government would try to end the slave trade and possibly try to abolish slavery. At the same time, southern delegations wanted slaves in their states to be counted as persons for the purpose of determining representation in the new House of Representatives. Northern delegates, realizing that southern support was crucial to the success of the new nation, finally agreed to two compromises over slavery: First, Congress would not have the power to prohibit the importation of slaves into the United States until 1808. Second, for purposes of representation in Congress (and the apportionment of direct taxes), each slave would count as three-fifths of a person.

2-5d The Signing of the Constitution

After three months of debate, Gouverneur Morris presented the final draft of the Constitution to the convention. On September 17, 1787, thirty-nine delegates representing twelve states placed their signatures on what they hoped would become the nation's new fundamental law (see Table 2-2). They then adjourned to the City Tavern to celebrate their

State	Signers
Connecticut	William S. Johnson; Roger Sherman
Delaware	George Reed; Gunning Bedford, Jr.; John Dickinson; Richard Bassett; Jacob Broom
Georgia	William Few; Abraham Baldwin
Maryland	James McHenry; Daniel of St. Thomas Jenifer; Daniel Carroll
Massachusetts	Nathaniel Gorham; Rufus King
New Hampshire	John Langdon; Nicholas Gilman
New Jersey	William Livingston; David Brearley; William Paterson; Jonathan Dayton
New York	Alexander Hamilton
North Carolina	William Blount; Richard Dobbs Spaight; Hubert Williamson
Pennsylvania	Benjamin Franklin; Thomas Mifflin; Robert Morris; George Clymer; Thomas FitzSimons; Jared Ingersoll; James Wilson; Gouverneur Morris
South Carolina	John Rutledge; Charles Cotesworth Pinckney; Charles Pinckney; Pierce Butler
Virginia	George Washington; John Blair; James Madison
Rhode Island	Boycotted the signing of the Constitution, claiming that small states, such as itself, would be unfairly treated

TABLE 2-2

Signers of the Constitution

INTERACTIVE TABLE

achievement and discuss a final challenge: Before the Constitution could become the supreme law of the land, it would have to be ratified by the states.

2-6 The Framers' Constitution

The Framers' Constitution was a brief document, only about four thousand words. It was not designed to spell out every detail of the new government, but rather to provide a structure; basic institutions; and a set of powers, principles, and prohibitions. The document reflected, naturally, those principles essential to the Framers' philosophy of government: consent of the governed, limited government, separation of powers, checks and balances, and federalism.

2-6a The Institutions of the New National Government

The first three articles of the Constitution, known as the **distributive articles,** defined the legislative, executive, and judicial branches, respectively, of the new government. The distributive articles divided the powers of government across three independent, co-equal branches in keeping with the Framers' commitment to the principle of the separation of powers.

Article I vested "all legislative Powers herein granted" in a "Congress of the United States." This was the lawmaking body, but the grant of power to make laws was intentionally limited. In addition to these specific powers, Article I, Section 8 contained a clause allowing Congress to "make all Laws which shall be necessary and proper for carrying into Execution the foregoing powers, and all other Powers vested by this Constitution in the Government of the United States, or in any Department or Officer thereof." The **Necessary and Proper Clause** would later emerge as perhaps the most significant language of Article I. (See the discussion of *McCulloch v. Maryland,* 1819, in Chapter 3, "Federalism: A Nation of States.") Congress gained through this clause much of the lawmaking power it now exercises.

Article II vested "the Executive Power" in the president of the United States. Article II, Section 2 spelled out the president's powers, the most significant of which are the powers to serve as **commander-in-chief** of the armed forces; make treaties with foreign nations,

distributive articles The first three articles of the Constitution, which define the legislative, executive, and judicial powers, respectively, of the national government.

Necessary and Proper Clause The final paragraph of Article I, Section 8 of the Constitution that allows Congress to make laws that are necessary and proper to further its enumerated powers.

commander-in-chief The constitutional role of the president as supreme commander of the armed forces.

▶ **advice and consent** The constitutional power of the Senate to ratify treaties and confirm presidential appointments.

with the **advice and consent** of the Senate; and appoint ambassadors, federal judges, and other high officials, again with the advice and consent of the Senate. Today, "advice and consent" refers to the two-thirds majority of the Senate that must approve treaties and presidential appointments. In no way did the language of Article II anticipate the power and prestige of the modern presidency. Although some Framers—most notably Alexander Hamilton—took a broad view of what constituted "executive power," most of them conceived of the president's role primarily as one of faithfully executing the laws passed by Congress.

Article III gave "the judicial Power of the United States" to "one supreme Court" and "such inferior courts as Congress may from time to time ordain and establish." Section 2 extended the judicial power to "all Cases . . . arising under this Constitution, the Laws of the United States, and Treaties made . . . under their Authority. . . ." Article III made no mention of what was to become the cornerstone of judicial power: the right to invalidate legislation found to be contrary to the Constitution. This power, known as judicial review, was assumed by the Supreme Court in a landmark decision in 1803 (see the discussion of *Marbury v. Madison* in section 2-8a, "Constitutional Change through Judicial Interpretation"). The Framers of the Constitution were aware of judicial review, but could not agree on whether the federal courts should be given this power. Some, including Alexander Hamilton, wanted the courts to be able to nullify acts of Congress that violated the Constitution. Others thought it dangerous to place the power to nullify legislation in the hands of appointed judges with life tenure. Ultimately, the Framers left the question of judicial review to be worked out in practice.

2-6b The System of Checks and Balances

Under the proposed Constitution, the president was authorized to veto bills passed by Congress, but Congress could override the president's veto by a two-thirds majority in both houses. The president was given the power to appoint judges, ambassadors, and other high government officials, but the Senate could reject presidential nominees to these positions. The president was made commander-in-chief, but Congress was given the authority to declare war, raise and support an army and a navy, and make rules governing the armed forces. The president was empowered to call Congress into special session, but was duty-bound to appear "from time to time" to inform Congress about the "state of the Union." These provisions were designed to create a perpetual competition between Congress and the executive branch for control of the government, with the expectation that neither institution would permanently dominate the other.

The Framers were concerned with not only the possibility that one institution might dominate the government but also that a popular majority might gain control of both Congress and the presidency and thereby institute a **tyranny of the majority.** An important feature of the system of checks and balances was the different terms for the president, members of the House, and U.S. senators. Representatives would be elected every two years; senators would serve for six-year terms. Presidents, of course, would hold office for four years. The staggered terms of the presidency and the Senate, in particular, were designed to make it difficult (although certainly not impossible) for a transitory popular majority to get and keep control of the government.

▶ **tyranny of the majority** Disregard of the rights of individuals or minority groups by the majority of the people in a society.

▶ **Articles of Confederation** The colonists' first attempt at a charter for the national government. Although the Articles were adopted by Congress in 1777, they were not ratified until 1781. In 1788, they were superseded by the U.S. Constitution.

2-6c Restrictions on the States

Article I, Section 10 imposed a series of restrictions on the state governments. States were prohibited from entering into treaties, alliances, or confederations among themselves or with foreign powers. They were also prohibited from coining their own money, imposing their own tariffs on imports and exports, and, most importantly, impairing the obligations of contracts. These restrictions on the economic powers of the states were a direct response to the conditions that existed under the **Articles of Confederation.**

2-6d Individual Rights

The Framers did not believe that a bill of rights was a necessary component of the Constitution, for three reasons:

- Because rights were founded in natural law, their existence did not depend on their enumeration in the Constitution.

- An enumeration of specific rights might imply that citizens lacked other rights not specified.

- The new national government was to be limited in power and thus would pose little threat to life, liberty, and property.

Yet, conversely, without creating a bill of rights, the Framers did recognize several rights in the text of the Constitution. Article I, Section 9 recognized the ancient common-law right to petition the courts for a writ of **habeas corpus,** a means by which an individual could challenge and, if successful, escape unlawful confinement. Section 9 forbade Congress from suspending the writ "unless when in Cases of Rebellion or Invasion the public Safety may require it."

Article I, Section 9 also prohibited Congress from passing bills of attainder and **ex post facto laws.** Article I, Section 10 imposed these same prohibitions on the state legislatures. A **bill of attainder** is a legislative act imposing punishment on a party without the benefit of trial in a court of law. An ex post facto law retroactively criminalizes some action that was not a crime when it was committed. The British Parliament had on occasion used both bills of attainder and ex post facto laws to punish opponents of the Crown. The Framers were well aware of these abuses of legislative power and wanted to make sure that neither Congress nor the state legislatures would succumb to them.

> ▶ **habeas corpus** A legal device by which an individual can go to court to challenge and, if successful, escape unlawful confinement.

> ▶ **ex post facto law** A legislative act that retroactively criminalizes some action that was not a crime when it was committed.

> ▶ **bill of attainder** A legislative act imposing punishment on a party without benefit of trial in a court of law.

Comparative Perspective

The French Constitution

The United States has been governed under the same Constitution since 1789, although it has been modified by formal amendments and changing judicial interpretations. In contrast, France has experimented with a variety of constitutions. Since 1789, France has experienced dictatorship, monarchy, and democracy. Over the past two centuries, it has had five republican regimes, each with its own constitution. The Constitution of the Fifth French Republic, adopted in 1958, has proven to be reasonably durable, but it has yet to outlast the Constitution of the Third Republic, which was in effect for sixty-five years (1875–1940). The current French Constitution, which has some similarities to both the U.S. Constitution and the British parliamentary system, provides for a powerful president, independent of the legislature and elected directly by the people. Unlike the U.S. president, however, the French president has the right to dissolve the assembly and call for legislative elections, as long as dissolutions are at least one year apart. The president nominates the premier (prime minister) who in turn selects the cabinet. The president is also empowered to submit referenda to the people and declare a state of emergency. Neither of these powers is vested in the American presidency. The French Constitutional Council supervises elections and referenda. It also rules on the constitutionality of any legislation before it is adopted, but considers constitutional questions only at the request of the president, the premier, or the president of the assembly. The courts are theoretically independent of the president and the assembly, but do not have the power to nullify laws or administrative actions.

2-6e An Undemocratic Document?

The Framers' Constitution contained a number of elitist elements that strike modern sensibilities as being downright undemocratic. In particular, many important choices were left to the elites of society rather than to the common people. First, Article I, Section 3 provided that members of the Senate would be chosen by the state legislatures rather than by the people directly. Second, the president was to be chosen not by direct popular election, but rather by the **electoral college** composed of delegates from the states. Third, federal judges were to be appointed, not elected, and would hold office for life. These elitist elements of the Constitution were controversial even in 1787. The more democratically minded Founders, such as Patrick Henry of Virginia, thought that the new Constitution should be rejected.

> **electoral college** The constitutional body that formally selects the president and vice president.

2-7 The Battle over Ratification

Today, U.S. citizens look to the Constitution as a statement of their national consensus—an expression of their shared political culture. But in 1787 the Constitution was a divisive political issue, and ratification was by no means a foregone conclusion. Interestingly, although the smaller states had been the obstacle at the Philadelphia Convention, opposition to ratification was most intense in the largest states: Massachusetts, New York, and Virginia. But division existed in every state.

Unlike the Articles of Confederation, the Constitution of 1787 did not require the unanimous consent of the states to be ratified. Instead, it would take effect after ratification by nine of the thirteen states. Rather than allow the state legislatures to consider ratification, the Constitution called for a popular convention to be held in every state. By rejecting a motion to hold another constitutional convention, the Framers presented the states with an all-or-nothing situation. These features, in addition to provisions for amending the Constitution later, were intended, in the words of Forrest McDonald, to "stack the deck" in favor of ratification.[14]

2-7a Federalists Versus Anti-Federalists

Supporters of the Constitution called themselves Federalists; opponents were dubbed Anti-Federalists. Federalists were found mainly in the cities, among the artisans, shopkeepers, merchants, and, not insignificantly, newspaper publishers. Anti-Federalist sentiment was strongest in rural areas, especially among small farmers. The Anti-Federalists were poorly organized and, consequently, less effective than their Federalist opponents. Moreover, they were constantly on the defensive. Because they were opposing a major reform effort, they were perceived as defending a status quo that was unacceptable to most Americans. Still, the Anti-Federalists had considerable support and succeeded in making ratification a close question in some states.

The most eloquent statement of the Anti-Federalist position was Richard Henry Lee's *Letters of the Federal Farmer,* published in the fall of 1787. Lee, a principal architect of the Articles of Confederation, thought that the proposed national government would threaten both the rights of the states and the liberties of the individual. Perhaps Lee's most effective criticism of the new Constitution was that it lacked a bill of rights. Lee pointed out that state constitutions, without exception, enumerated the rights of citizens vis-à-vis their state governments. The only conclusion Lee could draw was that the Philadelphia Convention and its handiwork, the Constitution, did not place a premium on liberty. However wrongheaded this criticism, it touched a nerve among the American people. Ultimately, the Federalists would only secure ratification of the Constitution by promising to support a series of amendments that would create a bill of rights.

Despite their popular appeal, *Letters of the Federal Farmer* and the other Anti-Federalist tracts were no match for the brilliant essays written by James Madison, Alexander Hamilton, and John Jay in defense of the Constitution. *The Federalist Papers* were published serially in New York newspapers during the winter of 1788 under the pen name Publius. Without question, *The Federalist Papers* helped to secure the ratification of the Constitution in the crucial state of New York. Yet *The Federalist,* as the collected papers are generally known, was much more than a set of time-bound political tracts. As historians Charles and Mary Beard recognized, it was "the most profound single treatise on the Constitution ever written." Accordingly, it ranks "among the few masterly works on political science produced in all the centuries of history."[15]

2-7b The Ratifying Conventions

Approximately three months after the close of the Philadelphia Convention, Delaware became the first state to ratify the Constitution. Within nine months after the convention, the necessary ninth state had signed on. But the two largest and most important states, Virginia and New York, became battlegrounds over ratification. Although the Constitution became the "supreme law of the land" when the ninth state, New Hampshire, approved it in June 1788, it was vital to the success of the new nation that Virginia and New York come on board.

At the Virginia ratifying convention, Patrick Henry, a leader of the Anti-Federalist cause, claimed that four-fifths of Virginians were opposed to ratification. But the oratory of Edmund Randolph, combined with the prestige of George Washington, finally carried the day. The Federalists won Virginia by a vote of 89–79. The news that Virginia had approved the new Constitution gave the Federalists considerable momentum. In July, New York followed Virginia's lead and approved the Constitution by 3 votes. The two holdouts, North Carolina and Rhode Island, not wanting to be excluded from the Union, followed suit in November 1789 and May 1790, respectively. The new Constitution was in effect and fully legitimized by "the consent of the governed."

After its ratification, the Constitution became an object of popular reverence—a sort of secular Bible. Yet, despite the widespread Constitution worship, the Constitution, like the Articles of Confederation that preceded it, had certain deficiencies. Of course, the Framers anticipated this problem and provided mechanisms for changing the Constitution. At the same time, these mechanisms were intentionally designed to make it difficult to change the Constitution. Because the Constitution represents the supreme and fundamental law of the land, amending the Constitution should be considerably harder than passing a statute. Otherwise, whenever a majority in Congress wanted to pass a law prohibited by the Constitution (for example, a law abridging the freedom of speech), they could easily change the Constitution to allow that law. Because the Constitution exists in large part to protect minority interests from abuse by the majority, mere majority approval is not enough.

2-8 Amending the Constitution

The two methods by which the Constitution can be amended are outlined in Article V. Both methods assign a formal role to the states. Most commonly, two-thirds of the members of each house of Congress propose an amendment, which must then be approved by three-fourths of the state legislatures. Thus, with this method, state legislatures around the nation must consider the proposed amendment, and a quarter of the states can block a change. In the 1970s, for example, opponents of the Equal Rights Amendment were able to concentrate on selected state legislatures and eventually succeeded in stopping the proposed amendment. The votes of certain state legislators in Illinois became pivotal as consideration of the amendment continued.

The second method of proposing an amendment to the Constitution has never been used. It allows two-thirds of the states to initiate the process by petitioning for a national constitutional convention. The logic of this second method is that it allows the states to overcome a stubborn Congress that might be unwilling to make widely supported changes in the Constitution. In either case, the Constitution cannot be altered without the participation of the state legislatures.

This difficulty of amending the Constitution prevents a "bandwagon effect" driven by short-term emotions. For example, politicians might react to popular outrage at constitutional interpretation by the courts and immediately suggest changing the Constitution. The amendment process gives opponents time to marshal their resources and make their arguments. It also allows them to target their opposition toward a small number of states. Merely having to face a drawn-out ratification process is enough to keep all but the most thoroughly considered constitutional changes from being formally proposed. For instance, in 1989, the Supreme Court held that flag burning was a legitimate form of political speech and declared unconstitutional a state law making flag burning a crime.[16] An immediate firestorm of reaction against the decision occurred. Not surprisingly, several members of Congress suggested an amendment that would specifically exempt flag burning from the protection of the Bill of Rights. As the debate continued, however, it became clear that there was much sentiment against tampering with the Bill of Rights in this way. The push for an amendment soon subsided, although the issue seems to resurface prior to every presidential election.

On the other hand, a workable constitution should not present insurmountable obstacles to change. When a clear consensus for changing the Constitution exists and no opposition group can argue effectively against it, amendments can, and do, pass. For example, the Twenty-Sixth Amendment, which established a national eighteen-year-old voting age, represented a near-consensus in American society and passed with little trouble in 1971. In all, the amendment process seems to strike an almost perfect balance. Efforts at change are infrequent and generally reflect shifts in very broad principles. With the exception of the Eighteenth Amendment, which outlawed the sale of alcohol, constitutional amendments have been accepted as part of the political fabric. Evidently, the American people approve of the process by which the Constitution is amended. When polled in 1987, 60 percent of a national sample said the process was "about right."[17]

The most glaring imperfection of the Constitution of 1787 was the absence of a bill of rights, a deficiency that almost derailed the ratification of the Constitution in Virginia and New York. When the First Congress adopted the Bill of Rights in 1789, it was making good on an agreement that had been instrumental in securing ratification. Although Congress was under no legal compulsion to act, most members believed that adding the Bill of Rights to the Constitution was desirable, either as an end in itself or as a means of engendering popular support for the new Constitution and government. James Madison, the prime mover behind the Bill of Rights in the House of Representatives, appealed to both the idealistic and pragmatic sentiments of his fellow members. In a speech on the House floor in June 1789, Madison said:

> It cannot be a secret to the gentlemen of this House that, not withstanding the ratification of this system of government . . . , yet there is a great number of our constituents who are dissatisfied with it, among whom are many respectable for their talents and patriotism and respectable for the jealousy they have for their liberty. . . . We ought not to disregard their inclination but, on principles of amity and moderation, conform to their wishes and expressly declare the great rights of mankind secured under this Constitution.[18]

After considerable debate, Congress adopted twelve amendments in the fall of 1789 and submitted them to the states for ratification. Ten of these amendments were promptly ratified and officially became part of the Constitution in 1791. Interestingly, one of the two "failed" amendments prohibited Congress from giving its members a pay increase that would go into effect before the next congressional election. The amendment was resurrected and finally ratified in 1992 amidst widespread public anger at Congress.

Guaranteeing States' Rights: The Tenth and Eleventh Amendments

▶ **sovereign immunity** Legal concept established in the Eleventh Amendment that grants states immunity from being sued in federal court by their own citizens or citizens from another state.

Although the term *Bill of Rights* refers collectively to the first ten amendments to the Constitution, only the first nine deal with individual rights. The Tenth Amendment was designed to reassure the state governments that powers not delegated to the new national government would be reserved to them. Similarly, the Eleventh Amendment was designed to limit the power of the federal courts to invade the **sovereign immunity** of the state governments—that is, their traditional protection against being sued in the courts without their consent. Thus, both the Tenth and Eleventh Amendments deal with **states' rights** and, accordingly, are examined in depth in Chapter 3, "Federalism: A Nation of States."

Correcting a Constitutional Malfunction: The Twelfth Amendment   The Framers of the Constitution did not anticipate, nor did they desire, the emergence of political parties. By the late 1790s, however, a two-party system was becoming established (the Federalists versus the Jeffersonians). Under the Constitution, the president and vice president were to be elected by the electoral college, which was made up of delegates from the states, rather than by the American people directly. The Constitution provided that the presidential candidate receiving a majority of votes in the electoral college would be elected president; the runner-up would become vice president. This procedure resulted in John Adams' having a "hostile" vice president in Thomas Jefferson (1797–1801). The Adams-Jefferson administration was anything but harmonious.

The electoral college malfunctioned badly in the next presidential election. In 1800, Thomas Jefferson and Aaron Burr, both of whom were Democratic-Republicans, received the same number of electoral votes (73), even though it was well known that Burr was seeking the vice presidency. Under the procedures outlined in Article II, Section 1, the election was thrown into the House of Representatives, which, much to Jefferson's chagrin, was controlled by the rival Federalist Party. To make matters worse, the ambitious Burr, no longer content to become vice president, tried to capture the presidency. After a battle in the House, Jefferson finally prevailed, but only after thirty-six ballots and securing the support of his old political enemy, Alexander Hamilton. The unpleasant episode prompted Congress to adopt, and the states to ratify, the Twelfth Amendment. Essentially, the Twelfth Amendment requires members of the electoral college to vote separately for the president and vice president. This method permits two individuals to run as a party ticket. The Twelfth Amendment became part of the Constitution on September 25, 1804, just in time for the next presidential election.

The Civil War Amendments   The impact of the Civil War (1861–1865) on American political culture, the institutions of government, and indeed the entire political system can hardly be overstated. The Civil War changed the Constitution in several ways, most obviously through the addition of three new amendments: the Thirteenth (1865), Fourteenth (1868), and Fifteenth (1870). The Thirteenth Amendment abolished slavery, thus reaffirming and extending President Abraham Lincoln's Emancipation Proclamation of 1863. The Fourteenth Amendment, among other things, prohibited states from denying persons within their jurisdictions **due process of law** and the **equal protection of the laws.** Due process of law refers to the legal procedures that must be observed before the government can deprive an individual of life, liberty, or property. Equal protection of the laws means that all citizens have an equal right to the various protections the law affords.

The primary motivation for the Fourteenth Amendment was to provide constitutional protection for the civil rights of the newly freed former slaves. Section 5 of the Fourteenth Amendment gave Congress the authority to enact "appropriate legislation" to enforce the broad guarantees of due process and equal protection. Finally, the Fifteenth Amendment guaranteed citizens of all races the right to vote in state and federal elections and, like the Fourteenth Amendment, authorized Congress to enforce the guarantee by appropriate legislation. The effect of the Civil War amendments was not immediate, but over the long run their influence has been profound. These amendments have served to protect not only the civil rights of African Americans and other minorities but also the civil rights and liberties of all Americans. In addition, by empowering Congress and the federal courts to protect civil rights against incursions by the state governments, these amendments had a tremendous impact on federalism.

Other Important Amendments   Twelve amendments have been added to the Constitution since 1870; the latest is the Twenty-Seventh Amendment, adopted by Congress in 1789 but not ratified until 1992. Although none of these amendments ranks in

> **states' rights** The doctrine that certain powers and responsibilities belong exclusively to the states and should not be interfered with by the national government.

> **due process of law** Legal procedures designed to ensure that life, liberty, and property cannot be arbitrarily or capriciously taken by government.

> **equal protection of the laws** Principle established by the Fourteenth Amendment that restricts states from arbitrarily discriminating against persons.

magnitude with the Bill of Rights or the Civil War amendments, several had a significant impact on the constitutional system. Three amendments—specifically, the Nineteenth (1920), the Twenty-Fourth (1964), and the Twenty-Sixth (1971)—expanded the right to vote to include groups that had previously been locked out of the political process. Accordingly, these amendments are discussed in section 2-8b, "Democratization of the Constitutional System."

The Sixteenth Amendment (1913) authorized Congress to "lay and collect taxes on incomes." This amendment was a direct response to an 1895 Supreme Court decision which held that Congress lacked the constitutional authority to impose an income tax.[19] By dramatically increasing the revenues of the national government, the Sixteenth Amendment facilitated the increasing responsibility (and power) that the national government assumed during the twentieth century. Accordingly, it must be considered an important modification of the constitutional system—a further departure from the limited role that the Founders envisioned for the national government.

> **Prohibition** The national policy in the 1920s barring the importation, production, or transportation of alcoholic beverages.

The Eighteenth Amendment (1919) prohibited the manufacture, sale, or transportation of alcoholic beverages in the United States. Congress implemented this amendment through the Volstead Act, which went into effect in 1920. This statute in essence attached criminal penalties to the prohibitions of the Eighteenth Amendment. **Prohibition** was brought about in large part by pressure groups, such as the Anti-Saloon Leagues, that believed alcohol abuse was a serious social problem that the national government should address. Prohibition was never popular or effective. Organized crime vaulted into the national consciousness as gangsters like Al Capone took over the business of importing and distributing liquor. In all, Prohibition was judged a tragic failure, and the Eighteenth Amendment was repealed by the Twenty-First Amendment in 1933 during the darkest days of the Great Depression. Prohibition was significant, however, in that it greatly increased the role of the federal government in law enforcement and crime control, a function previously left to the states. In a sense, Prohibition was the predecessor of the "war on drugs" being waged by the national government today.

The Twenty-Second Amendment, ratified in 1951, limited a president to no more than two consecutive terms. Before the election of Franklin Delano Roosevelt, who won four presidential elections (1932, 1936, 1940, and 1944), no president had sought a third term. In 1949, the Republican Congress reacted to Roosevelt's feat (as well as to the centralization of power in Washington that attended his presidency) by adopting the Twenty-Second Amendment. Ironically, in the mid-1980s, Republicans lamented that Ronald Reagan, a popular Republican president, was barred from seeking a third term. Some Republicans went so far as to call for the repeal of the Twenty-Second Amendment. When Reagan expressed no interest in a third term, the movement to amend the Constitution subsided.

2-8a Constitutional Change through Judicial Interpretation

In this chapter, you have read about constitutional changes that came about through the formal amendment process. Turn now to significant modifications in the constitutional system that came about through changes in the way the Constitution is interpreted. Constitutional interpretation has become the principal, but not exclusive, domain of the courts as a result of a key Supreme Court decision in 1803.

In *Marbury v. Madison* (1803), the Supreme Court asserted the power to review acts of Congress and declare them null and void if found to be contrary to the Constitution (see Case in Point 2-1).[20] Seven years later, the Court extended this power to encompass the validity of state laws under the federal Constitution.[21] The power of the federal courts to rule on the constitutionality of legislation is nowhere explicitly mentioned in the Constitution, although many commentators have tried to justify it in terms of the Supremacy Clause of Article VI. The Framers of the Constitution were not unanimous in their support for judicial review, but most likely expected the courts to exercise this power. In any event, the Supreme Court assumed this authority and, in so doing, greatly enhanced its role in the system of checks and balances. Moreover, the Court took on primary responsibility for interpreting the Constitution. In *McCulloch v. Maryland* (1819), Chief Justice John Marshall observed, "We must never forget, that it is a constitution we are expounding."[22] Mar-

---

Case in Point **2-1**

The Establishment of the Power of Judicial Review
Marbury v. Madison (1803)

After the national election of 1800, in which the Federalists lost the presidency and both chambers of Congress to the Jeffersonian Republicans, the Federalists tried to preserve their influence within the national government by expanding their control over the federal courts. The "lame duck" Congress, in which the Federalists held a majority, quickly passed the Judiciary Act of 1801, which was signed into law by President John Adams. The act created a number of new federal judgeships, which Adams would be able to fill with loyal Federalists. Congress also adopted legislation creating several minor judgeships for the newly established District of Columbia.

William Marbury was one of many Federalist politicians appointed to judicial office in the waning days of the Adams administration. Marbury's commission as justice of the peace for the District of Columbia had been signed by the president following Senate confirmation on March 3, 1801, Adams' last day in office. The responsibility for delivering the commission fell to Secretary of State John Marshall. For some reason, yet to be fully explained, the commission was never delivered.

Thomas Jefferson was sworn in as the nation's third president on March 4, 1801. The new secretary of state, James Madison, refused to deliver the commission to Marbury. Marbury filed suit against Madison in the Supreme Court, invoking the Court's **original jurisdiction**—that is, its power to hear cases that have not been previously decided by lower courts. In his suit, Marbury asked the Court to issue a **writ of mandamus,** an order directing Madison to deliver the disputed judicial commission.

The Supreme Court's presumed authority to issue the writ of mandamus was based on Section 13 of the Judiciary Act of 1789. Section 13 granted the Court the authority to "issue . . . writs of mandamus, in cases warranted by the principles and usages of law. . . ." According to Chief Justice John Marshall's opinion in Marbury, the Court could not issue the writ because the relevant provision of Section 13 was unconstitutional. Under Article III of the Constitution, Congress may regulate the appellate jurisdiction of the Court, but not its original jurisdiction. According to Marshall, Section 13 was invalid because it expanded the Court's original jurisdiction.

Thus, the power of judicial review was first asserted in a case involving a technical legal question. Since 1803, the power has been used to address much more important questions of public policy, such as abortion, racial segregation, and school prayer.

---

shall went on to observe that the Constitution "was intended to endure for ages to come, and consequently, to be adapted to the various crises of human affairs."[23] Clearly, Marshall had in mind that the courts would be principally responsible for making such adaptations.

The Constitution, *Laissez-Faire,* and the New Deal   A colossal struggle over the government's role in regulating the economy provides an excellent illustration of how a change in the way the Constitution is interpreted can affect government institutions and public policy making. The Framers of the Constitution believed in limited government, but they did endow the national government with the power to regulate interstate commerce. Under their **police power,** however, states had the authority to enact laws regulating economic activity for the purpose of promoting public health, safety, and welfare. At the same time, it is fair to say that the Framers did not expect either the federal or the state governments to attempt to manage the economy in any comprehensive way. Though not hardcore advocates of *laissez-faire* capitalism, in which the free market operates with no government intervention, the Founders did believe in the primacy of private enterprise.

After the Civil War, as the United States experienced rapid growth and change as a result of the Industrial Revolution, both the national and state governments began to enact measures designed to regulate the economy. By modern standards, these regulatory measures were relatively modest. Yet, beginning in the 1890s, a conservative Supreme Court limited the power of Congress to tax and regulate interstate commerce.[24] Moreover, the Court interpreted the Due Process Clauses of the Fifth and Fourteenth Amendments to create a barrier to federal and state legislation designed to regulate the industrial workplace. In case after case, the Court held that government efforts to regulate wages, working hours, and working conditions were violations of the liberty of both employers and employees. In *Lochner v. New York* (1905), the leading case of the era, Justice Rufus Peckham asserted that "the freedom of master and employee to contract with each other in relation to their

> **original jurisdiction**   The authority of a court of law to hear a case for the first time, usually for the purpose of conducting a trial or holding a hearing.

> **writ of mandamus**   A court order requiring a governmental official to carry out her official duties.

> **police power**   The power of the state to enact laws regulating economic activity for the purpose of promoting public health, safety, and welfare.

employment, and in defining the same, cannot be prohibited or interfered with, without violating the Federal Constitution."[25]

In 1929, the nation plunged headlong into the Great Depression. In 1932, Franklin D. Roosevelt was elected to the presidency on a promise to provide a **New Deal.** Roosevelt's New Deal consisted of unprecedented efforts by the federal government to regulate and manage the economy. The New Deal was enacted through a series of important statutes passed by Congress beginning in 1933. In a series of decisions between 1933 and 1937, the Supreme Court declared these statutes invalid. Although the particular reasons varied, the Court's essential objection was that these laws expanded the powers of the national government beyond the permissible scope delineated in the Constitution. Not surprisingly, Roosevelt, most members of Congress, and a substantial segment of the attentive public viewed the Court's decisions as unnecessarily obstructionist—even reactionary. Roosevelt began to refer to the Court as the "nine old men" whose "horse and buggy" views of the American economy were preventing the government from orchestrating a recovery.

In early 1937, Roosevelt proposed his infamous **Court-packing plan,** under which the president would be authorized to appoint one new justice to the Supreme Court for each current justice over the age of seventy. Although the Court-packing plan failed in Congress, the Supreme Court evidently got the message and in an abrupt turnaround in the spring of 1937 upheld the National Labor Relations Act, a key piece of New Deal legislation.[26] In the years to follow, the Court repudiated altogether the doctrines by which it had earlier blocked government efforts to regulate the economy. In rejecting these doctrines, the Court helped to bring about a veritable constitutional revolution.

As a result of the New Deal, President Lyndon Johnson's Great Society legislation of the 1960s, and various programs enacted under Republican as well as Democratic presidents, the national government has taken more and more responsibility for managing the economy and ensuring the economic well-being of the nation. This tremendous change in public policy, and in the power of government agencies, came about not through a formal amendment to the Constitution, but rather through changes in the way the Constitution was understood.

2-8b Democratization of the Constitutional System

The growth of government at all levels to meet demands engendered by economic and social change is perhaps the most obvious change in the constitutional system since its founding more than two centuries ago. Yet equally important is the **democratization** of the constitutional system, which simply means that the system has become more democratic than it was designed to be. Like other major changes in the constitutional system, this change has come about through both formal amendments and changes in constitutional interpretation. Even more fundamentally, though, the democratization of the constitutional system represents a profound change in American political culture.

Expanding Constitutional Protection of Liberty and Equality By protecting the rights of all citizens against the power of the national government, the Bill of Rights took a major stride in the march toward constitutional democracy. Certainly, the First Amendment, which protects the right of all citizens to speak freely and assemble and organize for the purpose of petitioning the government for a redress of grievances, has proved to be essential to American democracy. Without question, the Fourteenth Amendment, which provided broad protection for the civil rights of all Americans, must be regarded as a giant step forward in the evolution of American democracy. The Fourteenth Amendment guarantees, among other things, equal protection of the laws. This provision rests on the premise that individuals should be equal before the state, which is the fundamental principle of democracy.

> **New Deal** Policy initiative of President Franklin D. Roosevelt consisting of unprecedented efforts by the federal government to regulate and manage the economy.

> **Court-packing plan** Proposal by President Franklin D. Roosevelt in 1937 to expand the number of justices on the Supreme Court in order to create a Court majority likely to support his policies.

> **democratization** The process of making a political system more democratic.

Popular Culture and American Politics
The Grapes of Wrath

Henry Fonda in *The Grapes of Wrath*

The 1940 film *The Grapes of Wrath* dramatizes the plight of itinerant farm workers caught in the grip of the Great Depression.

©John Springer Collection / CORBIS

The Great Depression of the 1930s brought a fundamental challenge to the nation. The collapse of the banking system, massive unemployment, industrial stagnation, and the specter of millions of Americans waiting in bread lines shook the society to its foundations. To many, it seemed cold and heartless to think that individuals could succeed on their own in the face of such calamity. The question put to the American people in the presidential election of 1932 was whether government should move beyond its traditional limited role and provide help to Americans ravaged by the Great Depression. The electorate answered in a resounding "Yes," and the New Deal was under way.

The movie *The Grapes of Wrath* (1940) displayed a side of America not previously illuminated by Hollywood. The film's protagonists, the Joad family, faced injustice, hardship, unfairness, and cruelty fueled by greed as they moved from Oklahoma to California in search of opportunity. Their failures were not of their own making. Rather, they were the result of the economic system. America was not so much a land of small farmers as of "growers" who misused honest workers.

The federal government makes an appearance in *The Grapes of Wrath* in the form of a kindly agricultural agent running a work camp to help the Joads and others like them to survive. This was no faceless government bureaucrat, but rather a caring, almost saintly, gentleman. The image of America as a land of rugged individualism and limited government had faded. A new image of a benevolent, more active government came into focus. As tragic events dictated, the political system evolved. But the fundamental institutions of American democracy remained intact.

Enfranchising African Americans   In *Scott v. Sandford* (1857)—better known as the Dred Scott case—the Supreme Court ruled that persons of African descent were not, and could not become, citizens of the United States.[27] Indeed, they had no constitutional rights. This decision, which is now considered morally outrageous, was overturned by the ratification of the Fourteenth Amendment in 1868. The Fourteenth Amendment conferred citizenship on "all persons born or naturalized in the United States." It did not, however, specifically guarantee African Americans the right to vote. Congress corrected this oversight by adopting the Fifteenth Amendment (1870), which provides that "The right of citizens of the United States to vote shall not be denied or abridged by the United States or by any State on account of race, color, or previous condition of servitude."

The Constitution is not a self-executing document. Nearly a century passed before the promise of the Fifteenth Amendment was fulfilled. A number of states resisted the extension of the franchise to African Americans, and some adopted measures that frustrated black citizens' efforts to register and vote. Eventually, however, these impediments were swept away by Supreme Court decisions and acts of Congress, such as the landmark Voting Rights Act of 1965. These decisions and enactments involved both assertions of power by the national government vis-à-vis the states and changes in constitutional interpretation (for further discussion, see Chapter 5, "Civil Rights and the Struggle for Equality"). As a result of the enforcement of the Fifteenth Amendment, African Americans can register and vote without encountering legal and structural obstacles.

Direct Popular Election of the Senate   As noted in section 2-6e, "An Undemocratic Document?" the Constitution initially provided that members of the U.S. Senate would be elected by the state legislatures. The Seventeenth Amendment, ratified in 1913, required that the Senate be chosen directly by the people. The House of Representatives had proposed the amendment on several occasions, but the Senate had resisted. Finally, in 1912, after public opinion became aroused, the Senate relented. It took only one year for the states to ratify the measure, which had attracted widespread popular support. In reality, though, the Seventeenth Amendment merely formalized what had been occurring informally in half the states, where the legislatures routinely followed the will of the people expressed at the ballot box.

Women's Suffrage   The Nineteenth Amendment (1920), which guaranteed women the right to vote, was the culmination of a movement that began in the 1840s. But the Nineteenth Amendment applied only to voting. It said nothing about the numerous state and federal laws that discriminated against females in matters of property, marriage and divorce, employment, and the professions. In 1923, an amendment was introduced in Congress to provide wider constitutional protection for women's rights. Not until 1972, however, did Congress submit the Equal Rights Amendment to the states. After a protracted and, in some states, bitter struggle, the amendment failed to win ratification. But its failure did not leave women's rights without protection under the federal Constitution. The Equal Protection Clause of the Fourteenth Amendment has been interpreted to provide a substantial degree of protection against official, government-sponsored sex discrimination (see Chapter 5, "Civil Rights and the Struggle for Equality"). Moreover, Congress has used its enforcement powers under the Fourteenth Amendment to enact statutes that further protect women against discrimination.

Lowering the Voting Age   The Twenty-Sixth Amendment (1971) effectively lowered the voting age to eighteen in both state and federal elections. Congress had already decided in 1970 to lower the voting age in federal elections; the amendment came in response to a Supreme Court decision which held that a constitutional amendment was necessary to force the states to lower their voting ages.[28] Considerable impetus for lowering the voting age came from young men aged eighteen to twenty-one, who were eligible to be drafted into military service and sent to die in the jungles of Vietnam, but were unable to vote for or against the politicians who formulated policies like the draft and the conduct of the Vietnam War. The amendment was ratified quickly and with little opposition. Even state legislatures that supported maintaining the voting age at twenty-one were reluctant to deal with the costly administrative problems that would follow if the federal and state voting ages were different.

Eliminating Economic Restrictions on Voting

When the Constitution was framed, the states were given almost total discretion in determining eligibility to vote. They were limited only in that those who were deemed to be eligible to vote for members of the state house—technically, "the most numerous branch of the state legislature" —would be eligible to vote in elections to the U.S. House of Representatives. In all states, voting was restricted to white men of property, although specific property requirements varied somewhat. By the time Andrew Jackson was elected president in 1832, all states except New Jersey and North Carolina had abolished property requirements for voting.

One of the ways in which states limited the vote was through the **poll tax.** Throughout the nineteenth century, many states, especially in the South, charged a tax for the privilege of voting. Of course, the idea was to limit the participation of the poor, both black and white. In 1964, the Twenty-Fourth Amendment was added to eliminate the poll tax, which had already fallen into some disfavor. The amendment applied only to federal elections, however, and some states continued the practice. Two years later, though, the Supreme Court ruled that these state poll taxes violated the Fourteenth Amendment's Equal Protection Clause, and this device was effectively eliminated from the American political landscape.[29] The removal of the poll tax through formal constitutional change (the Twenty-Fourth Amendment) and the extension of this limitation to the states through constitutional interpretation signified a change in the American notion of political participation: Voting is for all citizens, not just the wealthy.

poll tax A fee paid for the privilege of voting.

Reapportionment: One Person, One Vote

The right to vote is devalued if one person's vote counts for less than the votes of other citizens. Unfortunately, this was the case before the 1960s. Congressional districts, state legislative districts, even local electoral districts (school boards, county commissions, and the like) were often grossly unequal in terms of population, a condition known as **malapportionment.** When districts are unequal, the influence of each voter in the more populous districts is diminished, and the influence of voters in the less populated districts is enhanced.

Historically, malapportionment of the state legislatures and U.S. House of Representatives favored the less populated rural districts over the more populated urban ones. Constituents from urban areas attempted to get the legislatures to reapportion themselves, but with little success. Finally, after it became clear that the legislatures were not going to act, the federal courts entered the "political thicket" of legislative apportionment. First, in the landmark case of *Baker v. Carr* (1962), the Supreme Court overturned a precedent that had prevented the lower courts from intervening in matters of apportionment.[30] Then, in *Reynolds v. Sims* (1964), the High Court held that state legislative districts had to be reapportioned according to the principle of **one person, one vote.**[31] Districts then had to be redrawn to be made equal in population. Other Supreme Court decisions extended this requirement to U.S. House districts and to districts for local governing bodies.

malapportionment The condition in which legislative districts are unequal in population.

Considered fairly revolutionary in the 1960s, **reapportionment** is now an accepted part of American political life. Every ten years, after the federal government completes its census, state legislatures reapportion themselves and the congressional districts in their respective states. Failure to do so inevitably means that they will be sued and ordered to undertake reapportionment by a federal court. Indeed, even when the legislature does reapportion itself, certain parties are bound to be displeased. Thus, lawsuits challenging reapportionment plans have become fairly routine in the federal courts. Although reapportionment can be tricky, both legally and politically, unquestionably the reapportionment revolution has rendered the political system more democratic. In a democracy—which rests, of course, on the premise that all citizens are equal before the state—no justification exists for one person's vote to count for more than another's. Political equality has thus become a fundamental aspect of American political culture.

one person, one vote Judicially recognized principle, derived from the Equal Protection Clause of the Constitution, that requires political districts to be made equal in population.

reapportionment The process by which legislative boundaries are redrawn to reflect changes in population.

2-9 Conclusion: Assessing the Constitutional System

The American Constitution is the oldest written constitution still in effect in the world. Its longevity can be attributed to a number of factors. One is its basic design, incorporating the separation of powers and federalism. This arrangement creates an inherent bias toward deliberation and consensus building and against quick government responses to social and economic problems. Given the gridlock that often occurs in Washington, especially during periods of **divided-party government** (when one party controls Congress and the other the presidency), some people have questioned the intelligence of that design. Yet no appreciable public demand exists to substitute a parliamentary system for the Framers' basic constitutional design.

At first glance, the Constitution has changed little over the nation's first two hundred years. The number of formal amendments is really quite small. Since the first ten amendments were ratified, which were a de facto part of the original document, fewer than twenty changes have been made. For the most part, these formal changes have dealt with structural corrections, the end of slavery, and the expansion of the franchise. A deeper examination, however, reveals that the constitutional system has undergone tremendous, even fundamental, changes. Notwithstanding the Founders' commitment to the ideal of limited government, government at all levels has expanded to address political demands engendered by social, economic, and technological change. A civil war, two world wars, a great depression, social unrest, and a four-decade-long cold war have had profound consequences for the constitutional system.

Three "megatrends" in American constitutional development can be identified:

- *The changing nature of federalism.* Over two hundred years, the relationship between the national government and the states has changed profoundly. Not only has the national government emerged as clearly dominant over the states, but the relationship between the national government and the states has become much more complex (see Chapter 3, "Federalism: A Nation of States").

- *The growth of government.* This phenomenon involves all levels of government, moving from the eighteenth-century model of limited government to the contemporary model in which government assumes ultimate responsibility for the social and economic well-being of the nation. We alluded to this megatrend in our discussion of the New Deal and the constitutional revolution of 1937 (see section 2-8a, "Constitutional Change through Judicial Interpretation"). We also discuss it in Chapter 3 and at various points in this book, especially Chapter 15, "The Federal Bureaucracy."

- *The democratization of the constitutional system.* The constitutional republic established by the Founders has become, through formal and informal changes, a constitutional democracy. This has occurred most notably through the achievement of universal suffrage, but also has involved structural changes to allow for greater citizen participation in government and make government more responsive to the popular will. These changes are highlighted throughout the book, but especially in Chapters 3, 5 and 6.

The political system has changed, the institutions of government have changed, and the political culture has changed. Yet the basic design of American government, conceived more than two hundred years ago, remains intact. It works reasonably well even though America now faces challenges that were unimaginable decades—let alone centuries—ago. Even in an age of mass communications, electronic media, and computer technology, the Constitution is capable of protecting individual rights and channeling the resolution of conflicts in a way that most citizens find acceptable. Through wars, depressions, and cultural revolutions, the Constitution has shown remarkable flexibility and adaptability. Even in the midst of the contemporary war on terrorism, its viability does not appear to be in jeopardy. Simply put, Americans continue to believe in their Constitution.

▶ **divided-party government**
A condition in which one political party controls Congress and the other party controls the presidency.

Questions for Thought and Discussion

1. Why were the leaders of the American Revolution not content to remain loyal British subjects?
2. What were the main reasons for the failure of the Articles of Confederation?
3. Why did the Framers of the U.S. Constitution reject the idea of a parliamentary system? What would the Framers say about the failure of legislation to pass because of the "gridlock" that sometimes develops when Congress is of one party and the president is of another?
4. How has the Constitution been adapted to cope with fundamental social and economic change?
5. In interpreting provisions of the Constitution that do not have obvious meanings, should contemporary Americans try to find out what the Framers of the Constitution intended and follow those intentions as closely as possible? Why or why not?

Practice Quiz

Note: You can find the correct answers to these questions by taking the quiz and then submitting your answers in the Online Edition. The program will automatically score your submission. If you miss a question, the program will provide the correct answer, a rationale for the answer, and the section number in the chapter where the topic is discussed.

1. _____ was the first agreement for self-government in America.
   a. The Constitution
   b. The Mayflower Compact
   c. The Articles of Confederation
   d. The Magna Charta

2. Published in 1748, _____ argued that the essential functions of government—legislative, executive, and judicial—must be separated into different branches of government.
   a. Montesquieu's *The Spirit of the Laws*
   b. Locke's *Two Treatises of Government*
   c. Hobbes' *Leviathan*
   d. Jefferson's *Notes on Virginia*

3. Which of the following most significantly influenced the delegates' view of constitutionalism?
   a. Das Capital
   b. Magna Carta
   c. Roman law
   d. The Napoleonic code

4. The fact that _____ was chosen to preside over the Constitutional Convention probably assisted in subsequent ratification efforts.
   a. James Madison
   b. Thomas Jefferson
   c. George Washington
   d. Benjamin Franklin

5. The first three Articles of the Constitution are referred to as _____.
   a. the Distributive Articles
   b. the Enumerated Articles
   c. the Articles of Faith
   d. the Articles of Separation

6. The two most basic organizing principles embodied in the Constitution are _____ and _____.
   a. the separation of powers; federalism
   b. federalism; republicanism
   c. humanism; rule of law
   d. separation of powers; republicanism

7. _____ is known as the "Father of the Constitution."
   a. Thomas Jefferson
   b. George Washington
   c. James Madison
   d. Benjamin Franklin

8. Which of the following concepts of _____ is most closely associated with the concept of separation of powers?
   a. parliamentary government
   b. checks and balances
   c. limited government
   d. rule of law

9. The power of judicial review was first articulated in _____.
   a. the Federal Judiciary Act of 1789
   b. the Supreme Court's decision in *Marbury v. Madison*
   c. the Court Reform Act of 1802
   d. Article II of the Constitution

10. Before the ratification of the Twenty-Fourth Amendment, many states imposed a _____ as a means to limit the participation of the poor in elections.
    a. literacy test
    b. residency requirement
    c. poll tax
    d. property tax

For Further Reading

Adler, Mortimer. *We Hold These Truths* (New York: Macmillan, 1987).

Banning, Lance. *The Sacred Fire of Liberty: James Madison and the Founding of the Federal Republic* (Ithaca, NY: Cornell University Press, 1995).

Beard, Charles A. *An Economic Interpretation of the Constitution of the United States* (New York: Macmillan, 1960).

Boorstin, Daniel J. *The Americans: The Colonial Experience* (New York: Random House, 1958).

Bowen, Catherine Drinker. *Miracle at Philadelphia* (Boston: Little, Brown, 1966).

Breslin, Beau. *The Communitarian Constitution* (Baltimore: Johns Hopkins University Press, 2004).

Bryce, James. *The American Commonwealth*, 3d. ed. (New York: Macmillan, 1911).

Ketcham, Ralph. *Framed for Posterity: The Enduring Philosophy of the Constitution* (Lawrence, Kansas: University of Kansas Press, 1993).

Madison, James, Alexander Hamilton, and John Jay. *The Federalist.* First published in 1787–1788; now available in numerous editions.

McDonald, Forrest. *The Formation of the American Republic, 1776–1790* (Baltimore: Penguin Books, 1965).

McGuire, Robert A. *To Form a More Perfect Union: A New Economic Interpretation of the United States Constitution* (Oxford: Oxford University Press, 2003).

Perry, Barbara. *Unfounded Fears: Myths and Realities of a Constitutional Convention* (Westport, CT: Greenwood Press, 1989).

Rossiter, Clinton. 1787: *The Grand Convention* (New York: Macmillan, 1966).

Schwartz, Bernard. *The Great Rights of Mankind: A History of the American Bill of Rights* (New York: Oxford University Press, 1977).

Storing, Herbert. *What the Anti-Federalists Were For* (Chicago: University of Chicago Press, 1981).

Vose, Clement E. *Constitutional Change* (Lexington, MA: Lexington Books, 1972).

Wood, Gordon S. *The Radicalism of the American Revolution* (New York: Vintage Books, 1993).

Endnotes

1. Samuel Eliot Morison, "The Mayflower Compact." In *An American Primer,* ed. Daniel J. Boorstin (Chicago: University of Chicago Press, 1966), p. 1.

2. Paul Kennedy, *The Rise and Fall of the Great Powers* (New York: Random House, 1987), p. 93.

3. See Gordon S. Wood, *The Radicalism of the American Revolution* (New York: Vintage Books, 1993).

4. Charles Francis Adams, ed., *The Works of John Adams,* vol. 10 (Boston: Little, Brown, 1856), p. 282.

5. Quoted in Catherine Drinker Bowen, *Miracle at Philadelphia* (Boston: Little, Brown, 1966), p. 4.

6. Quoted in Clinton Rossiter, *1787: The Grand Convention* (New York: Macmillan, 1966), p. 159.

7. Charles A. Beard, *An Economic Interpretation of the Constitution of the United States* (New York: Macmillan, 1960), p. 188.

8. Forrest McDonald, *We the People: The Economic Origins of the Constitution* (Chicago: University of Chicago Press, 1958).

9. John A. Garraty, *The American Nation,* 4th ed. (New York: Harper and Row, 1979), p. 123.

10. Robert A. McGuire, *To Form a More Perfect Union: A New Economic Interpretation of the United States Constitution* (Oxford: Oxford University Press, 2003), p. 30.

11. John P. Roche, "The Founding Fathers: A Reform Caucus in Action," *American Political Science Review,* vol. 55, 1961, pp. 799–816.

12. Thomas Hobbes, *Leviathan* (New York: Macmillan, 1947).

13. *The Federalist,* No. 47.

14. Forrest McDonald, *We the People* (Chicago: University of Chicago Press, 1958), p. 113.

15. Charles A. Beard and Mary R. Beard, *A Basic History of the United States* (New Home Library, 1944), p. 136.

16. *Texas v. Johnson,* 491 U.S. 397 (1989).

17. *CBS/New York Times poll,* May 1987. Respondents were asked, "Do you think it is too easy or too hard to amend the Constitution, or is the process about right?" Eleven percent responded "too easy," 20 percent responded "too hard," 60 percent responded "about right," and 9 percent were not sure.

18. Quoted in Charles S. Hyneman and George W. Carey, *A Second Federalist: Congress Creates a Government* (New York: Appleton-Century-Crofts, 1967), pp. 260–61.

19. *Pollock v. Farmer's Loan and Trust Co.,* 158 U.S. 601 (1895).

20. *Marbury v. Madison,* 5 U.S. (1 Cranch) 137 (1803).

21. *Fletcher v. Peck,* 10 U.S. (6 Cranch) 87 (1810).

22. *McCulloch v. Maryland,* 17 U.S. (4 Wheat.) 316, 407 (1819).

23. 17 U.S. (4 Wheat.) at 415.

24. In *Pollock v. Farmer's Loan and Trust Co.,* 158 U.S. 601 (1895), the Court invalidated an income tax measure passed by Congress. In *U.S. v. E. C. Knight Co.,* 156 U.S. 1 (1895), the Court substantially limited the scope of the Sherman Anti-Trust Act of 1890.

25. *Lochner v. New York,* 198 U.S. 45, 64 (1905).

26. *National Labor Relations Board v. Jones & Laughlin Steel Corp.,* 301 U.S. 1 (1937).

27. *Scott v. Sandford,* 60 U.S. (19 How.) 393 (1857).

28. *Oregon v. Mitchell,* 400 U.S. 112 (1970).

29. *Harper v. Virginia State Board of Elections,* 383 U.S. 663 (1966).

30. *Baker v. Carr,* 369 U.S. 186 (1962).

31. *Reynolds v. Sims,* 377 U.S. 533 (1964).

Federalism: A Nation of States

3

KEY TERMS

at-large election
Black Codes
block grants
board of commissioners
categorical grant
city manager
confederation
cooperative federalism
county manager
cutback
devolution
dual federalism
enumerated powers
federal system
fiscal federalism
general revenue sharing
grants-in-aid
home rule
implied powers, doctrine of
initiative and referendum
legislative proposal
marble cake federalism
Missouri Plan
municipal charter
nation-centered federalism
nonpartisan election
nullification, doctrine of
ordinances
reformed cities
secession, doctrine of
state-centered federalism
strong mayor-council system
Supremacy Clause
unfunded mandates
unreformed cities
weak mayor-council system

CHAPTER OUTLINE

3-1 The Idea of Federalism

When the United States was attacked by terrorists in September, 2001, the first government personnel to respond to the tragedy were the front-line troops of local government: firefighters and police officers. New York's mayor, Rudy Giuliani, was widely praised for his efforts in coordinating and leading the city's response to the tragedy. However, because the terrorist attack was an attack on the entire country, Americans looked to their national government in Washington, D.C., for a *national* response to the attack. In times of national crisis, Americans typically look to Washington for action.

Although local police and firefighters were the first to respond to the attacks, state and national agencies were not far behind. Indeed, within hours of the attacks, the Federal Emergency Management Agency (FEMA) was present on the scene of the attacks and helped to coordinate the national, state, and local responses. In the weeks that followed the attack of September 11, Americans saw government at all levels swing into action.

At the national level, Congress responded to the crisis with new legislation strengthening the powers of federal agencies to deal with suspected terrorists. President Bush promptly mobilized the military in an effort to destroy terrorist bases in Afghanistan. America's diplomatic corps, under the leadership of Secretary of State Colin Powell, worked tirelessly to assemble and maintain an international coalition in support of America's war on terrorism. National security and intelligence agencies worked behind the scenes around the globe to gather intelligence and forge alliances aimed at rooting out terrorist networks.

Various agencies of the national government, including the Federal Bureau of Investigation (FBI), the Immigration and Naturalization Service (INS), and the Federal Aviation Administration (FAA), were called on to dramatically upgrade domestic security. Even a new agency, the Office of Homeland Security (OHS), was hastily created within the executive office of the president to coordinate the national government's efforts in this area.

Although the principal thrust of America's war on terrorism came from the national government in Washington, national authorities worked closely with state and local agencies in the fields of law enforcement, transportation, public health, and civil defense. The frightening anthrax attacks of October 2001, in addition to numerous other terrorist threats, further galvanized intergovernmental cooperation. National authorities consulted and cooperated with governors, mayors, and other state and local officials to an extent never seen in this country.

What happened in the aftermath of September 11 can be viewed as a case study in American federalism. Essentially, *federalism* refers to a political system in which constitutional authority is divided between a national government and a set of provincial or state governments. The political system of the United States, from the time the Constitution was ratified in 1788 to the present, has been constructed on this basis. In the United States, the nation and the fifty states exist simultaneously as sovereign political entities. Although this arrangement has always been the case, the character of the federal system, and in particular the relationship between the national government and the states, has changed profoundly. As this chapter will make clear, our country has moved from a state-centered model of federalism to a nation-centered model. This chapter examines the development of American federalism from the founding of the American republic to the complex character of the contemporary system. The chapter also examines the structures and functions of state and local governments, which remain essential components of the federal system.

3-1a Inventing American Government

The United States of America officially became a nation when the Declaration of Independence was enforced by a successful revolutionary war against Great Britain. Having successfully asserted its independence, America was recognized as a member of the family of nations. Yet, in 1776, when independence was proclaimed, a formidable task of nation

Firefighters spray water on the smoking ruins of The World Trade Center, October 4, 2001.

AP Photo / Tony Gutierrez

building lay ahead. It would be some time before Rhode Islanders, Virginians, Pennsylvanians, Georgians, and New Yorkers would regard themselves first and foremost as Americans. Fortunately, they did have the essential materials from which to build a nation. Americans of all thirteen states shared a common language. Moreover, despite significant economic and social differences between North and South, Americans of the Revolutionary era shared the rudiments of a common political culture.

No real doubt ever existed that the thirteen former British colonies were to be the basic building blocks of the new nation. No one seriously argued that the former colonies should be left to fend for themselves as individual republics. Nor did any support exist for merging the colonies under one central government. The Articles of Confederation represented a temporary first attempt to find a middle ground between these undesirable extremes. As observed in Chapter 2, "The Development of American Constitutional Democracy," the Articles failed essentially because they had not allowed the central government enough power.

Of course, the fear of a centralized government had been, to a great degree, a major motivating force behind the Articles. The residents of what would become the United States had become accustomed to the colonies, many of which had unique histories. The idea of a larger unit was more than a little frightening. Nevertheless, the Framers of the Constitution were faced with the task of inventing an organizational scheme that combined a central government with the existing state governments that had evolved from the colonies. Their task was to divide power between these two levels in a way that was acceptable to enough residents of the states to ensure ratification. The **federal system** they created represented a uniquely American solution to the universal problem of governing.[1] In a federal system, authority and responsibility are divided between a central government and a set of regional governments. In the United States, federalism refers to the distribution of governmental power between the national government in Washington, D.C., and the fifty state governments.

3-1b Alternative Modes of Allocating Power

When the Constitution was written, two basic models existed by which power could be apportioned between the national government and the states: a *unitary system* and a **confederation.** The Framers rejected both of these alternatives, opting instead for a federal system.

▶ **federal system** A political system in which a division of authority and responsibility exists between a central government and a set of regional governments.

▶ **confederation** A political system in which the right to rule is vested in a league of states and the central government exists at the will of the states.

When the American federal system was created in 1787, it was altogether new. It is now recognized as a model that other countries forging new constitutions may choose to emulate.

Unitary Systems   In a unitary system, *sovereignty,* the right to rule, is vested in one central government. A government is sovereign if it is the seat of final authority. No other unit of government can eliminate or restructure it. In a unitary system, the central government cannot be altered by any agreement among the nation's smaller political units, such as cities, counties, states, or provinces. However, these smaller entities can be altered or eliminated by the central government—they do not have the protection that sovereignty brings. France and Japan are good examples of strong democracies that utilize unitary systems of allocating power.

In essence, had the Framers of the Constitution opted for a unitary government, they would have rendered the states no more than administrative units that were closer to the people and better able to deliver some services. Of course, a unitary system was never seriously considered. The experience with British rule had soured the Founders on the idea of a central government with unchecked power. The fact that the tyranny could come from a central government in America rather than from across the Atlantic was of little consolation. Moreover, in 1787, the states were sovereign entities, having been loosely held together since the Revolution by the Articles of Confederation. Because they were originally established as separate colonies, each with its own administrative machinery, the states became viable political entities after independence was declared. During the Revolution, each state adopted a constitution establishing a legislature, executive branch, and court system. The states had no intention of entirely surrendering their sovereignty to a new national government, and any constitution that required them to do so surely would not have been ratified.

Confederations   The existing alternative to the unitary system was one that had already been tried: a confederation. In a confederation, the states are sovereign and the central government is not. The central government exists only at the will of the states, which can eliminate or restructure it at will. This was essentially the situation under the Articles of Confederation.

If the experience with Britain made a unitary system unthinkable, the years under the Articles likewise eliminated a confederation from serious consideration. Without some independent authority, a central government would be too weak to function, and the chaos experienced under the Articles could be expected to continue. Clearly, creating another confederation would have doomed the new country to be a weak, fragmented collection of states. The realities of the world at that time mandated nationhood, which was not possible under a confederation.

The Federal Alternative   The Framers of the Constitution were both innovators and compromisers. Had they been otherwise, the Constitution they produced could not have been ratified. The federal system they adopted was a compromise between the advocates of a strong central government, such as Alexander Hamilton, and those, like George Mason, who favored strong states and a weak national government. Federalism was an innovation, based not on experiments that had been tried elsewhere, but rather on ideas that had been suggested by political philosophers of the Enlightenment.

In a federal system, both the states and the central government are sovereign. Neither can do away with the other nor alter the other's structure. Each has its own compact with the governed and its own role in performing the governing task. Both the national government and the states can act directly to affect the lives of individuals, although in different ways (see Figure 3-1). Of course, this shared sovereignty greatly complicates the process of governing. Any federal system involves overlapping functions and inevitable tensions between the national and state governments. Much of the history of the American political system reflects the tensions of competing national and state interests.

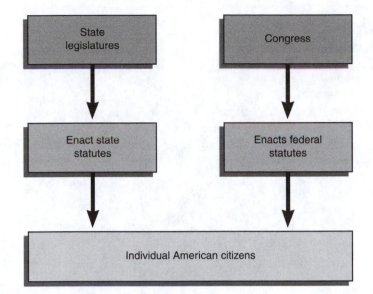

Figure 3-1
The Legal Status of the Individual in a Federal System

3-2 Federalism in the Constitution

At the time the Constitution was being written and discussed, the failed Articles of Confederation provided the only national structure. State governments, however, had continued to function. Because the Constitution was creating a new national (federal) government, it was reasonable to presume that this new government could do only what the Constitution specifically allowed. This presumption was very important, for some conflict over the respective roles of the new national government and the states seemed inevitable. When the state conventions ratified the Constitution, they were agreeing to let this new government take away some of their powers and responsibilities. Naturally, the states were apprehensive, and some were quite hesitant to ratify the Constitution. Advocates of states' rights insisted that the Constitution would have to be amended to make explicit the fact that the states were relinquishing only those powers delegated to the national government. This, of course, was the purpose behind the Tenth Amendment, which, along with the rest of the Bill of Rights, was adopted by the First Congress in 1789 and ratified by the states in 1791.

The fact that the proposed Constitution had to be ratified by nine states, voting individually as states, underlined the logic of the federal system. A bare majority in the five smallest states could have blocked the new government had they found it unsatisfactory. This routing of national decisions through states, as states, rather than through a "national" mechanism is a hallmark of the American system. In fact, the American people have no mechanism for making a purely national decision. In the Senate, states are equally represented. Even our presidential elections are conducted by the states. This system ensures a continuing role for the states as political units. As long as the states remain actors, they cannot be completely overshadowed, no matter how strongly the national government exerts its power.

3-2a Defining the Federal Relationship

The Constitution was ratified with the full knowledge that the new national government would have substantial but limited powers. The Tenth Amendment "reserved" to the states all powers not delegated to the national government. Therefore, the list of such delegated powers was of crucial importance (see Figure 3-2). The Framers defined the powers of the new government by carefully specifying the types of laws that Congress could enact. These **enumerated powers** are contained in Article I, Section 8 of the Constitution. They include

▶ **enumerated powers** Those powers that are expressly granted to Congress by the Constitution.

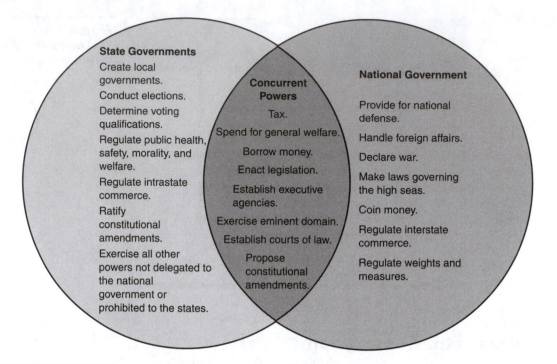

Figure 3-2
The Allocation of Powers between the National Government and the States: The Original Design

such tasks as collecting taxes, declaring war, providing for the national defense, coining money, regulating interstate commerce, establishing policies on immigration and naturalization, establishing a postal service, setting up a system of federal courts, and various other jobs associated with the administration of the new government. Most significantly, Article I, Section 8 permitted Congress to "make all Laws which shall be necessary and proper for carrying into execution the foregoing powers, and all other powers vested by this Constitution." This passage would turn out to be one of the most important in the Constitution.

As originally conceived, the national government was quite limited in scope. The states were clearly responsible for passing laws that defined criminal behavior; funded local roads, education, and sanitation; and regulated business. In a nutshell, the states were to have the *police power,* the power to make and enforce laws to protect the public health, safety, morality, and welfare.

Of course, the Constitution establishes only a broad framework for governing. It does not provide a detailed blueprint. Indeed, as one scholar has observed, the Constitution "virtually ensured continuing controversy about the respective roles of the national and state governments by creating sufficient ambiguity to leave many of the important questions unresolved."[2]

The Framers had no way of envisioning every possible situation Congress might face. The Necessary and Proper Clause in Article I, Section 8 seemed to anticipate this problem by providing Congress with some flexibility in lawmaking. But this provision would soon mean different things to different people. The ensuing battle over the meaning of the phrase "necessary and proper" would later determine the powers of the new national government *vis-à-vis* the states.

3-2b The Supremacy of Federal Law

Any federal system has to address the possible friction between the national and regional governments. The second paragraph of Article VI, known as the **Supremacy Clause,** makes it clear that federal laws and the U.S. Constitution take precedence over state laws and state constitutions when they are in conflict. The meaning of this clause seems straightforward. The laws of Congress are ultimately superior to the laws of the states, and the Supreme Court is likewise superior to the state supreme courts in determining the meaning of the

▶ **Supremacy Clause** The second paragraph of Article VI of the Constitution, which asserts the superiority of federal laws and the U.S. Constitution over state laws and state constitutions when they are in conflict.

U.S. Constitution. Although both the states and the national government are sovereign, the national government is superior when the two sovereigns conflict (assuming the national government is acting within the scope of its constitutional authority).

3-3 The Development of Federalism: The Founding to the Civil War

Whatever understandings may have existed when the Constitution was ratified, it did not take long for disagreements over the appropriate roles of the federal and state governments to arise. These types of disputes were almost inevitable, given the general, and sometimes rather vague, nature of the Constitution. The political culture supported two different views of what the new republic should be. One perspective, that of Thomas Jefferson, tended to envision a rural society with the national government playing a minimal role. Alexander Hamilton held a strikingly different vision, one of a country of shopkeepers and merchants involved in trade. This latter perspective supported a more active national government, playing a greater role in fostering interstate trade and protecting domestic markets from foreign competition. Jefferson's perspective soon evolved into a states' rights view of the Constitution, and Hamilton's became associated with a stronger central government. Together, they represented the two endpoints on a scale that defined the political discussion of the day. The politics of the era revolved around this debate, in much the same way as the politics of the mid-nineteenth century revolved around the issue of slavery and the politics of the 1960s revolved around civil rights and the Vietnam War.

3-3a Implied Powers and National Supremacy

The first major constitutional issue involving federalism concerned the economy. Alexander Hamilton, the first secretary of the treasury, believed that Congress needed to establish a national bank to promote economic development and strengthen the nation's economy. In 1791, Congress, acting largely at Hamilton's behest, created the First Bank of the United States. The bank acted as a clearinghouse of sorts for federal funds. The federal government was the bank's largest depositor and principal director.

From the outset, Thomas Jefferson objected to the bank as unnecessary and improper. Moreover, he believed that the bank was unconstitutional, going beyond what Congress could enact under Article I, Section 8. Jeffersonians charged that the bank was corrupt and was merely a tool enabling the Federalists to use the power of the national government for their own political and economic ends. In this regard, Jefferson was expressing the concerns of many rural residents who were suspicious of urban banking and trading interests. When the bank's charter expired in 1811, Congress, which was controlled by the Jeffersonians, opted not to renew it.

Within a few years, however, sentiment in Congress turned in favor of reestablishing the bank. Congress chartered the Second Bank of the United States in 1816. This new national bank was quite active, and many states became concerned that they would lose their state-chartered banks. In response, state legislatures moved to fight the national bank. The Maryland legislature enacted a law that imposed a heavy tax on the Baltimore branch of the Bank of the United States. But when presented with the state's tax bill, McCulloch, the cashier of the national bank at Baltimore, refused to pay. The state of Maryland filed suit and prevailed in the state courts, which upheld the payment order. McCulloch then appealed to the U.S. Supreme Court, which overturned the Maryland courts' decision.[3]

The Court based its decision in *McCulloch v. Maryland* on a broad interpretation of the Necessary and Proper Clause of Article I, Section 8. Although the power to charter a bank was not specifically mentioned in the enumeration of national powers, Chief Justice John Marshall believed that a bank was implied from the listing of powers involving taxation, credit, money, and the regulation of commerce. Thus, from Marshall's opinion in *McCulloch v. Maryland* emerged the **doctrine of implied powers,** one of the fundamental doctrines of American constitutional law.

> **doctrine of implied powers** A basic doctrine of constitutional law derived from the Necessary and Proper Clause of Article I, Section 8 (*McCulloch v. Maryland*, 1819). Under this doctrine, Congress is not limited to exercising those powers specifically enumerated in Article I but rather may exercise powers reasonably related to the fulfillment of its broad constitutional powers and responsibilities.

Having justified the action of Congress in establishing the bank, Chief Justice Marshall turned his attention to the Maryland tax. Because the national government was, under the Supremacy Clause of Article VI, "supreme within its sphere of action," the states had no power to impede the legitimate actions of the national government. Because the power to tax involved "the power to destroy," the state of Maryland was impeding, and quite possibly destroying, a legitimate enterprise of the national government. Having decided that creating a bank was a legitimate activity of the federal government, the Supreme Court had no trouble in forbidding Maryland, or any other state, from taxing it. *McCulloch v. Maryland* dealt a major blow to the forces of states' rights and substantially enlarged the powers of the national government.

The Supreme Court cemented its commitment to national supremacy with its 1824 decision in *Gibbons v. Ogden,* which affirmed the dominant role of the national government in the regulation of commerce.[4] In *Gibbons,* the Court struck down a New York law that granted a monopoly to operate steamboats in state waters. The law prevented a competitor from operating a ferry service between New York and New Jersey under a "coasting" license issued by the federal government. Writing for the Supreme Court, Chief Justice Marshall upheld the validity of the federal license and struck down the state monopoly. In an opinion reminiscent of *McCulloch v. Maryland,* Marshall expounded on the broad character of the federal power to regulate interstate commerce and the invalidity of state laws that collided with the federal power.

Both *McCulloch v. Maryland* and *Gibbons v. Ogden* were based on an interpretation of the Constitution that favored a stronger central government. These decisions allowed considerable discretion for Congress to respond to a changing society without worrying about whether its laws fit precisely within the list of enumerated powers in Article I, Section 8. This situation opened the door to broad federal legislation, especially in the twentieth century. Many laws Congress has passed in recent decades would not have been possible without the Supreme Court's broad interpretation of the Constitution in *McCulloch v. Maryland* and *Gibbons v. Ogden.*

3-3b The Civil War: A Battle between Two Ideas of Federalism

Without question, the fundamental social and political issue of the mid-nineteenth century was slavery. As noted in Chapter 2, "The Development of American Constitutional Democracy," the question of slavery was not effectively resolved at the Constitutional Convention of 1787. The issue was left to fester and eventually erupted into civil war when it became clear that the southern states were not going to relinquish what they thought was their "right" under the Constitution.

In the infamous Dred Scott decision in 1857, the Supreme Court gave support to the southern states' hard-line position.[5] In this complicated decision, the Court decided, among other things, that people of African origin or descent were not citizens of the United States at the time the Constitution was adopted; nor could they become citizens. Moreover, slaves were property, not persons with rights of their own. In the Court's view, when Congress outlawed slavery in certain territories under the Missouri Compromise of 1820, it deprived slaveholders in "free" territories of their "property" without due process of law. The decision was reviled in the North and celebrated in the South, showing how deepseated the regional cleavage was, even with respect to what the Constitution meant. Far from resolving the question of slavery, the Dred Scott decision revealed a basic division between the political cultures of the North and South.

The Doctrines of Nullification and Secession   As the increasingly democratic political culture of the United States became less and less hospitable to slavery, many in the South looked for a justification for continuing their way of life. Slavery had become very much identified with that way of life. Clearly, many leaders in the South felt loyalty not to

Profiles & Perspectives

Chief Justice John Marshall (1755–1835)

Print by J. H. E. Whitney after St. Memin. Copyright by Thomas Marshall Smith, Baltimore, Md. Copyrighted 1889 Jan. 29 / Library of Congress #LC-USZ62-8499

John Marshall was born in Germantown (now Midland), Virginia, in 1755. Although he received only two years of formal education, his father tutored him in literature and law. Marshall enlisted in the Continental Army and fought in a number of battles during the Revolutionary War. After the war, he entered the practice of law and soon developed a reputation as one of Virginia's most skilled attorneys. At George Washington's request, Marshall served in Congress from 1799 to 1800, where he emerged as a strong advocate for the policies of the Adams administration. After serving a brief term as secretary of state, Marshall was appointed chief justice of the United States by President Adams in 1801. Marshall, who served as chief justice until 1835, is universally acknowledged as one of the greatest jurists in this nation's history. Marshall wrote some of the most important opinions in American constitutional law, including the majority opinions in *Marbury v. Madison* (1803) and *McCulloch v. Maryland* (1819). The following excerpt from the majority opinion in *Cohens v. Virginia* (1821) shows Marshall's strong support for the federal government, the U.S. Constitution, and the federal judiciary against competing claims of states' rights:

> "That the United States form, for many, and for most important purposes, a single nation, has not yet been denied. In war, we are one people. In making peace, we are one people. In all commercial regulations, we are one and the same people. In many other respects, the American people are one; and the government, which is alone capable of controlling and managing their interests in all these respects, is the government of the Union. It is their government, and in that character, they have no other. America has chosen to be, in many respects, and to many purposes, a nation; and for all these purposes, her government is complete; to all these objects it is competent. The people have declared, that in the exercise of all powers given for these objects, it is supreme. It can then, in effecting these objects, legitimately control all individuals or governments within the American territory. The constitution and laws of a state, so far as they are repugnant to the Constitution and laws of the United States, are absolutely void. These states are constituent parts of the United States. They are members of one great empire—for some purposes sovereign, for some purposes subordinate."

More information, including related articles and books, can be found at http://www.marshall.edu/johnmarshall/.

the still youthful nation, but to their respective states and to the local political cultures those states were protecting.

Out of the growing division between the southern states and the national government emerged the **doctrine of nullification,** which held that a state could decide for itself whether it would recognize, and ultimately abide by, a law passed by the national government. The logical extension of this position was the **doctrine of secession**—the idea that a state could secede, or withdraw, from the Union. In seceding from the Union, the southern states were making the ultimate claim under a states' rights interpretation of the Constitution—the right to withdraw their ratification of the Constitution. Of course, in conducting the Civil War, President Abraham Lincoln used the power of the national government to implement his position that the states could not choose to leave the United States. Lincoln's position, which would prevail, was that after states had agreed to join the Union, their decision was irrevocable. In *Texas v. White*, issued four years after General Lee's surrender at Appomattox Courthouse, the Supreme Court pronounced, once and for all, that "[t]he Constitution, in all its provisions, looks to an indestructible Union, composed of indestructible States."[6]

The Victory of Nation-Centered Federalism   In addition to being a conflict over the morality of slavery, the Civil War was a contest between two visions of American federalism. The Union victory vindicated a **nation-centered federalism** and spelled the end of the **state-centered federalism** espoused by the South. By the end of the Civil War, the basic fabric of federalism had taken shape. Although the states were certainly major players, the federal government had become the first among equals. Its supremacy was well established, and the supreme role of the federal courts in resolving questions of federal and state power was ensured.

▶ **doctrine of nullification** Rooted in historical Southern culture, the belief that a state is sovereign and can decide for itself whether it will recognize, and ultimately abide by, a law passed by the national government.

▶ **doctrine of secession**   The doctrine that holds that a state can secede, or withdraw, from the Union.

▶ **nation-centered federalism** A federal system in which the central government is the dominant actor.

▶ **state-centered federalism** A federal system in which the states remain dominant over the central government.

3-4 Evolving Federalism in the Modern Era

In the wake of the Civil War, as the country changed from a mostly agrarian economy of farms and small towns to an urban, industrial society, the character of federalism continued to evolve in the direction of national dominance. Increasingly, the national government saw fit to move into areas of policy traditionally reserved to the states. In each instance, there was resistance, and sometimes sharp conflict. Each situation brought about a clash of political cultures, with local interests taking a states' rights position, usually to preserve deeply rooted patterns of dealing with public policy.

3-4a Civil Rights: A Case Study in Federalism

The Civil War ended in 1865. That same year, slavery was formally abolished throughout the United States by the ratification of the Thirteenth Amendment to the Constitution. Nevertheless, many states passed laws to perpetuate the secondary social and economic status of African Americans within their borders. The **Black Codes,** as they were called, limited the economic freedom and property rights of blacks and even denied them access to the courts of law. Congress responded by passing the Civil Rights Act of 1866, the first in a long line of federal civil rights laws. The Civil Rights Act of 1866 was designed to nullify the Black Codes, but many questioned whether Congress possessed the constitutional authority to act in this field. To alleviate these doubts, Congress proposed the Fourteenth Amendment, which was ratified in 1868.

> **Black Codes** Laws enacted by southern states following ratification of the Thirteenth Amendment that were aimed at perpetuating the secondary social and economic status of African Americans within their borders.

The Importance of the Fourteenth Amendment The Fourteenth Amendment prohibited the states from denying "any person" (a veiled reference to blacks) within their jurisdiction the equal protection of the laws, which is precisely what the Black Codes had done. Moreover, Section 5 of the Fourteenth Amendment gave Congress the power to enforce the Equal Protection Clause, as well as the other substantive provisions of the amendment, by "appropriate legislation." This language provided a firm constitutional foundation for congressional action in the civil rights field.

Although the Fourteenth Amendment and the Civil Rights Act of 1866 effectively dismantled the Black Codes, the southern states devised new means of legally subordinating blacks. These enactments, known as *Jim Crow laws,* took a multitude of forms. Whether mandating separate schools for black and white children or establishing segregated public facilities, these laws had the effect of keeping the races apart and restricting African Americans to menial positions. In addition, because the Constitution gave to the states the responsibility for conducting elections, the southern states were able to devise ways to keep blacks from voting. These measures were consistent with the dominant, traditional culture of the Deep South, which viewed persons of African descent as being inferior to whites. Look at Table 3-1 and imagine that you are a newly freed slave in the post–Civil War South. The column on the right describes how the Black Codes and Jim Crow laws affect your life.

The Jim Crow laws were passed in accordance with the rules of the states; that is, majorities of elected representatives voted to enact these laws, and state courts held that they were consistent with the state constitutions. In fact, many state constitutions explicitly required separation of the races. Despite the passage of the Thirteenth, Fourteenth, and Fifteenth Amendments, the U.S. Supreme Court did not have the will, or the means, to confront these state actions.[7] The prevailing political culture allowed the southern states to use state action to maintain their "way of life." This view prevailed until 1954, when, in the landmark decision in *Brown v. Board of Education,* the Supreme Court ruled that black citizens' rights to equal treatment under the law outweighed states' rights to maintain segregated school systems.[8]

The Development of a National Consensus on Civil Rights Initially, the Supreme Court's desegregation rulings were met with howls of disapproval. Governors of some southern states refused to abide by the Court's mandates. Many southerners resented what they felt was an unconstitutional intrusion into state affairs. In some places, such as

Situation	Effect of Black Codes	**T A B L E 3-1**
You want to farm your own land but are too poor to purchase any, so you try to rent some.	In Mississippi, you can't rent or lease land outside a city or town. Do you try to find work inside a town?	**Life under the Black Codes**
You live outside a town and need to pick up supplies at a store, or perhaps you're looking for work in a city.	In Opelousas, Louisiana, you are barred entry into cities and towns unless you have a note from your employer, stating your reason for being there and how long you are allowed to stay. If you are found in a city after 10 p.m., you will be locked up in the local jail.	
You live in Mississippi and have fallen in love with a white Northerner. You want to marry.	The Black Codes of 1865 in Mississippi outlaw interracial marriage, and you and your husband or wife can be imprisoned for life if you are caught.	
You and several friends, all over the age of eighteen, gather together for a political meeting.	You can be arrested for unlawful congregation and vagrancy, fined fifty dollars, and spend ten days in jail. White people associating with you and arrested at the same time pay two hundred dollars and can serve up to six months in jail. Why do you think there is such a difference?	
You live in Texas and witness a fight between two white men that leaves one severely injured. Surely it's your duty to testify at the trial, isn't it?	As a freeman in Texas, you cannot vote, hold office, sit on a jury, or testify in court except in cases involving other blacks.	

Data compiled from:
http://www.nilevalley.net/history/jim_crow_laws.html
http://afroamhistory.about.com/cs/jimcrowlaws/
http://www.tsha.utexas.edu/handbook/online/ articles/view/BB/jsb1.html

Little Rock, Arkansas, the reaction to desegregation was so violent that federal troops had to be mobilized to restore order. By the 1960s, the idea (if not the implementation) of desegregation had begun to gain acceptance, even in the Deep South. But in the 1970s, as federal courts began to mandate the busing of students to dismantle segregated public schools, white resistance flared up again. Interestingly, the most intense reactions to forced busing came not in Dixie, but rather in the big cities of the North and West.

The Supreme Court's pioneering decisions invalidating segregation in public schools were eventually followed and reinforced by congressional and presidential action. The most important of these efforts was the enactment of the Civil Rights Act of 1964, which, among other things, barred the transfer of federal funds to educational institutions (public or private) that practiced racial discrimination. By the 1980s, the political culture of the United States no longer supported the idea of racial segregation. Americans had come to accept the laws and court decisions that had been fostered by the national government to promote civil rights. No longer did any widespread sentiment exist for the old style of states' rights, under which state governments were free to discriminate against groups of their citizens. Americans had come to a consensus that equality under the law was a basic right.

3-4b "Electoral Federalism" and the Right to Vote

The Supreme Court's ruling in *Brown v. Board of Education* made clear that the federal courts would be willing to take an active part in overturning state systems that violated their citizens' constitutional rights. By the mid-sixties, Congress was also willing to cast a

Popular Culture and American Politics
Mississippi Burning

In the early 1960s, Mississippi, more than other state, came to symbolize white resistance to the civil rights movement. The state government, elected and controlled by the white majority, was hostile to the notion of equal treatment for its African-American citizens. But the U.S. Constitution, and in particular the Fourteenth Amendment, required equal protection of the laws without regard to race. When the state failed to live up to its responsibilities under the Fourteenth Amendment, the federal government stepped in. This instance of federalism in action was a recipe for conflict.

The burning cross came to symbolize the Ku Klux Klan's efforts to terrorize African Americans.
Stone / Getty Images

In 1964, three civil rights workers named Michael Schwerner, Andrew Goodman, and James Chaney were killed by members of the Ku Klux Klan in rural Mississippi. The story of their murders and the subsequent federal investigation is portrayed in the movie *Mississippi Burning* (1988). It depicts the hostility of southern whites to the idea of racial equality and toward the federal government's efforts on behalf of civil rights. The film involves two FBI agents (played by Gene Hackman and Willem Dafoe), who come to rural Mississippi to investigate the deaths of three civil rights workers who had been working in a voter registration drive. The local law enforcement authorities, reflecting the attitudes of the white majority, offer little help to the agents, who are resented for meddling in local affairs. Even though some of the local whites are horrified by the murder of the civil rights workers, they are caught up in a code of silence that frustrates the investigation. The local blacks, who have a good idea who committed the crimes, are terrorized into silence by the Ku Klux Klan. Ultimately, through good investigative work, the bodies of the victims are recovered and the perpetrators are arrested. *Mississippi Burning* suggests that segregation and official racism in the South could not have been broken without the intervention of the federal government. Thus, the film portrays the federal government in a positive, almost heroic light.

critical eye on the ways in which states had been conducting their elections. Historically, African Americans in some states had been denied an equal opportunity to register and vote. The passage of the Voting Rights Act of 1965 was the first major foray of the national government into the conduct of state and local elections, which had been always considered a state responsibility under federalism. The initial intent of this legislation was concerned with registering minority voters and eliminating devices that had been used to limit minority participation. In upholding the Voting Rights Act against a challenge brought by the state of South Carolina (one of the main targets of the legislation), the Supreme Court expressed hope that "millions of non-white Americans will be able to participate for the first time on an equal basis in the government under which they live."[9]

In 1980, the Supreme Court ruled that urban electoral systems could be invalidated under the Fourteenth Amendment (and the Voting Rights Act) *only* if it could be proved that they had been created with the intent to discriminate against minority voters.[10] This decision came down just before congressional hearings on the extension of the Voting Rights Act. When the extension was granted in 1982, Section 2 was amended to outlaw electoral systems that could be shown to lead to "minority vote dilution," regardless of any original intent to discriminate. This reworking of the Voting Rights Act led to a great surge in federal court involvement in the structures of local governments. As a result of litigation in this area, state and local governments are being held responsible for creating systems in which candidates preferred by blacks can be elected. In many cases, cities have been ordered by federal courts to change their form of government. Systems of electing city councils at-large, rather than by district, had been a major component of the early twentieth-century movement to reform American cities. These systems came under challenge in the 1980s under the Voting Rights Act on the ground that they were diluting the voting strength of minorities. At-large systems have proven to be difficult to defend legally, despite the fact that their original intent had not been to limit African American participation.

In addition, the federal courts have become embroiled in the drawing of district lines for Congress and state legislatures. For instance, to ensure the election of a black representative to Congress in North Carolina, a district was created that connects a number of predominantly black areas by including a two-hundred-mile length of interstate highway. The district that was created meanders across the entire state. However, in a controversial decision in 1995, the Supreme Court struck down the state's reapportionment plan. In the Court's view, vote dilution suffered by African-American voting in congressional elections throughout North Carolina is "not remedied by creating a safe majority-black district somewhere else in the State."[11] Under prevailing constitutional interpretation, states cannot make race the dominant factor in drawing district lines, but it can be considered along with other factors.[12]

3-4c Civil Liberties, State Action, and the Bill of Rights

As noted in section 3-2, "Federalism in the Constitution," the Bill of Rights was intended as a set of limitations not on the states, but rather on the national government. For protection of their rights from infringement by the state governments, citizens had to look to their respective state constitutions, as interpreted by the state courts. However, the adoption of the Fourteenth Amendment in 1868 created the legal basis for changing the relationship of the Bill of Rights to the states. In addition to forbidding states from denying "equal protection of the laws," Section 1 of the Fourteenth Amendment prohibited states from depriving anyone of life, liberty, or property "without due process of law" or abridging the "privileges and immunities of citizens of the United States." Although legal scholars have debated the intentions of the Framers of the Fourteenth Amendment, the Supreme Court eventually came to accept the idea that the Fourteenth Amendment "incorporated" most, if not all, of the protections of the Bill of Rights, making them enforceable against the state governments.

The Incorporation of the Bill of Rights   The first instance in which the Supreme Court accepted the doctrine of incorporation was in 1896, when it decided that the Fourteenth Amendment required state and local governments to provide "just compensation" to persons whose property had been taken for public use.[13] In essence, the Court decided that the Just Compensation Clause of the Fifth Amendment constituted an essential element of due process, and thus was binding on the states under the Fourteenth Amendment.

In 1925, the Supreme Court held that the First Amendment freedoms of speech and press were "among the fundamental personal rights and 'liberties' protected by the Due Process Clause of the Fourteenth Amendment from impairment by the states."[14] In 1940, the Court extended the doctrine of incorporation to include freedom of religion.[15] The First Amendment prohibition against "establishment of religion" was applied to the states in 1947.[16] By the late 1960s, virtually all the provisions of the Bill of Rights had been incorporated into the Fourteenth Amendment and thereby made applicable to the states.

The application of the Bill of Rights to the states was far more than a matter of legal abstraction. It permitted individuals who believed that their basic rights had been violated by a state government to challenge that government in a federal court.[17] This ability greatly expanded the supervisory power of the federal courts over the state governments. Although this dramatic expansion of federal judicial power met initial resistance, most Americans eventually came to accept the need for federal judicial supervision of state actions that

Controversy

Should the Electoral College Be Abolished?

Americans now consider our presidential elections as symbols of a deep national commitment to democracy. Yet the Framers of the Constitution, far less favorable toward democracy, provided for an indirect method of presidential selection, which became known as the electoral college. Under Article II, Section 1 of the Constitution, each state is authorized to appoint as many electors as it has senators and representatives in Congress. Of course, states use popular elections to "appoint" these electors. When a voter enters the voting booth, he or she is not voting directly for a candidate for president, but rather for a slate of electors who are pledged to support that candidate. To win the presidency, a candidate must receive a majority of the electoral votes cast; otherwise, the election is thrown into the House of Representatives. Of course, a candidate can "win" the popular vote nationwide and still lose the election in the electoral college. This situation occurred in 1876 and 1888, when the winning candidates, Rutherford B. Hayes and Benjamin Harrison, respectively, received fewer popular votes than their principal rivals, Samuel Tilden and Grover Cleveland. For many years, citizens have discussed whether the electoral college should be abolished. But, until recently, the discussion was more or less academic.

The 2000 presidential election renewed the controversy over the electoral college. Democrat Al Gore received more popular votes nationwide, but Republican George Bush won the electoral vote (after considerable dispute about who should receive Florida's 25 votes). Advocates of abolishing the electoral college argue that it is undemocratic. They think it ridiculous that a candidate who received fewer popular votes than his main rival should win the presidency. Before rushing to judgment on this issue, you need to think about the role that the electoral college was designed to play in the federal system. Specifically, you should ponder these questions:

- How would presidential elections change if the electoral college were abolished?
- Would the administration of elections, which is now a state and local function, have to be significantly nationalized?
- How would the abolition of the electoral college alter the balance of power in the federal system?
- Would the requisite three-fourths of the states be willing to ratify a constitutional amendment to abolish the electoral college? How would your state likely vote?

impinged on individual liberties. Liberty, like equality, came to be seen as a fundamental value that was not to be sacrificed on the altar of federalism.

The Rights of the Accused: A Case Study in Federalism   As a result of the nationalization of the Bill of Rights, the states gradually lost their ability to establish their own criminal justice policies. As late as the 1930s, some states routinely held trials in which the accused did not have legal counsel, even if the possible punishment after conviction included the death penalty.[18] Some states did not provide protection in their constitutions against double jeopardy, that is, being tried or punished twice for the same offense.[19] In many states, police could conduct searches and seizures that would have been considered to have violated the accused's Fourth Amendment rights had the searches been conducted by the national government.[20] By the 1960s, however, the Supreme Court had decided that most of the Bill of Rights applied to the states via the Fourteenth Amendment, including nearly all the provisions of the Fourth, Fifth, Sixth, and Eighth Amendments, which address the rights of the accused.

As a result of the Supreme Court's incorporation of the Bill of Rights into the Fourteenth Amendment, much more of a national set of policies is now in place in the criminal justice field. Most Americans are generally familiar with the exclusionary rule, which prohibits the use of illegally obtained evidence in a criminal trial,[21] and the Miranda warnings that police are required to provide criminal suspects before interrogating them.[22] Many Americans dislike the constraints that the courts have placed on the police under the Bill

Popular Culture and American Politics
Minority Report

By Chapman Rackaway

In a federal system, states and communities have enough freedom to experiment with new and innovative public policy initiatives. In the 2002 Tom Cruise movie *Minority Report,* a mythical future government engages in its very own—and very frightening—public policy experiment that could be adopted by the whole country.

The movie uses psychic visionary "pre-cognitives" to see murders that have not yet occurred. The seers then provide information to the Washington, D.C., "pre-crime" unit (headed by Cruise) that intercepts the potential criminal and arrests him or her for the crime before it happens.

Throughout the movie, a lesson in federalism appears. The movie even features a scene with an advertisement for a national referendum that would make the federal government adopt a pre-crime program of its own. Even though there is no national referendum allowance in the U.S. Constitution, the pre-crime idea could be used in an amendment to the Constitution. The movie's producers understood that federalism allows for local and state governments to take the lead on such projects and that the federal government can follow suit if it so chooses. Just as federal welfare reform in the 1990s was the extension of state programs in Wisconsin and Michigan, the movie portrays the successful D.C. pre-crime policy as a preview of a possible national adaptation of the program.

Even with the public policy lessons, the movie is still a Tom Cruise summer blockbuster. Wrongly accused of a pre-crime, Cruise must expose flaws in the pre-crime system, escape the law enforcement system, and clear his name. After the pre-crime system's flaws are brought to light, the program is scrapped and the national referendum fails.

The movie provides another lesson beyond federalism, as it raises some serious questions about civil liberties, which we discuss in Chapter 4, "Civil Liberties and Individual Freedom." Can the police obtain warrants and arrest people when no crime has actually been committed? What are a citizen's rights when the government knows what you will do before you do?

of Rights, but, at the same time, most of us take comfort in the fact that we do not live in a police state. When pressed, most Americans express support, at least in the abstract, for the idea of subjecting state criminal justice policies to the scrutiny of the federal courts.

Judicial Federalism You should not assume, however, that the relationship between the federal courts and the states consists entirely of the federal courts trying to make the states live up to their obligations to protect civil rights and liberties.[23] In recent years, as the federal courts have become more conservative as a result of judicial appointments by Republican presidents, a number of state courts have gone beyond federal judicial requirements in protecting the civil rights and liberties of their citizens. This statement is especially true with respect to the rights of persons accused of crimes. For example, what constitutes a reasonable search and seizure under the federal constitution may not qualify as reasonable under the relevant provisions of the New Jersey Constitution. You must not forget that states may provide more, but not less, protection to their citizens than is required by the U.S. Constitution.

3-4d Economic Regulation: An Historic Conflict in Federalism

In the late nineteenth century, the federal government began to assert its power to regulate interstate commerce, focusing first on railroads and manufacturing. The government's major concern was the emergence of large corporations that often combined to form monopolies, thus stifling competition and driving up rates and prices. Although some states had attempted to regulate railroad rates, state governments were generally incapable of dealing with large corporations with activities in many states. In 1886, the Supreme Court further hampered state regulatory efforts by ruling that an Illinois railroad regulation intruded on the commerce power of the national government.[24] While conservatives argued for a *laissez-faire* approach to the economy in general, increasing political pressure was brought to bear on the national government to act to stem the power of the large corporations.

In 1887, Congress adopted the Interstate Commerce Act, which created the Interstate Commerce Commission (ICC), the first permanent federal regulatory agency.[25] Though initially limited in its powers, the ICC marked the beginning of a trend toward the creation of national bureaucratic agencies to regulate facets of the economy. It also signaled the beginning of a new era of federal involvement in economic policy making, including areas traditionally regarded as state functions.

The Supreme Court and Federal Regulation of the Economy As noted in Chapter 2, "The Development of American Constitutional Democracy," the Supreme Court of the late nineteenth and early twentieth centuries resisted the trend toward federal involvement in economic policy. In one leading case, the Court struck down a federal law which prohibited the interstate shipment of goods manufactured by companies that used child labor beyond federal guidelines.[26] According to the Court, the federal law had invaded an area of policy reserved to the states under the Tenth Amendment. The Court was exercising one of its major roles: umpire of the federal system.

The Supreme Court continued to resist federal efforts to regulate the economy until the late 1930s. From the 1940s until the 1970s, the Court was dominated by liberal judges appointed by Democratic presidents. These judges brushed aside the Tenth Amendment and gave the federal government broad power to regulate commerce. Writing for the Court in 1941, Justice Harlan Fiske Stone observed that the Tenth Amendment "states but a truism that all is retained [by the states] which has not been surrendered [to the federal government]."[27] In recent years, however, a more conservative Supreme Court has moved to limit federal power somewhat vis-à-vis the states,[28] although the broad regulatory power of the federal government in the economic realm remains well established.

3-4e States, Cities, and the Federal Government: The Evolving Federal Relationship

The Constitution was written in an age when America was a country of farms and small towns whose inhabitants viewed cities with some suspicion, if not hostility. City residents were certainly in the minority. The first census showed that only one in twenty Americans lived in urban areas of more than 2,500 persons. The rest were little concerned with the services that city residents might want—fire and police protection, sanitary sewers, well-lighted streets, and public parks, for example.

By the early nineteenth century, urbanization had begun in earnest, with New York, Philadelphia, and Boston gradually becoming major urban centers. By 1820, nine cities had populations of more than one hundred thousand. The main growth in American cities took place in the late nineteenth and early twentieth centuries, however, when millions of immigrants flocked to American cities to work in factories. These people brought with them tremendous needs for governmental services, and they looked to the cities for help. Later, the urban migration included millions of blacks fleeing the rural South in search of decent jobs and an opportunity to live without the shackles of segregation. Naturally, they also looked to the cities for help.

Washington and the Cities   The Constitution does not mention cities. It did not have to, for cities were, and are, creatures of the states. States determine the means by which cities are created, their structure, the taxes they can collect, and the ways in which their boundaries can be enlarged. For most of our history, cities' fates were determined solely by the state legislatures. Before the 1930s, the relationship between the national government and the cities was limited to occasional, scattered public works projects. During the 1930s, the tremendous social and economic problems of the Great Depression overwhelmed the cities, and the states were not in a position to provide much help. As part of President Franklin D. Roosevelt's New Deal, the federal government established a number of programs to help urban residents because no other level of government was willing or able to meet their needs. Characterized by Roosevelt as "enlightened centralism," the New Deal programs provided work for urban residents, such as constructing public buildings, parks, and other facilities. These programs required the cooperation of the city governments because much of the federal funding was distributed through the local political structures.

Whereas the political culture of the nineteenth century would not have supported the idea of massive, direct federal aid to, and involvement in, the nation's cities, by the mid-twentieth century the political culture had changed markedly. People had become accustomed to the idea of looking first to Uncle Sam for solutions to social and economic problems. The political culture had become hospitable to the new federal role in distributing aid directly to the cities.[29] That support has evolved into an expectation and, consequently, federal aid to the cities is now institutionalized (see Table 3-2). When Hurricane Andrew struck Florida and Louisiana in August 1992, state and local governments expected that Washington would pay for most of the clean-up expenses. On September 17, 1992, their expectations were fulfilled as Congress appropriated, at President George H. W. Bush's request, more than $10 billion to pay for the damage wrought by the hurricanes and help people restore their homes and businesses. The same thing happened in 2004 as Florida was plagued by a series of devastating hurricanes. People expected federal aid to flow to local governments in the state to assist in the massive clean-up and restoration efforts and to buttress social services overextended by the social effects of the storms. Because 2004 was a presidential election year, and because Florida was expected to be a "battleground state," President George W. Bush wasted no time in coming to Florida to assure residents and civic leaders that federal assistance would be forthcoming.

TABLE 3-2

Cities' Fiscal Dependence on Federal Government, 1946–2000 (with Federal Funds Listed as a Percentage of Cities' General Revenue from Their Own Sources)

Year	Percentage of Cities' Governmental Revenue
1946	0.1
1952	1.2
1957	1.2
1962	1.8
1965	2.2
1967	2.7
1970	2.9
1972	4.0
1973	6.1
1974	7.1
1975	6.8
1976	7.6
1977	8.4
1978	9.0
1979	8.8
1980	8.2
1981	7.8
1982	6.7
1983	6.2
1984	5.7
1985	5.4
1986	4.7
1987	4.2
1988	3.5
1989	3.3
1990	3.2
1991	3.1
1992	3.1
1993	3.1
1994	3.3
1995	3.5
1996	3.3
1997	3.4
1998	3.4
1999	3.3
2000	3.2

Source: Data adapted from Harold W. Stanley and Richard G. Niemi, *Vital Statistics in American Politics 2003–2004* (Washington, CQ Press, 2003), p. 330.

The Federalism of the 1960s The programs of the New Deal were responses to the crisis of the Great Depression. By the early 1960s, the United States faced another set of urban problems. Affluent and middle-class city residents were moving in great numbers to the suburbs. This migration, which was greatly aided by federal mortgage and tax policies, left the cities with tremendous social and economic problems that they seemed unable to solve. As before, many looked beyond the states to the federal government for assistance. To complicate the situation, race became a major factor. As whites fled to the suburbs, many larger cities were increasingly inhabited by African Americans and other minorities. Issues thus became framed in racial as well as economic terms.

The political culture of the 1960s was quite different from that of the 1930s. The new generation was impatient with government officials, who seemed unable or unwilling to respond to increasing urban decay. Many believed poverty could be fought only by empowering the poor—that is, letting them play a major role in deciding how to spend federal antipoverty dollars. This feeling was somewhat understandable, considering the outcome of certain federal programs of the era. For instance, beginning with the Housing Act of 1949, Washington had spent a great deal of money on urban renewal projects that seemed to do little more than reduce available housing for the poor while benefiting developers and others in the local business community.

Federal dollars had been traditionally provided as **grants-in-aid,** in which federal money is allocated to a particular local project, usually after an application and review process. Before the 1960s, state and local governments could obtain federal grants without any meaningful involvement by those whom the grants were designed to benefit. The new grant-in-aid programs of the 1960s mandated the involvement of the poor in the application process as well as in deciding how the money would be spent after a grant was obtained.

> **grants-in-aid** Federal monies provided to state and/or local governments for particular projects, usually following an application and review process.

This new approach was embodied in a series of ambitious programs founded under the general umbrella of the "war on poverty," which President Lyndon Johnson was able to push through Congress in 1964 and 1965. The most controversial program was known as Model Cities.[30] Under this program, poor residents could elect representatives to decide how federal poverty funds could be spent. In many cases, this procedure bypassed city officials and gave them no say in how the money was spent. Not surprisingly, when it was discovered that the funds were sometimes spent in a questionable manner, Model Cities came under political fire.

One particularly troubling incident involved a Chicago street gang that used money obtained through the Model Cities program to purchase weapons. This episode and similar legendary excesses became embedded in the American political culture as evidence that a clumsy, inefficient national government was subverting traditional structures and values. The experiment of empowering the poor was abandoned as the country turned its attention away from the cities and toward the war in Vietnam. Even the explosive riots of the cities toward the end of the decade did little to rekindle interest in social programs. To the contrary, voters elected Richard Nixon to the presidency in 1968. Rather than call for new or revitalized federal programs to aid the inner cities, Nixon ran on a platform of restoring law and order.

> **general revenue sharing** Federal monies that were provided to state and local governments to be spent as elected officials saw fit. These funds were abolished in 1986.

The Nixon Retreat One of President Nixon's top priorities was to dismantle many of the social programs of the Johnson years. In some cases, his administration refused to spend money that Congress had appropriated for social programs. Foremost on his list of targeted agencies was the Office of Economic Opportunity, which had played a particularly active role in the attack on urban poverty. The Nixon administration sought to strengthen the state role along with that of elected officials by replacing many grants-in-aid with a new program—**general revenue sharing**—that went into effect in 1972. Revenue sharing provided states and cities with money that could be spent as elected officials saw fit.

This trend continued with the enactment of the Housing and Community Development Act of 1974, which replaced many **categorical grant** programs with **block grants.**

> **categorical grant** Federal monies provided to state and local governments for a narrowly defined purpose.

> **block grants** Federal monies provided to state and local governments that are to be spent in specified general areas, such as housing or law enforcement, but do not carry the restrictions and requirements of categorical grants.

Block grants are provided to state and local governments to be spent in specified general areas, such as housing or law enforcement; these grants do not carry the restrictions and requirements of categorical grants. The Nixon administration did not invent block grants, which had been in use for many years, but it did revitalize the concept, which was consistent with the administration's philosophy of shifting decision making from the national bureaucracy to state and local governments.

Under the Nixon administration, the relationship between the national government and the cities changed dramatically. Attempts at actively organizing the poor to act as spokespersons on their own behalf disappeared as federal money was channeled through existing power structures. Local elected officials were given more discretion than ever in deciding where the money would be spent. Of course, this policy also gave less discretion to bureaucrats in Washington.

Nixon's policies marked an important change in the federal system. They shifted power away from both the urban poor and the decision makers at the national level and toward state and local elected officials. This shift reflects an irony of our system. Often, minorities and the poor are the least able to assert themselves in local political systems, where the majorities enjoy superior resources. Yet these minorities can often bring sufficient power to bear at the national level to promote their interests. The Nixon years reflected a growing suspicion in American political culture about the national government's role in dealing with the cities. Although Jimmy Carter was a Democrat, his "outsider" presidency did nothing to change this antipathy toward Washington.

The Reagan–Bush Years and Beyond: From New Federalism to Devolution

The election of Ronald Reagan in 1980 had major consequences for the federal arrangement. Over the years, the cities had become quite dependent on federal aid. In fact, some communities relied on the federal government for the major part of their budget. In an early televised address to the nation, President Reagan stressed his commitment to reducing the federal government's size while recognizing and increasing the role of the states. However, Reagan's main contribution to the federal arrangement was the **cutback**. Whereas Nixon had given the states more discretion in how they spent the money they received from the national government, Reagan sought to reduce this funding altogether.

▶ **cutback**   An initiative of the Reagan administration to reduce the fiscal role of the federal government in state and local affairs.

The idea behind the Reagan approach was simple: If the states and cities want programs, they should pay for them. The federal government would do its part by eliminating costly rules and regulations—cutting the authority of federal bureaucrats. Some states moved to aid their cities in new and creative ways, but the ability of state governments to undertake major initiatives is limited. Three factors undercut their ability to provide much aid to the cities:

- *Politics.* Despite legislative reapportionment, the states have not been particularly hospitable to the interests of the cities. Quite often, urban delegations in the state legislatures find themselves outvoted by coalitions of rural and suburban representatives.

- *Money.* The states raise money through a variety of means, but, unfortunately, none can really compete with the federal income tax. The revenue from many types of taxes and fees does not increase as fast as the states' costs for basic programs. Moreover, the states must balance their budgets, leaving little room for new programs, especially in an age of fiscal austerity. Finally, state revenues are dependent on the national economy. In bad times, states find themselves in deep trouble.

- *Additional responsibilities.* During the 1970s, the federal courts began to hold the states responsible for the constitutional rights of prisoners in state facilities. In some cases, the courts even took over a state's correctional system until the state prison facilities met minimum standards. This situation put tremendous pressure on state budgets. In addition, the federal government imposed greater funding burdens on the states for health care. The states have the primary responsibility for

Case in Point 3-1

The Supreme Court as Umpire of the Federal System

United States v. Lopez (1995)

One of the many roles of the U.S. Supreme Court has been, historically, that of "umpire of the federal system." In numerous cases throughout history, the Court has had to rule on the scope of federal powers in relation to the powers of the states. According to prevailing constitutional theory, Congress does not possess open-ended legislative power, but must rely on its enumerated and implied powers under the Constitution. Congress has long relied on its power to regulate "commerce among the states" under Article I, Section 8 as a constitutional basis for legislating in areas once thought to be the domain of the states. Much modern federal legislation dealing with civil rights, the environment, and criminal justice is grounded in the Commerce Clause. The scope of this legislation was so vast that many observers came to believe that Congress could justify almost any legislation under the Commerce Clause. Virtually all human activity could be related in one way or another to interstate commerce.

Congress relied on the Commerce Clause when it adopted the Gun-Free School Zones Act of 1990. This law made it a federal crime to possess a firearm in or within one thousand feet of a school. Of course, most, if not all, of the states already had these types of prohibitions in their own laws. In a 5-4 decision, the Supreme Court declared the new federal law unconstitutional. Writing for the Court, Chief Justice Rehnquist asserted that the Gun-Free School Zones Act was "a criminal statute that by its terms [had] nothing to do with 'commerce' or any sort of enterprise, however broadly one might define those terms." Rehnquist observed that "if we were to accept the Government's arguments, we are hard-pressed to posit any activity by an individual that Congress is without power to regulate."

The *Lopez* decision was significant because it reversed a long-term trend in which the Court had been highly deferential to congressional reliance on the Commerce Clause. Moreover, *Lopez* shows that the Supreme Court's role as umpire of the federal system remains an important one more than two hundred years after the federal system was conceived.

funding Medicaid, which provides medical care to low-income residents. With medical costs escalating rapidly throughout the 1980s, states' Medicaid obligations doubled and sometimes tripled in just a few years.

Clearly, the Reagan revolution removed some of the regulatory burden from state and local governments. This freedom from federal oversight brought new responsibilities, however. States often found themselves in the front lines of defense against an onslaught of new social and economic problems without the ability to confront them effectively. To some degree, that was exactly what the Reagan revolution was about—reducing reliance on government, especially the federal government, to solve problems that many thought could be better handled through private action.

The election of George H. W. Bush in 1988 effectively added four more years to the Reagan era. State and local governments found themselves under increasing financial pressure through the early 1990s. The mounting federal debt effectively ruled out much in the way of increased aid from Washington. Meanwhile, the states and the cities were forced to raise taxes to maintain basic levels of services.

In the early 1990s, states and cities became increasingly vocal in objecting to a new phenomenon: unfunded mandates. **Unfunded mandates** are programs or policies that the federal government requires but does not fund. For instance, the federal Clean Water Act increased the water quality standards for rivers and streams in urban areas. The costs of meeting the increased standards were quite high, and virtually all had to be borne by city governments. Congress found this approach quite appealing, however, because it could appear to be responsive to national policy concerns by passing legislation while passing the cost on to other levels of government. For example, unfunded federal mandates cost Tennessee cities more than $164 million in 1993 alone.[31] A study of 134 cities conducted by the U.S. Conference of Mayors in 1993 found that federal mandates consumed, on average, nearly 12 percent of local budgets.[32] Los Angeles County, California, led the nation in federally mandated spending, laying out roughly $1 billion in 1993.[33]

Responding to widespread concern about unfunded mandates, Congress passed the Unfunded Mandates Reform Act (UMRA) in 1995. This legislation was designed to make

▶ **unfunded mandates**
Programs or policies that the federal government requires but does not fund.

it difficult for the federal government to make state and local governments pay for programs that they did not enact or even necessarily approve. Under the act, the Congressional Budget Office (CBO) is required to estimate the costs for any bill that would have an impact of $50 million on state and local governments. Any bill must provide funding to cover the cost of any new mandated spending in states and cities. However, the act did not apply to mandates existing at the time of its passage, and many conservatives complained that the act "lacked teeth."

The elimination of unfunded mandates was part of the Contract with America that helped the Republicans to gain control of Congress in 1994. One political buzzword of this period was **devolution,** the idea that federal power should be devolved to the state and local governments. The idea took hold not only in Congress, but within the Supreme Court's conservative majority in the mid-1990s (see Case in Point 3-1). The transfer of power and responsibility from the federal government to the states took place to some extent in the 1990s, but no one really expected a fundamental change in the character of modern federalism. And if some people did, they were disappointed. Despite some shifting of power and responsibility, the national government retains its dominant position in the political system, and it is difficult to imagine that it could ever be otherwise.

3-5 The Complex Character of Contemporary Federalism

The direct federal-city linkage is indicative of the complex nature of contemporary American federalism and the difficulty of dividing powers and responsibilities cleanly. The classical approach, called **dual federalism,** has never really characterized the American system. A more accurate description might be called **cooperative federalism,** with state and federal governments working together to deal with the problems of a growing and increasingly urban society. But some commentators point out that the cooperation has sometimes been less than abundant.

3-5a Areas of Federal-State Cooperation

Political scientist Morton Grodzins coined the term **marble cake federalism** to describe the mix of federal and state activities throughout the policy-making process.[34] This metaphor does fit much of the way the federal system works. In virtually any area of American public life, from roads to health care to education to law enforcement, the federal and state governments work side by side, if not always in perfect harmony. Of course, it is important to recognize that in most instances, the national government is the dominant partner, and when conflicts arise, the national government usually prevails.

Protecting the Environment Environmental protection is an area of public policy that nicely demonstrates the cooperative federal-state approach. Consider, for example, the Clean Air Act and the Clean Water Act. These federal statutes, enacted in the 1970s, represent the main thrust of the national effort to control air and water pollution. These acts are enforced primarily by the Environmental Protection Agency (EPA), a major federal regulatory agency, but states are given enforcement powers under these acts as well. The EPA works, in turn, with state agencies to develop implementation and enforcement plans. In 1995, responding to criticisms that their relationship was not always harmonious or productive, EPA and state officials agreed to establish the National Environmental Performance Partnership System (NEPPS). Consistent with prevailing attitudes about federalism in the mid-1990s, the new system sought to give states greater flexibility in the implementation of national environmental policies. It also sought to allow each state to focus its energies on the environmental problems that most affected it. Under the new system, the EPA and each state enter into an agreement that sets forth priorities, goals, strategies, and responsibilities. At least on paper, NEPPS is a an excellent example of cooperative federalism.

---

devolution In general, this term means "going back to how things once were," but in politics, it refers specifically to the movement to restore authority and autonomy to state and local governments.

dual federalism Classical characterization of the American federal system that recognizes strictly limited federal involvement in matters of traditional state and local concern.

cooperative federalism Characterization of the American federal system that emphasizes the cooperation and joint arrangements among the three levels of government.

marble cake federalism Characterization of the American federal system that emphasizes the shared responsibilities among levels of government in the policy process.

Law Enforcement   Usually, Washington plays a significant role in two areas: funding and coordination. Law enforcement provides a good example of both. For instance, because bank robbery violates both state and federal law, both the local police and the FBI become immediately involved. For all serious crimes, the federal authorities enter investigations when the suspect flees from one state to another to avoid prosecution.

In addition, Congress has established programs that provide funding (usually grants-in-aid) to state and local police departments. The funds often go toward the purchase of new computer systems or equipment. Under President Clinton's crime bill, which became law in September 1994, the federal government transferred money to cities to allow them to hire additional law enforcement personnel. State and local police work very closely with the federal databases to identify and track suspects. State and federal authorities often cooperate in conducting investigations and making arrests, especially where interstate criminal activity is involved.

The "war on drugs" provides many examples of cooperation among federal, state, and local agencies. Consider, for example, the marijuana-eradication programs that are under way in many states. These efforts are funded by the Office of National Drug Control Policy but are organized on a state-by-state basis. In each state, a task force under the leadership of the governor organizes an effort involving state and local law enforcement agencies, the federal Drug Enforcement Administration (DEA), and even the state's national guard. National Guard helicopters and other military equipment are used to locate marijuana patches and even indoor "grows." Searches, seizures, and arrests are then made by the law enforcement agencies involved. Depending on various factors, the persons arrested are prosecuted for drug offenses in federal or state courts.

Because federal and state laws overlap in regard to many crimes (the distribution of illicit drugs, for example), an accused criminal may be subject to prosecution in either state or federal court. In some instances, defendants are subject to prosecution in both state and federal courts. This was the case in 1992, when four Los Angeles police officers accused of using excessive force in the arrest of motorist Rodney King were prosecuted by both the state of California and the federal government. The police officers were acquitted in the state case, but two of them were convicted in a subsequent federal trial.

In the 2000 presidential election campaign, one issue of disagreement was whether the federal government should enact legislation against "hate crimes." A prominent example of a hate crime is the horrible incident that took place in Jasper, Texas, in 1999, when a black man, James Byrd, Jr., was dragged to his death behind a pickup truck. In fact, this incident was the topic of discussion in the campaign and the subject of a controversial television campaign ad. Candidate Al Gore cited the Byrd incident as an example of why federal legislation is needed. George W. Bush pointed out that the men responsible for the crime had been convicted of murder and punished severely under Texas law. In Bush's view, federal hate crimes legislation was unnecessary. But proponents of federal law claimed that state and local authorities were not always willing to enforce existing state hate crimes laws.

The general trend in recent decades has been for Congress to create new federal offenses to supplement the state criminal codes. An excellent example is the area of drug offenses in which there are now parallel prohibitions at the national and state levels. Although some critics object to the nationalization of the criminal law, state and local officials often appreciate the opportunity to enlist the support of federal law enforcement officials. And state and local prosecutors often turn drug cases over to federal prosecutors, because "the feds" often have greater resources and offenders are likely to be sentenced to longer prison terms under the very punitive federal drug laws.

Education   Traditionally, education was a matter of state and local concern. Beginning in the 1960s, however, the federal government became more involved in this area. Congress provided federal grants to states and local communities, but used this support to leverage control over various aspects of school administration. In the 2000 presidential election, education became a major topic of discussion, with both candidates pledging to improve a troubled educational system, albeit by very different means. Among other things, candidate

Comparative Perspective

Federalism in Yugoslavia and the Soviet Union

The United States has made federalism work, although not without considerable conflict. Other federal systems have not been so fortunate despite decades of formal government organization. The Federal Republic of Yugoslavia failed to function as a nation following the demise of the powerful Soviet Union in 1991. Yugoslavia's constituent parts never accepted each other or the legitimacy of the nation itself. Ancient loyalties based on religion and ethnicity overturned decades of enforced nationhood. Likewise, the supposed "federal" structure of the Soviet Union, which was always more show than substance, collapsed as Russians, Ukrainians, Georgians, and other ethnic groups asserted their separate, long-standing, and deeply held national identities. The Soviet Union and Yugoslavia, which were assembled by force from a number of smaller nations, never fully established national political cultures. In the early 1990s, both of these countries disintegrated. The lessons are clear: Decades of nationhood based on force can disintegrate virtually overnight unless the central government has legitimacy.

George W. Bush promised to return control of schools to the local level, a theme that has played well in recent decades, especially among conservatives. However, the No Child Left Behind Act of 2001,[35] which President Bush trumpeted as one of his major domestic policy successes, brought greater federal involvement in the field of education, much to the chagrin of conservatives.[36] It must be noted, though, that the new federal law made provisions for local control and flexible implementation, unlike many of the federal education policies of previous decades.

Welfare Historically, the federal government had little to do with matters of social welfare. That changed in the wake of the Great Depression, as President Franklin Roosevelt promised the American people a "New Deal." Part of the New Deal was the federal government assumption of responsibility for ensuring social welfare. This assumption grew dramatically in the 1960s as part of President Lyndon Johnson's Great Society program. The idea was to use the forces of government, primarily the federal government, to overcome poverty. Aid to Families with Dependent Children (AFDC) and other federal programs were funded primarily by the federal government, but the states were given primary administrative responsibility. Of course, with federal funding came federal control, which by the 1990s had become quite unpopular.

In 1996, the Republican-controlled Congress adopted, and President Clinton signed into law, the Personal Responsibility and Work Opportunity Reconciliation Act. The act dramatically changed the nation's welfare system. The old AFDC was replaced by a new program, Temporary Assistance for Needy Families (TANF). As the name of the program suggests, welfare assistance was made temporary, rather than a lifelong entitlement. The new program also emphasized job training to help move recipients off the welfare rolls and into gainful employment. Finally, welfare reform eliminated many of the federal controls and let states determine criteria for eligibility for welfare.

3-5b Fiscal Federalism

The brief discussions of education, law enforcement, and welfare in section 3-5a, "Areas of Federal-State Cooperation," highlight not only the cooperative relationship between the federal government and the states in certain programmatic areas but also the fiscal dependence of the states on Washington. As we have pointed out, states and cities have become dependent on federal dollars in a wide variety of areas, a dependency only partially reduced by the Reagan revolution of the 1980s and the devolution of the 1990s. But with funding comes control. Congress routinely attaches conditions to this aid. For example, in 1984,

Congress passed a law mandating that states raise their legal drinking age to twenty-one or forfeit a percentage of the federal funds they receive for highway construction. Of course, because Congress lacks the constitutional authority to raise the drinking age directly, a state could refuse to accept the money and keep its drinking age at a lower level. Realistically, however, states can ill afford to forgo this type of aid, as Congress knows perfectly well. As a result of these tactics, Congress can legislate a national policy in areas that traditionally belong to the states. When the state of South Dakota challenged the constitutionality of the 1984 act in the Supreme Court, it was informed that "objectives not thought to be within Article I's enumerated legislative fields . . . may nevertheless be attained through the use of the spending power and the conditional grant of federal funds."[37] By 2000, this use of the federal spending power had become so ingrained as a part of American federalism that few people even commented when Congress tied states' future highway funding to a reduction of the standard for driving under the influence of alcohol to .08 percent.

This nationalization of policy making reflects the increasing sense that our problems are of national scope and hence need national attention. Congress and the president often find themselves under some pressure to act, regardless of federal theory. The Los Angeles riots of 1992, for example, were regarded not just as reactions to local concerns, but as symptoms of national urban problems. Often, the quickest way to act is to require the states to take action, especially if additional laws are considered necessary. States and cities receive so much federal aid in so many areas that requiring state action as a condition of receiving federal funds is certainly an appealing strategy.

The dominance of federal dollars has become so complete that it has led to the use of the term **fiscal federalism** to describe the federal relationship based on money. In many ways, this term reflects the evolution of the American federal system. The emphasis on money is possible because the country's collective attention has been diverted from program differences rooted in state and regional variations. To a great degree, the United States has succeeded in developing a national political culture. Because the actions of the federal government changed the segregationist culture of the Deep South, regional and state differences in public policy have faded. Although some variation among the states persists, states in the future are unlikely to take actions designed to preserve themselves as distinct cultural entities.

> **fiscal federalism** A system under which the federal government uses money to induce state and local governments to enact certain policies.

3-6 The Contours of State and Local Government

Despite the centralization of power in Washington, D.C., the states continue to function as viable political entities. It is thus important to understand the structures and processes of state and local government. This book, which deals with American politics and government at the national level, can provide only a brief glimpse, of course, of state and local politics.

3-6a State Constitutions

Each state has its own constitution. Unlike the federal constitution, most state constitutions have been revised several times and amended frequently. For the most part, state constitutions are longer and more detailed than their federal counterpart. Nevertheless, all of them follow the basic principles of the federal constitution. All the state constitutions provide for separation of powers among the legislative, executive, and judicial branches of government. All of them employ some system of checks and balances among the branches. Every state constitution has a bill of rights patterned after the U.S. Constitution, although some state constitutions go considerably further in protecting individual rights.

All fifty state constitutions are similar in that all provide for the creation of local governments. Most states are divided into counties (in Louisiana, they are called parishes). The counties are merely subdivisions of the states; when the states were first established, they divided themselves into counties. Many functions of state government are organized by county, including the courts, taxation, licensure of business, regulation of land use, and, perhaps most significantly, education. States have also created a number of cities and towns

Popular Culture and American Politics
Model Illinois Government

By Chapman Rackaway

Have you ever wondered whether you might want to be a legislator yourself one day, affecting public policy in the most direct way possible, but you're not sure whether you want to go through the trouble of campaigning, winning office, and then doing the job of a state representative before deciding to run for office? College students in Illinois have the opportunity to test drive the job of state legislator in the Model Illinois Government (MIG) simulation.

The main idea behind MIG, founded by professors and students at Illinois community colleges in the early 1980s, was to give students in government classes an idea of the inner workings of a legislature. Since its beginning, MIG has expanded and now serves more than 200 participants every year in the simulation of state government.

For a week in late winter, students and faculty members get the run of the actual Illinois state capitol in Springfield to add to the simulation's reality. Students sign up to portray state legislators and senators, along with staffers, court judges, budget-writing bureaucrats, moot court attorneys, lobbyists, and newspaper reporters. Each year the MIG participants vote for the following year's executive branch, with a governor, lieutenant governor, secretary of state, attorney general, and treasurer. Each student has the opportunity to independently and as a group research bills, examine court cases, and study parliamentary procedure. Students may also sponsor legislation and write their own. During the simulation, delegates attend committee meetings, party caucuses, and legislative sessions to move bills through the legislature and onto the governor's desk. At the end of the simulation, a veto session is held in which both houses come together to consider overriding the governor's veto.

The event is a realistic and thrilling opportunity for students to experience the process of democratic government in a setting that allows the student to sit at the legislators' desks. They not only use the microphones, voting buttons, and behind-the-scenes meeting rooms, but also debate current issues facing the State of Illinois. They also have time to interact with students from other colleges from all over the state.

by special legislation. Cities and towns vary tremendously in their governing structures, powers, and responsibilities. All told, more than eighty-seven thousand local governments are in the United States, including counties, cities, towns, school districts, utility districts, and various other special districts.[38]

All state constitutions can be amended by **legislative proposal;** typically, a proposed amendment can be adopted by a two-thirds vote of the legislature followed by ratification by a majority vote of the state electorate. Most state constitutions permit the calling of a *constitutional convention* with the approval of the voters. The convention considers proposed amendments to the constitution, which, if approved, must be ratified by the people. Seventeen states permit their constitutions to be amended through a process named **initiative and referendum.** This process allows voters to initiate constitutional change by circulating a petition. If enough signatures are obtained, a proposal is placed on the ballot. The voters then decide whether to adopt the proposed change in the constitution. This process, though overtly more democratic, is highly controversial. Critics argue that it makes a state constitution too easy to amend and thus susceptible to transitory public passions. Some critics point to California, where numerous (and sometimes conflicting) changes have been made in the state constitution through initiative and referendum.

3-6b State Executive Branches

Because of the experience with British royal governors, the early colonies were wary of giving too much power to any executive, including a state governor. Consequently, state legislatures were the dominant institution in state governments. Throughout the nineteenth

legislative proposal
A means of amending a constitution whereby a legislative body proposes a constitutional amendment that must be ratified by some other authority.

initiative and referendum
One process by which a state constitution may be amended. Initiative refers to the act of petitioning the state government to put an issue before the voters in a referendum, or election.

Popular Culture and American Politics
The Governator

By Chapman Rackaway

Americans have always been fascinated by celebrity, and we have never been shy about voting for famous people. Early on, war heroes like George Washington, Andrew Jackson, and William Henry Harrison drew the attention and ballots of enough Americans to elect them to the nation's highest office. Even into the twentieth century, we elected Theodore Roosevelt and Dwight Eisenhower on the strength of their name recognition as great military leaders.

After World War II, we started paying less attention to soldiers and more to the people who played them in movies and on television. Today, our celebrities are movie stars and athletes. Ronald Reagan began as an actor, and other actors such as *The Love Boat*'s Fred Grandy and Fred Thompson turned to politics. Athletes such as Richard Petty, Jim Bunning, and Jack Kemp have also run for office at different times. In 2003, we added the name Arnold Schwarzenegger to the list.

The Austrian-born bodybuilder came to the United States in 1975 and immediately became a sensation in movies such as *Conan the Barbarian*. Schwarzenegger turned from B-movies to big-budget blockbusters such as *The Terminator* and *True Lies,* becoming America's top action star. Schwarzenegger used his popularity in small ways to help Republican politicians over time, even though he married Maria Shriver, who is related to America's Democratic royalty, the Kennedy clan. Pundits would often tout Schwarzenegger as a possible contender for the U.S. Senate, so it was not a surprise when he announced he would seek political office: the governorship of California.

California allows voters to recall elected officials, and in 2003 California voters recalled incumbent Gray Davis. Schwarzenegger jumped into a crowded field of almost 150 candidates, including former TV star Gary Coleman (Arnold from the 1970s series *Diff'rent Strokes*). Despite being the butt of regular late-night monologue jokes and more serious allegations of sexual harassment early in his career, California voters installed Schwarzenegger as their "Governator." As governor, Schwarzenegger has developed effective relationships with many interest groups that have given him leverage with the state legislature in getting progress on his aggressive budget-cutting agenda. Schwarzenegger now looks to follow in the footsteps of another actor-turned-California governor, Ronald Reagan. However, for voters to move Schwarzenegger to the White House, the Constitution would have to be changed because Schwarzenegger is not a natural-born U.S. citizen.

century, governors gained power, but a powerful reform movement around the beginning of the twentieth century was the major factor increasing the power of governors. Governors Woodrow Wilson of New Jersey, Charles Evans Hughes of New York, and Robert LaFollette of Wisconsin were among the leaders of this movement. In addition, recent changes over the past few decades have almost always increased the powers of governors, though the strength of the position still varies considerably from state to state.

Several factors contribute to a governor's strength:

- Does the governor have the power to veto legislation?
- Can the governor propose a budget?
- Does the governor have a line-item veto, which enables him or her to remove certain budget provisions without vetoing the entire bill?
- Does the governor have the ability to reorganize state agencies?
- Can the governor appoint other state executive officials and under what conditions?
- Does the governor have the staff and resources available to plan policy, develop legislative strategies, write a budget, and manage the bureaucracy?

Of these questions, the power over the budget is the most important. Generally, larger, more urban states have provided for a strong governor system, and southern and rural states have opted for a weak governor system. For example, Maryland, New Jersey, and New York are considered strong governor systems, and North Carolina, Alabama, and Vermont are considered weak governor systems.[39] Of course, this label refers to the position. Individuals occupying the office vary in their leadership skills and preferences.

Most, but not all, governors enjoy four-year terms with a limit of no more than two terms. Some states, such as Virginia, limit the governor to one term. In about half the states, the governor runs for office on the same ticket with the lieutenant governor, but in the others the two run separately. Therefore, the governor and lieutenant governor may be of opposite parties in the separately elected state systems. Unlike the president, who appoints his own cabinet, most governors must work with other executive officials who are elected on their own. About thirty states elect at least six different executive positions. For example, states may elect the attorney general (who is responsible for prosecuting crimes and representing the state in civil matters), a treasurer (who handles the state's finances), and a secretary of state (who oversees elections and keeps state records). In addition, numerous boards handle all kinds of issues, such as public schools, higher education, and utility regulation. These boards may be quite independent from the governor. The general trend of the past several decades has been to reduce the number of state executive officials who are elected independently, but most governors must deal with other executives who have their own political aspirations and ideological beliefs and the knowledge that they were elected on the basis of their own popularity rather than on the governor's.

State-Level Bureaucracies   One of the most important trends in state government over the past several decades has been the tremendous growth in the size of the bureaucracy. Because Congress has mandated that the states perform many policy tasks, such as handling medical care for the poor and welfare, the national government is partly to blame for the increase. But the states have also greatly expanded their own policy role. As a result of actions by both the states and the national government, the states have had to create many new agencies to implement policy. Most states have agencies responsible for public education, higher education, law enforcement, corrections, highway safety, health and human services, employment, revenue, transportation, and commerce and economic development. Collectively, the fifty state governments employ more than five million employees (not including employees of local governments).[40]

3-6c State Legislatures

State legislatures play a prominent role in the policy process, handling such issues as education, insurance, crime, health care, and transportation. State legislatures also provide policy innovation by trying different policy alternatives. Recently, state legislatures have undergone a number of changes. Both the operations of state legislatures and the campaigns of state legislators have become more professional. State legislatures have also become the focus of the movement to limit the number of terms that politicians can serve. Another change is the dramatic transformation of their membership: More women, African Americans, and Hispanics than ever now serve in state legislatures. Though their numbers are still less than their share of the population, all these groups have made dramatic gains over the past couple of decades. Furthermore, as they gain experience at the state level, these female and minority legislators may find greater opportunities at higher levels of office.

Bicameralism   With the exception of Nebraska, which has a unicameral legislature, each state has a bicameral legislature similar to the Congress with a lower house with more legislators than the upper chamber. Typically, the upper chamber is referred to as the "Senate," but the lower chamber goes by various names, such as the "Assembly," "General Assembly," "House of Delegates," or, most commonly, "House of Representatives." On average, the lower chamber has three times more members than the upper chamber. Unlike Congress, both chambers of state legislatures are based on population, but members of the upper chamber always represent more people than members of the lower chamber. State legislators represent geographic districts within the state. In many states, however, more than one member is elected from the same geographic district. About one-quarter of all lower chamber members are elected from multimember districts, and about 8 percent of state senators represent multimember districts.[41] Consequently, in some states a citizen may be able to vote for three state house members and two state senators in one district.

Legislative Sessions Most state legislatures now meet every year to propose new legislation, hold hearings, pass legislation, and conduct oversight of the state bureaucracy, but some states still limit the legislature to one session every two years. The biennial-session states (those that meet every other year) typically meet in January of odd-numbered years, and a few meet in even-numbered years. In most states, the governor can also call special sessions of the legislature to deal with a matter that either was not dealt with during the regular session or is so pressing that it cannot wait until the next regular session.

In about three-quarters of the states, the state constitution limits the number of days the legislature can meet; sessions range from 30 to 195 days. Some states even limit legislators' pay so that they will not have much incentive to try to extend the legislative session. Many legislative critics favor these limits on the state legislative calendar, believing that they keep meddlesome legislators from "messing with things" too much. On the other hand, legislators and many reformers find the limits troublesome because much legislation is passed at the last minute of a crowded legislative schedule. The tight schedule may prevent careful consideration of bills, and serious debate may be almost nonexistent.

Despite the time limits, the workload of most state legislatures has grown tremendously. In states with no time limits, such as California, Illinois, Massachusetts, Ohio, Pennsylvania, Wisconsin, Michigan, and New York, the annual legislative calendar ranges from seven to ten months per year.[42] In more than half the states, the legislature is almost continuously in session. In states that do have time limits, legislators must often resort to doing committee work during the interim period between legislative sessions. This committee work is essential to getting the work done during the limited legislative sessions.

Terms of Office and Legislative Pay Senators generally enjoy longer terms in office between elections than do the members of the lower chamber in the state legislature. The most common arrangement is a four-year term for senators and two-year terms for lower chamber members. Some senators, however, have only two-year terms, and a few lower chambers enjoy four-year terms. Generally, most state legislators are not well paid for the time they devote to getting elected and working in the legislature. On the low end of the scale, New Hampshire pays $200 for the two-year term. On the high end, California pays $99,000 per year plus a $121 per diem (by the work day) for expenses.[43] Generally, the more populous states pay their legislators well, and the smaller states tend to keep salaries low. In addition, most states provide some money for meals, lodging, and travel for the members while the legislature is in session.

Professionalization of State Legislatures State legislatures have become increasingly professionalized over the past couple of decades. More and more state legislators hope to stay in office from one term to the next. Many observers have lamented the slow decline in the number of citizen-legislators. Rather than just represent the people for a few years and then return to their previous occupations, many of the new breed of legislators seek a career in politics. Some hope for leadership positions in the state legislature, and others hope to use the legislature as a springboard to higher office, such as the governorship or a seat in Congress. One study has estimated that 20 percent of the state legislatures are controlled by professional legislators, another 20 percent are moving in that direction, and about 40 percent may be moving in that direction, although only 20 percent of states appear likely to continue to be dominated by citizen-legislators.[44]

To assist them in their efforts to make a career of politics, the legislators have more staff, perform more casework, and do more of the things necessary to stay reelected. Having a competent staff is extremely important to the professional legislator. Committee staff, leadership staff, researchers, and legal staff help the chamber perform the legislative functions of lawmaking, overseeing the bureaucracy, and developing a budget. In addition, the members of a legislator's personal staff play an extremely important role; those people assist the legislator in performing casework, communicating with constituents, sending newsletters and opinion polls to constituents, and handling press relations. Although personal staff members may provide some assistance on matters related to legislation, their most important function is to help the legislator stay in touch with potential voters.

State Legislative Campaigns   Campaigns for state legislative seats have increasingly followed the same pattern as congressional campaigns. Political partisanship is important, especially in the South, where Democrats still dominate almost all state legislatures. Most states outside the South are competitive for both major parties, though the Republicans dominate several Rocky Mountain states, such as Idaho, Wyoming, and Utah. One notable exception is Nebraska, which has a nonpartisan state legislature.

Generally, state legislators must endure two stages of an election to claim a legislative seat: First, they must win a primary within the party, and second, they have to beat the opponent from the other major party in the general election. Increasingly, these campaigns are using modern techniques, such as opinion polls, direct mail advertising and solicitation of campaign dollars, media consultants, radio and television advertising, and targeting of voters. Not surprisingly, the costs of campaigns have risen dramatically. In California, some state legislative campaigns have spent more than $1 million, but most state races cost far less than is spent in California. Nevertheless, one study of New Jersey found a tremendous increase in the costs of state legislative campaigns. In 1983, only thirteen candidates spent more than $100,000, but by 1991 more than thirty-four candidates spent more than $100,000 with three candidates spending more than $400,000.[45]

Generally, incumbents seeking reelection to state legislative races have been highly successful. Though state legislators are less likely to seek reelection than members of Congress, they are just about as likely to be reelected if they choose to run. About 90 percent of all incumbents seeking reelection are successful.[46]

All this may change in the near future, however, because by 1994 voter discontent had led sixteen states to adopt term limits. Though the term limits established by the states vary considerably, most limit the time that can be served in each chamber to between six and twelve years. Some require only a break in service for a couple of years, and others impose the limitation for life. In those states, members either have to retire or attempt to move on to other offices.

Proponents of term limits argue that the infusion of new blood rejuvenates the legislatures, keeps members from becoming entrenched in office, protects the idea of the citizen-legislator, and provides more competition for higher offices. Critics say that voters should be able to choose whomever they want for office; the legislature loses much of its experience and expertise; rapid turnover causes instability in state policy; and the legislature loses power to the governor and the bureaucracy.

3-6d The Interest Group Environment in the States

Historically, many state legislatures were dominated by a small number of interest groups that were important economically to the state. For example, the coal industry dominated the Kentucky and West Virginia state governments for decades; the sugar industry was an extremely powerful group in Hawaii; the oil industry was quite influential in Texas, Oklahoma, Louisiana, and Pennsylvania; and the railroads dominated many western states. This domination by a single group is no longer the case in most states. Public school teachers, bankers, labor unions, doctors, and government workers are now involved in state politics along with commercial, industrial, and agricultural interests. Indeed, the number of interest groups that are active at the state level has exploded over the past few decades.

Though close personal relations between traditional lobbyists and legislators are still important, the interest group environment has become much more professional in recent decades. Many interest groups have their own state headquarters and are hiring professional lobbyists and using more sophisticated lobbying techniques. Indeed, interest groups are at least partly to blame for the skyrocketing amounts of money that state candidates are raising for campaigns. Though almost all states have some laws requiring lobbyists to register, the strength of the laws and the degree to which they are enforced vary widely. Progressive states, such as California, have been most successful with lobbying and campaign reform, whereas southern states and some of the less populated states, such as Utah and Nevada, have been more lax.

3-6e State Court Systems

Each of the fifty state court systems is designed to settle cases arising under the laws of that state, which include the state constitution, the statutes enacted by the state legislature, the orders issued by the governor, the regulations adopted by various state agencies, and the **ordinances** (local laws) adopted by cities and counties. Nearly 90 percent of the court cases in this country are resolved in the state courts. They include criminal cases, where states prosecute people for committing crimes, and civil cases, where parties sue one another to settle legal disputes.

> **ordinances** Laws enacted by a local governing body, such as a city council or county commission.

No two state court systems are identical. They vary substantially in organization and administration; the procedures they follow in adjudicating cases; and the means whereby judges are selected, retained, and removed from office. Yet they also have many common features. Every state court system is equipped to conduct trials and to consider appeals from the outcomes of trials. Thus, every state court system has at least one tier of trial courts and at least one appellate court. A typical state court system is composed of four levels. At the bottom are trial courts of limited jurisdiction, which hear minor civil and criminal cases. At the next level of the hierarchy are trial courts of general jurisdiction, which decide major civil matters and more serious crimes. At the next level are the intermediate appellate courts, which consider routine appeals brought by losing parties in the trial courts below. At the top of the hierarchy is the state supreme court, which addresses the most important issues of state law. It is important to recognize that the decisions of the state supreme court are final with respect to questions of state law. Of course, state court decisions involving matters of federal law are subject to review by the federal courts. If a state or local law is challenged as being in violation of the U.S. Constitution, the federal courts may decide the issue.

Selection and Terms of State Judges At the time the U.S. Constitution was adopted, most state constitutions called for judges to be appointed by the governor. During the nineteenth century, new states coming into the Union tended to opt for popular election of their judges. Most of these elections were partisan in nature: Judicial candidates ran for office as members of a political party. In the early twentieth century, many states moved to nonpartisan judicial elections. In 1940, Missouri adopted a plan that has become the model for judicial selection reform throughout the states. The **Missouri Plan** works essentially as follows. First, a nonpartisan nominating commission interviews applicants for a judgeship and sends a "short list" to the governor. Presumably, all the individuals on the list are qualified to serve in the judiciary. The governor then appoints one of the nominees. After the term of office (which may range from four to eight years) has expired, the incumbent judge faces the voters in a retention election; that is, voters are asked to vote Yes or No on the question of whether the judge should be retained in office. Typically, judges who run in retention elections are retained, but occasionally they are ousted, because either the voters do not like their decisions or they have been implicated in some sort of scandal. The Missouri Plan, which is now used by most states to select some or all of their judges,[47] seems to be a reasonably successful approach to judicial selection. It incorporates the principle of merit selection, but also permits the people to retain a measure of control over their judiciary.

> **Missouri Plan** A plan for judicial selection and retention that originated in Missouri in 1940. The essential idea is that judges are selected and retained based on merit rather than on politics.

In all states except Rhode Island,[48] judges serve definite terms of office, although their terms vary from two to twelve years. In Alaska, for example, state supreme court justices are selected through the Missouri Plan, serve an initial term of three years, and then face the voters in a merit retention election. If they are retained, they serve a ten-year term, after which they are subject to another merit retention election.[49] The Alaska approach thus incorporates the element of popular accountability, but seems to place a premium on judicial independence. Assuming there is no misconduct, an Alaska supreme court justice has ten years in which he or she can serve without worrying too much about public opinion.

3-6f Local Governments

States are responsible for the delivery of most government services in the United States. These services include virtually everything except foreign policy and defense. States are responsible for most law enforcement, education, road building, and other major services. For the most part, these services are delivered by local governments, including school boards, utility districts, cities, and counties. Although all are important, the major political units within states are counties and cities.

Counties

Counties are the most basic form of local government. County boundaries are determined by the states and are rarely changed. The task of counties is simple: to deliver basic services to individuals, including education, law enforcement, and public health. Every county has a mechanism to provide public education, even if much or all of the funding comes from the state. In most counties, law enforcement is provided by a sheriff. Counties have other personnel who are responsible for road building, prosecuting criminals who violate state laws, and providing public health services.

> **board of commissioners** An elected body empowered to govern a county.

Although county government varies widely from state to state and often varies within states as well, two basic structures can be identified. The more traditional model is a small **board of commissioners** elected by the voters, usually from districts. The board, which operates without an elected executive, sets the budget and votes on county ordinances. The board also appoints various administrative officials. In most states, however, at least some heads of county departments are elected directly. They include the sheriff, who is almost always elected, as well as other officers ranging from court clerks to registrars of deeds and the trustees who handle the county's finances. In some states, legislatures have allowed counties to elect their own executives, who are responsible for running county departments and other basic administrative functions. Other counties have moved to a **county manager** form, in which a professional administrator is hired by the county commission to run the county departments.

> **county manager** A professional administrator hired by a county commission to oversee the administration of the county government.

The Need for Municipal Government

Virtually all cities and towns began as collections of houses, stores, and businesses, which at some point found that they needed more services than could be provided by their county government. As people demanded systems for sanitation, street cleaning, traffic control, fire protection, and other services, state legislatures developed mechanisms to allow them to form voluntary governmental units called cities or towns. These units are technically legal corporations.

> **municipal charter** An act of a state legislature creating a city and authorizing the creation of a city government.

When a city incorporates, it is granted a municipal charter. A **municipal charter** is a legal document that allows residents to form a city government. When a state grants a city a charter, it allows the city to raise money, hire workers, and make local laws. This charter specifies the process of electing city government officials and the basic structure of city government. Although the rules allowing cities to incorporate have been varied and complex, recent decades have witnessed a growth in the issuance of home rule charters. A **home rule** charter allows residents of a city to vote on a charter best suited to their city's conditions. Home rule means that a city can make governmental decisions without the approval of the state legislature. Even with home rule, however, the state sets broad limits on what a city can do. For instance, most states limit the types of taxes a city can impose on its citizens.

> **home rule** A municipal charter that allows a city to make governmental decisions without the concurrence of the state legislature.

The most crucial element of a municipal charter is the structure of government the city will have. Today, cities have three major options: the weak mayor-council, the strong mayor-council, and the city manager forms of government. A fourth form, the commission form, is found in only a few cities.

Mayor-Council Forms of Government   The predominant form of city government in early America was the **weak mayor-council system,** in which the mayor has limited powers. In this system, the city council has the power to hire and fire administrators. In many ways, the mayor's job in such cities is largely limited to performing ceremonial functions. Although these types of mayors can be influential, they are more often merely figureheads.

Many cities were not well served by the weak mayor system. Without a clear line of responsibility for administration, departments suffered from a lack of coordination. The **strong mayor-council system** of government was created to give the mayor responsibility for administration while the council retained legislative power. In this system, the mayor is much more than a ceremonial leader. He or she is responsible for the day-to-day operation of the city. Moreover, in many cities, the mayor has veto power over ordinances passed by the city council.

The Council-Manager Form   In the early 1900s, a new form of government, called the council-manager form, was proposed and adopted by a number of cities. It reflected a reform movement in city politics, which was driven by the desire to make city government more professional and less political. The council-manager form sought to professionalize city government by separating the administration of programs from politics. It accomplishes that goal by placing the city departments under a professionally trained **city manager** who is hired and fired by the city council. This model has proven to be very popular, especially with medium-size and rapidly growing cities. Usually, these cities have adopted the council-manager system as part of a reform package that also includes at-large, nonpartisan elections. In an **at-large election,** many or all members of the city council are elected from the city as a whole rather than from districts. In a **nonpartisan election,** no party labels are attached to the candidates on the ballot. Cities with managers, nonpartisan elections, and a substantial proportion of representatives elected at-large are known as **reformed cities,** and those with strong mayors, partisan ballots, and district elections of council members are often called **unreformed cities.**

Representation in Urban Politics   Although many cities have adopted at-large elections and nonpartisan ballots to increase professionalism, mounting evidence shows that the representation of minorities in these types of cities is minimized. If a city is 40 percent African American and elects representatives at-large, it may well end up with no African Americans on the council. For this reason, at-large systems have come under attack in many cities with substantial minority populations. The logic of an at-large system is simple and appealing. Members of the city council who represent the entire city should have the interests of the whole city in mind, and those who represent districts might be expected to protect only the interests of their districts. In the early twentieth century, urban reformers thought that cities would be better governed if at least some of the representatives were elected at-large. It is interesting to note that nowhere else in American politics are legislators elected to represent an entire political entity. In the U.S. Congress, for example, no senators or members of the House of Representatives are elected at-large from the entire country.

The paradox of local government is that although it is in many ways the closest government to its constituents and provides services that touch its citizens daily, Americans are quite ambivalent about it being too "political." Most state systems—and all national elections—are partisan. A great number of local governments are nonpartisan. Local elections are often held in years when no statewide or national races are held. The idea is simple: Isolate local politics. The results have been predictable. Interest in nonpartisan and at-large elections is low. Voter turnout lags far behind that in other elections. Ironically,

weak mayor-council system A form of city government in which the city council has the power to hire and fire administrators. In this system, the mayor's role is largely ceremonial.

strong mayor-council system A form of local government in which the mayor is responsible for the day-to-day operation of the city. In many cities, the mayor has veto power over ordinances passed by the city council.

city manager A professionally trained public administrator hired by a city council to oversee the day-to-day operations of the city government.

at-large election An election system in which representatives are chosen by voters in a vote from the whole community rather than from separate districts within the community.

nonpartisan election An election in which candidates are not formally affiliated with a political party.

reformed cities Cities that utilize a professional manager, nonpartisan elections, and at-large elections of a substantial proportion of the members of the city council.

unreformed cities Cities characterized by a strong mayor, partisan elections, and council members who represent districts within those cities.

the level of government that is closest to the voters is the one designed in many cases to minimize their interest and participation.

3-7 Assessing American Federalism

Clearly, the character of American federalism has changed dramatically since the Constitution was written in 1787. Yet the basic structure and fundamental principle of dual sovereignty remain reasonably intact. The national government cannot abolish the states, although the federal courts can redraw state legislative districts and even impose significant changes on local government structures. In most areas, the national government cannot dictate policy to the states, but it can, and does, coerce them to participate in national programs or abide by national policies. Still, the states remain more or less autonomous political entities that have enormous influence over the day-to-day lives of their citizens. Indeed, in some areas, such as education, health care, and the environment, some states have assumed leadership roles, adopting innovations that have served as models for other states (and even the federal government).

3-7a The Advantages of the Federal System

Despite enormous changes over the past two centuries, American federalism retains the basic advantages and disadvantages that are inherent in the federal arrangement. On the positive side, federalism allows government to be closer to the people. Despite the concentration of power in Washington over the past century, the federal system continues to provide a degree of decentralization. Imagine how much more concentrated power would be if the federal structure were abolished in favor of a unitary system! For someone living on Maui, in the Hawaiian Islands, traveling to Honolulu to petition the state government for a "redress of grievances" is more convenient (and considerably less expensive) than to make the several thousand-mile journey to Washington, D.C. Federalism is well suited to a country that spans a continent (and beyond).

Federalism also allows policies to be tailored somewhat to local and regional differences. For example, the state of Nevada, reflecting the traditional libertarian culture of the frontier, is much more permissive than most states with respect to the "vices" of prostitution and gambling. Similarly, Wyoming, which retains much of the political culture of the Old West, is much more permissive about the possession and use of firearms than is New York, for example.

Not only does federalism allow policies to reflect the different tastes and values that are found among the states, but it also allows the states to innovate and experiment with new policies and programs. In this sense, states can be viewed as "policy laboratories" where new ideas can be tested without committing the entire nation to a policy that may turn out to be ineffectual or counterproductive.

In the wake of the terrorist attacks of 9-11-2001, many people realized that federalism has another advantage. Suppose that Washington, D.C., were to be destroyed or contaminated by a nuclear or biological attack. It is somewhat comforting to realize that even if the national government were paralyzed, state and local governments would still be able maintain order and provide essential services.

3-7b The Disadvantages of Federalism

On the debit side of the ledger, federalism necessarily entails inefficiency in the implementation of national policies and the solution of national problems. States may be slow to act, and when they do, they may act in a fashion that contradicts what other states or the national government is doing.

Decentralization entails the diffusion of power, which is generally regarded as a good thing, but it also increases the opportunity for corruption. Contrary to commonly held stereotypes, the national government tends to be the least corrupt level of government because it conducts its business under the watchful eye of the mass media. State and local

What Americans Think About

The Power of the Federal Government

Do Americans believe that the federal government has too much power, not enough power, or about the right amount of power? The answer has changed somewhat over time. In 1992, the percentage of people thinking that the federal government had about the right amount of power declined sharply to 12 percent. The rest of America was sharply divided between those who believe the federal government has too much power and those who believe it has too little power.

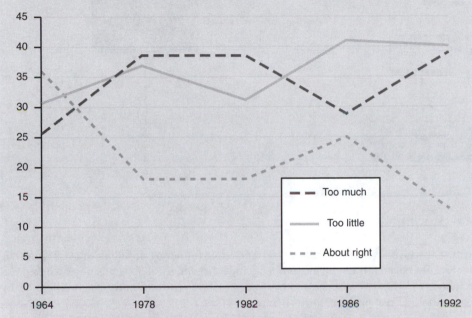

Source: Data adapted from Timothy J. Conlan, "Federal or State or Local: Trends in the Public's Judgment," *The Public Perspective* (Roper Center for Public Opinion Research), vol. 4, no. 2, January/February 1993, p. 3.

governments typically are subject to less intense media scrutiny. To be fair, though, state and local governments are probably now less corrupt than they were in the days of the powerful political machines and bosses.

Because states and local communities have primary governmental responsibility for the public welfare, the federal system permits what is sometimes an alarming variation in the degree of state and local support for education and social services. Traditionally, this variation extended also to civil rights and liberties, but this is less true now because of federal judicial oversight.

The inconsistencies of laws among the states and between the states and the federal government have made the legal system extremely complex. The complexity is apparent not only in the criminal law but also in rules of court procedure and jurisdiction, business law, family law, wills, estates, trusts, insurance, real property, licensure, environmental regulations, and zoning—the list goes on and on. Unquestionably, federalism has been a boon to lawyers. (Those planning to go to law school may see this as an advantage rather than a disadvantage of federalism!)

Finally, but not least significantly, federalism renders the American political system considerably less intelligible to the average citizen (see Figure 3-3). In a democracy, which puts a premium on citizens paying attention to and participating in their government, federalism adds much complexity. The average citizen may have difficulty figuring out what

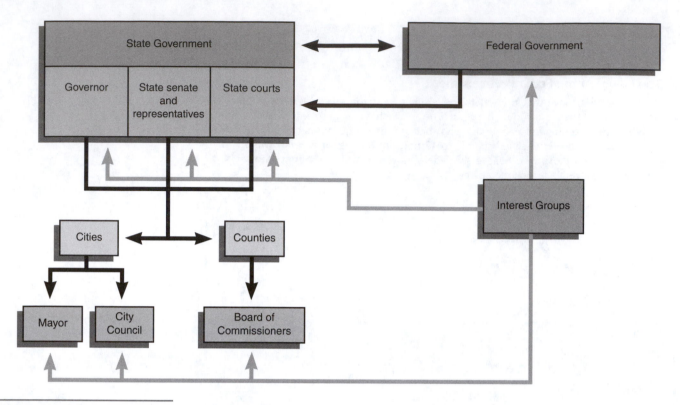

Figure 3-3
The American Political System Is Rendered Considerably More Complex by Federalism

agency at which level of government is responsible for acting or failing to act in a certain fashion. On balance, though, one must conclude that American federalism has worked reasonably well. There now appears to be no compelling justification for its abolition, or, for that matter, no real prospect for its demise.

3-8 Conclusion: Federalism and Political Culture

Like all societies, the United States has troubling divisions among its people: racial, ethnic, social, and economic. These divisions do not correspond now to states or regions. America has become a unified nation. Fostering this unity took a civil war, a monumental depression, two world wars, and a decades-long cold war, but it was finally achieved. Not only have crises brought the nation together, but advances in communications and transportation systems have also helped to foster identification with the national community. Today, a person may be born in one state, grow up in another, go to college in a third, move to a fourth to start a career, and finally move to a fifth state to enjoy retirement. This high degree of mobility erodes loyalties to states. In their place, one develops a loyalty to the nation. Whereas people living in the United States in 1787 thought of themselves primarily as Virginians or Marylanders or North Carolinians, people living in this country today think of themselves first and foremost as Americans. The development of the national identity has helped hold the system together during times of crisis; it also explains the emergence of the nation-centered model of federalism.

Since the Constitution was adopted, power in the American federal system has certainly tilted toward the national government. Nevertheless, the states have retained their political vitality and still play a significant role in the day-to-day lives of their citizens. Despite the nationalization of the American political culture, the states still approach their problems in a variety of ways. However, the variation is not of such magnitude or of such emotional import as to threaten the existence of the United States as a unified nation. The states still have vital roles in virtually every area of American public life. It remains as true today as when the Constitution was adopted: To understand the American political system, from the functioning of the criminal justice system to the conduct of elections to the construction and maintenance of highways, you must understand the unique nature of American federalism.

Questions for Thought and Discussion

1. Why did the Framers of the Constitution opt for a federal system rather than a unitary one?
2. How has the evolution of the federal system affected the civil rights and liberties of American citizens?
3. How does the federal government get the states to adopt policies they might otherwise not adopt?
4. Do Americans generally believe that the federal government has too much power, not enough power, or about the right amount of power?
5. In today's world, do the advantages of federalism outweigh the disadvantages?

Practice Quiz

Note: You can find the correct answers to these questions by taking the quiz and then submitting your answers in the Online Edition. The program will automatically score your submission. If you miss a question, the program will provide the correct answer, a rationale for the answer, and the section number in the chapter where the topic is discussed.

1. A _____ system of government is one in which sovereignty is vested solely in one central government.
   a. federal
   b. confederal
   c. unitary
   d. republican

2. Under the Articles of Confederation, the power to make major policy decisions _____.
   a. was vested in a national Congress
   b. was vested primarily in the states
   c. was vested in a national executive
   d. was vested in the Council of Revision

3. As originally envisioned, the power of the national government would be limited; however, judicial interpretation of the _____ Clause of Article I, Section 8 of the Constitution significantly increased the power of the national government.
   a. Supremacy
   b. Reserve
   c. Necessary and Proper
   d. Full Faith and Credit

4. In *Gibbons v. Ogden*, the Supreme Court _____ a New York law that granted a monopoly to operate steamboats in state waters.
   a. struck down
   b. upheld
   c. modified
   d. refused to review

5. Under the doctrine of _____, a state could decide for itself whether it would recognize, and ultimately abide by, a law passed by the national government.
   a. stare decisis
   b. reserved powers
   c. nullification
   d. secession

6. Which of these is not a concurrent power of federal and state governments?
   a. Borrow money.
   b. Tax.
   c. Establish courts of law.
   d. Regulate interstate commerce.

7. The Nixon administration sought to strengthen the state role in the federal system by replacing many federal grants-in-aid with a new program called _____.
   a. fiscal federalism
   b. general revenue sharing
   c. cooperative federalism
   d. financial revitalization

8. In the early 1990s, states and cities became increasingly vocal in objecting to _____, programs or policies that the federal government requires but does not fund.
   a. categorical grants
   b. noncategorical grants
   c. unfunded mandates
   d. revenue sharing

9. Political scientist Morton Grodzins has coined the term _____ to describe the mix of federal and state activities throughout the policy-making process.
   a. cooperative federalism
   b. marble cake federalism
   c. dual federalism
   d. fiscal federalism

10. With the sole exception of _____, every state has a bicameral legislature.
    a. Florida
    b. Texas
    c. Kansas
    d. Nebraska

For Further Reading

Berger, Raoul. *Government by Judiciary: The Transformation of the Fourteenth Amendment.* Cambridge: Harvard University Press, 1977.

Bowman, Ann O'Meara, and Richard C. Kearney. *The Resurgence of the States* (Englewood Cliffs, NJ: Prentice-Hall, 1986).

Conlan, Timothy J. *From New Federalism to Devolution: Twenty-Five Years of Intergovernmental Reform* (Washington, D.C.: Brookings Institution, 1998).

Elazar, Daniel J. *American Federalism: A View from the States,* 3d ed. (New York: Harper and Row, 1984).

Gittell, Marilyn. *State Politics and the New Federalism* (New York: Longman, 1986).

Greeve, Michael S. *Real Federalism* (Washington, D.C.: AEI Press, 1999).

Grodzins, Morton. *The American System* (New Brunswick, NJ: Transaction Books, 1983).

Leach, Richard H. *American Federalism* (New York: W. W. Norton, 1970).

Nagel, Robert F. *The Implosion of American Federalism* (New York: Oxford University Press, 2002).

Ostrom, Vincent. *The Meaning of American Federalism* (Institute for Contemporary Studies, 1999).

O'Toole, Lawrence. *American Intergovernmental Relations,* 3d ed. (Washington, D.C.: CQ Press, 2000).

Peterson, Paul. *The Price of Federalism* (Washington, D.C.: Brookings Institution, 1995).

Reagan, Michael, and John Sanzone. *The New Federalism,* 2d ed. (New York: Oxford University Press, 1981).

Riker, William H. *Federalism: Origin, Operation, Significance* (Boston: Little, Brown, 1964).

Simon, James F. *What Kind of Nation: Thomas Jefferson, John Marshall, and the Epic Struggle to Create a United States* (New York: Simon and Schuster, 2003).

Sundquist, James L., and David W. Davis. *Making Federalism Work: A Study of Program Coordination at the Community Level* (Washington, D.C.: Brookings Institution, 1969).

Walker, David Bradstreet. *The Rebirth of Federalism: Slouching Toward Washington,* 2d ed. (Washington, D.C.: CQ Press, 2000).

Endnotes

1. Samuel H. Beer, "Federalism, Nationalism, and Democracy in America," *American Political Science Review,* vol. 72, 1978, p. 11.

2. Lawrence J. O'Toole, "American Intergovernmental Relations: An Overview." In Lawrence J. O'Toole, ed., *American Intergovernmental Relations,* 3d ed. (Washington, D.C.: CQ Press, 2000), p. 5.

3. *McCulloch v. Maryland,* 17 U.S. 316 (1819).

4. *Gibbons v. Ogden,* 22 U.S. (9 Wheat.) 1 (1824).

5. *Scott v. Sandford,* 60 U.S. (19 Howard) 393 (1857).

6. *Texas v. White,* 74 U.S. (7 Wall.) 700 (1869).

7. See, for example, the Civil Rights Cases, 109 U.S. 3 (1883) and *Plessy v. Ferguson,* 163 U.S. 537 (1896).

8. The seminal case in this regard was *Brown v. Board of Education,* 437 U.S. 483 (1954), which is discussed at length in Chapter 5, "Civil Rights and the Struggle for Equality."

9. *South Carolina v. Katzenbach,* 383 U.S. 301 (1965).

10. *City of Mobile v. Bolden,* 446 U.S. 55 (1980).

11. *Shaw v. Reno,* 517 U.S. 899 (1995).

12. *Hunt v. Cromartie,* 532 U.S. 204 (2001).

13. *Chicago, Burlington and Quincy R.R. Co. v. City of Chicago,* 166 U.S. 226 (1897).

14. *Gitlow v. New York,* 268 U.S. 652 (1925).

15. *Cantwell v. Connecticut,* 310 U.S. 296 (1940).

16. *Everson v. Board of Education,* 330 U.S. 1 (1947).

17. The Eleventh Amendment, which would seem to prevent such challenges, was effectively circumvented by permitting individuals to sue state officials, rather than the states as sovereign entities.

18. See, for example, *Powell v. Alabama,* 287 U.S. 45 (1932).

19. See, for example, *Palko v. Connecticut,* 302 U.S. 319 (1937).

20. See *Wolf v. Colorado,* 338 U.S. 25 (1949).

21. See *Mapp v. Ohio,* 367 U.S. 643 (1961).

22. See *Miranda v. Arizona,* 384 U.S. 436 (1967).

23. William J. Brennan, "Guardians of Our Liberties—State Courts No Less than Federal." In *Views from the Bench: The Judiciary and Constitutional Politics,* eds. David M. O'Brien and Mark Cannon (Chatham, NJ: Chatham House, 1985).

24. *Wabash, St. Louis, and Pacific Railway Co. v. Illinois,* 118 U.S. 557 (1886).

25. Actually, the agency was abolished in 1995 after its regulatory functions were curtailed or transferred to other agencies.

26. *Hammer v. Dagenhart,* 247 U.S. 251 (1981).

27. *United States v. Darby,* 312 U.S. 100, 124 (1941).

28. See, for example, *United States v. Lopez,* 514 U.S. 549 (1995); *Seminole Tribe v. Florida,* 517 U.S. 44 (1996); *Printz v. United States,* 521 U.S. 898 (1997).

29. Christopher Hamilton and Donald Wells, *Federalism, Power, and Political Economy* (Englewood Cliffs, NJ: Prentice-Hall, 1990), p. 172.

30. The official name of the law was the Community and Demonstration Cities Act.

31. Pam Park, "Sasser to File Bill Easing Effect of Mandates," *Knoxville News-Sentinel,* October 27, 1993, p. A-5.

32. Marty Bauman, "Federal Mandates," *USA Today,* November 16, 1993, p. 15A.

33. Ibid.

34. Morton Grodzins, "The Federal System." In *The American Assembly: Goals for Americans* (Englewood Cliffs, NJ: Prentice-Hall, 1960), p. 250. Grodzins's "marble cake" metaphor is meant to contrast with the "layer cake" nature of classical federalism.

35. For official information on the law and the program it established, go to *http://www.ed.gov/nclb/landing.jhtml.*

36. See, for example, George F. Will, "Reelect Bush, Faults and All," *Washington Post,* October 31, 2004, p. B07.

37. *South Dakota v. Dole,* 483 U.S. 203 (1987).

38. U.S. Bureau of the Census, *2002 Census of Governments,* http://www.census.gov/govs/www/cog2002.html.

39. Thad L. Beyle, "Governors." In *Politics in the American States*, 7th ed., eds. Virginia Gray, Herbert Jacob, and Robert B. Albritton (Washington D.C.: CQ Press, 1999), pp. 210–211.

40. Harold W. Stanley and Richard G. Niemi, *Vital Statistics on American Politics, 2003–2004.* (Washington D.C.: Congressional Quarterly Press, 2003), p. 312.

41. Samuel C. Patterson, "Legislators and Legislatures in the American States." In *Politics in the American States*, 5th ed., eds. Virginia Gray, Herbert Jacob, and Robert B. Albritton (Glenview, IL: Scott, Foresman, 1990), p. 166.

42. Alan Rosenthal, "The Legislative Institution—In Transition and at Risk." In *The State of the States*, 2d ed., ed. Carl E. Van Horn (Washington, D.C.: Congressional Quarterly Press, 1993), p. 119.

43. National Conference of State Legislatures, "2000 State Legislator Compensation and Living Expense Allowances During Session" (Denver, CO: National Conference of State Legislatures, February 25, 2000.)

44. Rosenthal, "The Legislative Institution," p. 118.

45. Ibid., p. 126.

46. Patterson, "Legislators and Legislatures in the American States," p. 173.

47. See Larry C. Berkson, "Judicial Selection in the United States: A Special Report," *Judicature,* vol. 64, no. 4, October 1980, pp. 176–193. Data contained in this article were updated in 1992 and 1999 by Seth Andersen of the American Judicature Society and can be found on the AHS website, located at *http://www.ajs.org/js.*

48. In Rhode Island, state judges are appointed for life, just as federal judges are.

49. "Judicial Selection in the States: Initial Selection, Retention, and Term Length," American Judicature Society, on the web at *http://www.ajs.org/js/SelectionRetentionTerms.pdf.*

Civil Liberties and Individual Freedom

4

4-1 Individual Rights in a Democratic Society

In the United States, as in all the world's democracies, individuals possess certain basic rights. Indeed, the existence of individual rights is generally considered to be an essential element of democracy. Although the catalog of individual rights under American democracy is quite extensive, they can be summarized along two underlying dimensions: the right to be free from unreasonable interference in one's beliefs, associations, and activities and the right to equal treatment by the government and society. The former defines the realm of civil liberties, the subject of this chapter. The latter, which encapsulates the subject of civil rights, is dealt with in Chapter 5, "Civil Rights and the Struggle for Equality." In a nutshell, then, **civil liberties** deal with individual freedom; **civil rights** involve equality. These basic values—freedom and equality—are fundamental in not only American politics but also all democratic societies. Of course, as you shall see, considerable disagreement exists over the specific definition and application of these values. Moreover, because of their nature, civil liberties and civil rights issues put a great strain on the political system.

> **civil liberties** The freedoms protected by the Constitution and statutes—for example, freedom of speech, religion, and assembly.

> **civil rights** Legal protections against unreasonable discrimination.

Nothing strains the majority's support for civil liberties more than does a feeling of vulnerability, especially from enemies living within the society. In the wake of the terrorist attacks on America on 9-11-2001, government at all levels took stronger measures to protect domestic security. However, law enforcement agencies found themselves bound by legal limitations designed to protect the freedom and privacy of Americans. One such limitation was the federal law that limited wiretap requests to a specific telephone rather than to an individual who might be using a number of phones. At the urging of the Bush administration, Congress quickly and by a wide margin voted to ease this restriction. Although most Americans seemed to support the legislation, many cautioned against sacrificing civil liberties in the war on terrorism. Civil libertarians expressed concern that the civil liberties of all Americans might be sacrificed on the altar of domestic security. On the other hand, what good are civil liberties if no domestic security exists? The challenge to government, and especially to courts, is to strike a reasonable balance between these values, taking into account the changing circumstances of our national life.

4-1a Where Do Rights Come From?

The ideas of liberty and equality are embedded in the democratic political culture. Clearly, not all societies recognize liberty and equality as rights. In these societies, democratic institutions function poorly, if at all. Without a consensus in a society, rights do not exist or have no real meaning, regardless of any claims to the contrary. Often, the consensus is built on claims that a particular right comes from God or *natural law.*

Natural Rights In the view of the American Founders, as expressed in the Declaration of Independence, individuals "are endowed by their Creator with certain unalienable Rights," among which are "Life, Liberty and the pursuit of Happiness." In the Founders' view, these unalienable rights are inherent in human beings. They are given by natural law and discoverable by human reason. *Natural rights* are not granted by governments, but do depend on government for their security. Recalling John Locke's theory of the *social contract,* the Declaration of Independence further declares: "To secure these Rights, Governments are instituted among Men, deriving their just powers from the consent of the governed. . . ."

In the minds of the Founders, individual rights preceded, and were superior to, the powers of government. Therefore, government should be a vehicle to protect these rights and should have no authority to abridge them. At the same time, the Founders were well aware of the tendency of governments to infringe on, rather than protect, individual rights. This tendency could be found in all types of governments. In an authoritarian form, the infringement stemmed from tyrants as they sought to keep and expand their power. In a democracy, the threat was from the passions of citizens who sought to use the power of government to do their bidding at the expense of others.

An Evolving Social Contract   The more modern view of rights is that they are the legitimate claims that members of a civilized society may make to limit the actions of their government and each other. In this view, rights evolve along with the political culture of the society. Thus, what may not have been deemed a fundamental right in the eighteenth century, such as the right to be free from involuntary servitude, is universally regarded as fundamental in the early twenty-first century. The practice of witchcraft was grounds for execution in seventeenth-century New England. Although most people find witchcraft bizarre or even repugnant, it is now generally accepted that one has the right to practice witchcraft as long as it does not threaten the rights of others. The issue of abortion poses a more difficult question. On one side, abortion is condoned as an expression of a woman's right to control her own body. On the other side, it is condemned as the murder of innocent human beings. Abortion is an issue on which no societal consensus exists; hence, some people refuse to characterize it as a right, even though the courts have defined it that way.

4-1b Substantive and Procedural Rights

In the United States, the federal and state constitutions, backed by the power of judicial review, are the principal mechanisms by which the rights of individuals and minority groups are protected. Constitutional challenges to majority rule generally fall into two categories: challenges to the substance of a policy that the government has adopted and challenges to the procedures by which the government implements a policy. Through a number of provisions, the U.S. Constitution limits both what government may do and how it may do it. Government may not take actions that threaten the substantive rights of individuals, such as the right to free exercise of religion, nor may it take actions that threaten the life, liberty, or property of the individual without following due process of law. For example, a person accused of the crime of distributing obscene material might make a substantive constitutional challenge, based on the First Amendment, to the government's right to outlaw obscenity. The accused might also challenge the procedures used by the police in gathering evidence of the crime, claiming that they violated the Fourth Amendment prohibition against unreasonable searches and seizures.

Rights of the Accused   The overwhelming majority of constitutional challenges to government action are brought by individuals accused of crimes. Most of these cases involve procedural challenges. For the most part, their claims are made under the Fourth, Fifth, and Eighth Amendments, which prohibit unreasonable searches and seizures, compulsory self-incrimination and double jeopardy, and cruel and unusual punishments, respectively, or under the Sixth Amendment, which guarantees a speedy, public trial by an impartial jury, the right to confront witnesses, and the assistance of counsel. The Founders knew the potential for the criminal law to be used as an instrument of oppression. That is why they imposed limits on how police and prosecutors could do their job of ferreting out crime. Of course, every measure that protects the rights of the accused increases the probability that a guilty person will go free. In a society beset by crime, tremendous pressure exists to ignore or at least relax the rights of the accused, who by the very fact of being accused of a crime are accorded little sympathy by society.

4-2 Rights Protected by the Original Constitution

As noted in Chapter 2, "The Development of American Constitutional Democracy," the thirteen states comprising the newly formed Union experienced a difficult period of political and economic instability after the Revolutionary War. Numerous citizens, especially farmers, defaulted on their loans. Many were imprisoned under the harsh debtor laws of the period. To alleviate the plight of debtors, some state legislatures resorted to various measures, including making cheap paper money into legal tender, adopting bankruptcy laws, restricting creditors' access to the courts, and prohibiting imprisonment for debt. These policies, though now commonplace, were objectionable to the Framers of the Constitution, who regarded debts—indeed all contracts—as sacred. The Framers believed that serious steps had to be taken to prevent the states from forgiving debts and interfering with contracts in general.

It is fair to say that one of the motivations behind the Constitutional Convention of 1787 was the desire to secure overriding legal protection for contracts. Thus, Article I, Section 10 prohibits states from passing laws "impairing the obligation of contracts." The Contract Clause must be included among the provisions of the original Constitution that protect individual rights—in this case, the right of individuals to be free from governmental interference with their contractual relationships. By protecting contracts, Article I, Section 10 performed an important function in the early years of American economic development.

4-2a Habeas Corpus

Article I, Section 9 states that "the privilege of the Writ of Habeas Corpus shall not be suspended, unless when in Cases of Invasion or Rebellion the public Safety may require it." Grounded in English common law, the writ of *habeas corpus* gives effect to the all-important right of the individual not to be held in custody unlawfully. Specifically, *habeas corpus* enables a court to order the release of an individual found to have been illegally incarcerated. Although the right has many applications, it is used most commonly in the criminal context, when an individual is arrested and held in custody but denied due process of law.

In adopting the *habeas corpus* provision of Article I, Section 9, the Framers wanted not only to recognize the right but also to limit its suspension to emergency situations. The Constitution is somewhat ambiguous about which branch of government has the authority to suspend the writ of *habeas corpus* during emergencies. For example, President Lincoln unilaterally suspended the writ early in the Civil War, and Congress soon confirmed this decision by statute. During World War II, the writ of *habeas corpus* was suspended in the territory of Hawaii, allowing the military to take "necessary" measures to deal with persons of Japanese extraction without interference by the civilian courts.

These types of "emergencies" present real difficulties not only for *habeas corpus* but also for all devices that guarantee the liberties of individuals relative to the government. In wartime or during a riot, governments are under tremendous pressure to maintain security and order. Any society makes some provision, either explicitly or implicitly, for dealing with such situations. As reasonable and necessary as such provisions might seem, they are certainly subject to possible abuse. Those siding with potential enemies are not easily tolerated. Those appearing to side with countries with whom we are at war are often despised.

Federal Habeas Corpus Review of State Criminal Cases

The writ of *habeas corpus* is an important element in modern criminal procedure. As a result of legislation passed by Congress in 1867 and subsequent judicial interpretation of that legislation, a person convicted of a crime in a state court and sentenced to state prison may petition a federal district court for *habeas corpus* relief. The federal court is then permitted to review the constitutional correctness of the arrest, trial, sentencing, and punishment of the state prisoner. Here, as elsewhere, a state's criminal justice system must pass federal review to ensure that a prisoner's rights as a citizen of the United States are not violated by the state.

Under Chief Justice Earl Warren (1953–1969), the Supreme Court broadened the scope of federal *habeas corpus* review of state criminal convictions by permitting prisoners to raise issues in federal court that they did not raise in their state appeals.[1] The more conservative Court under Chief Justice Warren E. Burger (1969–1986) to some degree restricted state prisoners' access to federal *habeas corpus* relief.[2] Nevertheless, the frequency of federal *habeas corpus* cases challenging state criminal convictions prompted a movement in Congress to further restrict the availability of the writ. In 1996, Congress enacted the Antiterrorism and Effective Death Penalty Act, which, among other things, created a gatekeeping mechanism to reduce successive federal *habeas corpus* petitions. These new restrictions were upheld by the Supreme Court under Chief Justice William H. Rehnquist (1986–2005).[3] Federal *habeas corpus* review of state criminal cases still occurs, but is now less common. On the other hand, state courts have in recent years become more hospitable to the rights of the accused, so the need for federal oversight of state court convictions is no longer as compelling.

4-2b Bills of Attainder and *Ex Post Facto* Laws

The Constitution prohibits (in Article I, Sections 9 and 10) Congress and the states, respectively, from adopting bills of attainder. A *bill of attainder* is a legislative act that imposes punishment on a person without benefit of a trial in a court of law. For example, when Congress passed a law that prohibited members of the Communist party from serving as officers in trade unions, the Supreme Court declared the law unconstitutional, saying that Congress had inflicted punishment on easily ascertainable members of a group without providing them with a trial by jury.[4]

Article I, Section 9 also prohibits Congress from passing ex post facto laws. Article I, Section 10 imposes the same prohibition on state legislatures. Ex post facto laws are laws passed after the occurrence of an act that alter its legal status or consequences (see Case in Point 4-1). In 1798, the Supreme Court held that the ex post facto clauses applied to criminal but not to civil laws.[5] Thus, the ex post facto clauses do not prohibit retroactive laws dealing with civil matters. For an act to be invalidated as an ex post facto law, two key elements must exist. First, the act must be retroactive—it must apply to events that occurred before its passage. Second, it must seriously disadvantage the accused: The changes must be more than procedural; they must render conviction more likely or punishment more severe.

Case in Point **4-1**

The Prohibition against *Ex Post Facto* Laws

Carmell v. Texas (2000)

In 1997, Scott Carmell was convicted in a Texas court of sex crimes involving a child. Evidence showed that between 1991 and 1995 Carmell committed various sex acts with his stepdaughter, starting when she was only twelve years old. Carmell was sentenced to life in prison on two convictions for aggravated sexual assault and twenty years in prison on thirteen other counts. In May 2000, the U.S. Supreme Court reversed four of Carmell's convictions by a vote of 5–4. These convictions were for sexual assaults alleged to have occurred in 1991 and 1992, when Texas law provided that a defendant could not be convicted merely on the testimony of the victim unless she was under fourteen. At the time of the alleged assaults in question, the victim was fourteen or fifteen. The law was later amended to extend the "child victim exception" to victims under eighteen years old. Carmell was convicted under the amended law, which the Supreme Court held to be an unconstitutional *ex post facto* law. Writing for the Court, Justice John P. Stevens observed that "[u]nder the law in effect at the time the acts were committed, the prosecution's case was legally insufficient and [Carmell] was entitled to a judgment of acquittal, unless the State could produce both the victim's testimony and corroborative evidence." This case shows vividly how an ancient principle of law continues to have relevance.

4-3 The Bill of Rights

As discussed in Chapter 2, "The Development of American Constitutional Democracy," the failure of the Framers of the Constitution to include a more complete list of protected rights was a potential stumbling block to the ratification of the document. However, the Federalists and the Jeffersonians reached an agreement that led to the adoption of the Bill of Rights by the First Congress in 1789. Though not an exhaustive catalog of individual liberties, the Bill of Rights enumerates those freedoms that most concerned the Founders: the right to speak and write freely without governmental censorship, the right to assemble peaceably, the right to exercise one's religion without coercion or penalty, the right to be free from unwarranted arrest and prosecution, and the right to be secure in one's property, among others.

4-3a Nationalization of the Bill of Rights

As you have seen, when the Bill of Rights was ratified in 1791, it was widely perceived as limiting only the powers and actions of the national government. Through judicial interpretation of the Fourteenth Amendment, however, the Bill of Rights has been *nationalized*, or extended to the states. Section 1 of the Fourteenth Amendment imposed broad restrictions on state power, requiring the states to provide equal protection of the law to all persons, respect the "privileges and immunities" of citizens of the United States, and, most importantly, protect the "life, liberty, and property" of all persons. Specifically, the Fourteenth Amendment prohibited states from depriving persons of these basic rights "without due process of law." (For an extensive discussion of the civil rights implications of the Equal Protection Clause, see Chapter 5, "Civil Rights and the Struggle for Equality.")

The ratification of this amendment in 1868 provided an opportunity for the Supreme Court to reconsider the relationship between the Bill of Rights and state and local governments. Although no conclusive evidence exists that the Framers of the Fourteenth Amendment intended for it to "incorporate" the Bill of Rights and thus make the latter applicable to actions of state and local governments, the Supreme Court has endorsed a doctrine of selective incorporation by which most of the provisions of the Bill of Rights have been extended to limit actions of state and local governments.

The principal thrust of the process of **selective incorporation** is that, with few exceptions, policies of state and local governments are now subject to judicial scrutiny under the same standards that the Bill of Rights imposes on the federal government (see Table 4-1).

▶ **selective incorporation**
Judicial doctrine under which most of the provisions of the Bill of Rights are deemed applicable to the states by way of the Fourteenth Amendment.

T A B L E 4-1	Amendment	Supreme Court Case and Year
Supreme Court Decisions Incorporating Provisions of the Bill of Rights into the Fourteenth Amendment	First Amendment	*Fiske v. Kansas* (speech) 1927
		Near v. Minnesota (press) 1931
		Hamilton v. Board of Regents (free exercise of religion) 1934
		DeJonge v. Oregon (assembly) 1937
		Everson v. Board of Education (separation of church and state) 1947
	Fourth Amendment	*Wolf v. Colorado* (unreasonable searches and seizures) 1949
		Mapp v. Ohio (exclusionary rule) 1961
	Fifth Amendment	*Malloy v. Hogan* (self-incrimination) 1964
		Benton v. Maryland (double jeopardy) 1969
	Sixth Amendment	In *re Oliver* (right to public trial) 1948
		Gideon v. Wainwright (right to counsel) 1963
		Klopfer v. North Carolina (right to speedy trial) 1967
		Duncan v. Louisiana (right to jury trial) 1968
	Eighth Amendment	*Robinson v. California* (cruel and unusual punishment) 1962

Note: The Second, Third, and Seventh Amendments have not been incorporated. Also, the right to indictment by a grand jury (Fifth Amendment) and the prohibitions against excessive fines and bail (Eighth Amendment) have not been incorporated.

The prohibition of the First Amendment against the establishment of religion, for example, applies with equal force to a school board in rural Oklahoma and to the U.S. Congress. Likewise, the Eighth Amendment injunction against cruel and unusual punishments applies equally to high-profile federal prosecutions for treason and to sentences imposed by local courts for violations of city or county ordinances. Note, however, that in a few instances, such as those governed by the Sixth Amendment right to trial by jury, the Supreme Court has been willing to give the states slightly greater latitude than the federal government in complying with Bill of Rights requirements.

4-4 Protection of Private Property

As we have seen, protection of private property was a fundamental concern of the Framers of the Constitution. The authors of the Bill of Rights also expressed concern for private property rights. Specifically, the Fifth Amendment prohibits the federal government from taking private property for public use without just compensation. This prohibition has been extended to the state and local governments via the Fourteenth Amendment.[6] A state may use its power of eminent domain, for example, to create a lane of access across private property to the seashore to enhance recreational opportunities for the public. But if it does so, it must provide reasonable compensation to the property owners.[7]

The Due Process Clauses of the Fifth and Fourteenth Amendments prohibit the federal and state governments, respectively, from taking private property without due process of law. For example, a person whose property is being taken by the state is entitled to challenge the reasonableness of the state's action in court. The guarantee of due process also protects people against the arbitrary termination of government benefits.[8]

During the late nineteenth and early twentieth centuries, the Supreme Court routinely used the Due Process Clauses of the Fifth and Fourteenth Amendments to block legislation that regulated economic activities.[9] The theory underlying these decisions was that the Constitution protected free enterprise, or what the Court called "liberty of contract," from unreasonable interference by government. Thus, the Court struck down government efforts to regulate working conditions and establish minimum wages.[10] The modern Supreme Court has abandoned this doctrine, however, giving government at all levels broad powers to regulate the economy. Although hailed by many as progressive, this change in judicial perspective has disappointed those who regard government regulation of business as unnecessary and undesirable.

4-5 First Amendment Freedoms of Expression, Assembly, and Association

The First Amendment protects, among other things, freedom of speech and freedom of the press. Both of these freedoms are generally subsumed under the broader heading "freedom of expression." Freedom of speech has been rightly called "the matrix, the indispensable condition, of nearly every other form of freedom."[11] Justice Hugo L. Black, a champion of First Amendment rights on the Supreme Court, once wrote: "Freedom to speak and write about public questions is as important to the life of our government as is the heart to the human body."[12]

The Framers of the Bill of Rights understood that every utterance could be the mechanism through which an unpopular idea could become popular. Through the power of persuasion and the value of their ideas, minorities could eventually become majorities. But what if such ideas are considered dangerous? What if the expression of these ideas tends to undermine the very system that protects the freedom to hold unconventional ideas? During much of the first half of the twentieth century, many people believed that communism was a grave danger to American society. The courts often held that the federal and state governments acted appropriately in enacting laws restricting the activities of avowed Communists. Moreover, courts generally cooperated with attempts by Congress and some state legislatures to investigate and expose "subversive" or "un-American" activities on the far left. Especially with the decline of communism around the world and the demise of the Soviet Union, the issues of free speech are now very different. Nevertheless, individuals who claim First Amendment protections are still commonly perceived as those who would challenge "our way of life."

4-5a The Scope of Protected Expression

The Supreme Court has recognized that the underlying purpose of the First Amendment is to protect human communication from government interference. Thus, under current interpretation, the First Amendment protects not only speech and writing in their purest, most literal forms, but also a range of **symbolic speech** and **expressive conduct.** Wearing a political button, holding a sign, placing a bumper sticker on one's car—all are examples of symbolic speech or expressive conduct protected by the First Amendment. As you shall see, even burning the American flag qualifies as an act of expression that is subject to the protections of the First Amendment (see Case in Point 4-2).

It is important to realize that just because a particular form of conduct is expressive in nature does not mean that it is immune to government regulation or even criminal prosecution. The courts have recognized that certain types of expression are beyond the pale of the First Amendment. Even when the First Amendment does apply, courts often weigh the individual's interest in expression against countervailing societal interests. When expression is purely commercial or entertainment oriented, the courts tend to tolerate greater restrictions. For example, in 2000, the Court rejected a constitutional challenge to a local ordinance that restricted nude dancing in bars. The city of Erie, Pennsylvania, adopted an ordinance making it an offense for anyone to "knowingly or intentionally appear in public in a state of nudity." To comply with the ordinance, erotic dancers were required to wear pasties and G-strings. The owners of Kandyland, a club that featured all-nude erotic dancers, filed suit in a state court to challenge the constitutionality of the new ordinance. The Supreme Court upheld the ordinance, finding that the requirement that dancers wear pasties and G-strings was "a minimal restriction" that left dancers "ample capacity" to convey their erotic messages.[13]

> **symbolic speech**   An activity that expresses a point of view or message symbolically rather than through pure speech.

> **expressive conduct**   See symbolic speech.

Case in Point 4-2

Is Burning the American Flag an Exercise of Free Speech?

Texas v. Johnson (1989)

The most dramatic and controversial instance of expressive conduct to be afforded First Amendment protection is the public burning of the American flag as an act of protest. After burning the American flag on the street outside the 1984 Republican National Convention in Dallas, Gregory Johnson was prosecuted under a Texas law prohibiting flag desecration. Johnson was convicted at his trial, but his conviction was reversed by the Texas Court of Criminal Appeals, which held that Johnson's conduct was protected by the First Amendment. The U.S. Supreme Court agreed, splitting 5–4. Writing for the Court, Justice William Brennan observed that "[t]he expressive, overtly political nature of [Johnson's] conduct was both intentional and overwhelmingly apparent." Brennan rejected the argument that "the State's interests in preserving the flag as a symbol of nationhood and national unity justify [Johnson's] criminal conviction. . . ." Dissenting, Chief Justice Rehnquist challenged the idea that flag burning is a form of political speech, saying that "flag burning is the equivalent of an inarticulate grunt or roar that . . . is most likely to be indulged in not

to express any particular idea, but to antagonize others. . . ." Rehnquist stressed the "unique position" of the flag "as the symbol of our Nation, a uniqueness that justifies a governmental prohibition against flag burning. . . ."

The Supreme Court's decision in *Texas v. Johnson* (1989) was met with a firestorm of criticism. Conservatives were outraged by the ruling and shocked that two Reagan appointees to the Supreme Court, Justices Anthony Kennedy and Antonin Scalia, had concurred in the decision. Congress began debate on a proposed constitutional amendment that would remove flag burning from the protection of the First Amendment. The amendment failed, but Congress did adopt a new statute making it a federal offense to desecrate the American flag. However, like the state law struck down in *Texas v. Johnson,* the new federal statute was invalidated by the Supreme Court in *United States v. Eichman* (1990). Did the Court adopt the right interpretation of the First Amendment? Should freedom of speech include the right to burn the American flag?

4-5b The Prohibition against Censorship

The Founders wanted individuals to be able to speak their minds and publish their opinions without fear of government censorship. Thanks to the adoption of the First Amendment and the development of a political culture that supports the value of free expression, this country has been freer of censorship than most other countries, including many of the world's other democracies. From time to time, however, our government has sought to prohibit the publication of information or ideas deemed detrimental to the public interest. Quite often, these instances have involved considerations of national security. In a landmark case in 1971, the federal government attempted to prevent *The New York Times* and *The Washington Post* from publishing excerpts from a classified study titled "History of U.S. Decision-Making Process on Vietnam Policy" (the Pentagon Papers). The Supreme Court held that the government's effort to block publication of this material amounted to unconstitutional censorship.[14] The Court was simply not convinced that such publication—several years after the events and decisions discussed in the Pentagon Papers—constituted a significant threat to national security.

4-5c The Clear and Present Danger Doctrine

Societies strive to keep order in many ways. To many, it is appropriate for legislatures to pass laws to protect the community's moral climate. Others think that it is necessary to control "dangerous ideas" in times of crisis. To the degree to which these ends seem justified, the bounds of expression are not limitless. It is well established that the First Amendment does not provide absolute protection for freedom of expression. In a widely quoted Supreme Court opinion, Justice Oliver Wendell Holmes, Jr., once observed that "[t]he most stringent protection of free speech would not protect a man in falsely shouting fire in a theater, and causing a panic." Holmes concluded that "[t]he question in every case is whether the words used are used in such circumstances and are of such a nature as to create a clear and present danger that they will bring about the substantive evils that Congress has a right to prevent."[15] From the 1920s through the 1960s, this classic statement of the **clear and present danger doctrine** was the guiding principle behind most Supreme Court decisions having to do with the rights of political dissenters. The Warren Court modified the doctrine somewhat to allow greater leeway to free expression. In 1969, the Court held that "the constitutional guarantees of free speech and free press do not permit a State to forbid or proscribe advocacy of the use of force or of law violation except where such advocacy is directed to inciting or producing **imminent lawless action** and is likely to incite or produce such action."[16] Thus, the possibility that violence may erupt when an extremist addresses a hostile crowd is not enough to justify restrictions on free expression. The situation must be so dangerous that violence is inevitable unless the authorities intervene.

4-5d Fighting Words and Profanity

The courts have also recognized that **fighting words,** direct personal insults that are inherently likely to provoke a violent reaction from the person or persons at whom they are directed, are not protected by the First Amendment. In one historic case, the Supreme Court used the fighting-words doctrine to uphold the breach-of-the-peace conviction of a speaker who called a law enforcement officer "a damned fascist" and "a God-damned racketeer."[17] On the other hand, in another celebrated case, the Court refused to regard as fighting words an individual's public display of the slogan "F___ the draft."[18] After entering the Los Angeles County Courthouse wearing a jacket bearing that slogan, Paul Cohen was arrested for breach of the peace. In reversing his conviction, the Supreme Court noted that "No individual actually or likely to be present could reasonably have regarded the words on the appellant's jacket as a direct personal insult."

Profanity   Despite the Supreme Court's decision in *Cohen v. California*, a number jurisdictions retain laws proscribing profanity. Most of these laws were enacted long ago when prevailing attitudes in this area were much more conservative. Today profanity laws are

---

clear and present danger doctrine   The doctrine that the First Amendment protects expression up to the point that it poses a clear and present danger of bringing about some substantive evil that government has a right to prevent.

imminent lawless action   The First Amendment doctrine under which advocacy of lawlessness is protected to the point that lawless action is imminent.

fighting words   Direct personal insults that are inherently likely to provoke a violent reaction from the person or persons at whom they are directed; "fighting words" are not protected by the First Amendment.

seldom enforced, but when they are, defendants almost always raise a First Amendment defense. Consider the widely publicized case of the "cussing canoeist." When Timothy Boomer fell out of his canoe and into Michigan's Rifle River in 1999, he unleashed a torrent of profanity in a very loud voice. Boomer was arrested and convicted of violating an 1897 Michigan law that provided, "Any person who shall use any indecent, immoral, obscene, vulgar or insulting language in the presence or hearing of any woman or child shall be guilty of a misdemeanor." However, on appeal his conviction was overturned and the law was declared unconstitutional.[19]

4-5e Obscenity and Pornography

One of the more difficult First Amendment problems over the years has been the issue of pornography and obscenity. *Pornography* is the portrayal of sexual conduct, either in words, pictures, or performances, in a manner that many people find offensive. Obscenity is pornography that the law prohibits. Needless to say, pornographers are not a class of people accorded much respect. Many people are frustrated by any move to protect the right to produce, distribute, or possess material they deem to be morally reprehensible. Not surprisingly, severe tension develops when the many seek to use the instruments of government to promote a healthy moral climate, only to be challenged by the few, who want to pursue their own interests without regard for a moral climate they may not respect.

State and federal laws have long prohibited the production, sale, and even possession of obscene materials. The Supreme Court has held that such prohibitions are constitutional because obscenity is beyond the pale of the First Amendment. What, however, constitutes an obscene book, movie, or play? For years, the courts have struggled with the practical problems of defining obscenity. In the leading case on the subject, the Supreme Court has held that to be obscene, a particular work must meet a three-part test. Because the test is set forth in the Court's decision in *Miller v. California* (1973), it is called the **Miller test**.[20] To be obscene under this test, a particular work must be patently, or obviously, offensive. Second, it must appeal to a prurient, or unnatural, interest in sex. Finally, it must lack seri-

> ▶ **Miller test** A three-part test developed by the Supreme Court in *Miller v. California* (1973) to determine whether a particular work is obscene.

Popular Culture and American Politics

The People Versus Larry Flynt

By Chapman Rackaway

What are the acceptable bounds of adult content in American society? What is pornography, and what is legitimate material viewed by anyone of an appropriate age? Magazines featuring nude models might not seem to be the best subjects to frame a debate on freedom of speech, but the movie *The People Versus Larry Flynt* does exactly that.

Actor Woody Harrelson, previously famous for comic roles such as the TV series *Cheers* and the movie *White Men Can't Jump,* plays the strip club owner and magazine publisher. Flynt pushes against social mores and values with his *Hustler* magazine, which not only includes pictures but satire. The satire, ironically, is what gets Flynt in trouble and raises the free speech question.

In one issue of his magazine, Flynt publishes a parody of a liquor ad that asks about the first time a person tasted the drink, an obvious reference to losing one's virginity. The parody ad uses famed moralist Reverend Jerry Falwell as a subject and portrays him as having his first time incestuously. Falwell sues for defamation of character, and the suit goes all the way to the U.S. Supreme Court. In the end, the Court upholds Flynt's right to parody public figures such as Falwell, leading Harrelson's character, Flynt, to exclaim, "All I'm guilty of is bad taste!"

This film reminds us that when it comes to obscenity, there are no clear-cut rules for what protected free speech is and what it is not. Former Supreme Court Justice Potter Stewart's infamous admission regarding obscenity, "I don't know how to define it, but I know it when I see it," is a fair description of the story behind *The People Versus Larry Flynt.*

ous redeeming artistic, scientific, political, or literary value. Still, law enforcement agencies, prosecutors, judges, and juries struggle with the definition of obscenity. In many jurisdictions, the laws prohibiting obscenity go unenforced, except in the most extreme situations, because of the difficulty of proving the crime. Adult bookstores now abound, at least in big cities, and hard-core pornography is readily available in video rental stores and on the Internet. Clearly, societal attitudes, which ultimately drive the law, have changed dramatically in this area. With the exception of child pornography, which both the law and society condemn, sexually oriented expression has by and large achieved social and legal tolerance in this country.

Pornography on the Internet   In 1996, Congress adopted the Communications Decency Act (CDA), which made it a crime to display "indecent" material on the Internet in a manner that might make it available to minors. The American Civil Liberties Union brought suit to challenge the statute on First Amendment grounds. In *Reno v. American Civil Liberties Union*,[21] the Supreme Court invalidated the challenged provisions of the CDA. Writing for the Court, Justice John Paul Stevens concluded that, with respect to cyberspace, "the interest in encouraging freedom of expression in a democratic society outweighs any theoretical but unproven benefit of censorship." Some hailed the Court's decision as a virtual Declaration of Independence for the Internet. Others lamented that

---

Popular Culture and American Politics
Eminem

By Chapman Rackaway

Born Marshall Mathers in 1972, Eminem is the nickname of a white rapper who is as popular as he is divisive. Eminem has a unique style, rapping in patterns that are unlike anything other MC's have produced. Along with that style, Eminem says things that many others won't. In "The Real Slim Shady," one of Eminem's earliest hits, he accused his own mother of taking more drugs than he did. Drugs, misogynistic treatment of women, violence, and a negative attitude toward homosexuals have made Eminem the target of many people who would like to see his work banned.

The controversy over Eminem's lyrics continues, and although the controversy sells more records, his lyrics may inspire the same acts he describes in his songs. In 2003, David Pallester of South Shields, Britain, was arrested for the beating death of Richard Jones. Pallester claimed that he was listening to Eminem's group D12 and their song "Fight Music," which inspired him to kill Jones. Pallester was sentenced to life in prison, but during the court case, the prosecution made a connection between the music and Pallester's violent killing of Jones.

Eminem is merely the latest in a string of artists who have been called dangerous and had calls to ban them. Banning music is very infrequent, with two notable exceptions: Broward County, Florida, banned the explicit lyrics of 2 Live Crew in 1989, and Boston banned Olivia Newton John's single "Physical" in 1982. Although no outright bans of Eminem's music have been legislated in the United States so far, after singer Janet Jackson bared a breast at the 2004 Super Bowl, the Federal Communications Commission (FCC) has cracked down on material it considers indecent. To prepare for possible FCC action against him, in July 2004 Eminem and his record company, Interscope, announced plans to launch a censorship-free radio channel on the satellite provider Sirius in the fall.

There will always be controversial artists such as Eminem just as there will always be calls to ban them. The final decision on what is acceptable material for public purchase and exposure, though, always comes down to the committed and active members of a community who speak out on the issue. The political system provides the opportunity for supporters and opponents of controversial issues to have their voice heard and turned into public policy. Only by participating and speaking out can people who care either way on such issues make a difference.

Congress was prohibited from trying to protect children from the dangers of cyberspace. Now, largely as a result of the *Reno* decision, pornography is widely available on the World Wide Web. Theoretically, Internet pornography that rises (or sinks) to the level of obscenity can be prohibited, but little effort has been made to ferret out the obscene from the merely pornographic material on the Web. However, federal authorities (principally the FBI) have been aggressive in their efforts to combat child pornography in cyberspace. Those efforts received something of a setback in 2002 when the Supreme Court ruled that the child pornography laws could not be enforced against those who produce or distribute "virtual child pornography," that is, child pornography consisting of computer-generated images as distinct from real human subjects.[22]

4-5f Defamation

The laws of every state protect people against defamation of character. *Defamation* consists of making injurious, false public statements about someone. If the statements are made verbally, the offense is called *slander;* if they are made in writing, the offense is termed *libel.* An individual who is slandered or libeled may sue to recover actual and punitive damages for the injury to his or her reputation. The Supreme Court, however, has held that the First Amendment "prohibits a public official from recovering damages for a defamatory falsehood relating to his official conduct unless he proves that the statement was made with **actual malice**—that is, with knowledge that it was false or with reckless disregard of whether it was false or not."[23] Indeed, the Court has extended this prohibition to apply to all "public figures," not just to public officials.[24] This category includes all persons who have sufficient access to the media that they can effectively defend themselves against false charges. It is difficult, but not impossible, for a public person to prevail in a libel suit. This type of plaintiff has to show that the person being sued made the injurious statement with actual malice or reckless disregard of the truth. The rationale for making it hard for public persons to win defamation suits is that if it were easy to sue people for making false statements about others, public debate and criticism, especially in political matters, would be inhibited. On the other hand, many people now feel that certain elements of the media, in particular the supermarket tabloids, abuse their freedom under the First Amendment. Without the threat of libel suits, irresponsible publications may write whatever they want about celebrities.

> **actual malice** The deliberate intention to cause harm or injury.

4-5g The First Amendment and Electronic Media

Freedom of the press now involves much more than publication of newspapers, books, and magazines. With the advent of electronic media, the First Amendment guarantee of free expression has taken on new significance. Mass media now play an extremely important role in our daily lives, and certainly in the political life of the nation. Without question, the protection of the First Amendment applies to expression via electronic media, although in a somewhat diluted form.

From the inception of television and radio, the federal government has extensively regulated the broadcasting industry. Television and radio stations must obtain licenses from the Federal Communications Commission. Among other things, the FCC requires that television stations provide a "family hour" of evening programming and prohibits the broadcast of obscene programming at any time. Stations that violate these and other regulations are subject to having their licenses suspended, revoked, or not renewed. For the most part, the courts have upheld the policies and procedures of the FCC against a variety of challenges, some of which were based on the First Amendment.

The FCC rules against indecent programming do not apply to channels transmitted only by cable. Because cable stations do not, strictly speaking, engage in broadcasting, they are not subject to the regulations that affect the public airwaves. Consequently, cable companies may transmit programs to subscribers that would not be permitted on broadcast television. HBO, The Movie Channel, Showtime, and other premium channels routinely show R-rated movies that could not be shown on broadcast television without substantial

What Americans Think About

Freedom of Expression

Being in favor of free speech in the abstract is easier than when it means that some of our cherished beliefs or values are challenged. Strong, but not universal, support exists among the American people for allowing someone with unpopular views to speak in public. Similarly strong opposition exists to censoring books that express such views. Less support exists, however, for the idea of letting people who hold such views teach in a college or university where they can possibly have an impact on the minds of young people.

For many years, the General Social Survey has been asking Americans the following questions to gauge public support for civil liberties:

> There are always some people whose ideas are considered bad or dangerous by other people. For instance, somebody who … is against all churches and religion / admits he is a Communist / believes that blacks are genetically inferior / admits he is homosexual. If such a person wanted to make a speech in your community, should he be allowed to speak or not? Should such a person be allowed to teach in a college or university, or not? If some people in your community suggested that a book he wrote … should be taken out of your public library, would you favor removing this book or not?

Here are the results of the 1998 survey:

	Atheist	Communist	Racist	Homosexual
Allow to Speak	74%	67%	63%	81%
Allow to Teach	57%	56%	47%	74%
Keep Book in Library	69%	67%	63%	70%

Interestingly, more support exists for the First Amendment rights of people who are gay than for the rights of racists, Communists, and atheists.

You can go to the online version of this text to take the General Social Survey to see how your results compare with the rest of your class.

Source: Data adapted from the General Social Survey, 1998.

editing. Most cable companies now offer their subscribers X-rated programming on a pay-per-view basis. May a city enact an ordinance prohibiting a cable company from transmitting X-rated films to subscribers? Would the programming have to meet the legal test of obscenity before a court would permit a community to prohibit it? This question remains an open one, but the law is clearly evolving in the direction of granting protection to the suppliers of adult-oriented television programming, as long as it is made available only to those consumers who specifically choose to have access to such material.

4-5h Freedom of Assembly

Public assemblies have been and continue to be important mechanisms of political participation. From the assemblies on village greens before and during the American Revolution to the antiwar and civil rights demonstrations of the 1960s, public assemblies have played a key role in galvanizing public opinion. The political importance of free assembly is obvious; yet so too are the dangers that go along with assemblies by unpopular groups. Concern over public safety often prompts local authorities to take measures to restrict public assemblies. In 1977, when the American Nazi party announced plans to march through the predominantly Jewish town of Skokie, Illinois, the town council passed an ordinance prohibiting the march. The Nazis went to court and won a decision declaring the ordinance unconstitutional under the First Amendment.[25] On the other hand, the courts have consistently held that authorities may impose **reasonable time, place, and manner regulations** on public assemblies. The Supreme Court relied on this doctrine in 1983 in upholding a Washington, D.C., ordinance that prohibited assemblies within five hundred feet of foreign embassies.[26]

> ▶ **reasonable time, place, and manner regulations** Reasonable government regulations concerning the time, place, and manner of expressive activities protected by the Constitution.

Popular Culture and American Politics
Dale Earnhardt, Jr., Versus the FCC

By Chapman Rackaway

As previously mentioned, the Federal Communications Commission is the nation's arbiter of broadcast decency. Through these efforts, the government can even effect televised sports. Profanity is prohibited from broadcast airwaves, so over-the-air networks cannot air programs with nudity or other obscene material. HBO and other cable subscription services can bypass the FCC's rules on decency, but over-the-air broadcasters must comply. Broadcast networks such as CBS, NBC, and FOX cannot show nudity or air profane language. However, broadcasters sometimes push the limits of the FCC's prohibition on prurient matter—and sometimes they do it unintentionally.

During 2004's Super Bowl halftime show, singer Justin Timberlake exposed Janet Jackson's breast in front of millions of viewers, and afterward the FCC cracked down. CBS, which broadcast the game, was fined $500,000. Following the direction of leader Michael Powell, the FCC made clear it would aggressively enforce decency provisions. The FCC immediately broadened its scope, fining Clear Channel Communications almost a million dollars for Howard Stern's radio show (and later inspiring Stern to move his show to satellite radio) and threatening to go much further in its effort to remove what Powell considered indecent material.

Networks quickly began to "clean up" their programming, including even the steamier parts of daytime soap operas that have been a mainstay of broadcast television since its beginning. Other sports events were treated with ten-second delays to prevent any exuberant profanity from airing. Despite these efforts, NBC didn't bother with a delay for its NASCAR broadcasts, and at Talladega in October 2004, twenty-nine-year-old Dale Earnhardt, Jr., made an example of the reason NBC needed the delay. After winning the race, "Little E" uttered an expletive in Victory Lane, prompting NASCAR to fine him and take twenty-five championship points away from him. A parents group even called for the FCC to punish NBC for airing the Earnhardt curse. Even NASCAR, America's fastest-growing spectator sport, cannot avoid regulation by the FCC. No matter what interest you have, the government might be involved.

4-5i Freedom of Association

freedom of association
Although it is not explicitly mentioned by the Constitution, the courts have recognized the right to associate with people of one's choosing.

Although the Constitution makes no explicit reference to **freedom of association,** the courts have long recognized the right to associate with persons of one's choosing as an implicit First Amendment freedom. This freedom is very important in politics because it is the legal basis for the formation of political parties and interest groups. In a democracy, people must have the freedom to join (and leave) political groups of their own accord.

What about extremist groups? Does the First Amendment give a person the right to join the Ku Klux Klan or the Nazi party? Generally speaking, freedom of association applies to all groups, regardless of the content of their ideology or the nature of their political objectives. The only exception to this principle comes when groups are committed to the destruction of lawful governmental authority by force or violence. In these types of cases, the clear and present danger doctrine may permit government to infringe freedom of association. For example, Section 2 of the Internal Security Act of 1940, better known as the Smith Act, made it a crime merely to belong to the Communist party. In a 1961 decision, the Supreme Court upheld Section 2, but made clear that the prohibition applied only to active members of the Communist party who had a specific intent to bring about the violent overthrow of the U.S. government.[27] Under current constitutional doctrine, the government would have to show that lawless action by the group in question is imminent before the courts would permit restrictions on the group's freedom of association.

In recent years, state and local governments have utilized civil rights laws in an attempt to force social and civic groups to accept members of minority groups. By and large, these efforts have been successful. However, in the spring of 2000, the Supreme Court made national headlines when it invoked the doctrine of freedom of association in upholding the Boy Scouts' policy of refusing to allow openly homosexual men to serve as Scout leaders. The Court noted that "homosexuality has gained greater societal acceptance," but concluded that "this is scarcely an argument for denying First Amendment protection to those who refuse to accept these views." Although the Court's decision was strongly criticized by gay rights and other civil rights organizations, it was applauded not only by the Boy Scouts but also by many private groups who fear governmental interference with their activities.[28]

4-6 Freedom of Religion

The desire for religious freedom was one of the principal motivations for people coming to the New World. It is no accident that the Framers of the Bill of Rights placed freedom of religion first in the First Amendment: "Congress shall make no law respecting an establishment of religion or prohibiting the free exercise thereof. . . ." Freedom of religion as a constitutional principle has two distinct components: the prohibition against official establishment and the guarantee of free exercise.

4-6a Separation of Church and State

Some people believe that the Framers of the Bill of Rights intended, as Thomas Jefferson said, to erect a "wall of separation" between church and state. Others think that the Framers intended merely to prevent the national government from setting up one denomination as an official religion that the American people would be required to support. Although the intentions of the Framers of the Bill of Rights are debatable, the Supreme Court has opted for the stricter interpretation, saying that the First Amendment requires a wall of separation between church and state. And, although the First Amendment's Establishment Clause applies only to Congress, the Court has held that the principle of separation of church and state applies equally to state and local governments under the Fourteenth Amendment. More specifically, the Court has held that to survive a challenge under the Establishment Clause, a government policy must have a secular, or nonreligious, purpose; must neither inhibit nor advance religion to any significant degree; and must avoid excessive entanglement between government and religious institutions.[29]

Prayer in School
Prayer and Bible reading were common practices in America's public schools before the Supreme Court decisions of the early 1960s, in which these practices were invalidated.

Library of Congress #LC-USE35-132611. Prints & Photographs Division, FSA-OWI Collection.

Without question, the most controversial issues involving separation of church and state have arisen in the context of public schools. In a series of well-known decisions, the Supreme Court of the 1960s prohibited public schools from sponsoring religious exercises, including prayer and Bible reading.[30] In 1985, the Court reinforced and extended its school prayer decisions in striking down an Alabama law that required public school students to observe a moment of silence for the purpose of "meditation or voluntary prayer." And, in 1987, the Court invalidated a Louisiana law that forbade the teaching of the theory of evolution unless accompanied by instruction in creation science. The Court concluded that the principal purpose of the law was "to endorse a particular religious doctrine. . . ."[31] Although the contemporary Supreme Court is more conservative than the Court of the 1960s, it has maintained a commitment to the idea of strict separation of church and state in the public school setting. For example, in the spring of 2000, the Court struck down the practice of student-led invocations before high school football games.[32]

4-6b Religion, Government, and Ideology

The question of school prayer—indeed, the larger issue of the relationship between religion and government—is one that divides liberal and conservative ideologies. Liberals typically believe in strict separation of church and state, fearing that any government entanglement with, or endorsement of, religion constitutes a serious threat to liberty. Thus, liberals often attack practices such as using taxpayers' money to pay chaplains for state legislatures, placing nativity scenes and other religious symbols on public property, and even allowing churches to be exempt from paying property taxes.

Most conservatives, on the other hand, bemoan the increasing secularization of government and society. Many conservatives believe that inasmuch as both religion and government should foster public morality, the two are joined in a common cause. In the conservative view, government should find ways to enhance and encourage religious values and institutions. At the very least, government should be permitted to acknowledge the importance of religion in the social and political life of the nation. Thus, conservatives typically do not object to attempts to require public schools to teach the biblical account of creation alongside the theory of evolution or to the many policies and practices that mingle religion and public life. As noted at the beginning of this chapter, the dispute over the relationship of religion and government goes beyond clashing ideologies. It represents something of a cultural war in the United States between traditional and modern thinking and between rural and urban societies.

4-6c The Free Exercise of Religion

The reason the Framers of the Bill of Rights prohibited an official establishment of religion was not that they were opposed to religion. On the contrary, most Framers of the Bill of Rights—indeed, the overwhelming majority of those who founded this country—were deeply religious. Their principal motivation in separating church and state was to protect the free exercise of religion. The Founders were painfully aware of the bloody religious warfare that had plagued Europe for centuries. Compared to most European countries of the late eighteenth century, America already had tremendous religious diversity. Catholics, Jews, and Protestants of many denominations had come to this country seeking freedom from persecution and a chance to practice their beliefs in peace, without interference or coercion. Two hundred years later, the Free Exercise Clause of the First Amendment retains the importance it had to the founding generation. Indeed, given the increased religious pluralism of our society resulting from immigration from all over the world, the clause may be more important now than it was two hundred years ago.

What the Free Exercise Clause Does and Does Not Protect The Free Exercise Clause absolutely protects religious belief, and it grants extensive protection to solicitation and proselytizing by religious groups.[33] The most difficult problem of interpreting the Free Exercise Clause is determining the extent to which it protects unconventional religious practices. In 1879, the Supreme Court decided that the Free Exercise Clause did not protect a Mormon who practiced polygamy from prosecution for the crime of bigamy.[34] Although this decision has never been overturned, the modern Court tends to give wider berth to unconventional religious practices. For example, in 1972, the Court prohibited the state of Wisconsin from prosecuting a group of Old Order Amish who refused to send their teenage children to high school.[35] Yet the courts generally refuse to grant First Amendment protection to religious activities that offend the public morality or threaten people's health or safety. For example, courts have upheld laws prohibiting the use of poisonous snakes in religious exercises (a practice that still continues in remote parts of Appalachia). On the other hand, laws that outlaw socially undesirable practices only insofar as they are a part of religious ceremonies are subject to being declared unconstitutional. For example, in 1993, the Supreme Court struck down a Hialeah, Florida, ordinance prohibiting animal sacrifice in religious exercises. The law was aimed at the practice of Santeria, a mixture of ancient East African religions and Roman Catholicism that involves the sacrifice of live animals. The Supreme Court said that, in enacting the law, city officials "did not understand, failed to perceive, or chose to ignore the fact that their official actions violated the Nation's essential commitment to religious freedom."[36]

Popular Culture and American Politics
The Last Temptation of Christ

In 1988, Martin Scorsese's film *The Last Temptation of Christ* (based on the novel of the same title, by Nikos Kazantzakis) opened in the nation's theaters amid much controversy. Although other movies had portrayed the life of Jesus, none had raised such a furor. In Christian theology, Jesus is both God and man. The director portrayed Jesus (played by Willem Dafoe) confronting the temptations of his humanity. Most controversial was a dream sequence in which Jesus, while suffering on the cross, imagines what it would be like to live as an ordinary man. In this dream, Jesus is married to Mary Magdalene and has children by her. One scene shows the two of them making love. Although the love scene was shot in a guarded and restrained manner, it offended many Christians, especially those of a fundamentalist orientation. The film was condemned by many as a blasphemy, and theaters all over the country were picketed.

At one time some communities would have used some provision of state or local law to outlaw the showing of such a movie. Obviously, many Christians found the film to be offensive. Under current interpretation of the First Amendment, communities do not have the power to censor controversial films. However, those who thought the movie was inappropriate were perfectly free to express their opinion through demonstrations and picketing. The same commitment to First Amendment rights that prohibited a community from banning a movie supported people's right to peaceably assemble in protest. Some theater owners decided not to show the movie. However, for the most part, the controversy was settled as most are: Those who wanted to see the movie did so; those who opposed the movie had their say; and eventually all moved on to other concerns.

The controversy over *The Last Temptation of Christ* is somewhat reminiscent of the furor among Islamic fundamentalists over Salman Rushdie's book *The Satanic Verses*. Convinced that the book was a blasphemy, Iran's fundamentalist religious leaders put out a death warrant on the author, who was forced into hiding. But the two episodes have an important difference: In the United States, those who opposed the showing of *The Last Temptation of Christ* used peaceful means of protest prescribed by our laws. Religious leaders did not call for violence against those who made or showed the movie.

4-7 The Right to Keep and Bear Arms

right to keep and bear arms
Right protected by the Second Amendment to own and use firearms subject to reasonable regulation.

Most Americans believe that the Constitution protects their **right to keep and bear arms.** Yet the Second Amendment refers not only to the keeping and bearing of arms but also to the need for a "well regulated Militia." The Second Amendment provides: "A well regulated Militia, being necessary to the security of a free state, the right of the people to keep and bear arms shall not be infringed." The courts have generally interpreted the Second Amendment to allow broad governmental regulation of the sale, possession, and use of firearms. In one case, *United States v. Miller* (1939), the Supreme Court upheld a federal law banning the interstate transportation of certain firearms.[37] The defendant, who had been arrested for transporting a double-barreled sawed-off shotgun from Oklahoma to Arkansas, sought the protection of the Second Amendment. The Court rejected Miller's argument, asserting that "we cannot say that the Second Amendment guarantees the right to keep and bear such an instrument." In upholding a federal gun control act in a 1980 decision, the Court said:

> These legislative restrictions on the use of firearms are neither based on constitutionally suspect criteria, nor do they trench upon any constitutionally protected liberties. . . . [T]he Second Amendment guarantees no right to keep and bear a firearm that does not have "some reasonable relationship to the preservation or efficiency of a well regulated militia."[38]

gun control   Legislative attempts to regulate the sale, possession, use, and distribution of firearms.

As it's now interpreted, the Second Amendment does not pose a significant constitutional barrier to the enactment or enforcement of **gun control** laws, whether passed by Congress, state legislatures, or local governments. However, in May 2002, Attorney General John Ashcroft sent a letter to the National Rifle Association in which he argued that the Second Amendment conferred an individual right rather than a collective right to bear arms. This letter, along with the criticism accompanying it, demonstrated the divisions in American culture over the issues of gun ownership and the regulation of firearms.

When John Hinckley tried to assassinate President Ronald Reagan in 1981, Jim Brady, Reagan's press secretary, was seriously wounded. In the mid-1980s, Brady and his wife, Sarah, became the best-known advocates of national gun control measures. The Brady bill, as it came to be known, called for the imposition of a five-day waiting period for the purchase of a handgun; during that time, a background check would be conducted to see whether the purchaser was a convicted felon or had a history of mental illness. Hinckley, who had a history of mental problems, used a handgun he had purchased just a few days earlier with no background check in his attempt to assassinate the president of the United States. Even though President Reagan was a victim of this attack, he opposed the Brady bill

WEB EXERCISE

Visit these websites:

The National Rifle Association: *http://www.nra.org*

The Brady Campaign: *http://www.bradycampaign.org*

While you're looking at the websites or after you've seen both, think about the similarities and differences between them. Both groups are striving for broader support and political influence. How do these groups promote their causes and disparage opposing views? What kind of language is used at the websites, and what does it say about the organization, its audience, and its prospective supporters? How are the NRA and the Brady Campaign similar in their approaches to gaining support and political power? What kinds of people are they trying to reach? How do they target demographic groups with certain characteristics, and which groups are assumed to be more open to each cause? Based on your knowledge of these groups before looking at their websites, are you more likely to support one or the other? How did their arguments sway your opinion? If you already had a firm opinion on this topic, did reading these sites change your perspective in any way?

for many years. So did his successor, George Bush. But early in 1993, President Bill Clinton made clear that he supported the bill, and after much partisan wrangling, the Brady bill finally became law. Advocates of gun control hailed the victory, but called it a first battle in the war against easily available handguns. Opponents of gun control, such as the powerful National Rifle Association, lamented the passage of the Brady bill as a step on a slippery slope that would lead ultimately to the banning of privately owned firearms. The idea that gun ownership is a personal right is so deeply imbedded in American political culture that it is difficult to imagine the government's going too far in the gun control area.

4-8 Rights of Persons Accused of Crimes

Protecting citizens against crime is one of the fundamental obligations of government. In the United States, however, government must perform this function while respecting the constitutional rights of individuals. Courts of law are continually trying to balance the interest of society in crime control with the rights of individuals accused or convicted of crimes. Although violent crime has declined in recent years, the public remains quite fearful of crime. To some extent, this fear may be a function of continual frightening portrayals of crime in the media and popular culture. In any event, tremendous political pressure exists to "get tough" on criminals; courts of law are often blamed for coddling them.

4-8a Freedom from Unreasonable Searches and Seizures

The Fourth Amendment protects people from unreasonable searches and seizures conducted by police and other government agents. It requires that police have **probable cause** and obtain a **search warrant** from a judge before subjecting a person to a search for weapons, contraband, or other evidence of crime. Reflecting a serious concern of the Founders, the Fourth Amendment remains extremely important now, especially in light of the pervasiveness of crime and the national "war on drugs." In the twentieth century, the Fourth Amendment has been the source of numerous important judicial decisions and has generated a tremendous and complex body of legal doctrine. For example, the Supreme Court under Chief Justice Warren expanded the scope of Fourth Amendment protection to include wiretapping, an important tool of modern law enforcement.[39] In its landmark decision in *Mapp v. Ohio* (1961), the Warren Court also extended to the state courts the **exclusionary rule,** which prohibits the use of illegally obtained evidence at trial.[40] Since the 1970s, the Court has been more conservative in the Fourth Amendment area in an attempt to facilitate police efforts to ferret out crime. In several significant decisions rendered in the 1980s, the Court relaxed the probable cause and search warrant requirements and created a number of exceptions to the exclusionary rule. For example, in *United States v. Leon* (1984), the Court held that the exclusionary rule does not apply where police officers acting in good faith seize evidence on the basis of a warrant that is later held to be invalid.[41] Conservatives applauded the Court's newfound emphasis on law and order; liberals were outraged at the erosion of individual rights.

probable cause   Knowledge of specific facts providing reasonable grounds for believing that criminal activity is afoot.

search warrant   A court order authorizing a search of a specified area or person for a specified purpose.

exclusionary rule   Judicially created rule barring the use of illegally obtained evidence in a criminal prosecution.

Technology and the Fourth Amendment   The Fourth Amendment is one of the areas of law in which the impact of changing technology is most profound. Police are quick to employ new technological means of detecting illicit activities that are obscured from public view. One increasingly common device used in the "war on drugs" is the infrared thermal imaging device, which detects heat waves emanating from inside homes, greenhouses, and other structures. This type of device can provide a strong indication of whether marijuana is being grown inside the closed structure. Is the use of this type of device a "search," even if the officers using it are not physically positioned on a suspect's property? If so, officers must normally have probable cause and, if possible, must obtain a search warrant before employing the heat detector. The Supreme Court has held that any means of invading a person's "reasonable expectation of privacy" is considered a "search" for Fourth Amendment purposes.[42] The question is whether the use of thermal imagers by police violates a reasonable expectation of privacy. In 2001, the Supreme Court answered this question in the affirmative. In *Kyllo v. United States,* the Court held that the use of a "thermal imager" by law enforcement agents is a "search" within the meaning of the Fourth Amendment.[43] In this case, police had used the device without first obtaining a warrant to scan a home they suspected to be housing an indoor marijuana growing operation. Therefore, their search was invalid, and the case against Kyllo could not go forward. The *Kyllo* case is important because it shows how changing technology creates new and difficult Fourth Amendment problems. As technology in this area advances, courts will continue to confront these types of problems.

4-8b Protections of the Fifth Amendment

> **indictment** A formal criminal charge handed down by a grand jury.

The Fifth Amendment contains a number of important provisions protecting the rights of persons accused of crime. It requires the federal government to obtain an **indictment** from a **grand jury** before trying someone for a major crime. It also prohibits **double jeopardy,** or being tried a second time for the same offense after having been found not guilty. Additionally, the Fifth Amendment protects persons against **compulsory self-incrimination,** which is what is commonly meant by the phrase "taking the Fifth."

> **double jeopardy** The condition of being prosecuted or punished a second time for the same offense; prohibited by the Fifth Amendment to the U.S. Constitution.

In its well-known *Miranda v. Arizona* decision of 1966, the Warren Court interpreted the Fifth Amendment Self-Incrimination Clause to require police officers to advise criminal suspects of their constitutional right to remain silent.[44] Under *Miranda,* failure to provide the warning means that any admission made by the suspect cannot be used in court. This controversial decision has been somewhat limited by the Court in recent years, however. The Court has identified certain situations in which confessions that would have been suppressed under a strict reading of *Miranda* may nevertheless be used in evidence. As in the case of the Fourth Amendment, conservatives cheered and liberals bemoaned the departures from the precedents set by the Warren Court. In the spring of 2000, the Supreme Court reconsidered and reaffirmed its landmark *Miranda* ruling, suggesting strongly that the once-controversial decision is now firmly established as part of the legal landscape.[45]

> **grand jury** A group of twelve to twenty-three citizens convened to hear evidence in criminal cases to determine whether indictment is warranted.

> **compulsory self-incrimination** The requirement that an individual give testimony leading to his own criminal conviction; forbidden by the Fifth Amendment to the Constitution.

4-8c Sixth Amendment Rights

The Sixth Amendment is concerned exclusively with the rights of the accused. It requires, among other things, that people accused of crimes be provided a "speedy and public trial, by an impartial jury. . . ." The right of trial by jury is one of the most cherished rights in the Anglo American tradition, predating the Magna Carta of 1215. The Sixth Amendment also grants defendants the right to confront, or cross-examine, witnesses for the prosecution and the right to have "compulsory process" (the power of **subpoena**) to require favorable witnesses to appear in court. Significantly, considering the incredible complexity of the criminal law, the Sixth Amendment guarantees that accused persons have the "Assistance of Counsel" for their defense. The Warren Court regarded this right as crucial to a fair trial, holding that defendants who are unable to afford private counsel must be provided with counsel at public expense.[46] The Burger and Rehnquist courts have not significantly retreated from this holding, and most criminal defendants now rely on a **public defender** or other appointed counsel to represent them. One must realize, however, that in many areas of the country, public defender offices are underfunded and overburdened with cases. Even in jurisdictions where public defenders are well funded, the resources available to them seldom match those available to the prosecutor.

> **subpoena** A court order requiring a person to appear in court in connection with a designated proceeding.

> **public defender** An attorney appointed by a court or employed by a government agency whose work consists primarily of defending people who are unable to afford lawyers in criminal cases.

4-8d Freedom from Cruel and Unusual Punishments

> **cruel and unusual punishments** Torture and other barbaric punishments forbidden by the Eighth Amendment to the Constitution.

In prohibiting **cruel and unusual punishments,** the Framers of the Eighth Amendment were concerned with prohibiting the tortures that were common in Europe as late as the eighteenth century. The authors of the Bill of Rights probably had no expectation that the Cruel and Unusual Punishments Clause would be used to challenge the legality of the death penalty. After all, the Bill of Rights seems to assume the existence of capital punishment in its references to "capital" crimes and defendants being placed in "jeopardy of life or limb."

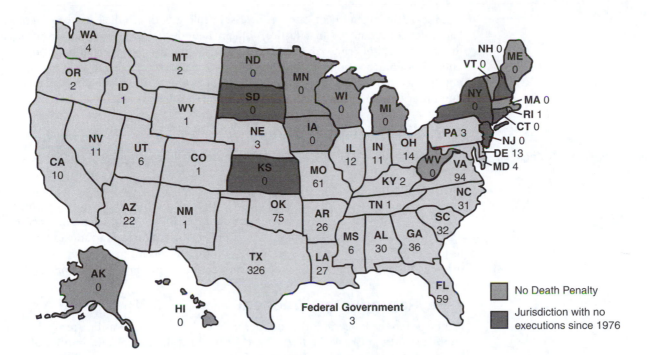

| | | | No Death Penalty |
| | | | Jurisdiction with no executions since 1976 |

Figure 4-1
U.S. Executions by State As of 2003

Source: Death Penalty Information Center, on the Web at *http://www.deathpenaltyinfo.org*

Yet the Supreme Court has said that the Cruel and Unusual Punishments Clause "must draw its meaning from the evolving standards of decency that mark the progress of a maturing society."[47] As the death penalty became controversial in the 1960s, courts invoked the Eighth Amendment to scrutinize capital punishment.

In a landmark 1972 decision, *Furman v. Georgia,* the Supreme Court struck down Georgia's death penalty.[48] Of the five justices who voted to invalidate the death penalty, only two held that capital punishment was inherently unconstitutional. For the other three justices in the majority, the problem was the manner in which the law permitted the death penalty to be imposed. Trial juries were given virtually unlimited discretion to decide when to impose capital punishment. The result, according to Justice Potter Stewart's opinion in *Furman,* was that the death penalty was "wantonly and . . . freakishly imposed."

In the wake of the *Furman* decision, the Georgia legislature rewrote the state's death penalty law. The new law, which became a model for many other states, provided a special procedural structure for judges and juries to follow in deciding who should get the death penalty (see Figure 4-1). The revised Georgia law requires a **bifurcated trial** for capital crimes: In the first stage, guilt is determined in the usual manner; the second stage deals with the appropriate sentence. To impose the death penalty, the jury must find at least one of several aggravating factors. The law also provides for automatic appeal to the state supreme court. The appellate review must consider not only the procedural regularity of the trial but also whether the evidence supports the finding of the aggravating factor and whether the death sentence is disproportionate to the penalty imposed in similar cases. The new law was upheld by the Supreme Court in 1976.[49] Subsequently, thirty-seven other states and the federal government adopted new death penalty statutes modeled after the law upheld in *Gregg.*

As crime rates rose during the 1960s and 1970s, public opinion became increasingly supportive of the death penalty. It was thus no surprise that the more conservative Supreme Court of the 1980s was willing to support capital punishment in the great majority of cases. Indeed, in the early 1990s, the Court took steps to prevent lower federal courts from interfering with the carrying out of death sentences imposed by state courts. For example, in January 1993, the Court refused to allow a lower federal court to stop an execution, even though several witnesses had come forward ten years after the fact to assert the innocence of the condemned man. In the Supreme Court's view, the question of guilt or innocence was a matter for the state courts that tried the individual and adjudicated his appeals.[50]

bifurcated trial A criminal trial with separate phases for determining guilt and punishment.

In Eighth Amendment cases, as in cases dealing with criminal justice generally, the Supreme Court under Chief Justice William Rehnquist has been much more oriented toward the goal of crime control than the goal of due process. Of course, as politics and public opinion ebb and flow, so do the tides of opinion on the nation's highest court. It is not inconceivable that, a decade from now, a more liberal Court might repudiate some of the conservative decisions now emanating from the federal bench.

4-9 The Right of Privacy

> **right of privacy** The right of an individual to make intimate personal decisions without undue interference by the government.

We come finally to one of the most controversial of all constitutional rights: the **right of privacy.** It is controversial for two reasons. First, the term *privacy* is nowhere mentioned in the Constitution. The right of privacy has been recognized by the courts as an implicit freedom. To some extent, this recognition is buttressed by the Ninth Amendment, which asserts the existence of rights not enumerated in the Bill of Rights. Yet critics charge that the right of privacy is nothing more than a judicial invention, unwarranted by the text or history of the Constitution. The second reason for the controversial nature of the right of privacy is its application to tough social issues, such as abortion, gay rights, and euthanasia.

4-9a Reproductive Freedom

Although foreshadowed in earlier decisions, the right of privacy was first recognized by the Supreme Court in *Griswold v. Connecticut* (1965).[51] Estelle Griswold, the director of Planned Parenthood in Connecticut, was convicted and fined $100 for aiding and abetting persons in using contraceptive devices, an offense under Connecticut law. The Connecticut courts upheld her conviction, rejecting the contention that the state law was unconstitutional. The Supreme Court struck down the Connecticut birth control law by a vote of 7–2, holding that it violated a constitutional guarantee of marital privacy. Seven years later, the Court ruled that the right of privacy was not limited to marital couples, but rather is a right enjoyed by all adults.[52]

The Supreme Court's 1973 ruling in *Roe v. Wade* is, without question, the modern Court's best-known and most controversial decision.[53] Norma McCorvey, also known as Jane Roe, was a twenty-five-year-old unmarried Texas woman who was faced with an unwanted pregnancy. Because abortion was illegal in Texas, Roe brought suit in federal court to challenge the constitutionality of the antiabortion statute. The district court declared the Texas law unconstitutional, but refused to issue an injunction against its enforcement. Roe appealed directly to the Supreme Court.

On appeal, the Supreme Court handed down a 7–2 decision striking down the Texas law. Justice Harry Blackmun wrote the Court's majority opinion, concluding that the right of privacy is broad enough to encompass a woman's decision to terminate her pregnancy. However, Blackmun noted, "the right [to abortion] is not unqualified and must be considered against important state interests. . . ." Although a fetus was not, in the Court's view, a "person" within the meaning of the Constitution, states would be permitted (except in cases in which the mother's life would be endangered by carrying the fetus to term) to ban abortion after "viability" (the point in gestation at which the fetus is capable of surviving outside the mother's womb). Dissenting, Justice Rehnquist wrote that "the fact that a majority of the States . . . have had restrictions on abortion for at least a century is a strong indication . . . that the right to an abortion is not 'so rooted in the traditions and conscience of our people to be ranked as fundamental.'"

Roe v. Wade touched off a firestorm of legal and political controversy that has not yet abated. As the Supreme Court became more conservative in the 1980s, support for *Roe v. Wade* among the justices began to erode. Prolife groups were disappointed, however, that justices appointed by Presidents Reagan and Bush—namely, Sandra Day O'Connor, Anthony Kennedy, and David Souter—refused to go along with a reversal of *Roe v. Wade*. At the same time, prochoice forces were alarmed at the degree to which the more conservative Court of the late 1980s and early 1990s permitted states to regulate abortion.[54] However, President Clinton's appointment of Ruth Ginsburg, an advocate of women's rights, to the Supreme Court in 1993 made it unlikely that the Court would move further in a con-

Hugo Black was born into humble circumstances, the son of a shopkeeper in rural Alabama. He went to the University of Alabama, where he completed a two-year undergraduate program in law. After serving as judge of a police court, Black ran for and was elected to the U.S. Senate, where he served two terms. In 1937, President Franklin D. Roosevelt nominated Black for a position on the Supreme Court. A national furor erupted when it was revealed that Black had been a member of the Ku Klux Klan for three years in the 1920s. Black was confirmed by the Senate nevertheless, and he went on to a distinguished thirty-four-year career on the High Court.

As a Supreme Court justice, Black took a strict view of the Bill of Rights. He was an adamant supporter of First Amendment rights, especially the freedoms of speech and press, which he regarded as absolute. But Justice Black objected to liberal interpretations of the Bill of Rights that recognized new rights. In a dissenting opinion in *Griswold v. Connecticut* (1965), Black objected to the Supreme Court's decision "finding" a right of privacy in the Bill of Rights. Black wrote:

> I realize that many good and able men have eloquently spoken and written, sometimes in rhapsodical strains, about the duty of this Court to keep the Constitution in tune with the times. The idea is that the Constitution must be changed from time to time and that this Court is charged with a duty to make those changes. For myself, I must with deference reject that philosophy. The Constitution makers knew the need for change and provided for it. Amendments suggested by the people's elected representatives can be submitted to the people or their selected agents for ratification. That method of change was good enough for our Fathers, and being somewhat old-fashioned I must add it is good enough for me.

Hugo Black retired from the Court in September 1971 and died a week later.
For more information, visit these sites:

http://www.ripon.edu/faculty/bowenj/antitrust/Black.htm;

http://foia.fbi.gov/foiaindex/black.htm.

Or, take a look at *Hugo Black: A Biography,* by Roger K. Newman (Cornelia & Michael Bessie/ Pantheon).

---

servative direction on the abortion issue. Indeed, this belief was borne out in the spring of 2000, when the Court struck down Nebraska's ban on partial-birth abortion. The Nebraska law in question defined partial-birth abortion as a "procedure in which the person performing the abortion partially delivers vaginally a living unborn child before killing the unborn child and completing the delivery." The Supreme Court, dividing 5–4, invalidated the law because it lacked an exception for the preservation of the health of the mother and imposed an undue burden on a woman's right to choose abortion.[55] Although many people are offended by the partial-birth abortion procedure, the Court pointed out that the real issue is the woman's right to choose, not the method by which abortion is performed.

Public opinion on abortion has remained fairly stable over the years. Survey research has shown that nearly 90 percent of the American people believe that abortion should be legal in cases in which the life of the mother is in jeopardy. About 80 percent believe that it should be available in cases of rape. A similar percentage supports legal abortion in instances of birth defects. Only about 40 percent support the idea that abortion should be available as a means of birth control.[56] Even though the opposition to abortion is intense, the idea of legalized abortion has taken hold in the American culture. The law is unlikely to ever return to the pre–*Roe v. Wade* state. Even if the Supreme Court were to overturn *Roe*, it would still be up to the state legislatures to decide whether to reinstate prohibitions against abortion that are now considered unconstitutional. And even then, state courts could declare these laws unconstitutional under their respective state constitutions. No doubt, if *Roe v. Wade* were overturned, some states would attempt to restrict abortion rights, but by no means would there be a nationwide prohibition on abortion.

4-9b Privacy and Gay Rights

If the right of privacy implies the right of an individual to make his or her own choices in matters of sex and reproduction, how can laws that prohibit homosexual activity be justified? That was the difficult question addressed by the Supreme Court in 1986.[57] Michael

Hardwick, a gay man living in Atlanta, was charged with committing sodomy with a consenting male adult in the privacy of his home. Although the state prosecutor decided not to take the case to the grand jury, Hardwick brought suit in federal court, seeking a declaration that the statute was unconstitutional.

The Supreme Court, dividing 5–4, upheld the Georgia law, refusing to recognize "a fundamental right to engage in homosexual sodomy." Writing for the Court, Justice Byron White stressed the traditional legal and moral prohibitions against sodomy. Responding to the argument that the state has no right to legislate solely on the basis of morality, White wrote that "law . . . is constantly based on notions of morality, and if all laws representing essentially moral choices are to be invalidated . . . , the Courts will be very busy indeed." Dissenting, Justice Harry Blackmun disputed the Court's characterization of the issue. For Blackmun and three of his colleagues, the case was not about a "fundamental right to engage in homosexual sodomy," but the more general right of an adult, homosexual or heterosexual, to engage in consensual sexual acts with another adult.

In the wake of the *Hardwick* decision, a number of state courts, relying on their state constitutions, struck down state laws prohibiting homosexual conduct. Indeed, the Georgia Supreme Court invalidated the very law that the U.S. Supreme Court upheld in the *Hardwick* case.[58] Of course, the Georgia court based its decision on the Georgia state constitution as distinct from the United States Constitution. Such decisions make an important point about civil liberties in the American federal system. The responsibility for protecting civil liberties rests not only with the Supreme Court and other federal courts; the state courts have an important role to play under their respective state constitutions.

The fact that a number of state courts invalidated their respective states' sodomy laws, combined with the liberalization of American attitudes on the subject of homosexuality in the 1990s, made it almost inevitable that the U.S. Supreme Court would reconsider and

Comparative Perspective

Civil Liberties around the World

How do other countries compare to the United States in the protection of civil liberties? A number of organizations compile data on the human rights performance of countries, including Amnesty International, Freedom House, and the U.S. State Department. One of the most credible sources of this information is the *World Human Rights Guide,* which uses forty indicators to measure every country's commitment to freedom. These indicators encompass cultural, social, economic, and personal aspects of freedom. They include the right to travel freely, the right to associate peacefully and assemble with others, freedom of religion, freedom of expression, freedom from arbitrary seizure of private property, and various manifestations of the right of privacy, as well as a number of rights related to the criminal justice system. Of course, not everyone in this country would agree with all the measures used. For example, the Guide gives positive credit for the abolition of the death penalty, the right of a minority group to use an ethnic language, and the right to engage in private homosexual conduct. Still, most Americans would consider most of the indicators consistent with the idea of human freedom.

In its 1992 edition, the *World Human Rights Guide* gave its highest ratings to Finland (99), Denmark, Germany, the Netherlands, New Zealand, and Sweden (98). The United States, which received a somewhat lower rating (90), is tied with Uruguay, Benin, Costa Rica, and Italy. Canada, the United States' neighbor to the north, received a rating of 94. Mexico, our neighbor to the south, received a rating of 64, which is only slightly above the average for all countries (62). The lowest ratings went to Iraq (17), the Sudan (18), North Korea (20), China (21), and Iran (22).

For more information on worldwide human rights issues, go to *http://www.hg.org/human.html*

Source: Adapted from Charles Humana, *World Human Rights Guide,* 3d ed. (New York: Oxford University Press, 1992).

overturn *Bowers v. Hardwick.* That is exactly what happened in 2003 when the Court, dividing 6-3, struck down a Texas law criminalizing "deviate sexual intercourse." Writing for the Court, Justice Anthony Kennedy summed up the Court's reasoning as follows:

> The case ... involve[s] two adults who, with full and mutual consent from each other, engaged in sexual practices common to a homosexual lifestyle. The petitioners are entitled to respect for their private lives. The State cannot demean their existence or control their destiny by making their private sexual conduct a crime. Their right to liberty under the Due Process Clause gives them the full right to engage in their conduct without intervention of the government. ... The Texas statute furthers no legitimate state interest which can justify its intrusion into the personal and private life of the individual.[59]

In his dissenting opinion, Justice Antonin Scalia accused the Court of signing on to "agenda promoted by some homosexual activists directed at eliminating the moral opprobrium that has traditionally attached to homosexual conduct." Scalia also predicted that the Court's decision would give greater impetus to the legalization of gay marriage, a prediction that was validated in 2004 (see Chapter 5, "Civil Rights and the Struggle for Equality").

Given the contemporary societal debate over the rights of gay men and lesbians, the legal battle over gay rights undoubtedly will continue, both in the courts and in the legislative branch of government. Ultimately, the issue will be resolved by the American people *en masse,* who must decide whether to maintain traditional attitudes of disapproval toward homosexuality or adopt a greater level of tolerance.

4-9c The Right to Die

For many years, going back to the famous Karen Quinlan case of the mid-1970s, state courts have recognized that the constitutional right of privacy grants a "right to die" in situations in which an adult is faced with an irreversible, terminal medical condition.[60] Thus far, the right to die has meant the right to force doctors to discontinue treatments that maintain life. Some courts have gone so far as to permit termination of feeding in order to induce death.[61] But where does one draw the line? Can we make a principled distinction between withholding medical care or food and water and active intervention to produce death? Are we moving inexorably down a slippery slope to the legalization of euthanasia? Some countries—most notably, the Netherlands—already have legalized euthanasia centers where people go to die. Would such a policy make sense for this country to emulate? If the right of privacy is the right to control one's own body, why shouldn't any competent adult have the right to commit suicide for any reason? Why should Dr. Jack Kevorkian, the so-called suicide doctor who is now serving a prison sentence for murder, be prosecuted for assisting terminally ill patients in taking their own lives? Courts and legislatures, indeed the American people, are still grappling with these difficult questions.

A real-life drama involving the right to die played out in the national spotlight in 2005. At the center of the drama was Terry Schiavo, a young woman who was in a "persistent vegetative state" due to brain damage she experienced fifteen years earlier. Terry's husband obtained a court order to remove the nasogastric tube that was providing Terry with water and nutrition. But Terry's parents, backed by pro-life organizations, objected to the removal of the tube and fought a protracted but ultimately unsuccessful legal battle to keep their daughter alive. Had Terry made a "living will," a binding declaration of her wishes, before she suffered the brain damage that rendered her unable to communicate, the long legal battle would have been avoided. Nearly all states now have laws allowing competent adults to make living wills. In the absence of such documentation, courts have to make hard decisions about what patients would prefer if they were unable to communicate, or they have to rely on the wishes of surrogates like husbands, parents, and siblings. When family members agree on what should be done, there is no problem. But when they are at odds, as was the case with Terry Schiavo's family, courts have to decide which family member's wishes are controlling. In Florida, the law stated that a spouse's wishes should be determinative, which is why the Florida courts sided with Terry's husband and against her parents. But, again, the struggle over the right to die is much more than a legal or political

Controversy

Civil Liberties, the USA Patriot Act, and the War on Terrorism

Most Americans understand that in time of war or national emergency, civil liberties claims must give way to considerations of national security. Certainly, that has happened many times historically, most notably during the Civil War and World War II. The terrorist attacks of 9-11-2001 and the subsequent "war on terrorism" raised this issue again, but in a very different context. The war on terrorism is an unusual war. The enemy is not a nation-state, and the enemy combatants are not conventional soldiers. The war on terrorism may go on for decades. Does the war on terrorism provide a justification for the curtailment of civil liberties?

Shortly after 9-11, Congress enacted the USA Patriot Act of 2001. The law significantly enhanced the powers of law enforcement and intelligence agencies to investigate suspected terrorists and other national security threats. For example, the law authorized law enforcement agencies to conduct a "sneak and peek" search of a residence—a search in which the occupants are not immediately informed, as long as the Attorney General has determined that the search is necessary to protect national security. The act also made it easier for federal officials to obtain wiretap orders and engage in other forms of electronic surveillance. It allowed government agents access to student records, library records, and even medical records. The law also provided for indefinite incarceration of non-U.S. citizens without any sort of trial, again as long as the Attorney General has determined such persons to be a threat to national security. The Patriot Act also removed legal barriers against the sharing of information by law enforcement and intelligence agencies.

During the 2004 presidential campaign, President Bush repeatedly extolled the virtues of the Patriot Act, which the White House said was "needed to stop terrorists before they strike, fulfilling America's duty to win the War on Terror." Civil libertarians took a very different view of the issue. The American Civil Liberties Union and numerous other organizations have been waging their own sort of war against the USA Patriot Act. They have tried to sway public opinion against the act. They have lobbied Congress not to renew the legislation, which was due to expire at the end of 2005. They have even gone to court to challenge the constitutionality of certain parts of the legislation. The future of the USA Patriot Act rests with federal judges and members of Congress, but these officials will likely be swayed both by public opinion and by events.

battle. It is ultimately a cultural struggle between traditional and modern, or postmodern, notions of individual rights and responsibilities.

4-10 Conclusion: Civil Liberties—A Question of Balance

Individual rights are widely seen as an indispensable feature of democracy. That is certainly true in the case of American democracy, in which individual rights are guaranteed by the U.S. Constitution. Yet individual rights exist in constant tension with majority rule, another essential feature of democracy. Individual rights must be balanced against legitimate societal interests in morality, order, public health and safety, and even national security. When policies reflecting these interests conflict with constitutional rights, the principal responsibility for striking a balance belongs to the courts. Yet the courts are influenced by the events of the day, by the other institutions of government, by public opinion, and, ultimately, by the political culture of the nation. At the same time, one must recognize that landmark court decisions—indeed, all political events—have an impact on the underlying political culture. Sometimes the political culture will evolve to accept, even embrace, court decisions that were once regarded as extremely controversial.

To many people, especially those of a conservative persuasion, American society has come to value individual rights to such a degree that the very fabric of society is now threatened. One can point to numerous examples—including gay rights, pornography, and legalized abortion—that many regard as undermining traditional values.

The American people are now alarmed by the persistent threat of terrorism. Naturally, people look to government to protect them against this and other threats to their security. In dealing with these types of threats, the danger exists that government will go too far in curtailing the rights and liberties of American citizens. Of course, it is the role of courts, applying the principles of the Bill of Rights, to see that this situation does not happen or at least to minimize the curtailment of freedom. It will be interesting to see whether, in the face of the terrorist threat, American political culture will come to value domestic security over individual liberty. More likely, society will continue to struggle to balance these competing values, and the law of civil liberties will ebb and flow accordingly.

Questions for Thought and Discussion

1. Could the Framers of the Bill of Rights have conceived of pornography as "speech" that would be protected by the First Amendment? What is the rationale for granting this type of expression a degree of constitutional protection?

2. What is meant by the term *hate speech*? Does it fall within the protections of the First Amendment? Does the First Amendment give a person the right to use racial and ethnic slurs in public?

3. To what extent does the First Amendment apply to the Internet? Does the First Amendment protect someone's right to put up a website devoted to propagating hatred against minorities? What if the site advocates violence against specific types of people and suggests means whereby such violence might be carried out?

4. Would the Second Amendment, which speaks of "the right to keep and bear arms," prohibit Congress from enacting a law generally prohibiting the sale and possession of all handguns?

5. Do the federal courts now favor the rights of the accused over the rights of crime victims?

6. Was the Supreme Court correct in finding a "right of privacy" in the Constitution?

7. Is Congress' recognition of Christmas as a national holiday a violation of the principle of separation of church and state? Why or why not?

8. Would a federal statute banning partial-birth abortion be likely to withstand constitutional scrutiny?

9. What arguments can be made for and against the constitutionality of the death penalty?

10. Are civil liberties seriously threatened by the government's efforts to prevent domestic terrorism?

Practice Quiz

Note: You can find the correct answers to these questions by taking the quiz and then submitting your answers in the Online Edition. The program will automatically score your submission. If you miss a question, the program will provide the correct answer, a rationale for the answer, and the section number in the chapter where the topic is discussed.

1. Freedom of _____ has been called "the matrix, the indispensable condition, of nearly every other form of freedom."
   a. religion
   b. speech
   c. the press
   d. assembly

2. Under current interpretation, "symbolic speech" is protected under the _____ Amendment.
   a. First
   b. Second
   c. Third
   d. Ninth

3. In *Texas v. Johnson* (1989), the Supreme Court struck down _____.
   a. a state law that made it illegal to burn the American flag
   b. a local ordinance that made it illegal to burn the American flag
   c. a federal law that made it illegal to burn the American flag
   d. all of the above

4. Under the doctrine of selective incorporation, _____.
   a. state constitutions may not contradict the U.S. Constitution
   b. state laws may not contradict federal laws
   c. with few exceptions, policies of state and local governments are subject to judicial scrutiny under the same standards that the Bill of Rights imposes on the federal government
   d. most federal laws are subject to judicial review under the same standards that the Bill of Rights imposes on the state governments

5. The Free Exercise Clause of the First Amendment prohibits government from interfering with _____.
   a. the mass media
   b. the right to keep and bear arms
   c. the right to freely assemble
   d. religious beliefs and practices

6. In 1919, Justice Oliver Wendell Holmes, Jr., first articulated the famous _____ test.
   a. clear and present danger
   b. clear and probable
   c. imminent lawless action
   d. bad tendency

7. Using a writ of *habeas corpus*, _____.
   a. a judge may deem it appropriate that a person accused be held immediately for sentencing even without the benefit of trial
   b. a higher court may call for the records of a lower court to determine whether any errors may have been committed by the lower court
   c. a court may order the release of a person who is found to have been illegally held in custody
   d. the president may suspend civil liberties during time of war or national emergency

8. The constitutional right of privacy was first recognized by the Supreme Court in _____.
   a. *Gideon v. Wainwright*
   b. *Brown v. Board of Education*
   c. *Griswold v. Connecticut*
   d. *Engle v. Vitale*

9. The Fourth Amendment protects citizens from unreasonable searches and seizures by requiring that judges issue search warrants only when _____ exists.
   a. clear and convincing evidence
   b. probable cause
   c. reasonable doubt
   d. moral certainty

10. In its landmark decision in _____, the Supreme Court held that confessions are inadmissible in a criminal trial unless police officers first advise suspects of their constitutional rights to remain silent and have a lawyer present during questioning.
    a. *Miranda v. Arizona*
    b. *Gideon v. Wainwright*
    c. *Mapp v. Ohio*
    d. *Griswold v. Connecticut*

For Further Reading

Abraham, Henry J., and Barbara A. Perry. *Freedom and the Court: Civil Rights and Liberties in the United States*, 8th ed. (Lawrence, KS: University Press of Kansas, 2003).

Amar, Akhil Reed. *The Bill of Rights: Creation and Reconstruction* (New Haven, CT: Yale University Press, 1998).

Ball, Howard. *The USA Patriot Act of 2001: Balancing Civil Liberties and National Security* (Santa Barbara, CA: ABC-Clio, 2004).

Berns, Walter. *The First Amendment and the Future of American Democracy* (New York: Basic Books, 1986).

Cole, David, James X. Dempsey, and Carole Goldberg. *Terrorism and the Constitution: Sacrificing Civil Liberties in the Name of National Security*, 2d ed. (New York: New Press, 2002).

Corwin, Edward S. *Liberty against Government* (Baton Rouge, LA: Louisiana State University Press, 1987.)

Dershowitz, Alan M. *The Best Defense* (New York: Random House, 1982).

Downs, D. A. *Nazis in Skokie: Freedom, Communication and the First Amendment* (South Bend, IN: Notre Dame University Press, 1985).

Epstein, Richard A. *Takings: Private Property and the Power of Eminent Domain* (Cambridge, MA: Harvard University Press, 1985).

Fiss, Owen M. *The Irony of Free Speech* (Cambridge, MA: Harvard University Press, 1996).

Foerstel, Herbert N. *Banned in the Media: A Reference Guide to Censorship in the Press, Motion Pictures, Broadcasting and the Internet* (Westport, CT: Greenwood Press, 1998).

Irons, Peter. *The Courage of Their Convictions: Sixteen Americans Who Fought Their Way to the Supreme Court* (New York: Penguin Books, 1990).

Levy, Leonard. *Emergence of a Free Press* (New York: Oxford University Press, 1985).

Lewis, Anthony. *Gideon's Trumpet* (New York: Vintage Books, 1964).

Newnan, John T., Jr. *The Lustre of Our Country: The American Experience of Religious Freedom* (Berkeley: University of California Press, 1998).

O'Connor, Karen. *No Neutral Ground: Abortion Politics in an Age of Absolutes* (Boulder, CO: Westview Press, 1996).

Rehnquist, William H. *All the Laws but One: Civil Liberties in Wartime* (New York: Vintage Books, 2000).

White, Welsh. *The Death Penalty in the Eighties* (Ann Arbor, MI: University of Michigan Press, 1988).

Endnotes

1. See, for example, *Fay v. Noia*, 372 U.S. 391 (1963).
2. See, for example, *Stone v. Powell*, 428 U.S. 465 (1976).
3. *Felker v. Turpin*, 518 U.S. 1051 (1996).
4. *United States v. Brown*, 381 U.S. 437 (1965).
5. *Calder v. Bull*, 3 U.S. (3 Dall.) 386 (1798).
6. *Chicago, Burlington and Quincy Railroad v. City of Chicago*, 166 U.S. 226 (1897).
7. *Nollan v. California Coastal Commission*, 483 U.S. 825 (1987).
8. *Goldberg v. Kelly*, 397 U.S. 254 (1970).
9. The leading case of this era is *Lochner v. New York*, 198 U.S. 45 (1905).
10. See, for example, *Adkins v. Children's Hospital*, 261 U.S. 525 (1923).
11. Justice Benjamin Nathan Cardozo, writing for the Supreme Court in *Palko v. Connecticut*, 302 U.S. 319 (1937).

12. *Milk Wagon Drivers Union v. Meadowmoor Dairies*, 312 U.S. 287 (1941).

13. *City of Erie et al. v. Pap's A M.*, 529 U.S. 277, 120 S.Ct. 1382, 146 L. Ed. 2d 265 (2000).

14. *New York Times Co. v. United States*, 403 U.S. 713 (1971).

15. *Schenck v. United States*, 249 U.S. 47 (1919).

16. *Brandenburg v. Ohio*, 395 U.S. 444 (1969).

17. *Chaplinsky v. New Hampshire*, 315 U.S. 568 (1942).

18. *Cohen v. California*, 403 U.S. 15 (1971).

19. *People v. Boomer*, 655 N.W.2d 255 (Mich. App. 2002).

20. *Miller v. California*, 413 U.S. 15 (1973).

21. *Reno v. ACLU*, 521 U.S. 844 (1997).

22. *Ashcroft v. Free Speech Coalition*, 535 U.S. 234 (2002).

23. *New York Times Co. v. Sullivan*, 376 U.S. 254 (1964).

24. *Curtis Publishing Co. v. Butts*, 388 U.S. 130 (1967).

25. *National Socialist Party v. Village of Skokie*, 432 U.S. 43 (1977).

26. *Boos v. Barry*, 485 U.S. 312 (1983).

27. *Scales v. United States*, 367 U.S. 203 (1961).

28. *Boy Scouts of America v. Dale*, 530 U.S. 640 (2000).

29. *Lemon v. Kutzman*, 403 U.S. 602 (1971).

30. See, for example, *Engel v. Vitale*, 370 U.S. 421 (1962); *Abington School District v. Schempp*, 374 U.S. 203 (1963).

31. *Edwards v. Aguillard*, 482 U.S. 578 (1987).

32. *Santa Fe Independent School District v. Doe*, 530 U.S. 290 (2000).

33. See, for example, *Cantwell v. Connecticut*, 310 U.S. 296 (1940).

34. *Reynolds v. United States*, 98 U.S. 145 (1879).

35. *Wisconsin v. Yoder*, 406 U.S. 205 (1972).

36. *Church of the Lukumi Babalu Aye, Inc. v. City of Hialeah*, 113 S.Ct. 2217 (1993).

37. *United States v. Miller*, 307 U.S. 174 (1939).

38. *Lewis v. United States*, 445 U.S. 55 (1980).

39. *Katz v. United States*, 389 U.S. 347 (1967).

40. *Mapp v. Ohio*, 367 U.S. 643 (1961).

41. *United States v. Leon*, 468 U.S. 897 (1984).

42. *Katz v. United States*, 389 U.S. 347 (1967).

43. *Kyllo v. United States*, 121 S.Ct. 2038 (2001).

44. *Miranda v. Arizona*, 384 U.S. 436 (1966).

45. *United States v. Dickerson*, 530 U.S. 428 (2000).

46. *Gideon v. Wainwright*, 372 U.S. 335 (1963).

47. *Trop v. Dulles*, 356 U.S. 86 (1958).

48. *Furman v. Georgia*, 408 U.S. 256 (1972).

49. *Gregg v. Georgia*, 428 U.S. 153 (1976).

50. *Herrera v. Collins*, 113 S.Ct. 853 (1993).

51. *Griswold v. Connecticut*, 381 U.S. 479 (1965).

52. *Eisenstadt v. Baird*, 405 U.S. 438 (1972).

53. *Roe v. Wade*, 410 U.S. 113 (1973).

54. *Webster v. Reproductive Health Services*, 492 U.S. 490 (1989); *Planned Parenthood v. Casey*, 112 S.Ct. 2791 (1992).

55. *Stenberg v. Carhart*, 430 U.S. 914 (2000).

56. For a nice summary of public opinion on abortion from 1965 to 2002, see Harold W. Stanley and Richard G. Niemi, *Vital Statistics on American Politics, 2003–2004* (Washington, D.C.: Congressional Quarterly Press, 2003), p. 160.

57. *Bowers v. Hardwick*, 478 U.S. 186 (1986).

58. *Powell v. State*, 510 S.E.3d 18, 26 (Ga. 1998).

59. *Lawrence v. Texas*, 539 U.S. 558, 578 (2003).

60. *In re Quinlan*, 355 A.2d. 647 (N.J. 1976).

61. See, for example, *Bouvia v. Superior Court*, 179 Cal. App. 3d 1127 (1986).

Civil Rights and the Struggle for Equality

5

KEY TERMS

affirmative action
apartheid
at-large voting
busing
civil rights movement
cracking
de facto segregation
de jure segregation
discrimination
equality of opportunity
equality of result
gerrymandering
grandfather clause
Jim Crow laws
judicial federalism
literacy test
majority minority districts
packing
proportional representation
racial profiling
separate but equal
sexual harassment
vote dilution
white primary

CHAPTER OUTLINE

5-1 Equality and American Democracy

One potential deficiency of democracy is the way majorities deal with minorities. An unfortunate but undeniable element of the human condition is the tendency of many people to distrust and dislike those who are not like them. Because the political system is the device by which a democratic society allocates its values, majorities tend to use political institutions to their benefit and to the detriment of minority groups. Left unchecked, this tendency can lead to the dehumanization of those who are different. "Difference" can be based on any number of criteria, including race, religion, gender, age, sexual orientation, physical disability, or political affiliation. The Founders, well aware of this "majority minority problem," placed institutional limits on the power of majorities.

At any time, any identifiable group faces the potential of discrimination. Although African Americans have been the most obvious victims of discrimination in America, other groups have been singled out for adverse treatment, often in times of war or threats of war. For instance, during World War II, Japanese Americans on the West Coast were "relocated" to detention camps as fears grew that they might engage in sabotage or espionage. In the wake of the terrorist attacks of September 11, 2001, many people feared that persons of Middle Eastern descent might be subjected to hate crimes or singled out for investigation by law enforcement authorities. In contemporary America, this type of treatment is characterized as a civil rights issue.

A *civil right* is a legal assurance of equal treatment by the society. Of course, a right is not self-executing—it has no meaning unless it is supported by a reasonable degree of societal consensus. For example, a right to equal treatment based on race did not exist in revolutionary America. It would take two centuries of social, economic, and political change, including a bloody civil war, before African Americans would acquire the right to equal treatment before the law. Even now, some people doubt whether African Americans have fully received equal treatment.

5-1a Equality and the Founding of the Republic

The term *democracy* did not elicit particularly positive reactions from elites in colonial America. The term brought to mind images of a mob, possibly driven by emotion, certainly motivated by self-interest, taking control of the machinery of government. Despite the physical separation of the colonies from Europe, there can be no denying the impact of European politics on American thinking and values. In France, the monarchy had been toppled in a revolution that shook the foundations of French society. Liberty and equality had been the watchwords of the French Revolution. In their name, virtually all institutions were shaken to the core. Blood truly flowed in the streets of Paris. Americans probably felt comfortable with the overthrow of the monarchy and the French aristocracy, but the chaos that followed was frightening. Thus, the prevailing political culture of late eighteenth century America did not foster either mass participation or equality, at least not in the ways these terms would come to be used in the latter part of the twentieth century.

Nevertheless, at the time the Constitution was written, majority and minority rights were matters of considerable concern. The Founders viewed minorities in terms of economic interests and, to some extent, religious cleavages, rather than racial or ethnic groups. There was, for instance, genuine fear of conflicts between debtors and creditors, and between farmers and merchants. The unique channeling of conflict through the systems of federalism and checks and balances was largely in anticipation of heightened passions among one or more of these groups. At the same time, the Framers of the Constitution showed little concern for the rights of racial and ethnic minorities or the rights of women.

The idea of equality has taken hold and expanded as the United States has become more of a democracy. Most Americans now believe in equality, at least in the abstract. Most accept the idea that all citizens should be equal before the law and equal before their government. Most Americans also believe in **equality of opportunity,** the idea that people should be given an equal chance to succeed in life. Of course, translating these abstract ideals into practical policies is difficult and often fraught with conflict. In making the laws

▶ **equality of opportunity**
Condition in which members of society are afforded an equal chance to succeed.

and policies that give concrete meaning to civil rights, citizens must confront the realities of group animosities, social and economic inequalities, and discrimination.

5-1b Two Faces of Discrimination

The term **discrimination** refers to the conscious or unconscious denial of equal treatment to a person based on his membership in some recognizable group. Discrimination can be public or private. This distinction is often of critical importance because a great deal of discrimination is not governmental, but is committed by private citizens pursuing their interests in the private sector. Discrimination by government and discrimination by private citizens must be confronted by very different strategies. State laws are passed by winning the approval of a majority in both houses of the legislature and obtaining the signature of the governor. These majorities are almost always reflective of majorities within the state, at least of those who have been granted the franchise. If a legislature decides to pass laws that limit the rights of minorities or place minorities in a separate, inferior category, what redress is there for the affected minorities? In the American system, they have two basic options. One strategy is to appeal to the majority to change the policy. The other strategy is to ask the courts to rule that the discriminatory laws themselves are invalid under the federal or state constitution.

It is much more difficult for a minority to successfully petition the majority to rescind a discriminatory law than to petition the courts to hold the law unconstitutional. Because legislatures are popularly elected, they reflect the dominant political culture. Most courts of law, however, are designed to be removed somewhat from popular sentiment, freeing them to invalidate discriminatory legislation. Yet, as you shall see in Chapter 14, "The Supreme Court and the Federal Judiciary," judicial decisions are rooted in the political culture. If the political culture is not reasonably amenable to the idea of minority rights, an appeal to the courts is not likely to succeed.

> **discrimination** The conscious or unconscious denial of equal treatment to a person based on her membership in some recognizable group.

The Question of Private Discrimination Discrimination by private citizens is not, in and of itself, a constitutional question. The federal and state constitutions prohibit only discrimination that is based on law or public policy, not private discrimination. If a landlord decides that she will not rent a house to an African-American family, that decision does not constitute a denial of the constitutional right to equal protection of the laws. The constitutional obligation to provide equal protection applies to government agencies and officials, but not directly to private actors. This reflects the larger principle that constitutions limit government and that constitutional rights are protections against adverse government action. The only way that private discrimination can be fought is by passage of a law that outlaws the discrimination. In other words, the legislature must act before the dispute can become a legal matter. Then, if the discrimination continues to occur, the affected party can obtain relief through the courts. But unless a law specifically prohibits the discriminatory act, the courts can provide little recourse. In the modern era, Congress and the state legislatures have enacted far-reaching legislation to combat the problem of private discrimination. Some have suggested that some of these laws go too far—that they combat discrimination at the expense of civil liberties. In some instances, the courts have agreed.[1] The essential problem is to strike an appropriate balance between people's freedom to express themselves and make their own decisions and everyone else's right to be treated fairly.

5-2 The Struggle for Racial Equality

The development of civil rights in the United States is linked historically with the evolving status of black Americans. The fundamental fact that defined the status of African Americans at the time of the Constitutional Convention was that they had been brought forcibly to this country to work as slaves. As slaves, African Americans were denied the most fundamental of human rights. Chief Justice Roger Taney's majority opinion for the Supreme Court in the infamous *Dred Scott* case (1857) asserted that persons of African descent "were not intended to be included under the word 'citizens' in the Constitution" and could therefore claim none of the rights and privileges which that instrument provides for and secures to citizens of the United States." In Taney's view, they were "a subordinate and inferior class of beings, who had been subjugated by the dominant race, and, whether emancipated or not, yet remained subject to their authority, and had no rights or privileges but such as those who held the power and the Government might choose to grant them."[2]

Of course, the racism reflected in the *Dred Scott* decision was not limited to the Supreme Court, but was also embedded in the political culture of the day, especially that of the South. Even in the North, calls for the abolition of slavery seldom implied the full participation of African Americans in American society.

The dehumanizing and wretched conditions that African Americans endured in the early and mid-nineteenth century are well known. Even freed slaves in northern states were accorded second-class citizenship at best. Although the Civil War and subsequent amendments to the Constitution formally abolished slavery and "guaranteed" the right to vote and equal protection of the law to the citizens who had been slaves, these rights were not readily forthcoming. As we have noted, rights are not self-executing, and African Americans found themselves in a society where both the power of government officials and the actions of private individuals made life incredibly unequal. Before African Americans could begin to enjoy full participation in American society, they had to overcome a vast array of institutions and policies that were geared against them. As minorities in a federal system, they faced both public and private discrimination at the local, state, and national levels. This discrimination took on a multitude of forms. It would be more than a century before the battle could even be fully joined, let alone won.

5-2a Civil Rights Measures Enacted after the Civil War

Slavery was formally abolished by the ratification of the Thirteenth Amendment to the Constitution in 1865. Three years later, the Fourteenth Amendment was ratified. This amendment had a number of important components. First, it effectively overturned the *Dred Scott* decision by announcing, "All persons born or naturalized in the United States, and subject to the jurisdiction thereof, are citizens of the United States and of the State wherein they reside." Second, in a clause that would play a major role in many civil rights cases in the following century, the Fourteenth Amendment provided: "nor shall any State deprive any person of life, liberty, or property, without due process of law; nor deny to any person within its jurisdiction the equal protection of the laws." The Fifteenth Amendment, ratified in 1870, forbade the United States, or any state, to deny the right to vote "on account of race, color, or previous condition of servitude." Known collectively as the Civil War amendments, the Thirteenth, Fourteenth, and Fifteenth Amendments provided a constitutional basis for the protection of civil rights. Not for many years, however, would the promise implicit in these amendments begin to materialize.

In addition to outlawing slavery, guaranteeing the right to vote, and prohibiting states from denying persons due process and equal protection of the law, the Civil War amendments granted Congress the power to adopt "appropriate legislation" to protect civil rights (see Table 5-1). In the decade following the Civil War, Congress passed a number of important civil rights statutes. One of these laws, the Civil Rights Act of 1875, attempted to eradicate racial discrimination in "places of public accommodation," including hotels, taverns, restaurants, theaters, and "public conveyances." This act was an ambitious one that, if enforced, would have represented a direct confrontation to the southern way of life.

During the Reconstruction Era, Congress enacted four major civil rights acts. Most provisions of these statutes remain important components of contemporary civil rights law.

The Reconstruction Era effectively ended by the close of the 1870s. By that time, little sentiment existed in the North for continuing what were viewed as punitive measures against the South. The states of the old Confederacy had chafed at the changes wrought in their region by Reconstruction. Southern state legislatures were quickly taken over by politicians who reflected the region's unreconstructed political culture.

Year	Civil Rights Act	Provision
1866	Civil Rights Act of 1866	Designed to invalidate the Black Codes enacted in the South during the Civil War, this statute provided that citizens of all races have the same rights to make and enforce contracts; sue and give evidence in the courts; and own, purchase, sell, rent, and inherit real and personal property.
1870	Civil Rights Act of 1870	Also known as the Enforcement Act, this statute made it a federal crime to conspire to "injure, oppress, threaten or intimidate any citizen in the free exercise of any right or privilege secured to him by the Constitution or laws of the United States." The statute also made it a criminal offense to deprive people of their constitutional rights through the authority of the state.
1871	Civil Rights Act of 1871	This statute made individuals acting under the authority of a state personally liable for acts violating the constitutional rights of others. Civil actions under this statute are commonly referred to as Section 1983 actions because the act is now codified at 42 U.S. Code § 1983.
1875	Civil Rights Act of 1875	This act, struck down by the Supreme Court in 1883, prohibited racial discrimination by places of public accommodation. This prohibition was ultimately accomplished by the Civil Rights Act of 1964.

T A B L E 5-1

Civil Rights Laws Passed during Reconstruction

INTERACTIVE TABLE

5-2b The Cementing of Second-Class Citizenship

With the ratification of the Civil War amendments, African Americans were formally granted citizenship, given the right to vote, and guaranteed "equal protection of the laws." But it is difficult to imagine how any group who had suffered the humiliation of slavery could be expected to participate effectively in American society under the best of circumstances. African Americans were without education, land, and property and certainly were not welcome in white society. It was soon clear, moreover, that any gains made in the post–Civil War period would be short-lived at best. Unfortunately, late nineteenth century America was not ready to welcome African Americans as anything but second-class citizens. Accordingly, the Supreme Court and the state legislatures rendered decisions that led to a two-tiered society based on race.

The Civil Rights Cases of 1883   In 1883, the Supreme Court struck down the key provisions of the Civil Rights Act of 1875, ruling that the Fourteenth Amendment limited congressional action to the prohibition of official, state-sponsored discrimination, as distinct from discrimination practiced by privately owned places of public accommodation.[3] This reading of the Constitution recognized an implicit right for private individuals to discriminate against other citizens. Moreover, this decision severely restricted the meaning of the Equal Protection Clause of the Fourteenth Amendment. It would be eighty years before Congress would again attempt to pass legislation outlawing this type of discrimination. Meanwhile, individuals were free to discriminate. The white-dominated political culture of the South, and to some degree the rest of the country, fully supported this type of discrimination.

The reality of life for African Americans was a separate and clearly substandard existence. Whatever freedom had been provided by the abolition of slavery was tempered by the social and economic realities of a two-tiered society. Whites would hire African Americans for only the most menial of jobs at the lowest pay. In the unlikely event that African Americans found themselves with any disposable income, they could spend it only at the few inferior establishments open to them. The mainstream of society was closed to African Americans. Moreover, not only were private individuals in positions of power not prevented from discriminating, but governments also provided active support for this way of life with a whole series of laws that gave the stamp of approval to racial segregation.

The Jim Crow Laws   Beginning in the 1880s, a number of state legislatures passed a series of laws that virtually mandated a dual society based on race. Most southern and border states changed their constitutions to require separate school systems. Laws required blacks and whites to ride in separate railroad cars, to use separate facilities in public buildings, and even to be buried in separate cemeteries. Courts of law maintained separate Bibles so that white witnesses would not have to touch the same Bible touched by black witnesses. The desire for total racial separation was so strong that segregation became a fundamental state policy enshrined in the state constitutions; as a result, later legislatures were unable to change the policy through simple majority votes.

The southern states did much more than establish a dual society. They also ensured a separate and very unequal society. Public schools provided for black children were clearly inferior. The few black colleges existed mainly for the purpose of training black teachers to work in all-black schools. These institutions were underfunded. No state-run black medical or dental schools existed, and African Americans were not allowed to attend the white professional schools. Thus, there was virtually no way to develop a black middle or professional class. The laws by which this separation was effected were known as **Jim Crow laws,** after a character in a popular minstrel show.

In 1896, the U.S. Supreme Court upheld the Jim Crow regime. In *Plessy v. Ferguson,* the Court was asked to review a Louisiana law mandating racial segregation on trains.[4] Homer Plessy, who was one-eighth black, brought the legal challenge to the Louisiana law. Plessy knew he would be arrested for refusing to give up his seat on the whites-only railroad car, but subjected himself to arrest in order to challenge the law in court. In the United States, a law cannot just be challenged as unconstitutional—the courts may strike down laws only when necessary to resolve a concrete case between opposing parties. In the case of a criminal law such as the Louisiana statute at issue in *Plessy,* a person must be arrested or face the real danger of prosecution before the courts will entertain a constitutional challenge.

Plessy was successful in getting the Supreme Court to review the Louisiana law, but he was profoundly disappointed with the Court's decision. Writing for the majority, Justice Henry Billings Brown asserted, "in the nature of things, [the Fourteenth Amendment] could not have been intended to abolish distinctions based upon color, or to enforce social, as distinguished from political, equality, or a commingling of the two races upon terms unsatisfactory to either." The Court would allow separate facilities for blacks as long as they were "equal." Justice John Marshall Harlan dissented, arguing that the "arbitrary separation of citizens on the basis of race" was tantamount to imposing a "badge of servitude" on African Americans. The following words from Justice Harlan's dissenting opinion set forth his idea of the "color-blind" Constitution:

> Our constitution is color blind, and neither knows nor tolerates classes among citizens. In respect of civil rights, all are equal before the law. The humblest is the peer of the most powerful. The law regards man as man, and takes no account of his color when his civil rights as guaranteed by the supreme law of the land are involved.

The Court's ruling in *Plessy v. Ferguson* would dominate the landscape of civil rights for half a century. The Court had put its blessing on a segregated society. In doing so, it had elevated the term **separate but equal** to the status of supreme law. In reality, of course, separate was rarely equal in a Jim Crow society. Not surprisingly, the *Plessy* decision deflated any hope that American political institutions would confront racial injustice. Fifty-eight years would pass before the Court would fully confront the contradictions of separate but equal.

▶ **Jim Crow laws**   Laws enacted by southern states following the ratification of the Fourteenth Amendment that were aimed at legally subordinating and segregating blacks from the white community. Laws passed in the late nineteenth century that required blacks and whites to be segregated.

▶ **separate but equal**   The legal principle established in *Plessy v. Ferguson* (1896) stating that racial segregation could be maintained as long as the facilities provided to each race were equal.

Electoral Disfranchisement   Even though a great many African Americans were registered to vote during Reconstruction, most had been taken off the voting rolls by the end of the nineteenth century. Although the Fifteenth Amendment was supposed to protect against the denial of voting rights by state governments, white-dominated state legislatures found a number of indirect means to keep African Americans from participating in the political process. One of these was the **grandfather clause,** which granted automatic and permanent registration to any person directly descended from someone who had voted before 1865. African Americans, who could not qualify for automatic registration because their ancestors were slaves, were required to take a **literacy test.** Given the state of education at that time, most blacks would have had a hard time attaining literacy. Moreover, these tests were given at the discretion of local election officials, who often required blacks to provide exact wording of large sections of the state constitution. Not surprisingly, whites who took the test were not required to demonstrate these levels of "literacy."

Another device that kept African Americans (and poor whites) from voting was the poll tax. This tax was literally a fee for the privilege of voting. Finally, another major impediment to the full participation of blacks in the political process in the South, where almost all blacks resided, was the one-party system. The Republican party, as the party of Abraham Lincoln and the Union, was virtually dead until the 1950s in the South. Therefore, the Democratic party enjoyed total dominance. Its nominees for state office and Congress were always elected overwhelmingly in the general elections. Because the party nominees were chosen in primary elections, the primaries were the real elections. The political parties were private organizations, which could have their own rules. In the South, the Democratic party excluded African Americans. Because they could not run in or vote in Democratic primaries, they were virtually excluded from office or even from casting a meaningful vote in an election. The U.S. Supreme Court upheld the **white primary** as late as 1927.[5]

The electoral situation for African Americans in the South was bleak, to put it mildly. In 1959, 159 counties in eight states had black majorities in their voting age populations. In 51 of these counties, fewer than 3 percent of blacks were registered to vote.[6] In some areas registration was next to impossible. In the unlikely event that blacks could pass the literacy test and pay the poll tax, they were allowed to vote only in a general election that played no role in determining who would be elected. Moreover, in most southern communities, the dominant political culture was sufficiently hostile to African-American participation to make any attempt to run this gauntlet an act of extreme bravery. Beatings and other forms of intimidation were common.

A Failure of Democratic Institutions   At the end of the nineteenth century, most African Americans lived in the South. They were citizens, but this status had little meaning. Southern state governments were dominated by white interests, which structured the rules of participation to keep blacks out of the decision-making arena. The few blacks who managed to make their way to northern states did not face the overt legal and political discrimination that plagued African Americans in the South, but in reality the political culture of the North did not provide much more support or opportunity than that of the South.

Before the mid-twentieth century, there was no sign of any national will to confront the South. Congress could do very little, in large part because southern senators, who tended to be reelected repeatedly, held positions of power. Nor did the Supreme Court show any real inclination to confront the states on their obvious violations of the Civil War amendments. Thus, by exploiting existing political institutions and procedures, the white majority was able to use the machinery of government to cement its superior status in society.

The Lack of Protest   From a contemporary standpoint, you might wonder why African Americans seemed to accept their second-class citizenship with minimal protest. For many years, defenders of the status quo were able to point to what appeared to be acquiescence on the part of African Americans. This type of interpretation was highly misleading, however. African Americans simply had no effective way to challenge the status quo. Blacks had no reason to think that they could ever enjoy equality with whites. African

grandfather clause   A legal provision limiting the right to vote to those persons whose ancestors held the right to vote before the passage of the Fifteenth Amendment in 1870.

literacy test   A test of reading and/or writing skills given as a condition for voting.

white primary   A primary election in which participation is limited to whites.

Americans were told in a myriad of ways that they should stay in their "place." No institution or politician dared articulate, let alone espouse, their cause. Any African American so foolish as to stray from her place faced a high likelihood of a violent visit from the Ku Klux Klan, which had been formed during Reconstruction as a secret society dedicated to the intimidation of blacks. This intimidation often took the form of murder, with lynching as the preferred mode of execution. African Americans, especially in the South, were virtually without hope.

Imagine that you live in the 1940s and are subject to Jim Crow laws. Table 5-2 shows how the applicable laws would govern your life.

5-2c The Decline of "Separate but Equal"

It was only a matter of time before state-mandated racial segregation would be challenged in the courts. It is not surprising that most of the major challenges involved the educational system. As noted in section 5-2b, "The Cementing of Second-Class Citizenship," most southern states had constitutionally mandated separate school systems, which kept African Americans in a social and economic straitjacket. Through the educational system, the machinery of state government was used to maintain existing social patterns and keep African Americans in low-paying jobs and out of the professions.

The Decline of Legally Mandated School Segregation   The battle against legally mandated segregated education was waged in the courts from the top down. The first successful cases challenged segregated graduate and professional education. Concentrating first on higher education was a sound approach for two reasons. First, the injustices at this level were so clear-cut that they could not be justified under the rather tenuous logic of separate but equal. Most often, a state had only one law school or medical school, and African Americans were not allowed to attend. Second, few whites were affected, and those affected were adults. The number of students and the emotional impact involved in these early cases were thus much less than in later battles involving elementary and high schools.

In 1950, the Supreme Court invalidated an attempt by the state of Texas to establish a separate law school for blacks. The Court found that the newly created law school at the Texas College for Negroes was substantially inferior in both measurable and intangible factors to the whites-only law school at the University of Texas. Consequently, the state had failed to live up to the requirement of the Fourteenth Amendment, which prohibited the states from denying "equal protection of the laws" to their citizens.[7] Of course, Texas argued unsuccessfully that it was entitled to run its educational system as it wanted and that the original intent of the Fourteenth Amendment, as ratified by the states in 1868, had nothing to do with the racial segregation of educational institutions.

The Supreme Court's Texas law school decision and other similar decisions rendered in the early 1950s marked the unraveling of the fabric of *Plessy v. Ferguson*. State educational systems clearly were not equal, and African-American plaintiffs increasingly found the federal courts to be sympathetic to their grievances. The courts were willing to take seriously the contention that the states were overstepping their role in the federal system by keeping blacks out of some educational institutions.

The *Brown* Decision   In the 1940s, the National Association for the Advancement of Colored People (NAACP) mounted a major challenge to segregated public schools by instituting lawsuits in a number of southern states. The NAACP's Legal Defense Fund at first concentrated its attack on the inequality of the separate school systems in these states. Then, under the leadership of its chief legal counsel, Thurgood Marshall (who would later be appointed to the Supreme Court by President Lyndon Johnson), the NAACP decided to confront directly the separate but equal foundations of the *Plessy* decision. These cases reached the Supreme Court in 1952, but because of the political magnitude of the issue, the Court asked for the cases to be reargued in 1953. On May 17, 1954, the Court unanimously struck down racial segregation in the public schools. Speaking for the Court in *Brown v. Board of Education,* Chief Justice Earl Warren declared that "in the field of public education,

Subject	Restriction
Nurses	No person or corporation shall require any white female nurse to nurse in wards or rooms in hospitals, either public or private, in which Negro men are placed (Alabama).
Pool and billiard rooms	It shall be unlawful for a Negro and white person to play together or in company with each other at any game of pool or billiards (Alabama).
Barbers	No colored barber shall serve as a barber [to] white women or girls (Georgia).
Burial	The officer in charge shall not bury, or allow to be buried, any colored persons upon ground set apart or used for the burial of white persons (Georgia).
Amateur baseball	It shall be unlawful for any amateur white baseball team to play baseball on any vacant lot or baseball diamond within two blocks of a playground devoted to the Negro race, and it shall be unlawful for any amateur colored baseball team to play baseball in any vacant lot or baseball diamond within two blocks of any playground devoted to the white race (Georgia).
Textbooks	Books shall not be interchangeable between the white and colored schools, but shall continue to be used by the race first using them (North Carolina).
Child custody	It shall be unlawful for any parent, relative, or other white person in this State, having the control or custody of any white child, by right of guardianship, natural or acquired, or otherwise, to dispose of, give or surrender such white child permanently into the custody, control, maintenance, or support, of a Negro (South Carolina).
Buses	All passenger stations in this state operated by any motor transportation company shall have separate waiting rooms or space and separate ticket windows for the white and colored races (Alabama).
Intermarriage	The marriage of a person of Caucasian blood with a Negro, Mongolian, Malay, or Hindu shall be null and void (Arizona).
Parks	It shall be unlawful for colored people to frequent any park owned or maintained by the city for the benefit, use and enjoyment of white persons . . . and unlawful for any white person to frequent any park owned or maintained by the city for the use and benefit of colored persons (Georgia).
Housing	Any person . . . who shall rent any part of any such building to a Negro person or a Negro family when such building is already in whole or in part in occupancy by a white person or white family, or vice versa when the building is in occupancy by a Negro person or Negro family, shall be guilty of a misdemeanor and on conviction thereof shall be punished by a fine of not less than twenty-five ($25.00) nor more than one hundred ($100.00) dollars or be imprisoned not less than 10, or more than 60 days, or both such fine and imprisonment in the discretion of the court (Louisiana).
Promotion of equality	Any person . . . who shall be guilty of printing, publishing or circulating printed, typewritten or written matter urging or presenting for public acceptance or general information, arguments or suggestions in favor of social equality or of intermarriage between whites and Negroes, shall be guilty of a misdemeanor and subject to fine or not exceeding five hundred (500.00) dollars or imprisonment not exceeding six (6) months or both (Mississippi).
Telephone booths	The Corporation Commission is hereby vested with power and authority to require telephone companies . . . to maintain separate booths for white and colored patrons when there is a demand for such separate booths. That the Corporation Commission shall determine the necessity for said separate booths only upon complaint of the people in the town and vicinity to be served after due hearing as now provided by law in other complaints filed with the Corporation Commission (Oklahoma).

T A B L E 5-2

Restrictions under Jim Crow Laws

Sources: Adapted from http://www.nilevalley.net/history/jim_crow_laws.html
http://afroamhistory.about.com/cs/jimcrowlaws/

*Profiles &
Perspectives*

**Thurgood Marshall
(1908–1993)**

Library of Congress
#LC-U9-1027-B-frame#11

Thurgood Marshall, the first African American to be appointed to the Supreme Court, was born in Baltimore in 1908. After graduating first in his class from Howard University Law School in 1933, Marshall became special counsel to the NAACP. As the most prominent lawyer working in the civil rights movement, Marshall won some thirty legal victories in the U.S. Supreme Court. By far, the most significant was *Brown v. Board of Education* (1954), in which the Supreme Court struck down laws mandating racial segregation in public schools. In 1961, President John F. Kennedy nominated Marshall to a position on the U.S. Court of Appeals. Despite the strenuous opposition of southern senators, Marshall was finally confirmed. In 1965, President Johnson appointed Marshall the U.S. solicitor general, in effect the government's chief advocate before the Supreme Court. Two years later, President Johnson appointed Marshall to the High Court, where he served until ill health forced his retirement in 1991. Marshall died of heart failure on January 24, 1993. His body lay in state in the Great Hall of the Supreme Court Building as thousands of Americans turned out to pay their last respects.

For more information, check out these links:

http://www.thurgoodmarshall.com/
http://www.oyez.org/oyez/resource/legal_entity/96/

the doctrine of 'separate but equal' has no place. Separate educational facilities are inherently unequal."[8]

The *Brown* decision of 1954 left open the question of how and when desegregation would be achieved. In a follow-up decision in 1955, the Court adopted a formula calling for the implementation of desegregation with "all deliberate speed," but the precise meaning of that phrase was not clear.[9] The Court recognized the magnitude of the task of desegregation in the South and wanted to give lower court judges some flexibility in responding to challenges to segregated schools. In many states, more than a decade passed before meaningful dismantling of segregated school systems was under way.

State Challenges to the Implementation of *Brown*   The political culture of the South in the 1950s harbored tremendous hostility to the idea of court-mandated desegregation. Some southerners saw integration of the public schools as tantamount to the breakdown of the social order. They looked to their state and local officials to fight implementation of the Brown decision. Many politicians based their careers on fighting the integration of public schools and universities. In 1956, 101 southern members of Congress signed The Southern Manifesto, in which they expressed their conviction that the Court had erred in the *Brown* decision and pledged to fight for its reversal.

Although the dominant political culture of the South was firmly opposed to school desegregation, the rest of the country was indifferent at best. President Dwight D. Eisenhower remained neutral on the merits of the *Brown* decision, but did say that as president he was obliged to see that the law of the land was enforced.[10] He soon had the opportunity to do so. In 1957, Governor Orval Faubus of Arkansas and other state and local officials sought to block the court-ordered desegregation of Central High School in Little Rock. The governor's action caused the Little Rock School Board to petition the federal district court for a delay in the implementation of its desegregation order. In reviewing the case, the Supreme Court refused to allow the delay. In an unusual step, the Court produced an opinion co-authored by all nine justices. The opinion issued a stern rebuke to Governor Faubus, reminding him of his duty to uphold the Constitution.[11]

The events surrounding the desegregation of Little Rock Central High School captured the attention of the nation. Governor Faubus refused to provide protection to the black students who were to attend the school. In fact, he tried to use the Arkansas National Guard to prevent them from entering the school. President Eisenhower took command of the guard and sent federal troops to the city to ensure the students' safety. As they approached the high school, the black students were spat on by a screaming mob of hostile whites. Pictures of the scene made the national news, and the story ran on the front page of magazines and newspapers across the country. The strategy of the white protesters backfired, however. The school was not only successfully integrated, but the scenes of hatred and intolerance also helped build support for the fledgling **civil rights movement** that had begun in earnest a few years earlier.

5-2d The Civil Rights Movement

The small group of lawyers who petitioned the courts for an end to state-sponsored segregated schools helped set in motion a movement that eventually led to equal citizenship for African Americans. Until the late 1940s, African Americans had had little reason to hope for an end to either private discrimination or the state-mandated segregation that had been sanctioned by the *Plessy* decision. Notably, the courts, the branch of government furthest removed from the passions of the majority, were the initial means of cutting through the laws and customs that supported the South's segregated way of life. As the courts began to strike down state laws as unconstitutional in the late 1940s and the Supreme Court prepared to reconsider the doctrine of separate but equal in the early 1950s, African Americans began to find reason for hope and to seek ways to challenge segregation at its roots.

To succeed, however, the civil rights movement would have to not only attract African Americans but also win white support. The bus boycott of 1955 in Montgomery, Alabama, did much to accomplish both objectives. The boycott began after Rosa Parks was arrested for refusing to move to the back of the bus, as required by a Montgomery city ordinance. Like Homer Plessy sixty years earlier, Parks committed an act of civil disobedience in order to dramatize an injustice. Unlike Plessy, however, Parks did not challenge her arrest in court. But her refusal to move to the back of the bus aroused the black community of Montgomery to institute a boycott of the city's buses. The boycott lasted more than a year, attracted attention across the nation, and sparked a new political movement.

The Role of Martin Luther King, Jr. Rev. Martin Luther King, Jr., first came to prominence in the Montgomery boycott and used its success to help create a national movement to gain basic civil rights for African Americans. King believed in nonviolent protest, which he employed not only to achieve change by inflicting economic hardship on discriminatory organizations but also to gain support among white citizens by demonstrating the justice of the cause and the legitimacy of its methods. King's tactics of civil disobedience became the mainstay of the civil rights movement of the 1950s and 1960s. Its targets were many. Among the first were the segregated eating establishments in many southern towns and cities. Blacks would occupy the stools and chairs at the counter and, after being refused service, would quietly remain seated until they were arrested for violating local ordinances prohibiting disorderly conduct or "refusing to disperse."

During the 1950s and early 1960s, the civil rights movement became a major component of American politics. Whites, who perceived that a politically active black minority would threaten their way of life, sometimes resorted to violence. Some incidents captured national attention. In 1963, a church in Birmingham, Alabama, was firebombed, killing three African-American children. Attempts to register blacks to vote were particularly likely to provoke a violent reaction. In 1963, three civil rights workers were slain near Philadelphia, Mississippi. Others were killed trying to register voters in Alabama and in other parts of the south. Again, the national media showed the rest of the country the barbarism of these acts and helped convert an indifferent white population into supporters of equal rights.

Some African Americans did not agree with King's strategy of nonviolent social protest to achieve integration. Leaders such as Malcolm X and H. Rap Brown followed in the tradition of Marcus Garvey in calling for a separate African-American community. They had no desire to be integrated into a white society that they perceived as evil and hostile.[12]

▶ **civil rights movement** The social movement of the 1960s aimed at ending racial segregation and achieving voting rights and other civil rights for African Americans.

Martin Luther King, Jr.
"I have a dream that my four little children will one day live in a nation where they will not be judged by the color of their skin, but by the content of their character."

Library of Congress #LC-USZ62-122992

Although most leaders of the civil rights movement rejected this approach, it remained popular among a significant minority of blacks, especially young men from urban areas.

American Political Culture and the Civil Rights Movement Ultimately, if the civil rights movement were going to achieve more than momentary or localized success, it would have to secure national legislation to protect the rights of African Americans. As you have seen, the federal courts were able to use the Equal Protection Clause of the Fourteenth Amendment to strike down discriminatory provisions of state law. Although their decisions were often unpopular, the courts were sufficiently removed from politics that they could act counter to public opinion, at least in the short term. Thus, through the courts, the American political system could correct certain fundamental injustices without assembling a majority in favor of change. But the courts could do only so much. As you have seen, a great deal of discrimination was private, and private individuals were not subject to the requirements of the Fourteenth Amendment. Therefore, if African Americans' rights were to be secured, a majority would have to be mobilized in support of national legislation. But the American political culture of the 1950s and early 1960s presented several obstacles to the enactment of civil rights legislation.

First, many southerners believed that their region and its lifestyle were under attack. To succeed, the movement would have to persuade southerners to abandon the racial separatism that had long been a fundamental part of their identity. Second, the movement would have to overcome the indifference of whites in other parts of the country. Although only the South had imposed segregation by law, African Americans throughout the country were often treated as socially inferior and were by no means the economic equals of whites, a situation that had not troubled most whites. Yet whites were the overwhelming majority in the United States, so their support would be needed if civil rights legislation were to be enacted. Would they be willing to limit their own power to discriminate against a minority? There have been few examples of racial and ethnic majorities voluntarily relinquishing power to struggling minorities, yet that would have to happen in the United States if the civil rights movement were to succeed. Finally, African Americans themselves would have to become involved in the political process to a much greater extent than in the past. Above all, as a minority in a fundamentally majoritarian political system, African Americans would have to find a way to demonstrate the injustice of the political culture and the need for change and at the same time avoid frightening whites.

5-2e The Civil Rights Act of 1964

The battle for a national civil rights law that would make private discrimination unlawful proved to be long and difficult. In June 1963, President John F. Kennedy formally asked Congress to pass a civil rights bill. His assassination in November 1963 may have temporarily delayed passage of the bill, but ultimately added momentum to the legislation. More important, however, was the ongoing spectacle of African Americans being subjected to brutal treatment in the South. By the time President Lyndon Johnson signed the Civil Rights Act of 1964 into law, Americans had come to a somewhat uneasy consensus that government action was necessary to prevent private discrimination as well as to cement the federal commitment to racial justice.[13]

The Civil Rights Act of 1964 was a far-reaching, even visionary piece of legislation, and it remains the foundation of national policy on the rights of minorities. The act's most important and controversial section, Title II, prohibited racial discrimination in "places of public accommodation" that affected interstate commerce, including restaurants, stadiums, theaters, and motels or hotels with more than five rooms. In adopting Title II, Congress relied on its broad constitutional power to regulate interstate commerce (Article I, Section 8) as well as its enforcement powers under the Fourteenth Amendment.

Ironically, Title II reversed the role of the courts and the states in civil rights matters. Before 1964, African Americans had looked to the courts to invalidate state laws that mandated segregation. In these types of cases, laws were the problem. After Congress passed national legislation to make individual acts of discrimination illegal, however, laws became the *solution* for African Americans and the *problem* for individuals who wanted to discriminate. This latter group then turned to the courts to invalidate laws that they felt improperly limited their freedom to discriminate.

In 1964, the Supreme Court upheld Title II, which had been challenged by the Heart of Atlanta motel, which had filed a suit to prevent the new policy from being enforced. The motel owners claimed that Title II was not designed to regulate interstate commerce and that, in any event, the motel should be immune because it was not primarily engaged in interstate commerce. The Supreme Court disagreed, ruling that Title II was a reasonable regulation of interstate commerce because racial discrimination by privately owned places of public accommodation constituted a serious impediment to interstate travel by blacks. The Court also held that the Heart of Atlanta motel was subject to the requirements of Title II because a substantial proportion of its clientele came from out of state.[14] In a related case, the Court held that Title II could be applied to a restaurant in Birmingham, Alabama, that also practiced racial discrimination. Even though most of the patrons of Ollie's Barbecue were locals, its foodstuffs and equipment had moved in interstate commerce.[15] In effect, the Supreme Court gave its blessing to a broad extension of federal power to regulate virtually any business in the country.

Without question, the public accommodations section of the Civil Rights Act of 1964 had an immediate impact on the lives of African Americans, especially in the South, where restaurants, motels, and hotels became available for the first time. In addition, stores removed the Colored and White designations from their drinking fountains and restrooms.

The Civil Rights Act did more than ensure equal access to restaurants and hotels. It also addressed these issues:

- *Voting rights* (Title I). The act limited the use of literacy tests. In particular, it made a sixth-grade education sufficient proof of literacy for purposes of voting registration.
- *Employment discrimination* (Title VII). Companies with twenty-five or more employees were forbidden from discriminating on the basis of race or sex in hiring and firing workers and granting pay and benefits.
- *School segregation* (Title IV). This provision allowed the U.S. attorney general to file suit to desegregate schools. Individual citizens then did not have to sue in the courts. Rather, they could complain to the U.S. Department of Justice, which could initiate legal action.
- *Denial of federal funds* (Title VI). Another important provision of the Civil Rights Act was the requirement that federal funding be withheld from any government or organization that practiced racial discrimination. Because virtually every public school and university system and almost all private colleges depend on federal funding, this provision has had an enormous impact.

Other Important Civil Rights Legislation Although the Civil Rights Act of 1964 was the most important modern civil rights legislation passed by Congress, other civil rights laws have also contributed to the nation's commitment to equality. Other legislation of the 1960s included the Voting Rights Act of 1965 and the Civil Rights Act of 1968, also known as the Fair Housing Act, which imposed criminal penalties on anyone selling or renting a house or apartment through a licensed agent who refuses to sell or rent on the basis of race or religion. Later legislation, including the Civil Rights Act of 1992, strengthened protection against discrimination in employment. President George Bush signed a compromise bill after first vetoing a similar measure that he had opposed as being too extreme in its demands on employers.

5-2f Dismantling Segregation: An Active Role for Government

State laws mandating separate school systems for blacks and whites were effectively rendered unconstitutional by the *Brown* decision. Although this segregation by law (*de jure* segregation)

> ▶ *de jure* **segregation** Racial segregation required or maintained by law.

Figure 5-1
Public Opinion among Whites on Neighborhood Integration, 1958–1990
Question: Would you move if black people came to live in great numbers in your neighborhood?

Source: Adapted from Harold W. Stanley and Richard G. *Niemi, Vital Statistics on American Politics,* 4th ed. (Washington, D.C.: CQ Press, 1994), p. 397.

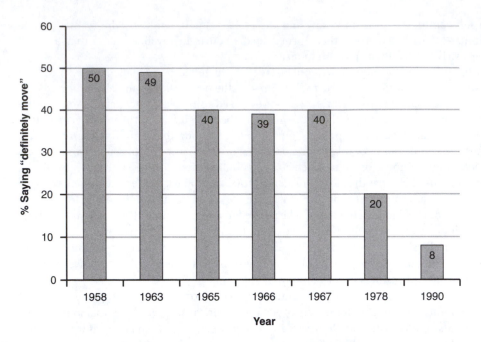

▶ *de facto* **segregation**   Racial segregation as a matter of fact.

soon became a thing of the past, blacks and whites remained largely separated due to long-established housing patterns and economic condition. The majority of white Americans (not only in the South) resisted the idea of integrated neighborhoods in the 1960s (see Figure 5-1). This *de facto* **segregation,** or segregation in fact, presented much more complex challenges. The demands for the elimination of state-sponsored separation had implied laws that were race neutral. Many people, however, thought that it was unrealistic and naive to expect that the mere elimination of officially sanctioned discrimination would result in real equal opportunity. President Johnson supported this view as he moved to implement the Civil Rights Act of 1964. In his commencement address at Howard University in 1965, Johnson said, "You do not take a person who for years has been hobbled by chains and liberate him, bring him up to the starting line of a race and then say 'You are free to compete with all the others,' and still justly believe you have been completely fair." Johnson was suggesting that government should take an active role in eradicating the vestiges of slavery and segregation. The policies that would flow from this new governmental role would prove to be enormously controversial.

The Busing Controversy   In the 1960s, many people in the civil rights movement came to believe that striking down laws requiring racially segregated schools was not enough. Stronger measures were needed to dismantle dual school systems, which often persisted in the absence of segregation laws. One such measure was to transport children by bus across school attendance zones to achieve a degree of racial integration. Of course, the idea of **busing** was extremely unpopular in white communities, and school boards were not inclined to take this type of action unless ordered to do so by a federal judge.

▶ **busing**   The transportation of students to ensure racial balance in the public schools.

In the late 1960s, the Board of Education of Charlotte–Mecklenburg, North Carolina, devised a desegregation plan to comply with the Supreme Court's mandate in *Brown v. Board of Education.* A federal district court rejected the plan, however, as not producing sufficient racial integration at the elementary level. The court adopted in its place a plan prepared by an outside expert that called for, among other things, establishing racial quotas, altering attendance zones, and busing students within the district. The Supreme Court unanimously approved the plan, even though it entailed "race-conscious remedies."[16] The Court made clear that a school system which has engaged in discrimination at some point in the past may be ordered to take remedial action to correct a persistent pattern of segregation. These remedies could include the busing of students.

Later, the Court clarified a point of contention, ruling that the court-ordered busing of students across school district lines is permissible only if *all affected districts* had been

Popular Culture and American Politics

Chapelle's Show

By Chapman Rackaway

Is it right to use racial epithets in a sketch comedy show for television? Is using the term *nigger* ever justified? Is the word a form of *de facto* discrimination, because it is a racially insensitive remark? What if the speaker is African American? Is the term so outright racist that it ought never be uttered? What does the use of the word have to say about race relations in this country and the social status of African Americans today? One successful stand-up comedian makes us ask all of those questions on his television show.

The place to look for answers is Comedy Central. On this cable network, comedian Dave Chapelle is the star of *Chapelle's Show,* and the African-American host consistently uses the term. But is it right to use a racially insensitive term if you don't intend it as an insult? Chapelle commonly calls other black actors and characters on his show *nigger.* Some believe, though, that using the term brings back images of slavery or a bygone era of discrimination. In two seasons, Chapelle has been both funny and controversial. He is not afraid to take on any sensitive issue, making fun of singer R. Kelly's legal troubles, 1970's funk icon Rick James, rapper Lil Jon, and MTV's *The Real World.*

Where *Chapelle's Show* forces us to ask some serious questions, though, is in the regular use of the word *nigger.* During the era of "gangsta" rap, with groups such as N.W.A. (Niggaz With Attitude) in the early 1990s, many rappers started to use the racist insult as a synonym for someone in touch with street and ghetto culture. But the word is still the same one used by racist Southern whites to denigrate African Americans. Now, Dave Chapelle uses the term to describe other black persons on his show.

The real question is, Does the messenger make a difference? The thirty-one-year old son of a Unitarian minister, Chapelle can use the word *nigger* without it being controversial, but a white comedian using the same term would be considered racist. Should we look at Chapelle's use of this word as a sign of solidarity with other African Americans or a double standard? Is the use of the word in popular culture just a sign of the times or a symbol of regression to an era of discrimination? Which is more important—the words or the speaker?

---

guilty of past discriminatory practices. If, for example, both city and county school systems had practiced discrimination in the past, students could be bused between the city and county school districts, even though the districts were administratively separate. However, when it was shown that the suburban districts surrounding the city of Detroit had not discriminated, even though Detroit clearly had, the Supreme Court did not allow a cross-district busing remedy.[17]

Busing proved to be quite controversial among both whites and blacks. In many instances, both resented the dismantling of their neighborhood schools. To make matters worse, many whites simply refused to attend schools where African Americans were in the majority and exercised their option of attending private schools. Often, systems where busing was ordered ended up more segregated than they had been previously. By the mid-to-late 1980s, the appeal of busing had diminished even within the African-American community as a result of these types of problems.

Busing is still in use for the purpose of school desegregation, but to a much lesser extent than twenty or even ten years ago. Around the country, school boards have moved decidedly away from busing as a means of desegregation, opting instead for devices such as magnet schools.[18] In some instances, judges have even ordered school districts to terminate busing.[19] It appears that Americans are now witnessing the demise of this grand social experiment. The busing experience is indicative of both the ambitious nature of desegregation policy and the difficulty of forcing results on a public that offers little support for the process. The public supported an end to segregation by law; it did not support government activism to achieve integration.

Popular Culture and American Politics
Do the Right Thing

Spike Lee's 1989 movie *Do the Right Thing* is a disturbing and ambiguous look at race relations in inner-city America. The story takes place on one city block in Brooklyn, New York, where most of the residents are African American. The grocery is run by a Korean family, and a pizza restaurant (Sal's Famous), run by an Italian-American family, is across the street. Sal is a good man. One of his sons is clearly a racist, and the other seems comfortable with the people in the neighborhood. The delivery man, Mookie (played by the director of the film, Spike Lee) seems ambivalent, a bridge between Sal's and the neighborhood.

Although everything seems comfortable enough in the neighborhood, tension is building. Someone notices that no black faces are on Sal's Hall of Fame, which contains only the pictures of famous Italian Americans. Soon, fatal confrontations involve the police, Sal, his family, and the residents of the neighborhood. The movie leads the audience to confront the complexities of race in modern America. Which is the proper strategy for African Americans—the nonviolence espoused by Martin Luther King or Malcolm X's "By any means necessary" strategy?

This film presents the complexity of race relations in America. The issues are no longer obvious, and actions are no longer easily classified. The battleground has shifted somewhat from the rural South to the large urban centers. New groups are now on the scene, and the focus is not so much on government action but rather on the businesses and opportunities. Part of the tragedy portrayed by *Do the Right Thing* is that both Sal and Mookie seem basically decent. They can communicate, but cannot quite understand each other. They certainly cannot agree on the "right thing."

5-2g Affirmative Action

Most commentators agree that Congress did not intend for the Civil Rights Act of 1964 to permit, let alone require, reverse, or correct, discrimination. Since that time, however, the act has come to be interpreted in a way that allows goals for the representation of members of racial minorities to be established. Not surprisingly, this extension of the original act has been extremely controversial. The policies by which federal agencies move to remedy past discrimination through the use of goals, quotas, timetables, and the like are examples of **affirmative action.** These programs usually involve some sort of special efforts to attract applicants for employment or to colleges or universities. Under pressure from federal agencies and/or courts of law, both private and public educational institutions have gradually developed affirmative action programs.

> **affirmative action**   A program under which women and/or persons of particular minority groups are granted special consideration in employment, government contracts, and/or admission to programs of higher education.

The *Bakke* Case   In the 1970s, the University of California at Davis established a program whose goal was to increase the number of minority physicians in the state. This program was rather typical of those established by many colleges and universities during the middle and late 1970s. Of course, admitting minority applicants inevitably kept others from being accepted. Not surprisingly, many of these excluded applicants felt that rejection on the basis of their race violated their rights to equal protection under the Fourteenth Amendment.

Allan Bakke, a white male, was not admitted to the Davis medical school, even though his test scores and grades were higher than those of most of the minority students who had been accepted to fill sixteen spaces that had been reserved for minorities. Bakke challenged the program in court, and the Supreme Court heard his case in 1978.[20] Many observers thought the Court would craft a clear ruling that dealt with the constitutionality of programs that allowed race as a consideration. Unfortunately, the Court's decision was not so clear-cut. It did order the University of California to admit Bakke. In addition, it ruled that the program under which he had been rejected was not constitutional because it reserved a fixed number of slots for minorities. In the Court's view, a fixed numerical quota was unacceptable. However, these types of programs would be acceptable if they established *goals* rather than quotas. In other words, a school could consider race as a factor in the decision to admit an applicant, but could not reserve a set number of places for members of a particular group.

Other Important Judicial Decisions   Employment discrimination involves somewhat different issues. Many companies established special hiring or training programs with the goal of increasing the number of minorities in higher-level positions. Kaiser Aluminum and Chemical Corporation had this type of program, which trained existing employees for higher positions in the company. Kaiser reserved half the slots in a training class for blacks. Bryan Weber, a white employee with more seniority than many African Americans who were chosen, filed suit. The Supreme Court held that these types of programs were acceptable because they were voluntarily established by private companies.[21]

In the late 1980s and throughout the 1990s a more conservative Supreme Court manifested a more critical posture toward affirmative action programs. For example, in 1989, the Court struck down a Richmond, Virginia, policy that set aside a certain proportion of city public works contracts for minority business enterprises. The Court based its decision largely on the fact that African Americans constituted a majority of the city population and held a majority of seats on the city council. Moreover, no evidence existed that the city had been discriminating against black-owned construction companies seeking public works contracts.[22] In 1995 the Court indicated that it would strictly scrutinize all affirmative action programs, whether local, state, or federal.[23] Writing for the Court, Justice O'Connor held that "all racial classifications, imposed by whatever federal, state, or local governmental actor, must be analyzed by a reviewing court under strict scrutiny. In other words, such classifications are constitutional only if they are narrowly tailored measures that further compelling governmental interests." This placed a heavy burden on government agencies to justify any sort of preferential treatment afforded to minorities.

Some commentators thought that the Court would move eventually to overturn its 1978 *Bakke* decision, but this turned out not to be the case. In 2003, the Court upheld an affirmative action program employed by the law school at the University of Michigan.[24] The decision made clear that affirmative action programs designed to enhance the diversity of student populations can survive strict judicial scrutiny. Thus, affirmative action remains legally viable, at least for the foreseeable future.

Affirmative Action and Presidential Politics   During the 2000 campaign, the presidential candidates George W. Bush and Al Gore sparred over the issue of affirmative action. Despite certain rhetorical devices designed to mask the candidates' differences on this issue, the two candidates clearly had fundamental disagreements about whether government should consider race as a factor in the distribution of benefits or opportunities. It was also clear that the new president's most profound impact on this issue would be made through his appointments to the Supreme Court because the affirmative action question would continue to appear on the judicial agenda. In fact, concerns over affirmative action were prominent in the Senate Judiciary Committee's rejection of Bush's nomination of Charles Pickering to the Fifth Circuit Court of Appeals. In 2004, however, the issue was barely mentioned in the context of the presidential election. By 2004, concern about the war in Iraq, international terrorism, and other national security issues had eclipsed this and many other domestic policy issues.

Public Attitudes Toward Affirmative Action   Affirmative action programs have been and remain highly controversial. Although many people feel that such programs are necessary to "level the playing field," others are troubled by any program that provides preferential treatment on the basis of group membership. The public is generally supportive of affirmative action, at least in principle, but a substantial percentage of Americans see it as unfair. Not surprisingly, these attitudes vary significantly by race (see Box 5-1).

| Box 5-1 | Public Attitudes toward Affirmative Action in Higher Education, by Race, 2003 |

"All in all, do you think affirmative action programs designed to increase the number of black and minority students on college campuses..."

"...are a good thing or a bad thing?"

	All Respondents	White Respondents	Black Respondents	Hispanic Respondents
Good thing	60%	54%	87%	77%
Bad thing	30%	35%	5%	17%
Don't know	10%	11%	8%	6%

"...are fair or unfair?"

	All Respondents	White Respondents	Black Respondents	Hispanic Respondents
Fair	47%	45%	58%	70%
Unfair	42%	43%	35%	27%
Don't know	11%	12%	7%	3%

Source: National telephone survey of 1,201 adults conducted by Princeton Survey Research Associates, April 30–May 4, 2003. Results obtained from The Pew Research Center for the People and the Press, http://people-press.org.

5-2h Racial Discrimination in Voting Rights

The American electoral system is the vehicle through which much societal discrimination has been buttressed. The systematic exclusion of African Americans from the electoral process was maintained through the early 1960s in many areas. As with the desegregation of the public schools, the process of opening political participation began in the courts. In 1944, the Supreme Court overruled one of its earlier decisions and struck down the infamous white primary as a violation of the Fifteenth Amendment.[25] Fifteen years later, however, the Court refused to invalidate the use of literacy tests.[26]

The Civil Rights Act of 1964 limited the use of literacy tests that had been employed by local officials to keep blacks from voting. In that same year, the states ratified the Twenty-Fourth Amendment, which outlawed the use of the poll tax in federal elections, and in 1966 the Supreme Court struck down the poll tax in state elections as a violation of the Fourteenth Amendment Equal Protection Clause.[27] Nevertheless, the participation of blacks was still quite limited. To some degree, the low level of voting was due to structural factors, but substantial evidence existed of a pattern of intimidation by local white officials who were unalterably opposed to the idea of blacks voting.

The reason for white intransigence was obvious. African Americans made up a substantial proportion of the population in most southern states—in many counties, they constituted a majority. If blacks were to turn out to vote in substantial numbers, they not only could threaten the political status quo but also might even be elected and take political control in some communities.

The Voting Rights Act of 1965   In 1965, Congress enacted the Voting Rights Act to ensure that African Americans would have access to the ballot box. The act outlawed the use of literacy tests as a condition of voting in seven southern states where black voting had lagged far behind that of whites. In addition, the act had a triggering mechanism by which federal registrars would be sent to any county in these states in which fewer than 50 percent of those of voting age were registered to vote in the 1964 presidential election.

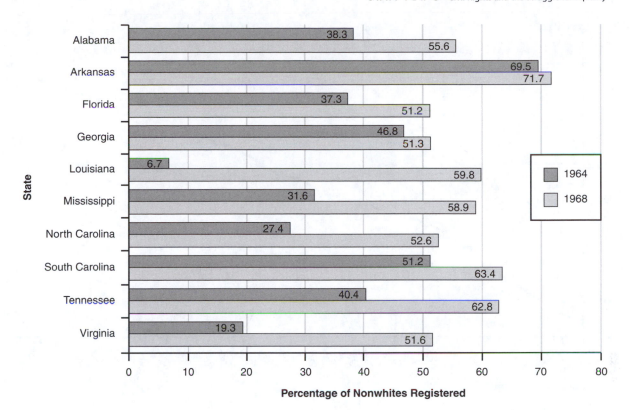

Figure 5-2

Percentage of Nonwhites Registered to Vote in the South, 1964 and 1968

Source: Adapted from Herbert Asher, *Presidential Elections and American Politics* (Chicago: Dorsey Press, 1988), p. 51.

The effect of the Voting Rights Act was dramatic. Black registration and voting increased dramatically. By the mid-1970s, blacks were voting in numbers that approached those of whites, and several thousand African Americans had been elected to state and local office (see Figure 5-2). The effects were profound. African Americans became such a force in southern politics that few politicians could afford to risk alienating them. The result was a new breed of white officeholders, epitomized by Governor Bill Clinton of Arkansas, who were sympathetic to the African-American community. Perhaps the best example of African-American voting power in the New South was the 1989 election of Douglas Wilder as governor of Virginia, the first African American to be elected governor of an American state.

Dismantling Institutionalized Electoral Discrimination The Voting Rights Act of 1965 was instrumental in increasing the number of African Americans who voted and held public office (see Figure 5-3). But voting rights have come to mean more than the right to cast a ballot. Indeed, if political jurisdictions and institutions are constructed in such a way as to minimize the impact of minority votes, members of these groups risk having the importance of their votes diluted.

The 1965 act did not specifically address actual electoral districts or the problem of **vote dilution.** Nevertheless, some districting practices clearly work to dilute minority votes in state legislatures, city councils, or congressional districts. This dilution can result from deliberately drawing district lines in such a way that minority voters are dispersed among a number of jurisdictions. The intentional dispersion of minority votes is called **cracking.** In another practice, known as **packing,** all minority voters are placed in one district. Though ensuring one minority representative, this practice dilutes the possibility of minority candidates' effectively contesting two or more seats.

At-Large Elections Minority votes can also be diluted because of the nature of the electoral system itself, which may or may not have been established with the intent of discrimination. The major culprit in this regard is the practice of electing representatives to

▶ **vote dilution** A situation in which the voting strength of racial or ethnic groups or both is significantly diminished.

▶ **cracking** A type of vote dilution that results from deliberate attempts to draw district lines in such a way that minority voters are dispersed among a number of districts.

▶ **packing** A type of vote dilution that occurs when all minority voters are placed in one district, thereby limiting the possibility of racial or ethnic residents from effectively contesting two or more seats.

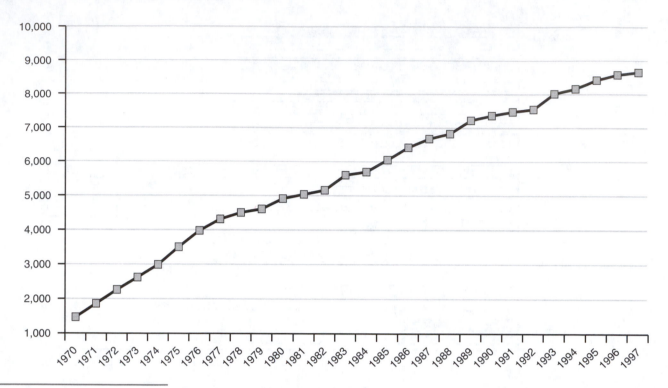

Figure 5-3
African-American Elected Officials (Federal, State, and Local), 1970–1997

Source: Adapted from Harold W. Stanley and Richard G. Niemi, *Vital Statistics on American Politics, 1999–2000* (Washington, D.C.: CQ Press, 2000), p. 56.

▶ **at-large voting** A system of voting in which all voters in a given community choose a set of representatives for the entire community, as opposed to a system in which the community is divided into districts and voters in those districts choose representatives only for those districts.

▶ **proportional representation** An electoral system in which the percentage of votes received by a given political party entitles that party to the same percentage of seats in the legislature.

city and county commissions and school boards by **at-large voting.** In at-large elections, representatives to a voting body are chosen in a vote from the entire community rather than from districts. For the most part, the intent of these systems was not to discriminate. In fact, at-large elections were established as part of the movement to reform city governments. Nevertheless, their impact has been in many cases discriminatory.

Since 1911, for example, the city of Mobile, Alabama, had used at-large elections to choose its three-member city commission. In the late 1970s, more than 35 percent of the city's residents were black, yet no African American had ever been elected to the city commission despite several attempts. Local residents brought a suit challenging the at-large system on the grounds that it had the effect of unfairly diluting the voting strength of racial minorities. In 1980, however, the Supreme Court held that unless one can prove discriminatory intent on the part of public officials, at-large voting systems do not violate the Constitution.[28]

Changes in the Voting Rights Act   Largely in response to the Supreme Court's decision in the Mobile case, the Voting Rights Act was amended in 1982 to apply to systems that could be shown to have discriminatory effects, regardless of their intent. The benchmark for judging the discriminatory effects of a given system would be the degree to which the votes of a racial minority were diluted. In a complex opinion in 1986, the Supreme Court held that Section 2 of the Voting Rights Act allowed the courts to require a city to change its voting system if African Americans were regularly frustrated in attempts to elect representatives of their choice.[29] The federal courts tend to find violations in systems where whites and African Americans vote in blocs for different candidates and the white-preferred candidate usually wins.

As a result of the changes in the Voting Rights Act and subsequent court decisions, many American cities have been involved in court cases that have led to changes in their form of government. When courts have found dilution, they have tended to replace at-large systems with districts drawn to ensure that minority voters make up a healthy majority of as many districts as possible. The courts have never recognized any group's right to a certain proportion of seats on any legislative body, however, as the idea of **proportional representation** of minorities is inconsistent with traditional American notions of representation.

The practice of creating districts to maximize the representation of minorities has been extended to state legislative and congressional districts. State houses have long had the responsibility for drawing district lines. Since the reapportionment decisions of the 1960s, redistricting has taken place every ten years—after each census. The redistricting process has long had a partisan political tone because the party controlling the legislature can ensure that the lines are drawn to benefit its electoral chances. This process of drawing district borders to reach a desired political end is called **gerrymandering.** Ironically, in the past, districts were gerrymandered to minimize the impact of minority voters; now, gerrymandering occurs to maximize minority influence!

> **gerrymandering** The process of drawing political district borders to advantage or disadvantage certain groups.

Under the Justice Department's interpretation of the 1982 Voting Rights Act, state legislatures must make every effort to create minority districts. This directive has led to legislative districts with very strange shapes. For instance, to create a congressional district with a safe African-American majority, the North Carolina legislature extended the boundaries of one district for hundreds of miles along an interstate highway to connect several concentrations of African-American voters. In 1996, the Supreme Court declared this plan unconstitutional, raising doubt about the Justice Department's policy of maximizing minority legislative districts.[30] In a related decision, the Court observed

> The Voting Rights Act, and its grant of authority to the federal courts to uncover official efforts to abridge minorities' right to vote, has been of vital importance in eradicating invidious discrimination from the electoral process and enhancing the legitimacy of our political institutions. Only if our political system and our society cleanse themselves of that discrimination will all members of the polity share an equal opportunity to gain public office regardless of race. As a Nation we share both the obligation and the aspiration of working toward this end. The end is neither assured nor well served, however, by carving electorates into racial blocs. "If our society is to continue to progress as a multiracial democracy, it must recognize that the automatic invocation of race stereotypes retards that progress and causes continued hurt and injury." . . . It takes a shortsighted and unauthorized view of the Voting Rights Act to invoke that statute, which has played a decisive role in redressing some of our worst forms of discrimination, to demand the very racial stereotyping the Fourteenth Amendment forbids.[31]

The Court's decisions left unclear whether this reverse gerrymandering would be permissible in the future. Critics of this type of gerrymandering applauded the Court's decision, but many people in the civil rights community lamented it, noting that this type of redistricting led to a great increase in the number of African-American representatives. In 2001, the Supreme Court addressed the constitutionality of North Carolina congressional districts again. This time, to the surprise of many observers, the Court upheld the plan in a close vote (5–4). Noting the correlation between race and political party identification, the Court held that the state legislature could not be faulted for drawing safe Democratic districts, even if these districts were overwhelmingly African American.[32] The decision only added to the uncertainty surrounding the creation of **majority minority districts**.

> **majority minority districts** Electoral districts in which the majority of voters are members of a racial minority.

5-2i Civil Rights for Other Racial and Ethnic Groups

During the latter part of the twentieth century, the United States became increasingly diverse. Increased immigration from Cuba, Mexico, and other Latin American countries, as well as from Asia, has created a different political landscape. To the degree that members of these groups identified with their ethnic heritage and groups were geographically definable, they faced problems of discrimination similar to those faced by African Americans.

Hispanics Some Hispanics face particular problems because they have entered this country illegally. As a result of their lack of documented citizenship, many are exploited and forced to work in low-paying jobs, such as picking fruits and vegetables. Moreover, many Hispanics, including those who are American citizens, face employment discrimination not unlike that experienced by African Americans.

In many ways, the struggle of African Americans for civil rights set the stage for the emergence of Hispanics as a political force. Faced with exploitation by growers in the Southwest, Cesar Chavez organized the United Farm Workers in 1962. Chavez understood the need to appeal to public opinion throughout the country to bring pressure for change. He developed the tactic of the nationwide boycott of certain farm products to dramatize his cause and create economic hardship for the growers.

In some states—in particular, those in the Southwest—individuals with Spanish surnames represented a strong potential political force. Registering to vote was often difficult, however, because of citizenship problems and language barriers. Hispanics are protected by civil rights and voting rights legislation, however. Under the 1982 amendments to the Voting Rights Act, states and cities must make every effort to see that Hispanic votes are not subject to dilution.

Although Spanish-speaking minorities benefited from legislation intended primarily for African Americans, language and citizenship issues seemed to demand specific legislation. In 1986, Congress passed the Simpson–Mazzoli Act. Under its provisions, individuals who could prove that they had been in the country for five years would be granted citizenship. In addition, American businesses were subject to criminal penalties if they knowingly hired illegal aliens. Fewer persons than expected applied for citizenship, however, and many immigrants, especially those from Mexico, continue to live without the basic protections of American society.

By the 1990s, Hispanic Americans had become a powerful force in American politics. Their influence should continue to increase because Hispanics are the fastest-growing minority group in the United States. The increase in numbers should lead to the continued election of more Hispanic officeholders and increased visibility in positions of power at the national level.

Native Americans   Native Americans have faced unique problems in the American system. Their existence was an impediment to the settlement of the United States, so they were systematically eliminated or forced to migrate westward. As late as the nineteenth century, many Anglo Americans viewed the "Indians," as they were mistakenly labeled, as less than fully human. Consequently, the concept of civil rights had no more meaning for Native Americans than it had for black slaves. As a result, about half the country's approximately 1.4 million Native Americans now live on reservations. These reservations represent the legacy of years of neglect by the federal government.

The federal government has always recognized Native Americans as a group with special status. Technically, reservations are sovereign, with Native Americans controlling their own destiny through separate political and legal systems. Their well-being, however, has been the responsibility of the Bureau of Indian Affairs within the U.S. Department of the Interior, which provides medical care and education to Native Americans on the reservations.

In many ways, Native Americans have endured suffering greater than that of any group in American society. They lag behind other minorities in education, income, and quality of housing. Native Americans also suffer through their lack of political clout. But they too built on the lessons of the civil rights movement. The American Indian Movement (AIM), founded in the late 1960s, articulated many Indian demands and dramatized their plight. Pressure from AIM and other groups helped bring about the passage of the American Indian Self-Determination and Educational Assistance Act in 1975. Native Americans demanded not only increased aid to the impoverished reservations but also an increased say in how the aid would be spent.

The struggles of Native Americans have left a long legal trail. Virtually every change in the status of Native Americans has been legitimized through a treaty. Many times, the claims of Native Americans are based on the implementation (or the failure of implementation) of treaties. Some treaties exempt a particular tribe from state and federal hunting and fishing regulations. Not surprisingly, others in the area are frequently upset with what they perceive as a dual standard that permits Native Americans to fish and hunt where and when non–Native Americans cannot.

In the early 1990s, many tribes attempted to raise money by experimenting with gambling on the reservations in areas where gambling was not otherwise permitted. In 1992, the federal government attempted to shut down these types of establishments near Phoenix, Arizona, but the courts ruled in favor of the tribes, citing their exemption under

Comparative Perspective

The Struggle for Racial Equality in South Africa

The first European settlers came to South Africa from the Netherlands in 1652. They established a colony and imposed slavery on many of the native African people. After Great Britain gained control of the colony in 1795, the British abolished slavery and recognized some degree of legal equality for blacks and "coloureds" (people of mixed African and Indian descent). The whites of Dutch ancestry, known as Boers, resented British rule and the changes it brought, and the resulting tensions eventually led to the Boer War (1899–1902). After defeating the Boers, the British established the Union of South Africa, which extended the territory under British rule. The Union of South Africa was administered by the British until 1931.

After the country's independence from British rule, the ruling white minority harshly suppressed the native black population, establishing a policy of **apartheid,** or strict racial segregation in every aspect of life. The official status of white supremacy was strengthened by the National party, which governed South Africa between 1948 and 1994. Under Prime Minister Hendrik Verwoerd, the government established nine "homelands" for the native black population. As long as blacks remained in these homelands, which were located in the least desirable areas of the country, they could exercise certain rights; elsewhere, their activities were strictly curtailed. Under apartheid, blacks were not permitted to vote, own land, travel, or work without permits. This policy generated strong protest, both from the native black population and the international community. In 1960, the government banned the African National Congress (ANC), which had been the leading organization in the struggle for black rights since its founding in 1912. After being banned, the ANC adopted a policy of armed struggle against the government. In 1964, Nelson Mandela, the leader of the ANC, was convicted of sabotage and sentenced to life imprisonment.

During the 1970s, apartheid became an international issue. Many countries refused to do business with South Africa until it changed its racial policies. During the regime of President P. K. Botha (1978–1989), the level of violence in the country escalated, leading to a declaration of a state of emergency. During the 1980s, the United Nations imposed international economic sanctions on South Africa. By the late 1980s, the attitude of South African whites began to change. The election of F. W. de Klerk in 1989 initiated a new era in South African politics. De Klerk ended the state of emergency, rescinded the ban on the ANC, and released Mandela, who had been jailed since 1964. Apartheid was officially abolished in 1991, although blacks were not given the right to vote. Mandela and de Klerk began negotiations designed to lead to a new constitution under which blacks would enjoy full citizenship. Two years later, in December 1993, the new constitution was approved by the white-dominated Parliament. For their joint efforts in working toward democracy, Mandela and de Klerk were awarded the Nobel Peace Prize in 1993.

The first elections in which blacks were able to vote were held in April 1994, and Mandela was elected president of the new South Africa. By the dawn of the twenty-first century, South Africa was able to achieve a reasonable level of political stability, although the nation still faced formidable social, political, and economic challenges.

> **apartheid** A legal system that requires strict racial segregation in every aspect of life.

earlier treaties. Although operating gambling casinos is controversial, it shows how much Native Americans on reservations desire to improve their standard of living and become more self-supporting and less dependent on the federal government.

Asian Americans   The United States has long been the home of many persons of Asian descent. Many were brought to the West to work on the railroads in the nineteenth century. Following the completion of the major east-west link in 1869, many Asians were subjected to exclusionary laws in San Francisco. The intent of the legislation was to rid the community of Asians, or at least keep them in an inferior economic and political status.

Overall, despite this early exploitation, Asian Americans were not subject to the pervasive discrimination that confronted African Americans. Nevertheless, in a shocking display of national hysteria, if not overt racism, more than one hundred thousand Japanese Americans were placed in internment camps during World War II. This "relocation" was accomplished without any pretense of due process. Nevertheless, the Supreme Court upheld the internment, citing the national emergency of the war.[33] Ultimately, in 1988, Congress recognized the injustice, formally apologized, and paid $20,000 compensation to each survivor of the internment. Yet the clear violation of fundamental constitutional rights by the federal government in the middle of the twentieth century stands as a stark reminder to Asian Americans of their former status as outsiders in American society.

In this century, many Asians have come to this country in search of economic opportunity. As is often the case when racially identifiable minorities share the same urban space, tensions developed between African and Korean Americans during the Los Angeles riots that followed the Rodney King verdict in 1992. Some African Americans claimed that Korean shopkeepers exploited their African-American customers, and many Korean businesses were apparently targeted for destruction and looting during the riots. Similar tensions had developed earlier in other cities. In the late 1980s, Asian Americans were also the victims of beatings and even murder at the hands of whites who were frustrated with the Japanese domination of the automobile business.

In many ways, Americans of Asian descent have adjusted quite well to American society. Whether as shopkeepers or professionals, by many measures Asian Americans have performed at levels surpassing those of all other groups. Many people credit this situation to the tight-knit family structures of Asian society and the strong work ethic of Asian families. Typically, Asian families place great emphasis on education, hard work, self-discipline, and saving for the future, all of which are values that help minorities achieve integration into the social and economic mainstream.

5-3 Sex Discrimination

Women were not accorded anything resembling equality at the time the American republic was founded. Even with the addition of the Bill of Rights and the Civil War amendments, the U.S. Constitution contained no explicit recognition of women's rights. Indeed, even the right to vote was not guaranteed until 1920, when the Nineteenth Amendment was ratified. Given the lack of women participants in the Constitutional Convention and, until quite recently, the dearth of women holding political office of any kind, there can be no doubt that women were intended to hold second-class citizenship at best. However, it would be simplistic to categorize this sort of systematic discrimination as merely an extension of the racism that defined the treatment of African Americans.

The inferior citizenship status of women in this country was certainly not unique to the United States. It was accepted virtually as a given because of deeply ingrained cultural norms. Western culture was patriarchal in nature. Men had long assumed a superior status within the whole structure of family and religion. Whereas the institution of slavery represented the exploitation of a whole people by another, the institutions surrounding the role of women were tightly woven into a cultural fabric so pervasive that the Founders could hardly be expected to see beyond it. Although one would be hard-pressed to find any race, tribe, or group of people whose cultural roots were grounded in submission to others, most women in the United States and elsewhere accepted their social status outside the political and economic mainstream almost without question.

Cultures evolve, however, and many individuals simply will never accept second-class treatment, regardless of the circumstances. As women began to challenge their status in American politics and the broader society, they faced a dual set of obstacles not unlike those faced by African Americans. First, the law kept women from full participation in society. Second, many individuals discriminated against women for their own reasons. To rectify the former problem, laws would have to be eliminated; to prevent the latter problem, new laws outlawing discrimination would have to be enacted.

Again, the situation is somewhat more complex than was the case for racial minorities. Although few people would accept the idea of basing discriminatory legislation on racial differences, many more might accept discriminatory laws based on gender differences.

Some laws that discriminate against women reflect long-standing customs that unfairly recognized men as the only legitimate owners of property. Others are grounded in the belief that biological differences justify discrimination. Some discriminatory laws are intended to protect women against sexual abuse, others regulate the role of women in the military, and still others govern the financial rights of men and women as they dissolve a marriage. Of course, the most visible and controversial laws deal with abortion. These controversies are all the more difficult because people's attitudes toward gender discrimination issues tend to be a function of their religious and/or philosophical beliefs rather than of their gender.

5-3a Women's Struggle for Political Equality

The beginnings of the women's struggle for political equality were rooted in the fight for the vote. Supporters of the vote for women were known as suffragists. After women were finally assured of the right to vote through the passage of the Nineteenth Amendment in 1920, however, the movement for women's political rights slowed dramatically. It was as though the vote had been seen as an end in itself rather than as a means of achieving greater societal change. Furthermore, the right to vote did not bring about many substantial changes in policy or a greater acceptance of women as public officeholders.

The modern women's movement took form in the 1960s. The movement adopted many of the tactics that had been employed successfully by African Americans in the civil rights movement, including marches, protests, demonstrations, and boycotts. Perhaps most memorable were public demonstrations in which feminists burned their bras as symbols of the constraints imposed on them by a male-dominated society.

Key Laws Affecting Women's Rights Congress responded to growing demands for legal equality between the sexes by passing the Equal Pay Act of 1963, the 1972 amendments to Title VII of the Civil Rights Act of 1964, and Title IX of the Federal Education Act of 1972. The first two statutes were aimed at eliminating sex discrimination in the workplace. The third authorized the withholding of federal funds from educational institutions that engaged in sex discrimination. These statutes have been an important source of civil rights protection for women and have given rise to a number of significant court decisions.

The Equal Rights Amendment Congress began considering a constitutional amendment guaranteeing equal rights for women as early as 1923. In 1972, the Equal Rights Amendment (ERA) had gathered enough support in Congress to be sent to the states, where three-fourths (or thirty-eight) of the state legislatures had to ratify the amendment before it could become part of the Constitution. The ERA was quite concise. It stated:

> *Section 1.* Equality of rights under the law shall not be denied or abridged by the United States or by any State on account of sex.

> *Section 2.* The Congress shall have the power to enforce, by appropriate legislation, the provisions of this article.

> *Section 3.* This amendment shall take effect two years after the date of ratification.

Initially, the ERA met with much enthusiasm and little controversy in the state legislatures. By 1976, it had been ratified by thirty-five of the necessary thirty-eight states. In the late 1970s, however, opposition to the ERA crystallized in those states that had yet to ratify. The opposition was led by Phyllis Schlafly, a conservative political activist who argued that the ERA and the other items on the feminist agenda would be destructive to the family and ultimately harmful to women. Although Congress extended the period for ratification until 1982, the amendment ultimately failed to win approval by the requisite number of states. However, roughly one-third of the states eventually amended their own constitutions to provide explicit protections against sex discrimination. In our federal system, state laws and constitutions may provide additional civil rights protections beyond those provided by federal laws and the U.S. Constitution.

Case in Point 5-1

Is Gender-Based Discrimination Inherently Suspect?

Frontiero v. Richardson (1973)

In the landmark decision *Frontiero v. Richardson* (1973), the Supreme Court upheld Lt. Sharron Frontiero's claim that the Air Force acted unconstitutionally in requiring women, but not men, to demonstrate that their spouses were in fact dependents for the purpose of receiving medical and dental benefits. The Court stopped short, however, of declaring gender-based discrimination to be "inherently suspect" and thus presumptively unconstitutional. Nevertheless, the Court made a strong statement on behalf of women's rights. Writing for a plurality of four justices, Justice William Brennan observed that "... since sex, like race and national origin, is an immutable characteristic determined solely by the accident of birth, the imposition of special disabilities on the members of a particular sex because of their sex would seem to violate 'the basic concept of our system that legal burdens should bear some relationship to individual responsibility'. ..." Although the Supreme Court has never declared that sex discrimination is inherently suspect, it has required government agencies to articulate very strong reasons to justify treating men and women differently. Rarely do such policies survive judicial review.

The demise of the ERA left constitutional interpretation in the field of sex discrimination largely in the domain of the Fourteenth Amendment. In 1976, the Supreme Court articulated a test for judging gender-based policies under the Fourteenth Amendment (see Case in Point 5-1). According to this test, to be constitutional, a gender-based policy must be substantially related to an important government objective. Applying this test, the courts have reached different results, sometimes upholding and at other times invalidating policies challenged as unconstitutional sex discrimination.

5-3b Women in Military Service

One of the most controversial issues in the area of sex discrimination is the role that women should play in the military. Opponents of the ERA argued that adoption of the amendment would result in women being drafted into combat, a prospect that many people still find unacceptable. In 1981, the Supreme Court upheld the constitutionality of the male-only draft registration law. Writing for the Court, Justice William Rehnquist stated that the exclusion of women from the draft "was not an 'accidental by-product of a traditional way of thinking about women.'"[34] In Rehnquist's view, men and women "are simply not similarly situated for purposes of a draft or registration for a draft." No doubt many would challenge Rehnquist's assumption, especially in light of the expanded role women played in the war against Iraq in 1991, and especially the current conflict in Iraq. But the question of women's role in the military and, in particular, whether they will ever be subject to the draft appear to have been left to Congress and the president to decide.

5-3c Sex Discrimination by Educational Institutions

Historically, many state-run colleges were single-sex institutions, but this situation began to change after World War II. By the late 1960s, when the Supreme Court became interested in sex discrimination as a constitutional question, almost all state colleges and universities had become coeducational. Yet some states continued to operate certain specialized institutions on a single-sex basis. In 1984, the Supreme Court required the Mississippi University for Women (MUW) to admit a male student to its all-female nursing school.[35] MUW tried to defend its policy of limiting enrollment to women as a type of affirmative action program. In her opinion for the Court, Justice Sandra Day O'Connor would have none of that, noting that nursing is not a field in which women have been traditionally denied opportunities. Quite to the contrary, it is a profession that has been stereotyped as "female." The Supreme Court could not find any substantial justification for the school's refusal to admit a qualified male applicant.

In 1996, the Court ruled that Virginia Military Institute (VMI), an all-male state-run military college, had to accept women as cadets.[36] Saying that the state of Virginia had to advance an "exceedingly persuasive justification" for the exclusion of women, the Court rejected the state's argument that admitting women would undermine the special character of the institution. The VMI ruling was the final nail in the coffin for single-sex higher education in this country.

An emerging issue of special concern to college students is whether universities can maintain sexually segregated athletic programs. Is the separate-but-equal doctrine appropriate when considering collegiate athletics? Suppose that a young woman wants to play football at a state university. Assuming that the university does not have a women's football program, does the Equal Protection Clause require the school to let the woman try out for the men's team? Although some may feel that these types of issues trivialize the Constitution, these matters tend to be far from trivial in the minds of people who are affected by the policies.

5-3d Women in the Workforce

Traditionally, the socially prescribed role of woman as wife and mother, combined with a protectionist attitude on the part of men, served to keep women out of the workforce in significant numbers although women were mobilized to fill jobs vacated by men during the two world wars. Now, most adult women are employed, at least part-time. Indeed, roughly half of all women with children under the age of one are employed outside the home.

Despite recent gains, women on average earn only about seventy cents for every dollar earned by men. This discrepancy is partially due to the fact that women are much more likely than men to be employed in relatively low-paying service, clerical, sales, and manufacturing jobs. They are still less likely than men to be doctors, engineers, accountants, lawyers, and the like, although the gender gap in the professions is narrowing. Finally, women have yet to gain access to the top-paying positions in corporations. Some have complained of a *glass ceiling*, an invisible barrier that keeps women out of top managerial positions.

Although women are not a minority—they comprise roughly 53 percent of the population—they have had to struggle as hard as minority groups to gain acceptance in the workplace. Early on, the issue was whether women should be permitted to work at all. Later the issue became which jobs, if any, were unsuitable for women. Then the issue became equal pay for equal work. In the 1980s, the issue came to be defined as equal pay for work of comparable worth. Women's groups argued that women should receive the same pay as men, even if their jobs were different, as long as the jobs entailed similar levels of education and experience. Critics of comparable worth argued that this idea could not be implemented without a massive program of government regulation or numerous lawsuits, either of which would be costly and disruptive to business. In the 1990s, the momentum behind the push for comparable worth declined. Today, the highest-priority issues for working women are access to affordable day care and workplace policies that accommodate childbearing and child-rearing. Although these issues are primarily economic and are not exactly questions of civil rights, they certainly are related to women's search for economic and social equality.

5-3e Affirmative Action on Behalf of Women

To facilitate the integration of women into the economic mainstream, federal, state, and even some local agencies have adopted a variety of affirmative action programs to benefit women. Employers that do business with government, as well as educational institutions that receive public funds, have been encouraged to adopt their own affirmative action programs. Like the policies that grant preferred status to African-American applicants, affirmative action programs that benefit women have been controversial and have even been challenged in court.

In 1987, the Supreme Court handed down a landmark decision on affirmative action for women. It upheld a program under which a woman had been promoted to the position of road dispatcher in the Santa Clara, California, Transportation Agency, even though a man had scored higher on a standardized test designed to measure aptitude for the job. The man who had been passed over for the job brought a lawsuit, claiming reverse discrimination, as Alan Bakke had done some years earlier. The Supreme Court rejected the plaintiff's claim, stressing that the affirmative action program was a reasonable means of correcting the sexual imbalance among the Transportation Agency's personnel, who were overwhelmingly male.[37]

In a somewhat different form of affirmative action, some cities and states have required all-male social and civic clubs to admit women. The courts have generally approved these types of measures, even though they are sometimes challenged as violating the concept of freedom of association, which is protected by the First Amendment. In a notable 1984 decision, a unanimous Supreme Court found that the state of Minnesota's interest in eradicating sex discrimination was sufficiently compelling to justify a decision of its human rights commission requiring local chapters of the Jaycees to admit women.[38] Later decisions of the Court extended this ruling to embrace chapters of the Rotary Club as well as private social clubs that served liquor and food to their members.

5-3f Sexual Harassment

> **sexual harassment**
> Unwanted sexual attention of a threatening, insulting, demeaning, or bothersome character.

In the 1980s, **sexual harassment** appeared on the public agenda as a civil rights issue. The sexual harassment issue has been particularly noticeable on college campuses, where it has entered the debate over questions related to dating, dormitory visitation, and student-teacher relationships.

The issue was aired in a particularly dramatic fashion when law professor Anita Hill appeared before the Senate Judiciary Committee in October 1991 to make allegations of misconduct against Clarence Thomas, who had been nominated by President Bush to a position on the Supreme Court. Hill alleged that Thomas, when he was chairman of the Equal Employment Opportunity Commission, made sexual advances toward her, told off-color jokes in her presence, and generally harassed her in a sexual manner. Thomas categorically denied the charges. Because little supporting evidence existed, the Senate ultimately approved Thomas' nomination to the Supreme Court. Many women believed that the all-male Senate Judiciary Committee had been insensitive to Hill and to the whole issue of sexual harassment. The Clarence Thomas–Anita Hill episode was apparently one factor that led women to run for public office in record numbers in 1992.

One survey conducted in 1991 found that 21 percent of women had experienced sexual harassment on the job.[39] In a 1992 survey, 57 percent of adults said that too little was being done to protect women against sexual harassment in the workplace.[40] It is now generally agreed that sexual harassment is unacceptable, but considerable disagreement exists over what exactly constitutes harassment. That uncertainty will be resolved in the courts.

In 1986, the Supreme Court ruled that sexual harassment in the workplace constituted unlawful gender discrimination in violation of federal civil rights laws.[41] In November 1993, the Supreme Court adopted a legal standard that makes it easier for victims of sexual harassment to sue in federal court.[42] The decision, joined by all nine justices (including Clarence Thomas), came in a case brought by Teresa Harris, who worked for a truck leasing company in Nashville. Harris complained that her boss subjected her to repeated comments and suggestions of a sexual nature. The federal judge who heard the case in Nashville described the boss' behavior as vulgar and offensive, but ruled that it was not likely to have had a serious adverse psychological effect on the employee. He dismissed the case before it could go to a jury trial. The court of appeals in Cincinnati upheld the district court's ruling. In reversing the lower courts, the Supreme Court, speaking through Justice Sandra Day O'Connor, said that it was not necessary for a plaintiff in a sexual harassment case to show "severe psychological injury." It is enough that the work environment would be perceived by a reasonable person as being "hostile or abusive." The Court's decision reinstated Harris' complaint, thus allowing the case to go before a jury in the district court. More important, the decision increased the likelihood that women (and men) who believe that they are victims of sexual harassment in the workplace will file and win federal lawsuits. Thus, the Supreme Court effectively put employers on notice that their conduct would be subject to judicial scrutiny. To avoid litigation, employers must have policies and training programs in place and must take immediate action whenever complaints are filed.

5-4 Other Civil Rights Issues

The concept of civil rights originated in the context of African Americans' struggle for equality. Later, the concept was extended to other racial and ethnic groups and to women. Yet many other groups in society have also experienced discrimination, and they too are seeking a place on the contemporary civil rights agenda. Among these groups are the elderly, the poor, the disabled, and gays and lesbians.

5-4a Age Discrimination

Discrimination against the young is usually not legally problematic because persons below the age of legal majority are presumed not to enjoy the full rights of citizenship. Most questions of age discrimination involve elderly Americans' claims that they have been discriminated against. Federal courts typically employ a "rational basis test" to determine the constitutionality of government policies that discriminate on the basis of age. Under this test, a restriction based on age must be rationally related to a legitimate government purpose in order to be upheld. This test is fairly lenient; most policies reviewed under this standard are ultimately upheld by the court. Most age discrimination cases are not constitutional cases, however. Instead, they are based on provisions of statutes enacted by Congress and the state legislatures. In 1967, Congress enacted the Age Discrimination in Employment Act, which bars companies that deal in interstate commerce or do business with the government from discriminating against their employees on the basis of age. In 1988, Congress enacted a measure that prohibits all organizations that receive federal funds from engaging in age discrimination. A substantial amount of litigation in the state and federal courts now deals with age discrimination by employers. These cases frequently grow out of attempts by companies to save money by dismissing people who are approaching retirement age. As our society ages, and people live and work longer, conflicts involving age discrimination will become more numerous and more intense.

5-4b Discrimination against the Poor

Clearly, neither the Constitution nor civil rights laws mandate anything resembling the equalization of economic conditions. American political culture supports the idea of equality of opportunity, but not the notion of **equality of result,** which is often equated with socialism. Welfare programs are thus seen not as matters of civil rights but rather as entitlements that, at least theoretically, may be terminated by majority rule. On the other hand, the courts have held that in some cases indigent persons have a constitutional right to public assistance. When a person who is unable to afford legal representation is charged with a serious crime, she is entitled to a lawyer at public expense. Failure to provide counsel to an indigent defendant is considered a violation of due process and equal protection of the law.[43]

> **equality of result** Condition in which wealth, power, and status are distributed equally among the members of a society.

Unequal Funding of Public Schools One of the most litigated civil rights issues since the 1970s has been the question of whether the methods by which many states fund their public schools are constitutional. Many funding systems are based on city or county property taxes and thus allow for tremendous variance among school districts in the amount of funds available to the schools. Critics of these types of inequalities argue that education is a fundamental right and that grossly unequal funding is a denial of equal protection of the law. In 1973, the Supreme Court rejected such a challenge to this method of funding public schools in Texas.[44] Note, however, that the Supreme Court's interpretation of the Fourteenth Amendment in this case in no way prevents state courts from adopting a contrary view of the relevant provisions of their state constitutions. Indeed, more than twenty state supreme courts have done exactly that in holding that disparities in funding

> **judicial federalism**   Principle under which state courts are free to interpret their state laws in a way that provides additional rights beyond those secured by federal law.

among school districts violate state constitutional requirements of equal protection. This trend nicely illustrates the principle of **judicial federalism,** under which state courts are free to interpret their state laws in a way that provides additional rights beyond those secured by federal law.

Restriction of Abortion Funding for Indigent Women   Another controversial equal protection issue reaching the courts in the late 1970s was the dispute over legislative efforts to cut off government funds to support abortions. In 1980, the Supreme Court upheld the Hyde Amendment, a federal law that severely limited the use of federal funds to support abortions for indigent women.[45] Writing for the Supreme Court, Justice Potter Stewart noted that "the principal impact of the Hyde Amendment falls on the indigent." Nevertheless, in Stewart's view, "that fact alone does not render the funding restriction constitutionally invalid, for this Court has held repeatedly that poverty, standing alone, is not a suspect classification." As in the case of public school funding, the Supreme Court essentially held that restricting public funding for abortions may not be egalitarian, but that it is not an inequality which offends the U.S. Constitution.

5-4c Discrimination against Persons with Disabilities

Although few laws overtly discriminate against them, persons with disabilities have always faced physical barriers as well as societal prejudice. For the most part, the Congress, not the courts, has taken the lead in recognizing the rights of persons with disabilities. On the other hand, the courts have not been completely insensitive to the rights of persons with disabilities. For example, in 1985, the Supreme Court struck down a zoning law that had been applied to prohibit a home for the mentally retarded from operating in a residential neighborhood.[46] The Court said that no rational basis for the ordinance existed. Rather, it appeared to be based solely on "irrational prejudice against the mentally retarded."

In passing the Voting Accessibility Act of 1984, Congress attempted to increase access to the polls for disabled persons. With the passage of Title V of the Rehabilitation Act of 1973 and the Education for All Handicapped Children Act of 1975, Congress attempted to remove barriers confronting persons with disabilities in employment and education. But the most significant legislation by far in this area is the Americans with Disabilities Act (ADA) of 1990. The ADA requires that

- Businesses provide reasonable accommodations to employees with disabilities (Title I).
- Public services, including public transportation systems, be made accessible to persons with disabilities (Title II).
- Newly constructed or remodeled places of public accommodation (stores, restaurants, hotels, etc.) be made accessible to persons with disabilities (Title III).
- Telecommunications services be reasonably accessible to persons with disabilities (Title IV).

Government agencies and private businesses have been forced to develop policies to comply with the dictates of the ADA. Unlike the Civil Rights Act, the costs of compliance with the requirements of the ADA can be quite substantial. State and local governments have objected to what they see as another set of unfunded mandates from the federal government. Businesses have been given tax breaks to ease the costs of compliance, but these costs remain substantial, and many businesses have been slow to comply. Of course, businesses that fail to comply with the ADA are subject to civil suit.

A person is considered disabled under the ADA if she has a physical or mental impairment that substantially limits her major life activities. Obviously, the ADA provides a fertile field for judicial interpretation because courts must decide what constitutes "reasonable accommodation," "reasonably accessible," "substantially limits," and so forth. Even though the policy originated in the legislative branch, much of the implementation is being done by the courts.

5-4d The Controversy over Gay Rights

Homosexuality has always been taboo in the Judeo–Christian moral tradition. Reflecting this taboo, the criminal laws that this country inherited from England made homosexual activity a serious offense. In the more permissive climate of the 1960s, homosexuals began to "come out of the closet," calling for an end to criminal prohibitions on their activities and for an end to discrimination based on sexual orientation. In the 1970s, gay men and lesbians began to organize and fight for legal rights, in much the same way as African Americans and women had done before them. Organizations such as the Lambda Legal Defense and Education Fund and the Gay and Lesbian Advocates and Defenders went to court to challenge laws they deemed to be discriminatory. They also lobbied Congress and the state legislatures to enact laws to prohibit private discrimination based on sexual orientation. Despite numerous setbacks, these organizations have been reasonably successful in both the legislative and judicial arenas. However, Americans continue to be divided on the issue of "gay rights" and the larger question of homosexuality. Indeed, gay rights is one of the defining elements of the "culture war" that erupted in the 1990s. Until there is a reasonable consensus within the culture, gay rights advocates will not be completely successful in their legal and political efforts. Of course, it is also true that by and large the mass media and popular culture have been sympathetic to the gay rights cause, and this has had profound effects on American attitudes. As societal attitudes become more tolerant and permissive, the gay rights agenda will continue to advance.

Gays in the Military In the early 1990s, one of the most controversial questions involving gay rights was the policy banning homosexuals from serving in the military. Should a person be disqualified from military service merely because of homosexual orientation, as distinct from homosexual acts? The military justified the ban as necessary to maintain discipline, morale, and good order in the armed forces. Gay and lesbian activists argued that the ban punished persons merely because of their status or orientation, without regard to their personal conduct or the quality of their service. The federal courts reached mixed results in a number of lawsuits challenging the ban, but the Supreme Court has never had the opportunity to rule on the matter.

During the 1992 presidential campaign, candidate Bill Clinton promised that, if elected, he would immediately issue an executive order rescinding the military's ban on homosexuals. Not surprisingly, Clinton received the overwhelming support of gay and lesbian voters in the election. After taking office in January 1993, President Clinton found himself embroiled in a controversy over his campaign pledge. Clinton's initiative met tremendous resistance not only from the military but also from Congress. Critics of the initiative argued that allowing openly gay individuals to serve in the military would damage morale and discipline and would present a host of practical problems. Supporters of the president's plan noted that the objections to gays in the military were strikingly similar to those raised in 1948 when President Harry S Truman moved to end racial segregation in the military.

In the midst of the controversy, public opinion appeared to side with the military, at least by a slight margin. A poll conducted by the *New York Times* and CBS in January 1993 found that 48 percent opposed permitting gays to serve in the military; 42 percent supported the idea.[47] Facing opposition of unexpected intensity, even from within his own party, President Clinton decided to delay issuance of the executive order for six months. He did, however, immediately order the military to refrain from inquiring into the sexual orientation of new recruits. Eventually, after holding hearings, Congress adopted a "don't ask, don't tell" policy proposed by the Clinton administration as a compromise. The firestorm of controversy that erupted over Clinton's initial proposal showed the lack of societal consensus on the issue of gay rights. But the eventual don't-ask, don't-tell compromise showed how even volatile, emotional issues can be resolved through discussion, debate, and negotiation. However, a series of federal appeals court rulings in 1993, all of which ordered the military to reinstate gays and lesbians who had been discharged, suggested that the ultimate decision on this controversial question would come not from Congress but rather from the

Supreme Court. However, the Supreme Court has yet to rule on this issue. Public opinion remains divided on whether gay men and lesbians should be permitted to serve in the military; so "don't ask, don't tell" appears to be a workable compromise, at least until the courts say otherwise.

Gay Rights before the Courts

Gay rights advocates did not win any significant victories in the Supreme Court until 1996. In that year, in *Romer v. Evans,* the Court struck down a state constitutional amendment disallowing "any minority status, quota preferences, protected status or claim of discrimination" on the basis of "homosexual, lesbian, or bisexual orientation."[48] Colorado voters had adopted Amendment 2 through a statewide referendum after a controversy erupted over the fact that some of the state's more liberal communities had adopted ordinances prohibiting discrimination on the basis of sexual orientation. In declaring the amendment invalid, the Supreme Court observed

> It is not within our constitutional tradition to enact laws of this sort. Central both to the idea of the rule of law and to our own Constitution's guarantee of equal protection is the principle that government and each of its parts remain open on impartial terms to all who seek its assistance. . . .

> . . . We must conclude that Amendment 2 classifies homosexuals not to further a proper legislative end but to make them unequal to everyone else. This Colorado cannot do. A State cannot so deem a class of persons a stranger to its laws.

In a sharply worded dissenting opinion, Justice Antonin Scalia argued that Amendment 2 was not adopted out of a popular desire to harm gays, but was instead "a modest attempt by seemingly tolerant Coloradans to preserve traditional sexual mores against the efforts of a politically powerful minority to revise those mores through use of the laws." Scalia attacked the reasoning of the majority, saying that the Court's opinion "has no foundation in American constitutional law, and barely pretends to."

Gay Rights Versus Associational Freedom

Current federal law does not prohibit discrimination based on sexual orientation with respect to employment, housing, or access to public accommodations.[49] It is important to remember that in a federal system, civil rights are not defined solely by federal law. State and local laws can provide significant protections in this area, and roughly one-third of the states and a number of cities and counties have enacted legislation along these lines. California law, for example, prohibits discrimination based on sexual orientation with respect to education, public accommodations, and public and private sector employment. California law also extends to same-sex "domestic partners" many of the legal rights normally afforded married persons.

One of the difficult questions arising under laws that forbid discrimination by places of public accommodation is defining "public accommodation." Traditionally, the term was used to refer to businesses that opened their doors to the general public, but recently some courts have found this definition to be too restrictive. In an effort to expand existing legal prohibitions against discrimination, gay rights activists have gone to court seeking to have certain private organizations declared public accommodations. One such case gave rise to a controversial Supreme Court decision involving the Boy Scouts of America.[50] James Dale had been dismissed from his position as an assistant scoutmaster after the organization learned that he was gay. Dale successfully sued the Boy Scouts in the New Jersey courts, which ultimately ruled that the Boy Scouts had violated a New Jersey law prohibiting discrimination by places of public accommodation. The New Jersey Supreme Court ruled that the Boy Scout organization constituted a "public accommodation" under New Jersey law, a ruling not subject to review by the U.S. Supreme Court. However, the U.S. Supreme Court took the case and ruled that the application of the state antidiscrimination law to the Scouts violated that organization's rights under the First Amendment. Splitting five to four, the Court held that the Boy Scouts' First Amendment freedom of association trumped the state's interest in advancing the cause of gay rights. Writing for the majority of justices, Chief Justice William Rehnquist opined

> We are not, as we must not be, guided by our views of whether the Boy Scouts' teachings with respect to homosexual conduct are right or wrong; public or judicial disapproval of a

tenet of an organization's expression does not justify the State's effort to compel the organization to accept members where such acceptance would derogate from the organization's expressive message.

Speaking for the minority, Justice John P. Stevens accused the Court of turning its prejudices into legal principles:

> That such prejudices are still prevalent and that they have caused serious and tangible harm to countless members of the class New Jersey seeks to protect are established matters of fact that neither the Boy Scouts nor the Court disputes. That harm can only be aggravated by the creation of a constitutional shield for a policy that is itself the product of a habitual way of thinking about strangers.

Critics of the decision, and there were many, argued that the Court was giving a green light to bigotry. But many in the private, not-for-profit sector applauded the Court for protecting a private organization from government control.

The Gay Marriage Issue As we noted in Chapter 4, "Civil Liberties and Individual Freedom," the Supreme Court in 2003 overturned one of its precedents and struck down a Texas law making private homosexual activity a crime.[51] The Court's decision in *Lawrence v. Texas* came after a number of state courts invalidated their own states' laws prohibiting private homosexual conduct by invoking privacy rights guaranteed by their respective state constitutions. Dissenting in *Lawrence,* Justice Antonin Scalia argued that the decision "dismantles the structure of constitutional law that has permitted a distinction to be made between heterosexual and homosexual unions, insofar as formal recognition in marriage is

---

Popular Culture and American Politics
Pedro Zamora and AIDS

By Chapman Rackaway

MTV launched reality television with its *The Real World* in May of 1992. The show placed seven young people of diverse backgrounds together in an apartment and showed the learning, lives, and conflicts as these different people are forced to live together and tolerate each other's personal flaws.

By the time of the third season, the show's producers wanted to show their social conscience on a more aggressive level. For the San Francisco season, they would put in not only the most obnoxious individual to ever live in a Real World house (Puck, forever famous for bad hygiene and ugly personality), but also the first HIV-positive person to be placed on a Real World cast: Pedro Zamora.

Pedro's story is a tragic one. At age 14, his mother died, and he turned to sex as an escape from the pain of his mother's passing. At the age of 17, Pedro went to participate in an American Red Cross blood drive at his high school. After testing, Pedro's blood was rejected by the screeners: Pedro then knew he was infected with HIV.

In the early 1990s, AIDS was still a subject very taboo to many people, and Pedro felt the conflict. "The toughest thing for me at the time was I didn't know what to think. Here I am in the doctor's office, and he is telling me that I am HIV positive, and I am thinking, 'No, that can't be,' because I believed people with AIDS were bad people, and they were dirty people, and they were going to die, and they were going to die fast. In my mind I thought, 'I am not dirty. I am not a bad person. I haven't done anything wrong. I can't be sick.'" Some were not ready either for Zamora's AIDS story or his openly gay relationship.

The prime-time romance between Zamora and Sean Sasser was the first real-life love affair involving two HIV-positive men that most Americans had ever seen. They were a team on camera and off, keeping the focus on the AIDS cause: educating Pedro's housemates, speaking to young people across the country, testifying before Congress. Sasser continues that work today. But without Pedro's presence on *The Real World,* a generation might not have been able to put a very human face on something very alien to them at the time—HIV and AIDS.

concerned." Whatever one thinks of Justice Scalia's position on the issue of gay marriage, his observation was borne out by a Massachusetts court decision declaring unconstitutional state laws limiting marriage to heterosexual couples. In a 4–3 decision handed down in November 2003, the Supreme Judicial Court of Massachusetts held that gay and lesbian couples should be entitled to marry in Massachusetts and set a six-month deadline for the state legislature to respond.[52] Chief Justice Margaret H. Marshall began her opinion for the court as follows:

> Marriage is a vital social institution. The exclusive commitment of two individuals to each other nurtures love and mutual support; it brings stability to our society. For those who choose to marry, and for their children, marriage provides an abundance of legal, financial, and social benefits. In return it imposes weighty legal, financial, and social obligations. The question before us is whether, consistent with the Massachusetts Constitution, the Commonwealth may deny the protections, benefits, and obligations conferred by civil marriage to two individuals of the same sex who wish to marry. We conclude that it may not. The Massachusetts Constitution affirms the dignity and equality of all individuals. It forbids the creation of second-class citizens. In reaching our conclusion we have given full deference to the arguments made by the Commonwealth. But it has failed to identify any constitutionally adequate reason for denying civil marriage to same-sex couples.

In 1999, the Vermont Supreme Court rendered a similar decision, but the Vermont legislature responded by adopting a statute permitting gay and lesbian couples to enter into "civil unions." Public opinion in Massachusetts opposed gay marriage per se, but was favorable toward the concept of civil unions.[53] However, the legislature was sharply divided and few seemed to be in a mood to compromise. Sponsors of a proposed amendment to the state constitution seeking to overturn the state supreme court's decision were not able to muster the requisite votes. Nor were there enough votes to legalize civil unions as an alternative to marriage. The legislative impasse resulted in the legalization of gay marriage in Massachusetts according to the deadline set by the court. Thus, in May 2004, officials in the Bay State began issuing marriage licenses to gay and lesbian couples.

It was inevitable, given the media attention to developments in Massachusetts, that the issue would erupt into a national controversy. The conflict escalated further in February 2004 when the mayor of San Francisco ordered city officials to begin issuing marriage licenses to same-sex couples in contravention of state law. Ultimately, the California Supreme Court held that the nearly three thousand gay marriages performed in San Francisco were unlawful, but the actions of the mayor helped to nationalize the controversy.

In his 2004 State of the Union address, President George W. Bush called on Congress to "defend the sanctity of marriage." In 1996, Congress had passed the Defense of Marriage Act (DOMA), under which states are not required to recognize same-sex marriages licensed by other states. But conservatives feared that DOMA might be declared unconstitutional by federal courts under the Full Faith and Credit Clause of the U.S. Constitution, which has long been interpreted to require states to recognize marriages licensed by other states. In February 2004, President Bush called on Congress to adopt a federal constitutional amendment defining marriage as "between one man and one woman." According to President Bush, the amendment would "fully protect marriage, while leaving the state legislatures free to make their own choices in defining legal arrangements other than marriage." According to national surveys taken at the time, most Americans opposed the idea of gay marriage, but only a minority supported the idea of amending the U.S. Constitution along the lines recommended by President Bush (see the following "What Americans Think About" feature).

Not surprisingly, this issue made its way into the presidential campaign. John Kerry opposed the idea of amending the Constitution, arguing that Congress should stay out of the matter entirely. Many observers were surprised when, in the late summer of 2004, President Bush's Vice President, Dick Cheney, seemed to echo Senator Kerry's sentiments on the issue. As the campaign entered the stretch run toward the November election, however, the issue was eclipsed by the war in Iraq and other foreign policy and defense issues. However, it should be noted that in 2004, voters in eleven states approved ballot measures to prohibit same-sex marriage. Voters who supported these measures voted by substantial margins in favor of President Bush. Although the issue of same-sex marriage clearly was

What Americans Think About

Gay Marriage

The following survey data from the Gallup Organization provide a recent snapshot of Americans' opinions on the issue of gay marriage:

"Do you think marriages between homosexuals should or should not be recognized by the law as valid, with the same rights as traditional marriages?"

Should Be Valid	32%
Should Not Be Valid	62%
No Opinion	6%

"Would you favor or oppose a constitutional amendment that would define marriage as being between a man and a woman, thus barring marriages between gay or lesbian couples?"

Favor	48%
Oppose	46%
No Opinion	6%

Note: Sample size=499. Margin of error is +/− five percentage points. For more public opinion data on gay marriage, go to *http://www.pollingreport. com/civil.htm.*

You can go to the online version of this text to take this poll and see your results compared to the rest of your class.

Source: Adapted from CNN/USA Today/Gallup Poll. July 19–21, 2004.

not a decisive one in terms of the presidential contest in most states, there is reason to believe that the Ohio ballot initiative banning same-sex marriage may have stimulated enough turnout among socially conservative voters to tip the election in Bush's favor in that crucial battleground state.[54]

As noted in Chapter 4, "Civil Liberties and Individual Freedom," homosexuality is an issue on which American culture has changed dramatically in recent decades. No doubt, public attitudes on gay marriage will continue to evolve, most likely in the direction of greater tolerance. Surveys consistently show that younger people are much more liberal on the issue of gay rights generally than are older Americans. However, gay rights should remain a "hot button" political and legal issue for some years to come.

5-5 Conclusion: Evolving Notions of Equality

Legal protection for civil rights can emanate from a number of sources. First and foremost, the U.S. Constitution, as amended after the Civil War, protects the right to vote and prohibits states from denying persons within their jurisdictions the equal protection of the laws. The Fourteenth Amendment also grants Congress the power to legislate in the field of civil rights. Using this power, as well as its broad powers under the Commerce Clause, Congress has enacted a number of important civil rights statutes, most significantly the Civil Rights Act of 1964 and the Voting Rights Act of 1965. Although these statutes are based on the authority of the Constitution, they go beyond the civil rights protections afforded by the Constitution in that they address discrimination by private individuals and corporations.

Many state constitutions contain provisions similar to the Equal Protection Clause of the Fourteenth Amendment. States that do not have these types of constitutional provisions may amend their constitutions to provide for this type of protection. Like Congress, state legislatures may enact statutes that protect civil rights from private discrimination as well as from discrimination by government agencies. Cities and counties may also adopt civil rights ordinances applicable within their jurisdictions. Of course, state and local civil rights laws may not conflict with federal protections. Under our federal system, however, states and localities are free to provide greater, but not lesser, protections to civil rights than are provided by federal law. And, of course, state and local laws may not, for the sake of fostering civil rights, violate individual liberties protected by the federal and state constitutions. When conflicts occur, it is generally up to the courts to sort them out. In doing this, courts attempt to strike a workable balance between equality and freedom, the two core values of our democracy.

Ultimately, though, questions of civil rights, as well as those of civil liberties, are determined not in courts of law but rather in the attitudes and opinions of Americans—in our political culture. The idea of rights is fundamental to American political culture. Our system is founded on the idea that individuals have rights that must be respected by other individuals, by the society generally, and certainly by government. One of the most fundamental rights of individuals is the right to equal treatment before the law and the state. Our society has taken two centuries to evolve to the point that it is willing to extend the right of equal treatment to African Americans and other racial and ethnic minorities as well as to women. Some would say that the evolution is incomplete—that American society still has a long way to go. Others would argue that we have moved beyond the ideal of equal protection of the law to a system in which preferred status has been institutionalized for certain protected groups and not others. In attempting to foster equality, society must avoid the dangers that can occur when group is pitted against group.

However well-intentioned and committed to civil rights American citizens may be, those commitments and intentions are always tested in times of war. In the wake of the terrorist attacks of 9-11-2001, America found itself again debating the scope and limits of civil rights protections. Under what circumstances, if any, should authorities be permitted to consider race or ethnicity as an element of a terrorist profile? Is it permissible for police or airport security personnel to be immediately suspicious of young, Arabic males? Although many Americans have no problem with **racial profiling,** especially in the context of the war on terrorism, others see this type of stereotyping as a real threat to civil rights. Here, as with many issues of law and policy, reasonable, well-intentioned people can and will disagree. Whatever one's perspective may be, it should be evident that the difficult and complex issues of civil rights will remain on the public agenda for quite some time, especially during America's war on terrorism.

▶ **racial profiling**   The use of a person's race or ethnicity as a factor in forming suspicion that he is involved in unlawful activity.

Questions for Thought and Discussion

1. Is affirmative action in hiring a necessary and just corrective to past discrimination, or does it amount to unjust reverse discrimination?

2. Should sex discrimination and race discrimination be judged by the same standards, or are these types of discrimination significantly different?

3. Should the federal civil rights laws be amended to forbid discrimination on the basis of physical or mental disabilities?

4. Does there need to be more legal protection for the rights of gays and lesbians? Should Congress add sexual orientation to the list of prohibited forms of discrimination?

5. What forms of discrimination beyond those mentioned in this chapter have the potential to become political and legal issues in the future?

Practice Quiz

Note: You can find the correct answers to these questions by taking the quiz and then submitting your answers in the Online Edition. The program will automatically score your submission. If you miss a question, the program will provide the correct answer, a rationale for the answer, and the section number in the chapter where the topic is discussed.

1. Chief Justice Roger Taney's opinion for the Supreme Court in _____ made it abundantly clear that blacks "were not intended to be included under the word 'citizens' in the Constitution."
   a. *Plessy v. Ferguson*
   b. *Sweatt v. Painter*
   c. *Gibbons v. Ogden*
   d. *Dred Scott v. Sandford*

2. Beginning in the 1880s, a number of state legislatures passed a series of laws, known as the _____, which virtually mandated a dual society based on race.
   a. Black Codes
   b. Civil Rights laws
   c. Jim Crow laws
   d. Civil War laws

3. The Supreme Court's decision in _____ overturned the "separate but equal" doctrine with respect to public education.
   a. *Sweatt v. Painter*
   b. *Brown v. Board of Education*
   c. *South Carolina v. Moyer*
   d. *Lyons v. Oklahoma*

4. For many years, the Democratic party in the South excluded African Americans from the electoral process through the use of _____.
   a. white primaries
   b. proportional electoral systems
   c. winner-take-all primaries
   d. multiparty district electoral systems

5. The military's present policy of don't ask, don't tell is aimed at protecting servicepersons who _____.
   a. have physical or mental handicaps
   b. have been divorced
   c. are gay
   d. have been convicted of a crime

6. The term _____ segregation is used to refer to that instance where segregation is maintained by law.
   a. *de jure*
   b. *de facto*
   c. *de novo*
   d. *de simplis*

7. In the 1970s, opposition to the Equal Rights Amendment (ERA) was led by _____, who argued that the ERA and the other items on the feminist agenda would be destructive to the family and ultimately to women.
   a. Patricia Ireland
   b. Phyllis Schlafly
   c. George Wallace
   d. Pat Buchanan

8. Which of the following terms refers to policies granting preferential treatment to members of traditionally disadvantaged minority groups?
   a. equal access
   b. equality of opportunity
   c. affirmative action
   d. equal protection

9. The _____, which prohibited racial discrimination in places of public accommodation, remains the foundation of national policy on the rights of minorities.
   a. Civil Rights Act of 1964
   b. 13th Amendment
   c. Hyde Amendment
   d. Supreme Court's decision in *Brown v. Board of Education*

10. The issue of sexual harassment was aired in a particularly dramatic fashion when _____ appeared before the Senate Judiciary Committee in 1991 to make allegations of misconduct against _____, who had been nominated to the Supreme Court.
    a. Anita Hill; Clarence Thomas
    b. Deborah Harry; Byron White
    c. Elizabeth Dole; David Souter
    d. none of the above

For Further Reading

Balkin, J. M., and Bruce Ackerman, eds. *What Brown v. Board of Education Should Have Said: The Nation's Top Legal Experts Rewrite America's Landmark Civil Rights Decision* (New York: NYU Press, 2001).

Chavez, Linda. *The Color Bind: California's Battle to End Affirmative Action* (Berkeley: University of California Press, 1998).

Finch, Minnie. *The NAACP: Its Fight for Justice* (Metuchen, NJ: Scarecrow Press, 1981).

Gerstmann, Evan. *The Constitutional Underclass : Gays, Lesbians, and the Failure of Class-Based Equal Protection.* (Chicago: University of Chicago Press, 1999).

Ginsburg, Ruth Bader. *Constitutional Aspects of Sex-Based Discrimination* (St. Paul, MN: West Publishing Co., 1974).

Glazer, Nathan. *Affirmative Discrimination: Ethnic Inequality and Public Policy* (New York: Basic Books, 1975).

Davidson, Chandler, and Bernard Grofman, eds. *Quiet Revolution in the South: The Impact of the Voting Rights Act 1965–1990* (Princeton, NJ: Princeton University Press, 1994).

Kluger, Richard. *Simple Justice: The History of Brown v. Board of Education and Black America's Struggle for Racial Equality* (New York: Vintage Books, 1977).

McGlen, Nancy E., and Karen O'Connor. *Women, Politics and American Society* (Upper Saddle River, NJ: Prentice-Hall, 1998).

Mezey, Susan Gluck. *In Pursuit of Equality: Women, Public Policy and the Federal Courts* (New York: St. Martin's Press, 1998).

Norell, Robert J. *Reaping the Whirlwind: The Civil Rights Movement in Tuskegee, rev. ed.* (Chapel Hill, NC: University of North Carolina Press, 1998).

Peltason, Jack W. 58 *Lonely Men: Southern Federal Judges and School Desegregation* (Urbana, IL: University of Illinois Press, 1961).

Thernstrom, Abigail, and Stephen Thernstrom. *America in Black and White: One Nation Indivisible* (New York: Simon and Schuster, 1997).

Wolters, Raymond. *The Burden of Brown: Thirty Years of School Desegregation* (Knoxville: University of Tennessee Press, 1984).

Woodward, C. Vann. *The Strange Career of Jim Crow* (New York: Oxford University Press, 1968).

Endnotes

1. See, for example, *R.A.V. v. City of St. Paul*, 505 U.S. 377 (1992), where the Supreme Court struck down a "hate crimes" ordinance on the ground that it unduly restricted speech protected by the First Amendment.
2. *Scott v. Sandford*, 60 U.S. (19 How.) 393 (1857).
3. The Civil Rights Cases, 109 U.S. 3 (1883).
4. *Plessy v. Ferguson*, 163 U.S. 537 (1896).
5. *Grovey v. Townsend*, 295 U.S. 45 (1927).
6. Wallace Mendelson, *Discrimination* (Englewood Cliffs, NJ: Prentice-Hall, 1962), p. 170.
7. *Sweatt v. Painter*, 339 U.S. 629 (1950).
8. *Brown v. Board of Education of Topeka, Kansas* (first decision), 347 U.S. 483 (1954).
9. *Brown v. Board of Education of Topeka, Kansas* (second decision), 349 U.S. 294 (1955).
10. Richard Kluger, *Simple Justice: The History of Brown v. Board of Education and Black America's Struggle for Racial Equality* (New York: Vintage Books, 1977), pp. 753–54.
11. *Cooper v. Aaron*, 358 U.S. 1 (1958).
12. Alex Haley, *The Autobiography of Malcolm X* (New York: Grove Press, 1966).
13. Hugh Davis Graham, *The Civil Rights Era: Origins and Development of National Policy* (New York: Oxford University Press, 1990).
14. *Heart of Atlanta Motel v. United States*, 379 U.S. 421 (1964).
15. *Katzenbach v. McClung*, 379 U.S. 294 (1964).
16. *Swann v. Charlotte–Mecklenburg Board of Education*, 402 U.S. 1 (1971).
17. *Millken v. Bradley*, 418 U.S. 717 (1974).
18. Stacy Teicher, "Closing a Chapter on School Desegregation." *The Christian Science Monitor*, July 16, 1999.
19. For example, on September 11, 1999, the Associated Press reported that a federal judge had ordered an end to busing in Charlotte–Mecklenburg, North Carolina, one of the school districts at the forefront of the conflict over busing three decades ago.
20. *University of California Board of Regents v. Bakke*, 438 U.S. 265 (1978).
21. *United Steelworkers v. Weber*, 433 U.S. 193 (1979).
22. *City of Richmond v. J. A. Croson Co.*, 488 U.S. 469 (1989).
23. *Adarand Constructors, Inc. v. Peña*, 515 U.S. 200 (1995).
24. *Grutter v. Bolinger*, 539 U.S. 306 (2003).
25. *Smith v. Allwright*, 321 U.S. 649 (1944).
26. *Lassiter v. Northampton County Board of Elections*, 360 U.S. 45 (1959).
27. *Harper v. Virginia State Board of Elections*, 383 U.S. 663 (1966).
28. *City of Mobile, Alabama v. Bolden*, 446 U.S. 55 (1980).
29. *Thornburgh v. Gingles*, 478 U.S. 30 (1986).
30. *Shaw v. Hunt*, 517 U.S. 899 (1996).
31. *Miller v. Johnson*, 515 U.S. 900 (1995).
32. *Hunt v. Cromartie*, 526 U.S. 541 (2001).
33. *Korematsu v. United States*, 323 U.S. 214 (1944).
34. *Rostker v. Goldberg*, 453 U.S. 57 (1981).
35. *Mississippi University for Women v. Hogan*, 458 U.S. 718 (1984).
36. *United States v. Virginia*, 518 U.S. 515 (1996).
37. *Johnson v. Transportation Agency of Santa Clara County*, 480 U.S. 646 (1987).
38. *Roberts v. United States Jaycees*, 468 U.S. 609 (1984).
39. *Newsweek*, October 21, 1991, p. 34.
40. University of Michigan, Center for Political Studies, National Election Study 1992.
41. *Meritor Savings Bank, FBD v. Vinson*, 477 U.S. 57 (1986).
42. *Harris v. Forklift Systems, Inc.*, 114 S.Ct. 367 (1993).
43. *Gideon v. Wainwright*, 372 U.S. 335 (1963); *Douglas v. California*, 372 U.S. 353 (1963).
44. *San Antonio Independent School District v. Rodriguez*, 411 U.S. 1 (1973).
45. *Harris v. McRae*, 448 U.S. 297 (1980).
46. *City of Cleburne, Texas v. Cleburne Living Center*, 473 U.S. 432 (1985).
47. "Public Views on Homosexuals in the Military," *New York Times*, January 27, 1993, p. A-8.
48. *Romer v. Evans*, 517 U.S. 620 (1996).
49. It should be noted that Executive Order 13087, issued by President Bill Clinton in May 1998, prohibited employment discrimination on the basis of sexual orientation by agencies within the executive branch of the federal government.
50. *Boy Scouts of America v. Dale*, 530 U.S. 640 (2000).
51. *Lawrence v. Texas*, 539 U.S 558, 578 (2003).
52. *Goodridge v. Department of Public Health*, 439 Mass. 665 (2003).
53. A *Boston Globe* poll, reported in that newspaper on February 12, 2004, indicated that 53 percent of Massachusetts' residents opposed gay marriage. However, 60 percent favored creation of "civil unions."
54. See James Dao, "Same-Sex Marriage Key to Some G.O.P. Races," *New York Times*, November 4, 2004, p. P4.

Public Opinion in American Politics

6

6-1 The Nature of Public Opinion

▶ **public opinion** The aggregation of individual opinions on issues of concern to the public.

▶ **pollsters** Professionals who conduct surveys aimed at measuring public opinion.

▶ **pundits** Knowledgeable political commentators in the mass media.

▶ **exit poll** A survey of voters exiting the voting place.

Public opinion is the aggregation of individual opinions on issues of concern to the public. Normally, people think of public opinion in the context of political issues, such as abortion, gay rights, or euthanasia. But anything that people think about or talk about or are interested in can become the stuff of public opinion. In a sense, public opinion is simply what **pollsters** measure through their surveys—whether it's people's approval or disapproval of the president's performance or their perceptions of what kind of person Elvis really was.[1]

Barely a day goes by that the American people are not presented with the results of a public opinion survey of some sort. The major television networks and newspapers often collaborate on national surveys (for example, CBS/*New York Times*, ABC/*Washington Post*, NBC/*Wall Street Journal,* and CNN/*USA Today*). Hundreds of other, smaller television stations and newspapers conduct their own polls from time to time. And, of course, thousands of surveys are performed each year by universities, public agencies, and research corporations. Survey research is now a major industry in this country. We, the people, are fascinated with what we, the people, think. Realizing the degree of this interest, the mass media provide us with a steady diet of polls and **pundits** explaining, analyzing, and interpreting polls. Thus, it was not at all surprising that immediately after the first Kerry–Bush presidential debate in 2004 the discussion quickly shifted from the debate itself to speculation regarding what the next polls would show.

Public opinion polls play a major role in political campaigns and elections. Potential candidates use these polls to "test the waters." Actual candidates use surveys to test messages, determine areas of support, and elicit voter concerns. The mass media use polls to track the public's preferences and perceptions and thereby enliven their coverage of campaigns. During a presidential campaign, television viewers and newspaper readers are treated to a steady diet of polling data. Media also use a particular species of survey, the **exit poll,** to "call" elections within minutes after the polls have closed and before all the returns have come in. Exit polls involve interviews with voters as they exit the voting place. Correctly done, this type of poll can provide an accurate assessment of who is winning the race before the votes are counted. However, in a close race, like the 2000 election, exit polls can be quite misleading (see the Controversy box, "The Use of Exit Polls to Call Elections" in section 6-4b).

In the 2000 election, elements of the mass media used exit polls in Florida to call the election for Vice President Gore. Unfortunately, the polling places had not yet closed in the Florida panhandle, which is located in the central time zone. Anecdotal evidence indicates that some people (nobody knows how many) were dissuaded from voting because they thought that the election was over in their state. As it tuned out, the race in Florida was much closer than the exit polls had predicted. Is it possible that George Bush might have received significantly more votes in Florida had the media not prematurely called the race for Gore? Certainly, many Bush partisans believed so.

Public opinion is critical in any time of national emergency, especially war. Most presidents have enjoyed strong levels of support at the initial stages of military conflict. George W. Bush's approval ratings soared to about 90 percent after the terrorist attacks of 9-11-2001, but declined dramatically in 2003. Americans usually rally around their president during wartime, unless the war bogs down with no successful conclusion in sight, a la Vietnam. The first President Bush enjoyed very high levels of support before, during, and immediately after the Gulf War in 1991, but saw his approval ratings slide following the war's successful conclusion, as Americans refocused on domestic issues. Presidential approval ratings are fluid and highly dependent on current events.

6-1a Public Opinion in a Democratic Society

Public opinion plays a special role in a democratic society because the essential democratic idea is that government should respond to the popular will. A democratic regime must be constantly aware of the demands and supports coming from the public. Yet even the most authoritarian of governments must be ever conscious of what its citizens think. A democracy exists to *respond* to the public, and an authoritarian system exists only if it can *control* opinion by limiting the spread of ideas that the regime considers dangerous or subversive. This control can be accomplished through some combination of **propaganda** and fear. Thus, any authoritarian system, whether it's the former Soviet Union or Fidel Castro's Cuba, pays a good bit of attention to public opinion. A democracy, on the other hand, is interested in responding to, rather than controlling, public opinion. That is not to say that leaders in democratic societies never engage in propaganda or fear mongering, for they certainly sometimes do. But that behavior is clearly at odds with the ideals of democracy.

> ▶ **propaganda** A government's promotion of its own policies or actions through the mass media.

6-1b Public Opinion and the U.S. Constitution

The Founders of the American republic realized the importance of public opinion. The campaign for the ratification of the Constitution was, in essence, a battle for public acceptance of a stronger central government. *The Federalist Papers* represented an effort to convince the public of the wisdom of the structures of federalism, separation of powers, and checks and balances. Yet the Founders also maintained a healthy fear of public opinion run amok. They foresaw dangers in the popular will, and the thought of government responding to transitory surges in public opinion led them to buffer majority wishes with governmental institutions designed to blunt popular passions.

The very constitutional structures that have come to be celebrated by the public were designed to temper the influence of transitory popular majorities on public policy while allowing policy to reflect a societal consensus. The Framers of the Constitution wanted to prevent government from acting under the pressures of fleeting popular passions, and they certainly wanted to protect the rights of individuals from what Alexis de Tocqueville called "the tyranny of the majority." The Founders probably never imagined that popular opinion could be gauged in any kind of systematic way or that the daily ebbs and flows of opinion would be of consequence to the system. Communication was so limited that only fundamental, lasting divisions in society could become issues among the mass citizenry.

Despite the intentions of the Founders, the American political system has become significantly more democratic over the more than two hundred years since America proclaimed its independence. The electoral franchise has been broadened to include all adults. Channels of political participation not envisioned (or desired) by the Founders have been opened up to the average citizen. Multiple sources of information (newspapers, magazines, radio, television and the Internet) have become available to the mass public. The expansion of channels of political participation and the proliferation of mass media have led to increased interest in public opinion, as candidates, journalists, and elected officials have all developed an urge to take the public's pulse. Whether attempting to predict election results or anticipating public support for a government initiative, analysts, journalists, and politicians now routinely seek the most current and accurate measure of public opinion. Public opinion has become a science as well as an industry, and shaping public opinion has become an art.

6-2 Public Opinion and American Political Culture

One way to think of public opinion in the United States, or in any liberal democracy, is as a marketplace of ideas. If American political institutions are functioning properly, by tempering majority rule with mechanisms to promote deliberation and protect minority rights, public discussion of issues should involve a free intellectual exchange. In the free marketplace, opinions compete for public acceptance. No opinion is automatically excluded from consideration merely because it is new, different, or unfamiliar. But, although this marketplace metaphor may be useful as an expression of the classical liberal ideas of tolerance and intellectual experimentation, it hardly describes the reality of American public opinion.

In the real world of public opinion, some opinions are taken much more seriously than others. The political culture of any society, by definition, places some limit on the range of alternatives that are subject to serious discussion. This situation is not the result of some sort of conspiracy. Rather, the degree to which human beings want to consider complex political alternatives is finite, limited by their experience. This statement does not mean that a political culture cannot evolve to make other alternatives legitimate; it just means that not every opinion or idea competes on a level playing field.

Contemporary public opinion in the United States must be understood in reference to fundamental shared American values. These values are a product of our history, religion, and geography. When Alexis de Tocqueville came to the United States in 1831, he was struck by Americans' efforts to reconcile two fundamental values—liberty and equality, which Europeans tended to view as being mutually exclusive. European societies were saddled with age-old divisions based on social class. The value of liberty usually applied only to the upper classes, who had resources and education and wanted to be free from government restraint. They tended to see equality as a threat to their liberty.

6-2a Individualism and Equality

The long journey to America and the subsequent movement westward greatly reduced the importance of social class as a meaningful concept of societal organization. Alexis de Tocqueville saw the "frontier" experience as crucial in the development of the values of individualism and social equality. Clearly, much of what is unique about American folklore and myth is related to the efforts of the pioneers who settled the continent and relied on family and friends to get through hard times. In the United States, individualism came to take on a meaning somewhat different from what it had meant in Europe. American individualism as a core value stresses self-reliance and individual responsibility. It seeks to minimize the role of the government, especially in matters related to private property. Every society differentiates what belongs in the public sphere from what belongs in the private sphere. Americans tend to stress the latter. For instance, few other societies seriously question the government's right to limit firearms. But many Americans are still convinced that they have a constitutional right to possess handguns with minimal government regulation. They have been successful at articulating and defending this perspective largely because of the core value structure that values the individual over the society.

Social equality is also a core American value. With rare exceptions, Americans have never had any use for royalty or titles of nobility. American popular culture—including music, magazines, movies, and TV shows—has always glorified the "common person" as opposed to the privileged. At the same time, this social equality has had meaning only within the multitude of groups accorded status within the society. Although the settlers had no use for the social stratification that served as a reminder of the European class system, they did not include African Americans among the constellation of groups whose members would be accorded social equality.

Individualism and self-reliance in the world of commerce have led to a commitment to capitalism as an economic system and an even stronger commitment to the institution of private property. In a capitalistic economic system, individual corporations rather than the government control the major means of production. Socialism, a system in which the government owns and operates major industries, has never had much appeal in the United States. Although Americans in the twenty-first century have come to accept a degree of government control of the economy, the basic structure of the American economy remains distinctly capitalist. The strong attachment to private property has led to many disputes over such issues as zoning, land-use planning, the regulation of signs, and the conservation of natural resources. Again, most Americans have come to accept the idea that government has a role to play in regulating the use of private property for the sake of the public interest. Still, whenever government proposes a specific project or policy that interferes with the private control of land, conflict is inevitable.

American individualism has led to a tenuous popular commitment to civil liberties. Yet particular claims of personal freedom are often more contentious than individualism in the abstract. To many people, individualism implies self-reliance, hard work, personal initiative, and responsibility. To others, personal freedom may involve behavior that is outside the social mainstream. The discussion of civil liberties in Chapter 4, "Civil Liberties and Individual Freedom," centered around the difficulty of protecting the expression of unpopular opinions in a majoritarian system. Nevertheless, most Americans remain committed to the ideals, if not always the application, of personal freedom.

6-2b Core Values: Elites and Masses

The American ambivalence toward personal freedom is a complex phenomenon that can best be understood in terms of elites and the masses. A **political elite** is a small group of individuals who have a greater amount of influence in a particular political arena than do those in the general population. Elites are usually, but not always, better educated and have higher incomes than their counterparts. Where there are elites, there are also masses. Masses are, by definition, much greater in number than elites. On any issue, the masses are those who do not possess any greater influence than others in a given area. For the most part, they are less educated and have lower incomes than those in the elite.

> **political elite** A small group of citizens who wield greater influence over politics than do average citizens.

In the United States, it is the educational elite who most seem to value the application of abstract notions of freedom of expression. This statement is not surprising considering the complexity of democratic institutions and the role of higher education in stressing tolerance, respect for differences, and the constitutional protections of individual rights. Evidence indicates that masses and elites are both committed in the abstract to the Bill of Rights. However, the more educated people in society tend to be much more supportive of the application of the Bill of Rights in particular situations. In a landmark study in 1964, Herbert McClosky found that although most Americans expressed support for the Bill of Rights, most of those who were less educated did not support its application to a number of situations, such as the right of a Communist to speak.[2] The political scientists Thomas Dye and Harmon Zeigler refer to the "irony of democracy"[3] as the fact that elites are more committed to democratic values than are the masses.[4]

6-3 The Opinions of Individuals

As you have seen, public opinion is the aggregation of what citizens think and feel about the people and policies associated with their government. These thoughts and feelings, which are conditioned by the society's core values, may or may not be expressed. To this point, we have treated public opinion from the perspective of the system as a whole. To understand how public opinion works in a system, however, we must first examine how individuals structure their thoughts and feelings about political objects.[5]

6-3a Values and Beliefs

People's opinions are built on their values, beliefs, and attitudes. **Political values** are basic sets of feelings about what ought to be and how people ought to behave. People hold a few basic values that form the foundation of other feelings and preferences about politics. An example of a political value is the fundamental "rightness" of equality.

> **political values** Basic sets of feelings about what ought to be and how people ought to behave.

Beliefs are less fundamental to individuals than their values. **Beliefs** can best be thought of as propositions about what is true or false. For example, some people believe that the death penalty deters crime; others do not. Although some people believe that private ownership of guns increases personal security, others believe that gun ownership is more likely to put a person in jeopardy. Most people now believe that smoking is detrimental to one's health. This widespread belief has developed as scientific evidence about the dangers of smoking has accumulated over the years.

> **beliefs** Ideas people hold about what is true or false.

Although science (including, supposedly, political science) is ideally based on a sharp distinction between what is true or false and what is right or wrong, the opinions of individuals in the real world are usually not based on a clear fact–value distinction. Indeed, beliefs about what is true or false are often based somewhat on values. For example, the extent to which people believe that "Democrats are better than Republicans for working people" depends on how they define better and worse, as well as on their assimilation of facts about Democratic and Republican behavior over the years.

Beliefs are more numerous than values, but they are still the basic building blocks of a person's opinion system. Whereas values may not be stated or realized by the individual, beliefs almost always are. Beliefs are not quite as enduring as values. Few people experience a fundamental shift in what they hold dear. Beliefs, on the other hand, may change with new information.

6-3b Attitudes and Opinions

▶ **attitudes**   More or less enduring orientations toward an object or situation and predispositions to respond positively or negatively toward that object or situation; attitudes are built on both values and beliefs.

Political attitudes are built on both values and beliefs. Political **attitudes** are "more or less enduring orientations toward an object or situation and predispositions to respond positively or negatively toward that object or situation."[6] That is, a person can have an attitude toward a particular minority group, toward the Republican party, or toward conservatives, for example. An attitude is a feeling that is not tied to a specific policy or situation. These types of feelings can stem from values and beliefs, but also from other nonpolitical areas of one's life. For instance, one's attitudes toward women's rights could stem from political values (for example, equality) and beliefs (for example, that women can do any job as well as men). However, a person's attitudes can also be affected by her experience with discrimination while attempting to establish a career.

▶ **affective response**   A response to the political world that is based on feelings.

Political attitudes are fundamentally different from values and beliefs. Attitudes represent an **affective response** to the political world. Affective reactions to politics are based on feelings. In contrast, beliefs represent a more **cognitive response** to politics. Cognitions are reactions based on one's logical processes. They represent the more rational way of thinking as opposed to the emotional. In reality, these distinctions are not always precise, and most individuals employ both affective and cognitive dimensions in coming to grips with the political world. In 1922, Walter Lippmann wrote about the interplay of cognitive and affective processes in the formation of opinions. In Lippmann's view, an individual's opinions "almost always consist of an intricate series of facts, as he has observed them, surrounded by a large, fatty mass of stereotyped phrases charged with his emotions."[7]

▶ **cognitive response**   A response to the political world that is based more on thought than on emotion.

▶ **opinions**   People's preferences or judgments about public issues and candidates.

Opinions are people's preferences and judgments about public issues and political candidates. One's opinions tend to be mixtures of thoughts and feelings toward persons and policies. They may directly reflect values, beliefs, and attitudes. People's fundamental religious values may be directly reflected in their opinions. For instance, opponents of legalized abortion often rely on and refer to religious precepts and symbols. But many pro-life advocates also state beliefs about the beginning of human life, which may or may not have a basis in a particular religious creed. Another person might express the belief that human life does not begin at conception in arriving at a pro-choice position. That person might also hold a negative attitude toward government involvement in people's private lives. These types of values, beliefs, and attitudes, taken in the aggregate throughout society, make up the contours of public opinion on the issue of abortion.

Individuals and groups of individuals who make up the multitude of publics in America create the base that gives rise to demands for government action. This base is continually changing, but the change is slowed by the relative stability of basic values. The nature of demands is complicated by the fuzzy boundaries that separate political attitudes from attitudes formed in nonpolitical areas of people's lives.

6-3c Ideology

Most people hold beliefs, opinions, and attitudes on a wide variety of issues and about a large number of political personalities. When someone's beliefs, attitudes, and opinions are organized into a coherent logical structure, we say that this person possesses an ideology. Political culture refers to the values, expectations, and ideas that are broadly shared in society. Ideology, on the other hand, refers to those ideas, or systems of ideas, that are in conflict in society. Moreover, ideology involves an agenda for action—a set of prescriptions for public policy making. Not everyone employs an ideology. Indeed, evidence indicates that

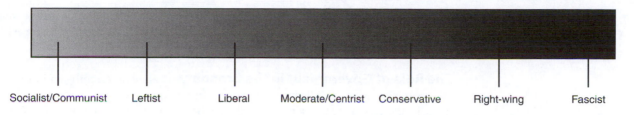

| Socialist/Communist | Leftist | Liberal | Moderate/Centrist | Conservative | Right-wing | Fascist |

Figure 6-1
The Liberal-Conservative Continuum

most people's beliefs, attitudes, and opinions are not highly constrained to any kind of logical order.[8] To the degree that individuals' beliefs have discernible patterns, however, they display some evidence of ideological thinking.

The Liberal-Conservative Continuum   The most common way of conceptualizing ideological differences is the one-dimensional liberal-conservative scale (see Figure 6-1). The continuum ranges from the radical label on the "far left" to the reactionary label on the "far right." Those in the middle are called *moderates* or *centrists*. The more familiar terms *liberal* and *conservative* apply to those whose ideologies are left and right of center, respectively.

Radicals believe that the established order is fundamentally corrupt or unjust. They would like to see an altogether new political and economic system, brought about by a revolution if necessary. Reactionaries are equally unhappy with the status quo, but they would like to return to some imagined golden age, or at least to a time when things were better for them or people like them. Both radicals and reactionaries tend to be impatient with or frustrated by the dominant political dialogue and with conventional forms of political participation. They often find ideological companionship by associating themselves with a fringe political group or even a religious cult. Not surprisingly, they find themselves "outside the conversation" on most issues, furthering their sense of isolation and lessening their identification with the political system.

The political dialogue in America is fairly moderate. Not many influential groups or spokespersons are on the far left or far right. Those that do exist seldom have access to the mass media to state their positions. However, the Internet has proven to be a perfect medium for dialogue among those on the fringes of the political system. However geographically isolated people may find themselves, most now have access to a computer and the Internet. The ability of people with minimal financial resources to communicate and organize over a wide geographic area gives just about any group, no matter how small, the opportunity to communicate, not only with each other but also with potential converts to their cause.

The liberal-conservative continuum has the advantages of simplicity and widespread familiarity. Not only political scientists but also commentators in the media and everyday citizens routinely use the terms *liberal* and *conservative* in describing people's views on issues. And, when surveyed, most people are able to place themselves on the spectrum. But what do liberal and conservative mean? These terms have been with us since their origin in the political philosophy of the late eighteenth and early nineteenth centuries. But so many

WEB EXERCISE

How do you view your political position? Where do you put yourself on the liberal-conservative scale? If you're not sure or are curious about how others might define you based on your views, go to http://www.studentcenter.org/tests/politicaltest.php and take the political self-test. Pay attention to the way the questions are worded: Did the way the questions were asked influence your answers? Did you receive the result you expected? Try taking the test again, changing your answers to aim for a specific classification. What does this test tell you about the criteria for being considered part of a particular political group? What does it tell you about political polling overall?

different varieties of liberalism and conservatism exist, and their public policy connotations have changed so much over the past two centuries, that defining them with any degree of precision is difficult.

The Role of Government in the Economy

In late nineteenth- and early twentieth-century America, the liberal-conservative debate centered around the role of government in the economy. Conservatives strongly defended the doctrine of *laissez-faire,* even though pure market capitalism had never really existed in this country. Liberals argued that in order to survive, capitalism had to evolve to permit the formation of labor unions, the creation of public welfare programs, and the government regulation of key industries. Conservatives accused liberals of embracing socialism; liberals chided conservatives for their insensitivity to the plight of workers and the poor. This debate was largely resolved by widespread popular acceptance of the New Deal and the welfare state created in the aftermath of the Great Depression. Although liberals and conservatives still argue about government's proper role in the economy, that debate is not now the principal component of liberal-conservative conflict.

Foreign Policy and Military Issues

Historically, foreign policy has been another important dimension of the liberal-conservative debate. After World War II, America's primary adversary became the Soviet Union and its communist allies. The United States established a policy of stopping the spread of Communism, by military force if necessary. In the early 1960s, this policy brought America into the ill-fated Vietnam War. Liberals and conservatives were divided over the war. Liberals, often called doves in the foreign policy context, argued first for limited involvement and later for withdrawal of our forces. Conservatives, or hawks, argued for a total commitment to win a clear military victory. Liberals and conservatives also divided over the issue of the growing antiwar movement. Liberals argued for tolerance of dissent and in many cases applauded the tactics of the protesters. Conservatives were outraged by what they perceived to be assaults on both patriotism and law and order.

In the 1970s and early 1980s, liberals and conservatives continued to argue about America's posture toward the Soviets and Communism in general. The specific issues were many and varied: the nuclear arms race; aid to anticommunist military dictatorships in Latin America; aid to rebels fighting Marxist governments in Nicaragua and Angola; and military intervention in Grenada, for example. Conservatives argued that the United States should continue building its military capabilities and confront Soviet expansionism and Communist insurgency wherever they threatened American interests. Liberals countered that America was investing too much in weapons and not enough in education, social programs, and environmental protection. The end of the cold war and the demise of the Soviet Union muted this aspect of the liberal-conservative debate, at least for a time. During the 1990s, liberals argued for swifter and deeper reductions in military spending; conservatives insisted that it was "still a dangerous world out there." The terrorist attacks of 9-11-2001 seemed to vindicate the conservative position. However, liberal voices were raised in objection to President George W. Bush's decision to invade Iraq and topple Saddam Hussein in the spring of 2003. Liberals decried the President's alleged deception of the American people in the run-up to the war as well as Bush's alleged violation of international law and contempt for international institutions. During 2003 and 2004, and most notably prior to the presidential election of 2004, the American left vehemently protested America's military campaign in Iraq and, at times, sounded downright dovish.

Pacifists object to war under any circumstances and stress the need for diplomatic resolution of all international conflicts. Post-modern American liberalism is characterized to a great extent by pacifism, although not all self-identified liberals would consider themselves pacifists. Certainly liberals are much more likely to embrace pacifism than are conservatives, who tend to believe that some disputes can only be resolved by force and that America is justified in using force against those who mean to do this country harm.

Civil Rights   Another historic element of the liberal-conservative debate has been civil rights. In the 1950s and 1960s, many conservatives opposed efforts to end segregated schools and other types of discrimination against blacks. Other, more moderate conservatives argued that although these types of practices were wrong, reform had to move at a pace slow enough for the American people to adapt. Liberals, on the other hand, championed the civil rights claims of African Americans and, later, of women, the poor, people with disabilities, and gays and lesbians. One major argument between liberals and conservatives is over affirmative action programs to aid minorities. Liberals argue that these types of programs are needed to remedy present and past discrimination. Conservatives tend to see affirmative action programs as unjustifiable "reverse discrimination."

Crime and Criminal Justice   Crime and criminal justice have been another point of division between liberalism and conservatism. Conservatives firmly believe in law and order. They believe that criminals should be punished harshly to drive home the message that society disapproves of their behavior. Finding conservatives who oppose capital punishment is difficult. Moreover, conservatives are highly critical of legal rules that hamper police and prosecutors in ferreting out crime and punishing criminals. The exclusionary rules that forbid the fruits of illegal searches and improperly obtained confessions from being used as evidence have been frequent targets of conservative ire. Liberals, on the other hand, as champions of the underdog, have tended to portray criminals as victims of an unequal and unjust society. They have called for the rehabilitation of criminals rather than harsh punishment. Liberals have tended to oppose the death penalty as barbaric and as racist in its application. As advocates of individual rights, they have looked to courts of law to maintain strict constraints on law enforcement. The mass public has tended to favor the conservative perspective on criminal justice. As crime rates rose in the 1970s and early 1980s, the public became impatient with the criminal justice system, which many regarded as excessively hampered by rules created by liberal judges. Consequently, many liberals backed away from their traditional positions on crime and punishment. This situation was certainly evident in 1994, when many liberal Democrats running for Congress ran TV ads stressing law-and-order themes. A number of liberals in Congress made a big show of their support for President Clinton's crime bill, which passed Congress in August 1994. The idea behind this legislation was to take the crime issue away from conservatives and Republicans.

Traditional Values and Institutions   To a great extent, the contemporary liberal-conservative debate is over the legitimacy of traditional values and institutions. In what they sometimes characterize as a cultural war, conservatives find themselves defending monogamy, traditional marriage, the nuclear family, and heterosexuality against what they perceive as a rising tide of barbarism. Liberals counter that they are not attacking these institutions per se, but rather an orthodoxy that denies the legitimacy of alternative lifestyles. In the liberal mind, such choices are to be made freely by individuals, not imposed by society.

The ground is continually shifting beneath this "cultural war." By the year 2000, voters in Vermont were embroiled in a controversy regarding the state's recognition of civil unions between same-sex partners. Churches were considering whether to ordain openly gay ministers and bishops. Gay and lesbian couples were having greater success in adopting children. In 2003, the Supreme Court held that private, consensual homosexual activity is protected by the Constitution.[9] By 2004, many states were considering whether to legalize gay marriage, and some conservative leaders pushed for an amendment to the U.S. Constitution to defend traditional marriage. The context will shift from time to time, as issues come to the fore and are resolved, but the underlying attitudes remain the same.

Ideology and Public Policy   Most public arguments about issues, from abortion to the role of women in society, have fairly well-recognized liberal and conservative positions. Box 6-1 compares the attitudes of liberals, moderates, and conservatives in the year 2000

Box 6-1	Issue Positions by Ideological Self-Identification, 2000

Abortion. "Which of the following best reflects how you feel about when abortion should be permitted?"

	Liberals	Moderates	Conservatives	All
By law, abortion should never be permitted.	7%	3%	13%	12%
The law should permit abortion only in case of rape, incest, or when the woman's life is in danger.	18%	30%	39%	31%
The law should permit abortion for reasons other than rape, incest, or danger to the woman's life, but only after the need for the abortion has been clearly established.	16%	24%	16%	15%
By law, a woman should always be able to obtain an abortion as a matter of personal choice.	58%	42%	29%	39%
Don't know; Other response.	1%	1%	3%	3%

Racial Discrimination in Employment. "Some people feel that if black people are not getting fair treatment in jobs, the government in Washington ought to see to it that they do. Others feel that this is not the federal government's business.... How do you feel?"

	Liberals	Moderates	Conservatives	All
Federal government should see to fair treatment	46%	37%	27%	35%
Not the federal government's business	20%	28%	42%	28%
Don't know; No interest in issue	34%	35%	32%	36%

The Role of Women in Society. "Some people feel that women should have an equal role with men in running business, industry and government. Others feel that women's place is in the home. Where would you place yourself on this scale or haven't you thought much about this?"

	Liberals	Moderates	Conservatives	All
Equal role for women	92%	84%	72%	78%
Women's place is in the home	4%	8%	13%	9%
Don't know	4%	8%	15%	13%

Source: Adapted from 2000 National Election Study, Center for Political Studies, University of Michigan, *http://www.umich.edu/~nes/*.

on abortion, employment discrimination, and the role of women in society. The tables show significant differences between self-identified liberals and conservatives on all three issues. On abortion, liberals are twice as likely (58 percent versus 29 percent) to believe that "a woman should always be able to obtain an abortion as a matter of personal choice." On the issue of employment discrimination, liberals are much more likely than conservatives (46 percent compared to 27 percent) to agree that the federal government should see to it that African Americans are treated fairly in matters of employment. And on the role of women, conservatives are three times more likely than liberals (13 percent to 4 percent) to say that "a woman's place is in the home."

In general, liberals tend to favor government spending (other than military spending) more than do conservatives. However, a difference in degree exists, with a good deal of consensus that spending on poor people should not be cut back. On the other hand, more pronounced differences become obvious when the subject is abortion, as indicated in Box 6-1. Liberals are much more likely to feel that the decision regarding abortion should be a personal choice. These questions represent the two dimensions of the liberal-conservative basis of ideology. Liberals are more likely to favor a more active government in dealing with economic disparities, but are less likely to favor government involvement in personal decisions.

People who identify themselves as liberal or conservative do not necessarily take consistently liberal or conservative positions on issues. There is no doubt that many people are

Social Issues

Figure 6-2
Fourfold Ideology Typology

Source: Adapted from William Maddox and Stuart A. Lilie, *Beyond Liberal and Conservative* (Washington, D.C.: Cato Institute, 1984).

confused about the labels and may identify themselves incorrectly in a survey. But many others simply don't fit neatly into a liberal-conservative dichotomy. A simple illustration suffices to explain why. A devout Roman Catholic may oppose legalized abortion and the death penalty on the grounds that both involve an immoral taking of human life. In her mind, the two positions are logically consistent, yet one of the positions (opposition to abortion) is conventionally seen as a conservative viewpoint, and the other (opposing the death penalty) is usually defined as a liberal perspective. The woman is not confused about her positions, but may be uncertain about which label, liberal or conservative, best applies to her. To answer the question, you would need to know where she stands on a whole range of issues. Of course, even after obtaining that information, she may not fit into the standard liberal-conservative framework. That would not, in itself, mean that she doesn't have an ideology, however.

Issues often become framed in different ways over time, and liberal and conservative positions become reversed on what would appear to be the same issue. A good example is the issue of American support for Israel. Although both parties have been strong supporters of the Jewish state, persistent strains of opposition to this support arose among many more conservative voters, especially those in the rural South. However, with President Bush's strong support of Israel during and following the suicide bombings of 2002, the strongest support for Israel came from traditionally conservative writers, and many liberals expressed a great deal more sympathy for the Palestinians. Moreover, Southern Protestants were the segment of the American electorate expressing the most support for the Israeli cause.

The invasion of Iraq in 2003 likewise confounded the usual ideological divisions. Most liberals were uneasy at best about the conflict and its conduct and were critical of the Bush administration's approach. The war revealed some divisions among conservatives, some of whom attributed the administration's policy to "neoconservatives" in the administration. Some traditional conservatives, like Rep. John Duncan (R-Tennessee), even voted against the resolution authorizing President Bush to go to war in Iraq.

A More Complex Model of Ideological Variance   A number of political scientists have argued that the liberal-conservative spectrum is inadequate because it fails to differentiate between social and economic issues. In an important 1984 book, William Maddox and Stuart Lilie argued that the liberal-conservative dichotomy should be replaced by a fourfold typology.[10] In this model, individuals are placed in one of four cells based on their attitudes to social and economic issues (see Figure 6-2). One who is liberal on social issues (abortion, affirmative action, gay rights, and the like) but conservative on economic issues (taxation, welfare programs, and regulation of business, for example) is classified as a **libertarian.** One who is conservative on social issues but liberal on economic issues is called a **populist.**

Libertarians believe in minimal government interference into the affairs of individuals. In their view, individuals ought to be free to pursue their own interests and act on their own moral judgments. Thus, libertarians espouse laissez-faire capitalism and oppose government efforts to regulate business. At the same time, libertarians are strong defenders of civil liberties, especially freedom of expression and the right of privacy.

Populism is not as easy to define. Populists believe that government should act to promote the welfare of the community as determined by majority rule. They are generally

libertarian   A person who is liberal on social issues but conservative on economic issues.

populist   A person who is conservative on social issues but liberal on economic issues.

receptive to government efforts to create jobs, protect domestic workers, and redistribute wealth from the rich to the rest of society. Populists historically have been rather unsympathetic to the rights of minority groups or individuals who appear to be "different."

The fourfold typology is useful to political scientists as an analytic device, but it has yet to catch on among the press or the public. One reason is that we have a two-party system in this country, for reasons we make clear in Chapter 8, "Political Parties." Although individuals within the parties vary ideologically, basically the Democrats tend to be liberals and the Republicans tend to be conservatives. No Populist party exists, and the Libertarian party, although viable, exists on the fringe. The terms *liberal* and *conservative* are for most purposes adequate to describe the distribution of ideological orientations in a political system dominated by two parties. For now, the liberal-conservative spectrum remains the primary means by which Americans discuss their ideological differences.

6-3d Political Socialization

Political socialization is the process by which people learn about their political world. Through this process, individuals develop patterns of attitudes and beliefs, which help shape the way they view the political world. Through political socialization, important facts, values, and processes of decision making are transmitted to new generations of Americans. Most political socialization occurs before adulthood. By the time people complete their education, they have probably acquired a **party identification,** meaning that they identify with a political party or consider themselves independents. They may have formed a conscious ideological orientation, a set of attitudes about various groups and issues, and a basic orientation toward authority. Moreover, by the time they reach adulthood, most people have developed their sense of commitment to community and likelihood of participating in politics.

> **party identification** The sense of belonging to a particular political party.

Political socialization explains much of the diversity that is fascinating about American politics. The incredible variation of opinion, belief, attitude, and participation is in large part a reflection of the myriad ways in which we all come to experience the political world. Of course, people's learning about politics is closely related to their social class, religion, and ethnicity. Each of these factors has its own effect on opinions and conditions the ways in which people are socialized. This conditioning effect can be seen in the ways the primary agents of political socialization operate: the family, the school, and one's peer groups.

Family The family plays the most important role in transmitting political values and orientations across generations. One way that parents teach children about politics is through explicit reference to and identification with various groups. No object of political orientation is more crucial to the political system than the political party. Children tend to take on the political party identification of their parents. Partisanship is learned in much the same way as religion is: Children soon learn that "we are" Catholic, Baptist, Methodist, Jewish, Muslim, or some other faith. On the other hand, some children may not hear anything about religion, and others hear only negative references about various religious groups. These messages help the child form a religious orientation that will likely last a lifetime. In the same way, many children hear that "we are" Democrats, Republicans, or Independents. In a sense, party identification is something like an attachment to a sports team. A child in New York City may grow up liking the Yankees and hating the Mets (or vice versa). This affinity may be inherited from the parents or perhaps from an older sibling. The attachment is never really pondered; that's just the way it is.

The family transmits values in both affective and cognitive ways. The specific information a child hears about political parties usually forms the base for later cognitive thinking. Thoughts such as "Democrats are good for the working person" and "Republicans are better in foreign affairs" may be somewhat simplistic, but they provide a *cognitive* basis for receiving and processing political information. Likewise, the child may hear statements about a political party, such as "They do not like people like us, and I can't stand them." These statements can make up the foundation for later *affective* reactions to politics.

The family communicates cognitive and affective information about liberals and conservatives in much the same ways as it transmits party affiliation. Although ideological identification is certainly a less enduring orientation than is party identification, with the decline in the importance of party labels, ideological labels have taken on added significance. Although children typically do not think of themselves as liberals or conservatives, they tend to hear more about these terms as they become teenagers.

Children learn from their families much more than affective and cognitive orientations toward various political individuals and groups. In many ways, their broader personal socialization can have an indirect effect on their later political opinions. A child's first experience with authority is with her parent or parents. Children are taught either to obey authority figures without question or perhaps to question and challenge any attempt at discipline. Societies vary greatly in the way authority is treated in the family. To some degree, societal patterns of child rearing explain different societies' attitudes toward government authority. The tradition of unquestioning obedience to authority figures in German families is one explanation for the widespread acceptance of Hitler's policies during the Holocaust period in Nazi Germany.[11] Attitudes learned in childhood toward authority can have an effect on later attitudes and beliefs toward civil liberties and proper police conduct. The lack of a relationship with one's father can apparently also lead to a low sense of **political efficacy,** the feeling that one can make a difference in politics.[12]

> **political efficacy**   The feeling that one can make a difference in politics.

Children first learn about politics through their perception of key personalities. At an early age, they become aware of—and usually have positive feelings toward—the president. This early view then evolves to one that mirrors the parents' position, with children of Democrats becoming somewhat critical of Republican presidents, and Republican children likewise being critical of Democratic presidents. Children growing up in homes without political dialogue miss much of this early adjustment. To some degree, the parents in these apolitical homes tend to have lower levels of income and education, and the father tends to be absent. Thus, the role of the family cannot be viewed in isolation from the effect of social class.

Considerable evidence indicates that lower-class families socialize their children differently than do middle- and upper-class families. The eminent political sociologist Seymour Martin Lipset has observed that the typical lower-class individual "is likely to have been exposed to punishment, lack of love, and a general atmosphere of tension and aggression since early childhood."[13] In Lipset's view, these experiences tend to foster, among other things, racial prejudice and political authoritarianism. Political scientists Thomas Dye and Harmon Zeigler have written that "[t]he circumstances of lower-class life . . . make commitment to democratic ideas very difficult."[14] One must remember, however, that these are only generalizations. Not all lower-class families share these characteristics, and not every citizen of lower-class origins develops antidemocratic attitudes. Nor are middle- and upper-class families devoid of racial prejudice and authoritarian inclinations.

School   Although parents play the primary role in transmitting party identification and attitudes toward authority, the school is responsible for teaching the rules and rituals of democracy and the specifics of the American political system. At first, much of the teaching is affective. Students learn the myths of the American Revolution and Civil War, developing positive attitudes toward individuals such as George Washington and Abraham Lincoln. Their earliest exposure to the symbols of American democracy may be through the pledge of allegiance to the flag.

For many children, the teacher is the first real authority figure outside the home. She may provide the first real discipline that many children have ever experienced. The teacher can therefore have a profound effect on learning, both directly, through teaching the symbols of nationhood, and indirectly, in her role as an authority figure. Depending on the nature of the class and the teaching style employed, children can develop different views of authority. At one time, schoolchildren in lower-income areas were likely to be taught a more structured obedience to authority, and middle-class children were encouraged to question and challenge authority figures. All schools are now experiencing great difficulty in teaching respect for authority. To some degree, this situation represents a change in educational philosophy. But this difficulty also reflects the more fundamental breakdown of authority in society. Schools can reinforce, at most, only what is transmitted through the family and the broader culture. They cannot, in and of themselves, teach values that are not being taught in the home or that are being contradicted in the popular culture.

In middle or junior high school, children learn about democratic institutions, through both classroom instruction in American history and repeated exposure to elections. Students there learn the basic institutions of American politics. In addition, virtually all classrooms and schools regularly hold elections to various posts. In high school, most students become comfortable with voting machines, with many holding mock elections corresponding to those held among their adult counterparts.

Many students who attend college take political science courses, which are required for graduation in a number of state college and university systems. In these courses, students learn fundamental notions of tolerance and acquire skills for evaluating various public policy alternatives. Moreover, college usually exposes students to a wide variety of ideas and cultures. This exposure is important in developing tolerance for diversity, which is not only imperative in contemporary pluralistic America but also essential for amassing intellectual capital to invest in one's later political life.

Peer Groups   The groups with whom individuals associate provide the third major agent of socialization in American politics. Although the family and the school have had their major effect by the time a child reaches adulthood, peer groups continue to affect political attitudes and opinions well into adulthood. Those who were raised in Democratic families, but work in groups that are largely Republican, such as investment bankers, are likely to change to become more like the groups they join. Likewise, children of Republicans who end up working in Democrat-dominated professions, such as the news media, are also likely to switch their partisan allegiance.

> **cognitive dissonance**   The psychological discomfort a person feels in trying to process contradictory feelings or thoughts.

Peer groups have a major influence on political attitudes for a number of reasons. First, people generally strive to reduce **cognitive dissonance,** which is the psychological discomfort, or dissonance, a person feels when trying to process contradictory feelings or thoughts.[15] Most people naturally come to terms with contradictory information by eliminating a source of confusion or discomfort. For instance, a young woman who was raised in a Democratic family but now works for a heavily Republican company would find it easier to change her party orientation than her career. Even the change from a Democrat to an Independent would lessen the stress she feels when involved in discussions with colleagues. That statement does not mean that she would not have firm convictions. A person's values and beliefs about the world evolve based on his own experiences and the viewpoints he develops.

6-3e The Effect of Other Socioeconomic Factors

Individuals vary greatly in their attitudes, opinions, beliefs, and values. To a great degree, the process of political socialization explains these differences. Though the agents of socialization are not particularly numerous, their effect varies depending on the situation. It is never possible to explain completely all the variation in political attitudes and opinions. Just knowing that Megan was raised by Republican parents, attended a good college, and now works at a public relations firm making $75,000 a year does not allow us to predict her attitudes or opinions with a high degree of certainty. The best an analyst can do is discern tendencies among different groups.

Social Class   Working-class families and schools in northern industrial cities socialize children differently than do upper-income families and schools in California suburbs. But social class has its own effect on attitudes apart from the socialization process. People of lower income and education make different demands on government. Those who are unemployed or employed in low-paying jobs are likely to place little value on the concept of minimal government. They likely look to government to create jobs and provide social services. On the other hand, those in the most educated social class are much more likely to support civil liberties and government funding for the humanities. Of course, lower-income and less-educated people tend not to participate in politics as frequently as people of higher income and more education. Their demands on the system are therefore likely to have less effect.

Religion   Religious affiliation can have a major effect on particular values and beliefs. A fundamentalist Christian in the rural South may feel that his religion implies values that lead him to demand that the local school board eliminate its sex-education program. Catholics traditionally opposed birth control and abortion, although American Catholics are now moving away from the church's official position on these issues. Many of the more mainline Protestant denominations have taken rather liberal stands on some social issues. In this area, some variance has occurred between the elites and the masses. The leaders of religious organizations of Methodists, Presbyterians, Lutherans, and Episcopalians have held more activist positions on many social issues than the membership as a whole.

Religion has always played a major part in shaping political values in America. Many people explicitly ground their political values in religious values; others make a point of keeping the two separate. Organized churches have often inspired their members to live in a way consistent with their teachings. At other times, churches have remained silent, preferring to concentrate on the private lives of members rather than take stands on public issues. Churches have had a major effect on both the nature and the expression of opinion. Black clergy played a major role in the civil rights movement, and they are still the most trusted leaders among African Americans.[16] In the 1980s, fundamentalist Protestants mobilized, often at the urging of ministers, to fight legalized abortion, gay rights, feminism, and other manifestations of secular humanism. Certainly, the power of religious leaders to inspire movements is indisputable, as is the practical value that a network of churches provides to a mass movement. Nevertheless, the tremendous variety of denominations and creeds in the United States makes the relationship between religion and political values a complex one. People of sincere religious feelings can be found on all sides of any given public issue.

Region   For the greater part of this country's existence, a person's region provided the best clues to her political attitudes. The unique history of the South, especially in regard to slavery and connected economic issues, meant that many national issues were viewed in terms of their effect on the region. Into the latter half of the twentieth century, Southerners were especially conscious of their regional identity, which, in many cases, had as much effect on their political opinions as social class and education did. Regional identity was especially pronounced during the civil rights movement of the 1960s.

Many issues have taken on a regional slant, and individuals often view policies in terms of the effect on their region. For instance, energy policies have different effects on oil-producing states in the Southwest than on oil-consuming states in the Northeast. Likewise, western states have a particular interest in water policy. Despite these lingering regional interests, the United States has become less a society of pronounced regional differences and more a society of different groups that cut across regions. The reason for this situation is quite simple: Technological advances have made this country so interconnected that communication is instantaneous and travel is forgiving of great distance. The nationalization of television has made regional isolation less and less a factor in shaping opinion. Public opinion and the underlying political culture have become much more homogeneous throughout the country.

Age   If region has lost much of its political clout, age seems to have taken on increased importance as a reference for public opinion formation. This factor parallels the rise in the proportion of the population that is over age sixty-five. Every generation of Americans has a distinct political history marked by certain **defining events.** Many younger adults do not fully appreciate the impact of the Great Depression or World War II on the attitudes of the

▶ **defining events**   Major events that shape and define one's response to the political world.

oldest Americans. Older Americans may not fully appreciate the impact of Vietnam or the civil rights movement on the baby boomers. The Great Depression likely made an entire generation of Americans more supportive of government programs designed to ensure old-age income security. The Vietnam War led a later generation to question authority, especially when the issue arises of committing American troops to conflicts overseas. Perhaps the events of September 11, 2001, will have their own effect on another generation. This effect could be manifested in a number of ways, including a greater likelihood of turning to government institutions as problem solvers or using pressure to limit immigration.

On the other hand, some evidence exists that all generations experience similar changes in attitudes as they age. As people acquire property, have children, and pay more taxes, they tend to become more conservative. Property owners and taxpayers feel that they have a greater stake in the system and tend to be suspicious of proposals for major economic change, especially if they think that it will cost them money. Parents tend to be protective of their children and, consequently, become more concerned about crime, violence, drugs, promiscuity, and other social problems that may threaten their children's well-being. Baby boomers who experimented with drugs and held negative attitudes toward the police in the 1960s and 1970s may find themselves sounding like their parents as they attempt to raise their own families. As a result, both generational and aging effects have an effect on the formation of political attitudes.

Race   In many ways, race has become the dominant factor in the formation of political attitudes and opinions. Although this statement is true among all groups, it is especially true for minority groups. African Americans are much more likely than whites to self-identify as liberals and Democrats. They are more likely to adopt liberal positions on civil rights and liberties issues, social welfare issues, and the rights of workers. They are much more likely to see government in positive terms—as a force for good in society rather than a nuisance. Yet, when it comes to social issues, such as abortion, gay rights, and the role of women, African Americans tend to be somewhat more conservative than whites. Box 6-2 compares attitudes across racial lines on three public issues in the year 2000. As suggested, African Americans are somewhat more conservative than whites on the issues of abortion and the role of women. But they are more than twice as likely as whites to believe that the federal government should see to fair treatment in matters of employment.

Gender   Although the United States has had a history of women's political activism since the nineteenth century, few issues were defined as women's issues before the women's movement of the late twentieth century. Today, differences in attitudes between men and women have led to something of a **gender gap** in voting, especially in presidential elections. In recent elections women have tended to be more supportive of Democrats; men have tended to favor Republicans. Box 6-2 compares attitudes across gender categories on three public issues in the year 2000. Interestingly, men and women do not differ all that much on the question of abortion. Not surprisingly, women are more likely than men to favor an equal role for women in society, but it is important to note than the great majority of men also take this position.

▶ **gender gap**   Differences in political attitudes and behavior between men and women.

Marital Status   As suggested earlier in section 6-3e, evidence indicates that married people with children are significantly more conservative than others in society. This group is potentially powerful on a whole range of social and economic issues, especially those that can be subsumed under the umbrella of family values. In the 1992 election, the Republicans tried to exploit their advantage on these types of issues to the married-with-children group. Most observers, however, thought that the Republicans failed to present a coherent appeal to this group while managing to alienate many women and single parents.

Box 6-2	Issue Positions by Sex and Race, 2000

Abortion. "Which of the following best reflects how you feel about when abortion should be permitted?"

	Males	Females	Whites	Blacks	All
By law, abortion should never be permitted.	10%	14%	11%	25%	12%
The law should permit abortion only in case of rape, incest, or when the woman's life is in danger.	32%	30%	31%	31%	31%
The law should permit abortion for reasons other than rape, incest, or danger to the woman's life, but only after the need for the abortion has been clearly established.	16%	15%	16%	10%	15%
By law, a woman should always be able to obtain an abortion as a matter of personal choice.	39%	40%	40%	32%	39%
Don't know; Other response.	3%	1%	2%	2%	3%

Racial Discrimination in Employment. "Some people feel that if black people are not getting fair treatment in jobs, the government in Washington ought to see to it that they do. Others feel that this is not the federal government's business.... How do you feel?"

	Males	Females	Whites	Blacks	All
Federal government should see to fair treatment	38%	33%	30%	64%	35%
Not the federal government's business	30%	28%	33%	6%	28%
Don't know; No interest in issue	32%	40%	37%	30%	36%

The Role of Women in Society. "Some people feel that women should have an equal role with men in running business, industry and government. Others feel that women's place is in the home. Where would you place yourself on this scale or haven't you thought much about this?"

	Males	Females	Whites	Blacks	All
Equal role for women	72%	81%	76%	67%	78%
Women's place is in the home	11%	9%	9%	19%	9%
Don't know	17%	10%	15%	14%	13%

Source: Adapted from 2000 National Election Study, Center for Political Studies, University of Michigan, *http://www.umich.edu/~nes/*.

6-3f Opinion Dysfunction

Any system of representative democracy is designed to process demands for government action. One gauge of the health of a political system is the degree to which its citizens believe what government officials say. Another is whether citizens trust that the system is in fact what it purports to be: Is a Communist system truly the "vanguard of the workers" that its leaders claim? Or is the American system as representative of the wishes of the majority and protective of the rights of the minority as our national and state leaders assert? If individuals do not trust their government or have little faith in the integrity of their system, they will fail to provide the level of support necessary to maintain its institutions over succeeding generations.

Alienation   A lack of trust in government can be both a cause and, to some degree, a product of political alienation. **Political alienation** is a feeling of distance from and hostility toward the political process. More than mere dislike of a particular political leader or policy, it is a deep-seated negative feeling about the entire political process. Although one can be actively alienated and freely express these types of feelings, alienation can exist without explicit realization or expression. Every society has some politically alienated individuals. Some people are generally alienated from all social institutions and would probably

> **political alienation** A feeling of distance from and deep-seated hostility toward the political process.

Popular Culture and American Politics
Saved

By Chapman Rackaway

Religion is well established as a central part of many people's lives, and it can even affect voting decisions. Contemporary popular culture tends not to look at religious faith favorably, and that often comes through in movies. In 2004, *Saved* joined the list of movies that skewer high school life but added a new twist by focusing on students who attend a Christian school. *Saved* follows a group of students who display various stages of struggle with their own religious beliefs. Mary (played by Jena Malone) sacrifices her virginity to her boyfriend, believing that God has told her it is the only way to keep him from becoming gay. Later she is stunned to discover that she's become pregnant. Former child actor Macaulay Culkin returns to acting as the wheelchair-bound Roland, who helps Mary adjust to her life and examine the conflicting feelings her pregnancy and faith give her. Mary also befriends the school's only Jewish student, Cassandra. Mary tries to hide her pregnancy from her social group, including the proselytizing Hilary Faye (played by singer Mandy Moore), but Hilary finds out, and Mary must reconcile her faith with the personal and social pressures she feels. Moore's character is not without her own struggles, as she attempts to convert Cassandra and become prom queen. Just as the relationship between the characters is complex, personal religious values are equally complicated. *Saved* shows how our choices are shaped by the values we hold, the institutions with which we affiliate, as well as by our interactions with our peers.

feel apart from any governmental system. For the most part, however, the level of political alienation in a society is reflective of the state of that society's political institutions. And most people would agree that high levels of political alienation do not reflect well on a given system. An alienated individual does not trust her government.

Political alienation increased dramatically in the United States between the 1960s and the 1990s. In the early 1960s, more than 70 percent of American adults felt that they could trust the national government most of the time. By 1996, only 32 percent felt that way. Despite some increase in recent years, trust in the government has clearly diminished greatly (see Figure 6-3).

Lack of Efficacy   Democratic institutions presuppose that citizens will support the basic rules by which decisions are made and that they will participate at least minimally in making demands on the system. When individuals feel that the system "does not listen to people like me" or that "people like me cannot make a difference," they suffer from a lack of political efficacy. A significant proportion of the American public could be categorized as lacking efficacy.

Clearly, someone who feels a lack of efficacy in his daily life is likely to feel the same toward political institutions (see Figure 6-4). Someone who feels powerless on the job, or powerless to obtain a job, will find it hard to feel much power in the political arena. Likewise, an individual who feels a lack of power and influence with people in personal settings may transfer that perspective to politics. It would be misleading, however, to automatically conclude that an individual's lack of political efficacy necessarily reflects deeper personal problems. In the aggregate, it may reflect a true state of affairs in some systems. Most citizens of Castro's Cuba may well feel that the government does not pay much attention to people like them, and, from all indications, their perception is correct. Feelings of a lack of efficacy could simply reflect on the individual, the system, or both.

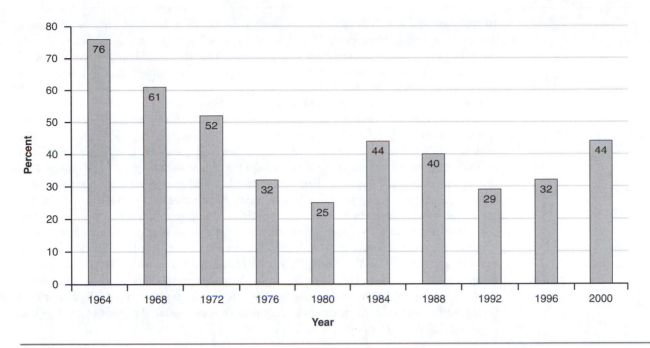

Figure 6-3
Percentage of Respondents Agreeing That They Trust Government in Washington "All of the Time" or "Most of the Time," 1964–2000

Source: Adapted from Center for Political Studies, University of Michigan, National Election Studies, 1964–2000.

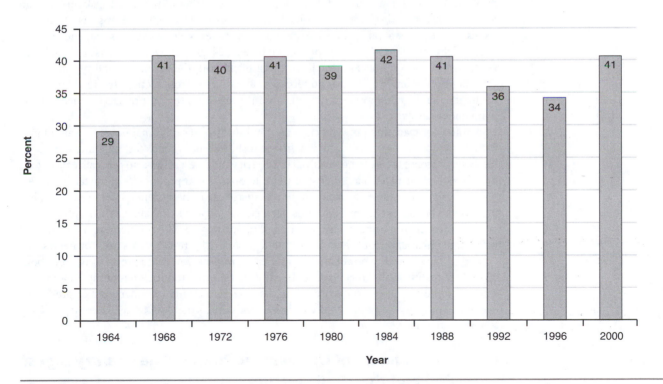

Figure 6-4
Percentage of Respondents Agreeing or Strongly Agreeing with the Statement "People like me don't have any say about what the government does," 1964–2000

Source: Adapted from Center for Political Studies, University of Michigan, National Election Studies, 1964–2000.

Intolerance   A democracy cannot work without an efficacious citizenry to make demands and provide support. Although the threat of opting out may endanger democratic institutions, the threat of those who make demands that would opt *others* out is every bit as dangerous. If a political culture does not support a reasonable degree of tolerance for others, it is doubtful that political institutions can do much more than stave off a majority who would use their power to limit the rights of a minority.

An abundance of evidence indicates that falling levels of efficacy are often followed by rising levels of intolerance among the same people. No better example exists than the rise of the Nazis in Germany following World War I. Working-class Germans felt dispirited and outside the political system in the Weimar Republic. They were brought back into politics through the appeals of Adolph Hitler. Unfortunately, those who would appeal to the downtrodden usually do so by providing a scapegoat. In the case of the Nazis, the principal scapegoat was the Jews. In this country, politicians looking to appeal to persons of low political efficacy have also been prone to scapegoating. African Americans, Jews, Asian Americans, and many other ethnic minorities have been the targets of these types of efforts. Following the attacks on the World Trade Center and the Pentagon in 2001, many people feared a wave of attacks on Muslim Americans along with intolerance for the expression of the Muslin religion. Surprisingly few attacks of this type or expressions of religious or cultural hostility occurred. American political culture has evolved to the point that the public expression of this type of animus is discouraged.

6-4 Measuring Public Opinion

For centuries, leaders have tried to know the will of their people. For the most part, these attempts have been haphazard and thus prone to error. Most nonscientific measurement of public opinion has been through key informants. A member of the state legislature may go to a certain coffee shop when he is back in his district. His conversations may touch on issues before the general assembly. Although these types of conversations may indeed provide insight into people's feelings on a given issue, the legislator would be wise to avoid generalizing beyond the folks at the diner. In all likelihood, they are not at all typical of the general population. Even if they do represent an accurate cross section, the tone and tenor of the dialogue could have as much effect on the attitudes they express as do their underlying beliefs and values.

Both politicians and nonpoliticians are continually observing what people say about politics. A member of a country club may find that she and her friends feel the same way about increasing income taxes on the wealthy. However, it would be a mistake to generalize these feelings into a statement such as "Everyone seems to oppose that proposed income tax increase."

Other attempts at measuring opinion may appear to be systematic and scientific, but may in fact be just as misleading. Consider a straw poll at a state fair. A **straw poll** is a survey in which the respondents decide whether to participate. The problem with a straw poll is the same as that encountered by a state legislator. The respondents are not necessarily typical of the rest of the population of interest. A **population** is the group of people about whom an analyst wants to generalize. Usually, that population includes adults in a nation, state, or some other political jurisdiction. If someone is trying to understand or predict an election, however, the population consists of registered voters or, better, those most likely to vote in that election.

6-4a The Dangers of Unscientific Polling: The *Literary Digest* Poll and the 1936 Election

The people whose opinions or attitudes are measured in any given attempt comprise the **sample** of a particular population. Virtually any attempt at public opinion measurement involves some sort of sampling. Measurements of opinion in which no attempt is made to ensure that the sample is representative of the population as a whole are nonscientific.

▶ **straw poll**   A nonscientific survey in which respondents take the initiative in deciding whether to participate.

▶ **population**   In survey research, the group of people about whom a survey is designed to generalize.

▶ **sample**   The group of people selected to be representative of a given population.

Although nonscientific sampling can provide some insights, the danger of making patently incorrect statements about the population is always present. Drawing incorrect conclusions about what a given population thinks can be risky—to a business looking to market new products, for example, or to a politician trying to get elected to public office.

Perhaps the most infamous example of the hazards of unscientific polling is the *Literary Digest* debacle of 1936. The *Literary Digest* had been polling the American people by mail and using the results to correctly predict presidential elections since 1916. Essentially, the magazine used telephone directories and lists of automobile owners to construct its sample. This method automatically biased the sample against the working class and poor because, in those days, few people who were not at least middle class could afford telephones and cars. After selecting a sample, the *Digest* mailed out millions of ballots. In 1936, based on a sample of nearly 2.4 million potential voters, the *Digest* predicted that the Republican challenger, Alf Landon, would defeat the incumbent, President Franklin D. Roosevelt, by a margin of 57 percent to 43 percent in the popular vote. Of course, FDR won the election handily, receiving almost 63 percent of the vote. Why was the *Digest's* prediction so wrong? First, despite its tremendous size, the sample was unrepresentative of the electorate. The response rate was a meager 22 percent, which exacerbated the problem of **nonresponse bias** (those who respond to a survey may hold different opinions from those who do not). Moreover, the survey was done in September, many weeks before the election. It had no way of detecting late shifts in voters' inclinations. The magnitude of the error in the *Literary Digest's* prediction convinced uninformed observers of the futility of polls. To more sophisticated observers, it only demonstrated the necessity of scientific survey research.

> **nonresponse bias** A situation in which those who respond to a survey hold different opinions from those who do not respond.

6-4b The Scientific Measurement of Opinion

One could say that George Gallup invented the modern polling industry. In 1935, Gallup founded the American Institute of Public Opinion at Princeton University. Although his background was in journalism and advertising, he had become interested in polling during the 1932 elections. He made a national reputation for himself by correctly predicting the outcome of the 1936 election. Even though his sample size was only a few thousand people, Gallup constructed a reasonably representative national sample by focusing on demographic traits, such as age, sex, region, and party affiliation. Over the years, Gallup refined his techniques, and the Gallup poll became a mainstay of American public opinion research. The Gallup poll continues under the direction of George Gallup, Jr., and is one of the most respected and influential survey research organizations.

Public opinion research has come a long way since its establishment by George Gallup, Elmo Roper, and a few others in the 1930s (see Table 6-1). This progress has been the result

1922	Walter Lippmann's influential book *Public Opinion* spawns scholarly interest in public opinion.
1933	The *Encyclopedia of Social Sciences* publishes its first article on public opinion.
1935	George Gallup establishes the American Institute of Public Opinion at Princeton University.
1936	Elmo Roper's *Fortune* poll is established.
1937	The *Literary Digest* poll erroneously predicts a Landon victory in the presidential contest. George Gallup, using more systematic sampling procedures, correctly predicts that President Roosevelt will win reelection.
1952	*Public Opinion Quarterly,* an academic journal dedicated to the scholarly study of public opinion, begins publication.
1956	The Institute for Social Research at the University of Michigan begins its periodic national election surveys.

TABLE 6-1

Milestones in the Development of Public Opinion Research

of both methodological and technological innovations. In technology, the two major developments have been in telecommunications and computers. Researchers can now gauge public opinion instantly using a large bank of telephone interviewers. Theoretically, an unlimited number of interviewers can perform computer-assisted telephone interviews with a minimum of difficulty and human error. Each interviewer sits at a computer terminal. The computer dials the phone number according to a predetermined sampling procedure. The interviewer, wearing a headset, reads the questions off the screen and enters data directly into the computer via the keyboard. This **CATI system** (for computer-assisted telephone interviewing) eliminates human errors in dialing phone numbers, recording responses to questions, and keypunching data into the computer. It also greatly speeds up the process, allowing researchers to conduct large-sample telephone surveys in hours or even minutes (depending on the number of interviewers and the number of questions to be asked). Yet, no matter how sophisticated the technology or how fast an organization can collect and analyze data, the research is worthless unless someone pays careful attention to the methodological requirements of scientific polling.

▶ **CATI system**   A computer-assisted telephone interviewing system.

Sampling   The first task in conducting a survey is choosing respondents. Those chosen to be questioned must be representative of the population about whom one wants to generalize. In virtually all cases involving the general population, interviewing every member of interest would be impossible or quite difficult. For instance, if a researcher wants to measure public opinion on an issue for Americans over the age of eighteen, she could hope to interview only a small proportion of that group.

Controversy

The Use of Exit Polls to Call Elections

As we noted in the Introduction to this book, tremendous controversy arose over the use of exit polls in leading the television networks to make early calls on the 2000 presidential election. Based partially on findings gleaned from people interviewed as they left the voting place, the Voter News Service (VNS), an organization funded by a consortium of news networks, projected that Al Gore had won Florida. This projection later was withdrawn, causing great concern, partly because at the time of the call, residents in Florida's central time zone had not yet finished casting their ballots.

In 2004, the exit polls suggested that John Kerry was going to defeat President Bush in a number of so-called "battleground states." As the returns came in, it was obvious that the exit polls were wrong. Why that was the case was a major topic of conversation in the media in the days following the election.

Why do exit polls fall short as a technique? The principle of "every voter has an equal chance of being selected" is violated, to a degree, and the chance of error increases. Analysts choose representative precincts at which to administer surveys to those who leave. To the degree that the representative precincts are not representative, the outcomes might be likewise not representative. But each "error" is compounded because each nonrepresentative precinct brings about a number of respondents. In a traditional phone survey, respondents are selected singly. One nonrepresentative respondent is likely to balance another. Much less chance for error exists with precincts as the unit. Moreover, the selection of respondents at a polling place depends to some degree on the interviewer. Interviewers have less discretion and less opportunity to color responses in a phone survey.

Exit polls have two advantages. First, only voters are interviewed, as opposed to likely voters in a phone survey. Second, the surveys occur on Election Day and tap the timeliest information. They have one related and important disadvantage: They miss completely those people voting early, by absentee ballot, or by mail. The numbers in these excluded categories have been growing rapidly in the past ten years.

The list of potential respondents from which respondents are chosen is the **sampling frame** for a particular survey. It could consist of listings of registered voters, students at a particular college, or published phone numbers. Often the survey researcher does not work from a true list, but rather from a list that theoretically exists. For example, in **random-digit dialing,** the last four digits in a phone number are randomly assigned to lists of telephone prefixes in a given area. This common practice allows a researcher to tap a broader sampling frame (the list of all phone numbers) than would be possible with listed numbers. A sampling frame should ensure that the sample that is eventually drawn will be representative of the population as a whole.

After a sampling frame is developed, the next step is creating a sampling plan. A **sampling plan** is the method of choosing a subset of the sampling frame that is representative of that frame. The best way to do that is by taking a **random sample,** or one in which every member of the sampling frame has an equal chance of being selected. An alternative is to take a **systematic sample,** or one in which every third, fourth, fifth, or whatever member of the sampling frame is selected. This method produces a good sample unless something is systematic about the sampling frame that makes every third, fourth, fifth, or whatever member different from others in the frame. In a case of this type, a random selection process is essential.

Question Writing

Question Writing   The wording of questions is, of course, crucial to a successful public opinion survey. In writing questions, analysts confront a fundamental challenge. They must construct a question that mirrors the phenomenon of interest, and they must provide the respondent with a set of alternative responses that mirror the range of opinions that exist in the population. The survey process must be as transparent as possible in translating attitudes into tabulated survey responses.

A good survey question measures only one attitude or opinion. Consider the question "Do you approve or disapprove of the way President Bush is handling the economy?" The response alternatives are balanced. **Balanced response sets** are desirable because they give no subtle cues that might lead the respondent. The question asks about one specific aspect of performance. This question would appear to be valid. An indicator has **validity** if it measures what it should measure. Another consideration is **reliability.** An indicator is reliable if it would produce the same response if it were asked again. You would have no reason to doubt the reliability of this question unless respondents really had no opinion, but felt obliged to provide one. For that reason, an interviewer should always make clear to the respondent that "Don't know" is an acceptable response.

Problems in Question Writing and Interpretation

Problems in Question Writing and Interpretation   Although selecting respondents is the necessary first step in producing a valid survey, the construction of questions to ask members of the sample is equally important. Unclear questions yield uninterruptible results. Biased questions lead to biased results. Let us return to the presidential approval-rating question discussed in section 6-1, "The Nature of Public Opinion." Consider this question: "Do you approve or disapprove of the way President Bush is handling taxation and jobs?" A respondent certainly might think that the president is doing a good job on one issue and a bad job on the other. This type of respondent might well say "Disapprove." But someone who disapproves of the president's performance on both issues would give the same answer. The analyst would be unable to reconstruct the original attitudes from the responses that are given. The overall figures in this type of case would provide artificially low evaluations. Asking about two phenomena in one question is using a **double-barreled question.** This type of question is certainly not valid, nor is it likely to be reliable.

The cardinal rule of question writing is a simple one: *Measure what you purport to measure.* The responses to a question should indicate what people really think, not something about the question itself. Consider the question: "Do you favor increasing taxes so

---

▶ **sampling frame**   The list of potential survey respondents from which the survey respondents are chosen.

▶ **random-digit dialing**   A survey technique in which respondents are chosen on the basis of phone numbers randomly generated by a computer.

▶ **sampling plan**   A method of choosing a sample to represent a given population.

▶ **random sample**   A sample in which every member of the sampling frame has an equal chance of being selected.

▶ **systematic sample**   A sampling plan in which every third, fourth, fifth, or nth member of the sampling frame is selected.

▶ **balanced response sets**   Sets of possible answers to a survey question in which the number of possible answers to one side of a question equals the number of answers to the other side of the question.

▶ **validity**   In survey research, a property of a question, meaning that it measures what it is designed to measure.

▶ **reliability**   In survey research, a property of a question, meaning that it would produce the same response if immediately asked a second time of the same respondent.

▶ **double-barreled question**   A survey question that presents two stimuli but allows only one response.

Born in New Haven, Connecticut, Louis Harris attended the University of North Carolina, where he majored in economics. After serving in the Navy during World War II, Harris worked as program director for the American Veterans Committee. In 1947, he joined Elmo Roper's polling organization and in 1956 founded his own firm, Louis Harris and Associates. As a pollster, Harris first achieved national recognition when his firm was hired to carry out polling for John F. Kennedy's presidential campaign. In 1962, Harris replaced Elmo Roper as the public opinion analyst for CBS News. Harris brought a new level of sophistication to polling, looking at not only the distribution of opinions on particular issues but also the underlying attitudes, values, and biases that helped shape people's opinions.

Writing in the *National Review* (February 14, 1975, p. 165), Harris responded to criticisms that his polls had been biased against the Nixon administration. He wrote:

"As a responsible polltaker, I, like a responsible reporter, must report the facts as they are in a given period, regardless who is pleased or displeased by what they say.... The Persians used to kill their messengers of bad tidings. Partisans in the mid-1970s have similar inclinations toward polltakers. This is part of the heat I am prepared to endure in my chosen profession."

▶ **social desirability bias** The bias resulting from a question being phrased in such a way that it elicits an answer that a person feels is the socially desirable response.

that the homeless could be provided with a place to stay?" Opposing an increase in taxes when the issue is framed in this way would be hard. A great many respondents would feel that they *should* answer in the affirmative. A question framed or phrased so that it seems to imply that a particular answer is preferred suffers from **social desirability bias.** A question is biased if it produces a response that is not a true indicator of the underlying opinion, attitude, belief, or value that it seeks to measure. In this example, an analyst using this type of question might report that the American people are more willing to pay taxes for programs for the homeless than they really are.

The most obvious example of social desirability bias is that of the intention to vote. When asked, almost all respondents say that they intend to vote in almost any election. At most, however, only about half the adult population casts ballots. People feel that they should vote and may intend to vote. These feelings and intentions are so bound up in the "ought to" of voting that responses to that question are useless in predicting a true vote. Asking for whom a person intends to vote does not present this problem. There is no socially desirable response that the respondent would feel compelled to provide to a neutral interviewer.

▶ **priming** A subtle biasing of a respondent's answer to a survey question caused by where the question is placed in the survey.

Another type of bias is subtler but just as likely to lead to false inferences. Responses to a question can be affected by its placement in the survey. Responses to any question can be biased by those questions asked previously, in a process called **priming.** That is why a survey about the presidential election usually begins with the key question: vote intention. If the vote intention question is asked after a series of questions on presidential job performance, respondents might be primed to match their vote intention to the candidate they had indicated was superior at the tasks presented in the survey. Respondents do not like to appear to give contradictory or irrational answers to questions. But a survey is an artificial process that may not replicate the respondent's own thought processes. She might decide to vote on the basis of other criteria than are measured in a survey.

6-5 Public Opinion and Public Policy

Clearly, public opinion is of fundamental importance in a democratic polity. Unless public policy bears some, albeit indirect, relationship to public opinion, a political system can hardly be called democratic. This statement does not mean, however, that public opinion

Model A

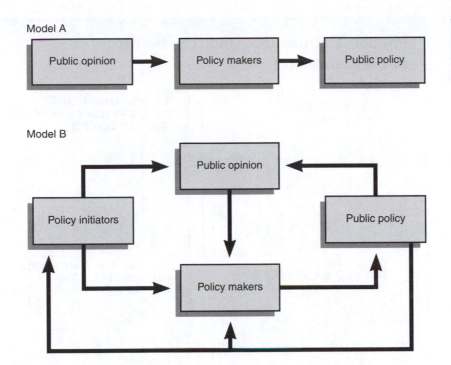

Model B

Figure 6-5
Alternative Models of the Role of Public Opinion in the Policy-Making Process

determines public policy directly. In every democracy, policy is made by leaders who respond to and shape public opinion.

6-5a Models of Public Opinion in the Policy Process

Consider the two alternative models of the policy-making process (see Figure 6-5). In Model A, which you might call the *traditional democratic theory model*, public opinion prompts policy makers to adopt policies to which, in turn, the public reacts. Although some might consider this model to be a good *prescription*, it is hardly a good *description* of how public policy is made in the United States—or in any of the world's democracies, for that matter. Model B is much more realistic. In this model, which you might call the *elite-pluralist model*, the policy process is initiated by activists, which are usually interest groups. These "policy initiators" get issues on the public agenda and help to frame the discussion of these issues. The activities of the initiators have direct influence on policy makers as well as on public opinion. Public opinion has a direct effect on policy makers. The policies that emerge from the process have a feedback effect on all the other elements of the model. Even though public opinion is not the prime mover, as it is depicted in Model A, it is still a crucial element of the process. Without public approval, policy decisions are not made or, if they are, do not survive over the long run.

6-5b Means of Communicating Public Opinion to Policy Makers

Policy makers learn of public opinion in a number of ways. Most pay close attention to the results of public opinion polls now routinely reported in the mass media. But they also heed phone calls and letters they receive from citizens directly. Policy makers tend to assume, with some justification, that those who take the time and trouble to contact them directly feel more intensely about an issue than most people who respond to a public opinion poll. Of course, that is why interest groups often mount phone-call and letter-writing campaigns. That is also why presidents in recent years have asked citizens who support their initiatives to contact their representatives in Congress. Presidents understand that members of Congress have staffs who tally the phone calls, cards, and letters their bosses receive.

Popular Culture and American Politics
Do You Know NAFTA?

Reprinted with permission, Steve Kelley, *The Times-Picayune,* New Orleans, LA

Survey research has become a staple of American political life. Politicians rely on polls. The news media are drawn to them, and the voters are fascinated by them. But nobody really likes polls. This cartoon touches a raw nerve within the survey research community. If you ask a question, you are most likely to get a response. But does that response really mean anything?

Americans have opinions on many issues. These issues are usually those that have been on the agenda for a while. For instance, most Americans know what they think about abortion. But some issues are so complex and inaccessible to the average American that any opinions they express may be fleeting. These expressions could represent a response to one bit of information, or they could represent a response to the interview process itself. The opinions expressed in this way have little or no meaning. Survey researchers can deal with this issue. They can first ask whether a respondent has heard or thought about an issue. The pollster whose work is represented in the cartoon has done his or her job well. At the time the poll was conducted, NAFTA (The North American Free Trade Agreement) did not mean much to many Americans.

6-5c Television and Radio Talk Shows

In the 1980s, a new programming format took hold in the American media: the call-in show. Millions of Americans watch *Larry King Live* on CNN or listen to Rush Limbaugh's syndicated radio show. These and other similar shows allow viewers or listeners, as the case may be, to call in and register their opinions. Often, the callers get into an argument with the host of the program or a guest. The format makes for lively television or radio. In the 1990s, these types of shows, especially talk radio, became a sort of ongoing

What Americans Think About

Polls

Polls have become prevalent in political campaigns and the media. Public officials make extensive use of polls to find out what different constituencies think about certain issues. But what do Americans think of polls? Do they tend to believe them? Do they think that polling is generally a good and useful thing? In a poll commissioned by *Time* and *CNN*, the firm Yankelovich Clancy Shulman, a leader in survey research, tried to find the answers to these questions. Their questions and results are reproduced here. In reviewing their findings, a question to ponder is whether respondents will be truthful when pollsters ask them about their feelings toward polls.

First, take the poll yourself by answering the questions posed by the pollsters, and then read the results.

Question 1: "Do you think political polling has a generally positive or generally negative influence on political campaigns?"

Question 2: "When you see polls saying which candidate is ahead, do you generally believe what the polls say or do you generally think they are wrong?"

Question 3: "Government officials sometimes use polls to find out what people think on the issues. In general, do you think this is a good practice or a bad practice?"

"Do you think political polling has a generally positive or generally negative influence on political campaigns?"

Positive	45%
Negative	40%
Not sure	15%

"When you see polls saying which candidate is ahead, do you generally believe what the polls say or do you generally think they are wrong?"

Believe polls	50%
Think they are wrong	39%
Not sure	11%

"Government officials sometimes use polls to find out what people think on the issues. In general, do you think this is a good practice or a bad practice?"

Good practice	72%
Bad practice	24%
Not sure	4%

You can go to the online version of this text to compare your results against the rest of your class.

Source: National survey of one thousand adults, conducted by telephone, October 15–17, 1990; the margin of error is +/– 3 percentage points. Results provided to the authors by Yankelovich Partners, Inc., Newport Beach, California.

national town meeting in which issues are discussed. Politicians have learned to pay attention to these programs as sources of information on the public mood. Though certainly not scientific measures of public opinion, these programs do provide politicians and other elites with an opportunity to learn what average people are thinking about politics. They also provide a channel of communication from the average person to the political elites. (This theme is explored further in Chapter 7, "Popular Participation in Politics.")

Comparative Perspective

Survey Research in China

In 1997, the Gallup Organization partnered with a research institute in the People's Republic of China to conduct the most ambitious and thorough public opinion survey ever attempted in that country. Researchers interviewed respondents in more than 3,700 households across all provinces. The survey found that China has made tremendous progress in economic development and modernization. Nearly nine in ten households in China now have TV sets. Half have telephones, 80 percent have washing machines, and almost 70 percent have refrigerators. The Chinese people manifest high levels of consumption of foreign goods. They express high levels of optimism about future economic prosperity. They also manifest a strong work ethic. When asked what statement comes closest to describing their basic attitude toward life, a majority (56 percent) chose "Work hard and get rich."

Public opinion research is a new phenomenon in the People's Republic. That the Chinese government is willing to permit this type of research to take place says something about the changes taking place in that country, which was once almost completely closed off to the outside world. Still, because China remains an authoritarian country, any representations of Chinese public opinion must be received with a degree of skepticism.

Source: Adapted from The Gallup Organization, Princeton, New Jersey.

6-6 Conclusion: The Dimensions of Public Opinion

Public opinion is fundamental in a democracy. Although public opinion may not be the prime mover in the policy-making process, it is a crucial element. Without public support, no policy—indeed, no democratic government—can survive for long. Public opinion is rooted in political culture and shaped by ideology. It is communicated to policy makers in a variety of ways, from informal, unscientific means to sophisticated scientific surveys.

Public opinion is not just a cause of political action; it is also an effect. Public opinion is affected by whatever the government does, whether it is the adoption of a new civil rights statute, the appointment of a new Supreme Court justice, or the making of a presidential decision to intervene militarily in another country. Indeed, public opinion is subject to some manipulation by those in power, through the strategic "leaking" of information to the media and by outright propaganda. In the United States, however, as in the other democracies of the world, public opinion has more influence over leaders than leaders have over public opinion.

Questions for Thought and Discussion

1. In general, do you think that people in government pay too much or too little attention to public opinion?

2. Does a preoccupation with public opinion mean that a government official or political candidate will ignore the interests and views of minorities?

3. In covering polls, do the mass media reflect or create public opinion?

4. How do politicians try to manipulate public opinion?

5. Is the study of public opinion an art, a science, or both? Why?

Practice Quiz

Note: You can find the correct answers to these questions by taking the quiz and then submitting your answers in the Online Edition. The program will automatically score your submission. If you miss a question, the program will provide the correct answer, a rationale for the answer, and the section number in the chapter where the topic is discussed.

1. Classical _____ has a negative view of human nature and is profoundly skeptical of the power of human reason.
   a. liberalism
   b. radicalism
   c. socialism
   d. conservatism

2. _____ tend to favor the welfare state.
   a. Liberals
   b. Radicals
   c. Reactionaries
   d. Conservatives

3. _____ plays the most important role in transmitting political values and orientations across generations.
   a. Schools
   b. The family
   c. The media
   d. Peer groups

4. Political _____ refers to the feeling that one can make a difference in politics.
   a. esteem
   b. alienation
   c. efficacy
   d. participation

5. A _____ is a survey where the respondents decide whether to participate.
   a. random sample survey
   b. straw poll
   c. modified random sample survey
   d. stratified poll

6. In 1936, the *Literary Digest* predicted that Republican Alf Landon would unseat incumbent president _____.
   a. Woodrow Wilson
   b. Herbert Hoover
   c. Franklin Roosevelt
   d. Harry Truman

7. The list of potential respondents from which respondents are chosen for the purpose of a survey is the _____.
   a. population
   b. random sample
   c. stratified random sample
   d. sampling frame

8. A survey question is said to be _____ if it produces a response that is not a true indicator of the underlying opinion, attitude, belief, or value it seeks to measure.
   a. valid
   b. biased
   c. reliable
   d. undependable

9. _____ is the psychological discomfort a person feels in trying to process contradictory feelings or thoughts.
   a. Attitude dysfunction
   b. Opinion dysfunction
   c. Cognitive dissonance
   d. Cognitive dysfunction

10. In surveys, _____ occurs when the pollster asks questions that can bias the questions that follow.
    a. social desirability bias
    b. priming
    c. pumping
    d. stripping

For Further Reading

Asher, Herbert. *Polling and the Public: What Every Citizen Should Know,* 5th ed. (Washington, D.C.: CQ Press, 2001).

Bogart, Leo. *Silent Politics: Polls and the Awareness of Public Opinion* (New York: John Wiley & Sons, 1972).

Devine, Donald J. *The Political Culture of the United States: The Influence of Member Values on Regime Maintenance* (Boston: Little, Brown, 1972).

Fiorina, Morris, Samuel J. Adams, and Jeremy C. Pope. *Culture War? The Myth of a Polarized America* (New York: Longman, 2004).

Folz, David H. *Survey Research for Public Administration* (Thousand Oaks, CA: Sage Publications, 1996).

Green, Donald, Bradley Palmquist, and Donald Schickler, *Partisan Hearts and Minds* (New Haven, CT: Yale University Press, 2004).

Halstead, Ted, and Michael Lind. *The Radical Center: The Future of American Politics* (New York: Doubleday, 2001).

Key, V. O., Jr. *Public Opinion and American Democracy* (New York: Knopf, 1961).

Lane, Robert E. *Political Ideology* (New York: Free Press, 1962).

Lippmann, Walter. *Public Opinion* (New York: Harcourt Brace, 1922).

Maddox, William, and Stuart A. Lilie. *Beyond Liberal and Conservative* (Washington, D.C.: Cato Institute, 1984).

Page, Benjamin, and Robert Shapiro. *The Rational Public: Fifty Years of Trends in Americans' Policy Preferences* (Chicago: University of Chicago Press, 1992).

Rubenstein, Sondra M. *Surveying Public Opinion* (Belmont, CA: Wadsworth, 1994).

Stimson, James A. *Public Opinion in America: Moods, Cycles and Swings,* 2d ed. (Boulder, CO: Westview Press, 1998).

Weisberg, Herbert F., Jon A. Krosnick, and Bruce D. Bowen. *An Introduction to Survey Research and Data Analysis,* 2d ed. (Glenview, IL: Scott, Foresman, 1989).

Yeric, Jerry L., and John R. Todd. *Public Opinion: The Visible Politics,* 2d ed. (Itasca, IL: Peacock, 1989).

Zaller, John R. *The Nature and Origins of Mass Opinion* (New York: Cambridge University Press, 1992).

Endnotes

1. Chet Flippo, "Burning Love," *Tennessee Illustrated,* July/August 1989, pp. 14–18.

2. Herbert McClosky, "Consensus and Ideology in American Politics," *American Political Science Review,* vol. 58, June 1964, pp. 361–82.

3. Thomas R. Dye and Harmon Zeigler, *The Irony of Democracy,* 12th ed. (Belmont, CA: Wadsworth, 2002).

4. In the 1970s, 1980s, and 1990s, the masses of American citizens manifested increased support for civil rights and liberties. As the nation now prosecutes the war on terrorism at home and abroad, some concern exists that public support for civil liberties may be eroding.

5. For an excellent survey of contemporary political science literature dealing with political attitudes and opinions, see Barbara Norrander and Clyde Wilcox, *Understanding Public Opinion,* 2d ed. (Washington, D.C.: CQ Press, 2001).

6. William Lyons and John M. Scheb II, "Ideology and Candidate Evaluation in the 1984 and 1988 Presidential Elections," *Journal of Politics,* vol. 54, May 1992, pp. 573–84.

7. Walter Lippmann, *Public Opinion* (New York: Harcourt Brace, 1922), p. 402.

8. See, for example, Philip E. Converse, "The Nature of Belief Systems in the Mass Public." In *Ideology and Discontent,* ed. David Apter (New York: Free Press, 1964).

9. *Lawrence v. Texas,* 539 U.S. 558 (2003).

10. William Maddox and Stuart A. Lilie, *Beyond Liberal and Conservative* (Washington, D.C.: Cato Institute, 1984).

11. Gabriel Almond and Sidney Verba, *The Civic Culture* (Princeton: Princeton University Press, 1963).

12. Robert Lane, *Political Ideology* (New York: Free Press, 1962).

13. Seymour Martin Lipset, *Political Man* (Garden City, NY: Doubleday, 1963), p. 114.

14. Dye and Zeigler, *The Irony of Democracy,* p. 152.

15. Leon Festinger, *A Theory of Cognitive Dissonance* (Stanford, CA: Stanford University Press, 1957).

16. A survey of 1,211 African-American adults conducted by Gordon S. Black Co., November 11–25, 1992, found that black churches were tied with the NAACP for first place in a ranking of groups effectively representing the interests of African Americans. Results reported in *USA Today,* February 19, 1993, p. 6A.

Popular Participation in Politics

7

7-1 Mass Participation in a Democracy

In a democracy, citizens are expected to participate in politics, although democratic theorists differ about the degree to which the mass public should be expected to get involved. Ideally, citizens participate voluntarily and with the expectation that their involvement will have some effect on what government does. Democratic institutions demand some minimal level of participation if they are to survive. Nevertheless, some upper limit seems to exist on the amount of participation that democratic institutions can process. Even assuming that this type of limit exists, though, it clearly has not been reached in the United States. Suffice it to say that a representative democracy—dependent on the orderly functioning of parties and interest groups and the actions of Congress, the presidency, and the courts—must inspire a healthy but manageable degree of popular participation beyond the exercise of the ballot.

Of course, any democratic system must channel participation through legitimate structures. In the United States, writing letters to public officials, contributing money to causes and campaigns, and assembling to conduct peaceful protests are all legitimate expressions of political preferences. Rioting, harassing one's opponents, and bribing public officials are also forms of political participation in that they serve to communicate preferences to those in politics. But these activities are outside the law and are almost universally regarded as illegitimate forms of political action. To the degree that people feel they must use illegitimate forms of participation to get their point across, democratic systems face serious crises.

7-1a Are People Political By Nature?

The ancient Greek philosopher Aristotle described man as a "political animal." For Aristotle, participation in politics was essential to make people fully human. The political scientist Robert Dahl, however, argues that citizens are not by nature political animals. Rather, Dahl maintains that citizens tend not to participate in politics to any extent until issues directly touch their lives.[1] Whether people are "political" by nature is of key importance to any discussion of political participation because much of the criticism of low levels of participation in the United States has at its core the belief that the system can be changed to bring about greater involvement. If people are naturally disinclined to participate, any such changes are doomed to failure.

7-2 Levels of Individual Participation

The fundamental form of participation in any democracy is voting. For many people, voting is the only form of participation. At the least, most people in a democracy should vote in most elections. The vote is the "official" input to the system, the device by which those who staff government are chosen. Political participation involves much more than voting, however. The political scientist Lester Milbrath has described political participation as a hierarchy ranging from the noninvolvement of the apathetics, or those who do not participate, to gladiatorial activities, such as running for office and working in campaigns (see Figure 7-1).[2]

7-2a Political Apathy

▶ **political apathy** Lack of interest in the political process.

Approximately 25 percent of the American electorate could be classified as apathetic.[3] These individuals essentially remove themselves from possible participation by failing to register to vote or registering but rarely, if ever, casting a ballot. **Political apathy** can stem from many causes. First, apathetics could be pleased with the status quo, and their lack of political involvement could reflect their satisfaction. Robert Kaplan has written that "apathy, after all, means that the political situation is healthy enough to be ignored."[4] But because most people in this category have lower levels of income and education, this explanation would seem to be insufficient. More likely, the vast majority of people in this cate-

Maximum Participation
(Highest resource demands)

Holding public office
Becoming a candidate for office
Raising money for a candidate or cause
Attending a caucus or strategy meeting
Becoming an active member of a political party or interest group
Contributing time to a political campaign
Attending a political meeting
Contributing money to a party, candidate, or PAC
Contacting a public official
Wearing a button or putting a sticker on a car
Calling a talk radio discussion show
Attempting to convince another to vote a certain way
Voting
Initiating a political discussion
Listening to political dialogue
Ignoring all political messages

Nonparticipation
(Lowest resource demands)

Figure 7-1
The Continuum of Political Participation

gory are alienated or lacking in political efficacy, or both (see Chapter 6, "Public Opinion in American Politics").

The apathetics have long been of interest to political candidates. Many candidates have made explicit appeals to those outside the mainstream of American politics, hoping to persuade them to participate. In 1972, George McGovern, the Democratic presidential nominee, made a series of appeals to those who had traditionally felt left out of American politics. His strategy failed, however, for one simple reason: Apathetics do not follow politics, and they have low levels of trust and efficacy. Therefore, any message targeted to apathetics is not likely to be heard or, if heard, not likely to be believed.

7-2b Spectator Activities

With few exceptions, a person who decides to play an active role in politics begins by voting. Voting is the fundamental act that separates those who are involved in politics from the apathetics, who are not. Thus, voting serves as the common denominator for all those who are active in the political community. It also serves as the base of the hierarchy of political participation. With voting at the base of the hierarchy are other activities that Lester Milbrath has called **spectator activities.**[5] (Although voting might not seem to be a spectator activity, it is certainly less active than running for office or working for a political campaign.) Like voting, the other activities at the base of the hierarchy are simple; they demand a minimum of effort, time, and political resources. Talking to other people about politics, wearing a campaign button, and putting a bumper sticker on a car are other examples of spectator activities. Note that none of these activities by themselves can have much effect on a political contest, but in the aggregate their effect can be significant.

Moving up the hierarchy of political participation, the number of people participating in each category declines. At the same time, however, a person who engages in an action partway up the hierarchy is likely to participate also in the lower activities. In other words, a person who votes may not participate in any other, more demanding activities. However,

> **spectator activities** The simplest kinds of political activities that demand a minimal amount of effort and a correspondingly low amount of political resources, for example, voting or wearing a political button.

Popular Culture and American Politics

http://www.punkvoter.org

By Chapman Rackaway

Rock musicians have a long history of being politically active. Popular protest songs sprang up in the 1960s as a response to the war in Vietnam and significant social changes. In the 1980s, Bruce Springsteen's "Born in the U.S.A." was a song motivated by political and social changes that the singer had observed. Popular 1970s' rock band Fleetwood Mac's "Don't Stop (Thinking About Tomorrow)" served as the campaign theme song for Bill Clinton's run for the presidency in 1992. Punk musicians, however, are normally associated with anarchy and apathy—very different from the politically aware and active nature of classic rock artists.

The idea of punks as uninvolved and uninterested might be changing. In 2004, the World Wide Web allowed for a loose coalition of punk musicians to band together and found the website Punkvoter.org. The goal of the website was to build a coalition to educate, register, and mobilize liberal voters, particularly young persons.

Along with other efforts to mobilize young citizens, such as MTV's "Choose or Lose/20 Million Loud" campaign and rapper/producer Sean "P. Diddy" Comb's "Vote or Die," Punkvoter.org created a comprehensive effort to push those who do not normally participate out to the polls. Punkvoter.org allied bands such as Anti-Flag, NOFX, The Dead Kennedys' Jello Biafra, Goldfinger, and Bad Religion posted guest columns on the site. The site uploaded flyers that visitors could download, print, and post. Punks affiliated with the site contributed songs to the albums "Rock Against Bush Volumes 1 and 2," released in April and August of 2004, and a tour of the same name with performances, voter registration drives, and promotion of liberal causes.

Music serves not only as a powerful form of personal expression but also one of political strength. With groups like Punkvoter.org, the goal is to involve people who would not normally become active in political causes. Youth voter turnout for the 2004 election might not have been driven significantly higher by efforts like those of Punkvoter.org, but as groups try to build younger voters' involvement in politics, those turnout numbers might increase.

a person who writes to a member of Congress is quite likely to have participated in less demanding activities, such as voting and discussing politics with others.

7-2c Political Activism

Other political activities demand much more effort than do spectator activities. Attending meetings or working for a campaign requires a considerable investment of time in the political process. Some people are **political activists** and participate in depth in the political arena by contributing large amounts of time and money either to a single cause or across a variety of causes. To the degree that these persons possess political resources, they can begin to have an effect on outcomes in a policy area. These persons become part of the attentive public for that issue. Others become involved across a number of issue areas. They may become associated with a political party and may even decide to seek public office.

Relatively few Americans decide to participate in politics at high levels. Perhaps only one in twenty could be classified as "active and attentive" (see Figure 7-2).[6] Thus, any given American has only about a 5 percent probability of being a member of the **active and attentive class.** From the perspective of the individual, that percentage may seem like relatively few (and it is), but in numbers, 5 percent of the American public means more than twelve million people. These 5 percent are active in political parties, provide leadership in civic organizations, join interest groups, and attend public meetings. During the 2000 presidential election campaign, only about 10 percent of Americans wore political buttons. Only about 6 percent made a political campaign contribution. Less than 5 percent attended a political meeting, and less than 3 percent actively worked in a campaign.

> **political activists** Those people who participate in depth in one political arena by contributing large amounts of time and money either to a single cause or across a variety of causes.

> **active and attentive class** Those persons who pay attention to politics and participate frequently in the political process.

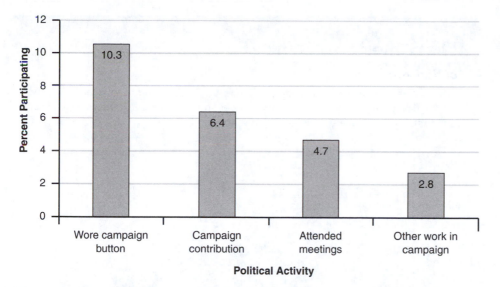

Figure 7-2
Levels of Participation in Political Activities Other than Voting during the 2000 Election Campaign

Source: Adapted from Center for Political Studies, University of Michigan, National Election Study 2000.

7-2d Deciding How Much to Participate

Deciding how much to participate in the political process is a complex decision. In making it, people consider not only the amount and type of political resources they possess but also the perceived costs and benefits of participation. This decision is not necessarily conscious. In fact, it may be more of a "nondecision" arrived at by default. That is, when individuals glance past a report of candidates' stands on complex political issues in their skims of local newspapers, they may, in effect, make a decision not to follow that election and not to care about the eventual winner. They are then much less likely to vote.

Political resources are the means of exercising influence that an individual or group can bring to bear in the political arena. In general, individuals' main political resources are much the same as their personal resources—money, time, communication skills, and personal connections. Of course, these resources tend to be cumulative; that is, people with one resource usually have others. Individuals holding important positions in society usually are highly educated and have many personal connections in addition to high incomes. On the other hand, those holding low-paying service jobs tend to have low levels of education, less money, little free time, and minimal interpersonal skills. Remember, however, that these patterns are not always true. Many people with minimal time, education, and money find that they have the power to lead and influence others. Malcolm X became a leader in the African-American community on the basis of his intelligence and ability to communicate, even though he had few political connections and only meager funds. He decided to use his considerable interpersonal and rhetorical skills to motivate others in the political arena. To Malcolm X, the benefits of participation were obvious. He saw participation as essential to changing the conditions African Americans faced in the United States. Likewise, his decision to enter politics had obvious costs: Politics dominated and eventually cost him his life.

Of course, most people do not have the charisma or communications skills of Malcolm X. Most people do behave rationally, however; that is, they decide to use their resources in the political arena if the benefits of doing so exceed the costs. The benefits of participation are many and varied. The most obvious benefit is that of fulfilling one's perceived citizen duty. Americans are socialized to vote, at the very least, and to take an active part in community affairs. Other benefits include the sense of helping to further a cause. A person who believes strongly that the natural environment is endangered may enjoy considerable personal benefits from contributing time and money to an interest group such as the Sierra Club or working to elect a candidate who strongly supports environmental causes.

In addition, other, more tangible benefits can be obtained. Many people participate because they think that they will fare better economically if their preferred party or candidate

> **political resources** The means by which an individual or group can affect the political process. Political resources include money, time, communication skills, and personal connections.

What Americans Think About

Political Participation

When polled, most Americans express an interest in politics and a sense of civic duty to vote. Political participation is viewed, of course, as socially desirable, which may lead some respondents to overstate their interest and sense of duty.

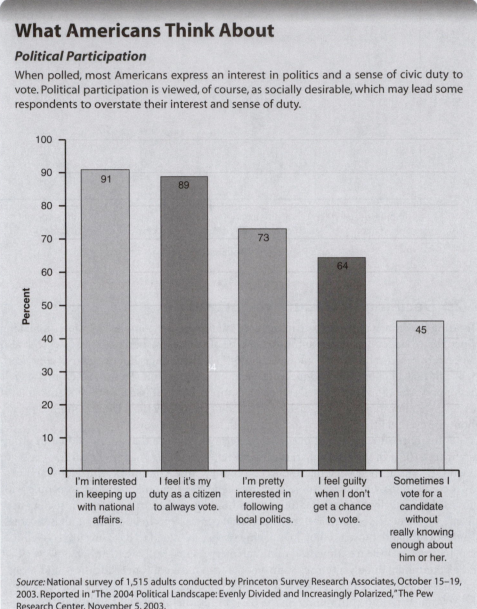

Source: National survey of 1,515 adults conducted by Princeton Survey Research Associates, October 15–19, 2003. Reported in "The 2004 Political Landscape: Evenly Divided and Increasingly Polarized," The Pew Research Center, November 5, 2003.

wins or if a certain policy is implemented. A wealthy industrialist may spend a lot of her resources in a presidential election because of the perception that her industry would fare better under one administration than another.

Every political act involves some costs. Although voting would seem to be a fairly low-cost activity, a voter must make the decision to register and invest time in following the issues or candidates in an election. Other activities cost considerably more in both time and money. Attending a meeting or playing a major part in a campaign takes considerable time and, in the latter case, requires a great deal of money. Many people who participated in Ross Perot's 1992 presidential campaign made significant commitments of time and money because they believed that they were part of a major movement to change the face of American politics.

7-3 Participation through Voting

Voting is the means by which political preferences are formally expressed in a democracy. Indeed, voting is, at least potentially, the most democratic of all forms of participation. For this to be the case, two essential conditions must be met. First, there must be universal suffrage; that is, all citizens must have the right to vote. Second, all votes must count equally. In *Gray v. Sanders* (1963), the Supreme Court observed, "The conception of political equality from the Declaration of Independence, to Lincoln's Gettysburg Address, to the Fifteenth, Seventeenth, and Nineteenth Amendments can mean only one thing—one person, one vote."[7] Writing for the Court in *Reynolds v. Sims* (1964), Chief Justice Earl Warren elaborated on this theme:

> The right to vote freely for the candidate of one's choice is of the essence of a democratic society, and any restrictions on that right strike at the heart of representative government. And the right of suffrage can be denied by a debasement or dilution of the weight of a citizen's vote just as effectively as by wholly prohibiting the free exercise of the franchise.[8]

In addition to being a means of expressing one's preferences, the act of voting seems to have intrinsic value for the voter. It increases one's sense of efficacy, encourages volunteerism, and strengthens citizenship.[9] Yet despite the essential character of voting in a democracy, and despite the intrinsic value of voting, many Americans choose not to vote. Certainly, Americans have a right not to vote if that is their preference. In the United States, the right to vote implies the right *not to vote,* and few commentators have suggested that voting should be compulsory.[10] Although few would insist that everybody should be required to vote, there is a growing sense that political participation through voting is lower than it ought to be in the United States.

7-3a Trends in Voting Turnout

Voter **turnout** can be defined as the number of people voting expressed as either a percentage of those registered to vote or a percentage of the voting-age population (VAP). Turnout has always been low in the United States compared to the other democracies of the world (see "Comparative Perspective"). Turnout peaked in 1960 when almost 63 percent of eligible Americans voted in the Nixon–Kennedy presidential election (see Box 7-1). Several factors contributed to this increase. Registration became somewhat easier over the first half of the twentieth century, and as more and more Americans completed high school, more had the background to understand the issues and follow campaigns. Finally, the trend toward a more urban society with an increasingly participatory culture and better communications also played a part. Nevertheless, the way elections are conducted and the necessity of formal registration kept voter turnout lower than in most other democracies.

Between 1960 and 2000, turnout for presidential elections declined by about eleven percentage points, from 65 percent to 54 percent. Had it not been for an increase in voting in the South, the decline would have been even greater.[11] Most of the change in the southern states was in response to the passage of the Voting Rights Act of 1965 and the tremendous increase in African-American registration and voting that ensued. By the end of the 1960s, virtually all the structural impediments to registration and voting had been removed. Ruy Teixeira lists eight major changes in the registration system that occurred between 1960 and 1988:

- The abolition of the poll tax
- The abolition of literacy tests
- Formal prohibitions against discrimination in registering voters
- The increased availability of bilingual registration materials
- The increased number of states allowing registration by mail
- A decline in residency requirements
- The moving of registration deadlines closer to elections
- The implementation of national standards for absentee registration

The removal of structural impediments, such as the outlawing of the poll tax and the easing of residency requirements, made voting much easier in the United States. Nevertheless, between 1972 and 1988, a steady decline in voter turnout occurred. In 1972, turnout was at 57% of VAP; by 1988 it had declined to 52%.

turnout The number of people voting either as a percentage of those who are registered to vote or as a percentage of the voting-age population.

Comparative Perspective

Levels of Voting Turnout in Presidential Elections around the World, 2000

Voter turnout in the United States is among the lowest in the developed democracies, regardless of how turnout is defined. In the 2000 presidential election, only 54 percent of voting-age Americans turned out to vote. Here are the comparable turnout rates in other countries for presidential elections held during 2000. What factors explain why countries vary so much in participation in elections?

Venezuela	47 %
Romania	54 %
Mexico	59 %
Haiti	61 %
Dominican Republic	65 %
Georgia	65 %
Russia	69 %
Croatia	74 %
Finland	77 %

Source: The International Institute for Democracy and Electoral Assistance.

In the 1992 presidential election, turnout spiked dramatically to 57 percent of VAP. In fact, the percentage of Americans voting in the 1992 election was greater than in any presidential election since 1972. Because no structural changes occurred between 1988 and 1992, this significant increase in turnout must reflect unique characteristics of the 1992 election. An obvious factor that made 1992 different was the independent candidacy of Texas billionaire H. Ross Perot. Perot's candidacy greatly increased interest in the election. For one thing, he offered an alternative to the two traditional parties. Second, his well-funded campaign, which drew heavily on his immense personal wealth, brought more people into the process. Finally, Perot's entry into the race made the outcome less predictable than it would have been otherwise.

In 1996, turnout fell back to 51 percent of VAP, slightly below the 1988 level. In 2000, there was an uptick, as turnout was about 54 percent of VAP. Although the turnout rate fluctuated somewhat from election to election, the average turnout in presidential elections from 1972 to 2000 was 54 percent of VAP. In 2004, a high-stimulus campaign produced a significant spike in turnout—59 percent of voting-age Americans cast ballots in the race between George W. Bush and John Kerry.[12] Both Democrats and Republicans worked hard to get their voters to the polls. However, the most interesting phenomenon in that election was the degree to which evangelical Christians turned out, not only to vote for President Bush, but also to support initiatives in eleven states to ban same-sex marriage. Voter turnout in 2004 was the highest in any presidential election since 1968 (see Box 7-1). President Bush's electoral victory in 2004 confounded the conventional wisdom that high-turnout elections favor Democratic candidates. Donald Green, a Yale political scientist, has observed, "The enduring legacy of the 2004 election is to demonstrate the potency of voter mobilization efforts."[13]

7-3b Who Votes?

Voting turnout varies somewhat by social group. For example, people with more education tend to vote more frequently than people with less education. The same is true of income: Higher income is positively associated with higher turnout. Young people (those in the 18–24 age bracket) are the least likely to vote of any age category. People in the 45–70 age bracket tend to vote the most.

In the 2000 election, only 43 percent of voters in the 18–29 age bracket turned out to vote. Because research suggested that younger voters would be more likely to support a Democratic alternative to President Bush, Democrats made tremendous efforts to mobilize

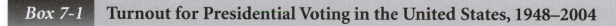

Box 7-1   Turnout for Presidential Voting in the United States, 1948–2004

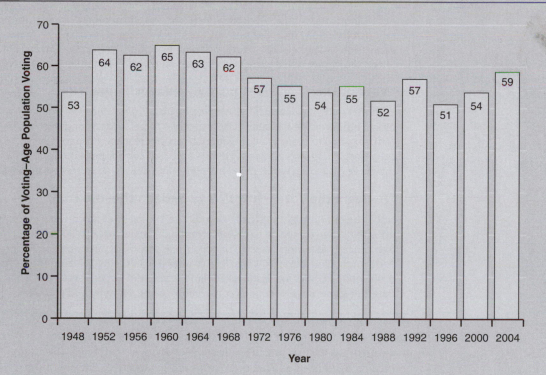

Sources: Data for 1948 through 2002 were obtained from Harold W. Stanley and Richard G. Niemi, *Vital Statistics on American Politics 2003–2004* (Washington, D.C.: CQ Press, 2003), pp. 12–13. The 2004 figure is taken from James Rainey, "Voter Turnout Highest Since 1968," *Atlanta Journal-Constitution,* November 4, 2004, p. B8.

younger voters in the 2004 election. As the Democrats hoped, turnout within this age bracket increased from 43 percent to 52 percent.[14] Moreover, exit polls indicated that 54 percent of these voters cast ballots for John Kerry. However, the increased turnout among younger voters was insufficient to counter the even greater turnout by other segments of the electorate that opted for President Bush. Given that overall turnout was 59 percent of VAP, the youth vote in 2004 was far from decisive.

Historically, women and minority groups voted in much lower proportions than white males. To a great extent, this disparity occurred because at one time women and minorities were not eligible to vote. Even after these groups were enfranchised, closing the gap took some time. No significant gap now exists between women and men—if anything, women are slightly more likely to vote than men. Something of a gap still exists between whites and nonwhites, but it is narrowing. The difference between whites and nonwhites is mainly attributable to differences in income and education. For example, middle-class blacks are just as likely to vote as middle-class whites.

Partisanship also has an effect on turnout. People who strongly identify with a political party tend to vote more than independents or weak partisans. Of the two major parties, Republicans tend to vote at higher levels than Democrats. These, of course, are only group tendencies. Individuals have to decide for themselves whether to vote.

7-3c The Individual Decision to Vote

The decision of whether to vote is a two-phase process. The first choice is whether to register. The second choice, open to those who have registered, is whether to go to the polls on Election Day and cast a ballot. Most states have made it much easier to register over the years. Much of this situation can be attributed to the Voting Rights Act of 1965, which

---

Popular Culture and American Politics

"Rock the Vote"   http://www.rockthevote.org

According to its website, "Rock the Vote is a non-profit, non-partisan organization, founded in 1990 in response to a wave of attacks on freedom of speech and artistic expression." Many celebrity artists, including Madonna, Tom Cruise, Queen Latifah, and Sheryl Crow, have donated their time to put on concerts and other Rock the Vote events.

"Vote or Die!"   http://www.citizenchange.com

With that pithy, if somewhat hyperbolic slogan, *Citizen Change,* an organization founded by rap producer Sean "P. Diddy" Combs, sought to persuade young people that voting is "hot, sexy and relevant to a generation that hasn't reached full participation in the political process." The organization's activities attracted considerable media attention and may have played some role in increasing turnout among young voters in 2004.

"Redeem the Vote"   http://www.redeemthevote.com/

Not to be outdone by the secular pop culture, the evangelical Christian community came up with its own campaign to mobilize young Christian voters in 2004. Through a series of free concerts featuring Christian bands such as Jonah 33, the Verbs, and Falling Up, Redeem the Vote attracted considerable attention in the mainstream media. As a non-profit, nonpartisan organization, Redeem the Vote did not endorse a particular candidate, but its message of cultural conservatism came through loud and clear.

---

made many restrictive practices illegal. Moreover, an unmistakable change in American political culture has occurred away from the perspective that only informed, supposedly "responsible citizens" should be allowed the privilege of voting to the perspective that all Americans have a right and responsibility to vote, regardless of their political knowledge or level of civic responsibility. Nevertheless, researchers estimate that even through the 1980s, the mere existence of registration laws depressed actual voting turnout by 14 percent.[15]

Current registration laws may not present much of a barrier to those who do intend to vote. Nevertheless, more than one in four Americans just do not register. Most states require some sort of waiting period, typically thirty days or so, although four states permit registration on Election Day. Many states now permit postcard registration or registration at locations other than the election commission or the courthouse. In addition, many groups, particularly African Americans, have worked quite hard to assist in registering voters, including many who would not have been likely to do so on their own.

In recent years, states have experimented with mail-in ballots and early voting in an effort to make voting easier and thus increase participation. To date, these efforts have met with only limited success. For a variety of reasons that we discuss in section 7-3d, "Explanations for Non-voting," many Americans simply do not want to be bothered by the simple act of voting.

Reasons for Failing to Register   Why do so many people choose not to register? Registration takes some forethought. No matter how simple the act may have become, it still involves a commitment of time and attention, even if only briefly. And many people believe that the cost of expending that amount of personal resources is still not worth the benefits they would derive from voting. Of course, few people make these cost/benefit calculations explicitly. Rather, whatever information they have received and digested about the political system, especially an upcoming contest, has not convinced them to go to the trouble of registering. Their reasons probably are related to their low sense of efficacy and civic duty. The political socialization process simply did not work for these people. The combination of family, school, and peer group influences failed to instill a feeling that voting is something a person "ought to do." Other people may not register because they distrust the whole political system or may lack the skills and interest needed to consume the information necessary to follow the political process.

7-3d Explanations for Nonvoting

As noted in section 7-3b, "Who Votes?" education is a major predictor of turnout. A person with a college degree is almost twice as likely to vote as a person without a high school diploma. We would expect, then, that as Americans generally become more educated, voting turnout would increase. In 1960, only about half of all adult Americans had graduated from high school, and fewer than one in ten had graduated from college. By 1988, more than three in four had graduated from high school, and two in ten had earned a college degree. Yet turnout has declined since 1960. Coupled with the increased ease in registration and the enfranchisement of the African-American electorate in the South, the observed decrease is even more dramatic. Clearly, an explanation is required.

As we discussed in Chapter 6, "Public Opinion in American Politics," Americans have become more cynical and alienated since the 1960s. The United States has seen a decline in levels of political trust and efficacy. People do not trust government as much as they used to, nor do they feel that their participation can make a real difference. People today are less likely to feel that they are members of a political community. The breakdown of community is related to many things, including the decline of cities, the increase in social mobility, the breakdown of the traditional family, reduced membership in labor unions, and the decline of organized religion. Society has become, to a great extent, a collection of disconnected individuals who lack interest in public affairs and do not feel a duty to participate in them.[16] For evidence that this affects voting behavior, one has only to consider the fact that individuals who have strong organizational affiliations, whether with churches, labor unions, civic groups, or political parties, are much more likely to participate in elections than those who do not have such ties.

The data in Box 7-2 shed some light on why people chose not to vote in 2004. The data come from a survey conducted at Harvard University shortly after the election. The most common reason cited by nonvoters for not voting was that they had moved recently and had not registered in their new location. This excuse seems weak, given that registration procedures have become easier and some states even permit same-day voting and registration. The second most common reason was that they did not like any of the candidates.

Box 7-2	**Reasons Nonvoters Gave for Not Voting in the 2004 Election**

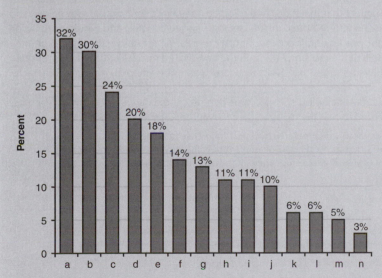

a. Moved recently and hadn't registered at my new location
b. Didn't like any of this year's presidential candidates
c. Was so busy that I did not have time to go to the polls
d. Didn't have any way to get to the polls on election day
e. Was disgusted with the election politics and didn't want to be involved
f. Politics are so complicated that I wasn't sure I understood it well enought to vote
g. Didn't quite know how to go about registering to vote
h. Not a U.S. citizen
i. The election outcome won't have much effect on my life
j. Not very interested in politics
k. Was planning to vote but the lines at the polls were so long that I decided not to vote
l. Thought I was registered, but when I went to vote I learned I wasn't and could not vote
m. Didn't want to register because that would put my name on the list for jury duty
n. Was worried that my right to vote would be challenged and I would not be allowed to vote

Source: National telephone survey of 1,010 adults conducted by the Joan Shorenstein Center on the Press, Politics and Public Policy at Harvard University's John F. Kennedy School of Government, November 3–7, 2004.

This reason, too, is not very compelling, as there were a number of candidates on the presidential ballot, representing a variety of parties and ideologies, not to mention congressional races, state legislative and gubernatorial races, and ballot initiatives. It is likely that many of those adopting this reason for not voting simply did not pay much attention to the election. Only 10 percent of respondents to the survey admitted not being very interested in politics. Patterns of political behavior suggest that the proportion of Americans who do not pay much attention to politics is, in fact, much higher than 10 percent.

7-3e Reforming the System

In 1993, Congress passed the Motor Voter Act, which requires states to register voters when they renew their driver's licenses. Because 90 percent of adults have licenses to operate motor vehicles, Congress anticipated that many more Americans would register to vote. The expectation was that turnout would increase by about 5 percent.[17] President George Bush had vetoed an earlier version, but during the 1992 campaign, Bill Clinton said that passage of the bill would be a high priority. The act that was finally adopted represented a compromise of sorts. Republicans fought to remove sections that would have also allowed registration at welfare offices. The Republicans felt that the legislation was an attempt to

Controversy

The 2000 Presidential Election and Political Protest

Confusion and anger surrounded the hand recounts that occurred following the 2000 presidential election tabulation in Florida. In a highly controversial decision, the Florida Supreme Court established November 26 as the deadline for any county to conduct a hand count. Democrat Al Gore had requested hand recounts in four counties, including the largest county in the state, Miami-Dade. Florida state law granted considerable discretion to the local three-member canvassing boards to decide whether these types of counts should continue. Miami-Dade officials had first agreed not to conduct the hand recount and then changed their minds and decided to proceed more than a week after the election day of November 7.

However, on November 24, members of the county canvassing board found themselves confronted with the seemingly impossible task of hand-counting hundreds of thousands of ballots in a couple of days. As they contemplated taking to a private room a subset of ten thousand ballots that machines had rejected, they were confronted with dozens of angry protestors who entered the courthouse and banged on walls and windows to stop what they thought was an unfair process. Shortly thereafter, the canvassing board unanimously decided to halt the recount. Although the board cited the lack of time, news reports immediately followed suggesting that the board was intimidated by the crowd, which many began calling a "mob."

Soon, Democrats—including the vice presidential candidate Joe Lieberman—began decrying the decision to halt the recounts. In a November 24 speech, he said:

"That is why I am deeply disappointed by reports of orchestrated demonstrations on Wednesday inside a state building, a government building, in Miami–Dade County, not just to express a point of view, but to disrupt and halt the counting of ballots.

"These demonstrations were clearly designed to intimidate and to prevent a simple count of votes from going forward.

"Shortly afterwards, one of the commissioners said, and I quote, 'We would be up there now counting,' end quote, if it weren't for those objections. He then joined his colleagues in deciding to give up the effort to count the ballots altogether.

"This is a time to honor the rule of law, not surrender to the rule of the mob."

Republicans characterized the protestors as merely exercising their First Amendment right to political protest. The question of appropriate versus inappropriate participation remained unanswered.

increase participation among those who were most likely to vote for Democrats. The actual long-term effects of the Motor Voter Act, if any, remain to be seen. However, Democratic hopes (and Republican fears) that the act would result in a massive influx of new Democratic voters into the electorate have not been realized.

In the incredibly close 2000 presidential election, many who thought that they had registered to vote through the program were indeed not registered because of breakdowns in communications among registrants, departments of motor vehicles, and county election commissions. This confusion was a byproduct of the (until recently) widely unrecognized decentralized electoral system in the United States. Much of the decisions involving the mechanics of voting take place at the county level, by county officials working within the constraints of county budgets. Until 2000 the fact that one jurisdiction might have opted for touch-screen voting machines while others had punch cards did not seem to have any consequence for the outcome of elections. The 2000 election brought intense public and media scrutiny to an area of governmental administration that had long been ignored.

7-3f Evaluating Nonvoting

Some would argue that a society in which a majority of citizens opt out of the political process is not a genuine democracy. Others worry about the stability of a political system characterized by widespread nonvoting. Seymour Martin Lipset, a well-known political sociologist, has argued that a society in which most citizens do not vote "is potentially more explosive than one in which most citizens are regularly involved in activities which give them some sense of participation in decisions which affect their lives."[18] Thomas Patterson, a distinguished political scientist, is among those who worry about the long-term impact of widespread nonparticipation on the system. Patterson questions whether self-government can be maintained when most citizens do not vote. In his view, "No stone should be left unturned in the effort to bring Americans back to the polls.[19]

7-4 Extraordinary Forms of Political Participation

Traditional democratic theory considers voting, political party affiliation, working in campaigns, and even running for public office to be the proper means of political participation in a democracy. **Modern pluralist theory** stresses interest group affiliation and activity. But numerous other activities can also be classified as political participation. Some may be regarded as unconventional, and others may be considered altogether illegitimate (see Figure 7-3).

> **traditional democratic theory**   Eighteenth- and nineteenth-century ideas regarding democratic citizenship, procedures, and institutions.

> **modern pluralist theory** Academic theory developed in the twentieth century that views democratic politics as a competition among interest groups rather than as a process dominated by one elite group.

Figure 7-3
Percentage of Americans Disapproving of Unconventional Forms of Participation

Source: Adapted from Samuel H. Barnes and Max Kaase, eds., *Political Action: Mass Participation in Five Western Democracies* (Beverly Hills, CA: Sage Publications, 1979), p. 545.

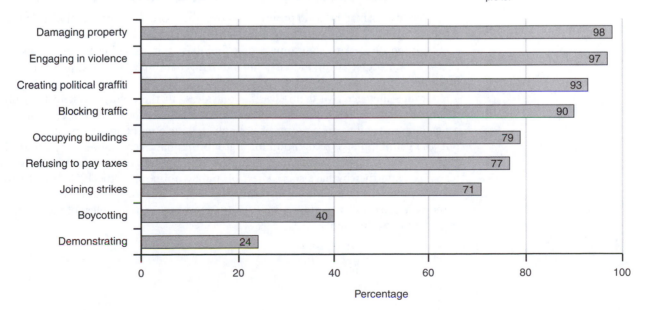

Form	Percentage
Damaging property	98
Engaging in violence	97
Creating political graffiti	93
Blocking traffic	90
Occupying buildings	79
Refusing to pay taxes	77
Joining strikes	71
Boycotting	40
Demonstrating	24

Percentage

Popular Culture and American Politics
Vote For Change Tour

By Chapman Rackaway

Participation in politics isn't always about voting or protesting. Sometimes, it's about going to a concert. In 2004, the PAC MoveOn.org organized a group of musicians across genres and age groups to perform forty shows in thirty cities as part of the Vote For Change Tour.

The artists on Vote For Change were a diverse group, from classic rockers John Mellencamp, Bruce Springsteen, and John Fogerty; to alternative godfathers R.E.M., grunge pioneers Pearl Jam, and country's Dixie Chicks; to hip-hop group Jurassic 5; to new artists such as Death Cab for Cutie, My Morning Jacket, Ben Harper, and Bright Eyes.

Many of the artists on the tour have been known for their politics. Pearl Jam's Eddie Vedder has been a prochoice advocate since the band burst onto the scene in 1991, and Dixie Chicks member Natalie Maines famously told a London audience in 2002 that she was ashamed President Bush was a fellow Texan.

The concerts were scheduled for a month prior to the November elections, and they were also strategically placed in hotly contested "battleground" states such as Ohio, Missouri, and Florida.

The more subtle message behind the tour's mention of "change" was to change the incumbent administration. MoveOn.org spent more than $50 million in the 2004 election to defeat President Bush, and the Vote For Change Tour reinforced that message. On MoveOn's website devoted to the tour, Dave Matthews discussed why he and his band played the tour, saying, "A vote for change is a vote for a stronger, safer, healthier America. A vote for Bush is a vote for a divided, unstable, paranoid America. It is our duty to this beautiful land to let our voices be heard. That's the reason for the tour. That's why I'm doing it."

The tour was unprecedented, as was the level of involvement from most of the musicians. Although rock music has been political for a long time, never before has a tour been organized for purely electoral purposes. Bruce Springsteen, always political in his music but rarely before outspoken about individual candidates, said, "I feel this is one of the most critical elections in my lifetime; this wasn't one that a concerned citizen felt comfortable sitting out."

7-4a Demonstrations, Marches, and Mass Protests

Demonstrations, marches, and protests have become more or less conventional elements of American politics, in large part because of their role in the civil rights and antiwar movements of the 1960s. Although some people find these activities objectionable, most realize that they are protected by the First Amendment guarantees of free expression and free assembly.

Groups that perceive themselves as "outsiders" in the political system typically use demonstrations, marches, protests, and other extraordinary forms of political action. Quite often, demonstrations are a means of not only making a point about a public policy issue but also gaining public recognition for a group that has been ignored. An extraordinary event like a march or protest is likely to capture the attention of the mass media, especially television, and thereby have some effect on public opinion. In the 1950s and 1960s, for example, the civil rights movement successfully used extraordinary activities—marches, demonstrations, and protests—to raise white Americans' consciousness of the injustices of racism and discrimination.

7-4b Riots

Sometimes, demonstrations, marches, and protests arise spontaneously in response to some decision or event. When no planning or leadership occurs, however, these activities carry a considerable risk of erupting into violence—rioting and looting. This was the case in south-central Los Angeles in 1992. People, mainly African Americans, took to the streets to protest the acquittal of several police officers accused of breaking the law in beating Rodney King, an African-American suspect who had been apprehended after a high-speed automobile chase. To many people in south-central Los Angeles, the police beating of King was just one more example of unwarranted brutality being inflicted on African Americans by a racist police department. They took to the streets to express their outrage. Unfortunately, the protest erupted into the worst riots the city had ever witnessed. The riots were exacerbated by the presence of armed gangs, who roamed the streets looting and victimizing innocent bystanders. The gangs deterred police from moving in and restoring order before the riot got out of control. Ultimately, calm was restored only after Governor Pete Wilson called in the National Guard.

Few would argue that riots are a legitimate form of political expression. Yet citizens must recognize that they are a powerful means of influencing public opinion and, ultimately, the government. Certainly, the race riots of the 1960s drew national attention to the conditions of the nation's inner cities and led to the enactment of public policies to alleviate those conditions. Similarly, in the wake of the riot of 1992, the Los Angeles Police Department was reformed and its leadership changed.

On the other hand, riots can have a counterproductive effect. One can credit the urban riots of the 1960s with helping to build support for the law-and-order–oriented candidacy of Richard Nixon in 1968. By 1968, many Americans had come to feel threatened by the rising tide of crime in the cities and by the general atmosphere of turmoil that pervaded the society. The riots certainly contributed mightily to this sense of uneasiness. The Nixon administration produced policies that many saw as contrary to the interests of urban minorities. Furthermore, the riots contributed to the phenomenon of "white flight" to the suburbs that ultimately worsened the problems of the cities by reducing their tax bases and making it more difficult for them to meet the needs of their residents.

Although no political system can tolerate rioting, most elites recognize rioting as an indicator that the system is not working. Rioting is certainly a collective political act that makes demands on the political system. At the least, it signals the participants' lack of faith in legitimate forms of political action. Elites respond to riots by demanding either more social control or increased aid to the cities. Conservatives typically call for law and order; liberals propose social programs. Government may do either or both of these things—they are not mutually exclusive. The urban riots of the 1960s led the federal government to enact tough new laws, such as the Anti-Riot Act of 1968. But they also led to more federal funding of programs designed to reverse urban decay.

7-4c Strikes and Boycotts

A **strike** is a collective decision by a large number of people to refuse to work in order to dramatize a situation or force those who are adversely affected to make some concession. In the United States, we associate strikes with labor unions. Strikes are not nearly as common now as they were fifty years ago, when the labor movement was in its infancy. Then, strikes were a means of forcing corporations merely to acknowledge and tolerate unions. Strikes now occur only when labor leaders and management teams are unable to settle on the wages and benefits to be provided under a collective-bargaining agreement.

Unknown in this country is the **general strike,** in which a large segment of the population refuses to work for a day to dramatize opposition to the government. This type of strike can paralyze a country: Shops close, factories shut down, and transportation systems

The Los Angeles Riots, 1992
The riots of 1992 were the worst Los Angeles had ever experienced.
© Peter Turnley / CORBIS

▶ **strike**   A collective decision by a large number of people to refuse to work in order to dramatize a situation or force those who are adversely affected to make some concession.

▶ **general strike**   Action taken by a large segment of the population in which people refuse to work for a day to dramatize their opposition to the government; not seen in the United States.

grind to a halt. This type of dramatic display of opposition can set in motion forces that bring down a regime. For example, in the Philippines in 1986, supporters of the presidential candidate Corazon Aquino staged a general strike to protest the reelection of President Ferdinand Marcos, who had been reelected in an atmosphere of pervasive fraud and corruption. Ultimately, after the Reagan administration shifted its support to the challenger, Marcos relinquished power and Aquino was declared president. Fortunately, in a democratic society with mechanisms for the orderly and periodic transfer of power, these types of extraordinary actions are seldom necessary.

A **boycott** is a collective refusal to purchase a particular good or service. Consumer groups unhappy with the safety or quality of certain products sometimes ask consumers to boycott particular companies. Groups displeased with the amount of sex and violence on television have been known to call for boycotts of companies that advertise during objectionable programs. Labor unions sometimes ask consumers to boycott companies with which they have grievances.

Perhaps the best-known example of an effective boycott took place in Montgomery, Alabama, in 1955. Rosa Parks, a black woman, was arrested for refusing to give up her seat in the whites-only section of a municipal bus. The Rev. Martin Luther King, Jr., the son of a well-known black minister in Atlanta, went to Montgomery and organized a boycott of the bus system by local blacks. The boycott, which lasted more than a year, was highly successful in dramatizing to the nation the issue of racial segregation. Eventually, the federal courts declared the segregated bus system unconstitutional.

> **boycott** A collective decision by a large number of people who refuse to purchase a particular good or service to dramatize opposition to the actions of particular companies.

7-4d The Question of Civil Disobedience

Certain forms of political actions are regarded as illegitimate by nearly everyone. Terrorism, assassination, extortion, intimidation—all may be politically motivated. Yet only the most militant radicals and reactionaries consider these types of actions to be an acceptable means of making a political point. Does political participation have to be confined to the boundaries of the law to be considered legitimate? **Civil disobedience** refers to the intentional breaking of the law to make a political point. Civil disobedience does not include actions that directly harm individuals. An assassination is not an act of civil disobedience; nor is bombing a building. Sometimes, civil disobedience does involve damage to property. More commonly, it entails one or more of these behaviors:

> **civil disobedience** The intentional breaking of the law to make a political point; does not include actions that directly harm individuals.

1. Trespassing on government or corporate property
2. Minor crimes against public order, such as disturbing the peace, disorderly conduct, unlawful assembly, or obstruction of vehicular traffic
3. Refusal to pay taxes or perform military service
4. Interference with public officials' performance of official duties

Civil disobedience has a long tradition in the United States, going back to the Boston Tea Party and other lawless actions by the American colonists to protest British rule. In the 1840s, the writer Henry David Thoreau refused to pay his poll taxes to protest American involvement in the Mexican War and the institution of slavery, both of which Thoreau considered immoral. Thoreau's act of civil disobedience became an icon in American political culture and has been invoked by successive generations of political activists who felt compelled to break the law for a perceived higher good.

In the 1960s, college students occupied campus administration buildings and refused to leave in order to protest the Vietnam War. In the 1970s, antinuclear activists trespassed on the grounds of power plants and government research facilities. In the early 1990s, members of Operation Rescue, a militant antiabortion group, violated court orders forbidding them from interfering with the operations of abortion clinics. All these activities are examples of civil disobedience. In each case, people broke the law on the ground that they were obeying a "higher law," whether it was the law of God or their own moral codes.

The question of civil disobedience is as old as politics itself. St. Paul believed that governments were ordained by God and that "whoever resisteth them, resisteth the ordinance

The civil rights movement began in Montgomery, Alabama, in 1955, when Rosa Parks refused to give up her bus seat to a white passenger.

Library of Congress #LC-USZ62-109426

of God."[20] On the other hand, St. Peter argued that people should "obey God rather than men."[21] Thomas Hobbes, rejecting the ability of human beings to know transcendental truth, argued that the duty to obey government was absolute. At the other extreme, anarchists deny the duty to obey any and all laws. Democratic thinkers have tended to argue for a duty to comply with the law if, and only if, the law is enacted by democratic procedures (see Case in Point 7-1). John Locke and Thomas Jefferson certainly believed that people have a right to overthrow government by force when that government no longer respects their inalienable rights. In fact, Jefferson wrote: "The tree of liberty must be refreshed from time to time with the blood of patriots and tyrants."[22]

7-4e Martin Luther King, Jr., and Civil Disobedience

The best-known exponent of civil disobedience in the twentieth century was Mohandas Gandhi, who used the technique of nonviolent resistance by the masses to win India's inde-

---

Case in Point **7-1**

Do Citizens Have a Constitutional Right to Violate an Unconstitutional Law?

Walker v. City of Birmingham (1967)

The Rev. Wyatt T. Walker, a leader in the civil rights movement, was held in contempt of court for defying an injunction prohibiting him from conducting a protest march in Birmingham, Alabama. The injunction was based on a Birmingham ordinance that forbade public demonstrations without a permit from the city. Civil rights leaders had attempted to obtain a permit, but had been denied. A local judge issued the injunction at the request of the city attorney without hearing arguments from the other side about the constitutionality of the ordinance.

The U.S. Supreme Court upheld the contempt citation by a 5–4 vote. Justice Potter Stewart wrote the opinion for the Court:

The rule that Alabama followed in this case reflects a belief that in the fair administration of justice no man can be judge in his own case, however exalted his station, however righteous his motives, and irrespective of his race, color, politics or religion. This Court cannot hold that petitioners were constitutionally free to ignore all of the procedures of the law and carry their battle to the streets. One may sympathize with the petitioners' impatient commitment to their cause. But respect for judicial process is a small price to pay for the civilizing hand of the law, which alone can give abiding meaning to constitutional freedom.

Although the Supreme Court upheld Walker's punishment for violating a court order, it later struck down the city ordinance on which the injunction was based.

pendence from British colonial rule. Gandhi's philosophy and methods of nonviolent civil disobedience influenced the American civil rights movement of the 1950s and 1960s, and especially the leader of that movement, Rev. Martin Luther King, Jr. In 1963, King led a protest march in Birmingham, Alabama. He and a number of civil rights leaders were arrested and jailed because they violated a court order prohibiting them from marching without a permit. Organizers of the march had, in fact, attempted to obtain a permit from Birmingham officials, but were denied. Believing that they had a constitutional right to assemble in a public forum to express their grievances, the organizers went ahead with the march. In a letter written from the Birmingham jail, King defended his group's exercise of civil disobedience. Like Thoreau and Gandhi before him, King argued that civil disobedience is proper when the law being violated is itself unjust, as long as the violator is willing to suffer the penalty for the act of disobedience. It is this willingness to accept punishment that dramatizes the sincerity of the belief in the injustice of the law. Breaking a law without being willing to face the consequences is not civil disobedience; it is merely lawlessness.

Anyone can easily understand civil disobedience in an authoritarian society where someone has no means of redressing grievances through democratic procedures. But how can anyone justify violating a law that has been adopted democratically? King's answer to this question was that black Americans had been denied the opportunity to participate in the political process. As far as blacks were concerned, the laws requiring racial segregation and other forms of discrimination had not been established democratically; hence, they had no obligation to obey them.

In his letter from the Birmingham jail, King justified civil disobedience in part on the ground that blacks in the South had been locked out of the political process. More recently, antiabortion protesters have frequently employed civil disobedience. How can these groups, who are not locked out of the political process, justify their violations of the law?

Profiles & Perspectives

Martin Luther King, Jr. (1929–1968)

Library of Congress, LC-USZ62-122992

The Rev. Martin Luther King, Jr., first gained national attention in 1955 by leading a yearlong boycott of the segregated busing system in Montgomery, Alabama. King subsequently established the Southern Christian Leadership Conference (SCLC), which became one of the most important organizations in the civil rights movement of the 1960s. Perhaps King's most memorable moment came in August 1963 when he delivered his famous "I have a dream" speech to a multitude of civil rights marchers in Washington, D.C. In 1963, King and a number of other civil rights demonstrators were arrested and jailed in Birmingham, Alabama. In a letter written from his jail cell in Birmingham, King sought to explain and justify the actions that led to his arrest:

> A law is unjust if it is inflicted on a minority that, as a result of being denied the right to vote, had no part in enacting or devising the law. Who can say that the legislature of Alabama which set up the state's segregation laws was democratically elected? Throughout Alabama all sorts of devious methods are used to prevent Negroes from becoming registered voters, and there are some counties in which, even though Negroes constitute a majority of the population, not a single Negro is registered. Can any law enacted under such circumstances be considered democratically structured?

King was awarded the Nobel peace prize in 1964, but his leadership of the civil rights movement began to be challenged by the more militant members of the movement. At the age of thirty-nine, King was assassinated on April 4, 1968, in Memphis, Tennessee, where he had gone to plan a multiracial Poor People's March. An escaped white convict, James Earl Ray, was convicted of the crime and sentenced to ninety-nine years in prison.

For more information, check out these websites:

King's papers and writings: http://www.stanford.edu/group/King/
Continuing King's work: http://www.thekingcenter.org/

You may also be interested in Dr. King's autobiography:

The Autobiography of Martin Luther King, Jr., by Clayborne Carson (editor) and Martin Luther King, Jr. (Time Warner, 2001).

They do so only on the basis of the moral rightness of their cause and the gravity of the evils they are fighting. To the committed environmentalist or antinuclear activist, trespassing or committing an act of vandalism to save the world from contamination or annihilation may seem necessary. To the committed prolife activist, violating a court order prohibiting interference with the activities of an abortion clinic may appear necessary to save the lives of unborn children. These committed activists may find it puzzling that others do not share their zeal or their willingness to flout the conventions of the law. Of course, if everyone did, anarchy would be the rule.

7-5 Social Movements

A **social movement** refers to the purposeful, directed actions of a large number of people attempting to achieve some collective purpose. Usually, that purpose is to bring about a major societal change that cannot be achieved through the ordinary channels of political participation. Social movements tend to attract people who feel disaffected and alienated. Perhaps they have been formally excluded from participating in politics, as women and African Americans once were. Or perhaps they feel that those in power are simply not interested in them or in what they have to say. Whatever the cause, social movements tend to be populated by "outsiders."

A social movement is distinguishable from a political party or an interest group in that a movement is not a formal organization. Nor is it limited to conventional forms of political participation. Social movements typically use unconventional tactics: demonstrations, marches, strikes, boycotts, and even civil disobedience. Some of the more militant elements of social movements may go even further, inciting riots, harassing opponents, and even committing acts of terrorism. Yet most people who join social movements are peace-loving,

> ▶ **social movement** The purposeful, directed actions of a large number of people attempting to achieve some collective purpose, for example, the civil rights movement.

Popular Culture and American Politics
Andrew Sullivan Blog

By Chapman Rackaway

Weblogs, or *blogs,* are an Internet-based source of information and opinion rapidly growing in popularity. In 2004, the major political parties provided onsite access at their conventions to bloggers who wrote about the events in real-time. For almost one hundred thousand readers a day, one of the best sites in the *blogosphere* is Andrew Sullivan's at www.andrewsullivan.com.

Sullivan has had a successful career writing on politics since moving to the United States from his native England. At the age of twenty-three, Sullivan interned at the center-left opinion magazine *The New Republic.* After taking a few years off to get his Ph.D. in political science from Harvard University, he returned to take over the job of editor at the age of twenty-seven.

Although Sullivan's slant is liberal, he is not afraid to deviate from the mainstream ideology. From his time at TNR through the growth and development of his blog in 2002, he has been not only a proponent for humanitarian military intervention in places such as Kosovo and the Sudan, gay marriage rights in the United States, and ending the war in Iraq; but also an outspoken opponent of liberal mainstays such as affirmative action and government-sponsored universal health-care coverage. In 2004, Sullivan took on the Bush administration's policies and strategies in going into Iraq, as well as the president's stand on a constitutional ban on gay marriage. Sullivan, who is openly gay, has made issues of homosexuality one of the primary components of his writing.

With more than a million visitors every month, Sullivan's site is a portal for many looking for news and insight in a new online world.

Popular Culture and American Politics
Radley Balko and TheAgitator.com

By Chapman Rackaway

Do you have a burning desire to share your opinions about politics with millions of people? Perhaps you are not a traditional Democrat or Republican and would like to publicize some political views that are outside the mainstream. If so, you might do what thousands of other (particularly young) people are doing and start your own *blog,* which is short for *weblog.* Blogs are Internet sites that post links to news reports and personal commentary. They are a rapidly growing political presence. Because younger people have adopted the Internet more quickly than others, it's no surprise that the universe of blogs, called the *blogosphere,* is populated mostly by younger people.

One very popular blog is Radley Balko's www.theagitator.com. A twenty-nine-year-old Saint Louis native, Balko moved to Washington, D.C., in 2000 to work for the libertarian CATO Institute and started the blog the following year to promote himself, his writing, and to improve his writing by daily postings.

Blogging is very different from typical news or opinion writing. It is a combination of posting links to other websites and placing commentary along with them. Balko says that a blog is a unique thing: "You should approach the blogosphere like you might approach the world's largest newsstand. You're going to get a little bit of everything—and varying degrees of credibility, talent, judgment, and of course every conceivable political persuasion." Balko's blog is a mix of classic liberal politics, observations on the Indianapolis Colts football team, and jokes about using monkeys as butlers. Always informative and entertaining, the blog gets about fifty thousand visits per day and is one of the most respected libertarian sites online.

Some consider bloggers to be people with political ambitions or personal axes to grind, but Balko says that blogging for him is about improving his own writing and developing his own ideology. He suggests that anyone considering a blog go ahead and start her own, "Do it, if for no other reason than to get your thoughts and feelings into word. If you want to be noticed, write every day. People come back more frequently when you reward them with new content. The best way to get noticed is to offer unique knowledge or a unique perspective."

► charismatic leader A leader who arouses fervent and enthusiastic support among his or her followers.

law-abiding citizens who believe strongly in something and feel that extraordinary effort is required to advance the cause.

Social movements are often grassroots uprisings. Yet although emphasizing mass action, movements tend to need charismatic leaders to galvanize people into action, to attract new adherents, and to bolster people's faith and courage when things go badly. In the United States, the best example of a **charismatic leader** of a social movement is the Rev. Martin Luther King, Jr. Grassroots uprisings can build slowly over time, or they can erupt spontaneously as massive popular reactions to certain events. For example, the incident at Three Mile Island nuclear power plant in 1979, when an accidental leak of radiation led to the evacuation of more than one hundred fifty thousand residents, helped to galvanize the antinuclear movement in the 1980s.

To understand social movements and their place in American politics, consider a number of the more significant movements that have taken place historically. Our examination begins in the early nineteenth century with the movement to abolish slavery and includes a number of recent movements, some of which are still important on the contemporary political scene. The survey is not intended to be exhaustive, but merely to highlight some of the more important social movements that have shaped American politics.

7-5a Abolitionism

Slavery was a point of contention in American society as early as the late eighteenth century. Abolitionist sentiment was particularly strong among Pennsylvania Quakers, who regarded slavery as an affront to their Christian ideals. At the Constitutional Convention of 1787, Northern and Southern delegates managed to reach a compromise on slavery for the sake of forming "a more perfect union." But the slavery issue would not go away. Congress struggled with the issue and managed to fashion a series of legislative compromises to hold the Union together. But the abolitionists, who regarded slavery as morally intolerable, would not be satisfied by anything short of total destruction of the "peculiar institution." Early on, abolitionists were not popular even in the North, where they were regarded as troublemakers and extremists. In the face of public opposition, they persisted, holding public rallies, giving speeches, writing essays, and publishing pamphlets and newspapers. Some even adopted more extreme tactics. In 1859, John Brown led a group of radical abolitionists in a raid on the federal garrison at Harper's Ferry, Virginia. Brown's plan was to obtain a large supply of arms to lead an uprising of slaves. The plan failed, and Brown was hanged for his actions. But John Brown began to be seen as a martyr within the abolitionist movement. Eventually, most people in the North began to agree that slavery was an evil that had to be eradicated. Ultimately, the question was resolved in favor of abolition by the bloody Civil War of 1861–1865. After more than fifty years of struggle, the abolitionists had prevailed.

7-5b Agrarian Populism

After the Civil War, farmers in the South, Midwest, and West experienced a long period of economic distress. At the same time, American industry was experiencing tremendous growth. By the 1880s, many farmers began to believe that they were being exploited by banks, railroads, and grain storage companies. The populist movement sought government control of these institutions and a number of other egalitarian policies, such as a progressive income tax and an expanded supply of cheap paper money. Out of this movement emerged the short-lived Populist party. Its leader, William Jennings Bryan, garnered 47 percent of the popular vote in the 1896 presidential election, but was narrowly defeated by the better-financed Republican candidate, William McKinley. Although by 1900 the Populist party had been subsumed by the Democratic party, the populist movement had a tremendous effect on American politics. Because it was instrumental in moving the country away from a *laissez-faire* economic policy to one of active government intervention, it helped pave the way for the New Deal of the 1930s and the creation of the modern welfare state.

7-5c The Labor Movement

In the late nineteenth and early twentieth centuries, the United States witnessed a colossal legal and political battle over the right of workers to form labor unions, organizations of workers that bargain collectively with management over the terms and conditions of employment. Corporate America vehemently, and in some cases violently, opposed the labor movement, which was sometimes characterized as a precursor to socialism. One of the first labor unions, the Knights of Labor, formed in 1869, embraced an extreme variety of socialism. Some early labor leaders, such as Eugene V. Debs, the president of the American Railway Union, adopted more conventional socialist views. But most unions have been more pragmatic than ideological. Samuel Gompers, the first president of the American Federation of Labor (AFL), embodied this pragmatism. According to Gompers, "Unions, pure and simple, are the natural organization of wage workers to secure their present material and practical improvement. . . ."[23]

The principal tactic of the labor movement was the strike, in which workers would walk off the job. In response to strikes, corporations would bring in nonunion workers, known disparagingly as scabs, to replace the strikers. Quite often, violence would erupt as scabs crossed picket lines to get to the workplace. Before workers obtained the legal right to form unions, to collectively bargain with management, and to strike if their demands were not satisfied, corporations would often enlist the aid of law enforcement authorities to arrest strikers or break up picket lines. Sometimes, the confrontations between the police and the strikers turned violent.

During the Great Depression of the 1930s, the labor movement grew in numbers and influence. The New Deal enacted under the leadership of President Franklin D. Roosevelt formally recognized the place of labor unions in the American economy. By the late 1930s, laws were adopted guaranteeing the rights of workers to unionize and collectively bargain with management over wages and other terms of employment. Although the right to unionize had been won, unions still had a major national agenda to advance. Foremost among these was the elimination of right-to-work laws, which made union membership optional in organized industries. Since the 1930s, labor unions have been politically active, primarily, but not exclusively, through the vehicle of the Democratic party. That affiliation was strained in 1993, however, when President Clinton, a Democrat, led the fight for Congressional approval of the North American Free Trade Agreement (NAFTA). Organized labor had fought hard against NAFTA, and most Democrats in Congress voted against it. But President Clinton prevailed by relying on a coalition of Republicans and conservative Democrats. Despite hard feelings among leaders of the labor movement, most of which were directed at President Clinton, organized labor has maintained its longstanding relationship with the Democratic party.

7-5d The Civil Rights Movement

It is hard to say exactly when the civil rights movement began. In the early twentieth century, the NAACP mounted a campaign of litigation challenging racial segregation in the courts. *Brown v. Board of Education* (1954), which invalidated segregated public schools, was the most significant political victory in that campaign. But the struggle for civil rights as a mass movement did not really begin until the latter part of the 1950s. Arguably, the modern civil rights movement began when Rosa Parks refused to give up her seat in the whites-only section of a Montgomery bus in 1955. The Montgomery bus boycott was the first in a series of mass political actions that began to typify the civil rights movement. Boycotts, demonstrations, marches—all were effectively employed by the movement. Even civil disobedience, principally in the form of sit-ins at segregated facilities, was successfully employed. The civil rights movement had a tremendous effect on American politics and social life. The adoption of the Civil Rights Act of 1964, the Voting Rights Act of 1965, and many other civil rights laws since then can be credited to the fact that the civil rights movement galvanized the conscience of America. Were it not for the movement, politicians—even liberal Democrats like President Lyndon Johnson, who pushed the Civil Rights Act through Congress—are unlikely to have manifested nearly as much concern for the civil rights of black Americans.

Before the mid-1960s, the civil rights movement employed strictly peaceful means, although opponents of the movement often practiced terrorism. The charismatic leadership of Martin Luther King, Jr., who embraced Gandhi's philosophy of nonviolent resistance, was instrumental in maintaining the peaceful character of the movement. By the mid-1960s, however, many black citizens began to believe that nonviolent protest was not enough—that more dramatic action was necessary. New, more militant voices began to be heard in the African-American community. After Dr. King was assassinated in Memphis in 1968, the militant voices began to appeal to an increasing number of black Americans. Radical groups, like the Black Panther party, went so far as to stage bank robberies and jailbreaks in an attempt to bring about revolution against the white-dominated society.

7-5e The Antiwar Movement

Another major contributor to the upheaval of the 1960s was the anti–Vietnam War movement that sprang up on college campuses in the mid-1960s. What started as a series of peaceful demonstrations and protests soon escalated into acts of civil disobedience, principally burning draft cards and refusing military service. Like the civil rights movement, the antiwar movement became more violent and militant as the 1960s progressed. Student protesters occupied university administration buildings, burned American flags, and even torched ROTC facilities. On some campuses, students clashed with police in violent riots. One of the most memorable, and bloodiest, episodes in the chronicles of the antiwar movement was the massive clash between demonstrators and police on the streets of Chicago during the Democratic National Convention during the summer of 1968. The Vietnam War had become the political issue of the year and threatened to tear the Democratic party apart. The protesters, led by the activists David Dellinger and Tom Hayden, assembled in Chicago in an attempt to persuade the Democrats to repudiate the war. When they learned that the convention attendees had rejected an antiwar plank in the party platform, the protesters marched to the convention hall, where they encountered legions of police officers. The ensuing battle was broadcast to the nation on live network television.

The antiwar movement helped solidify public opposition to the Vietnam War. Although the movement subsided after American forces left Vietnam, some of the more radical elements of the movement persisted throughout the 1970s. To some extent, the participants—and to a greater extent, the tactics—of the antiwar movement of the 1960s were revived by the antinuclear, environmental, and disarmament movements of the 1980s.

In late 1990, as America debated its response to Iraq's surprise invasion of Kuwait, many of the images of the 1960s' antiwar movement were rekindled as the more vocal opponents of military intervention assembled in America's cities to make their views known. Although the mass media gave these protests considerable attention, at least early on, the protesters had little effect on public opinion. If the Persian Gulf War of 1991 had dragged on into 1992 or 1993, and had the war bogged down into a Vietnam- or Korea-style stalemate, the number of antiwar protests, and their impact, would surely have grown markedly. Similarly, antiwar demonstrations on college campuses during the fall of 2001 had little effect on public support for America's "war on terrorism." As of January 2005, the American people were sharply divided regarding America's ongoing military activity in Iraq, but public opinion on this issue was driven more by daily media coverage of a continuing insurgency rather than by any sort of antiwar social movement.

7-5f The Women's Movement

People tend to think of the women's movement as a recent phenomenon. But women have a long history of organized political activity in this country. Women played an important role in the movement to abolish slavery. Many would trace the formal origin of the women's movement to the Seneca Falls Women's Rights Convention of 1848, which called for women to have equal rights in property ownership, trades, and educational opportunity. Most notably, the convention initiated the movement to secure the right to vote for women. In their struggle to achieve the right to vote, the suffragists engaged in a variety of political acts, not all of which were legal. In the early twentieth century, women played an important role in the temperance movement that led to the national prohibition of alcoholic beverages.

In the 1970s, a new wave of feminism swept the country. Feminists demanded liberation from a male-dominated society that they believed kept them in a position of subservience. It was in this climate that the Equal Rights Amendment, which had been proposed originally in 1923, was finally passed by Congress and sent to the states for ratification. The ultimate failure of the ERA to win ratification was not simply the result of male resistance, however. Many women evidently agreed with Phyllis Schlafly, who led the campaign against the ERA, that feminism is detrimental to the interests of women.

Despite the demise of the Equal Rights Amendment, women's groups in the 1980s and 1990s continued to push for policies to benefit women working outside the home. These groups demanded, and received, legal protection against sexual harassment on the job. Women's groups played a major role in the enactment of the Family and Medical Leave Act

Popular Culture and American Politics
Born on the Fourth of July

Oliver Stone's 1989 film *Born on the Fourth of July* is based on the true story of Ron Kovic, who was paralyzed as a result of wounds suffered in Vietnam and later became a famous antiwar activist. Eager to serve his country, Kovic volunteered for duty in Vietnam, fought bravely, and was severely wounded. Without the hope of walking again, he reconsidered his attitudes about the war and about his country. Kovic began to oppose the war and was instrumental in forming and leading the group Vietnam Veterans Against the War. The mere existence of this type of group illustrated the complexity of popular feelings toward the war because, traditionally, veterans of a conflict tended to be among its strongest supporters. Kovic gained the attention of millions of Americans by his efforts.

Kovic's ideal of service to his country had been smashed. However, it was replaced by another ideal: participation in the nation's discussion of what is right. In many ways, Kovic's story fits well with the myth of an ordinary citizen's achieving greatness by defying society's expectations. Kovic was convinced that Vietnam veterans needed a voice in policy making, first, in regard to the war, and second, in regard to treatment of veterans. By force of personality and with considerable political skill, he got the attention of the American public.

Oliver Stone's movie features Tom Cruise in the lead role. Stone won his second Best Director Oscar for *Born on the Fourth of July*.

---

of 1992, which requires employers to permit workers to take as many as twelve weeks of unpaid annual leave to deal with births, illnesses, and other family emergencies.

7-5g The Gay Rights Movement

One of the hallmarks of the 1960s was the sexual revolution, a broad cultural revolt against traditional sexual values and mores. Traditional values of modesty and chastity came under attack, both in popular culture (books, movies, plays, and music) and in everyday social life. To many people, virginity began to be viewed as a sign that a person was hopelessly old-fashioned, or even socially inept. Tolerance and experimentation became the watchwords of the times.

Out of the sexual revolution emerged a new openness with regard to homosexuality, which had long been taboo in Western culture. In the 1970s, people who were homosexual began to "come out of the closet," and heterosexuals began to express sympathy or tolerance rather than revulsion and condemnation. A new term, *gay*, was coined to replace more negative terms for being homosexual. That is not to say that animosity toward, or discrimination against, homosexuals disappeared. To the contrary, many gay men and lesbians who come out of the closet are still met by hostility and discrimination.

By the 1980s, gay men and lesbians had become politically aware and activated. They had even organized a number of interest groups to push for policy changes in the legislative and judicial branches of government at the local, state, and national levels. In particular, gays sought the repeal of sodomy laws that, although seldom enforced, technically made their sexual practices illegal. In the 1960s, 1970s, and 1980s, many states did do away with these types of laws, not so much as a result of political activity by gays, but rather because these statutes were widely regarded as outmoded. In a setback to the gay rights movement, however, the U.S. Supreme Court ruled in 1986 that state sodomy laws, as applied to homosexual conduct, did not violate the U.S. Constitution. In what gay rights activists regarded as an affront, the High Court said that gays have no right under the Constitution to engage in homosexual sodomy.[24] Subsequently, however, many state courts invalidated their own state sodomy laws based on state constitutional privacy protections. In 2003, the Supreme

Court, likely influenced by state court decisions as well as changing public attitudes, overturned its 1986 decision and declared unconstitutional a Texas law criminalizing homosexual conduct.[25]

More important than the demise of sodomy laws, however, is the effort by gay men and lesbians to acquire specific protection under civil rights laws. Some cities (for example, New York and San Francisco, where gays represent substantial voting blocs) have adopted ordinances specifically prohibiting discrimination on the grounds of sexual orientation. But gays have been less successful at the state and national levels. As of 1994, little sentiment seemed to exist in Congress or state legislatures to extend civil rights protections to gays. Indeed, in 1992, voters in Colorado adopted an amendment to the state constitution prohibiting the state legislature and courts from extending civil rights protection to gays. In 1996, however, in a major victory for gay rights, the U.S. Supreme Court struck down the amendment on the basis of the Equal Protection Clause of the Fourteenth Amendment.[26]

The other major objective on the gay rights agenda has been to persuade the government to put more effort into finding a cure for AIDS, not only because homosexuals disproportionately suffer from the disease but also because the disease exacerbates people's fears of homosexuality. One especially militant gay rights and anti-AIDS group, ACT UP, made headlines in the late 1980s and early 1990s by staging disruptive demonstrations and engaging in acts of civil disobedience. Whether these types of militant actions help or hinder the causes of gay rights and the fight against AIDS is debatable. But what is not debatable is that attitudes toward homosexuality have changed dramatically over the past several decades. The gay rights movement certainly is responsible for much of that attitudinal change.

By 2004, the agenda of the gay rights movement focused on the issue of marriage. Gay rights activists saw the legalization of homosexual marriage as a critical test of public acceptance of gays and lesbians. In November 2003, the Massachusetts Supreme Court ruled that the Massachusetts state constitution required that the legislature rewrite its statutes to provide marriage rights for gay couples. This set off a national discussion of gay marriage that led some local officials to perform weddings for gay couples. Although these marriages were later overturned, the "right to marry" a person of the same sex further widened the discussion of rights for gay and lesbian couples. Although at the end of 2004, the issue of gay marriage was still very much in flux, it was clear that there had been tremendous cultural change in this area over the preceding three decades.

7-5h The Christian Right

Periodic upsurges of political activity have occurred among fundamentalist Christians throughout American history. The most recent of these upsurges, which began in the late 1970s and continues now, has been referred to as the Christian Right. Most modern social movements—including the gay rights, environmental, antiwar, civil rights, and women's movements—have been oriented toward the ideological left: That is, participants in these movements have tended to be liberal or even radical in their overall political orientations. The Christian Right stands in sharp ideological contrast to these liberal-to-radical movements. The Christian Right is a conservative movement concerned primarily with sociomoral issues and "family values." Its agenda includes restoring prayer to the public schools, maintaining social and legal taboos on homosexuality, censoring pornography, and, above all, prohibiting abortion. Indeed, the Christian Right as a social movement overlaps considerably with the prolife movement, which is focused almost exclusively on the abortion issue.

The Christian Right is built on a network of fundamentalist preachers who exhort their congregations to become politically active. The movement has become adept at the arts of conventional politics: voter registration drives, lobbying, litigation, running candidates for public office, and fundraising. In the 1980s, the leadership of the Christian Right succeeded in mobilizing a large segment of the population that had been politically inactive. The Christian Right played an important role in the 1980 election and 1984 reelection of Ronald Reagan. In the late 1980s, the movement fragmented somewhat. Some conservative Christians supported Pat Robertson, a TV evangelist, for the Republican nomination in 1988. Others, including the Rev. Jerry Falwell, the founder of the Moral Majority and one of the leading spokespersons for the Christian Right, supported the more moderate candidate, George Bush (the elder). In 1992, many in the Christian Right looked to Pat Buchanan, a conservative TV commentator, who challenged incumbent President Bush for the Republican nomination. Buchanan's insurgency was eventually defeated, but at the price of some bitter feelings within the Republican party. In the 1992 general election, most conservative Christians supported George Bush, but some defected to the Independent Ross Perot, and still others voted for Bill Clinton, who was not shy about exploiting his "Christian credentials" as a member of the Baptist church. In the wake of the Democratic victory in 1992, the leadership of the NCR (New Christian Right) turned its attention to the local level, running candidates for school boards, city councils, and county commissions across America. During the mid-to-late 1990s, the Christian Right faded somewhat, but it certainly played an important (if not decisive) role in the election of George W. Bush in 2000. During the 2004 election cycle, the Christian Right emerged again, this time focusing its energies on President Bush's reelection and the attempt to prevent the legalization of gay marriage. No doubt President Bush's support for a constitutional amendment to protect traditional marriage helped to solidify his standing within the Christian Right. And without question, the Christian Right was instrumental in the approval of ballot initiatives in eleven states to ban gay marriage.

7-5i The Prolife Movement

The prolife movement draws much of its support from the Christian Right, although it is a distinctive phenomenon unto itself. The movement embraces a number of organized groups, such as Right to Life, Operation Rescue, and Rescue America. Right to Life is a conventional interest group, committed to lobbying, litigation, and influencing elections. Rescue America and Operation Rescue are direct-action groups that picket and sometimes blockade abortion clinics. Critics charge that these groups harass women going to clinics seeking abortions and try to intimidate doctors and other clinic personnel. Randall Terry, a leader of Operation Rescue, argues that most of his group's actions are specifically protected by the First Amendment. Of course, those on the other side of the issue believe that these actions constitute an interference with a woman's constitutional right to obtain, and a doctor's right to provide, an abortion.

In March 1993, the nation was shocked when Dr. David Gunn was shot and killed by an antiabortion protester outside a clinic in Pensacola, Florida. The killing was the most publicized of a number of lawless actions by fringe elements in the prolife movement. In other incidents, clinics have been bombed or vandalized, clinic staff members and doctors have been harassed—even stalked—and women seeking abortions have been confronted. Indeed, antiabortion activities have been successful in closing down many abortion clinics throughout the country. Although most people on both sides of the abortion issue deplore the violence that has infected the struggle over abortion rights, the very nature of the issue increases the likelihood that protest will become violent.

In 2001, the prolife movement focused on a new issue—stem cell research. Prolife activists opposed the use of stem cells obtained from human embryos, as they regard the destruction of a human embryo to be tantamount to homicide. In August 2001, President George W. Bush issued an executive order limiting the use federal funds to support research in this area to the seventy-eight embryonic stem cell lines then in existence. Opponents of the order insisted that new stem cell lines had to be created in order for research to progress. Stem cell research again became a national issue during the 2004 campaign as candidate John Kerry (as well as a number of celebrities) criticized President Bush's stand on the issue.

7-5j The Antiglobalism Movement

The changes in the communications and economic infrastructure during the last quarter of the twentieth century led to an increasingly global economy. This situation invariably led to a rise in business among multinational corporations and a host of treaties and agreements among nations to deal with this trade. By 2001, it had become difficult for any organization, such as the World Trade Organization or the International Monetary Fund, to hold meetings in Europe or the United States without massive protests staged by people convinced that the new global economy threatened the jobs or cultures of many people across the world in addition to the natural environment. Many involved in these protests saw themselves in the vanguard of what they hoped would become a new social movement. The protestors were a diverse mix, including black-masked anarchists, union members, Socialists, Communists, environmentalists, human rights activists, and self-styled radicals and activists of various bents and persuasions. The largest and most destructive protest of the institutions of the global economy took place in Seattle in 1999 at the time of the meeting of the World Trade Organization. More than fifty thousand protestors managed to keep many meetings from taking place. Their methods were not always peaceful. On the contrary, a good deal of property damage occurred, and many arrests were made. Some protestors manifested little understanding of the issues and institutions of globalization. For them, participation in the protest was a chance to experience some 1960s-style activism.

7-6 Conclusion: Participation and Political Culture

People can participate in politics in many ways, ranging from minimal spectator activities through active involvement in parties, campaigns, and interest groups to involvement in grassroots social movements and direct mass political action. The challenge to any democracy is twofold. First, the system must stimulate enough popular participation in politics so that it may continue to function as a legitimate "government by the people." Second, the system must maintain effective, legitimate channels of participation to avoid a groundswell of unconventional (and potentially violent) action that threatens to push the system into chaos. Although American democracy has struggled from time to time with the second of these challenges, for the most part political participation in the United States has been both conventional and peaceful. Many people would argue, however, that its citizens have been less successful in meeting the first challenge—engendering sufficient participation to be considered a true and vital democracy.

Americans tend to be quite proud of their political system. They are certainly proud of the Constitution and the freedoms enshrined in the Bill of Rights. They are convinced that America stands at the forefront of the world's democracies. Many Americans would be surprised to learn that the Founders did not intend for the political system to be a democracy and that many of the Framers of the Constitution equated democracy with mob rule. Most Americans now are not comfortable with the elitism that typified the Founders. Contemporary Americans are more comfortable with Abraham Lincoln's characterization of our political system as a "government of the people, by the people, and for the people." Certainly, that is what most Americans believe that our government should be. Yet, ironically, most Americans do not bother to vote in most elections. Even presidential elections generate barely a 50 percent voter turnout.

Part of the reluctance to register and vote stems from a cynicism about government. When polled, a majority of Americans are apt to say that they think the government is run by a "few big interests" that are more concerned with "looking out for themselves" than for the good of the people. Of course, when people do not participate in elections, they can hardly expect that their views will be taken into account. This is one of the paradoxes of American politics: Americans believe that their system was intended to be, and ought to be, a democracy. Yet they are reluctant to participate in the most basic of democratic institutions: the election. Two powerful elements of political culture are in conflict. Americans feel that they ought to vote. Thus, participation is fundamental to American political folklore. People often hear how Americans have fought and died to protect the right to vote.

But Americans are also skeptical about the role of government and somewhat cynical about politicians. In many ways, this cynicism is becoming as ingrained in the American character as is the obligation to participate. It is not surprising, then, that this discord in the culture has led to a relatively low level of voting.

Questions for Thought and Discussion

1. Why do Americans turn out to vote at lower rates than citizens in other democracies?
2. Does the right to vote include the right to have one's vote counted, even if the voter fails to follow instructions in the completion of the ballot?
3. With regard to forms of participation other than voting, is there an upper limit of mass participation beyond which a democracy cannot function?
4. Is it legitimate for a person to trespass on private property or block government buildings to draw attention to a political issue?

5. Has the environmental movement reached its peak in the United States? Is environmentalism likely to be more or less politically significant in the future?
6. Should people feel obligated to vote if they know nothing about the candidates or issues in an election?
7. Is there a minimal level of voter turnout for an electoral system to be considered democratic?
8. What social movements have been most effective in reshaping the American political agenda?

Practice Quiz

Note: You can find the correct answers to these questions by taking the quiz and then submitting your answers in the Online Edition. The program will automatically score your submission. If you miss a question, the program will provide the correct answer, a rationale for the answer, and the section number in the chapter where the topic is discussed.

1. The ancient Greek philosopher _____ described man as a "political animal."
   a. Socrates
   b. Thucydides
   c. Plato
   d. Aristotle

2. Most likely, political apathy is the result of _____.
   a. people being happy with the political system
   b. a feeling of alienation
   c. the decline in party identification
   d. satisfaction with the economic status quo

3. Since 1960, voter turnout in national elections in the United States _____.
   a. has declined
   b. has increased
   c. has fluctuated dramatically depending on the candidates
   d. has remained fairly constant

4. Although there has been a decline nationally in voter turnout, there has been an increase in turnout in the South. This has been primarily the result of _____.
   a. the passage of the Civil Rights Act
   b. the Supreme Court's decision in *Baker v. Carr*
   c. the Supreme Court's decision in *Bush v. Gore*
   d. the passage of the Voting Rights Act

5. People who are _____ are more likely to vote.
   a. poor
   b. well educated
   c. alienated
   d. young

6. Which of these has contributed most to the decline in U.S. voter turnout since 1960?
   a. Increased high school graduation rate
   b. Increased ease in registration
   c. Increased political alienation
   d. Increased enfranchisement of African Americans in the South

7. A _____ is a type of protest not seen in the United States in which a large segment of the population refuses to work in order to dramatize opposition to the government.
   a. coup d'etat
   b. general strike
   c. boycott
   d. sit-in

8. A _____ is the purposeful, directed actions of a large number of people attempting to achieve some collective purpose.
   a. general strike
   b. social movement
   c. boycott
   d. none of the above

9. Civil disobedience _____.
   a. is viewed by nearly all Americans as an unacceptable form of political participation
   b. includes the right to assassinate those leaders who are not sympathetic to one's claims
   c. has a long tradition in the United States
   d. is synonymous with anarchy

10. A massive protest against _____ took place in Seattle in 1999 during a meeting of the World Trade Organization.
    a. economic globalization
    b. racial discrimination
    c. agricultural subsidies
    d. Islamic extremism

For Further Reading

Barnes, Samuel H., and Max Kaase, eds. *Political Action: Mass Participation in Five Western Democracies* (Beverly Hills, CA: Sage Publications, 1979).

Branch, Taylor. *Parting the Waters: America in the King Years* (New York: Simon & Schuster, 1988).

Campbell, Angus, et al. *The American Voter* (New York: John Wiley and Sons, 1960).

Piven, Frances Fox, and Richard Cloward. *Why Americans Still Don't Vote and Why Politicians Want It That Way* (New York: Beacon Press, 2000).

Conway, M. Margaret. *Political Participation in the United States,* 3d edition (Washington, D.C.: CQ Press, 2000).

———, Gertrude A. Steuernagel, and David W. Ahern. *Women and Political Participation: Cultural Change in the Political Arena* (Washington D.C.: Congressional Quarterly Books, 1997).

Dalton, Russell J. *Citizen Politics in Western Democracies* (Chatham, NJ: Chatham House, 1988).

Goldberg, Robert A. *Grassroots Resistance: Social Movements in Twentieth Century America* (Belmont, CA: Wadsworth, 1991).

Miller, Warren E., and J. Merrill Shanks. *The New American Voter* (Cambridge, MA: Harvard University Press, 1996).

Patterson, Thomas E. *The Vanishing Voter* (New York: Vintage Books, 2003).

Putnam, Robert. *Bowling Alone: The Collapse and Revival of American Community* (New York: Simon and Schuster, 2000).

Teixeira, Ruy A. *The Disappearing American Voter* (Washington, D.C.: Brookings Institution, 1992).

———. *Why Americans Don't Vote: Turnout Decline in the United States, 1960–1984* (New York: Greenwood Press, 1987).

Verba, Sidney, and Norman H. Nie. *Participation in America: Political Democracy and Social Equality* (New York: Harper & Row, 1972).

Wattenberg, Martin P. *Where Have All the Voters Gone?* (Cambridge, MA: Harvard University Press, 2002).

Wolfinger, Raymond E., and Steven R. Rosenstone. *Who Votes?* (New Haven, CT: Yale University Press, 1980).

Endnotes

1. Robert Dahl, *Who Governs?* (New Haven, CT: Yale University Press, 1961), p. 225.
2. Lester Milbrath, *Political Participation: How and Why Do People Get Involved in Politics?* (Chicago: Rand McNally, 1965), p. 18.
3. Sidney Verba and Norman Nie, *Participation in America* (New York: Harper & Row, 1972), p. 119.
4. Robert Kaplan, "Was Democracy Just a Moment?" *Atlantic Monthly,* vol. 280, no. 6, December 1997.
5. Milbrath, *Political Participation,* p. 18.
6. J. R. Neuman, *The Paradox of Mass Politics* (Cambridge, MA: Harvard University Press, 1986), p. 11.
7. *Gray v. Sanders,* 372 U.S. 368, 380 (1963).
8. *Reynolds v. Sims,* 377 U.S. 533, 555 (1964).
9. Robert Putnam, *Bowling Alone: The Collapse and Revival of American Community* (New York: Simon and Schuster, 2000), p. 35.
10. In many democracies, from Australia to Uruguay, voting is viewed as an essential obligation of citizenship and is legally compulsory. In Australia, for example, citizens who fail to vote can be fined unless they can produce a satisfactory explanation for not voting.
11. Ruy Teixeira, *The Disappearing American Voter* (Washington, D.C.: Brookings Institution, 1992), p. 7.
12. James Rainey, "Voter Turnout Highest Since 1968," *Atlanta Journal-Constitution,* November 4, 2004, p. B8.

13. Ibid.
14. David C. King, "Youth Came Through with Big Turnout," *Boston Globe,* November 4, 2004; Eric Hoover, "Youth Turnout on Election Day Exceeded 1992 Peak, Scholars and Voting Groups Say," *Chronicle of Higher Education,* November 5, 2004.
15. G. Bingham Powell, Jr., "American Turnout in Comparative Perspective," *American Political Science Review,* vol. 80, March 1986, p. 17.
16. Teixeira, *The Disappearing American Voter,* p. 37.
17. Estimate by Thomas Mann, Brookings Institution, as reported in the *New York Times,* March 18, 1993, p. 1.
18. Seymour Martin Lipset, *Political Man* (Baltimore: Johns Hopkins University Press, 1981), p. 164.
19. Thomas E. Patterson, *The Vanishing Voter* (New York: Vintage Books, 2003), p. 186.
20. Romans 13:1–10.
21. Acts 5:29.
22. Thomas Jefferson, letter to William Stevens Smith, November 13, 1787.
23. Samuel Gompers, quoted in John M. Blum, et al., *The National Experience* (New York: Harcourt Brace & World, 1963), p. 438.
24. *Bowers v. Hardwick,* 478 U.S. 186 (1986).
25. *Lawrence v. Texas,* 539 U.S. 558 (2003).
26. *Romer v. Evans,* 517 U.S. 620 (1996).

Political Parties

8

8-1 The Role of Parties in a Democracy

A political party is "any continuing organization, identified by a particular label, that presents candidates for public office at mass elections."[1] Parties perform crucial functions in a democratic political system. They recruit political leadership, simplify and stabilize the political process, promote governmental organization, and foster coherent policymaking. Without parties, it would be difficult for democratic systems to choose their leaders and even more difficult for those chosen to implement the will of the people expressed through elections.

In the early 1940s, E. E. Schattschneider wrote that "political parties created democracy and modern democracy is unthinkable save in terms of the parties."[2] Perhaps he overstated the case, but contemporary political scientists tend to believe that democracies are *unworkable,* if not *unthinkable,* in the absence of political parties.[3]

When a country has two major parties, as in the United States, and one establishes clear dominance, that party is the **majority party.** The majority of citizens who express a party preference identify with this party. The majority party usually, but not always, has a majority of seats in the legislature. A party attains majority status by appealing to, and structuring programs for, a wide variety of interests. The **minority party** is the party that does not claim the allegiance of a majority of party identifiers. American politics has always had a major minority party that is striving to become the majority party. Basically, a minority party becomes a majority party whenever large groups defect from the majority. Many people who had previously not identified with a party may join these defecting groups. Whenever a massive, long-term shift occurs in voter allegiance from one party to another, a **partisan realignment** has occurred. A realignment suggests that an important change has taken place in the political culture and signals that the country is embarking on a new direction in public policy.

8-1a Functions of Parties

Political parties serve both to aggregate and to articulate interests. **Interest aggregation** is the process of bringing together various interests under one umbrella, and **interest articulation** is the process of speaking on behalf of these issue positions. Parties engage in both activities with the goal of winning elections.

In the United States, a person does not "join" a party. Rather, she simply identifies with it. A political party consists of those who hold office, seek office, and support those seeking office who identify with a common party label. These people all have the common purpose of winning office for themselves and/or other party members. The party label has meaning to these party identifiers, although the meaning is not necessarily the same for all identifiers. Although parties often stake out opposing policy positions and disagree over major issues, parties usually do not allow themselves to be identified in terms of a single issue. Rather, in order to win, they put together coalitions of voters attracted to various issues. A **coalition** is a loose collection of groups who join together to accomplish some common goal. Thus, parties provide a vital function in any democratic system. They promote compromise and cooperation among various interests. They allow the multiplicity of interests to find their voices, even though those voices may be somewhat muted.

The parties' tendency to promote compromise helps to ensure stability within the political system. In the United States, the Democratic party has traditionally represented a loose aggregation of diverse interests that might otherwise have little in common. For years, southern whites, Catholics, Jews, union members, African Americans, and various other ethnic groups were able to coexist in the party despite disagreements over social issues. The desire to achieve electoral victory enabled these groups to tolerate each other and find common interests. When this coalition fell apart, as it did during the Reagan era of the 1980s, the Republican party was able to win presidential elections convincingly, even though it remained the minority party.

Although parties structure alternative sets of public policy preferences on many issues, they can be expected to come together in any time of national emergency. Following the

majority party   The party with which the majority of citizens expressing a party preference identify.

minority party   A party that does not claim the allegiance of a majority of party identifiers.

partisan realignment   A massive long-term shift in voter allegiance from one party to another.

interest aggregation   The process of bringing together various interests.

interest articulation   The process of speaking on behalf of issue positions.

coalition   A loose collection of groups who join to accomplish some common goal.

September 11, 2001, attack on the United States, leaders of both parties embraced the president and quickly acted in almost total unanimity to provide President George W. Bush and his administration the legislation he needed to fund the military response and the increases in domestic security.

8-2 The Development of the American Party System

The Constitution does not mention political parties. This omission may be due to the Founders' fear that parties were a version of "factions," which they considered disruptive. Political parties "were widely regarded as hostile to the pursuit of a harmonious society and were seen as the agents of all manner of special interests."[4] Indeed, some thought that, by exacerbating political conflict, parties could place at risk the very survival of the new republic.[5] John Adams went so far as to assert that the emergence of political parties should be "dreaded as the greatest political evil under our Constitution."[6]

The first two articles of the Constitution addressed how members of Congress and the president, respectively, should be elected, but left the structure of campaigns to develop on their own. Likewise, although Article I outlines the powers of and limits on the Senate and House of Representatives, it says little about the organization of either chamber. Yet both the elective and legislative processes strongly implied the development of parties. In fact, it is difficult to imagine any but the smallest of nations conducting elections and passing legislation without political parties. Thus, even though the parties were basically inevitable in American politics, they have existed outside the formal constitutional framework.

As we noted, the Founders were wary of the influence of any organized group on the political process. Nevertheless, the first real attempt at organizing various interests for the purpose of affecting an election was to secure the ratification of the Constitution. The Federalists, including John Adams, George Washington, and Alexander Hamilton, strongly supported ratification. Those who opposed the ratification of the Constitution were known as Anti-Federalists. The Anti-Federalists represented a diverse set of interests and were united only by opposition to the Constitution. In four states—Virginia, New York, Pennsylvania, and Massachusetts—they came close to blocking ratification. Although the Anti-Federalists were too loosely organized to merit description as a political party, their opposition to the Federalists foreshadowed party competition and the emergence of the **two-party system**.

8-2a Parties in the Early Republic

The first president, George Washington, sought to avoid the formation of political parties by including diverse interests in his administration. What he got instead was severe factionalism *within* the administration. Alexander Hamilton, Washington's secretary of the treasury, was the major proponent of Federalist ideas. The Federalist program strongly supported banking and business and, by extension, the interests of the major cities. The centerpiece of the program was a national bank, which was desired by the business and banking interests.

Thomas Jefferson, whose views were sharply divergent from those of Hamilton's, was Washington's secretary of state. Jefferson became the spokesman for opposition to Hamilton's program within the administration. James Madison, who also opposed Hamilton's policies, led the opposition in Congress. Within a few years, the followers of Jefferson and Madison organized a political party under the name Democratic-Republicans. By 1796, both Federalist and Democratic-Republican candidates were presenting themselves to voters as members of opposing political parties. These party labels provided a cue to the voters. The voters could quickly determine the candidates' basic approach to government by their party affiliations. These early parties greatly simplified the task of voting in the fledgling republic by reducing complex issues to a simple choice. This reduction was vital if major issues were to be subject to rational decision making by government.

The Federalists won the presidential election of 1796, but Jefferson and the Democratic-Republicans won the election of 1800. The Federalists would not win another presidential

▶ **two-party system** A term used to describe the American political party system in which only two parties (Democrats and Republicans) have a realistic chance of controlling the government.

election. After Alexander Hamilton was fatally shot by Aaron Burr in 1804, the Federalist party went into a serious decline. The Federalists' opposition to America's involvement in the War of 1812, which proved to be both popular and successful, sealed their doom.

The Era of Good Feelings   After the disintegration of the Federalists, a brief period known as the Era of Good Feelings took place, when factionalism appeared to decline. During this period of one-party dominance, the Democratic-Republicans relied on a **congressional caucus** to choose their nominees for the presidency. A **caucus** is a meeting of all members of a legislature from a particular political party. This method ensured that the nomination decision would be dominated by party insiders. King Caucus, as it was called, was used to nominate Democratic-Republican presidential candidates from Jefferson in 1804 until the controversial decision to nominate William H. Crawford in 1824. The decision to nominate Crawford caused the other potential candidates—John Quincy Adams, Andrew Jackson, and Henry Clay—to launch their own campaigns. Adams and Jackson emerged as the eventual front-runners in the popular election, but no one earned a majority in the electoral college, throwing the election into the House of Representatives. Under the Constitution, the House can consider only the top three vote recipients in the electoral college. Henry Clay, who finished fourth in the electoral college, threw his support to John Quincy Adams, who had come in second. With Clay's support, Adams was able to win the election. The fact that Crawford, the caucus nominee, did not win the election, in addition to the perception of political corruption within Congress, led to the demise of King Caucus.

Andrew Jackson and the Origin of the Democratic Party   In the aftermath of the election of 1824, the Democratic-Republicans split into the National Republicans, championed by John Quincy Adams, and the Democratic-Republicans, who were led by Andrew Jackson. The Jackson wing, which would later evolve into the Democrats, became the dominant party, and supporters of Adams continued to offer competition. This period helped to redefine cleavages in the country. Jackson had appealed to working persons, exploiting class divisions and establishing the Democratic party as the party of the "common man." In addition, the Democrats took on a regional base in the South and the West and became the "majority party." This party began to develop an organizational base as candidates ran under its banner for state and local offices throughout the country. This party base was strengthened to some degree by the spoils system that Jackson championed. The **spoils system** is a system of staffing government that rewards supporters with jobs and contracts.

Democrats and Whigs   After Jackson came back to beat Adams in the election of 1828, the former Democratic-Republican party underwent a permanent split, which opened up an opportunity for other parties to join the fray. Many Democratic-Republicans who did not join the Jackson wing, along with people from other parties, created what became known as the Whig party. Its leaders were Daniel Webster and Henry Clay. Although the Whigs managed to elect William Henry Harrison in 1840 and Zachary Taylor in 1848, they continued to struggle as the minority party because of, in large part, their inability to unify their northern and southern branches. The Whig party was a viable minority party, however, in that it strongly contested major elections. The Whigs came to represent the interests of business and the eastern cities. In contrast, the Jacksonian Democrats directed their appeals to the "common man" and made structural changes to open up the party to wider participation.

8-2b Slavery and Party Realignment

The slavery issue split the parties in much the same way as it divided the nation. By the 1830s, those who were committed to ending slavery in the United States became organized under the abolitionist label. Under the leadership of William Lloyd Garrison, who wrote persuasively against slavery in his newspaper, *Liberator,* the nation confronted the issue on

congressional caucus A meeting of all those members of a legislature from a particular political party.

caucus A meeting of party members to discuss policy and direction, including the selection of presidential candidates.

spoils system A system of staffing government in which supporters are rewarded with jobs and contracts.

moral as well as economic and practical political terms.[7] The ensuing divisions led to the first great party realignment, which began in 1852 and continued for more than twenty-five years. The Democratic party had included both northerners and southerners. Andrew Jackson was unwavering in his insistence that slavery was allowed under the Constitution and that those who wanted to abolish it were suggesting changes that the Democrats found unacceptable. Later, his successor, Martin Van Buren, continued the Democrats' commitment to permitting slavery in the South.

The Whigs were less unified on slavery during the 1830s, when they were the **party out of power.** They were therefore less committed to the status quo and more likely to take the risk of establishing a new image.[8] In the 1840s and 1850s, first the Whigs and then the Democrats became increasingly split over the slavery issue. Out of the conflict emerged two parties dedicated to the abolition of slavery: the Liberty party and the Free Soil party. Slavery had effectively redefined the parties. The Whigs collapsed under the pressure, and the Democrats were weakened to a degree sufficient to make them vulnerable to the newly constituted Republican party.

> ▶ **party out of power** The party that does not control either the legislative or executive branch of government.

The Founding of the Republican Party   The Republican party was established in Ripon, Wisconsin, in 1854. It represented the interests of northern Whigs and Free Soil party members. This new party was clearly committed to the end of slavery. The Republicans nominated John C. Frémont for the presidency in 1856, but he received only 33 percent of the popular vote and lost the general election to the Democrat James Buchanan. In the years after Buchanan's victory, however, the Democratic party broke into rival factions over the slavery issue. By drawing support from antislavery Democrats, the Republicans soon became the majority party. Lincoln's election in 1860 and the ensuing Civil War left the Democrats as the minority party. They had split into southern and northern wings, and although the party survived, it was badly damaged.

The Republicans and Democrats have remained the two major political parties ever since the Civil War. For the most part, the Republicans have maintained their identity as the party of business. However, major shifts among great blocs of voters have periodically changed the nature of the parties. These shifts, or realignments, have come when the parties have reacted to major problems in society.

8-2c The Populist Revolt

The next great realignment of the parties came in the 1890s when widespread unhappiness with the economy was exploited by the Democrat William Jennings Bryan. The farmers, particularly hard hit, faced declining prices for their crops. The country was divided over monetary policy. The merchants of the East wanted to protect the price of gold. A new group, the Populists, led by Congressman Bryan of Nebraska, wanted to move to the silver standard, which they felt would benefit the farmers and other western interests. The election of 1896 split both parties around economic interests. Since the end of the Civil War, few major substantive issues had divided the two parties. This situation changed in 1896, with the Democrats' nomination of Bryan. Although the Republican candidate, William McKinley, won the election and the Republicans retained majority status, the interests that the parties aggregated and articulated shifted somewhat. In 1896, as in 1860, many voters shifted their allegiances. This was the second great **realigning election.** The cleavages in support were regional, with many states becoming one-party states.

> ▶ **realigning election** An election in which large numbers of voters change their allegiance from one party to another.

8-2d The Great Realignment of 1932

The two-party system remained stable from 1896 until the onset of the Great Depression in 1929. During this period, both parties mirrored the dominant political culture, which stressed minimal government intervention in the economy. Before the Great Depression, most Americans were not inclined to consider a large government role in the economy. But the depression changed the political culture and the political landscape for decades to come. The political parties changed to reflect the new political environment.

The depression of 1929 put millions of Americans out of work. Both in cities and on the farm, immense human suffering took place, and many feared that they would have no way to provide food or shelter for their families. President Herbert Hoover was constrained by the traditional ideology of the Republican party and was thus unable to offer the voters a reason to keep him in office to deal with the economic crisis. The Democratic candidate for president, Franklin Delano Roosevelt, offered a program that seemed radical at the time. Labeled the New Deal, it included a greatly increased role for government. Such programs as the National Recovery Administration (NRA), the Works Progress Administration (WPA), the Tennessee Valley Authority (TVA), and Social Security cast the federal government in the role of protecting citizens against economic ruin. The New Deal agenda also included price supports to help farmers, bank reform, and improved conditions for the nation's workers.

Beginning in 1932, the Democrats were able to assemble a viable coalition of voters. The elements of the New Deal coalition included southern whites, blacks and other ethnic groups, Catholics, and Jews. The party had the support of labor unions and residents of many large cities in addition to small farmers. The grand scope of their programs enabled the Democrats to appeal to a wide variety of constituencies. Roosevelt's appeal to the coalition was so strong that he was reelected to office in 1936, 1940, and 1944.

Holding the Democratic Coalition Together   Since the death of Roosevelt and the end of World War II, the Democrats have had much difficulty holding together their wide array of constituencies. For the most part, the Democratic party has remained the majority party, although it has experienced a number of serious challenges from the Republicans (see Figure 8-1). Despite being the minority party, the Republicans won the presidency in 1952, 1956, 1968, 1972, 1980, 1984, 1988, 2000, and 2004. Significantly, they gained control of both houses of Congress in 1994, leading some observers to speculate that the Republican party was on the verge of becoming the majority party in the United States. That, of course, has not happened. Indeed, by 2004 some political scientists were predicting the emergence of a new Democratic majority.[9] Due to the rise of the independent voter, it is unlikely that either party will maintain long-term political dominance in the future in the way that the Democratic party did in the decades following the great realignment of 1932.

The first shock to the New Deal coalition came from the civil rights movement. Roosevelt's successor was Harry S Truman, whose Fair Deal reached out to blacks in a way that concerned many southern whites. In 1948, many Southerners voted for a **third-party candidate** for president, Strom Thurmond, of South Carolina, whose party was called the Dixiecrats. Although Thurmond polled only about 2.5 percent of the popular vote nationally, his strong showing in the South earned him thirty-nine electoral votes. The Democrats were faced with a quandary that has concerned them ever since. How were they to appeal to southern whites and minorities at the same time? This tension produced another third-party candidate, George Wallace, who ran for president in 1968 and 1972. Both Wallace and Thurmond were southern Democrats who appealed to whites frightened by the civil rights movement.

The civil rights movement and its challenge to what was perhaps the strongest base of the Democratic party, southern voters, increased the tension between the national and the state and local elements of the party. The national Democratic party was increasingly liberal, although at the grassroots level in many areas the party remained conservative. **Grassroots party politics** are those activities that originate at the local level and work their way up through the party. They can be contrasted with policies that begin at the national level. The upshot of this conflict was that many Democratic voters chose to vote for Republicans and third-party candidates in presidential elections in which the national party seemed to them to be "out of touch."

The Democratic coalition has faced challenges beyond those connected with civil rights. Many in the party felt challenged by the lifestyle issues with which the party was forced to grapple in the 1960s. Writing in the late 1960s, the analyst Kevin Phillips foresaw

▶ **third-party candidate**
A candidate who runs for political office under some political party label other than Democrat or Republican.

▶ **grassroots party politics**
Activities that originate at the local level and work their way up through the party.

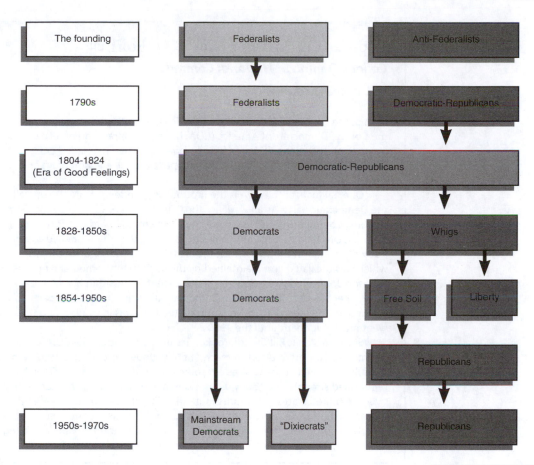

Figure 8-1
The Evolution of American Political Parties

an "emerging Republican majority" stemming from the dissatisfaction of many Catholic and working-class voters with the "intellectual" wing of the Democratic party, which seemed to be "soft on crime" and supportive of various nontraditional lifestyles.[10] Although most such voters did not change their party identification, many did, in fact, vote for Republican presidential candidates from the late 1960s to the late 1980s.

In fact, the Democrats were able to elect only two presidents between 1968 and 2004. The candidacies of Hubert Humphrey in 1968, George McGovern in 1972, Walter Mondale in 1984, Michael Dukakis in 1988, Al Gore in 2000, and John Kerry in 2004 failed to some extent because they were perceived to be "too liberal" on social issues. Much of the New Deal coalition deserted the Democrats during these elections, in large part because of uneasiness with the party's social policies. In fact, during this period the only successful presidential candidates were Jimmy Carter, of Georgia, and Bill Clinton, of Arkansas, southern governors who were able to keep southern and ethnic voters without alienating minorities and union members.

The Republican Coalition Since 1932   The Republican party has been the minority party since Roosevelt's victory in 1932. It has a more loyal constituency because the elements of its coalition have not been nearly as diverse or as quarrelsome as have the members of the Democrats' coalition. The Republican party has drawn its strength from white, suburban voters; Protestants; and small business. But divisions have also occurred among Republicans. In particular, the conservative elements of the party have been at odds with more mainstream views. Issues such as abortion have often divided these groups.

The Republicans have always had a smaller, but more closely knit coalition than the Democrats. This coalition can tolerate little shrinkage. When battles over core social issues,

Popular Culture and American Politics
College Democrat National Committee

By Chapman Rackaway

Both of the major political parties in America have college outreach organizations, and the College Democrats of America (CDA) has a proud tradition of its own. Like its Republican counterparts, the CDA was founded well before college-aged citizens had the right to vote. The CDA emerged in 1932 to help promote the election of Franklin Delano Roosevelt.

One hallmark of the CDA is the group's independence from the overall structure of the Democratic party. As an auxiliary, the CDA is partially funded by the Democratic National Committee (DNC) but has its own governing board and is housed separately from the DNC and its affiliated committees. The CDA's independence could have spelled its own downfall in the 1960s. In 1967, the CDA came out against the war in Vietnam, which was escalated and maintained by the incumbent Democratic president, Lyndon Johnson. Johnson did not appreciate the dissent from within his own party and, as a punishment for the CDA, used his authority within the Democratic party to withhold funding for the organization. Very quickly, the CDA was in trouble, and the organization went mostly dormant until the 1980s.

Since President Bill Clinton took office in 1992, though, the CDA has flourished. Clinton made a concerted effort to reach out to younger voters in his 1992 campaign, and as a result, he looked at the CDA as a resource and not a threat. The CDA subsequently rebounded strongly, and today it has more than five hundred chapters at universities all over the United States and counts more than fifty thousand members at those schools. Currently, the CDA also provides leadership opportunities to those students as part of the CDA's official structure. Eight national officers, all currently enrolled college students, serve the CDA in guidance, communication, and political outreach.

---

such as abortion, split the party, they almost always mean defeat in presidential elections. In 2000, the Republican candidate, George W. Bush, did his best to downplay the abortion issue, not only to hold his party together but also to avoid alienating prochoice independents, who might otherwise be favorably disposed to a Republican candidate. In 2004, the dominant social issue was gay marriage, and this played well for the Republicans. President Bush was able to take a conservative position on the issue without alienating many Republicans and also attracting some conservative Democrats and Independents.

8-3 The Contemporary Party System

The American party system is a loosely constructed two-party system built around a structure that mirrors the federal system. Most of the world's democracies have **multiparty systems.** In Great Britain, the major parties—Conservative and Labour—in some ways parallel the American Republican and Democratic parties. The British political parties are much more disciplined, however, with few party members voting against the leadership of the party in Parliament. Likewise, the British parties have more cohesive constituents. To some degree, the British pattern can be attributed to its unitary system of government as opposed to the U.S. federal system. In a unitary system, the national party does not need to be constructed on a base of state or local systems. Moreover, the British parliamentary system, in which the prime minister is chosen from the majority party in the legislative branch, has no counterpart to our "checks and balances."

The Founders constructed American national government to limit the power of factions. The party system reflects in many ways that desire to limit power. Just as the federal system retains states as policy-making units in government, the American party system retains state parties as policy-making units in party affairs. Just as the separation of powers

multiparty systems Political party systems in which several legitimate parties vie for control of the governmental system.

Popular Culture and American Politics
College Republican National Committee Profile

By Chapman Rackaway

Party politics has been open to young people since the late nineteenth century, but young people have been late to get on the bandwagon. Because people younger than twenty-one have been able to vote only since 1972, it's surprising that college-aged people have been formally involved in party politics for more than a century.

For Republicans, the College Republican National Committee (CRNC) is an opportunity to get involved in party politics and make contact with elected officials while still at a university. The College Republicans began in 1892 as the American Republican College League and has since grown into an organization boasting more than a hundred thousand members and chapters at more than a thousand college campuses in the United States.

The CRNC has a staff and leadership of ten people, all under the age of thirty, and most continue with their college careers while serving the College Republicans. The membership chooses a chairman every four years. The current chair, Eric Hoplin, is a graduate of St. Olaf College in Minnesota. Hoplin was previously head of the Minnesota CR chapter before he graduated in 2001.

Political party organizations recognize the vital role that young people can play in politics. Not only were young voters considered pivotal in electing Jesse Ventura governor of Minnesota in 1998, but they were also central to GOP gains in the U.S. House and Senate in 2002.

College party auxiliaries like the CRNC also provide the training ground for political professionals. Karl Rove is a previous CRNC chair, and the organization provides a field program with on-the-ground CRNC members assisting campaigns in battleground states. In 2004, the CRNC provided seven field operatives in Florida and six in Ohio. Training for the field operatives is also central to the organization. Its Fieldman School provides a crash-course in grassroots youth politics that trains College Republicans in four aspects of a mass-based youth effort: membership tables, the campus canvass, mock elections, and special projects. The CRNC claims that the Fieldman School had a major impact on many important races in 2002, including Minnesota, Missouri, and Georgia.

diffuses power between Congress and the president, the party system likewise diffuses the power of the parties to function as unified organizations.

8-3a Why Only Two Parties?

With rare exceptions, two political parties have always existed at the national level in the United States. This two-party system does not result from any direct design on the part of the Founders, who did not mention parties in the Constitution. The two-party system was not even consciously planned. Rather, it has flowed from other structural characteristics of American government as well as from American political culture.

The major reason for the two-party system has to do with the **winner-take-all** electoral system for president and Congress. In a winner-take-all electoral system, a party must capture the most votes in a district to obtain any representation in the government. For instance, a presidential candidate must win the most votes in a state before obtaining any electoral votes. In a winner-take-all system, a new party must win entire districts in a race for the House of Representatives before it has any representation in the House. It must win entire states before obtaining any Senate seats or accumulating any electoral votes for president. Thus, if a new party were to form and get 15 percent of the votes nationwide, it could easily end up with no House seats and win no electoral votes in a presidential contest. This system makes it hard for any new party to grow.

winner-take-all An electoral system in which a party must capture the most votes in a district to obtain any representation in the government.

Comparative Perspective

The Multiparty System in Italy

In 1922, Italy was taken over by the fascist dictator Benito Mussolini. During the 1930s and throughout World War II, Italy was allied with Nazi Germany. In 1946, three years after surrendering to the Allies, Italians voted to establish a democratic republic. Under the constitution of 1948, legislative power is vested in a bicameral parliament, which consists of a 630-member Chamber of Deputies and a 320-member Senate. With the exception of a few appointed members of the Senate, members of the parliament are elected directly by the people for five-year terms. Italy employs an electoral system which ensures that political parties receive proportional representation in the parliament—a political party will win a number of seats in the parliament proportionate to its share of the vote in the general election. Even a party that wins only 2 percent of the vote is ensured a few seats in the legislature. This system allows minor parties to proliferate. Italy now has more than thirty identifiable political parties. In the 1996 election, fourteen parties won seats in the parliament. This proliferation of small parties stands in sharp contrast to America's two-party system. On the positive side, Italian voters are offered more choices and can choose parties that more closely resemble their own views. On the negative side, politics in Italy are highly unstable, with governments changing hands frequently.

Another structural explanation for the two-party system is the difficulty third parties have experienced in getting on the ballot. Although the last two third-party candidates, John Anderson and Ross Perot, were listed on all fifty state ballots, the task continues to be quite difficult in some states. Indeed, in 1980, John Anderson had to sue election officials in some states to get his name on the ballot.[11]

Recently, the two-party system has been further cemented by the federal funding of presidential elections, established by the Revenue Act of 1971 and the Federal Election Campaign Act of 1974.[12] Since the 1976 election, the candidates representing the two major parties have received millions of dollars in federal funds to conduct their campaigns. A third party has difficulty obtaining the federal funding that the Democratic and Republican parties routinely receive. For example, in 1980, Independent John Anderson barely obtained the 5 percent of the popular vote in the general election that is needed to qualify for federal funds. Even if a third-party candidate qualifies for federal funds, the amount of funding is a fraction of what the major candidates receive. The major-party candidates' funding advantage makes it all but impossible for a third-party candidate to mount a viable campaign unless he has enormous personal resources, as did Ross Perot in the 1992 election.

In the 2000 presidential election, the 5 percent goal became of paramount importance in regard to Ralph Nader's candidacy. As the campaign drew to a close, surveys indicated an extremely tight race between Vice President Gore and his Republican opponent, George W. Bush. Moreover, Nader supporters came disproportionately from those who would otherwise have voted for Al Gore. Democrats, along with many in the media, began to put pressure on Ralph Nader to withdraw so as not to cost Mr. Gore the election. Meanwhile, many Nader supporters indicated that they were wavering in their support and considering a Gore vote. Nader steadfastly refused to ease up on his campaign, indicating that he was focused on building the Green party, under whose banner he ran. Clearly, to build a viable third party, the federal funding that would accompany the 5 percent total would be a crucial element. Nader supporters then faced a dilemma: Either vote for their first choice, Ralph Nader, and risk having their second choice, Al Gore, lose or vote for Al Gore and risk an outcome in which Ralph Nader would not receive enough votes to provide federal funding to the Green party in future elections. When the votes were cast, Nader did not get 5 percent. In many ways, the Nader dilemma underscores the almost impossible position of third parties in America's winner-take-all system.

What Americans Think About

The Two Major Parties

"Do you think there are any important differences in what the Republicans and Democrats stand for?"

	'64	'68	'72	'76	'80	'84	'88	'92	'96	'00
No Difference	44	44	44	42	34	30	35	35	35	33
Yes, a Difference	55	52	46	47	58	63	60	60	64	64
Don't Know	1	4	10	10	8	8	6	5	2	2

"Which party is better able to keep U.S. out of war?"

	'64	'68	'72	'76	'80	'84	'88	'92	'96	'00
Democrats	38	13	14	N/D	26	22	17	18	12	20
Same	46	50	50	N/D	51	48	52	59	69	60
Republicans	12	24	28	N/D	17	25	27	20	18	17
Don't Know	4	13	8	N/D	6	5	5	3	1	4

"Which party is more likely to favor a strong government?"

	'64	'68	'72	'76	'80	'84	'88	'92	'96	'00
Democrats	35	30	16	19	23	16	12	14	N/D	23
Same	19	26	32	38	28	27	20	28	N/D	19
Republicans	8	12	18	10	13	11	13	10	N/D	9
Don't Know	38	33	34	33	37	46	55	48	N/D	50

"Is one party more conservative?"

	'64	'68	'72	'76	'80	'84	'88	'92	'96	'00
Yes, Democrats	14	9	15	17	N/D	15	12	12	N/D	N/D
Yes, Republicans	59	63	57	54	N/D	53	57	57	N/D	N/D
No, Both Same, Don't Know	27	28	28	29	N/D	32	31	31	N/D	N/D

Source: Adapted from Center for Political Studies, University of Michigan, National Election Studies 1964–2000.

8-3b The Fate of Third Parties

Third parties have never won a presidential election in the United States. Nor have third parties remained a powerful force for more than a few years. The candidates and their supporters who have entered politics under the banner of a third party have usually done so out of frustration with the two major parties. For example, consider the Progressive party. Three totally different organizations were active under that name during the 1912, 1924, and 1948 presidential campaigns. The first Progressive party was also known as the Bull Moose party. Its candidate was the popular Theodore Roosevelt, who left the Republican party to oppose William Howard Taft in 1912. Roosevelt's platform contained many reforms that were later implemented by the major parties, including the right of women to vote and the direct election of U.S. senators. Though Roosevelt was not successful, his candidacy led to the election of the Democrat Woodrow Wilson. In 1924, another Progressive party was led by the Wisconsin senator Robert LaFollette. It too placed many items on the national agenda, including the recognition of labor unions. LaFollette carried only his home state of Wisconsin. Later, in 1948, Henry Wallace ran as a Progressive, but did not fare as well as Roosevelt or LaFollette.

Popular Culture and American Politics
Using Pop Culture in Political Campaigns

Every candidate who seeks his party's presidential nomination wants to make use of the symbols of American popular culture to get beyond complicated policy positions and communicate a simpler message. George W. Bush's election in 2000 was partially about a return to calmer, more orderly politics. Just eight years earlier, the message had been quite different.

The Clintons and the Gores had stood, and then danced, on the stage of the 1992 Democratic national convention. They wanted America to see them as candidates of change. The change they wanted to represent had more than a desired shift in policies: They wanted to be seen as representatives of a new generation— those born after the second world war.

These days, both political parties invariably have their nominees chosen well before the convention. Now the conventions are massive campaign rallies, with millions of Americans watching on TV. The party conventions have become a staple of pop culture—more entertainment than substantive politics.

Those who managed the 1992 Democratic convention knew the importance of cultural symbols. Even through the 1980s, the Democrats had clung to the symbols that had defined their party—the images of Franklin Roosevelt and the anthem "Happy Days Are Here Again." But voters born after the 1940s can hardly relate to the 1940s popular culture. They are, however, able to relate to the popular images of the 1970s and 1980s. By capping the convention with the Fleetwood Mac song "Don't Stop Thinking about Tomorrow," the Democrats were able to combine the symbols of their campaign with symbols of the broader culture. Although cultural symbols are not the stuff of election victories, those symbols can create a favorable climate for successful campaigns.

Pop culture is not always a positive benefit to a campaign. In 2004, the John Kerry campaign embraced Hollywood and the music industry, and the stars turned out in great numbers to perform benefit concerts and make guest appearances on Kerry's behalf. Some of the best-known celebrities to support the Kerry candidacy were Bruce Springsteen, Leonardo DiCaprio, Whoopi Goldberg, Sharon Stone, Chevy Chase, and John Mellencamp. Although the endorsements and appearances by celebrities attracted considerable media attention and infused much-needed money and energy into the Kerry campaign, the close association between Hollywood and the Democratic party became something of a liability. Many Americans, especially those of a conservative bent, react negatively to the values and lifestyles of Hollywood stars. In an election year in which "values issues" played an important role, the Kerry-Hollywood connection may well have been a net negative.

Third parties have been for the most part closely identified with charismatic leaders (see Table 8-1). That was certainly the case with Teddy Roosevelt in 1912. It was also true in 1968, when the Alabama governor George C. Wallace led the American Independent party in a national crusade against racial integration and other manifestations of modern liberalism. Decried by many as a demagogue, Wallace managed to earn nearly 14 percent of the popular vote in the 1968 presidential election. The Wallace candidacy was quite successful in foreshadowing the concern that many Americans felt about social issues. Many of these themes were later used with great success by Richard Nixon, Ronald Reagan, and George Bush.

The Rise and Fall of the Reform Party   In 1992, another charismatic individual, Texas billionaire H. Ross Perot, stepped onto the stage of American politics. His "party," originally named United We Stand, was little more than a hastily assembled organization to promote Perot's bid for the presidency. Perot's party was much more of an individual-centered organization than were any of the incarnations of the Progressive party. Nevertheless, with 19 percent of the popular vote in the 1992 election, Perot's candidacy was the

Third Party	Presidential Candidates
Bull Moose	Theodore Roosevelt ran for President as a member of the Bull Moose Party in 1912. The party platform contained voting reforms, promoting votes for women, and the direct election of Senators.
Progressive	Robert LaFollette ran on the Progressive Party ballot in 1924, emphasizing labor issues.
American Independent Party	George C. Wallace ran for President in 1968 as the American Independent Party candidate, campaigning against integration and modern liberalism.
United We Stand	H. Ross Perot's "United We Stand" party pushed for a balanced budget, tax reform, and campaign finance law reform in the 1992 election.
Green	Ralph Nader and the Green Party, promoting an environmentalist agenda, caused havoc in the 2000 election and was accused of splitting the Democratic vote.
Reform	As Perot's reform party splintered into diverse factions, Pat Buchanan ran as its Presidential candidate in 2000 with a conservative, isolationist platform.

T A B L E 8-1

American Third Parties

most successful third-party bid for the presidency since Teddy Roosevelt received 27 percent in 1912. Like Roosevelt in 1912, Perot forced the major parties and candidates to address issues and concerns that they might otherwise have chosen to ignore. Among Perot's priorities were balancing the budget, reforming the tax code, and strengthening campaign finance laws. In particular, Perot's 1992 campaign did much to put the federal budget deficit at the top of President Bill Clinton's priority list in 1993 and 1994. To some extent, the budget surplus of the late 1990s resulted from policies advocated by Ross Perot.

In 1995, Perot attempted to institutionalize his contribution to the American political dialogue by founding the Reform party. In 1996, the Reform party nominated Perot as its presidential candidate, to no one's surprise. However, Perot received only 8 percent of the popular vote in 1996, causing the party to fall into obscurity for nearly two years. In 1998, however, the Reform party scored a major success when one of its candidates, the former professional wrestler Jesse "The Body" Ventura was elected governor of Minnesota. After that, Ventura became the Reform party's de facto leader, although the party soon degenerated into factionalism. In 1999 and 2000, as the party prepared to nominate a candidate for president, it lacked any clear ideological direction. Rather, it was a hodgepodge of disaffected citizens and mavericks ranging from the billionaire Donald Trump to the Hollywood star Warren Beatty. In 2000, after a struggle for control of the party (and its federal matching funds), Pat Buchanan secured the Reform party nomination and barely registered in the presidential election. In the wake of this debacle, most observers declared the Reform party dead.

The Green Party   Green parties appeared in Europe in the 1970s and 1980s and in some countries, such as Germany and France, have had considerable success. Green parties are basically political parties centered around an environmentalist platform. In the United States, the Green Party espouses, according to its own publications, "ecological wisdom," grassroots democracy, social justice, feminism, and nonviolence.[13] It is an agenda well to the left of the Democratic party. The Green Party first appeared on the ballot in the United States in Alaska in 1990. In 1996, the longtime consumer activist and corporate critic Ralph Nader assumed leadership of the Green Party and in 2000 mounted a serious presidential candidacy. Although the Green Party has real ongoing appeal to a segment of Americans, Ralph Nader's successes in 2000 were more attributable to his strong name recognition and

TABLE 8-2

Major Third Parties' Share of the Presidential Vote, 1832–2004

Year	Party	Presidential Candidate	Percentage of Vote
1832	Anti-Masonic	William Wirt	8
1856	"Know-Nothings"	Millard Fillmore	22
1856	Secessionist Democrats	J.C. Breckenridge	18
1860	Constitutional Union	John Bell	13
1892	Populist	James B. Weaver	9
1912	Progressive (Bull Moose)	Theodore Roosevelt	27
1912	Socialist	Eugene Debs	6
1924	Progressive	Robert LaFollette	17
1948	States Rights	Strom Thurmond	2
1948	Progressive	Henry Wallace	2
1968	American Independent	George Wallace	14
1980	Independent	John Anderson	7
1992	United We Stand	Ross Perot	19
1996	Reform	Ross Perot	8
2000	Green	Ralph Nader	3
2004	Libertarian	Michael Badnarik	<1

dissatisfaction among some liberal Democrats with their party's candidate, Al Gore. In 2004, the Green Party and Nader parted company, and neither fared very well politically. Together, Nader and Green Party nominee David Cobb received less than 1 percent of the popular vote nationwide.

The Libertarian Party   The Libertarian party was founded in 1971 and held its first national convention one year later. In 1980, the Libertarian presidential candidate, Ed Clark, appeared on the ballot in all fifty states. By the 1990s, the party was firmly established on the American political scene. By 1996, the Libertarian party had become the first third party in American history to field a presidential candidate in all fifty states in three consecutive elections. In 2000, the Libertarian candidate, Harry Browne, again appeared on all fifty state ballots, although he garnered less than 1 percent of the popular vote nationwide. The Libertarian party has found a niche in American politics mainly because its ideologically consistent message calling for less government interference resonates with a significant segment of the electorate. The Libertarian party espouses free-market capitalism, advocates a noninterventionist foreign policy, and maintains a strong commitment to personal liberty.

Lesser Third Parties   Regardless of their limited potential to gather votes (see Table 8-2), the minor parties add a bit of spice to the political process. Most exist only at the presidential level and have no organizational structure. With the exception of the Libertarians, minor parties raise and spend little money. Although a few third parties manage to have a major effect in a particular election, many more linger for decades while capturing little interest or support. Many are on only a few state ballots. These parties come into existence outside the mainstream as a somewhat natural consequence of the fact that the two parties tend toward the center. Because "winning" is so unlikely, these third-party candidates are able to argue in favor of ideas that the major parties are afraid to touch. Later, these ideas often become part of the platforms of the major parties. Third parties fail to last, both because they are associated with individual candidates and because the system is so weighted in favor of two parties. But they do provide a valuable vehicle for protesting the status quo.

Third parties now tend to be narrowly ideological, basing their appeal on a fairly strict set of beliefs about government. Most are on the left side of the political spectrum. The parties arouse some interest, but they have a difficult time being taken seriously, mostly because their views are so far outside the mainstream. The Socialist and Socialist Workers parties are typical of these parties. The limited American appetite for socialism has greatly restricted their appeal, but they continue nevertheless. Other fringe parties represent conservative interests. These, too, have a difficult time being taken seriously, along with the potpourri of other parties, such as the Natural Law party and the Prohibition party.

8-4 Parties and the Governing Process

The parties have tremendous responsibility for government in the American system. When Bill Clinton was elected president in 1992, he campaigned as a New Democrat who could work with Congress to pull the federal government out of "gridlock." After the election was over, the parties were charged with the responsibility of governing rather than campaigning. For the first time in more than a decade, the Democrats held the presidency and a majority in both the House and the Senate. In this new political landscape, the Republican party had a complementary role, that of the **loyal opposition.** The role of the loyal opposition is to criticize the majority party, provide useful debate on legislation, and block the more extreme policies of the majority party. In 1994, however, the political landscape changed again. Republicans gained control of Congress, thus restoring divided-party government.

> ▶ **loyal opposition** The minority party in government. Its major roles are to criticize the majority party, provide useful debate on legislation, and block the more extreme policies of the majority party.

Divided-party government slows the policymaking process dramatically. A president has great difficulty getting his legislative agenda through a House or Senate controlled by the other party. When the opposition party controls the Senate, the consequences can be especially aggravating for a president; the Senate must approve judicial and other high-level appointments. Bill Clinton experienced frustration with the Republican-controlled Senate during his administration. Likewise, George W. Bush found himself facing a Senate controlled by Democrats early in his presidency. Slow Senate action, and often inaction, led to a tremendous backlog of judicial appointments. George W. Bush was unquestionably greatly relieved when the Republicans recaptured the Senate in the 2002 midterm elections. With Republicans in charge of both houses of Congress, President Bush had reason to believe that his agenda would be enacted. However, the war in Iraq and the 2004 election proved to be massive distractions for both the president and Congress. But Bush's victory over John Kerry in 2004 and the Republicans' solidifying majorities in both houses of Congress gave new life to the president's agenda in 2005.

8-4a The Party in Government

Elected officials are part of the **party in government.** The party in government consists of those officeholders from a particular party. Although party affiliation is crucial to the way the president and cabinet operate in office, they do not have to contend with members of the other party in day-to-day internal operations. At the same time, however, the president and cabinet have to be ever aware of their party in Congress and how it and the opposition in Congress will react. They also have to be sensitive to party identifiers in the electorate, most of whom were their supporters during the election.

> ▶ **party in government** The partisan-based activities of government officials.

Members of Congress are even more aware of their membership in the party in government. Congress is organized along party lines. The congressional Democrats and Republicans must take positions as party members. Above all, they must decide whether they will support positions of their party that are not in line with their own views or the views of their constituents in their district. Representatives and senators are also conscious of their role as supporters or opponents of the president's legislative proposals. Usually, members of the president's party in Congress are expected to support the president. However, this support cannot be assumed. For instance, in 1993, President Clinton could not persuade most Democrats to support the North American Free Trade Agreement (NAFTA). In fact, Richard Gephardt, the Democratic majority leader in the House of Representatives, and David Bonior, the House Democratic whip, led the opposition to NAFTA in Congress. Clinton won congressional support for NAFTA only by relying on a coalition of conservative Democrats and Republicans. Had the trade agreement not been negotiated principally by the Bush administration, Republican support might not have been forthcoming. The Democratic **party in Congress** did not deliver support for what the president wanted.

> **party in Congress**   The partisan-based activities of representatives and senators.

The party in government functions in a rather loose manner in modern American politics. Parties have weakened as institutions, and elected government officials face many pressures from organized interest groups. Pressures from party leaders to function according to a party agenda often are outweighed by perceived pressure from important groups and interests in a representative's state or district. For example, in early 1993, President Clinton proposed a complex BTU energy tax. The plan eventually was scrapped when Democratic senators from energy-producing states refused to go along with the Democratic leadership in the Senate, which was supporting the president. Clinton's later abandonment of the plan bothered many Democrats in the House of Representatives who had supported the president and the party despite their own misgivings about the plan's popularity in their district. In this case, the Democratic party in government was unable to operate with enough discipline to deliver a Democratic president's legislative program.

8-4b The Party in the Electorate

> **party in the electorate**   Voters who identify with a party label but do not participate in the party's day-to-day activities.

The **party in the electorate** refers to all those voters who identify with a party. In the United States, individuals do not formally express their party preference. The closest Americans come to making this type of declaration is when they register as Democrats or Republicans in those states that require voters to state a party preference to vote in a party primary. Most Americans express their party identification merely as a feeling. Thus, the Democratic and Republican parties in the electorate consist of those who say that they are Democrats or Republicans when asked "Are you a Democrat, a Republican, or an Independent?"

The party in the electorate refers to those voters who in national elections generally identify with a particular party. The term takes on less meaning between elections. The party in the electorate is mostly about electing candidates. Its official role is to nominate candidates for president. In that process, people participate as representatives of their parties, doing a party's main business: choosing who will run for office under its banner. Unofficially, the party in the electorate is the base on which the candidate hopes to build a winning electoral coalition.

Trends in Party Identification

Because Americans identify with, rather than join, political parties, the best way to determine the support for each party is to ask people "Do you consider yourself a Democrat, a Republican, or an Independent?" This measure, called party identification (see Table 8-3), is probably the best indicator of the status of the party in the electorate. When Americans answer this question, they are not necessarily indicating their voting preference in any particular election. Rather, they are expressing their affinity with one or the other party or, of course, a lack of affinity with either party. In many elections, voters choose a candidate from the opposite party. Over the long term, however, party identification is the best available indicator of how a person would vote in any election.

The University of Michigan has been regularly asking Americans about their party identification since 1952. The biggest change over the four decades has been the decline in those identifying with the Democratic party. The Republicans have remained the minority party throughout the period. The biggest increase has been among independents. These changes in the party in the electorate have not only influenced the outcomes of elections, but have also both reflected and changed the ways in which campaigns are conducted.

Party identification is a relatively stable and enduring force in American politics. With the exception of the 1964 election year, when Barry Goldwater pulled the Republican party further to the conservative end of the spectrum than many Americans were prepared to go,

TABLE 8-3	**Trends in Party Identification, 1952–2004**													
	'52	'56	'60	'64	'68	'72	'76	'80	'84	'88	'92	'96	'00	'04
Strong Democrat	22%	21%	21%	26%	20%	15%	15%	16%	18%	17%	17%	19%	19%	17%
Democrat	25%	23%	25%	35%	25%	25%	25%	23%	22%	18%	18%	18%	15%	15%
Independent Leaning Democrat	10%	7%	8%	9%	10%	11%	12%	11%	10%	12%	14%	14%	15%	17%
Independent	5%	8%	8%	8%	11%	13%	14%	12%	6%	11%	12%	10%	12%	10%
Independent Leaning Republican	7%	8%	7%	6%	9%	11%	10%	12%	13%	13%	13%	11%	13%	11%
Republican	14%	14%	13%	13%	14%	13%	14%	14%	15%	14%	15%	16%	12%	13%
Strong Republican	13%	15%	14%	11%	10%	10%	9%	10%	14%	14%	11%	10%	12%	16%
Other	4%	3%	4%	2%	1%	2%	1%	2%	2%	2%	1%	2%	2%	1%

Source: Adapted from Center for Political Studies, University of Michigan, National Election Studies 1964–2004.

year-to-year changes in party identification have been minor. However, in 2004, there is a very noticeable uptick in the percentage claiming to be "strong Republicans," which is certainly consistent with the outcome of the presidential and congressional elections of 2004.

The Rise of the Independent Voter   The most notable trend in party identification over the past four decades is the rise of the independent voter—the voter who identifies with no particular party. This is true not only in the United States, but also in most democracies around the world. "In almost all the advanced industrial democracies … the proportion of the population identifying with a particular party has declined in the past quarter-century, as has the strength of party attachments."[14] One reason for this phenomenon is the rise of mass media. Citizens no longer depend on parties for cues about issues and candidates. Rather, they get this information directly through the media. The prevalence of mass media has elevated the importance of a candidate's image while lessening the importance of that candidate's party affiliation. If voters have less need for partisan cues, they are less likely to form attachments to parties. Although the decline in partisan identification has affected both major parties, it has come more at the expense of the Democrats than the Republicans. It is important not to overstate this trend. Even in 2000, only 12 percent of the electorate identified themselves as straight independents, that is, not leaning toward either party.

8-5 The Structure of the National Parties

The political parties are organized around the American federal model. Unlike the federal system of government, however, the federal party system leaves much power at the state level. In fact, the national party offices are quite limited. There is little the national party offices can force the state or local parties to do. The national party has no control over who is nominated to run for an office under the party's name. Each state party controls the method of candidate nomination within the state. The national party also has little control over campaign finance. The national parties can provide assistance to the state parties or individual candidates, but the total amount of national party money spent in state and local races is a small fraction of all spending. Furthermore, after an individual is elected under the party banner, the party can do little to force that person to comply with the party's policy preferences.

The two major parties are organized with the national party at the top of the federal structure, but neither functions as a hierarchy, in the manner of the military or a business organization. Party leaders cannot issue commands that will be followed by the party members. A party is composed of individuals who are free to leave at any time. In fact, much of the party structure is composed of volunteers. Increasingly, the two major parties have hired professional staff members to perform organizational tasks on a day-to-day basis, but volunteers fill most of the decision-making positions. For the most part, not much of a party is in existence between elections. The party in most states has a small staff, and the national party has a somewhat larger staff, but most of the party organization lies dormant from election to election. In addition, the parties experience a great turnover in personnel from one election to another as volunteers choose to join or drop out because of their affection for a party's candidates.

8-5a The National Office

Both the Republican and Democratic parties conduct most of the national party's effort through the Washington offices of the national committee chair and the professional staff. The national chairperson is elected from among the members of the national committee. The national party chair appears regularly on television and radio news shows, defending the party's position or the position of major people within the party. Because the president acts as party leader, the chair of the president's party has less responsibility for maintaining party visibility, unity, and organization. The opposition party chair must provide a greater leadership role; several competitors within the party may be vying for power, so in the absence of a president from the party, the chair must protect the party's interests. In addition, the chair travels among the states, supporting candidates for state and national office, raising money for those campaigns, and building a **war chest** of funds for the next election. The party leader must have a complex set of skills, including being able to raise funds and assist in campaigns for important offices. In recent years, Terry McAuliffe, the Chairman of the Democratic National Committee from 2001 to 2004, best exemplified these traits.

> ▶ **war chest** The funds a political candidate accumulates to use for a campaign.

8-5b State Party Systems

Although the national parties garner much of the media attention, the state and local parties have historically been the most important element of each party. Each party has tremendous diversity across the states in terms of ideology and the issues that matter most to voters. For example, white Democrats in the South are much more likely to favor military spending and much less likely to support civil rights, gay rights, or social welfare than Democrats in the northeastern states or on the west coast. Republicans are more homoge-

---

Profiles & Perspectives

Terry McAuliffe (1957–   )

Photo courtesy Justin Paschal / Democratic National Committee

During the Clinton presidency, perhaps nobody was closer to the president than his longtime friend and supporter Terry McAuliffe, fundraiser extraordinaire for the Democratic party. A businessman with experience in real estate and insurance, McAuliffe has played for many years a key role in helping the Democratic party reach out to the business community. McAuliffe worked as a fundraiser for President Carter's reelection campaign in 1980 and for many other Democratic campaigns during the 1980s and 1990s. In 1996, he served as the national cochairman for the Clinton–Gore reelection campaign. McAuliffe played a major role in assembling corporate contributions to the 2000 Democratic national convention. Moreover, he was instrumental in arranging the finances for the Clinton's purchase of their house in Chappaqua, New York, before the former first lady's successful quest for the Senate. McAuliffe was elected the chair of the Democratic National Committee after President Clinton left office in January 2001. After assuming leadership of the DNC, McAuliffe said, "Our goal is to make the Democratic party the best-run, best-managed, best-organized, and best-funded political party in America." He also said, "When I decided to run for chair of the Democratic party, I did it for one reason: to win elections." McAuliffe's ascendance to power in the party highlighted both parties' increased role in raising money for campaigns and, to many observers, the increased need for campaign finance reform. McAuliffe's term as DNC Chairman ended after the 2004 presidential election, a contest that had to be extremely disappointing to McAuliffe. In the late fall of 2004, Democrats scrambled to find a suitable replacement. They would find it difficult to replace a party leader whose energy, organizational skills, and, above all, fundraising prowess were nothing short of amazing.

neous than Democrats, for the most part, but they also experience serious differences on issues such as abortion rights, school prayer, and other moralistic causes. Therefore, you cannot assume that all Democrats or all Republicans are the same.

Party Machines　The state parties also differ in history, party organization, and rules. Two of the historical factors that have been most influential in shaping state parties have been the presence of party machines and the progressive movement. **Party machines** are local party organizations that dominate elections in an area over a long period through a variety of both legal and illegal means. By distributing government jobs and contracts to loyal voters, the machines were able to keep many voters dependent on the party for their job security. Others received access to city services or direct assistance from the party. In some cases, machines resorted to illegal means of influencing elections, such as allowing loyal voters to cast more than one ballot, keeping dead voters on the voter registration lists so that others could use their names to vote more than once, or buying the votes of citizens. Two of the most notorious party machines were the Tammany Hall Democratic machine, in New York, and the Cook County machine, in Chicago, Illinois.

Party machines were most prevalent and most powerful at the turn of the twentieth century but then slowly began to lose their power. The expansion of the federal government since the Great Depression of the 1930s has taken away the machine's role of providing social service programs to loyal voters. The federal government is now involved in unemployment compensation, welfare, Social Security, and aid to families with dependent children, and anyone is eligible to receive the benefits regardless of party. Therefore, parties could not use the role of service provider as persuasively as they could before the New Deal programs. This loss made it difficult to hold voters in the fold.

The **progressive movement** also had an impact on the party machines. The progressive movement was an effort to reform government by eliminating fraud, corruption, and inefficiency. Like the founding generation, the Progressives were deeply suspicious of parties and sought to minimize their influence. The Progressives envisioned "a national community, in which new political institutions…would forge a direct link between public opinion and government representatives."[15]

Many government reforms favored by Progressives were direct assaults on the party machines. The **Australian ballot,** now used in American elections, allows voters to vote in secret and to choose between individuals of each party for each office. Because parties could no longer observe whether a voter cast a party ballot, the introduction of the Australian ballot made it more difficult to enforce party loyalty. The primary election is another reform that took power away from party leaders. Most state and local parties had used caucuses (party conferences) to determine the candidates the party would nominate for an office. Because the caucuses did not use secret voting, a well-organized machine could easily dominate the process. Primaries, however, take the decision out of the hands of the party leaders by allowing voters to choose party nominees through a **secret ballot.** Depending on the rules of the state, the primary may even allow independent voters to participate in a party's primary. Furthermore, in most states, the party cannot even control who is allowed on the ballot; the state establishes the rules for how a candidate is placed on the ballot.

Differences in Partisan Strength in the States　The strength of each party varies greatly from state to state. To understand partisanship in any state, one must examine its industrial development, urbanization, migration patterns, and the impact of historical events, such as the Civil War. The heavily industrialized states of the Midwest and Northeast have long had strong labor unions, so they also have had strong Democratic parties. Urban areas tend to have more minorities, which tend to be Democratic, so more urbanized states are more likely to have strong Democratic parties.

A large influx of new voters can affect a state's partisan orientation. For example, the migration of wealthy elderly people and Cubans into Florida has radically altered the state's politics. Wealthy senior citizens moving into the state from the North have made it more

party machines　Local party organizations that dominate elections in an area over a long period through a variety of both legal and illegal means, including distributing government jobs and contracts to loyal voters.

progressive movement　A movement during the early 1900s aimed at reforming government by eliminating fraud, corruption, and inefficiency.

Australian ballot　The secret ballot; used today in American elections, it allows secrecy for the voter and a choice between individuals of each party for each office.

secret ballot　See **Australian ballot**.

Republican. Because of their opposition to Fidel Castro, Cuban Americans are likely to be conservative voters. Both groups contributed to the emergence of the Republican party in Florida during the 1970s and 1980s. In 2000, these Cuban Americans supported by a large margin the candidacy of the Republican George W. Bush.

Historical events affecting partisanship can be either local or national. The Civil War is an example of a historical event that still influences partisanship in this country, particularly in the South. For most of the period from 1876 to the 1980s, the South was dominated by the Democratic party. Because Lincoln and the presidents during the Reconstruction period were all Republicans, the vast majority of white Southerners were Democrats. Black southerners were mostly Republican until the 1930s, when Roosevelt's New Deal legislation brought African Americans into the Democratic party. The Democrats' dominance in the South began to erode only as the Democrats in Washington began to push for civil rights legislation and social welfare programs in the 1960s. In the 1964 presidential election, the Republicans captured the majority of southern electoral votes for the first time in almost ninety years.

The South has continued to vote Republican at the presidential level since 1964, but until 1994 it remained heavily Democratic in state races and congressional elections. For example, the Democrats controlled a majority of the Congressional seats from the South, winning 90 of 147 seats in the 1992 election. In 1994, however, the Republicans won 77 of the southern seats (13 of 22 in the Senate and 64 of 125 in the House). The Republicans recently made great strides in states such as Florida and Texas, with Texas, Mississippi, and North Carolina each having two Republican U.S. senators for the first time since Reconstruction. By 2000, the Senate was evenly split at 50 for each party and the Republicans enjoyed a narrow 221–212 margin in the House of Representatives, with two members elected as Independents. The 2002 midterm elections saw the Republicans retake control of the Senate and extend their margin in the House. And in 2004, Republicans made additional gains, extending their margins to 55–45 in the Senate and 232–203 in the House. Most of these gains came in the South. By 2004, the once solidly Democratic South had become solidly Republican.

8-6 The National Party Conventions

> **national conventions**
> Meetings of party delegates to nominate their candidate for president. The conventions are also important in that they draw up the party platform, establish the rules that will govern the party, and select the new national committee.

The major political parties come alive at their **national conventions,** held every four years in the summer before the election for president takes place. These conventions are in many ways the only time the parties have a chance to present themselves to the American people. Since the 1950s, conventions have been televised. On occasion, they have provided viewers with excitement and entertainment. A successful convention is regarded as essential to the later electoral success of the party's candidate.

8-6a A Brief History of the Conventions

The first political convention was held in 1831 in preparation for the 1832 election. The Anti-Masonic party (a short-lived minor party) held the first national convention in 1831 in a Baltimore saloon and nominated a candidate to oppose Andrew Jackson, the incumbent Democratic president. Months later, the Whigs met in the same Baltimore saloon to nominate another opponent to Jackson. The Democrats held their first national convention in 1832 to confirm Jackson as their presidential nominee. In 1836, the Democrats met to confirm Jackson's chosen successor, Vice President Martin Van Buren. The Whigs chose not to have a convention but instead ran several candidates from different regions in the hope that they would prevent Van Buren from attaining a majority in the electoral college, thereby throwing the election into the House of Representatives. The Democrats prevailed, and Van Buren was elected.

Since 1836, the major political parties have routinely used conventions to choose the party's presidential nominee for the general election. The national party establishes rules for how many delegates are allowed from each state, the District of Columbia, and the territories. Generally, each state is allotted delegates in proportion to its percentage of the nation's population. Consequently, California, with nearly thirty million residents, received almost sixty times as many delegates to a convention in the 1990s as Wyoming, with less than half a million residents. The state party organizations determine how convention delegates from each state are chosen.

From 1832 to 1968, party leaders exerted much greater control over the conventions than has been the case since the 1970s. Indeed, state party leaders were crucial to the nomination of a presidential candidate. Two factors contributed to the power of the state leaders:

- *Most delegates were chosen by means of political caucuses, so they were part of the mainstream party organization.* The process of choosing convention delegates through a caucus system involves a complex organizational structure that begins with party supporters gathering in a series of local meetings all across a state. These local groups send a small number of delegates to a series of ever higher-level meetings that culminate in a statewide convention. The state convention determines the party rules for that state and selects its delegates to the national convention. Caucuses tend to be dominated by a small number of party activists. Because most states used caucuses until the 1970s, the vast majority of convention participants were professional politicians or party workers who had faithfully supported important political leaders. Furthermore, most delegates sent by a caucus system were not legally bound to support any particular candidate at the national convention. Therefore, the delegates could "shop around" at the convention to choose either a preferred candidate or the one with the greatest chance of defeating the other party's candidate.

- *The delegates from most states were generally more committed to the state's leaders than they were to the national party.* Patronage, a system that uses political support rather than merit as the basis of government hiring, was particularly useful in maintaining party loyalty. Because state leaders could command a large number of votes, presidential candidates had to bargain with them for the nomination. Most negotiations took place behind closed doors. At many conventions during these years, several ballots were needed to determine who would be the party's nominee.

8-6b The Rise of the Primaries

Wisconsin introduced the **direct primary** in 1903 as a device to involve more people in the nomination process. In a direct primary, party members vote for their preferred party nominee in a primary election that is held in the winter or spring before the party's national convention. Of course, the nomination of a presidential candidate reflects the federal system, with states having a good bit of discretion in how their convention delegates are chosen. Thus, it is not surprising that the state legislatures began to consider the primary as an alternative. By 1912, the Democrats were using presidential primaries in twelve states, and the Republicans were using them in thirteen states. The high point for primaries during this period came in 1916. More than 50 percent of all the Democratic delegates and almost 60 percent of the Republican delegates were chosen by primaries. But from 1920 through the election of 1968, fewer than 50 percent of the delegates were chosen by primaries in any given contest. Primaries fell from favor because of low voter turnout, their high cost, and the party leaders' desire to reassert their power over the nomination process. Case in Point 8-1 discusses the white primary, which is a system that excluded African Americans from party membership. The white primary was later struck down by the Supreme Court.

Types of Primaries   Primaries differ on a number of dimensions. Perhaps the most important distinction is between open and closed primaries. In an **open primary,** any voter can choose to participate in either primary merely by declaring her intention after entering the voting place. This system allows voters to cross over, or vote in the primary in which they sense the most excitement or in which they have the most interest. Most important,

> **direct primary**   An election held for the purpose of nominating a party's candidate for elective office.

> **open primary**   A type of direct primary in which any voter can choose to participate in either primary (Republican or Democrat) merely by declaring her intention after entering the voting place.

Case in Point **8-1**

The Death of the White Primary
Smith v. Allwright (1944)

In the early part of the twentieth century, southern states resorted to the infamous white primary as a means of keeping African Americans from exercising their right to vote in any meaningful sense. Until the 1960s, the "solid South" maintained a virtual one-party political system. In all but a few areas, nomination by the Democratic party was a guarantee of election. In fact, Republicans seldom bothered to run in the general elections. To keep blacks out of the political process, the Democratic party adopted in many states a rule excluding them from party membership. At the same time, state legislatures closed the primaries to everyone except party members. The Supreme Court had previously ruled that political parties were private organizations, not part of the government election apparatus. Consequently, through the white primary, blacks were effectively disenfranchised.

In the landmark case of *Smith v. Allwright* (1944), the Supreme Court overruled its own precedents and struck down the white primary as a violation of the Fifteenth Amendment. Writing for the Court, Justice Stanley Reed observed that the "opportunity for choice is not to be nullified by a State through casting its electoral process in a form which permits a private organization to practice racial discrimination in the election. Constitutional rights would be of little value if they could be thus indirectly denied."

▶ **closed primary** A type of direct primary in which a person must be registered as a Democrat or Republican to participate in the election to choose that party's nominee.

independent voters or voters from the other party can have as much effect on a party's nominee as that party's own voters. In contrast, in a **closed primary,** a person must be registered as a Democrat or Republican to participate in the election. Primaries also differ in the type of ballot voters confront after entering the voting booth. In some states, voters vote for delegates representing a candidate rather than vote for the candidate. In other states, the vote for the preferred candidate is a "beauty contest" that does not have any role in selecting delegates. In these states, party activists at a state convention choose delegates.

Advantages and Disadvantages of Primaries Versus Caucuses
The primary system offers several benefits over the caucus system:

- Voters can maintain the secrecy of their preferences for individual candidates in a primary, although doing so in a caucus is more difficult.
- A primary requires less time and energy for an individual to participate, so more people vote in primaries than attend party caucuses.
- A wider variety of people participate in primaries than in caucuses.

Because caucuses tend to be dominated by party activists, caucus participants are more extreme ideologically than primary voters. On the other hand, primaries are much more costly: The state has to pay for the election workers, voting booths, ballots, and other costs, and the candidates must pay for a campaign that reaches the millions of potential voters participating in a primary. Primaries also strip party leaders of their control over the nomination process. In some state and local elections, candidates have won the nomination even though state party leaders refused to endorse them. Delegates selected by primaries are also more likely to be required by law to vote in accordance with the results of the primary. This arrangement reduces the flexibility of the state's delegation at the convention. State party leaders no longer have as much opportunity to bargain with potential candidates.

8-6c Party Reform: 1968–2000

As late as 1968, most delegates to the national conventions were chosen by caucuses rather than through the primary system. That was the last year, however, that the caucus system delivered the nomination to the candidate of the party establishment. A number of dramatic events produced tremendous conflict within the Democratic party and led ultimately to a series of reforms that changed the nature of the party's nomination process. Early in the year, President Lyndon Johnson, beleaguered by protest against the Vietnam War and a poor showing in the New Hampshire primary, decided not to seek reelection. A number of candidates emerged to seek the Democratic nomination, including Hubert H. Humphrey, the incumbent vice president; Eugene McCarthy, a U.S. senator from Wisconsin; and Robert F. Kennedy, who represented New York in the Senate. Contrary to the Johnson administration, both Kennedy and McCarthy opposed continued American involvement in Vietnam. Kennedy and McCarthy tried to take their messages to the people directly by actively campaigning in state primaries. Many young people and others dissatisfied with traditional politics participated in these campaigns. These newcomers provided tangible assistance but also created an image of a new type of campaign that was not beholden to party insiders. In contrast, Humphrey decided to forgo the primaries and rely instead on his close ties to the party leadership throughout the states.

In the spring of 1968, both Martin Luther King, Jr., and Robert Kennedy were assassinated, creating turmoil throughout the nation but especially inside the Democratic party. Some of Kennedy's support went to Senator McCarthy; some went to a new candidate, Senator George McGovern, of South Dakota. In any event, Humphrey won enough delegates to secure the nomination. The Democratic national convention of 1968 was held in Chicago, where Mayor Richard Daley was determined to control the convention and deliver the nomination to Humphrey with a minimum of difficulty. The convention was a nightmare for the Democrats, with thousands of outraged protesters convinced that the party had ignored the wishes of the people in choosing Humphrey. Many saw the party nomination system as closed and even corrupt. Pressure to open up the process to more popular participation followed.

The Democratic party found itself in a precarious condition after the 1968 convention. Its traditional base had been shattered. Many union and blue-collar voters had bolted to the Republican candidate in response to the antiwar, procivil rights, and perceived radical direction of the Democratic party. Humphrey had run third during a good bit of the campaign, trailing both the eventual winner, Richard Nixon, and George Wallace, an independent candidate from Alabama. Southerners, most of whom had voted Democratic since the Civil War, were now defecting from the party. The once "solid South" appeared to have been lost.

In 1968, the party formed a commission, headed by George McGovern, to recommend changes in the rules of delegate selection.[16] Congressman Donald Fraser chaired the committee after McGovern resigned to seek the presidency. It issued its report in 1970 and has since been referred to as the **McGovern–Fraser Commission.** In essence, the McGovern–Fraser rules were designed to open the Democratic party to wider participation by women, minorities, and young people (see Figure 8-2). The rules also loosened the grip of traditional party bosses.

The rules suggested by the McGovern–Fraser Commission took effect in the 1972 presidential election. The major way the rules were enforced was by the convention's ability to judge the credentials of any delegation sent by a state. Any state whose delegation did not pass muster risked having an alternative delegation seated in its place. Rather than risk these types of challenges, the state parties pressured state legislatures to change the law determining the basis of selection. The easiest way to meet the McGovern–Fraser requirements was to institute a delegate-selection primary. More and more states opted for primaries, and the majority of delegates to the national convention are now chosen by primaries.

Somewhat ironically, the first Democrat to benefit from the rules changes was George McGovern. His nomination as the Democratic candidate for president in 1972 came from a convention that better reflected the racial and gender diversity of the country. Few party professionals were in attendance. The nomination, however, was doomed from the outset, because the American public was put off by the party it observed on television.

The Superdelegate System

The Democrats have repeatedly reformed their nomination process since the dismal showing of 1972. Nearly every convention has reformed the process in some way. One of the more significant changes was the introduction of the

> ▶ **McGovern–Fraser Commission** Part of the Democratic party reform movement of the 1970s that designed rules aimed at opening the party to wider participation by women, minorities, and young people. The rules also loosened the grip of traditional party bosses.

Figure 8-2
Major Reforms of the
McGovern–Fraser Commission

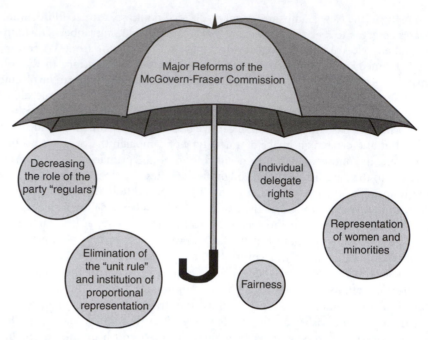

Fairness	All rules must be open and posted.
Elimination of the "unit rule" and institution of proportional representation	A state delegation cannot vote by majority rule to cast all its votes as a bloc. The final delegation should reflect choices made at the district levels.
Decreasing the role of the party "regulars"	The number of delegates the party committees of each state could send were limited, and elected officials would not receive automatic slots in the state delegation.
Individual delegate rights	No delegate can be compelled to cast a vote that was not the delegate's choice when selected.
Representation of women and minorities	Delegations from the states should reflect the racial and gender makeup of the state.

superdelegate Key party member, usually an elected official, who is not required to commit to a nominee until the national convention.

superdelegate system in 1984. Concerned that few party leaders had attended the 1976 and 1980 conventions, the party set aside a certain number of delegate spots for elected party officials. These superdelegates can be members of Congress, governors, or mayors. The superdelegates provide three main benefits for the party:

- First, because of their name recognition, their presence brings the party more media attention.
- Second, the support of a wide range of Democratic leaders gives a strong display of party unity.
- Because the superdelegates are not determined by primary elections and are not legally bound to vote for any particular party nominee, the superdelegates allow the national leaders of the party to have more control over the party than they had during the 1976 and 1980 conventions.

In 1986, the Democrats created another commission, the Fairness Commission, to study complaints that the convention was not allowing minority views to be truly reflected among the delegates who were selected. Jesse Jackson had won about 18 percent of the Democratic vote in 1984 but only 10 percent of the delegates to the convention. This phenomenon occurred because states had been required by party rules to ensure that a candidate who received 20 percent of the popular vote in a primary also received at least an equal percentage of the delegates. This percentage was changed to 15 percent for 1988, which had the effect of increasing the clout of second- or third-place candidates.

The Democratic Leadership Council and Super Tuesday   The increase in the number of primaries weakened the hold of the party professionals on the nomination process. Moreover, as the nominations of McGovern, Mondale, and Dukakis demonstrated, the process had become dominated by the more liberal states. For instance, Iowa, with its caucus, and New Hampshire, with its primary, are the first two states to begin the delegate selection process. This arrangement gives the Democrats of these states tremendous power in determining the nominee. Especially in Iowa, where only a small percentage of the party's voters even take the trouble to attend caucus meetings, moderate and conservative candidates seemed to be at a pronounced disadvantage.

In 1986, a group of southern Democrats decided to push for reforms that would give the South more clout in the nomination process and thereby increase the likelihood of a more moderate, and hence more electable, Democratic nominee. Their idea was to have the southern states hold their primaries on one day, early in the primary season. This idea proved popular with state legislatures throughout the South. In 1988, fourteen southern and border states moved their primaries to **Super Tuesday.**

Super Tuesday did not work as planned in 1988. Jesse Jackson received most of the votes of African Americans, offsetting to a large degree the strong showing of Tennessee Senator Al Gore, the more moderate of the candidates. Meanwhile, Michael Dukakis did well in Florida and Texas. Super Tuesday had little effect on the 1988 election. It did, however, play a major role in the nomination of Bill Clinton in 1992. Clinton emerged from Super Tuesday as the clear front-runner. Shortly thereafter, Clinton's main rival, former Senator Paul Tsongas, of Massachusetts, suspended his campaign because contributions were drying up. Even though Super Tuesday did not give Clinton enough delegates to clinch the nomination, it effectively delivered a knockout blow to the other candidates.

By 2000, Super Tuesday had declined dramatically in importance. Rather, the nominations of each party rested on issues peculiar to various states after the end of the New Hampshire primary. For instance, George W. Bush had to fight off a stronger than expected showing by John McCain, who had won in New Hampshire. The battle centered on two states, South Carolina and Michigan. In South Carolina, the issues centered around the confederate flag and its place in the state capitol building as well as around Bush's appearance at Bob Jones University. Michigan had changed its rules to allow any voter to vote in any party's primary. Although McCain won Michigan, largely with the help of Democrats who crossed over, Bush ultimately prevailed in securing his party's nomination. In 2004, George Bush's nomination by the Republicans was never in doubt, and John Kerry's nomination as the Democratic standard-bearer was all but assured before Super Tuesday.

> **Super Tuesday**   The second Tuesday in March when most southern states hold their presidential primaries.

Republican Reforms   Most reforms in the nomination process have taken place at the instigation of the Democratic party, mainly because the Democratic party includes a more diverse array of interests than the Republican party does. Thus, more interests are fighting for influence and representation. Republicans have not appointed commissions to study reform. Nevertheless, they have adopted many of the changes the Democrats have championed. Of course, new state laws, such as those creating primaries and Super Tuesday, have also affected them.

8-6d The Convention Delegates

The national convention held every four years during the presidential campaign serves as the supreme governing body for each national party. The conventions are composed of delegates from each of the fifty states, the District of Columbia, and the territories. In 2004, the Democrats had 4,353 delegates at their convention in Boston, and the Republicans had 2,509 delegates at their convention in New York City. The Republicans determine the number of delegates representing each state-by-state population. The Democrats employ a rule that apportions delegates on the basis of a combination of state population and how well the party performed in the last presidential election in the state. The two major parties vary greatly in their rules, structure, and method of choosing delegates to the convention.

In general, the delegates of both parties tend to be more extreme than the general electorate in their ideological persuasion. The Republican delegates tend to be more conservative and the Democratic delegates more liberal than those who identify with the parties. For example, in 1992, 24 percent of the self-described Democrats in a national survey identified themselves as being conservative, although only 5 percent of Democratic convention delegates self-identified as conservative. On the other hand, 8 percent of Republicans nationally identified themselves as liberals and only 1 percent of Republican convention delegates adopted the liberal label.[17]

Figure 8-3 profiles Democratic and Republican convention delegates in five presidential elections: 1968, 1976, 1992, 1996, and 2000. These numbers are really not surprising. Party activists enter politics because they tend to care about issues. Those who become delegates take these commitments to the convention. Those who run the conventions must take care, however, that the convention rhetoric is not too extreme for the tastes of the general public. That was apparently the case at the 1992 Republican national convention, where right-wing elements of the party made speeches that were not well received by the general public. This situation may have hurt George H.W. Bush somewhat in the 1992 general election.

In the 2000 campaign, Republican candidate George W. Bush did not allow an intolerant image to emerge. Quite to the contrary, he helped present an image of softness and inclusiveness—his so-called "compassionate conservatism." A significant number of African Americans and women graced the podium, with nary a word about the cultural warfare alluded to in 1992. Although Bush's attention to this image ultimately did little to increase his share of the African American vote, his softer approach did apparently ease the concerns of many moderate voters, especially women, who had helped lead to Republican defeats in the preceding two elections. Seeking reelection in 2004, Bush talked less of compassionate conservatism and instead stressed his leadership in the global war on terrorism and the need to stay the course in Iraq. Despite Democratic efforts to paint him as a right-wing extremist, Bush was able to maintain sufficient support from women, moderates and, significantly, from Hispanics. To a great extent, Bush's warm and friendly style helped offset negative characterizations in the media.

One issue that resonated during the primaries in 2000 but much less so during the general election that followed was campaign finance reform. Although there were no significant differences between the two parties' identifiers in the public, substantive differences existed between the two parties' delegates. Democratic delegates were much more likely to support reform than were those to the Republican convention.[18]

8-6e The Functions of the Conventions

The national convention chooses the party's candidates for president and vice president, determines the party platform, and establishes the rules governing the party for the following four years. Both parties use majority rule among the delegates to make most decisions, but in the modern campaign the presidential nominee of each party orchestrates much of what happens. Because the majority of delegates have already been pledged to vote for a particular candidate before the convention, no convention since 1968 has featured a wide-open contest that created any suspense. Because the eventual nominee controls the majority needed to win before the convention, the most important function of the convention is to provide the party with a tremendous advertising opportunity. The government contributes the financing for the convention for each of the two major parties, and the major networks provide hours of prime-time coverage. Each party uses its convention to demonstrate how it has rallied around the candidate, and the nominee usually enjoys a public opinion boost.

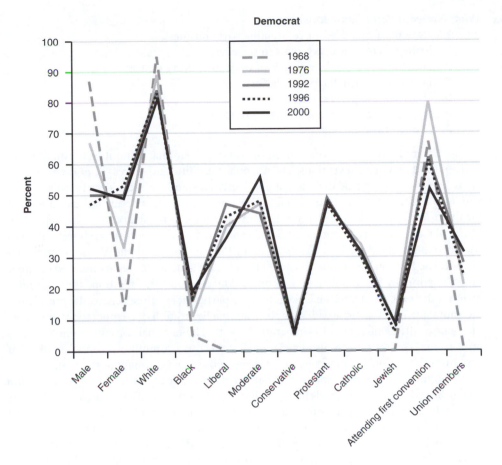

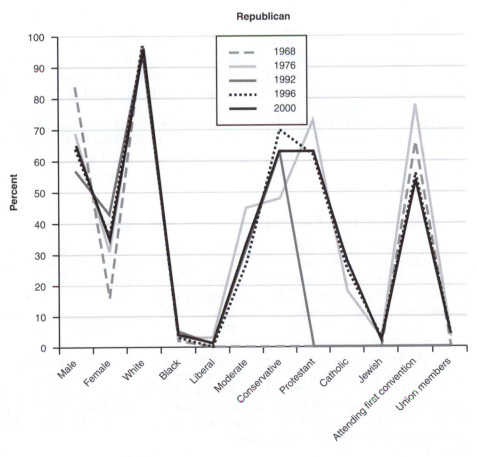

Figure 8-3
Profiles of Democratic and Republican Convention Delegates: 1968, 1976, 1992, 1996, and 2000

Source: Adapted from Harold W. Stanley and Richard G. Niemi, *Vital Statistics on American Politics 2003–2004* (Washington, D.C.: CQ Press, 2003), p. 75.

What National Party Conventions Do

1. Determine the rules for conducting party business.
2. Bring together diverse groups in the party.
3. Develop and provide exposure of upcoming party leaders.
4. Debate and write the party platform.
5. Showcase the party's image.
6. Nominate the president and vice president.
7. Launch the campaign.

Another function of the convention is choosing a national committee to run the party in the period between conventions. The national committee organizes the next convention, helps conduct the presidential campaign, formulates and publicizes party policies, and appoints a national chair. It can also fill any vacancies that may occur in the nominations for the office of president and vice president before the general election. The Republican National Committee is composed of a male and female member from each state, the District of Columbia, American Samoa, Guam, Puerto Rico, and the Virgin Islands. The Democratic National Committee is much larger; each state is allowed committee members in proportion to the number of its convention delegates. In addition, the committee includes the party leader in the U.S. House, the party leader in the Senate, the president of the Young Democrats, the president of the National Federation of Democratic Women, and the chair of the Conference of Democratic Mayors. The national committees meet at least once a year. The Democrats also have a smaller executive committee, composed of members from the national committee, which meets more often throughout the year.

> **party platform** A statement of a political party's goals and policies.

The **party platform,** a document that is developed at a party's national convention, establishes what the party stands for. Usually, the party's presidential candidate controls the process that creates the platform, but the final document is typically a compromise that may contain elements that are not even fully supported by the presidential candidate. Party members in Congress, the state legislatures, and the electorate are free to choose which aspects of the platform they support. The national party cannot force public officials to enact policy consistent with the platform.

Many people scoff at party platforms. No expectation exists in American political culture that parties should be bound by their platform promises. Indeed, cynicism about the platform has itself become a staple of the culture. Nevertheless, the platforms have tremendous symbolic importance for those who are intensely interested in the issues the platforms address. With the advent of various single-issue groups, some issues, such as abortion, generate tremendous interest.

The Republican and Democratic platform planks concerning abortion in 1992 showed the clear differences between the parties on this issue. The Republican plank, which was adamantly prolife, represented a victory for the conservative wing of the party. The president's wife, Barbara Bush, distanced herself from the plank, and the president never committed himself to pushing a "human life" amendment to the Constitution.

8-7 Decline and Revitalization of the Parties

> **dealignment** The movement of voters away from identifying with a political party.

As partisanship in the electorate eroded over the past few decades, most scholars lamented the slow death of political parties in America. Because political parties are seen as stabilizing forces within the political system that can make politicians more accountable to the voters and produce more coherent policies, the **dealignment** of our party system was seen as detrimental to democracy. Throughout the 1960s and 1970s, parties declined in importance as a voting cue for most citizens and as a defining theme of most campaigns. Increasingly, candidates rather than parties were the focus of campaigns. These **candidate-centered campaigns** were seen as lacking in accountability but overflowing with special-interest money, slick advertising campaigns, and too much mudslinging. The increasingly important role of television, political consultants, and large amounts of money made parties less influential. In addition, the Watergate scandal, which involved Republican President Nixon's administration, devastated the Republican party and caused declining levels of trust in government and both political parties.

> **candidate-centered campaigns** Campaigns for office that stress the personal characteristics of the candidates rather than the party.

To make matters worse, the campaign finance reforms of the early 1970s further eroded the parties' influence on campaigns, and the restrictions on party spending made many observers wonder why the parties themselves were not more visible actors in the 1976 presidential election between the Republican Gerald Ford and the Democrat Jimmy Carter.[19] This combination of factors seriously undermined the influence of parties, and many observers questioned whether parties could be revived.

The Watergate scandal and the resulting loss of the presidency in the 1976 election forced the Republicans to revamp the party by improving the resources and facilities needed to influence future campaigns. The Republicans became much more proficient at raising money, distributing money to candidates, and spending money on media resources and technology. The new forms of campaigning that developed during the 1980s required expensive equipment and expertise. The Republicans were the first to invest heavily in media support facilities, direct mail advertising, computer targeting of voters, and polling. The Republican national party had a technological advantage over the Democrats in terms of the assistance it could provide candidates. The Democrats had only begun to narrow this gap during the late 1980s and early 1990s.

In response to the limited role of parties in the 1976 presidential election, Congress changed the federal campaign-finance rules so that parties could raise and spend more money independently of the candidates. Because candidates were spending the money they raised on developing their own name recognition rather than communicating party interests, the parties had to fend for themselves. The campaign finance change that had the most effect was the creation of a legal loophole that allowed **soft money.** This change in the campaign finance laws permitted parties to raise and spend money for general political activities—such as bumper stickers, mass mailings supportive of the party but not a particular candidate, and phone banks urging potential party supporters to get out and vote—that are not covered by the limits on contributions to presidential or congressional candidates. As a result, individuals can give as much money as they want to the party, either state or national. Together, the two parties raised more than $168 million in soft money in the 2001–2002 election cycle.

> **soft money** The unlimited funds donated to political parties for the purpose of party-building activities, such as party bumper stickers, get-out-the-vote drives, and party mailings.

As a result of both parties' efforts to modernize and the legal change allowing soft money, the national parties of the 1990s were more influential than they were in the 1970s. The resurgence of the parties was threatened, however, when President Bush signed the campaign finance reform bill in 2002. Under campaign finance reform, parties are restricted in their ability to raise soft money. The effect it will have on the role of the parties remains to be seen, but the 2004 presidential campaigns suggest that the reforms weakened somewhat the ability of the parties to control campaign messages. In 2004, independent groups like MoveOn.org and the Swift Boat Veterans for Truth greatly eclipsed the role of the parties in supporting their preferred candidates.

8-8 Conclusion: Parties and Contemporary Political Culture

Many if not most Americans view political parties with suspicion, even scorn. This negative reaction is deeply rooted in American political culture. Most of the Founders were not fond of political parties even though many of them joined parties after they appeared on the scene around the turn of the nineteenth century. Most of George Washington's contemporaries agreed with him when he decried parties for provoking the "mischiefs of faction." Washington's view is still widely shared now because many people are turned off by partisan bickering and maneuvering. Americans seem to regard parties as, at best, a necessary evil.

With the advent of the media age, voters depend less on parties to structure their participation and guide their political choices. With the development of open primaries, party regulars have a rough time controlling the nomination process. At the November elections, Americans have little difficulty splitting their tickets and voting for candidates of different parties for different offices. All these factors conspire to weaken the parties and, some would say, debilitate government.

> **single-issue politics**
> Activities centered around one particular policy area, such as gun control or abortion.

American parties have been slow to respond to changing conditions. Their structure has remained essentially the same since the 1950s, when parties were the main vehicles many Americans had for participating in politics. On the other hand, interest groups (see Chapter 9, "Interest Groups") have been more creative in gaining members and in communicating with them. Unfortunately, this situation has led to an increase in **single-issue politics** and worked against forces that promote consensus in society.

Despite the loose and often contentious nature of the party coalitions, the American two-party system has been remarkably stable. The American party system does not always offer voters a clear policy choice, nor does it ensure that a coherent set of government policies will be pursued after the elections are over. Although the two-party system does not bring discipline to the governing process, it does act as a force for stability. As long as the two-party system exists, parties will be forced to bring together many groups if they are to hope to win elections. As American political culture strains under forces that isolate and separate groups of citizens, the much maligned two-party structure provides one of the few forces capable of drawing together groups of citizens.

Questions for Thought and Discussion

1. Why did the Framers not mention political parties in the Constitution?
2. Why have third parties not been more successful in the United States?
3. Are political parties necessary in a democracy? Are they desirable? Are they inevitable?
4. Why have so many states chosen to select delegates to the national party conventions through primaries rather than through party caucuses or state conventions? Is this trend good for American democracy?
5. What changes in the laws governing campaigns and elections would strengthen political parties?

Practice Quiz

Note: You can find the correct answers to these questions by taking the quiz and then submitting your answers in the Online Edition. The program will automatically score your submission. If you miss a question, the program will provide the correct answer, a rationale for the answer, and the section number in the chapter where the topic is discussed.

1. _____ are local party organizations that dominate elections in an area over a long period through a variety of both legal and illegal means.
   a. Grassroots machines
   b. Political machines
   c. Precincts
   d. Wards

2. The _____ attempted to reform government by eliminating fraud, corruption, and inefficiency.
   a. progressive movement
   b. populist movement
   c. Era of Good Feelings
   d. clean sweep

3. In _____ (1944), the Supreme Court struck down the white primary as a violation of the Fifteenth Amendment.
   a. *Baker v. Carr*
   b. *Smith v. Allwright*
   c. *Reynolds v. Sims*
   d. *Grovey v. Townsend*

4. The first political convention was held in 1831 by the _____ party.
   a. Democratic-Republican
   b. Democratic
   c. Whig
   d. Anti-Masonic

5. Wisconsin introduced the _____ primary in 1903 as a device to involve more people in the nomination process.
   a. direct
   b. open
   c. closed
   d. reformed

6. The primary purpose of the major parties' national conventions is to _____.
   a. nominate the party's chairperson
   b. establish and define the party's platform
   c. establish the rules that will govern the party
   d. nominate their candidates for president and vice president

7. The _____ was part of a Democratic party reform movement of the 1970s that designed rules aimed at opening the Democratic party to wider participation by women, minorities, and young people.
a. progressive movement
b. McGovern–Fraser Commission
c. Grace Commission
d. reform movement

8. The first great party realignment emerged from conflict over _____.
a. the populists' insistence on backing the federal money supply with a gold standard
b. slavery
c. the death of "King Caucus"
d. western expansion

9. The second great realigning election was precipitated by _____.
a. slavery
b. the populist movement
c. the death of "King Caucus"
d. World War I

10. A decline in party identification among the masses of voters is referred to as _____.
a. an electoral split
b. a realignment
c. a proportional split
d. a dealignment

For Further Reading

Aldrich, John H. Why Parties? *The Origin and Transformation of Party Politics in America* (Chicago: University of Chicago Press, 1995).

Beck, Paul Allen, and Marjorie Randon Hershey. *Party Politics in America*, 9th ed. (New York: Longman, 2001).

Burnham, Walter Dean. *Critical Elections and the Mainsprings of American Politics* (New York: W. W. Norton, 1970).

Diamond, Larry, and Richard Gunther. *Political Parties and Democracy* (Baltimore, MD: Johns Hopkins University Press, 2001).

Disch, Lisa Jane. *The Tyranny of the Two Party System* (New York: Columbia University Press, 2002).

Epstein, Leon. *Political Parties in the American Mold* (Madison, WI.: University of Wisconsin Press, 1986).

Gould, Lewis. *Grand Old Party: A History of the Republicans* (New York: Random House, 2003).

Keefe, William J., ed. *Political Parties and Public Policy in America* (Washington, D.C.: CQ Press, 1998).

Lublin, David. *The Republican South: Democratization and Partisan Change* (Princeton, NJ: Princeton University Press, 2004).

Maisel, L. Sandy, ed. *The Parties Respond: Changes in American Parties and Campaigns*, 4th ed. (Boulder, CO: Westview Press, 2002).

Milkis, Sidney M. *Political Parties and Constitutional Government: Remaking American Democracy* (Baltimore, MD: Johns Hopkins University Press, 1999).

Polsby, Nelson W. *Consequences of Party Reform* (New York: Oxford University Press, 1983).

Pomper, Gerald M., ed. *Party Organizations in American Politics* (New York: Praeger, 1984).

Price, David E. *Bringing Back the Parties* (Washington, D.C.: CQ Press, 1984).

Ranney, Austin. *Curing the Mischiefs of Faction: Party Reform in America* (Berkeley: University of California Press, 1975).

Rosenstone, Steven J., Roy L. Behr, and Edward H. Lazarus. *Third Parties in America*, 2d ed. (Princeton, NJ: Princeton University Press, 1996).

Sabato, Larry J. *The Party's Just Begun: Shaping Political Parties for America's Future*, 2d ed. (New York: Longman, 2001).

Sifry, Micah L. *Spoiling for a Fight: Third-Party Politics in America* (New York: Routledge, 2003).

Schlessinger, Arthur M. *A History of U.S. Political Parties* (New York: Chelsea House Publications, 2002).

Stonecash, Jeffrey M., Mark D. Brewer, and Mack D. Mariani. *Diverging Parties: Social Change, Realignment and Party Polarization* (Boulder, CO: Westview Press, 2003).

Sundquist, James L. *Dynamics of the Party System*, rev. ed. (Washington, D.C.: Brookings Institution, 1983).

Wattenberg, Martin P. *The Decline of American Political Parties, 1952–1996* (Cambridge, MA: Harvard University Press, 1998).

Witcover, Jules. *Party of the People: A History of the Democrats* (New York: Random House, 2003).

Endnotes

1. John Crittenden, *Parties and Elections in the United States* (London: Prentice-Hall, 1982), p. 3.

2. E. E. Schattschneider, *Party Government* (New York: Holt, Rinehart & Winston, 1942), p. 1.

3. John H. Aldrich, *Why Parties? The Origin and Transformation of Party Politics in America* (Chicago: University of Chicago Press, 1995), p. 3.

4. Jules Witcover, *Party of the People: A History of the Democrats* (New York: Random House, 2003), p. 3.

5. Joel H. Silbey, "From 'Essential to the Existence of Our Institutions' to 'Rapacious Enemies of Honest and Responsible Government': The Rise and Fall of American Political Parties, 1790–2000." In *The Parties Respond: Changes in American Parties and Campaigns*, 4th ed., ed. Louis Sandy Maisel (Boulder, CO: Westview Press, 2002), p. 4.

6. Quoted in Richard Hofstadter, *The Idea of a Party System: The Rise of Legitimate Opposition in the United States, 1789–1840* (Berkeley, CA: University of California Press, 1969), p. 2.

7. James L. Sundquist, *Dynamics of the Party System* (Washington, D.C.: Brookings Institution, 1973), p. 39.

8. Ibid., p. 44.

9. See, for example, John P. Judis and Ruy Teixeira, *The Emerging Democratic Majority* (New York: Scribner, 2004).

10. Kevin Phillips, *The Emerging Republican Majority* (New Rochelle, NY: Arlington House, 1969).

11. See *Anderson v. Celebrezze*, 460 U.S. 780 (1983).

12. For elaboration on this theme, see Micah L. Sifry, *Spoiling for a Fight: Third-Party Politics in America* (New York: Routledge, 2003).

13. See the Green party website, located at http://www.greens.org/na.html.

14. Larry Diamond and Richard Gunther, *Political Parties and Democracy* (Baltimore, MD: Johns Hopkins University Press, 2001), p. ix.

15. Sidney M. Milkis, *Political Parties and Constitutional Government: Remaking American Democracy* (Baltimore, MD: Johns Hopkins University Press, 1999), p. 5.

16. William J. Crotty, *Political Reform and the American Experiment* (New York: Thomas Y. Crowell, 1977), pp. 241–47.

17. The national survey results are from the 1992 National Election Study conducted by the Center for Political Studies at the University of Michigan. Ideological profiles of the 1992 convention delegates are reported in Harold W. Stanley and Richard G. Niemi, *Vital Statistics on American Politics*, 4th ed. (Washington, D.C.: CQ Press, 1994), p. 149.

18. Marjorie Connelly, "Delegates Out of Step with Public on Issue of Fund Raising," *New York Times*, August 17, 2000.

19. See Beth Donovan's article "Much-Maligned 'Soft Money' Is Precious to Both Parties," *Congressional Quarterly Weekly*, May 15, 1993, pp. 1195–98, for a discussion of reporters who made such comments about the political parties in the 1976 election. These comments, allegedly made by David Broder in the *Washington Post*, are considered one of the motivating factors influencing the 1979 legislation allowing soft money.

Interest Groups

9

9-1 What Are Interest Groups?

> **interest groups** Private organizations formed to advance the shared interest of their members.

Interest groups are private organizations formed to advance the shared interest of their members. In political science, an **interest** is simply something that someone wants to achieve—a goal or desire. Often, the shared interest that brings people together is economic—a desire to get a larger slice of the pie. But the interest of the group may be purely ideological—a wish to see public policy in a given area move in a liberal or conservative direction. To qualify as an interest group, an organization must have a political objective and be able to articulate that objective publicly.

> **interest** Something that someone wants to achieve from government; a goal.

Interest groups can be permanent or ephemeral. They can exist for many decades, like the American Bar Association, or for mere months, like the "Swift Boat Veterans for Truth." The latter group emerged in the late summer of 2004 to play a major role in changing the tenor of the presidential election campaign.

Interest groups attempt to advance their members' interests by influencing the policy-making process. As we shall see, they do this by lobbying decision makers, attempting to influence public opinion, and even engaging in litigation. Politics, from the perspective of interest groups, is basically a struggle to determine "who gets what, when and how."[1]

Although they have existed in one form or another since the founding of the Republic, interest groups have proliferated in recent decades. One explanation for this is the increasing diversity of American society and the increasing complexity and specialization of the American economy. The American people can be divided into so many different groups based on age, sex, race, ethnicity, language, religion, ideology, economic status, occupation, lifestyle. . . . The list goes on and on. Each of these cleavages gives rise to different political interests and hence to organizations created to further those interests.

9-1a Interest Groups and Political Parties

At the outset it is important to distinguish interest groups from political parties. As we saw in Chapter 8, political parties exist to recruit political leaders, mobilize voters in elections, and guide governance. Parties in the United States are large, undisciplined, ill-defined organizations that stand for broad, even vague, notions of what public policy ought to be. In their respective platforms, the two major parties address a wide range of policy issues, from abortion to health care to tax policy. Moreover, the parties bring together vast numbers of people who more or less support what the party represents.

By nominating candidates for public office and developing platforms that cover the spectrum of public-policy questions, parties present themselves to the electorate as virtual "governments in waiting." When a party does come to power, it must deal with all the issues of public policy, not merely those it finds convenient or feels strongest about. Moreover, the party in power expects that the voters will hold it responsible for the policies it enacts. Interest groups, on the other hand, are much more sharply focused in their objectives. Interest groups exist to get government to do what they want it to do. They are typically concerned with a fairly narrow range of issues. To a person interested only in the environment or in the issue of abortion or in preserving Social Security benefits for the elderly, for example, the appropriate interest group may hold considerably more appeal than becoming active in one of the major parties. Although political parties are responsible to all citizens, interest groups are responsible only to their members.

In recent years, the functional differences between parties and interest groups have become somewhat muddied. Increasingly, interest groups pursue their policy objectives indirectly by supporting candidates who share their objectives or philosophy. An excellent example of this is MoveOn.org, a liberal organization that focuses its efforts on securing electoral victories for Democratic candidates. In 2004, MoveOn.org played a major role in the political process by running television ads highly critical of President George W. Bush and his policies. Of course, other interest groups, such as the Swift Boat Veterans for Truth, engaged in the same strategy, but for the other side. Indeed, the role of these independent groups in the campaign and their alleged connections to the political parties and presidential candidates became an issue of public concern during 2004.

9-1b Interest Groups and American Society

Interest groups now occupy center stage in American politics; indeed, some would argue that they have replaced political parties as the primary institutions that mediate between the American people and their government. But interest groups are nothing new; they have a long history and are deeply rooted in American political culture. Writing in the 1830s, Alexis de Tocqueville noted that "Americans of all ages, all conditions, and all dispositions constantly form associations."[2] From the early days of the Republic, America was a nation of "joiners."

The tendency of Americans to join associations has lessened in the post-modern age. The average American today is less likely to join a civic group or a bowling league than was the case thirty or forty years ago. Today, most Americans live lives that are more private, more isolated, and more anonymous. Americans, on the whole, are less "public regarding" than they used to be, and few citizens have any real sense of community.[3] At the same time, the number of interest groups has proliferated, as Americans have learned how participation in such groups can be an effective means to advance their interests politically.

9-2 Interest Groups and American Democracy

The Founders referred to interest groups (as well as political parties) as "factions." According to James Madison, writing in *The Federalist* No. 10, a faction is "a number of citizens . . . who are united and actuated by some common impulse of passion, or of interest, adverse to the rights of other citizens or to the permanent and aggregate interests of the community." Madison observed that "the latent causes of faction . . . are sown in the nature of man." Yet Madison also noted that "[t]he most common and durable source of faction has been the various and unequal distribution of property." Madison also believed that factions would thrive under a republican form of government, writing that "liberty is to faction what air is to fire, an aliment without which it instantly expires. . . ." Nevertheless, in Madison's view, it would be foolish to try to prevent factions by restricting freedom. Madison wrote that "it could not be a less folly to abolish liberty, which is essential to political life, because it nourishes faction than it would be to wish the annihilation of air, which is essential to animal life, because it imparts to fire its destructive agency." Rather, in Madison's view, a constitution should be designed to prevent one faction from gaining control of the government. The fundamental design principles of the Constitution—federalism and separation of powers—were adopted to disperse power and ensure that no single faction could achieve dominance.

9-2a Interest Groups and the Constitution

The United States Constitution implicitly guarantees the right to form interest groups. The courts have long recognized that the First Amendment protects the right to join political associations for the purpose of petitioning government for a redress of grievances. In 1957, Chief Justice Earl Warren noted:

> Our form of government is built on the premise that every citizen shall have the right to engage in political expression and association. This right was enshrined in the First Amendment of the Bill of Rights. Exercise of these basic freedoms in America has traditionally been through the media of political associations. Any interference with the freedom of a party is simultaneously an interference with the freedom of its adherents. All political ideas cannot and should not be channeled into the programs of our two major parties. History has amply proved the virtue of political activity by minority, dissident groups.[4]

A year later, a unanimous Supreme Court recognized:

> Effective advocacy of both public and private points of view, particularly controversial ones, is undeniably enhanced by group association, as this Court has more than once recognized by remarking on the close nexus between the freedoms of speech and assembly. . . . It is beyond debate that freedom to engage in an association for the advancement of beliefs and ideas is an inseparable aspect of ... liberty.[5]

Case in Point 9-1

The Supreme Court Protects an Interest Group from Governmental Harassment

Bates v. Little Rock (1960)

The case *Bates v. Little Rock* grew out of the efforts of the National Association for the Advancement of Colored People (NAACP) to secure the desegregation of the public schools in Little Rock, Arkansas. In an effort to harass and intimidate the NAACP, the City of Little Rock sought to force the organization to produce lists of the names of the members of its local branches. Daisy Bates, the head of the Little Rock branch of the NAACP, refused to comply with the City's request and was convicted of violating the ordinance upon which the request was made. The U.S. Supreme Court reversed Bates' conviction and struck down the ordinance on which it was based. Justice Potter Stewart delivered the opinion of a unanimous Supreme Court, saying in part:

> Like freedom of speech and a free press, the right of peaceable assembly was considered by the Framers of our Constitution to lie at the foundation of a government based upon the consent of an informed citizenry—a government dedicated to the establishment of justice and the preservation of liberty.... Freedoms such as these are protected not only against heavy-handed frontal attack, but also from being stifled by more subtle governmental interference....
>
> On this record it sufficiently appears that compulsory disclosure of the membership lists of the local branches of the National Association for the Advancement of Colored People would work a significant interference with the freedom of association of their members. There was substantial uncontroverted evidence that public identification of persons in the community as members of the organizations had been followed by harassment and threats of bodily harm. There was also evidence that fear of community hostility and economic reprisals that would follow public disclosure of the membership lists had discouraged new members from joining the organizations and induced former members to withdraw. This repressive effect, while in part the result of private attitudes and pressures, was brought to bear only after the exercise of governmental power had threatened to force disclosure of the members' names.... Thus, the threat of substantial government encroachment upon important and traditional aspects of individual freedom is neither speculative nor remote....
>
> We conclude that the municipalities have failed to demonstrate a controlling justification for the deterrence of free association which compulsory disclosure of the membership lists would cause. The petitioners cannot be punished for refusing to produce information which the municipalities could not constitutionally require....

Similarly, Justice William Brennan, speaking for the Supreme Court in 1984, observed that "implicit in the right to engage in activities protected by the First Amendment [is] a corresponding right to associate with others in pursuit of a wide variety of political, social, economic, educational, religious, and cultural ends."[6] Of course, the reason that the courts have been called upon to make such pronouncements is that from time to time government agencies and officials have sought to suppress or interfere with unpopular advocacy groups (see Case in Point 9-1).

9-2b Pluralism

pluralism Democratic theory that conceives of politics as perpetual competition among interest groups.

Early in the twentieth century, political scientists began to develop a theory of American politics that came to be known as **pluralism.**[7] Pluralism stands in sharp contrast to classical republicanism and traditional democratic theory. Classical republicanism stressed the need for virtuous elites that would pursue the public interest. Traditional democratic theory stressed the need for elected officials to respond to the will of the majority. In contrast to these earlier theories, pluralism conceived of politics as the struggle among competing interest groups.

Pluralism presupposes that "all the active and legitimate groups in the population can make themselves heard at some crucial stage in the process of decision."[8] Public policy is thus nothing more than the government's response to group demands. Whereas the Founders saw factions as potentially mischievous and in need of regulation, the pluralists conceived of interest groups as necessary, desirable, and even virtuous. Their principal virtue was that they provided a vehicle for political participation beyond the formal and often insignificant exercise of voting. Pluralists viewed the perpetual interest-group struggle as having a stabilizing effect on the political system. Because people belong to multiple groups with overlapping interests, the intensity of conflict is reduced. The system tends toward a stable equilibrium that maximizes the greatest good for the greatest number. Moreover, the policy-making process is enhanced by the fact that policy makers have been exposed to multiple competing solutions to problems.

Many political scientists have questioned the assumptions and conclusions of pluralism.[9] Some have suggested that lurking behind the pluralist façade is a "power elite" that makes the important decisions.[10] Others have stressed the fact that not all groups in society are represented by organizations and that not all organizations are taken seriously by policy makers. As one scholar has observed, "the fact that some citizens by dint of their superior representation by organized interests seem to have a louder voice than others strikes many Americans as undemocratic."[11]

9-2c Hyperpluralism?

Some commentators believe that the American political system is suffering from **hyperpluralism,** a condition in which the prevalence of group demands makes it impossible for government to plan, deal with long-term problems, and make policies that further the public interest. Moreover, the constant barrage of interest-group demands undermines the rule of law. Perhaps the best-known exponent of this perspective is Theodore J. Lowi, whose book *The End of Liberalism* argues that pluralism, or **interest-group liberalism,** as Lowi calls it, has corrupted our politics and undermined our government. According to Lowi, "interest group liberalism has sought to solve the problems of public authority in a large modern state by . . . parceling out to private parties the power to make public policy."[12] Some critics of pluralism would go even further, arguing that the existence of numerous powerful interest groups causes the political system to bog down.[13] **Gridlock,** the inability of government to make or implement any decision, may be one of the consequences of hyperpluralism.

9-2d The Public Interest

Classical republican thinkers believed that the objective of government was the furtherance of the public interest. The *public interest* is one that is shared in common by all members of the society. The theory of pluralism rules out the idea of a public interest. It "portrays society as an aggregate of human communities, rather than as itself a human community; and it equally rules out a concern for the general good in practice by encouraging a politics of interest group pressures in which there is no mechanism for the discovery and expression of the common good."[14] In discussing the problem of the public interest, two questions must be posed. First, does such a thing as the public interest really exist, or is it merely an idealistic notion without any basis in reality? Second, assuming that the public interest does exist, what political mechanisms will allow it to be discovered and pursued? Increasingly, American politics is being defined in terms of groups and group membership. Table 9-1 provides a representative national sample of Americans as they rate a number of politically significant social groups.

> ▶ **hyperpluralism** A condition in which the prevalence of group demands makes it impossible for government to plan, deal with long-term problems, and make policies that further the public interest.

> ▶ **interest group liberalism** A term coined by the political scientist Theodore Lowi to describe the philosophy underlying American pluralism.

> ▶ **gridlock** The inability of government to make decisions that sometimes result from divided party control of the policy-making institutions.

	1992	1996	2000	2004
Whites	71.19	70.72	73.17	73.49
Poor people	70.55	69.96	70.10	73.25
Blacks	65.27	65.66	67.06	72.26
Hispanics	61.07	63.51	63.84	67.88
Environmentalists	67.68	63.04	64.09	66.03
Conservatives	55.78	59.84	58.64	60.49
Christian fundamentalists	54.89	53.60	52.32	57.60
Feminists	62.06	62.45	62.71	56.33
People on welfare	51.01	50.66	51.49	55.87
Liberals	50.99	51.62	54.56	55.40
Gay men and lesbians	37.74	40.35	46.87	48.52

TABLE 9-1

Public Attitudes toward Various Groups

The data reported are average scores on a "feeling thermometer," where 100 is most favorable and 0 is least favorable. Note that the least favored of these groups is gay men and lesbians, although there is considerable increase in their score from 1992 to 2004. Note also that the gap between whites and blacks shrinks over time.

Source: Adapted from Center for Political Studies, University of Michigan, 1992, 1996, 2000 and 2004 National Election Studies.

Protection of the natural environment is often cited as a good example of a public interest. Obviously, everyone has an interest in preserving the environment. But not everyone agrees on how seriously the environment is threatened or on how it can best be preserved or restored. Certainly, groups are sharply divided over who should pay the price to clean up the environment. Business? The consumer? The taxpayer?

Education provides another example. Most Americans agree in the abstract that education is a good thing. But what kind of education? Should it be compulsory? Again, who should pay to improve the educational system—the taxpayers or those directly benefiting by receiving an education? Of course, any group advocating any particular course of action with respect to education is likely to claim that its proposal is consistent with the public interest. What may be more accurate is to say that the proposal is in keeping with the group's perception of the public interest.

Is it meaningful, then, to talk about the public interest *as distinct from* the interest of one or more groups? If the public interest is defined as that good in which each member of society shares equally, whether he realizes it or not, we would be hard pressed to give a concrete example of the public interest. On the other hand, most people in society share certain interests—interests that transcend the narrow claims of particular groups seeking immediate gratification of their desires. Most people recognize the need to protect the environment, educate their children, and train workers to be more competitive in the global economy. Increasingly, people are aware of the long-term consequences of running a government that is ridden with debt. These interests may or may not be public interests in the truest sense of the term, but they are surely closer to the ideal of the public interest than, for example, an effort by a particular industry to gain a lucrative exemption from a regulation that applies to other similar industries. Unfortunately, these broader interests, especially when they are shared by people yet unborn, are often drowned out in the din of interest-group politics. Politicians looking to maintain power are most likely to listen to those who do the most to affect the outcome of the next election, whether by giving (or withholding) campaign funds or by mobilizing (or failing to mobilize) voters directly. It is difficult to get politicians to pay attention to issues that everyone regards as important but no one is organizing to articulate.

9-3 Organized Interests in the United States

Although obtaining an exact count is difficult, at least ten thousand interest groups exist in the United States. These groups may be divided into two basic categories: economic and noneconomic. This distinction reaches to the heart of interest articulation in a democracy. Economic groups exist mainly to use the political process to secure financial gains for their members. Other than supporting the basic economic philosophy of capitalism within the context of a market, economic groups do not have ideological preferences. Their members do not share core political values that drive their action. Rather, they share economic interests, which may indeed transcend ideological feelings. In contrast, noneconomic groups exist to articulate their values, not to advance material interests. Both economic and noneconomic groups are formed to advance the common interests of their members by influencing government policy. For the most part, leaders of interest groups do not seek government office.

9-3a Economic Groups

Economic interest groups include business organizations, trade associations, professional groups, and labor unions. These groups vary considerably in terms of their specific objectives, general ideological orientation, and political affiliation. Their number and importance reflect the major role that government at all levels plays in the regulation of economic activity. The role the federal government should play in regulating business has been debated since the founding of the Republic. Indeed, the "regulation of interstate commerce" clause of Article I, Section 8 of the Constitution made an active federal role a possibility that the Supreme Court's decision in *Gibbons v. Ogden* (1824) cemented as a reality.[15] In *Gibbons,* one of the key decisions of the nineteenth century, the Supreme Court took a broad view of Congress' power to regulate interstate commerce.

The first major economic issue facing the federal government, and one that is still important, was the **tariff,** a tax charged on products imported into a country. American industrial interests have often favored various tariffs because of the protection they provide. A tariff makes foreign goods more expensive relative to domestic products that are not subject to the tariff. Consumers or those needing to import goods for their businesses do not benefit from tariffs. In the late 1980s, many American interest groups, including those representing the troubled automobile and steel industries, fought for protective legislation. With few exceptions, these groups did not get what they wanted. The Bush administration and its successor, the Clinton administration, proved to be fairly committed to the concept of free trade.

▶ **tariff** A tax charged on products imported into a country.

Business Interests   Most businesses are set up as corporations. Legally, the corporation has an existence beyond the individuals that comprise it. Large corporations, such as General Motors, AT&T, and IBM, have many strategies for attempting to influence public policy that may have an effect on their interests. Hiring a lobbying firm or creating a political action office within the company is the most expensive strategy, but it also allows the firm to make individual decisions on the political issues most crucial to its interests. Many large corporations hire their own lobbyists to represent their interests. Estimates indicate that business groups account for more than half of all interest groups with offices in Washington, D.C.

In 2002, Enron Corporation declared bankruptcy and came under tremendous scrutiny for unsound business practices and possible securities fraud. Democrats in Congress questioned the role that Enron executives had played in helping the Bush administration craft its energy policy during 2001. Vice President Dick Cheney came under pressure to release details of any role that Enron officials might have played. The Bush administration decided not to release these details, making the argument that this type of release would harm future administrations' ability to get advice to inform policy making. The role of business interests will always be controversial in a democracy.

A second strategy is to join interest groups that advance either general business interests or narrower issues related to a particular industry. In the general category are such interest groups as the Chamber of Commerce and the National Association of Manufacturers. Examples of narrower groups are trade associations, such as the American Bankers Association or the National Beer Wholesalers Association. A firm incurs some costs of membership in these types of organizations, but the overall cost is less than individual political action by the corporation.

Another option that may be available is membership in professional associations, which are usually composed of individuals (although sometimes institutions also join) who have a common occupational interest. The National Realtors Association, the American Medical Association, and the American Bar Association (lawyers) are examples of professional associations. Because the membership is usually in the name of the individual worker, the firm may have only indirect input into the political goals of the organization, although it still receives at least some representation of its interests.

By combining memberships in the various types of economic groups, a corporation can greatly expand its ability to have its voice heard in Washington. For example, a large pharmaceutical company may be a member of the Chamber of Commerce and the National Association of Manufacturers for general business reasons, the National Association of Pharmaceutical Manufacturers for industry-specific representation, and the American Medical Association through the doctors it employs. Each organization may represent different interests of the company, use different means of influencing policy, and monitor different types of legislation or regulatory policy. The multiple layers of membership provide greater access to the system.

General Business Organizations   Among the oldest business groups in the United States is the Chamber of Commerce. Founded in 1912, the Chamber of Commerce is a national organization that embraces thousands of local Chambers of Commerce across America. The Chamber, which has become synonymous with the national business community, is dedicated to protecting the free enterprise system from government interference. In the 1980s and early 1990s, it worked hard to defeat efforts to have the national government mandate that businesses provide their employees with various benefits, such as family medical leave. Almost every community in the country has its own local Chamber of Commerce. Consequently, the national Chamber can mobilize a very large network of supporters who can influence local elected officials. Rather than have a stranger from a D.C. lobbying firm drop by the office of a member of Congress, a business leader from the member's hometown can personally deliver the Chamber's message. This personal touch makes it easier to gain access to influential political leaders.

The Chamber, as well as other business interests, has usually supported Republican presidential candidates over Democrats, and consequently, Republicans, such as Presidents Reagan and both Bushes, have been more sympathetic to the interests of the business community. When Bill Clinton was elected president in 1992, the Chamber of Commerce and other probusiness interest groups expressed concern about the direction that public policy would take under the new administration. These concerns were heightened on February 4, 1993, when Congress, at the urging of the Clinton administration, enacted a law requiring companies to give their workers as many as twelve weeks of unpaid leave per year to deal with births, adoptions, and serious illnesses within a worker's immediate family.

The Chamber of Commerce purports to represent the entire business community. It therefore takes stands on broad, business-related issues. These issues often involve an employer's relationship with its workers. The Chamber usually opposes (or at least seeks to weaken) legislation that increases the cost of hiring workers, such as increases in the minimum wage or mandatory health insurance. These issues typically pit the interests of business directly against those of labor. Taxes are another major Chamber concern. It almost always opposes increases in corporate taxes and other taxes that affect business operations across a wide variety of industries, such as the energy tax proposed by President Clinton in 1993.

Although President Clinton was generally perceived as hospitable to the interests of business, probusiness interest groups opposed many of the regulatory initiatives that emerged from the Clinton administration, especially from the Food and Drug Administration, the U.S. Forest Service, and the Occupational Safety and Health Administration. By and large, probusiness groups were pleased when Republicans took over the presidency in 2001 and were successful in securing various favorable policy changes.

Trade Associations   Of course, most business interests are not so universal. In fact, most business and corporate interests are relatively narrow. For example, the steel industry faced stiff competition in the 1970s and 1980s from foreign producers that had much lower labor costs and other overhead. Therefore, it was in the steel industry's interest to pursue tariffs on imported steel. Other American businesses took a different position on this issue. Higher prices on steel might help the steel industry, but the American auto industry, which uses large amounts of steel, wanted lower steel prices so that it could produce inexpensive cars to compete with foreign automakers. Consequently, general business organizations, such as the Chamber of Commerce and the National Association of Manufacturers, could not take a stance on this issue without alienating one set of members or the other. On the other hand, an organization with a narrower focus and a smaller membership that shares the same interest could pursue protective tariffs for the steel industry. **Trade associations** fill this important need for industries. American industries and businesses make most of their efforts to affect government through trade associations of companies producing the same type of goods or services.

Professional Associations   **Professional associations** are organizations of individuals employed, or self-employed, in a variety of skilled enterprises, such as medicine, law, accounting, and engineering. Professions generally limit their membership by granting licenses to practice. By state law, certain professional organizations are allowed to control their membership so that the public is protected against unqualified, incompetent individuals. Typically, the main task confronting any professional association is securing state action that confers professional status on its members. Often, major battles in state legislatures ensue between competing professional groups. For example, ophthalmologists, who have medical degrees, and optometrists, who are trained in colleges of optometry, are continually at odds over the degree to which the latter should be allowed to perform medical

▶ **trade associations**
Organizations that represent persons who possess common skills.

▶ **professional associations**
Organizations of people who are employed, or self-employed, in a variety of professions, such as medicine, law, accounting, and engineering.

procedures or prescribe drugs to their patients. Each group makes major contributions to candidates for state legislatures.

Although professional associations operate mostly at the state level on questions of licensing, they have an abiding interest in federal legislation that might affect the economic well-being of their members or the advancement of their professional agendas. Consider the Association of Trial Lawyers of America. In the first six months of 1992, this organization received more than $2.5 million in contributions.[16] One might wonder what interests trial lawyers have that would lead them to commit these types of resources to politics. But 1992 was an election year, with the presidency, one-third of the Senate, and all of the House up for election. The subject of legal reform was on the electoral agenda, with tremendous potential consequences for trial lawyers. For instance, imposing limits on the amounts that juries in civil cases can award for damages could have a substantial effect on the fees attorneys receive.

The best-known professional organizations are probably the American Bar Association (ABA), which represents lawyers, and the American Medical Association (AMA). During the 1950s and 1960s, the AMA raised tremendous amounts of money, which it used to successfully fight the passage of national health insurance legislation and to delay and change the provisions of medical insurance for the elderly (Medicare). Since the introduction of Medicare in 1965, the AMA and other associations of medical specialties have devoted great resources to its implementation by seeking to expand the definition of covered illnesses (such as adding mental illnesses or addiction treatments), working to increase compensation for services, and removing restrictions on the individual doctor's decisions about medical care for patients. The health insurance and medical cost reduction plan proposed by President Clinton in 1993 was another policy struggle with a potential impact of billions of dollars on the medical industry. The AMA, medical specialty organizations, hospital associations, insurance companies, and pharmaceutical manufacturers were actively involved in the policy debate, from the inception of the public hearings conducted by Hillary Rodham Clinton through the legislative debates in Congress.

In recent decades, public education has been an increasingly contentious national issue. By the 2000 presidential election, the appropriate role of public education and the desirability of limited publicly funded vouchers were at the forefront of the campaign and a major point of contrast between George W. Bush and Al Gore. The issue was clear: The Democrat Al Gore opposed any use of public money for vouchers for private education, and the Republican George W. Bush advocated providing vouchers to pupils in failing public schools for use in the school of their choice, including private schools.

The Gore position closely paralleled that of the National Education Association (NEA), the oldest, largest, and most influential of any organization dedicated to advocating for public education. This organization, which has more than 2.5 million members, has become one of the most critical organizations supporting the Democratic party. In fact, it sent 350 delegates and alternates to the 2000 national convention in Los Angeles.

The prominent role of the NEA in Democratic party politics has led many Republicans to refer to it and its state subsidiaries as teachers' unions. Not surprisingly, the NEA tends to see itself as a professional organization that advocates not only for the benefit of its members but also for broader public interest. The differences between the characterizations of the organization are important in affecting public opinion and, possibly, public support for NEA positions. Clearly, NEA opponents would like to dismiss its support of any position as merely self-serving and to undercut any perception of a position as stemming from professionals stating their best view of the public interest. Likewise, the NEA would rather be perceived as a professional association than as merely another labor union.

Organized Labor   This country experienced an epic battle in the late nineteenth and early twentieth centuries over the right of workers to form labor unions. The labor movement eventually won the battle, and in 1935 Congress adopted legislation that guaranteed the rights of workers to unionize and collectively bargain with management over wages and other terms of employment. The American Federation of Labor (AFL) was created in 1881 as a means of unifying diverse trade unions. The Congress of Industrial Organizations (CIO) was created in the late 1930s to provide representation for less-skilled industrial labor. In 1955, the AFL merged with the CIO to form an umbrella organization that, at its peak, represented more than 80 percent of union employees in this country.

After the right to unionize had been won, unions still had a national agenda to advance. Foremost among their goals was the elimination of **right-to-work laws,** which prevent labor agreements from requiring all workers to join the union. Because labor leaders know that some workers will choose not to get involved in the union, but will nevertheless profit from the higher wages and improved safety or other benefits won by the union, they prefer a system that requires all nonmanagement workers in a unionized company to join the union as a condition of employment. Therefore, unions have continuously fought to remove or prevent the passage of right-to-work laws. Most of this battle has taken place in the states.

The main rival to the AFL–CIO has been the Teamsters, who have broken with most of organized labor by occasionally supporting Republican candidates. In 1992, the Teamsters raised more campaign money than any other lobbying organization. They generally represent truck drivers and those involved in the transportation sector, although they also have organized other workers. The Teamsters, along with the United Mine Workers, have had to overcome a history of violence and corruption that has tarnished their image.

Since their inception, labor unions have been politically active. Generally, the unions have supported Democratic candidates, and Democrats have, by the same token, supported the interests of organized labor. Indeed, organized labor was a key element of the New Deal coalition assembled by President Franklin D. Roosevelt in the 1930s and maintained by the Democratic party for decades thereafter. In the 1960s, however, the close relationship between organized labor and the Democratic party began to break down, largely over the Democrats' liberal positions on social issues. The rank-and-file members of labor unions tend to be liberal—in fact, extremely so—on economic issues, and they tend to be somewhat conservative on social issues. In fact, the term *populist* may be a better description of the ideological orientation of organized labor.

The interests of workers, like those of business, are often specific to particular industries or trades. These unions attempt to influence legislation that might affect their industries or their relationship with their employers. For instance, the United Auto Workers (UAW) have long raised a large amount of money, much of which was used to try to influence Congress on issues related to the regulation of the automobile industry. Often, the UAW and American industry have the same interests. For example, both favor legislation limiting the number of cars that Japan can ship to the United States. In seeking legislation that is in their own economic interest, however, the UAW may be hurting the economic interests of other union members who must pay higher prices for cars.

Union density, the proportion of the nonagricultural work force belonging to unions, peaked in the mid-1940s at about 36 percent. Since then, union density has declined to around 14 percent.[17] Consequently, the political influence of organized labor has diminished considerably. Perhaps most embarrassing to organized labor was the landslide reelection of Ronald Reagan as president in 1984. The AFL–CIO endorsed and worked hard to elect Reagan's Democratic opponent, Walter Mondale, who was widely perceived as an old-fashioned prolabor Democrat. Because Mondale was negatively perceived as having been captured by special interests, many observers regarded the AFL–CIO endorsement as a liability rather than an asset to his campaign. Worse yet from the labor leaders' perspective, polls showed that only 52 percent of union families voted for Mondale in 1984.[18]

In the 1990s, the Democratic party worked hard to recapture the support of organized labor, but this effort was complicated by President Clinton's support of NAFTA and other free trade policies opposed by labor unions. NAFTA is an acronym for the North American Free Trade Agreement, which became effective on January 1, 1994. Essentially, the agreement reduced trade barriers that had limited commerce among the United States, Canada, and Mexico. Unions opposed NAFTA (as they oppose such agreements generally) because they believe that maintaining tariffs and other barriers to imports is necessary to preserve jobs in America. President Clinton, who styled himself as a New Democrat, generally supported the idea of free trade, much to the chagrin of organized labor.

The negotiations that led to NAFTA were begun under President George H.W. Bush in the late 1980s, but were finalized by Bush's successor, Bill Clinton. Because NAFTA changed

▶ **right-to-work laws** Laws that prevent labor agreements from requiring all workers to join a union.

▶ **union density** The proportion of the nonagricultural workforce belonging to unions.

many American trade laws, it had to be approved by both the House of Representatives and the Senate. Labor unions fought hard to get Congress to reject NAFTA, which they argued would cause American jobs to be exported to Mexico. Union spokespersons let it be known that they would work to defeat any member of Congress who voted in favor of NAFTA.

At first, it appeared that the unions would succeed. They found an unlikely ally in H. Ross Perot, the Texas billionaire who had run for president in 1992 as an independent candidate and had put together an impressive political organization named United We Stand. Throughout 1993, Perot spoke out against NAFTA at rallies around the country. As late as early November, public opinion was negative toward the agreement, although many people had not made up their minds. Perot's claim that NAFTA was dead in the House of Representatives appeared to be right. But a tremendous last-minute effort by the White House and other supporters of NAFTA resulted in a decisive shift in public opinion. Ultimately, NAFTA passed both the House and Senate by comfortable margins. Most Republicans in Congress supported NAFTA; indeed, their support was never really in doubt. The battle over NAFTA was really a struggle within the Democratic party, over which organized labor traditionally exercised strong influence. The fact that President Clinton, a Democrat, supported NAFTA and was able to get it through Congress showed the degree to which union influence over the Democratic party and the political process in general had declined.

Despite the decline of the labor movement, unions and their lobbyists remain quite active in politics, supporting measures to increase workers' benefits, improve the safety of the workplace, and protect domestic jobs against foreign competition. Union efforts tend to be successful only when their positions are supported by a substantial segment of the nonunion workforce. That was the case with the Family and Medical Leave Act, adopted in 1993. Unions supported the measure, and so did most nonunion employees. Unions also continue to be significant sources of financial support for Democratic candidates.

9-3b Noneconomic Groups

Over the past thirty years, the most rapidly growing segment of interest groups has been the noneconomic sector. The 1960s and early 1970s witnessed an explosion in single-interest, ideological groups and public interest groups that were largely liberal in nature. Conservative ideological groups responded with tremendous growth in the late 1970s and early 1980s.

WEB EXERCISE

Over the past ten years, graduate students at many major American and Canadian universities have organized unions to confront what many see as the unfair practices of university and college administrations. Perhaps graduate students and teachers at your school have organized a union, held public meetings or demonstrations, or gone on strike. Graduate student unions often include on their agendas improved benefits, such as insurance, child care, and pay. Students have affiliated with the United Auto Workers, the American Federation of Teachers, and the American Association of University Professors. Check out these websites:

The Coalition of Graduate Employee Unions: *http://www.cgeu.org*
The United Auto Workers: *http://www.uaw.org*
The American Federation of Teachers: *http://www.aft.org*
The American Association of University Professors: *http://www.aaup.org*

Take a look at the other side of the issue:

At What Cost? (Brown University): *http://www.geocities.com/brown_atwhatcost/*

What characteristics do the pro-union groups share? The anti-union groups? What kinds of tactics are used to persuade others of their position? What kinds of influence do these groups have, and how is it used? How does each group portray its opposition? Are you swayed by one argument or the other? What kinds of research are required in working for an interest group? How are gains made by interest groups? What would you do to gain public support?

Popular Culture and American Politics

Third Millennium

By Chapman Rackaway

Third Millennium was formally launched on July 14, 1993. This organization is the product of work done by several dozen people from across the United States.

In mid-March of 1993, Douglas Kennedy hosted a meeting of two dozen young leaders. There, an ideological cross-section of twenty- and thirty-somethings decided to issue a generational manifesto, laying out the concerns of the "rising generation," from the national debt and entitlement reform to the environment, crime, race relations, and education.

The Founders of Third Millennium did not have any particular experience starting or running a nonprofit organization. Many came from media backgrounds. Thanks to an anonymous $9,200 grant from a family foundation, however, Third Millennium was able to pay for a press conference, incorporate itself, and cover the cost of office supplies. It had no paid staff until early 1994.

By 1997, the organization had broken into the public spotlight with publication of a report titled "Free From FICA," which analyzed seven state and local retirement systems and compared their rates of return to Social Security. Third Millennium also testified before Congressional committees, prepared a Social Security legislative briefing from a younger citizen's perspective, and hosted a policy symposium on Capitol Hill.

Originally focused mostly on Social Security, Third Millennium soon branched out to cover a variety of issues important to younger citizens, such as lack of political candidates' attention to younger voters, Medicare, and political advertising's effect on young voter participation rates.

By 2003, the organization had expanded to offer unpaid internships in New York for young people seeking to get involved in political advocacy, and their policy areas expanded into attention toward the national debt. Although the organization does not see itself as a "Generation X version of AARP" because it doesn't have thirty million members, Third Millennium is one of a growing number of organizations actively voicing the concerns of younger voters in U.S. government.

Certainly, groups of both ideological types multiplied throughout both periods, but it is fair to say that the earlier period was characterized by the growth of liberal groups and the later period by the expansion of conservative groups. Nevertheless, a survey of the directory *Washington Representatives* shows that lobbyists working for economic interests still outnumber those working for noneconomic groups by nearly a four-to-one ratio. Noneconomic groups are interested in a range of topics, including the environment, school prayer, civil rights, abortion, and homelessness. Despite this range of issues, noneconomic interests can be loosely grouped into three categories: single-issue, broad ideological, and public interest groups.

> **single-issue groups**
> Organizations that focus their efforts on one particular policy area, such as gun control or abortion.

Single-Issue Groups   As their name suggests, **single-issue groups** are organizations focused on one particular policy area. Rather than push for a broad policy agenda, these types of groups may be concerned about only a few legislative proposals or regulations. Groups exist for almost every conceivable policy area. Although most are organized for action at the national level, many act only in certain states or local areas.

Two of the most prominent categories of single-issue groups in the 1980s were the abortion groups on both sides of the battle and the environmentalists. The National Abortion Rights Action League, on the side protecting legalized abortions, and the National Right to Life group, dedicated to the restriction and eventual criminalization of abortion, are two of the most influential groups in the abortion debate. Though the discussion may include religious issues, social welfare, and the state of the American education system, the fundamental issue for both groups is the legal availability of abortions in the United States.

The environmental movement has greatly expanded since the 1960s, and a bevy of groups have formed to cover a variety of specific issues within the overall concern for the environment.[19] Some national groups, such as the National Wildlife Federation and Green-

Profiles &
Perspectives

The National Rifle Association

Without question, gun ownership is deeply embedded in American political culture. Reflecting its revolutionary origins, the U.S. Constitution recognizes the "right to keep and bear arms." On the other hand, many people now believe that the easy availability of firearms contributes to the epidemic of violent crime that plagues this country. Obviously, gun owners have an interest in preventing the passage of laws that would make it more difficult or even illegal for them to possess and use their weapons. Nearly three million gun owners belong to an organization named the National Rifle Association (NRA).

The following is an excerpt from "A Brief History of the NRA," taken from the NRA website (*www.nra.org*):

> While widely recognized today as a major political force and as America's foremost defender of Second Amendment rights, the NRA has, since its inception, been the premier firearms education organization in the world. But our successes would not be possible without the tireless efforts and countless hours of service our nearly three million members have given to champion Second Amendment rights and support NRA programs. As former Clinton spokesman George Stephanopoulos said, "Let me make one small vote for the NRA. They're good citizens. They call their Congressmen. They write. They vote. They contribute. And they get what they want over time."

Although the original purpose of the NRA was to promote gun safety and education, in recent decades it has become an active force in American politics. The NRA consistently opposes any and all efforts at gun control, arguing that any restriction on the right to keep and bear arms will lead eventually to abolition of the right. For many years, the NRA prevented Congress from undertaking any serious attempt at gun control. The NRA is thus a powerful, although by no means invincible, interest group. In 1993, the NRA suffered a defeat when Congress enacted the Brady bill, which mandated a five-day waiting period for gun purchases. In 1994, many observers were surprised that Congress, over the strident opposition of the NRA, voted to adopt a ban on the sale and possession of certain military-style semiautomatic assault rifles. The leadership of the NRA characterized the Brady bill and the ban on assault weapons as a wholesale attack on the constitutional right to keep and bear arms.

Of course, not all gun owners believe that people should have a right to possess assault rifles, explosive bullets, or "Saturday night specials." Like any group of people, gun owners disagree among themselves about the degree of gun control that is necessary or desirable. Even members of the NRA disagree on the fine points of the gun control debate. As with most interest groups, the leadership is more extreme in its positions than is the rank-and-file membership.

peace, are concerned about a wide range of environmental issues both inside and outside this country. Other national groups focus on only a certain portion of the environment: The Sierra Club is organized to promote the protection of scenic areas, and People for the Ethical Treatment of Animals demands political action to protect animals from use in product testing and confinement in zoos and circuses. In addition, numerous groups form around local or even temporary issues, such as the ad hoc group of entertainment stars who tried to save Walden Pond in Massachusetts from development in the early 1990s. These various groups form coalitions from time to time to seek political action, and they also maintain their own, separate identities and causes.

Ideological Groups   Ideological groups promote a broader array of interests than do the single-issue groups. Civil rights groups, religious organizations, and broad political ideological groups are in this category. Several different types of civil rights groups exist. Some groups, such as the National Association for the Advancement of Colored People (NAACP) and Jesse Jackson's Rainbow Coalition, fight for legislation promoting racial equality in all facets of American life. Others, such as the National Organization for Women, fight for gender equality. More recently, groups such as ACT UP and Queer Nation have been formed to promote gay rights. The civil rights groups seek action in a wide variety of ways from the legislative, judicial, and administrative bodies at the national, state, and local levels of government.

Religious groups seek government action that fits their beliefs about how society should be organized. Religious fundamentalists, represented by such organizations as the Christian Coalition, have pushed for a more conservative ideological agenda, including outlawing abortion, allowing prayer in public schools, and preventing gays and lesbians from gaining protection under civil rights laws. Although the fundamentalist groups received more attention throughout the 1980s and 1990s, the Catholic Church and the mainline Protestant churches have always been active in a wide variety of issues. The Catholic Church has pushed for outlawing abortion (in agreement with the fundamentalist Protestants), but has also opposed the death penalty and advocated more liberal social welfare policy (in agreement with the more liberal and moderate Protestants). The Catholics and more liberal Protestants have also pushed for the United States to take a more aggressive stance in promoting human rights in other countries.

Other ideological groups exist just to advance a particular policy agenda. Groups such as the Americans for Democratic Action and the National Committee for an Effective Congress support a liberal agenda. The National Conservative Political Action Committee and the Fund for a Conservative Majority advocate conservative causes. Some members of these types of groups may have religious motivations, but the groups themselves are not specifically religious in nature.

> **public interest group**
> Organization that seeks a collective good, the achievement of which will not materially benefit the members of the organization.

Public Interest Groups Ideally, a **public interest group** is "one that seeks a collective good, the achievement of which will not selectively or materially benefit the membership or activists of the organization."[20] Whereas the ideological and single-issue groups are mass membership organizations, a public interest group may not be as concerned about having members. Often, charitable foundations or a few wealthy benefactors subsidize its actions. A key feature of public interest groups is that they are nonprofit organizations, so contributors receive tax deductions for contributions. This nonprofit status prevents the groups from maintaining political action committees (PACs) to support their causes, however. (PACs are discussed in detail in section 9-5a, "Influencing Elections.")

Public interest groups are usually composed of a small number of professionals who perform research on the topic, provide expert testimony at congressional hearings, and work to influence public opinion on an issue that is of no direct benefit to them. An example of this type of group is the League of Women Voters. The league promotes efforts to increase voter turnout. Other groups, such as Common Cause, seek reform in government. Recently, Common Cause has been heavily involved in the movement to limit the influence of PACs, curtail the perks received by government officials, and eliminate the wasteful pet projects of legislators. Other groups are less concerned about specific political battles and focus more on societal issues, such as homelessness, child welfare, and drug abuse.

9-4 Why Do People Join Interest Groups?

The simple answer to why people join interest groups is that they have a common interest. Farmers join an agricultural group because they have a stake in keeping commodity prices high and the costs of producing crops low. As you have read, groups serve a wide variety of economic and noneconomic interests—so many, in fact, that a group seems to be available for every conceivable common interest.

Shared interests alone do not seem to explain all types of interest groups, however. For example, more than ten thousand interest groups are in Washington, but almost none of them is a group representing the interests of homemakers, students, the homeless, or sports fans. Furthermore, even some of the largest interest groups, such as the American Medical Association and the National Association of Realtors, cannot persuade all potential members to join. Considering the importance often attached to the influence of interest groups in our political system, why don't all Americans participate in interest groups?

> **selective benefits** Benefits that are limited to individuals who are members of a particular group or organization.

> **free riders** Persons who enjoy the benefits of an organization's activity without having to contribute.

The Free Rider Problem In his classic book *The Logic of Collective Action* (1965), Mancur Olson argued that groups that pursue benefits for society at large, as opposed to **selective benefits** for their members, are not likely to succeed. These types of groups have difficulty recruiting and retaining members because anyone can benefit from the group's activities without joining. If individuals were to act purely on the basis of self-interest, they would prefer to be **free riders,** or persons who enjoy the benefits of an organization's activity without having to pay the costs.

For example, most Americans might agree that clean air is an important public policy, but a relatively small proportion of Americans are members of interest groups, such as the Sierra Club and the National Wildlife Federation, that push for environmental legislation. Any individual can evaluate the situation and realize that one person's $25 contribution to the organization will not affect the group's ability to influence politics. Furthermore, an individual knows that if the group is successful in affecting public policy, free riders cannot be prevented from taking advantage of the cleaner air that results from the group's activity. Thus, the individual has no incentive to join. If everyone reaches the same conclusion, however, the interest group will be either quite weak or nonexistent.

Despite the free-rider problem, people do join Common Cause, the Sierra Club, and other public interest groups. Indeed, the emergence and proliferation of these types of groups since the 1980s is one of the more interesting features of the political system. Why do people join these groups? Are they irrational? One answer is that interest groups may provide selective incentives to members. **Selective incentives** can be any private benefit that induces a potential member to join or a current member to stay in an organization. Clean-air legislation may not be enough of an incentive to get an individual to join the National Wildlife Federation, but selective incentives, such as a glossy calendar of wildlife scenes, a newsletter on wildlife preservation, bumper stickers displaying the member's support of a public good, or a T-shirt featuring an endangered species, may provide an individual with a tangible benefit that a nonmember could not receive. The benefit must be relatively inexpensive, or else it costs the interest group more than it receives from the individual.

▶ **selective incentives** Special inducements offered by organizations to their members.

Occasionally, however, selective incentives may be quite important to a potential member. For example, individuals in certain industries may not be able to obtain local government contracts unless they belong to a labor union. Similarly, an accountant who is not certified as a CPA will have a difficult time finding a job or obtaining clients. Therefore, economic groups may have selective incentives that are quite powerful in inducing potential members to join. This is one reason that narrow economic interests typically have an easier time forming interest groups than broad, public interests of a more ideological nature.

Not all selective incentives are economic in nature, however. Most political scientists understand that people do not act solely on the basis of immediate self-interest. Many people seem to have a need to be involved, to participate, to make a contribution, and to try to mold society to what they believe is right. Interest groups may provide intangible benefits associated with social interaction with other like-minded individuals or allow individuals to enhance their own sense of political efficacy by supporting a worthy cause.

Although these individuals may be extremely important in providing much of the funding and political activity for ideological groups, such as the prolife or prochoice movements in the abortion battle, political participation is fairly low in the United States. The low rate of political participation in noneconomic interest groups tends to confirm Olson's concerns about the free-rider problem. In turn, the free-rider problem reduces the effect that many public interest or noneconomic interest groups could have on the system.

At the same time, the free-rider problem is reduced by two other factors that influence the formation of interest groups. First, some individuals may be willing to take on enormous personal costs that exceed the personal benefits they obtain from a desired change in public policy. Through their willingness to take political action, these individuals, sometimes called **political entrepreneurs,** allow others to receive political benefits at a lower cost. Ralph Nader is an example; he was willing to spend thousands of dollars from his own pocket in the 1970s to form a consumer-protection interest group.

▶ **political entrepreneurs** Individuals who invest their own resources to establish interest groups, think tanks, institutes, and the like.

A second way in which the free-rider problem may be overcome is through the use of sponsorship. Many public interest groups do not have a large membership base, but they can rely on a relatively small number of benefactors, such as charitable foundations, wealthy individuals, or even the government, to maintain a staff of professional activists who pursue some political aim. For example, Marian Wright Edelman heads the Children's Defense Fund, an organization devoted to lobbying on behalf of children on health and social issues. The sixty million children in the United States are not members of the interest group. Instead, most of the group's funds come from a small number of large donors. Organizations that rely on sponsorships rather than on individual memberships are not as influenced by the free-rider problem. Rather than provide selective incentives to induce individuals to join, they are concerned about receiving grants and other large donations.

9-5 What Do Interest Groups Do?

In a nutshell, interest groups try to influence public policy. They do that in a variety of ways—some direct, some indirect. The groups may contact policy makers directly to try to persuade them to take a certain action or cast a vote in a desired direction. Or, they may try to influence the public to bring pressure on government to achieve a desired goal. Much of the activity of interest groups now has to do with supporting and opposing candidates for public office. Most activities undertaken by interest groups can be grouped into these categories:

- Influencing elections
- Fundraising
- Lobbying
- Influencing public opinion
- Targeting opposition
- Building coalitions
- Engaging in litigation

9-5a Influencing Elections

Increasingly, interest groups seek to influence campaigns and elections at all levels of government. They try to influence the positions that candidates take on issues and even the platforms that parties adopt at their conventions. Sometimes they even recruit political candidates. At the same time, candidates and campaign officials are paying more attention to interest groups. The reason is that interest groups can mobilize significant numbers of voters and can make substantial campaign contributions.[21]

political action committees (PACs) Organizations established by interest groups to support political candidates who support their agendas.

Political Action Committees Political action committees (PACs) are legal mechanisms through which interest groups funnel contributions to candidates for public office. For example, the MoveOn Political Action Committee, affiliated with the liberal group MoveOn.org, contributed more than $2 million to congressional campaigns in 2000, and more than $3.5 million in 2002. This money came from more than ten thousand individual contributors.[22] By concentrating and targeting money raised from individual contributors, PACs can have a significant effect on the political process.

During the 1940s, labor unions created organizations to funnel their contributions to candidates, often with such names as the United Automobile Workers' Committee for Political Education. Corporations could not form similar organizations until the enactment of the Federal Election and Campaign Act of 1971 (FECA). This legislation was supposed to be a reform. Its intent was to regulate the influence of business and labor interests, but the act had the unintended consequence of expanding the role of interest groups in the political process. Since the 1971 law went into effect, PACs have proliferated (see Figure 9-1).

In popular usage, the terms *PAC* and *interest group* are often used interchangeably; however, many interest groups do not have PACs. More than 10,000 interest groups are in Washington, D.C., and fewer than 4,200 PACs are registered with the Federal Election Commission (FEC). Most interest groups attempt to influence the political system without the benefit of a PAC.

A PAC performs two activities: Distribute funds to candidates for campaign purposes and spend money, separate from any candidate's campaign, to influence voters on an issue.

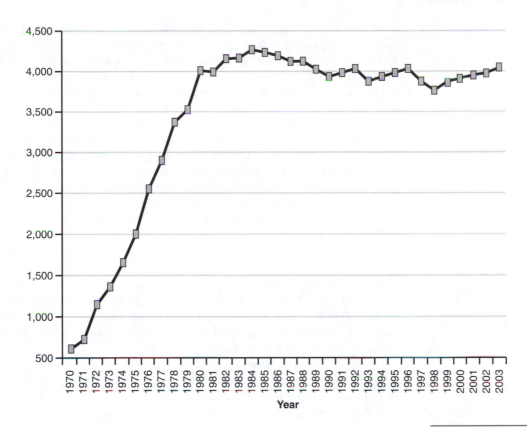

Figure 9-1
The Growth of PACs, 1974–2003

Source: Adapted from the Federal Election Commission.

The FEC defines a multicandidate PAC (which most PACs are) as one that has been registered for at least six months, has received contributions from more than fifty persons, and has made donations to at least five candidates for federal office. A multicandidate PAC cannot be formally tied to a political party, but, of course, most PACs have an ideological preference for the issues and candidates of one party or the other.

Any group of individuals can form a PAC by filling out the forms required by the FEC, filing the necessary quarterly reports, and following the FEC rules. These rules are numerous, but two in particular are important for all PACs. First, no PAC may contribute more than $5,000 to a candidate's campaign in any election (with a primary and general election considered separate elections). Also, no individual can donate more than $5,000 to any one PAC in a year. On the other hand, no limits exist on how much a PAC can spend independently from any particular candidate's campaign to influence voters. In 1976, the Supreme Court ruled in *Buckley v. Valeo* that it is unconstitutional to regulate independent expenditures by PACs.[23] Independent expenditures can be used to advertise support for or opposition to an individual. For example, in 1988 the National Rifle Association (NRA), which opposes gun control, advertised its opposition to the Democratic presidential candidate Michael Dukakis because of his support for legislation to control handguns. The NRA could not give the advertising money directly to the Bush campaign, but it could spend as much as it wanted to buy its own advertising.

The rules for PACs also vary by the type of PAC. The FEC divides PACs into six general groups:

1. Corporate
2. Labor
3. Trade or professional associations
4. Corporations without stock
5. Cooperatives
6. Nonconnecteds

The first five groups are considered connected PACs, or committees specifically tied to a particular organization. The organization can donate money, office space, and other support to the PAC for operating expenses, but cannot give to the PAC any money that will eventually go to candidates. Corporations and labor unions are forbidden from donating any money to presidential or congressional campaigns either directly from the organization's treasury or through contributions to a PAC. The money that a PAC gives to candidates or spends independently must be obtained from individuals in the organization. For example, the Teamsters union cannot donate money to DRIVE-PAC, the Teamsters' PAC. All funds the PAC donates to campaigns or spends independently on an election must come from the individual members of the union.

You can easily tell the affiliation of the connected PACs by their names. For example, corporate PACs are specifically tied to a particular company, such as General Motors or AT&T, and the PAC must use the name of the company. Other connected PACs are similar in that labor PACs use the name of the supporting union and trade PACs use the name of the supporting trade association. Nonconnected PACs are quite different in that they have no supporting organization. As their name suggests, these types of PACs cannot be connected (in a financial sense) to any other organization. The nonconnected category, therefore, has the widest range of possible ideological preferences and types of interest groups. Almost all the PACs of noneconomic interest groups are in this category. Examples of nonconnected PACs include the National Abortion Rights Action League PAC and the National Committee to Preserve Social Security PAC. Because nonconnected PACs do not have a parent organization providing operating expenses, many are strapped for funds. Often, all the money raised by a nonconnected PAC goes to meet operating expenses with none left over to make contributions to candidates.

Of the approximately 4,000 PACs in existence in 2002, the largest category was corporate. There were 1,528 corporate PACs, 1,055 nonconnecteds, 975 trade and professional association PACs, 320 labor PACs, 110 corporation-without-stock PACs, and 39 cooperatives.[24] Since 1980, the nonconnected category has been the fastest growing by far (see Figure 9-2). The number of nonconnected PACs has more than tripled since 1980, whereas the labor and trade categories grew by only 23 percent and the corporate by 75 percent. Because nonconnected PACs are usually single-issue groups with a narrow ideological focus, some observers have been alarmed by the rapid growth in the number of nonconnecteds.

Political action committees' overall spending in 1999 and 2000 provide a good measure of the activities of various interests in the 2000 presidential election, including congressional elections. The two biggest spenders were the National Rifle Association and Emily's List. However, union interests, ranging from municipal and state employees to the United Auto Workers and International Brotherhood of Electrical Workers (IBEW), were also quite active. The National Education Association and trial lawyers were major players in the Democratic party, and Elect Life supported prolife candidates, most of whom were Republicans.

Although some groups, such as the NRA, have long played a major role in electoral politics, the contours of group activity ebb and flow as the parties probe the limits of the law's limitations on soft money and various interests decide to invest more in the political process. The Realtor's PAC increased its spending more than any other political action committee between 1998 and 2000. However, the second- and third-greatest increases were shown by committees representing the political parties. The Democrats' PAC to Our Future and the Republicans' Keep Our Majority contributed a large amount to various candidates during the 2000 election cycle. In many ways, this phenomenon represented a strengthening of the parties as they flexed their money-raising abilities. These increases almost certainly paved the way for legislative passage of the 2002 campaign finance law (see Figure 9-2).

Other interests undoubtedly decided that they needed to play a much greater role in politics. Probably the most obvious among them was Microsoft, which almost quadrupled

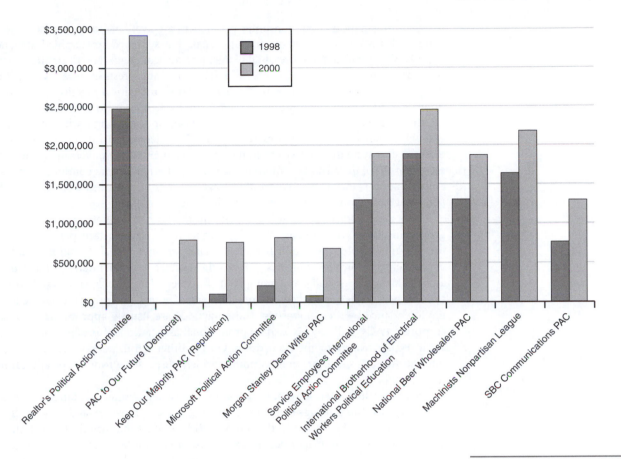

Figure 9-2
Greatest Increase in PAC Spending for Candidates (1998–2000)

Source: Adapted from the Federal Election Commission.

its candidate expenditures between 1998 and 2000. During this time, executives at Microsoft certainly must have rethought their earlier decisions to stay fairly removed from the political arena as they found themselves embroiled in a lengthy, expensive trial following the Justice department's filing of a lawsuit alleging that the company practiced anti-competitive business practices.

9-5b Fundraising

Fundraising is the most crucial activity undertaken by an interest group or PAC. To contribute to candidates or advertise its preferences through independent expenditures, a PAC must have money. The wealthiest PACs spend millions of dollars in each election cycle. Other interest groups must also raise money for the various activities they use to influence policy.

Generally, economic interest groups have an easier time raising funds than do ideological groups or public interest groups. For one thing, the free-rider problem is much more severe for noneconomic groups. Noneconomic groups are also more likely to depend on individuals for their funding than economic groups are. For example, the National Association of Manufacturers depends on businesses to contribute funds. On the other hand, Common Cause (a consumer-protection public interest group) refuses to accept business donations to avoid the appearance of being "bought off" by the companies it is supposed to be watching.

There are as many fundraising techniques as there are interest groups and innovative leaders. The most common method is **direct mail.** A 1984 survey of PAC leaders indicated that more than two-thirds of them use direct-mail solicitation.[25] Direct mail is popular for several reasons. First, finding potential donors is easy—numerous mailing lists that provide

▶ **direct mail** A technique used by interest groups to solicit funds directly from individuals or organizations.

detailed information about consumer preferences are available for purchase. Second, the wide availability and low cost of computers make it easy to produce sophisticated, targeted appeals. Third, through pictures, highly inflammatory language, and dramatic appeals that may stretch the truth ("Without you, we will have no rain forests in twenty years!"), groups can plead for money and also spread the word on their political positions. Fourth, after a donor has been found, continuing to send further solicitations to the same person is easy. On the other hand, direct mail entails high costs at the beginning until donors are found, and the response rate is often extremely low. For ideological interest groups, however, direct mail may be the only way to contact potential members. Conversely, economic interest groups have the advantage of knowing where potential donors conduct business or are employed; thus, they can avoid sending mass mailings to millions of people, only a small percentage of whom will be interested in the issue.

Other methods of fundraising depend on the type of interest group. Groups with a geographically concentrated membership frequently use face-to-face, personal requests for funds. For example, it would be feasible to make personal appeals to union members who are concentrated in a few factories. On the other hand, a national interest group would have a difficult time personally contacting all its members. Likewise, locally based groups may use seminars, rallies, special entertainment events, dinners, and other special events requiring attendance by their members. These methods are usually appropriate for labor and corporate PACs and may be used by professional associations if professional conventions are a regular feature of the occupation. On the other hand, nonconnected PACs, public interest groups, and other noneconomic, widely dispersed groups typically cannot use these methods.

Some wealthy interest groups may be able to use telephone solicitation or even media advertising for fundraising. These methods are expensive, however, and may be effective in only special cases. For example, the National Rifle Association may find it cost-effective to advertise nationally in magazines such as *Soldier of Fortune* because a large number of gun enthusiasts would see this type of advertisement. On the other hand, most groups would find that advertising in a weekly newsmagazine, such as *Time* or *Newsweek,* would be quite costly and reach such a diverse audience (with a low percentage of potential responses) that the money would be wasted.

9-5c Lobbying

▶ **lobbying** Any effort by an individual or group to contact public officials for the purpose of influencing their policy decisions.

The most basic, but also the most controversial, activity undertaken by interest groups is lobbying. **Lobbying** is any action taken by an interest group to let the government know how the members of a group feel about proposed or existing regulations or legislation.

Today interest groups commonly form coalitions to support or oppose policies in which they have a mutual interest. Thus, lobbying is often a cooperative enterprise. As one scholar of interest groups noted recently, "Organized interests fight their battles today largely in coalitions. Lobbying coalitions are also the building blocks out of which consensus within the Washington Beltway is built."[26]

Most interest groups have someone on staff who regularly watches both Congress and the administration to see whether any action is being taken on an issue affecting the common interests of the group. Many public interest and smaller ideological groups cannot afford to hire professional lobbyists to keep tabs on the government, although most economic groups and the larger noneconomic groups can. Typically, they either employ their own full-time lobbyist (or lobbyists) or contract with a public relations company or law firm that specializes in political activity.

Often, these firms work for a number of interest groups with different concerns—a necessity if conflicts between clients are to be avoided. These firms can spread some costs among their clients, such as the salary paid to a former government official "with connections" or the cost of buying and thoroughly evaluating all publications with information on congressional activity. Consequently, many corporations and trade groups find it more efficient to contract with these political "guns for hire" than to pay for their own staff.

The cost of obtaining information on what government is doing can be quite expensive. Congress passes hundreds of legislative bills every year out of the thousands that are proposed. In addition, the administrative agencies add thousands of pages of regulations every year to the *Federal Register,* a daily government publication of all new regulations. Although numerous publications, such as the *Congressional Quarterly Weekly Report* or the *Roll Call* newsletter, offer information on what has happened, often the most valuable information on what *may happen* cannot be obtained from publications. Then the experience and connections of a lobbyist come into play. That is also the reason that so many former members of Congress, administrative staffers, and White House assistants are employed by these political action firms. Concern over the "revolving door" between government service and employment by interest groups has caused both Congress in 1991 and President Clinton in 1993 to invoke rules barring their respective employees from taking jobs as lobbyists immediately after leaving either Congress or the White House.

Lobbying takes on many forms. The popular image of the lobbyist coercing a member of Congress into voting a particular way on a piece of legislation over a drink is largely false. The heavy demand on the average member's time, media scrutiny, and various ethics rules make such overt "arm twisting" less likely to occur in the modern Congress. The lobbyist's job is much more subtle and diverse. The most basic function is to transmit information to government officials in the legislative or executive branches. This transmitting may be done in several ways: direct conversations with a member of Congress, presentations to congressional or administrative staff members, publications in the media, or testimony in congressional committee hearings.

9-5d Grassroots Lobbying

One other important category of lobbying is **grassroots lobbying,** a fairly broad category of activity which can be defined as "any type of action that attempts to influence inside-the-beltway inhabitants by influencing the attitudes or behavior of outside-the-beltway inhabitants."[27] Typically, grassroots lobbying involves orchestrated personal contacts between constituents and a member of Congress. The most common grassroots tactic is the letter-writing campaign. Its aim is to flood the offices of targeted members of Congress, such as party leaders or committee chairpersons, with an overwhelming amount of mail or to have each individual write to the member representing her home district. Many interest groups routinely provide in their direct mail or regular publications some samples of letters or actual postcards that individuals can use. This way, individuals are spared the trouble of finding out bill numbers and names, congressional committees considering the bill, and the addresses of members of Congress.

When members of Congress agree with an interest group, the large volume of mail may provide a cover for the action they take. Members of Congress even occasionally explain a vote by mentioning that they received bags of mail or that the mail on one side of an issue outnumbered the mail on the other side. Thus, they treat the mail as an expression of public opinion even though only one side may have made a concerted effort. If a silent majority does not counteract the efforts of a determined minority on an issue, these types of campaigns can be effective.

If other, more formal means of lobbying are not effective, a group may turn to a different form of grassroots activity: political protest. Protests can take a number of forms: economic strikes, boycotts, marches, picketing, and sit-ins. Any activity that involves a number of people and will draw the media's attention can be used. The civil rights protests of the 1960s may be the most successful example of the use of this political tactic by a group that was largely denied access to the formal means of political influence. The sit-ins, boycotts,

> **grassroots lobbying** A form of lobbying in which interest groups attempt to get a large number of citizens to contact their own legislators directly and express their opinions on an issue.

and marches forced the issue on the national agenda, and the brutality witnessed by television viewers helped mobilize public opinion to support the passage of the Civil Rights Act of 1964 and the Voting Rights Act of 1965.

9-5e Influencing Public Opinion

Influencing public opinion is a crucial aspect of political strategy for many interest groups. It is particularly important for groups that do not have the resources to hire lobbyists or fund a PAC. When a group believes that its point of view would attract popular support if presented properly, it may adopt a public relations strategy. Ideological groups whose messages may have an effect on a large number of people are particularly likely to face this situation.

Formulating a public relations campaign can be quite difficult. The most direct approach is to buy media advertising. However, this option is expensive, it may appear to be biased, and sustaining interest in an issue through advertising is difficult. Most groups cannot afford even a limited advertising campaign. Therefore, most groups look for ways to obtain free media coverage. Some interest groups choose to fund research on the topic and later publish the results to make a point. For example, the Consumers' Union regularly tests various products for safety and then publicly releases the information. Another indirect method is to publicize the voting records of members of Congress. The Americans for Democratic Action (ADA), a liberal group, has issued a rating of all members of Congress each year since the 1960s. Using a scale from 0 to 100, the rating shows how often each member agreed with the group's position. Voters can assume that an ADA score of 100 indicates a liberal legislator. Finally, a group can provide the media with film footage, photos, or interviews of persons suffering from a situation that the group thinks should be remedied by government action. For example, an environmental group, such as Greenpeace, might provide the networks with footage of whales being killed or seal pups being clubbed. This type of graphic footage may be more effective at moving public opinion than a written argument would. Consequently, air time on the television news is a valuable commodity.

9-5f Targeting Political Opposition

One of the more important elements of any political strategy is to know one's opposition. In addition to observing government activity, a successful lobbyist must keep track of what

---

Profiles &
Perspectives

The American Civil Liberties Union

Founded in 1920, the American Civil Liberties Union (better known as the ACLU) has become America's leading interest group fighting for civil rights and liberties. The ACLU has always stood with the unpopular who are the targets of criminal prosecution or other forms of government action. It has defended the rights of atheists, abortionists, anarchists, pornographers, prisoners, racial minorities, students, gay men and lesbians, drug dealers, illegal aliens, Nazis, communists, and even members of the Ku Klux Klan. During the Cold War, the ACLU often stood up for the rights of persons accused of subversive activity, leading some to characterize the ACLU as a "communist front" organization. More recently, the ACLU has strongly criticized the federal government for some of its actions and policies in the "war on terrorism" following the attacks of September 11, 2001. The ACLU is one of the interest groups that rely heavily on litigation to achieve its objectives. At any time, the ACLU is party to numerous lawsuits in the state and federal courts.

Just 45 days after the September 11 attacks, with virtually no debate, Congress passed the USA PATRIOT Act. Many parts of this sweeping legislation take away checks on law enforcement and threaten the very rights and freedoms that we are struggling to protect. For example, without a warrant and without probable cause, the FBI now has the power to access your most private medical records, your library records, and your student records... and can prevent anyone from telling you it was done.

The Department of Justice is expected to introduce a sequel, dubbed PATRIOT II, that would further erode key freedoms and liberties of every American.

The ACLU and many allies on the left and right believe that before giving law enforcement new powers, Congress must first re-examine provisions of the first PATRIOT Act to ensure that is in alignment with key constitutional protections.

the political opposition has been doing and planning. You can find several good potential sources of information on the opposition: members of Congress and their staffers, other lobbyists, members of the interest group, the media, government hearings, administrators, and various people at social functions.

For many groups, the opposition may change from one issue to another. For example, in the same year, the United Auto Workers might oppose several different groups, such as the auto manufacturers, consumer safety groups, and even other unions, for different reasons. The union might oppose the auto manufacturers on worker safety issues, work with industry representatives against a consumer safety group to avoid new safety features on American cars that would raise the cost of American cars versus imports (and therefore possibly cost them jobs), and oppose the steel unions' efforts to obtain higher tariffs on steel (which would also raise the price of a car).

Groups often feed off their opposition. The actions or words of the opposition may be useful in motivating potential members to join or current members to become more active. The direct-mail solicitations sent by ideological groups commonly highlight the words or actions of some well-known politician on the other end of the ideological debate. Senator Edward Kennedy is a favorite target of conservative groups, just as the religious right is a frequent target of liberals, the same function for liberal groups. For example, the 1993 debates about gays in the military provided a great deal of material for conservative ideological groups seeking new members and contributions until this issue subsided in the late 1990s. In 2003 and 2004, the issue of same-sex marriage was exploited in much the same way.

9-5g Building Coalitions

Just as important as targeting the opposition is building coalitions with other interest groups. One interest group testifying at a congressional hearing does not suggest a strong current of public opinion on the issue, but if several lobbyists with different points of view, diverse constituencies, and a wide set of connections to the members of Congress appear, the issue is likely to be taken more seriously. Likewise, a coalition of groups is more likely to gain access to congressional offices, the media, and the administration.

Different groups will also have diverse resources and abilities. For example, Greenpeace, one of the more radical environmental groups, has a unique talent for drawing media coverage (see Table 9-2). Greenpeace does not have a PAC, however, and tends not

TABLE 9-2 **Membership, Budget, and Types of Activities of Selected Environmental Groups**

Name	Members	1988 budget	Lobbying	Litigation	Research	Media Outreach	Congress Testimony	Grassroots Activity	Education	Campaign Contributions	Grants and Awards	Direct Action
National Audubon Society	550,000	$30 million	x	x	x	x	x	x	x			
Greenpeace USA	800,000	$1.8 million	x		x	x	x	x	x			x
World Wildlife Fund	450,000	$20 million			x	x	x		x		x	
Sierra Club	443,000	$28 million	x	x		x	x	x	x	x	x	
Defenders of Wildlife	80,000	$3.5 million	x	x	x	x	x	x	x			
Clean Water Action Project	400,000	$4.5 million	x		x		x	x	x	x		

Source: Adapted from Foundation for Public Affairs, *Public Interest Profiles* (Washington, D.C.: Congressional Quarterly, 1992).

to use traditional channels of lobbying in Congress. Conversely, the Sierra Club, an older and more moderate organization, does have access to Congress and administrators. Thus, although the groups might agree on a particular environmental issue, they would use different tactics.

The coalitions that form among interest groups are often temporary and rather narrowly focused. The groups may have different goals and tactics that prevent permanent coalitions. Also, similar groups are competing for the same set of potentially interested citizens. For example, the National Committee to Preserve Social Security and the American Association of Retired Persons (AARP) both depend on senior citizens for most of their funds. Although both would oppose any proposal to reduce Social Security benefits, they would be rivals in claiming responsibility for defeating the legislation. Of course, the level of competition varies widely.

9-5h Litigation

The courts have increasingly become a focus for interest groups. One of the first interest groups to employ litigation to affect public policy was the NAACP. Through its Legal

Popular Culture and American Politics
The 2030 Center

By Chapman Rackaway

Many people shy away from involvement in interest groups because they think that politics is a game for older people. However, a number of groups seek to bring political advocacy to a younger audience and in turn encourage them to become more involved in America's political culture.

In 1997, the 2030 Center was founded (named for the ages of people in their twenties and thirties who would be the core and focus of the organization) to push for the economic interests of younger citizens. The 2030 Center's founders saw fewer employment opportunities for people just out of college and a general downturn in the economic fortunes of the young. The group has a strongly liberal lean: The group's primary purpose is to increase Social Security spending for future generations, and it features attacks on Bush administration privatization proposals and pictures of prominent Democratic politicians such as Al Gore and Bill Clinton.

Although Social Security might not seem to be an issue of much importance to college-age citizens, as many as 4.25 million Americans under age forty receive some form of Social Security benefit, either from loss of a parent or physical disability. As part of 2030's mission, the organization wants to protect and expand Social Security so the generations that currently pay in will be able to draw out the benefits when they are eligible. Not ironically, the year 2030 is also the year some government estimates suggest the Social Security trust fund will run out of money and be unable to pay benefits.

Despite the political bias, 2030 provides ground-floor opportunities for younger people to become directly involved in the political process. The 2030 Center's other main area of concentration is job growth. Its Jobs of the Future program lobbies for expanded protections for temporary, part-time, and service employment. While annual incomes for young adults have plummeted since 1972, pension coverage for workers age twenty-five or younger dropped one-third; for workers age twenty-five to twenty-nine, coverage dropped 15 percent, according to the Department of Labor. The jobs of the future hold little promise of improvement. Only 3.1 percent of temporary employees—half of whom are age twenty to thirty-four—have a 401(k) plan, and none have a pension through their employment. Similarly, only 18 percent of workers in small businesses (fewer than twenty-five employees) have any retirement plan. According to the Department of Labor, small businesses created 75 percent of all new jobs in 1995.

From conducting polls on younger voters' attitudes about Social Security to posting policy briefings on its website to testifying before Congress, the 2030 Center is an active voice for younger voters.

Figure 9-3
How Interest Groups Influence Policy

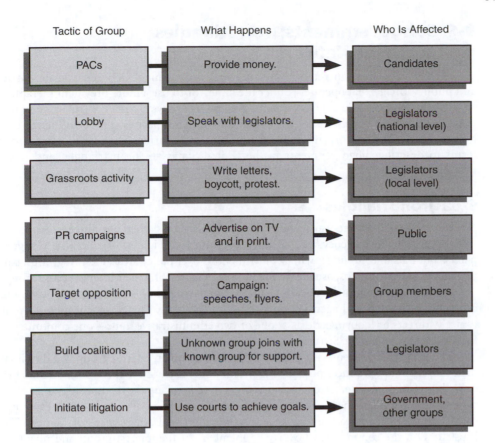

Tactic of Group	What Happens	Who Is Affected
PACs	Provide money.	Candidates
Lobby	Speak with legislators.	Legislators (national level)
Grassroots activity	Write letters, boycott, protest.	Legislators (local level)
PR campaigns	Advertise on TV and in print.	Public
Target opposition	Campaign: speeches, flyers.	Group members
Build coalitions	Unknown group joins with known group for support.	Legislators
Initiate litigation	Use courts to achieve goals.	Government, other groups

Defense and Education Fund, headed by Thurgood Marshall, the NAACP brought, and usually won, lawsuits challenging racial segregation and other civil rights violations. More recently, environmental and consumer groups have found litigation to be an effective means of advancing their interests.

Quite often, interest groups may not be direct parties to lawsuits because they lack standing to sue. The courts require the party who brings a lawsuit to have standing—that is, to be directly and adversely affected by the policy or situation being challenged in the suit. This requirement means that interest groups frequently have to find someone to serve as the plaintiff of record. After a suitable plaintiff is located, the interest group can provide legal representation and financial assistance. For example, in *Brown v. Board of Education*, the landmark school desegregation decision of 1954, the NAACP recruited the parents of Linda Brown to challenge school segregation in Topeka, Kansas. The Browns were the plaintiffs of record, but the NAACP was the driving force behind the lawsuit. Evidence indicates that more than half of all important constitutional law cases are sponsored in this way by interest groups.[28]

Amicus Briefs Another way in which interest groups use the courts to advance their interests is by filing **amicus curiae** briefs in cases in which they have a stake. Literally meaning "friend of the court," an *amicus* brief is filed by a person or group that is not a direct party to a case but wants to inform the court of its views on how the case should be decided. In a case involving a major social, political, or economic issue, many different groups may file *amicus* briefs (see Figure 9-3). Interest groups filed *amicus* briefs in more than half the noneconomic cases decided by the Supreme Court in the 1970s,[29] and this trend continues now.

▶ **amicus curiae ("friend of the court") briefs** Legal documents filed on behalf of organized groups that have an interest in the outcome of a case.

9-6 Subgovernments: Iron Triangles and Issue Networks

The term subgovernment refers to an informal arrangement between private parties and public officials that operates "under the table," or to use a more prevalent metaphor, "off the radar screen." Such arrangements are and have always been controversial in that they may provide largely unknown and unaccountable parties undue influence over public policy. Subgovernments may take a number of forms. The two most common terms to describe subgovernments in the United States are "iron triangle" and "issue network."

9-6a Iron Triangles

iron triangle A three-way relationship involving a legislative committee, an executive agency, and an interest group.

An **iron triangle** is a three-way relationship involving a legislative committee (or subcommittee), an executive agency, and an interest group (see Figure 9-4). Because Congress parcels out bills to committees with set jurisdictions over policy areas, interest groups, particularly economic groups, usually find that most bills affecting their interests pass through one congressional committee in each chamber. Similarly, policy is implemented by various cabinet departments and agencies, depending on the issue. Therefore, an interest group typically directs its lobbying efforts at one or two administrative units—one committee in the House and one in the Senate.

The iron triangle theory suggests that in the long run an interest group will dominate the subsystem that produces policy for a certain issue. Each of the three sets of actors gets something from the system, so no one has a reason to break up the relationship or let other actors into the system. The interest group provides the member of Congress with campaign contributions or volunteers, information on the policy, and other means of support. The legislators on the committee, who may be members of the interest group and may have many constituents who are involved in the group, either block unfavorable bills or push for legislation that the agency needs in order to implement policy favorable to the interest group. In addition, the committee passes the budget for the agency and is responsible for any legislative oversight. Big budgets, favorable legislation, and a minimum of interference from outside sources allow the agency to implement policy in a way that favors the interest group. Because most legislation must be reported by congressional committees before being considered by the entire chamber, the system is particularly successful at preventing action from taking place.

Other connections also exist between the agency and the interest group. Members of the interest group are typically the most informed potential appointees for administrative positions in the policy area, and over time an individual may hold various jobs in an industry, in the government agencies regulating the industry, in the economic interest groups representing the industry, in congressional or White House staff positions, or in the law and public relations firms that serve the interest groups.

Figure 9-4
The Iron Triangle

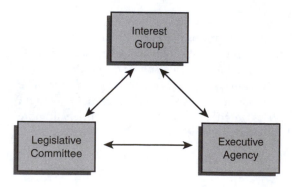

Consider the case of subsidies for tobacco farmers. The agriculture committees in the House and Senate are responsible for agricultural policy, including subsidies. The Agriculture department is the administrative body responsible for implementing farm policy. Senator Jesse Helms was the committee chairman from 1981 to 1986 and again assumed a leadership role in 1994 until his retirement in 2003. Senator Helms represented North Carolina, a state that relies on both tobacco farming and the manufacture of tobacco products. He received PAC money from several sources related to tobacco, such as the RJR corporate PAC and tobacco farming interests. In response to his state's economic interest and his connection to the interest groups supporting tobacco farming, Helms continued to push for tobacco subsidies and large budgets for the Agriculture department. The Agriculture department responded by working closely with tobacco farmers to help them qualify for subsidies. The tobacco interests may also have provided the senator or the Agriculture department with research that supports subsidies (such as the number of people employed in the industry, the volume of tobacco exports, and the plight of small farmers).

The issue was further muddled by the 1998 settlement between the tobacco companies and the states that provided for payouts to the states to compensate them for smoking-related health-care costs. The states agreed to drop lawsuits that had threatened to bring financial ruin to the tobacco industry in exchange for a twenty-five-year series of multimillion-dollar payouts that began in 2000. Moreover, tobacco companies agreed to spend almost two billion dollars on programs to discourage youth smoking and to eliminate advertising on billboards and displaying their logos on T-shirts and other merchandise. The entire settlement could exceed more than 200 billion dollars. In a sense, this agreement expanded the arena beyond the usual players, and the conflict was resolved in an unusual way.

Other interests, such as legislators concerned about health issues or the surgeon general, are not included in the policy subsystem. If a member of Congress is not on the committee that handles the policy, he is not likely to have much opportunity to affect it, particularly in the House, where more rigid rules prevent members from taking the initiative on matters outside the jurisdiction of the legislator's own committee. The surgeon general is excluded because that person has no say over the Agriculture department's budget or the legislation that provides the subsidies. Even the president may be frustrated in his attempts to fight the entrenched interests in an iron triangle. Because members of Congress, lobbyists, and career civil servants are in Washington for so long, they can usually wait out any temporary intrusions into the policy subsystem. A president has so little time to devote to a wide range of issues that no single administration can ensure that policy is implemented as it intended. The media and the public are even less likely to stay focused on an issue long enough to counter the iron triangle. Over time, an iron triangle can be quite effective at implementing policy in a favorable way and blocking any new initiatives.

9-6b Issue Networks

An **issue network** is a conglomeration of decision makers, activists, and experts in a particular policy area.[30] It is typically larger, more diverse, and more dynamic than the iron triangle (see Figure 9-5). In the issue network, relationships change, participants come and go, roles and levels of influence likewise change. An issue network in a particular policy area may involve governmental actors from several branches and several levels of government; activists and lobbyists representing numerous diverse interests; and experts from think tanks, consulting firms, and academia.

Because it is more inclusive and less insular than the iron triangle, the issue network is less objectionable to those who object to the undue influence of private actors over public policy. Today, the issue network may be a more realistic model of interest group influence in most policy areas.

> **issue network** A small group of political actors involved in a particular policy area.

Figure 9-5
An Issue Network

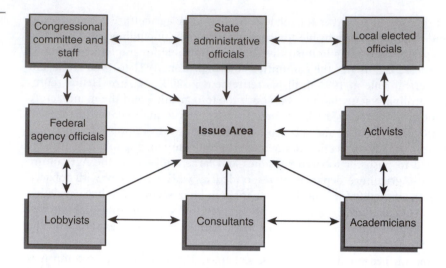

Comparative Perspective

Interest Groups in Japanese Politics

Interest groups are quite important in Japanese politics, but they operate differently than they do in the United States. Rather than pressure government from the outside, interest groups in Japan attempt to get their members elected to public office by affiliating with one of the political parties. Interest group leaders often hold seats in the Diet, or national legislature. Japanese farmers, for example, are well represented in the Diet by members of the Agricultural Cooperative Association. Labor unions, religious organizations, and consumer groups have similar representation. At any given time, as many as one-fifth of the members of the Diet may be formally affiliated with an interest group. Many more members may be regarded as sympathizers with particular interest groups. These sympathizers have close connections to interest groups, but do not hold formal positions in them.

Interest groups in Japan work closely with the political parties in orchestrating campaigns. Without question, interest groups have strong influence in the Japanese government. Indeed, the government actively cooperates with key interest groups in developing and implementing policy. Scholars may debate the openness of the Japanese interest group system, but no one doubts the groups' importance. Certainly, American government officials have become well aware of the centrality of interest groups in Japanese politics as they have tried to persuade the Japanese government to lower its trade barriers to American products, especially agricultural commodities. Although some groups in Japan favor free trade, the more powerful groups, especially the farmers, have steadfastly supported policies that keep American goods out.

9-7 Conclusion: Interest Groups and Political Culture

Interest groups are a subject of as much controversy as any phenomenon in American politics. Many believe that they foster and enhance political participation and are a desirable mechanism for ensuring representation and citizen involvement. Becoming involved in an interest group does not require an inordinate amount of time, energy, or money. By affiliating with an interest group, an individual can promote a particular cause directly. Unlike voting or getting involved in a political party, joining an interest group ensures that people's energies are focused on subjects that matter to them personally. Joining an interest group is an eminently practical form of political participation that appeals to America's pragmatic culture.

American political culture has become increasingly supportive of the articulation of individual demands through interest groups. At the same time, some commentators worry that the political system is becoming fragmented into small, narrowly defined groups that are increasingly unable or unwilling to compromise. Increasingly, critics of American politics lament that our political culture seems to place no emphasis on the needs of the community as opposed to the interests of the individual or small group.

Others believe that a political system built around interest groups, as the American system increasingly appears to be, is incapable of rational policy making that meets the long-term needs of society. Still others object to what they believe to be the conservative, probusiness bias of the interest group system. Regardless of one's evaluation of pluralist politics, interest groups clearly are playing an increasingly important role in this country's governance. Interest groups do not seek to govern, but in influencing those who do, interest groups can have a substantial impact on governance.

Questions for Thought and Discussion

1. Do interest groups have too much influence in the political process? What reforms might lessen their influence?
2. What effect has the proliferation of interest groups had on political parties in this country?
3. Why are some interest groups more successful than others in influencing policy making?
4. Does the proliferation of interest groups suggest changes in the underlying political culture?
5. What effect do political action committees have on congressional elections? What reforms, if any, are needed in the way that PACs operate?

Practice Quiz

Note: You can find the correct answers to these questions by taking the quiz and then submitting your answers in the Online Edition. The program will automatically score your submission. If you miss a question, the program will provide the correct answer, a rationale for the answer, and the section number in the chapter where the topic is discussed.

1. The right to join interest groups is guaranteed _____.
   a. by Article III of the Constitution
   b. has never been firmly established as a legal principle
   c. under the First Amendment of the Constitution
   d. in Article VI of the Constitution

2. Writing in the 1830s, Alexis de Tocqueville noted that _____.
   a. most Americans, like the Framers, were not fond of interest groups
   b. America was a nation of "joiners"
   c. Americans generally favored political parties over interest groups
   d. Americans, like most of the European countries, paid little attention to interest groups

3. According to the political scientist Theodore Lowi, _____ has corrupted our politics and undermined our government.
   a. interest-group liberalism
   b. factional government
   c. divided government
   d. none of the above

4. Classical republican theorists believed that the principal objective of government should be the furtherance of _____.
   a. property rights
   b. the public interest
   c. personal liberties
   d. majoritarian interests
   e. private interests

5. Which of the following is/are most likely to favor tariffs on imports?
   a. Domestic producers
   b. Labor unions
   c. Consumers
   d. All of the above
   e. a and b only

6. Generally speaking, labor union members tend to _____.
   a. support Democratic candidates
   b. support Republican candidates
   c. support legislation aimed at protecting the free enterprise system
   d. b and c

7. Which of the following groups has used the courts to further its cause?
   a. Civil rights groups
   b. Environmental groups
   c. Consumer groups
   d. All of the above
   e. a and b only

8. Formal organizations established by private groups to support candidates for public office are called _____.
   a. political action committees
   b. special interest groups
   c. electoral coalitions
   d. candidate support groups

9. _____ is the term used to describe that situation whereby government is unable to make or implement any decision.
   a. Pluralism
   b. Hyperpluralism
   c. Gridlock
   d. Interest group liberalism

10. The proportion of the nonagricultural work force belonging to unions is referred to as _____.
    a. labor intensity
    b. union density
    c. worker saturation
    d. collectivization

For Further Reading

Berry, Jeffrey M. *The Interest Group Society*, 3d ed. (New York: Longman, 1997).

——. *The New Liberalism: The Rising Power of Citizen Groups* (Washington, D.C.: Brookings Institution, 2000).

Cigler, Allan J., and Burdett A. Loomis, eds. *Interest Group Politics*, 6th ed. (Washington, D.C.: Congressional Quarterly, 2002).

Hayes, Michael T. *Lobbyists and Legislators: A Theory of Political Markets* (New Brunswick, NJ: Rutgers University Press, 1981).

Goldstein, Kenneth M. *Interest Groups, Lobbying and Participation in America* (Cambridge, UK: Cambridge University Press, 1999).

Lowi, Theodore J. *The End of Liberalism*, 2d ed. (New York: W. W. Norton, 1979).

Magleby, David B., and Candice J. Nelson. *The Money Chase* (Washington, D.C.: Brookings Institution, 1990).

Mahood, H. R. *Interest Groups in American National Politics* (Upper Saddle River, NJ: Prentice-Hall, 1999).

Moe, Terry M. *The Organization of Interests: Incentives and the Internal Dynamics of Political Interest Groups* (Chicago: University of Chicago Press, 1980).

Nownes, Anthony. *Pressure and Power: Organized Interests in American Politics* (Boston: Houghton Mifflin, 2000).

Olson, Mancur, Jr. *The Logic of Collective Action: Public Goods and the Theory of Groups* (Cambridge, MA: Harvard University Press, 1971).

Putnam, Robert D. *Bowling Alone: The Collapse and Revival of American Community* (New York: Simon & Schuster, 2001).

Rauch, Jonathan. *Demosclerosis: The Silent Killer of American Government* (New York: Times Books, 1994).

Rozell, Mark J., and Clyde Wilcox. *Interest Groups in American Campaigns: The New Face of Electioneering* (Washington, D.C.: Congressional Quarterly Books, 1998).

Sabato, Larry. *PAC Power: Inside the World of Political Action Committees* (New York: W. W. Norton, 1984).

Schlozman, Kay Lehman, and John T. Tierney. *Organized Interests and American Democracy* (New York: Harper & Row, 1986).

Sorauf, Frank J. *Money in American Elections* (Glenview, IL: Scott, Foresman, 1988).

Walker, Jack L. *Mobilizing Interest Groups in America: Patrons, Professions and Social Movements* (UMP, 1991).

Wolpe, Bruce E., and Bertram J. Levine. *Lobbying Congress*, 2d ed. (Washington, D.C.: CQ Press, 1996).

Endnotes

1. Harold D. Lasswell, *Politics: Who Gets What, When and How* (New York: McGraw-Hill, 1938).
2. Alexis de Tocqueville, *Democracy in America*, vol. 2 (New York: Vintage Books, 1954), p. 114.
3. Robert D. Putnam, *Bowling Alone: The Collapse and Revival of American Community* (New York: Simon & Schuster, 2001).
4. *Sweezy v. New Hampshire*, 354 U.S. 234, 250-251 (1957).
5. *N.A.A.C.P. v. Alabama*, 357 U.S. 449, 460 (1958).
6. *Roberts v. United States Jaycees*, 468 U.S. 609, 622 (1984).
7. Pluralist theory is generally thought to have begun with the publication of Arthur Bentley's seminal book, *The Process of Government* (1908).
8. Robert A. Dahl, *A Preface to Democratic Theory* (Chicago: University of Chicago Press, 1956), p. 137.
9. One of the best-known and most trenchant critiques is Grant McConnell, *Private Power and American Democracy* (New York: Knopf, 1966).
10. The classic exposition of this view is found in C. Wright Mills, *The Power Elite* (New York: Oxford University Press, 1956).
11. Anthony J. Nownes, *Pressure and Power: Organized Interests in American Politics* (Boston: Houghton Mifflin, 2001), p. 220.
12. Theodore J. Lowi, *The End of Liberalism*, 2d ed. (New York: W. W. Norton, 1979), pp. 43–44.
13. See, for example, Jonathan Rauch, *Demosclerosis: The Silent Killer of American Government* (New York: Times Books, 1994).
14. Robert Paul Wolff, "A Critique of Pluralism: 'Beyond Tolerance.'" In *The Dissent of the Governed: Readings on the Democratic Process*, eds. John C. Livingston and Robert G. Thompson (New York: Macmillan, 1972), p. 89.
15. *Gibbons v. Ogden*, 22 U.S. 1 (1824).
16. Information provided by the Federal Election Commission, on the Web at www.fec.gov.
17. According to the AFL-CIO website, "[t]he 16.3 million U.S. workers who belonged to unions in 2001 represented 13.5 percent of the total wage and salary workforce."
18. Harold W. Stanley and Richard Niemi, *Vital Statistics on American Politics*, 3d ed. (Washington, D.C.: CQ Press, 1990), p. 106.
19. See Ronald G. Shaiko, *Voices and Echoes for the Environment: Public Interest Representation in the 1990s and Beyond.* (New York: Columbia University Press, 1999).
20. Jeffrey M. Berry, *Lobbying for the People* (Princeton, NJ: Princeton University Press, 1977), p. 7.
21. For an excellent study of these trends, see Mark J. Rozell and Clyde Wilcox, *Interest Groups in American Campaigns: The New Face of Electioneering* (Washington, D.C.: Congressional Quarterly Books, 1998).
22. Information obtained from MoveOn.org website, http://www.moveon.org.
23. *Buckley v. Valeo*, 424 U.S. 1 (1976).

24. Harold W. Stanley and Richard Niemi, *Vital Statistics on American Politics 2003–2004* (Washington, D.C.: CQ Press, 2003), p. 102.

25. Larry Sabato, *PAC Power* (New York: W. W. Norton, 1984), p. 146.

26. Kevin W. Hula, *Lobbying Together: Interest Group Coalitions in Legislative Politics* (Washington, D.C.: Georgetown University Press, 1999), p. 2.

27. Kenneth M. Goldstein, *Interest Groups, Lobbying and Participation in America* (Cambridge, UK: Cambridge University Press, 1999), p. 3.

28. Karen O'Connor and Lee Epstein, "The Role of Interest Groups in Supreme Court Policy Formation." In *Public Policy Formation*, ed. Robert Eyestone (Greenwich, CT: JAI Press, 1984).

29. Karen O'Connor and Lee Epstein, "Research Note: An Appraisal of Hakman's 'Folklore,'" *Law and Society Review,* vol. 16, 1982, pp. 701–11.

30. See Hugh Heclo, *Issue Networks and the Executive Establishment* (Washington, D.C.: American Enterprise Institute, 1978).

The Mass Media

10

10-1 The Development of Mass Media

The **mass media** include the technologies and organizations that disseminate information to the mass public. This broad category can be divided into the print media and the electronic media. Also termed *the press,* the **print media** include newspapers, journals, tabloids, and magazines. The **electronic media** encompass radio, television, and, increasingly, the Internet. Although the media are often referred to as the fourth estate,[1] some have gone so far as to call them the fourth branch of government.[2] It is more accurate, however, to view the organizations that constitute the media as intermediary institutions, like political parties and interest groups. Like these other organizations, the mass media help to link government and the mass public, principally through the dissemination of political information. Far from being mere conduits of information, however, the media shape public perceptions of issues, candidates, and institutions. Ultimately, the media have a significant effect on American political culture by shaping the values, beliefs, and expectations of the citizenry.

10-1a The Print Media

During the Revolutionary Era, the press, consisting of small independent newspapers and pamphlets, played a vital role in facilitating political debate and in disseminating information. Indeed, the ratification of the Constitution was vigorously debated in not only the state ratifying conventions but also the press. The collection of essays known as *The Federalist Papers* first appeared as a series of newspaper articles analyzing and endorsing the new Constitution. Anti-Federalists also made wide use of newspapers in expressing their opposition to ratification.

Newspapers   The first newspapers in America were blatantly political. The *Gazette of the United States,* established in 1789, was decidedly Federalist in its political orientation. In contrast, the *National Gazette,* founded in 1791, was a Jeffersonian paper. These papers specialized in defending their partisans and criticizing (often unfairly) their political opponents. In adopting the First Amendment to the Constitution, which, among other things, guarantees freedom of the press, the Framers of the Bill of Rights were keenly aware that newspapers could not always be counted on to report stories fairly, accurately, and objectively. Yet they realized the vital importance of a free press to a free society and a republican form of government. In 1800, about two hundred small, independent newspapers were operating in the United States. By 1835, the number had grown to more than twelve hundred. In the 1830s, a new style of newspaper appeared: the penny paper. It was cheap, usually costing a mere penny. The penny papers were independent of political parties and were interested in much more than party politics. James Gordon Bennett's *New York Herald* was a good example of this new type of newspaper. The *Herald* was the precursor of the modern newspaper: It featured a society column, financial news, and a variety of local human interest stories in addition to political news.

Population growth, westward expansion, and the development of the telegraph and high-speed printing presses all contributed to a rapid proliferation of newspapers during the nineteenth century. By the 1890s, the number of newspapers in this country exceeded twelve thousand, a tenfold increase since the mid-1830s. As the newspaper industry grew, a new profession emerged: journalism. Like any profession, journalism took many years to develop a professional culture that dictated the norms governing how journalists should discover and report the news. By the twentieth century, a professional culture was emerging that stressed the need for accuracy, fairness, and impartiality. This professional culture was in part a response to a growing public concern over the press. In the late nineteenth and early twentieth centuries, yellow journalism, which emphasized the sensational with little concern for facts, became a popular style of newspaper reporting. This style of journalism, popularized by such newspapers as Joseph Pulitzer's *New York World,* appealed to the less educated but functionally literate segments of society: the working class and the masses of new immigrants.

---

mass media   The technologies and organizations that disseminate information to the public.

print media   That part of the media that includes newspapers, journals, tabloids, and magazines.

electronic media   That part of the media that includes radio, television, and computers.

Yellow Journalism   William Randolph Hearst's *New York Journal*, founded in 1885, was the epitome of **yellow journalism.** Hearst combined extreme sensationalism with political crusades, the most notorious of which was his effort to draw the United States into the Spanish–American War. In 1898, the *New York Journal* helped to whip up war fever by claiming, without solid evidence, that the Spanish had blown up the American battleship *Maine* in Cuba. Most historians now believe that the explosion on the *Maine* was accidental. But Hearst's claim, accompanied by an artist's rendering of the exploding ship, drove the nation into a war frenzy. Reportedly, Hearst sent the following message to artist Frederic Remington, who was on assignment in Cuba: "You furnish the pictures and I'll furnish the war."

The rising middle class, which was more educated and more reform-minded than the masses of workers and new immigrants, found Hearst's style of yellow journalism obnoxious. Eventually, yellow journalism gave way to the more objective, fact-conscious, and dispassionate style of reporting that now typifies the mainstream press. Since 1896, no other paper has represented this style better than the *New York Times*. Although some may find its calm, dispassionate, meticulous style boring, the *Times* is unsurpassed for the depth, breadth, and accuracy of its reportage. In terms of the extent of its coverage of American government and politics, the *Times* is rivaled only by the *Washington Post,* another of this country's most successful and most respected newspapers. Both are among the most widely read newspapers in this country (see Figure 10-1).

The Tabloids   Sensationalism, along with a less-than-fastidious concern for facts, remains the hallmark of the tabloid press. Publishers still find it profitable to appeal to people's appetites for the lurid, the morbid, and the outrageous. Many people buy the "supermarket tabloids," such as the *National Enquirer,* for entertainment; few take them at face value. Nevertheless, from time to time, celebrities who are the victims of false reports in the tabloids successfully sue for defamation of character. The possibility of being sued is evidently little deterrent to the tabloids, however. They can simply make too much money by publishing unflattering, and often untrue, stories about the rich, famous, and powerful. In the summer and fall of 1994, the tabloids feasted on the O. J. Simpson trial—easily the most

> ▶ **yellow journalism**
> Reporting that distorts or exaggerates facts to sensationalize the news.

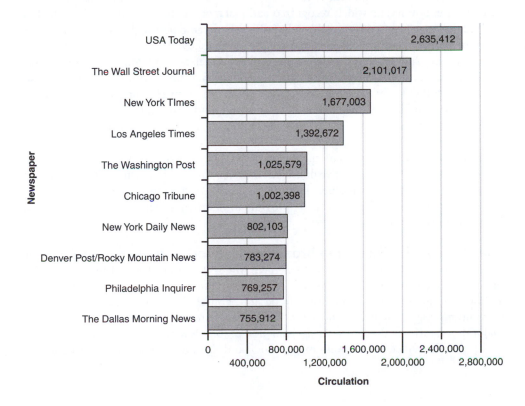

Figure 10-1
The Ten Largest Newspapers in the United States by Circulation, March 2004

Source: Audit Bureau of Circulations, on the Web at *http://www.accessabc.com.*

sensational criminal case in years. A decade later, Scott Peterson's double murder trial supplied similar fodder.

The Contemporary Mainstream Press   In sharp contrast to the tabloids, mainstream newspapers now depend on maintaining public trust. For the most part, journalists do a good job at that, at least by comparison with the yellow journalists of the nineteenth century. Even now, many people question the integrity of the press. Some critics question its impartiality, accusing the press of political bias of one kind or another. Conservatives have been especially vocal in accusing the mainstream press of liberal bias. Others, like Carl Bernstein, who along with fellow *Washington Post* reporter Bob Woodward broke the story of the Watergate cover-up, question the quality of the contemporary mainstream press. In Bernstein's view, "[t]he greatest felony in the news business today . . . is to be behind, or to miss, a major story, or more precisely, to seem behind, or to seem in danger of missing, a major story. So speed and quantity substitute for thoroughness and quality, for accuracy and context."[3] Bernstein suggests that the pressure to hurry the investigation and reporting of a story stems at least partially from the effect of the electronic media—television and radio—on the public's desire for instant information.

10-1b The Electronic Media

Radio was invented during the latter years of the nineteenth century. By the 1920s, commercial radio stations were being established in the United States. By 1930, this country had more than six hundred commercial radio stations, and nearly half of all households were equipped to receive their broadcasts. Television was invented during the 1920s—General Electric Co. and RCA began experimental television broadcasts in 1928—but did not become well established until the 1950s. In 1950, only 9 percent of households had television sets, but by 1960 the proportion had risen to 87 percent. Today, 98 percent of American households have television sets, and most households have more than one.

Talk Radio   Although radio is the oldest of the electronic media, it has been eclipsed by television in recent decades, especially for news. Many older Americans grew up listening to radio network news before the advent of the network television newscasts. Although the United States now has no widely recognized national radio newscast on this scale, radio has evolved into new forms, most notably **talk radio,** where radio personalities and their guests open the phone lines to callers who become part of the show.

> **talk radio**   Radio shows featuring discussion of public issues among a studio host, one or more invited guests in the studio, and the listening public.

   Talk radio stations exist in almost every major American city. Most of these stations feature local talk shows in addition to syndicated national shows with hosts such as Rush Limbaugh, Bill O'Reilly, Gordon Liddy, Michael Reagan, Sean Hannity, and Neal Boortz. These shows tend toward the conservative viewpoint and have quite loyal listeners. They have become an important source of news and commentary for people who are distrustful of the mainstream media. Although the medium is predominately conservative, in 2003 a group of unabashedly liberal commentators began planning a network—Air America—meant to counter this conservative domination. When this network, which went on the air in early 2004, did not draw listeners in numbers anywhere close to those of the more conservative programs, it did nonetheless provide an alternative vehicle to many listeners, especially in large markets.

The Three Major Television Broadcast Networks   By the 1940s, three major television-broadcasting networks had emerged: ABC, NBC, and CBS. As late as the 1970s, these big three networks dominated the coverage of national politics. News anchors such as Walter Cronkite and David Brinkley became household names and were accorded tremendous respect by most Americans. Their images are perpetually associated with the major news stories of the 1960s: the assassination of John F. Kennedy, the Vietnam War, the civil rights movement, the Apollo moon shots, and the 1968 Democratic convention in

Profiles & Perspectives

Rush Limbaugh (1950–)

AP Photo / Lennox McLendon

Much of the credit for the proliferation of talk radio must go to Rush Limbaugh. Every day, millions of Americans listen to three hours of comment, dialogue, and humor, all with a distinctive conservative flavor. Categorizing Limbaugh is hard. Does he provide entertainment or serious political analysis? Probably both. In any case, Limbaugh fills a unique niche in contemporary American politics.

Rush Limbaugh was born in Cape Girardeau, Missouri, in 1950. After many jobs in radio, from working as a disc jockey to working with a professional baseball organization, Limbaugh began his political commentary in Sacramento, California, in 1984. Limbaugh began his famous (or infamous, depending on your perspective) radio talk show in 1988. By late 1993, Limbaugh had twenty million listeners on more than six hundred stations, and his newsletter reached more than four hundred thousand subscribers. His book, *The Way Things Ought to Be,* became the fastest-selling hardback ever. He is also on the Internet at *http://www.rushlimbaugh.com*. During the 2000 presidential campaign, the site received millions of hits each day, making it one of the most popular political sites on the Web.

Limbaugh enunciates a clear conservative ideology, which includes a distrust of government, of course, and a particular dislike of liberals. He considers liberal programs to be ill conceived, but reserves his special scorn for what he regards as liberals' self-righteous, smug attitudes. Limbaugh feels that the press and academia are disproportionately filled with liberals, who have little use or respect for conservatives.

Following the election of Bill Clinton in 1992, Limbaugh began each radio and television show with the sarcastic phrase "America held hostage." Overtly partisan, Limbaugh is laudatory of Republicans and openly disdainful of Democrats. Limbaugh's favorite targets, aside from liberals in general, are environmentalists and feminists; he refers to them, respectively, as "environmentalist wackos" and "feminazis." According to Limbaugh, the national media are so biased that he is under no obligation to provide points of view other than his own. Many people disagree. However, he makes no bones about his intention of remaining the major conservative spokesperson in an increasingly complicated media age. About his personal style, which some find engaging and others find irritating, he says: "I combine irreverence and a sense of humor with serious discussion. Nowhere else does that happen.... If Ted Koppel opened with a comedy monologue, [you would think] 'Uh-oh, something's wrong here.' With me, people get both."

Source of quotation: "Limbaugh on Limbaugh," *U.S. News and World Report,* August 16, 1993, p. 35.

Chicago. Although the network news programs remain widely watched, they no longer dominate the media landscape.

During the 2004 presidential campaign, the role of the networks, in particular CBS, became the focus of much coverage and debate. In September, the network's popular and highly regarded *Sixty Minutes* aired a segment that relied on questionable documents to buttress the point that George W. Bush had received special treatment during his Vietnam-era National Guard service. Although the documents did not withstand minimal scrutiny, CBS continued to defend the broadcast for days before admitting that it could not vouch for the documents' authenticity. The event seriously undermined the credibility of both the network's main anchor, Dan Rather, as well as that of the network itself. It was a bitter pill for CBS to swallow. In the 1960s, with Walter Cronkite anchoring the evening news, CBS was the paragon of broadcast journalism.

Cable and Satellite TV   The 1960s saw the advent of cable television, which allowed consumers to receive many more channels. Cable TV was greatly spurred by the application of satellite communications in the 1970s and 1980s, making it possible for cable companies to receive and transmit to their subscribers a virtually unlimited number of channels. Of course, satellite technology makes it possible for consumers to bypass cable systems and receive satellite transmissions directly, as many people in rural areas now do with their small "dishes." With many more choices, television viewers are no longer confined to the big three networks for their political information (see Table 10-1).

TABLE 10-1	The Proliferation of the Electronic Media in the United States, 1930–2000			
Year	Number of Radio Stations	Percentage of Households with Radios	Number of TV Stations	Percentage of Households with TVs
1930	618	46	0	0
1940	850	82	0	0
1950	2,897	94	104	9
1960	4,389	95	626	87
1970	6,830	99	881	95
1980	9,235	99	1132	98
1990	10,671	99	1446	98
2000	12,717	99	1663	98

Source: Adapted from the Federal Communications Commission.

Twenty-Four-Hour Television News Networks   Cable television was originally designed to provide service to areas where traditional antennas did not provide adequate reception. The advent of satellite broadcasting, however, radically changed the nature of cable television. Still, the medium was mostly an extension of the entertainment function of television until 1981, when the Cable News Network (CNN) was launched. CNN altered the amount and the nature of politically oriented programming. For example, CNN was the only network to feature gavel-to-gavel coverage of the 1992 Democratic and Republican nominating conventions. CNN's *Crossfire* offered the cable-viewing public a steady diet of liberal-conservative dialogue on the issues and events of the day. Its nightly *Inside Politics* program highlighted breaking developments on the political scene. During the Gulf War, CNN provided almost constant coverage, including unprecedented reports from Baghdad as it was being attacked by the first air strike. Of course, it was not just the American public that had immediate access to these developments. World leaders, including Iraq's Saddam Hussein, tuned to CNN, using it as a source of worldwide information and communication. By 1992, approximately one in four adult Americans reported watching CNN at least "regularly."[4]

By the late 1990s, CNN had been joined by Fox News and MSNBC as the major purveyors of political information on cable and satellite TV. The main strength of the 24-hour news networks is their virtual nonstop coverage during major events and crises, such as the period following the attacks of September 11, 2001. In the days that followed, the major networks joined the cable outlets with nonstop coverage uninterrupted by commercials. Of course, millions of dollars were then in lost advertising revenue. In a week or so, the networks returned to regular programming, and the network news stations continued with almost continual coverage. All stations returned to their regular advertising patterns within two weeks of the incident.

Of course, only so much factual information can be relayed in a given period. This limitation has led to an increased emphasis on opinion-oriented programs modeled after CNN's *Crossfire*. Programs such as *Hardball* on MSNBC and *The O'Reilly Factor* on Fox News became popular in the late 1990s. These shows' ratings skyrocketed in the late 1990s as they focused on President Clinton's scandals and the impeachment saga. Millions tuned in nightly during the 2000 presidential election, especially during the thirty-five-day vote-counting controversy that followed. These shows created a new type of television personality, the "spinner," who appears on one show after another to give one side's perspective on the day's events and issues.

Popular Culture and American Politics

Jon Stewart and *The Daily Show*

By Chapman Rackaway

Can a comedian become the most trusted newsman in America? Maybe. Just ask Jon Stewart.

For millions of Americans—mostly college students and recent graduates—the only television talking head they trust is the forty-year-old Stewart, host of Comedy Central's *The Daily Show*. Even though the show's purpose is comedy, Stewart and his cast of reporters present a cynical and sometimes shockingly accurate picture of American politics today.

After *The Daily Show*'s first host, Craig Kilborn, left the desk to Stewart in 1999, the show truly began to take off. More politically minded than Kilborn, who treated the show like an interview program, Stewart quickly turned the show into the cynical, funny, but insightful look at politics that it is today.

Stewart began his career as a stand-up comedian, not a journalist. The New Jersey native worked the comedy circuit until landing a regular position on HBO's *The Larry Sanders Show* and a role in Adam Sandler's movie *Big Daddy*. Stewart's witty and critical style has found favor with the outlook of many young voters.

Stewart is fully aware of his position as an almost-anchor, but still concerned enough about democracy to point out the failings in other media. On October 24, 2004, Stewart went on CNN's *Crossfire,* a show about which he has often been critical for undermining the quality of American political discussion. When commentator Tucker Carlson turned the criticism on him, Stewart rebuffed, "You're on CNN. The show that leads into me is puppets making crank phone calls."

For better or for worse, *The Daily Show* is a program that Americans turn to for political information, an example of the new "infotainment" that shows up in television today. For a generation not convinced that politics relates to them, *The Daily Show* is perfect political commentary. A poll conducted in September 2004 even suggests that *Daily Show* viewers are very politically aware and knowledgeable. Poll respondents were asked six issue-related questions about the 2004 campaign, and *Daily Show* viewers averaged 3.59 correct responses, compared with 2.62 for people who watched no nightly comedy shows.

The Internet   Without question, the Internet is the most important development in mass media since the advent of television (see Figure 10-2). The Internet originated in 1969, when the Department of Defense sponsored a project to link mainframe computers at four universities. The proliferation of personal computers in the 1980s led to the creation in the 1990s of new hardware and software, allowing for all computers to be linked on a universal network. Since 1995, Internet connectivity and use have exploded. As of fall 2000, one firm estimated worldwide Internet use at more than 377 million people, with more than 161 million in the United States and Canada.

Virtually every government agency, media outlet, business, interest group, and political party has a presence on the Internet. What is unique about it is its interactive nature, which allows for information to be disseminated worldwide almost instantaneously. Obviously, the Internet is a tremendous political resource, especially as a tool of political mobilization. Ultimately, the Internet is a boon to democracy and a serious threat to authoritarian regimes. It also poses serious problems relative to national security. Because of its decentralized nature, the Internet is extremely difficult to regulate, much less control.

The Internet has led to the unprecedented availability of a variety of opinions. Every major (and most minor) newspaper's website makes available columnists previously available

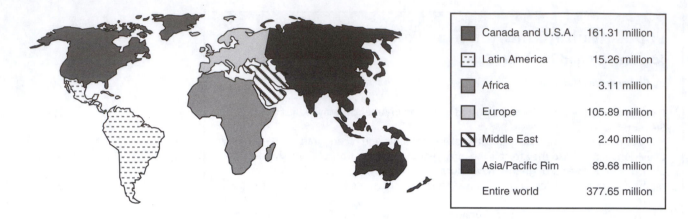

	Canada and U.S.A.	161.31 million
	Latin America	15.26 million
	Africa	3.11 million
	Europe	105.89 million
	Middle East	2.40 million
	Asia/Pacific Rim	89.68 million
	Entire world	377.65 million

Figure 10-2
Estimate of How Many People Use the Internet Worldwide

Source: Adapted from Nua Internet Surveys, September 2000.

> **bloggers** Slang term for people who operate "web logs," websites on which they and others comment on current issues and events of interest to them.

only to that newspaper's subscribers or those willing to make the trek to the library. Some influential outlets—such as *Salon, Slate,* and *Newsmax*—are available only on the Web. Likewise, influential media sources, such as Rush Limbaugh, regularly post written and audio files on their sites. Moreover, a number of sites, such as the Drudge Report, contain a wide number of links to newspapers and columns. The Internet has allowed many people who had to rely on one local newspaper for the column of the day to closely monitor thinking from any part of the political spectrum. This monitoring can even occur in real time rather than be delayed by a number of days.

The Bloggers By 2004, another Internet phenomenon further complicated and democratized the world of news delivery. Just about anyone could create a "web log," commonly known as a "blog," that allowed an individual to make use of readily available programs to easily create and maintain running commentaries about virtually any topic, including politics and world affairs. Thus, **bloggers** provided immediacy to raw, unfiltered news events along with their own running commentary. These blogs serve as yet another outlet for political news. This outlet just about completely eliminated any notion that the major networks could control the dissemination of news. Some bloggers, like Glenn Reynolds of *www.instapundit.com,* record hundreds of thousands of hits per day and have achieved virtual mainstream status. Reynolds, a law professor, libertarian, and one of the best-known architects of the "blogosphere," says that his principal interest is "the intersection between advanced technologies and individual liberty."[5] He likens the rise of the blogosphere to "the late 18th century environment of pamphleteers, numerous small ideological newspapers, and coffeehouse debates."[6]

10-1c The Ubiquitous Media

The American people are exposed to an amazing barrage of news, information, and entertainment through the mass media. Ninety-eight percent of American homes now have at least one television set, and 67 percent of these homes now subscribe to a cable TV service, giving them access to numerous channels. On average, Americans watch nearly eight hours of television a day.[7] Though watching television may adversely affect reading, most people still manage to at least peruse a newspaper every day.[8] Increasingly, Americans are relying on the Internet, both at home and at work, to stay current on political developments.

The Media Junkie Many Americans (including the authors of this book) have become media junkies. A *media junkie* turns on the television while she is making coffee at 6 a.m. While the coffee is brewing, the media junkie can peruse five or six channels to get updates on the weather, last night's sports scores, international political developments, local headlines, and the day's outlook for the stock market. Driving to work, the media junkie listens to NPR's *Morning Edition* or one of the many talk radio shows. At work, the media junkie is never far from the Internet, and probably has CNN's audio streaming

Glenn H. Reynolds of www.instapundit.com

through the computer. In meetings, the media junkie is checking her personal digital assistant, handy for breaking news, stock quotes, and email. On the way home from work, the media junkie again tunes into NPR's *All Things Considered* or some similar radio fare. Arriving at the house and sorting through the day's "snail mail," the media junkie simultaneously boots up the home computer and turns on the adjacent TV. Throughout the evening, the media junkie periodically surfs the Net, checks email, and "channel surfs" on cable TV. The number of media junkies is not really known, but it is at least sufficient to support a number of cable outlets, websites, and technologies that cater to them. The media junkie is addicted to electronic media, which tends to make her much better informed but much less well rested.

Immediacy of Information   The emergence of satellite and computer technology has given the mass media the capability to report, and often show visually, breaking news around the world with a minimum of lag time. An obvious example was the real-time broadcast of the terrorist attack on the World Trade Center in September 2001. People around the world were able to watch the second hijacked airliner crash into the tower. Millions of viewers watched in horror as the twin towers burned and occupants of the higher stories who were unable to escape the fire jumped to their deaths. Millions saw the towers collapse as people below ran for their lives. Never has a more horrifying event been captured live by the mass media. There's no doubt that the psychological and political impact of the terrorist attack was amplified by the immediacy of the television coverage. It is one thing to read about this type of event in a newspaper; it is quite another to watch it live on television.

Another dramatic example of this phenomenon took place in January 1991, when the cable TV news network CNN carried live, on-the-scene reports of American air strikes on Baghdad, Iraq. Three CNN reporters, armed with a television camera and a satellite uplink, broadcast pictures and descriptions of the air raid as it was taking place. Millions of people around the world, including President George Bush and the command structure in the Pentagon, were glued to the television screen that evening as CNN showed them the initiation of a war in real time. The George W. Bush administration decided to sharply reduce the media's access to the battlefield during the war in Afghanistan that began in late 2001, leading to some media criticism.

During the coverage of the 2000 presidential election, the cable news outlets—such as MSNBC, CNN, and Fox News—ran almost continuous coverage of all court proceedings and news conferences in addition to almost constant coverage of vote counting in a variety of places previously unfamiliar to most Americans. Viewers stayed glued to the drama by the tens of millions, chatting about now familiar election officials in Palm Beach and Broward counties and their vote-counting methods. Following a daily dose of this type of coverage, talking heads debated and analyzed the meaning of the day's events. All was available to Americans in real time.

The pervasiveness and immediacy of the electronic media have produced a much greater degree of global awareness among the American people. The revolution in electronic communications has produced more than an "information society," however. It has more or less led to the realization of the global village posited by the mass media guru Marshall McLuhan in the 1960s.[9] A rancher in remote Montana can now receive CNN through a satellite dish and watch live as American planes conduct air raids in Kosovo. People can view the same pictures simultaneously on the ground in Kosovo, even inside the compound under attack!

10-2 Mass Media in American Democracy

Mass media provide important sources of information about politics and government to the attentive public. Citizens interested in participating in the political process have access to an enormous quantity of information to inform their participation. Potential voters can see and hear candidates discuss issues and pundits discuss the candidates and their strategies. Citizens can observe the actions of their leaders and the workings of their government on a constant basis. To attentive citizens, the mass media provide a gold mine of information, although even the most sophisticated observers can sometimes feel overwhelmed by the sheer volume of information flowing through the media. In addition to their basic role of informing people, the mass media also perform a watchdog function, helping to keep politicians and other elites honest by exposing corruption, waste, deceit, and ineptitude. Hardly a day goes by that does not see some new revelation about an ill-conceived public policy, a poorly administered government program, or a scandal involving public officials.

10-2a Mass Media and Political Culture

The informational and watchdog functions performed by the mass media are essential in a democracy operating in a mass society. Of course, the mass media do more than inform and expose. They also provide entertainment. Music, movies, television series, and other types of entertainment programming do more than entertain, however. They serve as vehicles for the transmission of popular culture; that is, media reflect and help to shape the basic values, tastes, attitudes, desires, and expectations of the mass public. They even have an impact on political culture. One can argue that Americans' views of their leaders, and of their political institutions, have been and are being shaped by the mass media. When Vice President Dan Quayle launched his attack on the television series *Murphy Brown* and on

---

Popular Culture and American Politics
The Onion

By Chapman Rackaway

What kinds of headlines are these?

"American People Deemed Unfit to Govern"
"Republicans Seek to Privatize Next Election"

Internet readers know them instantly as content from *The Onion,* a print and online humor magazine that takes a decidedly cynical (and funny) look at politics. *The Onion* calls itself "America's Finest News Source," in a tongue-in-cheek way, but plenty of people do read it for its political commentary. *The Onion* is a satire of news, the way it is reported, and politics.

Founded in 1988 by University of Wisconsin students Tim Keck and Chris Johnson on an $8,000 loan from Keck's mother, *The Onion* has grown into a well-known and profitable venture. Originally a print alternative magazine for Wisconsin students, *The Onion* quickly gained a reputation and suddenly was sold on campuses all over the Midwest. In 1994, the original owners sold it to staffers at the paper, and when the new owners placed *The Onion* online in 1996, the secret was out all over the country. *The Onion* became a hit.

The Onion always manages to include some kind of political commentary in its weekly editions. One of the first notable stories in 1998 was "Clinton Deploys Vowels to Bosnia: Cities of Sjlbvdnzv, Grzny to Be First Recipients." The 2004 Presidential campaign also gave the writers plenty to work with, producing headlines such as "Kerry Makes Whistle-Stop Tour from Deck of Yacht," "Poll: Many Americans Still Unsure Whom to Vote Against," "Bush Vows to Pay Closer Attention to Needs of Non-Presidents," and "Citizens Form Massive Special Disinterest Group."

Even though the news is fictitious, *The Onion's* cynical look at politics expresses what many people think. Many Americans, for example, think television ads for candidates have become too negative and out of control. *The Onion* therefore took its reporting one step beyond with the story, "New Negative Ads Target Voters Directly." In the story, candidates and parties stop attacking each other, preferring instead to attack the voters, insulting them for their lack of attention to politics.

Although *The Onion* does not provide traditional news, it manages to show public attitudes toward politics in a funny and insightful way.

the "cultural elite" during the 1992 presidential campaign, he was acknowledging the power of the mass media to shape American culture.

10-2b Ownership and Control of the Mass Media

In this country, the mass media are almost entirely owned and operated by the private sector. The U.S. government has many official publications, but it does not own and operate an official newspaper. The government does contribute money to a public television network, the Public Broadcasting System (PBS), and to a public radio network, National Public Radio (NPR). But these entities are not under the direct control of government officials and cannot fairly be characterized as instruments of government propaganda.

Chain Ownership   Private ownership of the media has generally been regarded as important because private ownership means competition, in both the collection and dissemination of information and the points of view expressed. Although the mass media are almost entirely in private hands, the past several decades have seen a strong trend toward the **chain ownership** of newspapers, magazines, and radio and television stations. For example, the *New York Times,* one of the nation's largest newspapers, now owns the *Boston Globe* in addition to some forty small-town newspapers in thirteen states. Moreover, the past few decades have also seen the emergence of large companies that operate or control multiple media outlets. In fact, the New York Times Company is one of these, owning a number of magazines and television and radio stations in addition to its family of newspapers. The Gannett Company, which owns more than eighty daily newspapers, also owns sixteen radio stations and ten television stations. Similarly, the Times Mirror Company controls more than twenty newspapers and magazines, and fifty cable TV systems or television stations. Some critics of the mass media charge that this concentration of ownership reduces the diversity of information and opinions available to the mass public.

> **chain ownership**   Growing trend in the United States whereby different elements of the mass media are owned and operated by one parent company.

In addition to the issue of ownership and control is the question of the source of news and information available to newspapers and television and radio stations. Although most media outlets rely on reporters for information about local news, these outlets depend heavily on wire services and networks for national and international news. Of the roughly fourteen hundred television stations operating in this country, more than six hundred are affiliated with one of four major national networks: ABC, CBS, NBC, or Fox. Nearly every local newspaper relies on a major wire service, such as the Associated Press or United Press International, for national and international news, as do many television and radio stations. Despite the emergence of multimedia corporate giants, the demise of many small, independent newspapers, and the reliance on networks and wire services, the American media continue to have considerable diversity, in both the terms of information being reported and the commentary being offered.

10-2c Are the Mass Media Biased?

Conservatives and Republicans have long complained that the mainstream media, especially the three major television networks, are biased in favor of liberal policies and Democratic candidates. In the early 1970s, the Nixon administration went on the offensive against the "liberal media." In a highly publicized speech, Vice President Spiro Agnew attacked the press for what the administration perceived as unfair negativism toward its policies. In the 1980s, the Republican presidents Reagan and Bush continued to criticize the media, although in less strident terms than Agnew had used.

Were Republican and conservative suspicions of the media well founded, or were they merely expressions of political paranoia or hypersensitivity? One approach to investigating media bias has been to look at the political affiliations and ideological orientations of reporters and editors. For example, a survey conducted by the *Los Angeles Times* in 1984 found that only 26 percent of reporters and editors nationwide supported President Reagan's reelection. Of course, Reagan was reelected in a landslide, receiving 59 percent of the popular vote. The same survey found that only 17 percent of reporters and editors considered themselves to be conservative, whereas 55 percent identified themselves as liberal, which was nearly the reverse of the ideological orientation of the general population.[10]

As citizens, people who work in the media are entitled to their own preferences and affiliations. Most people believe that a strong sense of journalistic professionalism can mitigate the influence of a reporter's biases. The important question is not whether members of the media are biased, but whether their coverage of political issues and events is biased. A survey conducted in October 2004 by the Pew Research Center found that most voters believe that members of the news media let their biases influence their reporting.[11] Of course, the fact that most Americans believe this to be true does not make it so.

To answer the question of whether the perceived liberal bias of the media is real, Michael J. Robinson analyzed some six thousand news stories about the 1980 election, taken from both the print and electronic media. Robinson found no systematic liberal bias in either the selection or tone of the stories.[12] In a follow-up study of the 1984 election, Robinson did find some evidence of liberal or pro-Democratic bias in the media's coverage of the presidential campaigns, but concluded that the coverage had no appreciable effect on the voters.[13]

In November 1992, Mead Data Central and PR Data Systems examined news articles published by a sample of major newspapers during the period from September 1 through October 31. The researchers found that Bill Clinton received favorable coverage in approximately 45 percent of the articles dealing with his candidacy, and President Bush received favorable coverage in only 24 percent of the articles about his campaign. The researchers also found that President Bush was much more likely to receive negative treatment than either Bill Clinton or Ross Perot.[14]

During the 2000 election season, and especially during the post-election litigation, conservatives and Republicans chastised the mainstream media for their alleged favoritism toward the Democrat Al Gore. In December 2001, the former CBS reporter Bernard Goldberg released a controversial book that highlighted bias in the reporting of CBS news during his career, further adding to a general perception that the major networks had a liberal slant in their values and presentation of the news.[15]

In 2004, conservatives and Republicans continued to press the charge of liberal media bias. In particular, these critics focused their attacks on the *New York Times* and the three major television networks, all of which were accused of orchestrating their coverage of the war in Iraq and other events in order to damage President George W. Bush's chances for reelection. The scandal that erupted over CBS News' reliance on questionable documents in a *60 Minutes* story about President Bush's service in the National Guard helped to lend credence to charges of bias, at least as they were made against CBS.

In general, the American people have come to believe that there is a liberal bias in the mass media. As of 2004, according to a survey by the Gallup Organization, nearly half the adult population believed that the media were too liberal, while only 15 percent said they were too conservative (see What Americans Think About Media Bias).

It is important to recognize that not all criticisms of media bias come from the ideological right. Michael Parenti argues that right-wing attacks on the press "help the media maintain an appearance of neutrality and objectivity." In Parenti's view, the media are "complicit with the dominant powers" of society, which he defines as "big business and the executive power of government."[16] According to Parenti, the function of the media "is not to produce an alert, critical and informed citizenry but the kind of people who will accept an opinion universe dominated by corporate and governmental elites, almost all of whom share the same ideological perspective about political and economic reality."[17] Like other critics on the far left, Parenti faults the media for helping to maintain the dominance of the capitalist system. In the national conversation over media bias, Parenti's claims are like voices in the wilderness.

Assuming it exists, the liberal bias in the media is being attenuated by the proliferation of media outlets. After all, most local newspaper editors tend to the conservative side of the spectrum. And the proliferation of cable TV has led to an increasing diversity of views on

What Americans Think About

Media Bias

For the past several years, the Gallup Organization has been polling Americans on the issue of media bias. The results show that Americans are much more likely to believe that the media have a liberal bias than they are to believe they have a conservative bias.

Here is the question they posed: In general, do you think the news media is—too liberal, just about right, or too conservative?

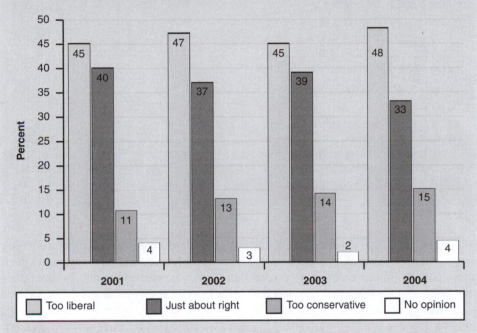

Legend: Too liberal | Just about right | Too conservative | No opinion

2001: 45, 40, 11, 4
2002: 47, 37, 13, 3
2003: 45, 39, 14, 2
2004: 48, 33, 15, 4

Source: Results based on national telephone surveys of adults by the Gallup Organization, conducted September 7–10, 2001; September 5–8, 2002; September 8–10, 2003; and September 13–15, 2004.

television. Conservative commentators, such as Sean Hannity, George Will, Fred Barnes, Robert Novak, Pat Buchanan, and John McLaughlin, are prominently featured on TV talk shows. The rise of talk radio has also contributed to the dissemination of conservative views through the electronic media. The talk-show host Rush Limbaugh, who is decidedly conservative in his orientation, is now (with the possible exceptions of Howard Stern and Don Imus) the best-known radio personality. In addition, an estimated 10 percent of all radio stations and 14 percent of all television stations are controlled by conservative Christian groups, somewhat offsetting the generally liberal character of the secular media. Finally, one cannot overstate the importance of the Internet as a medium for the dissemination of an amazing spectrum of viewpoints.

Politically Selective Consumption of Media With the proliferation of mass media, it is not difficult for a strongly opinionated consumer of mass media to select only those media outlets that conform to his political predilections. One whose orientation is strongly conservative is more apt to watch Fox News, whereas a more liberal individual is likely to be more comfortable with CNN. A survey conducted in October 2004 by the Pew Research Center found that 70 percent of regular Fox News viewers who planned to vote in the presidential election expected to vote for President Bush. On the other hand, 67 percent of regular CNN viewers preferred Senator Kerry. However, the entire sample of regular consumers of media was evenly divided between Kerry and Bush.[18]

WEB EXERCISE

Take a look at some of the following news sites on the Web. Compare the coverage of the same story among all the sources. What differences do you notice between them? How does the use of language differ from site to site in reporting on the same story? Do you notice any biases? Do you notice any differences in the levels and groups of readers each site is targeting? How do television news sites differ from print media in their coverage? Try looking up the newspapers or television news shows from smaller cities, perhaps in your hometown. How do smaller papers cover material? Do you detect a regional bias?

National print media

New York Times: http://www.nytimes.com
Washington Post: http://www.washingtonpost.com
USA Today: http://www.usatoday.com
Wall Street Journal: http://www.wsj.com

National television media

ABC News: http://www.abcnews.com
NBC News: http://www.nbcnews.com
CBS News: http://www.cbsnews.com
FOX News: http://www.foxnews.com/
CNN: http://www.cnn.com
MSNBC: http://www.msnbc.msn.com/

A libertarian can set aside time every day to listen to Neal Boortz on the radio. Even extremists of various kinds can find sources of news and commentary that appeal to them, although not through mainstream media. Rather, they go to the Internet. Without question, consumers of mass media, no less than buyers of groceries, benefit from choices in the marketplace. Truly informed citizens, however, draw their information from multiple sources. There appears to be a growing tendency for politically attentive and active citizens to "lock on" to those media outlets that reinforce their point of view. This may be one of the reasons for the greater polarization of politics in recent years, as well as the more overtly partisan commentary in the media. One wonders about the long-term effect on our political culture and, ultimately, the governability of the country.

10-3 Freedom of the Press: A Basic National Commitment

In no other country is the press as free from government censorship and control as it is in the United States. The idea of a free press, deeply rooted in Anglo-American legal and political culture, is expressed in the First Amendment to the U.S. Constitution, which explicitly prohibits government from abridging the freedom of the press. See Box 10-1 for a discussion and poll concerning the issue of censorship.

10-3a The Prohibition against Prior Restraint

> **prior restraint** An official act preventing the publication of a particular work.

> **injunction** A judicial order requiring a person to do, or refrain from doing, a designated thing.

English common law contributed an important concept to the development of freedom of the press in the United States: the prohibition against prior restraint. **Prior restraint** refers to censorship before the fact—preventing the press from publishing something the government doesn't like. In a landmark 1931 decision, the Supreme Court struck down a Minnesota law that permitted public officials to seek an **injunction** to stop publication of any "malicious, scandalous or defamatory" newspaper or magazine.[19] Officials in Minneapolis had used the law to suppress the publication of a small newspaper, the *Saturday Press,* which had strong anti-Semitic overtones and maligned local politicians. The law provided that after a newspaper was subjected to an injunction, further publication was punishable as contempt of court. The Supreme Court saw this mode of suppression as "the essence of

| Box 10-1 | Read a Censored Book Lately? | |

Do you recognize any of these books: *Lady Chatterley's Lover,* by D. H. Lawrence; *Catcher in the Rye,* by J. D. Salinger; *Harry Potter* titles, by J. K. Rowling; *Of Mice and Men,* by John Steinbeck; *The Handmaid's Tale,* by Margaret Atwood; *Lord of the Flies,* by William Golding; or *Song of Solomon,* by Toni Morrison? How about books by these authors—Judy Blume, Mark Twain, Alice Walker, Madeleine L'Engle, Roald Dahl, Stephen King, or Harper Lee? All have been challenged or banned by groups opposed to their content. Challenges have also been made to Internet sites and other forms of media.

Do you think that we should have stricter laws to control

Nudity or sexual content on television?	Yes	No
Violence on television?	Yes	No
The portrayal of substance abuse on television?	Yes	No
Pornography on the Internet?	Yes	No
Print pornography?	Yes	No
Information on the Internet about making weapons?	Yes	No
Print media on making weapons?	Yes	No
Information on the Internet about making drugs?	Yes	No
Print media on making drugs?	Yes	No

Do you think that the press should self-censor in cases of

Information relating to national security issues?	Yes	No
Information about individuals' private lives?	Yes	No
Information on specific details of unsolved crimes?	Yes	No

You can to to the online version of this text to see how your results compare to the rest of your classmates.

censorship" and declared the law unconstitutional. Though commenting with general approval on the rule against prior restraint, Chief Justice Charles Evans Hughes acknowledged that this restriction is not absolute. It would not, for example, prevent government in time of war from prohibiting publication of "the sailing dates of transports or the number and location of troops." In these and related situations, national security interests are almost certain to prevail over freedom of the press. But where is the line to be drawn? How far can the national security justification be extended in suppressing publication?

The Supreme Court revisited the question of prior restraint on the press in the sensational Pentagon Papers Case of 1971.[20] The Nixon administration attempted to prevent the *New York Times* and the *Washington Post* from publishing excerpts from a classified study about decision making on the Vietnam War. The newspapers had obtained the Pentagon Papers from Daniel Ellsberg, a defense analyst who worked in the Pentagon. In attempting to block the newspapers from publishing these classified documents, the federal government argued that considerations of national security outweighed the First Amendment interests of the press. The Supreme Court disagreed, however. By a 6–3 vote, the Court held that the effort to block publication of the Pentagon Papers amounted to an unconstitutional prior restraint on the press. Apparently, the Court was not convinced that publication—several years after the events and decisions discussed in the papers—constituted a significant threat to national security.

Does the First Amendment Protect Your Right to Publish Information on Making an H-Bomb?

The prior restraint issue arose again in 1979 when the federal government obtained a preliminary injunction against the magazine *The Progressive* in order to block publication of an article purporting to describe how to make a hydrogen bomb. In the meantime, however, another magazine published a similar article, with no apparent damage to national security. As a result, the case against *The Progressive* was dismissed and the injunction lifted.[21] The H-bomb article was ultimately published in November 1979. In light of the Pentagon Papers and *Progressive* cases, it is clear that although national security may theoretically justify a prior restraint, the national security interests at stake must be immediate and grave.

10-3b Libel Suits

> **libel** Defamation of character through published material.

Libel consists of injuring someone's reputation by reporting falsehoods about that person. Libel is not a crime, but rather a **tort,** the remedy for which is a civil suit for monetary damages. Libelous publications have traditionally been outside the scope of First Amendment protection. In a landmark 1964 decision, however, the Supreme Court articulated a new rule that afforded far greater protection to published criticism of official conduct.[22] This rule prevents a public official from winning a libel suit unless she can prove that the false statement was made with actual malice or **reckless disregard of the truth** (see Case in Point 10-1). As long as there is an absence of malice on the part of the press, public officials are barred from recovering damages for the publication of false statements about them. The Supreme Court justified the new rule as an expression of "a profound national commitment to the principle that debate on public issues should be uninhibited, robust, and wide-open."

> **tort** A civil wrong remediable through a lawsuit seeking monetary damages.

> **reckless disregard of the truth** Careless indifference to whether a story is true or false.

10-3c The "People's Right to Know"

In a democracy, does the public always have a right to know what its government is doing? Some would argue that our government violates democratic principles to the extent that it maintains secret information or conducts covert activities. According to this view, the proper role of the press is to oppose any government efforts at secrecy. The press thus "represents" the public by scrutinizing and publicizing the actions of government; accordingly, the people are better informed and are better able to evaluate their leaders. An active, adversarial press is therefore vital to democracy. Of course, not everyone shares this view.

Although press freedom is often advocated in terms of democratic principles and "the people's right to know," evidence exists that the American people do not always support the claims of the press against their government. For example, when reporters were excluded from the Grenada invasion of December 1983, an uproar of righteous indignation occurred in the media. However, an ABC News poll taken shortly after the invasion revealed that 67 percent of the public supported censorship of the news media when national security was at stake.

> **confidential source** A source of information whose identity is known only to the reporter.

10-3d Confidential Sources

The reporter's greatest asset (aside from the First Amendment) is the **confidential source.** The media therefore argue strenuously that the First Amendment gives reporters an

---

Case in Point **10-1**

A Landmark Decision Limiting Libel Suits by Public Officials

New York Times v. Sullivan (1964)

The landmark Supreme Court decision *New York Times v. Sullivan* came out of the civil rights struggle of the 1960s. L. B. Sullivan, a city commissioner in Montgomery, Alabama, brought suit against the *New York Times* for its publication of a paid advertisement highly critical of Montgomery officials for police responses to civil rights demonstrations. The Supreme Court disallowed the libel suit. As stated by Justice William

Brennan, who wrote the majority opinion, the First Amendment "prohibits a public official from recovering damages for a defamatory falsehood relating to his official conduct unless he proves that the statement was made with 'actual malice'—that is, with knowledge that it was false or with reckless disregard of whether it was false or not."

absolute privilege to maintain the confidentiality of their sources, a privilege similar to that claimed by lawyers with respect to their clients. On the other hand, prosecutors tend to argue that the public interest in finding the truth in a criminal prosecution outweighs a reporter's interest in maintaining the confidentiality of sources. Although some states have **shield laws** protecting journalists in these types of situations, others permit reporters to be held in contempt of court and confined for refusing to divulge their sources.

    In *Branzburg v. Hayes* (1972), the Supreme Court confronted a situation in which a newspaper reporter called to appear before a grand jury refused to identify certain persons he had seen using and selling illicit drugs.[23] The reporter had observed the illegal activities during an undercover investigation of the local drug scene. Citing the First Amendment, he refused to disclose his confidential sources to the grand jury. The Supreme Court sided with the grand jury, saying that "we cannot seriously entertain the notion that the First Amendment protects a newsman's agreement to conceal the criminal conduct of his source, or evidence thereof, on the theory that it is better to write about crime than to do something about it."

    Another problem relating to sources of information occurs when a reporter decides to reveal the identity of a source who has given information on the condition that his identity remain confidential. The Supreme Court addressed this problem in a case it decided in 1992. The controversy began when a political campaign worker provided a reporter with damaging information about a rival candidate on the condition that the worker's identity be kept secret. The newspaper made an editorial decision to publish the name of the source, who was fired by his employer as a result. The source sued the newspaper under a state law and won $200,000 in compensatory damages. The Supreme Court rejected the newspaper's argument that these types of suits were barred by the First Amendment, saying that "[t]he publisher of a newspaper has no special immunity from the application of general laws. He has no special privilege to invade the rights and liberties of others."[24]

> **shield laws** Laws that protect journalists from legal action when they refuse to divulge their sources.

10-3e The Special Case of Broadcast Media

The Framers of the First Amendment could not have foreseen the invention of radio and television, let alone the prevalence of these electronic media in contemporary society. Nevertheless, because television and radio are used to express ideas in the public forum, most observers would agree that the electronic media deserve First Amendment protection, at least to some extent. Yet since their inception, radio and television have been regulated extensively by the federal government. To operate a television or radio station, a person must obtain a license from the Federal Communications Commission (FCC); broadcasting without a license from the FCC is a federal crime (as operators of pirate radio stations have often discovered). In granting licenses, the FCC is authorized to regulate the station's frequency, wattage, and hours of transmission. To a lesser extent, the FCC also has the power to regulate the content of broadcasts. Station licenses come up for renewal every three years, and the FCC is invested with tremendous discretion to determine whether a given station has been operating "in the public interest."

The Fairness Doctrine   Since its creation by Congress, the FCC has required broadcasters to devote a reasonable proportion of their airtime to the discussion of important public issues. Until 1987, the FCC interpreted this statutory mandate to require broadcasters who aired editorials criticizing specific persons to provide notice to those persons and air time for rebuttal. The Supreme Court upheld this **fairness doctrine** in 1969.[25] The Court held that the FCC regulation had struck a reasonable balance between the public interest in hearing various points of view and the broadcaster's interests in free expression. Nevertheless, the fairness doctrine remained extremely controversial. It was finally repealed by the FCC in the summer of 1987. In the 1990s, a movement to revive the fairness doctrine appeared in Congress. Congress could, of course, pass legislation that would require the FCC to resurrect the fairness doctrine. But that has yet to happen.

> **fairness doctrine** A requirement by the Federal Communications Commission that allowed for equal opportunities for expression on controversial issues or policies.

Editorializing by Public Television and Radio Stations Electronic media in the public sector have been subject to more restrictive government regulations on editorializing. Based on a 1967 act of Congress, the FCC prohibited public radio and television stations from engaging in editorializing. However, the Supreme Court declared this ban unconstitutional.[26] Writing for a sharply divided Court, Justice William Brennan concluded that the "ban on all editorializing . . . far exceeds what is necessary to protect against the risk of governmental interference or to prevent the public from assuming that editorials by public broadcasting stations represent the official view of government." Nevertheless, most public television and radio stations minimize explicit editorializing, although conservative critics argue that the Public Broadcasting System and National Public Radio tend to offer programming that contains a liberal point of view.

Restrictions on the Content of Programming For many years, educators, psychologists, and children's advocacy groups have expressed concern about the amount of television that children watch and the kinds of messages they get through TV programs. Some are concerned about the portrayal of sexual conduct, which has become considerably more explicit and provocative over the years. Others object to the extreme commercialism of American television and believe that it fosters excessive materialism in children. In 1993, numerous critics, including the attorney general of the United States, Janet Reno, lashed out at the prevalence of violence on television. Coincidentally, in that same year, the public became alarmed about a rising tide of violence among young people. The year was punctuated with horror stories about toddlers being murdered by teenagers, teenagers bringing loaded guns to school, and, of course, unrelenting gang warfare in the nation's inner cities. Many people saw a connection between the constant barrage of TV violence and the increasingly violent behavior of the country's youth. Some called for restrictions on TV violence. Testifying before Congress, Attorney General Reno suggested that unless television producers and broadcasters voluntarily addressed this problem, the federal government might have to step in. According to a national survey reported in December 1993, about 60 percent of adults said they were offended by the amount of sex and violence on television; 55 percent responded in the affirmative when asked "Should the federal government regulate the amount of violence and sex on television?"[27]

In February 2004, the issue of indecency on the public airwaves reached a national crescendo after singer Janet Jackson experienced a "wardrobe malfunction" revealing one of her breasts during a halftime performance at the Super Bowl. The FCC received numerous complaints and levied a $550,000 fine against CBS for the incident. Two months later, the FCC imposed a fine of nearly $500,000 on Clear Channel Communications for airing sexually explicit content in a program by controversial "shock jock" Howard Stern. For his part, Stern relied on the First Amendment and claimed that the Bush administration was making him a political target. In late 2004, Stern announced plans to move his program to Sirius satellite radio, which is not under FCC jurisdiction. The Janet Jackson and Howard Stern incidents intensified a national conversation about indecency in mass media and popular culture.

To what extent may government regulate the content of television or radio programs without running afoul of the First Amendment? The courts have suggested that government regulation of the broadcasting industry is not necessarily equivalent to restrictions on the print medium. In a broad regulation that would almost certainly be declared unconstitutional if applied to a magazine or newspaper, the FCC has prohibited radio and television stations, whether public or private, from broadcasting "indecent" or "obscene" programs. In a highly publicized 1978 case, the Supreme Court reviewed this regulation as applied to a radio broadcast of a monologue by comedian George Carlin that discussed "seven dirty words you can't say on television." Attorneys for the radio station argued that the monologue in question did not meet the legal test of obscenity and therefore could not be banned from the radio by the FCC. The Supreme Court disagreed, observing that, "when the Commission finds that a pig has entered the parlor, the exercise of its regulatory power does not depend on proof that the pig is obscene."[28]

FCC regulations apply to broadcasters. Cable channels (as distinguished from broadcasts) are not subject to FCC content regulations. Whatever may not be shown on CBS or one of the other broadcast networks, therefore, may be shown on HBO, The Movie Channel, or other channels available exclusively to cable subscribers. Increasingly, there are calls for greater government regulation of pay-TV channels, with regard to both sexual content and violence. The widespread diffusion of new communications technology has thus generated new constitutional questions. However, American political culture has evolved (some might say degenerated) to the point that widespread tolerance now exists for this type of material in the mass media.

10-3f Constitutional Protection of the Internet

As we have already noted, the Internet is by its nature difficult to regulate and impossible for any single government to control. Nevertheless, some people believe that government should attempt to limit certain types of expression on the Net—for example, hard-core pornography and hate speech. Pornography is widespread on the Net, and numerous fringe groups have websites spouting hateful messages aimed at various groups in society. The constitutional question is whether the First Amendment protects this type of expression on the Net. The U.S. Supreme Court weighed in on this question in 1997. The preceding year, Congress passed the Communications Decency Act, which made it a crime to display "indecent" material on the Internet in a manner that might make it available to minors. In *Reno v. American Civil Liberties Union* (1997), the Court declared this statute unconstitutional on First Amendment grounds. Writing for the Court, Justice Stevens concluded that, with respect to cyberspace, "the interest in encouraging freedom of expression in a democratic society outweighs any theoretical but unproven benefit of censorship."[29] The decision was widely hailed by Internet users, and Congress has yet to make another attempt to regulate content on the Net.

10-4 Press Coverage of Government

The relationship between the press and government is often marked by confusion and hostility. Much of it can be attributed to the role of the press in a free society. Despite the wishes of those in government that newspapers and television report positive stories, the press has a basic duty to report the activities of government and politicians that are dishonest, inefficient, or corrupt. Members of the press see their role as "keeping the government honest" and providing citizens with enough information to enable them to make informed decisions when voting.

The press is also motivated by norms peculiar to its own culture. Journalists advance, and receive the admiration of their peers, by writing stories that have an impact, and the political stories with the most impact are those that expose government officials doing wrong. For example, the *Washington Post* reporters Bob Woodward and Carl Bernstein were catapulted to the top of their profession by exposing much of the Watergate scandal that eventually toppled the Nixon administration. Although positive, or at least noncritical, stories may be well received, the vast majority of career-building, breakthrough stories involve the exposure of some wrongdoing on the part of someone important.

Part of the conflict between politics and the press stems from the competitive nature of both institutions. Journalists compete to uncover stories about politicians, and politicians compete for the attention of journalists. Politicians feel that they "win" if they can obtain coverage that places them in a good light. Journalists win if they can claim credit for a good news story. Most good stories, however, do not reflect well on those seeking or holding office. Thus, tension is inevitable. Political officials and journalists need each other, but also try to use each other.

10-4a Coverage of the President

In May 2002, the broadcast and print news media were awash with stories raising questions about what warning President Bush might have had about the September 11 attacks on the World Trade Center and the Pentagon. No person in the world is the subject of as much media scrutiny as the president of the United States. This scrutiny has often angered presidents, some of whom have lashed out, or had others lash out on their behalf, at what they perceive as unfair or biased reporting. Probably the best known attack on the press came from Richard Nixon's vice president, Spiro T. Agnew. In 1969, after what the administration thought was excessively negative commentary following a televised presidential address, Agnew accused the press of being a small, liberal elite.

The relationship between the president and the press seems to progress through three phases. Many presidents experience what is called the honeymoon period at the beginning of their initial term. The honeymoon phase is characterized by cordial relationships, with the president accorded the benefit of the doubt and the press granted reasonable access to the functioning of government. Cabinet officials and others make themselves available for interviews, and television and newspaper reporters are likely to produce stories that highlight new people and programs.

Inevitably, this relationship evolves into another, more hostile, phase. Usually, it occurs after the new government proposes something controversial or makes a decision that is widely unpopular with some major group or interest. After the media focus on the controversy and pose questions that seem to legitimize the criticism, the administration often feels betrayed and unfairly portrayed. Either this hostility evolves further into a state of permanent hostility or both sides become conscious of the need for moderation.[30]

Perhaps no honeymoon was as brief as that enjoyed by President Bill Clinton in 1993. Clinton came into office well regarded by the press. In fact, he had been quite popular among the reporters who had covered his campaign, and he seemed at ease with the media during the period between his election and his inauguration. In fact, Republican critics continually cited the favorable treatment they felt Clinton was accorded as a candidate and as president-elect. In the first months of his administration, however, Clinton found himself under tremendous scrutiny by the press, much of it quite critical of his management style, decision-making processes, and consistency in handling controversial policy issues, including gays in the military and an unpopular proposed energy tax. Clinton was criticized for trivial matters, such as a $200 haircut from a Hollywood stylist, and for more serious mistakes, such as mishandling several key presidential appointments. By early June, not even a half-year into his presidency, Clinton was attacking the press and snapping at reporters. By the end of June, the president had held a press conference at which he made great efforts to mend the relationship. Thus, within a few months of taking office, President Clinton had moved through all three phases.

Although President Clinton may have not enjoyed his brief honeymoon with the media, he undoubtedly found it preferable to the extended coverage of the Monica Lewinsky scandal and the impeachment that flowed from it. The Drudge Report Internet site first revealed the scandal in January 1998 and later reporter Michael Isikoff in the mainstream *Newsweek* magazine. The Internet played a major role in shaping the discourse surrounding both the scandal and the impeachment. The incident was kept alive through constant discussion, dialogue, and speculation among the cable news stations and the morning news shows.

The Presidential News Agencies   Modern American presidents have a complex structure with which to represent their interests with the media. The White House director of communications, formerly known as the press secretary, regularly meets with the reporters assigned to cover the president. These reporters, known collectively as the **White House press corps,** can question the press secretary about policies. In addition, the press secretary provides announcements of appointments of new officials, policy initiatives, and other important news from the administration. President George Bush's press secretary, Marlin Fitzwater, enjoyed a fairly relaxed relationship with reporters. In contrast, President Bill Clinton's director of communications, George Stephanopoulos, was less open and more formal. Many thought that his relationship with the press was at least partly responsible for Clinton's early troubles. Stephanopoulos was soon replaced by David Gergen, a Republican who had worked in the Reagan White House. Gergen restored a friendlier atmosphere to the press room. The Office of Media Liaison works with editors from major newspapers and magazines to arrange more in-depth interviews than those provided to the

▶ **White House press corps**
Newspaper, radio, and television reporters assigned to cover the president on a day-to-day basis.

press corps. This method is a favored vehicle by which the president can reward news outlets that are favorable and punish those that are deemed to be overly critical.

The White House Press Corps   Of all the people who cover politics, the most widely recognized are the reporters of the White House press corps who cover the president for major television networks and newspapers. These reporters meet regularly with the press secretary to receive word of the president's schedule and impending policy decisions. Members of the White House press corps have often been accused of practicing **pack journalism,** or deciding which questions to ask and what stories to cover based on what other members of the press corps are doing. Considering the way the press corps routinely meets with the president or press secretary in the small press room at the White House and follows the president around the world, this phenomenon is hardly surprising. Nor is it surprising that members of the press corps sometimes develop confrontational relationships with the president. For example, Sam Donaldson, of ABC News, became well known for his tough questioning style. Although Donaldson is no longer a member of the White House press corps, his style is routinely emulated by others seeking to make a mark on American broadcast journalism.

The Press Conference   The most public way the president releases information is the most direct: the press conference. A **press conference** occurs when a president makes himself available for questioning by reporters, usually the White House press corps. The press conference is unique in that it provides the reporter, and usually the public, with unfiltered answers to questions framed by the press. Theodore Roosevelt is credited with the first press conference. Presidents use them to the degree that they feel they can control the agenda and the tone of the meetings. Consequently, presidents have held press conferences with varying frequency (see Figure 10-3).

▶ **pack journalism**   When reporters decide on what questions to ask and what stories to cover based on what other members of the press corps are doing.

▶ **press conference**   A media event in which a public official, candidate, or political activist holds a meeting with reporters to make announcements and answer questions.

Figure 10-3
Number of Presidential News Conferences, Herbert Hoover to George W. Bush (1929–2003)

Source: Adapted from Harold W. Stanley and Richard G. Niemi, *Vital Statistics on American Politics 2003–2004* (Washington, D.C.: CQ Press, 2003). p. 177.

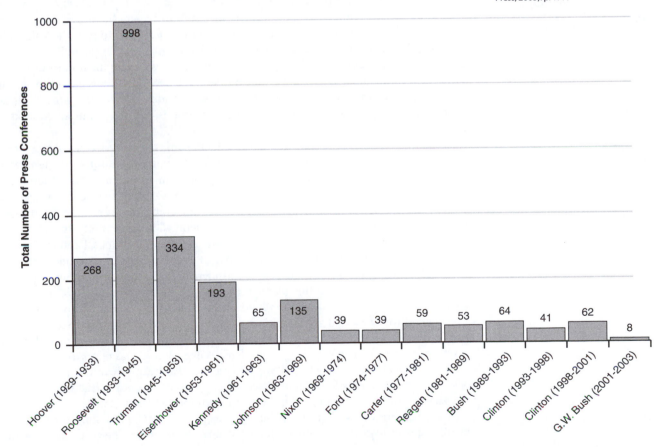

Most press conferences are videotaped, but the networks decide whether and when they will be aired. President Clinton held his first formal press conference in June 1993. Two networks, ABC and CBS, did not carry the conference, and NBC broadcast only the first half-hour. These decisions upset the Clinton administration. The networks' reason for not carrying the event was that it was "not news" in that they expected no new announcements or proposals. These judgment calls are always somewhat controversial because the networks try to balance their programming and news interests with their obligation to provide citizens with valuable information.

Press conferences usually follow a prescribed format. The president begins with a prepared statement regarding recent developments. He has some leeway to choose reporters he feels might be likely to ask friendly questions. He can avoid answering questions and quickly recognize another questioner before any embarrassing follow-up questions can be asked. But no president can completely control a press conference, and some find this format not to their liking. For this reason, President Clinton neglected to hold news conferences during the duration of the Lewinsky scandal and impeachment. A president experiences no real downside by avoiding news conferences because the general public is not particularly interested in them or even aware of their frequency.

Other members of the cabinet and high-ranking officials have briefing or background sessions to give details of an administration initiative. Officials often meet with reporters off the record to provide information. In these types of cases, the news stories cite "informed sources," but do not identify these sources by name. Because the stories are therefore released without attribution, the administration can use "deniability"; that is, the president can deny releasing the information or deny its truth.

Leaks and Trial Balloons   Presidential administrations have long complained about the problem of keeping secret information out of the media. The size of a presidential administration, the prevalence of the media, and the constant interaction between the two contribute to the leakage of information. Presidents and their top advisers often worry about **leaks** and sometimes take extraordinary measures to prevent them. For example, the Nixon White House created a special unit known as the "plumbers" to plug the leaks in its administration. The unit was headed by the White House aide Egil Krogh and included H. Howard Hunt and G. Gordon Liddy, both of whom were involved in the notorious Watergate scandal. Unfortunately, Nixon's plumbers went well beyond the confines of the law in trying to protect their president. Although most presidents have not gone to these extremes, all of them have tried, through various methods, to control unwanted leaks to the press.

Most leaks are unintentional and unwanted, but some are used strategically by presidents. Recent administrations have made frequent use of **trial balloons,** or the release, without attribution, of a proposed policy or appointment to the press with the idea of gauging public reaction. The advantage of this approach is that if the reaction is negative, the president can abandon the proposal without having ever officially advanced it. Like all information released without attribution, a trial balloon allows deniability. If the reaction is negative, however, the safer response is merely to abandon the proposal and move on.

The Clinton administration made great use of the trial-balloon method of gauging public opinion. The names of some people considered for the cabinet or other important appointments were floated in this manner. In some cases, the reactions were so negative that the names were withdrawn or never advanced. Following Zoe Baird's admission that she had employed an illegal alien as a housekeeper and failed to pay Social Security taxes, the reaction was so negative that she was forced to withdraw her name from consideration for attorney general. The next person considered, Kimba Wood, was never formally nominated. Rather, her name was released as a trial balloon. Her relatively minor problem with Social Security payments for a domestic employee proved so controversial that her name too was withdrawn, even though she had never been formally nominated.

Trial balloons can also involve policy options. When the Clinton administration was putting together its economic program, it let some members of the news media know that

leaks   The unauthorized release of information about a policy or appointment.

trial balloons   The release, without attribution, of proposed policies or appointments to the press for the purpose of gauging public reaction.

it was considering a value-added tax, a tax imposed on goods at every stage of their production and distribution. This tax was never proposed formally. The reaction to this release was sufficiently negative to derail any further consideration of the value-added tax. In many ways, the release of trial balloons is quite rational. Nevertheless, real dangers exist. Policy alternatives may not receive the discussion that formal proposals are accorded, and many complex policies may be abandoned before their advantages can be explained and debated. Moreover, people whose names are floated may be treated quite badly in that they are led to believe that they are to receive a major appointment, only to be passed over while suffering damage to their reputations during the vetting process. **Vetting** is the unofficial airing of a candidacy of an individual before an official nomination.

The media play a crucial role in the strategy of releasing trial balloons. One reason the strategy has become more popular in modern presidential politics is that it has become more feasible. The strategy requires a rapid circulation of information among opinion leaders and a quick reaction to the information released. Both would be impossible without modern television news shows, instant newspaper publishing, and radio talk shows. Only in the past two decades has mass communications technology begun to allow the general public to react immediately to a trial balloon.

▶ **vetting** Unofficial airing of a candidacy of an individual before an official nomination.

10-4b Covering Congress

Congress is arguably every bit as important an institution as the presidency, yet it seems to receive substantially less coverage on television, and what it receives is generally negative. This lack of positive coverage has done much to reduce the status of Congress in the mind of the public. Part of the problem is the difficulty the media have in covering Congress effectively. Portraying Congress in understandable terms is not easy, for a number of reasons. First, Congress is an institution of 535 members. The very size of the body makes it hard for the media to cover. Personalities and offices are numerous, and the procedures for making laws are quite complex. Producing understandable stories about isolated aspects of the process tends to be difficult for the media, especially television. In addition, because Congress reacts to and sometimes rejects presidential initiatives, it is often seen as being obstructionist. Although Congress may just be doing its job in the constitutional system, its actions are often portrayed in the media as petty and quarrelsome.

Although it receives less coverage than the presidency, Congress now has much more visibility than it once had. In 1979, the House of Representatives permitted live television coverage of floor proceedings and committee hearings. TV viewers now have unprecedented public access to the proceedings through the cable channel C-SPAN, which also broadcasts interviews and discussions on public-policy issues. In 1986, C-SPAN began Senate coverage too. Not many Americans put these broadcasts on their list of favorite programs. Nevertheless, for those few who are interested, the access to the workings of Congress is invaluable. These proceedings are available to all news services that want them.

The television coverage of Congress has been a decidedly mixed blessing for the institution's credibility. The impeachment of President Clinton was televised, beginning with the hearings of the House Judiciary committee, moving through the debate on the House floor, and ending with the Senate's shutting down its trial and failing to remove the president from office. Throughout the process, the public was treated to harsh rhetoric on both sides, highlighting the confrontational and highly personal nature of some issues.

Congressional Hearings Although an occasional congressional vote can capture the interest of the American people, the congressional hearing is best suited to television. Perhaps no political event drew the attention of Americans in the 1970s as did the Watergate hearings of 1974. On live television, a relatively small group of members of Congress looked into the break-in of the Democratic National Committee headquarters in the Watergate office building and the subsequent cover-up by the Nixon administration. This hearing attracted Americans for several reasons. First, the issues were clear-cut. Senator Howard Baker (R-Tennessee) repeated the question "What did the president know, and when did he know it?" Second, the committee included several easily recognizable personalities. Third, the events unfolded in a dramatic manner, especially with the news of the secret White House tapes of conversations that occurred in the Oval Office.

The Iran-Contra hearings of 1987 were not as well suited to live television coverage. For one thing, the issues were not so clear-cut. In fact, they were quite complex. The Reagan administration was being investigated by Congress for allegedly using profits from arms sales to the Iranian government to illegally fund the Contras, who were fighting the communist government of Nicaragua. The whole affair was particularly troubling because the arms sales were tied to the release of Americans held hostage in Lebanon. Although the president himself was never directly implicated, some members of his administration were later tried and convicted. But more memorable than the policy details were the personalities involved, particularly Oliver North. North, a Vietnam war hero who appeared in his Marine uniform before the committee, was able to capture the attention of the American people with his appealing attitude and can-do patriotic manner. In fact, North managed to put the committee somewhat on the defensive. Ultimately, although Congress found evidence of wrongdoing, it did nothing to penalize the White House.

In October 1991, another congressional hearing captured the attention of the American television-viewing public. President Bush, under pressure to nominate an African American to the Supreme Court, chose the conservative federal judge Clarence Thomas. The nomination, though controversial, was headed toward probable confirmation by the Senate until the law professor Anita Hill accused Thomas of having sexually harassed her ten years earlier, when she had worked for him at the Equal Employment Opportunity Commission. The Senate Judiciary Committee held televised hearings at which Hill and Thomas appeared. Again, the hearings were widely viewed by Americans and became the topic of national conversation. Congress emerged from the affair with its already low prestige tarnished further. It managed to appear excessively intrusive into Clarence Thomas' personal life and at the same time insensitive to the sexual harassment claims of Anita Hill. Women's groups were particularly incensed by the treatment that Hill received from the all-male Senate Judiciary Committee.

In 2004, Americans were highly attentive to the televised hearings of the 9-11 commission, which had been established by Congress to investigate the breakdowns in intelligence that allowed the plots that led to the terrorist attacks of September 2001 to go undetected. Americans watched as current Bush administration and former Clinton administration officials appeared before the commission to testify. No doubt, avid followers of the hearings were frustrated by the fact that many of the sessions were held in secret, including interviews with President George W. Bush and former President Bill Clinton. Given the magnitude of the terrorist attacks and their consequences for American policy, it was not surprising that much of the testimony became fodder for the presidential campaigns. And given the widespread distrust of government that exists in this country, it was also not surprising that many Americans chose to view the commission as an attempt to cover up rather than reveal the truth of what had taken place prior to 9-11-2001.

The process of passing legislation is perhaps the congressional duty that is hardest to frame to Americans. The problem is not that people lack interest in which laws are passed, but rather that the process just does not lend itself to media coverage. On the other hand, when Congress is performing its investigative role or fulfilling its advise-and-consent function, the media often can portray the process in an interesting and informative manner.

10-4c The Media and the Courts

By the nature of its task, the federal judiciary is the branch of government furthest removed from public access. Though actual trial proceedings are open to the public, judicial deliberations take place behind closed doors. State criminal courts have become less secretive in recent years with the gradual increase in the number of courts that allow cameras. The federal courts still do not permit cameras in the courtroom. Thus, when a sensational federal trial is reported on the evening news, such as the 1994 case of the Branch Davidians who were accused of murdering federal agents, viewers see an artist's sketches of the defendants,

Comparative Perspective

The British Press

As one of the world's best-established democracies, Great Britain has a strong cultural and legal commitment to the idea of a free press. Before the eighteenth century, however, the English press was strictly censored by Parliament and the Crown. In 1644, the poet John Milton penned *Areopagitica,* an eloquent argument for press freedom. A century later, a member of Parliament, John Wilkes, was expelled after attacking King George III in a periodical he edited. Eventually reinstated to Parliament, Wilkes became a champion of freedom of the press. From that point onward, the British press became steadily more free from government censorship or interference.

In 1702, England's first daily paper, the *Daily Courant,* began publication. The *Times of London,* founded in 1785, remains one of Britain's largest and most respected newspapers. By the nineteenth century, as the common people became literate, the English press began to reach the masses. Commenting on the widespread dissemination of newspapers, the nineteenth century English author Samuel Butler commented: "The most important service rendered by the press . . . is that of educating people to approach printed matter with distrust."

Many people now view the British press with distrust, if not abhorrence. The mainstream newspapers, like the *Times* and the *Manchester Guardian,* are being overshadowed by the tabloids, which operate with little if any sense of journalistic ethics. The English tabloids make their American counterparts, like the *National Enquirer,* look tame by comparison. The English tabloids revel in scandal, especially any connected with the private lives of the royal family. Evidently, the British people have a taste for the sordid and scandalous, especially if it involves the rich and powerful. A good many other Britons now find themselves embarrassed by the excesses of the tabloid press. As long as people buy these tabloids, however, their publishers feel no pressure to change their approach.

Take a look at some major daily British papers at these Web addresses:

The Observer: http://www.observer.co.uk
Guardian: http://www.guardian.co.uk
Independent: http://news.independent.co.uk
Times of London: http://www.timesonline.co.uk

Here are addresses for some of the more widely read tabloids:

Evening Standard: http://www.thisislondon.co.uk
Daily Telegraph: http://www.telegraph.co.uk

lawyers, and judge rather than a videotape of the proceeding. In many state cases, however, television viewers can see live or tape-delayed television coverage of events in the courtroom.

Commercial television has discovered the entertainment value of sensational criminal trials. Indeed, an entire cable channel, Court TV, is now dedicated to the live coverage and discussion of sensational cases now under way in the judicial system. In 1994, the public was riveted by media coverage of the trial of Lyle and Erik Menendez, who were accused of killing their parents, and the prosecution of Lorena Bobbitt, who was accused of malicious wounding after cutting off her husband's penis. Later in 1994, the public was subjected to a barrage of coverage of the O. J. Simpson case. Ten years later it would be the Scott Peterson murder trial. Without question, the public has a serious interest in learning about these types of cases. For the mass media, however, these cases are as much, if not more, about morbid entertainment as about keeping the public informed.

Covering the Federal Courts   Even though the federal courts—in particular, the Supreme Court—produce decisions that have a tremendous effect on society, the judicial process is a mystery to most Americans. Federal judges rarely give interviews. When they do, they do not discuss any substantive matters that might find their way into a decision. For this reason, television coverage of federal judges is not linked to personalities but rather to reporting the outcome of deliberations. The exception occurs when an individual is nominated to a position on the Supreme Court. Then, television and newspaper reporters become aggressive in examining the nominee's personality, ideology, and political affiliations and any potential embarrassing incidents from her past.

The major television networks and newspapers all have reporters and analysts who cover the Supreme Court. They report on, discuss, and analyze major decisions, especially those in which the public has a great interest, such as abortion and school prayer cases. The media are well represented at oral arguments before the Supreme Court. Members of the press pay close attention to the questions that the justices ask the lawyers who are arguing the cases. On the evening news, pundits speculate about how the Court will decide significant cases and how the justices will vote. Months later, when Supreme Court decisions are announced, they are often reported within minutes on CNN. Among newspapers, the *New York Times* provides the most in-depth coverage of the Court's decisions, often printing substantial excerpts from the opinions.

Covering the Supreme Court   The Supreme Court received unprecedented attention during the aftermath of the 2000 presidential election. The Court became involved twice in response to appeals of Florida Supreme Court decisions that had extended deadlines for hand recounts and overturned a circuit court judge who had ruled against further counts contesting the election. In both cases, the United States Supreme Court vacated or reversed the Florida Supreme Court decisions. The oral arguments that preceded these decisions were given unprecedented media attention. Although the justices refused to allow their deliberations to be televised, they did make a historic decision to allow audiotapes to be released soon after the close of the arguments. The tapes were eagerly awaited by all news organizations, including those of the broadcast networks, which interrupted regularly scheduled programming to play them. Americans seemed fascinated with the dialogue between the justices and the attorneys for Gore and Bush.

The Court's decision to stop the recounts and to bring an end to the controversy was released at 10 p.m. on December 12, only two hours before the deadline for states to send slates of electors free from congressional challenge. The complex and confusing decision, replete with a series of concurring and dissenting opinions, proved difficult for the new media to make sense of quickly. Americans were faced with the awkward spectacle of news analysts reading from the decision on live television while trying to decipher the decision's meaning "on the fly" and initially mistaking the decision as supporting further recounts under standards to be set by the Florida Supreme Court.

10-5 Coverage of Elections, Campaigns, and Candidates

Coverage of elections, campaigns, and candidates is a staple in the diet of American journalism, and most Americans follow this coverage to some degree (see Figure 10-4). Nevertheless, a majority of Americans believe that the press has too much influence over elections—in particular, the presidential contest. Moreover, a substantial and growing proportion of the public believes that the media do a poor job in covering the presidential race.

In a national survey conducted by the Times Mirror Center in January 1992, 58 percent of respondents said that the media has "too much" influence on who becomes president. In a similar survey conducted by the same firm in 1988, 51 percent had said "too much."[31] In 1992, the Gallup poll found that more than half of Americans believed that the media had done a fair or poor job in covering the presidential campaign.[32] In contrast, the Gallup poll found that only 10 percent thought that the press had done a fair or poor job in covering the Gulf War of 1991.[33]

Two themes surface when people are asked why they rate the media poorly: One is the tendency to focus on scandals, personalities, and problems of "character" rather than on the substantive issues facing the country, and the other is a widespread perception that the media are biased in one direction or another.

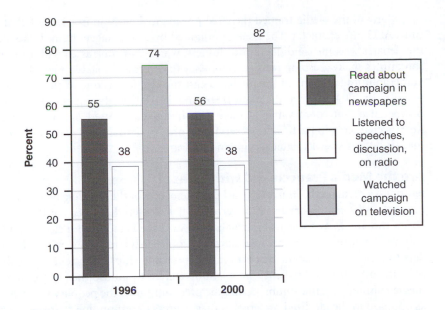

Figure 10-4
Americans' Attentiveness to the 1996 and 2000 Presidential Campaigns through the Media

Source: Adapted from Center for Political Studies, University of Michigan, National Election Studies, 1996 and 2000.

10-5a The Character Issue

In recent years, the question of "character" has taken on added importance. In the past, the press was able to avoid reporting on some issues, through a "gentleman's agreement" of sorts. For example, reportedly many members of the White House press corps were aware of President Kennedy's alleged extramarital relationships with women. But these stories were not reported at the time. Reporters of that era believed either that these types of stories were inappropriate subjects of news reports or that reporting the stories would express disrespect for the institution of the presidency. By the 1980s, however, the restrained relationship between the press and politicians, especially the president, had changed. The press now reports in detail on every aspect of the president's life, from personal habits to medical treatments. Nothing is immune from media coverage. The character of the president is continually subjected to public scrutiny. The same is true for presidential candidates.

In 1987, the Democratic presidential front-runner Gary Hart, of Colorado, was undone by the character issue. A *Miami Herald* reporter who had received a tip regarding Hart's impending rendezvous with a woman other than his wife staked out Hart's Washington residence. The subsequent story cast enough doubt on Hart's character that his candidacy was effectively ended. Hart's private life, once held to be off-limits to the media, had brought an end to a promising candidacy.

Character was again an issue for the Democrats during the 1992 presidential election. In the spring of 1992, Bill Clinton's candidacy was haunted by allegations that, as governor of Arkansas, he had had an affair with a woman named Gennifer Flowers. Flowers had released a tabloid interview in which she discussed some details of their alleged relationship. Clinton's candidacy suffered as a result of these accusations, which came out while he was campaigning for the all-important New Hampshire primary. In response, Clinton and his wife, Hillary, decided to confront the issue directly on the CBS News program *60 Minutes*. The appearance helped Clinton fend off the accusations and later regain his status as the leading Democratic candidate.

A *Newsweek* poll conducted in February 1992 found that most people disapproved of the way the press handled the allegations against Clinton. Indeed, 66 percent of those surveyed said that the adultery charges should not be a "significant issue" in the campaign, and 73 percent disapproved of the way the media were handling the candidate's "past and private life." Yet the same survey found that only 39 percent thought that Clinton was "personally honest," in contrast to 56 percent for Clinton's Democratic rival Paul Tsongas.[34] People may not have liked the media's coverage of the adultery charges, but this coverage seems to have had an effect on people's perceptions of Clinton's character. This perception endured well into Clinton's presidency and clearly hampered his performance as president.

Many in the media framed the 2000 presidential election in terms of character—this time, Al Gore's character. The issue, spotlighted by some exaggerations Gore made during the debates, was the candidate's truthfulness, which was contrasted with candidate Bush's sometimes shaky grasp on facts and tendency to commit verbal blunders. Both candidates' vulnerabilities led many in the media to cast the election as one of character versus competence. In 2004, many in the mainstream media continued to question George W. Bush's competence, but conservative elements in the media focused on questions about John Kerry's character, in particular his service record in Vietnam and whether he deserved the medals he was awarded after serving in that war.

Are the Media Preoccupied with Sleaze?   One of the harshest critics of the contemporary media is the journalist Carl Bernstein, one of the *Washington Post* reporters who broke the Watergate story in 1972. Bernstein has written that since the 1970s the press has "been moving away from real journalism toward the creation of a sleazoid infotainment culture." Bernstein chides the "new culture of journalistic titillation," which, he claims, panders to viewers and readers to boost ratings and readerships. Bernstein argues that "it is the role of journalists to challenge people, not merely to amuse them."[35] Defenders of the media counter with the argument that the press only gives the people what they really want as opposed to the idealized preferences they express in responding to surveys. The political scientist Darrell West has said that "people are both turned off by the media and attracted to it at the same time." According to West, if the media ignored scandals and stuck to substance, "it would probably be pretty boring."[36]

When the first hint of a scandal involving a candidate for high office comes to light, the press attacks like a school of sharks smelling blood in the water. The resulting feeding frenzy almost inevitably leads to the ruination of a political career. Talented people with something to contribute to governance can be lost to public life forever. But according to the political scientist Larry Sabato, the greatest impact of media feeding frenzies "is not in the winnowing of candidates but the encouragement of cynicism."[37] Clearly, public cynicism about politics, politicians, and government institutions has been on the steady increase over the past several decades. There is reason to believe that the media contribute to this cynicism, by not only showing the people their leaders "warts and all" but also dwelling on the lurid, the scandalous, and the sensational.

10-6 Mass Media and the Making of Public Policy

The media play a major role in what governments do and how they do it. Newspapers, and especially television reports, help prepare the public for an impending government initiative. Whether the issue is AIDS, the homeless, or starving people in a society far away, the images, especially as portrayed through television or print photojournalism, have a powerful effect on the American public. These images can build support among the public for government policies or lead to pressure from the public to pursue certain policies.

Because American media now have global reach, the content of American media reports can have global impact. This truth was brought home in the spring of 2005 when *Newsweek* magazine ran a story in its May 9 issue on the interrogation of prisoners captured in the ongoing war on terrorism. Since 2001, the United States has incarcerated hundreds of suspected terrorists and other "enemy aliens" at the American naval base at Guantanamo Bay, Cuba. In its story, *Newsweek* reported that American soldiers had flushed a copy of the Koran down a toilet as a psychological tactic in the interrogation process. The story caused an immediate upsurge of anti-American protest and violence throughout the Muslim world. At least nine people were killed in riots in Pakistan and other Muslim countries. Secretary of State Condoleezza Rice, who made a tour of the Middle East and Southern Asia in the week after the story broke, spent considerable time and energy performing "damage control." A week later, *Newsweek* retracted the story, admitting that the one source of the information had "backed away" from the account. But, by all accounts, serious damage had been done to American efforts to win "hearts and minds" in the Islamic world. Pakistan's foreign minister was quoted as saying that the retraction was "not enough" and that Muslims around the world had been "insulted" by the story. Pakistan's president, Pervez Musharraf, called on the United States to conduct "a thorough investigation into the reported sacrilege of the Holy Koran." Clearly, *Newsweek*'s retraction of the story had far less impact than the original report and many Muslims continued to believe the original story. Not only did the *Newsweek* story create an immediate problem for American diplomacy, it provided more ammunition to conservative critics of the media and probably further undermined the popular credibility of the mainstream press.[38]

10-6a Agenda Setting

Issues come and go in American politics. In many ways, the most important thing an interest group can do to further its cause is to place an issue on the agenda. Most often, this process involves gaining favorable media coverage, or at least the sort of coverage that dramatizes the issue and frames it in such a way that politicians feel that they must address it. For instance, much of the difficulty facing those who wanted the federal government to address the AIDS issue in the late 1980s and early 1990s had to do with getting the public to perceive AIDS as a crisis and one that the government should address. Although AIDS activists did not necessarily produce the legislative results they wanted, they were able to dramatize the issue in ways that the electronic media could portray. In one particularly poignant presentation, AIDS activists displayed a quilt bearing the names of Americans who had died of AIDS. The quilt was so large that it nearly covered the Mall between the Capitol and the Washington Monument.

In American politics, an issue or event can hardly be said to exist unless it receives attention by the media. The central importance of the media in political life is summed up in the following quotation about the need for media coverage of protests: "The first and foremost goal of all political protests is the same: to gain coverage by the media. Like a tree falling in the forest, a protest without media coverage goes unappreciated no matter how much noise it makes."[39]

Often, it is the members of the media themselves who help to place an issue on the public agenda. During 1992, Americans were bombarded with television images from faraway places. One set of pictures was particularly troubling: those showing children starving in Somalia. Few Americans knew where Somalia could be found on a map, and fewer still had any idea about the civil war that had made food distribution impossible. Yet the images were transfixing. The United States, as the world's single remaining superpower, seemed in a position to do something to help. Some people argued that the United States had no real national interest in Somalia. Nevertheless, President Bush ordered troops to the African country to restore enough order that relief could be provided. This decision had widespread bipartisan support. Nevertheless, it is doubtful that the intervention would have taken place if the American people, and their elected representatives, had not seen the horrible images of starving Somalis on television.

When Bill Clinton became president, he continued the American policy of providing security so that humanitarian organizations could feed the starving people of Somalia. However, that policy was soon complicated by the United Nations' effort to capture the warlord Mohammed Aidid. In what is widely referred to as Blackhawk Down, American troops were caught in a deadly battle with Aidid's forces, and seventeen Americans died. One dead GI was dragged through the streets. Soon, this image was beamed to startled and disgusted TV viewers in the United States. Again, images guided policy. This time, the message was different: "Get out."

Popular Culture and American Politics
Televised Presidential Debates

Senator John Kerry and President George W. Bush face off in a nationally televised debate during the fall of 2004.

The first nationally televised presidential debate took place in 1960 between incumbent Vice President Richard M. Nixon and Senator John F. Kennedy. Most political scientists agree that the debate gave a boost to Kennedy's candidacy. Fundamentally, the debate helped Kennedy in that he appeared on an equal plane with the incumbent Vice President. Interestingly, most people who heard the debate on the radio thought that Nixon had won, and most who saw the debate on TV perceived Kennedy as the victor. Clearly, Kennedy had the superior visual image. He was better looking than Nixon to begin with, and the harsh TV lights accentuated the difference. Moreover, Kennedy seemed at ease on camera, and Nixon did not.

The lesson of the Kennedy–Nixon debate was not lost on politicians and campaign managers. President Johnson saw no need to share a platform with his Republican chal-

10-6b Building Public Support for Particular Policies

In the days following the terrorist attacks on September 11, the major television networks broadcast nonstop coverage with few commercial interruptions. Weeks later, the cable news stations had developed regular coverage of the "war on terrorism." Many reporters and some anchors wore flag lapels. Clearly, the media supported the war effort and supported, in a general sense, the military response to the terrorist attack.

There was nothing novel about the approach the television networks took, although the intensity may have been heightened. In November 1991, an adviser to President George Bush said that television was "our chief tool" in building public support for the war against Iraq.[40] Bush had moved rapidly to send American troops to Saudi Arabia after the Iraqis had invaded Kuwait. Having been invited by Saudi King Fahd, Bush sought to stem any further advance by Iraqi forces. This effort was known as Operation Desert Shield. The operation evolved into Desert Storm, when the mission shifted from a defensive to an offensive posture with the goal of driving the Iraqis out of Kuwait. Following a passionate debate in

lenger, Barry Goldwater, in 1964. Nor did Richard Nixon believe that it was in his interest to debate Hubert Humphrey in 1968 or George McGovern in 1972. In 1976, President Gerald Ford did engage his Democratic challenger, Jimmy Carter, in a series of televised debates. Most observers agreed that Carter gave the better performance. He, of course, went on to win the presidency. In 1980, Carter was beaten decisively by Ronald Reagan, in both a televised debate and the election itself. In 1984, the incumbent Reagan faced the Democratic nominee Walter Mondale in two television debates. The first was disastrous for Reagan, who appeared slow and even confused. In the second debate, however, Reagan seemed more relaxed and more in command of the situation. He, of course, went on to win a landslide victory against Mondale.

In 1988, the debates between the Democratic candidate, Michael Dukakis, and the Republican nominee, George Bush, produced no decisive victor, although Bush went on to win the election by a substantial margin. In 1992, a series of three TV debates was televised. The 1992 debates were complicated by the presence of the independent candidate, Ross Perot, who stole the show with his down-home wit and humor. Because Perot's barbs were aimed more at President Bush than at Democrat Bill Clinton, the effect of the debate seems to have been to hurt Bush and help Clinton. Obviously, Clinton went on to win the election; the effect of the debates on the outcome was probably fairly minimal. Like other elements of pop culture, televised presidential debates seem to be as much, if not more, about entertainment than about educating the electorate about the candidates' positions.

In many ways, the 2000 presidential debates produced the most surprising results. It is probably fair to say that Al Gore never recovered from his performance in the first debate. He had entered the debates as a clear favorite, regarded by almost all observers as quite a good debater who was conversant with facts. George W. Bush, on the other hand, brought the opposite reputation, as a weak debater, somewhat uncomfortable as a speaker, and certainly not nearly as conversant with policy-relevant facts as was Vice President Gore. Most observers were stunned when Governor Bush clearly gained from the debate at the expense of Vice President Gore, who managed to alienate millions of viewers with his interruptions, sighs, and other negative reactions to his opponent. Governor Bush's relative calmness and avoidance of any verbal slips kept him alive and well at a time in the electoral process when many expected him to falter.

In 2004, the dynamics of the presidential debates were very different. In the first debate, President Bush appeared uneasy, even aggravated. He was also extremely inarticulate. In contrast, John Kerry seemed confident, poised, well-spoken, and very much in command of the issues. Although President Bush recovered somewhat during the next two debates, the damage had been done, as reflected in the considerable tightening of the race after the first debate. No president can afford to participate in such a debate and look "unpresidential."

January 1991, Congress voted to support military action against Iraq, providing President Bush with the authority to act militarily if the forces of Saddam Hussein did not leave Kuwait by January 15.

By all accounts, President Bush was extremely effective in using television to build the national consensus necessary to obtain the support of the Democratic-controlled Congress. By the time the United States engaged in military action in late January 1991, the president's approval rating exceeded 90 percent and support for military action was widespread. A major factor in rallying this support was the president's effective use of television. The president used the media at various stages of the process. In his first televised address to the nation, he explained the seriousness of the Iraqi invasion of Kuwait. His message was unequivocal, when he said that the invasion "will not stand." Thus, he quickly let the American public know that the conflict was serious and that he was committed to resolving it. In later speeches, Bush was clear on why the United States was involved and what the options were and that he was committed to using force to achieve his objectives. When the build-up, and later the war, began, Americans had been informed and involved at every step of the process.

For the first time, Americans were able to witness a historic congressional debate over whether to authorize the use of force, as the president requested, or continue economic sanctions with the hope that military force would not be necessary. The issues were debated openly for the American people, along with the rest of the world, to see. Although most Democrats voted to continue economic sanctions rather than approve the immediate use of force, President Bush was able to put together a majority in favor of using military force.

10-7 Conclusion: The Media—an Essential Part of the American Political System

It is generally acknowledged that the mass media have had and are having an important effect on American politics, but considerable disagreement exists over exactly what the effect is and whether it is desirable or undesirable. Surely one effect of mass media is to greatly accelerate the pace of political change. Events are reported instantaneously. Information flows back and forth from the mass public to decision makers and from one decision maker to another with amazing speed. Although everyone, including the attentive citizen, wants good information as soon as he can get it, a danger exists that the decision-making process may speed up to the point that human beings cannot cope with the pressures of making rapid decisions. Arguably, the quality of political decision making can suffer if individuals are not afforded enough time to digest facts, frame options, and calmly consider the consequences of adopting one alternative over another.

Mass media have become an integral part of the American political system. Our national political conversation is carried on through the mass media. It is impossible to imagine contemporary politics without television and radio and the Internet. Ever since the Kennedy–Nixon debate during the 1960 campaign, political actors who have not understood the media have eventually suffered for it. This understanding must be fluid. The mass media of today differ greatly from the media of the 1960s. Over the next several decades, media will probably take on forms that are difficult to imagine now.

Questions for Thought and Discussion

1. Generally speaking, is the American press too critical of government or not critical enough?

2. Does violence on television merely reflect violence in society, or does it encourage violent behavior? Should the government regulate the amount of violence on television? What constitutional problems might be raised by government regulation of TV violence?

3. Generally speaking, are the mass media biased against conservative ideas, policies, and politicians?

4. Would the government be justified in preventing a television network from reporting about an impending military operation if the report would jeopardize the success of the mission? Would this type of prohibition raise a constitutional problem?

5. Do the modern electronic media promote the candidacies of "outsiders," such as Ross Perot? Or does the cost of a modern media campaign prevent unconventional candidates from mounting serious challenges?

Practice Quiz

Note: You can find the correct answers to these questions by taking the quiz and then submitting your answers in the Online Edition. The program will automatically score your submission. If you miss a question, the program will provide the correct answer, a rationale for the answer, and the section number in the chapter where the topic is discussed.

1. Members of the White House press corps have often been accused of practicing _____ journalism, in which reporters decide on what questions to ask and what stories to cover based on what other members of the press are doing.
   a. yellow
   b. pack
   c. muckraking
   d. tinhorn

2. President _____ is credited for conducting the first press conference.
   a. Andrew Jackson
   b. Franklin Roosevelt
   c. Theodore Roosevelt
   d. John Kennedy

3. An unauthorized release of information to the press is referred to as a _____.
   a. trial balloon
   b. lead balloon
   c. hot air balloon
   d. leak

4. Which of the following is considered an example of a "supermarket tabloid"?
   a. *The National Enquirer*
   b. *The New York Times*
   c. *The Progressive*
   d. a and c

5. The _____ cable television channel routinely covers hearings in both the House and Senate in addition to interviews and discussions on public policy proceedings.
   a. CBN
   b. C-SPAN
   c. NPR
   d. The Public Television Network

6. The 1987 presidential bid of _____ (D-Colorado) was undone when a *Miami Herald* reporter broke a story detailing his rendezvous with Donna Rice.
   a. Michael Dukakis
   b. Lawton Chiles
   c. Jerry Brown
   d. Gary Hart

7. The first nationally televised presidential debate took place in 1960 between _____.
   a. John Kennedy and Lyndon Johnson
   b. Lyndon Johnson and Richard Nixon
   c. John Kennedy and Richard Nixon
   d. Lyndon Johnson and Barry Goldwater

8. In _____ (1972), the Supreme Court said that "we cannot seriously entertain the notion that the First Amendment protects a newsman's agreement to conceal the criminal conduct of his source, or evidence thereof, on the theory that it is better to write about crime than to do something about it."
   a. *Branzburg v. Hayes*
   b. *New York Times v. Sullivan*
   c. *New York Times v. U.S.*
   d. *Brandenburg v. Ohio*

9. To operate a television or radio station, a person must obtain a license from the _____.
   a. Interstate Commerce Commission
   b. Federal Communications Commission
   c. Federal Department of Communication
   d. Labor Department

10. During the presidential campaign of 1992, Vice President Dan Quayle attacked the popular television show _____.
    a. *The Simpsons*
    b. *Murphy Brown*
    c. *Roseanne*
    d. *Family Matters*

For Further Reading

Atherton, F. Christopher. *Media Politics: The News Strategies of Presidential Campaigns* (Lexington, MA: Lexington Books, 1984).

Bennett, W. Lance. *The Governing Crisis: Media, Money and Marketing in American Elections* (New York: St. Martin's Press, 1992).

———. News: *The Politics of Illusion*, 2d ed. (New York: Longman, 1988).

Berkman, Ronald, and Laura W. Kitch. *Politics in the Media Age* (New York: McGraw-Hill, 1986).

Broder, David S. *Behind the Front Page* (New York: Simon & Schuster, 1987).

Crouse, Timothy. *The Boys on the Bus* (New York: Ballantine, 1973).

Drudge, Matt, and Julia Phillips. *Drudge Manifesto* (New York: New American Library, 2000).

Goldberg, Bernard. *Bias: A CBS Insider Exposes How the Media Distort the News* (Washington, D.C.: Regnery Publishing, 2001).

Graber, Doris A. *Mass Media and American Politics*, 6th ed. (Washington, D.C.: CQ Press, 2001).

———. *Media Power and Politics*, 4th ed. (Washington, D.C.: CQ Press, 2000).

Halberstam, David. *The Powers That Be* (Champaign, IL: University of Illinois Press, 2000).

Kurtz, Howard. *Spin Cycle: Inside the Clinton Propaganda Machine* (New York: The Free Press, 1998).

Leighley, Jan E., *Mass Media and Politics: A Social Science Perspective* (Boston: Houghton Mifflin, 2004).

Nimmo, Dan, and James E. Combs. *Nightly Horrors* (Knoxville, TN: University of Tennessee Press, 1985).

Purvis, Hoyt. *The Media, Politics and Government* (Belmont, CA: Thomson/Wadsworth, 2001).

Ranney, Austin. *Channels of Power: The Impact of Television on American Politics* (New York: Basic Books, 1983).

Rosenstiel, Tom. *Strange Bedfellows: How Television and the Presidential Candidates Changed American Politics,* 1992 (New York: Hyperion, 1993).

Sabato, Larry. *Feeding Frenzy: How Attack Journalism Has Transformed American Politics* (New York: Free Press, 1991).

West, Darrell M. *The Rise and Fall of the Media Establishment* (Belmont, CA: Thomson/Wadsworth, 2001).

———., and John M. Orman, *Celebrity Politics* (Upper Saddle River, NJ: Prentice-Hall, 2003).

Endnotes

1. This reference stems from eighteenth century England: The "three estates" were the nobility, the commons, and the clergy.

2. Some commentators characterize the media as the fifth branch of government; the bureaucracy, the fourth.

3. Carl Bernstein, "The Idiot Culture," *The New Republic,* June 8, 1992, p. 24.

4. "The American Media: Who Watches, Who Listens, Who Cares," Times Mirror Center for People and the Press, Washington, D.C., 1992, p. 40.

5. Glenn H. Reynolds, http://instapundit.com/about.php

6. Glenn H. Reynolds, http://www.instapundit.com/, main page, blog posted October 14, 2004, 1:31 p.m.

7. See Harold W. Stanley and Richard G. Niemi, *Vital Statistics on American Politics 2003–2004* (Washington, DC: CQ Press, 2003), p. 173.

8. A 1992 study found that roughly 60 percent of adults read at least one newspaper daily. See *Multimedia Audiences Report* (New York: Mediamark Research, Spring 1992).

9. See Marshall McLuhan, *Understanding Media: The Extensions of Man,* 2d ed. (New York: New American Library, 1964); Marshall McLuhan and Quentin Fiore, *The Medium Is the Message: An Inventory of Effects* (New York: Bantam Books, 1967).

10. See S. Robert Lichter, Stanley Rothman, and Linda S. Lichter, *The Media Elite* (Bethesda, MD: Adler & Adler, 1986), pp. 38–41.

11. "Voters Impressed with Campaign, But News Coverage Gets Lukewarm Ratings," The Pew Research Center for People and the Press. October 24, 2004. On the web at http://people-press.org.

12. Michael J. Robinson, "Just How Liberal Is the News? 1980 Revisited," *Public Opinion,* February/March 1983.

13. Michael J. Robinson, "The Media in Campaign '84: Wingless, Toothless and Hopeless," *Public Opinion,* February/March 1985.

14. Press release issued by Mead Data Central and PR Associates, Inc., November 10, 1992.

15. Bernard Goldberg, *Bias: A CBS Insider Exposes How the Media Distort the News* (Washington, D.C.: Regnery Publishing, 2001).

16. Michael Parenti, *Inventing Reality: The Politics of the News Media,* 2d ed. (New York: St. Martin's Press, 1993), p. 6.

17. Ibid., p. 8.

18. "Voters Impressed with Campaign, But News Coverage Gets Lukewarm Ratings," The Pew Research Center for People and the Press. October 24, 2004. On the web at http://people-press.org.

19. *Near v. Minnesota,* 283 U.S. 697 (1931).

20. *New York Times Co. v. United States,* 403 U.S. 713 (1971).

21. *United States v. Progressive, Inc.,* 467 F. Supp. 990 (D.C.Wis. 1979).

22. *New York Times Co. v. Sullivan,* 376 U.S. 254 (1964).

23. *Branzburg v. Hayes,* 408 U.S. 665 (1972).

24. *Cohen v. Cowles Media Co.,* 111 S. Ct. 2513 (1992).

25. *Red Lion Broadcasting Co. v. FCC,* 395 U.S. 367 (1969).

26. *FCC v. League of Women Voters of California,* 468 U.S. 364 (1984).

27. National survey of 1,025 adults conducted by Scripps-Howard News Service and Ohio University. Results reported in Thomas Hargrove and Guido H. Stempel III, "Poll: TV Sex, Violence Irk 60 Percent," *Knoxville News-Sentinel,* December 26, 1993, p. A1.

28. *FCC v. Pacifica Foundation,* 438 U.S. 726 (1978).

29. *Reno v. American Civil Liberties Union,* 521 U.S. 844, 117 S.Ct. 2329, 138 L. Ed. 2nd 874 (1997).

30. Michael Grossman and Martha Kumar, "The White House and the News Media: Three Phases of Their Relationship," *Political Science Quarterly,* vol. 94, Spring 1979, pp. 57–73.

31. Surveys conducted by the Times Mirror Center for the People and the Press, reported in Elizabeth Kolbert, "As Political Campaigns Turn Negative, the Press Is Given a Negative Rating," *New York Times,* May 1, 1992.

32. George Gallup, Jr., ed., *The Gallup Poll: Public Opinion 1992* (Wilmington, DE: Scholarly Resources, Inc., 1993), p. 78.

33. George Gallup, Jr., ed., *The Gallup Poll: Public Opinion 1991* (Wilmington, DE: Scholarly Resources, Inc., 1992), p. 33.

34. *Newsweek* poll, conducted February 20–21, 1992. Results reported in "Wondering Who's Electable," *Newsweek,* March 2, 1992, pp. 24–26.

35. Bernstein, "The Idiot Culture," pp. 24–25.

36. Quoted in Kolbert, "As Political Campaigns Turn Negative, the Press Is Given a Negative Rating."

37. Larry Sabato, *Feeding Frenzy: How Attack Journalism Has Transformed American Politics* (New York: Free Press, 1991), p. 207.

38. Kamran Khan and John Lancaster, "Newsweek Retraction Has Hollow Ring for Some Pakistanis," Washington Post Foreign Service, May 17, 2005.

39. Jeffrey Berry, *The Interest Group Society,* 2d ed. (Glenview, IL: Scott, Foresman, 1989), p. 110.

40. Richard Haas, quoted in the *New York Times,* November 5, 1991.

Campaigns and Elections

11-1 The Importance of Elections

On November 3, 2004, the country knew that President George W. Bush had been elected to another four-year term. The night before had left a bit of uncertainty as the Ohio votes drifted in, but this election stood as a beacon of clarity when compared to the situation four years earlier. For more than a month following Election Day in 2000, there was great uncertainty about who had won. By the time Al Gore conceded the election to George W. Bush on December 13, the country had been through more than five weeks of almost non-stop news coverage and discussion. Even a year-and-a-half later, in May 2002, the Justice Department was considering filing voting rights lawsuits in counties and cities in three states regarding issues in the administration of the election. The extreme closeness of the contest highlighted the importance of presidential elections in this country. Those who worked in the 2000 campaigns or paid close attention to the media coverage might have felt that the 2000 election was more important than most. In truth, all presidential elections in the United States are of fundamental importance in charting the direction for the country.

Elections are fundamental to any democracy. They provide the mechanism through which the electorate communicates its preferences to government. Elections allow those who make the effort to vote to select those who will hold office. Moreover, elections hold public officials accountable to the people they govern. If officials do not perform their jobs to the satisfaction of a majority of the electorate, they are not reelected. Finally, elections perform the function of conferring legitimacy on the political system. If rulers are chosen in free and fair elections, they are widely perceived as having the right to rule. This perception of legitimacy is of critical importance. It is no wonder that shortly after George W. Bush's narrow, controversial victory in the electoral college in 2000, many Democrats and media commentators began to question the legitimacy of his presidency. In 2004, despite bitterness among Kerry supporters about the loss, there was no quarreling about the fact that Bush had won.

Anyone considering running for office, as well as anyone considering running a political campaign, must be aware of the variety of forces that converge during an election. One must consider a number of questions: Who will turn out to vote? What will the overall level of turnout be? What is the ideology of the two candidates, and whose ideology is more appealing to the voters? What are the key issues in the race, and how are these issues reflected in public opinion? What interest groups have a stake in the contest, and how will they seek to influence the outcome? How will the race be portrayed in the media? Indeed, will the media even take notice? Will the media be able to portray events in the lives of the candidates as scandals, thereby diverting attention from the substantive issues of the race? Finally, how will the political party organizations regard the campaign? How crucial is this election to the parties' overall national strategies? Will the parties provide assistance? The answer to each of these questions has a bearing on the outcome of the race.

11-1a Types of Elections

There are two basic types of elections: primary and general. In a **primary election,** a political party selects one candidate from a field of contenders to run against the nominees of other parties in a general election. In a **general election,** voters make the final choice of who will hold office. Parties can use a variety of methods to select the person to get their **nomination.** The most common are the primary election and the caucus. In a primary election, voters are asked to go to the polls to choose among the contenders for a party's nomination. In a caucus system, people affiliated with a party hold a meeting to select the party's nominee.

The complexity of the American federal system produces a great number of elections, held at different times, for different offices. In a given year, a citizen may be asked to vote in nomination contests and general elections for offices at the local, state, and national levels. These elections are often held at different times throughout the year. Thus, it is not surprising that turnout, especially for state and local elections, tends to be quite low. If as many

primary election   An election in which voters go to the polls to choose among the contenders for a party's nomination.

general election   An election in which voters choose among the nominees of various parties to determine who will be elected to public office.

nomination   The process by which a political party selects one candidate from a field of contenders to run against the nominees of other parties in a general election.

as 50 percent of those who are eligible turn out to vote in a state or local election, commentators are likely to describe the turnout as "high."[1]

In addition to voting for people for public office, Americans also participate in other types of elections, including *referenda,* elections in which voters make policy directly by changing laws, constitutions, or charters. This process takes place at the state level under guidelines set by the states. The U.S. Constitution does not contain any provision for a referendum at the national level. Two elections are held at the national level: presidential and congressional.

11-2 Presidential Campaigns and Elections

The presidential contest has two major phases. The first phase is the race for the Democratic and Republican parties' nominations. A candidate cannot reasonably expect to be elected president without first being nominated by one of the two major parties. Most people seeking the presidency are eliminated at this stage. The nomination phase culminates with the national conventions held by the two major parties during the summer of the election year. The second phase of the presidential contest is the general election, in which the party nominees are pitted against each other. Normally, the general election focuses on the Democratic and Republican nominees, but on occasion, as in 1992, a major third-party candidate receives a significant share of the vote. In 2000, the proportion of the vote going to the Green party candidate Ralph Nader was difficult to predict or foresee at various stages of the campaign.

11-2a The Nomination Process

The modern presidential nomination system is a long process that formally begins with the Iowa caucuses and New Hampshire primary in February of an election year and does not end until the party conventions in the summer. Candidates, however, must begin laying the groundwork for a campaign well before the month of February. Some candidates make informal visits to potential voters in the states of Iowa and New Hampshire at least a year or more before the event. Fundraising must start early, and an organization must be put together. Political parties provide minimal help to candidates during this phase. For all intents and purposes, the candidates are on their own. Despite the year or more of preparation and campaigning, most of the declared candidates in each party are eliminated less than a month after the first primary.

Getting Started   One of the more fascinating aspects of politics is observing which potential candidates decide to begin a campaign. Soon after a presidential election has taken place, political pundits begin mentioning people who might be likely candidates for the next presidential election. These political analysts are usually looking for several features in a potential candidate. First, the candidate must have some national or regional stature. Since 1960, four presidents have been state governors (George W. Bush, Clinton, Reagan, and Carter), three were former vice presidents (Johnson, Nixon, and George Bush), and one (Kennedy) was a senator when he ran for president, although several others also had congressional experience earlier in their careers. Of course, Al Gore was vice president when he ran against Texas Governor George W. Bush in 2000. The 2004 election was quite unusual with the Democratic nominees for both president and vice president being members of the U.S. Senate.

Another important consideration is the party of the current president. If the incumbent president is popular, few people from his own party may challenge him, and the best possible challengers from the other party may shy away from the race. Therefore, the incumbent's popularity at the midpoint in his term, after the midterm congressional elections, may be a decisive factor in who will consider a race. The other announced candidates can also influence whether someone will consider a bid for the presidency. Al Gore sought the presidency in 2000 in an unusual situation. The incumbent president, Bill Clinton, enjoyed high job-performance ratings. However, his personal approval ratings were quite

What Americans Think About

Presidential Campaigns

During the excitement of a presidential campaign, you can easily believe that virtually all Americans are emotionally involved in the election. However, you must remember that a substantial segment of society is largely indifferent to both the process and its outcome. According to the 1992, 1996, and 2000 national election studies, substantial proportions of the public were not really interested in the campaign and did not really care who would win the presidency. By 2004, polls showed increasing levels of interest. Certainly, the national election study conducted by the University of Michigan showed this to be the case (see results below). Still, four in ten adult Americans did not exercise their right to vote in the 2004 presidential election.

Campaign Interest

"Some people don't pay much attention to political campaigns. How about you? Would you say that you have been very much interested, somewhat interested, or not much interested in the political campaigns so far this year?"

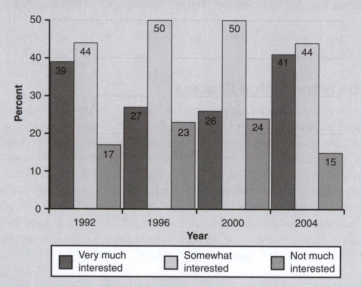

Outcome Interest

"Generally speaking, would you say that you personally care a good deal who wins the presidential election this fall, or that you don't care very much who wins?"

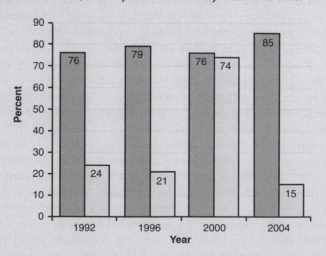

Source: Center for Political Studies, University of Michigan, National Election Studies, 1992, 1996, 2000 and 2004.

low, due in large part to the scandals that plagued him for several years. The Clinton factor caused confusion for the Gore campaign. Gore had to separate himself from Clinton personally but embrace his policy performance.

Several other factors influence the decision to enter the contest. What are the strengths of the candidate? Does the candidate have a good television appearance? Is the candidate a good public speaker? Does the candidate enjoy much name recognition outside her home state? Does the candidate have access to a good base of financial resources? Although resources can be developed over time, a strong position at the beginning improves the candidate's chances. Others, such as party leaders, potential opponents, and the media, must recognize these strengths so that the candidate can make a fast start from the gate.

At the same time, potential candidates have to consider their liabilities. Job performance and political failures are certainly relevant. In addition, has the potential candidate made any major blunders or had any personal problems that would provide the media with an opportunity for a "feeding frenzy" of "attack journalism?"[2]

Thomas Eagleton's psychiatric counseling quickly ended his bid for the vice presidency in 1972. Gary Hart's alleged affair with Donna Rice and Joe Biden's supposed plagiarism of others' speeches became sources of intense, negative media attention in 1988 and effectively ended each candidate's campaign for president. The possibility that these types of failings will end a campaign may have diminished somewhat because of Bill Clinton's survival and eventual triumph in 1992 despite feeding frenzies over an alleged affair, an allegation of pot smoking during his college years, and a charge that he dodged the draft during the Vietnam War. The late revelation that George W. Bush had a decades-old conviction for driving while intoxicated caused a disruption during the final week of the 2000 campaign.

Ultimately, the individual must decide whether to pursue the nomination. The party cannot draft nominees, and the national committee does not have enough central organization or political clout to recruit and nominate a candidate. Potential candidates must launch their own campaigns without much assistance from the party. Often, potential candidates float the possibility of a campaign as a trial balloon to test public reaction, but they must commit early enough in the process to begin raising funds.

Raising Money Raising money for a campaign is the most crucial aspect of a candidate's nomination strategy. It is sometimes called the first primary because the candidate with the most money at the time of the first primary typically wins the nomination. The candidate must begin with a base of money called seed money. **Seed money** is obtained from individuals and groups that are already closely associated with the candidate. For example, a cattle rancher from Texas is likely to rely on other ranchers to provide money early in the process to help jump-start the campaign. Members of Congress and national party leaders have already won other elections, and they usually have an established network of contributors who can help provide seed money. The seed money is used to form an organization, rent office space, buy office supplies, hire staff, contract with professional consultants, conduct surveys, and raise more funds.

> **seed money** Election funds used primarily to identify potential contributors to campaigns.

In particular, seed money is increasingly being used to develop more resources through direct mail. Direct mail fundraising involves buying or developing a list of potential contributors. The campaign then sends out to the targeted individuals as many requests as it can afford. The letter typically makes a dramatic appeal describing the candidate's strengths and explaining how he can correct the country's problems. It then asks for money. Even if a small proportion (2 or 3 percent) of the targeted group responds, the method can pay off well enough that the candidate can begin another mass mailing. This process can continue for some time. The candidate is also likely to go back to previous contributors after some time has passed. Millions of dollars can be raised in this fashion.

Candidates rely on other methods too. Fundraising events—such as thousand-dollar-a-plate dinners, cocktail parties, and celebrity galas—can be helpful, as can direct appeals after a speech by the candidate or at a reception for the candidate. The candidates can also use donations from interest groups, but it is important to note that political action committees (PACs) are not as important in presidential campaigns as they are in congressional campaigns. Candidates have also used paid advertising to ask potential donors to send in contributions. In the 1992 Democratic nomination process, Jerry Brown used an 800 number to bring in donations. George W. Bush raised in excess of $100 million for his successful bid for the presidency in 2000. His early success clearly discouraged many potentially strong opponents. For example, Elizabeth Dole pulled out of the race early while citing the difficulty of raising enough money.

By 2004 the newest method of money raising, the Internet, had matured to the point that one candidate, Howard Dean, used it to tremendous advantage to have by far the best funded primary campaign among those seeking the Democratic party presidential nomination. Websites such as MoveOn.org likewise helped raised substantial sums of money for John Kerry, the eventual nominee.

Overall, fundraising is the single most important activity for a presidential candidate in the modern era. The adage that it takes money to make money certainly applies to the need for seed money in a campaign. To do well in the early contests, the candidate must have enough money to hire a staff and pay for advertising. Early success can then be translated into momentum that will generate more press coverage and increase the number of people willing to contribute to the campaign. Because the government's public funding program matches individual contributions up to $250, a large number of donations in that category can be quite rewarding when the check from the government arrives after each new nomination contest.

Putting Together a Staff   The campaign staff includes four main groups. At the top are the candidate's closest advisers. They may be family members, personal friends, business associates, or previous campaign supporters. Often, these advisers are not paid, but some may be. They are usually part of the candidate's team from the beginning.

Second, modern presidential campaigns rely heavily on paid **consultants,** who include media relations experts, pollsters, advertising specialists, campaign strategists, and fundraising experts. These professionals have a particular expertise that they make available to different candidates in all kinds of elections. One of the first competitions is to see which candidate hires the best team of consultants. Because the candidate with the most money can pay for the best help and the best consultants want to continue their image of being winners, the reputation of the consultant team can serve as an early indicator of which candidate has the best chance of winning.

The other two groups involved in the campaign are the paid campaign staff and the volunteers. Though candidates increasingly rely on professional consultants for guidance at the highest levels, an extensive network of paid staffers still conducts much of the campaign's organizational tasks. The number of paid staffers may be quite small during the early stages of the campaign, and many of the workers travel from state to state as the primaries and caucuses take place. The volunteers are more likely to work for the local branch of the campaign during the period before their own state's primary or caucus. After the caucus or primary, the local office quickly goes dormant.

The Use of Polls   One of the first steps taken by a campaign is to assess the candidate's popularity and name recognition. Surveys are used to see what kinds of voters are aware of the candidate. They also examine what issues appeal to different voters. Typically, pollsters divide the population into groups according to whether they will participate in the nomination process and how likely they are to vote. This analysis can be used to determine which voters should be targeted by the candidate, what types of messages should be used in communicating with certain groups, what forms of media time should be purchased, and which opponents are most likely to provide the toughest competition. Most campaigns take several early polls to determine the viability of the candidate and to map strategy. Then, throughout the campaign, **tracking polls** are used to see how well the candidate performs over time and with different messages. Finally, as a primary or caucus approaches and the polls provide an idea of how well the candidate will do, the campaign begins **spin control** on the **expectations game.** Through spin control, the candidate's aides try to con-

---

▶ **consultants** Professionals who provide guidance to political candidates regarding such activities as polling, media relations, advertising, campaign strategies, and fundraising.

▶ **tracking polls** Technique employed to gauge how well political candidates perform over time.

▶ **spin control** An attempt by political candidates and their consultants to control the messages that the media communicate to the voters.

▶ **expectations game** The process in which political experts and the media establish who they think will win in a particular election.

trol the message that the media communicate to the voters. The expectations game is a matter of perception. Before a primary, political experts and the media predict how well the candidates will do, and a candidate who wins by a narrow margin may be characterized as a loser for failing to do as well as expected. Consequently, spin control is used to reduce expectations so that the media will positively report the results, whatever they are.

By 2000, the number of tracking polls had reached record levels. Each major network regularly released results of the horse race between the candidates, and each candidate relied on his own, more detailed surveys. The Bush campaign "leaked" internal numbers showing him with a lead in key states and close in others thought to be strong for Gore. Subsequently, Bush spent critical campaign time in California, and Gore campaigned hard in the critical state of Florida, where most independent polls showed a dead heat. Pundits questioned the wisdom of Bush's strategy, which appeared to be an effort to create a climate of impending victory. The later easy victory for Gore in California, along with other results, cast doubt on Bush's numbers. After the campaign was over, it appeared that Bush's strategy did not work. The national media polls had created the impression that Gore had pulled to a virtual dead heat. Meanwhile, Gore concentrated his efforts in an all-night blitz that ended in Tampa, Florida.

Building Momentum The first major event of the nomination process is the **Iowa caucus** (see Figure 11-1). Consequently, in most presidential election years, potential candidates practically live in Iowa. Because many candidates begin canvassing the state months before the caucus, active party members in the state have an excellent opportunity of meeting at least one candidate. Until the last few weeks before the caucus, candidates rely mainly on personal appearances as the main method of contacting voters. Because Iowa is the first test of the political viability of the candidates, the results can be important. A poor showing can eliminate a candidate from serious consideration. The expectations game depends largely on where the candidates are from and their name recognition. Generally, the established front-runner and any candidates from nearby states are expected to do better than others. In 1992, Senator Tom Harkin from Iowa was in the race, so the Democratic results were considered less important than usual. Harkin was expected to win a majority of votes, and he did. In 2000, the Republican John McCain made a controversial decision to skip the

> **Iowa caucus** The first major event of the presidential nomination process in which party members in Iowa meet to select delegates to the national party conventions.

Figure 11-1
Timetable to Election Day

Step 1:

The Iowa caucus is the first big test for candidates, and both the probable front-runners and less likely candidates spend much time "working" the state.

Step 2:

New Hampshire's early primary has been seen as a predictor for many elections, so after the Iowa caucuses are over, candidates head for New England.

Step 3:

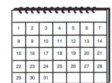

The next big date for potential presidential nominees is Super Tuesday, the second Tuesday in March. States in the South hold their primaries on this one day to strengthen the role of the South in the electoral process. By now the field of candidates has been narrowed by the contests in Iowa and New Hampshire, and only the best-funded and most-supported go on from here.

Step 4:

The Illinois, Michigan, and New York primaries fall after Super Tuesday, and candidates who have survived scramble for the large numbers of delegates from these states.

Step 5:

At the party conventions, nominees for president and vice-president are made, party platforms are established, and the gathering resembles a week-long infomercial pitching the surviving candidate and his campaign theme.

Iowa caucuses. McCain did not feel that he had the resources to mount a credible campaign in Iowa. This break with conventional wisdom later worked to McCain's advantage because he remained a viable candidate in later primaries.

The second major test is the **New Hampshire primary.** Its results may be more important than the Iowa caucus because it is a primary with more citizens participating. Usually held a week after the Iowa caucuses, the primary also receives tremendous media coverage. A dismal performance in both events effectively ends the chances of almost all candidates. Between 1972 and 1996, every Republican winner in the New Hampshire primary had gone on to win the party's nomination. However, in 2000, the ultimate winner, George W. Bush, lost to John McCain in New Hampshire. Bush's advantages in organization and money, though, ultimately overcame the McCain effort in New Hampshire. Nonetheless, McCain was able to extend the race with far fewer resources than Bush largely on the strength of the free media exposure that came with a New Hampshire victory.

Although the Democrats have had more exceptions, five of the last seven New Hampshire winners, including John Kerry in 2004, have gone on to win the nomination. Jimmy Carter's victory in 1976, when many analysts saw him as a long shot, gave his campaign tremendous momentum that eventually led to the Democratic nomination. If a candidate does not win, he must perform better than was expected by the political experts. Winning the expectations game can occasionally be enough for a candidate. Bill Clinton, for example, did not win in either Iowa or New Hampshire in 1992, but he won the expectations game. Early in the 2000 campaign, many people had thought that the challenger Bill Bradley had a good chance of defeating Gore in New Hampshire. Bradley was well known and respected in the region after having served as senator from New Jersey. However, he failed to score many points during his early debates with Gore and failed to mount a serious challenge to the incumbent vice president.

Narrowing the Field   Almost immediately after the New Hampshire primary, the candidates experience the effect of how well they performed. If they win in either state or beat the expectations game, they may receive a bounce in the national polls. More importantly, candidates with momentum can garner more contributions to keep their campaigns afloat. Contributors like to see that they are not wasting their money on a loser, so money flows toward the front-runners. The media also begin to focus attention on the candidates who appear to have a chance to win the nomination. Of the candidates chasing the front-runners, only the more controversial candidates, such as Jerry Brown in 1992 or Jesse Jackson in 1984 and 1988, continue to receive significant media attention. Several small states have caucuses and primaries in the week or so after the New Hampshire primary, and these events allow some previous losers to shine more brightly or front-runners to tighten their grip on the lead, but most of the attention then turns to Super Tuesday.

Super Tuesday   Super Tuesday is the second Tuesday in March. With a large number of delegates at stake on a single day, it was designed to be the most pivotal event in the nomination process. The original purpose of holding so many primaries on one day was to make the South more important in the Democratic nomination process, and Super Tuesday is generally seen as an excellent opportunity for a more conservative or moderate Democrat, such as Bill Clinton in 1992, to emerge with a large number of delegates. Typically, the race in each party is narrowed down to either one or two candidates after Super Tuesday. Because the large population of African-American voters in the South is mostly Democrats, it also rewards a candidate who appeals to those voters, such as Jesse Jackson in 1988 or Bill Clinton in 1992. In 2000, however, Super Tuesday was not so important. Al Gore had already locked up the race for the Democrats, and John McCain did not have the resources to contest many primaries. In 2004, Super Tuesday was again decisive, as John Edwards withdrew from the race after John Kerry all but locked up the nomination by winning nine of the ten primaries held on that day.

> ▶ **New Hampshire primary**
> The first primary in the presidential nomination process.

The Home Stretch   Shortly after Super Tuesday come the primaries in three large states with hundreds of delegates available: Illinois, Michigan, and New York. Because Super Tuesday is so crucial, most candidates have spent almost all their financial resources on advertising and campaigning in those states. After Super Tuesday, only the front-runners are generally able to replenish their campaign funds quickly. Consequently, even though hundreds of delegates are still at stake, the challengers have difficulty competing evenly with the front-runner in each party. Many challengers may have formally withdrawn by this point, and the rest are likely to be strapped for cash. Few second-place campaigns since 1972 have been able to continue after the New York primary in a seriously competitive mode. Even though California has the most delegates available in both parties, it has rarely had an effect on the nomination since 1972 because its primary comes at the end of the nomination season. Generally, the front-runner attempts to avoid any major embarrassments in the final few contests and begins to plan for the convention. Although a competitive nomination contest through the last few weeks is possible, one has not taken place recently.

The Convention: Culmination of the Nomination Process   At a national convention held during July or August, each party nominates its candidates for president and vice president. The conventions also determine the party platforms in addition to the rules by which the parties will govern themselves for the next four years. Both parties use majority rule among the delegates to make most decisions, including the selection of the nominee. Theoretically, with more than two candidates, a number of ballots could be needed before one candidate gets a majority. Indeed, in the past, numerous ballots were often required before the convention settled on a nominee. This multiple balloting made for a great deal of excitement and intrigue at the convention. But, in the modern era, the majority of delegates have already been pledged to vote for a particular candidate before the convention. No convention since 1968 has featured a wide-open contest that created any suspense. Because the eventual nominee controls the majority needed to win before the convention, the most important function of the convention is to provide the party with a tremendous advertising opportunity. The government provides the financing for the convention for both the major parties, and the major networks provide hours of free prime-time coverage.

As the party displays how it has rallied around the candidate, the convention can provide a significant public opinion boost to the party's nominee. That was apparently the case for Michael Dukakis in 1988, but the "bump" was short-lived and did not carry him through the election. In 1992, on the other hand, Bill Clinton's campaign orchestrated the convention to serve as a public relations coup that greatly boosted his public prestige and gave him considerable momentum heading into the general election contest. In 2004, support for incumbent president George W. Bush surged after the Republican convention, and Bush was able to sustain this momentum through the November election.

11-2b The General Election Campaign

The nomination process eliminates almost all the serious presidential candidates. Few third-party or independent candidates have had much of an effect on the general election (Ross Perot in 1992 was a notable exception), so the race generally comes down to the Democratic and Republican nominees. The acceptance speech by each candidate at the national party convention serves as the first official act of the general election campaign. This speech highlights the issues that the nominee intends to focus on throughout the campaign, communicates the candidate's vision for the country, and attempts to bring together the various elements of the party again after the nomination battles. Typically, the Democrats have held their convention first, and the Republicans have stayed out of the limelight during this time. The Republicans hold their convention later in the summer, and the Democrats let the Republicans take center stage during this time. Late August is regarded as the last opportunity for each campaign to plan its general election strategy. Labor Day weekend marks the beginning of an exhaustive fall campaign.

The Electoral Environment The political environment influences how the candidates prepare for the campaign. First, is the president running for reelection, or are both candidates hoping to fill an open seat? The incumbent president has the power of the entire administration at his disposal to influence voters, but he also has a record that must be defended. Generally, incumbents have done well. Sixteen incumbents have won reelection, whereas Bill Clinton was only the tenth challenger to beat an incumbent president.

The performance of the current administration is also important. Citizens consider the health of the economy, whether any scandals have taken place, and how well the president has protected national security. The incumbent president or the nominee of the incumbent president's party is likely to be held accountable by the voters for the economy, the ethical and moral conduct of the administration, and the maintenance of peace and security.

Another concern is the degree to which the president's party has been fractured. Because parties are loose coalitions of diverse factions with differing ideologies and issue positions, a party can easily experience disunity. Depending on how the dissatisfaction manifests itself, it can be devastating for the party's nominee in the general election. The causes of the split may be many. The nomination battle may have pitted one side against another. A particularly divisive issue may have become more salient. Poor performance by an incumbent president may have caused some to become dissatisfied. Or, personality problems between two individual party leaders may be at the source of a party break.

A party fracture can lead to three possible results. First, party supporters may abandon the party and vote for the opponent. For example, southern Democrats, who had supported the party since the Civil War, began voting for Republican presidential candidates in 1964 after the Johnson administration passed civil rights legislation and proposed further initiatives in that area. Second, voters may simply decide not to vote in a particular election. For example, the Democratic candidate Michael Dukakis' handling of Jesse Jackson in the 1988 campaign frustrated many African Americans. Although it is hard to determine how many voters decided not to vote as a protest, it is apparent that few African Americans chose to switch parties to vote for the Republican George Bush.

Third, a splinter group from a party may break off after the nomination process and support a candidate other than the original party nominee. For example, after having served as a Republican president from 1901 to 1909, Teddy Roosevelt became frustrated with the Republican nominee, William Howard Taft, in 1912. Consequently, Roosevelt decided to form a third party, the Bull Moose party, which was able to capture 27 percent of the vote. Because most of Roosevelt's supporters were Republicans, he took more voters away from Taft than from the Democratic nominee, Woodrow Wilson, who won the election. Many would argue that Ross Perot served a similar function in 1992. Though Perot was not as closely identified with the Republican party as Roosevelt had been in 1912, Perot's mostly conservative ideas tended to appeal more to Republican identifiers and independents (who had voted for Bush in large numbers in 1988) than Democratic supporters. The result was that the Republican George Bush received ten million fewer votes in 1992 than he had in 1988 and lost the election.

After these types of factors are taken into consideration, a campaign must consider several questions. First, what strategy will it use for campaigning in the states? Second, how can its financial resources best be used? Third, how can the campaign influence the image of the candidate that is presented in paid advertising and in the news? Finally, what issues are going to be most effective, and what positions should the candidate take on those issues?

State-by-State Strategies Because of the time and energy required to visit every state during the campaign, few modern campaigns send a candidate to every state. Instead, the campaigns target certain states for the vast portion of personal attention by the candidate, his/her running mate, and their families. Two factors influence the choice of states to be visited and the number of trips to each one. First, how many electoral votes does the state have? Because the electoral college reflects the number of people in a state, the most populous states have the most electoral votes. For example, California has 55 electoral votes; New York, 31; Texas, 34; and Florida, 27. Meanwhile, Alaska, the District of Columbia, Montana, North Dakota, South Dakota, Vermont, and Wyoming have only 3 electoral votes apiece. Considering that only 270 votes are needed to win in the electoral college, a candidate who takes just the four most populous states (with 142 votes) would have more than half the votes necessary for victory. Consequently, both candidates tend to devote a large share of their resources to the ten largest states.

Second, what is the likelihood of winning a given state? Each party carefully scrutinizes the past results of presidential, congressional, and gubernatorial elections to determine whether a state is a likely win, a potential win, or a likely loss. For example, Arizona, Kansas, and Utah have been conservative stalwarts for decades. Few Democratic presidential candidates would consider any of them a potential target for a win. On the other side, the District of Columbia, Massachusetts, and Minnesota have been steady supporters of the Democrats for decades. Though neither side completely writes off a state, no candidate wants to waste valuable resources on a lost cause. The result is that populous states receive much attention, but an average-size state may also garner attention if it is considered competitive.

The formulation of a state-by-state campaign strategy can be complicated by the presence of a strong third-party candidate, such as Ross Perot in 1992. In a two-way race, each candidate knows the strengths of the other, and both know that a vote gained is a loss for the other side. A third actor complicates the situation by allowing disgruntled members of the opposite party to choose someone else. Attacking just one opponent may not be enough. States assigned to the definite loss category could even become victories. For example, in 1992 Clinton was able to capture nine states that had voted Republican in at least the past six presidential elections. It is difficult to attribute all this showing to Perot's presence in the race, but it is interesting to note that Perot received a greater-than-average share (at least 20 percent) of the vote in six of the nine states.

In 2004, it was clear from the polling data which states would be the "battlegrounds" going into the general election. Thus, it was no surprise that both President Bush and his challenger, Senator John Kerry, spent most of their time on the campaign trail in Florida, Ohio, Pennsylvania, Michigan, Wisconsin, and a handful of other states. Ultimately, the 2004 election came down to Ohio, which opted for President Bush by a very narrow margin. The fact that the GOP put so much effort into GOTV (get out the vote) in Ohio was one of the reasons Bush was able to carry the state. The Democrats were also very successful in their GOTV efforts in Ohio. John Kerry received more votes in Ohio than either Al Gore or George Bush had received in 2000. Still, it was not enough.

Financing the General Election Campaign   Before the 1976 election, candidates could spend as much money as they could raise. From 1860 through the election of 1972, the winner of the election outspent the loser twenty-one of the twenty-nine times.[3] Fundraising was dominated by "fat cat" contributors who could give hundreds of thousands or even millions of dollars. Solicitors, or individuals with excellent personal connections that helped them raise millions, were vital to any presidential campaign.

A new era of campaign financing began in the 1970s. In a series of three major pieces of legislation, Congress created a new public funding system for presidential elections. The new system, which took effect for the 1976 election, provides candidates with millions of dollars of public funds during the general election; in exchange, the candidate must agree to forgo contributions from any other sources during the general election. In 1992, Clinton and Bush each received $56 million in public funds for the general election. This money goes directly to the candidate's campaign committee to spend on travel, advertising, staff salaries, consultant fees, and other necessary items. Advertising usually takes the largest share of the resources. The spending limit has two exceptions. First, the candidate's party can spend more than $10 million on behalf of the candidate during the election (or two cents per American of voting age). Second, the candidate can receive private donations to offset certain legal and accounting expenses that do not count against the limit.

Otherwise, the candidate cannot receive any money from PACs, individuals, or even family members during the general election campaign.

Candidates are not required to accept the public money. If they do not, they can spend as much money as they can raise. They still must abide by the $1,000 limit on individual contributions and the $5,000 limit on PAC contributions, but they can spend as much of their own money as they want. Ross Perot, for example, did not attempt to qualify for public funding in 1992 and spent tens of millions of dollars from his own resources to pay for his campaign.

Perot's case also illustrates another key feature of the public funding laws. Both major parties automatically qualify for public funding on the basis of their performance in the preceding election. Third-party and independent candidates, however, do not automatically qualify for funding. To qualify, a candidate must receive at least 5 percent of the total popular vote and be on the ballot in at least ten states. In addition, a third-party candidate receives the money after the election, which makes it rather difficult to run a successful campaign. Even if third-party candidates qualify for public funds, they are eligible for only part of the funding provided to the major-party candidates. After third-party candidates qualify, they become eligible for public funding in the next election.

The campaign laws in effect in 2000 also had two key exceptions. First, there were no limits on soft money. State party committees can raise unlimited funds for the purpose of party-building activities, such as party bumper stickers, get-out-the-vote drives, and party mailings. Because the presidential campaign tends to save its precious resources for advertising focused on the candidate rather than on the party in general, the law is designed to enhance the parties. In practice, however, it has become a loophole in the campaign finance regulations. The candidate and the national party committee actively seek unlimited contributions from individuals, which are then earmarked for the state parties. For example, in both 1988 and 1992, George Bush appeared at dinners where large contributors received more prestigious seats and were able to have their picture taken with the president. Many contributions were in the hundreds of thousands of dollars. Though this type of money is not under the direct control of the presidential candidate, it can be used for activities that generally help the party but also benefit the candidate.

Political action committees also enjoyed a loophole in the election laws. PACs could not donate money to a presidential candidate during the general election, but they could spend as much as they wanted on independent expenditures. Thus, a PAC could spend millions of dollars on advertising that attacked or supported a candidate as long as the PAC did not work with the campaign in developing the advertising. For example, in 1988, the National Security PAC spent more than $7 million on negative advertisements attacking the Democrat Michael Dukakis; among the ads was the Willie Horton advertisement, which has been described as the low point in one of the nastiest presidential campaigns ever. In this case, Bush benefited from the advertising, but was able to avoid responsibility for it because of the legal separation between his campaign committee and the PAC.

The campaign finance reforms of the 1970s changed presidential elections in four ways. First, the campaigns operated on more equal financial footing. Because Republicans had traditionally appealed to wealthier individuals, they usually enjoyed financial advantages over the Democrats until 1976. On the other hand, the increasing use of soft money had allowed the old inequality to reappear to some extent. The Republicans were the first to exploit the loophole, and they maintained sizable advantages over the Democrats in soft money until the 1992 election. In 1984, Reagan received $16 million to Mondale's $1 million, but Clinton and Bush were more equal in 1992. By the 2000 election, the parties had reached virtual parity in spending.

Second, in the first elections under the new laws, spending was reduced. The soft money loopholes, however, have allowed campaign spending to rise faster than the rate of inflation. Third, the limits on individual contributions severely constrained the "fat cat" contributors and initially somewhat reduced their role. The trend toward soft money, though, has allowed the fat cats to become major players again. Finally, the limits on spending have forced candidates to use campaign funds more carefully. Consequently, candidates are much more likely to focus their efforts on their own campaigns rather than on the party. Again, soft money has mitigated this effect by forcing the national committees to work with the state parties to raise and spend soft money. Thus, on one hand, the new restrictions have tended to separate the presidential campaign from the campaigns of other party members, including members of Congress and state officials; on the other hand, soft money has had the effect of increasing party cooperation.

Campaign Finance Reform of 2002   In May 2002, Congress passed, and President Bush signed, major campaign finance legislation. Campaign finance reform appeared on the national agenda during the late 1900s and throughout the nomination process and, to some extent, the general election in the 2000 presidential elections. Senator John McCain of Arizona mounted a strong challenge to the front-runner George W. Bush during the primaries. This challenge was largely built around McCain's commitment to campaign finance reform—in particular, around the bill he had cosponsored with Democratic Senator Feingold, of Wisconsin. Bush opposed the McCain–Feingold legislation. During the campaign, the issue again arose, with Al Gore favoring the McCain–Feingold bill.

President Bush took office in January, 2001, still expressing grave doubts about his old nemesis John McCain's finance reform package. The Republican House leadership helped delay consideration of the bill until 2002, when, following indications that President Bush would not veto the legislation, the House followed the Senate in passing legislation to restructure the regulation of contributions to candidates in federal elections.

The finance legislation signed into law in 2002 targets the use of soft money in campaigns. The soft-money process allows moneyed interests a mechanism for circumventing the limits on contributions by supposedly allowing unlimited contributions to "party building" activities. The legislation does increase the amount of hard money that can be contributed directly to candidates and to the party's local and national committees. However, its most controversial element is that it limits the ability of corporations and labor unions to run election ads for specific candidates during the last portion of campaigns. Many people speculated that the Supreme Court might invalidate this restriction on what many regard to be protected political speech, but that proved not to be the case.[4]

The 527s   In the wake of the McCain–Feingold campaign finance reform law, a new species of political creature evolved—the *527 group,* so called because they are governed by Section 527 of the federal tax code. Because they were not specifically covered by McCain–Feingold, 527s came to serve as vehicles for independent expenditures on behalf of candidates. Although they cannot endorse candidates, they render assistance by attacking opponents. These attacks are legal as long as there is no coordination between the group and a political campaign organization.

Two such groups played a prominent role in the 2004 presidential campaign. A liberal 527 known as MoveOn.org received a $5 million contribution from billionaire George Soros and proceeded to run television ads that were extremely critical of President Bush. On the other side of the fence, the Swift Boat Veterans for Truth attacked John Kerry's record of service in Vietnam and subsequent antiwar activities. Both MoveOn.org and the Swift Boat Veterans leveled charges against President Bush and Senator Kerry, respectively, that many people (including the candidates themselves) considered to be scurrilous and irresponsible. Bush, Kerry, Senator John McCain, and political notables across the land called for legal action to rein in these independent groups. But others argued that what these groups were doing was nothing more than to exercise their First Amendment rights, albeit in a way that many Americans found offensive.

The National Media Campaign   Two elements are essential in controlling the image of the candidate that is conveyed to the voting public. First, the campaign must manage the news media. Second, the campaign must develop a paid advertising schedule that allows the candidate to reveal personal strengths, attack the opponent's weaknesses, focus on a few issues, and provide a general theme of what the candidacy is all about.

Today, a successful campaign requires a skilled team of consultants who assist the candidate in managing the media. Because the mass media—including the television and radio networks, national newsmagazines, and major newspapers—send reporters and photojournalists to all campaign stops of both major candidates, the candidates can receive hours of free advertising throughout the campaign. In addition to being free, this advertising appears to be more unbiased and credible to the voters than paid advertising.

The Nixon campaign of 1968 was perhaps the first to effectively utilize media and advertising experts to manage the news. Now campaigns devote daily attention to the media. The candidate's schedule is designed so that the campaign stops on a given day are coordinated to develop a theme. The campaign staff carefully plans the events so that each one provides a suitable visual setting to reinforce the theme. For example, a factory might serve as the backdrop for a speech on the economy, and an aircraft carrier would be used for a defense policy theme. Because the campaign even controls the angle and position of the media's cameras at these types of events, any pictures that appear in the news present the image the campaign wants the viewer to see.

▶ **sound bite** A short media clip that provides a catchy phrase.

A major criticism of the modern media campaign is that it encourages simple messages that can be easily edited by television news producers. As a result, voters receive only a sound bite. A **sound bite** is a short clip, maybe ten to fifteen seconds long, that consists of a catchy phrase (such as "Read my lips: No new taxes") conveying a simple message. Candidates are not rewarded for providing the details of a complex policy or explaining why they think changes are necessary. A sentence or two attacking the opponent or a witty one-liner is more likely to make the news. Often, an attack is launched late in the afternoon so that it is aired on the evening network news and the opponent does not have time to respond. Though the strategic advantage of this type of move cannot be questioned, it falls somewhat short of the democratic ideal of an exchange of ideas that enables voters to make real choices between candidates.

Radio advertising has been around since Franklin D. Roosevelt's campaigns in the 1930s, and television has been a part of presidential campaigns since Eisenhower's first election in 1952. Since the enactment of the campaign finance legislation, paid advertising has become the main campaign tool, taking up most of the candidates' public funding. Typically, candidates spend as much as 90 percent of the public funds for television advertising, and as much as half of that amount may be saved for the last month or so of the campaign.

Advertising campaigns have increasingly adopted the best techniques Madison Avenue has to offer. Candidates work extensively with public speaking experts, acting professionals, makeup experts, hair stylists, and advertising consultants. Typically thirty seconds long, the advertisements carefully blend music and visually stimulating video clips with a simple theme. Expansive discussions of policy are avoided. Though the thirty-second ad provides slightly more time than the average sound bite, the candidate must still keep the message simple and focus on one theme. Strong campaigns coordinate the images and messages of the sound bites and the paid advertising.

Campaign consultants have developed a variety of techniques to assess how a message is being received by the public. The consultants usually test the potential effect of an ad before airing it by showing it to a group of viewers who are similar to the voters the campaigns are hoping to reach. After an ad has been shown on television, the consultants use surveys to assess its effect. Early in the campaign, the consultants try to find the "hot button" issues that are important to voters and develop the image and message that work well for the candidate. In the last weeks of the campaign, when there is little time for careful preparation, the consultants can move quickly with their advertising to respond to the opponent or even the media.

The Role of Issues in the Campaign   Though media campaigns tend to focus on personality and symbolism, issues still matter. Most voters are at least somewhat interested in a candidate's views on the issues, though they tend to react negatively to candidates who take extreme positions. Generally speaking, American political culture has fostered a preference for more moderate candidates than is the case in most other democracies. Americans have rejected the more extreme political ideologies, such as communism and fascism, and tend to elect moderate members of the two moderate parties that dominate American elections. Furthermore, from a strategic standpoint, if a candidate needs a majority to win (as is the case in the usual two-candidate election), the middle ground is most advantageous. With only two candidates, if candidate A places herself at the exact center of the ideological mainstream, her opponent is forced to choose a position to the left or right of center. After the opponent does so, all the voters on the other side (half the voters) plus the middle voter will choose candidate A. Candidate A will now have 50 percent plus one vote, the amount needed to win.

During the nomination process, a candidate has to please the voters in his party. Because the participants in primaries and, especially, caucuses tend to be more extreme than the average voter, candidates must often take more extreme positions during the nomination process. After the nomination is won, however, the candidate must attempt to appear more moderate to have a chance to win. Often, a candidate focuses on different issues in the nomination battle and the general election campaign. Occasionally, a candidate is caught by an opponent or the media in an attempt to soften or change a position. Becoming more moderate without appearing to "flip-flop" on the issues or seeming too "slick" can be difficult. Yet a candidate who does not appear moderate may be branded as an extremist. For example, in 1964, the Democrat Lyndon Johnson successfully portrayed the Republican Barry Goldwater as an extremist hell-bent on using nuclear weapons against the Soviet Union. In 1988, the Republican George Bush made Michael Dukakis look unpatriotic by attacking him for opposing a policy that would require children in the public schools to recite the pledge of allegiance.

Presidential Debates   The nationally televised debates that have become common in the past few elections provide a forum for greater depth than is possible in sound bites and thirty-second ads. Although debates are not required, a tradition has developed that the two major candidates should participate. One problem, however, is that no neutral organization exists that both parties will allow to conduct debates. Consequently, the rules, time, date, place, and number of debates are determined solely by negotiations between the two candidates' organizations. Typically, the front-runner is somewhat concerned about giving the opponent too many opportunities. Therefore, the incumbent, usually a Republican over the past thirty years, has been reluctant to take on the challenger in debates. Because he was behind in the polls, George H.W. Bush was the exception in 1992. He agreed to three presidential debates and one vice presidential debate that included both major-party candidates and Ross Perot's ticket. In 2000, candidate George W. Bush was eager to debate Vice President Gore. In 2004, incumbent President Bush was not so eager to debate John Kerry. Given Bush's lackluster performance in the three debates that did take place in 2004, the president's reluctance was easy to understand.

Though personality and style are important, the debates also provide a forum in which candidates can present their views on the issues. Winning candidates tend to be more moderate, or at least appear more moderate to a larger number of voters, than losing candidates. Though issues may not be the main focus of the modern American campaign, the positions that candidates take affect their chances of victory, and the art of position-taking is an important part of developing a winning image.

The three presidential debates between Al Gore and George W. Bush played a pivotal role in the 2000 elections. Before the debates, Gore had built a formidable lead in the polls, and most observers figured that his command of detail and experience in debate would serve him well against Bush, who lacked substantial debate experience or command of the details of policy. Bush's main advantage was that he faced minimal expectations. At the end of the three debates, most observers believed that Bush had helped himself considerably, not so much by displaying competence or expertise, but by force of personality, much like Ronald Reagan in the 1980s. Certainly, the narrowing gap in the polls and the extremely close vote on Election Day strongly suggest that the debates helped Bush.

In 2004, the situation was reversed. By most accounts, Senator John Kerry outperformed President Bush in the three debates between them. Even President Bush's supporters expressed dismay at how poorly he had performed, especially in the first debate. Still, Kerry's strong performance in the debates was not enough to secure victory in the November election.

11-2c The Electoral College Vote

On the first Tuesday in November, voters go to the polls to cast their votes for the presidential candidate of their choice. If these voters look carefully at the ballot, they notice that they are not voting directly for candidates for president. Rather, voters in each state are asked to choose a slate of individuals who will represent their state in the electoral college (see Figure 11-2). The electoral college is composed of electors who are chosen by each state. The method of choosing electors is determined by each state's legislature. Until 1800, in ten of the fifteen states, electors were chosen by state legislatures rather than elected directly by the people. By 1832, only South Carolina did not use a direct election. Since 1864, all states have chosen electors by direct elections. Almost all states (except Maine and Nebraska) use a winner-take-all system to determine the results. Under a winner-take-all system, all the electors from a state are awarded to the party that receives the most popular votes in the state. If two million persons vote for candidate X and two million and one voters choose candidate Y, candidate Y wins all the electoral votes from that state. Note that a majority of votes (50 percent plus one vote) is not needed to win. A plurality, or the most votes, is all that is necessary. Consequently, a close race in the popular vote may translate into a large margin of victory in the electoral college.

The number of electors from each state is equal to the number of its members of Congress. If a state has four House members and two senators, for example, it receives six electors. (The electors are not the same individuals as the congressional delegation, however.) Because the Congress consists of 435 House members and 100 senators, and the District of Columbia receives three electors, the electoral college was composed of 538 electors in 2004.

Figure 11-2
Electoral Votes per State for the 2004 Election

The electoral college system worked as planned in the first two presidential elections. As you have seen, however, the emergence of political parties, which had apparently not been envisioned by the Framers of the Constitution, revealed flaws in the system. After the contentious election of 1800, in which both Thomas Jefferson and his running mate, Aaron Burr, received the same number of votes in the electoral college, thereby throwing the election into the House of Representatives, Congress adopted the Twelfth Amendment, requiring electors to vote separately for president and vice president. If a presidential candidate does not receive a majority (270 votes now equals 50 percent plus 1 of the 538 electors) in the electoral college, the decision goes to the House, where each state delegation has one vote in choosing from the top three finishers. If a vice presidential candidate does not receive a majority of electoral votes, the Senate selects the vice president from the top two finishers.

On several occasions, the electoral college has either thwarted the national public's preference for a candidate, come perilously close to negating the outcome of the popular election, or has sent the election to the House of Representatives. The crucial election of 1860, which sent Abraham Lincoln to the White House and plunged the country into the Civil War, was one of these situations. The Democrats were divided over the issue of slavery. Consequently, four major candidates ran for president: Lincoln for the Republicans, Stephen Douglas for the main wing of the Democrats, John Breckenridge for a southern offshoot of the Democratic party, and John Bell for the Constitutional Union party, which drew its support from southerners committed to the preservation of the Union. Lincoln received less than 40 percent of the popular vote, but he carried eighteen northern states that enabled him to win the electoral college by twenty-eight votes. This pivotal election in our history was decided by only 25,000 popular votes. Lincoln won by 25,000 votes in New York, and its electors gave him a majority in the electoral college.

The election of 1876 also tested the limits of the system. The contest was between Rutherford B. Hayes, the Republican, and Samuel Tilden, the Democrat. Tilden had a 3 percent margin over Hayes in the popular vote (or 250,000 more votes), but Hayes beat Tilden by one electoral vote. Because the electoral college decides the winner, Hayes became the new president. The manner in which Hayes got that crucial vote was as important as the fact that the popular vote was circumvented by the electoral college. During the election, the Republicans had made massive attempts at voting fraud, and the Democrats had intimidated black voters in three hotly contested races in Florida, South Carolina, and Louisiana; both sides subsequently claimed the electors from those states. A special commission of five senators, five representatives, and five Supreme Court justices was formed to decide who had won. The commission voted along party lines (an 8–7 split in favor of the Republicans) to accept the electoral college votes submitted by Hayes' supporters in the three states. To

Controversy

Should Congress Mandate a National System for Conducting Federal Elections?

In the wake of the vote-counting fiasco that followed the 2000 presidential election, many observers called for an overhaul of the way national elections are administered in this country. Historically, national elections are administered by the states, which in turn rely heavily on local authorities. This system allows for tremendous variance in procedures. The paper ballots used in most Florida counties obviously had serious flaws. But a closer inspection of the administration of elections at the local level reveals numerous deficiencies. Should Congress mandate standardized balloting mechanisms and procedures? Can Congress do it constitutionally? What sorts of standards should be imposed? To what extent should federal officials be involved in the supervision of local elections personnel? What costs would be involved in federalizing the elections process? These are a few of the many questions to ponder when thinking about reform in this area.

Popular Culture and American Politics
Power

In the 1986 film *Power*, Richard Gere plays a political consultant who is in the process of putting together a successful campaign. Consultants are a relatively new phenomenon in American national politics. Although the national parties have their research staffs, individual candidates tend to have specially trained individuals who provide advice on strategy, tactics, and image. These consultants often are involved in more than one campaign. Although they tend to stick to one party, their loyalties are to the person paying their salaries. Their goal is simple: Win the election for that client.

The rise of consultants parallels in many ways the decline in the major parties. Most candidates for high office run their own campaigns. They do not necessarily cooperate with other candidates. Often, they run as party "outsiders." A political consultant in many ways provides the expertise that would otherwise be provided by the party. The candidates commission their own surveys, design their own advertisements, and ultimately present themselves to the voting public. When the contest is over, the consultants move on to other candidates for other offices.

Political consultants bring a tremendous amount of skill to the work. When they are successful, they become celebrities in their own right. Roger Ailes gained widespread recognition for his work on the George Bush campaign against Michael Dukakis in 1988. Likewise, James Carville was quite visible as the guru of the Clinton success over Bush in the following election. His hook was "It's the economy, stupid!" Anyone seeking national office in the United States looks to secure the services of a consultant.

get Congress to accept the commission results, Hayes promised the southern Democrats that he would end Reconstruction, which meant the end of military occupation and the beginning of the end for civil rights in the South.

On two other occasions, the popular vote winner lost in the electoral college. In 1888, Grover Cleveland, the Democratic incumbent, faced Benjamin Harrison, the Republican challenger. Grover Cleveland had a 1 percent lead in the popular vote (a 95,000-vote advantage), but he lost in the electoral college. Slim victories in two states—15,000 votes in New York and 3,000 in Indiana—gave Harrison the electoral college votes he needed to win. Finally, in one of the most controversial outcomes in American history, George W. Bush won the electoral college vote with a margin of two votes (271) but lost the popular vote by more than 300,000 votes to Al Gore.

Although Gore could have won in 2000 if only 500 people in Florida had voted differently, the country had often faced close electoral college calls. On several recent occasions, a small change in the votes in a few states could have thrown the election into the House of Representatives. In 1948, Truman won the election, but a shift of 12,500 votes in California could have prevented him from reaching a majority in the electoral college. Similarly, Kennedy in 1960 could have been denied an electoral college majority if just 9,000 votes had been different in Illinois and Missouri. In 1968, the Republican Richard Nixon received only 43.4 percent of the popular vote, but he garnered 301 electoral votes of 538 possible (56 percent), which was nearly 31 more than he needed to win (270). However, a 55,000-vote shift in New Jersey, New Hampshire, and Missouri would have thrown the election into a Democratically controlled House that might have chosen his Democratic opponent, Hubert Humphrey. In 1976, a switch of 3,687 votes in Hawaii and 5,559 votes in Ohio would have prevented Carter from achieving an electoral college majority.

11-3 Individual Voting Behavior

In any election, a candidate faces two fundamental challenges: to get potential supporters to register to vote, follow the campaign, and heed the candidate's message and to convince voters to make "the right choice." In developing strategies to achieve these goals, campaigns must take into account the forces that underlie the vote decision.

11-3a Party Identification

Party identification, the feeling of attachment that individuals have for a political party, is the major long-term force in American politics.[5] Most people develop party identification early in life, usually through parental influence. Though some people do change the party with which they identify, most keep this identification as a predisposition to vote for a certain party's candidates. For example, a Democrat is most likely to vote for the Democratic candidate in any given election. Other forces, of course, can cause this person to vote for the Republican candidate.

Party identification allows citizens to make sense of politics from a particular point of view. As a result, people do not have to process the vast amount of political information that comes to them in a campaign.[6] For instance, a woman who is committed to the Democratic party because of its stand on organized labor may feel that she does not have to pay close attention to all that the candidates say unless the Democratic candidate takes a different stand on labor issues. Likewise, a man who strongly agrees with Republican tax policy may not feel any need to reconsider his vote on a day-to-day basis.

Party identification tells us more about how people will vote than any other indicator. In any presidential campaign, the candidates must mobilize voters from their own parties. In 1992, on the other hand, 10 percent of Democrats voted for George Bush, and 10 percent of Republicans voted for Bill Clinton. In 2000, 11 percent of Democrats cast ballots for George W. Bush, and only 8 percent of Republicans voted for Al Gore. Likewise, in 2004, more than 90 percent of Republicans voted for President Bush, and more than 90 percent of Democrats voted for John Kerry. Because the electorate has more Democratic identifiers than Republican identifiers, the Republicans must do a better job than the Democrats in keeping their partisans if they want to win a presidential election.

Since the 1960s, the number of independents has steadily increased. This group has been quite instrumental in determining the winner of the presidential elections. In 1992, Bill Clinton won 42 percent of the independent vote, George Bush won 31 percent, and Ross Perot won 27 percent. This was the first time in more than a quarter of a century that the Democrat captured more of the independent vote than the Republican. In 2000, however, Independents again preferred the Republican candidate, albeit by a narrow margin (see Table 11-1). In 2004, Independents were split almost evenly between President Bush and Senator Kerry.

11-3b Issues

In any contested election, the voter is offered a choice between or among candidates. With rare exceptions, these competing candidates support different policies and take different positions on the issues. Moreover, even in cases in which the candidates do not take clear or differing stands on various issues, their party label gives important issue cues to the voter. Nevertheless, the role of issues in arriving at the vote decision is not clear, and political scientists have disagreed over the importance of issues in voting behavior.

Most observers agree that issues have played a major role in recent presidential elections. Ronald Reagan's victory in 1980 was widely viewed as a clear message from the electorate that a change in basic public policy was expected. A majority of voters had lost faith in the ability of the federal government to solve social problems. The electorate seemed to prefer a strong national defense and less government involvement in the economy. Clear differences existed between Reagan and the incumbent Democrat, Jimmy Carter. The electorate perceived these differences and acted accordingly.

Likewise, the 1992 election was widely seen as having been affected by economic issues. In fact, the Clinton campaign staff operated under the motto "It's the economy, stupid!" Issues have played a key role in many other presidential elections also. In 1968, many commentators attributed the success of Republican Richard Nixon to "the social issue,"

TABLE 11-1		Gore	Bush	Nader	Other
Presidential Voting among Various Groups, 2000	Male	42%	53%	3%	2%
	Female	54%	43%	2%	1%
	White	42%	54%	3%	1%
	African American	90%	9%	1%	0%
	Hispanic	62%	35%	2%	1%
	Asian American	55%	39%	4%	2%
	18–29	48%	46%	5%	1%
	30–44	48%	49%	2%	1%
	45–59	48%	49%	2%	1%
	60 and over	51%	47%	2%	0%
	Less than $15K	57%	37%	4%	2%
	$15K–30K	54%	41%	3%	2%
	$30K–50K	49%	48%	2%	1%
	$50K–75K	46%	51%	2%	1%
	$75K–100K	45%	52%	2%	1%
	Over $100K	43%	54%	2%	1%
	Married	44%	53%	2%	1%
	Not married	57%	38%	4%	1%
	Democrat	86%	11%	2%	1%
	Republican	8%	91%	1%	0%

Source: Adapted from exit polls conducted for CNN.

which was a summary of concerns about crime, the sexual revolution, and drug use.[7] The 1996 contest between Clinton and Bob Dole again centered on economic issues. Dole's signature campaign theme, an immediate cut in personal income tax rates, never did resound with the American public.

In 2000, Al Gore and George W. Bush disagreed on a number of domestic policy items. However, in many ways their differences were about details on an agenda with relative agreement on broad strokes. For instance, when Gore proposed a prescription drug benefit under Medicare, Bush responded with his own program. Both candidates put forth proposals for tax reduction. The difference was in the details, and the difference highlighted the historic themes of each candidate's party.

In 2004, the war in Iraq and "values" issues such as same-sex marriage were uppermost on the list of salient issues. Most observers believe that, in the absence of the Iraq war, President Bush would have won reelection handily. There is also good reason to believe that the issue of same-sex marriage, which helped to mobilize conservative Christians, contributed significantly, if not decisively, to President Bush's reelection.

Prospective and Retrospective Issue Voting
Issue voting can take place in two ways. With **retrospective voting,** voters look back at how well a candidate has done. In contrast, with **prospective voting,** voters look forward and predict how each candidate will perform in the future. Obviously, this type of voting is difficult to do, especially given the tendency of politicians to make campaign promises that are hard to keep.

In 1976, the Democratic challenger Jimmy Carter asked voters whether they were better off than they had been four years earlier. Obviously, Carter was asking voters to use retrospective voting to remove his opponent, Gerald Ford, from office. Unfortunately for

issue voting Voting on the basis of the candidates' positions on the policy issues addressed in the campaign.

retrospective voting A method of choosing between candidates in which voters look back and evaluate how the incumbent has performed.

prospective voting A method of choosing between candidates in which voters look forward and predict how the candidates will perform in the future.

President Carter, the challenger Ronald Reagan turned the tables by asking the same question four years later. In each case, the incumbent lost. In both cases, many voters concentrated on the incumbent's performance on economic issues.

On the other hand, a successful incumbent or a candidate closely associated with the incumbent often wants to put the discussion of the issues in retrospective terms. Both Ronald Reagan's 1984 reelection campaign and George Bush's 1988 campaign against Michael Dukakis called for a retrospective evaluation of the Reagan presidency. In 1992, however, President Bush's popularity was low. Not surprisingly, his campaign did not seek to frame the election on a referendum on the president's popularity. Instead, it tried to convince the voters to make a prospective evaluation of his opponent. Bill Clinton's campaign did more than seek a negative evaluation of the Bush presidency. It also sought to create an impression that such issues as health care, deficit reduction, job creation, and welfare reform needed attention that Bush would not provide. The campaign assumed that if Clinton could be successfully portrayed as the person who would address and resolve these problems, he would probably win the election. This strategy proved to be effective.

In 1996, President Clinton ran for reelection with an appeal to retrospective voting based on the success of the economy in the previous four years. Bob Dole was somewhat prospective in his use of a tax cut as his campaign centerpiece. Clearly, voters were not comfortable with changing presidents in the midst of a sound economy. The 2000 election was not quite as cut-and-dried. Vice President Al Gore was expected to make much of the success of the Clinton administration's record. The economy continued to grow over the following four years, and President Clinton's job approval ratings had remained high, even through the impeachment saga. However, Clinton's personal approval ratings were quite low. Gore made a strategic decision to minimize his identification with the Clinton years and made few direct appeals for retrospective voting. Rather, he asked voters to think ahead by proposing a wide range of new programs—most notably, a major entitlement for prescription drugs under the Medicare program.

The 2004 election was to a great extent a referendum on President George W. Bush's performance with respect to the economy, the war in Iraq, and the war on terrorism. Voters choices in that election correlated strongly with their assessments of Bush's performance in these key areas. Of course, those assessments also correlated strongly with party identification. It must be understood that both party loyalty and ideology (discussed in section 11-3c) color people's perceptions of a politician's performance in office. Those who identify strongly with the Democratic party are predisposed to assess negatively the performance of a Republican president. Among weak party identifiers, that predisposition is much less pronounced. Independents, of course, do not have such predispositions based on party affiliation, but their assessments of presidential performance may well be colored by their ideological orientations.

11-3c Ideology

Although voters' evaluations of a particular issue may vary, a citizen's ideology is a more enduring framework that helps her reach voting decisions. An ideology is an abstract view of the political world, with an underlying belief or set of beliefs that ties together various attitudes and opinions. The authors of *The American Voter*, which has become a classic in voting behavior research, found that few Americans could articulate an ideological position on politics.[8] Nevertheless, later research found that most voters could make some use of the liberal-conservative continuum in evaluating issues and candidates. The most educated and sophisticated voters do, in fact, use liberalism and conservatism as devices to order their positions on issues, which in turn influence their voting decisions.[9]

Though few Americans think in ideological terms, most Americans are familiar with ideological labels. By 1988, the Democratic presidential candidate Michael Dukakis, whose policies were certainly liberal, was not comfortable with the liberal label. In many ways, Americans have come to identify with the terms *liberal* and *conservative* in much the same way as they identify with political parties. The terms have taken on symbolic meaning. Many Americans, in fact, react to liberals and conservatives as groups of people and think of themselves as members of one or the other group. In 1988, the Bush campaign was successful in painting Dukakis as a member of a group ("the liberals") that many in the electorate did not like. Although George W. Bush often tried to portray Al Gore as a liberal who favored bigger government, he recognized that the liberal label had lost much of its power. Rather, the 2000 election campaign was framed more in personal and pragmatic than in ideological terms. Still, in 2000, 80 percent of self-identified liberals voted for Al Gore, and 81 percent of self-identified conservatives voted for George W. Bush. In 2004, the campaigns were more openly ideological. In particular, the Bush reelection campaign placed great stress on Senator Kerry's liberal voting record in the Senate. It was not surprising that in the election, 84 percent of conservatives voted for Bush and 85 percent of liberals voted for Kerry.[10]

11-3d Candidate Image

American politics has become increasingly about image. Much of this phenomenon can undoubtedly be attributed to television. A candidate can more easily project an image of what he is about in a thirty-second spot than describe complex policy positions. Many images do successfully embody issue positions, however. One of the more successful television spots used during the 1988 election was the Willie Horton ad. It showed a rather unflattering picture of an African American along with a long line of prisoners entering and leaving prison through a revolving door. The narrator explained that Michael Dukakis had supported weekend passes for some felons, which gave them the opportunity to commit horrible crimes like the rapes and murders that Horton had committed. The ad was widely condemned as appealing to racial prejudices. Nevertheless, for many people, the ad symbolized a wide range of domestic issue positions that came together to form an image of a Democrat who was "soft on crime."

In 2000, the National Association for the Advancement of Colored People (NAACP), which represents a key Democratic constituency, ran a controversial (but highly effective) TV spot linking the Republican George W. Bush to the hate-inspired dragging death of James Byrd, Jr., in Jasper, Texas, in 1998. The ad suggested that George W. Bush was soft on these types of "hate crimes." The ad reflected the prevailing mood in the African-American community, which voted overwhelmingly for Al Gore despite Bush's efforts in building a more "inclusive" Republican party.

In 2004, John Kerry suffered somewhat from an image of being aloof and out of touch with ordinary Americans. The Kerry campaign attempted to counter this by having the candidate go on a widely publicized goose-hunt a few weeks before the election. The image of Senator Kerry, an extremely wealthy liberal Democrat from Boston, dressed in camouflage and toting a shotgun was designed to connect with millions of hunters and gun owners across the country. Unfortunately for the Kerry campaign, the incident merely provided more fodder for the late-night comedians. Candidates must always take care not to be seen as trying to project a spurious image. Even without the assistance of the late-night comics, most voters are not taken in by such charades.

Party Image   **Party image** is the reaction people have toward a political party. Typical party images might be "The Republicans are the party of the rich" or "The Democrats are the tax-and-spend party." The party image is separate from that of the candidate. In the 1950s, party image was a powerful force in determining how Americans voted. The force of these images has faded somewhat as the parties have become less important in American politics. Still, the Republican party suffers somewhat from its white, Anglo-Saxon, Protestant image. The image is slowly changing, however, as Hispanics, Asian Americans, and Catholics are increasingly identifying themselves as Republicans.

Candidate Image   Although party image has waned somewhat as a short-term force, **candidate image** has become more and more important since the 1950s.[11] More than anything else, television is responsible for this change. Communicating an image of a candidate is much easier than projecting an image of a political party. Creating a negative image

▶ **party image**   The reaction that people have toward a political party.

▶ **candidate image**   The emotional reaction that people have toward a political candidate.

Popular Culture and American Politics

Wag the Dog

By Chapman Rackaway

Are political consultants and political image makers willing to do anything to make their clients look good (and electable)? How far will one of these consultants go to save a president? In the movie *Wag the Dog*, political fixers portray consultants as shifty characters who undermine the public faith in politics.

Roughly one week before the incumbent president stands for reelection, a scandal erupts that threatens to end his bid for a second term. Before the incident can completely undermine his voter base, the White House summons a shady consultant. Conrad Brean (played by Robert DeNiro) is the ultimate spin doctor. Brean has the ability to manipulate politics, the press, and the American people through deflection, diversion, and clever imagery.

Anticipating journalists operating like sharks in the water smelling blood and ready to feed, Brean smoothly diverts focus away from the president by creating a bigger and better story. He does so by manufacturing a war. He calls upon a Hollywood producer, Stanley Motss (played by Dustin Hoffman), who brings along an equally shady retinue of hangers-on, yes-men, and image makers. With Motss and his band of unlikely spin doctors, Brean manages to create, organize, and publicize a fictional war that turns attention away from the president's misdeeds and toward a mythical terrorist cell controlling a small foreign country.

The movie is full of sardonic humor, painting American politics as not only false but a product more of image than fact. *Wag the Dog* exposes the way politics, the media, and show business can sometimes use each other's methods in bad ways. In effect, the consultants in this movie "steal" the election: They manipulate the president's reelection through their diversionary tactics, undermining what American democracy means in the first place. The movie is a cautionary tale, to be sure, reminding us that not everything we see and hear on the news is completely real.

of the opposing candidate is also easier. Because of the advantages of projecting a candidate image as opposed to a party image, modern presidential campaigns have become candidate centered. Nixon's 1972 campaign for president, for example, was run totally independently of the Republican party structure. Calling itself the Campaign to Re-Elect the President, and known by its critics as CREEP, this organization was at least partially responsible for some of the excesses that led to the Watergate scandal.

Candidates establish their own images and try to paint unflattering images of their opponents in a number of ways. First, candidates can purchase advertisements, usually on television, to project themselves in positive terms and their opponents in negative terms. Second, they can make use of the existing news media by using photo opportunities and sound bites. A **photo opportunity** is an event staged with the hope that it will be photographed or filmed by the news media. If successful, photo opportunities and sound bites reflect positively on the candidate. Moreover, they appear in the news without cost to the candidate.

Candidate image has been crucial in most recent presidential elections. These images have been negative as well as positive. One of the most enduring images of the 1988 presidential campaign was that of Michael Dukakis riding in a tank. The Dukakis campaign originally arranged the filming as a photo opportunity, but the attempt backfired. Dukakis appeared ill at ease, and the Republicans soon used the image to ridicule Dukakis and highlight his lack of foreign policy experience.

Bill Clinton was able to convey a positive personal image during his two elections despite personal problems that had dogged him from his days as the governor of Arkansas, and, by 1996, added problems from scandals in his administration. Clinton had a unique

▶ **photo opportunity** An event staged with the hope that it will be photographed or filmed by the news media.

Figure 11-3
A Model of Voting Behavior

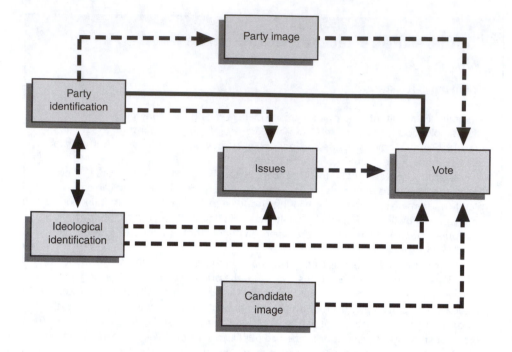

ability to connect with many Americans, especially African Americans, and to communicate a passion about the plight of ordinary citizens. Following his reelection, his image did suffer greatly from the Monica Lewinsky affair and the impeachment that followed. In 1992, the incumbent George Bush's image stood in contrast to that of then Governor Clinton's. Bush was unable to communicate a sense of concern for the economic uncertainty that many in the middle and working classes felt. He seemed somewhat distant and remote in contrast with Clinton's immediacy. Nowhere was this difference showcased more effectively than in the third debate, held in a talk-show–type setting. At one point, after awkwardly fielding a question about what needed to be done to get the economy moving, President Bush looked at his watch as though he were anxious to get away from the setting. Governor Clinton, on the other hand, was supremely comfortable in this type of setting. He made eye contact as he engaged each questioner and projected a level of communication with the "average voters" in attendance and, more importantly, with the millions of television viewers for whom the contrast became clear.

11-3e A Model of the Voting Decision

Figure 11-3 depicts a simplified model of the vote decision. The solid line represents a stronger link. Party identification has a strong, direct effect on the vote. It also affects the vote decision indirectly; that is, a voter's party identification has an effect on his image of the party, which in turn has an effect on the vote. Ideology, issues, and candidate image also play a role in the vote decision, but their influence is not as strong or direct as party identification.

11-4 The 1992 and 1996 Presidential Elections

Bill Clinton's victory in 1992 marked the first time the Democrats had captured the White House since 1976, when Jimmy Carter defeated Gerald Ford. Clinton received 370 electoral votes to 168 for George Bush, thus winning decisively in the electoral college. His electoral college coalition was broad based, as he was able to make inroads in the South while winning decisively in the Northeast, the industrial Midwest, and the West. However, his popular-vote total, though representing a clear victory, amounted to only 43 percent of the vote.

Clinton's victory with a low percentage of the vote was possible because of the strong showing of the third-party candidate Ross Perot. In many ways, Perot was instrumental in defining the tone of the campaign. His entry into the race energized the campaign at a time when both the Republicans' and Democrats' choices for the nomination had become clear. His later withdrawal during the Democratic convention catapulted the sagging Clinton candidacy into a lead it never relinquished. Perot's unique use of the talk-show circuit was quickly copied by Bush and Clinton, creating expectations for accessibility that will probably endure for many years.

The 1992 presidential campaign began in earnest as the fall approached. The Clinton campaign focused on the economy and the need for change. The Bush campaign had great difficulty developing a theme. Bush strategists were convinced that the best way to win was to increase Clinton's negative evaluation, especially by stressing the "character issue." Meanwhile, Perot decided to reenter the race. Both Clinton and Bush were hesitant to attack Perot, fearing they would alienate his supporters. Much of Perot's efforts seemed to be aimed more at Bush than at Clinton, however. Throughout the fall, Clinton enjoyed a commanding lead in the polls, followed by Bush, with Perot gaining ground. Moreover, Clinton's vice presidential choice, Al Gore, was well received, and Dan Quayle was still trying to overcome his weak image.

The televised debates offered Bush his best chance to change the momentum of the campaign. Much disagreement ensued over the format. Eventually, the candidates agreed on three debates among the presidential candidates (including Perot) with one vice presidential debate. The formats would vary, with one debate to include the participation of a panel of voters. By most accounts, however, Bush placed last in the eyes of viewers. He was not particularly comfortable with the more open format. Both Clinton and Perot were able to score points: Clinton for his familiarity with a wide range of issues and Perot with his folksy, direct style. As Election Day neared, many observers were predicting a fairly comfortable Clinton victory.

Although Clinton received only 43 percent of the popular vote in 1992 (as compared with 37 percent for Bush and 19 percent for Perot), he obtained a clear victory in the electoral college. Clinton won thirty-seven states (in addition to the District of Columbia) and received 370 electoral votes, a clear majority. Perot, despite his strong showing in the popular vote, won no electoral votes. Clinton was able to garner votes in areas where recent Democratic presidential candidates had failed. In the 1980, 1984, and 1988 elections, Ronald Reagan and George Bush had established a Republican stronghold in the West and the South. It served as their base throughout the campaign. In 1992, however, President Bush found himself doing so poorly in California, mainly because of the weak economy, that he basically "wrote off" the state as unwinnable.

Early in the 1992 campaign, Clinton strategists sought to put together a coalition that would allow them to win the industrial Northeast and Midwest while making inroads in the South and the West. This strategy required an appeal to traditional Democratic voters, including southerners and union members. It involved strong support from those running for state and local office. Although many had kept their distance from Walter Mondale in 1984 and Michael Dukakis in 1988, Democrats at the grassroots level were active in their support of Clinton. Clinton won by successfully dismantling the coalition that had supported Reagan and Bush. The key to his victory was his ability to appeal to those Democrats who had left the party for the preceding three elections.

In many ways, Bill Clinton was successful in parlaying the Democratic party's advantage in party identification into victory by convincing the voters to cast votes based on both retrospective and prospective perspectives. In addition, he was able to overcome his initial disadvantage in candidate image by casting himself as someone who cared more about the problems facing Americans. George Bush, on the other hand, ran a flawed campaign that lacked a clear theme and failed to inspire much enthusiasm. No doubt, he was hurt by Perot's candidacy. Nevertheless, the state of the economy, health care, and the condition of the cities troubled many Americans, who saw Bush as unable or unwilling to focus on a domestic policy agenda.

President Clinton successfully sought reelection in 1996. Unlike the case in 1992, and later in 2000, the 1996 election was never in doubt. Bob Dole, the Republican nominee, was

Profiles & Perspectives

James Carville (1944–)

AP Photo / Suzanne Plunkett

During the 1990s, James Carville enjoyed probably the greatest visibility ever for a political consultant. During Bill Clinton's successful 1992 presidential campaign, Carville was often seen in the "war room" in Little Rock. Carville's down-home appearance and demeanor seemed to fascinate the media. He coined the phrase "It's the economy, stupid," which became the theme of the campaign. Even his personal life captured the interest of the media. In a literal example of politics making strange bedfellows, in 1993 Carville married Mary Matalin, a high-level Republican strategist and the former cohost of CNN's *Crossfire*.

James Carville, Jr., was born in Georgia, but went to college at Louisiana State University. In his own words, Carville "drank, chased a lot of coeds, and got into a lot of fights." After being asked to leave the university after only two years, Carville joined the Marines. He later finished his degree at LSU and also earned a law degree there. But he was bored by practicing law. His mother said that he was "the worst lawyer in the world." Carville found his vocation when he managed the campaign of a lawyer-colleague who was running for city judge. From that point on, Carville's career has consisted of helping Democrats win political contests. His big break came in 1986, when he helped Robert Casey win a surprise victory in the race for the Pennsylvania governorship. Carville later worked the same magic in helping Harris Wofford get elected to the Senate in 1990. In that contest, he successfully exploited Pennsylvanians' frustration with the health-care system. Not surprisingly, health-care reform became a major Clinton campaign theme in 1992. After the 1992 election, Carville enjoyed easy access to the White House. Although serving as a trusted Clinton adviser, he continued to be very much in demand as a campaign consultant.

Carville continued to be highly visible in the late 1990s, especially in his efforts in defending President Clinton during the Monica Lewinsky scandal. Carville became a regular on many television talk shows and could always be counted on for colorful, passionate, and highly partisan commentary. After the election of George W. Bush in 2000, Carville's visibility declined somewhat, although he remained quite active as an author and a commentator. In the spring of 2002, Carville began appearing as a regular cohost of CNN's *Crossfire* program, which was well-suited to his highly aggressive style of argumentation.

---

a decorated veteran of World War II who barely survived serious combat injuries that left him with the limited use of one arm. Dole resigned from the U.S. Senate, giving up his leadership role as the Republican majority leader to devote his full effort to the campaign. He got off to a rough start in New Hampshire, where he trailed the conservative talk show host and columnist Pat Buchanan in a close contest and barely edged out the former education secretary Lamar Alexander for second.

Dole overcame the New Hampshire embarrassment in the primaries that followed and by Super Tuesday was the clear victor. Buchanan could not appeal to much more than a quarter of the Republican base, and Alexander's candidacy never did catch on despite his message that Bob Dole was fundamentally not electable in a general election contest. Despite misgivings among many rank-and-file Republicans who saw some truth in Alexander's remarks, Dole played successfully on the loyalty of Republicans who felt that Dole deserved the nomination for his long years of service to the country and the party.

The 1996 general election campaign lacked much excitement or suspense. Ross Perot captured the nomination of the Reform party, but did not generate the enthusiasm or support that he had four years earlier and was never a factor in the outcome. Dole never connected with voters or articulated a clear alternative vision to that of the incumbent. His main issue, a tax cut, did not resonate well. Moreover, when compared with the younger, media-savvy Bill Clinton, Dole came across as inaccessible and removed from lives of most voters.

President Clinton positioned himself in opposition to the leadership of the Republican party, who had badly miscalculated in a confrontation with the president that had led to a shutdown of the federal government in 1995. The showdown helped Clinton and the Democrats frame the Republicans as mean-spirited and their budgetary policies as insensitive. Clinton began the campaign early, before the national conventions during the summer. Many early ads were paid for by the party under the soft-money, "party building" loophole in the campaign finance laws. Others were sponsored by unions. These early ads were quite effective and were not countered by the Republicans or by the Dole campaign. Although many people doubted the wisdom of the early campaign, the Clinton preemptive strike was quite effective. In many ways, Dole never recovered. He trailed in the polls throughout the convention period and until the end of the campaign, ultimately losing by 379–159 in the electoral college and 49 percent to 41 percent (Perot had 9 percent).

11-5 The 2000 Cliffhanger

The presidential election of 2000 was the closest and most controversial in modern American history. The turnout of 51 percent represented a slight increase over the turnout in 1996, but fell short of the 1992 election, in which Ross Perot's candidacy had injected more interest in the process.

Before election night, much discussion occurred regarding the closeness of the election. On the eve of the election, most publicly released tracking polls showed George Bush with a slight lead over Al Gore, although the difference was within the margin of error, making the election too close to call. Most projections regarding the electoral college were likewise close or "too close to call." In the last weeks of the election, both campaigns shifted to a massive get-out-the-vote campaign directed at their supporters.

The Bush campaign and the Republican party sent out millions of direct mail pieces and made millions of calls to their supporters. Gore and the Democrats not only made mail and phone contacts but also stressed their core support in the African-American community. The vice president spent the weekend at prayer breakfasts and in churches in the black community.

The controversy over the eventual outcome was presaged by the earlier returns and exit poll projections from the Voter News Service (VNS), a company funded by the major television networks along with the Associated Press. When most of Florida's polls closed at 7 p.m. Eastern time, VNS soon provided data that led the networks to project that Gore had won the state's twenty-five electoral votes. Most observers had previously highlighted the importance of Florida for each campaign. When combined with the projections of a Gore victory in Pennsylvania and Michigan, the Florida call could not have contributed to any enthusiasm among Bush supporters. However, as the vote counting proceeded in Florida, it became obvious that the projection had been premature and Florida was placed in the too-close-to-call category. As the evening progressed and states continued to report, Florida loomed as the state whose electoral votes would ensure victory for either candidate.

Early in the morning following, the networks declared Bush to have won the Florida vote—and the election. Both candidates quickly moved to play out their expected roles. Gore called Bush to concede, and each prepared to address their followers at their respective campaign headquarters along with the millions watching on television. However, as the last precincts reported in Florida, the race tightened dramatically, with the final unofficial count indicating fewer than 2,000 votes separating the two. Moreover, in Palm Beach County, a growing cry was heard of widespread voter frustration with a "confusing" ballot. A Gore staffer in Florida reached the vice president's party as Gore was on his way to address the crowd at his Nashville headquarters to urge him not to publicly concede. Gore agreed, and called an incredulous Governor Bush in Austin again to retract his earlier concession. The networks again classified Florida as too close to call, and an amazed and confused American public still did not know who their next president would be. By dawn, a confused American public faced a totally confused situation, with Gore leading by a tiny margin in the national tabulation, or popular votes, and all eyes focused on Florida.

The weeks that followed were unique in American politics, highlighting the federal nature of the system. Gore had won the national popular vote. He led in the electoral college without the Florida vote. He and his campaign leaders were convinced that they had really won Florida if people who turned out to vote had their intentions measured, but that many were "disenfranchised" by confusing ballot procedures involving punch card ballots. On the other hand, Bush supporters were as least as convinced that Governor Bush had won. Bush had won the initial machine count and the subsequent recount, although the recount had reduced his margin to about 300 votes.

Popular Culture and American Politics
Election

By Chapman Rackaway

Election might seem to be a typical teen movie, *American Pie* with a political plot. However, the movie is much more. Tracy Flick (played by Reese Witherspoon) is the annoyingly smart super student at Carver High. She also happens to be having an affair with a teacher, Mr. Novotny. Tracy decides to run for class president, and it appears she will run unopposed as a testament to her dedication. Mr. McAllister (played by Matthew Broderick) is a very student-focused teacher who is appalled at the idea of an uncontested election. McAlister also sees a white-ballot victory for Tracy as a bonus for Novotny, whom he cannot stand. Mr. McAllister bribes the stereotypically portrayed dumb jock Paul Metzler (played by Chris Klein) to run against her to make his point about the importance of contested elections in a democracy. Paul's entry enrages Tracy, who wants nothing more than to win. The plot is complicated by Paul's sister Tammy, who runs as well as revenge for stealing her girlfriend. The election becomes a bitter three-way fight and a parable for the uglier personal side of politics.

After a close and hard-fought race, Mr. McAlister counts the votes. Even though he appeared to have no agenda, McAlister throws away some votes for Tracy and manipulates the results to ensure that Paul wins the vote.

The movie's director, Alexander Payne, managed to make a movie that was eerily similar to the 2000 presidential election in a number of ways. And *Election* was released a full year prior to the disputed real-life contest. The movie features a third-party spoiler, a popular but reputedly dim-witted candidate who gets by on charm alone, and allegation of fraud in vote counting.

The film is a typically cynical look at American politics, but Payne manages to show the nuances of the situation and how seemingly well-intended efforts can backfire and spiral into an ugly cycle of deception.

11-5a Florida's Post-Election Contest

Vice President Gore decided to challenge the Florida outcome by taking advantage of the state's somewhat confused system of election laws and specifying the challenge in three heavily populated Democratic counties in the southeastern part of the state along with one other, Volusia, which is further north along the East Coast. Florida law allowed a candidate to protest an election and request a recount on a county-by-county basis. However, counties had to file their votes with the secretary of state within a set period after which the secretary could accept returns at her discretion. Following that, a candidate could contest an election outcome in state court in the capital city of Tallahassee.

Florida law did not anticipate anything like the situation that existed in November of 2000. As in most states, the laws were a patchwork of sometimes-contradictory elements that had evolved in response to isolated problems rather than a comprehensive integrated package. The laws left great power to various state and county officials, all of whom had been elected on a partisan ballot. In this case, the official most under the spotlight was the governor, Jeb Bush, the brother of George W. Bush. The governor immediately recused himself from the process. However, others remained, including Katherine Harris, the Republican secretary of state, who had co-chaired George W. Bush's campaign in Florida and served as a delegate to the Republican national convention. The state attorney general, Democrat Bob Butterworth, who played a lesser role, had held a similar position with the Gore campaign. At the county level, where the decision whether to recount had to be made in the protest phase, the three-member canvassing boards all were elected on a partisan ballot.

The partisanship inherent in the process created a climate of distrust among all involved. Democrats dominated the boards, especially in three of the larger counties Gore chose to protest. Thus, the request for this type of recount lost Gore a potential upper hand in the battle for public support during the protest. To this criticism, the Gore response was that the Bush campaign could have mounted similar protests in Republican counties. Of course, any challenge mounted by the winner would strike many as irrational. The Bush team decided to avoid this type of challenge and to instead work to avoid any further hand recounts as unnecessary and unwarranted.

The tone was then set for a five-week war of the words, with the Democrats' count-every-vote mantra countered by the Republicans' the-legal-votes-have-been-counted version. Most of this verbal warfare centered on ballots that the machine counts missed that would have to be counted by hand if "voter intent" could be determined. The voter could have voted for more than one candidate in an election, thus invalidating the ballot as an overvote. Officials had no way to discern voter intent from this type of ballot. Many in Palm Beach County had claimed that they had been confused by the ballot and cast these types of overvotes in attempts to vote for Gore. Likewise, many African Americans in Duval County claimed to have likewise mistakenly overvoted, also in an attempt to vote for Gore. These types of voter errors could not be legally addressed after the fact, and apart from a failed attempt to force a revote in Palm Beach County, were not the subject of much of the legal wrangling in the election aftermath.

The real battle of the ballots regarded "undervotes," in which machines were unable to register a voter preference. Florida law, along with that of most other states, had been interpreted by its courts as requiring that the "intent of the voter" be determined by the county canvassing board when election outcomes were in doubt. However, the criteria used to examine these types of ballots had never been specified by Florida courts and were left to be applied by each county. Of course, the failure of a machine to determine a vote could have reflected a voter decision to skip the contest. Preelection surveys had shown that about 1 percent of the electorate in Florida wanted to abstain from the presidential election while voting for other contests down the ballot.

Many of Florida's counties, including the three challenged by Gore, used punch card ballots that exacerbated the many problems with improperly cast ballots. All voters were instructed to punch the holes, or chads, corresponding to their preference all the way through and to make sure that any hanging chads were removed. However, many voters did not follow these instructions and left their punch cards with partially removed chads that machines did not count. Other ballots often had mere indentations, called dimpled chads, or pregnant chads. No consensus in law or in practice stated whether this type of mark reflected the clear intent of the voter. A person could make a good case that this type of mark might just as well reflect a voter's change of mind after thinking that she might cast a vote for one person and later deciding to abstain from making a choice. Many wanted to count any mark, or crease, observable by a candidate's name, but others felt that counting dimples and creases was in fact creating votes rather than counting them.

The post-election drama in Florida came to a head with the request for hand recounts in Volusia, Broward, Palm Beach, and Miami–Dade counties. After some initial uncertainty, the canvassing boards in all the counties decided to move ahead with recounts. However, only one, Volusia County, was completed by the deadline specified in Florida law—November 14—when all counties were required to forward their updated totals to the secretary of state, the Republican Katherine Harris. The law did allow the secretary to accept later returns at her discretion. At this point, the legal wrangling brought in yet another set of players, members of the Florida Supreme Court. All seven members of the Court were appointed by Democratic governors (one jointly appointed by the Republican Jeb Bush). The Court had made a number of controversial decisions that led to conflict with the Republican-dominated state legislature.

Following a lower-court decision that would allow Ms. Harris to use discretion that was not arbitrary, the Florida Supreme Court ruled that Ms. Harris must accept all vote totals turned in by Sunday November 26. The Court ordered her not to certify a winner in the election until after this date. The logic of the Court's ruling was that it was clarifying a contradiction in Florida law that permitted hand recounts but required that votes be turned in within five days of the election. Republicans had argued that the Court should not interfere with the legislative timetable and that by doing so, the Court was performing a legislative function. They also noted that the legislature allowed for a contest period following the certification date, at which time the issue could be further argued until the secretary of state would face the December 12 deadline for a state's electors to be certified and cast ballots that would be free from congressional challenge. Democrats had countered with the argument that past court decisions had stressed that gleaning the intent of voters was of paramount importance. The Court unanimously agreed with the latter argument, to a great extent couching its decision to alter the legislatively mandated timetable in language from the preamble to the Florida Constitution. However the decision of the Democrats to push to extend the protest period at the expense of the contest period would prove to be a grave miscalculation. Given the rapidly changing legal and political environment, thinking beyond the next day's court case was extremely difficult for either side.

11-5b The Counting

The next ten days were among the most bizarre in American political history. Three counties had the task of deciding whether to conduct their hand recounts and, if so, how. Two counties, Palm Beach and Broward, began their counts with different and somewhat shifting criteria, and Dade stopped and started its count before later deciding not to continue. Florida law did mandate that recounts in the protest period consider all votes cast. Each of the counties' canvassing boards faced the task of examining hundreds of thousands of ballots. This task was performed in full public view under the watchful eyes of not only partisan observers but also the constant gaze of millions of viewers on national cable news channels. (See Figure 11-4 for an example of a hypothetical election recount.)

Of course, the rules for counting were the key element of the counting, and local canvassing boards decided these rules with Democratic majorities. Given the overwhelming Democratic majorities in Broward and, to a lesser degree, in Palm Beach, a more liberal counting standard would clearly work to Gore's advantage. That is, if the canvassing boards considered any discernible mark as a vote, a greater chance existed that any uncounted ballot would yield a vote for Gore rather than for Bush. This was especially likely to be true in Palm Beach because many intending to vote for Gore later said that the ballot had confused them. Moreover, for any questionable ballot the final decision fell into the hands of a Democratic-dominated three-person board. Moreover, all were operating with full knowledge of the running total. The Gore team was confident that it would find the votes it needed, and the Bush team was upset over a process that centered in such a Democratic enclave in possibly determining the outcome of the election in not only Florida, but also, by extension, the country. The 2000 presidential election showed every prospect of being determined by a small number of actors with their own political agendas.

Not surprisingly, the counting process was fraught with controversy. Broward's board was the most partisan of the three and soon began to consider that almost any discernable ballot perforation be counted as a vote. In one widely broadcast memorable scene, two members of the board indicated that they could not discern a preference. A third member, however, a Democrat, indicated that she could see a prick of light coming through next to Gore. The chairperson, another Democrat, first could not see anything, but after some alternative views, agreed. The Republican buried his head in his hands, and the ballot was counted as a vote for Gore. Gore picked up more than 500 votes from the Broward recount. To be sure, not all the ballot decisions resembled the one just described. However, the process did little to convince many observers of the possibility of those involved from either side of operating free from unconscious bias.

If the situation in Broward County did little to ameliorate fears of partisan agendas, Palm Beach may have helped a bit, at least from the perspective of those favoring Bush. The Democratic chair Charles Burton led his board to consider a criterion that took in the totality of the circumstances in determining voter intent. If a voter had not managed to punch through the chad for president, but had done so for all other contests, the ballot was not counted as a vote. However, if the voter had failed to punch through the chad for any

Figure 11-4
Hypothetical Recount Example

(To view this figure, please go to the online text.)

In this hypothetical exercise, Ms. Smith, a Democrat, leads Mr. Rodriguez, a Republican, by 231 votes after a machine count of the 1 million votes cast in the state. Questions have been raised about whether the voting machines missed valid votes. Some counties use the punch-card system, while other counties use the optical-scanner system. Punch-card ballots that were partially punched or only dimpled were not counted. The optical-scanner machines may have been missed ballots that were filled out with pen rather than pencil or had stray marks or other discrepancies. These ballots, if they exist, can be counted only by hand.

Due to the small margin of votes between the candidates, a recount is necessary. You decide which rules should be used to recount the ballots. Select one rule from each column that you believe should be used to count votes, and then click the Show Final Count button.

contest on the ballot, but merely indented each preference, the presidential preference was counted as a vote. That criteria ultimately would have netted Gore significantly more votes in the recount. However, the recount was not completed in time to meet the newly extended deadline recently set by the Florida Supreme Court.

As though the situation were not confused enough, Dade County presented another bizarre set of circumstances. Unlike those in the other two counties in south Florida, Gore carried Dade by only a small margin (53 percent). It was never clear from the initial samples that the hand recount would ultimately yield much of an advantage, especially if the "Palm Beach standard" for ballot counting were employed. After first deciding not to recount, and then to recount, the Dade board found itself unable to contemplate counting more than 700,000 ballots by hand in the remaining days. It did consider, for a time, counting only the approximately 10,000 undervotes. However, in another widely broadcast scene, the board began a move to a room out of public view to consider the hand count of undervotes. In minutes, hundreds of protestors began pounding on windows and demanding to observe the proceedings. Soon, the canvassing board announced that it was terminating any hand recount because it could not finish by the deadline. Democrats immediately charged that the board had been intimidated by a "mob." Republicans scoffed at the characterization of the protest as a mob. At the time the recount in Dade was ceased, Gore had picked up well over a hundred votes. However, these votes had been gained in the most Democratic precincts, and many thought that any full count would not have yielded much of an advantage for Gore.

One other issue surfaced while the counties scurried to complete their recounts. Florida allowed citizens living overseas or serving in the military to request ballots and, as long as the ballots were sent by Election Day, to be counted for up to ten days after the election and before counties filed them with the secretary of state for inclusion with the statewide totals. Considering that these ballots play no part in the determination of most outcomes, little attention has traditionally been paid to these votes. However, for obvious reasons, the two to three thousand ballots that were expected could be critical in 2000. There was fairly widespread agreement that these votes would tend to favor George W. Bush. In a public relations disaster, Gore campaign attorneys sent memos to Democratic observers in each county to challenge military ballots for a variety of reasons, including the lack of a postmark. However, people serving overseas often do not have a way to see that a postmark is applied. Many ballots were challenged and eliminated. Bush gained another 600 votes from overseas ballots, giving him a lead of 930 votes before any hand recounts.

When the deadline approached, Secretary of State Harris announced that she would not accept the results from Palm Beach County that missed the five o'clock specification even though the count was on target to be completed within hours. This decision angered Democrats who thought that she had it within her discretion to accept the results, further exacerbating the partisan ill will on both sides. The final numbers, including the controversial hand recounts from Broward County, left Bush in the lead by approximately 500 votes. This total was certified, and Ms. Harris convened the state canvassing board to pronounce Bush the winner of Florida's 25 electoral votes and to certify Bush's electors to the electoral college.

11-5c The Contest Period: The Courts Take Over

The entire recount procedure had taken place under the extension of the protest period mandated by the Florida Supreme Court. The Bush campaign asked the United States Supreme Court to review the Florida Supreme Court's decision. To the surprise of many, the Supreme Court decided to hear the case. The Bush legal team made a number of legal arguments. One, that the different counting methods by the state violated the Equal Protection Clause of the Fourteenth Amendment by treating voters unequally across the state, was not immediately examined. The Court did rule unanimously, though, in an unsigned *per curium* decision that the Florida Supreme Court's ruling extending the date for the counting of ballots could not be made on the basis of the Florida Constitution, but rather required justification as an interpretation of conflict in Florida statutes. The U.S. Supreme

Court vacated and remanded the earlier Florida Supreme Court decision pending clarification.[12] Considering that Gore still trailed following the hand recount done under the now vacated ruling, the issue appeared to be closed. However, the contest period still remained.

In Florida, a candidate who trailed after the protest period and certification could contest the outcome of the election in circuit court in Tallahassee if he or she could bring into doubt enough questionable ballots as to put the final outcome in doubt. As was the case in most of the litigation in this highly unusual situation, the law was not clear, having developed through court interpretation of scattered cases around limited statutory language. Gore contested the failure of Dade County's canvassing board to count the undervotes as well as the criteria used to hand count ballots in Palm Beach County. In addition, he contested a questionable use of original rather than machine-recounted votes in another county.

Judge Sanders Sauls was assigned the case in Tallahassee. Gore's position, as advocated by the lead attorney David Boies, was clear: The questionable ballots should be brought to Tallahassee, and counting should begin immediately. The justification for counting before any testimony and ruling was simple: The November 12 deadline was less than two weeks away, and time was short. The Bush response was simple: No justification for a partial recount of mere undervotes existed under Florida law, so any ballot recount should not be limited to undervotes, but rather apply to all ballots. Moreover, given the statewide nature of the contest, any recount should be statewide in nature and not limited to a few counties, and any recount should use consistent standards from county to county. Finally, the Bush team, led by Barry Richard, argued that no proof had been offered that there was any reason to look at any ballots. Boies countered that his team had contested only certain ballots, that the ballots were sufficient in number to affect the outcome, and that these ballots were in effect the evidence the Court should consider.

Judge Sauls ruled that all ballots from Dade and Palm Beach counties be trucked to Tallahassee. Millions followed the ballots' progress on a moving truck as the trial began. The Gore team called voting experts and statisticians to demonstrate problems with the punch card ballot system that could have led to voters having difficulty registering their preferences and leading to less-than-fully-punched ballots that machines would not count. Judge Sauls ultimately did not agree, and ruled that the Democrats had not made their case in justifying further recounts of the questionable ballots. Again, the issue appeared to be settled. The only way for Gore to get further recounts was through an appeal to the Florida Supreme Court to overrule Judge Sauls. Not many observers thought that this appeal was likely. Sauls' decision seemed to leave few avenues for appeal.

The drama would not end so soon. In a surprising and contentious 4–3 decision, the Florida Supreme Court overruled Judge Sauls and ordered an immediate statewide recount to begin immediately of all undervotes in each Florida county with the exception of Palm Beach and Broward. There, they ordered the secretary of state to accept the late figures from Palm Beach County along with those from Broward. However, the court provided no direction regarding what standards should be used, again leaving that major decision to canvassing boards in each county. The counting of Dade ballots got under way in Tallahassee, and other counties' canvassing boards met to develop a process for counting undervotes in their counties.

11-5d The U.S. Supreme Court Ends the Process

The Bush campaign attorneys immediately sought relief from the United States Supreme Court to stop the new wave of hand recounts. On December 9, five Supreme Court members agreed to order the recounts stopped immediately pending a full hearing of the case. The halt was ordered on the basis of "irreparable damage" that could occur to the Bush campaign if counting continued without clear standards that produced an outcome that could later be determined to have been based on an improper process.

The Court later heard oral arguments in the case known simply as *Bush v. Gore* (see Case in Point 11-1). The audiotapes of this argument were released amid great public inter-

Case in Point 11-1

The Supreme Court Ends the Presidential Deadlock

Bush v. Gore (2000)

On December 12, 2000, the United States Supreme Court effectively resolved the 2000 presidential election when it decided the case of *Bush v. Gore*. The following is an excerpt from the *per curiam* (unsigned) opinion issued by the Court:

> Upon due consideration of the difficulties identified to this point, it is obvious that the recount cannot be conducted in compliance with the requirements of equal protection and due process without substantial additional work. It would require not only the adoption (after opportunity for argument) of adequate statewide standards for determining what is a legal vote, and practicable procedures to implement them, but also orderly judicial review of any disputed matters that might arise. In addition, the Secretary of State has advised that the recount of only a portion of the ballots requires that the vote tabulation equipment be used to screen out undervotes, a function for which the machines were not designed. If a recount of overvotes were also required, perhaps even a second screening would be necessary. Use of the equipment for this purpose, and any new software developed for it, would have to be evaluated for accuracy by the Secretary of State, as required by [Florida law].
>
> The Supreme Court of Florida has said that the legislature intended the State's electors to "participat[e] fully in the federal electoral process," as provided in 3 U. S. C. §5. That statute, in turn, requires that any controversy or contest that is designed to lead to a conclusive selection of electors be completed by December 12. That date is upon us, and there is no recount procedure in place under the State Supreme Court's order that comports with minimal constitutional standards. Because it is evident that any recount seeking to meet the December 12 date will be unconstitutional for the reasons we have discussed, we reverse the judgment of the Supreme Court of Florida ordering a recount to proceed.
>
> Seven Justices of the Court agree that there are constitutional problems with the recount ordered by the Florida Supreme Court that demand a remedy.... The only disagreement is as to the remedy. Because the Florida Supreme Court has said that the Florida Legislature intended to obtain the safe-harbor benefits of 3 U. S. C. §5, ... remanding to the Florida Supreme Court for its ordering of a constitutionally proper contest until December 18— contemplates action in violation of the Florida election code, and hence could not be part of an "appropriate" order authorized by [Florida law]....
>
> None are more conscious of the vital limits on judicial authority than are the members of this Court, and none stand more in admiration of the Constitution's design to leave the selection of the president to the people, through their legislatures, and to the political sphere. When contending parties invoke the process of the courts, however, it becomes our unsought responsibility to resolve the federal and constitutional issues the judicial system has been forced to confront....

est. The Court ruling that followed late on the evening of December 12 brought an end to the five-week post-election battle, but not to the controversy. In a complicated split decision, the Court ruled that the Florida Supreme Court decision specifying the recounts without standards violated equal protection standards under the U.S. Constitution and that the case should be remanded to the Florida Supreme Court so that consistent standards could be applied. Seven of the nine justices agreed with that proposition. However, by a 5–4 margin, the Court also agreed that Florida law mandated that electors be chosen by December 12 and that there was time for the Florida Supreme Court to use appropriate due process, specify standards, and allow for recounts to occur to meet that deadline.[13] The effect of the ruling was to end any recounting, leaving Bush in the lead, with electors already certified and with no further options for Gore. The election was decided. When the electors cast their votes on December 18, Bush had 271 electoral votes, one more than the 270 he needed to win.

11-6 The 2004 Election

The 2004 campaign was the most engaging, and also the most divisive, that the country had experienced since 1968. Throughout the campaign, polls showed that public interest in the campaign was very high and that Americans had strong feelings about the incumbent president, George W. Bush. The media coverage of the campaign was extensive, if not always impartial; the political rhetoric on both sides was often vitriolic; and the race went down to the wire. In 2004, more than $600 million were spent on political ads on radio and TV, more than twice as much as in 2000. Because both sides worked so hard to mobilize voters, and because Americans were more engaged in the campaign than they had been in many years, voter turnout was significantly (though not dramatically) higher. Contrary to widespread expectations and conventional wisdom, the higher turnout helped the Republican candidate. Fortunately, the election was decided by the next day, and the nation was spared a protracted and stressful post-election challenge.

11-6a The Candidates

President George W. Bush took office in January 2001 under a cloud of suspicion. A poll taken just prior to President Bush's inauguration found that almost a quarter of Americans believed that Bush had "stolen the election."[14] Many Democrats, especially Democratic members of Congress, seemed determined not to work with the new president. From January to August of 2001, George W. Bush found his job as president to be very rough sledding. However, the terrorist attacks of 9-11 would have an enormous impact on the country's perception of its president. Widely praised, even by Democrats, for his handling of the crisis, President Bush's approval ratings skyrocketed. Despite the terrible economic fallout from 9-11, President Bush might well have maintained these high approval ratings and been reelected easily in 2004, were it not for his fateful decision in 2003 to invade Iraq and depose Saddam Hussein. Although the war went well initially, and Saddam's government readily collapsed, American forces encountered tremendous difficulties in maintaining public order, rebuilding the country, and establishing a new government. By the summer of 2003, amidst a growing insurgency in Iraq, the chorus of criticism of the president at home grew louder and louder. By 2004, it was clear that the Democrats would look to use the difficulties in Iraq to defeat George W. Bush at the polls.

By March of 2004, Senator John Kerry of Massachusetts emerged from a field of ten Democrats to all but secure his party's nomination. Given his liberal voting record in the Senate, where he had served since 1984, and his record of antiwar protest after returning from two tours of duty in Vietnam, many observers thought that he was ill-suited to challenge President Bush, especially in the American heartland. But polls pitting Senator Kerry against President Bush showed that the two were virtually tied in March of 2004. At that point, President Bush appeared to be extremely vulnerable.

Another perceived liability for President Bush was the incumbent Vice President, Dick Cheney. Cheney had been a lightning rod for controversy in the previous three years and was not well regarded by the public. When John Kerry chose his main Democratic rival, Senator John Edwards of North Carolina, to be his running mate, the contrast between the vice presidential candidates could not have been more pronounced. The young, handsome, and charismatic Edwards brought energy to the campaign and offered hope that the Democrats might do better in the South than they had fared in recent presidential contests. Ultimately, that hope would prove unfounded, as the Kerry/Edwards ticket would be defeated throughout the South, even in Edwards' home state.

The Nader Non-Factor Many Democrats blamed Green Party candidate Ralph Nader for Al Gore's narrow defeat in the 2000 election. Most Democrats were chagrined when Nader announced his intention to run again in 2004. Although the Green Party did not nominate Nader, and Democrats worked hard to keep him off the ballot, this idiosyncratic gadfly refused to go away. In the end, his candidacy would be a non-factor. Nationally, he would get less than 1 percent of the vote.

11-6b The Issues

After 9-11, terrorism became the overriding national issue. Prior to the Iraq invasion in 2003, Americans across the political spectrum gave President Bush high marks for his conduct of the war on terror. President Bush sought to link the invasion of Iraq to the war on terror by stressing the need to secure Saddam Hussein's supposed weapons of mass destruction lest they fall into the hands of terrorists. The fact that no stockpiles of chemical or biological weapons were found in Iraq after American troops captured the country took a tremendous toll on President Bush's credibility. Some, like filmmaker Michael

Moore, whose inflammatory documentary *Fahrenheit 9/11* became a blockbuster in the summer of 2004, accused the president of deceiving the American people in an effort to justify his obsession with invading Iraq.

The War in Iraq

The war in Iraq dominated the 2004 campaign. The unrelenting media coverage of the war, most of which brought bad news, placed President Bush on the defensive. Senator Kerry, who had actually voted to authorize the president to go to war (and then later voted against funding the war) seized the opportunity to use the war in his effort to defeat the president. Calling the war in Iraq "the wrong war at the wrong time" and a "massive distraction" from the war on terrorism, Kerry hammered away at George Bush's most vulnerable position. Kerry's message resonated with those who had opposed the war in Iraq from the beginning, but was much less successful in persuading others. Kerry's claim that, if elected president, he could do a better job in bringing the war in Iraq to a successful conclusion was met with widespread disbelief. The fact that he had voted against going to war against Iraq in 1991, then voted for the resolution authorizing the Iraq War in 2003, and then only a few months later voted against the bill to fund that war helped fuel criticisms that he was "dovish" or, worse, a "flip flopper." Kerry's claim that, if elected president, he would be able to secure greater assistance in Iraq from America's allies was likewise greeted with considerable skepticism. How could he, as president, convince allies to commit resources to a war that he did not personally support? Although he went to great lengths to explain his position on Iraq, many voters were left with the impression that Kerry's position was incoherent. On the other hand, voters seemed to know where President Bush stood on Iraq, even if they disapproved of his decision to go to war in the first place.

The Economy

After 9-11-2001, the economy tanked. Consumer spending, especially in the areas of tourism and travel, declined markedly. Unemployment rose dramatically as industries laid off workers. However, by 2003 the economy had turned around significantly. President Bush claimed that tax cuts enacted by Congress at his urging had stimulated the economy and moved the country out of recession. Democrats countered by focusing on the massive budget deficits created by declining government revenues resulting from the tax cuts and the greatly increased spending on defense and homeland security after 9-11.

Despite the overall improvement of the economy in 2003 and 2004, in some areas of the country the economic situation remained rather grim. Ohio, which would prove to be a pivotal state in the election, lost 200,000 jobs between 2000 and 2004. Its unemployment rate going into the 2004 election was two points higher than the national figure. Most Democrats believed that President Bush's alleged mismanagement of the economy, including his "irresponsible" tax cuts, and his alleged support for corporate "outsourcing" would be a powerful issue for them in states like Ohio.

"Values Issues"

Survey research conducted throughout 2004 showed that voters who believed that the economy was the most important issue favored John Kerry over George Bush by a substantial margin. But the research also showed that most Americans were troubled by what they perceived to be a decline in morality. The Republicans were able to capitalize on this sentiment, which has always been particularly pronounced among evangelical Christians. Indeed, President Bush's chief strategist, Karl Rove, targeted four million evangelical Christians who had failed to support Bush in 2000. The strategy focused on an issue of great concern to social conservatives—the legalization of homosexual marriage. Republicans in eleven states, including the pivotal state of Ohio, succeeded in placing on the ballot proposals to ban same-sex marriage. All eleven of these proposals were adopted, even in a relatively liberal state like Oregon, where 57 percent of voters supported the ban on gay wedlock. In Ohio, evangelical Christians turned out in record numbers to vote for the ban. In so doing, they also cast their ballots for George Bush. Some found it ironic, and others outrageous, that such an issue would play such a crucial role in the election. In the end, the Democrats underestimated the degree to which ordinary

Figure 11-5
2004 Election Results by State

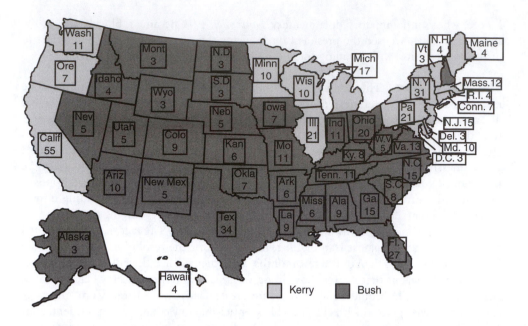

Americans were suffering from culture shock after seeing televised images of same-sex weddings in San Francisco and Massachusetts. Karl Rove understood.

11-6c The Voters Decide

Americans of all political persuasions became increasingly anxious as Election Day approached. The polls suggested that the race was extremely tight, too close to call. Americans who watched the returns come in after polls began to close at 7 p.m. Eastern Time expected a long night. Many expected that the race would be so close that post-election recounts and legal challenges would be inevitable and that the outcome might not be known for weeks. As it turned out, it was a long night, as the winner did not emerge until the following morning. But there was to be no post-election contest a la 2000. And for that the country was greatly relieved.

All of the factors that always come into play in presidential elections impacted the outcome of the 2004 race. Partisanship, ideology, race, gender, social class, geography—all of these came into play. So did issues such as terrorism, Iraq, the economy, tax policy, and gay rights. Also important were voters' perceptions of character and credibility, as well as assessments of their own circumstances and the overall condition and direction of the country. Whereas some voters were driven primarily by one or two of these factors, others found their decision making to be unusually complex. In the end, the country decided to give President Bush four more years in the White House. The national popular vote was 51 percent for Bush, 48 percent for Kerry, and 1 percent for Nader and miscellaneous other minor candidates (see Figure 11-5). The all-important electoral vote was much closer though. President Bush won the electoral vote 286 to 252. As noted in section 11-6b, it all came down to Ohio, which Bush won by fewer than 150,000 votes. Had Kerry won Ohio, the electoral vote would have been 272 to 266 in Kerry's favor.

11-7 Congressional Campaigns and Elections

A comparison of congressional and presidential elections reveals both differences and similarities. The format is the same in that it has a nomination process and a general election. Candidates for the U.S. Senate are nominated through statewide primaries; House candidates are nominated though primaries held in each House district. The Republican and Democratic nominees who emerge from these primaries face off in the general election. The two major parties tend to dominate almost all congressional elections as they do most presidential elections. Name recognition and public approval are just as important to congressional candidates as they are to presidential candidates. On the other hand, the political environment, membership turnover, effect of incumbency, and nature of campaign financing are quite different.

All House members must run for reelection every two years. The two senators from each state have six-year terms that start and end at different times so that they usually do not come up for reelection at the same time. The two-year cycle of House elections overlaps with the four-year presidential term and the six-year senatorial term so that every even-numbered year has a congressional election. The 1992 election year was known as the presidential election year, but all 435 House members and at least 33 senators were also up for election. The 1994 election year was known as a midterm election because it occurred at the midpoint between presidential elections. Consequently, the president was not up for election, but 435 House members and at least 33 senators were. Every two years, a House member must withstand the possibility of a nomination battle against a fellow party member and then survive a general election against a challenger from the opposing party.

One of the most salient features of congressional elections in the past five decades is the surprising lack of turnover from year to year. On average, since 1950 more than 90 percent of the House members who have desired reelection have been successful. The Senate has been a bit more volatile, but since 1960 senators have enjoyed an average reelection rate of more than 75 percent. The various factors contributing to the high rates of electoral success and low rates of turnover for members of Congress are known as the **incumbency advantage.** Members of Congress have a variety of resources available for improving their name recognition and public approval. The government provides free mail, free travel to the district, free long-distance telephone calls, district offices, staff to assist the legislators with constituent service, and the power to secure government projects that provide jobs and money for their districts. Because the features that contribute to the incumbency advantage are so much a part of the nature of Congress as an institution, this topic is discussed in detail in Chapter 12, "Congress."

> ▶ **incumbency advantage** The various factors contributing to the high rates of electoral success and low rates of turnover for members of Congress.

11-7a Financing Congressional Campaigns

A potential challenger faces a formidable task in squaring off against an incumbent member of Congress. The government has provided at least two years, and in many cases decades, of funding to the incumbent for activities that increase name recognition and good feelings with voters. If this advantage is not enough to drive away most people, they must also consider the huge advantage the incumbent usually has in raising money for campaigns.

Because so much of the average campaign is conducted over the television or radio airwaves, running for Congress is enormously expensive. The average amount spent per candidate in 1992 was $197,000 in the House. This figure, however, is misleading in that winners of a House seat spent $550,000 on average. The average Senate candidate spent $1.1 million. The total amount spent represents a 52 percent increase in campaign spending since 1990. By 2000, Congressional candidates had raised more than $800 million, greater than a 39 percent increase over 1998. In 2000, the New Jersey senate candidate David Corsine spent a record $45 million on his successful campaign.[15]

Incumbents enjoy five main advantages in raising campaign funds:

1. Interest groups want access to power, and incumbents are already in power and likely to stay there.
2. An incumbent member of Congress has been a winner at least once. People like to know that they are not wasting their money on someone with no chance of winning, and incumbents quickly pass this test.
3. Because incumbents have already been winners, they have been able to develop a successful fundraising organization.
4. An incumbent's previous contributors can be canvassed again for money.
5. Incumbents usually have money in the bank well before the campaign has even begun.

Money is important to all candidates, but challengers have the greatest need for money and the most difficulty in raising it. Because challengers must overcome the incumbency advantage, they must spend hundreds of thousands of dollars even to be considered serious candidates. The ability to raise money is probably the best indicator of a challenger's chances of winning. For example, from 1984 to 1990, only forty-five House challengers on average in each election were able to raise as much as $300,000. Of these well-funded challengers, 20 percent (or 35 of the total 180 in the four elections) were able to win against an incumbent. On the other hand, only seven of the hundreds of challengers who raised less than $300,000 won an election. Successful challengers spent an average of $500,000.[16]

Sources of Money   Members of Congress have four sources of campaign funds:

- Individuals
- PACs
- Party organizations
- Their own personal finances

Members of Congress are not eligible for the public funding that presidential candidates receive. The Federal Election Campaign Act of 1974 placed a limit of $1,000 on the amount individuals can contribute to a campaign for each election and a $5,000 limit on PAC contributions per candidate per election. Many more individuals than PACs give money to candidates, but PACs tend to give more money each time they contribute and donate money to many more candidates in any one election year. Individuals give a larger total amount of money to all congressional candidates than PACs, but PACs are much more important for the average incumbent. In 1992, 44 percent (or $263,500) of the total funds raised by incumbents came from PACs versus only 26 percent (or $149,700) for the successful challengers.[17]

For the election cycles 1975 through 1998, PACs contributed between 40 and 50 percent of their total receipts to congressional campaigns. During this period, total PAC contributions to congressional candidates increased more than ninefold, from about $23 million to nearly $200 million per election cycle.

Party money tends to be not that important in most races. On the other hand, family money and loans can be quite important. Personal finances tend to make up a much larger share of a challenger's funds than they do for the average incumbent. Often, challengers must rely on family money and loans to get their campaigns started. If they lose, they may never be able to pay off the loans. The winning challengers in 1992 averaged $65,500 of debt in the House and $266,073 in the Senate.[18] After winners are successful, however, they quickly begin to accrue the benefits of being an incumbent. PACs almost immediately turn their attention to the new members and begin making contributions (see Table 11-2). In 1992, from Election Day until the end of December, PACs donated $1.2 million to new members.[19]

PACs and Congressional Campaigns   Members of Congress have experience and access to power that people, particularly interest groups, want. Well before the campaign starts in the summer of an election year, the member must start raising money. PACs provide the most readily available funds at this time. As you have seen, the more than four thousand PACs are organizations that exist solely to raise and spend campaign money on behalf of some issue of interest to the donors. PACs with a specific economic interest, such as the American Medical Association's concern about legislation affecting the health-care industry, are the most common and best-funded groups. Therefore, most PAC money available to legislators is tied to a particular economic interest.

This PAC money tends to flow to members who can be most influential on bills affecting that economic interest. Because Congress assigns bills to various committees based on their subject matter, interest groups know which legislators are most likely to be able to help or hurt their cause. Consequently, PAC money tends to be concentrated on members of the

Election Cycle	($ Millions)	
1975–1976	22.6	**TABLE 11-2**
1977–1978	34.1	
1979–1980	60.2	**PAC Contributions to**
1981–1982	87.6	**Congressional**
1983–1984	113.0	**Candidates,**
1985–1986	139.8	**1975–2002**
1987–1988	159.2	
1989–1990	159.1	
1991–1992	188.9	
1993–1994	189.6	
1995–1996	217.8	
1997–1998	219.9	
1999–2000	257.2	
2001–2002	282.0	

Source: Adapted from Harold W. Stanley and Richard G. Niemi, *Vital Statistics on American Politics 2003–2004* (Washington, D.C.: CQ Press, 2003), p. 99.

relevant committees. For example, members of the Agriculture Committee would receive, on average, more PAC money from farming interests than from other members. Although the wealthier PACs, such as the American Medical Association, can spread their money around, most focus their money on the better investments available in certain committees.

Because the jurisdiction of congressional committees does not change significantly from year to year, the PACs can concentrate on certain members, and committee members know that they have a steady source of funds from a core group of PACs. One outcome of this relationship is that PACs tend to shower much more money on incumbents than on challengers. This statement is especially true for economic interest groups, which tend to donate much more money to incumbents than do ideological interest groups. Of the $659 million spent by all congressional candidates in the 1992 election, $180 million of it came from PACs. Most of the PAC money, $127 million, went to incumbents. Of the top twenty recipients of PAC money in the Senate, eighteen were incumbents, and fifteen of them won reelection. All the top twenty PAC recipients in the House were incumbents, and fifteen of them also won reelection.

Another advantage of incumbents is that they can stockpile their campaign funds over time. If a member has a relatively easy campaign one year, it would be wise to save some of the money raised this year for the next campaign. Because individuals and PACs are limited in how much money they can give a candidate in any one election ($1,000 for an individual and $5,000 for a PAC), a member can receive only so much help from any one source in a given year. Therefore, members take contributions every year and build up a war chest for future tough campaigns. Some members have amassed war chests of more than a million dollars. For example, at the end of 1992, David Dreier, a Republican representative from California, had $2,026,019 cash on hand, and Dan Rostenkowski, a Democrat from Illinois, had $1,245,721 in his war chest.[20] When you consider that the House candidate who ranked fortieth in total spending in 1992 spent $1,086,152, you can easily see how valuable a large war chest can be. Potential challengers know that they will have a difficult time raising as much money as the incumbent during the campaign, and few can match funds with a large war chest.

The large advantage that incumbents have in campaign financing scares off many qualified potential challengers. Most challengers are aware that they have to either spend large sums of their own money or borrow heavily to start a campaign. Of the $659 million spent in the 1992 elections, $54 million was either lent to or contributed by the candidate personally. Almost all this personal funding was done by challengers or candidates in open races with no incumbent. These financing advantages combined with the other benefits of incumbency, such as the franking privilege and congressional staff, help explain why reelection rates of more than 90 percent have been routine in recent decades (see Table 11-3).

11-7b National Trends and Local Context

Thomas P. "Tip" O'Neill, a former speaker of the house, once stated that "all politics is local." The tremendous attention that legislators give to local problems through constituency service is clear evidence that they understand this maxim. Members spend as much time as possible in their district speaking to groups, such as the Kiwanis and Rotary Club, visiting local schools, and attending public functions of all types to enable constituents to get to know them. Members must develop a unique "home style" that fits both their personality and the local culture. This home style is used to develop trust between the constituents and the member so that the legislator can effectively communicate with the district and rely on the trust she has built up to survive tough elections.[21] Sometimes, despite the member's best efforts, the partisanship and political ideology of the local culture make it impossible for her to retain the seat.

National Events and Congressional Elections   The effect of national events on congressional races has been extensively studied by political scientists. Three factors stand out as most important:

- *Bad economic conditions generally hurt the party of the president.* A recession (when economic income growth falls and unemployment rises) in the months before an election generally results in a loss of seats in Congress for the president's party.

TABLE 11-3					
1999–2000 Financial Activity of Senate and House General Election Campaigns (January 1, 1999– October 18, 2000)	**No.**	**Total Receipts**	**Total Disbursements**	**Average Receipts**	**Average Disbursements**
Senate					
Democrats	32	$178,138,888	$161,266,389	$ 5,566,840	$ 5,039,575
Incumbents	11	$ 39,618,416	$ 28,904,018	$ 3,601,674	$ 2,627,638
Challengers	16	$ 45,613,784	$ 43,150,294	$ 2,850,862	$ 2,696,893
Open seats	5	$ 92,906,688	$ 89,212,077	$18,581,338	$17,842,415
Republicans	33	$146,837,255	$135,231,307	$ 4,449,614	$ 4,097,918
Incumbents	18	$ 78,803,908	$ 71,984,213	$ 4,377,995	$ 3,999,123
Challengers	10	$ 16,940,467	$ 14,267,814	$ 1,694,047	$ 1,426,781
Open seats	5	$ 51,092,880	$ 48,979,280	$10,218,576	$ 9,795,856
House					
Democrats	371	$235,308,296	$192,163,049	$ 634,254	$ 517,960
Incumbents	204	$150,534,048	$117,628,695	$ 737,912	$ 361,360
Open seats	32	$ 28,999,200	$ 25,750,691	$ 906,225	$ 804,709
Republicans	359	$234,529,537	$189,561,716	$ 653,286	$ 528,027
Incumbents	196	$168,269,518	$132,230,711	$ 858,518	$ 674,646
Challengers	132	$ 32,594,248	$ 28,542,530	$ 246,926	$ 216,231
Open seats	31	$ 33,665,771	$ 28,788,475	$1,085,993	$ 928,660

Source: Federal Election Commission

Alternatively, average or even strong economic growth may not help the president's party. Voters seem more willing to punish poor performance than to reward good results.

- *Another issue is the popularity of the president.* Many factors contribute to the president's job approval ratings, including the economy, foreign policy, scandal, relations with Congress, and personal factors. Typically, the president's party loses congressional seats in the midterm election. In the ten midterm elections between 1954 and 1990, the party that controlled the White House lost an average of twenty-three seats in the House and three in the Senate. The president's popularity affects how badly his party performs in the midterm election. In fact, many observers see the midterm election as a referendum on the president's job performance. That was certainly the case in 1994, when President Clinton's sagging approval rating cost the Democrats control of both the House and Senate.

- *In presidential election years, the president's own political survival not only depends on his popularity but also influences whether the president has coattails.* Presidents are said to have strong **coattails** if they can bring several new party members into Congress in a presidential election year. Because of the decline in partisanship, recent presidents have had weaker coattails than their predecessors. In fact, the Republicans controlled the presidency for twenty of the twenty-four years from 1969 to 1993, but the Democrats dominated the House throughout the entire period and controlled the Senate for eighteen of those years. This period of divided government suggests that congressional elections are no longer tied as closely to the popularity of presidents as they were for most of the first two centuries of the republic.

▶ **coattails** A presidential candidate's influence on the election of other members of the same party who are running for Congress.

Scandals Scandals can also influence congressional elections. The 1972 Watergate scandal involving the Republican administration of Richard Nixon led to a massive infusion of 91 new members in Congress in 1974 with the Democrats taking 49 of the 55 House seats that changed from one party to the other. Some would argue that the House bank scandal contributed to the large number of new legislators elected in 1992. Many members had written checks that would have bounced because of insufficient funds had they been deposited in an ordinary bank. In similar circumstances, most citizens would have to pay large fees and possibly suffer damage to their credit ratings, so some people saw the special treatment as proof that Congress is out of touch with the American public. Of the 46 members with more than a hundred overdrafts, 54 percent retired or lost. Of the 269 members who had any rubber checks, 77 (or 29 percent) retired or lost.

Congressional Elections: 1994 and Beyond Although many observers expected the Republicans to do well in the 1994 midterm congressional elections, only the most wildly optimistic Republicans would have predicted the magnitude of the Republican victory. Riding a wave of voter anger directed mainly at Democratic incumbents, the Republicans added eight Senate seats and fifty-three seats in the House. Consequently, the Republicans gained control of both the House and the Senate for the first time since 1954. The scope of the Democratic loss was underscored by the defeat of Tom Foley, the previous speaker of the house, and Jim Sasser, who was in a position to become the majority leader of the Senate. On the day after the election, President Clinton held a news conference in which he acknowledged some responsibility for the defeat. Clinton pledged to work with the new Republican leadership in an attempt to govern from the ideological center. No one expected that to be easy, however, as the parties in Congress had become more polarized and the Republicans were not in a mood to compromise. Although some commentators referred to the Republican victory as a tidal wave, it was more like an earthquake that dramatically changed the shape of the political landscape in Washington.

The zenith of Republican congressional domination came in 1994 with their nationalization of the midterm election. The Democrats gradually reduced the Republican advantage,

Comparative Perspective

Buying Elections—The United States and Thailand

In November 1993, the Republican Christine Whitman won the New Jersey governorship in a close election. The election may have been decided by the fact that urban African Americans, who normally vote Democratic, turned out to vote at a lower level than expected. A few days after the election, people were shocked when Whitman's campaign manager, Ed Rollins, claimed that campaign funds had been spent to "suppress" the urban African-American vote in the election. An angry Democratic party brought a lawsuit seeking to have the results of the election invalidated. In the midst of the furor, Rollins recanted, saying that he had lied about his original claim. Ultimately, the Democrats dropped their suit and the controversy subsided.

In this country, an attempt to buy an election is a major scandal. Yet at one time these types of practices were quite common, especially in the big cities run by political machines. Of course, many reformers would now argue that the American system of campaign finance has a corrupting influence on elections. Is it fair to say that elections in this country are for sale?

In Thailand, where democracy is still in its infancy, overt vote buying is standard operating procedure. Party activists routinely dispense gifts ranging from live ducks to movie tickets, lipsticks, and cash in the hope of currying favor with potential voters. In one province in 1993, a candidate was reported to have paid tailors to sew for villagers. In another province, a political party offered prospective voters free dental care. In a country where the annual per capita income is only about $1,500, these types of favors can make a strong impression. In remote villages, vote buyers may be the only connection that people have with the government in Bangkok. A reform effort is under way, and some candidates have pledged to forgo vote buying. But refraining from buying votes is difficult if an opponent is doing so, especially if the race appears to be close.

however, until 2000, when they came within six seats of winning the House and tying in the Senate. Despite their success in 1994, the national Republican Party did not attempt to run a national congressional campaign but rather joined the Democrats in running a district-by-district series of races stressing local as well as national issues. In 2002 and 2004, the Republicans were able to reverse recent Democratic gains and consolidate their hold over the House. As the new Congress began its work in 2005, Republicans held 230 of the 435 seats in the House.

Although George W. Bush won the presidency in 2000, the Democrats regained control of the United States Senate.[22] Their control was short-lived, however, because Republicans regained control in the 2002 midterm elections, albeit by the narrowest margin (51–49). In 2004, Republicans extended their control of the Senate by picking up four seats, including the seat formerly occupied by the minority leader, Tom Daschle of South Dakota. As of 2005, there were fewer Democrats in the Senate than at any time since 1938, when the Democrats held only 39 seats.

Recent congressional selections reveal a nation closely divided between Democratic and Republican voters with a substantial bloc of Independent voters willing to swing back and forth in their support of Republican and Democratic congressional candidates. The political landscape in the first decade of the twenty-first century is such that neither party can expect to maintain firm control of Congress over the long term.

11-7c The Perennial Campaign

Because members of the House of Representatives are up for reelection every two years, they always seem to be running for office. The public gets tired of congressional races and tends to be more interested in presidential contests, which occur only once every four years and involve major national issues. Not surprisingly, then, voter turnout tends to be quite low in most midterm elections, when no presidential race is taking place to stimulate interest. On the other hand, interest groups pay close attention to all congressional races. Members of Congress are continually in search of money from PACs. The public is more or less aware of this phenomenon, and it contributes to the low public regard for Congress as an institution.

11-8　Conclusion: Campaigns, Elections, and American Political Culture

Americans have been faulted for their low turnout in elections. Citizens in other democracies tend to turn out to vote at much higher levels. To some extent, the relatively low level of turnout in the United States reflects the alienation and cynicism of voters. But it is also a function of the complexity of the American electoral process and the sheer number of elections in which citizens are asked to participate. The American system of elections places a great burden on the average citizen, a burden that many are not willing to bear.

Most observers would agree that the process by which our leaders are chosen is too complicated and time-consuming. Furthermore, the immense sums of money required to wage a successful campaign deter many potentially qualified candidates from seeking office. Proposals for reform are made from time to time, but few have much chance of being adopted. The current structure is deeply embedded in American political culture.

American political culture is committed to the idea of representative democracy. No matter how bitter the campaign, Americans are taught to accept the outcome of an election and respect the legitimacy of the process. If more and more people become disaffected and choose not to vote, however, or if people participate begrudgingly, believing that the process is corrupt, it is only a matter of time before the system faces serious challenge. Thus, it came as a great relief to many when the 2004 presidential election was decided in a timely way, was widely perceived as fairly contested, and most Americans accepted the outcome.

Questions for Thought and Discussion

1. Should the United States have a national presidential primary in which each party chooses its presidential nominee? If this type of primary were instituted, what would the consequences be for the two major political parties?
2. How much weight should Americans give to the "character issue" in deciding whether to vote for a presidential candidate? Do the mass media give too much or too little attention to the character issue?
3. Considering that more Americans identify with the Democratic party than with the Republican party, why have Republicans been so successful in winning the presidency?
4. Should the electoral college be abolished? What would have to happen to bring about a movement to do away with it? Who might support this effort? Who would be likely to oppose it?
5. Should congressional campaigns be reformed to give incumbents less of a financial advantage than they now enjoy?

Practice Quiz

Note: You can find the correct answers to these questions by taking the quiz and then submitting your answers in the Online Edition. The program will automatically score your submission. If you miss a question, the program will provide the correct answer, a rationale for the answer, and the section number in the chapter where the topic is discussed.

1. Elections in which voters make policy directly by changing laws, constitutions, or charters are called _____.
   a. referenda
   b. direct elections
   c. general elections
   d. none of the above

2. The term describing the various factors contributing to the high rates of electoral success and low rates of turnover for members of Congress is the _____.
   a. turnover factor
   b. incumbency advantage
   c. iron triangle
   d. ADA rating

3. In the 2000 presidential election, African Americans voted overwhelmingly for _____.
   a. George W. Bush
   b. Pat Buchanan
   c. Al Gore
   d. Ralph Nader

4. A _____ is short clip, perhaps ten to fifteen seconds long, that provides a catchy phrase conveying a simple message.
   a. sound bite
   b. trial balloon
   c. leak
   d. spin spot

5. Political candidates in _____ spend more time campaigning for office than any other of the world's democracies.
   a. Great Britain
   b. Japan
   c. the United States
   d. Canada

6. On average, since 1950, more than _____ of the House members that have desired reelection have been successful at winning it.
   a. 60 percent
   b. 70 percent
   c. 80 percent
   d. 90 percent

7. The American presidential contest is marked by two significant phases: the _____ process and the _____ election.
   a. vetting; general
   b. referendum; electoral college
   c. induction; general
   d. nomination; general

8. The Constitution assigns the administration of elections to _____.
   a. Congress
   b. the state and local governments
   c. the Federal Election Commission
   d. the Department of Justice

9. _____ is the most crucial aspect of a presidential candidate's nomination strategy.
   a. Spin control
   b. Choosing a running mate
   c. Creating photo opportunities
   d. Raising money

10. The state with the greatest number of electoral votes is _____.
   a. California
   b. Texas
   c. Florida
   d. New York

For Further Reading

Alexander, Herbert. *Financing Politics: Money, Elections, and Political Reform,* 4th ed. (Washington, D.C.: Congressional Quarterly, 1992).

Asher, Herbert. *Presidential Elections and American Politics,* 5th ed. (Pacific Grove, CA: Brooks/Cole, 1997).

Ayengar, Shanto, and Stephen Ansolabehere. *Going Negative: How Political Advertisements Shrink and Polarize the Electorate* (New York: Free Press, 1996).

Bartels, Larry M. *Presidential Primaries and the Dynamics of Public Choice* (Princeton, NJ: Princeton University Press, 1988).

Campbell, Angus, Philip E. Converse, Warren E. Miller, and Donald E. Stokes. *The American Voter* (New York: John Wiley & Sons, 1960).

Cook, Rhodes. *The Presidential Nominating Process: A Place for Us?* (Lanham, MD: Rowman and Littlefield, 2003).

Crotty, William, and John S. Jackson. *The Politics of Presidential Selection,* 2d ed. (New York: Longman, 2001).

Fiorina, Morris P. *Retrospective Voting in American National Elections* (New Haven, CT: Yale University Press, 1988.)

Flanagan, William H., and Nancy H. Zingale. *Political Behavior of the American Electorate,* 9th ed. (Washington, D.C.: CQ Press, 1998).

Jacobson, Gary C. *The Politics of Congressional Elections,* 5th ed. (New York: Longman, 2000).

Magelby, David. *Financing the 2000 Election* (Washington, D.C.: Brookings Institution Press, 2001).

Nie, Norman H., Sidney Verba, and John R. Petrocik. *The Changing American Voter* (Cambridge, MA: Harvard University Press, 1979).

Polsby, Nelson W., and Aaron Wildavsky. *Presidential Elections: Contemporary Strategies of American Electoral Politics,* 10th ed. (New York: Chatham House, 2000).

Popkin, Samuel L. *The Reasoning Voter: Communication and Persuasion in Presidential Campaigns* (Chicago: University of Chicago Press, 1991).

Sabato, Larry. *Overtime! The Election 2000 Thriller* (New York: Longman, 2001).

Smith, Bradley A. *Unfree Speech : The Folly of Campaign Finance Reform* (Princeton, NJ: Princeton University Press, 2001).

Sorauf, Frank J. *Inside Campaign Finance: Myths and Realities* (New Haven, CT: Yale University Press, 1988).

Toobin, Jeffrey. *Too Close to Call: The Thirty-Six-Day Battle to Decide the 2000 Election* (New York: Random House, 2002).

Wayne, Stephen J. *The Road to the White House, 2000: The Politics of Presidential Elections* (New York: Bedford/St. Martin's Press, 2000).

White, Theodore H. *The Making of the President 1960* (NewYork: Atheneum,1961).

Endnotes

1. Voting turnout in a local primary election can run as low as 10 percent. Normally, turnout in local elections is in the 20 to 30 percent range.

2. Larry Sabato, *Feeding Frenzy: How Attack Journalism Has Transformed American Politics* (New York: Free Press, 1991).

3. Herbert A. Asher, *Presidential Elections and American Politics,* 5th ed. (Pacific Grove, CA: Brooks/Cole, 1992).

4. *Federal Election Commission v. Beaumont,* 539 U.S. 146, (2003).

5. Angus Campbell, Phillip E. Converse, Warren E. Miller, and Donald E. Stokes, *The American Voter* (Chicago: University of Chicago Press, 1960).

6. Asher, *Presidential Elections and American Politics,* p. 61.

7. See, for example, Kevin Phillips, *The Emerging Republican Majority* (New Rochelle, NY: Arlington House, 1969).

8. Campbell, Converse, Miller, and Stokes, *The American Voter.*

9. William Lyons and John M. Scheb II, "Ideology and Candidate Evaluation in the 1984 and 1988 Presidential Elections," *Journal of Politics,* May 1992.

10. Data for both 2000 and 2004 are taken from exit polls. Results reported in Marjorie Connelly, "How Americans Voted: A Political Portrait," *New York Times Week in Review,* November 7, 2004, p. 4.

11. Samuel A. Kirkpatrick, William Lyons, and Michael Fitzgerald, "Candidates, Parties and Issues in the American Electorate: Two Decades of Change," *American Politics Quarterly,* July 1975.

12. *Bush v. Palm Beach Canvassing Board,* 531 U.S. 98 (2000).

13. *Bush v. Gore,* 531 U.S. 98 (2000).

14. Survey conducted January 15–16, 2001, by the Gallup Organization.

15. Federal Election Commission (*www.fec.gov*).

16. David Price, *The Congressional Experience: A View from the Hill* (Boulder, CO: Westview Press, 1992), p. 28.

17. Beth Donovan and Ilyse J. Veron, "Freshmen Got to Washington with Help of PAC Funds," *Congressional Quarterly Weekly,* March 27, 1993, p. 723.

18. Ibid., p. 724

19. Ibid., p. 723.

20. Michael Barone and Grant Ujifusa, *The Almanac of American Politics 1994* (Washington, D.C.: National Journal, 1993), pp. 1453, 1461.

21. Richard Fenno, *Home Style: House Members in Their Districts* (Boston: Little, Brown, 1978).

22. The Democrats were aided by the defection of Republican Jim Jeffords of Vermont, who after winning reelection as a Republican in 2000, declared that he would thereafter be an Independent, although he voted much more with the Democrats than the Republicans during the period 2001–2004.

Congress

12-1 The National Legislature

In a democracy, the governmental institution that enacts the laws is referred to as the legislature. In the United States, the national legislature is the Congress, which is made up of two chambers: the House of Representatives and the Senate. In addition to adopting laws governing the nation, Congress has the responsibility to see that the laws it passes are administered by the executive branch in the ways that Congress intended when it passed them. Moreover, members of Congress represent the citizens who live in the areas that elect them and are expected to provide service to their constituents. Congress is also occasionally required to act in a judicial fashion, such as when considering whether to impeach and remove the president or a federal judge. Finally, Congress has certain electoral powers because it is required to choose the president and vice president if no candidate secures a majority of the electoral college vote.

12-1a The Congressional System Versus the Parliamentary System

The American system of government differs considerably from the parliamentary system of Great Britain and most European countries. A parliamentary system is organized around more centralized and disciplined political parties, and the legislative branch is clearly superior to the executive. In England, a person runs for Parliament as a candidate of the Labour, Conservative, or Liberal party. The candidates are chosen and approved by their respective parties, and members of Parliament are expected to vote with their parties when laws are being considered. The majority party in Parliament chooses the prime minister, who along with the cabinet wields executive power. But, unlike the American president, the prime minister and the cabinet are directly accountable to the Parliament. Thus, no separation exists between the lawmaking and administrative branches of a parliamentary system. This system stands in stark contrast to the American congressional system (or presidential system, as it is sometimes called). In this country, congressional candidates seek office as Democrats or Republicans, but they may run with or without the blessing of the official party structure. After members of Congress are in office, they vote with their parties most of the time, but they are in no way bound to do so. Presidents need the support of Congress to get legislation passed, but presidents, unlike prime ministers, do not rely on members of the legislature to stay in office. In fact, a politically astute president can sometimes

With its cornerstone placed in 1793, the Capitol has been the meeting place of the United States Congress since 1801. Before that time, Congress met in New York (1789–1790) and Philadelphia (1791–1800).

increase his status by opposing the actions of a Congress controlled by the opposition party. President Clinton enjoyed his greatest popularity when Republicans held majorities in both the House and the Senate, especially when the House impeached him.

Although presidents and the Congress are not bound together as are the chief executive and legislature in a parliamentary system, they often act very much in concert in times of national emergency. For instance, following the September 11, 2001, terrorist attacks, Congress voted almost unanimously to support President Bush in approving the use of military force against Osama bin Laden's al-Qaeda terrorist network. These eras of cooperation are often short lived. By May 2002, many Democrats were openly questioning the way in which the president and his administration had dealt with information about potential terrorist threats before September 11.

12-1b Congress and the Two-Party System

Many parliamentary systems are structured so that minor political parties can win seats in the legislature. Typically, candidates run nationwide with a provision that a party will win a number of seats in proportion to its share of the popular vote. In the United States, the electoral system is quite different. All members of the U.S. Congress are elected from **single-member districts;** that is, only one person represents a particular geographic area. This statement is certainly true of the House of Representatives, where each member represents a district carved out of a state. The number of districts in a state depends on its population. In the Senate, of course, two senators represent each state, but the two senators' terms in office are staggered. Thus, states are single-member districts in the sense that only one candidate wins a Senate seat in each election. It is virtually impossible for candidates from minor political parties to win seats in Congress. With rare exceptions, all members of Congress are from either the Democratic or Republican party. The two-party system in Congress frustrates certain voters, who may wish for clearer alternatives to the Democrats and Republicans. Most observers agree, however, that the two-party system promotes stability in politics and policy making.

> **single-member districts**
> Electoral system in which only one person represents a particular geographic area.

12-2 Functions of Congress

The delegates to the Constitutional Convention of 1787 had two purposes in mind in restructuring the Congress. First, they wanted a forum in which legislators could deliberate on the conditions of the nation, debate policy alternatives, and carefully consider the plans and actions of the government. Second, the Founders intended for the legislators to represent the people who placed them in office. To allow members to pursue the policy development aspect of the job, the Constitution gives Congress broad powers over the economy and taxation, oversight of the bureaucracy, and some influence over foreign affairs. To ensure that members could feel free to express their opinions, the Constitution prevents the executive branch and the judiciary from arresting members for their debate on the floor of Congress. The Constitution also allows members to devise their own rules for conducting business in Congress. Combined with the power to develop a budget, this self-governance feature later resulted in Congress' providing itself with staff members, a library, offices, research agencies, and other resources necessary for conducting legislative business.

In addition to this deliberative function, the Congress is also charged with representing the people. Because the judicial branch and the bureaucracy are appointed and the president is elected by the entire nation, the only way local interests are heard in the national government is through the members of Congress. The Constitution provides for this relationship through the method of frequent elections. A House member is elected every two years from a district that elects only one legislator to the House. Senators are chosen every six years by states, but each state has two senators whose terms in office are staggered. Before the ratification of the Seventeenth Amendment in 1913, senators were chosen by the state legislatures, but they have since been chosen in statewide popular elections. Because of the longer span of time between elections for senators versus representatives, it

Comparative Perspective

Representation in the Israeli Knesset

Every democracy must define the manner in which the public is represented in its legislative body. The United States has opted for winner-take-all single-member districts for the House of Representatives and Senate. Each member of Congress represents a geographically defined area. Each election produces only one winner for that particular seat. If a party is to achieve representation in Congress, it must win a series of seats outright. A party that finishes with 30 percent of the vote nationwide without winning any particular election outright does not earn any seats in Congress. These results are one reason that the United States has a two-party system rather than a multiparty system.

Other countries use different systems of representation. Some systems are predicated on the idea that a party earning, for example, 30 percent of the vote nationwide should get 30 percent of the seats in the legislature. This system is called proportional representation. One country that has this type of system is Israel. Israelis vote for a slate of candidates put forward by each party. Candidates do not represent any particular geographic area. Because the Knesset (the Israeli parliament) has 120 seats, each party can have as many as 120 candidates on its slate. After the votes are counted, the seats are apportioned to the parties based on the proportion of the vote. Each party that receives as many as 1 percent of the votes cast is entitled to a seat in the Knesset.

This type of system ensures representation of virtually all viewpoints. Israel has a great many diverse parties, largely because almost every party with any support at all finds itself represented in government. Eleven parties are now represented in the Knesset. With so many parties, obtaining a majority is quite difficult, however. Thus, the party with the most votes has to form a coalition with one or more minor parties to have the majority it needs to form a government. Proportional representation leads to quite a different type of legislative body than does the single-member district representation utilized by the U.S. Congress. Politics in the Israeli Knesset, for example, are less stable and less predictable than in the U.S. Congress.

In 2002, the coalition government led by Prime Minister Ariel Sharon was severely tested as Israeli public opinion became sharply divided over the government's military response to the Palestinian suicide bombings and the larger question of Palestinian statehood. Sharon faced the constant threat that his government would collapse because of right-wing defections from his governing coalition. The mechanism used to bring down a government is the motion of no confidence, which requires sixty-one votes to succeed.

---

is generally thought that the Founders intended for the representatives to be closer and more responsive to the people than senators.

The problem, however, is that these two functions—deliberation and representation—often are not compatible. Policy deliberation requires lots of time. Good policy making requires careful research, much debate, input from concerned citizens and those affected by the policy, and the development of substantial expertise. This activity keeps the legislators in Washington. On the other hand, representation of the people can also be quite demanding. A member must spend time visiting constituents in the district (which may be thousands of miles from D.C.), responding to inquiries (including letters, phone calls, and personal visits), and, to secure reelection, campaigning actively in the district. The representation function claims much of the legislator's time and energy. Therefore, a member must make trade-offs between these two functions in terms of time and energy.

12-2a Representing Constituents

Representation is a central issue in considering the functions of Congress, but this concept has multiple dimensions. One dimension is referred to as **descriptive representation.** In other words, does the membership of Congress look like the American people in terms of gender, race, religion, age, education, and occupation, for example? Do all identifiable social groups have a member in the legislature?

▶ **descriptive representation**
One of the various roles of Congress in which the membership in the legislative body is expected to reflect the key demographic characteristics of the population.

Members of Congress are overwhelmingly white, male, Christian, highly educated, wealthy individuals. A large number are lawyers, and most have been politicians for years or even decades. Females, ethnic minorities, religious minorities, and blue-collar workers have fewer legislators (in percentage terms) than their share of the population. This situation leads many people to question whether Congress is good at providing descriptive representation. Because representation is an abstract concept that involves an individual's own subjective feelings, descriptive concerns may have a powerful effect on how people feel about the government and the American system. Therefore, the look of Congress may influence the levels of political trust and participation in the system.

Recent decades, although not altering the preceding description, have certainly seen a more diverse Congress. The 108th Congress that took office in January 2003 had 37 African Americans, 23 Hispanics, 73 women, 8 Asian Pacific Islanders, and 2 Native Americans. There is every reason to believe that the diversity of Congress will continue to increase, although not at the pace that many critics of the current Congress would prefer.

Symbolic Representation

Symbolic Representation   Representation also involves a symbolic component. People must believe that they are being represented, and symbolism can be used to increase the likelihood that people will feel this way. Televised sessions of Congress, public discussions of issues on television talk shows, and newsletters from members to their constituents are examples of activities that may cause voters to feel that they are being represented. For others, elections and campaigns for office may provide enough symbolic reassurance of the representation function. Members of Congress are quite aware of the importance of symbolism, and they take every opportunity—such as giving speeches at high schools or providing a flag that has flown over the Capitol to a school—to encourage the voters' belief that they are being represented. These activities come under the heading of **symbolic representation.**

Service Representation

Service Representation   The process of making government services available to the people and allowing individuals to believe that government is there for them is referred to as **service representation.** Because the federal bureaucracy is so large, embracing hundreds of agencies and thousands of programs, the rules can be overwhelming. Accordingly, legislators help individuals and organizations (such as businesses, schools, or even city governments) in obtaining government services. Members of Congress routinely handle a variety of requests. High school students may ask for help in obtaining information for a research paper. An injured person may ask for assistance in obtaining disability insurance payments from the Social Security Administration. A business owner may need help in obtaining a check from a government agency for services performed for the government. The process of providing this type of help is known as **casework.**

When a member of Congress intercedes with an administrative agency on behalf of a citizen, the member is performing the role of an **ombudsman** (see Box 12-1). Because the demand for constituency service has increased so dramatically in this century, the members themselves cannot possibly handle all the requests. Nevertheless, the members recognize that providing these services can have potential electoral benefits. Voters may be opposed to a member's policy decisions, but few will be angry and some will be extremely happy if the member helps a senior citizen get her Social Security check. Because the members of Congress control the federal budget, they have chosen to take this opportunity to please voters by providing funding for staff and district offices for each member. The large personal staff that each member receives free of charge from the government performs almost all the casework, but the member reaps the benefits of performing the service role.

Competing Models of Policy Representation

Competing Models of Policy Representation   Policy representation requires that a legislator make policy decisions that are best for her constituents. But what does "best for constituents" mean? A legislator who adopts the **trustee style of representation** is one who makes policy decisions based on what she thinks is best. The member can be removed from office if the voters do not agree with her view of what is best, but as each vote occurs, the member makes an independent decision. Conversely, a legislator who embraces the

---

symbolic representation A style of representation in which a legislator employs various symbolic strategies to make people feel that they are playing a significant role in the political process.

service representation A style of representation in which a legislator emphasizes providing services to his constituents.

casework   The activities a legislator engages in to help constituents obtain government services.

ombudsman   An official who investigates and tries to resolve problems that people have with public agencies.

policy representation A style of representation in which the legislator makes policy decisions that are best for her constituents.

trustee style of representation   A style of representation in which a legislator makes policy decisions based on her own values rather than on the demands of constituents.

Box 12-1   Congressional Representation

Increasingly, women and minorities are playing leadership roles in American business and government.

Republican Senator (and former Nebraska football coach) Tom Osborne autographing a copy of his book, *On Solid Ground*, for students.

AP Photo / Will Kincaid

Providing constituent service might even include giving information to a college student for a term paper.

© Royalty-Free / CORBIS

As an ombudsman, a member of Congress might assist a veteran with obtaining government benefits and services.

AP Photo / Joe Marquette

▶ **delegate style of representation**   A style of representation in which a legislator votes in a manner consistent with constituents' preferences.

delegate style of representation acts on what he thinks the constituents in the district want. The delegate is not worried about making the best decision in terms of how well the policy will work or how much it costs or whether the president wants it; rather, the delegate is nothing more than a translator of citizen preferences into final congressional votes.

Some people would argue that a delegate is not capable of providing any kind of leadership; only a trustee has the kind of leeway to make difficult votes on issues that may not be politically popular. For example, the civil rights bills of the 1960s were not favored by a majority of Americans, so a legislature full of delegates would not have passed these antidiscrimination laws. Because some legislators chose to do what they personally thought was best for the country, the Civil Rights Act of 1964, the Voting Rights Act of 1965, and the Fair Housing Act of 1968 were passed in the face of contrary public opinion polls. Of course, few legislators would subscribe to either view of representation in the purest sense. Legislators, because they are pragmatists for the most part, choose whichever style they think is best for a given occasion.

Overall, each form of representation contributes to an understanding of how Congress works, although service representation stands out for the pervasive manner in which it influences the way members shape the institution and their own time. Policy representation, however, may be the most important in understanding how well Congress governs the country. If the Congress appears to do no more than what is now popular with the people calling in to radio talk shows, it appears to lack leadership. On the other hand, if Congress forces too much unpopular policy onto the electorate through the trustee role, it appears out of touch with the people. Either extreme leaves members of Congress vulnerable to attack.

12-2b Making Laws

The Framers of the Constitution wanted a strong legislature to be the keystone of the new national government. Thus, the Constitution gave the new Congress much broader powers than the legislature that existed under the Articles of Confederation. These constitutional powers may be divided into two broad categories:

- *Enumerated powers:* Include those powers mentioned specifically in the Constitution.
- *Implied powers:* Include those powers inferred from general language in the founding document.

Enumerated Powers   Although the enumerated powers of Congress are spelled out in a number of provisions scattered throughout the Constitution, most of the key powers are provided in Article I, Section 8. They include the powers to

- Lay and collect taxes
- Borrow money
- Provide for the common defense and general welfare of the United States
- Declare war
- Raise and support an army and a navy
- Regulate the militia when called into service
- Regulate commerce among the states
- Control immigration and naturalization
- Regulate bankruptcy
- Coin money
- Fix standards of weights and measures
- Establish post offices and post roads
- Grant patents and copyrights
- Establish tribunals "inferior to the Supreme Court"

The Constitution did not confer on Congress the police power—the general authority to make laws for the protection of the public welfare. Under our country's federal system, this responsibility was vested in the state and local governments. But over the years, the enumerated powers of Congress, especially its power to regulate interstate commerce, have been broadened substantially by congressional action and judicial acceptance. For example, Congress is not empowered to prohibit prostitution per se, but it may make transporting persons across state lines for purposes of prostitution a crime by drawing on its broad power to regulate interstate commerce.[1] Congress has invoked the commerce power to make policy in many areas ranging from environmental protection to organized crime to civil rights. Judicial acquiescence to this type of legislation led many observers to believe that the commerce power had been converted into a virtual police power. However, in recent years the Supreme Court has imposed some boundaries around Congress' use of the commerce clause. In one important case, by a 5–4 margin the Court struck down the 1990

Gun Free Schools Act, which had made it a federal crime to take a gun within one thousand feet of a school.[2] Still, Congress' power under the Commerce Clause is broad indeed.

Constitutional Amendments Conferring Power on Congress   Several constitutional amendments confer additional powers on Congress. Importantly, the Sixteenth Amendment permits Congress to "lay and collect taxes on incomes from whatever source derived, without apportionment among the states." This amendment nullified an earlier Supreme Court decision striking down an income tax imposed by Congress. A number of constitutional amendments endow Congress with the power to legislate in support of civil rights and liberties. For example, the Thirteenth, Fourteenth, and Fifteenth Amendments permit Congress to enforce civil rights through "appropriate legislation." The Nineteenth Amendment removes gender as an impediment to voting, and the Twenty-sixth Amendment lowers to eighteen the voting age in state and federal elections. Both amendments contain clauses permitting Congress to enforce their terms by "appropriate legislation."

Implied Powers   Congress obviously now exercises far more powers than are specifically enumerated in the Constitution. The Necessary and Proper Clause (Article I, Section 8, Clause 18) permits Congress to "make all laws which shall be necessary and proper for carrying into Execution the foregoing powers, and all other powers vested by this Constitution in the Government of the United States. . . ." This clause has been interpreted to provide Congress with a vast reservoir of implied powers. Under the doctrine of implied powers, there is scarcely any area in which Congress is absolutely barred from acting because most problems have a conceivable relationship to the broad powers and objectives contained in the Constitution. Thomas Jefferson, an opponent of the doctrine of implied powers, perceived as much in 1790 when he wrote a memorandum to President George Washington, saying "To take a single step beyond the boundaries thus specially drawn around the powers of Congress is to take possession of a boundless field of power, no longer susceptible of any definition." The constitutional powers of Congress, although not exactly "boundless," are now certainly far greater than most of the Founders could have imagined.

12-2c Controlling the Purse Strings of Government

The single most time-consuming issue on the legislative calendar in any year is the federal budget. In Article I, Section 7, the Constitution requires that all "bills for raising revenue shall originate in the House of Representatives; but the Senate may propose or concur with amendments as on other bills." As with any other bill, the president may veto appropriations bills, and Congress may override the veto. In addition, Congress has important powers over the budget and economy through such powers as the ability to lay and collect taxes, pay the debts and provide for the common defense and welfare of the United States, borrow money, coin money, and pay for a navy and an army. Without this power over the purse, Congress would not be effective in its struggles with the president, the bureaucracy, or the states.

By custom, the president sends an annual budget proposal to Capitol Hill, and Congress has also established its own complex organizations and rules for dealing with the federal budget. Each year, the president's staff in the Office of Management and Budget provides a detailed plan that can number in the tens of thousands of pages, and Congress has its own set of estimates, established by the Congressional Budget Office. Congress considers the president's recommendations, and it may choose to alter the president's proposal, reject it, or pass its own alternative.

The Budgetary Process   Congress divides its budgetary process into three parts. The Appropriations Committees in the House and Senate consider how the money will be spent for each executive department and program. The Ways and Means Committee in the House and the Finance Committee in the Senate decide how the revenue will be raised (or, in other words, who will pay the taxes). Finally, the budget committees in each chamber

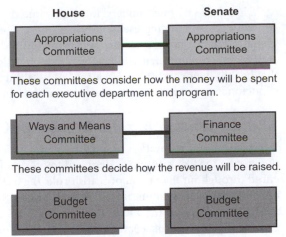

House   **Senate**

| Appropriations Committee | Appropriations Committee |

These committees consider how the money will be spent for each executive department and program.

| Ways and Means Committee | Finance Committee |

These committees decide how the revenue will be raised.

| Budget Committee | Budget Committee |

These committees establish the overall spending and revenue levels.

Figure 12-1
How Money Moves through the Federal Bureaucracy

establish the overall spending and revenue levels. All details, however, are still worked out in the Revenue and Appropriations Committees. Consequently, you can easily imagine that the money committees are the most influential and desirable of all legislative committees. Of course, the full chamber (House or Senate) must approve all proposals made by its committees. Ultimately, both chambers must pass the identical budget before it can be sent to the president for approval (see Figure 12-1).

Particularism and the Pork Barrel   The annual budget deficits that occurred from 1969 to 1997 focused much more attention on this function of Congress. One result is that the congressional budgeting procedures became increasingly controversial. Despite four major overhauls of the budget process since 1974, some critics still maintain that the major problem is that members engage in **particularism,** where a member of Congress considers legislation only in terms of how it affects the home district. Particularism means that rather than consider whether the nation needs something, such as a permanent space station, members vote for it only if they can get some of the contracts in their districts.

The **pork barrel** is a pejorative term suggesting that an expenditure is not only particularistic but also wasteful. The term refers to a government project or spending measure that benefits a certain legislator's constituency. Most people would agree that a Coast Guard station in the middle of a desert would be wasteful spending, but most of the time it is difficult to get people to agree on what is "pork." A congressional district's new six-lane highway through a town of only ten thousand people may appear to be pork barrel spending to an outsider, but to the residents of the community the new highway means jobs and economic growth in addition to enhanced public safety and convenience.

Any efforts to curtail pork barrel expenditures are particularly difficult in times of budget surplus. Even though the Republicans controlled both the House and Senate during the 106th Congress, they found themselves adding many questionable items to the final appropriations bill at the end of the session in late 2000. In a speech on the Senate floor, Senator John McCain (R-Arizona), a longtime critic of pork barrel spending, claimed that "[t]ens of billions in pork barrel and special-interest spending have been packed into these appropriations bills, as well as numerous provisions pushed by Capitol Hill lobbyists that the American public will not know about until after these bills become law." McCain complained that "all of this maneuvering and horse trading has been conducted behind closed doors, away from the public eye, bypassing a process whereby all of my elected colleagues could evaluate the merit of each budget item." McCain's comments were not so much directed at the pork barrel spending for Fiscal Year 2001, but rather at the underlying particularism engaged in by his colleagues, including many who had been critical of excessive spending. McCain was especially critical of further pork barrel spending in the spending bills for FY 2002 that were added following the September 11, 2001, terrorist attacks.

particularism   Situations in which a member of Congress considers legislation only in terms of whether it produces tangible benefits for her home district.

pork barrel   A pejorative term for wasteful government spending that provides benefits to particular congressional districts.

However, one must understand that some degree of particularism is the inevitable consequence of how representation in Congress (especially the House) is structured. A member's first concern is for the well-being of his district (or state in the case of the Senate). Members show their concern by obtaining federal money for projects and programs that benefit their constituents. In an age of fiscal surpluses, little pressure exists (other than condemnation from mavericks like Senator McCain) to control pork barrel spending.

12-2d Maintaining the System of Checks and Balances

The principle of separation of powers, which is a fundamental part of the philosophy underlying the Constitution, is designed to prevent tyranny. Because of the abuses experienced throughout the period of British rule, the executive branch was particularly suspect of being capable of tyrannical acts. Therefore, the Founders were quite concerned with providing Congress with the ability to place checks on executive power. Despite this effort to provide the principle of separation of power with some teeth, each branch has the responsibility to maintain the balance. Historically, Congress has had to hold its ground against persistent encroachment by the executive branch. Typically, presidents have asserted their powers most vigorously during times that demanded stronger and more decisive government leadership. Thus, the Civil War and the Great Depression provided Abraham Lincoln and Franklin D. Roosevelt, respectively, with the greatest opportunities for expanding the powers of the president at the expense of the Congress.

The Constitution has provided several methods for Congress to maintain checks on the other two branches. The most powerful check has already been discussed: the power of the purse. Neither the judiciary nor the executive branch is capable of doing anything without money. Of course, Congress does not have complete control over the budget because of the presidential veto.

Checking the Chief Executive Congress can check presidential powers by several means. First, it can override a presidential veto by a two-thirds vote in each chamber. Second, all presidential appointments to either executive or judicial positions are subject to confirmation by the Senate, where a simple majority must vote to confirm. Third, the Senate must approve of all presidential treaties with other nations by a two-thirds vote. Fourth, Congress is responsible for oversight of the bureaucracy. Congress performs **oversight** when it examines the actions of the various departments and agencies to see whether they are executing the laws in a manner consistent with the intent of the legislature.

▶ **oversight** Congressional supervision of the various executive departments and agencies.

Finally, Congress can impeach the president or any executive officer. The term *impeachment* technically refers to the action of the House of Representatives in adopting one or more articles of impeachment by a majority vote. To be removed from office, the impeached official must be convicted of "high crimes or misdemeanors" by the Senate. Only twice in our history have presidents been impeached, but both Andrew Johnson and Bill Clinton were acquitted by the Senate (see Chapter 13, "The Presidency," for additional discussion).

Checking the Court The legislature spends much more time on maintaining checks on executive power than on judicial power, but its contacts with the judiciary can be quite dramatic, as evidenced by the Clarence Thomas confirmation hearings in 1991. Thomas, a federal appeals court judge, was nominated by President George Bush to succeed Justice Thurgood Marshall, who had just retired from the Supreme Court. When allegations of sexual harassment were made against Judge Thomas by Anita Hill, who had worked for Thomas when he chaired the Equal Employment Opportunity Commission, the nomination was almost derailed.

Congress influences the judiciary in a number of ways. One way is through the judicial appointment process. All presidential nominations to the federal courts must be approved by the Senate. Usually, the confirmation hearings held in the Senate Judiciary Committee are less sensational than the Clarence Thomas–Anita Hill saga. The Senate is mainly interested in the qualifications and ideology of the person nominated. The Senate is unlikely to approve a nominee whose qualifications are seriously questioned or whose ideology is unacceptable to the majority of senators. This confirmation function, which the Constitution refers to as "advise and consent," helps shape the judiciary and, ultimately, the decisions that emerge from it.

Congress can attempt to undo judicial decisions in two ways. Court decisions based on the interpretation of a statute can be countered by amending the statute. Judicial decisions based on interpretation of the Constitution can be nullified by amending the Constitution itself. The latter is difficult to accomplish because it requires not only passage by a two-thirds vote in both chambers of Congress but also ratification by three-fourths of the states. Nevertheless, four times in our country's history, particular Supreme Court decisions have been reversed through the adoption of a constitutional amendment.[3]

The ultimate weapon that Congress may use against the judicial branch is impeachment. No justice of the Supreme Court has ever been removed from office by Congress. In 1801, Justice Samuel Chase was impeached by the House, but he was narrowly acquitted in the Senate. The Chase proceeding set quite an important precedent: Federal judges are not to be impeached unless they are guilty of "high crimes or misdemeanors." Political differences between the Court and the Congress are not a proper basis for impeachment.

12-3 The Institutional Development of Congress

The first Congress in 1789 was composed of sixty-five House members and twenty-six senators. Each House member represented thirty thousand citizens. After a majority of legislators arrived in New York City, the first capital, legislative business began. Indeed, the First Congress began working before the inauguration of President Washington in April 1789. Some of its first concerns were the internal organization of each chamber, the issue of tariffs, the organization of the federal courts, and what title to use when addressing the president. Vice President John Adams, in his dual role as president of the Senate, pushed for discussion of the presidential title. Some of the suggested titles were His Mightiness the President of the United States of America and Protector of Their Liberties, His Highness, or His Mighty Highness. Several legislators scoffed at such pretensions. They referred to Adams as His Rotundity in mocking his proposals and eventually settled on a simpler title suggested by James Madison: the President of the United States.[4]

In the first few sessions of Congress, few formal rules or institutions constrained the legislators. Most of the action took place on the floor of each chamber. There were no permanent committees, and most of the debate on each bill was conducted on the floor. Ad hoc, or temporary, committees were formed as they were needed to work out the details of a bill. In one session, there were 350 ad hoc committees. Not until Thomas Jefferson's presidency, from 1801 to 1809, did Congress establish permanent, standing committees. The committees did not have fixed jurisdiction over a policy area, however, so they had little opportunity to block legislation or radically change proposals. Most committee chairs were considered close allies of President Jefferson. Through his "lieutenants" in the legislature, the president was able to dominate congressional actions.

Another important characteristic of the early Congress was that legislators were amateur politicians who would spend only a few years in Congress and then return to their district and continue their chosen professions. After the capital was moved to the new town of Washington, few people were interested in spending much time in a little town full of mosquitoes, high temperatures, and high humidity during the summer. Membership in Congress changed quite frequently. About half the House members in the second Congress were new. The average tenure of a member in the first ten Congresses was only four years. The legislative session was just a few months long, and by today's standard, few bills were discussed. Typically fewer than two hundred bills were considered in each of the first ten sessions of Congress.

Important differences also existed between the two chambers. Senators were chosen by state legislatures at that time, so they also differed somewhat in their attitudes. The Senate was much more of a "gentleman's club." It kept most of its meetings secret, and it was viewed as somewhat of an executive council in that it conferred more directly with administrative

Popular Culture in American Politics
Mr. Smith Goes to Washington

Frank Capra's classic 1939 film *Mr. Smith Goes to Washington* portrays the quintessential hard-working American, decent and honest, taking on the rich and the powerful.

When Senator Sam Foley dies, the power structure discusses who can be trusted to protect a pet project. The state's senior senator, Joseph Paine, desperately wants to keep scrutiny away from a corrupt dam construction project that would benefit a small group of connected people. He wants to make sure that whoever replaces Senator Foley will not cause trouble. Jefferson Smith (played by Jimmy Stewart) seems like a suitable patsy. He is a hero, having played a major role in putting out a forest fire around the town of Sweetwater. But he is naïve in the ways of politics.

When Mr. Smith is appointed by the governor to fill out the term of the departed senator Foley, those in the power structure are not worried. They are convinced that the simple-minded Mr. Smith will not ask too many questions or cause any trouble. Of course, their confidence is misplaced. Mr. Smith goes to Washington and refuses to go along. He is awed by the grandeur of the capital and soon finds himself supporting a boy's camp that threatens the corrupt dam project. He is then cynically framed by others in the Senate, but, despite incredible odds, conducts a climactic filibuster in which he finally defeats his corrupt senate colleague. American idealism and basic values of citizenship are victorious.

Although modern-day audiences might have a hard time finding *Mr. Smith Goes to Washington* believable, they certainly would have little trouble imagining some corruption in Congress. Jefferson Smith represents an American icon, a principled individual in a tainted institution.

Americans do tend to think well of their own representative while thinking badly of Congress as a whole. People like to think that their own representatives are like Mr. Smith, even if they suspect that the institution is corrupt.

officers. By 1794, the Senate had removed the secrecy rule, but it still remained a much less active organization than the House. Senator John Quincy Adams wrote in his diary that "the year which this day expires has been distinguished in the course of my life by its barrenness of events."[5] The Senate proposed less legislation, spent less time in committees, and received less public attention than the House.

12-3a An Evolving Institution

Throughout the nineteenth century, the legislature changed from a largely disorganized body with few committees, no parties, and little stability in membership into a more professional, organized assembly. In 1810, the War Hawk faction, led by Henry Clay, won the congressional elections. Consequently, Clay was elected Speaker, and he quickly asserted himself by expanding the powers of the office. He was the first speaker to make appointments to permanent committees independently from the president. He also established five House committees to oversee expenditures in the federal bureaucracy. One author notes that by 1814 "the committee system had become the dominant force in the chamber."[6] The committees became the congressional workhorses slogging through the grudging details of legislation. But the speaker retained tight control over appointments to committees and their jurisdictions. From 1810 to 1910, the speaker exerted tremendous control over the House.

The legislative workload also changed dramatically. In the Twelfth Congress, about 400 measures were introduced, but by the Twenty-fourth Congress in 1835, more than 1,100 measures were being proposed. In the Sixtieth Congress, which met from 1907 to 1909, more than 38,000 proposals were introduced. Until the 1820s, Congress usually passed more than 50 percent of the proposals. But, as the total number of measures introduced grew, the percentage of bills that were passed dropped quite dramatically. By the twentieth century, fewer than 10 percent of the proposals, on average, were passed in Congress.

Differences between the House and the Senate became more important politically during this time. Because of the equal representation of the states in the Senate and the rising tensions between the North and the South over the issue of slavery, the Senate became the primary battleground for legislative disputes over regional differences. Also, because it had no single leader as powerful as the Speaker in the House, the Senate maintained a bit more independence from tight leadership control. The Senate's committees evolved a bit more slowly than the system in the House, but the Senate also never had to experience a battle between its members and leaders like the one the House experienced in 1910.

The Strong Committee System   Until the twentieth century, most Speakers of the House had been relative amateurs. Of the thirty-three speakers before 1899, twenty-five had fewer than eight years of service in the House before moving into the top position. None had more than fourteen years of service before being elected speaker. Between 1899 and 1999, however, no speaker was elected who had fewer than fifteen years of experience.[7] Almost all of them had at least twenty years of service before .being chosen as speaker. Because of the powerful position that speakers had assumed in the House, the position became more prestigious. But as speakers increasingly centralized their control over the House, other members became frustrated with the system.

In 1910, House Republicans revolted against their leader, Speaker Joe Cannon. Cannon had been speaker since 1903 and had wielded strong powers. He appointed committees, picked committee chairs, set the legislative calendar, decided who would get to speak on the floor during debate, and determined who would get to reconcile legislative differences with the Senate on conference committees. The speaker's readiness to punish members who did not agree with him precipitated the revolt. In some cases, he had either failed to promote to a chair a member with the greatest seniority or had stripped a chair of his position.

The outcome of the insurgency against Cannon was a committee system that was much more independent of the speaker. The committees would now enjoy a fixed jurisdiction over a particular policy area no matter how the speaker felt about the issue. Furthermore, **seniority** on a committee (the number of years served continuously on the committee) would determine the ascent to leadership regardless of the member's relationship with the speaker. Committees would also have more power over their own, internal rules of organization. Finally, the speaker would no longer control appointments to the committees. The Ways and Means Committee, the committee responsible for tax policy, would now decide committee appointments. The overall effect of the revolt was that committee chairs became power brokers within the system who could make or break a bill.

▶ **seniority**   The number of years served continuously on a given committee; a key criterion in making committee assignments.

Decentralization and Fragmentation   The strong committee system continued to control the House of Representatives until the 1970s. By that time, however, an undercurrent of dissent had been developing over the abuses of power by committee chairs. Because seniority determined who received the chair, members from safe seats were more likely to serve enough time to become a chair. A **safe seat** is a representative's district that is so one-sided that it always elects a member of the same party to the House. These types of seats were especially common in the South from the 1870s until the 1960s. Because the Republicans were the party of Abraham Lincoln and the Union in the Civil War, the South had few Republican politicians until the Democrats became involved with the civil rights movement in the 1960s. Consequently, many chairs in both chambers were southern Democrats who were quite conservative, particularly on civil rights issues. Many northern Democrats who were elected in the 1960s and 1970s felt stymied by a system that prevented them from pushing for civil rights, social welfare policy, and other liberal reforms. These new members were aware of the need to establish their own leadership credentials for election purposes. Also, these members were influenced by the political culture of the time, which was one of change and of questioning authority. This influx of new members conspired against the power structure and brought on the most important reforms of Congress since 1910.

▶ **safe seat**   A representative's district that is so one-sidedly partisan that it always elects a member of the same party to the House.

A series of reforms were instituted in the 1970s, but the three most important for congressional procedure were the elimination of the automatic seniority rule for becoming a chair, the institution of multiple referral, and the establishment of the so-called Subcommittee Bill of Rights. The Democrats in the House determined that seniority would still matter in determining rank within a committee, but they now ruled that a majority of votes among just the Democrats in the House could remove a chair. Though this rule has been used on few occasions, it has provided a powerful tool for constraining the power of chairs.

The **multiple referral system** also undermined the power of the chairs. Before the 1970s, a bill would go to only one committee to be considered. If the committee chair chose to ignore the bill, it would simply die in committee. If the bill was complex enough that it involved more than one issue area and another committee might be interested in influencing the legislation, there was no way for more than one committee to consider the bill. Multiple referral, however, allowed more than one committee to influence a piece of legislation. This move decentralized power in Congress by allowing more members access to legislation. Although this practice arguably made the process more democratic, it was also much more chaotic and inefficient. The practice was abolished in 1995 in favor of a **sequential referral system,** under which the speaker can refer a bill to another committee after one committee has finished with it. Alternatively, the speaker can refer parts of bills to separate committees, but cannot send an entire bill to more than one committee at a time.

The final major reform of the 1970s was the Subcommittee Bill of Rights. House Democrats also brought about this change. It removed several powers from the committee chair and secured certain powers and resources for the subcommittee. The subcommittees, or smaller units of the full committee, are responsible for considering one segment of the broad range of issues considered by the full committee. Subcommittees allow a small group of members an excellent opportunity to become experts in a particular policy area and to become influential on that issue. By guaranteeing them the right to their own rules, staff, jurisdictions, and funding, this reform allowed these small groups to have much greater leeway than was previously possible under the strong committee chair system. Combined with the other changes of the 1970s, these reforms decentralized power in Congress substantially. Pushing legislation through the House would become much more difficult for party leadership and the president.

Because senators have always enjoyed more access to debate and policy changes on the floor of the chamber, they have never felt compelled to make such massive changes in the Senate's rules. Because all senators have equal standing in amending a bill, what happens in committees is not as crucial as it is in the House. Therefore, the Senate's rules have not undergone such dramatic reform. Subcommittees became more important in the Senate in the 1970s, but they still do not play the prominent role that they do in the House. Although the Senate's system of committees and subcommittees is less decentralized than that of the House, it has always provided greater opportunity for individual members to influence policy.

12-4 The Members of Congress

In our discussion of descriptive representation in section 12-2a, "Representing Constituents," we posed this question: How closely does Congress resemble America? Throughout its history, members of Congress have been wealthier and better educated than the average American. The two most prominent professions throughout the years have been the law and business. Most members have also been older than the average citizen, and most have been Christians. The average age of all representatives elected in 1994 was 52 years old, while the average age of senators was 58. Some commentators talked about the new blood that was injected into Congress after the 1992 and 1994 elections, but the average age dropped by less than half a year. Of the 535 representatives and senators elected in 1994, all except about 10 percent were Christians. Most of the rest were Jewish. In 1993, Roman Catholics formed the largest single religious group, with about 30 percent of the members.

Considering the restrictions on any type of political participation by females throughout most of the nineteenth century and the denial of political participation to most

---

▶ **multiple referral system**
Technique employed by the House of Representatives in which more than one committee could consider a piece of legislation. This practice was abolished in 1995 in favor of a sequential referral system.

▶ **sequential referral system**
System under which the Speaker of the House of Representatives can refer a bill to another committee after one committee has finished with it.

minorities in this country until the 1960s, it is not surprising that most members have been white males. Female representation has increased steadily since women gained the right to vote in 1920. The representation of African Americans has witnessed two distinct periods of involvement, and other minorities have only recently seen an infusion of members.

12-4a Female Representation

During the 2000 New York senatorial campaign, many observers commented on the fact that Hillary Rodham Clinton could become New York's first female senator. Her subsequent victory over the Republican Rick Lazio did propel her into a small but growing group of female senators. Although more than half the population is female, women never made up more than 10 percent of Congress until 1993. In 1973, it had fourteen female representatives and no female senators. By 1983, it still had only twenty-one female representatives and two female senators. The number of women on the ballot changed dramatically in 1992, however. In an election year dubbed the Year of the Woman, more than one hundred females won their party's nomination for a congressional seat. After all the elections in November 1992 and the races to fill vacant seats in 1993, a total of forty-eight women were in the House and six were in the Senate. The 1994 elections resulted in victories for forty-nine female representatives and eight female senators. By 2004, fourteen females represented their states in the Senate along with fifty-nine in the House. Obviously, women have made substantial progress in penetrating this elite realm, but clearly they still have a long way to go to reach parity with men.

12-4b Minority Representation

When Barack Obama (D-Illinois) was overwhelmingly elected to the U.S. Senate in November 2004, he became the only African American in that body. African-American representation has experienced two distinct eras. The first was in the Reconstruction period, after the Civil War. The Thirteenth, Fourteenth, and Fifteenth Amendments to the Constitution passed in the years immediately after the war abolished slavery, conferred citizenship on all persons regardless of race or color, and guaranteed the right to vote regardless of race. Because the black population was heavily concentrated in the South, blacks were able to win seats in states where their voting rights were traditionally denied. Two African-American senators, both from Mississippi (one ironically filling the seat abandoned by Confederate President Jefferson Davis before the war) were elected during the Reconstruction period. Twenty black representatives were elected from the South between 1870 and 1901. Because Lincoln and his party opposed slavery and southern secession, all African-American representatives throughout this period were Republicans.

Despite the gains made during Reconstruction, discriminatory practices—such as the poll tax, literacy tests, and grandfather clauses—eventually prevented any new black representatives from being elected to Congress between 1901 and 1929. From 1929 until the 1960s, Congress had no more than five African Americans, and all were from outside the South. The Voting Rights Act of 1965 and the Twenty-fourth Amendment, which banned the poll tax in federal elections, radically improved black turnout in the South, and the number of black legislators slowly began to rise. By 1973, fifteen African Americans were in the House and one was in the Senate. By 1983, the numbers had only improved slightly to twenty in the House and zero in the Senate. In 1982, however, an amendment to the Voting Rights Act made a radical change in the way districts could be drawn after the 1990 census. In effect, a state legislature had to increase the number of minority seats in the state no matter how the lines had to be drawn. If a state with ten House members had a 20 percent African-American population, the state would have to make every effort to produce two districts that had a majority of African Americans. The law was at least partially responsible for raising the total from twenty-five House members in 1992 to thirty-seven voting members and one nonvoting member from the District of Columbia in 2004.

Other minorities did not experience the same rise and decline of representation during the Reconstruction period. All their gains have occurred in this century (see Table 12-1).

TABLE 12-1

Female and Minority Representation in Congress, 1971–2004

House	Number of Representatives		
	Female	Black	Hispanic
92nd (1971–72)	12	12	5
93rd (1973–73)	14	15	5
94th (1975–76)	18	16	5
95th (1977–78)	18	16	5
96th (1979–80)	16	16	6
97th (1981–82)	19	16	6
98th (1983–84)	21	20	10
99th (1985–86)	22	19	11
100th (1987–88)	23	22	11
101st (1989–90)	25	23	11
102nd (1991–92)	29	25	10
103rd (1993–94)	48	38	17
104th (1995–96)	49	39	18
105th (1997–98)	51	37	18
106th (1999–2000)	58	39	19
107th (2001–02)	59	36	19
108th (2003–04)	59	37	23

Senate	Number of Senators		
	Female	Black	Hispanic
92nd (1971–72)	1	1	1
93rd (1973–74)	0	1	1
94th (1975–76)	0	1	1
95th (1977–78)	0	1	0
96th (1979–80)	1	0	0
97th (1981–82)	2	0	0
98th (1983–84)	2	0	0
99th (1985–86)	2	0	0
100th (1987–88)	2	0	0
101st (1989–90)	2	0	0
102nd (1991–92)	2	0	0
103rd (1993–94)	6	1	0
104th (1995–96)	8	1	0
105th (1997–98)	9	1	0
106th (1999–2000)	9	0	0
107th (2001–02)	13	0	0
108th (2003–04)	14	0	0

Source: Adapted from Harold W. Stanley and Richard G. Niemi, *Vital Statistics on American Politics 2003–2004* (Washington, D.C.: CQ Press, 2003), p. 207.

Hispanics have had only thirty total legislators in this country's history, but seventeen were elected in 1994, and two nonvoting members are from the territories of Puerto Rico and the Virgin Islands. Hispanics enjoyed the same benefits as African Americans in the application of the 1982 Voting Rights amendments to the redistricting process. Although two Hispanics served as senators in the past, the Senate has none now. The proportion of Hispanics in the Congress is 3.9 percent, but 9 percent of the general population is Hispanic. Asian Americans, the third-largest minority in the United States, are also underrepresented.

12-5 How Congress Is Organized

The Constitution is largely silent on how Congress should conduct its business. It says that the House has the right to "choose their speaker and other officers" and "The Vice President of the United States will serve as the President of the Senate, but shall have no vote, unless they be equally divided." Indeed, the Senate that took office in January 2000 found itself in that predicament, with incoming Vice President Dick Cheney the potential tie-breaking vote.

The Senate can choose other officers, including a president pro tempore, who presides over the Senate "in the absence of the Vice President." It also states that each chamber must publish a "journal of its proceedings" and that each chamber "may determine the rules of its proceedings." How a bill passes in each chamber is not explained. No mention is made of committees or subcommittees. As is the case on many constitutional issues, the Founders provided a great deal of flexibility to allow future generations to shape the Constitution to their needs. Consequently, the organization of Congress has changed dramatically over time.

12-5a Leadership

Exerting leadership in either chamber of Congress is difficult in the modern age. Individual senators have always had a great deal of freedom to frustrate leaders trying to get legislation passed, but increasingly the House has also become a complex environment for leadership. The gradual breakdown of partisanship in the electorate that has increasingly caused members to run candidate-centered campaigns has also allowed members greater freedom from the party leadership. When parties were the dominant factor in campaigns,

---

Popular Culture and American Politics
Bulworth

By Chapman Rackaway

In the movie *Bulworth,* Senator Jay Bulworth (played by Warren Beatty) has become completely disillusioned with all of the lying, cheating, and money-grubbing aspects of politics. He decides that because he cannot end his own life, he must find another way. After buying a lucrative insurance policy, he hires an intermediary to put out a contract on the Senator. Bulworth is empowered by the freedom of knowing his life is about to end, so he decides to tell people all the things he has been secretly thinking but afraid to express. Beatty's character sets about destroying his reputation and showing people the darker side of politics by delivering racist and hate-filled speeches to the public. Bulworth's plan works well until he falls in love with an African-American woman, Nina (played by Halle Berry). With a heady mixture of hip-hop and political criticism, Bulworth's rapping politician isn't afraid to say anything he wants and offend anyone he wants to.

Beyond the basic critique of politics in America, the movie offers even more discussion of race in the United States. Bulworth's rap-speech-tirades highlight economic inequalities between the races in America and raise the question of whether wealthy white people can advocate effectively for reducing racial inequalities today. Simultaneously, Bulworth effectively manages to look behind the veneer of political attempts to bridge racial gaps and show the arrogance of white politicians in their perspective on African Americans in society today.

Ironically, as Bulworth's comments grow progressively more blunt, his popularity grows. Bulworth begins to regret his decision to put out the suicidal hit contract. Life becomes a pleasure as the senator defies societal conventions, smoking marijuana and showing public affection to his interracial paramour. An insightful and biting commentary on American politics in general and race relations specifically, *Bulworth* is an important political film.

the party leaders could use more coercion to force the rank-and-file members to stay in line with the party. The modern Congress, however, is composed of 535 individual enterprises who are in the business of getting reelected. Toeing the party line for a president or speaker who cannot do much to influence one's reelection opportunities is not the highest priority for the modern member of Congress who is most interested in the game of survival. The modern congressional leader cannot be a tyrant. Rather, the modern leader is forced to negotiate, compromise, and work to form coalitions to get legislation passed. One member has stated, "Once in a while we need more than good leadership—we also need good followership."[8]

Leadership in each chamber is divided along party lines. Each party in each chamber has its own caucus. The **party caucus** is an organization composed of the members of one party in each chamber, although the organization is not formally part of the legislature. The caucus is used to determine how leaders will be chosen and how committee assignments will be made. Soon after an election and before the next session of Congress has met, each party in each chamber convenes a meeting of its caucus to choose its leaders and form a committee to determine party choices for the standing committees of Congress. The actual committee assignments and the election of the speaker or president pro tempore must occur on the floor of each chamber, but the party decisions are routinely approved by the majority on the floor. Practically, though not formally, each party makes the decisions on committee assignments of its own members. The majority party, by virtue of its numerical dominance, always wins a floor vote on the position of Speaker in the House and president pro tempore in the Senate.

House Leadership The speaker is the most important leadership position in the House. The Constitution does not require that the speaker be a member of Congress. However, that has always been the case. The speaker's power peaked at the turn of the twentieth century, but it is still a powerful position. Through the party leadership on the Rules Committee, the speaker controls the schedule for all House business. The speaker also has the power to recognize members during debate. Perhaps most important in the media age, the speaker has become the spokesperson for the majority party in the House. When the president has been of the opposite party (as was the case from 1981 to 1993, when Democrats controlled the House and Republicans were in the White House, and as it was in 1994 to 2000, with a Democratic president and a Republican Congress), the role of the speaker has been particularly important. Although Newt Gingrich was unquestionably the key player in the Republican victory in 1994, his stewardship of the Republican majority was not nearly so effective. Indeed, the leadership's miscalculation in confronting President Clinton on the shutdown of the government in 1995 played a key role in rebuilding Clinton's popularity for his successful reelection bid in 1996.

Next to the speaker, the two highest-ranking leaders of the House are the majority leader and the majority whip. The **majority leader** is the second-highest-ranking leader of the majority party. While the speaker presides over floor debate from the podium at the front of the House, the majority leader controls the party's efforts on the floor. Like the speaker, the majority leader and majority whip are elected by the party caucus. Typically, a member moves from one job to another as positions become vacant, but it is possible for other party leaders to contest the election. The **majority whip** is responsible for closely watching party members to determine how they plan to vote and whether they will be in attendance for a vote. The whip is the "eyes and ears" of the party leadership. The whip is also responsible for notifying members in advance of important legislation. Each bill has a floor manager who controls debate for just that bill. The floor manager works closely with the majority leader in pushing the legislation through the chamber. This job calls on strong persuasive skills and a keen ability to count votes. In the late 1990s, these types of skills earned the Republican whip Tom Delay the nickname "the hammer."

The minority party also has its own leader and whip. Because the majority party controls floor debate, the minority leadership has less effect on legislation. The minority lead-

party caucus An organization that is composed of members of one party in each chamber of the Congress but is not formally part of the legislature. The caucus is used to determine how leaders will be chosen and how committee assignments will be made.

majority leader The leader of the dominant party in each chamber of Congress. The majority leader in the House is second in rank to the Speaker. In the Senate, the majority leader is more powerful in that he is responsible for scheduling bills for debate.

majority whip A member who ranks just below the majority leader. The whip's duties include monitoring how party members plan to vote and notifying members of important legislation.

ership works with the majority leadership in arranging the legislative calendar, but it also works against the majority party in attempting to defeat the majority's legislative agenda.

One can easily underestimate the importance of which party is the majority party. The Democrats controlled both Houses of Congress for the better part of a half-century before the Republicans captured the House and the Senate in the important 1994 midterm election. During their decades of control, the Democrats were able to staff and run important committees and support functions. In many ways, their control over day-to-day congressional functions helped bring about their demise. One example, the Congressional post office, often served as a no-interest "bank" for many (mostly Democratic) members. The ensuing scandal greatly scarred the Democratic party. After the Republicans' ascendance, they pledged a more open administration of the House.

The Rise and Fall of Newt Gingrich

The nature of the presidency has always highlighted the personality of the person holding the office. If anything, this phenomenon has been heightened in the age of television. Ronald Reagan personalized the office in a unique way. Bill Clinton was in many ways a "celebrity president," viewed by many almost as a movie or rock star. But Congress, by its nature, a mass institution of 535 members, is not usually framed in personal terms. Even its leaders have not traditionally been well known by the general public. However, the campaign of 1994 changed all that.

The Democrats controlled the House of Representatives for a half-century before the Republicans won a landmark majority in 1994. The landmark victory could be attributed to many factors. Voters were apparently dissatisfied with the direction of the first two years of the Clinton administration, which had struggled with a failed national health-care proposal. The Republican leader, Newt Gingrich, of Georgia, successfully challenged the maxim that "all politics is local" by nationalizing the campaign around a Contract with America. The vast majority of Republican Senate and House candidates signed on to this commitment to bring change to the way Congress worked and to support specific legislation in a number of areas. This national strategy captured the attention of Republican supporters, who turned out in greater numbers than their Democratic counterparts. The victory catapulted Newt Gingrich in the job he had always wanted—Speaker of the House of Representatives. He was *Time* magazine's 1995 Man of the Year. An historian by training, Gingrich saw himself as a major historical figure.

Yet by 2000 the Republicans were struggling to hold on to their majority. Bill Clinton had resurrected his image in 1996 in large part on the basis of his epic budget battle with Gingrich, whose strategic decision to play a high-stakes poker game with the president proved to be his undoing. Gingrich, so successful in his behind-the-scenes role in creating the 1994 victory, had become a visible public figure and, in many ways, the best thing that happened to Bill Clinton. Gingrich became a symbol of Republican "excess" and "extremism" to which Clinton and the Democrats could position themselves. Soon, Gingrich was more of a political liability than a benefit. He was censured for mishandling the finances of his own political action committee (PAC).

Gingrich's political demise was as much personal as it was ideological. Ironically, his downfall came in the midst of another classic conflict between the Republicans and Clinton: the impeachment battle of 1999. The president was under attack for behavior stemming from personal, moral shortcomings. Yet Gingrich was strangely silent. He had been having a relationship with an aide, and his marriage had ended. Bill Clinton retained his presidency buttressed by continuing high levels of public support, while Gingrich resigned as speaker and also from Congress.

To replace Gingrich as speaker, the Republican caucus chose a much less visible and controversial figure, Representative Dennis Hastert, of Illinois. The contrast could not be more stark. Although Gingrich is visionary, pugnacious, and confrontational, Hastert is pragmatic, reserved, and more conciliatory. Whereas Gingrich sought the national spotlight, Hastert is more content to stay behind the scenes. Whereas Gingrich was an easy target for Democrats, the personable Hastert does not inspire partisan rancor.

Barack Obama, who represents Illinois in the U.S. Senate, is widely considered to be a rising star in the Democratic party. He won his Senate seat in a landslide in 2004. Prior to that, Obama represented the south side of Chicago in the Illinois legislature for less than seven years. In 2003, The Democratic Leadership Council named Obama one of its "100 Democratic Leaders to Watch." In 2004, he was selected to deliver the keynote address at the Democratic National Convention in Boston. Without question, Obama's political ascendancy has been meteoric. Some have even mentioned his name as a future presidential candidate. Obama's appeal crosses party and racial lines. Indeed, more than one million Illinois voters who cast ballots for Obama in 2004 also voted to reelect President Bush. In the wake of John Kerry's ill-fated run for the presidency, many Democrats stated publicly the need for the party to nominate candidates who can speak to moderates and independents. Obama appears to fit that prescription. In his keynote speech at the 2004 Democratic Convention, Obama praised his country for offering him an opportunity to achieve greatness:

> I stand here today, grateful for the diversity of my heritage, aware that my parents' dreams live on in my precious daughters. I stand here knowing that my story is part of the larger American story, that I owe a debt to all of those who came before me, and that, in no other country on earth, is my story even possible.

Leadership in the Senate

The Senate is quite different from the House in that it has no speaker. The vice president officially serves as the presiding officer of the Senate, but vice presidents rarely perform this role except at the beginning of a session, at the president's State of the Union address to Congress, or in the case of a tie vote. Otherwise, the president pro tempore, a member elected by the rest of the Senate, serves as the presiding officer on a day-to-day basis. Often, the president pro tempore passes the power of the chair over to another senator on a temporary basis. The powers of the president pro tempore are in no way similar to the speaker's in the House, and they never have been. The position is not even considered the most powerful in the Senate.

The majority leader is the most powerful figure in the Senate, but still has less power than the speaker in the House. Because the rules of the Senate allow individual legislators considerable freedom to propose legislation or speak on a bill, the majority leader cannot push a bill through the Senate as easily as the speaker can in the House. The majority whip in the Senate performs much the same role as the whip in the House.

The minority party leader has more leeway to frustrate the majority in the Senate than the minority leader has in the House. Therefore, when the House, Senate, and presidency are all controlled by one party (as was the case in 1993), the Senate minority leader becomes the "point person" for the opposition. For example, during the first Clinton term, the Senate minority leaders Bob Dole (R-Kansas) and Trent Lott (R-Mississippi) assumed the role of leading the Republican opposition, not just in Congress but also in the country. Dole resigned to run for president in 1996. Although he lost, Republicans gained control of the Senate, allowing Trent Lott to become the majority leader.

The 2000 Election and the Jeffords Defection

The election of 2000 left the Senate split evenly—fifty Democrats versus fifty Republicans. That was the first time in more than one hundred years that the Senate had been split down the middle. The even split necessitated a "power sharing" arrangement between the Republican and Democratic leadership. Because ties in the Senate are broken by the president of the Senate (who is also the vice president of the United States), and because the president of the Senate is Republican Vice President Dick Cheney, the Republican leader Trent Lott remained as majority leader; the Democrat Tom Daschle remained as minority leader. However, the two leaders agreed to have equal committee memberships and equal staff payrolls. Senator John Breaux, a conservative Democrat from Louisiana, observed, "Power sharing was the first real test of bipartisanship in the new fifty-fifty Senate, and we passed."

House of Representatives	Senate	**TABLE 12-2**
Dennis Hastert (R-Illinois), Speaker of the House	Bill Frist (R-Tennessee), majority (Republican) leader	**Leadership of the House and Senate (2005)**
Tom Delay (R-Texas), majority (Republican) leader	Mitch McConnell (R-Kentucky), majority (Republican) whip	
Roy Blunt (R-Missouri), majority (Republican) whip	John Kyl (R-Arizona), chair, Republican policy committee	
Deborah Pryce (R-Ohio), chair, Republican conference	Rick Santorum (R-Pennsylvania), chair, Republican conference	
Nancy Pelosi (D-California), minority (Democratic) leader	Harry Reid (D-Nevada), minority (Democratic) leader	
Steny Hoyer (D-Maryland), minority (Democratic) whip	Richard Durbin (D-Illinois), minority (Democratic) whip	
Bob Menendez (D-New Jersey), chair, Democratic caucus	Barbara Mikulski (D-Maryland), Democratic conference secretary	

The power-sharing arrangement did not last long enough to allow an assessment, however. In May 2001, Senator James Jeffords, of Vermont, miffed at some of President Bush's legislative agenda and clearly angry at what he regarded as pressure from the leadership, announced that he was switching from the Republican party to Independent status. In making this switch, he also decided to vote with the Democrats on organizational matters. The upshot was an unprecedented change in control from the Republicans to the Democrats. As a result of the Jeffords defection, Democrats were in a position to exert considerable control over the legislative process. They chaired committees, and, as we have noted, the prerogatives of chairmanship are considerable. For instance, Senator Edward M. Kennedy's (D-Massachusetts) leadership of the Judiciary Committee enabled him to have a major effect on confirmation hearings for President Bush's nominees to the federal bench.

The 2002 Midterm Elections The Democrats' hold on the Senate leadership proved to be short-lived. In November 2002, voters across the country went to the polls in the midterm congressional elections. The result of these contests was that the Republicans won fifty-one seats in the Senate, allowing them to resume control (see Table 12-2). In what was widely seen as a referendum on President Bush and the "war on terrorism," Republicans also strengthened their hold on the House of Representatives. Coming out of the midterm elections, the Democrats were reeling. Although Tom Daschle remained in charge of Senate Democrats, House minority leader Dick Gephardt announced that he would not seek a new term as the leader of the House Democrats. This situation created a contest between the liberal wing and the moderate wing of the party for control of the House. Representative Nancy Pelosi, a liberal Democrat from California who held the post of House Democratic whip under Gephardt, became the front-runner for the position. But she was challenged by thirty-four-year-old Harold Ford, Jr., an African-American representative from Memphis, Tennessee, who represented the more moderate wing of the party. Pelosi won the position, but the challenge from Washington revealed a rift within the party that would not be easily healed.

The 2004 Election President George W. Bush's decisive win in 2004 was accompanied by significant Republican victories in the congressional races. In the House of Representatives, Republicans picked up four seats, increasing their margin of control to 231–202 (with two Louisiana races still to be decided in runoffs in December.)[9] The Republicans picked four seats in the Senate, including one in South Dakota where Tom Daschle, the Democratic minority leader, was defeated by Republican challenger John Thune. The only bright spot for the Democrats was the election of Barack Obama to an Illinois seat formerly held by Republican Peter Fitzgerald. Obama, widely regarded as a rising star in the Democratic party, became only the third African American to be elected to the Senate since Reconstruction. Asked to account for the Republicans' strong showing in recent congressional elections, Obama observed, "Republicans have been successful in framing themselves as the defender of American traditions, religious traditions, family traditions. And I think that they have successfully painted the Democrats all too often as contrary to those values."[10]

12-5b Committees

Although most of the leadership's influence over legislation is exerted on the floor of each chamber, most of the actual work that goes into making legislation occurs in the standing committees of Congress. Though never mentioned in the Constitution, temporary committees for working out the details of legislation were routinely used in the early Congresses. By Jefferson's presidency, some committees were made permanent. After the revolt against Speaker Cannon in 1910, committees were given fixed jurisdiction over particular issues and control over their own rules for conducting business. The committee system had always been important, but since 1910 it has been the dominant institutional feature of Congress.

Four types of committees are in Congress. By far the most important are the standing committees. **Standing committees** possess authority to consider legislation within a fixed policy domain. For example, the Ways and Means Committee in the House considers all tax legislation proposed in the House. Although there are some exceptional means of passing legislation that has not been through the proper committee, almost all major pieces of legislation must pass in committee before reaching the floor of the House. That is not true for the Senate, however. Some bills never pass through the Senate committee system. See Table 12-3 for the list of standing committees of Congress.

Another important type of legislative committee is the conference committee. A **conference committee** exists only temporarily when the two chambers need to reconcile dif-

> **standing committees** Those congressional committees that possess the authority to consider legislation within a fixed policy domain; the most important committees in Congress.

> **conference committee** Congressional committee that exists only temporarily when the two chambers need to reconcile differences between two versions of the same bill.

T A B L E 12-3 **Standing Committees of Congress (As of the 108th Congress)**	**House of Representatives**	**Senate**
	Agriculture	Aging
	Appropriations	Agriculture, Nutrition and Forestry
	Armed Services	Appropriations
	Banking	Armed Services
	Budget	Banking, Housing and Urban Affairs
	Commerce	Budget
	Education and the Workforce	Commerce, Science and Transportation
	Government Reform	Energy and Natural Resources
	House Administration	Environment and Public Works
	Intelligence	Ethics
	International Relations	Finance
	Judiciary	Foreign Relations
	Resources	Governmental Affairs
	Rules	Health, Education, Labor and Pensions
	Science	Indian Affairs
	Small Business	Intelligence
	Standards of Official Conduct	Judiciary
	Transportation and Infrastructure	Rules and Administration
	Veterans' Affairs	Small Business
	Ways and Means	Veterans' Affairs

ferences between two versions of the same bill. Both chambers must pass exactly the same version of a bill before it can go to the president to be signed into law. If the House and the Senate have passed different versions, they may agree to form a conference committee composed of an equal number of representatives and senators who will work out the differences. If the two sides cannot agree, the bill dies. Sometimes, the conference committee agrees, only to find that the compromise will not pass the House or Senate. That was the case in 1994 with President Clinton's crime bill. House Republicans objected to the increased social spending added to the bill by the conference committee. The bill passed the House only after this spending was scaled back. Later, the revised compromise bill faced considerable opposition in the Senate, but it eventually passed there too.

The other kinds of committees are less important to the passage of legislation. **Select committees,** or **special committees,** are temporary panels that allow members to investigate a problem and make recommendations for legislation. The special committees do not have the power to propose or pass legislation, however. Likewise, **joint committees** have no legislative authority. Members from each chamber sit on joint committees that deal with special topics of interest to Congress as a whole. For example, a joint committee oversees the Library of Congress. Joint committees are more administrative in nature and do not propose or pass legislation.

Subcommittees have become an increasingly important part of the committee system in Congress, particularly in the House. **Subcommittees** are units that exist within a full standing committee to consider one narrow issue within the overall policy area considered by the full committee. For example, the Foreign Affairs Committee has a subcommittee for each different region of the world, and the Agriculture Committee has subcommittees for different sectors of the farming economy, such as livestock, commodities, and crops.

Subcommittees play a more important role in the House than in the Senate. Because representatives sit on fewer committees than senators and more people are on each full standing committee, representatives are more likely to focus attention on subcommittee work. Almost all the House committees make extensive use of their subcommittees, but some Senate committees spend little time in subcommittee consideration of a bill.

12-5c Staff

Congress employs more than twenty-five thousand people (see Figure 12-2). The functions performed by these employees include security, maintenance, research, clerical help, and assistance with casework. The Capitol Police Force and Architect's Office hire more than three thousand workers to provide physical support of the Capitol grounds, and the four agencies that provide general legislative support have more than ten thousand employees. The remainder work either directly for members on their personal staffs or on committee or leadership staffs.

Each member of Congress, regardless of party affiliation or seniority, receives an allowance for personal staff. In 1999, House members received $632,355 to hire personal staff. The average size of a representative's staff is 14 full-time employees; in the Senate, it is 34. The member may use these employees for many activities, including scheduling, handling mail, performing clerical work, answering phones, helping to formulate policy, meeting with administrators, dealing with lobbyists, or helping to negotiate with other legislators. On the whole, however, the personal staff members devote most of their time and attention to helping the legislator deal with constituents. Staff members handle most casework requests. The House has more than 6,000 full-time personal staff members, and the Senate employs more than 3,400.

Personal staff members provide a wide range of services, such as organizing the member's schedule, handling the mail, answering the phones, assisting with legislation, and representing the member at an assortment of meetings. Their most important function is working to maintain good relations with the constituents in the district. Considering that the member can hire more than twenty persons in either Washington or the home district, you can easily see how a large amount of casework can regularly be provided to the district. Of course, each member's fondest hope is that all assistance provided to a constituent will be rewarded in the future with a vote.

select committees
Temporary panels that allow members to investigate a problem and make recommendations for legislation.

special committees See **select committees**.

joint committees
Congressional committees that have no legislative authority but instead exist for the purpose of carrying out administrative duties; committees made up of members from both chambers of Congress.

subcommittees Smaller units of full committees that are responsible for considering smaller segments of the broad range of issues considered by the full committees.

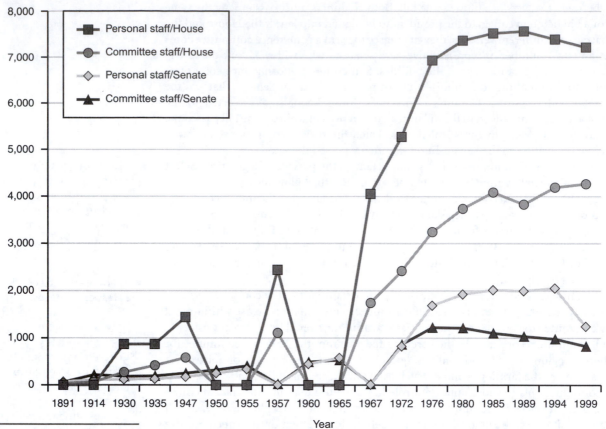

Figure 12-2
Increase in Congressional Staff, 1930–1999

Note: Lines on the 0 axis indicate data not available for that year.

Source: Adapted from Norman J. Ornstein, Thomas E. Mann, and Michael J. Malbin, *Vital Statistics on Congress 1999–2000* (Washington, D.C.: AEI Press, 2000), pp. 130–31.

In addition to staff allowances, each member also receives funding for an office in Washington and at least one office in the home district. The allocation for the home office depends on local cost factors and the number of people the member represents. Senators tend to get more money because they represent more people and have larger districts, in terms of physical space, than representatives. The allowance provides for office rental, furnishings, communication equipment (such as telephones and fax machines), stationery, and other office necessities. The total cost per House member now approaches $200,000. In the Senate, the cost ranges from $127,000 to $470,000.[11]

Of the personal staff provided to members, about 45 percent in the House and 30 percent in the Senate, on average, work in the district rather than in Washington.[12] Although it is difficult to evaluate how much the constituent service role affects the job of the average Washington staffer, the vast majority of the time spent by the district staffers is clearly devoted to the continuous care of the legislator's constituents.

Most members, however, are not willing to rely exclusively on staff resources for maintaining voter contact. Because the maxim among congressional candidates is that all politics is local, members want to spend time in the district personally. To allow this, the members have provided themselves with a travel allowance. In the early 1970s, the rules allowed reimbursement for a set number of trips back to the district, although members now have an overall budget allowance that does not limit the number of trips. Most members, if they care to do so, can fly home to the district on the government's tab every weekend during the session. Considering that few official meetings take place on Monday mornings or Fridays, many legislators spend only Tuesday, Wednesday, and Thursday in Washington. The rest of the week can be spent in the district, making public appearances that look good to voters or raising money for the next campaign.

Committee and Leadership Staff In addition to members' personal staff, each chamber provides staff for the committees, the leadership, and officers of the chamber.

Because most of the personal staff members are busy helping the legislator with constituents in the district, the committee staff must provide most of the assistance on research and policy formulation. The House has approximately fourteen hundred full-time committee staffers, and the Senate employs just fewer than one thousand. In addition, the leadership needs extra assistance in establishing the legislative schedule, arranging party caucuses, and organizing the party's legislative strategy. The House and Senate each have more than one hundred leadership staff positions. Each chamber also hires officers of the chamber, such as the parliamentarian, the doorkeeper, and the clerk. These officers perform the administrative tasks of keeping the institution running.

12-5d Agencies Providing Assistance to Congress

Three main agencies assist Congress in investigating the bureaucracy, providing research on legislation, producing a budget, and assessing technological advances. For the most part, the thousands of workers in these agencies allow the legislature to be less reliant on the executive branch for sources of information.

The Library of Congress has nearly five thousand employees who provide the legislature with one of the most complete library collections in the world. The library is open to the public, and it specializes in providing research to Congress through the Congressional Research Service (CRS). The CRS was founded in 1914, as the Legislative Reference Service, to provide nonpartisan research to members of Congress. Any member can make almost any kind of request. The CRS provides long-term research on policy, but it does not make recommendations. It also spends time responding to smaller requests by members for historical or statistical references for a speech or letter to a constituent. CRS reports on most topics are available to the public through members of Congress.

The Government Accountability Office (GAO), known prior to 2004 as the General Accounting Office, performs oversight of the bureaucracy for Congress. In particular, the GAO investigates how money appropriated by Congress has been spent. Many scandals on excessive government spending, such as five-hundred-dollar toilet seats on a military plane or one-hundred-dollar screwdrivers, have been uncovered by GAO studies. The GAO, developed in 1921, is the largest congressional support agency, with more than five thousand employees.

The Congressional Budget Office (CBO) was also a product of the 1970s reforms (see Figure 12-3). The 1974 Budget and Impoundment Control Act was passed in response to

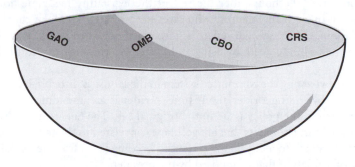

Figure 12-3
Acronym Soup

GAO The Government Accountability Office performs oversight of the bureaucracy for Congress. In particular, the GAO investigates how money appropriated by Congress has been spent. If Congress buys a thirty-thousand-dollar pencil sharpener, for example, the GAO finds out.

CRS The Congressional Research Service provides nonpartisan research to members of Congress. Any member can make almost any kind of request. The CRS provides long-term research on policy, but it does not make recommendations. It also spends time responding to smaller requests by members for historical or statistical references for a speech or letter to a constituent. If Senator Tolstoy needs to know when Franklin Roosevelt's dog Asta first moved into the White House, for example, the CRS find out.

CBO The Congressional Budget Office provides Congress with assessments of the economic and budgetary impact of policy proposals. Its numbers usually differ from those of the OMB, and much time is spent arguing over which numbers are correct.

OMB The Office of Management and Budget provides the president with assessments of the economic and budgetary effect of policy proposals.

what the Democrats in Congress viewed as an abuse of power by President Nixon in his handling of the budget. As part of an effort to assert greater influence on the budget process and to rely less on the executive branch for the details needed to form budget policy, Congress formed the CBO. The CBO, which has about 225 employees, provides Congress with assessments of the economic and budgetary effect of policy proposals. The assumptions developed by the CBO for assessing the budget are often in conflict with the president's numbers, which are developed by the Office of Management and Budget (OMB). One of the annual rituals of the budget process is a battle over whose numbers (the CBO's or the OMB's) should be used. During the 1980s, the Democrats controlling Congress became increasingly reliant on the CBO numbers rather than trust the Reagan or Bush OMB numbers. Beginning in 1993, Congress and President Clinton agreed to use a common set of assumptions for developing budgets.

12-6 How Congress Makes Laws

Over the years, the process by which Congress passes a bill has become increasingly complex. In the first few Congresses, most debate on legislative details took place on the floor of each chamber with few formal rules and no permanent committees. Since the 1990s, however, most bills must pass through a complicated maze of committees, subcommittees, and legislative calendars just to reach the floor of one chamber. If a bill passes on the floor, it must begin a similar process in the other chamber. Then differences between the House and Senate versions of the bill must be ironed out. Finally, the bill must pass the scrutiny of the president, who must either accept or reject the bill in its entirety.

Before describing the policy process, we must point out how much the rules and institutions of the two chambers differ. In general, the House is much more structured than the Senate. Because of a tradition of more deliberation on the floor of the Senate, the fact that representatives are more numerous than senators, and the absence of a filibuster in the House, a senator has much more freedom to debate, amend, and vote on all parts of a bill. The House restricts who can speak on a bill, how long someone can speak, and whether someone can propose any changes in the bill through amendments. Unless a representative is a party leader, she will have few chances to speak during floor debate. The most likely opportunity will come during the consideration of a bill that was originally debated in a committee of which the representative is a member. Otherwise, a representative has access to the floor only during the period when noncontroversial measures are considered or during the hours after the rest of the legislature has gone home. At this point, the floor is open to any member who cares to speak to a couple of cameras in front of an empty room. Conversely, all senators have equal access to speak, propose amendments, or even talk a bill to death by using a filibuster. No rules exist to control speech on the Senate floor.

In addition, bypassing the committee system in the House is difficult, but a senator can do so quite easily by adding a rider at any time. A **rider** is an amendment to a bill that is not directly related to the policy issue in the original bill. The Senate allows this, but the House permits only amendments that are germane (or related to the same topic). Senators may use riders to attach to a bill that is certain to become law a favorite pork barrel project or a piece of legislation that is opposed by the president.

Because of these differences, no senator has an excuse for not "speaking his mind" on a bill or amendment. Therefore, senators must be prepared to speak on a wider variety of issues than most representatives. Furthermore, because only a hundred senators deal with as many issues as the House, discuss almost as many bills as the House, and participate in nearly as many committee and subcommittee meetings as the House, senators spend less time on formulating details than representatives do. Representatives are much more likely to specialize in a particular policy area that is considered in their committee or subcommittee assignments. Because of their limited access to most bills on the floor, representatives must become experts in a particular policy area to gain influence in the chamber.

▶ **rider** An amendment to a bill that is not directly related to the policy issue in the original bill.

12-6a Bill Referral

The first step in enacting legislation is to have a member of Congress place a copy of a bill in the hopper. Though the media often speak of the president's proposing legislation, only a member of Congress can introduce a bill. On average, about ten thousand bills are proposed in each two-year Congress.

Before any action can be taken, the bill must be referred to one of the standing committees. In the House, the speaker has control over this process, but the parliamentarian, a staff person responsible to the speaker, routinely handles most referrals. In the Senate, the presiding officer formally controls referral, but the Senate parliamentarian handles most cases. Because committees have a fixed jurisdiction over bills in a particular policy area, there is not much discretion on most bills. After a bill has been referred, the committee chair is responsible for deciding whether it will receive any action. Most bills simply die of neglect in committee. Of the 7,732 bills proposed in the 105th Congress (1997–1999), only 394 were enacted into law.[13] The overwhelming majority of these bills died in committee.

12-6b Committee Action

In most House committees and some Senate committees, a subcommittee of the full committee first considers the bill. For example, all bills relating to agriculture are referred to the House Agriculture Committee; a bill on subsidies to tobacco farmers goes to a subcommittee on farm commodities. The subcommittee likely holds a public hearing in which experts from government, think tanks, industry, and interest groups can testify on the bill and discuss any problems with current regulation or the absence of government intervention. Next, the subcommittee holds a **markup session** in which members of the subcommittee revise the bill—sometimes drastically and sometimes only slightly. The reason they call it a markup is that they literally cross out the sections they do not like.

The subcommittee then sends the bill to the full committee, where the bill may again receive a hearing and markup. The final step in the committee process is the committee report on the bill. The committee expresses its sentiments in the report, which may be as long as a thousand pages. The committee issues a majority report that usually provides reasons for passing the legislation, a minority report, and additional or supplemental views.

> ▶ **markup session** Session of a congressional subcommittee in which members literally mark up bills by crossing out provisions they do not support.

12-6c Getting a Bill to the Floor

Bills take different paths to get to the House and Senate floors. The House uses a **Rules Committee** to establish when a bill will be placed on the legislative calendar, how much debate will be allowed, and whether amendments will be permitted. The resolution specifying this type of information is forwarded from the Rules Committee to the House floor. A majority on the floor must approve the rule.

In contrast, the Senate uses negotiations between the majority and minority party leadership to determine when a bill will be debated. There are no limits on debate or the number of amendments. Often, the Senate uses **unanimous consent agreements** as a means of establishing some format for considering a bill, but these types of agreements are quite fragile. Any senator may block this type of agreement to expand debate or add an amendment. Because of the Senate's more open rules, it is much more difficult for party leadership or the president to steer a bill through that chamber.

> ▶ **Rules Committee** Powerful House committee that establishes when a bill will be placed on the legislative calendar, how much debate will be allowed, and whether amendments will be permitted.

> ▶ **unanimous consent agreements** Agreements made in the Senate as a means of establishing a format for considering a bill.

12-6d Dislodging Bills from Committees

Both the House and Senate have procedures whereby bills can be dislodged from committees that have taken no action on them. In the House, 218 members (50 percent plus one) must sign a discharge petition. In the Senate, dislodgment can be effected through an ordinary floor motion, which of course requires a majority vote. These dislodgment rules are seldom invoked. In the House, the Speaker often brings a bill to the floor when the number of members signing the petition approaches the necessary majority. In the Senate, there really is no need to move for dislodgement because Senate rules allow a bill to come to the floor as an amendment to another bill already under consideration.

12-6e Calendars

After a bill reaches the floor in the House, it is placed on a particular calendar. The calendars are used to divide legislation into noncontroversial minor bills and major bills. Each calendar has a set schedule during the month, and each has its own rules. Note that much of the legislation that Congress passes ends up on the minor bills' calendars. More than one-third of all public laws are commemorative in nature. They could include bills naming a certain date to be National Cheese Day or congratulating the New York Yankees for winning the World Series (again). Administrative actions include electing a Speaker or determining a date of adjournment. Of the substantive bills, fewer than twenty-five would be considered major pieces of legislation, such as the Clean Air Act or the welfare reform bill.

The Senate uses only two calendars to divide up its workload. The Executive Calendar deals with treaties that must be ratified and presidential nominations, such as cabinet secretaries and federal judges, who must be confirmed. The Calendar of Business is the general calendar that can be used for any other legislation.

The leadership does not have to provide advance notice of the agenda for the following week, but it has become customary for the majority party leadership to notify other members. The agenda is discussed on the floor; a notice is printed in the *Daily Digest* and the Congressional Program Ahead; and the party whips are responsible for sending out whip notices, whip advisories, and whip issue papers on forthcoming legislative action.

12-6f Floor Procedure

House consideration of a bill entails five basic steps. First, the floor must accept the resolution that lays out the rule granted by the Rules Committee. Second, the House places itself into the Committee of the Whole. The **Committee of the Whole** is a device used by the House to expedite consideration of a bill. In essence, the full House can then act as though it were a committee. The advantage is that the House can then follow several rules that are more lenient than the full-chamber rules, such as a smaller number of legislators who must be present for business in order to proceed (called a **quorum**), a five-minute rule on debate of any amendment, and an easier process for closing debate.

After taking itself out of the Committee of the Whole, the floor moves into general debate. Generally, one hour of debate is allowed. Each party has a floor manager, usually a member from the committee with original jurisdiction over the bill, who controls the time for the party. For the most part, committee members dominate the time set aside for debate. The floor manager is extremely important to the passage of the legislation because consideration of the bill can be obstructed or delayed in numerous ways. A hostile member can propose numerous amendments, require recorded votes for every amendment, demand quorum calls so that time must be taken for each member to check in, or ask for a complete reading, word for word, of the bill and its amendments. Because time is such a precious commodity in a tightly packed schedule, delays can cause the party leadership to abandon a bill.

After general debate, the amendment process occurs. What happens at this stage is determined largely by the rule that was passed for the bill. The Rules Committee could have established a closed rule that allows no amendments. A modified rule is also possible. The modified rule may determine who can amend a bill or what sections may be amended or how many amendments are allowed. An open rule allows all proposed amendments to be considered. Each section of the bill is announced, and each amendment affecting that section is considered. Each amendment receives only five minutes for the proponent to speak and five minutes for any opponents. The amendments can vary in importance and in the level of change being proposed. Some amendments change only a few words of minor consequence. Others may be designed to kill the entire bill. The floor manager has the responsibility to fend off the more hostile amendments.

The final consideration of the bill divides the amendments into recorded and non-recorded blocs. The nonrecorded amendments are usually not controversial and are passed

> **Committee of the Whole** A device used by the House to expedite consideration of a bill.

> **quorum** The minimum number of members of a legislative body required in order to transact business.

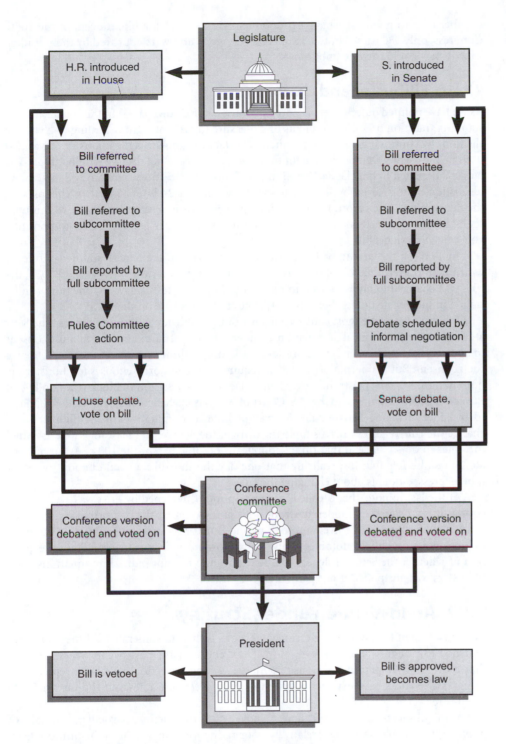

Figure 12-4
How a Bill Becomes a Law

Source: William F. Hildenbrand and Robert B. Dove, "Enactment of a Law: Procedural Steps in the Legislative Process" (Washington, D.C.: Government Printing Office, 1982), p. 233.

with a voice vote. All members present simply yell out their voting preference, and the chair determines whether the ayes or nays have won. A standing vote, in which each member stands to be counted for one side or the other, is also possible. The recorded votes on more controversial amendments have been cast by **electronic voting** since 1973. Each member has a personalized card (somewhat like a bank ATM card) that allows access to one of the voting machines in the chamber. The member inserts the card and pushes a button for Yes, No, or Present But Not Voting. The vote on the final bill also uses the electronic voting method. In the 106th Congress (1999–2000), the House recorded 603 total votes, and the Senate cast 298.

Overall, the legislative process includes a series of obstacles that can prevent the passage of a bill (see Figure 12-4). Many observers have noted that the process provides a

▶ **electronic voting** The process by which members of Congress cast recorded votes electronically.

number of veto points at which any opponent can try to kill a bill. Indeed, in the 106th Congress, only 580 passed both chambers of Congress and were approved by the president so that they could become public laws.

12-6g Filibuster and Cloture

As we have pointed out, the Senate and the House set their own rules. In the Senate, a long-standing tradition permits opponents of a measure to prevent it from coming to a vote on the floor by continuing debate indefinitely. This tactic is known as the filibuster. It was first used in 1841 when Democrats sought to prevent a vote on a bill dealing with banking. The tactic is depicted in the classic 1939 film *Mr. Smith Goes to Washington,* in which a young idealistic Senator played by Jimmy Stewart filibusters for 24 hours and then collapses on the Senate floor. The record for a speech by one Senator is actually 24 hours, 18 minutes, set by South Carolina Senator Strom Thurmond, who in 1957 led a filibuster to prevent a vote on a civil rights bill.

In 1917, at the urging of President Woodrow Wilson, the Senate adopted a rule by which cloture (termination of debate) could be imposed by a two-thirds vote. In 1975, the rule was changed to allow cloture to be imposed by 60 votes. Today, any measure can be stalled in the Senate unless there are sixty votes to force a vote on the floor.

In recent years, the most controversial use of the filibuster has been to prevent the Senate from voting on judicial nominations. Under the Constitution, the Senate must consent to any judicial nomination by the president, and only a simple majority is required to give such consent. But a supermajority of 60 is required is the minority chooses to filibuster the nomination. In 2005, frustration over Senate Democrats' decision to block votes on five of President Bush's nominees to the U.S. Court of Appeals led Senate majority leader Bill Frist to consider changing Senate rules to exempt judicial nominations from filibusters. To change the rule requires only a simple majority of the Senate, and Frist may well have had the votes to do so, since at that time Republicans occupied 55 of the 100 seats in the Senate. But some Republicans, realizing that one day the shoe likely would be ion the other foot, expressed doubts about changing the rules.

At the last minute, the so-called "nuclear option" threatened by Frist was averted by a compromise fostered by moderates from both parties. Under the compromise the Senate would vote on three of the five nominations and Senators would agree to use the filibuster to block votes on judicial nominees only "in extraordinary circumstances." Thus, the question of whether the Senate rules should be changed to exempt judicial nominations from filibusters was postponed if not permanently avoided.

12-7 An Institution under Scrutiny

The most salient feature of congressional elections is that most members, if they want, are returned to Congress after every election. The trend over the past twenty years has been that more than 90 percent of House members seeking reelection have been returned to Congress. Senators have experienced slightly lower reelection rates, but the vast majority are also reelected.

Many observers have found these turnover rates disquieting, particularly in light of public opinion polls showing a relatively poor rating for Congress as an institution. Even most members of Congress make fun of the institution when they are talking to constituents in the district.

Congressman Les Aspin once quipped, "I don't care what my district thinks of Congress as long as fifty-one percent of it likes me."[14] Americans do tend to distinguish between Congress as an institution and their own particular representatives. A *New York Times*/CBS News survey conducted in 1994 found that while only 25 percent of people surveyed approved of Congress' performance as an institution, 56 percent approved of the performance of their own representative.[15] There are two main reasons for this paradox. First, an institution that requires compromise for any action to take place will naturally frustrate many observers without dimming their view of a particular member of the organization. Citizens may think that their representative is doing the right thing but that she is being stymied by all the other "no-good" politicians in Washington.

A second reason that individual members emerge unscathed from the criticism of the institution is that they work hard to create a good image of themselves to their constituents. One main feature of the modern campaign is that candidates run their own enterprises in getting elected. The parties are not nearly as active in campaigns as they once were, and candidates must raise their own money, create their own campaign organizations, and determine their own positions on policy. The move from a party-centered campaign system at the turn of the twentieth century to a candidate-centered campaign system during the 1960s has dramatically altered the electoral process. Elections are no longer quite as easy to interpret in terms of national partisan trends. Each congressional election year is composed of 435 individual House elections and thirty-three or thirty-four Senate elections rather than one broad statement on national partisan preferences. Members have learned how to survive in Washington even when Congress as an institution is berated, the presidency changes from one party to the other, or policy failures, such as the savings-and-loan crisis of the early 1990s, occur. Members rely on two main methods for survival: using the advantages of incumbency and raising large sums of money. (For a discussion of campaign finance as it relates to congressional elections, see Chapter 11, "Campaigns and Elections.")

12-7a The Advantages of Incumbency

Because of the constitutional requirement that Congress control the purse strings, members of Congress have been able to use government funds for a variety of expenditures that have become quite useful to individual members in their quest to stay in office. The institutional support—such as the franking privilege, paid personal staff, travel allowances, and government-funded offices in Washington and the home district—that each member receives regardless of party, age, or experience is known as the incumbency advantage. However, this incumbency advantage cannot always overcome a damaged candidate. Following his admission that he had an extramarital relationship with a missing Congressional intern, Congressman Gary Condit (D-California) found his popularity sinking amid devastating national media attention. In December 2001, he declared that he would seek reelection the following year despite criticism by his party leader, Dick Gephardt, and the Democratic governor of California, Gray Davis. He was defeated in the Democratic primary by one of his former staff members.

The Franking Privilege   The **franking privilege** is the power of any member of Congress to sign (or to have the printer reproduce his signature on) any piece of mail and have it delivered without cost to the member. The use of this power is limited in that members cannot mail campaign materials on the frank, but they can send letters, public opinion polls, or newsletters about policy discussions or what the member has been doing in Washington or the district. Although the member's literature cannot directly say "vote for me," one would have difficulty finding any comments in a newsletter that would not make the legislator's parents proud. The use of this privilege has grown dramatically. In the 1950s, fewer than 45 million pieces of mail were sent, but by the 1980s an average of more than 600 million deliveries were made; the high was 925 million pieces in the 1984 election year. In 1994, more than 363 million pieces of franked mail were sent at a cost of nearly $53 million.[16] In recent years, however, public concern over the privileges of Congress has led to a reduction in the amount of franked mail. Still, the franking privilege remains a major aspect of incumbency advantage.

> ▶ **franking privilege**
> The power of any member of Congress to sign or have a printer reproduce her signature on any piece of mail and have it delivered, without cost to the member.

12-7b The Constant Campaign

The main purpose of all this institutional support is to allow the member to maintain continual contact with her constituents. A politician never wants to be accused of "not being in touch with the people." To survive in a political system that lacks strong party ties, relies heavily on mass media, and requires large amounts of money to win elections, the average member of Congress must run a continual campaign from the minute one election ends until the next. Because voters do not pay close attention to politicians or elections, members must do everything possible to keep their names before the public. Name recognition is difficult to attain through a few advertisements during a campaign, when so many other politicians are blanketing the airwaves, so a legislator must engage in a continual effort throughout the two- or six-year term. Travel home, personal staff, and district offices help maintain name recognition through casework and personal contact.

12-7c Proposals for Reform

Public confidence in Congress is undeniably at an all-time low. One reason is the widespread perception that members are interested only in getting themselves reelected and raising money for that purpose. But Congress has a poor public image for several other reasons, including the intractable federal debt, the gridlock of the late 1980s and early 1990s, and a series of scandals that rocked Capitol Hill during the same period. Particularly damaging were revelations in 1991 that some representatives had badly abused their privileges in the bank and restaurant that the House operated exclusively for its members.

perks Tangible benefits received by members of Congress, such as subsidized medical care.

Curtailing Members' Perks   Widespread dissatisfaction with Congress has led to several proposals for reform, some of which have come from within the institution itself. But Congress has a difficult time coming to grips with reform. The reasons for this difficulty are numerous, but the most obvious is that members do not want to take steps that will reduce the benefits of holding office and, most importantly, their electoral advantage over challengers. One thing that is most irritating to the public is the **perks** that members of Congress receive: their expense allowances, travel budgets, subsidized life and health insurance, free tax preparation, subsidized restaurants, free health club, free parking, free haircuts, free office decorations, free use of photography and recording studios, discounts on official merchandise, and so on. Although some perks have been curtailed in recent years, they have helped foster the impression that members of Congress are out of touch with the people they represent. Moreover, they lend credence to the perception that the entire institution is corrupt.

Campaign Finance Reform   Critics argue that it is unseemly for members of Congress to have to continually raise money for reelection—money that tends to come from wealthy contributors and political action committees who clearly expect something in return. Whether or not this obsession with fundraising is a corrupting force, the public certainly perceives it that way. In addition, few quality challengers can raise the funds to compete with incumbents, thus contributing to the low rate of turnover in Congress. A variety of proposals have been put forth, including public financing of campaigns, prohibiting contributions from PACs, placing spending limits on candidates, mandating free media access to challengers, and restricting contributions from outside the candidate's district. All these options are controversial, and none can be assumed to have the desired effect. Moreover, under the present circumstances, a majority of incumbents in either chamber or party is highly unlikely to be mustered to support any of these measures. Furthermore, even presidents feel somewhat limited in pushing for reform. For example, President Clinton favored campaign finance reform in 1994, but he was reluctant to push it for fear of alienating key members he needed to support his crime bill and health-care agenda. The bipartisan McCain–Feingold bill introduced in the 106th Congress would put serious limitations on the use of soft money in all federal races.

During the 2000 presidential election campaign, the Republican candidate and senator John McCain chose campaign finance reform as his signature issue. Although he ultimately was defeated by George W. Bush, McCain promised to introduce legislation at the onset of the 107th Congress. Clearly, the issue had reached the political front burner, if not among the general public, then certainly among many in the media and those holding public office.

What Americans Think About

Congress

Part of conventional political wisdom says that Congress as a whole is ill-regarded by the American people. However, as these Gallup poll data show, Congress in recent years recovered a substantial measure of public approval, reaching a peak in January 2002 (shortly after the terrorist attacks of September 11, 2001).

Question: Do you approve or disapprove of the way Congress is handling its job? (The graph shows the percentage expressing approval.)

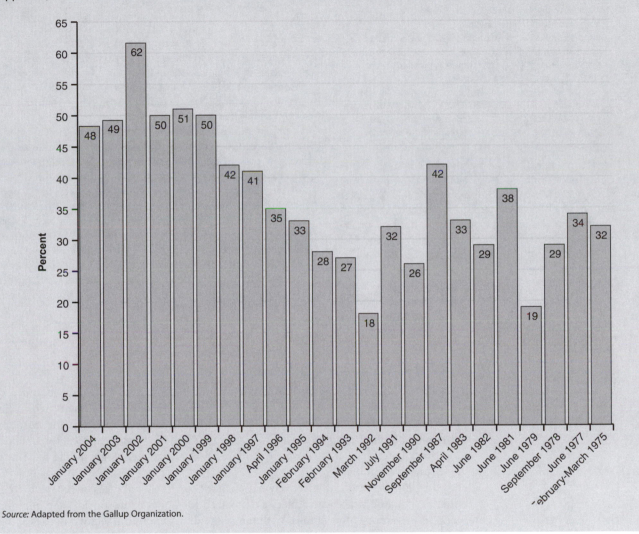

Source: Adapted from the Gallup Organization.

Term Limits   During the early 1990s, there was considerable interest in the idea of limiting the number of terms that members of Congress can serve (see Case in Point 12-1). A variety of proposals surfaced calling for various limits on the number of consecutive terms that members of the House and Senate would be eligible to serve. All these proposals had a common purpose: to remove the professional politician and restore the concept of citizen-legislator. More than twenty states adopted measures that would in some way limit the terms of members of their congressional delegations. Typically, these measures limited senators to two terms (twelve years) and House members to three, four, or six terms (six, eight, or twelve years). However, none of these measures prevented any member of Congress from seeking reelection because in 1995 the Supreme Court struck down the state-by-state approach to term limits for members of Congress.[17]

Case in Point 12-1

The Supreme Court Strikes Down Congressional Term Limits

U.S. Term Limits v. Thornton (1995)

In November 1992, Arkansas voters amended their state constitution to limit the number of elections in which one person could run for the United States Senate or House of Representatives. The amendment provided:

(a) Any person having been elected to three or more terms as a member of the United States House of Representatives from Arkansas shall not be certified as a candidate and shall not be eligible to have his/her name placed on the ballot for election to the United States House of Representatives from Arkansas.

(b) Any person having been elected to two or more terms as a member of the United States Senate from Arkansas shall not be certified as a candidate and shall not be eligible to have his/her name placed on the ballot for election to the United States Senate from Arkansas.

The State of Arkansas defended the measure as an exercise of its constitutional authority to determine the "times, places and manner" of elections. In a suit brought by Arkansas voters, the U.S. Supreme Court declared this measure unconstitutional. Writing for a sharply divided bench, Justice John Paul Stevens began by observing that the Constitution sets forth qualifications for membership in the Congress. Article I, Section 2, clause 2, provides

No Person shall be a Representative who shall not have attained to the Age of twenty five Years, and been seven Years a Citizen of the United States, and who shall not, when elected, be an Inhabitant of that State in which he shall be chosen.

Similarly, Article I, Section 3, clause 3, provides

No Person shall be a Senator who shall not have attained to the Age of thirty Years, and been nine Years a Citizen of the United States, and who shall not, when elected, be an Inhabitant of that State for which he shall be chosen.

In his opinion for the Court, Justice Stevens claimed that the Framers of the Constitution intended "that neither Congress nor the states should possess the power to supplement the exclusive qualifications set forth in" Article I. He further observed that "[a]llowing individual states to craft their own qualifications for Congress would . . . erode the structure envisioned by the framers."

In dissent, Justice Clarence Thomas argued that "[n]othing in the Constitution deprives the people of each state of the power to prescribe eligibility requirements for candidates who seek to represent them in Congress. . . . And where the Constitution is silent, it raises no bar to action by the states or the people." In its majority opinion, the Court recognized cogent arguments on both sides of the term limits issue. It concluded, however, that an issue of this magnitude must be referred to the formal process by which the Constitution is amended. Immediately after the *Thornton* decision was rendered, supporters of term limits pledged renewed efforts to achieve a constitutional amendment to limit the tenure of members of Congress. That, of course, has not transpired.

Presumably, imposing term limits on all members of Congress would require a constitutional amendment along the lines of the Twenty-second Amendment, which limits presidents to two consecutive terms. Political scientists often question the wisdom of attempting to limit congressional terms, citing the need for stable political leadership. On the other hand, regular turnover in Congress would likely enhance public trust in that beleaguered institution.

In 1994, Republicans effectively nationalized congressional races by having their candidates sign a Contract with America that called for Congress to consider the question of term limits, among other things. With the resounding Republican victory, the advocates of term limits were optimistic that the issue would finally make it to the congressional agenda. Ironically, though, the magnitude of the Republican victory in 1994 was itself an argument for the electorate's ability to impose term limits through the ballot box.

12-8 Conclusion: Assessing Congress

Congress is a complex institution that has changed dramatically since its founding. The idea of the citizen-legislator has long been abandoned for the professional legislator, with a staff and support system that rival those of a corporate executive. As Congress has evolved as an institution, however, it has come into difficult times. Congress is unloved and unap-

Controversy

Are Term Limits for Congress a Good Idea?

The ancient Greek philosopher Aristotle believed that individual rotation in office was healthy for the political system. During the Roman republic, no citizen could hold any office more than once in his lifetime. During the Renaissance, the Constitution of Venice made officeholders ineligible for reelection until a term equal to that of their office had passed. Under the Articles of Confederation, members of Congress could serve for only three annual terms during a six-year period. During the Constitutional Convention of 1787, the Virginia Plan provided that members of the House of Representatives would be ineligible for reelection for a period to be determined by the convention. That proposal was ultimately rejected by the convention, which was swayed by Alexander Hamilton's argument that rotation "would be a diminution of the inducements to good behavior . . . and tempt sordid views and peculation" by elected officials considering prospects for employment after their terms expire. Hamilton further claimed that term limits would deprive the country of "the experience of wisdom gained by an incumbent, perhaps just when the experience is needed most."

Now, because of the advantages of incumbency, little turnover typically occurs in Congress. Accordingly, many members become "professional legislators." Advocates of term limits for Congress argue that longtime incumbents lose touch with their constituents and become corrupt captives of interest groups. These reformers believe that limiting the terms of members of Congress will restore the idea of the citizen-legislator who makes the rules knowing that she will soon return to private life and live under those rules. Opponents of term limits object to the idea of depriving voters of the right to vote for the candidate of their choice. If the voters of a particular state or district believe that an incumbent senator or representative is doing a good job, shouldn't they have the right to return her to office?

The prevailing view among political scientists is that by limiting members' terms, the influence of unelected bureaucrats and congressional staff members would be increased. What would be the effect of removing the possibility of accumulating seniority? Who would assume leadership roles? Would not the Congress become even more fragmented and chaotic than it is now? These serious questions must be considered before enacting a measure that would affect all Senate and House seats for years to come.

preciated by the American people, who see it as constantly bickering and unable to rise above in-fighting.

During the twelve years of the Ronald Reagan and George H.W. Bush presidencies, Congress was often accused of contributing to gridlock. Many people were pleased to see divided-party government end when the Democrats won the presidency in 1992. However, divided government returned when the Republicans gained control of both houses of Congress in the dramatic midterm elections of 1994. Yet President Clinton and the Republican Congress managed to achieve some major policy accomplishments, most notably in the realms of fiscal policy, foreign trade, and welfare reform.

Though Congress as an institution is still held in relatively low regard, individual members of Congress tend to have reasonably good relationships with their constituents. Those who want to be reelected usually are. The incumbency advantage comes at a steep price, however. The money it brings to the incumbent inevitably commits him to special interests. Even if the commitment is only to grant some access to hear the interest's point on an issue, the appearance of corruption has done much to convince many Americans that the institution is not deserving of their respect.

Paradoxically, although it was designed to be "closest to the people," Congress remains the least loved and respected of the institutions of government.

Questions for Thought and Discussion

1. Should members of Congress vote according to what they think is best for the country, or should they follow what they think their constituents want?

2. How can a member of Congress accurately determine what her constituents want? Should all constituents' opinions count equally?

3. Are term limits for members of Congress a good idea? If so, what limits should be imposed?

4. Why is Congress less trusted and respected than the other two branches of the national government? What reforms might improve Congress' public image?

5. What changes in the ways Congress operates would create more party discipline in voting on legislation? Is more party discipline desirable?

6. How did Republican control of Congress from 1994–2004 affect the way in which the institution is perceived by the mass public?

Practice Quiz

Note: You can find the correct answers to these questions by taking the quiz and then submitting your answers in the Online Edition. The program will automatically score your submission. If you miss a question, the program will provide the correct answer, a rationale for the answer, and the section number in the chapter where the topic is discussed.

1. Those who argue that legislators ought to act as trustees often do so because _____.
   a. trustees, unlike delegates, can provide leadership
   b. trustees, unlike delegates, have the necessary latitude to make difficult votes
   c. trustees, unlike delegates, are the only true translators of citizen preferences
   d. a and b

2. The _____ powers of Congress are those mentioned specifically in the Constitution.
   a. enumerated
   b. implied
   c. inferred
   d. inherent

3. The _____ Amendment allows Congress to "lay and collect taxes on incomes from whatever source derived, without apportionment among the states."
   a. Fifteenth
   b. Sixteenth
   c. Seventeenth
   d. Nineteenth

4. As interpreted by the courts, the _____ Clause of Article I, Section 8 of the Constitution provides Congress with a vast number of implied powers.
   a. Supremacy
   b. Necessary and Proper
   c. Speech and Debate
   d. Privileges and Immunities

5. The Appropriations Committees in the House and Senate _____.
   a. consider how money will be spent for each federal government program
   b. consider how revenue will be raised
   c. establish the overall spending and revenue levels of the federal budget
   d. monitor the office expenses of each representative

6. The Ways and Means Committee in the House and the Finance Committee in the Senate _____.
   a. consider how money will be spent for each government program
   b. consider how revenue will be raised
   c. establish the overall spending and revenue levels of the federal budget
   d. monitor the office expenses of each representative

7. The term _____ refers to that situation whereby a member of Congress considers legislation only in terms of how it affects his home district.
   a. *parochialism*
   b. *paternalism*
   c. *particularism*
   d. *parentalism*

8. Within the system of checks and balances, Congress' most significant power is _____.
   a. its ability to override presidential vetoes
   b. its ability to propose constitutional amendments
   c. its power of the purse
   d. its power to regulate interstate commerce

9. Congressional oversight occurs _____.
   a. when Congress examines the decisions of the Supreme Court to determine whether they are interpreting the laws in a manner consistent with the intent of the legislature
   b. when Congress examines the decisions of the lower federal courts to determine whether they are interpreting the laws in a manner consistent with the intent of the legislature
   c. when congressional committees examine various departments and agencies to determine whether they are executing laws in a manner consistent with the intent of the legislature
   d. all of the above

10. The most important leadership position in the House of Representatives is the _____.
    a. Speaker of the House
    b. majority leader
    c. majority whip
    d. chair of the Rules Committee

For Further Reading

Aberbach, Joel D. *Keeping a Watchful Eye: The Politics of Congressional Oversight* (Washington, D.C.: Brookings Institution, 1990).

Adler, E. Scott. *Why Congressional Reforms Fail* (Chicago: University of Chicago Press, 2002).

Baker, Ross K. *House and Senate* (New York: W. W. Norton, 1989).

Benjamin, Gerald, and Michael J. Malbin, eds. *Limiting Legislative Terms* (Washington, D.C.: CQ Press, 1992).

Boller, Paul. *Congressional Anecdotes* (Oxford: Oxford University Press, 1991).

Brady, David, and Craig Volden. *Revolving Gridlock: Politics and Policy from Carter to Clinton* (Boulder, CO: Westview Press, 1998).

Davidson, Roger H., and Walter J. Oleszek. *Congress and Its Members,* 9th ed. (Washington, D.C.: CQ Press, 2004).

Dodd, Lawrence C., and Bruce I. Oppenheimer, eds. *Congress Reconsidered,* 8th ed. (Washington, D.C.: CQ Press, 2004).

Fenno, Richard F. *Home Style: House Members in Their Districts* (Boston: Little, Brown, 1978).

Fiorina, Morris. *Congress: Keystone of the Washington Establishment,* 2d ed. (New Haven, CT: Yale University Press, 1989).

Mayhew, David R. *America's Congress: Actions in the Public Sphere, James Madison Through Newt Gingrich* (New Haven, CT: Yale University Press, 2002).

Oleszek, Walter J. *Congressional Procedures and the Policy Process,* 6th ed. (Washington, D.C.: CQ Press, 2004).

Price, David E. *The Congressional Experience: A View from the Hill* (Boulder, CO: Westview Press, 1993).

Rae, Nicol, and Colin Campbell, eds. *New Majority or Old Majority? The Impact of Republicans on Congress* (Lanham, MD: Rowman and Littlefield, 1999).

Sinclair, Barbara. *Unorthodox Lawmaking,* 2d ed. (Washington, D.C.: CQ Press, 2000).

Strahan, Randall. *New Ways and Means: Reform and Change in a Congressional Committee* (Chapel Hill, NC: University of North Carolina Press, 1990).

Sundquist, James L. *The Decline and Resurgence of Congress* (Washington, D.C.: Brookings Institution, 1981).

Thompson, Dennis F. *Ethics in Congress* (Washington, D.C.: Brookings Institution, 1995).

Wilson, Woodrow. *Congressional Government* (Boston: Houghton Mifflin, 1885).

Endnotes

1. *Hoke v. United States,* 227 U.S. 308 (1913).
2. *United States v. Lopez,* 514 U.S. 549 (1995).
3. *Chisholm v. Georgia* (1793) was overturned by the Eleventh Amendment; *Scott v. Sandford* (1857) was overturned by the Thirteenth and Fourteenth Amendments; *Pollock v. Farmer's Loan and Trust Co.* (1895) was overturned by the Sixteenth Amendment; and *Oregon v. Mitchell* (1970) was overturned by the Twenty-sixth Amendment.
4. Paul Boller, *Congressional Anecdotes* (Oxford: Oxford University Press, 1991) p. 4.
5. As quoted by Ross K. Baker, *House and Senate* (New York: W. W. Norton, 1989), p. 35.
6. William N. Chambers, *Political Parties in a New Nation* (New York: Oxford University Press, 1963), p. 194.
7. In 1999, Representative Dennis Hastert (R-Illinois) was elected Speaker of the House after serving in the House for only thirteen years, but this occurred only after his predecessor, Newt Gingrich (R-Georgia), resigned his leadership position and gave up his seat in the Congress after the Republican party's disappointing performance in the 1998 midterm elections.
8. Quoted in the *Congressional Record,* 100th Congress, first session, December 3, 1987, p. 3.

9. Actually, one seat credited here to the Democrats is occupied by an independent from Vermont who generally votes with the Democrats.
10. William Branigin, Dan Morgan and Thomas B. Edsall, "GOP Adds to Majority with Wins in South," *Washington Post,* Wednesday, November 3, 2004.
11. Roger H. Davidson and Walter J. Oleszek, *Congress and Its Members,* 7th ed. (Washington, D.C.: CQ Press, 2000), p. 154.
12. Norman J. Ornstein, Thomas E. Mann, and Michael J. Malbin, *Vital Statistics on Congress 1999–2000* (Washington, D.C.: AEI Press, 2000), p. 126.
13. Davidson and Oleszek, *Congress and Its Members,* 7th ed., p. 233.
14. Quoted in the *Washington Post,* June 22, 1975.
15. New York Times/CBS News national survey of 1,161 persons, conducted September 8–11, 1994. Margin of error is ±3 percentage points. Results reported in *New York Times,* September 13, 1994, page A-8.
16. Davidson and Oleszek, *Congress and Its Members,* 7th ed., p. 156.
17. *U.S. Term Limits v. Thornton,* 514 U.S. 779 (1995).

The Presidency

13-1 The President: Personification of American Government

When President George W. Bush spoke to the nation on the evening of September 11, 2001, after the horrific terrorist attacks on the United States, many Americans saw him in a new light. Most had felt lukewarm at best toward the new president after his controversial victory in the 2000 election. Even some of his supporters wondered about his ability to lead. Those fears were greatly dispelled in the days that followed 9-11-2001. In responding to the crisis, the President appeared resolute, compassionate, and competent to the vast majority of Americans, as reflected in public approval ratings as high as those enjoyed by any president. In a crisis, Americans immediately look to the president for leadership. That almost instinctive public response to a crisis provides the occupant of the Oval Office an opportunity for greatness. Of course, not all presidents are able to rise to the occasion.

Even during normal times, the president is the personification of American government. When people think of a country, they often think of the person who is the leader of that country. The leader, whether elected or unelected, comes to symbolize much of what that system is about. Throughout the world, people think of the U.S. government in terms of the president. When Iranians in the 1970s and 1980s and Iraqis in the 1990s and early 2000s took to the streets to protest the actions of the United States, they often carried pictures of the president—Jimmy Carter, George Bush, and George W. Bush, respectively. Certainly, anyone who is asked to name great Americans of any period would sprinkle her responses with a generous portion of presidents. In popular culture, presidents help define historical eras and patterns of politics. For example, President John F. Kennedy symbolized the energy, idealism, and optimism that were cresting as American society entered the 1960s. On the other hand, a reference to the Carter years, 1977–1981, conjures up images of inflation, ineptness, and malaise. Mention the Reagan years and people think of economic growth—or the deficit, or greed, depending on their ideological predisposition. The Bush years (1989–1992) remind many people of success in the Gulf War coupled with a disinterest in an economic slowdown. Mention the Clinton years (1993–2000) and people think of almost amazing economic growth coupled with a sense of moral decline.

This personalization of politics and the use of presidential images to denote political eras are not surprising. Of the three branches of government, only the executive branch can be so easily captured in an image. This image has taken on even more political clout with the advent of the electronic media. It is hard to imagine any American who could not recognize a picture of the president. In fact, the American president is probably the most recognizable presence in the world. Hence, despite its coequal constitutional status with the Congress and the Supreme Court, the executive branch has in many ways become the "first among equals" in national government.

13-1a The Many Roles of the President

The realities of international affairs and the United States' role as a major world power have inevitably tended to strengthen the presidency (see Box 13-1). Yet major areas of disagreement still occur over the proper scope of the president's power. Nevertheless, Americans invariably look to the White House for leadership and action when they want government to act. Because Americans expect their president to be a problem solver, they tend to judge presidents harshly when problems linger unresolved. Accordingly, despite President Bush's overwhelming popularity at the close of the Gulf War, he was defeated for reelection a little more than a year later, in part because he was perceived as not being sufficiently engaged in solving domestic problems.

Head of State   The American president has tremendous resources with which to attack problems. But these resources have to support the president in an ever-increasing number of roles. The president is, of course, the head of state who represents this country symbolically at home and abroad. It is in this role, which is most like that of a monarch, that the president appears most impressive and majestic. This is why Americans were so distressed when they saw television coverage of President Bush becoming ill at a state din-

President George W. Bush addressing the nation from the Oval Office on the night of September 11, 2001.

AP Photo / Doug Mills

ner in Japan in 1992. When the president is on stage representing this country, we like to think of him as being superhuman.

Chief Executive   The president is the chief executive, which means that he is responsible for running the massive federal bureaucracy. That means putting together a team of people, called the administration, who occupy the top positions in the executive departments and agencies. It also means putting together a White House staff to help the president manage the government.

The tremendous growth of government in the twentieth century, especially since the 1930s, has greatly increased the resources of the presidency. But it has also increased the difficulty and complexity of being the nation's chief administrator. No single human being, no matter how much staff she is provided, can stay on top of what the federal government is doing at any given time. A president must strive for some reasonable middle ground. President Carter was criticized for trying to micromanage the executive branch. On the other hand, President Reagan was often characterized as being out of touch with what was going on in his administration. After assuming the presidency in January 2001, George W. Bush gave the impression that he would not be overly detail-oriented, but rather would work with the Cabinet with Vice President Cheney more involved in legislative and administrative matters. Of course, this arrangement changed dramatically in September 2001, when President Bush took on the details of military and diplomatic policy while Cheney assumed a clearly subordinate, even barely visible role.

Crisis Manager   The president also now plays the role of crisis manager. The president must be able to act quickly and effectively when events around the world dictate an American response. When Saddam Hussein's Iraq annexed its tiny neighbor Kuwait in August 1990, thereby threatening the world's oil supply, world leaders looked to the United States, and ultimately to George Bush, to respond to the crisis. Sometimes, crises at home require immediate action. The president is expected to lead the government's response to national disasters, such as Hurricane Andrew, which devastated much of South Florida in 1992. Although President Bush was given high marks by most commentators for his quick, decisive action in response to the crisis in Kuwait, he received a less positive assessment for the

Box 13-1   The Many Roles of the American President

As the chief executive, the president needs to show a certain amount of control and personal involvement with major issues. At the onset of his presidency, George W. Bush delegated so many tasks to his vice president that Dick Cheney was becoming known as the co-president.

AP Photo / Eric Draper

After the September 11 terrorist attacks, the president's role as crisis manager became more apparent as George W. Bush led efforts to console and reassure Americans at home while planning retaliatory strikes.

© Reuters NewMedia Inc. / CORBIS

The role of commander-in-chief is a large one: In addition to instigating and directing warfare, the commander-in-chief creates and reviews military policies and governs the military establishment. Bill Clinton's involvement as commander-in-chief included working for better treatment of gays serving in the armed forces.

AP Photo / Greg Gibson

When the president meets with leaders of other nations, as shown in this picture of Bill Clinton meeting with Britain's Tony Blair, he wears the hat of chief diplomat and foreign policy maker, working to improve relations between the United States and other nations in addition to assisting other countries in their diplomatic pursuits.

AP Photo / PA

Box 13-1   *continued*

Although the president does not actively debate bills on the floor of the Senate or House, he is the chief legislator, supporting, approving, and vetoing an enormous amount of legislation each year.

AP Photo / Doug Mills

Being the leader of his party is another role the president must fulfill. Although making the State of the Union address is one of the less-partisan activities involved, Republicans everywhere look to George W. Bush as the head of their party.

AP Photo / J. Scott Applewhite

federal government's response to Hurricane Andrew. Most observers gave President Clinton high marks for his response to the Oklahoma City bombing in 1995. Perhaps the highest grade for crisis management would be reserved for George W. Bush's response to the terrorist attacks of September 2001.

George W. Bush was given high marks for his handling of the September 11, 2001, terrorist attacks on America. Perhaps his most memorable single act was his appearance at the scene of the fallen trade towers, when in response from a person in the crowd yelling "I can't hear you," he yelled back, "I can hear you, and the world can hear you" while draping his arm over the shoulder of a firefighter standing next to him. Often, these spontaneous actions are the most effective in sealing a bond between a leader and the rest of us.

Commander-in-Chief   The Constitution makes the president commander-in-chief of the armed forces. Obviously, in time of war, the president is "first among generals." In a development probably not foreseen by the Framers of the Constitution, the role of commander-in-chief has come to mean that the president has the power to initiate war and to direct its progress. But being commander-in-chief means much more than that. The president has the primary responsibility for setting the military policy of the United States and governing its massive military establishment. For example, President Harry S Truman issued an executive order desegregating the military after World War II. In 1993, President Bill Clinton tried to fulfill a campaign promise by issuing an executive order lifting the ban on gays in the military, but he soon discovered that key members of Congress had other ideas. Ultimately, the president was forced to compromise with those who wanted to maintain the ban.

Chief Diplomat and Chief Foreign Policy Maker   By virtue of both constitutional text and history, the president is the nation's chief diplomat. He is under unrelenting pressure to represent the United States effectively on the world stage. Moreover, he is accorded primary responsibility for both making and implementing this country's foreign policy. And since the demise of the Soviet Union, the United States is the only superpower in the world. As the chief diplomat and principal foreign policy maker of the world's greatest power, the president is necessarily cast in the role of the leader of world leaders. He is expected to lead the way in finding solutions to problems such as the civil war in the former Yugoslavia. George Bush felt extremely comfortable in this role. Bill Clinton, on the other hand, struggled with the complexities and dilemmas of foreign policy and world leadership during his first two years in office. He later developed a comfort level with foreign policy, but left office without the clear foreign policy legacy that he would have liked to achieve.

George W. Bush's journey to Europe in May 2002 represented some of his first major actions as chief diplomat and foreign policy maker. He negotiated an agreement with Russian president Vladimir Putin to drastically cut back on nuclear arms. While in Russia, President Bush made clear that he wanted Congress to overturn legislation that put Russia in a disadvantaged trading position with the United States. On that same trip, President Bush met with other European leaders to shore up support for American policy in the Middle East and, in particular, toward Iraq.

Chief Legislator   Although the Constitution formally places the legislative power of the national government in Congress, the president has come to be regarded as the chief legislator. Even though the president does not formally participate in the legislative process, Congress looks to him to set the legislative agenda. Americans expect the president, not Congress, to initiate major policies. Unlike George Bush, who was faulted by his critics for failing to provide leadership in domestic policy, Bill Clinton came to Washington with an ambitious legislative agenda that spanned health care, welfare, crime, and the economy. He failed in his signature legislative goal—health-care reform—in 1993 despite having Democratic majorities in both houses of Congress. He later embraced some of the policies enunciated by the Republican Congress that took over in 1994; the most notable, welfare reform. However, Clinton's most skillful performance in the role of chief legislator may well have been his active role in marshalling bipartisan support for the North American Free Trade Agreement (NAFTA) in 1993. George W. Bush took an active role in promoting an economic stimulus package in 2001 and in proposing legislation to support his war on terrorism after September 11.

Party Leader   Finally, the president is the symbolic leader of his party. Though others run the party organization, the electorate tends to think of the party in terms of the president's policies, appointments, decisions, and leadership style. Failure to lead effectively, with the attendant loss of popularity, can potentially harm members of his party signifi-

---

Popular Culture and American Politics
The West Wing

One of the most successful prime-time television dramas in recent years is NBC's *The West Wing*. The highly rated show provides a glimpse of the inner workings of the White House, focusing on the president, the first lady, the press secretary, and the top staffers. In its debut season (1999–2000), *The West Wing* won nine Emmy awards, including the award for outstanding dramatic series. The success of the show can be attributed to three factors: its first-rate cast, which includes Martin Sheen, Allison Janney, John Spencer, and Stockard Channing; its clever and sophisticated scripts, written by the show's creator (Aaron Sorkin) and others; and the mass public's insatiable appetite for drama and intrigue, especially involving the rich and powerful. As the most powerful actor on the world stage, POTUS (president of the United States) is obvious material for prime-time drama. The difficulty, which the creators of *The West Wing* have overcome, is making a television drama about the White House credible. One way in which this credibility is achieved is by basing scripts on real-world problems, issues, and events. Some topics addressed by the show include terrorism, civil rights, abortion, gun control, the death penalty, drug and alcohol abuse, campaign finance reform, and illegal immigration.

cantly, especially as they seek election or reelection. At the same time, the president is expected to limit his partisan activities. Being party leader thus presents the president with a dilemma. But facing dilemmas—and finding a way to resolve them—is what being president is all about.

When the president appears every January to report to Congress on the "state of the Union," as required by the Constitution, he is acting as head of state, chief legislator, and party leader. When the president enters the House chamber for the speech, everyone, regardless of party affiliation, stands to applaud the leader of the country. During the speech, the president sets forth the broad outlines of his legislative agenda. Media pundits watch carefully to see how Democrats and Republicans, who sit on opposite sides of the main aisle, are responding to the president's message. After the speech is over, the networks provide time for a leader of the opposing political party to respond. Presidents generally dislike this practice because they do not want their State of the Union messages to be viewed in such partisan terms.

13-2 The Constitutional Basis of the Presidency

Perhaps the most glaring weakness of the Articles of Confederation was that they did not provide for any real leadership in the national government. All members of the Congress represented individual states. No one represented the nation as a whole. No one provided leadership. Clearly, some type of chief executive was needed if the United States was to function effectively as a nation.

13-2a Creating the Presidency

The delegates to the Constitutional Convention of 1787 agreed on the need for an executive authority in the new national government they were creating. They were also in agreement that the executive should be a separate, independent branch of government—they did not want a parliamentary system. As with other matters at the convention, though, the delegates disagreed over the nature, structure, and powers of the executive branch (see Figure 13-1). Some delegates preferred a weak administrator, whose main function would be to faithfully execute the laws passed by Congress. Others, most notably Alexander Hamilton, wanted an executive endowed with significant independent powers and capable of

---

Profiles &
Perspectives
———————

John F. Kennedy
(1917–1963)

AP Photo

The American president is not only the leader of his nation but also the most important leader in the world community. People all over the world pay attention to what American presidents say and do. When President Kennedy took office on January 20, 1961, he was profoundly conscious of this fact. In the depths of the cold war, Kennedy used his inauguration speech to send a message to America's allies and enemies abroad. The new president said:

> Let the word go forth from this time and place, to friend and foe alike, that the torch has been passed to a new generation of Americans, born in this century, tempered by war, disciplined by a hard and bitter peace, proud of our ancient heritage, and unwilling to witness or permit the slow undoing of those human rights to which this nation has always been committed, and to which we are committed today at home and around the world. Let every nation know, whether it wishes us well or ill, that we shall pay any price, bear any burden, meet any hardship, support any friend, oppose any foe to assure the survival and the success of liberty.

More than forty years after John Kennedy's assassination in 1963, Americans still look back at his brief presidential administration with admiration and affection. Clearly, Kennedy possessed two characteristics of greatness: vision and charisma.

For more information about John Kennedy, check out these websites:
Past presidents at the White House site:
   http://www.whitehouse.gov/history/presidents/jk35.html
The John F. Kennedy Library:
   http://www.jfklibrary.org/

Figure 13-1
Potential Presidencies

Legislatively Elected Presidency
A president elected by and dependent on the legislature wouldn't be the kind of strong president the Founders wanted. What kinds of pressures would such a president be under? How might the legislators push and pull him or her to act?

Plural Presidency
A plural presidency would have given us more than one president. What would happen if they couldn't decide? What would happen if they argued all the time? On the other hand, what if they worked well together? What would the benefits of a plural presidency have been?

?

One-Term Limit Presidency
Proponents of election by national legislature wanted to limit the president to one long term in office. Some feared, perhaps, that a president elected to a long-term presidency might become unreliable with the trust placed in him or her, could abuse his or her power, or could do the opposite and be a much-admired figure. Knowing what you do about the uses and abuses of power, why do you think the Founders hesitated in creating a president with a long term?

Short-Term Presidency with Term Limits
Those who favored election by other means (nonlegislative) preferred to allow the president to serve two or more shorter terms. How would a president manage the duties of the office while thinking about re-election more often? What are the benefits of shorter terms with limited or unlimited terms?

providing vigorous national leadership. Writing in *Federalist* No. 70, Hamilton articulated his view of the presidential office:

> There is an idea, which is not without its advocates, that a vigorous executive is inconsistent with the genius of republican government. . . . Energy in the executive is the leading character in the definition of good government. It is essential to the protection of the community against foreign attacks; it is not less essential to the steady administration of the laws, to the protection of property . . . ; [and] to the security of liberty against the enterprises and assaults of ambition, of faction and anarchy.

The Framers of the Constitution opted for a middle ground. The Constitution they drafted seemed to contemplate a president who would be capable of acting independently, but who would also be answerable to the Congress. The president would be endowed with significant constitutional powers, but these powers would be well defined and limited. In the more than two hundred years since the Constitution was ratified, the presidency has changed more dramatically than either the legislative or the judicial branch of the national government. The presidency has grown in size, scope, and power beyond anything ever contemplated in the late eighteenth century. But even with these changes, the president is no king and must still answer to the Congress, the courts, and, ultimately, the American people.

A Single Executive?

A number of delegates at the Constitutional Convention of 1787 favored a multiple executive in which presidential power would be shared by three or more individuals. The delegates, who had recently participated in a successful revolution against the British Crown, were reluctant to create an institution that could degenerate into a monarchy. But the knowledge that George Washington would assume a central role of leadership greatly reduced these fears. Ultimately, the delegates opted for a single executive.

Of course, a single executive is more likely to become a tyrant. This fear motivated many people to suggest limiting the president to a single term of seven years or to two three-year terms. Still others maintained that the president, in concert with the Supreme Court, should function as a "council of revision," which would decide on the constitutionality of acts of Congress. Neither of these proposals was adopted. In the end, the Constitution prescribed a four-year term for the president, with no limit on the number of terms that one individual could serve. The Constitution said nothing of a council of revision, but it did give the president the authority to veto acts of Congress of which he disapproved.

13-2b Presidential Terms

George Washington, as the first president, displayed both the leadership and self-restraint that the American people expected. He established an important precedent by refusing to seek a third term, a tradition that survived until Franklin D. Roosevelt was elected to a third term in 1940, followed by a fourth term in 1944. Roosevelt died in office in 1945, and the Republican party gained control of both chambers of Congress after the 1946 elections. Reacting to Roosevelt's break with tradition, Congress then proposed the Twenty-second Amendment, which was ratified in 1951, prohibiting future presidents from being elected to more than two consecutive terms. In the aftermath of Ronald Reagan's popular first term and landslide reelection in 1984, Republicans began to urge the repeal of the Twenty-second Amendment. This consideration was short-lived, however. The nation soon became preoccupied with the Iran-Contra affair and other problems during Reagan's second term.

Presidential Succession and Disability   The constitutional problem of presidential succession has troubled generations of Americans. The problem first arose in 1841 when President William Henry Harrison died after only a month in office. The immediate question was whether Vice President John Tyler would assume the full duties and powers of the office for the remaining forty-seven months of Harrison's term or serve merely as acting president. Unwilling to settle for less than the full measure of presidential authority, Tyler set an important precedent, which has been followed by the eight other individuals who have succeeded to the office because of the death or resignation of an incumbent president.

The related problem of presidential disability has proved more perplexing. Several presidents have been temporarily disabled during their terms of office, giving rise to uncertainty and confusion about the locus of actual decision-making authority. For example, President Woodrow Wilson was seriously disabled by a stroke in 1919 and for a number of weeks was totally incapable of performing his official duties. No constitutional provision existed at that time for the temporary replacement of a disabled president. The result was that Wilson's wife, Edith, took on much of the responsibility of the office, an arrangement that evoked sharp criticism.

The problem of presidential disability is addressed by the Twenty-fifth Amendment, ratified in 1967. This amendment, proposed in the aftermath of the assassination of President Kennedy in 1963, establishes, among other things, a procedure under which the vice president may assume the role of acting president during periods of presidential disability. The amendment provides alternative means for determining presidential disability. Section 3 allows the president to transmit to Congress a written declaration that he is unable to discharge the duties of the office, after which the vice president assumes the role of acting president. The vice president continues in this role unless and until the president can transmit a declaration to the contrary. If, however, the president is unable or unwilling to acknowledge his inability to perform the duties of the office, the vice president and a majority of the cabinet members are authorized to make this determination.

The Order of Presidential Succession

The order of succession to the presidency is as follows:

Vice President	Secretary of Labor
Speaker of the House	Secretary of Health and Human Services
President Pro Tempore of the Senate	Secretary of Housing and
Secretary of State	Urban Development
Secretary of the Treasury	Secretary of Transportation
Secretary of Defense	Secretary of Energy
Attorney General	Secretary of Education
Secretary of the Interior	Secretary of Veterans Affairs
Secretary of Agriculture	Secretary of Homeland Security
Secretary of Commerce	

13-2c Removal of the Chief Executive

The ultimate constitutional sanction against the abuse of presidential power is impeachment and removal from office. *Impeachment* refers to an action of the House of Representatives in which that body adopts, by at least a majority vote, one or more articles of impeachment accusing a sitting president of "high crimes and misdemeanors." An impeached president is then tried before the Senate, at least two-thirds of which must so vote in order to remove the president from office.

Only twice in U.S. history have presidents been impeached, but in neither case was the president removed from office. President Andrew Johnson was impeached by the House of Representatives in 1868 but narrowly escaped conviction by the Senate. President Richard M. Nixon almost certainly would have been impeached and convicted had he not resigned the presidency in 1974. Nixon's role in the Watergate cover-up had become clear; he had even been named by a federal grand jury as an "unindicted co-conspirator." In 1998, the House of Representatives impeached President Clinton, charging him with perjury and obstruction of justice. After trial, the Senate acquitted him of both charges, and he remained in office to fill out his term.

The Andrew Johnson Impeachment President Andrew Johnson was impeached solely for political reasons, stemming from his clash with Congress over Reconstruction policy. His ultimate acquittal can be attributed to the fact that he had not committed indictable offenses, although many in Congress were willing to interpret quite broadly the "high crimes and misdemeanors" language in the Constitution. As America matured through the twentieth century, however, it became clear that American political culture set certain guidelines for the impeachment of a president, who would have to commit some serious breach of ethics or law to be impeached. The public would not support the removal of a popularly elected president by a Congress inspired by purely political motives.

The Impeachment of Bill Clinton In January 1998, the nation became immersed in one of the most prolonged and intense presidential scandals in American history. The events leading to the eventual impeachment of President Clinton in 1998 began to unfold behind the scenes in a sexual harassment lawsuit filed by Paula Corbin Jones, a former worker in Arkansas state government during Clinton's tenure as the governor of that state. Jones' attorneys sought to query President Clinton about other alleged sexual relationships. The Supreme Court, in *Clinton v. Jones,* allowed this questioning to take place, accepting Jones' lawyers' arguments that the president could answer questions in this civil suit without interfering with his presidential duties.

On January 17, 1998, Clinton submitted to questioning and became the first president to testify in a civil lawsuit while serving as president. During this testimony, the president was asked specifically about having had an affair with Monica Lewinsky. Clinton denied a sexual relationship with Lewinsky, who had also denied an affair during an earlier deposition. However, word of a relationship had begun to spread. A Lewinsky friend and confidant, Linda Tripp, approached the independent prosecutor Ken Starr with tape recordings. Starr, who had long been involved in investigating alleged wrongdoings in the Whitewater case, sought and received approval from Attorney General Janet Reno to launch an inquiry into the Lewinsky matter.

The story of a sexual relationship between the president and a young White House intern, Monica Lewinsky, first appeared on the Internet in the *Drudge Report,* which had become aware of a story about to break in *Newsweek.* The story soon became the focus of massive media and public attention. President Clinton addressed the nation on January 26 with the following statement:

> I want to say one thing to the American people. I want you to listen to me. I'm gonna say this again. I did not have sexual relations with that woman, Miss Lewinsky. I never told anybody to lie. Not a single time. Never. These allegations are false. And I need to go back to work for the American people. Thank you.

Popular Culture and American Politics
The Contender

By Chapman Rackaway

The process of impeaching and removing presidents and vice presidents is politically volatile and difficult, but so is the possibility of nominating people to replace them. Just as we place informal standards on what personal characteristics and failings invalidate a potential candidate when running, when a replacement for a resigned or deceased vice president is nominated, what possible scandals or indiscretions might invalidate that candidacy?

Since the Monica Lewinsky scandal exploded in 1998, issues of sexual impropriety have become common in discussions of politics. What personal indiscretions are a matter of public record, and which ones are not important in the way a political leader carries out his or her job? In *The Contender,* the film asks:"What if a female nominee for vice president had an indecent sexual past?" After the sudden death of the vice president, sitting president Jackson Evans (played by Jeff Bridges) picks a replacement. He decides against picking the popular governor of Virginia and instead makes the radical choice of Senator Laine Hanson (portrayed by Joan Allen) to become the nation's first female vice president.

Congressman Shelly Runyon (played by Gary Oldman) is a powerful ally of Virginia's Governor Hathaway and the man who will oversee Hanson's confirmation. Runyon digs into Hanson's personal life and finds evidence that in college, Hanson participated in an alcohol-fueled orgy as part of a sorority initiation. When faced with this scandal, Hanson refuses to respond to the attacks, causing a political crisis leading to further shocking revelations. Runyon blocks Hanson's confirmation while her voting record and personal past become the fodder for talk radio and news broadcasts, calling her capabilities into question. Throughout the ordeal, Hanson refuses to bring up the issue or discuss it, referring to it as a private matter.

In addition to its approach to politics, *The Contender* raises issues about personal privacy for all people, not just political figures. What issues are fair game, and what are purely personal, in an age when ever more information is available publicly?

Not surprisingly, many Republicans and some Democrats pointed to the Lewinsky mess as indicative of President Clinton's lack of moral fiber. The president's defenders, while decrying the president's apparent lack of judgment, sought to frame the issue as a private one between the president and his family. Many defenders sought to exploit the president's continuing high approval ratings by shifting the focus to the independent counsel Ken Starr. First Lady Hillary Rodham Clinton, appearing on NBC's *Today* program, blamed a "vast right-wing conspiracy" bent on destroying her husband.

Ken Starr convened a grand jury to look into the matter, especially whether the president had committed perjury in his testimony in the Paula Jones case. By the summer, many had testified before the grand jury, including President Clinton, who eventually testified from the White House on August 17. By this time, Judge Susan Webber Wright had dismissed the original Jones lawsuit and Ms. Lewinsky had admitted the affair. Following his testimony, the president addressed the nation to admit the affair and to seek forgiveness.

The president's problems grew worse in September when Ken Starr prepared a lengthy, detailed report and submitted it to the House Judiciary Committee. The committee conducted somewhat acrimonious debate before large television audiences before voting along party lines to recommend that the House vote to impeach on all counts. Meanwhile, the country remained divided. Although most citizens condemned the president's behavior, a clear majority did not favor impeachment. To many, the true villain was Ken Starr, who was vilified for his relentless pursuit of the Clintons and excessive concentration of the more prurient aspects of the Lewinsky affair.

The debate in the House reflected much of the acrimony that had surfaced in the Judiciary Committee. Many Democrats urged censure rather than impeachment. The discussion and subsequent vote occurred along party lines. The House eventually voted to impeach on two counts: perjury and obstruction of justice. On December 20, 1998, William Jefferson Clinton became the second president to be impeached.

In many ways, the trial in the Senate the following January was anticlimactic. It was clear from the beginning that the Republican leadership in the Senate saw impeachment as a losing political proposition in the climate of high approval ratings for the president. Facing almost no chance of mustering the necessary two-thirds to convict, the trial was short-lived. Ultimately, the House impeachment managers failed to achieve a majority on either count, allowing President Clinton to serve out the remainder of his term. The president was hardly vindicated, however. In April, Judge Wright held the president in contempt for giving misleading testimony in the Jones case. Finally, in his last day in office in January 2001, President Clinton agreed to a plea bargain with the new special prosecutor, Robert Ray. In this agreement, Clinton admitted to providing misleading testimony and agreed to surrender his license to practice law in Arkansas.

13-3 The Scope and Limits of Presidential Power

pardons Acts of executive clemency by which persons who have committed crimes are absolved of their guilt.

Article II, Section 1 of the Constitution provides that the "executive power shall be vested in a President of the United States." Sections 2 and 3 enumerate specific powers granted to the president. They include the authority to appoint judges and ambassadors, veto legislation, call Congress into special session, grant **pardons,** and serve as commander-in-chief of the armed forces. Each of these designated powers is obviously a part of "executive power," but that general term is not defined in Article II.

13-3a Competing Theories of Presidential Power

In the early days of the Republic, James Madison and Alexander Hamilton engaged in the first of what was to be a long series of sharp disagreements among constitutional theorists about the proper scope of presidential power. Madison argued that presidential power is restricted to those powers specifically listed in Article II. By contrast, Hamilton argued that the president enjoyed broad power. He believed that "the general doctrine of our Constitution . . . is that the executive power of the nation is vested in the President; subject only to the exceptions and qualifications which are expressed in that instrument." Madison maintained that if new exercises of power could be continually justified by invoking inherent executive power, "no citizen could any longer guess at the character of the government under which he lives; the most penetrating jurist would be unable to scan the extent of constructive prerogative." These competing theories correspond to quite different notions of the proper role of the president in the newly created national government. Although Madison envisaged a passive role for the president, who would faithfully execute the laws adopted by Congress, Hamilton viewed the presidency in more activist terms.

stewardship theory A theory of presidential power holding that the president is authorized to do whatever he believes to be necessary as long as it is not prohibited by the Constitution.

constitutional theory A theory of presidential power holding that the president cannot exercise any power unless it can be traced back to the Constitution.

The Stewardship Theory of Presidential Power The debate over the scope of presidential power was by no means confined to the early years of the Republic. A vigorous debate took place early in the twentieth century between those who espoused the **stewardship theory** and those who embraced the **constitutional theory** of presidential power. The constitutional theory, derived from Madison's ideas, finds its best and most succinct expression in the words of President William Howard Taft. In his view, the president can "exercise no power which cannot be fairly and reasonably traced to some specific grant of power or justly implied and included within such express grant as proper and necessary to its exercise." The stewardship theory, the modern counterpart to Hamilton's perspective, was best encapsulated by President Theodore Roosevelt. In his view, the Constitution permits the president "to do anything that the needs of the nation [demand] unless such action [is] forbidden by the Constitution or the laws." According to this perspective, the president is a steward empowered to do anything deemed necessary, short of what is expressly prohibited by the Constitution, in the pursuit of the general welfare for which he is primarily responsible.

American constitutional history has, for the most part, vindicated the views of Hamilton and Roosevelt. Although some observers advocate scaling down the modern presidency, few truly expect this type of diminution to occur. The problems of modernization, the complexities of living in a technological age, and the need for the United States as a superpower to speak to other nations with a unified voice and respond quickly to threats to the national security have forced us to recognize the stewardship presidency as both necessary and legitimate. The inherent vagueness of Article II has facilitated this recognition.

The Supreme Court and Presidential Power   The Supreme Court has been, for the most part, willing to allow the expansion of executive power. But on occasion the Court has invalidated particular exercises of executive power that it found excessive under the Constitution. For instance, in 1952, the Court disallowed President Truman's effort to have the government take over and operate the steel industry to prevent a stoppage of production caused by a steelworkers' strike (see Case in Point 13-1).[1] In a dramatic decision during the summer of 1974, the Court unanimously ruled against President Nixon's claim that he had a right to withhold his tape recordings from Congress during the Watergate crisis.[2]

Another important instance in which the Court imposed limits on the stewardship presidency was in the Pentagon Papers Case of 1971.[3] In the most celebrated case arising from the Vietnam controversy, the Court refused to issue an injunction against newspapers that had come into possession of the Pentagon Papers, a set of classified documents detailing the history of American strategy in Vietnam. Basing his position on inherent executive power and not on any act of Congress, President Richard M. Nixon sought to restrain the press from disclosing classified information that, he argued, would be injurious to the national security. The Court, obviously skeptical of the alleged threat to national security and sensitive to the values protected by the First Amendment, refused to defer to the president.

13-3b The President's Powers to Limit Congress

Under the Constitution, the American president has substantial powers to provide a check on congressional action. These checks can become the subject of considerable testiness,

---

Case in Point **13-1**

The Supreme Court Says "No" to President Truman

Youngstown v. Sawyer **(1952)**

In December 1951, President Harry S Truman was informed that negotiations between labor and management in the steel industry had broken down. Concerned about the consequences of a stoppage in steel production, for both the domestic economy and the Korean War effort, Truman acted to delay a strike by referring the issue to the Wage Stabilization Board for further negotiation. By April 1952, further negotiations were clearly fruitless, and the workers announced their plans to strike. To prevent this situation, Truman ordered Secretary of Commerce Charles Sawyer to seize the steel mills and maintain full production. Not surprisingly, this action was challenged in the courts, and soon the issue was before the Supreme Court.

Much to President Truman's displeasure, the Supreme Court refused to allow the government to seize and operate the steel plants. Writing for the Court, Justice Hugo Black rejected inherent executive power as a justification for Truman's order. The Court was clearly swayed by the fact that Truman acted not only without congressional approval but also irrespective of implied disapproval. In considering the Taft–Hartley bill, Congress had rejected an amendment that would have given the president a power similar to the power Truman exercised in seizing the steel mills. Thus, the Steel Seizure Case was by no means a wholesale repudiation of the stewardship theory of presidential power—rather, it was a reminder that the steward's authority is neither entirely self-derived nor without limitation. Moreover, the decision served notice to the chief executive that his actions, at least in the domestic sphere, are subject to judicial scrutiny.

especially when the president is from one party and Congress is controlled by the other. This phenomenon, known as divided-party government, has occurred with regularity since 1968 (although in 2000 the Republicans captured the presidency and kept a slim lead in the House of Representatives while having to rely on Vice President Cheney's potential tie-breaking vote to maintain control of the Senate). American political culture has created the term *gridlock* to denote both the division and the resulting frustration. Many people, and not just Democrats, were relieved when Bill Clinton won the presidential election of 1992. To many, this victory meant the end of gridlock because Democrats would control both the executive and legislative branches of government. But President Clinton soon discovered, much to his chagrin, that Congress has a mind of its own. To some extent, gridlock is a function of the constitutional design as the president and Congress respond to their differing constituencies.

The Power to Veto Legislation   Under Article I, Section 7 of the Constitution, "every bill" and "every order, resolution or vote to which the concurrence of the Senate and the House of Representatives may be necessary" must be presented to the president for approval. This "presentment" requirement has only three exceptions. It does not apply to:

- Actions involving a single chamber, such as the adoption of procedural rules.
- Concurrent resolutions, such as those establishing joint committees or setting a date for adjournment.
- Proposed constitutional amendments adopted by Congress.

The president has ten days (not counting Sundays) in which to consider legislation presented for approval. The president has several options:

- Sign the bill into law, which is what usually occurs.
- Veto the bill, which can be overridden by a two-thirds majority of both chambers of Congress.
- Neither sign nor veto the bill, thus allowing it to become law automatically after ten days.

▶ **pocket veto**   A means of vetoing legislation whereby the president refuses to sign a bill passed by Congress during the last ten days before it adjourns, thus preventing the bill from becoming law.

A major exception applies to the third option, however: If Congress adjourns before the ten days have expired and the president still has not signed the bill, it is said to have been subjected to a pocket veto. The beauty of the **pocket veto** (at least from the president's standpoint) is that it deprives Congress of the chance to override a formal veto. This device was first used by President James Madison in 1812.

The veto was rarely used until after the Civil War. President Andrew Johnson (1865–1869), who was at odds with Congress over Reconstruction, vetoed more bills than any of his predecessors. In fact, Johnson vetoed twenty-nine bills in four years, whereas all previous presidents combined had vetoed only fifty-nine bills. Johnson's use of the veto power was one of the reasons the House of Representatives impeached him. He survived his Senate trial because there was no clear evidence of wrongdoing on his part. Using the veto, even using it unwisely, is not an impeachable offense!

Franklin D. Roosevelt used the veto more frequently than any other president in history. During his almost thirteen years in office, Roosevelt issued 635 vetoes. Amazingly, only 9 of these were overridden by Congress. By contrast, Gerald Ford had 12 of his 66 vetoes overridden. Of course, Ford, a Republican, was facing a hostile Congress in which the Democrats controlled both chambers, whereas Roosevelt, a Democrat, had the luxury of having a Congress controlled by the Democrats throughout his tenure. More recently, President Bush used the veto 46 times and was overridden only once, even though he faced a Democratic Congress. Bush's Democratic successor, Bill Clinton, did not veto any bills passed by Congress during his first year in office. In this respect, Clinton's first-year experience was similar to that of Jimmy Carter's, who vetoed only one bill during his first year. See Table 13-1 for a listing of the presidential vetoes from 1789 to 2005.

TABLE 13-1

Presidential Vetoes, 1901–2005

Years	President	Regular Vetoes	Vetoes Overridden	Pocket Vetoes	Total Vetoes
1789–1797	Washington	2	0	0	2
1797–1801	Adams	0	0	0	0
1801–1809	Jefferson	0	0	0	0
1809–1817	Madison	5	0	2	7
1817–1825	Monroe	1	0	0	1
1825–1829	J. Q. Adams	0	0	0	0
1829–1837	Jackson	5	0	7	12
1837–1841	Van Buren	0	0	1	1
1841–1841	Harrison	0	0	0	0
1841–1845	Tyler	6	1	4	10
1845–1849	Polk	2	0	1	3
1849–1850	Taylor	0	0	0	0
1850–1853	Fillmore	0	0	0	0
1853–1857	Pierce	9	5	0	9
1857–1861	Buchanan	4	0	3	7
1861–1865	Lincoln	2	0	5	7
1865–1869	A. Johnson	21	15	8	29
1869–1877	Grant	45	4	48	93
1877–1881	Hayes	12	1	1	13
1881–1881	Garfield	0	0	0	0
1881–1885	Arthur	4	1	8	12
1885–1889	Cleveland	304	2	110	414
1889–1893	Harrison	19	1	25	44
1893–1897	Cleveland	42	5	128	170
1897–1901	McKinley	6	0	36	42
1901–1909	T. Roosevelt	42	1	40	82
1909–1913	Taft	30	1	9	39
1913–1921	Wilson	33	6	11	44
1921–1923	Harding	5	0	1	6
1923–1929	Coolidge	20	4	30	50
1929–1933	Hoover	21	3	16	37
1933–1945	F. Roosevelt	372	9	263	635
1945–1953	Truman	180	12	70	250
1953–1961	Eisenhower	73	2	108	18
1961–1963	Kennedy	12	0	9	21
1963–1969	L. Johnson	16	0	14	30
1969–1974	Nixon	26	7	17	43
1974–1977	Ford	48	12	18	66
1977–1981	Carter	13	2	18	31
1981–1989	Reagan	39	9	39	78
1989–1992	G. Bush	29	1	17	46
1993–2000	Clinton	36	2	1	37
2001–2005	G. W. Bush	0	0	0	0

Source: Adapted from Harold W. Stanley and Richard G. Niemi, *Vital Statistics on American Politics 2003–2004* (Washington, D.C.: CQ Press, 2003), p. 260.

However, after the Republicans captured Congress in 1994, President Clinton was no longer in the position of working with a friendly Congress unlikely to pass legislation leading to a veto. The new Speaker, Newt Gingrich, had an activist conservative agenda for the Congress stemming from the Contract with America that Republicans used successfully to gain control of the House. Bill Clinton was not shy about using, or threatening to use, his veto power, and, although the Republicans had control, they did not have the supermajority they needed to override presidential vetoes. During his eight years in the White House, Bill Clinton used the veto thirty-six times; Congress overrode his veto only twice.

An Item Veto?   The veto is a blunt instrument of presidential power, in that presidents must accept or reject a piece of legislation as a whole. Recent presidents—most notably, Ronald Reagan and George Bush—called for a constitutional amendment providing the president with a **line-item veto,** a power exercised by many state governors. A line-item veto is a veto of only part of a particular bill as opposed to a veto of the entire piece of legislation. Supporters of the item veto argue that it would allow the president to control the swelling federal budget more effectively. Arguably, a line-item veto would also allow the president to defeat the congressional tactic of attaching disagreeable riders to bills the president basically supports. In 1994, Republican Congressional candidates called for the line-item veto in their Contract with America. In 1996, Congress passed it into law. However, it was short-lived. Six members of Congress challenged it as an unconstitutional surrender of Congress' authority and violation of the separation of powers (see Case in Point 13-2). In a 6–3 ruling, the Supreme Court struck down the item veto, noting that the Constitution allows the president to exercise only the options of signing legislation or vetoing it, but not the authority to strike specific items with legislation approved by Congress.[4] The ruling upset both the president and key Republicans in Congress who saw the line-item veto as necessary to control Congress' propensity to spend.

Many observers believed that the idea of a presidential line-item veto died with the Supreme Court's decision in 1998. Yet, in his first press conference after winning reelection in 2004, President George W. Bush resurrected the idea. "I do believe there ought to be budgetary reform in Washington. I would like to see the president have a line-item veto again, one that (can pass) constitutional muster."[5] Exactly how a statute could be drawn to "pass constitutional muster" remained unclear, but a Democratic spokesman for the House Appropriations Committee said, "It's probably something that some real clever lawyers can get around."[6]

Impoundment   Another controversial presidential check on the legislative branch is **impoundment,** or the refusal to allow the expenditure of funds appropriated by Congress. The first instance of impoundment occurred in 1803 when President Thomas Jefferson

> **line-item veto**   A reform measure aimed at curbing congressional spending that would allow the president to veto specific items within a piece of legislation without vetoing the entire bill.

> **impoundment**   The refusal of the president to allow an expenditure of funds appropriated by Congress.

Case in Point **13-2**

The Supreme Court Strikes Down the Line-Item Veto

Clinton v. City of New York (1998)

Objecting to President Clinton's use of the line-item veto to eliminate certain federal funds from its hospitals, the city of New York and other interested parties filed lawsuits challenging the constitutionality of the Line-Item Veto Act of 1996. In a 1998 decision, the Supreme Court, by a vote of 6–3, invalidated this controversial statute. Justice Stevens, writing for the majority, maintained that "repeal of statutes, no less than enactment, must conform" to Article I, Section 7 of the Constitution. This section established "a single finely wrought and exhaustively considered procedure" for passing laws. Stevens asserted that "the Line-item Veto Act authorizes the President himself to affect the repeal of laws, for his own policy reasons, without observing" required constitutional procedures. In a concurring opinion, Justice Kennedy sharply criticized Congress for what he regarded as a transgression of the principle of separation of powers. Kennedy declared that "abdication of responsibility is not part of the constitutional design." Justice Scalia dissented in an opinion joined by Justices O'Connor and Breyer. "There is not a dime's worth of difference," Scalia insisted, between permitting the president to cancel a project by using the line-item veto and allowing him to spend money at his discretion. In a separate dissent, Justice Breyer characterized the line-item veto as an acceptable "experiment" that posed no threat to "the liberties of individual citizens."

withheld $50,000 that Congress had allocated to build gunboats to defend the Mississippi River. Jefferson's purpose was merely to delay the expenditure, primarily because the Louisiana Purchase, completed shortly after Congress appropriated the money for gunboats, minimized the need for defenses along the Mississippi. During the remainder of the nineteenth century, presidents rarely invoked Jefferson's precedent. In 1905, Congress gave the president statutory authority to engage in limited impoundments to avoid departmental deficits. In 1921, Congress extended this authority to allow the president to withhold funds to save money in case Congress authorized more than was needed to secure its goals. Although Congress provided for a limited power of impoundment, these concessions to the president did not significantly undermine Congress' basic power of the purse.

Richard Nixon, however, extended the power of impoundment beyond acceptable limits. Nixon not only used impoundment to suit his budgetary preferences but also attempted to dismantle certain programs of which he disapproved. The most notorious example was the Office of Economic Opportunity (OEO), which Nixon tried to shut down by refusing to spend any of the funds Congress had designated for the office. (Congressional and public pressures forced Nixon to capitulate on the OEO issue.) In one of his far-reaching uses of the impoundment power, Nixon ordered the head of the Environmental Protection Agency (EPA), Russell Train, to withhold a substantial amount of money allocated for sewage treatment plants under the Water Pollution Control Act of 1972. Particularly disturbing to some members of Congress was that Nixon had originally vetoed the act and Congress had overridden the veto. Thus, Nixon was seeking to have his way by impounding funds despite the wishes of a two-thirds majority of Congress.

Largely in response to the Nixon administration's unbridled use of impoundment, Congress adopted the Congressional Budget and Impoundment Control Act of 1974. Although the act recognizes a limited presidential power to impound funds, it requires the president to inform Congress of the reasons for an intended impoundment and provides for a bicameral legislative veto to prevent the president from proceeding.

13-3c The Powers of Appointment and Removal

Long before the advent of the modern stewardship presidency, it was obvious that presidents could not be expected to fulfill their duties alone. As presidential power has expanded, so too have the size and complexity of the executive branch. Originally, Congress provided for three cabinet departments—State, War, and Treasury—to assist the president in the execution of policy. The executive establishment now has fifteen cabinet departments in addition to a plethora of agencies, boards, and commissions in the executive establishment. In 1790, fewer than a thousand employees worked for the executive branch; that number now has grown to approximately three million. Although almost all these are civil service employees, the president directly appoints some two thousand upper-level officials.

Although the Constitution permits some upper-level officials in the executive branch to be selected solely at the discretion of the president and some to be appointed solely by the heads of departments, the more important federal officials are to be appointed by the president with the advice and consent of the Senate. In the case of appointments requiring senatorial consent, the president nominates a candidate, awaits Senate approval by majority vote, and then commissions the confirmed nominee as an "officer of the United States."

Although the Constitution is reasonably clear on the subject of the presidential appointment power, the issue of removal of an appointed official has been rather problematic. Obviously, the president has a strong interest in being able to remove those appointees whose performance displeases him. However, the Constitution addresses the question of removal only in the context of the cumbersome impeachment process. It is unlikely that the Framers intended that an administrative official whose performance is unacceptable to the president be subject to removal only by impeachment. Given the difficulty of this method of removal, this type of limitation could paralyze government.

Most observers agree that officers of the United States can be removed by means other than impeachment—except for judges, whose life tenure (assuming good behavior) is guaranteed by the Constitution. The problem is the role of Congress in the removal of executive officers. Given that the Constitution requires senatorial consent for certain presidential appointments, is it not reasonable to expect Congress to play a role in the removal of these officials? The Supreme Court's decisions in this area suggest that the legality of presidential removal of an official in the executive branch depends on the nature of the duties performed by the official in question. Officials performing purely executive functions may be removed by the president at will; those performing quasi-legislative or quasi-judicial functions can be removed only for cause. Legitimate cause includes malfeasance (wrongful conduct) or abuse of authority.

13-3d The Power to Grant Pardons

President Gerald Ford's full and unconditional pardon of former President Richard Nixon following the Watergate affair may have been politically unwise, but it was unquestionably constitutional. Article II, Section 2 states that the president shall have the power to "grant reprieves and pardons for offenses against the United States, except in cases of impeachment." Although impeachment proceedings were initiated against President Nixon, his sudden resignation foreclosed any possibility of impeachment, let alone conviction by the Senate. Whether or not they liked the idea, most observers agreed that President Ford acted constitutionally in issuing the pardon to Nixon.

The pardoning power came under tremendous scrutiny in early 2001 following outgoing President Clinton's controversial pardons issued in the last days of his administration. Although many pardons raised eyebrows, one was particularly troubling—that of the fugitive billionaire Marc Rich. Although the power to pardon is absolute and unconditional, both the House and the Senate held hearings to investigate the circumstances surrounding the pardon, including the failure of the president to consult with the prosecuting attorneys in the case and, most especially, the role of Mr. Rich's ex-wife, Denise Rich. Ms. Rich had played a major role in fundraising for the president, Hillary Clinton for her senate campaign, the Democratic National Committee, and the Clinton Library. President Clinton's impolitic use of the pardoning power met with substantial public disapproval. According to a Gallup poll, 62 percent disapproved of the pardon, and only 20 percent approved of it. Worse, 58 percent believed that the pardon was made in "return for financial contributions."[7] The Rich pardon scandal further damaged former President Clinton's public image and helped to ensure that his legacy would be defined primarily in terms of scandal. The important point is that even though a president has the constitutional authority to take a certain action does not mean that the action is immune to criticism.

Amnesties   Although the presidential pardon was traditionally thought to be a private transaction between the president and the recipient, it did not prevent President Jimmy Carter from granting **amnesty**—in effect, a blanket pardon—to those who were either deserters or draft evaders during the Vietnam War. President Carter's amnesty was not challenged in the courts; neither was it criticized on constitutional grounds, although many considered it to be an insult to those who had fought and died in Vietnam. Note that Congress has traditionally granted amnesty to those who deserted or evaded service in America's wars.

> **amnesty**   A blanket pardon given to a large group of lawbreakers.

13-3e Executive Privilege

Beginning with George Washington, presidents have asserted a right to withhold information from Congress and the courts. Known as **executive privilege,** this "right" has been defended as inherent in executive power. Indeed, it must be defended as such because it is mentioned nowhere in the Constitution. Scholars are divided over whether the Framers foresaw this type of power in the presidency, but the point is moot in light of two centuries of history supporting executive privilege and explicit Supreme Court recognition.

Although the term *executive privilege* was coined during the Eisenhower administration of the 1950s, the practice dates from 1792. In that year, President Washington refused to provide the House of Representatives with certain documents it had requested relative

> **executive privilege**   The right of the president to withhold certain information from Congress or a court of law.

to the bewildering defeat of military forces under General St. Clair by the Ohio Indians. Washington again asserted the privilege in 1795 when the House requested information dealing with the negotiation of a peace treaty with Great Britain. A few years later, President Thomas Jefferson, once a sharp critic of Washington's approach to the presidency, would rely on inherent executive power in defying a subpoena issued during Aaron Burr's trial for treason in 1807.

Later presidents invoked executive privilege primarily to maintain the secrecy of information related to national security. Presidents Truman, Eisenhower, Kennedy, and Johnson all found occasion to invoke the doctrine to protect the confidentiality of their deliberations. Nevertheless, the power of executive privilege did not become a major point of contention until the Nixon presidency.

President Clinton's claims of executive privilege in limiting evidence in the Lewinsky matter was later the basis of one of the charges in his impeachment hearings. Ken Starr and House Republicans on the Judiciary Committee concluded that Clinton's privilege claims amounted to an abuse of power. However, the full House did not concur and failed to impeach Clinton on that count.

The Watergate Controversy   During his first term (1969–1973), President Richard M. Nixon invoked executive privilege on four separate occasions; others in the Nixon administration did so in more than twenty instances. But after his landslide reelection in 1972, Nixon and his appointees routinely employed executive privilege to evade queries from Congress regarding the Watergate break-in and subsequent cover-up. Although Nixon was able to use executive privilege to withhold information requested by Congress, he was unable to avoid a subpoena issued by the federal courts at the request of the Watergate special prosecutor Leon Jaworski. Earlier, Nixon had fired Archibald Cox, Jaworski's predecessor, when Cox refused to back down in his efforts to subpoena the infamous tapes on which Nixon had recorded conversations with other people involved in the Watergate scandal. In an episode that became known as the "Saturday night massacre," Nixon fired Attorney General Elliot Richardson and Assistant Attorney General William Ruckelshaus, both of whom refused to follow the president's order to dismiss Cox. Ultimately, Cox was dismissed on the order of Robert H. Bork, who was the solicitor general at the time. Although there was no question of Nixon's constitutional authority to dismiss Cox—who was, after all, an employee of the Justice Department—the dismissal was politically disastrous: The Saturday night massacre led Congress to consider the possibility of impeaching the president. Succeeding Archibald Cox, Leon Jaworski pursued the Watergate investigation with just as much enthusiasm as his predecessor. When the federal district court denied Nixon's motion to quash a new subpoena obtained by Jaworski, the question of executive privilege went to the Supreme Court.

In a severe blow to the Nixon administration, the Supreme Court ruled unanimously that the tapes had to be surrendered.[8] Recognizing the legitimacy of executive privilege, the Court nevertheless held that the needs of criminal justice outweighed the presidential interest in confidentiality in this case. The Court refused to view executive privilege as an absolute presidential immunity from the judicial process. Thus, the Court asserted the primacy of the rule of law over the power of the presidency. Although Nixon reportedly was tempted to defy the Court's ruling, wiser counsel prevailed and the tapes were surrendered. Shortly thereafter, recognizing the inevitable, Richard Nixon resigned the presidency.

13-3f The Power to Make Foreign Policy

Scholars have written of the "two presidencies."[9] One aspect of the presidency, concerned with domestic affairs, is severely limited by the Constitution, the courts, and Congress. The other aspect of the presidency, involving foreign affairs and international relations, is less susceptible to constitutional and political constraints. Although the thesis may have been overstated, the basic point is valid. Throughout American history, Congress, the courts, and the public have been highly deferential to the president in the conduct of foreign policy. Although some commentators suggest that a serious reading of the Constitution indicates that the Framers intended for Congress to play a greater role in foreign policy, the demands of history, more than the intentions of the Framers, determine the roles played by the institutions of government.

Another factor contributing to presidential dominance of foreign policy inheres in the distinctive structures of Congress and the executive branch. Congress is composed of 535 members, each representing either a state or a localized constituency. In contrast, the president represents a national constituency. American political culture supports the idea that the president alone should speak for the nation in the international arena.

The "Sole Organ" in the Field of International Relations?

In *United States v. Curtiss-Wright Export Corporation* (1936), the Supreme Court placed its stamp of approval on the primary power of the president in the realm of foreign affairs, referring to the president as the "sole organ of the federal government in the field of international relations."[10] Many would challenge the Court's sweeping endorsement of presidential power to make foreign policy; few would argue that the president should be subject to no constitutional limitations in making and executing the foreign policy of this nation. Clearly, though, the degree of freedom afforded the president in the field of foreign policy has been substantial indeed.

In the wake of Vietnam and Watergate, and fueled by revelations about covert activities by the Central Intelligence Agency (CIA) during the 1960s, Congress in the 1970s adopted a series of laws limiting presidential power to employ covert means of pursuing foreign policy objectives. Moreover, during the 1980s, members of Congress began to get personally involved in diplomatic affairs by making trips to foreign countries that were not approved by the White House. For example, Speaker of the House Jim Wright (D-Texas) launched his own "peace mission" to Central America during the mid-1980s, when the Reagan administration was actively supporting rebels fighting the Marxist government of Nicaragua. Needless to say, President Reagan and his advisers were not amused by what they saw as an encroachment on the role of the executive. Similarly, Reagan was irritated when Senator Richard Lugar (R-Indiana) went to the Philippines in 1986 to investigate allegations of fraud in the elections that kept President Ferdinand Marcos, a longtime ally of the United States, in power. The White House had originally supported Marcos' claim to a legitimate electoral victory, but it had to retreat from its support of Marcos based in part on statements made by Senator Lugar. Clearly, the president had been upstaged and embarrassed by a U.S. senator acting on his own in the foreign policy arena. Although nothing is illegal about these types of activities on the part of members of Congress, they are not likely to curry favor with the White House and in fact may generate considerable political ill will.

The Iran–Contra Scandal

In the 1980s, when Congress learned of CIA efforts to support the Contras battling to overthrow the Marxist government of Nicaragua, it adopted the Boland Amendments, a series of measures restricting the use of U.S. funds to aid the Contras. The Reagan administration attempted an "end run" around the Boland Amendments by secretly selling weapons to Iran and using the profits to aid the Contras. When the operation was uncovered, an outraged Congress conducted an investigation that included the testimony of Lt. Col. Oliver North, a staff member of the National Security Council who was heavily involved in the covert operation. North was convicted of perjury and obstruction of justice, but his conviction was overturned on appeal in 1991.

Although the Iran–Contra affair was a blow to the credibility and prestige of the Reagan administration, it remains shrouded in legal uncertainty. It is not clear whether the administration violated the Boland Amendments, although little doubt exists that it sought to undermine the policy objective behind the amendments. Second, given the Supreme Court's pronouncements in *United States v. Curtiss-Wright* (1936), a serious question exists about the extent to which Congress may exercise control over presidential actions in the foreign policy sphere. Clearly, Congress may impose restrictions on the expenditure of government funds because Congress possesses the "power of the purse." May Congress prevent the president from carrying out a foreign policy objective through "creative enterprises," however, such as the deal to sell weapons to Iran?

Troubling constitutional questions involving the allocation of powers in the field of foreign policy are unlikely to be resolved in the courts of law. Rather, as "political questions," they are apt to be resolved in the court of public opinion. As the underwhelming public response to Iran–Contra demonstrates, the American people are not particularly troubled by broad presidential latitude in the foreign policy arena. Indeed, American political culture has always glorified the heroic individual who leads the community out of crisis.

13-3g The Specifics of Conducting Foreign Affairs

Although presidential authority in international relations rests in large part on inherent executive power, the Constitution also enumerates specific powers important in the everyday management of foreign affairs. Article II, Section 3 authorizes the president to receive ambassadors and emissaries from foreign nations. In effect, it provides the president the power to recognize the legitimate governments of foreign nations. This power is of obvious importance in international relations, as attested by Franklin Roosevelt's recognition of the Soviet government in the 1930s, Truman's recognition of Israel, Kennedy's severance of ties with Cuba, and Carter's recognition of the People's Republic of China.

Treaties   In addition to the authority to recognize foreign governments, the president is empowered by Article II to make treaties with foreign nations, subject to the consent of the Senate. A **treaty** is an agreement between two or more nations, in which they promise to behave in specified ways. The atmospheric nuclear test-ban treaty negotiated under President Kennedy's leadership, the SALT I treaty reached with the Soviets during the Nixon presidency, and the Panama Canal treaty negotiated during the Carter administration illustrate the importance of the treaty-making power.

> **treaty** An agreement between two or more nations containing promises to behave in specified ways; U.S. treaties require ratification by a two-thirds vote of the Senate.

In the early 1990s, treaties dealing with issues of international trade emerged as more important than agreements dealing with strategic issues or arms control. The North American Free Trade Agreement (NAFTA) and the General Agreement on Tariffs and Trade (GATT), both of which were negotiated in 1993, dramatically altered the climate for international business. In essence, these treaties lowered barriers to imported goods and services, thus facilitating trade among nations. Most economists predicted positive economic consequences for the world community. President Bill Clinton, whose first year in office was marred by a number of foreign-policy problems, gained considerable stature as a world leader by presiding over the successful conclusion of these treaties. This success abroad also had a positive effect on Clinton's approval rating at home, which rose to 56 percent in December 1993, a level of public support that Clinton had not enjoyed since he took office the preceding January.[11]

Executive Agreements   Like treaties, **executive agreements** require certain national commitments. These types of agreements, however, are negotiated solely between heads of state acting independently of their legislative bodies. Most of these agreements involve minor matters of international concern, such as specification of the details of postal relations or the use of radio airwaves. In recent years, however, the executive agreement has emerged as an important tool of foreign policy making. It enables the president to enter into an agreement with another country without the need for Senate approval, as is constitutionally required in the case of treaties.

> **executive agreements** Agreements between the United States and one or more foreign countries, entered into by the president without the necessity of ratification by the Senate.

Perhaps the most dramatic recent use of the executive agreement was President Jimmy Carter's agreement with Iran that secured the release of fifty-two American hostages in early 1981. The agreement negated all claims against Iranian assets in the United States and transferred claims against Iran from American to international tribunals. In 1981, the Supreme Court upheld the validity of Carter's executive agreement.[12] The Court found in the Emergency Powers Act of 1977 sufficient presidential authority to cancel claims against Iran. Finding no statutory authority for the transfer of claims to an international tribunal, the Court held that Congress had tacitly approved the president's actions by its traditional pattern of acquiescence to executive agreements. Thus, merely by being used, a power that is thought by some to conflict with the Constitution can gain legitimacy.

13-3h Presidential War Powers

Presidential dominance in international affairs is not limited to or based on the formalities of recognizing and striking agreements with other governments. Essential to the president's foreign policy role is the tremendous power of the American military, over which the Constitution makes the president commander-in-chief. Force is often threatened, and sometimes used, to protect American allies and interests, maintain national security against possible attack, or defend the nation against actual attack. The success of American foreign policy would be severely limited if the Constitution curbed the nation's ability to respond effectively to threats against its interests or security. On the other hand, the Constitution was designed as a limitation on the power of our government.

The Framers of the Constitution attempted to provide some limitation on the war-making power, as they did with government power in general, by dividing power between the president and Congress. Although Article II recognizes the president as commander-in-chief, Article I provides Congress with the authority to declare war. Does this mean that a formal declaration by Congress is the only way the United States can get into a war? Evidently not. The military conflicts in Vietnam and Korea qualify as wars; yet in neither case did Congress issue a formal declaration of war. When the United States was attacked by Islamic terrorists in September 2001, President George W. Bush rhetorically declared that the United States would wage a "war on terrorism." President Bush did not seek, and Congress did not pass, a declaration of war. But Congress did adopt a resolution authorizing Bush to use military force against the terrorists and those states that harbor them.

Presidential power to commit military forces to combat situations in the absence of a formal declaration of war has a long-standing heritage. It was first exercised in 1801, when Thomas Jefferson sent the U.S. Marines to "the shores of Tripoli" to root out the Barbary pirates. In 1846, James K. Polk sent American troops to instigate a conflict with Mexico that Congress formally approved by declaring war. In 1854, Franklin Pierce authorized a show of American force that led to the total destruction of an entire city in Central America. During the Civil War, Abraham Lincoln exercised broad war powers to prevent the dissolution of the Union. Look at the regions of the world in the map shown in Figure 13-2 to learn more about actions by presidents as commander-in-chief.

The Vietnam War   Lacking a formal declaration of war by Congress, the Johnson administration maintained that inherent presidential power essentially included the power to make war. In the Gulf of Tonkin Resolution of 1964, Congress gave limited authority to the president to take whatever actions were necessary to defend the government of South Vietnam and American interests and personnel in the region. The resolution was adopted in response to an alleged attack on American ships operating near North Vietnam. Later evidence indicated that the attack was at least exaggerated and was perhaps contrived to force Congress to sanction the growing American involvement in Southeast Asia. It was not long before the war expanded far beyond anything envisioned by Congress in 1964. In a later development in the Vietnam conflict, President Nixon's covert war in Cambodia certainly fell beyond any authority granted the president by the Gulf of Tonkin Resolution. Amidst the harsh strains of sometimes violent antiwar protest, calmer voices began to be heard questioning the legality of the war effort.

During the Vietnam era, the Supreme Court had ample opportunity to rule on the constitutionality of the war, but it declined to do so, viewing the issue as a "political question."[13] The Court drew some criticism for this deferential posture. However, the Court likely would have also been attacked if it had chosen to review the constitutionality of the Vietnam War. It certainly would have been criticized more harshly if its ruling had been adverse to the president. In any event, the influence of the courts over the conduct of wars,

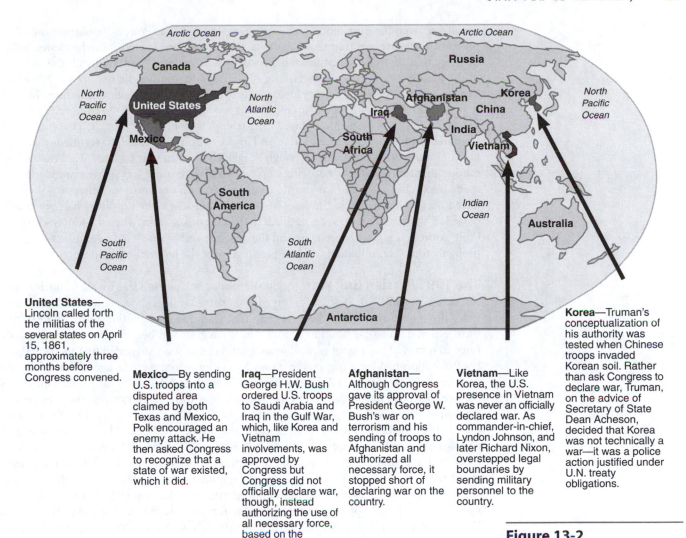

United States—Lincoln called forth the militias of the several states on April 15, 1861, approximately three months before Congress convened.

Mexico—By sending U.S. troops into a disputed area claimed by both Texas and Mexico, Polk encouraged an enemy attack. He then asked Congress to recognize that a state of war existed, which it did.

Iraq—President George H.W. Bush ordered U.S. troops to Saudi Arabia and Iraq in the Gulf War, which, like Korea and Vietnam involvements, was approved by Congress but Congress did not officially declare war, though, instead authorizing the use of all necessary force, based on the auspices of existing U.N. treaties.

Afghanistan—Although Congress gave its approval of President George W. Bush's war on terrorism and his sending of troops to Afghanistan and authorized all necessary force, it stopped short of declaring war on the country.

Vietnam—Like Korea, the U.S. presence in Vietnam was never an officially declared war. As commander-in-chief, Lyndon Johnson, and later Richard Nixon, overstepped legal boundaries by sending military personnel to the country.

Korea—Truman's conceptualization of his authority was tested when Chinese troops invaded Korean soil. Rather than ask Congress to declare war, Truman, on the advice of Secretary of State Dean Acheson, decided that Korea was not technically a war—it was a police action justified under U.N. treaty obligations.

Figure 13-2
The President's War Powers
Presidents have often used their authority as commander-in-chief to take military action in other parts of the world and closer to home.

foreign or domestic, is minimal at most. The reason in large part is that the courts really do not have any way to make presidents abide by their decisions.

The War Powers Resolution   In the waning days of the Vietnam War, Congress began to question the unbridled conception of presidential war powers. In 1973, Congress adopted the War Powers Resolution over the veto of President Nixon. The act was designed to limit the president's unilateral power to send troops into foreign combat. It requires the president to make a full report to Congress when sending troops into foreign areas, limits the duration of troop commitment without congressional authorization, and provides a veto mechanism whereby Congress can force the recall of troops at any time.

Serious questions have arisen about the constitutionality of the War Powers Resolution. Yet because Congress has not yet invoked the resolution, the courts have had no occasion to address the question of its constitutionality. The War Powers Resolution is unlikely to ever be subjected to judicial review because it is unlikely to ever be invoked against the president. Even if the resolution were invoked and litigation resulted, the courts probably would view the matter as a political question. In 1982, a federal judge dismissed as "political" a lawsuit brought by members of Congress against President Reagan. The members were attempting to get the courts to invoke the War Powers Resolution to prevent the Reagan administration from providing military aid to the government of El Salvador.[14]

Aside from the question of its constitutionality, the War Powers Resolution is probably not an effective constraint on the presidential war power. Indeed, it can be viewed as little more than a symbolic gesture of defiance from a Congress displeased with the conduct of the Vietnam War. The existence of the War Powers Resolution did not prevent President Reagan from employing military force in pursuit of his foreign-policy objectives. Reagan sent the U.S. Marines into Beirut and even used naval gunfire against the rebels in the Lebanese civil war. Reagan employed U.S. troops to topple the Marxist government of Grenada. And he ordered an air strike on Libya to punish the Khadaffi regime for its support of international terrorism. Although Reagan chose to comply with the War Powers Resolution in all three cases by notifying Congress of his actions, it was still the president who made the decisions to send troops into hostile situations. Congressional disapproval would have made no difference in the cases of Grenada and Libya; the hostilities had practically ceased by the time Congress was notified. In the case of Lebanon, when the ninety-day time limit expired, Congress chose to extend the deadline rather than face an embarrassing and probably futile confrontation with the president over the removal of the troops.

The 1991 Persian Gulf War

Soon after Saddam Hussein's Iraq invaded and annexed Kuwait in August 1990, President George Bush ordered military forces into Saudi Arabia in a defensive posture. When it became clear that Iraq had no intention of leaving Kuwait, Bush ordered a massive buildup of forces in the region and began to threaten the use of force to remove Iraqi troops from Kuwait. Bush's critics soon suggested that the War Powers Resolution had been triggered because American troops were in a situation of imminent hostility. Yet Congress did not attempt to "start the clock" under the resolution. When the president did finally decide to move against Iraq in January 1991, he first obtained a resolution from Congress supporting the use of force. Had Bush refused to obtain congressional approval, it would have been interesting to see whether and how Congress would have asserted itself. Little question exists, however, of whether Bush's decision to seek congressional approval ultimately enhanced political support for the war. The war was executed with overwhelming force, resulting in minimal losses to allied forces. Iraq, which suffered enormous losses in both life and property, capitulated quickly. In the wake of the war, President Bush's approval ratings soared to levels not seen since the end of World War II. Presidential popularity is a volatile phenomenon, however, and Bush's approval ratings dropped steadily during the remainder of 1991, culminating in his defeat in the presidential election of 1992.

Somalia and Haiti

Acting without the authorization of Congress, President George Bush sent troops to Somalia in December 1992. The purpose of the mission was to restore order in the war-torn African country, whose people were suffering from a terrible famine. Citing humanitarian reasons, President Clinton chose to continue the mission. But after American troops were drawn into deadly skirmishes with members of one of the warring factions, public and congressional support began to deteriorate. Faced with declining political support, President Clinton had little choice but to withdraw the troops. Although the Somalia mission was generally not regarded as a success, Clinton could place the blame for the failure on the shoulders of the preceding administration.

In the fall of 1994, the Clinton administration sent American troops to Haiti to restore the government of President Jean-Bertrand Aristide, who had been ousted by a military coup. The justification for the mission was twofold: Foster democracy in our hemisphere and protect our borders against a flood of refugees. Nevertheless, the public did not want American troops to go to war in Haiti. Fortunately, a last-minute diplomatic mission headed by former President Carter managed to persuade the military dictators to surrender power. Thus, rather than invade Haiti, American troops went in unchallenged and succeeded in restoring President Aristide. As 1994 came to a close, the mission in Haiti appeared to be succeeding, and the troops started coming home. Leaders of the Republican-controlled Congress, who had never supported the Haiti mission, demanded an immediate end to American military involvement.

Bosnia and Kosovo   President Clinton's main foray into international relations took place in the Balkans, where the breakup of Yugoslavia followed the disintegration of the old Soviet Union in the 1980s. In 1995, President Clinton committed troops to help keep the peace in Bosnia, where deeply rooted conflict between Christians and Muslims had led to widespread fighting and the loss of life. Later, the world focused its attention on a particularly destructive outbreak of fighting in Kosovo, a province of Yugoslavia that bordered on Albania.

In Kosovo, the problem was again ethnic in nature. By the late 1990s, enough Muslim Albanians had moved to Kosovo to put the Christian Serbs in minority status. The Serbs, supported by the government in Belgrade, began especially harsh treatment of the Albanians in 1998, including widespread rape and murder. Soon the world witnessed the agonizing spectacle of hundreds of thousands of refugees on the road to Albania where many who made it suffered in squalid refugee camps. The Serbian Yugoslav leader, Slobodan Milosevic, was urged by NATO to withdraw his troops from Kosovo or face military action. When Milosevic failed to comply with NATO demands, the United States, along with some of its allies, responded with a bombing campaign in Yugoslavia. Eventually, the Yugoslav government withdrew its forces from Kosovo, and refugees returned to an uneasy peace brokered by troops from Europe, Russia, and the United States.

Afghanistan and the War on Terrorism   When Islamic militants flew hijacked airplanes into the World Trade Center and the Pentagon in September 2001, they were continuing a series of terrorist acts aimed at the United States. In the 1990s, these acts included attacks on American embassies in Africa and military housing in Saudi Arabia and the suicide attack on the USS Cole in Yemen. President George W. Bush responded to the 9-11 attacks by assembling a worldwide coalition and demanding that the Taliban government in Afghanistan turn over Osama bin Laden, the leader of the terrorist effort, to the United States. When the Afghan leader Mullah Omar refused, the United States began a relentless bombing campaign that led to the victory of the opposition Northern Alliance and other groups in overthrowing the Taliban. This effort was clearly the beginning of a new era in U. S. policy. This war, unlike those in Bosnia, Kosovo, and the first Gulf War, was supported by the vast majority of the American people and by an overwhelming majority in Congress.

The war in Afghanistan was, by most accounts, a success. The Taliban was defeated and al Qaeda forces dispersed. A new transition government was installed in Kabul. In the fall of 2004, Afghans went to the polls in that country's first-ever democratic election. A fledgling democracy had taken root in a country with no history of democracy. On the other hand, Mullah Omar and bin Laden evaded capture, and many of the Taliban and al Qaeda operatives escaped into the lawless areas of northwest Pakistan.

Of course, no one (including President Bush) knew in 2002 what the scope of the war on terrorism would be. After the Taliban was overthrown, what other states might come under military attack? The president argued that Iraq was a terrorist state, and many people speculated on imminent military action to remove Saddam Hussein. Meanwhile, major conflicts between Israel and the Palestinians further strained the United States' ability to focus on any one conflict. How long would the war on terrorism last? Clearly, it would be a war unlike any other.

The war on terrorism raised other questions. In November 2001, President Bush announced that the United States would make use of military tribunals to try noncitizens accused of terrorism. Although most people conceded that this practice was permissible under the Constitution, many in the media and in Congress were highly critical of Bush's plan. Some complained that although Bush might technically have the power in his role as commander-in-chief, he should be more specific regarding the circumstances under which tribunals would be used and the procedures they would follow. Others worried that using military commissions to try accused terrorists sent the wrong message to the world: that America was abandoning its historic commitment to the ideal of due process. These questions continued when captured Taliban and al Qaeda personnel were brought to the American naval base at Guantanamo Bay, Cuba, for detainment in 2002.

The War in Iraq At President George W. Bush's urging, Congress in October 2002 authorized military action against Iraq. President Bush praised the resolution, declaring that "America speaks with one voice" on Iraq. But Americans were far from united on this issue. Invoking painful memories of the Vietnam War, Senator Robert Byrd (D-West Virginia) asserted, "This is the Tonkin Gulf resolution all over again. Let us stop, look and listen. Let us not give this president or any president unchecked power. Remember the Constitution."[15] President Bush sought to link the invasion of Iraq to the war on terrorism by stressing the need to secure Saddam Hussein's supposed weapons of mass destruction (WMDs) lest they fall into the hands of terrorists. The fact that no stockpiles of chemical or biological weapons were found in Iraq after American troops captured the country took a tremendous toll on President Bush's credibility. Had those weapons been found in Iraq, the president's decision to go to war would have been largely vindicated, and he might well have been politically unassailable. The failure to find WMDs made the president extremely vulnerable, and Democrats would seek to exploit that vulnerability during the 2004 campaign.

The unrelenting media coverage of the war, most of which brought bad news, placed President Bush on the defensive. Of course, despite bad news from Iraq, President Bush was able to secure reelection. Within days after the election, American forces launched an offensive in Fallujah, a city controlled by insurgents opposed to American occupation and the interim Iraqi government supported by the United States. Although the offensive was successful in meeting its specific objectives, it by no means brought an end to the insurgency. An Associated Press poll taken after the election showed that achieving stability in Iraq was the voters' top priority.[16] Clearly, this would be President Bush's most daunting challenge as his second term began. In its post-election issue, *Time* magazine stated the case bluntly: "The bloody mess in Iraq remains George W. Bush's No. 1 responsibility and the one most likely to define his presidential legacy."[17]

13-3i Domestic Powers during Wartime

Just as serious as the constitutional question over who has the power to *make* war is the question of the extent of presidential power within our borders *during* wartime. Do the president's **inherent power** and duty to protect national security override constitutional limitations and the rights of citizens? The Supreme Court's answer to the question has been mixed.

> ▶ **inherent power** The power existing in an agency, institution, or individual by definition of the office.

The "Relocation" of Japanese Americans during World War II
Early in World War II, President Franklin D. Roosevelt issued orders authorizing the establishment of zones from which persons the military considered to be security risks could be expelled or excluded. Congressional legislation supported Roosevelt's orders by establishing criminal penalties for violators. Under these executive and congressional mandates, General DeWitt, who headed the Western Defense Command, proclaimed a curfew and issued an order excluding all Japanese Americans from a designated West Coast military area. The exclusion order led first to the imprisonment of some one hundred twenty thousand persons in "assembly centers" surrounded by barbed wire. Later, these Japanese Americans were removed to "relocation centers" in rural areas as far inland as Arkansas. Although these actions were justified at the time on grounds of military necessity, overwhelming evidence indicates that they were in fact based on the view that all Japanese Americans were "subversive" members of an "enemy race." In spite of the blatant racism reflected in these policies, the Supreme Court upheld both the curfew and the exclusion order.[18] A majority of the justices concluded that, under the pressure of war, the government had a compelling interest justifying such extreme measures. It has now been well established that the forced relocation of thousands of Japanese Americans was not justified on grounds of military necessity and was motivated largely by racial hostility. In 1988, Congress belatedly acknowledged the government's responsibility for this gross miscarriage of justice by awarding reparations to survivors of the internment camps.

Peacetime Threats to National Security
During peacetime, presidential responses to perceived domestic threats to the national security are not as likely to win

judicial approval. A good example is the Nixon administration's extensive wiretapping and other forms of electronic surveillance directed at American citizens during the late 1960s and early 1970s. The Supreme Court held that these activities, which were conducted without prior judicial approval, offended the Fourth Amendment prohibition against unreasonable searches and seizures.[19] The Court rejected the Nixon administration's argument that inherent executive power permitted the government to take these actions to obtain intelligence regarding foreign agents acting in the domestic sphere. In 1978, Congress buttressed the Court's decision by adopting the Foreign Intelligence Surveillance Act, which requires government agents to obtain a search warrant before subjecting American citizens to electronic surveillance for the purpose of foreign intelligence.

Detention of American Citizens Suspected of Terrorism   Two months after the terrorist attacks of 9-11-2001, President George W. Bush signed an executive order authorizing the creation of military tribunals for the detention, treatment, and trial of certain noncitizens in the war against terrorism. After the invasion of Afghanistan, hundreds of foreign nationals suspected of fighting for al Qaeda were detained at the U.S. naval base at Guantanamo Bay, Cuba. One of these individuals was Yaser Hamdi, a Saudi national who was also an American citizen because he was born in New Orleans. When military officials discovered that he was an American citizen, they moved him to a military prison in the United States. He was not charged with a crime, but held incommunicado as an "enemy combatant." Hamdi sought a writ of habeas corpus in the federal courts, challenging the legality of his detention. The Bush administration argued that the president had authority as commander-in-chief to detain enemy combatants, even American citizens, and that such detentions were not subject to judicial review.

Commenting on the case, former Justice Department official David Rivkin observed that it was "absolutely, clearly, constitutionally permissible, as a matter of international law, for an enemy combatant, lawful or unlawful, detained in the course of open hostilities, to be held on any charges proffered, for the duration of this particular conflict."[20] Taking the opposite view, Georgetown University law professor Mark Tushnet observed, "The difficulty with the administration's position is that, at least as applied to U.S. citizens, it poses a threat to essentially anyone who the administration chooses to call an enemy combatant."[21] In June 2004, the Supreme Court decided the case of *Hamdi v. Rumsfeld*.[22] The Court stopped short of ruling on the constitutional questions pertaining to presidential power, but did say that Hamdi was entitled to a fair and impartial hearing to determine the factual basis of his detention. Subsequently, Mr. Hamdi renounced his American citizenship and was deported to Saudi Arabia. A similar case, *Rumsfeld v. Padilla*, was dismissed on technical grounds.[23] The Supreme Court managed, at least in the near term, to avoid the troubling constitutional questions raised by indefinite military detention of American citizens suspected of terrorism.

13-4 The Structure of the Presidential Office

The responsibilities of the presidency are so vast, and the expectations of the American people so great, that one person cannot possibly exercise the powers of the presidency. Clearly, the president needs help, which he gets from a variety of supporting offices within the executive branch.

Throughout the first 140 years of the Republic, the president had only a small staff. Not until 1857 did Congress even pass a provision allowing the president to hire a full-time clerk. Early presidents relied mostly on their cabinet members and a few close personal advisers to help them form policy. With the emergence of a more active presidency during Franklin Roosevelt's tenure in office, however, greater staff resources were required. Three main sources of staff assistance are now available to presidents:

- The White House staff
- The Executive Office of the President
- The Cabinet

Presidents generally rely most heavily on the members of the White House staff. They are the president's closest advisers. Cabinet members do not have as much daily access to the president, who usually relies less heavily on them than on the White House staff or the Executive Office of the President.

13-4a The White House Staff

The president usually places his closest advisers in positions on the White House staff. In selecting these staffers, the president does not have to worry as much about their public reputation as he does in choosing members of the cabinet. Congress allows the president great latitude in choosing White House staff, but occasionally rejects cabinet nominees. Each president also has the power to organize the White House staff in whatever manner he chooses. Some have preferred tightly organized structures with only a few close advisers at the top, and others have designed open structures allowing much greater access to the president.

The most important position in the White House is the **chief of staff.** The chief of staff is viewed as the president's right-hand man. Usually, the chief of staff controls the president's calendar, limits access to the president, manages the staff, and helps the president in all aspects of domestic and foreign policy. The most important qualification for the position is loyalty to the president. The chief of staff often serves as the bad guy for the president so that the president can maintain a likable reputation. H. R. Haldeman argued that "Every president needs a son of a bitch, and I'm Nixon's. I get what he wants done, and I take the heat instead of him."[24] Because the chief of staff must say no to so many people, he often serves as a lightning rod for the president. Many have eventually fallen from power because of a scandal: Sherman Adams, Eisenhower's chief, left after being accused of taking gifts from a lobbyist; Haldeman was disgraced by Watergate; and John Sununu, George Bush's chief, was forced out after media attention focused on his use of government jets for private purposes. This job is not easy, and few have made it through an entire four-year presidential term.

The White House staff had grown to more than five hundred people by the time George H.W. Bush took office in 1989. The shape of the organization changes with every president, but generally the president has an adviser who coordinates domestic policy, a liaison staff that lobbies Congress for the president, and a press secretary and a communications director who coordinate public relations and press relations. Any services the president needs in performing the many aspects of the job are essentially provided by the White House staff.

13-4b The Executive Office

The Executive Office of the President (EOP) was formed in 1939 with thirty-seven employees. By 1992, it had grown to more than fifteen hundred employees. Most EOP employees work in the Executive Office Building, a structure right next to the White House. The EOP includes several different units; the three most important are the National Security Council (NSC), the Council of Economic Advisers (CEA), and the Office of Management and Budget (OMB). The National Security Council, formed in 1947, assists the president in handling crises in the international arena. The NSC is composed of the president, the vice president, the secretary of defense, and the secretary of state. The staff of the NSC helps the president interpret the massive amount of information on international events that flows into the White House. The NSC staff appraises the quality of the information, filters out the less meaningful and unsubstantiated stories, and packages the information in a way more useful to the president. The NSC works closely with other parts of the bureaucracy, such as the Department of Defense and the CIA.

The Council of Economic Advisers assists the president in evaluating economic trends and formulating economic policy. Composed of three economists appointed by the president, the council prepares an annual President's Economic Report that analyzes economic

▶ **chief of staff** The head of the White House staff; the person responsible for controlling the president's calendar and advising the president on all aspects of domestic and foreign policy.

developments. The council is designed to help the president anticipate potential weaknesses in the economy and devise policy to maintain economic growth.

The Office of Management and Budget, originally called the Bureau of the Budget, was formed in 1921. The OMB prepares the president's budget proposal to Congress, helps push the proposal through Congress, and analyzes the effect of all new programs on the national debt. Because of the central role the budget plays in the legislative agenda, this power alone would make the OMB one of the most influential units within the federal bureaucracy. The OMB, however, has gained over time other responsibilities that have greatly expanded its power. Franklin Roosevelt, after taking the bureau out of the Treasury department and placing it in the EOP, required that all new agency proposals receive clearance through the OMB before being sent to Congress. This centralized clearance procedure greatly enhanced the bureau's power. Later, President Reagan required that all new agency rules proposed by the bureaucracy must also receive OMB approval before they can take effect. This combination of budget influence, clearance for agency proposals to Congress, and review of agency rule making has made the OMB the single most important tool for presidential control of domestic policy.

13-4c The Cabinet

The president's cabinet consists of the heads of the major executive departments. Originally, the cabinet consisted of the attorney general and the secretaries of state, war, and treasury. The cabinet now includes the heads of the fifteen major executive departments in addition to certain other high-level executive officials. At one time, the cabinet members were close advisers to the president, but their role has gradually changed as the bureaucracy has grown, the powers of the president have expanded, and expectations of the president have increased. The bureaucracy is composed of three million civilian employees with a multitude of programs, so the cabinet members do not have the time to assist the president on a day-to-day basis. Furthermore, recent presidents have not always completely trusted their cabinet members, for two reasons. First, cabinet members are often chosen for public relations reasons. Presidents, particularly Democrats, are concerned about the symbolism of the appointments. Features such as ethnicity, gender, geographic origin, membership in an interest group, ideological orientation, and prominence within the party are all considered by the president in making an appointment. Because of the concern for balancing the cabinet along these lines, a president may have to seek out people he does not know. Because their prominence gives them an independent power base, cabinet members are not usually part of the president's inner circle of advisers.

A second factor reducing the power of cabinet members as presidential advisers is that many recent presidents have not trusted the bureaucracy, and they are suspicious that cabinet members may be "captured" by the interests they represent. Presidents Nixon and Reagan, in particular, believed that much of the bureaucracy had a liberal, pro-government stance that would thwart their conservative policies if given a chance. If a president has a choice between relying on advice from a White House staffer who has been loyal for a number of years or a cabinet secretary who was only recently brought on the team and may be more sympathetic to the interests of the agency she manages, the president is likely to choose the staffer. Cabinet members are especially likely to be excluded from the most important strategic planning when the president is already hostile toward the programs and political aims of their agency or department.

The influence of a cabinet member ultimately depends on the president. In some cases, such as when Robert Kennedy was John F. Kennedy's attorney general, cabinet members can be extremely influential, but often they are not. The bureaucracy retains access to large volumes of information, expertise, experience, and policy ideas, but often presidents do not fully utilize it because of the lack of trust, the rivalry between agencies, and the vast number of points where information can be cut off on the way to the president. On the other hand, control of the bureaucracy is one of the most important, and most difficult, functions of the president.

Popular Culture and American Politics
Dave

By Chapman Rackaway

Would you be willing to portray a body double for the President of the United States for just one night? How about three months? In the hilarious comedy *Dave,* starring Kevin Kline, the main character is faced with the choice of impersonating the president. Kline's character, Dave Kovic, is a temporary employment agency owner who looks remarkably like the president. The look-alike factor gives Dave an inside look at the harder parts of being the country's most powerful person.

Dave is recruited by the Secret Service to body double for the president one night. That night, President William "Bill" Harrison Mitchell is involved in an extramarital affair and has a stroke, falling into a coma. Secretly, the president is rushed back to the White House and placed on life support. Instead of announcing the event to the public, Chief of Staff Bob Alexander (played by Frank Langella) convinces Dave to extend his temporary role in the president's guise. Reluctantly, Dave agrees.

In the following months, "President" Dave changes the culture inside the White House. The First Lady, long estranged from the president, falls for Dave and the feeling is mutual. Dave calls his accountant, Murray Blum (played by Charles Grodin), to help him rearrange budget priorities to fund homeless shelters for kids, and brings a new energy and enthusiasm to the job. As Dave becomes more comfortable in the job, he disagrees with Alexander, eventually firing him. The former chief of staff then releases information that President Mitchell had been involved in financial improprieties that threaten the presidency and forces Dave to testify before Congress.

The job of president might seem full of power, fame, and even glamour, but the movie *Dave* manages to put a real human face on the job while making us laugh at the same time.

13-5 The Functioning Presidency

Although the Constitution has granted the president a variety of powers that permit decisive leadership on foreign policy, it is less generous on the domestic front. Presidents are more likely to become bogged down in battles with Congress over domestic policy. This likelihood can be politically dangerous to a president because legislative gridlock may create the appearance that the president is indecisive or incapable of leadership. In turn, this perception may adversely affect his chance of reelection, ability to get legislation passed, and place in history.

If the president wants to have a long-term effect on domestic policy, he must work with Congress to pass legislation, although the Constitution has provided the president with few resources. The Constitution gives the president the veto power and the right to "give to the Congress information of the state of the Union, and recommend to their consideration such measures as he shall judge necessary and expedient." The veto does provide the president with leverage over legislation, but it is a difficult tool for the president to use in all but the most extreme cases. Because the president must veto the entire bill, this tool is not useful for working out differences of opinion on the details of legislation.

Most of the president's influence over lawmaking has evolved over time as presidents have expanded on the duty to report on the "State of the Union." Most presidents in the first century of the Republic did not use the State of the Union speech or their power to recommend legislative measures as a means of creating their own policy agenda. Some presidents actively attempted to control congressional action on legislation, but most did not. Though the increase in presidential influence over Congress evolved over time, the presidency of Franklin D. Roosevelt radically changed the president's role in the policy process. Partly because of his political ideology but largely because of the devastating economic conditions of the Great Depression, Roosevelt came into office with the most active

Comparative Perspective

The Russian Presidency

In 1917, Russia transitioned from a monarchy into a communist dictatorship that lasted until the Soviet Union collapsed in 1991. Russia's experience with democracy is of very recent vintage. On December 12, 1993, Russian voters went to the polls to approve a new constitution, which established a powerful presidency to be filled through popular election. In adopting the new charter, the Russian people signaled their desire to live under a democratic system.

Boris Yeltsin became the first president of the new Russian republic. Under the new constitution, Yeltsin and future presidents could serve only two four-year terms. Like his American counterpart, the Russian president is the head of state and commander-in-chief of Russia's armed forces. Under the new constitution, the Russian president has strong appointment and nomination powers. Moreover, the president has the power to dissolve the Parliament and call for new elections. At the same time, executive power is limited. The Parliament may refuse to confirm some presidential appointments. Like the U.S. Congress, the Russian Parliament also has the power to impeach the president and may override the president's veto of legislation. Like Bill Clinton, Boris Yeltsin survived an impeachment effort, in 1999.

In approving their new constitution, the Russian people edged closer than ever to democracy. But considering Russia's long history of authoritarian rule, many observers were pessimistic about whether the new constitution would succeed. Russian political culture is in many ways the mirror image of that of the United States. Whereas Americans fear authority and dictatorship, Russians fear anarchy and excessive personal freedom. Can Russians place limits on their president? Does Vladimir Putin, who succeeded Boris Yeltsin as president in 2000, understand that political opposition is part of the democratic process? During his reelection campaign in 2004, Putin's critics charged that he engaged in "dirty tricks" toward his rivals. Nevertheless, he was reelected easily, winning 71 percent of the votes. Subsequently, Putin took steps to further consolidate his power, leading to fears that Putin might be taking Russia backward toward authoritarianism.

legislative agenda ever proposed by a president. His first hundred days in office were so productive that they have served as a measure for assessing the efforts of all other presidents. The public now expects the president to come into office with a set of policy preferences that he wants to see enacted.

13-5a The President's Legislative Agenda

The president's **legislative agenda** is the primary tool available for securing and extending his power. Passage of the agenda is the key to the president's effort to be reelected to a second term and to secure his place in history. These goals along with any campaign promises from his first election are often the primary motivation for what the president places on the agenda and moves to the top of his priority list. For example, President Reagan's top priority in 1981 was enacting tax cuts. Reagan first proposed these cuts during the campaign of 1980, and the administration assumed that they would stimulate economic growth that would aid Reagan's reelection bid in 1984. Of course, the president's political ideology and vision of good policy also shape the nature of his policy proposals. For example, even though President George Bush claimed that education was high on his agenda in 1989, he was not interested in creating any costly new programs. Current events also influence the agenda. For example, the oil shortages and huge energy price increases of the 1970s forced President Carter to make energy policy a priority.

Beyond formulating an agenda, the president must push Congress to act on his proposals. That is not an easy job because Congress is a complex organization with a heavy workload separate from the president's agenda. Negotiating with Congress over policy has become increasingly difficult as Congress has become more fragmented and decentralized. Furthermore, because of the decline of partisanship, the president cannot even rely on his

> **legislative agenda** The set of policy goals the president wants to pursue through congressional legislation.

own party members to fully support all aspects of his agenda. President Clinton certainly experienced this phenomenon repeatedly during his first two years in office.

President Clinton had a wide-ranging agenda after taking office in 1993. Most observers later questioned his strategy of beginning his term with such controversial issues as gays in the military and national health-care reform. Both were controversial, and in both cases no obvious consensus was formed in either the public or the Congress. President George W. Bush, on the other hand, began his term in 2001 with issues around which he could more easily build: an education initiative and a substantial tax cut.

Political Context   Several factors influence the political situation facing the president. First, does the president have an electoral mandate? Second, does the president face a friendly Congress with a majority of his own party members or a hostile Congress with a majority of the opposition party? Third, is the president at the beginning of a term, late in the first term, or in the second term in office?

Candidates have been propelled into the White House by a wide variety of margins. Some presidents, such as Clinton in 1992, are elected with less than 50 percent of the popular vote, whereas others, such as Johnson in 1964 and Reagan in 1984, received approximately 60 percent of the popular vote. A strong showing in both the popular vote and the electoral college is viewed as a **landslide.** A landslide lends tremendous credibility to a president's claim of a mandate. A **mandate** is the idea that the people have spoken in an election and that they support the president so strongly that they want his agenda to pass. Though the concept of a mandate is so vague that almost every president can claim he has one, if most people believe the claim, it can be a powerful tool in Congress. To use a mandate successfully, the president as a candidate must have expressed a clear set of ideas that form an agenda. This step is important because the president must be able to identify what the people were saying they wanted. Obviously, it is a game of perception, but, nevertheless, the more others believe that the president's victory represented people's approval of a particular set of ideas, the more likely the president will be able to translate a mandate into political capital in Congress. This capital is crucial to passage of the president's agenda.

In no case was a lack of a mandate more obvious than in George W. Bush's election in 2000 and his subsequent inauguration in 2001. Not only did Bush lose the popular vote, the newly appointed chair of the Democratic National Committee, Terry McAuliffe, stated his strong belief that Bush had not legitimately won in Florida. However, President Bush, after assuming office, began his administration without any indication that he held office without public support. After President Bush narrowly won reelection in 2004, some of his supporters characterized the outcome as a "mandate," but few neutral observers could agree with that characterization. Today, with the people of the United States so sharply divided ideologically, landslide elections are unlikely. But a mandate requires more than a "squeaker" like the 2004 election.

The Partisanship of Congress   The partisan makeup of the Congress dramatically affects the likelihood of the president's legislative success. Presidents are much more successful when their party has a majority in each chamber. From 1955 to 1994, the Democrats controlled the House of Representatives, so no Republican president since Eisenhower has enjoyed an easy ride in the House. The Senate was Democratic every year from 1955 to 1994 with the exception of the six years from 1981 to 1987. This six-year period of Republican control of the Senate was quite beneficial to President Reagan in that it gave him a strong ally in his battles with the Democratic House. Unlike Reagan, Republicans Nixon, Ford, and George Bush had to work with hostile Congresses that were not only willing to defeat or ignore the presidential agenda but were also likely to pass their own measures. Ford and Bush both made extensive use of the veto power in staving off Democratic legislation; and Congress overrode many of Ford's vetoes, though only one of Bush's. Until 1968, when Nixon was elected president and the Democrats retained control of Congress, divided-party government in this country was rare. But in twenty of the twenty-four years between 1968 and the inauguration of Democrat Bill Clinton, presidents have had to deal

---

landslide   An overwhelming electoral victory.

mandate   The idea that the voters, through a resounding electoral victory, are sending a clear signal that they want the president to enact his policy preferences after taking office.

with Congresses in which at least one chamber had a majority of the opposite party. This long period of divided government made presidential leadership of Congress even more difficult. George W. Bush was unquestionably extremely pleased in November 2002 when Republicans regained control of both houses of Congress.

In devising a strategy for getting his agenda passed, a president can divide each chamber of Congress into four partisan groups:

1. Strong party loyalists of the president's party
2. Weak party loyalists
3. Weak opposition-party members
4. Strong opposition-party members

The president can count on strong party loyalists to be supportive in most legislative battles and strong opposition-party members to almost always work against his agenda. The two decisive groups are the moderates in each party. Most of the president's efforts to put together coalitions to pass his agenda focus on the two moderate groups. For example, President Reagan in 1981 faced a Democratic majority in the House, but he was able to put together successful coalitions. He achieved them by keeping his party in line and wooing conservative Democrats, particularly Southerners known as the Boll Weevils.

In 1995, President Clinton faced an especially daunting task in dealing with a Congress that had just come under Republican control via the 1994 midterm elections. In the wake of the Republican victory, the magnitude of which no one had expected, Clinton appealed for cooperation and pledged to "govern from the center." However, the Republicans, who were feeling their oats after capturing both houses of Congress for the first time since 1954, were in no mood to compromise. Rather, they looked eagerly to the 1996 presidential election that they hoped would return the White House to Republican control. Of course, that was not the case. By the end of his term, Clinton's relationship with Congress had plummeted, pushed downward by impeachment, vetoes, and battles that either threatened to shut down, or did in fact shut down, the federal government.

George W. Bush's relationship with Congress, although beginning on a high note, showed signs of deterioration during 2002. The Senate, under the leadership of Tom Daschle after the defection of Vermont Senator Jim Jeffords in 2001, turned down some of the president's judicial appointments and delayed consideration of others. Following his reelection victory in 2004 and Daschle's loss in South Dakota, President Bush could look forward to a slightly more Republican Senate under new leadership, but with no assurance of success in overcoming the threat of a filibuster in the Senate for any judges deemed too conservative by the Democratic leadership.

The Importance of Timing   The timing of a new proposal is extremely important for a president. Even a president who enjoys congressional majorities realizes that a mandate does not last for long. A president must "move it or lose it" in trying to use the mandate to push legislation through Congress in the first hundred days, sometimes referred to as the **honeymoon period.** During the early days of the term, the president still enjoys the benefits of the electoral victory. The press treats a new president with a bit more deference, the members of Congress are still somewhat taken by the new person in the White House, and the general mood is one of high expectations of the new administration. Members of the president's party are likely to believe the president has a mandate, and electorally vulnerable members of the opposition party may be more likely to go along with the president. Recently, the honeymoon period has been getting progressively shorter for each new president as the press has become more aggressive, the Congress has become more independent, and the public has become more cynical about politics. For example, Dave Barry, a national humor columnist, was already referring to the Clinton presidency as the "failed Clinton administration" even before Clinton had taken office!

Many questioned whether George W. Bush would have much of a honeymoon period following his contentious election in 2000. However, after assuming office, President Bush embarked on what many in the media referred to as a "charm offensive" with congressional

honeymoon period   The first one hundred days of a presidential administration in which Congress, the media, and the public give the president more leeway in pushing his policy agenda.

Democrats. Bush attended a Democratic caucus and invited many Democrats to the White House. The initiative seemed to disarm many Democrats and set a decidedly more pleasant tone, at least at the beginning of the term.

Because of the honeymoon phenomenon, presidential proposals are much more likely to pass if they are presented in the first year of the president's first term, and the earlier in the year, the better. One study has shown since 1961 that almost three-fourths of all presidential proposals introduced in the first quarter of the first year have been passed, but only one-fourth of the proposals made in the last six months of the first year have been successful.[25] David Stockman, the budget director for President Reagan in 1981, dramatically emphasized this point: ". . . if bold policies are not swiftly, deftly, and courageously implemented in the first six months, Washington will quickly become engulfed in political disorder . . . a golden opportunity for permanent conservative policy revision and political alignment could be thoroughly dissipated before the Reagan administration is even up to speed."[26]

The first year stands out as the greatest legislative opportunity for a president. The second year is dominated by political maneuvering in Congress by members of each party preparing for the midterm congressional elections. Though the president is not on any of the midterm election ballots, his performance usually affects the congressional elections. The president's party generally loses seats in the midterm elections. The loss of seats can be devastating for the president if he was already working with a bare party majority or creating fragile coalitions between his party and the moderates of the other party. The third year may be difficult if the midterm losses were too large. The fourth year is usually dominated by the presidential election with primaries and caucuses starting in February. Consequently, passage of major legislation is unlikely.

A second term is likely to be much different from the first term. The president is immediately tagged with the title of **lame duck** because he cannot run for a third term. Furthermore, a second-term president usually does not enjoy the benefits of a mandate or a honeymoon period. Typically, items from the first-term agenda that were not passed are left over for the second term. Neither the Congress, the media, nor the public accepts these leftovers as the basis for a mandate. Unless the president has pushed for new legislation in the campaign, major legislative initiatives are unlikely to be undertaken in the second term. By the last couple of years of the second term, the Washington community usually begins to ignore the president and starts focusing its attention on the election of a new president.

▶ **lame duck** An elected official who cannot or will not return to office after her current term expires.

13-5b Power and Persuasion

Despite labels such as the leader of the free world and the most powerful man on earth, the president cannot just issue commands and expect action. Richard Neustadt, a prominent political scholar, argues that "presidential power is the power to persuade."[27] The president has to rely on cooperation from a number of individuals in the political system to get anything done. The president relies on a large White House staff to implement his strategies, but they may not respond perfectly to his requests. Though the president is the head of the administration, the bureaucracy is so large, complex, and, in some cases, legally independent that the president cannot expect policy to be implemented as planned without close supervision, occasional negotiation, and lots of persuasion. Congress is even more independent and willing to aggressively counter the president's wishes. It requires even greater powers of persuasion than the rest of the government. President Harry S Truman expressed the limits on presidential power in describing how Dwight Eisenhower would feel after taking the office after having been a general: "He'll sit here and he'll say, 'Do this! Do that!' And nothing will happen. Poor Ike—it won't be a bit like the Army. He'll find it very frustrating."[28]

The power of persuasion depends on both the rhetorical skills and political savvy of the president. It involves both the public perception of the president and behind-the-scenes action. A popular president is more likely to be persuasive, but he also has to know how to use his skills. Bargaining with other political leaders, knowing when to compromise, building coalitions that are strong enough to survive but not so large that the president wastes resources, and choosing priorities are vital political skills. Considering the complexity of

Congress and the independence of its members, the president has difficulty even knowing which leaders need to be targeted for action.

President Lyndon B. Johnson was known as a master of the legislative game. Through his years of experience in the House and Senate, he had developed a keen sense of how to keep friends happy, never burn bridges with foes, and massage the egos of all of them. A president can help persuade members to stay focused on his agenda through a variety of means, and Johnson was a master of these techniques. One way that presidents can maintain good relations with Congress is through the provision of personal amenities, sometimes known as the "Johnson treatment." For example, Johnson was known for keeping track of members' birthdays, anniversaries, and other significant events along with some of their personal preferences. When he needed a key vote or wanted to reward a member for loyalty, he would offer the presidential seats to the opera on the member's anniversary. Sometimes, the president can attract or retain a key vote by simply making a big display of bringing a legislator to the White House for a personal meeting to demonstrate the member's influence and importance. Although these amenities and personal attention often do not change a hostile member's vote, they help the president focus attention on his agenda and keep loyal members in line.

At other times, a president may need to make more serious overtures to a member of Congress. The president may have to trade votes with a member, release funding for a special project in the member's district, or make legislative concessions. This kind of "horse trading" costs the president more in political terms than the personal-amenities approach, but when it is essential to attain the necessary majority, the president must decide whether the cost is worthwhile. Often, the president must decide whether "half a loaf" is better than none. That this type of trading goes on is a clear indication that the president must continuously work to persuade and cannot simply command.

If all else fails, a president may resort to arm-twisting to keep members in his legislative coalition. But presidents have little to use as threats. Members of Congress enjoy independent power bases supported by congressional committees, personal staffs, the incumbency advantage, and campaign fundraising techniques that do not rely on the party. Therefore, a president has difficulty bullying a member of Congress. Some subtle techniques, however, are useful against members of the president's party and electorally vulnerable members of the opposition (see Figure 13-3). The president can apply direct pressure to a party member by using party financial, technical, and media assistance as a carrot to get a key vote. The president can also use indirect pressure on either group of legislators by contacting interest groups and influential constituents and asking them to apply pressure, either financial or otherwise, on a member. If the president is nationally popular or at least performed well in a member's district in the last election, a presidential visit to the district can be used as either a carrot or a stick. For members of the same party, a visit by a popular president may be useful in the next election. For members of the opposite party, a visit by the president in support of a challenger may be quite a credible threat that may give the president leverage in bargaining for a member's vote.

"Going Public" As Neustadt's argument about persuasion suggests, popular presidents are more likely to be influential. This concern over presidential popularity has resulted in nearly continuous polling of the public's approval of the president's handling of the job. Because of the number of polls and continual attention to polls by the press, public, and Congress, the president is increasingly facing a "perpetual election."[29] This perpetual election has a dramatic effect on the president's influence. Several studies have shown a strong relationship between presidential popularity and presidential success in Congress. Popularity enhances a president's ability to enact his agenda and avoid vetoes.[30]

Because of its importance for legislative success, presidents focus tremendous resources on "going public."[31] Press conferences, nationally televised presidential addresses, personal appearances, sound bites on the national news, and aggressive courting of the press are all part of the president's appeal to the voters to support his policies and place pressure on Congress. Franklin D. Roosevelt was one of the first to make extensive use of

Figure 13-3
Presidential Success in Congress during the First Year

Source: Adapted from Congressional Quarterly.

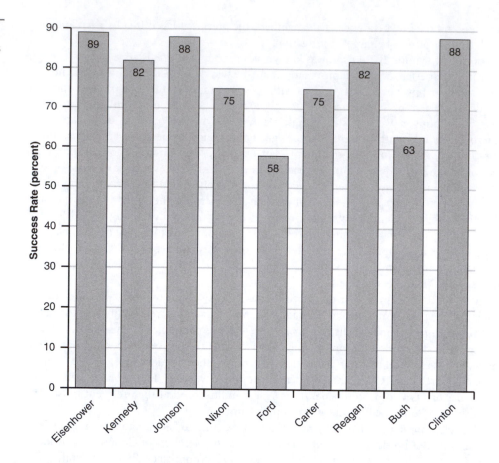

national addresses by broadcasting his "fireside chats" on the radio. Television greatly expanded the president's ability to reach the public. Many view President Reagan, a former actor, as the most successful president in exploiting the mass media and the strategy of going public. Dubbed the Great Communicator, he was quite effective in making national appeals to the public and asking voters to pressure their representatives to support his programs. Because of his personal appeal, he was able to maintain high levels of public support throughout most of his two terms despite a severe recession early in his first term, the bombing of the U.S. Marine compound in Lebanon that killed nearly 250 Marines, and the Iran-Contra scandal.

Not surprisingly, presidents are most successful when they are popular. Generally, the pattern has been one of initially high public support during the honeymoon period immediately after the first election followed by a gradual decline in support throughout the term. If a president is reelected, he usually benefits from a brief period of higher support followed by another gradual decline. Of course, this general pattern is greatly affected by events, and the numbers move up and down almost continuously over time. The public expects the government to provide, in general, peace, security, and prosperity in this country. As one study of the presidency argues, "the public punishes the President more than members of Congress if expectations are not met."[32]

One of the worst things that can happen to a president's public approval is an economic downturn.[33] Severe recessions have always had a negative effect on public approval. On the other hand, a crisis can have a positive effect on public approval. For example, before the Iraqi invasion of Kuwait in 1990, President George Bush's public approval numbers were slightly less than 60 percent. After the Iraqi army had been thoroughly routed by the allied forces in early 1991, Bush's public approval ratings skyrocketed to almost 90 percent. However, the deepening recession, the Los Angeles riots, and the lack of any new legislative initiatives combined to cause his approval numbers to drop sharply to less than 40

Controversy

The Bush Administration Response to Hurricane Katrina

In late August of 2005, Hurricane Katrina struck the Gulf Coast just east of New Orleans. The resulting damage was horrific, especially for Mississippi's coastal communities. While New Orleans at first appeared to have dodged the bullet, the levees that protect the city from the Mississippi River and Lake Pontchartrain gave way. Because New Orleans lies below sea level, nearly the entire city was flooded. By the end of the day following the passing of the storm 80% of New Orleans was under filthy water, much of it 8 or more feet deep. The power went off. The sewer system backed up. The water system became contaminated. The communication infrastructure failed completely. All services broke down. Essentially, the city ceased to function.

While most of the city's residents had evacuated prior to the storm's landfall, tens of thousands of people were stranded inside the city. Hundreds of people had to be rescued from their homes by boat or helicopter. Thousands of people gathered in miserable conditions in the Superdome and around the convention center without power, water, food, or the basics of sanitation. Millions of people around the world watched via television as increasingly desperate people, overwhelmingly poor and African American, were left to fend for themselves without any discernable governmental presence. It took three days after the storm passed for National Guard troops and evacuation busses to arrive. During this time lawlessness and violence had steadily escalated. Survivors told frightening tales of rapes, shootings, and looting by armed gangs.

The response to the New Orleans disaster by local, state, and especially federal authority was widely condemned in the press and by many in politics. President George W. Bush, along with Michael Chertoff secretary of homeland security, and Michael Brown, director of the Federal Emergency Management Agency (FEMA), found themselves under tremendous criticism for delays in responding to the crisis. Americans seemed shocked that their own government seemed unprepared for a scenario that had been long discussed among disaster planners. Many speculated that the concern for terrorism had eclipsed a concern for national disasters. Others suggested that racism played a role in the government's lackluster response.

In the weeks following Hurricane Katrina, President George W. Bush's approval ratings reached their lowest point since he took office in January 2001. Obviously, the public perception of the President's handling of the Hurricane Katrina disaster contrasted sharply from its view of how the President responded to the 9-11 terrorist attacks.

percent by the time his campaign for reelection began in 1992.[34] Although the public may not always reward the president for what is going well in the country, they are usually quick to punish the president for any problems, especially economic ones. In turn, public approval influences how successful a president will be in achieving legislative success.

Bill Clinton was a master of going public. His ease before the camera and natural style of communication helped bolster his image among voters throughout his presidency despite his having to defend himself against an almost constant stream of criticism regarding a variety of scandals. Even during impeachment, Clinton was able to maintain a high job rating despite quite a low personal approval rating (see Figure 13-4).[35]

13-5c The Budget

Although the president's relationship with Congress has always been difficult, the deficit problems of the 1980s and 1990s exacerbated the tensions between the two branches and the two parties. In the late 1990s and 2000, the tension eased as the deficit was replaced by a surplus for the first time in three decades. Unfortunately, the surplus did not last long: Government expenditures increased in response to the terrorist attacks of 9-11-2001, and the economic downturn produced lower-than-expected government revenues.

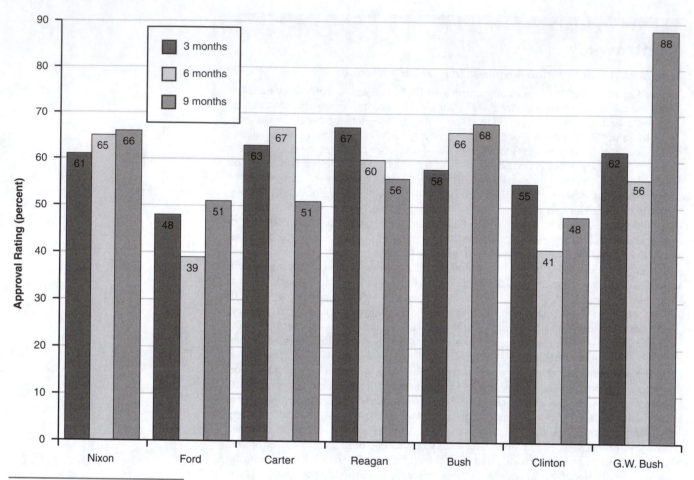

Figure 13-4
Presidential Approval Ratings
(after Three Months, Six Months,
and Nine Months)

Source: Adapted from surveys by the Gallup
Organization.

The budget process is complex and slow; it extends over several different stages involving the president's budget proposal, negotiations over the general shape of the budget, tax considerations, deliberations on appropriations to each different program, the actual expenditure decisions, and oversight of the manner in which the money was used. Furthermore, budget considerations influence every major legislative decision. No new program may be discussed without assessing its effect on the national debt.

Unfortunately, despite the central nature of budget policy in the legislative calendar, the system is not well designed for producing coherent policy. The president has only limited constitutional tools, such as the veto and the right to recommend legislation, to deal with a Congress that divides power between two chambers that are further divided into several committees and subcommittees with power over the budget. The Constitution does not provide for a joint bargaining process among the president, the House, and the Senate. The budget must originate in the House, pass in each chamber in identical form, and be submitted to the president for signing or a veto. The president has a potent weapon in the veto power, but it is a clumsy tool for fighting with Congress over the details of a budget. If Congress passes the president's budget and he does not care for some of the spending decisions, his only choice is to either defeat the entire bill or accept the entire document including the less-preferred parts.

In 1990, President George Bush chose to let the government close down for a weekend rather than accept a budget plan that he did not like. National parks closed, government workers were told to stay home from work, and no government checks were mailed out. The president and Congress were both within their constitutional rights in fighting for a desirable budget, but the battle did not look good to the average citizen. The deadlock was to many observers just another symptom of a dysfunctional political system. Both Congress and the president paid a price, in terms of public trust in government, for the provisions of the bill.

President Clinton utilized the budget battle with congressional Republicans to great advantage in 1995 following the Republican victories in 1994. By allowing the Republicans to take the blame for the government shutdown, Clinton was able to skillfully use his communications advantages as president to cast congressional leaders, especially House Speaker Newt Gingrich, as extremists. Many observers attributed Clinton's subsequent election to his ability to recast himself following his battle with Congress.

13-6 Evaluating Presidential Performance

Americans love rankings and ratings. Not surprisingly, scholars like to rate presidents. In 1982, they were polled and their ratings tabulated.[36] The scholars' three favorites were Abraham Lincoln, George Washington, and Franklin D. Roosevelt. Lincoln's greatness was in his leadership and steadfastness through the nation's greatest crisis, the Civil War. Washington's greatness derived from having presided over the creation of a new republic and setting the tone for how the presidency should be conducted. Roosevelt's claim to greatness rests on his decisive leadership through the two greatest challenges this country faced in the twentieth century: the Great Depression and World War II.

According to the survey of scholars, the two worst presidents were Warren G. Harding and Richard Nixon. Harding's main failure was the widespread corruption of his administration—most notably, the infamous Teapot Dome scandal. Nixon, on the other hand, was accused of abusing the power of the presidency. His primary failure was his handling of a very troubling event: the Watergate scandal. Even worse was his cover-up of the whole enterprise. Nevertheless, though little can be offered in defense of Harding, one can find much in Nixon's administration to praise. He negotiated an end to America's involvement in the Vietnam War, made progress in controlling nuclear weapons, and established an important relationship with the People's Republic of China.

When polled in 1991, the American people rated Washington, Lincoln, and Roosevelt among the greatest presidents.[37] But, interestingly, the public gave its highest rating to John F. Kennedy (who did not make the scholars' top ten). To some extent, Kennedy's ongoing popularity is a function of his charisma, his oratorical skill, and the degree to which he inspired America to strive for a "new frontier." Without question, his untimely death at the hands of an assassin has also buttressed his standing in the public mind. One might wonder how Kennedy would be regarded now had he not been assassinated three years after being elected.

Americans tend to think of the great presidents as those who brought an activist approach to the office—what political scientist James David Barber has called the "active-positive" presidency.[38] In Barber's framework, an active-positive president brings a high level of energy and excitement to the office and derives pleasure from being president. He is characterized by a general openness and flexibility and has a warm and engaging personality. Moreover, he has a strong drive to lead and to be judged a success by others. Certainly, John Kennedy exemplified this approach to the office, as did Franklin Roosevelt.

Perhaps a fairer way to evaluate presidents is to determine whether they achieved the goals they set for themselves during their campaigns. Ronald Reagan did not have an activist conception of the presidency. Indeed, he wanted to scale down the activities of the national government. Yet most would agree that, despite certain problems and setbacks, Reagan's presidency was a successful one. Whether Reagan will go down in history as a great president remains to be seen, but strong indications show that history will regard Reagan quite favorably. Certainly, the mass public now renders a favorable judgment of President Reagan.[39] To his many admirers, Reagan was the president who stood up to the Soviet Union and hastened the end of the cold war.

13-6a Evaluating the Clinton Presidency

During the first two years of the Clinton presidency, Republicans in Congress had simply sought to block the president's agenda. The Democrats who controlled Congress at the time kept Republican proposals from being considered. After gaining control of the House

What Americans Think About

The Performance of Modern Presidents

Public-opinion surveys routinely show that Americans think of John F. Kennedy, Abraham Lincoln, and Franklin D. Roosevelt as the greatest presidents in United States history. In averaging the approval ratings for presidents since Harry Truman, you see that Kennedy comes out on top, with an average approval rating of 70 percent. President Truman is lowest, at 45 percent.

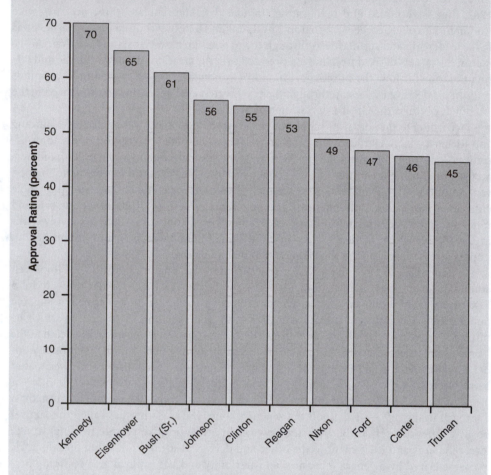

Note: Figures are average approval ratings for entire term in office.

Source: Adapted from Gallup polls; see David W. Moore, "Clinton Leaves Office with Mixed Public Reaction," *Gallup News Service,* January 12, 2001.

of Representatives in 1994, Republicans were at last in a position to set the legislative agenda. But it remained for President Clinton to react, perhaps with the veto, to what the Republicans sought to do. In some instances, the president used the veto, but in others he was able to reach agreement with Congress. Ultimately, much of the success of the Clinton presidency is attributable to the fact that he was able to work with the Republican Congress in establishing policy, at least before the impeachment saga of 1998–1999. Bill Clinton's presidency was marked by dramatic highs and lows—impressive accomplishments and devastating scandals. Although the judgment of history has yet to be written, the American people by and large expect Clinton to go down in history as a good, if not great, president. At the same time, the public expects Clinton to be remembered more for scandals than for his accomplishments.[40]

Bill Clinton must be given credit for presiding over a vibrant economy and for working with Republicans to bring about welfare reform. He left office, however, without a signature foreign policy accomplishment to serve as a centerpiece of his legacy despite spending a good deal of the latter part of 2000 trying to broker yet another peace agreement between Israel and the Palestinians. As his term ended, it appeared that Clinton's legacy might well be framed in terms of his personal scandals. The probability of such a legacy increased substantially in the wake of Clinton's leaving office. This exit was mired in controversies concerning questionable pardons and gifts to the first couple.

13-6b Assessing George W. Bush's Presidency

By most standards George W. Bush's first term did not appear to be successful as he approached the election of 2004. His approval rating hovered at or slightly below the 50 percent mark deemed critical for any president seeking reelection. The economic recovery seemed to be stalling out, and the war in Iraq was generating increasingly negative headlines. George W. Bush had assumed office in early 2001 with a full agenda, including reforming Social Security, cutting taxes, and adding a prescription drug component to Medicare. He also brought an expectation that he would unite, rather than divide, the country and reduce partisan fighting. By the end of his first term, he could claim to have worked with the Democrats in Congress to pass "No Child Left Behind" legislation, to have developed a prescription drug policy, to have cut taxes, but not to have managed to close the partisan divide or to have done much with Social Security.

What the president, or anyone else, could not have foreseen, was the terrorist attacks of September 11, 2001. Most observers give President Bush high marks in the way in which he led the country in the aftermath of the attacks. In the understandable wave of concern for national security Congress approved the USA PATRIOT Act by an overwhelming margin. By the end of his first term, the PATRIOT Act and its implementation was a point of strong controversy, with many in and out of government decrying its impact on civil liberties while others pointed to the lack of a second attack.

It is difficult to assess any presidency at the halfway point. One experiencing a disruption like that of 9-11 presents even greater problems. George W. Bush's reelection demonstrated at least a tentative positive review by the American people. At the very least, George W. Bush has accomplished some of his objectives. Given that his most pressing goal is the achievement of a stable and democratic Iraq, it may be many years before George W. Bush's presidency can be adequately assessed.

13-7 Conclusion: Assessing the Presidency as an Institution

American political culture has always been somewhat ambivalent in regard to executive power. The Articles of Confederation did not even provide for a chief executive. The debate among the Framers at the Constitutional Convention made clear that their greatest fear was a tyrant. They carefully devised a method of selecting presidents that was far from the people; the president was to be chosen by a deliberative body picked by state legislatures. On the other hand, the American people have always loved heroes and have looked to heroic individuals to lead the country through times of crisis. The American people have come to expect a great deal from their presidents. Yet presidents, like all other officials in this country, operate with an elaborate set of legal and political constraints.

Not surprisingly, American presidents have trouble maintaining their popularity. The political scientist Paul Light has argued that the job has become a "no-win presidency."[41] The president is limited by the structures originally intended to limit the office. Moreover, he must face the pressure of living up to the expectations to excel in a multiplicity of roles, many of which are in conflict. By most accounts, George Bush (the elder) excelled at the military and diplomatic aspects of his presidency. He was widely perceived as unsuccessful as chief legislator, however, and, in the view of some Republicans, as party leader. Bill Clinton was highly successful as party leader and chief legislator, though his performance in the foreign policy realm was less stellar. At the beginning of his second term as president, George W. Bush appeared to be most successful as crisis manager, chief diplomat, and commander-in-chief, which few would have expected before his becoming president. Here, as in many areas of political life, unforeseen events dictate unexpected roles and responses.

Questions for Thought and Discussion

1. Is the American presidency too powerful, or is it not powerful enough?

2. Is it better for the country if the same party controls the presidency and Congress?

3. Should the president be given the power to veto specific lines in an appropriations bill?

4. Was President Bush (the elder) constitutionally required to obtain consent from Congress before initiating Operation Desert Storm in 1991?

5. Who was the greatest president since World War II? What makes a great president?

6. Did Congress have good grounds for impeaching President Bill Clinton in 1998? Did the Senate make the correct decision in acquitting him?

7. Should the Constitution be amended to require Senate approval of presidential pardons?

8. How will the Clinton presidency be regarded by historians fifty years from now?

9. How does the administration of George W. Bush differ from that of Bill Clinton?

10. How do the leadership styles of George W. Bush and Bill Clinton compare and contrast?

Practice Quiz

Note: You can find the correct answers to these questions by taking the quiz and then submitting your answers in the Online Edition. The program will automatically score your submission. If you miss a question, the program will provide the correct answer, a rationale for the answer, and the section number in the chapter where the topic is discussed.

1. The power of a president to reject a bill and thus prevent it from becoming law is called the _____ power.
   a. removal
   b. presentment
   c. veto
   d. impoundment

2. The ultimate constitutional sanction against the abuse of presidential power is _____.
   a. impoundment
   b. impeachment
   c. presentment
   d. oversight

3. The _____ Amendment limits the tenure of presidents to two four-year terms.
   a. Twenty-sixth
   b. Fourteenth
   c. Twenty-second
   d. Twenty-seventh

4. The only president to be elected to more than two terms is _____.
   a. Franklin Roosevelt
   b. George Washington
   c. Woodrow Wilson
   d. Thomas Jefferson

5. As _____, the president is responsible for managing and running the federal bureaucracy.
   a. chief executive
   b. head of state
   c. commander-in-chief
   d. chief legislator

6. Unlike today, early presidents relied primarily on their _____ and a few close personal advisors to make policy.
   a. cabinet
   b. chief of staff
   c. White House staff
   d. vice president

7. The powers of the presidency are less susceptible to constitutional and political restraints in those areas that affect _____.
   a. social spending
   b. foreign policy
   c. domestic policy
   d. civil rights

8. A president's legislative success is likely to be greatest during _____.
   a. the last year of his first term
   b. the first year of his first term
   c. the last year of his second term
   d. the year after the midterm elections

9. The use of an executive agreement allows the president to circumvent the power of _____.
   a. the Congress in the treaty ratification process
   b. the House in the treaty ratification process
   c. the Senate in the treaty ratification process
   d. the State Department in the treaty ratification process

10. In making decisions, contemporary presidents rely most heavily on _____.
    a. the White House staff
    b. the cabinet members
    c. the vice president
    d. congressional leaders

For Further Reading

Barber, James David. *The Presidential Character,* 4th ed. (Upper Saddle River, NJ: Prentice-Hall, 1992).

Bond, John R., and Richard Fleisher. *The President in the Legislative Arena* (Chicago: University of Chicago Press, 1990).

Campbell, Colin, and Bert A. Rockman. *The George W. Bush Presidency: Appraisals and Prospects* (Washington, D.C.: CQ Press, 2004).

Edwards, George C., III. *Presidential Influence in Congress* (San Francisco: W. H. Freeman, 1980).

Fisher, Louis. *The Politics of Shared Power: Congress and the Executive,* 4th ed. (College Station, TX: Texas A&M University Press, 1998).

Hess, Stephen. *Organizing the Presidency,* 2d ed. (Washington, D.C.: Brookings Institution, 1988).

Kernell, Samuel. *Going Public: New Strategies of Presidential Leadership,* 3d ed. (Washington, D.C.: CQ Press, 1997).

Kessel, John H. *Presidents, the Presidency and the Political Environment* (Washington, D.C.: CQ Press, 2001).

Light, Paul. *The President's Agenda,* 3d ed. (Baltimore: Johns Hopkins University Press, 1999).

Maraniss, David. *First in His Class* (New York: Simon and Schuster, 1995).

McPherson, James M. *Abraham Lincoln and the Second American Revolution* (New York: Oxford University Press, 1991).

Milkus, Stanley, and Michael Nelson. *The American Presidency: Origins and Development, 1776–1998,* 4th ed. (Washington, D.C.: CQ Press, 2003).

Nelson, Michael, ed. *The Evolving Presidency: Addresses, Cases, Essays, Reports, Resolutions, Transcripts, and Other Landmark Documents, 1787–2004* (Washington, D.C.: CQ Press, 2004).

Neustadt, Richard E. *Presidential Power: The Politics of Leadership from FDR to Carter* (New York: John Wiley & Sons, 1980).

Pika, Joseph A., and John A. Maltese. *The Politics of the Presidency,* 6th ed. (Washington, D.C.: CQ Press, 2004).

Schlesinger, Arthur, Jr. *The Imperial Presidency* (Boston: Houghton Mifflin, 1973).

Waterman, Richard W., ed. *The Presidency Reconsidered* (Itasca, IL: Peacock Press, 1993).

Endnotes

1. *Youngstown Sheet and Tube Co. v. Sawyer,* 343 U.S. 579 (1952).
2. *United States v. Nixon,* 418 U.S. 683 (1974).
3. *New York Times v. United States,* 403 U.S. 713 (1971).
4. *Clinton v. City of New York,* 524 U.S. 417 (1998).
5. Quoted in Sean Higgins, "President Revives Idea for a Line-Item Veto to Help Curb Spending," *Investor's Business Daily,* November 22, 2004.
6. Ibid.
7. Jeffrey M. Jones, "Bill Clinton's Image Suffers as Americans Criticize Pardon," *Gallup News Service,* February 22, 2001.
8. *United States v. Nixon,* 418 U.S. 683 (1974).
9. See, for example, Aaron Wildavsky, "The Two Presidencies." In *The Presidency,* ed. Aaron Wildavsky (Boston: Little, Brown, 1969), p. 230.
10. *United States v. Curtiss-Wright Export Corp.,* 299 U.S. 304 (1936).
11. As reported by Tom Brokaw on the "NBC Nightly News," December 15, 1993.
12. *Dames and Moore v. Regan,* 453 U.S. 654 (1981).
13. *Massachusetts v. Laird,* 400 U.S. 886 (1970).
14. *Crockett v. Reagan,* 558 F. Supp. 893 (D.C.D.C. 1982).
15. "Senate Approves Iraq War Resolution," *CNN,* October 11, 2002, http://archives.cnn.com/2002/ALLPOLITICS/10/11/iraq.us/.
16. Will Lester, "AP Poll: Stable Iraq Tops Voter Priorities," *Associated Press,* November 7, 2004.
17. Johanna McGeary, "The Number One Priority," *Time,* November 15, 2004, p. 66.
18. See *Hirabayashi v. United States,* 320 U.S. 81 (1943); *Korematsu v. United States,* 323 U.S. 214 (1944).
19. *United States v. United States District Court,* 407 U.S. 297 (1972).
20. Quoted in Bill Mears, "Supreme Court Looks at 'Enemy Combatants,'" CNN.com, April 28, 2004.
21. Ibid.
22. *Hamdi v. Rumsfeld,* 124 S.Ct. 2633 (2004).
23. *Rumsfeld v. Padilla,* 124 S.Ct. 2711 (2004).
24. Quoted in Benjamin I. Page and Mark P. Petracca, *The American Presidency* (New York: McGraw-Hill, 1983), p. 169.
25. Paul Light, *The President's Agenda* (Baltimore: Johns Hopkins University Press, 1982), p. 44.
26. Ibid., p. 45.
27. Richard Neustadt, *Presidential Power* (New York: John Wiley & Sons, 1980), p. 10.
28. Ibid., p. 9.
29. See Richard A. Brody and Benjamin I. Page, "The Impact of Events on Presidential Popularity." In *Perspectives on the Presidency,* ed. Aaron Wildavsky (Boston: Little, Brown, 1975).
30. See George C. Edwards III, *Presidential Influence in Congress* (San Francisco: W. H. Freeman, 1980); Douglas Rivers and Nancy Rose, "Passing the President's Program: Public Opinion and Presidential Influence in Congress," *American Journal of Political Science,* vol. 29, 1985, pp. 183–96.
31. See, generally, Samuel Kernell, *Going Public: New Strategies of Presidential Leadership,* 3d ed. (Washington, D.C.: CQ Press, 1997).
32. John R. Bond and Richard Fleisher, *The President in the Legislative Arena* (Chicago: University of Chicago Press, 1990), p. 2.
33. Compare Henry C. Kenski, "The Impact of Economic Conditions on Presidential Popularity," *Journal of Politics,* vol. 39, 1977, pp. 764–73; Douglas A. Hibbs, "On the Demands for Economic Outcomes: Macroeconomic Performance and Mass Political Support in the United States," *Journal of Politics,* vol. 34, 1982, pp. 426–62; K. Monroe, "Presidential Popularity: An Almon Distributed Lag Model," *Political Methodology,* vol. 7, 1981, pp. 43–70.
34. See Kernell, *Going Public.*
35. During the Lewinsky scandal, President Clinton's approval rating ranged from 73 percent in December 1998 to 53 percent in May 1999. During 1999 and 2000, his approval rating ranged in the high 50s to low 60s. The average approval

rating for the entire Clinton presidency was 55 percent. These approval ratings are based on regular surveys conducted by the Gallup Organization and can be accessed at www.gallup.com.

36. Arthur Murphy, "Evaluating the Presidents of the United States," *Presidential Studies Quarterly,* vol. 14, 1984, pp. 117–26.

37. George H. Gallup, Jr. *The Gallup Poll: Public Opinion 1991* (Wilmington, DE: Scholarly Resources, 1992).

38. James David Barber, *The Presidential Character,* 3d ed. (Englewood Cliffs, NJ: Prentice-Hall, 1985).

39. A survey conducted in early 2001 by the Gallup Organization found that the mass public is now most likely to regard Ronald Reagan as the greatest president ever. See Wendy W. Simmons, "Reagan, Kennedy and Lincoln Receive the Most Votes for Greatest U.S. President," Gallup News Service, February 19, 2001. As we note earlier in section 13-6, a 1991 Gallup survey identified John F. Kennedy as the leading choice.

40. David W. Moore, "Clinton Leaves Office with Mixed Public Reaction," Gallup News Service, January 12, 2001.

41. Paul Light, *The President's Agenda,* rev. ed (Baltimore: Johns Hopkins University Press, 1991), p. 202.

The Supreme Court and the Federal Judiciary

14

The "Marble Temple," the impressive structure the Supreme Court has occupied since 1935.

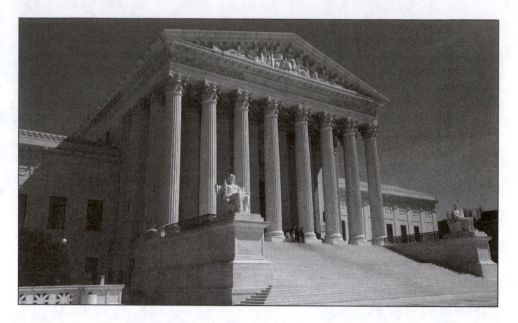

14-1 The "Least Dangerous Branch"

One of the principal deficiencies of the national government under the Articles of Confederation was that no court of law was capable of resolving disputes between states or between citizens of different states. Early in the Constitutional Convention of 1787, the delegates unanimously adopted a resolution calling for the creation of a national judiciary. Yet the Constitution they produced said little about the structure, powers, and functions of the third branch of government. Nevertheless, Alexander Hamilton assured the nation that the judiciary would be the "least dangerous branch" because it would have "no influence over either the sword or the purse; no direction of the strength or of the wealth of a society; and can take no active resolution whatever." In Hamilton's view, the judicial branch "may be truly said to have neither force nor will, but merely judgment."[1]

The "mere judgment" of the federal courts has become a much more important source of government power than Hamilton or the other Framers of the Constitution ever could have envisioned. In the modern era, the "least dangerous branch" has become more or less coequal to the Congress and the executive branch. In part, this increased importance has come about because the federal courts have emerged as the referee in the ongoing struggle for power between Congress and the president and between the national government and the states. It is also because great questions of public policy are often framed as legal questions for the courts to decide. As Alexis de Tocqueville observed in 1835: "Scarcely any political question arises in the United States that is not resolved, sooner or later, into a judicial question."[2] That statement proved unusually prophetic in December 2000, when the Supreme Court decided *Bush v. Gore*, which effectively determined the outcome of the presidential election.[3]

14-1a The Power "To Say What the Law Is"

The mainstay of judicial power is the authority to interpret the law. The federal courts interpret the statutes enacted by Congress and the regulations promulgated by federal agencies. On occasion, the courts must also interpret executive orders issued by the president and treaties the United States has made with foreign governments. Quite often, the law that must be interpreted to decide a case is vague, ambiguous, or incomplete, particularly with federal statutes. Congress, or any legislature, has difficulty writing a law that provides clear, precise guidance for the courts in all future situations. Moreover, the politics of the legislative process often results in vague, ambiguous, or even self-contradictory statutes because Congress is seeking to satisfy different constituencies with different views about what the law should contain. Ultimately, the courts must decide what a particular provision of a statute really means in the context of a given set of facts. In assigning meaning to statutes, the courts rely heavily on **precedent**—a law will be interpreted in the way it has already been interpreted. In the absence of precedent, however, a court must use its own discretion to decide the meaning of an unclear law. In doing so, a court, in a sense, makes law. The more Congress leaves the meaning of a statute open to conflicting interpretations, the greater the likelihood that the federal courts will have to engage in lawmaking. With Congress having to make laws dealing with increasingly complex issues, the meaning of legislation is often decided, not surprisingly, in the courts.

> ▶ **precedent**   A judicial decision on a point of law giving direction to or authority for later cases presenting the same legal problem, although involving different parties.

Judicial Review   In addition to their power to interpret statutes, regulations, and so forth, the federal courts possess the power to interpret the U.S. Constitution and to invalidate laws and policies that are found to be contrary to the Constitution. This aspect of judicial power, known as judicial review, is a uniquely American invention. Although English common-law courts exercised the power to make law in some instances, no English court claimed the authority to nullify an act of Parliament. Though judicial review is normally associated with the U.S. Supreme Court, nearly all courts of law in this country also possess this power. In fact, judicial review had already been exercised by a few state courts before the adoption of the U.S. Constitution. The Framers, however, did not resolve the question of whether the newly created federal courts should have this power. Article III is silent on the subject. It remained for the Supreme Court, in a bold stroke of legal and political genius, to assume this power for itself and the rest of the federal courts. That bold stroke occurred in *Marbury v. Madison* (1803),[4] the first great case in American constitutional law (see Case in Point 14-1). In *Marbury*, the Supreme Court struck down as unconstitutional a provision of the Judiciary Act of 1789.[5] Writing for the Court, Chief Justice John Marshall asserted the primacy of the courts in interpreting the Constitution and statutes, observing, "It is emphatically the province and duty of the judicial department to say what the law is."

In the two centuries since the *Marbury* decision, nearly 200 federal statutes, or provisions thereof, have been declared unconstitutional by the Supreme Court. The Court has also invalidated about twelve hundred state and local laws. More than half these declarations have come since 1960, showing the increased activism of the modern Court. When Congress, a state legislature, or a city council debates pending legislation, it must consider whether the law as written will survive judicial review. Failure to exercise due care in the drafting of legislation increases the probability that it will be challenged in court and ultimately invalidated. Of course, it is not unheard of for legislators to enact a law that they know will be struck down in the courts in order to satisfy a certain constituency. When that happens, the legislature can take credit for passing the measure and blame the courts for striking it down.

Although the courts sometimes invalidate popular legislation, the American public is generally supportive of judicial review, at least in principle. Yet, from time to time, it is criticized as antidemocratic. Clearly, judicial review is counter-majoritarian, by definition. Whether it is antidemocratic depends on one's definition of *democracy*. If democracy is defined not just in terms of majority rule, but also in terms of individual and minority rights, a case can be made that judicial review is eminently democratic. Some commentators even argue that judicial review is necessary to ensure that the right to vote is not infringed and that channels of political participation remain open to citizens.[6] To the extent that courts use their power to invalidate legislation to maintain the integrity of the democratic process, judicial review is consistent with democracy. On the other hand, when courts employ judicial review merely to impose their own public policy preferences without a sound basis in constitutional interpretation, one can argue that democracy is being usurped.

In making a determination about what the law means and applying it to a concrete situation, a federal court often makes an important public policy decision. Certainly, that was the case in 1973 when the Supreme Court interpreted the right of privacy under the Constitution to be broad enough to allow a woman to choose to terminate an unwanted

Chief Justice John Marshall
(1755–1835)

Hulton | Archive by Getty Images

Case in Point 14-1

An Excerpt from Chief Justice John Marshall's Opinion for the Supreme Court in *Marbury v. Madison* (1803)

... Certainly, all those who have framed written constitutions contemplate them as forming the fundamental and paramount law of the nation, and consequently, the theory of every such government must be, that an act of the legislature, repugnant to the Constitution, is void.

This theory is essentially attached to a written constitution, and is, consequently, to be considered, by this Court, as one of the fundamental principles of our society. It is not, therefore, to be lost sight of, in the further consideration of this subject.

If an act of the legislature, repugnant to the Constitution, is void, does it, notwithstanding its invalidity, bind the courts, and oblige them to give it effect? Or, in other words, though it be not law, does it constitute a rule as operative as if it was a law? This would be to overthrow, in fact, what was established in theory; and would seem, at first view, an absurdity too gross to be insisted on. It shall, however, receive a more attentive consideration.

It is, emphatically, the province and duty of the judicial department, to say what the law is. Those who apply the rule to particular cases, must of necessity expound and interpret that rule. If two laws conflict with each other, the courts must decide on the operation of each.

So, if a law be in opposition to the Constitution; if both the law and the Constitution apply to a particular case, so that the court must either decide that case, conformable to the law, disregarding the Constitution; or conformable to the Constitution, disregarding the law; the court must determine which of these conflicting rules governs the case: this is of the very essence of judicial duty.

If then, the courts are to regard the Constitution, and the constitution is superior to any ordinary act of the legislature, the Constitution, and not such ordinary act, must govern the case to which they both apply.

Those, then, who controvert the principle, that the Constitution is to be considered, in court, as a paramount law, are reduced to the necessity of maintaining that courts must close their eyes on the Constitution, and see only the law.

This doctrine would subvert the very foundation of all written constitutions. It would declare that an act which, according to the principles and theory of our government, is entirely void, is yet, in practice, completely obligatory. It would declare, that if the legislature shall do what is expressly forbidden, such act, notwithstanding the express prohibition, is in reality effectual. It would be given to the legislature a practical and real omnipotence, with the same breath which professes to restrict their powers within narrow limits. It is prescribing limits, and declaring that those limits may be passed at pleasure....

The judicial power of the United States is extended to all cases arising under the Constitution. Could it be the intention of those who gave this power, to say, that in using it, the constitution should not be looked into? That a case arising under the Constitution should be decided, without examining the instrument under which it arises?

This is too extravagant to be maintained.

In some cases, then, the constitution must be looked into by the judges. And if they can open it at all, what part of it are they forbidden to read or to obey? ...

...[I]t is apparent, that the framers of the Constitution contemplated that instrument as a rule for the government of courts, as well as the legislature.

Why otherwise does it direct the judges to take an oath to support it? This oath certainly applies in an especial manner, to their conduct in their official character. How immoral to impose it on them, if they were to be used as the instruments, and the knowing instruments, for violating what they swear to support!

... Why does a judge swear to discharge his duties agreeable to the Constitution of the United States, if that constitution forms no rule for his government? If it is closed upon him, and cannot be inspected by him?

If such be the real state of things, this is worse than solemn mockery. To prescribe, or to take this oath, becomes equally a crime.

It is also not entirely unworthy of observation, that in declaring what shall be the supreme law of the land, the Constitution itself is first mentioned; and not the laws of the United States, generally, but those only which shall be made in pursuance of the Constitution, have that rank.

Thus, the particular phraseology of the Constitution of the United States confirms and strengthens the principle, supposed to be essential to all written constitutions, that a law repugnant to the Constitution is void; and that courts, as well as other departments, are bound by that instrument....

pregnancy.[7] The Court's landmark decision in *Roe v. Wade* effectively legalized abortion in this country, a major public policy pronouncement. Although *Roe* stands as a legal landmark, the Supreme Court and other federal courts have also made important policy pronouncements in numerous other cases. Thus, public policy making must be regarded as a major function of the federal judiciary.

14-1b Rules Governing the Resolution of Legal Disputes

Few would deny that the courts play an important role in the policy-making process. Yet one must understand that courts make policy in a manner that is unique to the judiciary. Federal judges are not simply legislators in black robes. First, courts are limited to deciding

Comparative Perspective

Judicial Review in Germany

Although it has roots in English common law, judicial review is an American invention. In most of the world's democracies, legislative bodies—not courts—have the final word on constitutional questions. In recent decades, however, a number of democratic countries have adopted varying forms of judicial review. After World War II, Germany adopted a new constitution providing for judicial review of legislation. The Federal Constitutional Court in Germany is now regarded as the "supreme guardian of the constitution," and its constitutional decisions are endowed with "final binding force." Unlike American courts, however, the German Federal Constitutional Court is not limited to "cases or controversies." Thus, it may render advisory opinions requested by other courts and the Bundestag, the Federal Assembly. Other German courts do not possess the power of judicial review. When constitutional questions arise during litigation, other courts may request a ruling from the Federal Constitutional Court. By the end of 1995, the Federal Constitutional Court had declared more than three hundred statutory provisions to be null and void. Although the idea of judicial review is foreign to the Germanic legal tradition, most observers would agree that judicial review has played an important role in the establishment and maintenance of a viable democracy in Germany. In particular, the Federal Constitutional Court has played a significant role in the reunification of East Germany and West Germany, which had been divided at the end of World War II.

legal disputes and may address only the policy questions that arise in the context of those disputes. A court cannot undertake to make a ruling except in response to a dispute that individuals or groups bring before it. Second, courts observe rules and doctrines that limit the way in which they decide legal disputes. Finally, in certain areas of public policy, such as taxing and spending, foreign affairs, and military policy, the courts have limited, if any, involvement.

Jurisdiction   In law, the **plaintiff** is a party who files a complaint alleging wrongdoing on the part of a **defendant,** who must either admit to the wrong or defend against the accusation. A **civil case** begins when a plaintiff brings a lawsuit, usually seeking monetary damages for an injury that occurred as a result of the defendant's actions. A **criminal case,** on the other hand, begins when the government prosecutes someone for allegedly committing a crime. Of course, not all civil and criminal cases find their way into the federal courts; indeed, the overwhelming majority of cases originate and are finalized in state courts. For a case to be brought into the federal courts, it must qualify under federal jurisdiction. **Jurisdiction** is, quite simply, the authority of a court of law to hear and decide a case. A court must have jurisdiction, both over the subject matter of a case and the parties to a case, before it may proceed to adjudicate that controversy. The jurisdiction of the federal courts is determined by both the language of Article III of the Constitution and statutes enacted by Congress.

Standing   Ever since the Supreme Court refused to give legal advice to President George Washington, it has been well established that the federal courts do not render **advisory opinions** on hypothetical questions. If the president wishes advice on a legal matter that involves the government, he consults with the attorney general, who heads the Justice department. If a member of Congress wants a legal opinion on a public matter, she consults with a staff attorney on the relevant congressional committee. The federal courts issue rulings and opinions only as they are necessary to resolve real cases or controversies between adverse parties.

It follows from the **case or controversy principle** that one may not invoke the jurisdiction of a federal court without standing. To have **standing,** a party must have suffered, or be about to suffer, an injury. The injury need not be physical in nature; it may be economic or

▶ **plaintiff**   The party initiating legal action.

▶ **defendant**   A party charged with a crime or against whom a civil action is brought.

▶ **civil case**   A judicial proceeding, outside the criminal law, by which a party seeks to enforce rights or to obtain redress for wrongs, usually seeking monetary damages.

▶ **criminal case**   A judicial proceeding in which a party is accused of a crime.

▶ **jurisdiction**   The authority of a court of law to hear and decide a case.

▶ **advisory opinions**   Judicial opinions, not involving adverse parties in a "case or controversy," that is given at the request of the legislature or executive. The U.S. Supreme Court has a long-standing policy of not rendering advisory opinions.

▶ **case or controversy principle**   Article III of the U.S. Constitution extends the federal judicial power to actual cases or controversies, not to hypothetical cases or abstract questions of law.

▶ **standing**   The legal requirement that a party must have suffered, or be about to suffer, an injury in order to bring suit. The injury need not be physical in nature; it may be economic or even aesthetic.

Popular Culture and American Politics
The Napster Fight

By Chapman Rackaway

The Internet has opened up access to information for millions of people, but there have also been some unintended consequences of the information autobahn's open nature. Anyone with a high-speed Internet connection and the proper file-sharing service can break the law, even if she has the best of intentions. File sharing has raised the issue of copyright law infringement and whether sharing files online is legal.

The controversy started in 1999, when college student Shawn Fanning developed computer software that allowed users on multiple computers to share files with each other. Napster, taken from Fanning's nickname, was born. Immediately, people began downloading the free sharing software, and with music ripped onto computers from CDs, users were able to share music files with each other.

Napster (and other similar file-sharing services such as Gnutella, LimeWire, and WinMX) was great for college students who could seek songs online and download them, burn them onto CDs, or upload them to MP3 players, but the Recording Industry Association of America (RIAA) took exception to the practice of music sharing. Because downloaders paid no fees to share music, the effect was similar to rampant copying of music. Recording companies and musicians received no compensation for downloads, and the RIAA claimed the practice infringed on the copyrights the artists and companies held. Some musicians, like Metallica drummer Lars Ulrich, spoke out against the practice as stealing.

In 2003, the RIAA began to file suits against file sharers. Although Bertelsmann Music Group (BMG) had purchased Napster and rebuilt it into a pay-for-download service, people were still illegally sharing music over the Internet, and the RIAA sued. Most defendants settled with the organization and agreed not to download illegally, but some services still allow for downloading without paying for the music or movies that are shared. The fight will continue, but with Apple's pay-to-download iTunes service having recently sold its ten millionth song, music file sharing has become a legitimate business.

even aesthetic. For example, a person who has been convicted of a federal crime clearly has standing to challenge the conviction on appeal. The injury the person has sustained is the punishment that follows conviction. In some situations, a person may even have standing to bring a federal lawsuit to prevent the enforcement of a criminal law if being prosecuted under the law would violate his constitutional rights. In this case, the injury would arise from the infringement of constitutional rights. A resident living in a community in which a toxic waste dump will be located would probably have standing to challenge the legality of the dump's intended location. Having standing to sue or to appeal has nothing to do with ultimately winning the case, however. It means only that a suit may be brought.

Political Questions Even though a litigant may have standing and meets all the other technical requirements, the federal courts may still refuse to consider the merits of the dispute. Under the **doctrine of political questions,** cases may be dismissed if the issues they present are regarded as extremely "political" in nature. Of course, in a broad sense, all the cases that make their way into the federal courts are political in nature. The political questions doctrine really refers to those issues that are likely to draw the courts into a political battle with the executive or legislative branch or are simply more amenable to executive or legislative decision making.

The doctrine of political questions originated in an 1849 decision in which the Supreme Court refused to take sides in a dispute between two rival governments in Rhode Island—one based on a popular referendum and the other based on an old royal charter. Writing for the Court in that case, Chief Justice Roger B. Taney observed that the argument

▶ **political questions, doctrine of** Legal principle which holds that cases may be dismissed if the issues they present are extremely "political" in nature and would be answered more appropriately by either the legislature or executive branch.

Controversy

Bush v. Gore: The Supreme Court Enters the Political Thicket of the 2000 Presidential Election

The Supreme Court takes a certain risk whenever it intervenes in a political controversy. Intervening in the presidential election of 2000 was a colossal risk for the Court. With the country so sharply divided on the question of who should be president and who in fact won the pivotal state of Florida, it was inevitable that no matter how the Supreme Court decided *Bush v. Gore,* a substantial proportion of Americans would regard the Court's decision as illegitimate. Of course, few Americans would even read the opinions produced by the Justices. Their evaluation of the Court would depend primarily on the outcome. For those who watch the Court closely, the decision was not surprising. Ample precedent exists for the Court to involve itself in political contests, although never had the Court intervened in a presidential election. The Court's decision (supported by seven justices) that the standardless manual recount process under way in Florida violated the Equal Protection Clause of the Fourteenth Amendment was certainly a plausible, if not universally compelling, argument. The real controversy surrounds the Court's holding (supported by a bare majority of five) that time would not permit an orderly recount according to constitutionally adequate standards. In a bitter dissenting opinion, Justice Ruth Ginsburg asserted that "the Court's conclusion that a constitutionally adequate recount is impractical is a prophecy the Court's own judgment will not allow to be tested. Such an untested prophecy should not decide the Presidency of the United States." The question that students should ponder is this: Would the decision have come out the same way had the interests of the parties been reversed? Unfortunately for the Court, many people believe that the answer to this question is "No." In his dissenting opinion, Justice John Paul Stevens suggested that *Bush v. Gore* would damage the Court's reputation:

> Time will one day heal the wound to that confidence that will be inflicted by today's decision. One thing, however, is certain. Although we may never know with complete certainty the identity of the winner of this year's Presidential election, the identity of the loser is perfectly clear. It is the Nation's confidence in the judge as an impartial guardian of the rule of law. . . .

in the case "turned on political rights and political questions."[8] Not insignificantly, President John Tyler had agreed to send in troops to support the charter government before the case ever went to the Supreme Court.

Perhaps the best-established application of the political questions doctrine is the federal courts' unwillingness to enter the fields of international relations, military affairs, and foreign policy making. This unwillingness was demonstrated in 1970 when the Supreme Court dismissed a suit challenging the constitutionality of the Vietnam War.[9] It was also invoked in 1982 when a federal district judge in Washington, D.C., dismissed a suit brought by members of Congress challenging President Reagan's decision to supply military aid to the government of El Salvador.[10]

In December 2000, some observers thought the Supreme Court would dismiss *Bush v. Gore* on the basis of the political questions doctrine. That expectation proved to be wrong, of course. Although the issues posed in that sensational case were as politically charged as legal issues can be, they were really not the types of issues the modern court has avoided through the political questions doctrine. Since the early 1960s, the Supreme Court has shown a willingness to enter the "political thicket" of campaigns, elections, and voting systems. Most accept the Court's role in policing the democratic process, but certainly many people (especially Democrats) were shocked and dismayed by the Court's closely divided decision in *Bush v. Gore.* Harvard law professor Alan Dershowitz went so far as to accuse the Court of hijacking the election.[11] According to Vincent Bugliosi, "the Court committed the unpardonable sin of being a knowing surrogate for the Republican Party instead of being an impartial arbiter of the law."[12]

Popular Culture and American Politics
Philadelphia

By Chapman Rackaway

In 1994, AIDS was a subject that still brought up significant controversy. Many still believed AIDS to be a disease only associated with drug addicts and homosexuals. Director Jonathan Demme wanted to tell a different AIDS story, and he succeeded with the movie *Philadelphia*. Demme's own life was partly the inspiration for *Philadelphia*: Demme's friend Juan Botas discovered he was HIV positive and that led Demme to research the AIDS epidemic and the way it affected people on the job. Demme was most interested in stories like Clarence B. Cain's. Cain, an associate in a Philadelphia law firm, was fired two weeks after telling his superiors about his HIV. Cain took his case to a federal court and won a settlement of $157,000. As society's attitudes about AIDS were changing, Demme was making his movie. *Philadelphia* would manage to change the American dialogue about AIDS.

In the movie, Tom Hanks plays a Philadelphia-based lawyer named Andrew Beckett. Beckett is a closeted gay man who has tried to hide his homosexuality from his conservative bosses. Hanks' character contracts AIDS, which compounds the trouble he has in trying to keep his secret. Beckett's bosses fire him, and he then takes the case to court. To make the parable about homosexuality sharper, Beckett's lawyer (played by Denzel Washington) has fears about AIDS and is himself a homophobe. Washington's character, Joe Miller, has to overcome his fears and preconceived notions to adequately defend Beckett and have his job restored.

Philadelphia won two Academy Awards, a testament to making a powerful movie that never preaches but sensitively shows the intricacies of a subject that produces significant controversy. Ironically, the movie based on a court case was itself later the subject of a legal fight. Geoffrey Bowers was an attorney at the world's largest law firm and lost his job after revealing he had AIDS. Bowers' family later sued Demme and distributor Tri-Star pictures, claiming that *Philadelphia* was based on Bowers' life, and therefore they were owed royalties. Tri-Star settled as the case went on, admitting that Bowers' story was a partial inspiration for the movie.

The Importance of Precedent   As you have seen, a number of important doctrines limit access to judicial decision making, chief among them standing and political questions. Likewise, a number of important doctrines apply when a federal court has reached "the merits" of a case (the substantive legal question to be resolved) and has to render an interpretation of the law. Most fundamental is the **doctrine of** *stare decisis* ("stand by decided matters"), which refers to the fact that American courts rely heavily on precedent. A longstanding tradition in American courts of law stipulates that they should follow precedent whenever possible, thus maintaining stability and continuity in the law. Justice Louis Brandeis once remarked, "*Stare decisis* is usually the wise policy, because in most matters it is more important that the applicable rule of law be settled than that it be settled right."[13]

Devotion to precedent is considered a hallmark of American law. Obviously, following precedent limits a judge's ability to determine the outcome of a case in the way that she might choose if it were a matter of first impression (a case in which an issue arises for the first time; thus, there is no precedent to follow). Although the doctrine of *stare decisis* applies to constitutional and statutory interpretation, numerous examples exist of the Supreme Court departing from precedent in constitutional matters. Perhaps the most famous **reversal** is *Brown v. Board of Education* (1954), in which the Supreme Court repudiated the "separate but equal" doctrine of *Plessy v. Ferguson* (1896). The separate but equal doctrine had legitimated racial segregation in this country for nearly six decades. Beginning with the *Brown* decision, official segregation was abolished as a denial of the equal protection of the laws required by the Fourteenth Amendment.

▶ *stare decisis*, **doctrine of** Literally, "to stand by decided matters." The legal principle which holds that past decisions should stand as precedents for future decisions.

▶ **reversal**   A higher court's decision to overturn the decision of a lower court.

14-2 The Federal Court System

Article III of the Constitution provides that "[t]he judicial Power of the United States, shall be vested in one supreme Court, and in such inferior Courts as the Congress may from time to time ordain and establish." Thus, Congress was given the power to create and, to some extent, control the federal court system (see Figure 14-1). When the First Congress convened in early 1789, its first order of business was the creation of a federal judiciary. Not all members of Congress saw the need for lower federal courts, however. Some preferred that state courts, which had existed since the American Revolution, be given the power to decide federal cases. But the advocates of a federal court system prevailed, and the Judiciary Act of 1789 became law. The Judiciary Act laid the foundation for the contemporary federal court system.

14-2a The Supreme Court

Although Article III provided for the Supreme Court, it was not officially established until the adoption of the Judiciary Act. The act provided for a Court composed of a chief justice and five associate justices. The Supreme Court was given the authority to hear certain appeals brought from the lower federal courts and the state courts. The Court was also given the power to issue various kinds of orders, or **writs,** to enforce its decisions. But the Court's powers remained somewhat vague, and its role in the governmental system was unclear. Like many aspects of the new Constitution, the role and powers of the Court had to be worked out in practice.

> **writs** Court orders requiring or prohibiting the performance of some specific action.

14-2b The United States District Courts

At the base of the hierarchy created by the Judiciary Act of 1789 were the district courts, which were given limited jurisdiction. The Judiciary Act established thirteen district courts, one for each of the eleven states then in the Union and one each for the parts of Massachusetts and Virginia that were later to become the states of Maine and Kentucky, respectively. Above the district courts were the circuit courts, which were given broader jurisdiction, including the authority to hear suits between citizens of different states. The circuit courts were not staffed by their own judges. Rather, judges of the district courts sat alongside Supreme Court justices, who were required to "ride circuit." Given the difficulty of travel in late eighteenth-century America, it is not surprising that Supreme Court justices regarded their circuit-riding duties as onerous. Eventually, Congress responded to their complaints, reduced the justices' circuit-riding responsibilities, and staffed the circuits with their own judges. In 1911, the circuit courts were abolished; their responsibilities were transferred to the district courts.

Figure 14-1
The Federal Court System

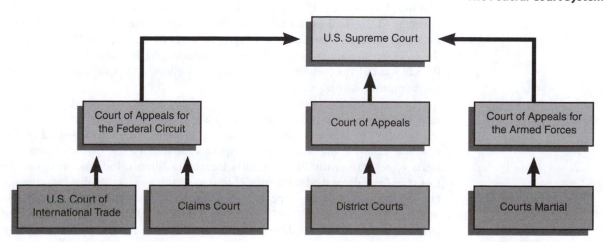

Figure 14-2
Growth in the Federal Caseload, Cases Filed in U.S. District Courts, 1950–2002

Source: Adapted from the Administrative Office of the United States Courts.

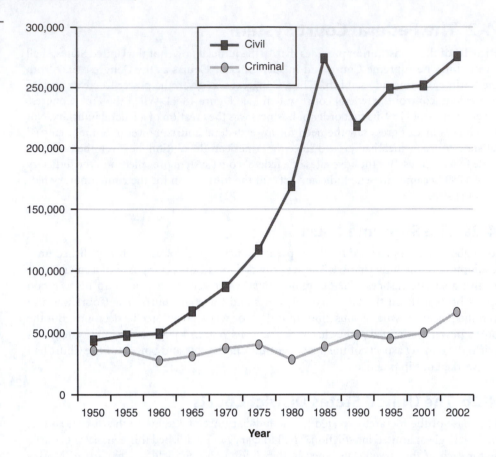

The district courts remain the major trial courts in the federal system. Their principal task is to conduct trials and hearings in civil and criminal cases arising under federal law. Normally, one federal judge presides at such hearings and trials, although federal law permits certain exceptional cases to be decided by panels of three judges. Ninety-four federal judicial districts now exist, with each state allocated at least one. About a third of the states, mainly in the West, have only one district. Most states have two districts. Some—including Tennessee, Florida, Georgia, Illinois, and North Carolina—have three. California, New York, and Texas are the only states with four federal judicial districts. The district courts' caseload has expanded dramatically in recent decades, especially in the filing of civil cases (see Figure 14-2).

14-2c The United States Courts of Appeals

The Judiciary Act of 1789 authorized the party who lost at trial to appeal the ruling to the Supreme Court. As the caseload of the federal courts proliferated, the Supreme Court was unable to handle the number of routine appeals it was receiving. In 1891, Congress created the U.S. courts of appeals to handle routine federal appeals. Not only did this action reduce the caseload of the Supreme Court, but it also allowed the Court to concentrate on the more important cases.

Like the district courts, the U.S. courts of appeals are organized geographically. The nation is divided into twelve circuits, with a number of federal judicial districts comprising each circuit. Each court of appeals hears appeals from the federal districts within its circuit. For example, the U.S. Court of Appeals for the Seventh Circuit, based in Chicago, hears appeals from the district courts located in Illinois, Indiana, and Wisconsin. The Court of Appeals for the District of Columbia Circuit, based in Washington, has the important function of hearing appeals from numerous quasi-judicial bodies in the federal bureaucracy (see Chapter 15, "The Federal Bureaucracy"). A federal circuit court, not to be confused with the D.C. circuit court, hears appeals from certain specialized courts.

Appeals in the circuit courts are normally decided by rotating panels of three judges, although under exceptional circumstances these courts decide cases *en banc,* meaning that all judges assigned to the court participate in the decision. On average, twelve judges are assigned to each circuit, although the number varies according to caseload.

14-2d Specialized Federal Tribunals

As federal law has become more complex, Congress has over the years provided for a number of specialized courts. The U.S. Claims Court is responsible for adjudicating civil suits for damages brought against the federal government. The U.S. Court of International Trade adjudicates controversies between the federal government and importers of foreign goods. Finally, the Tax Court performs the important function of interpreting the complex federal tax laws and deciding who prevails in disputes between citizens or corporations and the Internal Revenue Service. Appeals from the Claims Court, the Court of International Trade, and the Tax Court are directed to the Court of Appeals for the Federal Circuit, which represents the thirteenth federal circuit court (again, not to be confused with the D.C. circuit court).

Under the Uniform Code of Military Justice, crimes committed by persons in military service are prosecuted before courts-martial. In 1950, Congress created a civilian court, the U.S. Court of Military Appeals, to review criminal convictions rendered by **courts-martial.** In 1994, Congress changed the name of the court to the Court of Appeals for the Armed Forces. Cases before this tribunal are decided by a panel of five judges.

> **courts-martial** Military courts established to conduct trials of persons in military service alleged to have committed crimes.

14-2e Appointment of Federal Judges

All federal judges, including Supreme Court justices, are appointed by the president, with the consent of the Senate, to life terms. The grant of life tenure was intended to make the federal courts independent of partisan forces and public passions so that they could dispense justice impartially according to the law. There is no question that life tenure has the effect of insulating the federal judiciary from political pressures. In the view of many lawyers and litigants who have dealt with the federal courts, life tenure also allows some judges to become haughty, arrogant, and even authoritarian. Yet a strong consensus remains that the Framers' plan for a life-tenured judiciary still makes good sense. In any event, no serious public support exists for changing the system.

Presidential Nomination of Judicial Candidates   The fact that federal judges are life-tenured makes a president's judicial appointments extremely crucial. Yet, given the numbers of federal judges to be appointed in a typical term, presidents have to rely heavily on others to locate nominees. Lower federal court appointments are heavily influenced by patronage, although ideology and, increasingly, race and gender considerations play a role in the selection process. Under the custom known as **senatorial courtesy,** senators from the president's party have traditionally exercised significant influence in the selection of judges for the district courts within their states. Senatorial courtesy has been less important in the nomination of individuals to the courts of appeals and almost irrelevant in the selection of Supreme Court nominees.

> **senatorial courtesy** The tradition of allowing senators from the president's party to exercise significant influence in the selection of judges for the district courts located within their states.

Recent presidents have moved away from reliance on home-state senators and increasingly turned to the Justice department for help in identifying nominees. This change has been coincident with an increased emphasis on the ideology of nominees, as against treating judgeships solely as patronage. Another factor that has lessened the influence of the Senate in the selection process is the concern for increasing the diversity of the federal bench, which, until recently, has been the exclusive preserve of white males. There is reason to believe that allowing senators to pick nominees has helped to maintain the "good old boy network" and undermine efforts to increase the ethnic, racial, and sexual diversity of the judiciary. Although Presidents Carter, George Bush (the elder), and Clinton made clear that they wanted to appoint more women and members of minority groups to the courts (see Figure 14-3), some women's and minority groups have been dissatisfied with the pace of change.[14]

Figure 14-3
Number of Women and Minorities Appointed to Federal Judgeships: Presidents Johnson through Clinton

Source: Adapted from Stanley, Harold W., and Richard G. Niemi, *Vital Statistics on American Politics 2003–2004* (Washington, D.C.: CQ Press, 2003), pp. 281–83.

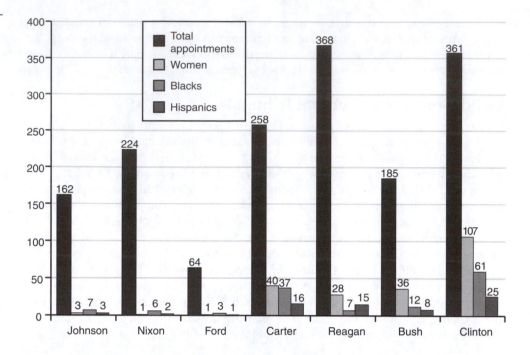

The Senate Confirmation Process

Under the Constitution, the Senate must give its "advice and consent" to presidential nominations to the federal courts. The confirmation process begins in the Senate Judiciary Committee, which conducts a background investigation and then holds a public hearing on the nomination. During the hearing, the nominee appears before the committee to answer questions. Other individuals, often representing interest groups with a perceived stake in the appointment, testify in favor of or in opposition to confirmation. At the conclusion of the hearing, the Judiciary Committee votes on a recommendation to the full Senate. The Senate almost always follows the committee's recommendation.

The Bork Controversy

On July 1, 1987, President Ronald Reagan touched off a national debate by nominating the federal appeals court judge Robert H. Bork to succeed Justice Lewis Powell on the Supreme Court. With Powell's departure, the Supreme Court appeared to be evenly split between liberal and conservative blocs. One vote would be enough, or so it was widely believed, to tip the balance one way or another in any given case. Liberals feared, rightly or wrongly, that Bork, a judicial conservative, would create a conservative majority on the Supreme Court. Unfortunately for President Reagan and his nominee, the Democratic party had regained control of the Senate in the 1986 midterm elections. What transpired was a battle between Senate Democrats and the Reagan administration over the future direction of the Supreme Court.

A long parade of interest groups lined up to testify for and against Bork in the Senate Judiciary Committee. Liberal groups—including feminists, abortion rights activists, environmentalists, civil libertarians, and labor unions—united to wage an extremely effective lobbying and media campaign against Judge Bork. They painted him as a reactionary who, if confirmed, would work to strip Americans of their constitutional rights. Conservative groups, somewhat on the defensive, argued that Bork would help restore the proper balance to government by acting on the premise that in a democracy, legislators—not judges—should make policy. The highlight of the hearings was the testimony of Bork himself, who obliged the committee with detailed discussions of his views on constitutional interpretation. As the hearing continued over twelve days, public opinion began to shift against Bork. The Senate Judiciary Committee narrowly recommended rejection of the nomination, and the full Senate followed suit. The vote on the Senate floor was 58–42, the largest margin by which a Supreme Court nominee has ever been rejected by the Senate.

Profiles & Perspectives

Justice Ruth Bader Ginsburg (1933–)

Collection, The Supreme Court Historical Society / Photographed by Robin Reid, Reid Photography.

Ruth Bader Ginsburg was born in New York City in 1933. She graduated from Cornell University in 1954 and received her law degree from Columbia University in 1959. Ginsburg began her legal career as a clerk (staff attorney) for U.S. District Court Judge Edmund Palmieri. In 1963, she became a professor in the law school at Rutgers. In 1972, Ginsburg joined the law faculty at her alma mater. As counsel for the American Civil Liberties Union in the 1970s, Ginsburg argued and won a number of important women's rights cases before the Supreme Court. Collectively, these cases dramatically changed the law regarding sex discrimination.

In 1980, President Jimmy Carter appointed Ginsburg to the U.S. Court of Appeals for the District of Columbia, perhaps the most important federal judicial position short of the Supreme Court. As an appeals court judge, Ginsburg developed a reputation as a fair-minded jurist who analyzed cases thoughtfully and thoroughly. President Bill Clinton's choice of Ginsburg to succeed Justice Byron White on the Supreme Court in 1993 was well received by the press, the legal community, most interest groups, and, most importantly, the Senate.

In her most important opinion to date, *United States v. Virginia* (1996), Justice Ginsburg explained why the Supreme Court struck down the Virginia Military Institute's policy of refusing to admit women:

> VMI ... offers an educational opportunity no other Virginia institution provides, and the school's "prestige"—associated with its success in developing "citizen–soldiers"—is unequaled. Virginia has closed this facility to its daughters and, instead, has devised for them a "parallel program," with a faculty less impressively credentialed and less well paid, more limited course offerings, fewer opportunities for military training and for scientific specialization. VMI, beyond question, "possesses to a far greater degree" ... "those qualities which are incapable of objective measurement but which make for greatness in a ... school," including "position and influence of the alumni, standing in the community, traditions and prestige." Women seeking and fit for a VMI-quality education cannot be offered anything less, under the State's obligation to afford them genuinely equal protection.

For more information on Ruth Bader Ginsburg:

The Supreme Court: http://www.supremecourtus.gov/
Supreme Court biography: http://www.supremecourthistory.org/justice/ginsburg.htm

The Clarence Thomas Ordeal   In one of the most bizarre spectacles ever seen in American politics, President George Bush's nomination of Judge Clarence Thomas to the Supreme Court in 1991 was nearly derailed by allegations of sexual harassment. The law professor Anita Hill appeared before the Senate Judiciary Committee to testify that Thomas had sexually harassed her when they worked together at the Equal Employment Opportunity Commission in the early 1980s. The nation watched on live television as Hill detailed her charges and Thomas vehemently denied each one. Ultimately, the Judiciary Committee passed the nomination to the Senate without recommendation. The Senate approved Thomas by the vote of 52–48, one of the closest judicial confirmation votes in history.

President Clinton's Supreme Court Nominations   When Justice Byron R. White retired in 1993, President Bill Clinton was given an opportunity that Democratic presidents had not had since Lyndon Johnson nominated Thurgood Marshall to the Court in 1967. After a three-month-long search for a candidate, Clinton settled on the federal appeals court judge Ruth Bader Ginsburg. Ginsburg, who became famous arguing women's rights cases before the Supreme Court in the 1970s, easily won confirmation by the Senate.[15] In her first decade on the Court, Ginsburg firmly positioned herself within the Court's liberal bloc.

President Clinton's second and final opportunity to shape the Supreme Court came in 1994 when Justice Harry Blackmun retired. Clinton again chose to elevate a federal appeals court judge, selecting Judge Stephen G. Breyer. Like Ginsburg, Breyer easily won Senate confirmation[16] and joined the liberal wing of the Court.

Presidential Predictions of Judicial Behavior   Presidents have no way to predict with certainty what their judicial nominees will do after they have been confirmed.

What Americans Think About

The U.S. Supreme Court

Surveys conducted by the Gallup Organization suggest that Americans' confidence in the Supreme Court was highest during the late 1980s, ebbed in the early 1990s, and then rebounded somewhat in the late 1990s.

Percentage Expressing "A Great Deal" or "Quite a Lot" of Confidence in the Court

May 1973	44	March 1991	48
May 1975	49	March 1993	44
January 1977	46	March 1994	42
April 1979	45	April 1995	44
November 1981	46	May 1996	45
August 1983	42	July 1997	50
October 1984	51	June 1998	50
May 1985	56	June 1999	49
July 1986	54	June 2000	47
July 1987	52	June 2001	50
September 1988	56	June 2002	50
September 1989	46	June 2003	47
August 1990	47		

Source: Adapted from the Gallup Organization.

Although most judges perform more or less as expected, presidents are not always happy with their judicial appointments. Dwight D. Eisenhower once remarked that his nomination of Earl Warren to become Chief Justice in 1953 was "the biggest damn fool mistake I ever made." Eisenhower was reacting to the liberalism of the Warren Court as manifested in cases like *Brown v. Board of Education* (1954). As a moderate conservative, Eisenhower found himself at odds with many of the Warren Court's rulings.

14-2f Impeachment of Federal Judges

The only means of removing a federal judge or Supreme Court justice is through the impeachment process provided in the Constitution. First, the House of Representatives must approve one or more articles of impeachment by at least a majority vote. Then, a trial is held in the Senate. To be removed from office, a judge must be convicted by a vote of at least two-thirds of the Senate.

Since 1789, the House of Representatives has initiated impeachment proceedings against fewer than twenty federal judges, and fewer than ten of them have been convicted in the Senate. Only once has a Supreme Court Justice been impeached by the House. In 1804, Justice Samuel Chase fell victim to President Jefferson's attempt to control a federal judiciary largely composed of Washington and Adams appointees. Justice Chase had irritated the Jeffersonians by his haughty and arrogant personality and his extreme partisanship. Nevertheless, no evidence existed that he was guilty of any crime. Consequently, Chase narrowly escaped conviction in the Senate.

The Chase affair set an important precedent: A federal judge may not be removed simply for reasons of partisanship, ideology, or personality. Thus, despite strong support in ultraconservative quarters for the impeachment of Chief Justice Earl Warren during the

1960s, there was never any real prospect of Warren's removal. Barring criminal conduct or serious breaches of judicial ethics, federal judges do not have to worry that their decisions might cost them their jobs.

14-3 The Supreme Court and Public Policy: A Brief History

The Supreme Court is now the most visible and prestigious court of law in the United States—indeed, in the entire world. Many of its decisions have an enormous effect on public policy and, ultimately, on the daily lives of Americans. That was not always the case, however. The Court began as a vaguely conceived tribunal, with no cases to decide and no permanent home. Over the years, as the Court's caseload increased, so did its prominence and prestige. Eventually, the Court found a home in the Capitol, although its chambers were less than spectacular. In 1935, the Court moved into its own building, the majestic marble structure across the street from the Capitol. In this "marble temple," the Court hears arguments, holds conferences, and renders decisions on important matters, all the while shielded from the glare of television lights, the stress of press conferences, and the demands of lobbyists.

The first chief justice of the United States was John Jay, a former chief justice of the New York state supreme court and the author of several of *The Federalist Papers*. During Jay's tenure as chief justice, the Court decided few important cases and enjoyed little prestige. The one truly important decision of the Jay Court, *Chisholm v. Georgia* (1793), was overruled by the adoption of the Eleventh Amendment to the Constitution.[17] Somewhat disgusted, Jay resigned from the Court in 1795. When President John Adams asked Jay to resume his duties as chief justice in 1800, Jay refused, saying that the Court lacked "energy, weight, and dignity."[18]

14-3a The Marshall Court

When John Adams could not get John Jay to resume the chief justiceship, he turned to his secretary of state, John Marshall. Marshall became chief justice in 1801 and held the position until his retirement in 1835. No other individual has had more of an effect on the Supreme Court than Marshall. Under his leadership—indeed, dominance—the Court established its credibility and prestige. Moreover, the Marshall Court set many of the basic precedents of American constitutional law in decisions that still affect the outcome of litigation.

As we noted in section 14-1a, "The Power 'To Say What the Law Is,'" the Supreme Court assumed the power of judicial review in the landmark case of *Marbury v. Madison* in 1803. The *Marbury* decision was the only instance in which the Court under Chief Justice Marshall used its power of judicial review to strike down an act of Congress. The Marshall Court did, however, use its power of judicial review to strike down a number of state laws in some important cases. Perhaps the most important of these was *McCulloch v. Maryland* (1819), in which the Court invalidated an attempt by a state to tax a branch of the Bank of the United States.[19] Nearly as important was *Gibbons v. Ogden* (1824), in which the Court struck down a New York law granting a monopoly to a steamboat company in violation of a federal law granting a license to another company.[20] The decisions in *McCulloch* and *Gibbons* were not only important as assertions of power by the Supreme Court, but were also instrumental in enlarging the powers of Congress vis-à-vis the states. In addition to asserting the power to invalidate state laws, the Marshall Court established its authority to overrule decisions of the highest state appellate courts on questions of federal law, both constitutional and statutory. Thus, under Marshall's leadership, the Supreme Court asserted, expanded, extended, and consolidated its power.

14-3b The Civil War Era

Under John Marshall's successor, Chief Justice Roger B. Taney, the Court damaged its credibility and prestige by an unwise use of judicial review. It occurred in the infamous Dred Scott decision of 1857, the first case since *Marbury v. Madison* in which the Court struck down an act of Congress.[21] In 1820, in an attempt to solve the slavery issue, Congress had adopted the Missouri Compromise, which admitted Missouri to the Union as a *slave state* (one in which slavery would be legal), but prohibited slavery in the western territories north of thirty-six degrees, thirty minutes latitude. In *Dred Scott*, the Supreme Court ruled that the Missouri Compromise arbitrarily deprived slave holders of their property rights and therefore violated the provision of the Fifth Amendment that prohibits government from depriving persons of property without "due process of law." Moreover, the Court held that Congress lacked any power to regulate slavery. This bold exercise of judicial review, well received in the South but roundly condemned in the North, probably hastened the start of the Civil War. In any event, the decision was rendered null and void by the adoption of the Thirteenth and Fourteenth Amendments to the Constitution after the Civil War.

14-3c The Age of Conservative Activism

Judicial review again became a subject of political controversy in the late nineteenth and early twentieth centuries as the Supreme Court exercised its power to limit government activity in the economic realm. During this age of conservative activism (1890–1937), the Court often interpreted the Constitution as prohibiting the governmental regulation of business and other types of progressive reform. For example, in 1895, the Court gutted the Sherman Anti-Trust Act, which Congress had passed in 1890 to curtail industrial monopolies.[22] That same year, the Court struck down a new federal tax on the incomes of the wealthiest Americans, evidently viewing the tax as a manifestation of socialism.[23] The best-known decision of the period is *Lochner v. New York* (1905), in which the Supreme Court struck down a state law regulating working hours in bakeries.[24]

Throughout the early twentieth century, the Supreme Court continued to use its power of judicial review to frustrate state and federal attempts at economic regulation. In 1918, for example, the Court struck down an act of Congress that sought to discourage the industrial exploitation of child labor.[25] In another notable decision in 1923, the Court invoked the "freedom of contract" doctrine it had developed in *Lochner v. New York* and similar cases to invalidate a law authorizing a minimum wage for women and children working in the District of Columbia.[26] This tendency to insulate *laissez-faire* capitalism from government intervention brought the Supreme Court, and its power of judicial review, under an increasing barrage of criticism from populists and progressives.

14-3d The Constitutional Battle over the New Deal

The age of conservative activism entered its final phase in a constitutional showdown between the Supreme Court on one side and Congress and the president on the other. In 1932, in the depths of the Great Depression, Franklin D. Roosevelt was elected president in a landslide over the Republican incumbent, Herbert Hoover. Roosevelt promised the American people a "new deal" from the federal government. A bold departure from the traditional theory of *laissez-faire* capitalism, the New Deal greatly expanded the role of the federal government in the economic life of the nation. Inevitably, the New Deal faced a serious challenge in the Supreme Court, which in the 1930s was still dominated by justices with conservative views on economic matters.

The first New Deal program to be struck down was the National Recovery Administration (NRA). The NRA, the centerpiece of the New Deal, was a powerful government agency with the authority to regulate wages and prices in major industries. In 1935, the Supreme Court held that in passing the act that created the NRA, Congress had gone too far in delegating legislative power to the executive branch.[27] Between 1935 and 1937, the Court declared a host of other New Deal programs unconstitutional.

President Roosevelt responded to the adverse judicial decisions by trying to "pack" the Court with new appointees. Although the infamous Court-packing plan ultimately failed to win approval in Congress, the Supreme Court may have gotten the message. In an abrupt turnabout, the Court approved a key New Deal measure. In 1937, the Court upheld the controversial Wagner Act, which guaranteed industrial workers the right to unionize and bargain collectively with management.[28] The Court's sudden turnabout was the beginning of a constitutional revolution. For decades to come, the Court would no longer interpret the Constitution as a barrier to social and economic legislation. In the late 1930s and 1940s, the Court permitted Congress to enact sweeping legislation affecting labor relations, agricultural production, and social welfare. The Court exercised similar restraint with respect to state laws regulating economic activity.

14-3e The Warren Court

The modern Supreme Court's restraint in the area of economic regulation was counterbalanced by a heightened concern for civil rights and liberties (see Case in Point 14-2). This was especially the case under the leadership of Earl Warren, who served as chief justice from 1953 to 1969. The Warren Court had an enormous effect on civil rights and liberties. Its most notable decision was *Brown v. Board of Education* (1954), in which the Court declared racially segregated public schools unconstitutional.[29] In *Brown* and numerous other decisions, the Warren Court expressed its commitment to ending discrimination against blacks and other minority groups.

The Warren Court used its power of judicial review liberally to expand the rights of not only racial minorities but also persons accused of crimes, members of extremist political groups, and the poor. Moreover, the Court revolutionized American politics by entering the "political thicket" of legislative reapportionment in *Baker v. Carr* (1962) and subsequent cases.[30] In what proved to be the least popular of its many controversial decisions, the Warren Court rendered a series of rulings striking down prayer and Bible-reading exercises in the public schools as a violation of the First Amendment requirement of separation of church and state.[31] Without question, the Warren era represents the most significant period in the Supreme Court's history since the clash over the New Deal in the 1930s. The Warren Court has been praised as heroic and idealistic; it has also been denounced as lawless and accused of "moral imperialism."

Case in Point **14-2**

Miranda v. Arizona (1966): A Symbol of the Warren Court's Revolution in Criminal Justice

Police arrested Ernesto Miranda, a twenty-three-year-old man with a ninth-grade education, and charged him with raping an eighteen-year-old woman. At the police station, the victim picked Miranda out of a lineup. Two officers then took Miranda to a room where they interrogated him. After first denying his guilt, Miranda eventually confessed to the crime. Following his conviction, Miranda appealed on the ground that his confession had been coerced.

The Supreme Court granted a review, consolidating Miranda's appeal with three other cases involving the admissibility of confessions. The Court reversed Miranda's conviction, holding that his confession had been improperly admitted into evidence. The Court held that, henceforth, police must advise suspects of their right to remain silent and their right to have counsel present during interrogation. Failure to provide these warnings will result in the suppression of a confession, even if it is deemed reliable. These new requirements were based on the Court's conclusion that "without proper safeguards the process of in-custody interrogation . . . contains inherently compelling pressures which work to undermine the individual's will to resist and to compel him to speak where he would not otherwise do so freely." In a bitter dissent, Justice Byron White complained that "[i]n some unknown number of cases the Court's rule will return a killer, a rapist or other criminal to the streets . . . to repeat his crime whenever it pleases him."

The Miranda decision became a hallmark of the Warren Court's concern for the rights of criminal suspects and a focal point for criticism of the Court by advocates of law and order. Some observers expected that the more conservative Supreme Court under Chief Justice Rehnquist would overturn the *Miranda* decision if given the opportunity. But in *Dickerson v. United States* (2000), the Supreme Court reaffirmed its landmark *Miranda* decision. Writing for the Court, Chief Justice Rehnquist observed: "Whether or not we would agree with Miranda's reasoning and its resulting rule, were we addressing the issue in the first instance, the principles of *stare decisis* weigh heavily against overruling it now." Evidently, the *Miranda* decision is here to stay.

14-3f The Burger Court

President Nixon's appointment of Chief Justice Warren E. Burger and three associate justices had the effect of tempering the liberal activism of the Warren Court. In numerous cases, the Burger Court limited the decisions of the Warren Court, especially in the criminal justice area. Yet, despite the predictions of some critics, the Burger Court did not stage a counterrevolution in American law. Indeed, it was the Burger Court that handed down the blockbuster decision in *Roe v. Wade* (1973), effectively legalizing abortion throughout the United States. Even Chief Justice Burger, who was clearly much more conservative than his predecessor Earl Warren, concurred in *Roe v. Wade*. Moreover, in a series of decisions beginning with the landmark *Bakke* case of 1978, the Burger Court gave its approval to affirmative action programs to remedy discrimination against minorities. Support for affirmative action is hardly indicative of a reactionary court.

14-3g The Rehnquist Court

In the 1980s, the Supreme Court became increasingly conservative as older members retired and were replaced by justices appointed by Presidents Reagan and George Bush (the elder). In 1986, Associate Justice William Rehnquist was elevated to Chief Justice when Warren E. Burger retired. The Rehnquist Court continued the Burger Court's movement to the right, although it did not dismantle most of what was accomplished by the Warren Court in the realm of civil rights and liberties. Indeed, the Court's 5–4 decision in *Texas v. Johnson* (1989), in which the Court struck down a state law making it a crime to burn the American flag, was surprisingly reminiscent of the Warren era.[32] With the retirements of Justices William Brennan and Thurgood Marshall, both of whom were members of the majority in *Texas v. Johnson,* the Rehnquist Court moved further away from the civil liberties commitments of the Warren Court. During the 1990s, the Court's most important effect was in limiting the powers of the national government vis-à-vis the states.[33]

One "Court watcher" observed that the Rehnquist Court was "the most conservative Supreme Court since before the New Deal."[34] This may well have been the case, yet it was a Court that rendered liberal decisions with some regularity, due largely to the moderate orientations of Justices Sandra Day O'Connor and Anthony Kennedy. Not only did these justices prevent the Court from overruling *Roe v. Wade*,[35] they provided crucial votes in cases upholding "gay rights,"[36] maintaining a strict separation of church and state,[37] and recognizing the rights of detainees in the war on terrorism.[38] The Rehnquist Court was indeed a conservative Court, but not nearly as conservative as it might be but for President Clinton's two appointments (Ginsburg and Breyer) and the fact that two of three of President Reagan's appointees (O'Connor and Kennedy) turned out to be less conservative than many expected.

After the Rehnquist Court? Going into the 2004 presidential election, most observers believed that whoever won would likely appoint one or two new members to the Court. For some voters, the future direction of the Court was an important consideration in deciding between candidates Kerry and Bush. Indeed, within days after the 2004 election, the Court announced that Chief Justice Rehnquist was undergoing treatment for thyroid cancer. Immediately, commentators began to speculate as to whom President George W. Bush would nominate to replace Rehnquist. Would he seek to elevate Justice Scalia or Justice Thomas and thereby create a conflict with the Democrats in the Senate? Or would he choose a more moderate current justice such as Anthony Kennedy? And whom would President Bush nominate to fill the vacancy created if Scalia, Thomas, or Kennedy were elevated to Chief Justice? Would he seek a clearly conservative nominee, as his supporters on the right would prefer? Or would he adopt a more moderate course in the hopes of avoiding a contentious fight with the Democrats?

In June 2005, as the Supreme Court ended its 2004 term, Court watchers were surprised when Chief Justice Rehnquist announced his intention to remain on the court despite his ill health. They were further surprised when Justice Sandra Day O'Connor announced her retirement. Within weeks, President Bush nominated conservative D.C. Appeals Court Judge

John Roberts to succeed O'Connor. But just as the Senate confirmation hearings were set to begin in early September, Chief Justice Rehnquist died. President Bush decided to nominate Judge Roberts to the Chiefjusticeship and promised to name a successor to Justice O'Connor within a very short time. With two nominations to the Supreme Court pending, the Senate braced for a tough partisan battle over the future direction of the Supreme Court.

14-4 Supreme Court Decision Making

The Supreme Court's first session was held in February 1790. It had no cases on the docket and adjourned after ten days. During its first decade (1790–1801), the Court met twice a year for brief terms beginning in February and August. Over the years, the Court's annual sessions have expanded along with its workload and its role in the political and legal system. Since 1917, the Court's annual term has begun on the "first Monday of October." Until 1979, the Court adjourned for the summer, necessitating special sessions to handle urgent cases arising in July, August, or September. Since 1979, however, the Court has stayed in continuous session throughout the year, merely declaring a recess for a summer vacation. Still, the Court observes an annual term beginning on the first Monday of October.

The Constitution permits Congress to decide how many justices will serve on the Court. Initially, Congress set the number at six, but in 1807 the Court was expanded to include seven justices. In 1837, Congress increased the number of justices to nine. During the Civil War, the number of justices was increased to ten. Since 1869, the membership of the Court has remained constant at nine.

14-4a The Court's Internal Procedures

The overwhelming majority of cases the Supreme Court hears come by way of writs of **certiorari** (pronounced "SIR-she-o-rary"), which the Court grants at its discretion. The losing party in a lower court may apply for a writ of certiorari from the Supreme Court as long as the case involves a substantial federal question and the party seeking review has exhausted all other avenues of appeal.

> **certiorari** Literally, "to be informed." An order from a higher court to a lower court to send up the record in a particular case so that it may be reviewed.

Granting Certiorari   A grant of certiorari from the Court requires the affirmative vote of at least four justices, the so-called **rule of four.** Getting four justices to agree to review a case is not easy. Each justice is entitled to evaluate a petition for certiorari according to his or her own criteria. However, most justices would seem to follow the criteria enumerated by Justice Sandra Day O'Connor, who has indicated that she considers "the importance of the issue, how likely it is to recur in various courts around the country, and the extent to which other courts considering the issue have reached conflicting holdings on it."[39]

> **rule of four**   The requirement that at least four justices of the Supreme Court agree before the Court will grant certiorari in a given case.

The chances of the Supreme Court granting certiorari in a given case are slim. The odds are somewhat improved if the case originated in a federal court. The chances are even better if the party seeking review is the federal government. Of the more than 7,500 petitions for certiorari coming to it each year, the Court normally grants review in only a couple hundred. In an average term, fewer than one hundred cases are treated as full-opinion decisions. It is difficult to overstate the importance of the fact that the Supreme Court's appellate jurisdiction is almost entirely discretionary. Because the continuous stream of certiorari petitions contains a wide range of policy questions, the Court is able to set its own agenda. Agenda setting is, of course, the first phase in any institutional policy-making process. Figure 14-4 summarizes the Court's decision-making process.

Briefs of Counsel   Parties to cases slated for review are required to submit **briefs,** which are written documents containing legal arguments in support of a party's position. By Supreme Court rule, briefs are limited to fifty pages. In addition to the briefs submitted by the direct parties, the Court may permit outside parties to file *amicus curiae* briefs. Amicus briefs are often filed on behalf of organized groups that have an interest in the outcome of a case. Examples of interest groups that routinely file amicus briefs in the Supreme Court are the American Civil Liberties Union (ACLU), the National Association for the Advancement of Colored People (NAACP), the National Rifle Association (NRA), and the American

> **briefs**   Written documents containing legal arguments in support of a party's position.

Figure 14-4
**Internal Procedures of the
Supreme Court: How a Review
Is Made**

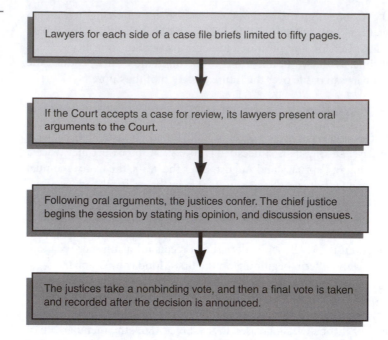

Lawyers for each side of a case file briefs limited to fifty pages.

If the Court accepts a case for review, its lawyers present oral arguments to the Court.

Following oral arguments, the justices confer. The chief justice begins the session by stating his opinion, and discussion ensues.

The justices take a nonbinding vote, and then a final vote is taken and recorded after the decision is announced.

Medical Association (AMA). The federal government often files *amicus* briefs in cases that have national policy significance.

> **oral argument** A public hearing in which lawyers for both parties appear before an appellate court to make verbal presentations and answer questions from the bench.

Oral Argument   After the briefs are submitted, the case is scheduled for **oral argument,** a public hearing where lawyers for both sides appear before the Court to make verbal presentations and, more importantly, answer questions from the bench. The oral argument is the only occasion on which lawyers in a case have any direct contact with the justices. Oral arguments are normally held on Mondays, Tuesdays, and Wednesdays beginning on the first Monday in October and ending in late April. Oral argument on a given case is usually limited to one hour. Four cases are argued before the Court on any given oral argument day. Representatives of interest groups and the media often attend the oral argument, hoping to learn something about the Court's predisposition with respect to the case under consideration or something about the general leanings of the justices, especially the most recent appointees.

Conference   Within days after a case is orally argued, the justices discuss it in private conference. Conferences are usually held on Wednesdays, Thursdays, and Fridays. At conference, the chief justice opens the discussion by reviewing the essential facts of the case at hand, summarizing the history of the case in the lower courts, and stating his view about the correct decision. This practice gives the chief a chance to influence his colleagues, an opportunity that only a few occupants of the office have been able to exploit. It is well known, however, that Chief Justice Charles Evans Hughes was on occasion able to overwhelm other members of the Court with a photographic memory that gave him command over legal and factual details.

After the chief justice has presented the case, associate justices, speaking in order of seniority, present their views of the case and indicate their votes about the proper judgment. This original vote on the merits is not binding, however, and justices have been known to change their votes before the announcement of the decision. The final vote is not recorded until the decision is formally announced.

The Judgment of the Court   In deciding a case that has been fully argued, the Court has several options. First, the Court may decide that it should not have granted review in the first place, whereupon the case is dismissed. Of course, this situation rarely occurs. Alternatively, the Court may instruct the parties to reargue the case, focusing on somewhat different issues; in this case, the matter is likely to be carried over to the next term and final decision delayed for at least a year.

If the Court decides to render judgment, it either will **affirm** (uphold) or **reverses** (overturn) the decision of the lower court. Alternatively, it may modify the lower court's decision in some respect. Reversal or modification of a lower court decision requires a majority vote; a quorum is six justices. A tie vote (in cases in which one or more justices are unable to participate) always results in the affirmance of the decision under review.

Supreme Court Opinions   After a judgment has been reached, it remains for the decision to be explained and justified in a written **opinion** or opinions. In the early days of the Court, opinions were issued *seriatim*—each justice would produce an opinion reflecting his views of the case. John Marshall, who became chief justice in 1801, instituted the practice of issuing an Opinion of the Court, which reflects the views of at least a majority of the justices. The **Opinion of the Court,** referred to as the **majority opinion** when the Court is not unanimous, has the great advantage of providing a coherent statement of the Court's position to the parties, the lower courts, and the larger legal and political communities.

It must be understood, however, that even a unanimous vote in support of a particular judgment does not guarantee that an Opinion of the Court will be issued. Justices can and do differ on the rationales they adopt for voting a particular way. Every justice retains the right to produce an opinion in every case, either for or against the judgment of the Court. A **concurring opinion** is one written in support of the Court's decision; a **dissenting opinion** disagrees with the decision.

Dissenting opinions, although indicative of intellectual conflict on the Court, are important in the development of American law. It is often said that "yesterday's dissent is tomorrow's majority opinion." Although the time lag is much longer than the saying suggests, a number of examples exist of dissents being vindicated by later Court decisions. More frequently, of course, a dissenting vote is merely a defense of a dying position. The modern Supreme Court has seen a dramatic rise in the frequency of dissenting opinions, reflecting both the increased complexity of the law and the demise in consensual norms in the Court itself. The modern Court has become less of a collegial decision-making body and more like "nine separate law firms."

In an effort to obtain a majority opinion, the chief justice, assuming that he is in the majority, either prepares a draft opinion himself or assigns the task to one of his colleagues in the majority. If the chief is in dissent, the responsibility of opinion assignment falls on the senior associate justice in the majority. Sometimes, in a 5–4 decision, a majority opinion may be "rescued" by assigning it to the swing voter, that is, the justice who was most likely to dissent. On the modern Court, the task of writing majority opinions is more or less evenly distributed among the nine justices. However, majority opinions in important decisions are more apt to be authored by the chief justice or a senior member of the Court.

After the opinion has been assigned to one of the justices, work begins on a rough draft. At this stage, the law clerks play an important role by performing legal research and assisting the justice in writing the opinion. When a draft is ready, it is circulated among the justices in the majority for their suggestions and, ultimately, their signatures. A draft opinion that fails to receive the approval of a majority of justices participating in a given decision cannot be characterized as the Opinion of the Court. Accordingly, a draft may be subject to considerable revision before it attains the status of majority opinion.

The Supreme Court announces its major decisions in open court, usually late in the term. A decision is announced by the author of the majority or plurality opinion, who may even read excerpts from that opinion. In important and controversial cases, concurring and dissenting justices also read excerpts from their opinions. When several decisions are to be announced, the justices making the announcements speak in reverse order of their seniority on the Court. After decisions are announced, summaries are released to the media by the Court's public information office. Word of an important Supreme Court decision now often spreads across the nation within minutes of being handed down.

affirm   A higher court's decision to uphold the decision of a lower court.

reversal   A higher court's decision to overturn the decision of a lower court.

opinion   A written statement accompanying a judicial decision, authored by one or more of the judges supporting or dissenting from the decision.

Opinion of the Court   An opinion announcing both the decision of the court and its supporting rationale. The opinion can be either a majority opinion or a unanimous opinion.

majority opinion   An opinion joined by a majority of judges or justices on a collegial court.

concurring opinion   An opinion written by a judge agreeing with the decision of the court, which may or may not agree with the rationale adopted in the majority opinion.

dissenting opinion   An opinion by a judge or justice setting forth reasons for disagreeing with a particular decision of the court.

14-4b Factors That Influence the Court's Decisions

Political scientists who have studied Supreme Court decision making have amassed considerable evidence that the Court's decisions are influenced by the ideologies of the justices. This belief is inferred from regularities in the voting behavior of the justices—mainly, the tendency of certain groups of justices to vote as **blocs.** In the late 1980s, for example, the Court was divided into two opposing ideological camps: a liberal bloc composed of Justices Brennan, Marshall, Blackmun, and Stevens; and a conservative bloc composed of Justices Rehnquist, White, O'Connor, Scalia, and Kennedy. In the early 1990s, the Court became increasingly dominated by justices with conservative ideologies. Perhaps the most significant recent ideological shift on the Court occurred when Justices William Brennan and Thurgood Marshall, both staunch liberals, retired in 1990 and 1991, respectively. Their replacements, David Souter and Clarence Thomas, are considerably more conservative. President Clinton's appointment of Justices Ginsburg and Breyer in 1993 and 1994, respectively, moderated the Court's movement to the right.

Although observers tend to characterize Supreme Court decisions and voting patterns in simplistic liberal-conservative terms, judicial "ideology" may well include more than general political attitudes or views on specific issues of public policy (for example, school prayer or abortion). It may also embrace philosophies regarding the proper role of courts in a democratic society. At least for some justices, considerations of **judicial activism** versus **judicial restraint** may weigh as heavily as policy preferences in determining how the vote will be cast in a given case. Justices inclined toward activism are more likely to support the expansion of the Court's jurisdiction and powers and are more likely to embrace innovative constitutional doctrines. Activists are less likely than restraintists to follow precedent or defer to the judgment of elected officials. Judicial activists also are more prone to see cases in terms of their public policy significance rather than as abstract questions of law.

The Political Environment   In addition to the ideologies of the justices, a number of political factors influence Supreme Court decision making (Table 14-1 provides selected characteristics of the Justices of the Supreme Court). Although the Supreme Court is ostensibly a counter-majoritarian institution, public opinion may occasionally influence the Court. Certainly, ample evidence exists that the actions, or threatened actions, of Congress and the president have an effect on Court decisions. And, in a constitutional system that emphasizes checks and balances, one should not expect that it would be otherwise. The political environment unquestionably imposes constraints on and provides stimuli to, and support for, Supreme Court decision making.

The Internal Politics of the Court   Finally, the Court's decision making is intensely political in the sense that the internal dynamics of the Court are characterized by conflict,

---

blocs   Groups of decision makers in a collegial body who usually vote the same way. In judicial politics, the term refers to groups of judges or justices on appellate courts who usually vote together.

judicial activism   Judicial philosophy that embraces innovative constitutional doctrines and supports the expansion of the Court's jurisdiction and powers.

judicial restraint   Judicial philosophy which holds that judges should exercise power cautiously and show deference to precedent and to the decisions of other branches of government.

T A B L E 14-1						
Selected Characteristics of the Justices of the Supreme Court	**Justice**	**Joined Court**	**Prior Position**	**J.D. Degree From**	**Political Party**	**Appointing President**
	William H. Rehnquist*	1971	Asst. Attorney General	Stanford	Republican	Nixon
	John Paul Stevens	1975	U.S. Court of Appeals	Northwestern	Republican	Ford
	Sandra Day O'Connor	1981	Arizona Court of Appeals	Stanford	Republican	Reagan
	Antonin Scalia	1986	U.S. Court of Appeals	Harvard	Republican	Reagan
	Anthony M. Kennedy	1987	U.S. Court of Appeals	Harvard	Republican	Reagan
	David H. Souter	1990	New Hampshire S.C.	Harvard	Republican	Bush
	Clarence Thomas	1991	U.S. Court of Appeals	Yale	Republican	Bush
	Ruth B. Ginsburg	1993	U.S. Court of Appeals	Columbia	Democrat	Clinton
	Stephen G. Breyer	1994	U.S. Court of Appeals	Harvard	Democrat	Clinton

* Elevated to chief justice in 1986 by President Reagan.

bargaining, and compromise—the essence of politics. These activities are difficult to observe because they occur behind the "purple curtain" that separates the Court from its attentive public. Conferences are held in private, votes on certiorari are not routinely made public, and the justices tend to be tight-lipped about what goes on behind the scenes in the "marble temple." Yet from time to time, evidence of the Court's internal politics appears in the form of memoirs, autobiographies, and other writings of the justices and in the occasional interviews the justices and their clerks give to journalists and academicians.

14-4c Checks on the Supreme Court

The concept of checks and balances is one of the fundamental principles of the U.S. Constitution. Each branch of the national government is provided with specific means of limiting the exercise of power by the other branches. For example, the president may veto acts of Congress, which do not become law unless the veto is overridden by a two-thirds vote in both chambers. Although the federal courts, and the Supreme Court in particular, are often characterized as guardians of the Constitution, the judicial branch is by no means immune to the abuse of power. Accordingly, the federal judiciary is subject to checks and balances imposed by Congress and the president. In a constitutional system that seeks to prevent any agency of government from exercising unchecked power, even the Supreme Court is subject to external limitations.

Constitutional Amendment   By far the most effective means of overruling a Supreme Court or any federal court decision is for Congress to use its power of amendment. If Congress disapproves of a particular judicial decision, it may be able to override that decision through a simple statute, but only if the decision was based on statutory interpretation. In *Grove City College v. Bell* (1984), for example, the Court was called on to interpret Title IX of the Education Amendments of 1972, which prohibited sex discrimination by educational institutions receiving federal funds. In *Grove City,* the Court interpreted Title IX narrowly so as to limit a potential plaintiff's ability to sue a college or university for sex discrimination.[40] Congress disapproved of the Court's interpretation of Title IX and effectively nullified the decision by adopting the Civil Rights Restoration Act of 1988 over President Reagan's veto. Because *Grove City College v. Bell* was based on a statute rather than on the Constitution, Congress could overrule the Court by simply amending the statute.

Congress has much more difficulty in overriding a federal court decision based on the U.S. Constitution. Indeed, Congress alone cannot do so. Ever since *Marbury v. Madison,* the U.S. system of government has conceded to the courts the power to authoritatively interpret the nation's charter. A Supreme Court decision interpreting the Constitution is therefore final unless and until one of two events occurs. First, the Court may overrule itself in a later case, which has happened numerous times. Historically, the most notable example was the repudiation of official racial segregation in *Brown v. Board of Education* (1954). The only other way to overturn a constitutional decision of the Supreme Court is through constitutional amendment. This method is not easily done because Article V of the Constitution prescribes a two-thirds majority in both chambers of Congress followed by ratification by three-fourths of the states. Yet four times in our country's history, specific Supreme Court decisions have been overturned in this manner, beginning with a 1793 decision that was reversed by the adoption of the Eleventh Amendment.[41] The infamous *Dred Scott* decision was overturned by the ratification of the Fourteenth Amendment in 1868. The income tax decision of 1895, alluded to in section 14-3c, "The Age of Conservative Activism," was reversed when the Sixteenth Amendment was ratified in 1913.

The most recent instance of a Supreme Court decision being overturned by constitutional amendment took place in 1971. In 1970, Congress enacted a statute lowering the voting age to eighteen in both state and federal elections. The states of Oregon and Texas filed suit under the original jurisdiction of the Supreme Court seeking an injunction preventing the attorney general from enforcing the statute with respect to the states. The Supreme Court ruled that Congress had no power to regulate the voting age in state elections.[42] The

Twenty-sixth Amendment, ratified in 1971, accomplished what Congress was not permitted to do through simple statute.

Over the years, numerous unsuccessful attempts have been made to overrule Supreme Court decisions through constitutional amendments. In 1983, an amendment providing that "[t]he right to an abortion is not secured by this Constitution," obviously aimed at *Roe v. Wade,* failed to pass the Senate by only one vote. In 1971, a proposal designed to overrule the Warren Court's controversial school prayer decisions fell twenty-eight votes short of the necessary two-thirds majority in the House of Representatives. In his 1980 presidential campaign, Ronald Reagan called on Congress to resurrect the School Prayer Amendment, but Congress was unwilling to give the measure serious consideration.

The most recent example of a proposed constitutional amendment aimed at a Supreme Court decision dealt with the emotional public issue of flag burning. As we noted in section 14-3g, "The Rehnquist Court," in 1989, the Court held that burning the American flag as part of a public protest was a form of symbolic speech protected by the First Amendment. Many, including President George Bush (the elder), called on Congress to overrule the Court. Congress considered an amendment that read, "The Congress and the States shall have power to prohibit the physical desecration of the flag of the United States." Votes were taken in both chambers, but neither achieved the necessary two-thirds majority. In the wake of the failed constitutional amendment, Congress adopted a statute making flag desecration a federal offense. As it had done with the Texas law in 1989, the Supreme Court declared the new federal statute unconstitutional.[43]

The Appointment Power   The shared presidential–senatorial power of appointing federal judges is an important means of influencing the judiciary. For example, President Richard Nixon made a significant impact on the Supreme Court and on American constitutional law through his appointment of four justices. During the 1968 presidential campaign, Nixon criticized the Warren Court's liberal decisions, especially in the criminal law area, and promised to appoint "strict constructionists" (widely interpreted to mean "conservatives") to the bench. Nixon's first appointment came in 1969, when Warren E. Burger was selected to succeed Earl Warren as chief justice. In 1970, after the failed nominations of Clement Haynsworth and G. Harold Carswell, Harry Blackmun was appointed to succeed Justice Abe Fortas, who had resigned from the Court in a scandal in 1969. Then, in 1972, Nixon appointed Lewis Powell to fill the vacancy left by Hugo Black's retirement and William Rehnquist to succeed John M. Harlan, who had also retired. The four Nixon appointments had a definite impact on the Supreme Court, although the resulting swing to the right was less dramatic than many observers had predicted.

More recently, Presidents Reagan and George Bush moved the Court further to the ideological right by their appointments of Justices O'Connor (1981), Scalia (1986), Kennedy (1987), Souter (1990), and Thomas (1991). When Justice Byron White announced his retirement in 1993, President Clinton was given the opportunity to reverse the conservative trend by appointing a more liberal justice to the Court. Clinton chose the federal appeals court judge Ruth Bader Ginsburg to fill the vacancy. Widely seen as a moderate-to-liberal judge, Ginsburg won confirmation easily in the Senate. The year 1994 saw the departure of Justice Harry Blackmun, who had been on the Court since 1970. President Clinton appointed Judge Stephen G. Breyer, of Boston, to fill the vacancy. The appointments of Ginsburg and Breyer prevented the Court from moving further to the right.

Without question, the shared presidential–senatorial power to appoint judges and justices is the most effective means of controlling the federal judiciary. Congress and the president may not be able to achieve immediate results using the appointment power, but they can bring about long-term changes in the Court's direction. The appointment power ensures that the Supreme Court and the other federal courts may not continue to defy a clear national consensus for long.

14-4d Enforcement of Court Decisions

Courts generally have adequate means of enforcing their decisions on the parties directly involved in litigation. Any party who fails to comply with a court order, such as a subpoena

Popular Culture and American Politics
Courts in Film

Americans have always been fascinated with what goes on in the courtroom. It is not surprising that courtroom dramas are a staple of the popular culture. Some of the most popular television series have been based on what happens in the courtroom, including *Perry Mason, Matlock, L.A. Law, Civil Wars, Law & Order, The Practice,* and *Boston Legal.* Countless films have been based on courtroom dramas—some of them real, others fictitious. Some of the most interesting are shown in this list:

Film	Year	Starring
12 Angry Men	1957	Henry Fonda
Anatomy of a Murder	1959	Jimmy Stewart and Lee Remick
Inherit the Wind	1960	Fredric March and Spencer Tracy
To Kill a Mockingbird	1962	Gregory Peck
And Justice for All	1979	Al Pacino
The Verdict	1982	Paul Newman
Marie	1985	Sissy Spacek
Reversal of Fortune	1990	Ron Silver and Jeremy Irons
Presumed Innocent	1990	Harrison Ford
Class Action	1991	Gene Hackman and Mary Elizabeth Mastrantonio
The Client	1994	Susan Sarandon and Tommy Lee Jones
A Time to Kill	1996	Matthew McConaughey and Samuel L. Jackson
The Rainmaker	1997	Matt Damon
A Civil Action	1998	John Travolta and Robert Duvall
Erin Brockovich	2000	Julia Roberts

All these films deal with sensational civil or criminal trials. What happens in courts of appeal, including the U.S. Supreme Court, does not lend itself as readily to portrayal on the screen or TV. A few made-for-TV movies have been made about important Supreme Court decisions, including *Roe v. Wade* (1989), starring Holly Hunter as Jane Roe, and *Separate but Equal* (1991), which features Sidney Poitier as Thurgood Marshall and deals with the landmark case *Brown v. Board of Education* (1954).

Several films in the mystery genre deal indirectly with the Supreme Court. One of the best known is *The Pelican Brief,* based on the John Grisham novel of the same name. This 1993 film, starring Julia Roberts, tells an unlikely story about a law student who holds the answer to the assassination of two Supreme Court justices. Another film along the same lines is *Suspect* (1987), starring Cher and Dennis Quaid, in which the villain turns out to be a judge!

Few films deal with the Supreme Court as an institution. Perhaps the best known is *First Monday in October* (1981), which stars Jill Clayburgh and Walter Matthau. Clayburgh's character plays the first woman appointed to the High Court. Matthau plays a somewhat cranky senior justice whose views on the issues are decidedly more liberal than those of his new female colleague. Predictably, the two come into conflict but eventually develop a close friendship. The film is interesting in that it does try to provide a glimpse of what happens inside the "marble temple."

or an injunction, may be held in **contempt of court.** The Supreme Court's decisions interpreting the federal Constitution are typically nationwide in scope. For this reason, they automatically elicit the compliance of state and federal judges. Occasionally, one hears of a stubborn federal judge who, for one reason or another, defies a Supreme Court decision, but this phenomenon, although not uncommon in the early days of the Republic, is now an eccentric curiosity.

▶ **contempt of court**
An action that embarrasses, hinders, or obstructs or is calculated to lessen the dignity of a judicial body.

Courts have greater difficulty enlisting the compliance of the general public, especially when they render unpopular decisions. Despite the Supreme Court's repeated rulings against officially sponsored prayer in the public schools, these activities now continue in some parts of the country. Even after three decades, the Warren Court's school prayer decisions have failed to generate broad public acceptance. Without the assistance of local school officials, the Court can do little to effect compliance with its mandates regarding school prayer unless and until an unhappy parent files a lawsuit.

14-5 Conclusion: Assessing the Judicial Branch

Courts are both legal and political institutions. As legal institutions, they decide cases by following set procedures, applying legal rules, and following legal precedents. As political institutions, they are involved in the authoritative allocation of values, the resolution of conflict, the determination of "who gets what," and the making of public policy. How the courts exercise their political role, however, can be a great source of controversy. In earlier decades, liberals chided the courts for employing judicial review to thwart progressive economic policies. Today, criticism of judicial activism is more likely to come from conservatives who believe that liberals have come to rely on the courts to achieve social policies they could never achieve through legislatures. In both instances the underlying question is: What is the role of a court in a constitutional democracy? The easy answer is that the courts should follow the rule of law and permit the people's elected representatives to legislate as long as legislation does not conflict with constitutional principles. But there is a more difficult question lurking within this easy answer. How should constitutional principles be understood and applied to contemporary issues? On this profound question, liberals and conservatives often disagree. This is why ideology is an important consideration in deciding who should be appointed to the bench and, especially, who should serve on the highest court in the land.

The power and prestige of the Supreme Court—indeed, of the entire federal judiciary—have grown tremendously over the past two centuries. It is no exaggeration to say that the Supreme Court now stands as the most influential tribunal in the world. Nevertheless, the Court works within a constitutional and political system that imposes significant constraints on its power. The Supreme Court can, and often does, speak with finality on important questions of constitutional law and public policy. But it must consider the probable responses of Congress, the president, and, ultimately, the American people. In the long run, the power of the Supreme Court depends on its acceptance within the political culture. Diffuse support for the federal courts is fairly strong, certainly relative to public support for Congress. But this support could be jeopardized by a series of court decisions that run counter to public opinion. Most people are willing to accept court decisions that they do not agree with from time to time, but a continual series of decisions that run counter to the political culture could undermine the legitimacy of the courts as institutions. Of course, the system of checks and balances works to ensure that the federal courts do not stray too far from the ideological mainstream for too long.

American government, especially at the national level, is vastly more powerful and pervasive than the Framers of the Constitution could have imagined. The increased authority of the federal judiciary has kept pace with the growth of governmental activity generally, but it has not placed the Court in a dominant position in the American system of government. Although judges, because they are human beings, are not immune to corruption or the abuse of power, and courts sometimes overstep their traditional bounds, those who worry about the prospect of "government by judiciary" are exaggerating judicial power. Although the federal courts have formidable powers, they cannot raise an army, start a war, create a new government program, or raise anyone's taxes. More than two hundred years after the ratification of the Constitution, Alexander Hamilton's characterization of the federal judiciary as the least dangerous branch of the national government still remains credible.

Questions for Thought and Discussion

1. Is the power of judicial review consistent or inconsistent with the ideals of democracy?
2. Should federal judges have to stand for reelection periodically as most state judges do?
3. How important is it that the federal judiciary mirror the diversity of society?
4. In reviewing presidential nominees to the Supreme Court, what factors should the Senate consider? Is the ideology of the nominee a legitimate consideration?
5. Is it possible for federal judges to determine the intentions of the Framers of the Constitution? How is this done? In interpreting the Constitution, should judges be limited by the intentions of the Framers?
6. Was the Supreme Court justified in intervening in the disputed 2000 presidential election in Florida? Do you agree or disagree with the Court's decision in *Bush v. Gore*?

Practice Quiz

Note: You can find the correct answers to these questions by taking the quiz and then submitting your answers in the Online Edition. The program will automatically score your submission. If you miss a question, the program will provide the correct answer, a rationale for the answer, and the section number in the chapter where the topic is discussed.

1. The major trial courts in the federal court system are the
   _____.
   a. circuit courts
   b. district courts
   c. courts of appeals
   d. claims courts

2. In the U.S. Courts of Appeals, cases are usually heard by panels of _____ judges.
   a. three
   b. five
   c. seven
   d. nine

3. The first Chief Justice of the United States was _____ of New York.
   a. Oliver Wendell Holmes
   b. John Marshall
   c. Charles Evans Hughes
   d. John Jay

4. Following its decision in *Marbury v. Madison* (1803), the Supreme Court did not strike down an act of Congress until its 1857 decision in _____.
   a. *McCulloch v. Maryland*
   b. *Gibbons v. Ogden*
   c. the Dred Scott case
   d. *Lochner v. New York*

5. According to the authors of this book, the most important case of the Warren Court era was _____.
   a. *Brown v. Board of Education*
   b. *Mapp v. Ohio*
   c. *Miranda v. Arizona*
   d. *Terry v. Ohio*

6. Which of the following Supreme Court nominees was not confirmed by the Senate?
   a. Ruth Bader Ginsburg
   b. Robert Bork
   c. Clarence Thomas
   d. Stephen Breyer

7. Interest groups can affect Supreme Court policy making by
   _____.
   a. directly lobbying the justices through personal contacts
   b. indirectly lobbying the justices through letters and other write-in campaigns
   c. filing *amicus curiae* briefs
   d. filing writs of *habeas corpus*

8. The tradition of allowing Senators from the president's party to exercise significant influence in the selection of judges for the federal district courts located within their states is known as senatorial _____.
   a. deference
   b. preference
   c. courtesy
   d. reciprocity

9. If the Supreme Court refuses to review a lower court decision,
   _____.
   a. the lower court decision is overturned
   b. the lower court decision remains undisturbed
   c. the case is declared as a mistrial
   d. the question is declared moot

10. The idea that judges should exercise power cautiously and show deference to precedent and to the decisions of other branches of government is known as judicial _____.
    a. restraint
    b. review
    c. activism
    d. originalism

For Further Reading

Baum, Lawrence. *The Supreme Court,* 8th ed. (Washington, D.C.: CQ Press, 2004).

Bork, Robert H. *The Tempting of America: The Political Seduction of the Law* (New York: Free Press, 1990).

Carp, Robert A., and Ronald Stidham. *The Federal Courts,* 3d ed. (Washington, D.C.: CQ Press, 1998).

Dershowitz, Alan M. *Supreme Injustice: How the High Court Hijacked Election 2000* (New York: Oxford University Press, 2001).

Epstein, Lee, and Jack Knight, *The Choices Justices Make* (Washington, D.C.: CQ Press, 1998).

Garraty, John A., ed. *Quarrels That Have Shaped the Constitution,* rev. ed. (New York: Harper & Row, 1987).

Glick, Henry R. *Courts, Politics and Justice,* 3d ed. (New York: McGraw-Hill, 1993).

Irons, Peter. *A People's History of the Supreme Court* (New York: Penguin Putnam, 2000).

Lamb, Charles M., and Stephen C. Halpern, eds. *The Burger Court: Political and Judicial Profiles* (Urbana, IL: University of Illinois Press, 1991).

Lazarus, Edward. *Closed Chambers: The Rise, Fall, and Future of the Modern Supreme Court* (New York: Penguin Books, 1999).

Leuchtenburg, William E. *The Supreme Court Reborn: The Constitutional Revolution in the Age of Roosevelt* (New York: Oxford University Press, 1996).

Murphy, Walter. *Elements of Judicial Strategy* (Chicago: University of Chicago Press, 1964).

O'Brien, David. *Storm Center: The Supreme Court in American Politics,* 2d ed. (New York: W. W. Norton, 2000).

O'Connor, Sandra Day. *The Majesty of the Law: Reflections of a Supreme Court Justice* (New York: Random House, 2003).

Rehnquist, William H. *The Supreme Court,* rev. ed. (New York: Knopf, 2001).

Schwartz, Bernard, with Stephen Lesher. *Inside the Warren Court* (Garden City, NY: Doubleday, 1983).

Schwartz, Herman, ed. *The Rehnquist Court: Judicial Activism on the Right* (New York: Hill and Wang, 2002).

Slotnick, Elliot E. *Judicial Politics,* 3d ed. (Washington, D.C.: CQ Press, 2005).

Starr, Kenneth W. *First Among Equals: The Supreme Court in American Life* (New York: Warner Books, 2002).

Wasby, Stephen L. *The Supreme Court in the Federal Judicial System,* 3d ed. (Chicago: Nelson Hall, 1988).

Woodward, Bob, and Scott Armstrong. *The Brethren: Inside the Supreme Court* (New York: Simon & Schuster, 1979).

Endnotes

1. Alexander Hamilton, *The Federalist,* No. 78.

2. Alexis de Tocqueville, *Democracy in America,* ed. Phillips Bradley (New York: Knopf, 1944), vol. 1, p. 280.

3. *Bush v. Gore,* 531 U.S. 98 (2000).

4. *Marbury v. Madison,* 5 U.S. 137 (1803).

5. An excellent account of the political context surrounding *Marbury v. Madison* can be found in Jean Edward Smith, *John Marshall: Definer of a Nation* (New York: Henry Holt Co., 1996), Chapter 13.

6. See, for example, John Hart Ely, *Democracy and Distrust: A Theory of Judicial Review* (Cambridge, MA: Harvard University Press, 1980).

7. *Roe v. Wade,* 410 U.S. 113 (1973).

8. *Luther v. Borden,* 48 U.S. 1 (1849).

9. *Massachusetts v. Laird,* 400 U.S. 886 (1970).

10. *Crockett v. Reagan,* 558 F. Supp. 893 (D.C.D.C. 1982).

11. See Alan M. Dershowitz, *Supreme Injustice: How the High Court Hijacked Election 2000* (New York: Oxford University Press, 2001).

12. Vincent Bugliosi, "None Dare Call It Treason." *The Nation,* January 18, 2001.

13. *Burnet v. Coronado Oil and Gas Co.,* 285 U.S. 393 (1932), dissenting opinion.

14. For example, the George H.W. Bush administration (1989–1992) appointed 182 federal judges. Nearly 19 percent of those appointees were women, and 5.5 percent were African Americans.

15. The vote was 96–3.

16. The vote was 87–9.

17. *Chisholm v. Georgia,* 2 U.S. 419 (1793).

18. Quoted in Sandra F. VanBurkleo, "John Jay." In *The Oxford Companion to the Supreme Court of the United States,* ed. Kermit L. Hall (New York: Oxford University Press, 1992), p. 447.

19. *McCulloch v. Maryland,* 17 U.S. 316 (1819).

20. *Gibbons v. Ogden,* 22 U.S. 1 (1824).

21. *Scott v. Sandford,* 60 U.S. 393 (1857).

22. *United States v. E. C. Knight Co.,* 156 U.S. 1 (1895).

23. *Pollock v. Farmer's Loan and Trust Co.,* 158 U.S. 601 (1895).

24. *Lochner v. New York,* 198 U.S. 45 (1905).

25. *Hammer v. Dagenhart,* 247 U.S. 251 (1918).

26. *Adkins v. Children's Hospital,* 261 U.S. 525 (1923).

27. *A. L. A. Schechter Poultry Corp. v. United States,* 295 U.S. 495 (1935).

28. *National Labor Relations Board v. Jones and Laughlin Steel Corp.,* 301 U.S. 1 (1937).

29. *Brown v. Board of Education,* 347 U.S. 483 (1954).

30. *Baker v. Carr,* 369 U.S. 186 (1962).

31. See, for example, *Abington School District v. Schempp,* 374 U.S. 203 (1963).

32. *Texas v. Johnson,* 491 U.S. 397 (1989).

33. See, for example, *United States v. Lopez,* 514 U.S. 549 (1995); *Printz v. United States,* 521 U.S. 898 (1997).

34. Herman Schwartz, "Introduction." In *The Rehnquist Court: Judicial Activism on the Right,* ed. Herman Schwartz (New York: Hill and Wang, 2002), p. 13.

35. See *Planned Parenthood v. Casey,* 505 U.S. 833 (1992).

36. *Romer v. Evans,* 517 U.S. 620 (1996); *Lawrence v. Texas,* 539 U.S. 558 (2003).

37. See, for example, *Santa Fe Independent School District v. Doe,* 530 U.S. 290 (2000).

38. *Rasul v. Bush,* 124 S Ct 2686 (2004).

39. Sandra Day O'Connor, *The Majesty of the Law: Reflections of a Supreme Court Justice* (New York: Random House, 2003), p. 5.

40. *Grove City College v. Bell,* 465 U.S. 555 (1984).

41. *Chisholm v. Georgia,* 2 U.S. 419 (1793).

42. *Oregon v. Mitchell,* 400 U.S. 112 (1970).

43. *United States v. Eichman,* 496 U.S. 310 (1990).

The Federal Bureaucracy

15

15-1 Bureaucracy and the Growth of Government

When the first Congress convened in 1789, the United States consisted of thirteen states stretching along the Atlantic coast. The economy was primarily agricultural, and most of the nation's four million people lived in rural areas. The pace of life was slow. Little was expected from the national government. Consequently, government was small and seldom touched people's lives directly. In 1792, the federal government had approximately eight hundred employees. The total expenditures of the new national government until that time were around $4 million, and the national debt left over from the Revolutionary War stood at just over $77 million. Thus, during the early days of the Republic, the national government essentially followed the dictum often attributed to Thomas Jefferson: "That government is best which governs least."[1]

As the nineteenth century began, the federal government concerned itself mostly with the regulation of foreign trade, internal improvements such as canals and "post roads," and the protection of the national security. Such functions as social welfare and education were left to the state and local governments, which, in turn, tended to leave matters of social welfare and education to neighborhoods, churches, and families. Perhaps most fundamentally, the dominant political culture regarded individuals as responsible for their own problems in addition to their own good fortunes. When Alexis de Tocqueville visited America in the 1830s, he was surprised to find so little in the way of government agencies. Tocqueville concluded that in America, "society governs itself for itself."[2]

Of course, things are quite different now. The United States stretches across the continent and beyond into the islands of the Pacific. The nation's population exceeds three hundred million. The United States is the only nation in the world that is now both a military and an industrial superpower. The American people now live in gigantic metropolitan areas—restless hubs of transportation, communications, and business. The pace of life has become extremely quick. Although Americans enjoy a standard of living undreamed of by the Founders, we also experience collective problems that did not greatly trouble the eighteenth century: environmental degradation, crime, racial conflict, and social disorganization, to name just a few. Most Americans now look to government, especially to Washington, D.C., to address these problems. Consequently, the annual federal budget is more than $2 trillion; the national debt exceeds $7 trillion.[3] Although the federal government was downsized somewhat under the Clinton administration, the number of federal employees is in the neighborhood of 2.8 million, not counting the armed forces (see Figure 15-1). Perhaps as many as ten million other individuals make their living indirectly from the national government, as consultants or contractors.

The roughly 2.8 million civilian employees of the federal government staff an enormous bureaucracy encompassing fifteen major government departments and some fifty independent regulatory commissions, executive agencies, and government corporations. In the past four decades, more than two hundred fifty new agencies or bureaus have been added to the federal bureaucracy. Although some consolidation has taken place, few agencies have been eliminated. In all, the national government now has more than two thousand identifiable units. All these bureaucratic entities exist to meet some demand that the American people, or particular interests within society, have made on the national government. (Table 15-1 shows a sampling of federal agencies.)

The extensive bureaucratization of American government has led some commentators to refer to contemporary government as the administrative state.[4] More than simply a collection of offices, the **modern administrative state** consists of "vast, interconnecting webs of complicated administrative systems, regulatory procedures and nameless bureaucrats."[5] Given what government is now expected to do, from agricultural inspection to space exploration, bureaucracy is both necessary and inevitable. Indeed, one can argue that the "administrative state is very much a central factor, perhaps *the* central factor, influencing what happens in contemporary life."[6] Elements of this administrative state often appear to take on a world of their own. This sometimes leads to a very public discussion of its accountability. When President George W. Bush appointed Congressman Porter Goss (R-

▶ **modern administrative state**
The highly bureaucratic nature of American government in the modern era, in which day-to-day functions of government are performed by bureaucratic agencies.

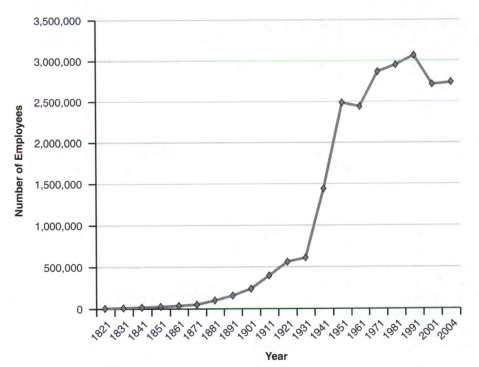

Figure 15-1
Growth in Federal Civilian Employment by Decade, 1821–2004

Source: Adapted from Office of Personnel Management.

Florida) to head the Central Intelligence Agency (CIA) in the fall of 2004, the consensus among most observers was that he was put in place with a clear mandate to provide accountability to what had been perceived as an agency that was out of control.

15-1a What Is Bureaucracy?

A bureau is a government agency or office. Although the term **bureaucracy** literally means "government by agency," the term is commonly employed to describe the collection of agencies a government creates to impose regulations, implement policies, and administer programs. *The American Heritage Dictionary* defines bureaucracy as "administration of a government chiefly through bureaus staffed with nonelective officials."

Bureaucracy is a universal phenomenon among advanced societies with well-established governments. The German sociologist Max Weber argued that bureaucracy exists in the modern world because it is the most rational way of organizing efforts to achieve collective goals. Whether or not Weber was right, bureaucracy is an inextricable component of modern government.

In the United States, bureaucracy is found at every level of government: local, state, and national. And bureaucracy may be found in all three branches of government—executive, legislative, and judicial. To simplify matters somewhat, this chapter focuses on the collection of agencies that constitute the executive bureaucracy of the national government in addition to the numerous agencies officially classified as independent—that is, not formally part of any of the three branches of government. Indeed, many observers think of the entire executive bureaucracy as a virtual fourth branch of American national government.[7] Constitutionally speaking, this characterization may be incorrect. But considering the difficulties that both the president and Congress can have in controlling agency action, the characterization makes sense.

The federal bureaucracy may seem remote, impersonal, and impenetrable. It is, after all, a large group of American citizens doing a wide variety of jobs for the federal government, from a ranger riding on horseback through a national park to a clerk entering data at a computer terminal inside a massive government building in Washington. The people who operate the federal bureaucracy can be placed in two categories. **Political appointees,**

▶ **bureaucracy** The collection of agencies a government creates to impose regulations, implement policies, and administer programs.

▶ **political appointees** Those members of the bureaucracy who hold the highest executive positions and are appointed by the president.

TABLE 15-1 **A Sampling of Federal Government Agencies**

USAID (http://www.usaid.gov)	USAID is an independent federal government agency that receives overall foreign policy guidance from the secretary of state. The agency works to support long-term and equitable economic growth and to advance U.S. foreign policy objectives by supporting economic growth, agriculture, and trade; global health; and, democracy, conflict prevention, and humanitarian assistance.
CIA (http://www.cia.gov)	The Central Intelligence Agency's mission is to support the president, the National Security Council, and all officials who make and execute the U.S. national security policy, by • Providing accurate, comprehensive, and timely foreign intelligence on national security topics • Conducting counterintelligence activities, special activities, and other functions related to foreign intelligence and national security, as directed by the president
EEOC (http://www.eeoc.gov)	The Equal Employment Opportunity Commission was created in the historic Civil Rights Act of 1964. This act was an omnibus bill addressing not only discrimination in employment but also discrimination in voting, public accommodations, and education.
FCC (http://www.fcc.gov)	The Federal Communications Commission was established by the Communications Act of 1934 and is charged with regulating interstate and international communications by radio, television, wire, satellite, and cable. The FCC's jurisdiction covers the 50 states, the District of Columbia, and U.S. possessions.
SEC (http://www.sec.gov)	The primary mission of the U.S. Securities and Exchange Commission is to protect investors and maintain the integrity of the securities markets.
NEH (http://www.neh.gov)	The National Endowment for the Humanities is an independent grant-making agency of the United States government dedicated to supporting research, education, preservation, and public programs in the humanities.
Peace Corps (http://www.peacecorps.gov)	The Peace Corps has three goals: • Help the people of interested countries in meeting their need for trained men and women. • Help promote a better understanding of Americans on the part of the peoples served. • Help promote a better understanding of other peoples on the part of Americans.
Smithsonian Institution (http://www.si.edu)	The Smithsonian is an independent trust instrumentality of the United States holding more than 140 million artifacts and specimens in its trust for "the increase and diffusion of knowledge." The Institution is also a center for research dedicated to public education, national service, and scholarship in the arts, sciences, and history. The Smithsonian is composed of sixteen museums and galleries and the National Zoo and numerous research facilities in the United States and abroad.
United States Customs Service (http://www.customs.gov)	The United States Customs Service ensures that all imports and exports comply with U.S. laws and regulations. The Service collects and protects the revenue and guards against smuggling and is responsible for these tasks: • Assess and collect Customs duties, excise taxes, fees, and penalties due on imported merchandise • Interdict and seize contraband, including narcotics and illegal drugs • Process persons, baggage, cargo, and mail and administer certain navigation laws • Detect and apprehend persons engaged in fraudulent practices designed to circumvent Customs and related laws • Protect American business and labor and intellectual property rights by enforcing U.S. laws intended to prevent illegal trade practices, including provisions related to quotas and the marking of imported merchandise; enforcing the Anti-Dumping Act; and, by providing Customs Recordations for copyrights, patents, and trademarks • Protect the general welfare and security of the United States by enforcing import and export restrictions and prohibitions, including the export of critical technology used to develop weapons of mass destruction, and preventing money laundering • Collect accurate import and export data for the compilation of international trade statistics
The Voice of America (VOA) (http://www.voa.gov)	The Voice of America (VOA) is an international multimedia broadcasting service funded by the U.S. government. VOA broadcasts more than 900 hours of news, informational, educational, and cultural programs every week to an audience of some 91 million people worldwide. VOA programs are produced and broadcast in English and 52 other languages through radio, satellite television, and the Internet.

who hold the highest executive positions, come and go with changing presidential administrations. **Career civil servants** who occupy the middle-management, professional, technical, and clerical positions—obtain their jobs on the basis of merit and are protected from being fired for political reasons.

15-1b Bureaucracy in American Political Thought

Whereas the classical liberals of the Enlightenment called for minimal government as a means of promoting individual freedom, liberal theorists of the late nineteenth and early twentieth centuries sought to justify a broader role for government. Social theorists, such as John Dewey, advocated an expanded governmental role in part to realize the ideal of equality in an economy in which gross disparities exist between rich and poor. For modern liberal economists, like John Maynard Keynes, a greater degree of government intervention is necessary to avoid the wild swings between periods of dramatic growth and periods of recession, or even depression. According to the Keynesian perspective—dominant during the New Deal era—the very survival of capitalism depends on successful government management of the economy. In the decades following the New Deal, the American intellectual community, as exemplified in the work of the economist John Kenneth Galbraith, embraced the concept of proactive government—that is, government committed to progress through regulation, the redistribution of wealth, and planning. In the 1960s, President Lyndon Johnson's Great Society program was based squarely on the assumptions of modern liberalism.

15-1c The Conservative Aversion to Bureaucracy

Conservatives are highly critical of the mammoth bureaucracy that has developed in Washington to implement the policies and programs of modern liberalism. Conservatives view bureaucracy as unnecessary meddling in people's lives, especially in their economic activities. The modern conservative criticism of bureaucracy stems from a pervasive distrust of government and a deep-seated skepticism about what government can do to promote justice, welfare, and progress. Indeed, one fundamental point of division between liberals and conservatives now is their differing view of the role and capabilities of government.

Former President Ronald Reagan was, without question, the most conservative president the United States had seen in decades. Throughout his career in government, which began as the governor of California in the 1960s, Reagan remained sharply critical of big government, "liberal" programs, and the bureaucracy created to implement them. In his 1981 inaugural address, Reagan famously observed, "Government is not the solution to our problem; government is the problem."

As president, Reagan sought to scale down the national government and return decision making to the state and local levels. During his first term, he attempted to have Congress abolish the newly created Department of Education, which he saw as both unnecessary bureaucracy and a federal encroachment on a traditional local function. In failing to abolish the department, Reagan learned what political scientists have long known: *After bureaucracy is created, it is virtually impossible to do away with it!* As one well-known student of public administration has put it, "Government activities tend to go on indefinitely."[8]

Despite the Reagan Revolution of the 1980s, most Americans now continue to view the national government as responsible for the social and economic well-being of the nation. As a practical matter, however, the influence of pluralist politics (the interplay of organized interests) has been even more important in creating and maintaining bureaucracy. You only have to consider the success of numerous interest groups in shaping, perpetuating, and often enlarging government programs created (at least in theory) to advance the public interest. Students of American politics have long recognized that government regulators are apt to be more influenced by the interests of those they regulate than by abstract notions of responsible government.

> **career civil servants**
> Members of the bureaucracy who occupy the middle-management, professional, technical, and clerical positions; career civil servants obtain their jobs on the basis of merit and are protected from being fired for political reasons.

What Americans Think About

The Federal Bureaucracy

Americans are not particularly fond of the federal bureaucracy. Indeed, a dislike of bureaucracy is part of American political culture. According to the following survey data, most Americans believe that federal workers are underworked and overpaid. At the same time, however, most people who have had recent contact with a federal agency were satisfied with the performance of the federal officials with whom they dealt.

Harder Workers

"Overall, who do you think works harder—people in federal government jobs or people in similar jobs outside the government?"

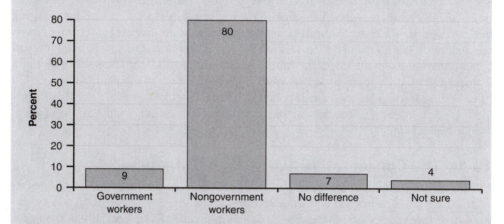

Size of Government

"How about the number of people employed by the federal government: In general, do you think the federal government employs too many people or too few people to do the work that must be done?"

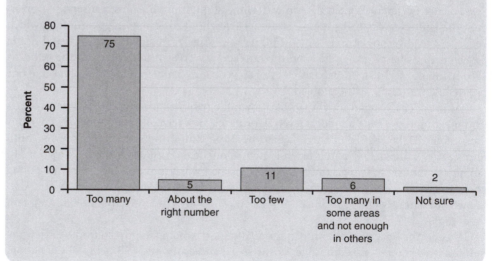

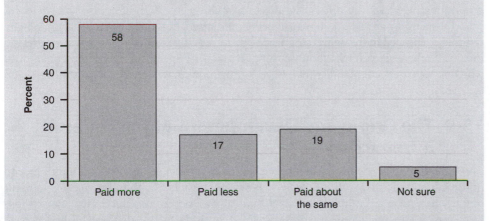

Income

"Do you believe that federal employees are paid more, less, or about the same as people in similar jobs outside the government?"

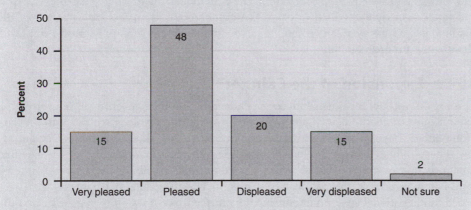

Satisfaction

[Asked only of those who had contact with a federal agency during the past year]
"Overall, would you say you were pleased with the conduct of the government worker or workers you dealt with? Would you say you were very pleased/displeased or just pleased/displeased?"

Source: Adapted from a national telephone survey of 603 adults, conducted January 15–16, 1994, by the Social Science Research Institute at the University of Tennessee, Knoxville. The margin of error is ±4 percentage points at the 95 percent confidence level.

15-1d Bureaucracy in American Political Culture

Although Americans over the past decades have come to look to Washington to solve their social and economic problems, bureaucracy remains a dirty word in American political culture. To say that an organization is bureaucratic, or to call someone a bureaucrat, is obviously not a compliment. Although most people recognize the necessity of bureaucracy, Americans are deeply critical and suspicious of it. In common parlance, bureaucracy is synonymous with delay and waste—with red tape[9] and the runaround. The business community (particularly small business) tends to be especially vocal in complaining about government regulations and record-keeping requirements. "Anyone who has ever attempted to operate a small business in this country is well aware of the difficulties (not to mention costs) associated with compliance with myriad laws and regulations."[10]

Suffice it to say that American political culture, which has long valued localism and the popular control of government, is not hospitable to bureaucracy. Yet the basic reason that bureaucracy exists is to achieve goals that the people, through their elected representatives, have set for government in the modern age. The American people may dislike bureaucracy, but most of them understand that, given what they expect from government, bureaucracy is inevitable. Yet most also believe, rightly or wrongly, that the federal bureaucracy is beset by "waste, fraud, and abuse." Unfortunately, waste, fraud, and abuse, when they do exist in government agencies, are difficult to detect and eliminate. And, of course, efforts to cut wasteful spending are always subject to being politicized, especially when the agency being targeted is engaged in the delivery of needed social services. As one commentator observed in 2003, "Whenever you talk about [cutting] mandatory spending, it's spun by the groups who oppose true accountability that we are trying to take away entitlements for those who are needy."[11]

15-2 The Origin and Development of the Federal Bureaucracy

The Constitution says nothing about the president's cabinet, let alone a mammoth federal bureaucracy. Article II, Section 2 merely allows the president, with the advice and consent of the Senate, to appoint "public ministers" and all other officers of the United States whose appointments are not herein otherwise provided for, and which shall be established by law." In Article I, Section 6, the Constitution does mention "the Treasury," which became one of the three executive departments established by Congress in 1789. In addition to the treasury, President George Washington's administration consisted of two small departments—the Department of State and the Department of War (now the Department of Defense)—and the office of attorney general. Thomas Jefferson, the first secretary of state, had only nine people working for him at the State department. The Department of War had fewer than eighty civilian employees. Alexander Hamilton, the first secretary of the treasury, had a somewhat larger staff. In all, the first Washington administration employed about eight hundred people.

15-2a Expansion of the Cabinet

Throughout most of the nineteenth century, the idea of limited government prevailed. The national government remained relatively small and did not involve itself much in the lives of the American people. The existing executive departments (state, war, treasury, and attorney general, which became the Justice department in 1870) performed only the essential functions of government. Social welfare and economic regulation were not considered legitimate concerns of the national government. The three new departments that were added to the national government during the nineteenth century—the post office and the departments of the interior and agriculture—did not represent a significant change in public expectations of the national government.

The Post Office   In 1790, Congress created the post office and placed it under the jurisdiction of the Treasury department. Much of the growth of the federal bureaucracy during the early nineteenth century is attributable to the expansion of the post office, which grew as the nation expanded westward. The post office became so large and so important that in 1829 Congress removed it from the treasury and made it a separate department. The postmaster general was made a member of the cabinet. In 1970, the Post Office department was converted into the U.S. Postal Service, an independent agency governed by an eleven-member board, and the postmaster general was removed from the cabinet.

The Department of the Interior   In 1849, President James K. Polk signed a bill creating the new Department of Interior to take charge of the millions of acres of land being acquired by the federal government in the West. Moreover, the Interior department, through its Bureau of Indian Affairs, was to handle relations with the Native Americans who lived on much of this land. The Interior department was also given the responsibility of conducting the decennial census mandated by the Constitution, a function originally performed by the Treasury department.[12] In 1916, the National Park Service was set up within the Department of the Interior to administer the growing number of national parks and monuments. The park service now operates more than three hundred national parks, monuments, historic sites, battlefields, cemeteries, parkways, and recreational areas, encompassing nearly eighty million acres of public land.

The Department of Agriculture   The Department of Agriculture was established in 1862 to promote food production on the nation's farms. President Abraham Lincoln and Congress created the new department to ensure that the Union Army would have a steady food supply during its war with the Confederacy. Originally, the department assisted farmers through research, planning, and various service programs. It now assists consumers by inspecting and grading meat products. The department also administers the food stamp program, a major welfare program for the poor. The U.S. Forest Service, a bureau within the Department of Agriculture, manages federally owned forest lands, many of which are leased to private companies for logging.

15-2b Emergence of the Regulatory State

Before the twentieth century, the federal bureaucracy was concerned primarily with the essential functions of government and secondarily with providing services to citizens. In the late nineteenth century, America experienced a period of rapid industrialization. Factories and mills sprang up everywhere, mines were dug to extract coal and iron, and railroads were built to carry goods and people westward. At the same time, waves of immigrants looking for better lives were streaming in from Europe. Many immigrants took jobs in mines, mills, or factories or worked on the railroads. Wages were low, and working conditions were often miserable. Children worked side by side with their parents. Those who subscribed to the principle of *laissez-faire* argued that government should not intervene on behalf of workers or consumers. Unrestricted capitalism would, over the long run, produce the greatest good for the greatest number of people. On the other side of the issue were reformers backed by throngs of workers, many of whom were beginning to exercise their right to vote. Pressure was growing for the national government to become actively involved in the regulation of the economy.

The Interstate Commerce Commission   In 1887, Congress created the Interstate Commerce Commission (ICC), the first independent regulatory commission of the national government. The ICC was independent in the sense that commissioners held their positions for fixed terms rather than simply served at the pleasure of the president. The ICC was created, largely at the behest of the nation's farmers, to control price fixing and other unfair practices by the railroads. Over time, the ICC's jurisdiction was expanded to include the trucking industry, bus lines, and even oil and gas pipelines. The ICC controlled rates and enforced antidiscrimination laws in these industries. When these industries were deregulated in the 1980s, there was no longer any need for the commission. The ICC was finally abolished in 1995.

The Department of Labor   Concerns over the plight of the nation's workers led to the creation of the Department of Labor in 1913. The department's mission is to administer programs and enforce laws that improve working conditions and advance employment opportunities. Now, the Department of Labor, through the Bureau of Labor Statistics, compiles important data on the American economy, including the consumer price index and the unemployment rate. The Occupational Safety and Health Administration (OSHA), an agency within the Department of Labor, was established in 1970 to develop and enforce regulations for the safety and health of workers in major industries. Congress has given OSHA the power to make rules that are "reasonably necessary or appropriate to provide safe and healthful employment and places of employment." One of OSHA's principal concerns now is the exposure of workers to hazardous chemicals. OSHA routinely inspects workplaces and issues citations to companies that fail to comply with its regulations. Labor unions and environmentalists strongly support OSHA in these activities, although business interests often resent OSHA's "meddling."

The Federal Trade Commission   In 1914, Congress established the Federal Trade Commission (FTC) as an independent agency, like the ICC. The FTC's creation was supported not only by consumers but also by small businesses threatened by unfair competition from large-scale monopolies. The FTC was charged with maintaining free and fair competition, specifically by enforcing antitrust laws and preventing deceptive advertising. A major concern of the FTC is now the labeling and packaging of products. The FTC is empowered to investigate claims of unfair practices. It may issue cease-and-desist orders if it finds these types of claims to be valid. It may even file suit in federal court against companies deemed to be acting unlawfully.

15-2c Emergence of the Welfare State

No single event in American history had more of an impact on the growth of the federal bureaucracy than did the election of Franklin D. Roosevelt to the presidency in 1932. Roosevelt won the election by promising the American people a "new deal" to cope with the massive poverty and unemployment brought on by the Great Depression. Under the New Deal, Roosevelt and the Democratic Congress established public works programs, such as the Civilian Conservation Corps and the Works Progress Administration, in addition to a variety of regulatory programs affecting agriculture, banking, and heavy industry. All these programs required new bureaucracies, and the size of the federal government grew dramatically as a consequence. The Supreme Court declared unconstitutional several of the laws that established these regulatory programs.[13] The result was a showdown between the president and the Court, which Roosevelt finally won when the Court, perhaps fearing retaliation by Congress and the president, abruptly changed direction in what has been referred to as the "constitutional revolution of 1937." Roosevelt's four-term presidency, which lasted from 1933 until his death in 1945, firmly established the legitimacy of the modern regulatory state.

Although the Constitution authorized Congress to spend money to promote the general welfare, the federal government had traditionally left social welfare problems to the state and local governments. But the Great Depression of the 1930s overwhelmed the ability of state and local governments to provide relief and created widespread demands for the national government to get involved. These demands led to the passage of the Social Security Act of 1935, the federal government's first major foray into the realm of promoting social welfare. The Social Security Act established retirement insurance for older Americans, provided unemployment compensation for laid-off workers, and provided federal supplements to state and local welfare programs. The enactment of the Social Security Act signaled the emergence of another face of modern government: the welfare state.

The Great Society   In 1965, President Lyndon B. Johnson, a lifelong Democrat and admirer of Roosevelt, launched a broad range of initiatives to achieve what he called the Great Society. Unlike the New Deal, which was conceived during a time of national crisis, the Great Society program was introduced during a period of economic vitality. The president's theme was that America could afford to do a better job of taking care of its people. Johnson, who had been elected in a landslide over the conservative Republican Barry Goldwater, felt that he had a mandate from the American people to enact this program, and Congress evidently agreed. In short order, Johnson proposed and Congress adopted the Medicare program, which provides health insurance for Americans over sixty-five, and Medicaid, which provides health care for the poor. At Johnson's request, Congress greatly increased funding for Aid to Families with Dependent Children (AFDC), which had been established by the Social Security Act in 1935 as a means of helping children whose fathers were deceased. From 1965 to 1969, the federal government doubled the money it spent on AFDC, and the number of AFDC recipients increased by almost 60 percent.

The administration of Social Security, Medicare, Medicaid, and AFDC required a large-scale bureaucracy. Before 1979, these programs were administered by the Department of Health, Education and Welfare, which had been established during the Eisenhower administration. The national government's social welfare programs are now run by the Department of Health and Human Services, which in monetary terms is the largest of the executive departments.

In addition to expanding social welfare programs, Johnson's Great Society program also called for an increased federal role in a number of other areas traditionally relegated to state and local governments: education, transportation, and housing. The Department of Health, Education and Welfare assumed the responsibility of administering the greatly increased federal grants to local schools, but new bureaucracies were created to handle the increased federal role in housing and transportation. In 1965, Congress established the Department of Housing and Urban Development (HUD) to administer programs that provide federal aid for housing and community development. Acting under the mantle of "cooperative federalism," HUD subsidized state and federal low-income housing projects. The Department of Transportation (DOT) was created in 1967 to coordinate policies and administer the transportation programs of the national government, especially urban mass-transit systems.

15-2d Growth of Government during the 1970s

Under President Richard M. Nixon (1969–1974), the Social Security program was expanded, wage and price controls were instituted in an attempt to control inflation, and a number of new regulatory programs were initiated, most significantly in the areas of environmental protection, occupational safety and health, and consumer product safety. Indeed, the period of the early 1970s has been called the Golden Age of Regulation, as new federal agencies generated volumes of new regulations to protect workers, consumers, and endangered species.

By far the most significant bureaucratic development of the Nixon years was the creation of the Environmental Protection Agency in 1971. With its broad responsibilities for environmental protection, the EPA quickly became a focal point for political controversy, as environmentalists, business interests, and state and local officials sought to advance or protect their interests. From the outset, critics in business and industry charged that the EPA was imposing unreasonable policies that would threaten the economic health of the nation. On the other hand, environmentalists have often accused the EPA of dragging its feet in the face of political resistance to environmental progress.

In response to the energy crisis of the 1970s, President Carter persuaded Congress in 1977 to enact legislation creating the Department of Energy. The department brought together various federal programs and offices, including the nuclear weapons program previously housed in the Department of Defense. By assuming cabinet-level status, the new agency dramatized the importance of the energy issue at a time when future energy supplies were in doubt.

The most significant bureaucratic development of the Carter years was the creation of the Department of Education in 1979. The new department was essentially carved out of the existing Department of Health, Education and Welfare, which was renamed Health and Human Services. The creation of the Department of Education highlighted the increasing federal role in public education, an area that, before the 1960s, had been the nearly exclusive preserve of state and local governments.

15-2e The Reagan Revolution

The election of Ronald Reagan to the presidency in 1980 was a watershed event in American political history. Reagan rode a wave of discontent in American society. To a great extent, the public was frustrated with the performance of the economy which, shocked by spikes in oil prices, had experienced high levels of inflation combined with recession. Reagan also exploited a degree of popular dissatisfaction with the federal government. Reagan's strongest support came from the business community, which demanded relief from government regulation it regarded as excessive and oppressive. The Reagan administration came to Washington with a clear agenda of reducing the size and scope of the federal government, at least in domestic affairs. The administration sought to curtail regulatory activity and even deregulate industries altogether. It sought to reduce the size of federal welfare programs. President Reagan went so far as to call for the abolition of the recently created departments of education and energy. In his 1981 inaugural address, Reagan observed, "Government is not the solution to our problem; government is the problem."

Under President Reagan (1981–1989), the budgets of social services and regulatory agencies were reduced, but not without tremendous political resistance. The number of new regulations being issued by the federal bureaucracy declined, and entire industries were deregulated. But Reagan's proposals to eliminate the Department of Education and the Department of Energy never gained real traction. As we noted in section 15-1c, "The Conservative Aversion to Bureaucracy," once created, bureaucracy is extremely difficult to dislodge. Moreover, during the Reagan years, the defense budget was increased dramatically, and with it, the number of civilians working for the Pentagon. Despite President Reagan's commitment to downsizing the federal government, federal civilian employment continued to rise during the 1980s, albeit at a slower rate. Federal spending, mainly in the area of defense, rose dramatically and helped to create the massive budget deficits that became the defining political issue of the 1980s.

15-2f Reinventing Government? Bureaucracy in the Clinton Years

A staple of presidential campaigns is that candidates promise to go after the wasteful, inefficient, or corrupt bureaucracy. Many presidents have tried to reform the bureaucracy, most with limited success. Shortly after taking office in January 1993, President Bill Clinton appointed Vice President Albert Gore to head a task force named the National Performance Review. Operating under the banner of "reinventing government," Gore and his staff spent six months scouring the federal bureaucracy for waste, inefficiency, and needless or silly regulations. In reporting his findings to the press, Gore displayed a souvenir of his inquiry. Referred to officially as an "ash receiver, tobacco, desk type," Gore's memento was nothing more than a glass ashtray, the kind found in offices and restaurants everywhere. Along with the ash receiver, Gore produced ten pages of federal regulations detailing the procedures government agencies must go through to procure the item. The regulations also contained an interesting requirement for testing the ashtray. First, the ashtray is placed on a maple plank exactly 44.5 millimeters thick. It is then struck with a hammer and steel punch, the point of which is ground to a specified angle. The ashtray must break into no more than thirty-five glass shards, each of which must be at least 6.4 millimeters on any three of its adjacent sides.[14] The National Performance Review generated considerable publicity for the Clinton administration.

During the 2000 presidential campaign, Al Gore made numerous references to the success of the government in reducing federal government employees. Some critics maintained that many of the numbers Gore used as indicators of government reduction in fact reflected cutbacks in the military and its civilian support staff. Moreover, the number of private contractors doing business with the government increased significantly as government functions were increasingly "outsourced." Needless to say, government was hardly reinvented during the Clinton–Gore administration. It would be a rare thing indeed for a president to be able to effect such radical change.

15-2g George W. Bush, the Federal Bureaucracy, and the War on Terrorism

As a Republican, President George W. Bush came to Washington with considerable skepticism of the federal bureaucracy. Yet, as is often the case with presidents, uncontrollable events would have a powerful effect on the president's relationship with the bureaucracy. After the terrorist attacks of September 11, 2001, President Bush found himself leading the

Popular Culture and American Politics
Office Space

By Chapman Rackaway

A common stereotype of bureaucracy is an organization dominated by inept managers and red-tape reports. Creativity and even a person's own life are drowned out in a sea of foolish coworkers, petty political fights, and meaningless forms—just like the picture most of us have of government bureaucracy. Although it is set in a for-profit corporation and not government, one movie captures the view of bureaucracy that many people hold: *Office Space.*

Directed by *Beavis and Butthead* creator Mike Judge, the movie features Ron Livingston's character Peter, who is disillusioned in his job as a mid-level paper-pusher for a large company. Peter is swamped by a boss with seemingly no intelligence who constantly asks Peter to work overtime and is agitated by constant reminders about the covers of his TPS reports. His girlfriend, played by Jennifer Aniston, is humiliated by the bureaucracy-like situation at her own job at a chain restaurant. Employees are required to wear at least thirteen "pieces of flare" (buttons, squirting flowers, and other items). Her boss chastises her for wearing only thirteen pieces, asking her whether she wants to be the type of person who does just enough to get by.

Both of the characters' frustrations turn around as Peter begins to miss work and randomly terrorize the office. When the company brings in consultants to reorganize personnel and fire people, Peter sees his chance to be fired as he wants. Ranting against the corporation in his meeting with the consultants, they instead see a creative mind ready to take on higher level responsibilities. Immediately, we realize the name Peter is appropriate because the character is a living example of the Peter Principle: He has risen to his level of incompetence, a common criticism of the bureaucracy.

A hilarious look at how dysfunctional any organization can be, *Office Space* is a lesson about bureaucracy, even if the government is never mentioned in the movie.

federal government's efforts to improve domestic security. In this capacity, President Bush interacted with government agencies at all levels. At first Bush seemed to be profoundly impressed by the government's response to the new crisis. He praised the actions of government agencies and supported their requests for additional resources. Bush even used his constitutional and statutory powers to create a new federal office, the Office of Homeland Security, based in the Executive Office of the President, to coordinate federal, state, and local efforts to make the country safe from terrorism.

By the summer of 2002, it had become apparent that there were serious problems with the federal government's homeland security operations. They included serious deficiencies in the Immigration and Naturalization Service, inadequacies in the Customs Service, and an overall lack of coordination among federal law enforcement and intelligence agencies. Many members of Congress called for an overhaul of the national homeland security apparatus. President Bush eventually came to support this idea and the result was the Homeland Security Act of 2002, creating a new Cabinet-level department: the Department of Homeland Security. After signing the bill into law in late November 2002, Bush nominated Tom Ridge, who had been serving as Director of the temporary Office of Homeland Security, to head the new department.

The creation of the new department represented the largest reorganization of the Executive Branch in the past five decades. It merged more than twenty existing federal agencies, including the Secret Service, the Coast Guard, the Customs Service, and the Immigration and Naturalization Service, into a new department with more than one hundred seventy-five thousand employees. While the creation of the new department signaled the high priority now assigned to homeland security, the construction of the new department would not be easy. It required the merger of agencies with different computer systems, different operational styles, different leadership structures, and different agency cultures. President Bush called the creation of the new department an "immense task"' that would "take time and focus and steady resolve." Senate Republican leader Trent Lott (R-Mississippi) called it a "monstrous undertaking." President Bush proposed a budget of $38 billion for homeland security in FY 2003, up dramatically from $19 billion in 2002. But most observers expected the budget of the new cabinet-level department to soar in the years to come.

In the spring of 2002, the Federal Bureau of Investigation (FBI) came under increasing scrutiny following the revelation that people in senior positions in the agency did not follow through on field agents' concerns about suspected terrorist activities before 9-11-2001. Testifying before the Senate Intelligence Committee in May 2002, FBI Director Robert Mueller admitted that the FBI could have done a better job in piecing together information from the field. Much of the discussion of the FBI's performance and its perceived weaknesses centered on the nature of its bureaucracy. Many expressed the opinion that those promoted to leadership positions were overly interested in "playing it safe" to advance their careers while the best agents remained in the field without promotion to positions of greater authority. The FBI experience pointed to a perennial bureaucratic pathology: The organization loses sight of its mission as people in the organization work to maintain their own status and power within. In response to mounting criticism of the FBI, Director Mueller and Attorney General John Ashcroft (Mueller's boss) announced sweeping structural and procedural changes in the agency. What they hoped for as well, but what is always more difficult to achieve, was *cultural change* within the FBI.

15-3 The Structure of the Federal Bureaucracy

> ▶ **independent agencies**
> Government agencies located outside the fifteen major executive departments. Examples include the Interstate Commerce Commission and the Federal Reserve Board.

The federal bureaucracy now encompasses fifteen major executive departments and a host of **independent agencies.** Each of these departments or agencies is responsible for administering programs, collecting information, or making and enforcing regulations within a specific area of public policy. Unfortunately for the student of American politics, the dividing lines of responsibility and authority in the federal bureaucracy are not always clear. Often, agency responsibilities overlap so that several agencies within the bureaucracy are working on the same issue or problem. For example, more than a hundred different agencies or bureaus of the national government have some responsibility for education policy. Usually, federal agencies cooperate in making policy or running programs, but not always! Just as well-known rivalries exist among the military services, rivalries exist within the federal bureaucracy. Sometimes, these rivalries even occur between bureaus located within the same department.

The fragmented responsibility, interagency rivalries, and, above all, generally unwieldy character of the massive bureaucracy have led presidents to try to reorganize the executive branch. These efforts have been, at best, only moderately successful. Perhaps the most ambitious plan was launched by President Nixon, who wanted to combine all the more than fifty independent agencies into four new executive departments. Nixon was interested in not only simplifying the bureaucratic structure but also achieving more presidential control over the independent agencies. Unfortunately for Nixon, too many powerful, entrenched interests supported the status quo, and the plan never got off the ground.

15-3a The Cabinet-Level Departments

The executive branch is organized into fifteen major departments, each of which is headed by a secretary who is a member of the president's cabinet (see Table 15-2). Although secretaries are primarily accountable to the president, who appoints and may fire them without notice, they are also somewhat accountable to Congress, which appropriates the funding for their departments.

Offices within these major departments are called bureaus, or agencies. In some departments, the bureaus and agencies are closely controlled by the appointed officials at the top of the hierarchy. In others, the political appointees at the top find it quite difficult to control the activities that go on "under" them. The appointed leaders often find that the

TABLE 15-2	The Fifteen Cabinet-Level Departments 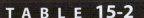

Department (year established)	Contact info	Number of Civilian Employees, 1990 (in thousands)	Number of Civilian Employees, 2003 (in thousands)	Difference, 1990–2003
Agriculture (1862)	14th St. and Independence Ave., SW Washington, DC 20250 202-720-8732 http:// www.usda.gov	123	99	-24
Commerce (1913)	14th St. and Constitution Ave., NW Washington, DC 20230 202-482-2000 http://www.doc.gov	70	37	-33
Defense (1789 as the Department of War; name changed in 1947)	The Pentagon Washington, DC 20301 703-545-6700 http://www.defenselink.mil	1,034	664	-370
Education (1979)	400 Maryland Ave., SW Washington, DC 20202 202-401-2000 http://www.ed.gov	5	5	0
Energy (1977)	1000 Independence Ave., SW Washington, DC 20585 202-586-5000 http://www.energy.gov	18	16	-2
Health and Human Services (1953 as Health, Education, and Welfare; renamed HHS after Education was spun off in 1979)	200 Independence Ave., SW Washington, DC 20201 202-619-0257 http://www.dhhs.gov	124	67	-57
Homeland Security (2002)	http://www.dhs.gov	N/A	152	+152
Housing and Urban Development (1965)	451 7th St., SW Washington, DC 20410 202-708-1112 http://www.hud.gov	14	11	-3
Interior (1849)	1849 C St., NW Washington, DC 20240 202-208-3100 http://www.doi.gov	78	71	-7
Justice (1789)	950 Pennsylvania Ave., NW Washington, DC 20530 202-514-2000 http://www.usdoj.gov	84	101	+17
Labor (1913)	200 Constitution Ave., NW Washington, DC 20210 202-219-5000 http://www.dol.gov	18	16	-2
State (1789)	2201 C St., NW Washington, DC 20520 202-647-4000 http://www.state.gov	26	32	+6
Transportation (1966)	400 7th St., SW Washington, DC 20590 202-366-4000 http://www.dot.gov	67	59	-8
Treasury (1789)	1500 Pennsylvania Ave., NW Washington, DC 20220 202-622-2000 http://www.ustreas.gov	159	132	-27
Veteran's Affairs (1989)	810 Vermont Ave., NW Washington, DC 20420 202-273-5400 http://www.va.gov	248	225	-23
TOTALS		2,068	1,687	

Source: Office of Personnel Management.

Controversy

George W. Bush's Cabinet Nominations

George W. Bush began his presidency in January 2001 under challenging circumstances. All eyes were on his cabinet nominees, and many wondered whether he would respond to strong suggestions from Democrats and many in the media that he appoint moderates to head the nation's departments. The importance of a president's cabinet decisions cannot be understated. The heads of the federal departments supervise the day-to-day work of government. They carry out the president's priorities. They are where the policy "rubber" meets the road. So, it was not a surprise to many that Bush nominated the conservatives John Ashcroft for attorney general, Linda Chavez for secretary of labor, and Gale Norton to head the Department of the Interior. Although Chavez had to withdraw her nomination when it was revealed that she had housed and possibly employed an illegal alien, Bush did not give any ground on the other nominees.

In a frenzy reminiscent of the campaign against President Reagan's 1987 nomination of Judge Robert Bork to the Supreme Court, liberal groups pulled out all the stops to defeat the Ashcroft nomination. The rhetoric became intemperate, as often happens when the policy stakes are high and the political blood begins to boil. Patricia Ireland, the head of the National Organization for Women, called Ashcroft "the extremist's extremist." Ralph Neas, of People for the American Way, said that Ashcroft was "the very worst executive-branch nominee ever." Democrats in Congress, buoyed by their supporters among various interests, saw Ashcroft's nomination as a challenge to be confronted. During the Senate confirmation hearings, Democratic senators grilled the conservative Ashcroft on his views on abortion, civil rights, and the law. Ultimately, though, Ashcroft survived the ordeal, winning confirmation by a vote of 58–42. Through the first Bush term, Ashcroft remained a controversial figure. It was no surprise when he resigned his position after the 2004 election.

The Interior nominee Gale Norton also proved to be somewhat controversial because some of her earlier environmental positions included support for mining, logging, and oil drilling on public lands and opposition to the Endangered Species Act. Not surprisingly, she was stridently opposed by almost all environmental interest groups, who referred to her as a James Watt disciple, a reference to President Reagan's controversial Secretary of the Interior. Like Ashcroft, Norton survived the confirmation process (the vote was 75–24) and became the first woman to head the Department of the Interior. Like John Ashcroft, Gale Norton remained at her post throughout the first Bush term. Unlike Mr. Ashcroft, however, she did not resign her position after the 2004 election.

Why such a keen interest in these cabinet posts? The director of a cabinet-level department not only has a great deal of discretion in what issues to pursue and how they should be pursued but also takes on great symbolic import. In American politics, symbol is often more important than substance.

---

careerists in their departments have adopted an agency point of view rather than the administration's agenda.[15]

> **agency point of view**
> Attitude of bureaucrats that stresses the protection of their own agency's budget, powers, staff, and routines, often at the expense of what elected officials may want.

The **agency point of view** stresses protection of the agency's budget, powers, staff, and routines, often at the expense of what elected officials may want. Agencies become quite protective of their "turf" and set in their ways. Presidents and their cabinets come and go, but career bureaucrats seem to stay on forever! The longevity of careerists within a particular bureau or agency is one reason that agencies develop their own, distinctive culture. For example, one study has shown that more than 80 percent of the career civil servants at the highest ranks have risen through the same agency.[16] It is no wonder that they believe in the goals of the agency and the societal need for its programs. In fairness, one must recognize that not everyone working in an agency subscribes to the agency point of view. Many agency managers truly believe that they are working for the public good.[17]

15-3b The Independent Agencies

Congress created the first independent agency in 1887 when it established the Interstate Commerce Commission. Since then, more than sixty other independent agencies have been established. These agencies can be divided into three rough categories: regulatory commissions, government corporations, and administrative agencies (see Table 15-3). The categories are rough because all the independent agencies engage in administration and many of them have some degree of regulatory authority. These agencies are independent in two senses. First, because they are located outside the fifteen major executive departments, they are not under the authority of a member of the cabinet. Second, the heads of these agencies, usually multimember boards or commissions, are appointed by the president for set terms of office. In most cases, they cannot be fired until their terms have expired.[18] This arrangement was intentional—the idea was to give the agencies a degree of freedom from

TABLE 15-3
U.S. Government Independent Agencies by Type

Regulatory Commissions

Commodity Futures Trading Commission	Federal Maritime Commission
Consumer Product Safety Commission	Federal Reserve Board
Environmental Protection Agency	Federal Trade Commission
Equal Employment Opportunity Commission	National Labor Relations Board
Federal Communications Commission	Nuclear Regulatory Commission
Federal Election Commission	Postal Rate Commission
Federal Housing Finance Board	Securities and Exchange Commission

Government Corporations

Export–Import Bank of the United States	Pension Benefit Guaranty Corporation
Federal Deposit Insurance Corporation	Resolution Trust Corporation
Government National Mortgage Association	Tennessee Valley Authority
National Railroad Passenger Corporation (Amtrak)	U.S. Postal Service
Pennsylvania Avenue Development Corporation	

Other Independent Agencies

ACTION	Merit Systems Protection Board
Administrative Conference of the United States	National Aeronautics and Space Administration
African Development Foundation	National Archives and Records Administration
Arms Control and Disarmament Agency	National Credit Union Administration
Central Intelligence Agency	National Foundation on Arts and Humanities
Commission on Civil Rights	National Mediation Board
Farm Credit Administration	National Science Foundation
Federal Emergency Management Agency	National Transportation Safety Board
Federal Housing Finance Board	Occupational Safety and Health Review Commission
Federal Labor Relations Authority	Office of Personnel Management
Federal Mediation and Conciliation Service	Peace Corps
Federal Mine Safety and Health Review Commission	Railroad Retirement Board
Federal Retirement Thrift Investment Board	Selective Service System
General Services Administration	Small Business Administration
Government Printing Office	Smithsonian Institution
Inter-American Foundation	Tennessee Valley Authority
International Trade Commission	United States Information Agency
International Development Cooperation Agency	United States Postal Service

presidential pressure. Much to the chagrin of presidents, this arrangement promotes the development of an agency point of view.

The independent agencies slide in and out of public view. The Federal Communications Commission (FCC), charged with regulating the airwaves, became the subject of controversy in 2004 when it became much more aggressive in policing radio and television programming. After Janet Jackson's infamous "wardrobe malfunction" during the 2004 Super Bowl halftime show, the FCC imposed record-level fines on CBS and its affiliates. FCC Chairman Michael Powell defended the FCC's action, saying, "As countless families gathered around the television to watch one of our nation's most celebrated events, they were rudely greeted with a halftime show stunt more fitting of a burlesque show."[19] When radio personality Howard Stern, the subject of numerous fines for violating the FCC's decency rule, finally abandoned the public airwaves for satellite radio in 2004, he was unmerciful in his criticism of the agency and its chair, Michael Powell. Speaking to thousands of cheering supporters in late 2004, Stern screamed, "Down with the FCC! They have ruined commercial broadcasting."[20]

15-4 Functions of the Bureaucracy

The functions of the bureaucracy can be divided into three broad categories: administration of programs, rule making, and adjudication of disputes. Every agency is involved to some degree in administration—at the least, it has to run itself. Many agencies have been given responsibility for managing government programs designed to meet some social or economic need: for example, agricultural subsidies, veterans' hospitals, school lunch programs, space exploration, delivery of mail, and construction of highways, among others. Some agencies are designed to manage and supervise aspects of the entire federal bureaucracy. For example, the General Services Administration manages and supplies government buildings, the Government Accountability Office keeps tabs on agency budgets, and the Office of Personnel Management supervises the hiring of federal employees.

15-4a Rule Making

The broad role now played by the national government makes Congress' job in passing needed legislation much more difficult. The sheer magnitude of problems demanding congressional attention and the practical difficulties of drafting sound regulations now limit Congress' ability to legislate comprehensively, much less effectively. Indeed, this complexity and impracticability, coupled with the pluralistic politics of the legislative process, make it difficult for Congress to fashion rules with any measure of precision. At the same time, the tortuous process of passing legislation makes it difficult for Congress to respond promptly to changing conditions. Thus, Congress has come to rely more and more on "experts" for the development, and the implementation, of regulations. These experts are found in a host of government departments, commissions, agencies, boards, and bureaus that comprise the modern administrative state.

Delegation of Legislative Power   Through a series of broad delegations of its legislative power, Congress has transferred to the federal bureaucracy much of the responsibility for making and enforcing the rules and regulations deemed necessary for a technological society (see Table 15-4). Frequently, the **enabling legislation** creating these agencies provides little more than vague generalities to guide agency rule making. These delegations of power may be desirable or even inevitable, but they do raise serious philosophical and constitutional questions. Most fundamental is the question of representative government. No one votes for the bureaucrats at OSHA who make regulations that affect millions of American workers and businesses.

The Americans with Disabilities Act (ADA) of 1990 provides a recent example of legislative delegation. The ADA, which built on the existing body of federal civil rights law, mandates the elimination of discrimination against individuals with disabilities. A number

▶ **enabling legislation**
Statutory provisions defining the function and powers of government agencies.

T A B L E 15-4

The Major Federal Regulatory Agencies

Agency	Year Created	Functions
Food and Drug Administration (FDA)	1907	Regulates the safety of food, drugs, and cosmetics
Federal Reserve Board (The Fed)	1913	Controls money supply; attempts to stabilize the economy; sets bank reserve requirements
Federal Trade Commission (FTC)	1914	Attempts to prevent false and misleading advertising; monitors business practices affecting fair competition
Federal Deposit Insurance Corporation (FDIC)	1933	Insures deposits in participating banks
Federal Communications Commission (FCC)	1934	Regulates interstate telephone service, cellular phones, broadcasting, and cable television
Securities and Exchange Commission (SEC)	1934	Regulates securities markets, such as the stock market
Federal Power Commission, renamed the Federal Energy Regulatory Commission (FERC) in 1977	1935	Regulates natural gas and oil pipelines and natural gas prices and issues hydroelectric dam licenses
Atomic Energy Commission, changed to Nuclear Regulatory Commission (NRC) in 1975	1947	Licenses and regulates nuclear power plants
Federal Aviation Administration (FAA)	1958	Regulates airline safety
Occupational Safety and Health Administration (OSHA)	1971	Protects workers' safety and health in the workplace
Consumer Product Safety Commission	1972	Regulates the safety of consumer products; recalls unsafe products from the market
Environmental Protection Agency (EPA)	1972	Regulates air, water, and noise pollution

Note: The first federal regulatory commission, the Interstate Commerce Commission, was abolished in 1995. Its functions were transferred to other agencies.

of federal agencies, including the Department of Justice, the Department of Transportation, the Equal Employment Opportunity Commission (EEOC), and the Federal Communications Commission (FCC), are given extensive regulatory and enforcement powers under the act. One of the many regulations that have been adopted in support of the statute is a final rule prohibiting discrimination on the basis of disability in the provision of state and local government services, which was published in the *Federal Register* by the Justice department. Twenty-nine pages of the *Federal Register* of July 26, 1991, are devoted to this one rule. Various agencies' regulations implementing the ADA fill hundreds of pages of the *Federal Register.*

Article I of the Constitution vests "all legislative power" in the Congress. When Congress delegates legislative power to the executive branch, it can be viewed as violating the implicit separation of powers. In 1935, the Supreme Court struck down an act of Congress on the grounds that it delegated too much legislative power to the bureaucracy without adequate policy guidance.[21] Since then, the Court has not invalidated any federal laws on this basis. In effect, the courts have given Congress *carte blanche* to delegate policy-making authority to the bureaucracy.

Normally, the federal courts permit agencies to interpret their statutory authorities broadly. For example, the Supreme Court has held that the Internal Revenue Service is empowered to revoke the tax-exempt status of private schools that practice racial discrimination, even though the text of Section 501(c)(3) of the Internal Revenue Code suggests otherwise.[22] However, in 2000, the Supreme Court dealt a major blow to the Clinton administration when it held that the Food and Drug Administration did not have the authority to regulate tobacco products (see Case in Point 15-1). The Court ruled that the

Does the Food and Drug Administration Have the Power to Regulate Tobacco Products?

FDA v. Brown and Williamson Corporation **(2000)**

Under federal law, the Food and Drug Administration (FDA) has the authority to regulate "drugs" and "devices." In 1996, the FDA adopted regulations governing the promotion and labeling of tobacco products. The regulations were concerned specifically with making these products less accessible to children and adolescents. FDA based its regulatory authority on the grounds that nicotine is a drug and tobacco products are devices that deliver nicotine to the body. Brown and Williamson, a leading manufacturer of tobacco products, filed suit challenging the FDA's authority in this area. The federal district court upheld the FDA's authority, but the Court of Appeals reversed, holding that Congress had not granted the FDA jurisdiction over tobacco products. Dividing 5–4, the Supreme Court also ruled against the FDA. Although the Supreme Court normally defers to agency interpretations of statutes, it concluded that Congress clearly had not intended to give the FDA the authority to regulate tobacco products. Of course, as a matter of statutory interpretation, the Court's decision can be overturned by ordinary legislation clearly authorizing the FDA to regulate tobacco.

FDA has misinterpreted the power granted by Congress under the Food, Drug and Cosmetics Act.[23]

Procedures for Adoption of Rules   Although Congress has delegated broad rule-making authority to the bureaucracy, it has also stipulated the procedures that must be followed in making rules and applying them to concrete cases. These procedures are spelled out in the Administrative Procedures Act (APA), first enacted in 1946 and later amended. The APA requires that the time, place, and procedures for agency rule making be published in the *Federal Register* and that interested parties be afforded the opportunity to submit written arguments to the agency before a proposed rule is finally adopted. Once adopted by the agency, the final rule must be published in the *Federal Register*. In most cases, agencies are required by law to conduct formal public hearings before adopting rules, and they must give the public an opportunity to comment on the proposed rules. Of course, even when a hearing is held, the interests that are adversely affected by a new rule often claim that the agency's rule-making procedures were inadequate.

15-4b Adjudication of Disputes

Controversies often arise as agencies attempt to apply their rules to affected parties. Before an agency enforces a decision that adversely affects a person, group, or company, it must follow a process provided for in the Administrative Procedures Act. In these instances, agencies take on a judicial, or "quasijudicial," character. Indeed, some agencies employ administrative law judges (ALJs) to decide disputes. Although less elaborate than a civil or criminal trial, a hearing conducted by an ALJ is a formal legal proceeding with its own rules and procedures. Agencies and affected parties are usually represented by counsel, testimony and other evidence are presented, and the losing party has the right to appeal the ALJ's decision to the federal courts. And the agencies do not always win these disputes. Although the ALJs are technically the employees of the agency for which they work, they are required by law to act as independent arbiters. Indeed, the law provides that no punitive action may be taken against ALJs for making decisions that run counter to their agencies.

15-5 Staffing the Bureaucracy

In *The Federalist* No. 86, Alexander Hamilton observed, "The true test of a good government is its aptitude and tendency to produce a good administration." Be that as it may, in the early days of the Republic, federal employees were chosen largely on the basis of political patronage. This practice of hiring the political supporters and cronies of the president came to be known as the spoils system, from the adage "To the victor belongs the spoils." Though practiced in greater or lesser degree by all the early presidents, the spoils system

WEB EXERCISE

Visit these links to federal bureaucracy websites. As you look at some of these sites, consider these questions:

- How many redundancies or overlaps do you see among agencies?
- If you were in charge of cutting back on government agencies, what criteria would you use to eliminate or combine agencies?
- Which would you cut or change?
- Are there any agencies you think we could do without?
- Imagine for a moment that Reagan had been successful in eliminating the Department of Education. After visiting that department's website, how do you think the removal of this cabinet post might have affected your education?
- How might your education be different from that of a student in a neighboring state?

Executive Office of the President (EOP)

White House; http://www.whitehouse.gov
Office of Management and Budget (OMB); http://www.whitehouse.gov/omb
United States Trade Representative (USTR); http://www.ustr.gov

Cabinet-Level Departments

Department of Agriculture (USDA); http://www.usda.gov
Department of Commerce (DOC); http://www.doc.gov
Department of Defense (DOD); http://www.dod.gov
Department of Education; http://www.ed.gov
Department of Energy; http://www.energy.gov
Department of Health and Human Services (HHS); http://www.os.dhhs.gov
Department of Homeland Security; http://www.dhs.gov/dhspublic/
Department of Housing and Urban Development (HUD); http://www.hud.gov
Department of the Interior (DOI); http://www.doi.gov
Department of Justice (DOJ); http://www.usdoj.gov
Department of Labor (DOL); http://www.dol.gov
Department of State (DOS); http://www.state.gov
Department of Transportation (DOT); http://www.dot.gov
Department of the Treasury; http://www.ustreas.gov
Department of Veterans Affairs; http://www.va.gov

Selected Independent Agencies

Board of Governors of the Federal Reserve System; http://www.federalreserve.gov
Central Intelligence Agency (CIA); http://www.odci.gov
Commodity Futures Trading Commission (CFTC); http://www.cftc.gov
Consumer Product Safety Commission (CPSC); http://www.cpsc.gov
Environmental Protection Agency (EPA); http://www.epa.gov
Equal Employment Opportunity Commission (EEOC); http://www.eeoc.gov
Federal Communications Commission (FCC); http://www.fcc.gov
Federal Deposit Insurance Corporation (FDIC); http://www.fdic.gov
Federal Election Commission (FEC); http://www.fec.gov
Federal Emergency Management Agency (FEMA); http://www.fema.gov
Federal Energy Regulatory Commission (FERC); http://www.ferc.gov
Federal Labor Relations Authority (FLRA); http://www.flra.gov
Federal Trade Commission (FTC); http://www.ftc.gov
General Services Administration (GSA); http://www.gsa.gov
Merit Systems Protection Board (MSPB); http://www.mspb.gov
National Aeronautics and Space Administration (NASA); http://www.nasa.gov
National Archives and Records Administration (NARA); http://www.nara.gov
National Credit Union Administration (NCUA); http://www.ncua.gov
National Endowment for the Arts (NEA); http://www.arts.endow.gov
National Endowment for the Humanities (NEH); http://www.neh.fed.us

continued

WEB EXERCISE — continued

National Mediation Board (NMB); http://www.nmb.gov
National Railroad Passenger Corporation (AMTRAK); http://www.amtrak.com
National Science Foundation (NSF); http://www.nsf.gov
National Transportation Safety Board (NTSB); http://www.ntsb.gov
Nuclear Regulatory Commission (NRC); http://www.nrc.gov
Office of Personnel Management (OPM); http://www.opm.gov
Peace Corps; http://www.peacecorps.gov
Securities and Exchange Commission (SEC); http://www.sec.gov
Selective Service System (SSS); http://www.sss.gov
Small Business Administration (SBA); http://www.sbaonline.sba.gov
Social Security Administration (SSA); http://www.ssa.gov
Tennessee Valley Authority (TVA); http://www.tva.gov
United States Agency for International Development (USAID); http://www.usaid.gov
United States Arms Control and Disarmament Agency (ACDA);
http://www.state.gov/www/global/arms/index.html
United States International Trade Commission (USITC); http://www.usitc.gov
United States Postal Service (USPS); http://www.usps.gov

was elevated to an art form by President Andrew Jackson. Jackson defended the system as necessary to the implementation of presidential will. In his view, federal officials should be loyal supporters of the president and must remain totally dependent on the president to keep their jobs if the president is to be assured that his policies will be carried out.

By the 1880s, criticism of the spoils system was reaching a crescendo. Reformers argued that the system fostered incompetence and inefficiency. They believed that being a good federal official required much more than being a friend of the president's—it required ability, dedication, and special training. Reformers were calling for the creation of a **meritocracy,** a system in which officials are recruited, selected, and retained on the basis of demonstrable merit.

▶ **meritocracy**   A hiring system in which officials are recruited, selected, and retained on the basis of demonstrable skills.

15-5a The Civil Service

The assassination of President James A. Garfield by a frustrated federal job seeker in 1881 spurred Congress to enact civil service reform. The Pendleton Act of 1883 forbade the firing of a federal employee for failing to contribute to a political campaign (a common practice at that time). Moreover, the act created a bipartisan Civil Service Commission to oversee a new federal meritocracy. As a result, approximately 15 percent of federal offices were to be staffed on the basis of competitive examinations, commonly referred to as the civil service exam. After the passage of the legislation, presidents routinely used expansions of the civil service system to protect their political appointees. After a worker was included under civil service, both the person and the job remained in the system. This practice led to a slow increase in the number of workers in the civil service system. Thus, by 1952, after further expansion by the Truman administration, the merit system covered more than 90 percent of all federal jobs.

As a result of reports in 1949 and 1955 by the Hoover Commission, the federal civil service was streamlined, and the operations of numerous agencies were consolidated under the General Services Administration. In an effort to further separate the civil service from partisan politics, Congress enacted the Hatch Act in 1940, which prohibited federal civil service employees from actively participating in or even contributing money to political campaigns. The Hatch Act was criticized by many as an infringement on the First Amendment rights of federal employees. Nevertheless, the act was upheld by the federal courts against constitutional challenges based on the First Amendment.[24] In 1993, Congress amended the Hatch Act to allow for greater political activity by federal employees. Republicans were critical of this change because most federal employees have traditionally sup-

*Profiles &
Perspectives*

**Woodrow Wilson
(1856–1924)**

Library of Congress
LC-USZ62-85704

Woodrow Wilson was born in Staunton, Virginia, on December 28, 1856. Growing up, Wilson lived in Augusta, Georgia; Columbia, South Carolina; and Wilmington, North Carolina. He graduated from Princeton University in 1879 and received a master's degree from Princeton three years later. Wilson studied law at the University of Virginia in 1881 and practiced law in Atlanta during 1881 and 1882. In 1886, he received his Ph.D. from Johns Hopkins University in Baltimore. He then took a teaching position at Bryn Mawr College. From 1888 to 1890, Wilson taught at Wesleyan, and in 1890 he returned to his alma mater, Princeton, as the professor of jurisprudence and political economy. In 1902, Wilson became the president of Princeton. In 1910, he was elected the governor of New Jersey. Two years later, with the aid of William Jennings Bryan, Wilson was nominated for president of the United States and won the 1912 election. He was narrowly reelected four years later on the slogan "He kept us out of war." In April 1917, after four American ships were sunk by the Germans, Wilson secured a declaration of war against Germany. After the Allies won the war, Wilson pushed for a League of Nations, but the necessary treaty was rejected by the Senate in 1920. Wilson died in Washington on February 3, 1924. He had been an invalid since October 1919, when he suffered a stroke.

Though his presidency is generally associated with issues of war and foreign relations, Wilson the political scientist contributed significantly to the emerging field of public administration, which is essentially the theory and practice of bureaucracy. In a paper published in 1887, Wilson wrote that public administration ought to be "removed from the hurry and strife of politics." Indeed, in Wilson's view, "administration lies outside of the proper sphere of politics. Administrative questions are not political questions. Although politics sets the tasks for administration, it should not be suffered to manipulate its offices." Wilson further claimed, "Bureaucracy can exist only where the whole service of the state is removed from the common political life of the people, its chiefs in addition to its rank and file. Its motives, its objects, its policy, its standards, must be bureaucratic." Thus, Wilson was a strong advocate of civil service reform on the principle of meritocracy: "A body of thoroughly trained officials serving during good behavior we must have in any case: that is plain business necessity."

Source of quotations: Woodrow Wilson, "The Study of Administration," *Political Science Quarterly*, vol. 2 June 1887.

ported the Democrats. Allowing greater political participation by federal employees helps the Democratic party, although the effect is probably not that great.

The Civil Service Reform Act of 1978 As the federal bureaucracy grew in size, complexity, and authority, presidential appointees charged with running the major departments found themselves relying more and more on senior civil service personnel. Because almost all these people had come up through the ranks within that department, they tended to have an agency point of view that often differed from the president's political agenda. Presidents of both parties became concerned that they might be losing control of the bureaucracy. These concerns led to the enactment of the Civil Service Reform Act of 1978. The act created the Senior Executive Service, an echelon of approximately eight thousand top managers who can be hired, fired, and transferred more easily than civil service personnel. The idea was to place top department and bureau managers more directly under the control of the president's appointees. More than two decades later, it does not appear as though the 1978 law has had much effect on the federal bureaucracy. Few members of the Senior Executive Service are fired or transferred. Cabinet members still complain about departments adopting an "agency point of view" rather than the president's.

15-6 Presidential Control of the Bureaucracy

Most recent presidents have entered office with strong suspicions about the bureaucracy. At a minimum, the bureaucracy is a large, unwieldy organization that must be pushed, pulled, pleaded with, threatened, and persuaded into enacting the goals of the president. Moreover, conservative presidents see a bureaucracy full of workers dedicated to the social welfare system and the power of government regulation. Because all recent conservative presidents have campaigned against the perceived excesses of the social welfare system and the prevalence of regulation, their hostility toward much of the bureaucracy is easy to understand. On the other hand, liberals distrust the close relationship between interest groups and government agencies. Liberals also fear that the rigidity of the organization and job safety of the individuals will create obstacles to any new ideas or policy changes. At the same time, all presidents realize that they must rely on the bureaucracy to carry out their wishes and that they depend on the bureaucracy for information. Given the bureaucracy's control over information, technical expertise, close relations with members of Congress, ties with interest groups, and long-term security, presidents may feel that this reliance on the bureaucracy makes them vulnerable.

Presidents have developed three main strategies for dealing with the bureaucracy. First, a president can appoint high-level bureaucrats who are in agreement with him on issues related to the agency's functions. Second, the president can establish a counterbureaucracy within the White House composed of close advisers who will watch over the shoulders of the bureaucrats. Third, the president can depend on policy organizations within the White House to develop new policy. Each of these three methods has its advantages and short-comings.[25]

15-6a Presidential Appointment and Removal Powers

The powers of removal and nomination are the best tool a president has for asserting control over a stubborn bureaucracy. Presidents control appointments to only 1 percent of all bureaucratic jobs, but the jobs in question are leadership positions at the top of the federal bureaucracy. When a president enters office, it is now assumed that the political appointees of the former president who hold most of the top positions will resign so that the new president, even if he is of the same party, can leave his own imprint on the bureaucracy. Presidents have always insisted on broad power to remove officials in their administrations. With respect to the top-level officials in the major executive departments, the president unquestionably has unbridled removal powers. These officials—secretaries, assistant secretaries, and undersecretaries—are widely understood to be political appointees who serve at the president's pleasure.

In an attempt to force the bureaucracy to adopt its political agenda, the Reagan White House exercised tight control over the process of top-level executive appointments. The Reagan people scrutinized all candidates for high-level administrative posts to ensure that they shared President Reagan's conservative views about the role of the federal government. In some cases, Reagan appointed persons whom he knew were opposed to the programs they would be charged with administering. For example, Anne Burford Gorsuch, who opposed the enforcement of many antipollution regulations, was appointed as director of the Environmental Protection Agency. Rather than confront Congress to try to change the legislation, Reagan sought to avoid controversy by appointing someone who would make the laws less effective by not enforcing them.

In contrast, the Clinton White House was less concerned about ideology and more concerned about diversity in making its bureaucratic nominations. Of course, the Clinton administration was much more liberal than its Republican predecessors, but it was also more diverse in terms of race and gender. This increased diversity reflected Clinton's campaign promise to make his administration "look like America."

Although cabinet and subcabinet officials are subject to immediate presidential firing, civil service employees can be fired only for cause, and displeasing the president is not necessarily cause for dismissal. Of course, presidents are seldom aware of the activities of civil service personnel because they occupy the middle and lower rungs of the administrative hierarchy.

Removal of Officials in the Independent Agencies   The independent agencies and commissions pose a more difficult question of presidential removal authority, one that the courts have struggled with over the years. For example, in 1935, the Supreme Court considered whether President Franklin D. Roosevelt could fire a member of the Federal Trade Commission (FTC) solely on policy grounds.[26] In 1931, President Herbert Hoover reappointed William Humphrey to serve on the FTC. According to an act of Congress,

Humphrey's seven-year term was subject to presidential curtailment only for malfeasance, inefficiency, or neglect of duty. When Roosevelt took office, he fired Humphrey, believing that the goals of his administration would be better served by people of his own choosing. Although Humphrey died shortly after his removal, the executor of his estate brought suit to recover wages lost between the time of removal and the time of his death. In deciding the case, the Supreme Court held that executive officials performing strictly executive functions could be removed at will by the president. In the case of regulatory commissions, like the FTC, however, Congress had created a quasi-legislative body designed to perform tasks independently of executive control. Thus, the Court said that Congress could regulate the removal of these officials.

In 1958, the Supreme Court expanded on this holding, saying that the unique nature of independent agencies requires that removal must be for cause, whether or not Congress has so stipulated.[27] The latter case involved a member of the War Claims Commission who had been appointed by President Harry S Truman and who was removed for partisan reasons by President Dwight D. Eisenhower. In disallowing Eisenhower's actions, the Court stated that "it must be inferred that Congress did not want to have hang over the Commission the Damocles' sword of removal by the President for no other reason than that he preferred to have on the Commission men of his own choosing." Thus, the legality of presidential removal of an official in the executive branch depends on the nature of the duties performed by the official in question. Officials performing purely executive functions may be removed by the president at will; those performing quasi-legislative or quasi-judicial functions can be removed only for cause (see Figure 15-2).

Establishing a Counterbureaucracy in the White House   Some presidents have not seen appointment and removal as a strong enough strategy in dealing with the bureaucracy. Mostly, they are concerned that even when an appointee takes office as a loyal supporter of the president's position, over time the appointee will begin to take on an agency point of view. This socialization into the culture of the agency or bureau has several facets. The high-ranking civil servants still provide most of the information and policy alternatives to the appointees. Furthermore, the appointees must work within the bureaucracy on an everyday basis, and they may begin to be more worried about their own turf than the president's agenda, particularly in the area of budget battles. The appointees also work within a small community of persons with an interest in that area: interest groups, members of Congress, policy experts, and other bureaucrats.

To help ensure responsiveness from career civil servants, President Richard Nixon employed a "counterbureaucracy strategy." Because he distrusted the bureaucracy, Nixon

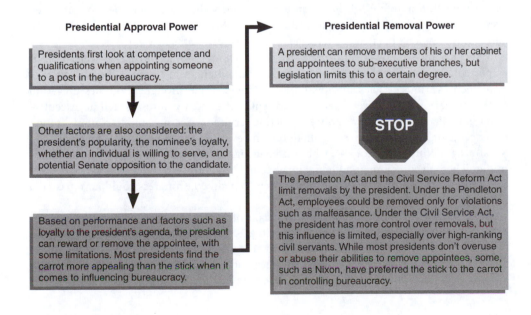

Presidential Approval Power

Presidents first look at competence and qualifications when appointing someone to a post in the bureaucracy.

Other factors are also considered: the president's popularity, the nominee's loyalty, whether an individual is willing to serve, and potential Senate opposition to the candidate.

Based on performance and factors such as loyalty to the president's agenda, the president can reward or remove the appointee, with some limitations. Most presidents find the carrot more appealing than the stick when it comes to influencing bureaucracy.

Presidential Removal Power

A president can remove members of his or her cabinet and appointees to sub-executive branches, but legislation limits this to a certain degree.

STOP

The Pendleton Act and the Civil Service Reform Act limit removals by the president. Under the Pendleton Act, employees could be removed only for violations such as malfeasance. Under the Civil Service Act, the president has more control over removals, but this influence is limited, especially over high-ranking civil servants. While most presidents don't overuse or abuse their abilities to remove appointees, some, such as Nixon, have preferred the stick to the carrot in controlling bureaucracy.

Figure 15-2
Presidential Means of Controlling Bureaucracy through Appointment Power

established groups within the White House to keep watch on the different bureaus and agencies. The advantage of this system was that Nixon knew that he could trust his counterbureaucracy. These people worked in the White House and thus were not as influenced by the bureaucratic culture. Ironically, this strategy proved ineffective. Even though the top-level agency personnel were Nixon appointees, they were treated as outsiders by the counterbureaucracy in the White House. Clashes cropped up between the two groups, and they had difficulty cooperating to formulate policy or communicate information. As one scholar explained, "the experience of the Nixon years clearly demonstrates that these two approaches (appointment strategy and counterbureaucracy) do not go together. A strong White House staff interested in managing the executive branch is likely to weaken the role of the cabinet officer and vice versa."[28]

White House Policy Organizations

President Nixon also used another strategy to influence the bureaucracy. Rather than rely only on his counterbureaucracy, he appointed a new Office of Telecommunications Policy (OTP) that was responsible for promoting his views in the fast-growing and important area of telecommunications technology. Although the Federal Communications Commission (FCC) existed to handle these types of policies, the OTP served as an "action-forcing mechanism" to shake things up in the policy area.[29] The advantage of this strategy was that Nixon had a like-minded individual running the OTP. Because the FCC is relatively independent from the president, this strategy allowed Nixon greater influence in the area than he would have had otherwise. The disadvantage was that policy development became confused, bogged down in turf wars, and incoherent. Neither group wanted to share information with the other. This strategy is not likely to be effective over the long term. Ultimately, a new president can easily eliminate any temporary White House office, whereas a more permanent, bureaucratic agency would enjoy congressional protection.

Other Presidential Tools for Controlling the Bureaucracy

The president also has a variety of other tools, both formal and informal, that assist him in controlling the bureaucracy. The president's most powerful formal tool is the budget. Because of the budget deficits rampant in the 1980s and 1990s, the budget process has become a dominant force in the policy process. Presidents have increasingly relied on the Office of Management and Budget (OMB) to formulate budget policy. Though Congress may or may not accept the president's budget plan, any bureau or agency wants to avoid budget cuts proposed by the OMB. This threat alone may be enough to convince a stubborn bureau to abide by the president's policy wishes. In addition, any new legislative proposals an agency wants must be cleared by the OMB prior to proposal to Congress. Moreover, since the Reagan administration, the OMB has been used to review the budgetary effect of proposed agency rules. Although the primary justification of OMB review is cost control, this review allows the president, in effect, to veto agency rules or programs he opposes.

Another formal power is the executive order. Though not as forceful as legislation or as permanent, executive orders can require certain changes in the way the bureaucracy implements various policies. President Truman, for example, brought about desegregation of the military by executive order. More recently, President Clinton issued an executive order liberalizing the military's policy restricting service by gay men and lesbians. Clinton's order came only after extensive negotiation with key members of Congress—in particular, Senator Sam Nunn (D-Georgia), who was chairman of the Senate Armed Services Committee. These negotiations resulted in an agreement to adopt a don't-ask, don't-tell policy through executive order. Of course, had it been so inclined, Congress could have passed a bill stating a different policy.

The president has numerous informal means of influence. A president can influence a bureau's legislative proposals by using his prestige to publicly support the agency's request. A president can lend even greater support to an agency's proposal by pushing for it in a State of the Union address to Congress or other public speeches. A popular president may also use personal visits to reward a bureaucracy for its efforts. The chief executive can also use his "bully pulpit" to attack the bureaucracy. This threat alone may sway some bureaucrats to adopt the president's positions.

15-7 Congressional Control of the Bureaucracy

Although Congress has found it necessary or expedient to delegate much of its legislative authority to the executive branch, it has attempted to maintain control over executive decisions arising out of the exercise of delegated authority. Keep in mind that executive agencies in many cases do not just promulgate but also implement and enforce regulations, the traditional concept of separation of powers notwithstanding. Thus, Congress has attempted, through a variety of mechanisms, to retain control over agency discretion. These mechanisms can be divided into two general categories: formal actions employing the legislative powers of Congress and oversight of the bureaucracy.

15-7a Legislative Tools

Congress has numerous legislative tools to use in controlling the bureaucracy. Legislation is a cumbersome method because of the difficulty of forming coalitions and the time required to pass a bill, but it is a powerful method. Congress may pass new legislation or attach amendments to other legislation changing certain policies. It may also use its power over the purse to threaten an agency with loss of funding if it does not cooperate. Of course, if Congress is extremely dissatisfied with the performance of a particular agency, it may rewrite the statute that created the agency in the first place. By amending the appropriate statute (or statutes), Congress may enlarge or contract the agency's jurisdiction in addition to the nature and scope of its rule-making authority. Congress could even shift the responsibility for policy from a difficult agency to another, more cooperative one.

The Senate can also influence the bureaucracy through its approval of the president's bureaucratic nominations. Though most nominees are approved by the Senate, the hearings that are held can be used to grill a nominee extensively about a particular policy, organizational structure, or management method. Sometimes, these hearings are concerned more with the battle between the president and Congress than with the qualifications of the nominee, but they also send a message to the bureaucracy about congressional preferences.

One of the more interesting, and certainly the most controversial, of the mechanisms by which Congress has sought to control the bureaucracy is the legislative veto. In existence since the early 1930s, the **legislative veto** is a device whereby Congress, one chamber of Congress, or even one congressional committee can veto agency decisions that are based on delegated authority. A legislative veto provision is written into the original act delegating legislative power to an executive agency. The provision requires that before an agency rule can take effect, it must be approved by Congress. Some provisions require Congress to vote on the measure before it takes effect, but others simply state that the rule will not take effect until Congress has had ninety days in which to consider and possibly reject the regulation. Because legislative vetoes do not always involve bicameral passage and presentment to the president, however, the Supreme Court has said that they are unconstitutional unless they pass both chambers of Congress and are signed by the president.[30] Nevertheless, many legislative veto provisions remain on the books, although no court will enforce them.

> **legislative veto** A device whereby Congress, one chamber of Congress, or even one congressional committee can veto agency decisions that are based on delegated authority.

15-7b Legislative Oversight

Because the bureaucracy is so large and has so many different programs, Congress has had to develop an institutional process, known as *oversight,* to keep track of the bureaucracy and the implementation of policy. Congress divides the task among the different standing committees according to issue area. For example, the Armed Services Committee performs oversight on the Department of Defense. Oversight involves hearings in which bureaucrats have to defend their actions publicly; investigations by the Government Accountability Office and the Congressional Budget Office; annual reports from the bureaucracy to Congress; informal meetings; and responses to demands from the media, constituents, or interest groups. Congress may be concerned about whether policy implementation was consistent with congressional wishes, how the bureaucracy handles individual cases, whether the policy works, how well the bureaucracy serves its customers, or whether money is being wasted.

The more active oversight process has been likened to a police patrol. Under a police patrol system, legislators actively search for problems in the bureaucracy by routinely conducting investigations. In general, most observers do not believe that members of Congress engage in a great deal of police patrol oversight. A less active style in which members of Congress wait for others—such as interest groups, constituents, or the media—to alert them to problems with the bureaucracy has been compared to a fire alarm system. The fire alarm system requires much less work on the part of members, and they can look like heroes when they step in to fix the problem.[31] Congress routinely engages in more fire alarm oversight than police patrol. Some observers argue that the problem with this system is that through constant vigilance, police patrols may prevent some problems within the bureaucracy, but with fire alarm oversight, a problem must become serious enough to cause someone to pull an alarm before Congress gets involved.

15-8 Legal Constraints on the Bureaucracy

Like Congress, the federal courts play an important role in supervising the federal bureaucracy. A fundamental question arising in many cases is whether an agency has acted beyond the scope of its jurisdiction as defined by Congress. In addition to the substantive issues of agency jurisdiction and rule-making authority, administrative actions may raise significant procedural questions. Agency decisions must follow procedural guidelines, so as to prevent arbitrary and capricious action and to safeguard the rights of parties.

Federal agency procedures are generally based on statutory requirements—most notably, the Administrative Procedures Act (APA) of 1946. In addition to the requirements of the APA, the federal courts have applied the Due Process Clause of the Fifth Amendment when statutory procedures have been deemed inadequate to ensure fairness or to protect the rights of individuals. When a federal court reviews an agency decision, it generally attempts to dispose of the case on statutory grounds; for example, by interpreting the APA rather than reach the constitutional due process issue.

15-8a Public Access to Agency Information

Government agencies maintain tremendous stockpiles of information. In a society in which information is power, citizens often want to gain access to these types of data. Although the courts have never held this type of access to be a matter of constitutional right, Congress has created a statutory right of public access under the Freedom of Information Act of 1966 and a right of individual access under the Privacy Act of 1974. Although these acts create exemptions for certain types of secret information, such as sensitive national security material, they nevertheless represent a significant attempt to open up the process of modern governance to the ordinary citizen.

Government in the Sunshine   Much of what bureaucracies do occurs behind the scenes, away from the hot lights of television or the probing questions of interest group spokespersons. In an effort to open the bureaucracy to public scrutiny, Congress passed the Open Meeting Law in 1976. The law requires all meetings and hearings conducted by the bureaucracy to be open to the public, except where matters of diplomacy, national security, military affairs, or trade secrets are being discussed. Moreover, meetings must be announced in advance. The Open Meeting Law parallels the **sunshine laws** that have been adopted by most states. The effort to open up the bureaucracy and "let the sun shine in" is generally applauded by citizens and scholars alike.

▶ **sunshine laws** Laws that require most bureaucratic organizations to open their meetings to the public.

Whistle Blowing   One of the most important constraints on bureaucracy is the ability of people within an agency to "blow the whistle" when the agency is acting improperly. Waste, fraud, and mismanagement that cost taxpayers money are the most common problems revealed by **whistle blowers.** Sometimes, the issue goes beyond economics, however, as in the case of workers at nuclear power plants reporting their safety concerns. Of course, whistle blowers run the risk of being punished, formally and informally, by their superiors and colleagues. They can be fired, stripped of their responsibilities, or even deprived of their security clearances. Most difficult perhaps for whistle blowers is being shunned by their coworkers. A 1988 survey found that two-thirds of government workers expressed concern that they would suffer reprisals if they "blew the whistle."[32]

Perhaps the most famous whistle blower in American politics was A. Ernest Fitzgerald, a Pentagon financial analyst who was fired after he told Congress about the extreme cost overruns on the C-5A transport plane being built by Lockheed. Fitzgerald spent a decade in court and incurred more than a million dollars in legal fees before he was able to win back his civil service job. Fitzgerald's case helped place the issue of whistle blowing on the congressional agenda. Recognizing the need to protect whistle blowers, in 1988 Congress passed the Whistleblower Protection Act. President Reagan vetoed this legislation, but his successor, George Bush, signed the bill into law in 1989. The law provides for awards of as much as $250,000 to individuals who blow the whistle on cost overruns by government contractors. The law encourages whistle blowers to come forward by providing financial incentives and legal protection.

> **whistle blowers** Individuals working for either the government or a company under government contract who expose corruption, violations of the law, and environmental abuses within an organization.

15-9 Do Bureaucracies Respond to the Public Interest?

Because the American democracy relies on the bureaucracy to implement the decisions of its elected officials, one major concern with bureaucracy is whether it responds to the public interest. Two of the major theories of the way bureaucracies interact with other political actors in the policy process suggest that a small group of individuals dominates the process at the expense of broader political control by the president and all members of Congress.

15-9a Iron Triangles and Issue Networks

Iron triangles are small policy systems composed of the members of Congress on a particular subcommittee or committee with jurisdiction over an issue, leaders of the interest groups affected by the policy, and the agency responsible for implementing the program. The agency stays in the system because the legislators control the bureaucracy's budget, can stifle unfavorable legislation, and protect the agency from extensive oversight. Because members of Congress choose which committees they prefer and stay on the same committee for years, the system can be maintained over time. Presidents or other outside actors may influence the policy for short periods when the issue is controversial and in the public eye, but the iron triangle can outlast most intrusions and control the administration of the program during normal times.

Somewhat similar to iron triangles but including more people and somewhat less reviled are issue networks, which are composed of a small group of political actors involved in a particular policy area.[33] They include bureaucratic leaders, congressional staff members, interest groups, the media, academics, and researchers in the Washington think tanks who regularly interact on a given issue. Issue networks are not as exclusive as iron triangles, but they do dominate the policy process. A different network exists for each different policy area. In general, expertise and information tend to be the keys to influence within a policy network. Individuals move between the different jobs within the issue network, so the network develops its own language and political culture. Access to others within the network and to key decision makers is crucial to influence, but some individuals may be influential regardless of their official position. In general, power is fragmented, and the bureaucracy may fill the void by trying to develop coalitions of support for certain policies. Most observers would view the issue network as more inclusive than an iron triangle. Furthermore, it may be more likely to serve the public interest than an iron triangle.

Comparative Perspective

Bureaucracy in the People's Republic of China

The People's Republic of China has the world's largest and most powerful bureaucracy. China's bureaucracy has ancient origins, but as recently as the late nineteenth century the country was administered by some two thousand civil servants. More than twenty-seven million Chinese now hold some sort of position in the state (national) bureaucracy, and many more hold positions at the local level. The structure of the Chinese bureaucracy is both vertically and horizontally complex. The state council encompasses three vice premiers, nine state councillors, and more than forty ministries, each of which is comparable to a major executive department in the American national government. In addition to this mammoth structure, the system has numerous other "administrations," bureaus, offices, and institutes. Similar complex structures exist at the provincial and local levels.

Chinese officials have three ranks indicating their status in the system: their formal administrative title, their position within the Communist party, and their civil service grade. As in most bureaucracies, few officials are dismissed, disciplined, or demoted for inefficiency or incompetence. In China, as in other authoritarian systems, bureaucrats are more likely to be penalized for political reasons. During the infamous Cultural Revolution of the 1960s, Chinese bureaucrats were routinely purged for ideological impurity. These days, China's government is more stable and more conservative. But in a country making great strides in economic development, the concern is more about the strangling effect of bureaucracy on enterprise. To start a business, an entrepreneur in China needs the approval of a government agency. About half of all government officials are involved on a day-to-day basis in administering China's burgeoning economy.

In China, a quiet debate is now taking place at the highest levels of the government over how the bureaucracy can be streamlined. In the early 1980s, the Chinese leader Deng Xiaoping set out to reduce the size of the bureaucracy by one-third. Nevertheless, between 1982 and 1988, although the Chinese work force grew by 20 percent, the number of government and party officials grew by 59 percent. As the Chinese experience indicates, bureaucracy is not only hard to eliminate but also difficult to keep from growing.

15-10 Conclusion: Assessing the Bureaucracy

It is fair to say that the United States has a mammoth bureaucracy that exercises formidable powers. It is not accurate to characterize the bureaucracy as all-powerful or out of control, as some of the more extreme critics of the administrative state are prone to do. To be sure, the federal bureaucracy is large, powerful, and unwieldy, but like all institutions of American government, it is subject to a system of checks and balances. These checks and balances are not spelled out in the Constitution, for the Framers did not anticipate the emergence of a large-scale bureaucracy. Rather, they are a natural outgrowth of the constitutional and statutory powers of Congress, the president, and the courts.

No one is particularly happy with the federal bureaucracy now. Liberals often see the bureaucracy as the protector of corporate interests. Conservatives tend to view the bureaucracy as "big government" meddling where it does not belong. Presidents are often frustrated that the executive branch seems to have a mind of its own. Members of Congress are sometimes disappointed in the way in which legislation is (or is not) implemented. The average person, irrespective of ideology, is likely to believe that the bureaucracy is wasteful, inefficient, and too powerful. This view of the bureaucracy is firmly established in the political culture. Even our popular culture is filled with negative portrayals of bureaucrats and bureaucracies.

Some expert commentators have also been very critical of the federal bureaucracy, although their critiques seldom resemble popular perspectives on the subject. Many have called for dramatic reorganizations of the executive branch with an emphasis on "flattening the pyramid"—reducing the layers of hierarchy.[34] But many political scientists have defended the federal bureaucracy, charging that popular perceptions of inefficiency and incompetence are based more on myth than reality.[35]

From time to time, government leaders attempt to reform the bureaucracy, as in the case of the National Performance Review under the Clinton administration. These attempts at reform seldom accomplish all that they set out to do. Despite occasional reform efforts, the public continues to perceive the bureaucracy as the epitome of waste, fraud, and abuse. What citizens should keep in mind in evaluating their bureaucracy is what our society would look like without the rules, programs, and services the bureaucracy represents. To the person struggling to maintain a small business, the prospect of less government regulation and red tape could be appealing. But to an industrial worker risking injury on the job, the prospect of curtailing OSHA plant inspections might be more than a little worrisome. Much of what the bureaucracy does has come in response to public demands for the government to address some serious problem. Most of these problems do not go away, but instead require continuing attention. As the aftermath of September 11 demonstrates, particularly in reference to the FBI and the CIA, the nature of bureaucracy itself has become a problem, with its inevitable internal politics and interagency jealousies. This problem often cries out for attention from the public and its elected officials.

Questions for Thought and Discussion

1. Why do Americans generally dislike bureaucracy?
2. Is it possible to imagine a democracy in a mass society without bureaucracy?
3. Can the federal bureaucracy be made more efficient? More accountable? More representative of the American people? To what extent are these goals consistent with one another?
4. Why has Congress found it necessary or desirable to delegate so much regulatory authority to the federal bureaucracy?
5. Do the federal courts do an effective job of ensuring that the bureaucracy respects individual rights and liberties?

Practice Quiz

Note: You can find the correct answers to these questions by taking the quiz and then submitting your answers in the Online Edition. The program will automatically score your submission. If you miss a question, the program will provide the correct answer, a rationale for the answer, and the section number in the chapter where the topic is discussed.

1. Much of the growth of the bureaucracy during the nineteenth century was attributable to the growth of the _____.
   a. post office
   b. Department of War
   c. Department of State
   d. Department of Justice

2. The Department of _____, created in 1849, is responsible for managing the national parks system.
   a. Labor
   b. Health and Human Services
   c. the Interior
   d. Indian Affairs

3. The Hatch Act, enacted in 1940, prohibited federal civil service employees from _____.
   a. actively participating in political campaigns
   b. taking a private-sector job in an industry directly affected by the employee's former government service
   c. working past the age of seventy
   d. none of the above

4. The Civil Service Reform Act of 1978 created the _____, an echelon of approximately eight thousand managers who can be hired, fired, and transferred more easily than civil service personnel.
   a. Presidential Management Staff
   b. Federal Government Management Staff
   c. Senior Executive Service
   d. Presidential Elite Corps

5. Operating under the banner of _____, Vice President Al Gore and his staff spent six months documenting waste, inefficiency, and needless regulation in the federal bureaucracy.
   a. efficiency now
   b. government for the people
   c. reinventing government
   d. that government is best that governs least

6. The heads of the fifteen major executive departments comprise the _____.
   a. Executive Office of the President
   b. White House staff
   c. presidential caucus
   d. president's cabinet

7. The Administrative Procedures Act deals with the two basic types of agency decision making: rule making and _____.
   a. adjudication
   b. enforcement
   c. licensure
   d. policy making

8. President Andrew Jackson defended his use of the spoils system on the grounds that it _____.
   a. promoted good will between the masses and the elites
   b. was necessary to ensure the implementation of presidential will
   c. promoted racial and ethnic equality
   d. promoted social and economic equality

9. Congressional checks on the bureaucracy include _____.
   a. passing legislation that may threaten the life of the agency or its funding
   b. the Senate's role in the confirmation process
   c. the legislative oversight function
   d. all of the above

10. The _____ was passed by Congress in an attempt to encourage government employees to report cost overruns by government contractors.
   a. Whistleblower Act
   b. Pentagon Act
   c. Government Contractors Act
   d. Fitzgerald Act

For Further Reading

Aberbach, Joel D. *Keeping a Watchful Eye: The Politics of Congressional Oversight* (Washington, D.C.: Brookings Institution, 1991).

DiIulio, John J., Gerald Garvey, and Donald L. Kettl. *Improving Government Performance: An Owner's Manual* (Washington, D.C.: Brookings Institution, 1993).

Dodd, Lawrence C. *Congress and the Administrative State*, 2d ed. (Boulder, CO: Westview Press, 1998).

Downs, Anthony. *Inside Bureaucracy* (Boston: Little, Brown, 1967).

Goodsell, Charles. *The Case for Bureaucracy: A Public Administration Polemic*, 4th ed. (Washington, D.C.: CQ Press, 2003).

Gormley, William T., Jr. *Taming the Bureaucracy: Muscles, Prayers and Other Strategies* (Princeton, NJ: Princeton University Press, 1989).

Heclo, Hugh. *A Government of Strangers* (Washington, D.C.: Brookings Institution, 1974).

Ingraham, Patricia Wallace. *The Foundation of Merit: Public Service in American Democracy* (Baltimore: Johns Hopkins University Press, 1995).

Kerwin, Cornelius M. *Rulemaking: How Government Agencies Write Law and Make Policy*, 3d ed. (Washington, D.C.: CQ Press, 2003).

Kettl, Donald F. *The Transformation of Governance: Public Administration for Twenty-First Century America* (Baltimore: Johns Hopkins University Press, 2002).

Light, Paul C. *The True Size of Government* (Washington, D.C.: Brookings Institution, 1999).

Meier, Kenneth J. *Politics and The Bureaucracy: Policymaking in the Fourth Branch of Government*, 4th ed. (Fort Worth, TX: Harcourt College Publishers, 2000).

Osborne, David, and Ted Gaebler. *Reinventing Government: How the Entrepreneurial Spirit Is Transforming the Public Sector* (New York: Plume Books, 1993).

Pressman, Jeffrey L., and Aaron B. Wildavsky. *Implementation*, 3d ed. (Berkeley: University of California Press, 1984).

Rourke, Francis E. *Bureaucracy, Politics and Public Policy*, 3d ed. (Boston: Little, Brown, 1984).

Seidman, Harold. *Politics, Position, and Power: The Dynamics of Federal Organization*, 5th ed. (New York: Oxford University Press, 1997).

Shapiro, Martin. *Who Guards the Guardians? Judicial Control of Administration* (Athens, GA: University of Georgia Press, 1988).

Stillman, Richard J. *Creating the American State: The Moral Reformers and the Modern Administrative World They Made* (Tuscaloosa, AL: University of Alabama Press, 1998).

———. *The American Bureaucracy*, 3d ed. (Belmont, CA: Thomson/Wadsworth, 2004).

Wilson, James Q. *Bureaucracy: What Government Agencies Do and Why They Do It* (New York: Basic Books, 1991).

Yates, Douglas. *Bureaucratic Democracy: The Search for Democracy and Efficiency in American Government*, 2d ed. (Cambridge, MA: Harvard University Press, 1987).

Endnotes

1. Although it does not appear in his writings, the following quotation has been attributed to Thomas Jefferson: "That government is best which governs the least, because its people discipline themselves." Later, in his essay *Civil Disobedience* (1846), Henry David Thoreau wrote, "I heartily accept the motto—'That government is best which governs least;' and I should like to see it acted up to more rapidly and systematically."

2. Alexis de Tocqueville, *Democracy in America* (New York: Vintage Books, 1945), vol. 1, p. 59.

3. Office of Management and Budget, online at www.whitehouse.gov/omb.

4. See, for example, Gary Lawson, "The Rise and Rise of the Administrative State," *Harvard Law Review*, vol. 107, 1994, p. 1231.

5. Richard J. Stillman, *Creating the American State: The Moral Reformers and the Modern Administrative World They Made* (Tuscaloosa, AL: University of Alabama Press, 1998), p. 3.

6. Ibid.

7. See, for example, Kenneth J. Meier, *Politics and The Bureaucracy: Policymaking in the Fourth Branch of Government*, 4th ed. (Fort Worth, TX: Harcourt College Publishers, 2000).

8. Herbert Kaufman, *Are Government Organizations Immortal?* (Washington, D.C.: Brookings Institution, 1976), p. 76.

9. The term *red tape* derives from the strips of red tape once used by the British government to bind bundles of official papers. The term now connotes needlessly complicated and time-consuming bureaucratic rules and procedures.

10. John M. Scheb and John M. Scheb II, *Law and the Administrative Process* (Belmont, CA: Thomson/Wadsworth, 2005), p. 11.

11. Susan Mosychuk of Citizens Against Government Waste, quoted in Christine Hall, "House GOP Targets Waste, Fraud in Government Programs," *CNS News*, May 21, 2003. On the web at http://www.cnsnews.com.

12. Today, the census is conducted by the Bureau of the Census, an agency within the Department of Commerce.

13. See, for example, *Schechter Poultry Corp. v. United States*, 295 U.S. 495 (1935); *United States v. Butler*, 297 U.S. 1 (1936); *Carter v. Carter Coal Co.*, 298 U.S. 238 (1936).

14. See Joe Klein, "The Vice-President's Ashtray," *Newsweek*, August 16, 1993, p. 27.

15. William A. Niskanen, Jr., *Bureaucracy and Representation* (Chicago: Aldine-Atherton, 1971), p. 38.

16. Hugh Heclo, *A Government of Strangers* (Washington, D.C.: Brookings Institution, 1974), pp. 117–18.

17. Barry Z. Posner, and Warren H. Schmidt, "An Updated Look at the Values and Expectations of Federal Government Executives," *Public Administration Review*, vol. 54, January/February 1994, pp. 20–24.

18. *Wiener v. United States*, 357 U.S. 349 (1958).

19. CBS Stations Fined $550,000 for "Wardrobe Malfunction,'" Associated Press, September 22, 2004.

20. Verena Dobnik, "Stern Blasts FCC at Satellite Promotion," Associated Press, November 18, 2004.

21. *Schechter Poultry Corp. v. United States*, 295 U.S. 495 (1935).

22. See *Bob Jones University v. United States*, 461 U.S. 574 (1983).

23. *FDA v. Brown and Williamson Corp.*, 529 U.S. 120 (2000).

24. See, for example, *United States v. Harris*, 216 F.2d 690 (5th Cir. 1954).

25. Francis E. Rourke, "The Presidency and the Bureaucracy: Strategic Alternatives." In *The Presidency and the Political System*, ed. Michael Nelson (Washington, D.C.: CQ Press, 1984).

26. *Humphrey's Executor v. United States*, 295 U.S. 602 (1935).

27. *Wiener v. United States*, 357 U.S. 349 (1958).

28. Richard P. Nathan, *The Administrative Presidency* (New York: John Wiley & Sons, 1983).

29. Francis E. Rourke, "The Presidency and the Bureaucracy: Strategic Alternatives," p. 354.

30. *Immigration and Naturalization Service v. Chadha*, 462 U.S. 919 (1986).

31. Mathew McCubbins and Thomas Schwartz, "Congressional Oversight Overlooked: Police Patrols Versus Fire Alarm," *American Journal of Political Science*, vol. 28, 1984, pp. 165–79.

32. Survey reported in Bob Cohn, "New Help for Whistle Blowers," *Newsweek*, June 27, 1988, p. 43.

33. See Hugh Heclo, "Issue Networks and the Executive Establishment." In *The New American Political System*, ed. Anthony King (Washington, D.C.: American Enterprise Institute, 1978).

34. See, for example, Paul C. Light, *Thickening Government: Federal Hierarchy and the Diffusion of Accountability* (Washington, D.C.: Brookings Institution Press, 1995).

35. See, for example, Kenneth J. Meier, *Politics and The Bureaucracy: Policymaking in the Fourth Branch of Government*, 4th ed.; Charles Goodsell, *The Case for Bureaucracy: A Public Administration Polemic*, 4th ed. (Washington, D.C.: CQ Press, 2003).

Domestic Policy and the Policy-Making Process

16

16-1 What Is Public Policy?

public policy Whatever government attempts to do about an issue or problem.

policy-making process The process by which public policy is produced.

Public policy is whatever government attempts to do about an issue or problem. Public policy is produced through the long, complicated **policy-making process.** To understand how any particular government policy emerges from the broad array of options available, you must understand both the rules of the game and the social, cultural, and economic conditions that shape the policy debate. The institutions, rules, and political actors involved in the policy-making process largely determine the shape of any particular policy, although the political environment plays a crucial role in determining what options are considered relevant for discussion. The politics of the policy-making process do not occur in a vacuum: The prevailing values of the culture combine with events and the nature of an issue to either expand or contract the set of alternatives available to policy makers.[1] Furthermore, because the Constitution established a flexible system of government that could change over time, the political culture changes even the rules of the game. The changing political culture continually places pressures on political actors and institutions to adapt to the new environment. In turn, institutions change, the policy process remains fluid, and new issues enter the public debate over the proper role of government.

As the culture changes, some policy alternatives become irrelevant or even unthinkable, and new possibilities emerge in other areas. For example, the enslavement of millions of African Americans was a relevant topic of policy debate fewer than 150 years ago, but would now be considered morally repugnant for political debate. In the reverse direction, culture can change to allow new ideas to enter the policy debate. For example, the dominant values of capitalism, individualism, and self-reliance would have prevented mainstream political leaders of the nineteenth century from even considering government-provided health care for all individuals. The political culture inhibited these types of ideas from emerging in the public debate.

From time to time, technological advances provide new policy alternatives that did not previously exist. For example, before the 1950s, no one had reason to consider whether the U.S. government should engage in space exploration. But the cultural values that emerged from the frontier tradition, westward expansion, and the idea of manifest destiny allowed Americans to consider the policy of sending astronauts to the moon. Considering the cost, the absence of tangible benefits for most Americans, and the numerous social needs of the society competing for scarce resources, this policy could have been quite controversial. Instead, from the 1950s until it encountered difficulties in the 1980s, the space program enjoyed some of the strongest support of any government program. The space race became a strong symbol of American values and abilities to many citizens, and, consequently, the political culture accepted this new policy.

By 2000, however, government at all levels had begun to deal with difficult questions about high technology, especially questions related to the Internet. The U.S. Justice department, along with several state attorneys general, prevailed against Microsoft Corporation in a case in which a federal district judge ruled that Microsoft had violated the nation's antitrust laws.[2] This case, like many others, dealt with the application of laws enacted many decades earlier to a continually evolving marketplace. The dynamics of policy making in the computer–Internet age often make for a rough juxtaposition of twentieth century remedies and twenty-first century problems.

16-2 The Policy-Making Process

The complex policy-making process involves nearly every aspect of the American political system that has been discussed in this book. The political culture shapes both the rules of the game and the policy debate. The Constitution, reflecting the political culture of the late eighteenth century, establishes the broad foundation for the way the policy process will be carried out, although the specifics of the process have undergone major changes over time. The federal structure embodied in the Constitution adds considerable complexity: multiple avenues of access, subtle differences in the political cultures of the states, different policy processes within each state, and quite different policy outcomes within different states.

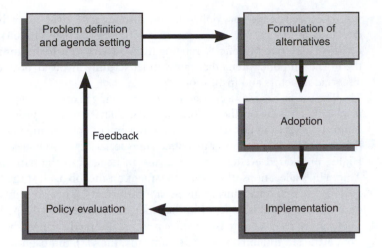

Figure 16-1
The Traditional Model of the Policy-Making Process

Access to the process is guaranteed by the civil liberties U.S. citizens enjoy—in particular, the First Amendment—and the number of people who can participate has been expanded by the various civil rights movements. The political parties, interest groups, media, and public opinion polls are all avenues through which demands can be placed on the policy system. The four major political institutions—Congress, the president, the courts, and the bureaucracy—provide the forum for making decisions and implementing policy. Nearly every political actor is also involved in evaluating the results of policy and formulating new policies or policy changes.

The traditional policy-process model suggests that a policy must first become part of the national debate in the **problem definition** and **agenda setting** stage (see Figure 16-1). Next, different alternatives must be suggested, discussed, and researched in the **formulation of alternatives** stage. After the discussion of alternatives, the government must make a decision in the **adoption** phase of the process. Then the policy must be carried out in the **implementation** stage. Finally, **evaluation** of the policy occurs. If the assessment of the policy shows that it was ineffective, too costly, unconstitutional, or unpopular or that it has other problems, the process starts over as problem definition and agenda setting begin anew. The process can become stuck at any stage, but after a policy decision is made, implementation typically occurs and feedback and a reassessment of the policy start the process over.[3]

16-2a Problem Definition and Agenda Setting

One enduring value of American culture has been that individuals are responsible for their own actions and for dealing with their own problems. Individualism is the basis of our capitalist economic system. Like the frontier settlers who relied on their own initiative to survive the harsh conditions they faced, individuals are expected to take responsibility for their own livelihood and accumulation of material gains. Both this frontier mentality and capitalist economic beliefs have contributed to the American notion that most problems are private and should be solved by the individual. Occasionally, however, some problems afflict enough individuals, become severe enough, or require some kind of group action to warrant attention as a public problem. President Lyndon Johnson put the elimination of poverty on the public agenda through his Great Society initiatives of the 1960s.

The first step for any group demanding a new public policy is to convince others that their problem is a public problem rather than an individual problem. For example, the observation that more than forty million Americans did not have medical insurance in 2000 could be seen as either a private problem or a public problem. If it is a private problem, government obviously has no role. If it is a public problem, it may be because of income inequality, discrimination by insurance companies, or a major flaw in the health-care system.

> **problem definition** The initial phase of the policy-making process in which different political actors attempt to show that a problem is a concern that government can take some action to remedy.

> **agenda setting** The stage of the policy-making process when different political actors attempt to get an issue in the public view so that government officials will take policy action.

> **formulation of alternatives** The stage of the policy-making process when political actors propose various policies to overcome the public problem.

> **adoption** The phase of the policy-making process when a decision is made to deal with a public problem; the most common form of adoption is a legislative enactment, although the other branches of government and the bureaucracy may also play a key role at this stage.

> **implementation** The stage of the policy-making process when an adopted policy is carried out.

▶ **evaluation**   The stage of the policy-making process when the policy is assessed. If the assessment shows that the policy was ineffective, too costly, unconstitutional, or unpopular or that it has other problems, the process starts over at the problem-definition stage, and agenda-setting begins anew.

▶ **national agenda**   A compilation of those issues that deserve national attention.

▶ **systemic agenda**   The issues that are generally viewed as deserving of public attention and as legitimate concerns of government. Generally, the systemic agenda contains abstract ideas that merit discussion.

▶ **institutional agenda**   The set of issues being actively considered by some governmental authority.

The need for a new policy is sometimes made clear more by events than by the demands of any group. The occurrence of the September 11, 2001, attacks brought into question a myriad of policies, ranging from airport security to immigration to the role of the FBI. Each policy arena that came under scrutiny involved, both directly and indirectly, a myriad of actors and institutions.

The media can play a crucial role in convincing people that a public problem exists and in placing an issue on the national agenda. Television news programs identify problems, radio and television talk shows discuss government policies and national concerns, and the network evening news programs often run special series on issues confronting the nation. Highly publicized events can also thrust an issue onto the national stage. For example, Anita Hill's allegations of sexual harassment on the job against the Supreme Court nominee Clarence Thomas during his Senate confirmation hearings in 1991 brought tremendous attention to this issue, which had long been ignored by the public and policy makers. The charges received intense media coverage, and the hearings, shown on network television, attracted millions of viewers. Similarly, the O. J. Simpson case in 1994 focused the attention of the nation on the issues of spouse abuse and domestic violence.

After an issue gains attention, it moves onto the **national agenda.** The national agenda can be divided into two types: the systemic agenda and the institutional agenda.[4] The **systemic agenda** consists of all issues generally believed to deserve public attention and to be legitimate concerns of government. In general, the systemic agenda contains abstract ideas that merit discussion. The **institutional agenda** is the set of issues being actively considered by some governmental authority. The different levels and branches of government may have their own different institutional agendas. Each state may have its own agenda, and each branch may be considering different issues. In the late 1980s, for example, education and welfare reform made their way to the systemic agenda. They were the subject of numerous newspaper and magazine articles, television and radio talk shows, and public opinion polls. By the 1990s, specific proposals began to emerge on the institutional agenda. Congress and the state legislatures began to consider legislation. During the 2000 presidential election, both candidates made a priority of creating a prescription drug benefit for older Americans. Four years earlier, the topic had not been broached by either party during the campaign. Nor was it considered during the succeeding congressional sessions. Nonetheless, the issue in 2000 was not whether the federal government would move to provide the benefit, but rather the timing and the nature of that benefit.

Policy through Inaction   An issue that reaches the institutional agenda does not necessarily move any further into the policy process. In effect, *some* policy is made by the government's taking no action. For example, the U.S. policy on the creation of a national high-speed railroad network has been made by the absence of any action by Congress or the president. In contrast to the European Economic Community and Japan, the U.S. government does not plan to finance or encourage the development of these types of trains. No president has vetoed a bill on high-speed train funding; no bill has ever been voted on by Congress. In effect, the policy has been made through government inaction. Early in his presidency in 2001, President George W. Bush decided not to move to regulate carbon dioxide emissions from power plants despite having earlier pledged to do so during the campaign. Again, a policy decision was essentially implemented through inaction rather than through action.

16-2b Formulation of Policy Alternatives

After a problem has been identified, possible solutions must be devised. Everyone may agree that illiteracy is a major problem, but how can it be solved? Numerous political actors may propose different policies to overcome the public problem. The president, the cabinet, and the other top officials of the executive departments, members of the legislature, and candidates for office are obvious sources, but often they borrow their ideas from others. Interest groups are always willing to share their ideas for policy solutions. Friendly legislators or bureaucrats may be quite willing to promote the interest group's policy proposal.

Similarly, numerous **think tanks** in Washington employ policy specialists, scientists, and lawyers to conduct research on various topics and propose policy changes. Some think tanks with a general ideological orientation (for example, the liberal Brookings Institution and the conservative American Enterprise Institute) investigate a wide range of topics. Most Washington think tanks, however, focus on a particular policy area. For example, the Rand Corporation focuses on issues related to national security and defense. In addition to trying to define the problem and place it on the national agenda, these groups offer their preferred policy alternatives to anyone who will listen.

The term *policy formulation,* with its suggestion of an orderly process of careful deliberation, is a bit misleading. Although most policy alternatives start out as logically constructed proposals based on careful analysis of the problem, the nature of democratic politics often leads to compromises that may frustrate all sides. Proposals by new candidates for office, interest groups, think tanks, and other participants from outside government are likely to reflect their political preferences in an idealized world. Typically, these types of proposals must be changed to have any chance of becoming policy. From the hundreds of thousands of proposals, usually only ten to twenty thousand bills are proposed in a two-year session of Congress. Of these, only a few hundred are passed. Most policy alternatives are never considered by Congress, and often the policies that take effect do not reflect any particular alternative proposed in the early stages of the policy process.

16-2c Adoption

A policy can be adopted in several different ways, none of which is final in that an existing policy may be changed over time. Perhaps the most important method is the legislative process at either the state or national level, although the bureaucracy and the courts also play an important role in the adoption of policy. Major new national policy initiatives, such as the Social Security Act in 1935, the Clean Air Act of 1970, Clinton's national health-care proposal of 1994, and welfare reform in 1998 almost always take the legislative route, however.

The nature of decision making in Congress greatly influences the adoption of policy. Legislative decisions require bargaining among diverse interests leading to compromises that may not be consistent with the policy alternatives laid out in the preceding stage. The division of policy responsibilities among various legislative committees may also make it difficult to form coherent policy. For example, a committee concerned with health may fight against cigarette smoking, whereas an agriculture committee, concerned about tobacco farmers, provides incentives to farmers to grow more tobacco. Another impediment to policy adoption is the complex structure of Congress that allows a bill to be killed at various points. Because all bills must be approved by both chambers of Congress and the president and because most major bills must also pass through two or more congressional committees, a bill is far more likely to fail than to pass. Congress therefore tends to favor the status quo, and policy changes incrementally (in small steps over time).

Policy may also be heavily influenced by the different groups placing demands on each legislator. Most importantly, the nature of the member's district may encourage the member to consider policy from a perspective other than what is best for the nation as a whole. Because legislators are elected in separate geographic districts, a member's policy decision is likely to be more heavily influenced by the preferences of the groups that elected the member than by the national interest. Consequently, a bill that benefits the legislator's district is likely to receive the legislator's vote, regardless of the bill's other merits. The efforts of interest groups to sway legislators may also prevent them from considering all policy alternatives. For example, the National Rifle Association has long been seen as the main obstacle to gun control despite public opinion favoring some controls on handguns and semiautomatic weapons.

Judicial Policy Making   Congress and the state legislatures have not been the only source of policy making: The courts have been active in creating policy in such areas as civil liberties and civil rights. The courts have historically been the most important forum for

> **think tanks**   Groups that employ policy specialists, scientists, and lawyers to perform research on various topics and propose policy changes.

the protection of individual liberties against government power and the rights of any kind of minority against the majority. Though Congress was active in supporting civil rights after the Civil War and during the 1960s, many of the most important policy decisions on such issues as desegregation, criminal justice, and equal employment opportunities have been made by the courts as they have decided legal disputes. For example, the current U.S. policy on abortion was initiated in the judicial arena—in particular, through the Supreme Court's 1973 decision in *Roe v. Wade*[5] (see Case in Point 16-1).

Adoption of New Policies by the Bureaucracy   Though most new policy decisions are made by Congress or the courts, the bureaucracy can create new policy as it administers legislation. Because most laws passed by Congress contain only general guidelines about the way the policy should be shaped, agencies must create rules for implementing the policy. Although legislation provides the goals and basic structure, agency rule making provides most of the details on how policy will be carried out. For example, the Americans with Disabilities Act (ADA) of 1990, which mandated the elimination of discrimination against individuals with disabilities, gave extensive regulatory and enforcement powers to a number of federal agencies, including the Department of Justice, the Department of Transportation, the Equal Employment Opportunity Commission, and the Federal Communications Commission. These agencies have adopted numerous rules to achieve the broad objectives of the ADA. In the areas of civil rights, education, the environment, public health and safety, transportation, energy, and many others, public policy is often made through bureaucratic agency rule making.

16-2d Implementation

Regardless of which institution adopts it, the policy must be carried out by either the federal or state bureaucracies. For most issues other than national security, the policy must be publicized. Indeed, one of the government's ongoing problems is the way to alert all people who could be affected by a new policy or a change in current policy. All new regulations are published in the *Federal Register,* a huge document regularly issued by the government, but how many citizens ever read it? Often, agencies use the media, mass mailings, and posted notices in government buildings to inform citizens of new policies affecting their

Case in Point **16-1**

Abortion—the Ultimate Example of Judicial Policy Making?

Roe v. Wade (1973)

Norma McCorvey, also known as Jane Roe, was a twenty-five-year-old, unmarried Texas woman who faced an unwanted pregnancy. Because abortion was illegal in Texas, Roe brought suit to challenge the constitutionality of the state's abortion law. A federal district court declared the Texas law unconstitutional but refused to issue an injunction blocking its enforcement. On appeal, the Supreme Court issued a 7–2 decision striking down the Texas law and prohibiting it from being enforced. The Court concluded that the constitutional right of privacy was broad enough to encompass a woman's decision to terminate her pregnancy. The Court noted, however, that "the right [to abortion] is not unqualified and must be considered against important state interests...." Although a fetus was not, in the Court's view, a "person" within the language of the Constitution, states would be permitted (except in cases in

which the mother's life was endangered by carrying the fetus to term) to ban abortion after "viability" (that point in pregnancy when the fetus is capable of surviving outside the mother's womb). Dissenting, Justice Byron White wrote that "the Court perhaps has authority to do what it does today; but in my view its judgment is an improvident and extravagant exercise of the power of judicial review...." Justice William Rehnquist argued that "to break pregnancy into three distinct terms and to outline the permissible restrictions the State may impose in each one ... partakes ... of judicial legislation...." Critics of the decision charged the Court with acting like a legislative body; supporters cheered the Court for upholding the constitutional rights of women. The Court has been struggling with the abortion issue ever since. Did the Supreme Court go too far in *Roe v. Wade?*

rights or making benefits available to them. Sometimes, the government requires private businesses to notify people of a new policy. For example, most large companies must post notices informing employees of their rights in such areas as equal employment opportunity, minimum wage standards, and worker safety.

The enactment of the policy also requires some type of action by the bureaucracy. Policies involving criminal conduct, taxes, and civil rights require the government to enforce the law. For example, the Internal Revenue Service (IRS) is one of the most feared enforcers of a government policy—the payment of income, corporate, and other taxes. If it is regulatory policy, the agency must establish a means of forcing businesses or individuals to take actions consistent with the law. The Environmental Protection Agency (EPA), for example, is charged with administering environmental laws, such as the Clean Air Act Amendments of 1977 and 1990. In some cases, to implement the law, the EPA has had to develop new techniques for measuring pollution and its effects.

The provision of entitlements such as Social Security benefits, disability insurance, and welfare requires a different kind of structure. Rather than focus on how to force citizens or businesses to comply with a law, the agency must figure out how to give out benefits to all who are eligible for the program. To implement these types of policies, an agency must distribute information to the public so that qualified persons will be aware of the benefits; establish a process for receiving and reviewing applications; develop a system of appeals for persons who are initially denied benefits; create a process of reviewing, processing, and storing relevant information about the recipients; and initiate a process for discontinuing benefits when persons are no longer eligible. Administering this type of program requires a tremendous amount of paperwork and supervision, so agencies involved in the provision of social welfare benefits are usually among the largest agencies. Other than the Defense department, three of the four largest departments in the federal government are primarily devoted to the provision of benefits to various groups: Veterans' Affairs, Health and Human Services, and Agriculture.

The Importance of State and Local Governments   Like the federal bureaucracy, state agencies are responsible for administering policy. Of course, any policy decisions made by a state's legislature or courts must be implemented by its own bureaucracy, although the state agencies are also involved in implementing federal policies through the model of *cooperative federalism* (see Chapter 3, "Federalism: A Nation of States"). For example, the Social Security Administration's disability insurance program is funded by the federal government, although initial applications for benefits are made at a state office. Applicants turned down twice by the state office can appeal the decision to a regional office of the Social Security Administration (SSA). Thus, the state must share the burden of processing the applications if it wants its citizens protected by the disability program.

Likewise, the federal government has frequently used *unfunded mandates* to force states, local governments, and businesses to comply with its policy wishes. For example, under the Clean Water Act, cities were forced to take expensive measures to prevent rainwater from mixing with untreated sewage. Although the cities had to spend millions of dollars to modify their sewer systems to meet this requirement, the federal government provided none of the money. According to the National Conference of Mayors, which strongly opposed unfunded mandates, compliance with the Clean Water Act and related regulations was costing local governments more than $1 billion per year by 1993.[6] Through both congressional action and executive orders issued by President Clinton, the federal government has restricted the imposition of new unfunded mandates, much to the relief of state and local governments. However, the financial burdens of existing mandates, such as those emanating from the Americans with Disabilities Act, remain in effect.

Congressional and Judicial Oversight of the Bureaucracy   In addition to the difficulty of coordinating action by federal, state, and local administrative officials, implementation is further complicated by the continual supervision of bureaucratic actions by Congress and the courts. Congress influences implementation in three ways:

1. At least one committee in each chamber of Congress has responsibility for oversight of the agencies under its jurisdiction. The committees monitor the actions of the agency through hearings, investigations, and informal inquiries; sometimes, investigative reports by other actors, such as the media, may trigger a committee response.

2. Individual members of Congress routinely intervene in policy administration when they are asked to do casework for their constituents. For example, a local business struggling with new rules created by an agency may plead with its local legislator for help.

3. Congress can pass new laws affecting the policy or change the budget for the agency responsible for administering the policy. Although enacting a new law is a cumbersome method of influencing the bureaucracy, the threat of congressional action may cause bureaucrats to reconsider their actions. A potential budget cut can be quite a credible threat.

The courts can also change the way a policy is administered. Although agencies that enforce regulations (the IRS) or determine eligibility for benefits (the SSA) are required to have a formal internal review process, any persons not satisfied with the outcome can appeal to the courts. Relatively few do so, however; for example, of the nearly 1.3 million people initially denied Social Security disability benefits in 1992, fewer than 5,000 pursued their appeals to the courts. If the courts decide that an agency has misinterpreted congressional intent in applying the policy, they may require a change in the way the policy is administered. Also, for some policies, the courts are the main institutions responsible for administration. For example, the bankruptcy laws are largely administered by the courts, which hear cases filed by businesses or individuals seeking protection from their creditors.

16-2e Policy Assessment

The most fundamental question that can be asked about any policy is "Does it work?" In some cases, the answer may be obvious. The policy of ignoring the environmental costs of manufacturing was revealed as woefully inadequate by the dramatic pictures during 1970 of the Cuyahoga River in Cleveland *burning*. Most policies cannot be so easily evaluated, however. Even though policy analysts use a variety of advanced techniques, such as cost-benefit analysis, statistics, economic analysis, and mathematical modeling, assessment usually results in a confusing picture. At times, the data are bad or no one has collected the right kinds of information. Gathering information about the effects of a policy takes time, but no one likes to keep dumping money into a program that is not working while waiting for a policy evaluation. Besides, evaluation can be so complicated that two independent analysts using different assumptions can give contrasting opinions on the results of the same policy. Typically, most programs have some positive results—some intended and others unintended—and some negative effects that were not anticipated or desired.

Every policy area has a network of specialists who closely monitor the implementation of the policy and assess whether it seems to be working. These networks include members of Congress who sit on the committee with responsibility for the bill, congressional staffers, academics, members of think tanks, bureaucrats, interest group lobbyists, and individuals working within the policy area. The issue network typically has its own language and methods of analysis that allow insiders to interact.

Most policy evaluation is conducted by members of this issue network. Assessments by government specialists are likely to carry the most weight in policy discussions. The Government Accountability Office, the Congressional Research Service, the Office of Management and Budget, the inspector general for each department, and research specialists within each department provide most of the official policy analysis. Private sources also produce a wide variety of reports and analyses, although they typically have a more difficult time in gaining the attention of those who "matter."

Because policies often do not work as expected and because conditions change, policy evaluation usually identifies new areas of concern that need to be placed on the national agenda. Thus, the information gained from the evaluation process can be used as **feedback** within the system. In a sense, the policy cycle is complete because this feedback leads back to the agenda-setting stage. Getting policy revisions on the national agenda can be just as difficult as placing a new policy there. Nevertheless, because few truly new policy issues appear on the agenda at any one time, most items on the agenda are revisions of existing policy.

Because each policy-making institution has a limited amount of time, energy, and other resources to devote to new or revised policies, only a limited number of the many proposals on the national agenda can be considered at one time. If constituents or interest groups complain about policy problems to state legislators or members of Congress, the legislators may pay more attention to policy evaluations that make the point more systematically. The media have even more power to bring policy failures to the public agenda. Though they may omit subtle and complex details, the media can dramatically portray the basic point of a policy analysis by adding pictures and making it more human.

Although the implementation and policy-evaluation stages of the policy process may appear tedious and dull to the average citizen (or student), interest groups that can benefit from changes in policy are quite aware of what is happening at this stage. Media coverage and public attention are greatest at the adoption stage, but much of the fine-tuning of policy takes place in relative obscurity. Insiders can then play a more important role in the process than may appear possible during the more public aspects, such as presidential campaigns, presidential addresses to Congress, or battles in Congress. The policy process is much more complex, time-consuming, and frustrating than policy statements presented during debates, political speeches, news sound bites, or campaign advertising would lead us to believe.

16-2f The Involvement Model of the Policy Process

The traditional model of policy making views public input as a component of the process before the adoption stage. In reality, public opinion is important throughout the process. But most members of the mass public are not attentive to most aspects of policy making. In contrast, numerous interest groups get involved in the process, no matter what issue is being considered. These groups are sometimes referred to as **stakeholders** because they stand to win or lose as a result of the policy decision. Accordingly, the model of the process needs to be refined to take into account the importance of stakeholders at every stage of the process. A better model of the policy process is the **involvement model,** which stresses the importance of activist groups at every stage (see Figure 16-2). Although the involvement model applies to all areas of policy making, it is a particularly good description of the way

> **feedback** Information from the public that leads to the reassessment of a particular policy output.

> **stakeholders** The groups in the policy-making process that stand to win or lose as a result of a policy decision.

> **involvement model** Conception of the policy-making process that stresses the importance of activist groups at every stage of the process.

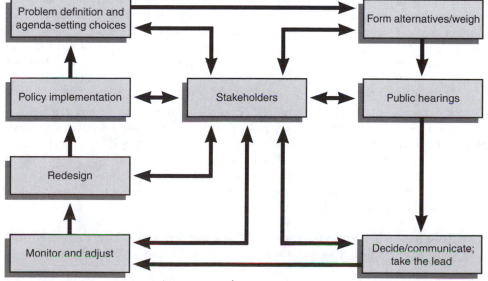

Figure 16-2
The Involvement Model of the Policy-Making Process

policy is made on environmental issues. Numerous groups on both sides of an issue, all well armed with factual and scientific data, interact with policy makers at every stage of the process, from agenda setting through assessment. Environmental groups have been especially adept at using the Freedom of Information Act and open-meeting laws to make the process accessible.

16-3 The Domestic Agenda

The domestic agenda includes numerous issues. Each of them is important, at least to some segment of the public. Among the most important issues on the domestic agenda over the past several decades have been crime and criminal justice, the environment, education, and social welfare. These issue areas remain important and are now attracting considerable activity. In the 1992 presidential election, the issue of health-care reform came onto the public agenda, largely at the initiative of the candidate Bill Clinton, who used the issue against President George Bush. By the time of the 2000 election, the issue had morphed from an overall reform of the health-care system to a more modest prescription drug benefit for older Americans. In 1996, Bob Dole, the Republican challenger, proposed a 10 percent across-the-board cut in income taxes. Although this suggestion failed to inspire much support among voters, George W. Bush revived the idea of tax cuts four years later. Not only did the issue "take" in 2000, but a major tax cut also became the signature item on Bush's policy agenda in 2001. After Congress passed two of President Bush's tax cut proposals during Bush's first term, the issue remained alive in the 2004 campaign, with Democrats attacking the tax cuts as helping to swell the budget deficit and disproportionately favoring the wealthiest Americans. After his reelection in 2004, President Bush announced an ambitious domestic policy agenda to include reforming the Social Security system and overhauling immigration policy.

Domestic issues always figure prominently in a presidential election, even when, as in 2004, the nation is involved in a controversial war abroad. The following survey of domestic policy concerns is not intended to be comprehensive, nor does it focus on the most salient policy issues of 2005. Rather, it is an overview of issues that have remained on the domestic agenda for the last several decades. These prominent issue areas are crime and criminal justice, the environment, health care, education, social welfare, and immigration.

16-3a Crime and Criminal Justice

Every day, a story about some type of crime seems to make the evening news. Most often, the crimes described on television news reports are violent in nature, involving death or injury to one or more victims. Increasingly, violent crimes are being committed by teenagers armed with weapons once confined to battlefields and police arsenals. The National Crime Victimization Survey found that 23.7 percent of the nation's households experienced some form of criminal victimization in 1991. Fortunately, by 2003 the proportion of households victimized by crime declined to roughly 15 percent. However, the crime problem still loomed large. Persons over the age of 12 experienced approximately 24 million violent and property crimes in 2003. In the nation's largest cities such as Chicago and Washington, D.C., nearly 50 percent of residents expressed fear of crime in their communities.[7]

One does not need to look at a public opinion poll to know that Americans remain concerned about crime and expect their government to do something about it. Of course, the principal responsibility for criminal justice rests with the state and local governments. Most crimes are offenses against state law and are therefore investigated by state and local law-enforcement agencies and prosecuted in state and local courts. But the national government also has its own criminal justice system, designed primarily to address criminal activity that is interstate or international in scope.

The Role of the National Government in Assisting Local Law Enforcement

The national government has attempted to assist state and local agencies in fighting the war against crime. During the 1970s, state and local law enforcement agencies were able to modernize their equipment and facilities by utilizing funds made available through federal grants from the Law Enforcement Assistance Administration. For decades, state and local enforcement agencies have been able to get assistance from the Federal Bureau of Investigation, which maintains the best crime lab in the world, in identifying perpetrators and helping solve difficult cases. In 1994, in response to rising public concern about crime and violence, Congress passed a comprehensive crime bill that, among other things, provided funds to local governments to hire as many as an additional one hundred thousand police officers. The 1994 crime bill also fostered widespread adoption of community-oriented policing, a style of police work in which officers are encouraged to develop relationships with schools, recreation centers, nonprofit organizations, and other community institutions. Local police departments that adopted the community policing approach were rewarded with federal dollars to hire new officers, establish new programs, and obtain new equipment. After September 11, 2001, the emphasis of the Justice Department shifted to counterterrorism, and community policing faded into the background.

The Role of the Courts in Setting Crime Control Policy   The federal courts have a major role in setting public policy dealing with crime, for both the federal and state criminal justice systems (see Figure 16-3). The federal courts, and in particular the Supreme Court of the 1960s and early 1970s, interpreted the Bill of Rights to greatly increase the legal protection of persons suspected, accused, and convicted of crimes. Perhaps the best-known cases were the Supreme Court's 1961 *Mapp* decision prohibiting the use of illegally obtained evidence in criminal trials[8] and its 1966 *Miranda* decision requiring police to inform suspects of their rights before conducting interrogations.[9] In addition, the Court expanded defendants' rights in such areas as the right to counsel, double jeopardy, and the right to challenge state convictions in federal court. Critics charged that the net effect of these decisions was to handcuff the cops and compound the growing problem of crime. By the late 1960s, public opinion began to reflect this attitude. Since the 1960s, the Gallup poll has routinely asked people "Do you think that the courts in this area deal too harshly or not harshly enough with criminals?" In April 1965, 48 percent said "not harshly enough." By January 1969, 74 percent said "not harshly enough" (see Figure 16-3). Judicial decisions expanding defendants' rights certainly had something to do with this changed perception of the courts.

Figure 16-3
Public Opinion toward the Nation's Criminal Courts, 1965–2002

Source: Adapted from Harold W. Stanley and Richard G. Niemi, *Vital Statistics on American Politics 2003–2004* (Washington, D.C.: CQ Press, 2003), p. 164.

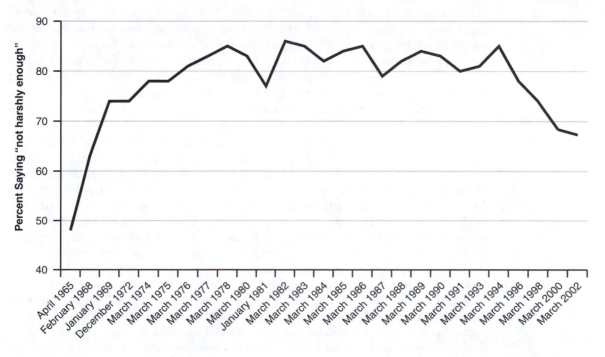

The new public skepticism toward the courts manifested itself in popular culture too. Numerous movies of the 1970s and 1980s portrayed judges as virtual co-conspirators with the criminal element. A prime example is the *Dirty Harry* series, in which Clint Eastwood plays a tough, streetwise cop with a big gun and a knack for using it effectively. Officer Harry Callahan, or "Dirty Harry," is always in trouble with the police department for acting in a fashion considered reckless. But he (and the audience) knows that what Dirty Harry does on the street is necessary and justified, even if judges might find his actions unlawful.

The national government's approach to crime became considerably more punitive in the 1980s and 1990s. Sentences were stiffened, prison space increased, and the death penalty authorized for a number of crimes. The Supreme Court has facilitated, if not endorsed, this get-tough law-and-order stance by loosening some of the constraints on searches and seizures and the use of illegally obtained evidence. Clearly, in the 1980s, the national government got the message that the American people wanted harsher measures against crime. Still, in the early years of the twenty-first century, crime remains at or near the top of the public's list of concerns, and many question whether government can really do much about it.

Gun Control   Without question, the prevalence of guns—especially handguns—in this society contributes to the problem of violent crime. In no other society are guns as readily available. The Constitution protects the right of law-abiding citizens to "keep and bear arms," but it also permits reasonable regulation of the sale and use of firearms. Most Americans do not support drastic measures, such as an attempt to ban the sale of guns (see Figure 16-4). The right to bear arms is not only part of the constitutional tradition, it is also well entrenched in political culture. Moreover, many Americans feel that they need weapons to protect themselves and their families against criminals. One in seven Americans has used a gun in self-defense.[10] And many people believe that, in the words of a prominent bumper sticker, "if guns are outlawed, only outlaws will have guns." It has been estimated that more than fifty million Americans own more than two hundred million guns legally.[11] With so many guns already in circulation, many believe that criminals will always have access to an illegal gun market. But only a small minority, represented by the National Rifle Association (NRA), opposes any and all efforts at gun control. Surveys routinely show that a majority of Americans favor some restriction on the availability of handguns, assault rifles, and armor-piercing bullets. One survey conducted by the Gallup organization in late 1993 even found that most gun owners favored banning assault weapons and cheap handguns.[12] Since 1973, the Gallup poll has asked the question "Would you favor or oppose a law which would require a person to obtain a police permit before he or she could buy a gun?" As recently as March 2002, eight in ten Americans favored laws to require people to obtain permits before buying guns (see Figure 16-4).

In March 1991, former President Ronald Reagan shocked many of his conservative admirers by endorsing a bill pending before Congress that would require a five-day waiting period on the purchase of handguns. The purpose of the waiting period was to allow for a background check on the prospective buyer, with the goal of prohibiting convicted felons or persons with a history of mental illness from buying a gun. The legislation was known as the Brady bill, after James Brady, President Reagan's press secretary who was shot during the assassination attempt on Reagan in 1981. Brady was severely incapacitated as a result of his wounds. His wife, Sarah, began an arduous campaign on behalf of the bill. Of course, the NRA has long opposed these types of measures, and as one of the most effective lobbying groups, it has always had tremendous influence in Congress. During the 1992 presidential campaign, Bill Clinton expressed his support for the Brady bill. A year after Clinton was elected, Congress passed the Brady bill, but only after Senate Republicans ended a filibuster against the measure. Speaking to the press after the bill passed, Jim Brady expressed his delight but said that the bill was only the first step in a long journey. Opponents of gun control, on the other hand, worried that the bill might represent just that—a first step down a legislative road that would lead ultimately to the banning of firearms. Of

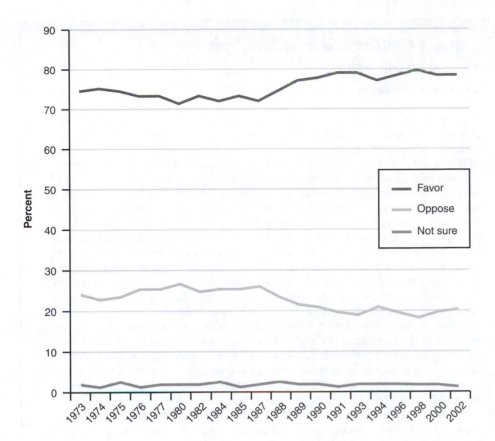

Figure 16-4
Public Opinion on the Issue of Gun Control, 1973–2002

Source: Adapted from Harold W. Stanley and Richard G. Niemi, *Vital Statistics on American Politics 2003–2004* (Washington, D.C.: CQ Press, 2003), p. 163.

course, given the strong public support for the "right to keep and bear arms," that prospect is highly unlikely. The more pressing question is whether the Brady bill, now that it is law, is doing enough to curb the availability of firearms for criminal purposes.

The debate of guns was heightened following a series of school shootings that captured the attention of media in the 1990s. The mass shootings at Columbine High School outside Denver, Colorado, in April 1999 placed the related issues of alienated youth and access to guns at the top of the national agenda. The gun the shooters used had been purchased at a gun show, bringing immediate efforts to tighten legislation dealing with the sale of guns at the shows. However, despite the concern and apparent support for various elements of gun control among the public, Democrats quietly dropped much of their rhetoric about gun control during the 2000 campaign. Moreover, following another school shooting in March 2001 in Santee, California, little discussion of gun legislation took place. This latter shooting brought another item to the agenda: bullying of students by their peers. The reason was that the student who allegedly perpetrated the shooting had been the victim of bullying and teasing by his classmates. The national discussion that ensued focused on ways that school authorities could intervene with students early on to prevent these types of problems before they escalated into violence.

The War on Drugs Another factor that contributes to the prevalence of crime in this country is the drug problem. The use of drugs such as opium, cocaine, and marijuana is not new; indeed, these drugs were widely used, and legal, in the nineteenth century. In the twentieth century, these and other drugs were made illegal under state and federal laws. Before the 1960s, use of these drugs was confined to a small subculture in the big cities—jazz musicians, beatniks, and the like. But in the 1960s, middle-class young people, mainly college students, began to experiment with these drugs and with hallucinogens like LSD, mescaline, and psilocybin. The use of hallucinogens and marijuana came to be a significant feature of the "hippie" counterculture of the 1960s. In the 1970s, cocaine and marijuana

Popular Culture and American Politics
Bowling for Columbine

By Chapman Rackaway

Why do violent acts seem to happen more often in America than in other countries? That question guides filmmaker Michael Moore's *Bowling for Columbine.* Made in the aftermath of the tragic school shootings in Littleton, Colorado, the movie poses politically charged and vital questions about violence as a part of America's cultural fabric.

Moore approaches the Columbine question primarily from an attitude critical of the Second Amendment and gun ownership in America. Focusing mostly on the prevalence and availability of guns, along with the politically potent National Rifle Association's lobbying efforts, the movie casts the United States as a nation in love with guns, even if the result is incredible violence. The movie pointedly takes the NRA to task. Moore accuses NRA president Charlton Heston of pressing forward with a rally in Denver just after the Columbine tragedy despite the request of that city's mayor to cancel, even though the film clip used to attack the NRA in *Bowling for Columbine* was from a rally the previous year in Charlotte. Moore even concludes the movie with a scathing interview of Heston. Although Moore never blames guns for violence, the insinuation is blunt.

Guns aren't the only angle from which Moore examines the violence issue, however. He returns to his hometown of Flint, Michigan, to show how lack of economic opportunities for young people contribute to the violent culture in which they live, and at least raises the question of whether media drive the violence. He even goes so far as to interview singer Marilyn Manson for his opinion on "copycat" violence that might be inspired by movies such as *The Matrix* or Manson's own music.

There is no question that Moore has a political agenda in the movie, but interestingly he never makes the case to ban or increase restrictions on gun sales. He leaves the conclusions up to the viewer. Even if you disagree with Moore's take on the roots and effects of violence in America or his questionable manipulation of video to make his points, you will be challenged by his treatment of this sensitive subject.

---

entered the social mainstream, complementing alcohol as "recreational drugs." The term *partying* came to be synonymous with drinking and using drugs. By the 1980s, an epidemic of illegal drug use in society was taking place. Students in high school—even junior high—had ready access to drugs. In the inner cities, drug use was rampant, especially among young people. In America, it had become "cool" to "get high."

The social consequences of widespread drug abuse became painfully obvious in the 1980s. Numerous studies, and even more numerous media stories, drove home to the American people the fact that the drug epidemic was ruining lives, contributing to violent crime, making education more difficult, and costing the economy untold millions in lost productivity and health care. By the mid-1980s, the public looked to Washington to deal with the crisis. Washington's response was to declare "war" on drugs.

Since the mid-1980s, the federal government has waged a war on drugs by interdicting drug imports, increasing punishment for people convicted of drug offenses, and instituting drug testing for many federal employees. The federal government's efforts are coordinated by the Office of National Drug Control Policy, located within the Executive Office of the President. The federal effort has been mirrored at the state level, with many states and communities adopting a policy of "zero tolerance" for illegal drug use and stepping up law enforcement efforts. One notable aspect of the war on drugs is the high level of interagency cooperation at all levels of government. For example, the ongoing effort to eradicate domestic marijuana production involves various state and local law enforcement agencies, the federal Drug Enforcement Administration, and even units of the National Guard.

The war on drugs has resulted in a significant decline in casual drug use among the middle class. In the inner city, where poverty and gang violence are prevalent, illegal drugs are still readily available and widely used. In the 1990s, some commentators (including some conservatives) questioned whether the results of the war on drugs justified the commitment of public resources being used to wage it. Some even called for the legalization of drugs. In their view, prohibition has not worked, so efforts should be focused instead on prevention and rehabilitation. But this view has not gained much sympathy from the public or from policy makers.

Under the Clinton administration, the war on drugs continued but was eclipsed by a number of other domestic and foreign policy priorities. Conservative critics, such as the former drug czar Bill Bennett, faulted President Clinton for not making the drug war a greater priority and for not using the "bully pulpit" to provide rhetorical leadership. As Bennett noted in a March 2001 TV interview, Clinton's most memorable statement on the issue of drugs was "I didn't inhale."[13] In the same interview, Bennett called on President George W. Bush to reinvigorate the war on drugs and claimed that, contrary to conventional wisdom, the drug war had been successful in reducing the regular use of illicit drugs by 45 percent since 1985. Bennett praised the recent emphasis on treatment and rehabilitation, but argued that vigorous criminal enforcement is needed to leverage drug users into court-supervised rehab programs.

Many people now doubt the viability of the war on drugs. Despite years of billion-dollar spending on interdiction, drugs still seem to find their way to the marketplace to meet the demand. Despite tough drug laws, often with mandatory sentences, there seems to be no shortage of those willing to sell *and* consume drugs. This frustration was highlighted in the recent hit movie *Traffic*, which suggested the hopelessness of the drug war. But despite widespread frustration with the war on drugs, few seriously advocate legalizing drugs. Finding an effective approach to deterring illicit drugs will continue to present a major public policy challenge into the foreseeable future.

16-3b The Environment

During the 2000 presidential election, the campaign candidates Bush and Gore disagreed over whether the United States should allow oil drilling in the Arctic national wildlife reserve in Alaska. Despite his victory in the election that followed, President George W. Bush was unable to convince Congress of his position despite assurances that the oil could be tapped without environmental degradation. Even the heightened sensitivity to the country's oil dependence that accompanied the September 11 attacks did little to help build a consensus for drilling. Americans have become uneasy about any risk to the environment.

WEB EXERCISE

Some people feel that governmental policies are contradictory. If the government as a whole supports personal autonomy and choice, where do the rights of the individual end and the rights of the state begin? If a person is in charge of her own body, the argument says, shouldn't she be able to choose to die or choose to take drugs? Take a look at some websites on policy issues and then consider these questions:

At what point do you think the government should regulate personal behavior? What kinds of work do the Hemlock Society and Planned Parenthood do to influence policy? Consider the proposals of legalizing drugs: How does the policy reflect on the policy makers? What kinds of arguments can be made for both sides? Do you see a conflict in the laws that ban so-called soft drugs and the work lawmakers do to protect the tobacco industry?

For more information:

In 2003, the Hemlock Society changed its name to "End-of-Life Choices." Here is the link to their website:
http://www.compassionandchoices.org/

Planned Parenthood (reproductive rights):
http://www.plannedparenthood.org

The DEA's position on legalization of drugs can now be found at:
http://www.usdoj.gov/dea/ongoing/legalization.html

From the dawn of civilization, human activities have resulted in some degree of pollution and environmental destruction. Since the industrial revolution, however, pollution has become a major problem, especially in highly urbanized areas. The growth of giant cities, which generate an incredible volume of human waste and garbage, is one aspect of the problem. So too is the prevalence of automobiles, which emit a number of pollutants into the air. Factories contribute to both air and water pollution as they discard their waste products. The widespread use of fertilizers and pesticides in agriculture contributes to pollution of rivers, lakes, and streams as these chemicals are carried off the land by the rain. And the common use of synthetic fibers that do not decompose when they are disposed of further contributes to the problem. As a result, the capacity of the natural environment to safely absorb the waste products of mass, industrialized society has been severely taxed.

Problems of pollution were noticed by some as early as the late nineteenth century, but not until the 1960s did pollution get on the policy agenda in the United States. By then, pollution had begun to be a major health problem in some areas. In many cities, the air was not fit to breathe, and waterways were unsafe for swimming, fishing, or water supplies. By the 1960s, scientists had accumulated evidence linking various pollutants to human health problems, including cancer and birth defects. In the late 1960s and early 1970s, an environmental movement sprang up in the United States, and before long government responded with a number of policy initiatives. Richard Nixon was the first president to make the environment part of his legislative agenda. In his State of the Union address in 1970, Nixon observed that the great challenge of the 1970s was to "make peace with nature and begin to make reparations for the damage we have done. . . ."[14]

The National Environmental Policy Act   The first major environmental policy produced by the national government was the National Environmental Policy Act (NEPA) of 1969. NEPA required all federal agencies to produce an environmental impact statement before implementing any policy that may be harmful to the environment. The requirement is merely procedural—it sets no standards indicating the degree of environmental impact that is acceptable. But NEPA has become a major weapon in the arsenal of environmental groups, which can bring lawsuits challenging the adequacy of an agency's efforts to determine the environmental impact of proposed projects or policies.[15] An agency can be delayed for years, even decades, by litigation of this kind. At some point, the agency may give up entirely.

Air Pollution Control   During the industrial revolution, the main cause of air pollution was the burning of coal. By the 1960s, the major problem had become the automobile. Fumes from the exhaust pipes of millions of cars were the main reason that many American cities became enshrouded in an ugly and noxious haze called smog. The Clean Air Act of 1970 established national air-quality standards, charging the Department of Transportation (DOT) and the EPA with establishing and enforcing regulations to clean up emissions from automobiles and stationary sources of air pollution. Throughout the 1970s and 1980s, the "big three" U.S. automakers (Ford, Chrysler, and General Motors) complained loudly about DOT standards for auto emissions. The big three, which were facing increasingly tough competition from Japanese automakers, argued that it was economically impossible for them to meet federal air-pollution standards. Congress, led by representatives from states where automobile manufacturing constituted a significant part of the employment base, responded by weakening emission standards.

By 1977, the EPA, which had been charged by the Clean Air Act with identifying toxins contained in industrial emissions, had identified only seven toxins. Environmentalists complained that hundreds of toxins exist and that the EPA was dragging its feet. In 1977, Congress responded by enacting a set of amendments to the Clean Air Act. The 1977 legislation established somewhat stricter standards for air quality. Still, environmentalists argued that the federal government should do more to ensure clean air. Business groups, in addition to some in organized labor, complained that moving too rapidly in the environmental area would have a detrimental effect on the economy. They pointed out that clean air costs money, in the form of either higher taxes or higher costs to consumers. Business leaders argued that forcing American industry to meet tougher air-pollution standards would make it less competitive with industries in countries that have no requirements of this type.

During the 1980s, the Reagan administration took the side of business groups concerned about the economic effect of environmental regulation. The administration cut the budgets of a number of agencies charged with cleaning up the environment. Environmentalists complained that the EPA was "under-staffed, under-funded and under Reagan." By the end of the decade, air pollution from automobiles was even worse than it had been in the 1960s. Although automobile engines had become cleaner and more efficient, the number of cars on the road had grown dramatically.

In his successful 1988 presidential campaign, George H.W. Bush promised to be the "environmental president." Though environmental groups generally criticized his administration for being too conservative, Bush won high marks from environmentalists and the general public for his efforts on behalf of the Clean Air Act Amendments of 1990. These amendments renewed and strengthened the Clean Air Act, imposing tougher standards for tailpipe emissions and instituting the first measures designed to control acid rain. The 1990 law also required industrial plants that emit any of some 200 toxins to cut their emissions of those substances to the average level of emissions for the twelve cleanest comparable plants. The law also called for the phasing out of chlorofluorocarbons (CFCs), widely used in refrigeration devices and aerosol cans, in order to protect the Earth's ozone layer.

Many business groups opposed the Clean Air Amendments of 1990, arguing that the legislation would dampen economic growth and cost numerous jobs. Yet the public, although not fully aware of the costs, was highly supportive of the legislation, as it tends to be with any public policies aimed at protecting the environment. In 1992, the candidate Bill Clinton capitalized on the public's desire for environmental protection by making it a major theme of his campaign. Clinton's selection of the Tennessee senator Al Gore as his running mate was due, at least in part, to the fact that Gore was considered a champion of the environmental movement.

The Clinton administration supported strict enforcement of air pollution policies and focused a good deal of attention on greenhouse gases and global warming. In 1997, Vice President Al Gore symbolically signed the Kyoto Protocol, which set specific guidelines for the reduction of six of these gases. However, the Clinton administration never submitted the treaty to the Senate for ratification. Prior to the negotiation of the treaty, the Senate adopted, by unanimous vote, a resolution opposing the Protocol on the ground that it "would result in serious harm to the economy of the United States."

Environmentalists overwhelmingly supported Al Gore in his bid for the presidency in 2000. During the campaign, it became clear that George W. Bush had clear differences with Gore on environmental matters regarding just how far to extend environmental protections when adverse consequences for the economy were possible. In March 2001, President Bush changed his mind on one key issue—the regulation of carbon dioxide gases from power plants, in announcing that he would not support their regulation. In making the decision, he disagreed with his EPA director, Christine Todd Whitman, citing recent electricity shortages and power outages. Throughout his first term, President George W. Bush drew fire from environmentalists for this and other related policy positions.

Dealing with Water Pollution   The pollution of oceans, bays, lakes, rivers, and streams also became a major concern in the 1960s. Water pollution comes from a number of sources, including sewage generated by cities, waste water produced by industry, toxins from waste dumps and landfills that leach into the water table, and rainwater that runs off from residential areas and farmlands, carrying fertilizers and pesticides into streams, rivers, and lakes. Finally, the problem of acid rain occurs when rain passes through an atmosphere laden with pollutants such as sulfur dioxide. Over time, acid rain can change the acidity of lakes, killing fish and other wildlife.

The first major federal response to the problem of water pollution was the Water Pollution Control Act of 1972, commonly known as the Clean Water Act. The act was designed to control water pollution and regulate industrial and other discharges into navigable waters. The primary motivation for the legislation was concern over the terrible pollution of the Great Lakes and rivers in the Northeast. Because these waterways are in close proximity to urban and industrial centers, they had been severely polluted by sewage and industrial waste. Among other things, the act provided federal grants to municipalities to upgrade their sewage-treatment capabilities. It also encouraged interstate cooperation for the prevention and control of pollution. Since the enactment of the law, water quality has improved markedly in many areas, largely because of improved municipal sewage treatment. Despite significant progress since the 1970s, water pollution remains a serious concern.

The Problem of Waste Disposal At one time, cities routinely dumped raw sewage into rivers, bays, and oceans. As a result of advances in technology, in addition to public concern that led to state and federal mandates, sewage is now subjected to treatment that renders it reasonably safe to be emptied into waterways. Solid waste, however, is becoming a serious problem for the United States. Most cities still deposit their garbage in open-air dumps, although many now use sanitary landfills where layers of garbage are covered with earth. Some cities use incinerators to burn flammable refuse, although some environmental groups object to this practice. Because of the shortage of landfill space, many communities are now recycling aluminum, glass, plastic, and newspaper, all of which can be reprocessed into useful products. Increasingly, cities and states are instituting voluntary recycling programs, and some communities are moving toward mandatory recycling.

In our advanced industrial society, the disposal of toxic waste is a serious problem. Toxic waste includes heavy metals, such as mercury and lead, and various compounds that are byproducts of industrial processes. Toxic waste is often stored in metal drums and deposited underground, but metal containers corrode and eventually leak, causing pollution of groundwater. Radioactive waste, produced as byproducts of nuclear power generation and nuclear weapons research, poses a particular problem because of both its lethal nature and its longevity. Radioactive waste is now stored deep underground, which is clearly preferable to dumping it in the ocean.[16] Yet this method of disposal is not entirely satisfactory to environmentalists or people living in those areas.

Congress has adopted a number of important laws dealing with hazardous waste. The Resource Conservation and Recovery Act (RCRA) of 1976 was designed to encourage the states, through grants, technical assistance, and advice, to establish standards and provide for civil and criminal enforcement of state regulations. The EPA sets minimum standards requiring the states to enact criminal penalties against any person who knowingly stores or transports any hazardous waste to an unlicensed facility or who treats this type of waste without a permit or makes false representations to secure a permit. The Toxic Substances Control Act of 1976 authorizes the EPA to require testing and to prohibit the manufacture, distribution, or use of certain chemical substances that present an unreasonable risk of injury to health or the environment and to regulate their disposal. Although the act depends primarily on civil penalties, a person who "knowingly" or "willfully" fails to maintain records or submit reports may be prosecuted in federal court.

In 1980, Congress enacted the Comprehensive Environmental Response, Compensation, and Liability Act (CERCLA), commonly known as the Superfund law. Its purpose is to finance the clean-up of sites damaged by hazardous waste and provide for civil suits by citizens injured by improper waste disposal. As revised in 1986, the act requires notice to federal and state agencies of any release of a "reportable quantity" of several hundred hazardous substances. CERCLA also provides for the EPA to promulgate regulations for the collection and disposal of solid wastes. Like many other federal environmental laws, CERCLA imposes criminal sanctions for certain violations. Not only can companies be sued, but executives can also be prosecuted for violating the law.

Forests, Wetlands, and Endangered Species Environmentalists have long warned of the dangers of deforestation stemming from the uncontrolled logging of the nation's forests. Forests not only provide a renewable source of timber, but they also provide an essential habitat for a wide variety of plant and animal species, some of which are endangered. Wetlands—also known as swamps, marshes, and bogs—are equally important to the ecosystem. They not only provide a wildlife habitat, but they also help to filter toxins out of water that trickles into underground water supplies. Yet, throughout our country's history, wetlands have been drained and filled to allow for development.

In the 1970s, environmentalists succeeded in getting the conservation of forests, wetlands, and endangered species on the public agenda. Environmentalists scored a major victory with the adoption of the Endangered Species Act of 1973. Nevertheless, many environmentalists were not satisfied with the legislation or its enforcement. In 1991 the World Resources Institute predicted that if current trends continued, one-fourth of all plant and animal species existing in the mid-1980s would be extinct within 25 years. In response, Congress began considering revisions of the Endangered Species Act in 1994.

No federal law specifically protects forests or wetlands. Conservationists, therefore, have had to focus their efforts on the endangered species that live in these habitats. The public lands that are designated as national forests may be leased to private companies for mining and logging. Yet, under the Endangered Species Act of 1973, the federal government may not lease public lands for activities that would further threaten designated endangered species. For example, conservationists in the Northwest have used the Endangered Species Act to stop the logging of forests on the grounds that it threatens the habitat of the northern spotted owl, an endangered species. Although conservationists are concerned with saving the spotted owl, their main objective is to protect the old-growth woodlands from logging. Of course, logging companies, sawmills, and paper companies, in addition to the people employed in these enterprises, strenuously object to the "intrusion" of the federal government into their livelihoods. They also resent the environmentalists who, in their minds, put owls and trees before people.

In the early 1990s, the National Research Council, an environmental think tank, accused the U.S. Forest Service, the agency within the Department of Agriculture that manages the national forests, of promoting timber production at the expense of the environment. In response, the Forest Service announced that it would do everything possible to adhere to the position that "a forest is . . . a refuge of biological diversity and an indicator of the health of the planet." Before the release of the report, the Forest Service had already unveiled a new master plan calling for a substantial reduction of logging in national forests by 1995. Environmentalists have therefore succeeded in winning some measure of protection of national forests from logging, not only in the Northwest but also throughout the country. However, 80 percent of the nation's timber production comes not from national forests but rather from private lands.

During the 2000 election campaign, candidate George W. Bush made an issue of drilling in the Alaskan National Wildlife Reserve (ANWR), suggesting that he supported this type of drilling and was convinced that it could be done in such a way as to protect wildlife, including moose herds that grazed there. Al Gore and the Democrats soundly criticized the suggestion as environmentally irresponsible. However, the public appeared receptive to the idea, as evidenced by a poll conducted for the *Christian Science Monitor* in October 2000.[17] With the California energy crisis of 2001, and widespread concern about America's energy supply, political support mounted for drilling. But by 2005, no consensus had emerged in Congress to allow drilling in ANWR to proceed.

16-3c Health-Care Policy

Probably no aspect of public policy in the United States came under as much scrutiny in the 1990s as health care. In 1990, Harris Wofford, an underdog Democratic candidate for the U.S. Senate, exploited dissatisfaction with health care to win a clear victory over the well-known Republican (and former Pennsylvania governor and U.S. attorney general) Richard Thornburgh. The architect of this campaign was James Carville, who later became Bill Clinton's chief campaign strategist in 1992. Not surprisingly, candidate Clinton made health-care reform a centerpiece of his presidential campaign. The issue was twofold: the rising cost of medical care and the desire for everyone to have access to the health-care system.

What Americans Think About

Federal Spending Priorities

"If you had a say in making up the federal budget this year, for which of the following programs would you like to see spending increased and for which would you like to see spending decreased? Should federal spending on _____ be increased, decreased, or kept about the same?"

Program	Percentage Saying "Increase"
Public schools	77%
Dealing with crime	69%
Social Security	65%
Child care	64%
Dealing with illegal immigration	55%
Aid to poor people	54%
AIDS research	53%
Environmental protection	51%
Building and repairing highways	38%
Aid to Blacks	18%
Welfare programs	17%
Food stamps	16%
Foreign aid	9%

Source: Center for Political Studies, University of Michigan, National Election Study 2000.

In the 1990s, health care came to the forefront of American politics. In many ways, it lies at the intersection of competing elements of political culture. The American medical establishment has long fought to preserve a free-market approach to medical care. In the United States, the major cost of health care has always been borne by the citizen, most often through insurance provided by the employer. Although this system had provided what is arguably the finest health care in the world, it had become quite costly to those providing insurance and frightening to those unable to obtain coverage. As a result, this free-market approach is increasingly being questioned by those who argue that medical care should not be provided just to those with the ability to pay. Most advanced countries think of medical care as a responsibility of government, not of the private sector. Although countries provide health care in different ways, most commonly a government agency provides health care without cost to the citizen. Britain has utilized the National Health Service since the 1940s. Physicians and other health-care professionals work for the government. The program is quite costly, however, and providing quality care has presented many problems. Few in the United States have advocated a government-run health-care system. Nevertheless, there has been continual pressure to involve the government in making sure that those who cannot afford health care are able to receive treatment.

Medicare　By the 1960s, a majority of Americans favored government-guaranteed medical care for people over age sixty-five. Nevertheless, the medical community, represented by the American Medical Association (AMA), lobbied hard for years against the passage of legislation that would establish **Medicare.** Congress finally approved Medicare in 1965 and provided for the program to be funded by a payroll tax to be split between employers and employees. Although Medicare did not pay all costs, it quickly became the major source of funding for medical care for the elderly.

▶ **Medicare** Congressional program approved in 1965 that provided for a payroll tax to be split between employers and employees to fund medical care for the elderly.

Medicare costs have been escalating rapidly for a number of reasons. First, medical breakthroughs have created quite expensive treatments not previously possible. Second, the number of elderly Americans has increased rapidly over the past three decades and is expected to grow even more in the first quarter of the twenty-first century. Moreover, people are living longer, which means that they are utilizing more resources. Finally, the government has extended coverage to treatments not previously covered, such as mental illness. In 1983, Medicare was changed in an attempt to control costs. Until then, the government had provided reimbursements based on the cost of the service, as claimed by the hospital or physician, plus an add-on. Under the new system, a schedule of set prices was established, which helped cut back on the growth in cost. Nevertheless, costs continued to escalate rapidly. By 1992, employers and employees were paying Medicare taxes on a much greater proportion of their incomes than ever.

By the early 2000s, the major issue facing Medicare was the lack of prescription drug benefits. Many older Americans found themselves overwhelmed by the rapidly escalating cost of medicines. Although everyone agreed that the cost to the system of any drug benefit would be very substantial, both Democrats and Republicans offered plans. George W. Bush and Al Gore had disagreed on the proper approach during the 2000 presidential election campaign. In December 2003, President Bush signed the Medicare Prescription Drug, Improvement and Modernization Act, which gave prescription drug benefits to seniors and people with disabilities. The act, which also expanded choices and provided other benefits to recipients, was touted by President Bush as the most significant improvement to Medicare in nearly forty years. Democrats complained that the plan was confusing and too costly to patients. Fiscal conservatives, including many in the Republican party, objected to the tremendous cost of the new benefit. In January 2004, the Bush administration released a report projecting the cost of the new Medicare plan to exceed $530 billion over ten years, which was one-third more than the administration's initial estimates.[18]

Medicaid   The other major government health-care program is Medicaid. Unlike Medicare, **Medicaid** is a joint program between the states and the federal government. The national government provides matching funding, but states decide who is eligible under their definitions of medically indigent. Medicaid costs have soared throughout the life of the program. In most states, payments for this coverage of the poor have grown faster than any other part of the state budget. In addition, many people, though not eligible for Medicaid, still do not have medical insurance. Many employers do not provide health insurance, especially for part-time workers. Some people without coverage choose not to purchase insurance, but many cannot afford it. Often, these individuals simply go to hospital emergency rooms when they need medical attention. The extremely high cost of this treatment is passed on to paying customers, most often through high insurance premiums. In the late 1990s, approximately a million people were dropped from Medicaid because the formulas for coverage did not keep up with increases in earned income.

> **Medicaid**   A joint program between the states and the federal government whereby the national government provides matching funding, but the states decide which indigent persons are eligible for medical care.

By the 1990s, the nation's health-care system, largely financed through employer-provided health insurance and supplemented by the public funding of care for the poor and the aged, was clearly in trouble. Though nobody questioned the quality of care available for those who could get it, the system had major problems. First, the costs of insurance were increasing to reflect the costs of care and the costs of providing care to those who could not pay. Many companies were forced to cut coverage for retirees or reduce the size of their full-time workforce, in part because of the costs of insurance coverage. In addition, American corporations found that their mounting insurance costs made it hard to compete with foreign companies. By 1993, an estimated $1,000 of the cost of a new automobile went to pay workers' insurance costs. Finally, Americans were paying much more for health insurance per capita than people in any other country in the world.

The Clinton Health-Care Proposal   Following his inauguration in 1993, President Clinton moved quickly to fulfill his campaign promise of revamping the nation's health-care system. First Lady Hillary Rodham Clinton was put in charge of a major effort to propose new legislation. Throughout the first six months of the year, with the aid of the policy adviser Ira Magaziner, she put together a task force and held hearings in various cities. Many interest groups, especially physicians and insurance companies, complained that they did not have sufficient input into the forthcoming plan. As the process continued to unfold, it became clear that the suggested reforms would not include a centralized system of health care like that in Britain but rather would be a form of **managed competition.** In a managed competition system, many health providers compete with each other to sign up individuals and businesses under a set of rules and regulations set by the government.

> **managed competition**
> President Clinton's proposal for a health-care system in which many health-care providers compete with each other to sign up individuals and businesses under a set of rules and regulations set by the government.

When President Clinton unveiled his plan in September 1993, it had two major components. First, it was structured to bring all Americans under the private insurance system. This was to be accomplished by requiring all employers to provide coverage. Small businesses not providing insurance would receive a government supplement. These small businesses, along with other Americans, regardless of their health status, would be placed in "pools" that would negotiate with competing groups providing insurance for the best price for coverage of those in the pools. Every American would then receive a full package of health coverage benefits. These benefits would follow individuals from job to job or even from employment to unemployment. Moreover, nobody could be turned down because of a preexisting condition.

The second prong of the Clinton proposal dealt with cost control. The proposed changes would be quite expensive. Clinton realized that Americans would not support any major increase in the general tax rate to pay for his program (though a majority indicated they would accept at least a moderate increase). Therefore, he proposed putting a lid on the Medicaid and Medicare programs, limiting the growth in payments to half their rate of increase over the preceding decade. This cost containment was to be accomplished in a number of unspecified ways, which generated considerable criticism. President Clinton stressed reducing costs in paperwork and controlling premiums for health insurance within managed-care provider networks.

During the latter part of 1994, Congress considered, but did not pass, bills based on the Clintons' proposal. By the fall of 1994, public support for large-scale reform had evaporated. Ultimately, the failure of Congress to get behind President Clinton's version of health-care reform can be traced to the public's distrust of government and aversion to bureaucracy, and may have contributed to the Republicans' decisive victory in the 1994 midterm elections. There was not much stomach for major health-care reform throughout the rest of the 1990s, and neither candidate made it a major issue in the 2000 campaign. However, during the campaign, candidate Bush was put on the defensive when queried about the relatively large proportion of uninsured people in Texas. Instead, the discussion centered more around the nature of any prescription drug plan to aid the elderly. In 2004, Democratic candidate John Kerry tried to make health care a campaign issue, but it was eclipsed by other concerns, not the least of which was the ongoing war on terrorism.

Health-Care Policy and American Political Culture The health-care dilemma facing national policy makers reflects the dual nature of American political culture when it comes to domestic policy. A commitment to the values of free enterprise and individual choice has kept the United States from joining most countries, and virtually all developed countries, in assigning health care to the government. But frustration with pricing and availability has led many Americans to demand that government "do something" about health care. Clinton's promise to change the system struck a positive chord in the campaign, but Americans did not seem ready for a government-run system. Many also did not seem ready to pay the costs associated with a managed-care system or to give up some of their options under the previous system. As with other policy issues, the political culture gave rise to both the demand for change and the limitations surrounding the discussion of the change.

Popular Culture and American Politics

John Q

By Chapman Rackaway

Would you take people hostage to make sure someone you loved got medical care that would save his life? Faced with that kind of choice in the movie *John Q*, John Q. Archibald (played by Denzel Washington) does the unthinkable: He holds a hospital emergency room hostage.

In the movie, Washington plays a typical middle-class father. When his son Michael (played by Daniel E. Smith) falls seriously ill, Archibald's troubles begin. Michael collapses while playing baseball, and tests confirm that his heart is failing. Doctors inform Archibald that Michael needs a heart transplant. Archibald's insurance company informs him that his policy will not cover the cost of the transplant. Archibald cannot pay for the transplant, and thus Washington's character is thrust into the middle of a terrible choice: do something drastic or watch his child die. Archibald barricades himself inside the emergency room with doctors and other patients who are waiting for treatment themselves. The police are called, and a hostage negotiation scenario plays out against a backdrop of concerns over health care.

The real villain in the movie is the health insurance company that steadfastly refuses to pay for Michael's transplant. As increasing numbers of Americans are losing health insurance or finding their benefits limited, and in light of President Clinton's failed universal health-care proposal of the 1990s, the fiction of *John Q* becomes ever more a legitimate fear that ordinary Americans hold.

16-3d Education Policy

In the United States, primary and secondary education has always been a responsibility of the state and local governments. Local school boards set school district policies. The major state role has been to set standards and provide funding. The federal government has traditionally played a minor role. Its greatest effect on state and local schools has been through the courts. Its most crucial role has been the dismantling of segregated schools following the *Brown v. Board of Education* decision in 1954. The federal government has also undertaken a number of programs to provide money to needy districts. One of the most visible has been the school lunch program. Students from low-income families are eligible for reduced or even free lunches and breakfasts at school. Other federal monies are available on a grant basis. One program aids school districts where federal facilities are located as compensation for the students added to the system.

In 1979, during the Carter administration, the Department of Education was established, giving its director cabinet rank. Since then, its budget has grown dramatically, reflecting the increased federal role in education. In 1980, the department's budget was about $14 million; by 2000, it had surpassed $35 million. Although the Department of Education has the fewest employees of any of the fifteen cabinet-level departments, it spends large sums on grants to local school districts. Local school districts, many of which are cash-starved, jump at the chance for federal dollars. But strings are attached, allowing federal officials to dictate policy in such matters as special education and school discipline. Critics of the federal role in education resent this sort of "meddling" in what was once an exclusive state and local matter. Others have called for abolition of the Department of Education as a means of cutting unnecessary bureaucracy. Still, the secretary of education has a "bully pulpit" from which to push the policies of the current administration. During the 1980s, William Bennett, President Reagan's secretary of education, used his position to draw attention to the declining performance of the public schools. Bennett urged a return to discipline and the "three Rs."

Growing Concern for Educational Quality   Throughout the 1980s, concern for the performance of American schools grew. Despite an ever-increasing commitment of public funds, most provided by state and local governments, educational performance continued to decline. Many urban school districts experienced dropout rates in excess of 50 percent. Drugs and crime were rampant in many schools, and more and more shooting incidents occurred. Although liberals called for more financial support for public schools and an equalization of funding between wealthy and poor school districts, conservatives argued that the problem has to do with the structure of the public schools. Conservatives believe that the private sector should be able to provide affordable alternatives to the public schools. Under the current system, private schools are beyond the financial reach of most parents.

By the 1990s, the issue of **school choice** had become one of the major public-policy issues facing the nation. For the most part, the discussion took place in the school districts. School choice can be approached in a variety of ways. The usual device is through the use of vouchers. A school **voucher** is a grant to the parents of school-age children that can be used at any school, public or private. The idea behind vouchers is to introduce competition into public education. Proponents of vouchers argue that they will force the public schools to become more efficient in using their resources and more effective in educating their students. Opponents counter that only the worst students would be left in the public schools and that private schools would not have to meet the same standards that the traditional public school system meets.

The school choice dilemma is difficult for most Americans to resolve. Americans have long had a firm commitment to the public schools. In fact, the myth of the frontier school, often with one room, is firmly rooted in American culture. In the past, schools provided a chance for everyone. As society grew more complex, however, many people began to think of public education as a large, inflexible, and inefficient self-serving bureaucracy. Modern American culture is not kind to institutions with this type of image. The idea of choice is therefore quite appealing. In November 1993, however, California voters soundly rejected a proposition to establish a voucher system. Teachers' unions mounted an effective media campaign to convince voters that the plan was unworkable and would destroy the public education system.

Although it might be argued that education is among the most fundamental national concerns, education policy on most matters is set at the local and state levels. There is no constitutional or philosophical reason that health-care policy has been "nationalized" and education policy has not. The main reason that education has remained a local concern is that the local control of education has become a fundamental part of the American political culture, probably because of education's role in transmitting values. Real fear exists that a national set of values might be imposed on the curricula of school districts around the country. The decentralized nature of American education makes national reform difficult to achieve. Although health-care reform can be accomplished through presidential and congressional action, educational reform must take place through the actions of fifty state legislatures and thousands of independent school districts. Take the poll in Box 16-1 to see where you stand on the issues of health-care and school vouchers as compared to the rest of your class.

By the 2000 election campaign, vouchers were very much on the political agenda. George W. Bush favored an approach that provided vouchers to parents of children in failing school districts as a last resort when schools could not perform. The National Education Association, a major supporter of Democratic candidates, strongly opposed the concept of vouchers, making the argument that this approach would drain dollars from the public schools. Gore concurred. Following his narrow victory, President Bush introduced education legislation early in 2001, but seemed willing to compromise on the voucher issue, especially if any legislation tied federal aid to a strong testing program.

"No Child Left Behind"   When George W. Bush campaigned in 2000 as a "compassionate conservative," a number of political commentators wondered what this would

---

▶ **school choice**   A policy whereby parents and students maintain the right to choose the school, public or private, that the children will attend.

▶ **voucher**   A grant to the parents of school-age children to be used at any accredited school, public or private.

Box 16-1	**Health Care and Schools Poll**		

Health-care systems

Do you think the United States should have some kind of national health-care system for all citizens?	*Yes*	*No*
Would you be willing to pay higher taxes to have a national health-care system?	*Yes*	*No*
Do you think you should have a choice in health-care programs?	*Yes*	*No*
Do you think that income should determine how much you pay for health care? (Should people who make more money pay more?)	*Yes*	*No*

School vouchers

Do you think that the government should be able to use tax money to help lower-income students attend private schools?	*Yes*	*No*
Do you think that students at poorly performing schools should have the option to go to other public schools by using vouchers?	*Yes*	*No*
Do you think that providing vouchers will force public schools to become more competitive and become better places of learning?	*Yes*	*No*

You can go to the online version of this text to take this poll and compare your results to the rest of your classmates.

mean in terms of policy proposals if Bush were elected. The No Child Left Behind Act of 2001 was the one signature domestic policy accomplishment during Bush's first term. President Bush went so far as to describe the new law as the "cornerstone of my administration." In enacting the law, Congress reauthorized the Elementary and Secondary Education Act (ESEA), the main statutory basis for federal involvement in K–12 education. Under ESEA, the federal government funds about 7 percent of the cost of education borne by state and local governments. Federal aid to public schools has always had strings attached. Federal funds provide the leverage by which the Department of Education imposes various regulations on local education authorities. Most school districts have been willing (albeit reluctantly) to accept federal control as the price of receiving federal finds. What No Child Left Behind did was to force public schools to demonstrate adequate yearly progress toward a state-defined level of proficiency. Although President Bush has touted the program as a landmark in education reform, it has been assailed by critics, both on the right and on the left. Liberals generally protested that the program was grossly underfunded and accused President Bush of trying to exploit the education issue for political gain. Conservatives expressed horror at the degree to which No Child Left Behind brought yet another wave of federal intervention into what was historically a state function with a high level of local control.

Higher Education   Other than the military service academies, no colleges and universities are operated by the federal government. Nevertheless, Washington has played a significant role in aiding higher education. Many state universities were aided by grants from the sale of public lands under the Morrill Act of 1862. This legislation helped establish many state universities as centers for the study of agriculture. These universities are now known as land grant universities because their initial funding was based on monies generated by the sale of federal lands.

Recently, the federal role in higher education has been more indirect, with aid going to students through such devices as Pell grants or to the universities for specific research projects. In the latter case, the university or college recovers funds for "overhead," which goes beyond the specific cost of the research. Federal funding has become an important component of most college and university budgets. For example, in 1988, the University of Illinois obtained more than 30 percent of its budget from grants and contracts, most of which came from federal agencies.[19] During the 1991 fiscal year, federal spending on college- and university-based research exceeded $10 billion.[20] This funding gives federal agencies significant leverage to achieve national policy goals. Foremost among these policy goals have been equal opportunity and affirmative action. Institutions found not to be in compliance risk the loss of all federal funding. Federal regulations have affected hiring at all levels in addition to the provision of equal opportunities for men and women in intercollegiate athletics.

16-3e Welfare Policy

One major task modern governments accomplish is that of aiding the needy. This is the basic component of what is referred to as *welfare*. Countries that have extensive programs to aid the poor and other groups of people desiring or requiring assistance are known as *welfare states*. Western European countries, most of which have generous welfare programs, are often referred to in this way. In these countries, individuals are provided with "cradle to grave" health care and other benefits. For instance, in the Netherlands, workers can qualify for government benefits if they suffer stress on the job. By and large, Americans have never bought into the notion of a welfare state. As a result, compared to other countries, the United States commits a far smaller part of its economy to social welfare programs.

The degree to which a society is willing to provide assistance through the public sector reflects a people's basic orientation toward personal responsibility. A country whose culture stresses self-reliance and individual responsibility is not likely to embark on a broad program of government assistance to individuals. On the other hand, a people whose culture stresses the group as opposed to the individual will find it a natural extension of government aid. Welfare, possibly more than any other government expenditure, expresses the fundamental character of a society.

Americans have never been open to the idea of the welfare state. The individualistic basis of American political culture has never really legitimized state responsibility for the well-being of individuals. With the increased social problems of the latter part of the twentieth century, however, many have looked to government to take a more active role in providing a social safety net. The Great Depression, which began in 1929, was instrumental in redefining the American perspective on welfare. The tumbling economy put millions of people out of work. Existing local welfare programs, which barely supplemented family and church efforts, were totally unable to provide needed help. Many Americans looked ahead to a future of poverty. Under the aegis of the New Deal, the Roosevelt administration greatly expanded the role of the government in providing what has come to be called a safety net. A **safety net** is a guaranteed level of support beneath which individuals are not allowed to fall.

> **safety net** A guaranteed level of support beneath which individuals will not be allowed to fall.

The idea of a safety net and the role of government in overcoming poverty was further stressed during the 1960s, when President Lyndon Johnson proposed programs that were collectively oriented toward achieving the Great Society. The idea was to use the forces of government, primarily the federal government, to overcome poverty. Although the impetus was clearly from the national government, the focus was always federal in nature—that is, most of the programs would receive substantial federal funding but be administered by the states.

The Great Society initiative was inextricably bound to the civil rights movement that was reaching its zenith with the passage of the Civil Rights Act of 1964 and the Voting Rights Act of 1965. Yet it was clear to many people that a right to political participation was somewhat hollow without a guarantee of a basic standard of living. The notion of a right to a certain standard of living implied a series of payments or services that would allow the individual—and especially the individual recipient's children—to escape from poverty. These programs were wide-ranging, including subsidized housing, income assistance, early childhood education, and nutritional programs.

Social Security: The Third Rail of American Politics? The centerpiece of New Deal social policy was Social Security. It remains among the most significant social policies ever established by the federal government. Enacted in 1935, in the depths of the Great Depression, Social Security was designed as a social insurance program to provide

Comparative Perspective

European Governments and Social Welfare Spending

Americans are not fond of the idea of a welfare state. Part of the political mythology of this country is that welfare programs are beset by waste, fraud, and abuse. Yet the U.S. government spends a lower percentage of its annual budget on welfare than do the democracies of Europe. To some extent, the reason is that social welfare in the United States is also supported by state and local programs. Still, the American welfare state is far less generous than its European counterparts. In the United States, welfare spending represents about 28 percent of the federal government's expenditures. In Sweden, the figure is more than 55 percent, and in most European countries it is in the 40 percent range.

In the 1990s, European governments began to reconsider their generous welfare programs. Chancellor Helmut Kohl, of Germany, was especially critical of a welfare system he blamed for undermining the German work ethic that produced the miraculous post–World War II recovery in that country. Throughout western Europe, governments tried to find ways to reduce the tremendous cost of their welfare programs without seriously hurting the people who have come to depend on them. Of course, this goal is difficult to achieve, both economically and politically.

benefits for elderly retirees. Over time, the program has expanded to include disabled workers and the surviving spouses and dependent children of covered workers who die. Social Security now covers more than 90 percent of the American work force. Every month, the Social Security Administration mails checks to some forty-five million beneficiaries. Virtually everyone has a stake in the system, which is why it has become something of a sacred cow.

Social Security is funded through a payroll tax paid by employees and employers. In 2000, salaries up to approximately $76,200 were subject to the tax. Thus, this tax is not progressive. A person making $1 million pays the same amount as a person making $76,200. The reason is partly that Social Security has been conceptualized more as an insurance program than as a welfare program. It was not designed to collect based on the ability to pay or to provide benefits based on need. It's an entitlement: Everyone who pays into the system is entitled to a pension. As a result, millionaires over sixty-five receive Social Security benefits whether they need them or not. The problem is that the ratio of payers to beneficiaries has been steadily declining (see Figure 16-5). At some point (probably around 2032), the system will become insolvent.

For some time, critics have been calling on Congress to reform the system. The choices are stark: Increase payroll taxes, reduce benefits, means-test beneficiaries, or raise the retirement age. None of these options is politically palatable. Social Security has become the political equivalent of the third rail on the subway train: Touch it and you get fried. Politicians are loath to discuss the issue because they fear that opponents will use it against them with the voters. The elderly population, which votes at a high percentage, has been particularly vulnerable to campaign tactics designed to scare people into thinking that a competing candidate wants to cut their Social Security benefits. In particular, Democrats have been quite effective in using these types of tactics against Republicans. President George W. Bush waited until he had secured reelection in 2004 to raise the serious issue of Social Security reform. When he did, not only were his proposals immediately attacked by Democrats, but neutral observers doubted his ability to move Congress on this most sensitive subject. By the midway point of 2005, little progress had been made on this front.

Federal Welfare Programs   Most Americans, although they would not appreciate being labeled welfare recipients, receive some sort of aid from the federal government. Most homeowners benefit from tax breaks on mortgage interest. Many farmers get subsidies

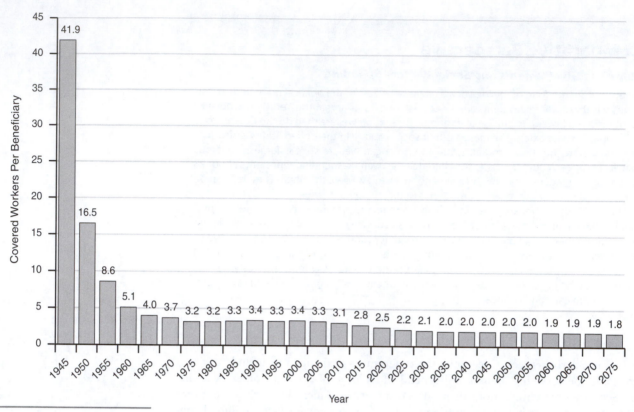

Figure 16-5
Ratio of Covered Workers to Social Security Beneficiaries, 1945–2075

Source: Adapted from 2000 OASDI Trustees Report, available online at http://www.ssa.gov.

▶ **means test**   The requirement that a recipient who benefits from a program demonstrate financial need for the benefits.

for a variety of crops. Virtually all Americans over age sixty-five receive Social Security benefits and Medicare coverage. College students benefit from low-interest loans that are subsidized and guaranteed by the federal government. Yet these programs are not conventionally thought of as welfare. That label is reserved for programs designed to help the poor.

At the federal level, the three main programs to aid the poor are Temporary Assistance for Needy Families (formerly known as Aid to Families with Dependent Children), Supplemental Security Income (SSI), and food stamps. SSI was established by an amendment to the Social Security Act in 1972. Unlike Social Security, SSI is funded from the general treasury. The program provides funds to low-income Americans who are elderly, blind, or disabled. Again, unlike with Social Security, eligibility for SSI is based on a means test. A **means test** requires a recipient who benefits from a program to demonstrate financial need for the benefits. As of December 2000, approximately 6.6 million Americans were receiving SSI payments.

In 1964, Congress passed the Food Stamp Act. Funded from general revenue, and administered by the U.S. Department of Agriculture (which also administers the school lunch program and the Women, Infants, and Children Care program), this program provides stamps redeemable at grocery stores for food items. During FY 1999, an average of 7.7 million households per month benefited from the program. The program distributed nearly $16 billion in food vouchers during FY 1999.

Although allegations of waste, fraud, and abuse have been directed from time to time at food stamps and SSI, for the most part these programs have been well-managed and have continued to enjoy strong public support. The same cannot be said for Aid to Families with Dependent Children. Until Congress passed the Welfare Reform Act of 1996, AFDC was the mainstay of American welfare. First created in 1935 under the Social Security Act, AFDC was expanded during the 1960s. By the late 1960s, the burgeoning federal welfare rolls had become an explosive political issue. But AFDC was always more of a social issue than an economic issue. AFDC came under growing criticism as contributing to the decline of the nuclear family. Evidence existed that AFDC rules encouraged husbands and fathers to leave the home. In the 1990s, the grim statistics on welfare dependency lent credence to these

Controversy

Hurricane Katrina: A Shock to the Policy Process

From time to time a cataclysmic event jolts government into dramatic action. In late August of 2005, Hurricane Katrina devastated the Gulf Coast and caused the flooding of New Orleans. In a televised speech on September 15, 2005, President George W. Bush accepted responsibility for the federal government's inadequate response theretofore and promised an investigation of why the government's immediate response to the disaster was uncoordinated, slow and inadequate. Speaking from Jackson Square in the heart of New Orleans' French Quarter, the President outlined a series of new proposals, including:

- A mammoth public works program to rebuild infrastructure.
- Reimbursement of state governments for health care expenditures resulting from the treatment of hurricane evacuees.
- Establishment of "worker recovery accounts" providing money for job training, education and child care.
- An Urban Homesteading Act to make federal lands available to low-income citizens for new home sites.

The most dramatic element of the President's speech was his promise to confront the deep-seated poverty of the Gulf Coast "with bold action." Bush noted that this poverty "has roots in a history of racial discrimination, which cut off generations from the opportunity of America."

By September 15, 2005, Congress had already appropriated $62 billion for disaster relief, but those funds were expected to last only a couple of months. Estimates as to the total cost of rebuilding of the Gulf Coast, resurrecting the city of New Orleans, and protecting it from future flooding ran into the hundreds of billions of dollars. For more than a fiscal challenge, Hurricane Katrina would challenge policymakers at all levels and in all agencies of government to find practical solutions to a host of social, economic, technological, and environmental problems that might in many parts of the world seem insurmountable.

arguments. The number of families with no male head of household had increased markedly throughout society, but the increase had been most dramatic among the poor. Women who went on AFDC to support their children found it difficult to break the cycle of welfare dependency.

The costs of welfare dependency may have been more than economic. In the 1990s, a growing consensus indicated that the breakdown of the traditional, nuclear family was contributing to a variety of social problems, including crime, illiteracy, teenage pregnancy, and the use of illicit drugs. Critics of welfare believed that these problems could be lessened, if not alleviated altogether, by reforming the welfare system. In fact, many people thought that the welfare system—and in particular, AFDC—was in fact causing these problems. By the end of 1994, both President Clinton and the new Republican leadership in Congress were committed to reform.

Welfare Reform   The solution to the problems with AFDC was the Welfare Reform Act of 1996. This major legislation ended AFDC and replaced it with a series of block grants to the states. Much of the "action" regarding welfare was therefore moved from Washington to state capitals around the nation. This phenomenon extended a trend begun in the early 1990s when a number of states were granted waivers under AFDC to experiment with programs that limited the number of years a person could receive welfare payments and limited these types of payments to people who received job training or were seeking employment. Under the new legislation, states received funds under the Temporary Assistance for Needy Families (TANF) block grant program. To qualify for these types of funds, states were required to create programs that moved people from welfare to work. By

Figure 16-6
Parental Advisory Label
Responding to widespread
concern about sex and violence in
pop music and videos, the
recording industry agreed to place
this label on CDs containing sexual
and violent content.

Popular Culture and American Politics
Government, Kids, and the Entertainment Industry

Many commentators have long expressed concern about the messages children receive through the popular culture. In recent years, parents, educators, and psychologists have voiced particular concern about sex and violence in the media. Movies, television programs, and even music videos consumed by young people are heavily laden with sexual images and violence. Most troubling are images of sexualized violence. Although no one is certain what effects these types of images have, few would argue that this type of exposure is beneficial to young people. What, if anything, should government do about it? Obviously, constitutional limitations (the First Amendment) exist on policies aimed at the content of mass media and pop culture. So far, the political response has been limited to pressure exerted by Congress and influential politicians in an effort to persuade corporations that produce and market these types of materials to police themselves. In the 1960s, this approach led to the movie rating system sponsored by the Motion Picture Association of America and the National Association of Theatre Owners. In the 1980s, a group of "Washington wives" led by Tipper Gore criticized the music industry for offensive song lyrics involving sex, violence, and the occult. Their efforts, and especially congressional hearings into the matter, led to the parental-advisory labels for music (see Figure 16-6).

In 1997, the television industry established a television ratings system similar to that developed by the Motion Picture Association. All television programs are now rated according to six categories: Y (suitable for all children), Y7 (suitable for children 7 and under), G (suitable for all ages), PG (parental guidance recommended), 14 (parents strongly cautioned), and M (for mature audiences only). Still, many critics continue to express concerns about the sex, language, and violence contained in many television programs that air during times that kids are likely to be viewing.

Senator Joe Lieberman (D-Connecticut) has called on the entertainment industry to elevate the content of movies, television programs, and video games for young people. Some in the industry reacted with hostility, even going so far as to equate Lieberman with Senator Joe McCarthy and Lieberman's crusade with the "witch hunts" and blacklists of the Red Scare period. Others in the industry responded more positively, if not because Lieberman's criticisms touched a moral nerve, then because they feared that the failure to self-regulate might lead to government censorship. All these issues raise a difficult question: What is the proper role of government, if any, in policing the popular culture?

In the 1980s, the artists "targeted" by Tipper Gore's group included Prince, Vanity, Madonna, Judas Priest, AC/DC, Motley Crüe, Twisted Sister, Def Leppard, Cyndi Lauper, and the Mary Jane Girls. Controversy now swirls around Eminem and various rap artists.

all accounts, the move has been successful. By 2000, most states had significantly slashed their welfare rolls under the 1996 legislation.

16-3f Immigration Policy

The United States is a land of immigrants. The nation's motto, *E pluribus unum,* means "Out of many, one." In the earliest years of the Republic, most immigrants were welcome. Of course, the overwhelming majority of these immigrants were from Great Britain and western Europe. Later, Congress passed laws encouraging immigration from Europe while discouraging Asians. Laws passed at the end of the nineteenth century and beginning of the twentieth century set quotas on immigrants from some countries, especially those in eastern Europe, while encouraging those from western European countries, such as Britain and Germany. These types of quotas were set in the 1929 National Origins Act, which limited total annual immigration to one hundred fifty thousand. Only forty-five thousand could come from eastern and southern Europe. Following the suspension of the National

Origins Act after World War II, Congress passed the McCarran–Walter Act in 1952. This act shifted concern from racial to ideological considerations as potential immigrants were questioned about their possible Communist leanings.

The latter half of the twentieth century and the aftermath of the Red Scare brought about a wholesale change in immigration policy. The major legislative pillar of this change was the Immigration Act of 1965. The act, while lifting country-by-country limits, placed significant limits on legal immigration from Latin America through its specification of limits by hemisphere. Legislation since that time has allowed the president to declare an emergency period in which to allow the immigration of refugees—those suffering in their own country because of their race, religion, or beliefs. By the 1980s, the difficulty of obtaining legal immigrant status, especially when combined with America's demand for cheap labor, had led to a great wave of illegal immigration from Mexico. Congress, in passing the 1986 Immigration Reform and Control Act, made a policy decision to deal indirectly with the problem by levying sanctions on those who illegally employ people in the country.

By 2004, more than a million legal immigrants were entering the United States each year, supplemented by a third as many who come illegally. The basic legislation affecting present-day immigration is the 1996 Immigration Act, which beefed up border patrols. The intent of the act is to put teeth into limits on immigration across the Mexican border. Another approach is denial of state and federal benefits to illegal immigrants. The state of California, by means of an amendment to its constitution, set these types of limits in 1994. This strategy is also accomplished through parts of welfare reform passed by Congress and signed into law by President Clinton in 1996. This legislation eliminated all except emergency benefits for those in the country illegally.

Following the terrorist attacks of 2001, attention shifted from the flood of illegal immigrants from the South to the set of policies that had allowed nineteen people to legally enter the United States with the intent of causing massive death and destruction. Many who enter the country do not declare their intent to immigrate, but rather to stay in the country a short time for education or work purposes. These people apply for visas and are overseen by the Immigration and Naturalization Service (INS). The INS has long been overwhelmed by the difficulty of keeping track of those who enter the country under these types of circumstances. In 2002, Congress tightened the oversight of these individuals by requiring colleges and universities to notify the INS if someone holding a student visa from a designated terrorist country.

16-4 Conclusion: Politics and Policy Making

When polled, most Americans consistently say that their government spends too much on domestic policy and social programs. Yet the level of government support for these programs, in addition to the level of taxation needed to fund them, is substantially lower than in other Western democracies. The American commitment to the free market and individual self-reliance, although somewhat weaker than during the nineteenth century, will not permit government to expand the welfare state much beyond its current dimensions.

Americans clearly are concerned about domestic issues, such as crime, education, and the environment. Increasingly since the early twentieth century, Americans have looked to government to address these problems. But widespread skepticism now exists about whether government can do anything about them. The natural turn to government following the terrorist attacks of 2001 may spread to other problem areas, although that turn might ultimately depend on the degree of confidence generated by government's performance.

Substantial support exists among the American people for solutions that depend not on government but rather on individuals acting freely in the marketplace. Proposals for educational vouchers to promote school choice certainly come under this heading. Moreover, the realization is growing that many of society's worst problems are cultural maladies beyond the effective reach of public policies. Nevertheless, government can do meaningful things. Unfortunately, most of them cost money. Government decisions on how to spend, and how much to spend, are discussed in the next chapter.

Questions for Thought and Discussion

1. What role should government play in ensuring that Americans have adequate health care?
2. Can the American welfare system be reformed? Should it be reformed? How?
3. Who are the stakeholders in the environmental policy area? How do their actions affect the nature of environmental policy in the United States?
4. Can the American public education system survive without major reform? What is the appropriate role for the federal government?
5. Can the federal government provide the social services that Americans demand without massive increases in the federal debt?

Practice Quiz

Note: You can find the correct answers to these questions by taking the quiz and then submitting your answers in the Online Edition. The program will automatically score your submission. If you miss a question, the program will provide the correct answer, a rationale for the answer, and the section number in the chapter where the topic is discussed.

1. Those persons who stand to win or lose from policy decisions are referred to as _____.
   a. interest groups
   b. attentive publics
   c. issue publics
   d. stakeholders

2. The _____ is a compilation of those issues that have come to the attention of policy makers at the national level.
   a. national agenda
   b. congressional agenda
   c. president's agenda
   d. public's platform

3. In the traditional model of policy making, the initial phase of the policy-making process consists of _____.
   a. setting the agenda
   b. evaluating the performance of existing policies
   c. formulating policy alternatives
   d. convincing the public to accept particular policy outcomes

4. _____ are groups that employ policy specialists, scientists, and lawyers to perform research on various topics and propose policy changes.
   a. Interest groups
   b. Think tanks
   c. Issue publics
   d. Attentive publics

5. Most crimes in the United States are investigated and prosecuted by _____.
   a. the federal government
   b. the federal courts
   c. state and local governments
   d. the FBI

6. Public opinion polls tend to show that a majority of Americans _____.
   a. opposes any restrictions on gun ownership and purchase
   b. favors some restriction on the availability of guns
   c. favors a total ban on the sale and possession of handguns
   d. favors laws requiring all citizens to own firearms

7. _____ has been called the third rail of American politics: Touch it and you get fried.
   a. Medicaid
   b. The GI Bill
   c. The Clean Air Act
   d. Social Security

8. Bill Clinton's decision to choose Al Gore as his running mate in the 1992 presidential election was motivated, at least in part, because Gore was considered a champion of _____.
   a. educational vouchers
   b. the natural environment
   c. gun control
   d. the rights of the unborn

9. The health-care program known as Medicaid targets which of the following groups?
   a. Persons over sixty-five years of age
   b. Social Security recipients
   c. The medically indigent
   d. All of the above

10. Under the Welfare Reform Act of 1996, Aid to Families with Dependent Children was recast as _____.
    a. Temporary Aid to Needy Families
    b. Medicaid
    c. the Women and Infant Care Program
    d. Americans United for Prosperity

For Further Reading

Anderson, James. *Public Policymaking: An Introduction,* 4th ed. (Boston: Houghton Mifflin, 2000).

Derthick, Martha. *Policy Making for Social Security* (Washington, D.C.: Brookings Institution, 1979).

Dye, Thomas R. *Top Down Policymaking* (Washington, D.C.: CQ Press, 2001).

Heidenheimer, Arnold J., Hugh Heclo, and Carolyn Tech Adams. *Comparative Public Policy,* 3d ed. (New York: St. Martin's Press, 1990).

Gore, Al. *Earth in the Balance: Ecology and the Human Spirit* (Boston: Houghton Mifflin, 1992).

Kingdon, John. *Agendas, Alternatives and Public Policies,* 2d ed. (Boston: Addison Wesley, 1995).

Kraft, Michael E., and Scott R. Furlong. *Public Policy: Priorities, Analysis and Alternatives* (Washington, D.C.: CQ Press, 2004).

Murray, Charles. *Losing Ground: American Social Policy, 1950–1980* (New York: Basic Books, 1984).

Page, Benjamin. *Who Gets What from Government* (Berkeley: University of California Press, 1983).

Palumbo, Dennis J. *Public Policy in America: Government in Action* (New York: Harcourt Brace Jovanovich, 1988).

Peters, B. Guy. *American Public Policy: Promise and Performance*, 6th ed. (Washington, D.C.: CQ Press, 2004).

Rosenbaum, Walter. *Environmental Politics and Policy*, 6th ed. (Washington, D.C.: CQ Press, 2004).

Vig, Norman J., and Michael E. Kraft. *Environmental Policy: New Directions for the Twenty-First Century*, 5th ed. (Washington, D.C.: CQ Press, 2003).

Wilson, James Q. *The Politics of Regulation* (New York: Basic Books, 1980).

Endnotes

1. Robert A. Dahl, *A Preface to Democratic Theory* (Chicago: University of Chicago Press, 1956), pp. 132–33.

2. In July 2001, the U.S. Court of Appeals for the District of Columbia upheld the district court's ruling that Microsoft had violated antitrust rules by holding a monopoly in the personal computer (PC) operating systems market. In October 2001, the Supreme Court denied a Microsoft request to review the case. Subsequently, the Justice department and Microsoft reached an agreement to settle the case.

3. See Charles O. Jones, *An Introduction to the Study of Public Policy*, 2d ed. (North Scituate, MA: Duxbury Press, 1977), and James E. Anderson, *Public Policymaking: An Introduction* (Boston: Houghton Mifflin, 1990) on the dynamic process of public policy making.

4. Roger W. Cobb and Charles D. Elder, *Participation in American Politics: The Dynamics of Agenda-Building*, 2d ed. (Baltimore: Johns Hopkins University Press, 1983).

5. *Roe v. Wade*, 410 U.S. 113 (1973).

6. Marty Bauman, "Federal Mandates," *USA Today*, November 16, 1993, p. 15A.

7. See U.S. Department of Justice, Bureau of Justice Statistics, Crime and Victim Statistics, 2003. Online at http://www.ojp.usdoj.gov/bjs/cvictgen.htm

8. *Mapp v. Ohio*, 367 U.S. 643 (1961).

9. *Miranda v. Arizona*, 384 U.S. 486 (1966).

10. Dennis Cauchon, "Gun Owners Back Controls," *USA Today*, December 30, 1993, p. 1A.

11. See "Gun Owners Don't Fit Stereotypes," *USA Today*, December 30, 1993, p. 5A.

12. Gallup poll conducted December 17–21, 1993. Results reported in *USA Today*, December 30, 1993, p. 5A.

13. William Bennett, in an interview with Bill O'Reilly, Fox News, March 14, 2001.

14. Quoted in Richard E. Cohen, *Washington at Work: Back Rooms and Clean Air* (New York: Macmillan, 1992), p. 13.

15. The seminal court case in this area is *Citizens to Preserve Overton Park, Inc. v. Volpe*, 401 U.S. 402 (1971).

16. On October 17, 1993, it was reported that Russia had just dumped thousands of tons of nuclear waste into the Sea of Japan, much to the chagrin of the Japanese government.

17. The poll explored a broad range of energy issues with a cross-section of 803 likely voters in the United States. By a margin of 54 percent to 38 percent, respondents favored the development of the Alaskan Wildlife Reserve. Reported by the *Christian Science Monitor*, October 18, 2000.

18. Robert Pear, "Medicare Drug Benefit Cost Soars," *New York Times*, January 30, 2004.

19. Virginia Gray, Herbert Jacob, and Robert B. Albritton, *Politics in the American States*, 5th ed. (Glenview, IL: Scott-Foresman, 1990), p. 471.

20. Chronicle of Higher Education, August 25, 1993, p. 5.

Economic Policy

17-1 The Contours of Economic Policy

Although free enterprise and self-reliance have long been staples of American political culture, the Great Depression of the 1930s convinced Americans that government has a significant role to play in managing the economy and promoting the general welfare. A great many observers gave a good bit of credit for the economic boom of the 1990s to the wise stewardship exhibited by Alan Greenspan in his role as chairman of the Federal Reserve. Few suggested that the downturns of 2000 were a recipe for less government oversight. Rather, Enron Corporation's fall into bankruptcy led to cries for more, rather than less, government regulation of corporate business practices.

Government programs are now a reality at every level of government. The federal government is seen as problem-solver for the nation and the manager of the nation's economy. The management of the economy involves three major areas of public policy: **fiscal policy** (taxing and spending), **monetary policy** (control of the money supply), and **trade policy** (regulating trade with other countries). Each is extremely important to the economic vitality of the United States. Yet in each area, the government can do only so much effectively. Government now plays a crucial role in the economy, but it is by no means omnipotent or omnicompetent. Moreover, profound differences still exist among Americans concerning what role government should play and what policies it should pursue. Liberals generally favor a broader role for government; conservatives tend to favor more reliance on the marketplace.

> **fiscal policy** The government's taxing and spending policies.

> **monetary policy** Government policy aimed at controlling the supply of money and controlling interest rates.

> **trade policy** The set of rules governing trade between the United States and other countries.

17-1a The Political Context

All economic policy making, whether it is fiscal, monetary, regulatory, or trade policy, involves clashes among opposing ideologies. Usually, the two major political parties assume opposing ideological stances, with the Democrats taking the liberal side and the Republicans espousing a conservative position. Economic policy making also typically involves intense activity by interest groups. Sometimes, this activity is ideologically driven; more often, it occurs because certain groups stand to gain and other groups stand to lose if a particular policy is adopted. Indeed, economic policy making is at the center of the vortex of American politics, with competing ideas, personalities, and groups whirling around in seemingly perpetual motion.

Although the process of economic policy making is a source of political conflict, it takes place within an overarching consensus about the limits of government's role in the economy. As in other areas of policy and politics, American political culture imposes parameters on the discussion of policy options and directions. Although Americans may disagree over specifics, most of them assume the essential desirability of the capitalist system. Thus, with the exception of a few people at the ideological extremes, no support exists for radical change in how economic policy is made or what it seeks to accomplish. Of course, political culture changes over time. American political culture has evolved quite markedly with respect to government intervention in the economy. Measures such as minimum wage laws that seemed heretical to many in the nineteenth century now seem commonplace. Social Security, which was viewed as fairly radical when it was introduced in 1935, is now the sacred cow of American politics. Before we examine fiscal, monetary, and trade policy in some detail, let us take a closer look at how American political culture has changed with respect to government's role in the economy.

17-2 From *Laissez-Faire* to Interventionism

One central tenet of American political thought at the time of the founding of the United States was the doctrine of *laissez-faire*, a French term meaning literally "leave it alone." In economics and political science, the term refers to the theory that the economy functions best when government does not interfere. According to the theory, the economy operates on its own with strong competitors pushing out the weak. Even though weak competitors, either individuals or businesses, may suffer, the "invisible hand" of market forces ensures that the economy performs efficiently. The economy grows, and eventually everyone benefits from the competition for scarce resources.

The idea that society as a whole would benefit if individuals act in their own self-interests was first advanced by Adam Smith in his book *The Wealth of Nations.* This book, first published in 1776, greatly influenced American political thought. From the Constitutional Convention of 1787 until the Great Depression of the 1930s, the *laissez-faire* doctrine was the central concept guiding the development of the American economy. To be sure, government began to intervene in the economy in the nineteenth century, but the intervention was minimal and confined to certain industries. For the most part, the market economy operated without government intervention.

Beginning in the mid-nineteenth century, Marxism posed a fundamental challenge to the ideas of free market capitalism. Marxists called for government control of economic institutions in order to benefit the masses of people, especially the workers, whom they regarded as exploited by capitalism. Although Marxism never gained the sympathies of the American people, it did have a profound influence on American intellectuals. American liberalism, which had traditionally been opposed to government control of the economy, came to reject *laissez-faire* and embrace the idea of activist government. It would take a cataclysmic event, however, to sell the idea of activist government to the American people.

The Great Depression that began with the stock market crash of 1929 shocked the American political culture. Economic desperation led millions of Americans to rethink the role of government in the economy. Leading intellectuals of the day, such as the British economist John Maynard Keynes, argued that government could use policies and programs to stimulate the economy. **Keynesian theory** became the basis for the New Deal in the 1930s. One principal thrust of the New Deal was the use of massive government spending to stimulate the economy. The success, or perceived success, of these policies led to the institutionalization of Keynesianism as the cornerstone of American economic policy. Even a Republican president, Richard Nixon, was able to comment in the early 1970s that "we are all Keynesians now."

President Nixon's observation was true in the sense that a new political consensus had emerged to allow government to assume managerial responsibility for the American economy. But it would be a mistake to ignore the real, and sometimes profound, philosophical differences that exist in our society regarding the role of government in economic affairs. A substantial segment of the population—well represented in the business community, the Republican party, and in think tanks like the Cato Institute—still believes in minimizing government involvement in the economy. At the opposite end of the spectrum are Americans, like those in the left wing of the Democratic party, who believe that government should increase its control of economic life. As usual, most Americans, because they are pragmatists rather than ideologues, are somewhere in the middle. They accept a role for government, but they also recognize that economic prosperity has come about largely through private enterprise.

17-2a The Business Cycle

Before the Great Depression of the 1930s, the economy operated without constant management by the government. Everyone was aware that the economy was subject to a continuous **business cycle** of economic growth followed by **recession** or **depression.** During the growth periods of the cycle, businesses hire more workers, produce more goods, expand their capacity for making more goods, and purchase more materials and services from other businesses. During these boom periods, the prices paid for both materials and labor rise as businesses compete for scarce resources necessary to increase their profits. This increase in prices is known as **inflation.** Inflation makes the money that a person now holds worth less than it was before the inflation. With an annual inflation rate of 10 percent, something that now costs $100 will cost $110 a year from now.

Because buyers cannot buy as many products or services for the same amount of money, they usually consume less after inflation. If enough people react this way, businesses start to have too many products still sitting in inventory. The businesses must therefore

Keynesian theory   A theory which holds that the state of the economy is the result of the relationship between the demand for goods and the productive capacity of the economy.

business cycle   The alternating periods of economic growth and recession that mark a capitalist economy.

recession   A mild slowdown of economic activity.

depression   A severe decline in economic activity characterized by extremely high unemployment, a high rate of bankruptcies, and a general decline in the value of assets.

inflation   A decline in the purchasing power of money.

What Americans Think About

Who Gets Credit for Economic Growth

In a survey taken in the late spring of 2000, the Gallup Organization found that Americans were more likely to give credit for recent economic growth to private industry and to the Federal Reserve than to the Clinton administration. Congress was least likely to receive credit.

"For each of the following, please indicate how much credit, if any, they deserve for the positive state of the economy in the past few years: a great deal, a fair amount, not much, or none at all. How about . . . ?"

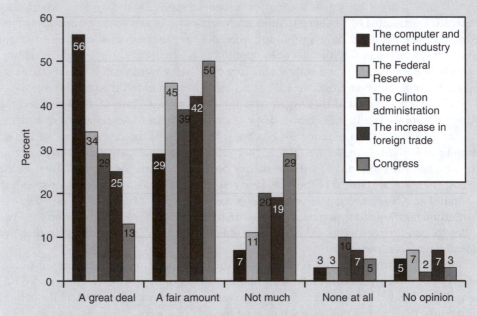

Source: Adapted from the Gallup Organization, national survey of 1,021 adults, June 22–25, 2000.

reduce their levels of production to avoid losing too much money or going out of business. Typically, companies respond to these types of downturns by firing employees, laying them off, or not replacing workers who leave. The combined effect on the economy produces high unemployment, declining salaries, and a large number of bankruptcies. Known as a recession in a mild case or a depression in the most severe cases, the economic slump creates great hardship for many people. Despite the suffering, the *laissez-faire* principle argues that the government should stay out of the way and allow the "invisible hand" to correct the economic problems. Eventually, the economy bottoms out, businesses start growing again and hiring more workers, and the business cycle begins anew. Thus, the business cycle was regarded as an almost natural process of revitalization of the economy.

Keynesian theory holds that public policy can be used to smooth out the ups and downs of the business cycle. To a great extent, that is what fiscal and monetary policies are about. Before the stock market decline in 2000 and 2001, many people thought that the government's ability to manage the economy along with other technological advances had allowed the country to move beyond the business cycle. Some thought that a reasonably high rate of growth could continue without periodic episodes of economic stagnation. This assessment was at least a bit premature, if not just wrong. By 2001, the business cycle indeed appeared to be alive and well, much to the chagrin of investors in the stock market. Worried investors, consumers, businesspeople, and workers looked to government to use

Popular Culture and American Politics
Wall Street

In Oliver Stone's 1987 film *Wall Street,* Gordon Gecko (played by Michael Douglas) makes no apologies for his insatiable appetite for money. "Greed is good," he tells the audience at a stockholders' meeting. Gecko makes his money buying and selling companies. When he buys a company, he usually plans to take it apart and sell it piece by piece. People lose jobs they have had for their entire adult lives. Factories shut down. And Gecko gets rich. The pain was real. But so were the results. American business had tremendous inefficiencies. People like Gecko were wringing out the fat and making the country competitive. Or so they said.

Thinking of this sort of unbridled economic activity usually leads to thoughts of the 1980s and the presidency of Ronald Reagan. It was an era of great economic growth. It was also an era of great economic change. The leveraged buyout, in which investors borrow tremendous amounts of money to purchase whole companies, became almost commonplace. Regulation seemed a bit lax. High rollers prospered. Fraud and deception were not uncommon. Some, like Gecko in the movie, later went to jail.

People still disagree on the economics of the 1980s. Critics contend that many fortunes were made by rearranging existing wealth. They point out that the traders who prospered created nothing themselves. Defenders counter with the argument that American industry needed a shaking up and a shaking out. Whatever the truth, America seemed to sour on this type of wheeling and dealing by the end of the decade.

the tools of fiscal and monetary policy—specifically, cutting taxes and interest rates—to stave off recession.

Supply-Side Economics   In the late 1970s, a school of economic thought known as **supply-side economics** caught the attention of the conservative wing of the Republican party, which had long been dissatisfied with Keynesian thought and its application in American fiscal policy. In particular, Republican presidential candidate Ronald Reagan adopted this new perspective, which argued that cutting taxes, rather than increasing spending, is the best way to stimulate the economy and eventually increase government revenues. The idea is that when tax rates are too high, people are discouraged from investing in enterprises that create jobs and wealth. Therefore, even if government revenues are lessened in the short run, they would increase in the long run because the income from newly created jobs would produce more revenue than was lost by cutting the tax rates. Ronald Reagan found that this economic idea had tremendous political appeal in the 1980 presidential election. Reagan won election on a promise to cut taxes, reduce government spending, balance the budget, and, at the same time, build up America's military power. In 1981, President Reagan signed into law a tax cut based on the supply-side theory. Most economists agree that the Reagan tax cuts did help to stimulate the economy and produce sustained economic growth during the 1980s.

> **supply-side economics**   A school of economic thought which holds that a reduction in government taxation will stimulate the economy so that government revenue will eventually increase, thus reducing the deficit.

The terrorist attacks of September 11, 2001, had an immediate and profound effect on the American economy. The fear, uncertainty, and lack of confidence were palpable. However, the economy had been approaching a recession for months, and the stock market, already harmed by the bursting of the "dot-com bubble," had fallen sharply before the attacks. Prior to the stock market crash of 2000, many observers speculated that the country had evolved to a "new economy" without business cycles. It would soon be apparent that the business cycle was alive and well, however, as the economy slipped into a recession in the latter half of the year.

In early 2001, Congress, at the urging of President George W. Bush, passed an economic stimulus package that included payments of $600 to every household that paid federal income taxes in the preceding year. However, in December 2001, President Bush and Republican leaders found themselves in a heated political battle with Democrats regarding the nature of any further stimulus measures. As a general matter, Republicans tend to favor policies under which taxpayers retain more resources then they can either spend or invest. Democrats tend to favor higher rates of taxation accompanied by government efforts to stimulate the economy through spending programs. Both parties agree on one thing, however: When the economy cycles downward, the federal government has a role to play in helping to reverse the downturn.

17-3 Fiscal Policy

The implementation of public policy almost always costs money. This statement is true whether the national government is seeking to reduce crime, wage "war" on illicit drugs, protect civil rights, strengthen the military, or improve the highway system. Sometimes, the national government passes on the costs of policies to state and local governments in the form of unfunded mandates. At other times, it merely imposes costs on business, which are then passed on to consumers in the form of higher prices for goods and services. Most often, however, the national government must pay at least some of the cost of its programs directly. This money comes from the national treasury and, ultimately, from the American taxpayer.

The Constitution places the "power of the purse" in the Congress. Congress is responsible for passing a budget allocating public monies for specific purposes. The federal budget is really the centerpiece of the public policy process in the United States. It is through the budgetary process that government sets national priorities. Those policies and programs deemed most important are allocated the most money. This process of raising money and deciding how and where to spend it is the realm of fiscal policy. In a nutshell, fiscal policy includes all the questions surrounding taxation and expenditures.

Fiscal policy involves more than setting national priorities and funding programs to achieve them. Maintaining a healthy economy is one of the most important concerns of government. Politicians, especially presidents, know that when the economy worsens, so do their chances for reelection. Not everyone agrees that government can or should manage the economy, but for the better part of this century, the federal government has tried to do just that. One of the ways in which government has attempted to manage the economy is through the federal budget. Government has used spending to try to stimulate the economy in times of economic slowdown. By pumping federal dollars into a certain area of the economy—for example, the construction industry through public works projects—the government attempts to stimulate economic activity and initiate a recovery. Alternatively, government may cut taxes in the hope that taxpayers will use their additional money for investment or consumption and thereby stimulate the economy. Regardless of which approach is used—increasing spending or cutting taxes—fiscal policy often involves some effort to manage the economy.

The Politics of Fiscal Policymaking   In recent years, fiscal policy has dominated the political environment in Washington with an annual battle between the president and Congress over taxation and government spending. Presidents have sought to impose their political preferences while Congress has struggled to maintain its constitutional power of the purse. A president may propose new programs, try to cut old programs, and generally attempt to leave his own imprint on the shape of government. Individual members of Congress, meanwhile, seek to create their own programs, protect existing programs, and maintain the institution's independence from the executive branch. The effort to form a budget in the face of these conflicting goals has led to protracted and often hostile standoffs between the legislative and executive branches. For example, in 1990, Republican President George H.W. Bush chose to let the government close down for a few days rather than sign the budget that the Democratically controlled Congress preferred. National parks and all government offices performing almost every government function except security and

Popular Culture and American Politics

New America Foundation

By Chapman Rackaway

Where can you find "the greatest American thinkers under 40," according to *The Economist* magazine? The answer is the New America Foundation, an organization dedicated to changing public political debate by bringing new, bright, and young voices into the dialogue.

The foundation was created and is chaired by Ted Halstead, an aggressive policy entrepreneur who founded his first think tank, "Redefining Progress," when he was just twenty-five years old. Since its inception in 1999, the New America Foundation has developed a niche outside the conservative-liberal mainstream of political discourse through its nontraditional emphasis on young voices.

In just a few years, the foundation has had a tremendous amount of success, with more than fifteen hundred published articles by fellows and staff of the foundation, as well as thirteen full-length books. The foundation's staff of more than twenty fellows research, publish, and speak about technology, global manufacturing, political participation, education policy, human rights, property rights, space exploration, and a variety of other topics. Some cutting-edge policy areas get full treatment from the foundation: To promote a more fair and efficient allocation of the airwaves, New America's Spectrum Policy Program opposes efforts to privatize the airwaves and advocates requiring commercial licensees to pay market value for their use of the spectrum. The foundation's Tax Policy Program seeks to end the practice of America's largest taxes punishing work and saving, because the revenues raised are far short of those needed, and even as income inequality has grown, the overall tax code has become less progressive. All the foundation's fellows working on such policies are under the age of forty.

In their efforts to empower new voices, the foundation offers many opportunities to young people. Students can apply for internships with the foundation in Washington, D.C., and graduates can apply for fellowships. A foundation fellow receives a stipend, along with research and publication and broadcast assistance, plus a health plan for D.C.-based fellows.

With younger people less likely than ever to involve themselves in political discourse, groups like the New America Foundation provide opportunities for those who want to become involved but don't know the first step to take.

national defense were closed for several days. Partial government shutdowns happened again in 1995 and 1996 as President Clinton and the Republican-controlled Congress could not agree on how much to spend on various programs.

In the mid-1990s, the inability to produce a budget became a symbol to many people of what was wrong with our political system: partisan bickering, institutional struggles over power, political gridlock, and staggering amounts of government debt. Sensing a decline in public confidence, Congress and President Clinton arrived at a landmark bipartisan budget deal in 1997 calling for strict limits on spending. The 1997 budget agreement set the stage for the surpluses of the late 1990s. It also showed how policymakers can, in a crisis, bridge political differences, especially when they have a mutual interest in doing so.

Although it may make some Americans uncomfortable, the budget process will always be highly conflictual. The budget process is the only occasion when Congress and the president attempt to reconcile the conflicting political ideologies of the various factions of our society into a coherent set of priorities. The policy makers must decide how much money they will spend, how they will obtain the funds, who will provide the revenues, and how they will allocate the scarce set of resources available to them. Almost every policy decision is influenced by its effect on the budget, and no new government program can be implemented without a funding decision. Because a budget attaches a price tag to each possible policy goal, it forces politicians to make choices between alternative policy outcomes.[1] The price tags, however, are uncertain estimates of future costs. Policy makers develop a budget for the future that establishes a contract for the way resources will be allocated based on a sophisticated but highly speculative set of assumptions about individual behavior of the affected citizens, the health of the economy, and the methods used for policy implementation. Consequently, the budget process is a complex series of steps involving several different actors and a continually changing set of rules governing the final expenditure of funds.

17-3a The Budget Process

The Framers of the Constitution assigned to the Congress most of the responsibility for producing a budget. Early on, Congress developed all taxation and appropriations legislation with the final approval of the president. Cabinet secretaries made direct requests to Congress for their own department's funding, and there was little centralized control of the system. Although the budget process has evolved over time, and short periods of presidential dominance occurred during wars, this system of congressional budget control existed until the early twentieth century. In 1913, Congress began delegating some of its powers to executive agencies, and in 1921 the passage of the Budget and Accounting Act established a new role for the president in the budget process. A new Bureau of the Budget (later known as the Office of Management and Budget, or the OMB) was created so that the president could propose a budget to the Congress. Since that time, the basic procedure has been a two-stage process: The president proposes a budget, and then Congress reacts to the president's proposal. The specific rules governing the process have changed numerous times since 1921 as Congress and the president have struggled for power, new programs have been created, and deficit spending has gotten out of control. In general, over time, the budget process has seen a gradual shift in power from the legislative branch to the executive. More recently, Congress has attempted to restore some of its influence over the process, and much of the conflict between the two branches since the 1970s has been a result of this attempt.

The Nature of the Budget Arriving at the federal budget is now a complex process. It includes the president's budget, a congressional version, the final plan that is signed by the president, and finally the implementation of the plan, which requires continual adjustments. In a sense, the budget is a living document that is continually changing throughout the budget battle and during the year of implementation. The period in which the budget is implemented is the **fiscal year** (FY). The fiscal year begins on October 1 each year and ends on September 30. A fiscal year is known by the year in which it ends. For example, the FY 2006 budget applies to the period from October 1, 2005, to September 30, 2006.

The money the government expects to receive during the fiscal year is known as **budget receipts,** or **revenue.** Because most receipts come from taxes on individual income and to a lesser degree on corporate income, the estimate of receipts available for government spending is highly dependent on how well the economy performs. On the other side of the ledger, the government has two different methods of accounting for spending. **Budget authority** is how much government agencies are allowed to spend in implementing their policy programs. The actual amount the agencies are expected to spend is known as **budget outlays.** The two spending concepts differ in that authority for spending may extend beyond one particular fiscal year. An agency may have unspent authority left over from a previous budget that will allow greater outlays in this year than would be possible with the current year's authority. For example, some military projects, such as a new aircraft carrier or nuclear submarine, take longer than a year to build, so authority is granted in one year although the outlays on the project may extend over several years. This difference between outlays and authority can be confusing, and it usually results in slightly different estimates of how much the government spends.

An important aspect of the budget is whether the levels of spending and revenue match. If revenues exceed spending, the government experiences a **surplus.** If spending

fiscal year The period in which the budget is implemented.

budget receipts See **revenue**.

revenue The money the government expects to receive during the fiscal year.

budget authority The amount government agencies are allowed to spend in implementing their policy programs.

budget outlays The actual amount of money agencies are expected to spend in a given fiscal year.

surplus The amount that revenues exceed spending in a fiscal year.

during a fiscal year exceeds revenues, the government has a **deficit.** If a deficit occurs, the government must borrow money from the private sector by selling bonds that promise that the government will repay the amount borrowed plus interest at some later point. If the annual deficits are not matched by equal levels of surpluses in other years, the government begins to accumulate **debt.** The national debt, therefore, is an accumulation of all past years' deficits minus all surpluses. Each time budget outlays exceed revenues, the government debt grows.

> **deficit** When spending exceeds revenues in a fiscal year.

> **debt** An accumulation of all past years' deficits minus all surpluses.

The President's Budget   The Office of Management and Budget (OMB) assumes most of the responsibility for developing the president's budget proposals. Each spring, the OMB begins work on the budget proposal by consulting with the president and considering the budget requests of each agency. For example, the FY 2000 budget proposal was first considered in the spring of 1999. Because the president's budget is typically unveiled to Congress and the public in February of the year in which the budget begins (1999 for the FY 2000 budget), a president in his second through eighth years of office has plenty of time to prepare a budget. In contrast, a newly elected president (particularly one from a party different from the preceding president, as was George W. Bush in 2001) must begin preparing a budget proposal before even taking office and still usually needs additional time to present all the details of the proposal. For example, President Bush presented a short version of his FY 2002 budget in February 2001, less than a month after his inauguration.

The budget proposal is a president's most important statement of his priorities. It becomes the most important piece of legislation on the congressional calendar. Consequently, the president, the OMB, and all government agencies pay careful attention to its development. Each agency devotes considerable resources to influencing the president and the OMB during the development of the budget proposal. It may seem odd that a cabinet secretary needs to lobby the president, the chief of staff, or the OMB director for favorable budgetary considerations, but it is absolutely crucial to each agency and department. Almost every agency wants greater resources for its pet projects, to sustain employee morale, and to assert power, but the OMB and the president must reconcile the demands for more money with the revenue projected to be available and the president's priorities.

In February (or April, for new presidents), the budget proposal is released to the public in a carefully orchestrated ceremony designed to gain maximum media coverage. To assist the press, presidents have usually presented their new budgets at noon on a Monday, although the initial version of the budget is ordinarily distributed to the White House press corps on the preceding Friday (with a vow of silence until Monday) so that reporters can prepare their stories.[2] Mondays are good days for gaining the public's attention, and the early afternoon time slot works well for the television evening news programs. The lead time for reporters is crucial for favorable attention because the budget proposal is huge and takes some time to scrutinize. In addition to the *Budget of the United States* (the main document), the government usually prints two shorter versions of the budget, a separate appendix (of two thousand pages) on the details of budget authority and outlays, *Special Analyses* of specific topics on revenue or spending policy, books about historical aspects of budgeting, books about the spending for particular programs, a management document about efforts to cut government waste, and books about government procurement (or purchasing decisions) for each department.

The president's budget becomes the starting point for congressional considerations of the budget and future negotiations between Congress and the president over the final budget numbers. Because the Democrats controlled at least one chamber of Congress throughout the twelve years of Republican control of the presidency under Ronald Reagan and George Bush, congressional leaders often regarded the president's budget proposal as "dead on arrival." To dramatize this point and to mock his congressional opponents, President Reagan had copies of his budget taken to Capitol Hill in an ambulance in 1987.[3] Despite congressional independence, the president's budget dominates the news after its release, and most discussions in Congress are in relation to whether particular program numbers should be more or less than the president's proposal (see Figure 17-1).

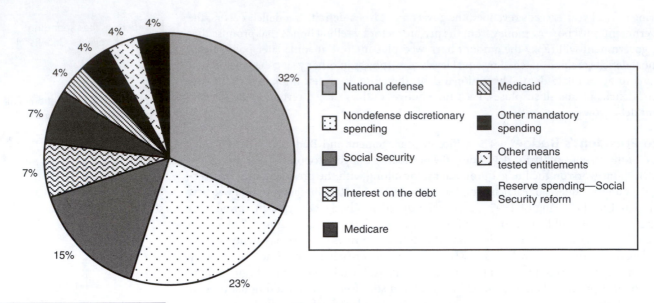

Figure 17-1
Where Does the Money Go?

Source: Adapted from Congressional Budget
Office, 2001, The Budget and Economic
Outlook: Fiscal Years 2002–2011.

▶ **revenue bills** Legislative acts
aimed at raising the money
the government intends to
spend.

▶ **authorization** Legislative
approval of a program.

▶ **appropriations** Money
allocated by Congress for the
purpose of funding
government programs.

Congressional Budget Procedures The congressional budget procedure involves dozens of committees and subcommittees that must decide on taxes, budget authority, appropriations, and the reconciliation of the budget (see Figure 17-2). Reforms in the 1970s, 1980s, and 1990s placed new limits on congressional action on the budget, but basically Congress must take three steps.

First, **revenue bills** must be passed. In the House, the Ways and Means Committee has jurisdiction over all bills dealing with taxes, tariffs, and other means of raising revenues. Because of its ability to revise tax codes, the Ways and Means Committee wields a powerful position within Congress, and it is one of the most sought-after committee assignments. The Finance Committee considers all revenue measures in the Senate. Like any bill, tax legislation must pass through the appropriate committee in each chamber before being approved on the floor; then, all differences between the two chambers' versions must be worked out before the bill is sent to the president for signing.

On the spending side, two main actions are required. First, a program must receive **authorization.** About twenty committees in the House and fifteen in the Senate consider legislation authorizing government programs. For example, the Public Works Committee in the House can pass legislation approving the construction of new dams. Of course, as with any bill, the entire House, the Senate, and the president would have to concur. At this point, the new dams have been authorized, but no money has been appropriated to fund construction.

Before any money can be released to fund the program, an **appropriations** bill that provides funding for the program must be passed. All the different areas of government spending are covered by thirteen regular appropriations bills, which are considered by the Appropriations Committees in each chamber. Even if an authorization bill has been passed by Congress and signed by the president, the policy cannot be implemented until it receives funding from an appropriations bill. Because the Appropriations Committees work out all the details of spending for each bill, they are considered the most powerful committees in their respective chambers. This is also the point where the president's proposals are most likely to be changed as members of Congress push through their own favorite projects. Even though the executive agencies have already fought for funding within the executive branch when the OMB assembles the president's budget proposal, they are not likely to receive favorable funding in the final appropriations bills unless they also work to win support on the Appropriations Committees.

One major problem with this system is that one set of committees makes spending decisions and another forms tax policy. This division of labor is efficient in that it reduces the leg-

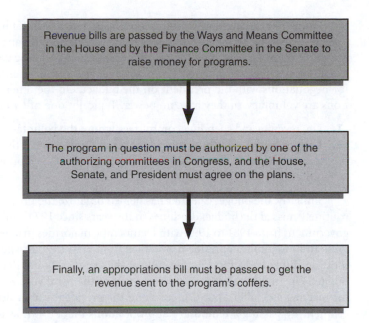

Figure 17-2
Congressional Budget Procedures

islature's workload, provides time for extensive hearings and review of the bills, and allows legislators to specialize and develop expertise on a certain subject; however, it also prevents the coordination of efforts and reduces policy coherence. Until recently, Congress did not have a method of coordinating budget decisions or establishing overall budget priorities.

To respond to the lack of coordination in budget policy and to counter the power of the president, Congress enacted the Budget and Impoundment Control Act of 1974. Congress had grown increasingly impatient with the loss of budgetary control to the executive, but a series of disagreements over spending between the Democrat-controlled Congress and Republican President Richard Nixon helped push the legislation to the forefront. The supporters of the bill also escaped powerful opposition to the passage of budget reform by carefully avoiding confrontation with the powerful chairs of the Appropriations Committees (in both chambers), the Ways and Means Committee (in the House), and the Finance Committee (in the Senate), who played crucial roles in the budget process. Rather than eliminate their committees, take away any power, change their rules for decision making, or combine the responsibilities of the committees, the act created a new Budget Committee in each chamber. The Budget Committee would be a permanent committee with the responsibility of coordinating the budget process by setting overall budget targets for spending and revenue.

The act also changed the budget process by creating a new Congressional Budget Office (CBO) and developing a new annual calendar for passing the budget. The CBO has provided Congress with valuable information on the budget that has allowed Congress to verify presidential estimates and generate independent proposals for spending and taxation. The revised schedule for passage of the budget was designed to make the process more orderly. Under this schedule, the president proposes a new budget by January; both chambers pass a budget resolution by April 15 on the broad guidelines for revenue targets and spending targets; and Congress passes a binding resolution on the budget by September 15. The Budget Committees are responsible for establishing the initial targets for revenues and spending that will be embodied in the budget resolutions of April and September. The first budget resolution establishes targets on spending and revenues, but if new legislation affects the budget or key parts of spending bills or revenue bills violate the first resolution, either the second budget resolution must reflect the new numbers, or a reconciliation act becomes necessary. A reconciliation is in order when Congress or the president does not accept any of the changes made between the first and second budget resolutions. If reconciliation occurs, Congress must go back to either the revenue or the appropriations process to make the changes necessary to achieve the targets in the first budget resolution.

The 1974 reforms have met with mixed success. The CBO has proved useful to Congress by providing an independent source of information. Because the Budget Committees are mostly composed of members of the revenue and spending committees, their presence has allowed some coordination of the revenue and spending efforts and provided a basis for negotiations with the president on the budget. On the other hand, the budget resolutions are voluntary, so they have no power. Typically, one of two things happens:

1. The revenue and spending committees ignore the voluntary targets; or
2. The resolution is nothing more than a reflection of what the revenue and spending committees have already decided independently of each other or the Budget Committee.

> **continuing resolution**
> Legislative act that temporarily continues the current level of funding for a program until an annual budget can be passed.

Similarly, the budget calendar has helped organize the process, although Congress has routinely missed the budget deadlines in the years since 1974. During the period of divided government from 1981 to 1993 with Democratic majorities in at least one chamber of Congress and a Republican president, and then from 1995 to 2000 when the roles were reversed, most deadlines had almost no meaning as the Democrats and Republicans battled over the budget. One might think that the beginning of the fiscal year would create some pressure for meeting a deadline, but Congress and the president can avoid shutting down the government by passing a temporary appropriations bill, known as a **continuing resolution,** that continues funding until a permanent budget can be passed. When Congress and the President cannot agree, either can risk shutting down the government by failing to pass or sign a continuing resolution.

Continuing resolutions are widely considered to be a poor method of financing government. First, because the bills are rushed through at the last minute, they do not allow time for careful scrutiny or much debate. In 1982, Senator Thomas Eagleton (D-Missouri) observed that the process was a "hectic, frantic, helter-skelter way of doing the nation's business . . . [that] made a mockery of the Senate tradition as 'the world's greatest deliberative parliamentary body.'"[4] Second, because the continuing resolution must pass to keep the government from shutting down, every legislator realizes that it is an excellent opportunity to attach a provision appropriating funds for a pet project in the legislator's district or state. Because Senate rules allow amendments to any bill but the House does not, senators can much more easily add goodies to a continuing resolution. Consequently, continuing resolutions encourage higher levels of pork barrel spending but little policy deliberation.

17-3b Raising Revenue

Government spending presupposes revenue. Raising revenue is the other side of the fiscal policy coin. The major portion of the federal government's income is derived from the federal income tax (see Figure 17-3). Before the ratification of the Sixteenth Amendment in 1913, the United States had no federal income tax. The Sixteenth Amendment, by creating the basis for massive federal revenues, laid the groundwork for modern, activist government.

The federal income tax is *progressive,* which means that people pay a higher proportion of their income on taxes as their incomes increase. This tax is levied on income deemed to be taxable, after various exemptions are taken into account. Income is divided into brackets, and income in each bracket is taxed at rates that increase as the brackets increase. These rates are known as marginal rates, by which each person's income is taxed at higher rates as her income increases. Income higher than $100,000 is taxed at a higher rate than income lower than $25,000.

The nature of the brackets is always contentious and reflects the parties' philosophies regarding the role of government in redistributing income. Republicans generally favor lowering rates for the top bracket, and Democrats generally see lowering these types of rates as providing an unneeded windfall for higher-income taxpayers. As of 2000, the tax code used five tax brackets, starting at 15 percent and ending at 39.6 percent. As a result of tax relief enacted during George W. Bush's first term, the highest rate was reduced to 35 percent, and a new 10 percent rate was created for the lowest-income taxpayers.

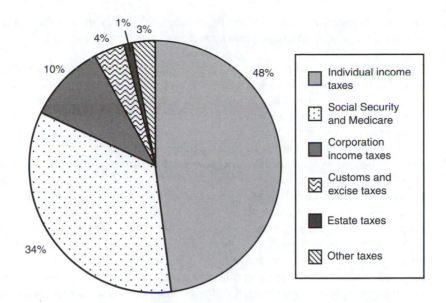

Figure 17-3
Where Does Government Revenue Come From?

Source: Adapted from Congressional Budget Office, 2001, The Budget and Economic Outlook: Fiscal Years 2001–2011.

Most income tax is paid by using payroll withholding through deductions from taxpayers' paychecks. This method increases tax compliance and provides the government with a steady stream of revenue throughout the year. Income not realized through payrolls cannot be deducted in this manner. This other income from investments or from personal service contracts must also be paid throughout the year by paying quarterly estimated taxes.

Social Security and Medicare Taxes   The federal government takes in its second-largest amount of income through the Social Security tax. This tax, otherwise known as the payroll tax, is paid by all wage earners on incomes up to a ceiling. This tax, unlike the individual income tax, is not progressive. It is intended to fund Social Security retirement payments and Medicare payments. Each person has her own Social Security and Medicare accounts. Because all wage earners pay Social Security and Medicare payroll taxes and those at the bottom of the income ladder often pay no income tax, more people pay the payroll tax than the individual income tax. Today, the Social Security payroll tax is 6.2 percent of annual wages under $72,600. The payroll tax for Medicare is 1.45 percent of annual wages, with no upper limit. Employers must match their employees' Social Security and Medicare tax payments.

Other Taxes   The federal government collects about 10 percent of its taxes from taxes on corporations. This somewhat controversial tax is often seen as a tax on consumers who pay taxes that are "passed through" to them. Many corporations have successfully lobbied various exemptions to this tax. Another controversial tax is the estate and gift tax. Until it was changed in 2001, the estate tax had to be paid on estates worth more than $675,000. The Economic Growth and Tax Relief Reconciliation Act of 2001 increased the exclusion amount to $3.5 million in 2009 and repealed the estate tax altogether beginning in 2010. Democrats complained bitterly that this measure, promoted by President George W. Bush and Republicans in Congress, favored the wealthiest Americans. Republicans countered by arguing that lowering these taxes would promote investment and lead to economic growth which, in the long run, would benefit everyone.

The capital gains tax has long troubled many, mostly conservative, critics. This tax is paid on transactions that result in a profit, such as from the sale of stock or real property. Some see this as a double taxation because taxes were paid on the income that was used to purchase the asset in the first place. The rates on capital gains were reduced in 1997. However, President Bush did not include a capital gains reduction in his 2001 tax proposals, perhaps because many see capital gains taxes as falling primarily on wealthy taxpayers.

However, as more and more Americans acquire stock (today the number exceeds 60 percent), reducing taxes on capital gains becomes politically more palatable.

Taxpayer Relief In 1997, President Clinton and the Republican-controlled Congress agreed to pass legislation to lower taxes by approximately $100 billion over five years. This strategy was accomplished by cutting $151 billion and imposing new taxes of $56 billion. The legislation contained a number of major cuts, including a $500-per-child tax credit, lower capital gains rates, IRA and education tax credits, and lower estate and gift taxes. This legislation marked a response to a number of commitments from both parties. However, a third of the cuts were balanced by increases in taxes on tobacco, airline travel, and a variety of corporate transactions.

Tax policy was hotly debated during the 2000 election campaign. Following his election, President George W. Bush placed tax reduction at the top of his legislative agenda. His proposals centered on a $1.6 trillion tax cut to be phased in over a ten-year period. Originally proposed in 1999 during a period of economic growth and projected budget surpluses, the Bush plan was grounded in the logic that the overpayment of taxes should be returned to those who were paying it. Although Bush proposed eliminating the marriage penalty, among other suggestions, the plan's centerpiece was an across-the-board lowering of tax rates. Democratic critics countered with the argument that the tax cut was too large and would go disproportionately to wealthier taxpayers.

George W. Bush's Tax Cuts On May 26, 2001, Congress passed, and President George W. Bush subsequently approved, the Economic Growth and Tax Reduction Reconciliation Act of 2001. The act reduced **marginal tax rates** from 39 percent to 35 percent, 36 percent to 33 percent, 31 percent to 28 percent, and 28 percent to 25 percent. The legislation also expanded the "earned income credit" for married taxpayers filing jointly and doubled the "child tax credit" to $1,000 per child. Because the tax cuts were made retroactive to 2000, the government mailed a refund check to everyone who paid taxes the previous year. Married filers received $600, and singles got $300. The rationale was to stimulate an economy suffering from stagnation following the stock market declines in 2000 and 2001. Most analyses agree that the tax refunds did have a stimulative effect, although there is disagreement as to the magnitude of the stimulus.

As we noted in section 17-2a, "The Business Cycle," the terrorist attacks of 9-11-2001 had an extremely detrimental effect on economic activity in this country. Business travel and tourism slowed substantially, consumer spending declined significantly, and the nation suffered a tremendous decline in employment. President Bush responded by proposing yet another tax relief bill, the Jobs and Growth Tax Reduction and Reconciliation Act, which Congress adopted in 2003. During the 2004 presidential campaign, President Bush's tax cuts became a political issue as Democrats blamed them for the ballooning federal deficit. John Kerry, John Edwards, and other Democratic candidates also painted the tax cuts as "giveaways" to the rich, because higher income taxpayers received greater reductions in tax rates. Of course, under our progressive income tax system, wealthier Americans pay a higher proportion of their incomes in taxes.

According to a report released by the Congressional Budget Office in August 2004,[5] the effective federal income tax rate[6] for all households in 2001 was 21.5 percent. As a result of the Bush tax cuts, that rate fell to 19.6 percent in 2004. The bottom 20 percent of taxpayers saw their effective tax rate lowered from 5.4 percent to 5.2 percent. The middle 60 percent of taxpayers received reductions in effective tax rates from 15.4 percent to 14.7 percent. The top 20 percent saw their effective tax rate fall from 26.8 percent in 2001 to 23.8 percent in 2004. According to these data, wealthy taxpayers did benefit from the Bush tax cuts more than low- and middle-income taxpayers. But they still paid substantially higher income tax rates than low- and middle-income households.

Analyses performed by conservative think tanks such as the Heritage Foundation suggested that, if made permanent, the Bush tax cuts would result in stronger economic growth, reductions in unemployment, and, ultimately, significantly higher revenues for the

▶ **marginal tax rates** Different tax rates that apply to different levels of income. That is, one pays a certain rate on income up to a certain point and a higher rate on income above that point. Our progressive income tax system is constructed in this way.

federal government.[7] Liberal think tanks like the Brookings Institution predicted that making the tax cuts permanent would result in much higher budget deficits and result in significantly higher interest rates, thus depressing economic growth.[8]

17-3c Debts, Deficits, and Surpluses

When President George W. Bush took office in January 2001, he could look forward to projected budget surpluses well into the future. His proposed tax cuts fit well within the constraints of the projections. However, just as these optimistic projections replaced those that preceded them, they too proved to be short-lived. The downturn in the economy, especially as exacerbated by the terrorist attacks of September 2001, again led to projections of deficits rather than surpluses.

Even when a surplus was projected, it was easy to forget about the federal debt, which today stands at more than $7 trillion (see Table 17-1). The dramatic rise in the federal debt was the major policy problem of the 1980s and 1990s. Despite the 1974 budget reforms and the election of a president (Reagan) in 1980 who was publicly committed to balanced budgets and reduced government spending, the national debt grew from around $1 trillion in 1980 to more than $7 trillion today.

Though visualizing this much money is difficult, consider that the current federal debt amounts to nearly $27,000 per person in the United States, or more than $80,000 per family. President Clinton dramatically described the growth of the debt in his first address to Congress in February 1993, when he said, "I well remember twelve years ago when President Reagan stood at this podium and told you and the American people that if our debt

Year	Total Public Debt	U.S. Population	Debt per Capita
1799	$82,976,294	5,170,556	$16.05
1809	$53,173,218	7,046,741	$7.55
1819	$91,015,566	9,398,596	$9.68
1829	$48,565,407	12,543,263	$3.87
1839	$3,573,344	16,649,110	$0.21
1849	$63,061,859	22,700,435	$2.78
1859	$58,498,381	30,687,000	$1.91
1869	$2,545,110,590	37,906,000	$67.14
1879	$2,298,912,643	48,866,000	$47.05
1889	$1,249,470,511	61,289,000	$20.39
1899	$1,436,700,704	74,318,000	$19.33
1919	$25,484,506,160	105,003,065	$242.70
1929	$16,931,088,484	121,878,000	$138.92
1939	$40,439,532,411	131,028,000	$308.63
1949	$252,610,000,000	149,188,000	$ 1,693.23
1959	$287,465,000,000	177,073,000	$ 1,623.43
1969	$365,769,000,000	202,736,000	$ 1,804.16
1979	$829,470,000,000	225,106,000	$ 3,684.80
1989	$2,868,039,000,000	247,397,000	$11,592.86
1999	$6,357,759,000,000	266,640,400	$23,843.94
2004	$7,497,665,000,000	281,400,000	$26,644.15

TABLE 17-1

The Federal Debt, 1799—2004

Source: Adapted from U.S. Department of the Treasury, Bureau of the Public Debt, on the Web at http://www.publicdebt.treas.gov.

was stacked in thousand-dollar bills, the stack would reach sixty-seven miles into space. Well, today that stack would reach 267 miles."[9] Today, the stack would reach more than 300 miles.

One might question how such a large amount of debt could have come into existence. The simple answer is that the government ran massive deficits in the 1980s and early 1990s. Between 1961 and 1997, only one year, 1969, showed a surplus, but the deficit reached the $100 billion mark only one time before 1982. The more complicated answer involves tax cuts, a massive defense buildup during the 1980s, spending increases, uncontrollable expenditures, and the growing interest on the debt. In 1981, President Reagan proposed and successfully pushed through Congress legislation to cut income taxes. As a consequence of the 1981 Economic Tax Recovery Act, the government lost a total of $750 billion, or $150 billion a year for five years, in revenues it would otherwise have received.[10] At the same time, President Reagan proposed quite a large increase in the defense budget. He doubled the defense budget between 1980 and 1986, and the total military outlays for the eight fiscal year budgets he planned were more than $2 trillion.[11]

Although Democrats were quick to blame "Reaganomics" for the growth of the federal debt, policies established in the 1980s created the basis for the rapid economic growth in the 1990s. As the economy grew at a rapid rate during the 1990s, so did government revenues, allowing for budget deficits to be eliminated by 2000. The balanced budget was short-lived, however, as the economic downturn of 2001–2002 slowed government revenues. Even if the surplus is restored under more favorable economic conditions, paying off the massive public debt would take many years. Indeed, the desired time frame for paying down the debt was one element of disagreement between the George W. Bush administration and its Democratic critics during the tax debate of 2001. Democrats suggested accelerated payments and a smaller tax cut; Bush countered that paying the debt down "too fast" would cost money because of the penalties associated with the early payment of long-term obligations.

Some economists have argued that no proof exists that government debt has hurt the economy. But, if $7 trillion of debt has not caused massive economic problems, what level would? Some economists argue that the American economy can grow fast enough to make the current debt seem as small in retrospect as a debt of a few hundred billion dollars would seem now. They point out that the American economy is quite different from the economies of the small, less developed countries that experienced severe debt problems in the 1980s. Furthermore, they maintain that foreign investment in this country, which increases as our government seeks to finance the public debt, is good for our economy. More foreign investment means more research, more productive capability, and lower borrowing costs than would be possible without outside money.

17-4 Monetary Policy

Monetary policy is the control of how much money is in circulation in the economy. Economists known as **monetarists** believe that proper management of the money supply is the principal factor influencing inflation, recession, and economic growth. Monetarists think that fiscal policy alone cannot deal with the ups and downs of the business cycle. Nor can politicians be trusted to apply fiscal policy in a responsible fashion. Monetarists believe that the proper government role is less direct. By controlling the money supply, government influences but does not dictate private decisions on investment and enterprise. For example, if the goal is to create jobs, a fiscal policy approach would be to cut taxes or increase spending on public works programs, or both. A monetary approach would be to lower interest rates, making it easier for people to obtain the credit needed to start new businesses or expand existing ones.

17-4a The Federal Reserve Board

In the United States, monetary policy is set principally by the Federal Reserve System (better known as "the Fed"). The Fed is governed by a seven-member board of governors,

▶ **monetarists** Economists who believe that proper management of the money supply is the principal factor influencing inflation, recession, and economic growth.

Comparative Perspective

Central Banks in Other Countries

In the United States, the Federal Reserve System serves as a central bank. The United States is not alone in having a central bank. All the world's more advanced countries have central banks, charged with controlling their country's money supply. Central banks are almost invisible to the general public; they are banks for the banking industry. Central banks play a major role in international trade and economics by buying and selling currencies from other countries. The first country to establish a central bank was England. The Bank of England was created in 1694 to manage England's national debt. By the nineteenth century, the Bank of England had begun to regulate interest rates. Napoleon established France's national bank in 1800. Known as the Banque de France, it was nationalized in 1945, one year before Britain nationalized its central bank.

National banks in advanced capitalist countries perform much the same function—they deal with foreign currencies and set interest rates. However, each country's history and political culture set limits on the range of alternatives a bank may consider. Consider Germany, for example: Its central bank, the Deutsche Bundesbank, functions much like the U.S. Federal Reserve System, but with a slightly different emphasis. Germany experienced extreme levels of inflation during the 1920s that helped build public support for Adolf Hitler and the Nazi movement. As a result, German monetary policy is heavily weighted in the direction of controlling inflation. Germany was so concerned with inflation that it was willing to suffer a near depression when West Germany reunified with East Germany after the collapse of the Soviet Union. East Germany was badly in need of capital, which called for a policy of low interest rates. Yet the Bundesbank held a tight rein on the money supply, keeping interest rates high and inflation low. Some critics thought that Germany overreacted in its excessive fear of inflation. But to many Germans, uncontrolled inflation is something to be avoided at all costs. In any event, the Bundesbank's approach to German reunification illustrates the tremendous effect that monetary policy can have on people's everyday lives.

---

located in Washington, D.C. The governors are appointed to fourteen-year terms by the president with the consent of the Senate. The board of governors runs the system in tandem with representatives of twelve regional Federal Reserve banks. The presidents of the regional banks are elected by their respective boards of directors, who are in turn selected by the directors of the commercial banks that are members of the system. All banks chartered by the federal government must belong to the Federal Reserve System. Thus, it is an unusual mixture of private and public power, leading a member of Congress to describe it as "a pretty queer duck."[12] The structure of the Federal Reserve System ensures that it is to a great extent independent from the president and Congress. Indeed, the Fed, created in 1913, is a product of the Progressive Era, when politics was regarded as the enemy of good policy making. This independence, however, runs counter to traditional notions of representative democracy, in which policy is made by elected officials, or at least those accountable to them. Not surprisingly, therefore, Congress has often been frustrated by the secrecy and independence that typify Fed decision making. For example, in late 1993, the House Banking, Finance and Urban Affairs Committee, chaired by Henry Gonzales (D-Texas), conducted hearings reviewing Federal Reserve System practices. In an effort to increase accountability and open the process to greater public and congressional scrutiny, Gonzales threatened to change the way Fed governors are selected. In response to the threat from Congress, the Federal Reserve System took steps in 1994 to reduce the secrecy of its operations.

The Federal Reserve System uses several devices in setting monetary policy, including its **open-market operations,** which involve the purchase and sale of government securities. The most important device the Fed uses to set monetary policy is the **discount rate.** The discount rate is simply the rate of interest Federal Reserve banks charge to lend money to

open-market operations Measures used by the Federal Reserve to regulate the money supply in the economy.

discount rate The rate of interest that Federal Reserve banks charge to lend money to the private banks that are members of the Federal Reserve System.

The Federal Reserve Building, Washington, D.C.

the private banks that are members of the Federal Reserve System. Changes in the discount rate influence interest rates throughout the economy. If the discount rate increases, interest rates go up and borrowers are less willing or able to seek loans. If less money is being lent, less is going into circulation, so the money supply is reduced. When the governors of the Federal Reserve System believe that the money supply is growing too fast and that inflation is about to rise, they increase the discount rate. Conversely, if the economy is in a recession, the Fed is likely to lower the discount rate and increase the supply of available money, thus "heating up" the economy.

In the 1990s, more Americans than ever began to follow the role of the Federal Reserve in setting the discount rate. A spate of cable channels devoted considerable attention to the ups and downs of the stock market, with one channel, CNBC, devoted to covering the markets during each weekday. Much of this attention focused on what the Federal Reserve System would do in regard to interest rates. The Federal Reserve was seen as a prime mover in setting the climate for future profits for companies. Everyday citizens began to speculate on whether chairman Alan Greenspan would act to change rates. That intense observation of the Fed and speculation as to its impending actions continue unabated today.

17-5 Trade Policy

Foreign policy is about more than military confrontations, political crises, and humanitarian missions. It is also about creating an international environment that is favorable to a country's economic interests. Every country wants to sell its goods to other countries, but not all countries are willing to allow foreign goods to be sold within their borders on an equal footing with domestically produced products. Since the early 1990s, one of the most crucial issues of foreign policy, and not just for the United States, has been international trade.

The United States, as a country with both Atlantic and Pacific ports, has always paid close attention to trade. Although the political and economic culture of the United States would seem to support open trade, tremendous pressure to protect domestic industries from foreign competition has always existed. This apparent contradiction between free market ideology and actual policy can be attributed to the self-interest of manufacturers. Americans value the concepts of the free market and free enterprise. However, individual self-interest, which is a major part of free enterprise philosophy, often leads threatened industries to lobby the government to reduce or eliminate competition from abroad. The

*Profiles &
Perspectives*

**Alan Greenspan
(1926–)**

Federal Reserve Board of
Governors

Alan Greenspan was born in 1926, the only child of the stockbroker Herbert Greenspan and his wife, Rose. The younger Greenspan's parents divorced when he was only four, leaving him to be raised in the Washington Heights area of New York City by his mother and grandparents. Always fascinated by numbers and baseball, he "took" to music and entered the Julliard School, intending to pursue a career as a musician. Young Greenspan played the clarinet and the saxophone and joined the Henry Jerome swing band as a jazz musician. The band toured the country in the 1940s. In 1952, he briefly married Joan Mitchell, who introduced him to the author Ayn Rand, who had a profound effect on his thinking through her philosophy of "enlightened selfishness." Despite her influence, however, Greenspan retained a pragmatic approach to economics. He soon joined with his partner William Townsend to form a company that provided economic forecasts to industry. Greenspan later returned to finish his education, eventually earning a Ph.D. from New York University in 1977.

Greenspan joined the Nixon administration after renewing a friendship with his old friend Leonard Garment, a Nixon campaign advisor. Greenspan served as Nixon's director of policy research. In 1974, just before his resignation, Nixon nominated Greenspan to be the chairman of the Council of Economic Advisers.

The election of Jimmy Carter in 1976 led to Greenspan's return to the private sector. However, when the Republicans recaptured the White House in 1980, President Reagan appointed Greenspan to chair the Commission on Social Security Reform. This choice put Greenspan in a position to replace Federal Reserve Chairman Paul Volcker when Reagan decided to change chairpersons in 1987. Shortly after his confirmation, Greenspan had to deal with a plunge in the Dow Jones Industrial Average, which fell more than 500 points in October of that year. He then made it clear that he would do whatever was necessary to calm the financial markets. The stock market recovered quickly with minimal damage to the economy. He has served as chair of the board of governors of the Federal Reserve System since his appointment by President Reagan in 1987.

In his years as chairman of the Federal Reserve, Alan Greenspan has enjoyed support from both Democrats and Republicans. He served during the Clinton administration, soon developing a close working relationship with the president. During the long bull market of the 1990s, Greenspan kept a watchful eye on inflation. His decisions on rates were followed closely, along with any comments he might make on the direction of the economy. His decision to raise rates in late 2000 as a move against inflation drew criticism from many people in the financial and investment community who maintained that this rate increase was not necessary. The subsequent slowdown in economic growth led the Federal Reserve to begin reducing rates in 2001 with the hope of avoiding recession. As the economy recovered and picked up steam in 2004, the Fed raised rates slightly to stave off any threat of inflation.

For more information on Alan Greenspan, check out these websites:
The Federal Reserve: http://www.federalreserve.gov
Ayn Rand: The Ayn Rand Institute: http://www.aynrand.org
The Objectivist Center: http://www.objectivistcenter.org

tension between free trade and protectionism has been a staple of American policy from the beginning of the Republic.

17-5a Tariffs

A *tariff* is a tax on goods that are brought to one country from another. Although tariffs do raise some money, their primary goal is to discourage trade. Because the amount of the tariff must be added to the cost of the item when it is sold in the United States or another consuming country, producers in the consuming country are at an advantage. If the tariff is sufficiently large, the real effect is to cut off imports of the item. Although tariffs can be placed on the use of ports and other facilities, by the seventeenth century, most countries chose to collect tariffs on goods as they entered the country.

Most of the Founders were familiar with the work of Adam Smith, the Scottish economist whose 1776 book *The Wealth of Nations* revolutionized economic thought. Smith argued that unrestricted international trade would benefit all countries involved. Accepting this theory, the Framers of the Constitution left the regulation of commerce to the federal government and banned the taxation of exports by the states. Many fortunes were made from trade between the founding of the Republic and the beginning of the twentieth century. However, most of the energy of the United States was focused on building internal markets. At the turn of the twentieth century, foreign trade was still a small part of the American economy.[13] When the Great Depression hit America in 1929, a great deal of sentiment for protecting U.S. industries was expressed. The vehicle for this protection was the Smoot–Hawley Tariff Act, which became law in 1930. With the passage of Smoot–Hawley, tariffs reached their highest level. Not surprisingly, other countries responded with tariffs of their own. Most economists now view the trade war that resulted from the Smoot–Hawley Act and the retaliatory tariffs by other countries as a major factor contributing to the severity and longevity of the Great Depression. World War II effectively quashed any notion of free trade among all nations. From the end of the war until now, however, the trend has been toward open trade.

This statement does not mean, however, that a number of industries have not managed to convince Congress to establish tariffs to protect them from competition. Winners and losers appear whenever an industry is protected with a tariff. The winners, of course, are those who can sell their products at a much higher price. The losers are just about everybody else in society, who must pay higher prices. It would then seem that Congress would not enact tariffs. After all, consumers have many more votes than the industry wanting protection. The cost of a tariff, however, is spread over many consumers who may not be politically activated by this cost. A small increase in the price of any single item has a negligible effect on their lives. For the producers, however, the tariff can make the difference between a profitable business and being put out of business altogether. Producers, in addition to labor unions, often become politically active to protect their interests. In 2002, much to the chagrin of free trade advocates and many conservatives, President Bush gave in to pressure from domestic steel producers and imposed tariffs on steel imports to the United States. Many predicated retaliatory actions, especially in Europe, where the immediate response was to create a list of American products that could be subject to tariffs. The tariffs were scheduled to remain in effect until 2005, but were lifted prematurely in December 2003 after the World Trade Organization ruled that they violated international trade agreements.

17-5b Trade Policy with Japan

Despite the protection provided to some industries, the United States has kept its markets quite open by international standards. During the 1970s and 1980s, a number of previously healthy American industries suffered greatly as inexpensive but high-quality imports flooded into the United States. The textile industry was particularly hard hit, as workers in many Asian countries produced clothing for much lower wages than those paid to workers in the United States. The electronics industry was also badly hurt. By the end of the 1980s, Americans were producing few television sets and no videocassette recorders. Japan, and later South Korea and Taiwan, had cornered the market on most of the electronic entertainment industry.

The automotive industry also suffered greatly at the hands of the Japanese. American automakers enjoyed virtually complete control of the market throughout the 1960s. Unfortunately, the lack of competition led to problems with quality. American cars came to be regarded by consumers, at home and abroad, as inferior products. In addition, American automakers were slow to recognize the growing consumer demand for smaller, fuel-efficient automobiles. The Japanese were quick to fill the gap. Soon, their cars were everywhere and were widely perceived to be of higher quality. Though American automobiles had closed much of the quality gap by the end of the 1980s, the industry decline had cost hundreds of thousands of American jobs.

Although the Japanese were exploiting America's relatively open imports market, Japan maintained strict control over the importation of American goods ranging from computers to rice. Throughout the 1980s, American presidents engaged in negotiations with the Japanese government in the hope of persuading the Japanese to open their markets to American goods. Despite some limited successes, the Japanese market remained much more closed to American goods than the American market was to Japanese goods. In 1994, the Clinton administration attempted to "get tough" with the Japanese, first threatening sanctions and then, after threats failed, imposing penalties on certain Japanese imports. The political situation was difficult for leaders on both sides of the Pacific. Neither wanted a trade war, which would be bad for both economies, but neither side wanted to look as though it was caving in to the other. This situation is the reality of trade negotiations: The political and economic considerations are bound up together.

17-5c Trade with China

China has become a major player, both politically and economically, on the world stage. As it has moved away from Communist-style central planning and embraced elements of capitalism, its economy has boomed. In the 1990s, China became a source of many products, especially textiles and small manufactured products, consumed in the United States. At the same time China became increasingly receptive to American products and to American businesses that wished to open branches in that country. However, concern about China's authoritarian government and human rights policies led many in Congress to resist policies under which the United States and China would have an unrestricted trading relationship known as Most Favored Nation (MFN) status. In 2000, Congress and the Clinton administration agreed on legislation granting China permanent normal trade relations status. This landmark legislation capped the Clinton administration's accomplishments in moving trade policy in the direction of free trade and away from protectionism.

Today, controversy persists over trade with China. More and more manufactured goods consumed in the United States are produced in China, not just textiles and other low-tech products, but computers, televisions, DVD players, and the like. America's trade imbalance with China is tremendous, as Americans consume more Chinese products than Chinese consume American-made goods. In August 2004, America's trade deficit with China reached a record $18.1 billion.[14] However, in recent years China has made its markets more accessible to American agricultural products, automobiles, and telecommunications services. Some economists predict that in the long run, as China develops economically and its people have more disposable income, trade between China and the United States will become more balanced. Unless and until that happens, trade with China will continue to be a major political issue in the United States.

17-5d Landmark Free Trade Agreements

Since the founding of the Common Market in 1958, Europe has been moving toward a unified economy devoid of tariffs and border controls. The removal of these trade barriers has promoted tremendous economic growth in Europe over the past several decades. The success of the Common Market has led to demands for a similar arrangement among the countries of the Western Hemisphere. During the George Bush administration, a significant step was taken as Mexico, Canada, and the United States worked out an agreement to allow free trade in North America. The North American Free Trade Agreement (NAFTA) was not final when President Bush left office. It remained for his successor, Bill Clinton, to carry the process forward through congressional approval. During the 1992 campaign, Clinton expressed cautious support for NAFTA with the caveat that additional "side agreements" would have to be negotiated with Mexico to ensure worker safety and environmental protection. These side agreements were reached during 1993, and NAFTA was submitted to Congress for approval. There, it faced tremendous opposition, especially from organized labor. Unions argued that the agreement would result in American jobs being shipped to Mexico, where labor is cheap. During the 1992 campaign, the independent candidate Ross Perot made much the same argument, referring to a "giant sucking sound" as American jobs moved south to Mexico. Proponents of NAFTA argued that it would promote growth throughout the continent and ultimately increase the number of American jobs. They also argued that NAFTA would create a better economic environment in Mexico, lessening the pressure for Mexicans to emigrate illegally to the United States.

Because NAFTA required changes in American laws, it had to be approved by both the Senate and the House of Representatives. As the treaty came before Congress in the fall of 1993, public opinion was sharply divided, with opposition to the treaty much more intense than support for it. The climate of public opinion changed, however, when the White House launched an intense campaign for NAFTA. The high point of the campaign was a debate on CNN's *Larry King Live* between Vice President Al Gore and Ross Perot. Most commentators believed that Gore won the debate, and public opinion shifted dramatically in its aftermath. Reflecting the more favorable climate of pubic opinion, both chambers of Congress approved NAFTA by a comfortable margin, giving President Clinton a great victory. Whether NAFTA represented a victory for the American people, both as consumers and workers, is something that will have to be assessed over the long term. Early indications are positive in that there seem to be more winners than losers.

The General Agreement on Tariffs and Trades (GATT) aroused much less controversy. In December 1993, seven years after negotiations had begun, trade representatives from 117 nations agreed on a package of reforms intended to dramatically lower import barriers around the world. GATT cuts tariffs on thousands of products, reduces government subsidies, and expands the rules of world trade to cover agricultural commodities and services. Most economists thought that GATT would create jobs and jump-start the troubled global economy, which had been mired in recession since the late 1980s. Clearly excited about the agreement, President Clinton called it "an early Christmas gift." American farmers were equally excited about the prospect of selling their products in the world market on a level playing field. So were most American manufacturing firms. Of course, not everyone was happy. In the United States, environmentalists complained that GATT lacked provisions protecting the environment. In Asia, rice farmers protested vociferously at the prospect of having to compete with cheaper American rice. But, in public policy making—indeed, in politics generally—*someone* is always unhappy.

Although the globalization of the economy through the adoption of free trade pacts remains controversial, most Americans have come to accept the idea that globalization is both inevitable and desirable. A national survey conducted in 2002 found that 52 percent of Americans supported "free trade between the United States and other countries," whereas only 25 percent opposed it.[15] When the question is more specifically focused on NAFTA and other particular agreements, the level of support declines, however. A 2004 poll found that only 44 percent of Americans believed that NAFTA and the WTO were "a good thing for the United States," whereas 37 percent said they were "a bad thing."[16] Despite lukewarm public support for NAFTA and serious opposition from organized labor, the Bush administration proceeded to extend the NAFTA pact to include other Central American countries. That agreement, called CAFTA (Central American Free Trade Agreement), was finalized in 2004 and was expected to go before Congress for approval in early 2005.

Without question, international trade will continue to be a political issue in the United States for the foreseeable future.

17-6 Conclusion: Politics, Policy, and the American Economy

Everyone wants the economy to be vibrant and healthy. And most Americans have come to accept a governmental role in ensuring economic prosperity. Perhaps the most significant change in American political culture since the founding of the United States has been the increased acceptance of government intervention in the economy. But the public does not comprehend the complexities of the economy or the difficulties in fashioning and implementing policies that will manage it successfully. In overseeing America's massive and dynamic economy, the national government has taken on a gigantic responsibility that is not easily shouldered.

Policy makers try to manage the economy through fiscal and monetary policy. The control of the money supply through the management of interest rates is the principal responsibility of the Federal Reserve. Congress and the president also try to manage the economy through the selective use of taxing and spending, but it is fair to say that most members of Congress are more interested in the political effects of their fiscal decisions than in sound economic policy. Over the years, politicians have tried to appease voters by supporting popular spending programs without raising taxes or, in some cases, even while lowering them. The result was a federal debt of gargantuan proportions.

In the 1990s, a consensus developed in the electorate that the massive federal debt was a threat to the long-term health of the economy. Politicians began to get the message that the American people wanted their government to move in the direction of a balanced budget. In fact, a balanced budget amendment was a central feature of the Republicans' Contract with America in 1994. In 1997, the Republican-controlled Congress worked out a landmark budget agreement with President Clinton featuring limits on discretionary spending. By 1998, the whole discussion regarding the economy had been recast. The growing economy of the 1990s had created a budget surplus expected to extend at least ten years into the future. Both parties responded by agreeing to cut taxes during the 2000 election. When George W. Bush proposed a $1.6 trillion tax cut in 2001, the Democrats agreed in concept, but disagreed on the amount and focus of the cuts. Likewise, after Bush's reelection in 2004, Democrats responded negatively when the president proposed permanent cuts in taxes on dividends and capital gains. While Republicans touted the benefits of reducing government burdens on capital formation, Democrats predicted swelling deficits and a debt spiraling out of control. As usual, economic policy was being forged on the anvil of partisan conflict.

Questions for Thought and Discussion

1. Should the Federal Reserve Board be made more accountable to the president and Congress? Why or why not?
2. Can the national debt be substantially reduced? How? With what consequences?
3. Richard Nixon once said "We are all Keynesians now." Does bipartisan agreement on the principles of Keynesian economics exist?
4. Is supply-side economics dead? Why or why not?
5. What can the federal government do to create jobs? Is this best done through monetary or fiscal policy? Why?

Practice Quiz

Note: You can find the correct answers to these questions by taking the quiz and then submitting your answers in the Online Edition. The program will automatically score your submission. If you miss a question, the program will provide the correct answer, a rationale for the answer, and the section number in the chapter where the topic is discussed.

1. It took _____ to convince American citizens that the government had a significant role to play in stimulating the economy and creating jobs.
   a. the Industrial Revolution
   b. Reaganomics
   c. the Great Depression
   d. World War II

2. _____ policy includes all the questions involving taxation and expenditures.
   a. Monetary
   b. Fiscal
   c. Trade
   d. Regulatory

3. The doctrine of *laissez-faire* is most closely associated with the economist _____.
   a. Adam Smith
   b. John Maynard Keynes
   c. John Kenneth Galbraith
   d. Thomas Malthus

4. Under the principles of _____ economics, government can spend more money during times of recession to stimulate the economy.
   a. *laissez-faire*
   b. Keynesian
   c. supply-side
   d. Austrian

5. Members of the Federal Reserve Board are appointed by the president with the consent of _____.
   a. the Council of Economic Advisors
   b. the Office of Management and Budget
   c. the Senate
   d. Congress

6. An important device the Federal Reserve Board uses to set monetary policy is the _____.
   a. discount rate
   b. inflation rate
   c. exchange rate
   d. unemployment rate

7. The _____ assumes most of the responsibility for developing the president's budget proposals.
   a. Federal Reserve Board
   b. Council of Economic Advisors
   c. Office of Management and Budget
   d. Department of the Treasury

8. In 1974, Congress enacted the _____ to respond to the lack of coordination in budget policy and to counter the power of the presidency in the budgetary process.
   a. Gramm–Rudman–Hollings Act
   b. Budget and Impoundment Control Act
   c. Deficit Reduction Act
   d. Balanced Budget Act

9. A budget _____ occurs when spending exceeds revenues.
   a. deficit
   b. appropriation
   c. surplus
   d. reallocation

10. _____ occurs when there is a decrease in the purchasing power of money.
    a. Unemployment
    b. A trade deficit
    c. A general deficit
    d. Inflation

For Further Reading

Bhagwati, Jagdish. *In Defense of Globalization* (New York: Oxford University Press, 2004).

Gilder, George. *Wealth and Poverty* (Oakland, CA.: ICS Press, 1993).

Gosling, James J. *Budgetary Politics*, 3d ed. (New York: Brunner-Routledge, 2002).

Greider, William. *Secrets of the Temple: How the Federal Reserve Runs the Country* (New York: Simon & Schuster, 1987).

Kettl, Donald. *Deficit Politics: The Search for Balance in American Politics*, 2d ed. (New York: Longman, 2002).

Leonard, Herman B. *Checks Unbalanced: The Quiet Side of Public Spending* (New York: Basic Books, 1986).

Reich, Robert B. *The Work of Nations: Preparing Ourselves for 21st Century Capitalism* (New York: Knopf, 1991).

Rubin, Irene S. *The Politics of Public Budgeting*, 4th ed. (New York: Chatham House, 2000).

Samuelson, Robert. *The Good Life and Its Discontents: The American Dream in an Age of Entitlement* (New York: Times Books, 1996).

Schick, Allen. *The Federal Budget: Politics, Policy and Process* (Washington, D.C.: Brookings Institution, 2000).

Schier, Steven. *A Decade of Deficits* (Albany: State University of New York Press, 1992).

Shuman, Howard. *Politics and the Budget*, 3d ed. (Englewood Cliffs, NJ: Prentice-Hall, 1992).

Stiglitz, Joseph E. *Globalization and Its Discontents* (New York: W.W. Norton, 2003).

Weidenbaum, Murray L. *Business, Government and the Public*, 4th ed. (Englewood Cliffs, NJ: Prentice-Hall, 1990).

Wildavsky, Aaron, and Naomi Caiden. *The New Politics of the Budgetary Process*, 5th ed. (New York: Longman, 2003).

Witte, John F. *The Politics and Development of the Federal Income Tax* (Madison: University of Wisconsin Press, 1985).

Wolf, Martin. *Why Globalization Works* (New Haven, CT: Yale University Press, 2004).

Endnotes

1. Aaron Wildavsky, *The New Politics of the Budgetary Process*, 2d ed. (New York: HarperCollins, 1992), p. 2.

2. Howard E. Shuman, *Politics and the Budget*, 3d ed. (Englewood Cliffs, NJ: Prentice-Hall, 1992), p. 3.

3. Ibid.

4. *Washington Post*, December 21, 1982, p. A-13.

5. Congressional Budget Office, "Effective Federal Tax Rates Under Current Law, 2001 to 2014," August 2004.

6. Effective household tax rates are determined by dividing taxes paid by total household income.

7. William W. Beach, Ralph A. Rector, Rea S. Hederman, Jr., Alfredo B. Goyburu, and Tim Kane, "The Candidates' Tax Plans: Comparing the Economic and Fiscal Effects of the Bush and Kerry Tax Proposals." The Heritage Foundation Center for Data Analysis Report #04-09, September 20, 2004.

8. William G. Gale and Peter R. Orszag, "The Budget Outlook: Projections and Implications," *The Economists' Voice*, vol. 1, no. 2, article 6, 2004.

9. William J. Clinton, "Presidential Address," printed in *Congressional Quarterly Weekly*, February 20, 1993, p. 399.

10. Howard E. Shuman, *Politics and the Budget*, p. 280.

11. *Economic Report of the President* (Washington, D.C.: U.S. Government Printing Office, 1991), pp. 376–77.

12. Former Congressman Wright Patman (D-Texas), quoted in William Greider, *Secrets of the Temple: How the Federal Reserve Runs the Country* (New York: Simon & Schuster, 1987), p. 50.

13. John Steele Gordon, "Land of Free Trade," *American Heritage*, July/August 1993, p. 52.

14. "China' Sales Boost Trade Gap," CBS News, October 14, 2004.

15. Survey conducted May 8–13, 2002, by Techno Metrica Institute of Policy and Politics. Results reported in *Investor's Business Daily* and *Christian Science Monitor*.

16. Survey conducted by Princeton Survey Research Associates International, July 8–18, 2004, for the Pew Research Center and the Council on Foreign Relations. Results available online at www.pollingreport.com/trade.htm.

Foreign Policy and National Defense

18

18-1 The Importance of Foreign Policy and National Defense

The United States, despite being flanked by two oceans, cannot afford to think of itself apart from the rest of the world. The events of September 11, 2001, cemented the fact that American interests are never separable from those of other nations and cultures, no matter how seemingly remote and distant. The question is not whether the United States will deal with other countries, but rather in what manner and with what goals.

foreign policy The decisions that one country makes in its dealings with other countries.

national defense The policies and strategies that guide a nation's military forces.

The term **foreign policy** refers to the decisions that one country makes in its dealing with other countries. **National defense** refers to the policies and strategies that guide a nation's military forces. Foreign policy and national defense have always been fundamental concerns for every nation, sometimes involving national survival itself. As the scholar Hans Morgenthau put it, "[t]he most elementary function of the nation-state is the defense of the life of its citizens and of their civilization."[1] The existence of the United States is not now immediately threatened by war, but foreign policy and national defense remain high on the national agenda. Of particular concern is the ongoing threat of terrorism to the United States, it allies, and American interests around the world. Closely related to that concern is the need to stem the proliferation of nuclear weapons and other weapons of mass destruction. Another high-priority objective is fostering a climate of international trade that promotes the continued success of the American economy. These concerns are heightened by the fact that the world is shrinking—technology is increasing the extent to which nations interact with one another. With closer interaction come new challenges and new problems, but also new opportunities. The potential for international conflict is increased, but so too is the possibility of cooperation.

When Bill Clinton was on the campaign trail in 1992, he hammered President George Bush for ignoring domestic concerns and focusing all his attention on international affairs. As president, Clinton soon learned that American presidents are necessarily involved in international relations, even though it often conflicts with their domestic priorities. President Clinton must have wondered what he could have accomplished on the domestic scene were it not for the foreign policy crises in Bosnia, Haiti, Somalia, Russia, and Cuba that clamored for his attention during the first two years of his presidency. But no president, regardless of campaign rhetoric or personal goals, can afford to ignore foreign policy. America's role as the one true superpower in the world demands no less than continual attention to international affairs on the part of the president.

Ironically, the tables were somewhat turned in 2000 when Vice President Gore ran against George W. Bush. Gore prided himself on his encyclopedic knowledge of foreign policy buttressed by his experience as a senator and then as vice president. Bush, unlike his father, was focused on such domestic policy issues as taxes and education while never having demonstrated much interest in international affairs or diplomacy. Bush supporters were nervous about his ability to deal effectively with questions regarding international policy during the presidential debates. Pundits expected Bush to stumble while trying to pronounce names of international leaders. Bush did not stumble, but handled the foreign policy debate competently, if not brilliantly. And, as had been the case eight years earlier, foreign policy came to occupy a relatively minor role in the 2000 presidential election.

The lesson seemed clear. Without the specter of the cold war, Americans remain focused on the domestic rather than international political arena. This lack of public focus does not detract from the complexity of the United States' role in the world. Rather, it reflects the difficulty of framing the complex as opposed to the simple. The international political arena remains a maze of economic, military, religious, and cultural forces that are a constant challenge to those making policy. That was made abundantly clear following the terrorist attacks of September 2001. Following an election in which foreign policy concerns were relegated to the back burner, Bush had been in office less than a year before finding himself in the midst of a complex international situation. For the first time in more than half a century, America had been attacked on its own soil. President Bush's response, the launching of a war on international terrorism, would reflect both America's collective outrage and the complexity of the international situation.

In 2002, President Bush dealt with a series of critically important foreign policy matters, including, but certainly not limited to

- The prosecution of the war on terrorism, which involved the assembly and maintenance of a fragile international coalition.
- An escalating conflict in the Middle East involving Israel, the Palestinians, and the surrounding Arab countries.
- America's new relationship with post-Soviet Russia, including the negotiation of a new treaty reducing stockpiles of nuclear weapons in Russia and the United States, in addition to Russia's entry into a partnership with NATO.
- An increasing level of tension between India and Pakistan over the disputed Kashmir region. The situation was all the more dire because both sides were capable of using nuclear weapons.
- Rising tensions with North Korea stemming from that country's decision to go forward with a covert nuclear arms program in violation of an agreement that had been negotiated during the Clinton administration.
- Mounting concerns about possible weapons of mass destruction in Iraq and, more specifically, Iraq's refusal to cooperate fully with international inspectors looking for such weapons.

Like every president in the modern era, George W. Bush soon discovered that foreign policy is the chief concern of the president no matter how much emphasis he wants to place on the domestic agenda. By 2003, especially after the president's fateful decision to invade Iraq and depose its dictator, Saddam Hussein, foreign policy had become the overriding issue in American politics. In 2004, despite the Democrats' initial attempt to focus voters' attention on economic problems at home, Iraq and the global war on terrorism would dominate the national conversation leading up to the presidential election.

18-1a Political Culture and America's World Role

America was not always a superpower. Indeed, in its early history, the United States was a rather minor actor on the world stage. To most Americans in the late eighteenth and early nineteenth centuries, that was fine. Most people at that time were quite content for the United States to stay out of world politics. As the nineteenth century progressed, the United States became a more active and more important player in world affairs. Much of this increased activism was caused by changes in the American economy and population, both of which expanded dramatically after the Civil War. American political culture began to change to accept a more active role abroad for the United States. Nevertheless, public opinion was, at least early on, opposed to American involvement in both World War I and World War II. Events overtook public opinion, however, and the United States became involved (see Figure 18-1 for current opinion on U.S. involvement in world affairs). America emerged from its successful participation in these wars as a superpower, with a massive economy and an enormous military machine. American power and influence were now being exercised and felt around the globe. The failure of the United States to achieve a military victory in Vietnam caused many Americans to rethink America's role in the world. Vietnam rekindled a debate that is a perennial feature of American political culture: Should the United States look outward toward the rest of the world or inward toward its own problems and needs?

18-2 The Evolution of American Foreign Policy

American foreign and defense policy have evolved through a number of distinct stages. In the earliest stage, the United States followed a policy of isolation from the rest of the world. As the United States grew economically and geographically, so did its influence in the international arena. The United States began to dominate the western hemisphere, both politically and militarily. As the twentieth century dawned, America emerged as a major player

Figure 18-1
Public Opinion on U.S. Involvement in World Affairs
"Do you think the U.S. should take the leading role in world affairs, take a major role, but not the leading role, or take a minor role, or take no role at all?"

Source: The Gallup Organization.

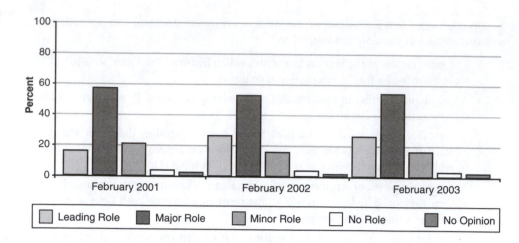

on the world stage, capable of projecting its military power anywhere on the globe. After two world wars, the United States became a superpower, one of two political and military giants that dominated world politics. The other superpower, the Soviet Union, represented quite a different style of political and economic organization—a Communist dictatorship committed to support worldwide revolution against the capitalist system. For four decades, the United States and the Soviet Union engaged in a struggle for supremacy that involved the creation of tremendous military arsenals capable of destroying the entire world many times over. Though the two rivals never directly engaged in war, the Soviet-American struggle, or **cold war,** as it was called, provided the backdrop to numerous regional conflicts from Vietnam in the 1960s to Afghanistan in the 1980s. During the cold war, all foreign and military policy decisions, and many domestic-policy decisions, were colored by the standoff between the United States and its allies on one hand and the Soviet bloc on the other. When the Soviet Union finally collapsed in the early 1990s, the cold war ended and the United States embarked on a new era in foreign and military policy. As the new era began, the United States was left as the only real superpower, striving to define and pursue its national interests amidst a world that was changing daily.

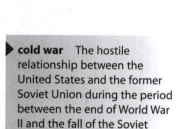

cold war The hostile relationship between the United States and the former Soviet Union during the period between the end of World War II and the fall of the Soviet Union in the 1990s.

18-2a The Origins of American Foreign Policy: 1789–1900

During the early days of the Republic, a strong consensus existed among political elites that America should avoid entanglements with foreign nations. In his farewell address in 1796, President George Washington admonished the nation to "steer clear of permanent alliances with any portion of the foreign world." Washington's warning was well received by the dominant political culture of the day, which viewed America as a haven from the wars, persecutions, and rivalries that had long characterized European politics. In the late eighteenth century, most Americans were quite happy for the United States to be politically isolated and economically self-sufficient. This philosophy, which became known as **isolationism,** still has strong appeal in American political culture, although it is no longer dominant.

isolationism The belief that U.S. foreign policy should be marked by political isolation and economic self-sufficiency; dominant foreign policy theme during the early days of the Union.

The Monroe Doctrine In a message to Congress in 1823, President James Monroe signaled that American foreign policy was entering a new phase. The **Monroe doctrine** stated that North and South America were no longer open for colonization by European countries and that the United States would object to any European intervention in the Americas. Although never formally recognized in international law, the doctrine was relied on several times and became a cornerstone in U.S. foreign policy. At first, the Monroe doctrine was welcomed by Latin American countries struggling for independence. Eventually,

Monroe doctrine President James Monroe's proclamation that North and South America were no longer open for colonization by European countries and that the United States would reject any European intervention in the Americas. It was never accepted as international law.

though, it became viewed with suspicion by Latin American countries that feared domination by the United States.

As the nineteenth century progressed, Americans began to believe in the idea of **manifest destiny,** the doctrine that the United States had the right to expand its territory and influence throughout North America. This belief reflected a growing feeling of confidence among the American people. America was expanding, both geographically and economically, and Americans were starting to look outward to the world. The world that once seemed threatening and corrupt now seemed to hold opportunities, especially for business. Americans, who saw their new country as a haven from the dangerous games of European politics, were beginning to think that the United States was destined to become a great nation, a model for the rest of the world to follow.

Although westward expansion may have seemed to be a matter of manifest destiny to Americans, it produced conflict, first with Mexico and later with Spain. In 1845, the United States annexed Texas, which was claimed by Mexico. In the two-year war that ensued, the United States defeated Mexico and acquired not only Texas but also California and most of what is now the southwestern United States. The Pacific Northwest was acquired peacefully by a settlement with Great Britain in 1846, and the territory of Alaska was purchased from Russia in 1867.

> **manifest destiny** The doctrine that the United States had the right to expand its territory and influence throughout North America.

18-2b The Emergence of the United States as a World Power

By the end of the nineteenth century, the United States had developed a formidable navy capable of projecting American power around the world. In 1898, that power was used to destroy the Spanish empire. The Spanish–American War began after the United States demanded that Spain withdraw from Cuba. One week after Spain declared war, a U.S. naval squadron defeated the Spanish navy in Manila harbor, in the Philippines. Several weeks later, when the Spanish fleet attempted to escape from Cuba, it too was destroyed. On July 17, 1898, American forces captured Santiago, Cuba, ending the war. In the peace treaty, the Spanish freed Cuba and ceded Puerto Rico, Guam, and the Philippines to the United States. Flexing its military muscle in the Pacific, the United States also annexed the Hawaiian Islands in 1898.

Interventionism   As the United States emerged as a world power, it began to use its military might to intervene in the domestic conflicts of other countries. For example, President Theodore Roosevelt intervened in a civil war in Panama to foster the construction of the Panama Canal, claiming that the United States had the right to impose order in Latin America. In 1904, in an important extension of the Monroe doctrine, Roosevelt stated that a conflict in Latin America could require U.S. military action to forestall European intervention. This policy was relied on extensively by Presidents William Howard Taft and Woodrow Wilson to justify U.S. military involvement in the Caribbean. The practice of using American military power, or the mere threat of military action, to achieve American interests abroad is known as **interventionism.** Critics of the practice often refer to it as **gunboat diplomacy.** Americans remain divided about how and when their government should intervene militarily in foreign disputes.

> **interventionism** The practice of using American military power, or the threat of military action, to achieve American interests abroad.

The Impact of Two World Wars   Despite the efforts of President Woodrow Wilson to keep the United States out of World War I, the nation entered the war on the side of the French and British in 1917. After the successful conclusion of the war, the United States reverted to an isolationist policy. Concerns about the growing power and imperial designs of Nazi Germany in the 1930s were not enough to persuade most Americans that the United States should enter World War II. But the surprise attack by Japanese airplanes on the American base at Pearl Harbor in December of 1941 created an immediate consensus that America should enter the war. Ultimately, America's role proved to be decisive, especially in the Pacific theater of the war. Germany and Japan were defeated. America, along with the Soviet Union, assumed the role of superpower.

> **gunboat diplomacy** The use of the threat of military force as a tool in international relations.

18-2c The Cold War

In July 1945, President Harry S Truman met with Soviet Premier Joseph Stalin and British Prime Minister Winston Churchill at Potsdam, Germany, to decide the fate of postwar Germany. The Allies agreed to divide Germany into American, British, Soviet, and French occupation zones. The area occupied by the Soviets eventually became the country of East Germany, a Communist dictatorship closely allied with Moscow. The remaining parts of Germany became the Federal Republic of Germany, a country based on Western-style democracy and capitalism and allied closely with the United States. The division of Germany remained a point of contention between the United States and the Soviet Union for decades, until Germany was reunified in 1990.

Not only East Germany, but also most of Eastern Europe fell under Soviet control in the wake of World War II. In a speech at Westminster College in Fulton, Missouri, in 1946, Winston Churchill warned that an "iron curtain" had descended across Europe (see Figure 18-2). The **iron curtain** metaphor became a symbol of the threat posed by the Soviet Union and its allies. The **Truman doctrine,** enunciated in 1947, was aimed at keeping Greece and Turkey outside the iron curtain. Speaking to a joint session of Congress, Truman asserted, "It must be the policy of the United States to support free peoples who are resisting attempted subjugation by armed minorities or outside pressures."

Responding to the Soviet domination of Eastern Europe, the United States undertook the reconstruction of war-ravaged Western Europe through a massive infusion of economic aid known as the **Marshall Plan.** Advocated by Secretary of State George C. Marshall in 1947, the program funneled more than $12 billion in American aid to Europe between 1948 and 1951. In addition to providing economic aid, the United States established a strong military alliance with the democracies of Western Europe. Established in 1949, the **North Atlantic Treaty Organization (NATO)** guaranteed the collective security of its twelve member nations: Belgium, Canada, Denmark, France, Great Britain, Iceland, Italy, Luxembourg, the Netherlands, Norway, Portugal, and the United States.[2] The United States, as principal sponsor of NATO, maintained bases in many of the NATO countries, and throughout the Pacific. These bases allowed for the rapid projection of American military power to almost any point on the globe.

The principal justification for the maintenance of a strong American military presence throughout the world was the cold war that developed between the United States and the Soviet Union. The Soviet Union had come into being in the twentieth century as Russia, which had been ruled by a Communist party dictatorship since 1917, and built an empire throughout Eastern Europe and Central Asia. Although never as economically powerful as the United States, the Soviet Union emerged victorious from World War II with a massive military machine and a goal of world domination. With Soviet backing, Communist dictatorships came to power in the war-ravaged countries of Eastern Europe. With the exception of Albania and Yugoslavia, these countries became the dependable military and political allies of the Soviet Union, joined together by a treaty known as the **Warsaw Pact** (1955). For decades, the formidable armies of the Warsaw Pact stood poised to do battle with the forces of NATO on the plains of central Europe. Fortunately, this battle, which many expected to produce Armageddon, never took place.

In addition to military buildups on both sides, the cold war was characterized by intense economic and political competition and chilly, sometimes hostile, diplomatic relations. Throughout the 1950s, 1960s, and 1970s, the Soviets supported Communist insurgencies and dictatorships around the world, from southeast Asia to the Caribbean basin. Convinced that the spread of communism represented a real threat to American values and interests, in the early 1950s the United States committed itself to a **policy of containment** of communism.[3]

The Korean War The American commitment to containing the spread of communism led to the Korean War. During World War II, American and Soviet forces liberated Korea from occupation by Imperial Japan. At the end of the war, Korea was divided at the 38th parallel into Soviet and American occupation zones. The Communist government of

---

iron curtain Metaphor coined by Winston Churchill that became a symbol of the threat posed by the Soviet Union and its allies during the cold war.

Truman doctrine Foreign policy stance enunciated in 1947 by President Harry Truman, who asserted, "It must be the policy of the United States to support free peoples who are resisting attempted subjugation by armed minorities or outside pressures."

Marshall Plan Economic effort by the United States aimed at rebuilding Europe after World War II.

North Atlantic Treaty Organization (NATO) Anti-Soviet military alliance established in 1949 that guaranteed the collective security of its twelve member nations: Belgium, Canada, Denmark, France, Great Britain, Iceland, Italy, Luxembourg, the Netherlands, Norway, Portugal, and the United States.

Warsaw Pact The former military alliance of Eastern European Communist regimes that was originally formed to counter the establishment of NATO.

policy of containment Dominant foreign policy theme following World War II in which the United States sought to prevent the Soviet Union from expanding its sphere of influence.

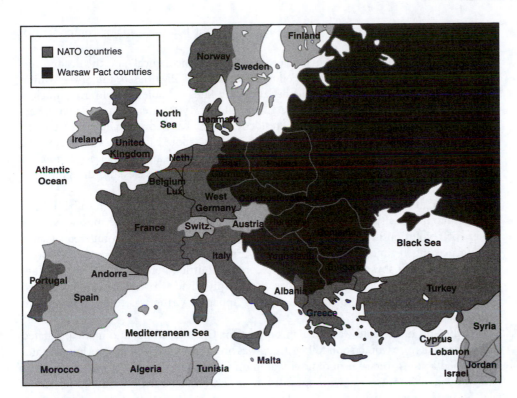

Figure 18-2
Cold War Europe

North Korea was aligned with the Soviet Union; capitalist South Korea aligned itself with the United States. When North Korean forces invaded the South in 1950, the United Nations authorized member nations to aid South Korea. China, which had been taken over by the Communists in 1947, joined the battle on the North Korean side. After the initial Communist advance was repelled, most of the fighting bogged down around the 38th parallel. A ceasefire was declared on July 27, 1953. The war ended in stalemate, but the United States and its allies had prevented a friendly government from falling under Soviet domination.

Cuba Like many countries in Latin America, Cuba was governed during the 1950s by an unpopular dictator, Fulgencio Batista. Like many traditional dictatorships, the corrupt Batista regime ran the country for its own benefit with little concern for the welfare of the Cuban people, most of whom lived in abject poverty. Havana, the Cuban capital, became a playground for American tourists and a haven for organized crime. Although mobsters and rich tourists reveled in decadence, an uprising began in the countryside. Led by Che Guevara and Fidel Castro, this uprising grew into a full-fledged civil war, and Castro assumed control of the government in 1959.

At first, Castro gave every indication of being committed to democratic values. Soon, however, it became apparent that he planned to establish a Marxist-Leninist state in Cuba. The prospect of a Communist country just ninety miles from Florida was viewed as a serious threat to American national security. The cold war was at its height, and the growing relationship between Cuba and the Soviet Union was seen as unacceptable. But America's first effort was a disaster. In 1961, the United States supported a group of anti-Castro Cubans who launched a failed attempt to overthrow the Castro regime. On April 17, about 1,500 Cuban exiles who had been trained and supplied by the Central Intelligence Agency (CIA) were defeated by Castro's forces at the Bay of Pigs. This situation marked a crisis point in American foreign policy. Castro seemed entrenched; contrary to the expectations of the American intelligence community, Cubans did not rise in revolt when the invasion took place. The United States had on its doorstep a neighbor that was friendly with the opposing superpower, the Soviet Union. Many feared Cuba would pose a threat to the security of all of Latin America. Eliminating this threat became a major component of American foreign policy.

Cuba's friendship with the Soviet Union was at first ideological, and then economic. Finally, it was a military friendship. Following the Bay of Pigs fiasco, the Soviet Union secretly began building in Cuba missile-launching sites capable of delivering nuclear weapons to targets inside the United States. In October 1962, after the missile launchers were detected by American spy planes, President John F. Kennedy demanded their withdrawal. Kennedy issued an ultimatum to Soviet Premier Nikita Khrushchev to remove the missiles and imposed a blockade on all shipping to Cuba. After an intense week of nuclear brinkmanship, the Soviets gave in and agreed to remove the missiles and dismantle the launchers.

Following the Bay of Pigs invasion and the missile crisis, relations with Cuba did not provide an opportunity for direct military action. However, the Cubans became active promoters of revolution in Africa and Latin America. The United States countered by supporting existing regimes, especially in Latin America. Quite often, these regimes were authoritarian, with abysmal human rights records and little interest in democratic values or institutions. The American people became sharply divided over whether the United States should support dictatorships whose only apparent virtue was their opposition to communism.

At the end of the cold war, Russian support for Cuba dried up, and many predicted that Castro's demise would soon follow. Cuba was an economic disaster. The United States maintained a controversial economic embargo on Cuba that prevented American citizens and companies from trading with it. Castro, however, consolidated his hold on power. In fact, he used American hostility to buttress his support among the Cuban population. Many Americans believed that ending the embargo would bring about pressures for democracy among Cubans as they participated in the new economic opportunities that would present themselves with the lifting of the embargo.

The American relationship with Cuba has long been a staple of the politics of Florida. The large number of refugees from Cuba who had settled in the Miami area maintained a great hostility to the Castro regime. Any presidential candidate thinking of eliminating the sanctions would have to face the consequences of an angered Cuban community that could make the difference in who would capture Florida's haul of electoral votes.

The American relationship with Cuba and its consequences for domestic politics came to the forefront of American domestic politics in 2000 with the Elian Gonzalez situation. Elian's mother had fled Cuba with her son, but died at sea off the Miami shore. Two fishermen rescued young Elian who was then placed with relatives in Miami. Elian's father in Cuba wanted him to come back. Soon, an epic battle began. The Miami Cuban community wanted Elian to stay in Miami and grow up under the care of his relatives. Fidel Castro demanded the boy's return. Ultimately, Attorney General Janet Reno approved and oversaw a plan that led to armed federal agents entering the relatives' house and seizing the boy, who was later reunited with his father and returned to Cuba.

The War in Vietnam

Before World War II, Vietnam was a French colony. It was occupied by the Japanese during the war, and when the Japanese were ousted by the Allies, many Vietnamese decided that it was time for Vietnam to govern itself. In 1946, a guerrilla war was launched against the French colonial rulers, who were finally defeated in 1954. At the Geneva Conference of 1954, Vietnam was divided into two separate countries, much as Korea had been partitioned a decade earlier. War soon erupted in South Vietnam as Communist guerrillas, known as the Viet Cong, attempted to overthrow the South Vietnamese government and unify the country under Communist rule.

▶ **domino theory** The belief that if one country becomes Communist, neighboring countries will follow like falling dominoes.

As early as 1954, President Dwight D. "Ike" Eisenhower had warned of the Communist threat in Southeast Asia, where Vietnam is located. Indeed, it was in this context that Ike articulated the **domino theory,** the idea that if one country becomes Communist, neighboring countries will follow like falling dominoes. Beginning in 1961, the United States supplied military advisers to South Vietnam. It soon became apparent that the situation

WEB EXERCISE

The Libertad Act (also known as the Helms–Burton law), passed in 1996, strengthened the embargo against Cuba. It provides for a total embargo of Cuba until the United States decides that Cuba's government has taken a turn toward democracy. Many people feel that as a result of the hardship caused by the embargo—under which Americans cannot officially travel to Cuba and American medicines and food supplies cannot be sold to Cuba, for example—the people of Cuba will be inspired to take action against the rule of Fidel Castro. Other people feel that the embargo hurts Cubans and will do little to encourage change in the politics of the country. Take a look at some sites on both sides of the issue:

The Libertad Act (from the State department):
  http://www.state.gov/p/wha/rls/fs/2001/2596.htm
CNN coverage of George W. Bush's May 2002 speech on Cuba:
  http://fyi.cnn.com/2002/fyi/news/05/20/bush.cuba/
Transcript of the May 2002 speech by George W. Bush:
  http://fyi.cnn.com/2002/ALLPOLITICS/05/20/bush.cuba.transcript/index.html
Cuba News:
  http://www.cubanet.org/cubanews.html
The Cuban American National Federation (CANF):
  http://www.canfnet.org/
The Cuba Center:
  http://www.cubacenter.org/
Directorio (Cuban Revolutionary Democratic Directorate):
  http://www.directorio.org

How do you think the embargo affects the leaders of Cuba? Working-class people? Would lifting the embargo give more power to Castro, or do you think that a U.S. presence would contribute to the opposite and assist in change? If you owned a business and wanted to sell or manufacture in Cuba, how do you think the presence of your business would influence the government, the economy, and the everyday lives of Cuban citizens? One Cuban group (CANF, see the preceding website) is essentially a government-in-exile, based in Miami, Florida. If you were a member of the Cuban government-in-exile, how would you pressure the U.S. government to act in regard to Cuba?

was becoming dire. The Kennedy administration concluded that more American involvement would be necessary to save the imperiled South Vietnamese government. President Kennedy could not know, nor would he live to see, just how great the American commitment would become and how many lives would be sacrificed in a losing cause.

After President Kennedy was assassinated in November 1963, the Johnson administration inherited the Vietnam problem. President Lyndon B. Johnson decided to escalate American involvement. After U.S. Navy ships allegedly were attacked in the Gulf of Tonkin in 1964 by North Vietnamese gunboats, Johnson asked Congress to authorize future military action in Vietnam. As is usually the case when a foreign country launches an attack on U.S. forces, the resolution passed overwhelmingly. The Gulf of Tonkin Resolution gave Johnson the authority to "take all necessary measures to repel armed attack against the forces of the United States and to prevent further aggression."

Some people now reasonably believe that the alleged attack in the Gulf of Tonkin never took place or was greatly exaggerated, or that American ships were operating inside North Vietnamese territorial waters when they were confronted by enemy gunboats. Whatever the reality was, and no one will probably ever know for sure, Congress and the American people were quite willing to go along with the Johnson administration's plans for increased military action in Vietnam. America had never lost a war, and few Americans could imagine that the American military could not prevail against the small, impoverished Communist North Vietnam or its guerrilla supporters in the South, the Viet Cong.

After the passage of the Gulf of Tonkin Resolution, the Vietnam War rapidly escalated. When Johnson took office, roughly six thousand American troops were in Vietnam. By

June 1965, the number had swelled to seventy-four thousand. By 1968, the peak of American involvement, more than half a million military personnel were deployed in or around Vietnam. As early as 1965, signs indicated that the war was going badly. Some advisers and commentators, known as hawks, wanted the United States to use massive force against North Vietnam. A few of the most extreme hawks even suggested that nuclear weapons might be in order. Others, known as doves, thought that America should cut its losses and begin to disengage. President Johnson rejected both alternatives, opting for a middle course that proved to be ineffective and politically divisive. As early as the fall of 1965, organized demonstrations against the war began to take place on college campuses. By 1968, the American people had become deeply divided over a war that was beginning to look like a bottomless pit. Americans continued to fight and die, seemingly without effect.

The defining event in terms of American public opinion was the **Tet offensive** of February 1968. After being assured by the generals that the war was being steadily won, Americans watched in horror as the nightly news showed films of Viet Cong guerrillas attacking posts throughout South Vietnam with renewed strength. Even the American embassy in Saigon, the South Vietnamese capital, came under attack. Although the Tet offensive was a military defeat for the Viet Cong, the American public soon turned against the war. President Johnson shocked the nation by refusing to seek reelection, and the Democratic party ripped itself apart over the war issue.

Johnson's Republican successor, Richard Nixon, pursued a policy of "Vietnamization," that is, turning the war effort over to the South Vietnamese. In 1972, American forces began pulling out of Vietnam pursuant to an agreement reached with North Vietnam. By this time, fifty thousand Americans had died in Vietnam; the American people had had enough. After the American presence ended, the South Vietnamese forces began to crumble. Finally, in 1975, Saigon fell to invading North Vietnamese troops. Vietnam was unified under Communist rule. From the American point of view, a decade-long war fought to contain communism had failed. From the perspective of many Vietnamese, the war against Western colonialism that had begun in 1946 had finally been won.

The Vietnam War had major repercussions on American society, on political culture, and certainly on American foreign policy during the 1970s. The credibility of military and political leaders had been severely damaged. Young people increasingly questioned and challenged authority figures. Americans' faith in their institutions had been shaken as illustrated in Case in Point 18-1. The **bipartisan consensus** that had existed since World War II about America's role as leader of the "free world" was shattered. Liberals and Democrats called for America to look inward again, to address such domestic problems as racism, poverty, and illiteracy. They called for new efforts to protect national security through peaceful cooperation rather than military confrontation with America's Communist adversaries.

The United States became involved in the Vietnam War without clear goals. The first major explanation to the American people about American involvement came well into the conflict, when President Johnson asked for and received congressional support through the Gulf of Tonkin Resolution. Public opinion was at first supportive, but as the war dragged on without victory, the public became increasingly skeptical. Eventually, a majority of the American people became opposed to continued U.S. involvement. The United States fought most of the war without much assistance from other countries. Most importantly, the war dragged on for better than a decade, with more than fifty thousand American dead.

After two decades had passed and the cold war was over, the bad blood between the United States and Vietnam had simmered. In 1995, President Clinton announced the normalization of relations with Vietnam, saying that the time had come to bind up the wounds from the war. In 2000, President Clinton arrived in Hanoi for a historic visit, the first American president to visit Vietnam since Richard Nixon's visit in 1969. The Clinton visit signaled the close of one of the most tragic chapters in American history.

Détente   The term **détente** means the relaxation of tensions between nation-states. The term is often applied to the early 1970s when relations between the United States and the Soviet Union improved. Much of the credit for achieving this détente goes to President

---

Tet offensive   The defining event of the Vietnam War, when the Viet Cong attacked posts throughout South Vietnam, including the American embassy in Saigon.

bipartisan consensus   Agreement between the two major political parties about the basic outline of American foreign policy.

détente   The relaxation of tensions between nation-states; the period in the late 1960s and 1970s when relations improved between the United States and the Soviet Union.

Case in Point 18-1

Can the Government Censor the Press on National Security Grounds?

New York Times v. United States (1971)

In 1971, the Supreme Court was asked to decide which was more compelling: the First Amendment guarantee of a free press or the Nixon administration's concern that national security was being threatened. The case involved the Pentagon Papers, which were the product of a top-secret government study of U.S. involvement in Vietnam from the end of World War II through 1968. The papers revealed that policy makers had grossly miscalculated and that the government had continually resisted the full disclosure of American military activities in Southeast Asia. In 1971, Daniel Ellsberg, a disaffected Pentagon employee, leaked the Pentagon papers to the *New York Times,* which began to publish a series of articles based on them. The Nixon administration went to court and obtained an injunction against the *New York Times* on the grounds that further publication jeopardized national security. In reviewing the case, the Supreme Court reversed the lower court and invalidated the injunction, splitting 6–3. In his opinion concurring in the decision, Justice Hugo Black wrote that "paramount among the responsibilities of a free press is the duty to prevent any part of the government from deceiving the people and sending them off to distant lands to die of foreign fevers and foreign shot and shell." Dissenting from the Court's decision, Justice Harry Blackmun wrote that "Article II . . . vests in the Executive Branch primary power over the conduct of foreign affairs and places in that branch the responsibility for the Nation's safety."

Richard Nixon who, though certainly not a dove, had a pragmatic view of foreign policy. Nixon believed that the two superpowers had to learn to live with one another or face nuclear extinction. Indeed, the most notable achievements of détente were arms limitations agreements negotiated between Moscow and Washington during the late 1960s and early 1970s. Chief among these were the Nuclear Nonproliferation Treaty (1968) and the Strategic Arms Limitation Treaty or SALT I (1972). Among other things, SALT I imposed a five-year freeze on testing and deployment of intercontinental ballistic missiles (ICBMs) and submarine-launched ballistic missiles. Though SALT I by no means ended the nuclear arms race, it did slow the race temporarily and allowed many people around the world to breathe a sigh of relief.

18-2d The 1980s: The Twilight of the Cold War

After the Soviet invasion of Afghanistan in 1979, relations between the two superpowers worsened. A political crisis in Poland, which the Soviets believed had been encouraged by the United States, an escalation of the arms race, and President Ronald Reagan's tough anti-Communist rhetoric brought an end to détente in the early 1980s, as the United States and the Soviet Union remained bitter adversaries. Rhetoric was sharp and hostile on both sides. The relationship improved significantly, however, after President Reagan met with the new Soviet leader Mikhail Gorbachev at a **summit conference** in Geneva, Switzerland, in 1985. Reagan and Gorbachev met privately for five hours and emerged with a personal relationship of mutual trust and respect that changed the tone of Soviet–American relations. This new relationship gave impetus to ongoing negotiations to limit the arms race between the superpowers. Ultimately, these negotiations would bear fruit after the collapse of the Soviet Union in the early 1990s.

> **summit conference**   A meeting between the highest officials of two or more governments.

Latin America: Flash Point for Conflict in the 1980s   Latin America includes the twenty countries of South and Central America and the Caribbean, where Spanish, Portuguese, and French are generally spoken. This region has been of great concern to the United States for the past hundred years. The area's poverty and history of unstable governments have made it a natural target for Communist movements. These revolutionary efforts have sprung up among the local populations, but were aided by the Soviet Union and Cuba. The United States has always been fearful of major social and political upheaval in its own backyard. Thus, containment of these movements was a central part of American foreign policy during the cold war years.

Although much of American policy toward the rest of Latin America from the 1960s through the 1980s was dictated by Cuba, the United States has had a major policy interest in the rest of Latin America, especially Central America, for more than a century. In the 1980s, this interest was focused on Nicaragua and to a lesser degree on El Salvador. In the 1970s, Nicaragua, like most other Central American countries, was run by a dictator, Anastazio Somoza. The rebel leader, Augusto Sandino, with his guerrilla fighters, mounted continuing attacks on the Somoza government until Somoza was forced to flee the country in 1979. The rebels, who became known as Sandinistas, formed a government led by Daniel Ortega, who was elected president in 1984. The Sandinistas were of great concern to the United States, which feared that they would encourage unrest throughout the rest of Latin America.

The Sandinistas nationalized a number of industries, including banking and mining. They also canceled elections that they had promised. In response, the United States supported an opposition movement known as the Contras, who were fighting against the Sandinistas. This support proved highly controversial in the United States for a number of reasons. First, many Contra leaders had occupied positions in the corrupt Somoza government. Second, the Contras' tactics were often dubious, and many accused them of being terrorists. Third, the Contra presence forced the Sandinista regime to use many of its resources for defense. Finally, many Americans were afraid that the United States would get bogged down in "another Vietnam." On the other hand, the Soviets were clearly aiding the Sandinista government, which, like Castro's in Cuba, was Marxist in nature. Moreover, the war in Nicaragua had spilled over to neighboring El Salvador, where Marxist rebels were seeking to overthrow the American-backed government. This backing, like that of the Contras, was controversial in the United States. Some evidence showed that the government of El Salvador was using "death squads" to terrorize the rebels' supporters.

During the 1980s, the Reagan administration strongly favored aid to both the Contra rebels and the government of El Salvador. Most congressional Democrats wanted to bring an end to that aid. In 1985, Congress turned down Reagan's request for more aid to the Contra rebels. Nevertheless, the administration secretly forwarded aid to the Contras in the form of proceeds from illegal arms sales to Iran. In 1987, Congress began hearings on this arrangement, which became known as the Iran–Contra affair. A special prosecutor was appointed, numerous congressional hearings were held, and several Reagan appointees ultimately were indicted on criminal charges.[4] The Iran–Contra scandal was a major embarrassment to the Reagan administration and a thorn in the side of President George Bush, who repeatedly denied any involvement in the affair.

The tension in Nicaragua eased in 1990 when the Sandinistas allowed elections. The opposition candidate, Violeta de Chamorro, defeated Ortega, but the Sandinistas continued to dominate the police and army. Nevertheless, with the Contras effectively disbanded and the end of aid from the old Soviet Union, Nicaragua was assigned a much lower priority on the American foreign policy agenda. Likewise, with a peace treaty between the government and the rebels in El Salvador, Latin America ceased to be an area of major foreign policy concern. However, concern about drug trafficking and "narcoterrorism" in the region remains high.

18-2e Foreign Policy after the Cold War

From the end of World War II to the breakup of the Soviet Union in the early 1990s, American diplomatic and defense policy was focused on containing Soviet expansion and achieving victory over communism. With the end of the cold war, those objectives were no longer relevant, and these changes, along with the budget deficit, led to cutbacks in military spending. Yet people still faced great challenges to peace in the world. At the end of the Bush administration and the beginning of the Clinton administration, people around the world looked to the United States to put a stop to regional conflicts and to step in when the combatants or other countries in the region could not resolve the situation themselves.

The Gulf War   The ancient nations that border the Persian Gulf have been in conflict since early in the twentieth century. The disputes tend to involve boundaries and the status of various ethnic and religious factions. After the fall of the Shah of Iran in 1979, Iran became a fundamentalist Islamic state that sought to export its revolution to other countries. Iranian-backed Islamic fundamentalism has become a major concern of governments throughout the Middle East, especially Egypt, Saudi Arabia, and the other pro-Western Arab states.

In 1980, Iran and Iraq, which were historic enemies, became involved in a protracted and bloody war. During that same year, Saddam Hussein took control of the Ba'ath party, the governing political party in Iraq. Hussein escalated the war with Iran by using chemical weapons against both the Iranians and the rebellious Kurds in his own country. Because of the American fear of Iranian extremism, the United States, while remaining officially neutral in the conflict, adopted measures that favored Iraq. Saddam Hussein began to believe that the United States would not stand in the way of his territorial ambitions, which included the annexation of tiny, oil-rich Kuwait.

In July 1990, Iraq accused Kuwait of tapping into an oil field in an area that both countries claimed. Apparently thinking that the rest of the world, especially the United States, would not take action, Hussein's forces stormed across the border on August 2 and quickly overran Kuwait, claiming it as the "thirteenth province" of Iraq. This invasion marked the first challenge to the United States in the post-cold war era. Its task was made easier because Iraq had no protector. The Soviet Union, though not enthusiastic about the use of military force against its longtime friend, agreed not to interfere with any military efforts launched by the United States and its allies.

The interests of the United States were certainly threatened by the Iraqi invasion, which endangered the supply of oil flowing to the United States, Europe, and Japan (see Figure 18-3). A disruption of the oil supply could have a disastrous effect on the economies of the industrial world. President Bush first took action to defend Saudi Arabia, although making it clear that the invasion "would not stand." After extensive discussion with his military and foreign policy advisers, Bush sent American forces to Saudi Arabia and instituted a massive blockade of Iraqi shipping in the hope that economic hardship would force Iraq to withdraw from Kuwait.

The United States was not alone in Operation Desert Shield, as the defense of Saudi Arabia was called. President Bush put together a multinational force under the guise of the *new world order,* the term he coined to describe world politics after the cold war. To demonstrate that the United States had international support for its stand against Iraq, the president worked hard to ensure that the force included soldiers from as many countries as possible, including Arab states such as Egypt and Syria. Other nations agreed to respect the boycott of Iraqi oil. Despite the great economic pressure, Saddam Hussein refused to pull out of Kuwait.

Figure 18-3
How the Iraq Invasion Might Have Caused You to Have a Bad Vacation

Iraq invades Kuwait and—without US intervention—Saudi Arabia. Iraq seizes control of the oil fields, oil refineries, and all other aspects of oil production and export in those countries.

Oil prices jump to four times the normal rate.

Oil companies raise gas prices to eight dollars per gallon to cover the cost of crude oil.

You go from paying sixteen dollars to fill up your car to one-hundred-fifty dollars for a full tank. You wait in long lines at gas stations because of shortages and you miss a class because of a long wait one day. Your grade drops a point because of the missed class.

Over the winter break, you have to stay at college in the dorm because oil prices are so high that airlines aren't running, it costs too much to drive, and you have to make some money to pay for the gas you need just to get around town.

You miss turkey and trimmings, and you don't even get the CD you want because the CD cases are made of petroleum products and the CD costs triple the normal amount, and your parents can't afford to make an extra trip to the mall anyway.

With Hussein digging in, President Bush increased the number of troops in the Gulf area to half a million by the end of 1990. War was beginning to seem inevitable, but the American public was somewhat ambivalent about using American troops to liberate Kuwait. Some questioned whether Americans should die for Kuwait and its undemocratic, repressive regime. Others were concerned about shedding blood for oil. Against this backdrop of uncertainty, President Bush asked Congress for a vote authorizing the use of force by the United States in applying the United Nations sanctions against Iraq. On January 12, 1991, the House of Representatives approved the resolution by a vote of 250–183. In the Senate, which acted the same day, the vote was much closer: 52–47.

On January 16, the United States and its allies began a tremendous air assault on Iraq, marking the transition from Desert Shield to Desert Storm. This attack, which relied heavily on new high-technology "smart bombs," quickly overwhelmed the Iraqi air defenses. The air war, with its immediate, somewhat exhilarating victory, was quite popular in the United States. President Bush's popularity skyrocketed. Weeks later, the United States began a massive ground assault. In less than a week, the Iraqi troops were defeated and in disarray. For all practical purposes, the war was over.

By most standards, the war against Iraq was a textbook military operation. First, the president quickly communicated America's position to the public. Second, he clearly articulated the goals for the action. Third, diplomacy was used to convince other countries to share the financial and military responsibility. Fourth, troops were withdrawn after the mission was accomplished. Finally, American losses were quite light. Of course, not everyone approved of all aspects of the conflict. Many were critical of the decision not to pursue fleeing Iraqi troops and destroy Saddam Hussein. Bush's successor, Bill Clinton, had to threaten the use of force against Iraq in 1994 when Saddam Hussein again threatened Kuwait. Although Hussein backed down, many people complained again about Bush's decision not to "finish off" Hussein in 1991.

The U.S. experience in the Gulf stands in stark contrast to its use of military force in Vietnam. Many suggested that the Gulf War marked the end of the "Vietnam syndrome," or the fear of many Americans of becoming involved in another conflict like the Vietnam War. Some commentators had thought that the syndrome might limit the ability of the United States to respond militarily with a massive show of force. The Gulf War demonstrated that a successful limited engagement was possible. Moreover, the Gulf War reassured many of America's allies that the United States was capable of assuming world leadership within the framework of international law.

18-2f Military Actions in the 1990s

In many ways, George Bush's success in the Gulf War put more pressure on the United States to intervene in other conflicts. In 1992, U.S. troops were sent to Somalia to supervise the distribution of international food aid designed to end the starvation there. Once that was accomplished, however, a smaller American military force remained to assist United Nations forces in trying to capture the dominant warlord and bring about some sort of political stability. In the infamous "Blackhawk Down" incident, 18 U.S. soldiers were killed and 73 were wounded in a failed effort to capture the warlord. The incident produced a furor in the United States after television broadcasts showed images of an American soldier's body being dragged through the streets of Mogadishu. In the wake of this furor, President Clinton was forced to withdraw U.S. forces from Somalia. The failed mission to Somalia raised anew old questions about the limits of America's ability to intervene in the affairs of other countries.

What then would be the basis of post–cold war American foreign policy? Would it be the maintenance of world order? A policy based on maintaining order would certainly lead to American involvement in a variety of conflicts. Or would the policy be to take action only when American national security is threatened? Under this approach, the United States would refrain from intervening in most skirmishes around the world. By the end of 1993, the Clinton administration was moving toward a policy of "enlargement," which had as its goal the expansion of free-market democracies throughout the world. At the same

What Americans Think About

America's Military Might

Do you feel that it's important for the United States to be number one in the world militarily, or that being number one is not that important, as long as the U.S. is among the leading military powers?

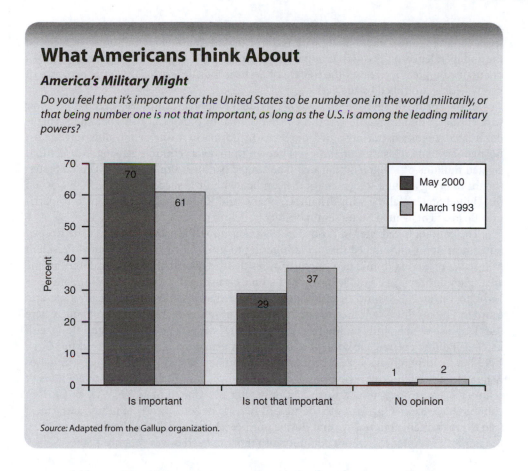

Source: Adapted from the Gallup organization.

time, the administration's ambivalence about international involvement seemed to contradict its broader policy goals.[5]

The Crisis in Haiti   Haiti's history is one of poverty and repression. François Duvalier, or "Papa Doc," ruled the country until his death in 1971. He was succeeded by his son, Jean-Claude, also known as "Baby Doc," who was forced from power in 1986. In 1991, a Catholic priest named Jean-Bertrand Aristide was elected president. Later that year, Aristide was ousted by the military. The United Nations called for Aristide to be restored and imposed an economic embargo on Haiti. The dictators agreed to restore Aristide to power, but later reneged. In 1993, thousands of Haitian refugees left for Florida in makeshift rafts. This situation prompted President Clinton in 1994 to issue an ultimatum to the military dictatorship: Restore Aristide or face an invasion. The threat ultimately succeeded, but only when an invasion was imminent. American troops were sent to Haiti to maintain order until the democratically elected government could be reinstalled. The Haiti policy was controversial from the beginning. Conservatives and Republicans questioned whether President Aristide deserved American support. Moreover, they asserted that America's vital interests were never really at stake.

The Balkans   Although the fall of the Soviet Union was a great victory for decades of American military and foreign policy, the consequences were widespread. The power vacuum created with the decline of Soviet power created great pressure on a number of countries. One was Yugoslavia, a Communist state created from a number of ethnically diverse people, many of whom bore tremendous enmity toward the other. This hostility was based on centuries-old religious differences—ancient hatred between the Albanian Muslims and the Christian Serbs—in addition to the politics of the first and second world wars. When the area eventually exploded, the United States played a major role in trying to create an atmosphere that could lead to peace and an end to bloodshed. The major American role was in Bosnia-Herzegovina, which became an independent country after Yugoslavia disintegrated. The United States, along with most of the international community, recognized the independence of Bosnia-Herzegovina in April 1992. However, neighboring Serbia maintained a great interest in the welfare of Serbs in Bosnia, especially in the province of Kosovo, long controlled by the Serbs.

In the spring of 1992, Serbia, led by President Slobodan Milosevic, entered into war with Bosnia. The idea was to create a Greater Serbia. In pursuit of this goal, the Serbian-dominated Yugoslavian army aided the Serbs in Bosnia in a war of intimidation against Bosnian civilians. This intimidation was known to many as ethnic cleansing, conflict that created millions of refugees in the area. The United Nations, along with the United States, sought to bring about a settlement of the conflict, with little success until May 1994, when the United States—along with Britain, Germany, and Russia—supported a plan to partition Bosnia. The United States sent monitors to help keep the uneasy peace.

The conflict flared later in Kosovo in 1998. A group of Muslims known as the Kosovo Liberation Army announced that it was fighting to unify Kosovo with Albania. President Milosevic, of Serbia-dominated Yugoslavia, reacted by dispatching Serbian forces to the area. They again engaged in the practice of ethnic cleansing in an effort to intimidate non-Serbs to leave. This ethnic cleansing included systematic terrorism, especially rape and murder. The result was another stream of millions of refugees, this time to Albania, where they languished in horrid conditions in camps by the border. The United States, along with its NATO allies, entered the conflict to avoid an international catastrophe, and in March 1999 began to bomb against Serbian targets, eventually including the Serbian capital of Belgrade. Eventually, Milosevic conceded after massive damage to his country. Millions of refugees began to return to Kosovo, but only after the United States, NATO, and Russia committed peacekeeping forces to the area. At the end of 2002, nearly ten thousand American troops remained in Kosovo and Bosnia in a peacekeeping role. But by the end of 2004, the number of American troops committed to those countries was roughly 2,500.

18-2g Foreign Policy Challenges at the Beginning of the Twenty-First Century

The conflicts in the Balkans demonstrated the difficulty of post-cold war foreign policy. Ancient conflicts, long suppressed, were not solvable by traditional means, but only by interposing others between the combatants. The United States, as the world's only superpower, often finds itself involved in conflicts that do not appear to directly involve its national interest. That situation often creates pressure to try to resolve a conflict without clear criteria for choosing among competing conflicts. President Clinton apologized in 1999 for the United States' failure to become involved in a peacekeeping role in an especially bloody ethnic conflict in Rwanda. During the 2000 election, the candidate George W. Bush expressed his intent not to enter conflicts without a clear American interest and a clear exit strategy. However, Bush indicated that he did support American bombing in the Kosovo conflict.

Russia In March 2001, first the United States and then Russia expelled fifty of the other's diplomats from their respective countries. The United States took its action in response to the revelation that Russia had long been involved with the accused spy Robert Hannsen, an FBI agent who was arrested for espionage earlier that year. The end of the cold war certainly did not bring an end to Russian and American desire to gain knowledge of the other's secrets. Major issues remain between the two countries.

American leaders in both parties have remained concerned about the old Soviet nuclear arsenal. Americans have an interest in fighting nuclear proliferation and in eliminating excess plutonium. The security of Russia's nuclear stockpile has become a major concern, not so much for what the Russians might do, but rather to keep the weapons out of the hands of terrorists.

The nature of European security has become another flash point between the two countries. Russia has never been comfortable with the expansion of the North Atlantic

Controversy

Military Intervention in the Balkans

With the collapse of the Soviet Union and the end of the cold war, U.S. foreign policy lost its focal point and no longer centered on the struggle against communism. In the post-cold war era, regional conflicts have come to the fore. Perhaps none of these is more pressing than the situation in the former Yugoslavia. This federation of Bosnia and Herzegovina, Croatia, Serbia, Slovenia, and other countries had bound together people with long-standing hatreds. In Bosnia, the bad blood stemmed principally from religious differences traceable to centuries-old Turkish conquests, when many residents of the area converted to Islam. These Muslims lived throughout the area with the Serbs, who remained Christian. After the breakup of Communist Yugoslavia in 1991, the Serbs controlled the old Yugoslavian army. When the world recognized the new sovereignty of Bosnia, Croatia, and Serbia, war immediately broke out among the three countries. The worst conflicts took place in Bosnia, where invading well-armed Bosnian Serbs, aided by Serbia, began a series of attacks on the Muslim population. Though all sides were guilty of atrocities, the Serbs apparently embarked on a campaign of genocide against the Muslims. They surrounded the Bosnian capital, Sarajevo, and inflicted heavy casualties on the civilian population there. Americans saw much of this horror on the nightly news. In January 1994, in one of the most heart-wrenching incidents, children sledding in the snow came under deliberate mortar fire. Americans watched as children were carried into the hospital with severed limbs and other bloody injuries. Americans listened as one boy told of seeing his friend's head blown off. Many wondered how America and its NATO allies could permit the slaughter to continue.

The United States faced a dilemma. Should it intervene to stop the violence? In 1991 and 1992, President George Bush resisted using American military force. Those counseling against intervention asked whether U.S. interests were involved and suggested that the United States might become bogged down in the mountainous terrain in a war it could not win. Others countered that a world power is obliged to come to the aid of people threatened with extinction. Although the candidate Bill Clinton decried the Bush administration's lack of action, President Clinton decided against military involvement beyond some airlifting of supplies. By early 1994, the debate had become centered on whether to try to divide the region into Serb and Muslim areas. By this time, President Clinton had seemed to place most of the responsibility on the warring parties. On January 25, 1994, Clinton was quoted in the *New York Times:* "I don't think that the international community has the capacity to stop people within that nation from their civil war until they decide to do it." In 1995, the warring parties signed a peace accord brokered by the Clinton administration. American troops did go to Bosnia, but only as part of a multinational peacekeeping force authorized by the United Nations.

In 1999, President Clinton authorized American war planes to bomb Serbian military targets in Kosovo, a province of Yugoslavia beset by civil war. Subsequently, American military forces went into Kosovo as part of a NATO peacekeeping mission. In 2000 and 2001, Muslim rebels moved from Kosovo into neighboring Macedonia, creating the real prospect of a wide Balkan war. In the United States, critics of American involvement in the Balkans wondered whether we could extricate ourselves from the conflict.

What should be U.S. policy regarding American military intervention abroad? Should we intervene only when our vital interests are at risk, or should we use our military power for humanitarian purposes?

Treaty Organization (NATO). Relations were further challenged by the conflict in Bosnia and the bombing that followed. Russia has long had a relationship with the Serbs and, despite their participation in the postwar peacekeeping force in Kosovo, were never happy with NATO's bombing campaign.

Another challenge to American foreign policy is Russia's relationship with her own minorities. In the late 1990s, Russia sought to prevent Muslim rebels in Chechnya from breaking away from Russia. In putting down the rebellion, the Russians used brutal tactics that offended many in the United States. The Clinton administration was troubled by the conflict and the nature of the Russian military effort. Russia, on the other hand, saw the Chechnya conflict as part of its own domestic agenda. The multiethnic nature of Russia made future conflicts of this type highly likely.

The terrorist attack on the United States in September 2001 had immediate consequences for America's relationship with Russia. President George W. Bush immediately reached out to Russian President Vladimir Putin for support, which was immediately forthcoming. Implicit in Russia's support for America's war on terrorism was an understanding that the United States would be less critical of Russia's efforts to deal with Islamic insurgency in Chechnya. Old adversaries now found unity in a new struggle: the fight against Islamic extremism. This unity was further cemented when President Bush met with Russian President Putin in May 2002 to sign a major arms-reduction agreement. Following that meeting, President Putin attended a meeting of NATO and discussed a role for Russia in the organization. This feat was an amazing one, considering that the reason NATO was created was to contain Russian expansionism.

By 2005, the relationship between Russia and the United States was again becoming strained. Many in the United States became concerned about indications that President Putin was not serious about building democracy in his own country. Alarm bells sounded in January 2005 when it was learned that Russia was planning to sell advanced SCUD missiles to Syria, a development that threatened to further destabilize an already unsettled situation in the Middle East. In May 2005, President George W. Bush flew to Moscow to meet with President Putin to express American concerns over Russian policies but also to maintain a personal relationship that both leaders seemed to value.

China Because China now ranks among the world's great powers, it necessarily occupies a prominent place on America's foreign policy agenda. China and the United States have experienced an uneasy relationship since the Tiananmen Square massacre in 1989, when the Chinese government brutally suppressed a pro-democracy uprising in Beijing. China's continued harsh treatment of its dissidents, in addition to its persistent refusal to allow its people religious freedom, runs counter to the values of American political culture. On the other hand, the explosive growth of the Chinese economy has opened up important opportunities for American business. China has become a major trading partner with the United States, and many American businesses have opened offices and stores in China. Many argue that allowing free commerce between the United States and China will cause China to become more sympathetic to Western political values, and signs show that it has happened to some extent. On the other hand, critics of China's human rights record argue that a continuing commercial relationship should depend on China's willingness to embrace Western human rights values. For its part, the Chinese government consistently tells these critics to mind their own business, insisting that China's internal affairs should be of no concern to the rest of the world.

The Clinton administration tried to walk the tightrope between demands for increasing business with China and demands to force China to improve its human rights record. In May 1993, President Bill Clinton issued a statement giving the Chinese one year to show improvement or risk China's Most Favored Nation (MFN) status, which allowed Chinese exports to enter the United States under the lowest tariff rates. In the spring of 1994, Secretary of State Warren Christopher offended Chinese leaders with his continual references to human rights and the treatment of dissidents. American businesspeople in China expressed concern about American pressure, fearing that American companies would be greatly hurt if trade between the countries were curtailed. In May 1994, Congress renewed China's Most Favored Nation status. The decision was praised by American companies eager to do business with China, but was sharply criticized by human rights groups.

In 1997 and 1998, mounting evidence showed that China had illegally funneled money into President Clinton's 1996 election campaign. In 1999, American warplanes accidentally bombed the Chinese embassy in Belgrade, Yugoslavia, as part of a NATO military campaign against Serbian actions in Kosovo. Needless to say, the Chinese were not amused. In 2000, scientists at the Los Alamos national laboratory reported that secret information had been compromised and ultimately made available to China. All these developments increased the level of tension between the two countries, but nevertheless, Congress, with the strong support of the Clinton administration, granted China permanent normal trade relations status in 2000.

In 2001, tensions between the United States and China increased again as the George W. Bush administration considered whether to approve the sale of several high-tech destroyers to Taiwan, a sale strongly opposed by China. Since the enactment of the Taiwan Relations Act in 1979, American policy has been to assist Taiwan in meeting its defense needs. Yet the sale of high-tech warships threatened to worsen the relationship with China, something the Bush administration did not want to happen. From 2002 to 2005, the relationship between China and the United States remained a cool one. China opposed U.S. intervention in Iraq and continued to talk tough to the Taiwanese government. At the same time, economic and cultural ties between China and the United States continued to expand. Clearly, American–Chinese relations will occupy a central place in American foreign policy making for some time to come (see Table 18-1).

The Middle East   Ever since the creation of the State of Israel in 1948, conflict has existed between the Israelis and their Arab neighbors, including four wars, numerous "uprisings," and countless acts of terrorism. Since 1967, the conflict has focused on the Israeli occupation of the West Bank of the Jordan River, which is the place where the major Palestinian cities are located. Palestinians and other Arabs have demanded that Israel withdraw from these territories. Israel has steadfastly refused to do so until a plan could be worked out to guarantee Israel's security. Moreover, Israel has antagonized its Arab neighbors by building settlements in the occupied territories, suggesting to some that it intended to eventually annex these areas.

Although consistently supporting Israel, both politically and militarily, the United States has also attempted to broker peace. In 1978, President Carter brokered the Camp David accord, a landmark peace agreement between Israel and Egypt. In 1995, Israel signed a peace agreement with Jordan, another of its Arab adversaries, and in 1999 the Clinton administration held peace talks between Israel and Syria, which have technically been in a state of war since 1967.

		T A B L E 18-1
1989	Tensions between the United States and China increase when China brutally strikes down the pro-democracy protests at Tiananmen Square.	**U.S.–China Relations**
1993	President Clinton gives China one year to improve its human rights record or face losing Most Favored Nation (MFN) trading status.	
1994	Warren Christopher offends the Chinese during a State department visit with repeated queries on human rights issues; Congress renews MFN status.	
1996	China may have funneled money to President Clinton's campaign funds.	
1997–1998	An investigation of China's funding Clinton's campaign takes place.	
1999	During a military strike in Yugoslavia, the United States bombs the Chinese embassy in Belgrade.	
2000	The Los Alamos scientist Wen Ho Lee is accused of passing on secrets to the Chinese. Jailed and dismissed from his post, he is later released by the FBI. China is granted permanent normal trading status.	
2001	Tensions arise between the United States and China over the United States' consideration of selling military goods to Taiwan, which the United States views as an independent country and China sees as a "rogue province" belonging to China.	

Although much progress had been made in forging peace in the Middle East, the conflict between Israel and the Palestinians remains intense. The intense nature of the conflict comes from competing claims for the same real estate, especially the city of Jerusalem. Bargaining is difficult because the conflict involves ethnic and religious differences, not merely political and economic ones. Despite immense effort, the Clinton administration was unable to broker a peace agreement between the Israelis and the Palestinians, leaving this problem for the Bush administration. When George W. Bush assumed the presidency in 2001, he faced an ever-increasing cycle of terrorism by Palestinian militants followed by tough Israeli military responses.

No one on any side of the conflict expected that the Bush administration would succeed where the Clinton administration had failed, and most observers seemed reconciled to the fact that the quest for Middle East peace would remain elusive for years to come. However, the attacks of September 11, 2001, focused world attention on terrorism and the appropriate response when it occurs. Following a devastating series of suicide bombings in crowded Israeli gathering places and on buses that occurred in December, the United States refused to condemn Israel for its response of using missiles to attack symbols of Arafat's authority in Palestinian territory. As 2001 came to an end, the prospects for peace between the Israelis and the Palestinians appeared bleaker than at any time since the early 1970s. During the spring of 2002, the situation deteriorated dramatically as a wave of Palestinian suicide bombings led Israel to launch a harsh military campaign in the West Bank. The world looked on in horror as battles raged in refugee camps and around the Christian church that sits on the site in Bethlehem where Jesus is believed to have been born. President Bush sent Secretary of State Colin Powell to the Middle East to try to broker peace, but without much success. In fact, the administration's critics did not hesitate to label the mission a failure. Few observers across the political spectrum believed that peace would come to the Middle East any time soon, but virtually all agreed that the United States needs to remain "engaged" in the region.

One of the principal stumbling blocks on the road to peace in the Middle East was Israel's steadfast refusal after 2002 to deal with Palestinian leader Yasser Arafat, who the Israelis believed could not be trusted. Arafat's death in the fall of 2004 opened a new window of opportunity for peace, and the Bush administration immediately signaled its willingness to reopen the stalled peace process. The Israelis expressed cautious optimism, but reiterated their insistence that the Palestinians select new leadership that would renounce terrorism and deal with Israel in good faith. As one observer noted, that put "the burden squarely on the Palestinians to turn themselves into a model partner before the U.S. or Israel will stretch out a hand."[6]

In January 2005, Palestinians went to the polls to choose a successor to Yasser Arafat. Their overwhelming choice was Mahmoud Abbas, widely regarded as a moderate. Both Israel and the United States welcomed Mr. Abbas' election. Commentators around the globe suggested that a new opportunity for peace was at hand. Abbas called for an end to terrorism, but was unable to prevent militants from launching terrorist attacks within days after the election. Israel responded by stepping up military operations in Gaza and threatening to cut ties with Mr. Abbas. Mr. Abbas then ordered Palestinian security forces to use force to prevent militants from attacking Israeli targets. Given the tremendous cleavages within Palestinian society, particularly that between moderates who favor the peace process and are willing to live side by side with Israel and radicals who favor continued "armed struggle," expectations for peace in the near future are difficult to justify.

18-3 The War on Terrorism and the War in Iraq

Islamic extremism had been growing for many years in the Middle East. In particular, Islamic militants focused their outrage at America's support for Israel in its long-running conflict with the Palestinians. During the 1980s and 1990s, Islamic terrorists struck at American interests around the world, including terrorist attacks in Yemen, Saudi Arabia, Lebanon, Tanzania, Kenya, and even New York City. The first attack on the World Trade Center in 1993, delivered by means of a truck bomb, failed to bring down the twin towers.

Profiles & Perspectives

**Colin Powell
(1937–)**

DEC 448/08 Bettman/Corbis

Colin Powell served as the chair of the Joint Chiefs of Staff under George H. W. Bush and as the secretary of state under George W. Bush a decade later. In January 2001, the Senate confirmed Powell as secretary of state. In doing so, it placed Powell in the highest position in American government ever achieved by an African American.

Colin Luther Powell was born in Harlem in New York City in 1937. His parents had come to the United States from Jamaica. Powell grew up in the South Bronx in a mixed neighborhood. There, he attended the public schools, graduating from Morris High School in 1954. Then he attended the City College of New York, where he joined the Reserve Officers Training Corps (ROTC) and later commanded his college ROTC unit. After his graduation in 1958, with a degree in geology, Powell received a commission of second lieutenant in the United States Army. His long and distinguished army career had begun.

In 1962, Powell married Alma Johnson, of Birmingham, Alabama. He then went to serve as an adviser to the South Vietnamese government. He returned to Vietnam in 1968. He was rewarded with a purple heart. Powell returned to resume his schooling at George Washington University, where he received an MBA in 1971. Soon thereafter, he began his political service with a White House fellowship. He stayed in government with the Carter administration, where he held positions in the Department of Defense. President Ronald Reagan appointed Powell to the post of national security adviser in 1987. Two years later, President George Bush named Powell to be the chair of the Joint Chiefs of Staff.

Powell gained national attention as a major adviser to President Bush during Operation Desert Storm, the war against Iraq that followed the Iraqi invasion of Kuwait. Powell was given credit for a major role in the successful outcome of that war. Following the war in Iraq, Powell was often cited as a potential candidate for the Republican nomination for president in 1996. However, he never put his hat in the ring, despite poll numbers that indicated he would have made a strong candidate. He was willing, however, to serve in George W. Bush's cabinet. His nomination was widely heralded and supported by members of both parties.

As secretary of state, Colin Powell played a major role in assembling and maintaining an international coalition in support of the United States' war on terrorism. He also assumed the leading role in the attempt to broker peace in the Middle East, perhaps the most difficult undertaking of his career. Ever the good soldier, he forcefully argued President George W. Bush's case for the invasion of Iraq in 2003 and stayed on as secretary of state until after Bush's reelection in 2004 even though many observers felt that he was among the cabinet officials least supportive of the war effort.

It also seemed to have little impact on America's collective consciousness and very little impact on public policy.

The attacks of 9-11-2001 achieved the terrorists' goal—to demonstrate to America that its enemies could strike with devastating impact at its most important assets. It was not long before the attacks were traced to Osama bin Laden's al Qaeda network. Eventually, bin Laden himself would admit to having planned and ordered the attacks. In an interview with Hamid Mir, a Pakistani journalist, bin Laden offered his justification for 9-11:

> America and its allies are massacring us in Palestine, Chechnya, Kashmir, and Iraq. The Muslims have the right to attack America in reprisal. … The September eleven attacks were not targeted at women and children. The real targets were America's icons of military and economic power.[7]

September 11 was a wake-up call to Americans. No longer would the United States ignore the threat of Islamic extremism. President George W. Bush immediately launched a war on al Qaeda. President Bush successfully enlisted the support of Russia, the European powers, and even many Islamic countries in this effort. He threatened military action against any nation-state that harbored or supported terrorists. In assembling an international coalition to prosecute the war on terrorism, President Bush was able to draw upon a wave of international sympathy for the United States in response to the attacks of 9-11. Unfortunately, the complexion of world opinion would change drastically over the next few years, due primarily to President Bush's decision to invade Iraq in 2003. Although President Bush characterized the invasion of Iraq and toppling of Saddam Hussein as part of the larger war on terrorism, many critics at home and abroad disagreed with that characterization. The Iraq War would greatly erode international support for the United States and would endanger the president's bid for a second term in office. Although President Bush was able to win a second term in a narrow victory over his Democratic opponent, the war in Iraq loomed over his second term as a potential foreign policy disaster. Clearly, stabilizing the situation in Iraq and establishing some sort of reasonably democratic government there would be the number-one challenge facing the Bush administration in 2005 and beyond.

18-3a The War in Afghanistan and the Hunt for Osama bin Laden

The United States military was pressed into action in Afghanistan to root out Osama bin Laden and his al Qaeda terrorist network, which had effectively taken over that impoverished and war-torn nation. Within three months, the al Qaeda forces in Afghanistan were routed and the extremist Taliban government, which had given al Qaeda sanctuary, was toppled. Far from expressing jubilation, President George W. Bush warned Americans that the war on terrorism would go on for years. In fact, plenty of evidence showed that al Qaeda forces had moved across the border to Pakistan, where they showed signs of regrouping. Midway through 2002, the situation was further complicated by heightened tensions between Pakistan and India that stemmed from violence in the disputed Kashmir region. Fortunately, cooler heads in both countries prevailed, and the threat of war between these two nuclear powers subsided, at least for the time being.

During 2003 and 2004, American forces, aided by soldiers from Germany, Japan, and other allied states, maintained an active presence in Afghanistan, working to keep the Taliban at bay and continuing to hunt for the elusive Osama bin Laden. American civil affairs specialists helped Afghans rebuild their infrastructure, including roads, water treatment facilities, hospitals, and schools. They also helped recruit and train police officers and other public servants. American military personnel helped train and equip a new Afghan army. They also provided security for Afghan officials, supply convoys, and international aid workers. All the while, American special forces searched remote mountain areas of Afghanistan for remnants of al Qaeda and the Taliban. By the fall of 2004, American military and civil affairs operations in Afghanistan were costing American taxpayers more than $750 million per month.

In October 2004, despite threats of violence from terrorists, some eight million of ten million Afghans eligible to vote went to the polls to choose a president. President Bush pointed to Afghanistan's first ever national election as a symbol of the progress that country had made toward stability and democracy. Hamid Karzai, who was elected president of Afghanistan by a decisive majority, vowed to continue that progress, but made it clear that his government would continue to require international support and an American military presence for years to come.

18-3b Iraq: A New Front in the War on Terrorism or a Massive Distraction?

Although Afghanistan was the first battlefield in the war on terrorism, Iraq loomed as a major problem in 2002. Many in the George W. Bush administration and beyond were convinced that Saddam Hussein was continuing to develop and stockpile chemical weapons, which he had used in the past against Kurds and Iranians and had promised to destroy after losing the Gulf War in 1991. There was even some reason to believe that Iraq might have a covert nuclear weapons program. Relying on intelligence that ultimately proved to be faulty, President Bush became convinced that Saddam Hussein had to be removed from power to prevent the spread of weapons of mass destruction to terrorist hands.

In October 2002, Bush won the support of Congress, which adopted a resolution authorizing the use of force against Iraq. After an intense diplomatic effort, the United States persuaded the United Nations Security Council to adopt a resolution demanding that Saddam Hussein produce an accounting of all weapons of mass destruction and give weapons inspectors unfettered access to suspicious sites. Facing imminent military action

Popular Culture and American Politics

Fahrenheit 9/11

By Chapman Rackaway

With a list of successful and thought-provoking movies to his credit, such as *Roger and Me* and *Bowling for Columbine,* Michael Moore has developed a reputation as a modern-day muckraker. Moore's biggest cinematic splash came in 2004, though, with the release of *Fahrenheit 9/11.*

The movie was almost never released. Produced by Miramax (a company owned by Walt Disney Corporation), the movie was set to be distributed by Disney's powerful theater channels, but Disney refused to release the film. Miramax owners Harvey and Bob Weinstein actually bought the distribution rights from Disney and contracted Lions Gate films to handle distribution. A month's delay for the movie meant more publicity, which in turn brought attention and viewers. Over the release weekend, the film grossed $21.8 million, which is more than *Bowling for Columbine* grossed over its entire cinematic run.

An outspoken liberal and critic of President George W. Bush, Moore made his most brazen attack on a subject yet with *Fahrenheit 9/11.* In the movie, Moore takes constant shots at the Bush administration and its policies post–9/11. No aspect of Bush's presidency is spared from Moore's jaundiced eye: starting with the disputed Florida ballots from which Bush emerged as the 2000 presidential election winner and continuing on through the wars in Afghanistan and Iraq. Moore's usual style of pop culture cross-references and sarcastic humor mostly takes a back seat in favor of a polemical assemblage of soundbites, visuals, and commentary. Gone are the traditional Moore tactics of entertaining story development and humor that allow him to make political points, except for the movie's funniest scene, in which Moore recites the USA PATRIOT Act over a public address system mounted in an ice cream truck as he drives around Washington, D.C.

One of the film's central points is that the Bush and bin Laden families are tied together with financial arrangements that belie Bush's stance on terrorism and undermine his post–9/11 rhetoric. Moore accuses Bush of smuggling Osama bin Laden's relatives out of the United States immediately after the 9/11 attacks. Using documentary footage and Moore's own perspective, *Fahrenheit 9/11* is one of the most impactful and politically charged films ever made.

---

by the United States and a strong consensus in the world community, Hussein accepted the U.N. demands. However, his government continued to act evasively and defiantly with respect to international demands. Despite the staunch opposition of Germany, Russia, and France, President Bush decided to go forward with a military invasion of Iraq. He sought to assemble a "coalition of the willing" to assist in the effort, but it was clear from the outset that America would go it alone if necessary. When the invasion began in late March of 2003, two hundred fifty thousand American troops were joined by forty-five thousand British, two thousand Australian, and two hundred Polish soldiers. These forces made quick work of the invasion and were able to take Baghdad, Iraq's capital city, and depose Saddam Hussein within a month. What President Bush and most Americans did not realize at the time was that the real challenges remained ahead.

Although international support for the invasion of Iraq was never strong, Americans were generally supportive of President Bush's decision to use military force to remove Saddam Hussein. Americans were well aware of Saddam's history of aggression against his neighbors in the region, his brutal repression of his own people, as well as his genocidal campaigns against Kurds and Shiites. But, above all, Americans were concerned about the possibility that Saddam's weapons of mass destruction might find their way into the hands of terrorists bent on attacking American cities. When no such weapons were found in Iraq after the invasion had succeeded, political attacks on President Bush increased. Some opponents charged that he had intentionally misled the world about Saddam's weapons. Senator Ted Kennedy (D-Massachusetts) went so far as to accuse President Bush of invading

Iraq solely for political gain. Given the drastic decline in President Bush's approval rating during 2003 and 2004, the invasion of Iraq proved to be an enormous political liability for the president going into the 2004 election.

In the latter part of 2003 and continuing throughout 2004, elements of Saddam Hussein's regime, aided by foreigners streaming across the borders from Iran, Jordan, and Syria, mounted a bloody insurgency against American occupation forces and the interim government they installed. Insurgents used bombings, ambushes, assassinations, kidnappings, and other terrorist methods to harass American forces, intimidate Iraqis who might be inclined to support the new government, and drive foreign companies and relief agencies out of the country. Despite the capture of Saddam Hussein in December 2003 and the formal transfer of sovereignty to the new Iraqi government in June 2004, the insurgency continued to grow. Eighteen months after the fall of Saddam's regime, efforts to reconstruct the country remained at a virtual standstill.

Iraq became the principal issue in the 2004 presidential election. Throughout the campaign liberals and Democrats railed at the president for launching a war to remove nonexistent weapons of mass destruction. Those who believed that President Bush knew that Saddam's weapons did not exist and went ahead with the war anyway castigated Bush for deceiving the American people. Some who supported the decision to go to war but objected to the way it was carried out accused the president and his administration of incompetence. Even conservatives criticized President Bush's decision to invade Iraq. Pat Buchanan, a conservative pundit and former presidential candidate, said, "Iraq is the worst strategic blunder in our lifetime."[8] Politically, it was certainly a blunder for President Bush, who likely would have been reelected fairly easily without the albatross of Iraq hanging around his neck.

When the invasion of Iraq began in March of 2003, most Americans supported the decision to go to war. Nearly two years later, after it was clear that no stockpiles of weapons of mass destruction would be found, and given the continuing bloody insurgency, public opinion had changed dramatically. A CNN–Gallup survey conducted in mid-January of 2005 found that 52 percent of Americans believed that invading Iraq was a mistake; 47 percent said it was not. Despite elections to be conducted in Iraq later that month, 38 percent of those surveyed said they expected that U.S. troops would remain there for the foreseeable future.[9] Whether invading Iraq and deposing Saddam Hussein were really blunders in American foreign policy and, if so, how much, may take years to fully assess.

18-4 How American Foreign Policy is Made

The Constitution is clear in assigning the responsibility for foreign policy to the national government. However, it is not so clear in regard to the roles of the president and the Congress. The making of American foreign policy is necessarily complicated by the separation

---

Popular Culture and American Politics
The Sum of All Fears

Based on a novel by Tom Clancy, the movie *The Sum of All Fears* strikes a raw nerve in the American psyche. In the film, terrorists detonate a nuclear device during the Super Bowl in an effort to start a war between the United States and Russia. The plan almost works, except that the CIA analyst Jack Ryan is able to convince both powers to stand down at the last second. When the novel was penned in the early 1990s, people did not worry much about terrorism on American soil. After 9-11-2001, the scene in which Baltimore is devastated by a nuclear explosion is frighteningly realistic. However, as in most American movies in the action-adventure genre, the heroic individual, one who is something of a loner and an iconoclast, saves the day. *The Sum of all Fears* is unsettling, but also reassuring in that Jack Ryan is on the job. Americans clearly believe in the threat of nuclear terrorism, but do they believe in "Jack Ryan"?

Popular Culture and American Politics
Toby Keith Versus the Dixie Chicks

By Chapman Rackaway

The post–9/11 war on terrorism has divided Americans on whether President Bush has followed the correct course of action, and that division has spilled over into a feud between two of country music's most popular acts.

Country singer Toby Keith released the controversial pro-war anthem "Courtesy of the Red, White, and Blue" in late 2002. In an interview after its release, the Dixie Chicks' lead singer, Natalie Maines, made her distaste of the song public. "Don't get me started," Maines said. "I hate it. It's ignorant, and it makes country music sound ignorant. It targets an entire culture—and not just the bad people who did bad things. You've got to have some tact. Anybody can write, 'We'll put a boot in your ass.' But a lot of people agree with it." Keith said nothing in response to Maines' quote at the time, but it would not be long before the feud became nasty.

At a concert in London in March of 2003, Maines told the audience, "Just so you know, we're ashamed the president of the United States is from Texas." The band members also call Texas home. With the Iraq War moving forward at that time, Maines was expressing concern and displeasure with the administration's policies. The uproar back in the United States was immediate and sharp. Many radio stations stopped playing Dixie Chicks records, and fans boycotted the band and refused to buy albums released by Maines and her bandmates.

Keith and the Dixie Chicks then went on to feud with words—both spoken, and written on T-shirts. Keith said he would "bury" the Dixie Chicks in terms of popularity and compared sales of their CDs and singles. At subsequent events, the Dixie Chicks wore T-shirts taking an obvious shot at Keith. Keith responded with his own T-shirts, which were just as subtle.

Considering the gender gap in recent politics, it is appropriate that the male representative in the feud supported the Republican president, whereas the women opposed him—similar to vote results from the 2000 election. With a nation divided on the war on terrorism, though, the feud was just a very public example of the same discussion people are having in this country every day.

of powers. Much of the conflict about foreign policy has been about the appropriateness of presidential action. Throughout American history, Congress, the courts, and the American public have been highly deferential to the president in the conduct of foreign policy. Some commentators believe that the Framers intended for Congress to play a greater role in the foreign policy process, but it has not worked out that way. For the most part, Congress takes a back seat (see Case in Point 18-2).

Presidential Dominance   In *The Federalist* No. 75, Alexander Hamilton observed that foreign policy is different from domestic policy in that it requires "secrecy, decision and dispatch" in addition to a "steady and systematic adherence to the same views. . . ." Hamilton used these premises to argue for presidential domination in foreign policy making. Congress, in his view, was incapable of meeting these criteria.

Congress is composed of 535 members, each representing either a state or a district within a state. Only the president represents the nation as a whole. This arrangement gives the president more credibility in speaking for the United States in the international arena. The Supreme Court has placed its stamp of approval on the primary power of the president in the realm of foreign affairs, referring to the president as the "sole organ of the federal government in the field of international relations."[10] Although this statement may be an exaggeration, it is fair to describe the presidency as the *dominant organ* of the federal government in international relations.

Case in Point 18-2

The Supreme Court Recognizes Broad Presidential Power in the Field of International Relations

United States v. Curtiss-Wright (1936)

In May 1934, Congress adopted a joint resolution authorizing the president to forbid American companies from selling munitions (under such limitations and exceptions as the president might determine) to the warring nations of Paraguay and Bolivia. Additionally, Congress provided for criminal penalties for those violating presidential prohibitions. Shortly after this resolution was adopted, President Franklin D. Roosevelt issued an executive order imposing an embargo on arms sales to the belligerent countries. In 1936, the Curtiss-Wright Export Corporation was indicted for conspiring to sell arms to Bolivia in violation of the embargo. Curtiss-Wright sought to avoid prosecution by arguing that Congress had unconstitutionally delegated its lawmaking power to the president because the resolution allowed the president to make the specific rules controlling arms shipments.

Even though it had taken a tough stand on the issue of delegation of legislative power just one year earlier (see *Schechter Poultry Corporation v. United States*, in 1935), the Supreme Court refused to find anything unconstitutional in the *Curtiss-Wright* case. The Court distinguished between two classes of power, domestic and foreign, and held that the rule against legislative delegation applied only to the former. Furthermore, the Court suggested that the president would have inherent power to impose this type of an embargo, even without an authorizing resolution from the Congress. Expounding on presidential primacy in foreign affairs, the Court referred to the president as the "sole organ of the federal government in the field of international relations." This phrase has been repeated ever since as a justification for unfettered presidential action in the foreign policy area.

Historically, most major foreign policy initiatives have been associated with presidents, and most of these initiatives were launched and carried out without significant congressional participation. The Vietnam War was certainly a "presidential war." Richard Nixon was the major actor in the American decision to establish a relationship with China. Though George Bush consulted with Congress to build support for the Gulf War, the initiative was clearly his. Likewise, foreign policy failures are associated with presidents. The Iranian takeover of the U.S. embassy in November 1979 and the subsequent failed rescue attempt in April 1980 were viewed as Jimmy Carter's crisis, and his inability to end the crisis was a major factor in his failure to win reelection.

18-4a The Foreign Policy Infrastructure

Although the president is the dominant player, he cannot make foreign policy alone. After policy is made, the president must depend on others to carry it out. Given the enormity of American interests and responsibilities in the world, the president must depend on a host of advisers, staff members in the White House, and agencies within the executive branch.

The State Department   Established in 1789, the State department is the oldest cabinet-level department. The secretary of state, who heads the department, is the highest-ranking member of the cabinet. Although the secretary of state must be confirmed by the Senate, she reports to the president. The secretary has a major role in making foreign policy. Presidents vary in the degree to which they grant the secretary of state quite a public role. Often, secretaries of state are closely associated with a particular policy initiative. For instance, when President George Bush undertook a strategy to bring the Israelis and Palestinians to the peace table, Secretary of State James Baker traveled extensively around the Middle East, talking with the leaders of the various countries. He was closely identified with the peace effort in the minds of Americans in addition to those in the Middle East.

▶ **intelligence**   Information about activities in other countries that is used in making foreign-policy decisions.

Intelligence Agencies   Presidents need good information, or **intelligence,** about activities in other countries to help them make foreign policy decisions. Because virtually all policies that deal with other countries involve at least the possibility of military action, and all involve the use of intelligence, the president regularly consults with officials from

Comparative Perspective

Foreign Policy in the People's Republic of China

American foreign policy is usually cast in terms of a principle. For most of the cold war, that principle was the containment of communism. After the fall of the Soviet Union, President George Bush attempted to define a new concept, the *new world order*, that would govern American relations with other countries. American foreign policy has represented perceived American interests, which have sometimes been defined in reaction to the actions of other countries. But rarely has the United States shaped its policies in an attempt to please the rulers of other countries.

The leaders of China have felt no such aversion to framing their policies to suit the United States. In the days after its violent suppression of the student rebellion in Tiananmen Square in 1989, China desperately wanted to maintain economic relations with the United States. China was especially concerned with keeping its Most Favored Nation designation, which it needs for trade. But American revulsion toward the massacre led many members of Congress to argue that China should be punished.

In 1990, China made a number of foreign policy initiatives aimed at repairing the damage. First, it used its influence to get the Khmer Rouge (an extremist Communist group waging guerrilla warfare in Cambodia) to go along with a United Nations peace plan designed to bring peace to Cambodia. China even pledged to suspend arms shipments to its former ally. The United States clearly approved. Second, China voted with other members of the United Nations to support sanctions against Iraq. In addition, the Chinese agreed to suspend their lucrative arms sales to Iraq. Both actions were clearly in support of American policies. Arguably, the good faith showed by China played a major role in keeping lines of trade open between the countries. Two of China's major foreign policy initiatives seemed planned largely to please a potential trading partner. China's foreign policy, once driven by Communist ideology, was apparently being driven largely by the desire for economic development.

As the century turned, China sent signals that it wanted to "reunify" with Taiwan, which had been independent since the Chinese Revolution. Tensions in the region escalated as sabers were rattled on both sides of Taiwan Straits. To China, Taiwan was important symbolically, in addition to economically and militarily. However, China had to face the prospect of provoking the United States, which was pledged to aid in the defense of Taiwan.

both the defense and intelligence establishments. The intelligence establishment includes agencies within each branch of the armed forces as well as within several of the Cabinet-level executive departments.

The major intelligence agency is the Central Intelligence Agency (CIA), established in 1947. Its mission is to gather intelligence outside the United States. As a member of the National Security Council, the Director of the CIA often plays an important role in foreign policy deliberations. In the Iran–Contra affair of the mid-1980s, the CIA, led by William Casey, was involved in the scheme to provide military hardware to Iran in exchange for that country's help in obtaining the release of American hostages held in Lebanon. The money from the sale would go to the Contra rebels fighting the Marxist Sandinista government in Nicaragua. Congress had prohibited this type of aid in the Boland Amendments. As noted in section 18-2d, "The 1980s: The Twilight of the Cold War," the Iran–Contra affair mushroomed into a major scandal.

In the wake of the 9-11 terrorist attacks, the CIA was faulted for not assembling the intelligence that would have allowed federal authorities to prevent the catastrophe. Part of the problem seemed to lie with the intelligence bureaucracy in which intelligence-gathering responsibilities were spread over a number of agencies and there was little communication among intelligence, immigration and law enforcement agencies. Another reason for the failure was the grossly inadequate "human intelligence" coming from the Arab world. In recent decades, American intelligence agencies had emphasized hi-tech intelligence and had allowed the old fashioned means of intelligence gathering to wither. But old-fashioned human intelligence may be the best way to uncover plots like that which led to the 9-11 attacks.

The CIA again became the focus of controversy in 2004 when it became apparent that the Agency's assessment of Iraqi dictator Saddam Hussein's capabilities with respect to chemical, biological and nuclear weapons had been way off target. Because the Bush Administration had placed so much emphasis on deposing Saddam Hussein in order to control the threat posed by his weapons of mass destruction, the intelligence failure proved to be politically costly (although not fatal) to President Bush.

Congress and the Bush Administration responded to growing concerns about America's intelligence capabilities, or lack thereof, by overhauling the system in 2004. A new position, that of Intelligence Czar, was created to oversee and coordinate activities across fifteen separate intelligence agencies. The new Intelligence Czar would report daily to the president, a function traditionally performed by the Director of the CIA. Clearly, the overhaul represented a demotion of sorts for the CIA Director, and not everyone was convinced that the reorganization would result in better intelligence being provided to the White House and the congressional leadership. But everyone agrees, after the events of the past several years, that improving America's intelligence capabilities is of crucial importance.

The Military　The president also works closely with the military in creating foreign policy. What was originally called the War Department was renamed the Department of Defense in 1949. The head of this department, the secretary of defense, works with the secretaries of each of the armed services, especially the chair of the Joint Chiefs of Staff. The secretary of defense is a civilian, and the chair of the Joint Chiefs of Staff is the nation's top military officer. These individuals work closely together in conducting military operations and advising the president about any decision to embark on military action. During the Gulf War in 1991, Richard Cheney, the secretary of defense, and Colin Powell, the chair of the Joint Chiefs, were responsible for the implementation of the military strategy for driving the Iraqis from Kuwait. See how a percentage of Americans rated their military, as well as other various institutions, in the fall of 2000 in Figure 18-4.

Figure 18-4
Americans' Ratings of Various Institutions

In the fall of 2000, researchers at the University of Michigan asked a representative sample of Americans to indicate their feelings about a number of American institutions, using a "feeling thermometer" on which one hundred is the most favorable rating and zero is the least favorable. The military received the highest rating, indicating the high degree of trust and confidence that Americans have in their military establishment.

Source: Adapted from Center for Political Studies, University of Michigan, National Election Study 2000.

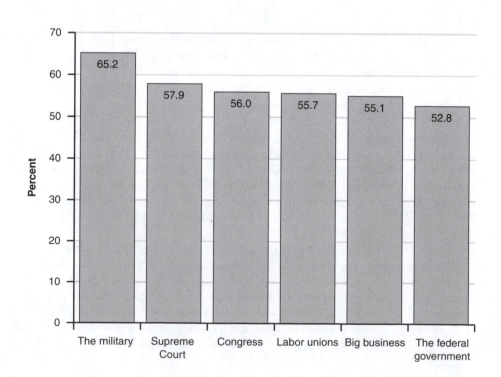

The National Security Council   The main body that advises the president on foreign policy is the National Security Council (NSC), which is a part of the Executive Office of the President. The NSC was created in 1947 to coordinate policy. It includes the president, the vice president, the secretary of defense, and the secretary of state. They are advised by the chair of the Joint Chiefs of Staff and the CIA director. The NSC meets regularly to advise the president and formulate strategy for foreign affairs. The NSC has offices in the basement of the White House and is readily accessible to the president in times of foreign policy crises.

18-4b Defining the National Interest

Any foreign policy decision inevitably involves a definition of the national interest. Of course, the nature of this national interest is quite complex. Probably the most clear-cut measure of **national interest** is protection against a military threat from another country (see Figure 18-5). The 1962 Cuban missile crisis came about in response to a clear threat to the security of the United States. The almost universal support for the tough action taken by President Kennedy can be largely attributed to the nature of the threat: Americans understood it. A threat to American national security is therefore seen as a threat to the country's national interest.

Politicians often define the national interest in ways that are not nearly so clear-cut. An action that does not pose a direct military threat to the United States may well endanger its economic well-being. Many argued that the action taken in the Gulf War of 1991 was based on a threat to our economic system. Saddam Hussein would control a significant segment of the world's oil had Iraq been able to annex oil-rich Kuwait. Moreover, he threatened to attack Saudi Arabia, the world's largest oil producer. The crisis in the Gulf threatened the economies of the advanced industrial world and, in that sense, certainly threatened the national interest of the United States. Whether our national security was threatened certainly depended on one's definition of national security. Nevertheless, though some complained that Americans would die to protect the interests of oil companies and the royal families of small sheikdoms across the world, most Americans supported President Bush's decision to commit American troops to liberate Kuwait from the Iraqis.

▶ **national interest**   The idea that the country has long-term foreign policy interests, such as protection against invasion or maintenance of energy supplies.

Figure 18-5

U.S. Defense Spending, 1940–2008, As a Percentage of All Federal Outlays and Gross Domestic Product

Note: Data for 1999–2004 are estimates. *Source:* Harold W. Stanley and Richard G. Niemi, *Vital Statistics on American Politics 2003–2004* (Washington, D.C.: CQ Press, 2003), pp. 346-47.

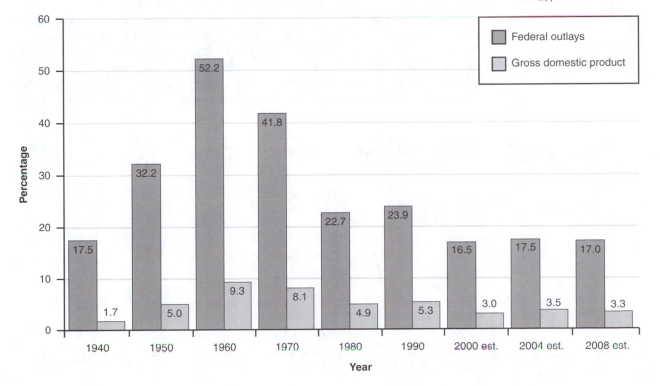

Morality as a Basis for Intervention Abroad The United States, as the foremost democratic world power, often finds itself in a position of taking military and diplomatic action on the basis of moral concerns. Many have argued that the United States has an obligation to push other countries to respect the **human rights** of their citizens, even when human rights abuses abroad have no direct effect on American military or economic security. For example, President Jimmy Carter believed that morality should play a major part in U.S. policy. He pressured the Soviet Union to improve treatment of its Jewish minority and to allow Jews to leave the country if they wanted. Carter also pressured military dictatorships in Latin America and elsewhere to improve their human rights records in order to continue receiving American aid.

Much of the controversy surrounding human rights stems from the different ways various cultures define human rights. In the United States, we tend to think of human rights in terms of freedom of speech, press, religion, and the other protections enshrined in our Bill of Rights. In other countries, especially developing countries, people may think of human rights more in terms of the necessities of life—food, clothing, shelter, and health care. Other countries often resent the imposition of American values under the mantle of concern for human rights.

18-4c Foreign Aid

The most obvious method of implementing foreign policy is through military action. Nevertheless, a country can affect outcomes in other countries in other ways. For years, the United States and other countries have provided **foreign aid** to countries for a variety of purposes (see Table 18-2). During the cold war, a great deal of U.S. aid was directed to countries that seemed to offer strategic advantages against the Soviet Union. A good bit of this aid was for military hardware. The United States also maintained a policy of strong financial support for Israel. This aid had two purposes. First, America has long supported Israel in its drive to achieve security as a state. In addition, because the Soviets were supplying other Middle Eastern countries, such as Syria and Iraq, with massive armaments, the United States felt the need to counter Soviet influence in the region. In addition, after Egypt agreed to a peace treaty with Israel in 1979, the United States began sending substantial aid to Egypt. Although Egyptian moderation in the Islamic world is an important aspect of U.S. support, aid to Egypt is closely linked to American concern for Israeli security.

Most American foreign aid is directed to the world's developing countries. The United States has supported a number of massive relief efforts to meet emergencies. This aid is provided in a variety of ways. Much is distributed through private agencies, like CARE. Some aid is provided through government agencies, especially the Agency for International Development (AID), and much is given indirectly through American government contributions to the World Bank or various other regional development banks. These banks tend

> **human rights** Basic political and religious freedoms in addition to the right to equal treatment under the law and the right to due process of law.

> **foreign aid** A policy of assisting other countries both economically and militarily.

TABLE 18-2	The total bill was $19.4 billion dollars.	
Principal Recipients of U.S. Foreign Aid, 2005	Israel	$2.56 billion
	Egypt	$1.84 billion
	Afghanistan	$1.38 billion
	Sudan	$311 million
	Jordan	$250 million
	Pakistan	$200 million
	Haiti	$50 million
	Lebanon	$35 million
	Cyprus	$13.5 million

Source: Foreign Aid Watch, www.foreignaidwatch.org/

to provide loans, rather than cash grants, to developing countries. Often, the receiving countries have difficulty repaying loans, creating further international monetary problems.

In 2002, Treasury Secretary Paul O'Neill toured Africa to study the effectiveness of U.S. aid dollars. The trip stirred up some controversy because O'Neill suggested loans rather than grants as the most effective way to deal with the continent's poverty. He also questioned the effectiveness of a great deal of foreign aid in the past, suggesting that much of the spending was wasted in graft and inefficiency.

The American people have never been particularly fond of foreign aid. They tend to think that the money is wasted or goes to undeserving, even corrupt, politicians, bureaucrats, and military rulers around the world. Most Americans know that the United States is the largest donor of foreign aid in absolute terms, handing out more than $19.4 billion in 2005. But few realize that as a percentage of gross national product (GNP), American foreign aid is surpassed by that of most other industrialized nations. In 1990, U.S. foreign aid amounted to roughly 0.16 percent of GNP. In contrast, Norway's foreign-aid payments in 1990 represented about 1.17 percent of its GNP. Even Japan's foreign aid was twice that given by the United States in terms of percentage of GNP.[11] It is important to recognize that the unpopularity of foreign aid among Americans stems from several factors, including distrust of governments and dislike for compulsory giving. When the Tsunami disaster struck Southeast Asia in January 2005, Americans were extremely generous in terms of private giving to relief organizations. Americans are much more likely to support giving to the Red Cross for disaster relief than providing aid to a foreign regime.

Aid to Russia   In the early 1990s, American policy makers struggled with the question of whether to provide economic aid to Russia and the other countries that comprise the former Soviet Union. President George Bush supported aid to Russia as a means of promoting the move toward democracy and free enterprise in the former Soviet Union. Bush's position was maintained by President Clinton and supported strongly by former President Richard Nixon. Many Americans, including some in Congress, felt uncomfortable with the prospect of giving aid to a former enemy. Others believed that any assistance was likely to disappear into the inefficient Russian economy and corrupt bureaucracy. Congress did approve a measure of economic aid as part of an overall plan of support to Russia by the United States, Japan, and the European allies. This aid never approached what had been requested by Russian President Boris Yeltsin, however, and the aid that was provided seemed to have little effect. Critics of aid to Russia gained momentum in early 1994 when Aldrich Ames, a CIA official, was arrested on charges of spying for the Soviet Union and, later, Russia. In fact, the Ames affair resulted in some damage to the Russian–American relationship, which was undergoing stress as a result of Russian support for the Serbs in the civil war in Bosnia and President Yeltsin's movement away from economic reform.

18-4d The Power to Make War

War is the ultimate tool of foreign policy. Democracies tend to be hesitant to resort to war, and rightfully so. The Framers of the U.S. Constitution, although not "democrats" in the modern sense, certainly wanted to prevent the nation from being thrust into war without a firm national consensus. Thus, they provided, in Article I, Section 8, that Congress has the power to declare war. Of course, the nature of the military and of military conflict has changed greatly since the founding. In the late eighteenth century, the constitutional division of responsibility for committing the nation to war was logical and clear. The Congress could declare war, and the president, as commander-in-chief, would conduct that war. After war was declared, the president would be "first among generals, first among admirals." But he did not have the power to start the war; that power belonged to the Congress.

As the nature of war changed and the speed of international events increased, however, the whole concept of "declaring war" became obsolete. In Korea, Vietnam, the Gulf War, and the other conflicts of the latter half of the twentieth century, the president took responsibility for involving American troops without the benefit of a declaration of war by Congress. The role of Congress was clearly secondary. In response to the increasingly dominant

Popular Culture and American Politics
The Draft Revival Bill Controversy

By Chapman Rackaway

The Internet is a great place to communicate and get information. It's also a giant rumor-spreading machine, an effective place to start and disseminate disinformation. Sometimes, those rumors can inspire Congress to act.

In the summer of 2004, an email that began circulating expressed great concern over a clandestine resurgence of the military draft. The email claimed that the George W. Bush administration was pushing through Congress a pair of bills that would require men and women between the ages of eighteen and twenty-five to serve in a military or public service capacity for two years, starting in the spring of 2005. The email cited some compelling statistics: a $28 million increase for the Selective Service's budget in 2004 and a Pentagon effort to fill draft board positions numbering twenty thousand nationwide. The timing of the email was important—right in the middle of a presidential campaign in which the Iraq War was a central issue.

There was only one major problem with the email: It was completely false. The bills referenced in the email were real, but they were introduced almost two years before the email was sent out and the Bush administration was not behind them. Liberal Democrats who wanted to make a point about the racial and economic bias among active membership in the volunteer army sponsored the bill in 2002, well before the Iraq War was even being considered. Republican leadership ignored the bill until the email circulated, and they then brought up the bill with the express motive of killing it. Even the bill's House sponsor, Representative Charles Rangel of New York, voted against the measure. The Selective Service's entire budget is less than the amount the email claimed its budget was increased. For two years, the agency's budget has remained flat at $26 million.

Always remember that emails are great not just for communicating but also for scams. Bill Gates won't give you a thousand dollars to forward emails to everyone you know, and the draft isn't coming back. Don't believe everything you read in your email.

presidential role, Congress enacted the War Powers Resolution of 1973. The resolution requires the president to notify Congress within forty-eight hours after committing U.S. military forces into combat situations or where hostilities are imminent.

Serious questions have arisen about the constitutionality of the War Powers Resolution. But because Congress has not yet invoked the resolution, the courts have had no occasion to rule on its constitutionality. Even if it were invoked and litigation resulted, the courts probably would view the matter as a "political question" (see Chapter 14, "The Supreme Court and the Federal Judiciary"). To date, the War Powers Resolution has not proved to be a significant limitation on presidential war powers. Nor has it proved to be a major weapon in Congress' arsenal of powers. It is just as true now as it was before the adoption of the War Powers Resolution that the best way for Congress to force the withdrawal of American forces from a particular war is to cut off funding for the operation. As in other areas of policy, Congress' most potent weapon is the power of the purse.

18-4e The Role of the United Nations

American foreign policy is always conducted in the context of various organizations and agreements. The most important international organization is the United Nations. The United Nations, headquartered in New York, replaced the League of Nations in 1945. The move to establish the United Nations came from the Allies fighting the Germans and Japanese in World War II. The U.N. charter was created at a conference in San Francisco. Originally, the organization had 51 members. Today, 191 nation-states are members of the U.N.

All member states of the United Nations have seats in the General Assembly, but most important decisions are made by the Security Council, which has fifteen members. Five of these members are permanent: the major powers of Britain, France, China, the United States, and Russia. Any of the five permanent members can veto any proposal. Vetoes were common during the cold war years, when the Soviet Union used its veto to frustrate the plans of the Western powers. The veto has also been used extensively by the United States to protect Israel from U.N. sanctions and condemnations.

The United Nations has served as a forum for discussion and debate and occasionally for peacekeeping and war efforts. Although its effectiveness was limited during the cold war, it has become much more active in the 1990s, spearheading efforts to encourage peace in Bosnia and Somalia. Given its limited resources and firepower, these efforts have had limited success. The United Nations has also provided the moral authority for U.S. military action. For example, even though the effort to liberate Kuwait from Iraq was primarily a U.S. action, it was conducted under the U.N. banner. Likewise, America's military intervention in Haiti in 1994 was conducted with the approval of the United Nations.

Conservative Americans have long been suspicious of the U.N., which they tend to regard as little for than a forum for the expression of anti-American sentiments. Liberals and moderates have been more supportive of the institution, which at least provides a convenient venue for the conduct of diplomacy and sometimes works as a vehicle for international cooperation. A poll conducted in September 2000 found that 81 percent of Americans believed that it is important "for the United States to cooperate with other countries by working through the United Nations."[12]

The Oil for Food Scandal During the 1990s, the United Nations administered a program under which Iraq, which was subject to a strict regime of sanctions, was permitted to sell oil to purchase food, medicine, and other essential goods. In 2004, revelations of financial improprieties in the Oil for Food program hurt the reputation of the United Nations, especially in American public opinion. In November 2004, a Senate committee began what columnist Robert Novak predicted could be "the most explosive congressional investigation in years."[13] The initial investigation revealed that U.N. administrators allowed billions of dollars from the oil sales to go to Saddam Hussein and that some of that money was used to purchase weapons. What remained unclear at the end of 2004 was the degree to which high U.N. officials, including Secretary General Kofi Annan, were aware of the improprieties and permitted them to continue. It was clear, however, that the U.N. bureaucracy was less than cooperative in responding to congressional requests for documents. With allegations swirling and suspicions mounting, Novak declared, "The United Nations and its secretary-general are in a world of trouble."[14]

18-5 Conclusion: Foreign Policy and National Defense in the Twenty-First Century

The years between the end of World War II and the fall of the Soviet empire were dominated by the cold war. America's military forces and its relations with other countries were based on a bipolar world, with Soviet and American spheres of influence. For years, the political culture of the United States was favorable to a large, powerful military with the capability of defending the country against a Soviet nuclear attack. Moreover, the presence of hundreds of thousands of Soviet troops in Eastern Europe was a constant threat to American allies there, especially West Germany. The result was a large U.S. military equipped to fight a conventional war in Europe and prepared to reply to any nuclear attack. With the demise of the Soviet Union, the American armed forces are necessarily undergoing major changes.

International conflict did not disappear with the Soviet threat. The power vacuum created by the breakup allowed long-festering conflicts to erupt in local and regional fighting. And, of course, the American military is now involved in an open-ended war on terrorism around the globe. This situation poses great challenges to the American military, which was scaled down significantly after the end of the cold war. The emphasis now is on a leaner military force that can deploy quickly. Some critics believe that the military has become too lean and is spread too thin around the world. But even if a large, cold war–type force were desirable, it is no longer economically possible for this country to maintain this type of force.

Despite the scale-down of its forces, the United States remains the world's dominant military power. However, "the foundations of power have been moving away from the emphasis on military force and conquest."[15] Most observers would agree that America's national security depends as much on economic vitality as it does on military capabilities. And maintaining a strong economy depends in large part on maintaining a healthy, well-functioning society. In the long run, no country can maintain a strong economy unless its people are ready, willing, and able to work and have the technology and the skills to work productively in an increasingly competitive world marketplace. The challenge to American government in the twenty-first century is to address the tremendous problems that beset this society: crime, illiteracy, drug abuse, poverty, low educational attainment, and, of course, inadequate health care for millions of Americans. By so doing, the United States can maintain a vibrant economy, a formidable military, and strong political influence in the international arena.

Questions for Thought and Discussion

1. What was the effect of the end of the cold war on American foreign policy?
2. Did the Framers of the Constitution intend for Congress to play a coequal role with the president in making foreign policy?
3. To what extent should the United States let humanitarian concerns drive its foreign policy?
4. The breakup of the Soviet Union has allowed age-old ethnic conflicts to emerge. What role should the United States play in dealing with these conflicts?
5. To what extent will international trade dominate the foreign policy agenda in the coming decades?
6. How will the war on terrorism change America's relationships with its allies and former adversaries?

Practice Quiz

Note: You can find the correct answers to these questions by taking the quiz and then submitting your answers in the Online Edition. The program will automatically score your submission. If you miss a question, the program will provide the correct answer, a rationale for the answer, and the section number in the chapter where the topic is discussed.

1. In a message to Congress in 1823, President _____ stated that North and South America were no longer open for colonization by European countries and that the United States would object to any European intervention in the Americas.
   a. Woodrow Wilson
   b. James Monroe
   c. James Madison
   d. Andrew Jackson

2. The _____ involved an effort to rebuild Western Europe following World War II.
   a. Truman Plan
   b. cold war
   c. Marshall Plan
   d. Triple Alliance

3. _____ coined the term *iron curtain* to refer to the threat of the Soviet Union and its Communist allies in Eastern Europe.
   a. Harry Truman
   b. Winston Churchill
   c. George Marshall
   d. Neville Chamberlain

4. The term _____ is often used to describe the relationship between the United States and the Soviet Union following the period beginning with the end of World War II and the fall of the Soviet Union.
   a. détente
   b. proxy warfare
   c. cold war
   d. none of the above

5. NATO is a collective security agreement between the United States and _____.
   a. the United Nations
   b. Japan
   c. the countries of Eastern Europe
   d. a number of other democratic nations

6. The highest-ranking member of the president's cabinet is the _____.
   a. chair of the National Security Council
   b. secretary of state
   c. chair of the Joint Chiefs of Staff
   d. secretary of defense

7. The nation's top military officer is the _____.
   a. secretary of defense
   b. chair of the Joint Chiefs of Staff
   c. president
   d. secretary of state

8. In *The Federalist #75*, Alexander Hamilton argued for _____ dominance in foreign policy making.
  a. legislative
  b. presidential
  c. judicial
  d. bureaucratic

9. The term _____ means the relaxation of tensions between nation-states.
  a. *détente*
  b. *bipartisan agreement*
  c. *gunboat diplomacy*
  d. *accord*

10. The practice of using American power to achieve American interests abroad is known as _____.
  a. internationalism
  b. isolationism
  c. interventionism
  d. manifest destiny

For Further Reading

Allison, Graham, and Gregory F. Treverton, eds. *Rethinking America's Security: Beyond War to New World Order* (New York: W. W. Norton, 1992).

Ambrose, Stephen, and Douglas Brinkley. *Rise to Globalism*, 8th ed. (New York: Penguin Putnam, 1997).

Christopher, Warren. *In the Stream of History: Shaping Foreign Policy for a New Era* (Palo Alto, CA: Stanford University Press, 1998).

Ferguson, Niall. *Colossus: The Price of America's Empire* (New York: Penguin, 2004).

Hastedt, Glenn. *American Foreign Policy: Past, Present and Future*, 5th edition (Upper Saddle River, NJ: Prentice-Hall, 2000)

Hook, Stephen W., John Spanier, and John W. Spanier, *American Foreign Policy Since World War II*, 16th ed. (Washington, D.C.: CQ Press, 2003).

Huntington, Samuel. *The Third Wave: Democratization in the Late 20th Century* (Norman, OK: The University of Oklahoma Press, 1993).

Jentleson, Bruce W. *American Foreign Policy: The Dynamics of Choice in the 21st Century* (New York: W.W. Norton and Co., 2000).

Keegan, John. *The Iraq War* (New York: Knopf, 2004).

Luttwak, Edward. *The Pentagon and the Art of War* (New York: Simon & Schuster, 1985).

Nixon, Richard M. *Seize the Moment: America's Challenge in a One-Superpower World* (New York: Simon & Schuster, 1992).

Nuechterlein, Donald E. *America Recommitted: A Superpower Assesses Its Role in a Turbulent World*, 2d ed. (Lexington, KY: University Press of Kentucky, 2001).

Nye, Joseph S., Jr. *The Paradox of American Power: Why the World's Only Superpower Can't Go It Alone* (New York: Oxford University Press, 2002).

Silverstein, Gordon. *Imbalance of Powers: Constitutional Interpretation and the Making of American Foreign Policy* (New York: Oxford University Press, 1996).

Snyder, Richard C., H. W. Bruck, Burton Sapin, and Valerie Hudson. *Foreign Policy Decision Making (Revisited)* (New York: Palgrave Macmillan, 2002).

Woodward, Bob. *The Commanders* (New York: Simon & Schuster, 1991).

Woodward, Susan. *Balkan Tragedy: Chaos and Dissolution after the Cold War* (Washington, D.C.: Brookings Institution, 1996).

Endnotes

1. Hans J. Morgenthau, *The Purpose of American Politics* (New York: Knopf, 1960), p. 169.
2. Greece and Turkey joined NATO in 1952; West Germany joined in 1955; Spain followed suit in 1982. In 1966, France terminated the integration of its military into NATO forces.
3. The policy of containment was originally proposed in a 1947 article written by George Kennan under the pen name Mr. X. See "The Sources of Soviet Conduct," *Foreign Affairs*, vol. 25, 1947, p. 556.
4. Caspar Weinberger, who was Reagan's secretary of defense, and several others who were indicted for their roles in Iran–Contra, were pardoned by President George Bush on Christmas Day, 1992, a month before Bush left office.
5. Christopher Layne and Benjamin Schwarz, "How Marxist Is Our Foreign Policy?" *New York Times*, October 3, 1993, p. 15.
6. Johanna McGeary, "Who Will Lead Them Now?" *Time*, November 22, 2004, p. 49.
7. Quoted in Peter Bergen, "The Long Hunt for Osama," *Atlantic*, October 1, 2004.
8. Patrick J. Buchanan, "Coming Home," *The American Conservative*, November 8, 2004.
9. CNN–Gallup poll of 1,007 adults conducted January 14–16, 2005. The margin of error is +/– three percentage points. Results reported on CNN, January 17, 2005.
10. *United States v. Curtiss-Wright Export Corp.*, 299 U.S. 304 (1936).
11. Data are provided by the Organization for Economic Cooperation and Development.
12. Survey conducted by Program on International Policy Attitudes, September 2000. For more information on this and other similar surveys, go to http://www.americans-world.org/digest/global_issues/un/un1.cfm.
13. Robert Novak, "The Senate Versus the U.N., *Chicago Sun-Times*, November 28, 2004.
14. Ibid.
15. Joseph S. Nye, Jr., *The Paradox of American Power* (New York: Oxford University Press., 2002), p. 5.

The Declaration of Independence

In Congress, July 4, 1776

When in the course of human events, it becomes necessary for one people to dissolve the political bands which have connected them with another, and to assume the Powers of the earth, the separate and equal nation to which the Laws of Nature and of Nature's God entitle them, a decent respect to the opinions of mankind requires that they should declare the causes which impel them to the separation.

We hold these truths to be self-evident, that all men are created equal, that they are endowed by their Creator with certain unalienable rights, that among these are Life, Liberty, and the pursuit of Happiness. That to secure these rights, Governments are instituted among Men, deriving their just powers from the consent of the governed. That whenever any Form of Government becomes destructive of these ends, it is the Right of the People to alter or to abolish it, and to institute new Government, laying its foundation on such principles and organizing its powers in such form, as to them shall seem most likely to effect their Safety and Happiness. Prudence, indeed, will dictate that Governments long established should not be changed for light and transient causes; and accordingly all experience hath shown, that mankind are more disposed to suffer, while evils are sufferable, than to right themselves by abolishing the forms to which they are accustomed. But when a long train of abuses and usurpations, pursuing invariably the same Object evinces a design to reduce them under absolute Despotism, it is their right, it is their duty, to throw off such Government, and to provide new Guards for their future security.—Such has been the patient sufferance of these Colonies; and such is now the necessity which constrains them to alter their former Systems of Government. The history of the present King of Great Britain is a history of repeated injuries and usurpations, all having in direct object the establishment of an absolute Tyranny over these States. To prove this, let Facts be submitted to a candid world.

He has refused his Assent to Laws, the most wholesome and necessary for the public good.

He has forbidden his Governors to pass Laws of immediate and pressing importance, unless suspended in their operation till his Assent should be obtained; and when so suspended, he has utterly neglected to attend to them.

He has refused to pass other Laws for the accommodation of large districts of people, unless those people would relinquish the right of Representation in the Legislature, a right inestimable to them and formidable to tyrants only.

He has called together legislative bodies at places unusual, uncomfortable, and distant from the depository of their public Records, for the sole purpose of fatiguing them into compliance with his measures.

He has dissolved Representative Houses repeatedly, for opposing with manly firmness his invasions on the rights of the people.

He has refused for a long time, after such dissolutions, to cause others to be elected; whereby the Legislative powers, incapable of Annihilation, have returned to the People at large for their exercise; the State remaining in the mean time exposed to all dangers of invasion from without and convulsions within.

He has endeavored to prevent the population of these States; for that purpose obstructing the Laws of Naturalization of Foreigners; refusing to pass others to encourage their migrations hither, and raising the conditions of new Appropriations of Lands.

He has obstructed the Administration of Justice, by refusing his Assent to Laws for establishing Judiciary powers.

He has made Judges dependent on his Will alone, for the tenure of their offices, and the amount and payment of their salaries.

He has erected a multitude of New Offices, and sent hither swarms of Officers to harass our People and eat out their substance.

He has kept among us, in times of peace, Standing Armies without the Consent of our legislature.

He has affected to render the Military independent of and superior to the Civil Power.

He has combined with others to subject us to a jurisdiction foreign to our constitution, and unacknowledged by our laws; giving his Assent to their Acts of pretended Legislation;

For quartering large bodies of armed troops among us;

For protecting them, by a mock Trial, from Punishment for any Murders which they should commit on the Inhabitants of these States;

For cutting off our Trade with all parts of the world;

For imposing taxes on us without our Consent;

For depriving us in many cases, of the benefits of Trial by jury;

For transporting us beyond Seas to be tried for pretended offences;

For abolishing the free System of English Laws in a neighboring Province, establishing therein an Arbitrary government, and enlarging its Boundaries so as to render it at once an example and fit instrument for introducing the same absolute rule into these Colonies;

For taking away our Charters, abolishing our most valuable Laws, and altering fundamentally the Forms of our Governments;

For suspending our own Legislatures, and declaring themselves invested with Power to legislate for us in all cases whatsoever.

He has abdicated Government here, by declaring us out of his Protection and waging War against us.

He has plundered our seas, ravaged our Coasts, burnt our towns, and destroyed the lives of our people.

He is at this time transporting large armies of foreign mercenaries to compleat the works of death, desolation, and tyranny, already begun with circumstances of Cruelty & perfidy scarcely paralleled in the most barbarous ages, and totally unworthy the Head of a civilized nation.

He has constrained our fellow Citizens taken Captive on the high Seas to bear Arms against their Country, to become the executioners of their friends and Brethren, or to fall themselves by their Hands.

He has excited domestic insurrections amongst us, and had endeavored to bring on the inhabitants of our frontiers, the merciless Indian Savages, whose known rule of warfare is an undistinguished destruction of all ages, sexes, and conditions.

In every stage of these Oppressions We have Petitioned for Redress in the most humble terms: Our repeated Petitions have been answered only by repeated injury. A Prince, whose character is thus marked by every act which may define a Tyrant, is unfit to be the ruler of a free people.

Nor have We been wanting in attention to our British brethren. We have warned them from time to time of attempts by their legislature to extend an unwarrantable jurisdiction over us. We have reminded them of the circumstances of our emigration and settlement here. We have appealed to their native justice and magnanimity, and we have conjured them by the ties of our common kindred to disavow these usurpations, which, would inevitably interrupt our connections and correspondence. They too must have been deaf to the voice of justice and of consanguinity. We must, therefore, acquiesce in the necessity, which denounces our Separation, and hold them, as we hold the rest of mankind, Enemies in War, in Peace Friends.

WE, THEREFORE, the Representatives of the UNITED STATES OF AMERICA, in General Congress Assembled, appealing to the Supreme Judge of the world for the rectitude of our intentions, do, in the Name, and by Authority of the good People of these Colonies, solemnly publish and declare, That these United Colonies are, and of Right ought to be FREE AND INDEPENDENT STATES; that they are Absolved from all Allegiance to the British Crown, and that all political connection between them and the State of Great Britain, is and ought to be, totally dissolved; and that as Free and Independent States, they have full Power to levy War, conclude Peace, contract Alliances, establish Commerce, and to do all other Acts and Things which Independent States may of right do. And for the support of this Declaration, with a firm reliance on the Protection of Divine Providence, we mutually pledge to each other our Lives, our Fortunes, and our sacred Honor. . . .

Resolved, That copies of the Declaration be sent to the several assemblies, conventions, and committees, or councils of safety, and to the several commanding officers of the continental troops; that it be proclaimed in each of the United States, at the head of the army.

The Articles of Confederation

To all to whom these Presents shall come, we the undersigned Delegates of the States affixed to our Names send greeting.

> Articles of Confederation and perpetual Union between the states of New Hampshire, Massachusetts-bay Rhode Island and Providence Plantations, Connecticut, New York, New Jersey, Pennsylvania, Delaware, Maryland, Virginia, North Carolina, South Carolina and Georgia.

Art I. The Stile of this Confederacy shall be "The United States of America."

Art II. Each state retains its sovereignty, freedom, and independence, and every power, jurisdiction, and right, which is not by this Confederation expressly delegated to the United States, in Congress assembled.

Art III. The said States hereby severally enter into a firm league of friendship with each other, for their common defense, the security of their liberties, and their mutual and general welfare, binding themselves to assist each other, against all force offered to, or attacks made upon them, or any of them, on account of religion, sovereignty, trade, or any other pretense whatever.

Art IV. The better to secure and perpetuate mutual friendship and intercourse among the people of the different States in this Union, the free inhabitants of each of these States, paupers, vagabonds, and fugitives from justice excepted, shall be entitled to all privileges and immunities of free citizens in the several States; and the people of each State shall free ingress and regress to and from any other State, and shall enjoy therein all the privileges of trade and commerce, subject to the same duties, impositions, and restrictions as the inhabitants thereof respectively, provided that such restrictions shall not extend so far as to prevent the removal of property imported into any State, to any other State, of which the owner is an inhabitant; provided also that no imposition, duties or restriction shall be laid by any State, on the property of the United States, or either of them.

If any person guilty of, or charged with, treason, felony, or other high misdemeanor in any State, shall flee from justice, and be found in any of the United States, he shall, upon demand of the Governor or executive power of the State from which he fled, be delivered up and removed to the State having jurisdiction of his offense. Full faith and credit shall be given in each of these States to the records, acts, and judicial proceedings of the courts and magistrates of every other State.

Art V. For the most convenient management of the general interests of the United States, delegates shall be annually appointed in such manner as the legislatures of each State shall direct, to meet in Congress on the first Monday in November, in every year, with a power reserved to each State to recall its delegates, or any of them, at any time within the year, and to send others in their stead for the remainder of the year.

No State shall be represented in Congress by less than two, nor more than seven members; and no person shall be capable of being a delegate for more than three years in any term of six years; nor shall any person, being a delegate, be capable of holding any office under the United States, for which he, or another for his benefit, receives any salary, fees or emolument of any kind.

Each State shall maintain its own delegates in a meeting of the States, and while they act as members of the committee of the States.

In determining questions in the United States in Congress assembled, each State shall have one vote.

Freedom of speech and debate in Congress shall not be impeached or questioned in any court or place out of Congress, and the members of Congress shall be protected in their persons from arrests or imprisonments, during the time of their going to and from, and attendance on Congress, except for treason, felony, or breach of the peace.

Art VI. No State, without the consent of the United States in Congress assembled, shall send any embassy to, or receive any embassy from, or enter into any conference, agreement, alliance or treaty with any King, Prince or State; nor shall any person holding any office of profit or trust under the United States, or any of them, accept any present, emolument, office or title of any kind whatever from any King, Prince or foreign State; nor shall the United States in Congress assembled, or any of them, grant any title of nobility.

No two or more States shall enter into any treaty, confederation or alliance whatever between them, without the consent of the United States in Congress assembled, specifying accurately the purposes for which the same is to be entered into, and how long it shall continue.

No State shall lay any imposts or duties, which may interfere with any stipulations in treaties, entered into by the United States in Congress assembled, with any King, Prince or State, in pursuance of any treaties already proposed by Congress, to the courts of France and Spain.

No vessel of war shall be kept up in time of peace by any State, except such number only, as shall be deemed necessary by the United

States in Congress assembled, for the defense of such State, or its trade; nor shall any body of forces be kept up by any State in time of peace, except such number only, as in the judgement of the United States in Congress assembled, shall be deemed requisite to garrison the forts necessary for the defense of such State; but every State shall always keep up a well-regulated and disciplined militia, sufficiently armed and accoutered, and shall provide and constantly have ready for use, in public stores, a due number of filed pieces and tents, and a proper quantity of arms, ammunition and camp equipage.

No State shall engage in any war without the consent of the United States in Congress assembled, unless such State be actually invaded by enemies, or shall have received certain advice of a resolution being formed by some nation of Indians to invade such State, and the danger is so imminent as not to admit of a delay till the United States in Congress assembled can be consulted; nor shall any State grant commissions to any ships or vessels of war, nor letters of marque or reprisal, except it be after a declaration of war by the United States in Congress assembled, and then only against the Kingdom or State and the subjects thereof, against which war has been so declared, and under such regulations as shall be established by the United States in Congress assembled, unless such State be infested by pirates, in which case vessels of war may be fitted out for that occasion, and kept so long as the danger shall continue, or until the United States in Congress assembled shall determine otherwise.

Art VII. When land forces are raised by any State for the common defense, all officers of or under the rank of colonel, shall be appointed by the legislature of each State respectively, by whom such forces shall be raised, or in such manner as such State shall direct, and all vacancies shall be filled up by the State which first made the appointment.

Art VIII. All charges of war, and all other expenses that shall be incurred for the common defense or general welfare, and allowed by the United States in Congress assembled, shall be defrayed out of a common treasury, which shall be supplied by the several States in proportion to the value of all land within each State, granted or surveyed for any person, as such land and the buildings and improvements thereon shall be estimated according to such mode as the United States in Congress assembled, shall from time to time direct and appoint. The taxes for paying that proportion shall be laid and levied by the authority and direction of the legislatures of the several States within the time agreed upon by the United States in Congress assembled.

Art IX. The United States in Congress assembled, shall have the sole and exclusive right and power of determining on peace and war, except in the cases mentioned in the sixth article—of sending and receiving ambassadors—entering into treaties and alliances, provided that no treaty of commerce shall be made whereby the legislative power of the respective States shall be restrained from imposing such imposts and duties on foreigners, as their own people are subjected to, or from prohibiting the exportation or importation of any species of goods or commodities whatsoever—of establishing rules for deciding in all cases, what captures on land or water shall be legal, and in what manner prizes taken by land or naval forces in the service of the United States shall be divided or appropriated—of granting letters of marque and reprisal in times of peace—appointing courts for the trial of piracies and felonies committed on the high seas and establishing courts for receiving and determining finally appeals in all cases of captures, provided that no member of Congress shall be appointed a judge of any of the said courts.

The United States in Congress assembled shall also be the last resort on appeal in all disputes and differences now subsisting or that hereafter may arise between two or more States concerning boundary, jurisdiction or any other causes whatever; which authority shall always be exercised in the manner following. Whenever the legislative or executive authority or lawful agent of any State in controversy with another shall present a petition to Congress stating the matter in question and praying for a hearing, notice thereof shall be given by order of Congress to the legislative or executive authority of the other State in controversy, and a day assigned for the appearance of the parties by their lawful agents, who shall then be directed to appoint by joint consent, commissioners or judges to constitute a court for hearing and determining the matter in question: but if they cannot agree, Congress shall name three persons out of each of the United States, and from the list of such persons each party shall alternately strike out one, the petitioners beginning, until the number shall be reduced to thirteen; and from that number not less than seven, nor more than nine names as Congress shall direct, shall in the presence of Congress be drawn out by lot, and the persons whose names shall be so drawn or any five of them, shall be commissioners or judges, to hear and finally determine the controversy, so always as a major part of the judges who shall hear the cause shall agree in the determination: and if either party shall neglect to attend at the day appointed, without showing reasons, which Congress shall judge sufficient, or being present shall refuse to strike, the Congress shall proceed to nominate three persons out of each State, and the secretary of Congress shall strike in behalf of such party absent or refusing; and the judgement and sentence of the court to be appointed, in the manner before prescribed, shall be final and conclusive; and if any of the parties shall refuse to submit to the authority of such court, or to appear or defend their claim or cause, the court shall nevertheless proceed to pronounce sentence, or judgement, which shall in like manner be final and decisive, the judgement or sentence and other proceedings being in either case transmitted to Congress, and lodged among the acts of Congress for the security of the parties concerned: provided that every commissioner, before he sits in judgement, shall take an oath to be administered by one of the judges of the supreme or superior court of the State, where the cause shall be tried, 'well and truly to hear and determine the matter in question, according to the best of his judgement, without favor, affection or hope of reward': provided also, that no State shall be deprived of territory for the benefit of the United States.

All controversies concerning the private right of soil claimed under different grants of two or more States, whose jurisdictions as they may respect such lands, and the States which passed such grants are adjusted, the said grants or either of them being at the same time claimed to have originated antecedent to such settlement of jurisdiction, shall on the petition of either party to the Congress of the United States, be finally determined as near as may be in the same manner as is before prescribed for deciding disputes respecting territorial jurisdiction between different States.

The United States in Congress assembled shall also have the sole and exclusive right and power of regulating the alloy and value of coin struck by their own authority, or by that of the respective States—fixing the standards of weights and measures throughout the United States—regulating the trade and managing all affairs with the Indians, not members of any of the States, provided that the legislative right of any State within its own limits be not infringed or violated—establishing or regulating post offices from one State to another, throughout all the United States, and exacting such postage on the papers passing through the same as may be requisite to defray the expenses of the said office—appointing all officers of the land forces, in the service of the United States, excepting regimental officers—appointing all the officers of the naval forces, and commissioning all officers whatever in the service of the United States—making rules for the government and regulation of the said land and naval forces, and directing their operations. The United States in Congress assembled shall have authority to appoint a committee, to sit in the recess of Congress, to be denominated 'A Committee of the States', and to consist of one delegate from each State; and to appoint such other committees and civil officers as may be necessary for managing the general affairs of the United States under their direction—to appoint one of their members to preside, provided that no person be allowed to serve in the office of president more than one year in any term of three years; to ascertain the necessary sums of money to be raised for the service of the United States, and to appropriate and apply the same for defraying the public expenses—to borrow money, or emit bills on the credit of the United States, transmitting every half-year to the respective States an account of the sums of money so borrowed or emitted—to build and equip a navy—to agree upon the number of land forces, and to make requisitions from each State for its quota, in proportion to the number of white inhabitants in such State; which requisition shall be binding, and thereupon the legislature of each State shall appoint the regimental officers, raise the men and cloath, arm and equip them in a solid-like manner, at the expense of the United States; and the officers and men so cloathed, armed and equipped shall march to the place appointed, and within the time agreed on by the United States in Congress assembled. But if the United States in Congress assembled shall, on consideration of circumstances judge proper that any State should not raise men, or should raise a smaller number of men than the quota thereof, such extra number shall be raised, officered, cloathed, armed and equipped in the same manner as the quota of each State, unless the legislature of such State shall judge that such extra number cannot be safely spread out in the same, in which case they shall raise, officer, cloath, arm and equip as many of such extra number as they judge can be safely spared. And the officers and men so cloathed, armed, and equipped, shall march to the place appointed, and within the time agreed on by the United States in Congress assembled.

The United States in Congress assembled shall never engage in a war, nor grant letters of marque or reprisal in time of peace, nor enter into any treaties or alliances, nor coin money, nor regulate the value thereof, nor ascertain the sums and expenses necessary for the defense and welfare of the United States, or any of them, nor emit bills, nor borrow money on the credit of the United States, nor appropriate money, nor agree upon the number of vessels of war, to be built or purchased, or the number of land or sea forces to be raised, nor appoint a commander in chief of the army or navy, unless nine States assent to the same: nor shall a question on any other point, except for adjourning from day to day be determined, unless by the votes of the majority of the United States in Congress assembled. The Congress of the United States shall have power to adjourn to any time within the year, and to any place within the United States, so that no period of adjournment be for a longer duration than the space of six months, and shall publish the journal of their proceedings monthly, except such parts thereof relating to treaties, alliances or military operations, as in their judgement require secrecy; and the yeas and nays of the delegates of each State on any question shall be entered on the journal, when it is desired by any delegates of a State, or any of them, at his or their request shall be furnished with a transcript of the said journal, except such parts as are above excepted, to lay before the legislatures of the several States.

Art X. The Committee of the States, or any nine of them, shall be authorized to execute, in the recess of Congress, such of the powers of Congress as the United States in Congress assembled, by the consent of the nine States, shall from time to time think expedient to vest them with; provided that no power be delegated to the said Committee, for the exercise of which, by the Articles of Confederation, the voice of nine States in the Congress of the United States assembled be requisite.

Art XI. Canada acceding to this confederation, and adjoining in the measures of the United States, shall be admitted into, and entitled to all the advantages of this Union; but no other colony shall be admitted into the same, unless such admission be agreed to by nine States.

Art XII. All bills of credit emitted, monies borrowed, and debts contracted by, or under the authority of Congress, before the assembling of the United States, in pursuance of the present confederation, shall be deemed and considered as a charge against the United States, for payment and satisfaction whereof the said United States, and the public faith are hereby solemnly pledged.

Art XIII. Every State shall abide by the determination of the United States in Congress assembled, on all questions which by this confederation are submitted to them. And the Articles of this Confederation shall be inviolably observed by every State, and the Union shall be perpetual; nor shall any alteration at any time hereafter be made in any of them; unless such alteration be agreed to in a Congress of the United States, and be afterwards confirmed by the legislatures of every State.

And Whereas it hath pleased the Great Governor of the World to incline the hearts of the legislatures we respectively represent in Congress, to approve of, and to authorize us to ratify the said Articles of Confederation and perpetual Union. Know Ye that we the undersigned delegates, by virtue of the power and authority to us given for that purpose, do by these presents, in the name and in behalf of our respective constituents, fully and entirely ratify and confirm each and every of the said Articles of Confederation and perpetual Union, and all and singular the matters and things therein contained: And we do further solemnly plight and engage the faith of our respective constituents, that they shall abide by the determinations of the United States in Congress assembled, on all questions, which by the said Confederation are submitted to them. And that the Articles thereof shall be inviolably observed by the States we respectively represent, and that the Union shall be perpetual.

In Witness whereof we have hereunto set our hands in Congress. Done at Philadelphia in the State of Pennsylvania the ninth day of July in the Year of our Lord One Thousand Seven Hundred and Seventy-Eight, and in the Third Year of the independence of America.

The Constitution of the United States of America

We the People of the United States, in Order to form a more perfect Union, establish Justice, insure domestic Tranquility, provide for the common defence, promote the general Welfare, and secure the Blessings of Liberty to ourselves and our Posterity, do ordain and establish this Constitution for the United States of America.

Article I

Section 1. All legislative Powers herein granted shall be vested in a Congress of the United States, which shall consist of a Senate and House of Representatives.

Section 2. (1) The House of Representatives shall be composed of Members chosen every second Year by the People of the several States, and the Electors in each State shall have the Qualifications requisite for Electors of the most numerous Branch of the State Legislature.

(2) No Person shall be a Representative who shall not have attained to the age of twenty-five Years, and been seven Years a Citizen of the United States, and who shall not, when elected, be an Inhabitant of that State in which he shall be chosen.

(3) Representatives and direct Taxes shall be apportioned among the several States which may be included within this Union, according to their respective Numbers, which shall be determined by adding to the whole Number of free Persons, including those bound to Service for a Term of Years, and excluding Indians not taxed, three fifths of all other Persons. The actual Enumeration shall be made within three Years after the first Meeting of the Congress of the United States, and within every subsequent Term of ten Years, in such Manner as they shall by Law direct. The Number of Representatives shall not exceed one for every thirty Thousand, but each State shall have at Least one Representative; and until such enumeration shall be made, the State of New Hampshire shall be entitled to chuse three, Massachusetts eight, Rhode Island and Providence Plantations one, Connecticut five, New York six, New Jersey four, Pennsylvania eight, Delaware one, Maryland six, Virginia ten, North Carolina five, South Carolina five, and Georgia three.

(4) When vacancies happen in the Representation from any State, the Executive Authority thereof shall issue Writs of Election to fill such Vacancies.

(5) The House of Representatives shall chuse their Speaker and other Officers; and shall have the sole Power of Impeachment.

Section 3. (1) The Senate of the United States shall be composed of two Senators from each State, chosen by the Legislature thereof, for six Years; and each Senator shall have one Vote.

(2) Immediately after they shall be assembled in Consequence of the first Election, they shall be divided as equally as may be into three Classes. The Seats of the Senators of the first Class shall be vacated at the Expiration of the second Year, of the second Class at the Expiration of the fourth Year, and of the third Class at the Expiration of the sixth Year, so that one third may be chosen every second Year; and if Vacancies happen by Resignation, or otherwise, during the Recess of the Legislature of any State, the Executive thereof may make temporary Appointments until the next Meeting of the Legislature, which shall then fill such Vacancies.

(3) No Person shall be a Senator who shall not have attained, to the Age of thirty Years, and been nine Years a Citizen of the United States, and who shall not, when elected, be an Inhabitant of that State for which he shall be chosen.

(4) The Vice President of the United States shall be President of the Senate, but shall have no Vote, unless they be equally divided.

(5) The Senate shall chuse their other Officers, and also a President pro tempore, in the Absence of the Vice President, or when he shall exercise the Office of the President of the United States.

(6) The Senate shall have the sole Power to try all Impeachments. When sitting for that Purpose, they shall be on Oath or Affirmation. When the President of the United States is tried, the Chief Justice shall preside: And no Person shall be convicted without the Concurrence of two thirds of the Members present.

(7) Judgment in Cases of Impeachment shall not extend further than to removal from Office, and disqualification to hold and enjoy any Office of honor, Trust or Profit under the United States: but the Party convicted shall nevertheless be liable and subject to Indictment, Trial, Judgment and Punishment, according to Law.

Section 4. (1) The Times, Places and Manner of holding Elections for Senators and Representatives, shall be prescribed in each State by the Legislature thereof; but the Congress may at any time by Law make or alter such Regulations, except as to the Places of chusing Senators.

(2) The Congress shall assemble at least once in every Year, and such Meeting shall be on the first Monday in December, unless they shall by Law appoint a different Day.

Section 5. (1) Each House shall be the Judge of the Elections, Returns and Qualifications of its own Members, and a Majority of each shall constitute a Quorum to do Business; but a smaller Number may adjourn from day to day, and may be authorized to compel the Attendance of absent Members, in such Manner, and under such Penalties as each House may provide.

(2) Each House may determine the Rules of its Proceedings, punish its Members for disorderly Behaviour, and, with the Concurrence of two thirds, expel a Member.

(3) Each House shall keep a Journal of its Proceedings, and from time to time publish the same, excepting such Parts as may in their Judgment require Secrecy; and the Yeas and Nays of the Members of either House on any question shall, at the Desire of one fifth of those Present, be entered on the Journal.

(4) Neither House, during the Session of Congress, shall, without the Consent of the other, adjourn for more than three days, nor to any other Place than that in which the two Houses shall be sitting.

Section 6. (1) The Senators and Representatives shall receive a Compensation for their Services, to be ascertained by Law, and paid out of the Treasury of the United States. They shall in all Cases, except Treason, Felony and Breach of the Peace, be privileged from Arrest during their Attendance at the Session of their respective Houses, and in going to and returning from the same; and for any Speech or Debate in either House, they shall not be questioned in any other Place.

(2) No Senator or Representative shall, during the Time for which he was elected, be appointed to any civil Office under the Authority of the United States, which shall have been created, or the Emoluments whereof shall have been increased during such time; and no Person holding any Office under the United States, shall be a Member of either House during his Continuance in Office.

Section 7. (1) All Bills for raising Revenue shall originate in the House of Representatives; but the Senate may propose or concur with Amendments as on other Bills.

(2) Every Bill which shall have passed the House of Representatives and the Senate, shall, before it become a Law, be presented to the President of the United States; If he approve he shall sign it, but if not he shall return it, with his Objections to that House in which it shall have originated, who shall enter the Objections at large on their Journal, and proceed to reconsider it. If after such Reconsideration two thirds of that House shall agree to pass the Bill, it shall be sent, together with the Objections, to the other House, by which it shall likewise be reconsidered, and if approved by two thirds of that House, it shall become a Law. But in all such Cases the Votes of both Houses shall be determined by Yeas and Nays, and the Names of the Persons voting for and against the Bill shall be entered on the Journal of each House respectively. If any Bill shall not be returned by the President within ten Days (Sunday excepted) after it shall have been presented to him, the Same shall be a Law, in like Manner as if he had signed it, unless the Congress by their Adjournment prevent its Return, in which Case it shall not be a Law.

(3) Every Order, Resolution, or Vote to which the Concurrence of the Senate and House of Representatives may be necessary (except on a question of Adjournment) shall be presented to the President of the United States; and before the Same shall take Effect, shall be approved by him, or being disapproved by him, shall be repassed by two thirds of the Senate and House of Representatives, according to the Rules and Limitations prescribed in the Case of a Bill.

Section 8. (1) The Congress shall have Power To lay and collect Taxes, Duties, Imposts and Excises, to pay the Debts and provide for the common Defence and general Welfare of the United States; but all Duties, Imposts and Excises shall be uniform throughout the United States;

(2) To borrow Money on the credit of the United States;

(3) To regulate Commerce with foreign Nations, and among the several States, and with the Indian Tribes;

(4) To establish an uniform Rule of Naturalization, and uniform Laws on the subject of Bankruptcies throughout the United States;

(5) To coin Money, regulate the Value thereof, and of foreign Coin, and to fix the Standard of Weights and Measures;

(6) To provide for the Punishment of counterfeiting the Securities and current Coin of the United States;

(7) To establish Post Offices and post Roads;

(8) To promote the Progress of Science and useful Arts, by securing for limited Times to Authors and Inventors the exclusive Right to their respective Writings and Discoveries;

(9) To constitute Tribunals inferior to the supreme Court;

(10) To define and punish Piracies and Felonies committed on the high Seas, and Offenses against the Law of Nations;

(11) To declare War, grant Letters of Marque and Reprisal, and make Rules concerning Captures on Land and Water;

(12) To raise and support Armies, but no Appropriation of Money to that Use shall be for a longer Term than two Years;

(13) To provide and maintain a Navy;

(14) To make Rules for the Government and Regulation of the land and naval Forces;

(15) To provide for calling forth the Militia to execute the Laws of the Union, suppress Insurrections and repel Invasions;

(16) To provide for organizing, arming, and disciplining, the Militia, and for governing such Part of them as may be employed in the Service of the United States, reserving to the States respectively, the Appointment of the Officers, and the Authority of training the Militia according to the discipline prescribed by Congress;

(17) To exercise exclusive Legislation in all Cases whatsoever, over such District (not exceeding ten Miles square) as may, by Cession of particular States, and the Acceptance of Congress, become the Seat of the Government of the United States, and to exercise like Authority over all Places purchased by the Consent of the Legislature of the State in which the Same shall be, for the Erection of Forts, Magazines, Arsenals, dock-Yards, and other needful Buildings;—And

(18) To make all Laws which shall be necessary and proper for carrying into Execution the foregoing Powers, and all other Powers vested by this Constitution in the Government of the United States, or in any Department or Officer thereof.

Section 9. (1) The Migration or Importation of such Persons as any of the States now existing shall think proper to admit, shall not be prohibited by the Congress prior to the Year one thousand eight hundred and eight, but a Tax or Duty may be imposed on such Importation, not exceeding ten dollars for each Person.

(2) The Privilege of the Writ of Habeas Corpus shall not be suspended unless when in Cases of Rebellion or Invasion the public Safety may require it.

(3) No Bill of Attainder or ex post facto Law shall be passed.

(4) No Capitation, or other direct, Tax shall be laid, unless in Proportion to the Census or Enumeration herein before directed to be taken.

(5) No Tax or Duty shall be laid on Articles exported from any State.

(6) No Preference shall be given by any Regulation of Commerce or Revenue to the Ports of one State over those of another; nor shall Vessels bound to, or from, one State, be obliged to enter, clear or pay Duties in another.

(7) No Money shall be drawn from the Treasury, but in Consequence of Appropriations made by Law; and a regular Statement

and Account of the Receipts and Expenditures of all public Money shall be published from time to time.

(8) No Title of Nobility shall be granted by the United States: And no Person holding any Office of Profit or Trust under them, shall, without the Consent of the Congress, accept of any present, Emolument, Office, or Title, of any kind whatever, from any King, Prince or foreign State.

Section 10. (1) No State shall enter into any Treaty, Alliance, or Confederation; grant Letters of Marque and Reprisal; coin Money; emit Bills of Credit; make any Thing but gold and silver Coin a Tender in Payment of Debts; pass any Bill of Attainder, ex post facto Law, or Law impairing the Obligation of Contracts, or grant any Title of Nobility.

(2) No State shall, without the Consent of Congress, lay any Imposts or Duties on Imports or Exports, except what may be absolutely necessary for executing its inspection Laws: and the net Produce of all Duties and Imposts, laid by any State on Imports or Exports, shall be for the Use of the Treasury of the United States; and all such Laws shall be subject to the Revision and Control of the Congress.

(3) No State shall, without the Consent of Congress, lay any Duty of Tonnage, keep Troops, or Ships of War in time of Peace, enter into any Agreement or Compact with another State, or with a foreign Power, or engage in War, unless actually invaded, or in such imminent Danger as will not admit of Delay.

Article II

Section 1. (1) The executive Power shall be vested in a President of the United States of America. He shall hold his Office during the Term of four Years, and, together with the Vice President, chosen for the same Term, be elected, as follows:

(2) Each State shall appoint, in such Manner as the Legislature thereof may direct, a Number of Electors, equal to the whole Number of Senators and Representatives to which the State may be entitled in the Congress: but no Senator or Representative, or Person holding an Office of Trust or Profit under the United States, shall be appointed an Elector.

The Electors shall meet in their respective States, and vote by Ballot for two Persons, of whom one at least shall not be an Inhabitant of the same State with themselves. And they shall make a List of all the Persons voted for, and of the Number of Votes for each; which List they shall sign and certify, and transmit sealed to the Seat of the Government of the United States, directed to the President of the Senate. The President of the Senate shall, in the presence of the Senate and House of Representatives, open all the Certificates, and the Votes shall then be counted. The Person having the greatest Number of Votes shall be the President, if such Number be a Majority of the whole Number of Electors appointed; and if there be more than one who have such Majority, and have an equal Number of Votes, then the House of Representatives shall immediately chuse by Ballot one of them for President; and if no Person have a Majority, then from the five highest on the List the said House shall in like Manner chuse the President. But in chusing the President, the Votes shall be taken by States, the Representation from each State having one Vote; a quorum for this Purpose shall consist of a Member or Members from two thirds of the States, and a Majority of all the States shall be necessary to a Choice. In every Case, after the Choice of the President, the Person having the greatest Number of Votes of the Electors shall be the Vice President. But if there should remain two or more who have equal Votes, the Senate shall chuse from them by Ballot the Vice President.

(3) The Congress may determine the Time of chusing the Electors, and the Day on which they shall give their Votes; which Day shall be the same throughout the United States.

(4) No Person except a natural born Citizen, or a Citizen of the United States, at the time of the Adoption of this Constitution, shall be eligible to the Office of President; neither shall any Person be eligible to that Office who shall not have attained to the Age of thirty five Years, and been fourteen Years a Resident within the United States.

(5) In Case of the Removal of the President from Office, or of his Death, Resignation, or Inability to discharge the Powers and Duties of the said Office, the Same shall devolve on the Vice President, and the Congress may by Law provide for the Case of Removal, Death, Resignation or Inability, both of the President and Vice President, declaring what Officer shall then act as President, and such Officer shall act accordingly, until the Disability be removed, or a President shall be elected.

(6) The President shall, at stated Times, receive for his Services, a Compensation, which shall neither be increased nor diminished during the Period for which he shall have been elected, and he shall not receive within that Period any other Emolument from the United States, or any of them.

(7) Before he enter on the Execution of his Office, he shall take the following Oath or Affirmation:—"I do solemnly swear (or affirm) that I will faithfully execute the Office of President of the United States, and will to the best of my Ability, preserve, protect and defend the Constitution of the United States."

Section 2. (1) The President shall be Commander in Chief of the Army and Navy of the United States, and of the Militia of the several States, when called into the actual Service of the United States; he may require the Opinion, in writing, of the principal Officer in each of the executive Departments, upon any Subject relating to the Duties of their respective Offices, and he shall have Power to grant Reprieves and Pardons for Offenses against the United States, except in Cases of Impeachment.

(2) He shall have Power, by and with the Advice and Consent of the Senate, to make Treaties, provided two thirds of the Senators present concur; and he shall nominate, and by and with the Advice and Consent of the Senate, shall appoint Ambassadors, other public Ministers and Consuls, Judges of the supreme Court, and all other Officers of the United States, whose Appointments are not herein otherwise provided for, and which shall be established by Law: but the Congress may by Law vest the Appointment of such inferior Officers, as they think proper, in the President alone, in the Courts of Law, or in the Heads of Departments.

(3) The President shall have Power to fill up all Vacancies that may happen during the Recess of the Senate, by granting Commissions which shall expire at the End of their next Session.

Section 3. He shall from time to time give to the Congress Information of the State of the Union, and recommend to their Consideration such Measures as he shall judge necessary and expedient; he may, on extraordinary Occasions, convene both Houses, or either of them, and in Case of Disagreement between them, with Respect to the Time of Adjournment, he may adjourn them to such Time as he shall think proper; he shall receive Ambassadors and other public Ministers; he shall take Care that the Laws be faithfully executed, and shall Commission all the Officers of the United States.

Section 4. The President, Vice President and all Civil Officers of the United States, shall be removed from Office on Impeachment for, and Conviction of, Treason, Bribery, or other high Crimes and Misdemeanors.

Article III

Section 1. The judicial Power of the United States, shall be vested in one supreme Court, and in such inferior Courts as the Congress may from time to time ordain and establish. The Judges, both of the supreme and inferior Courts, shall hold their Offices during good Behaviour, and shall, at stated Times, receive for their Services, a Compensation, which shall not be diminished during their Continuance in Office.

Section 2. (1) The judicial Power shall extend to all Cases, in Law and Equity, arising under this Constitution, the Laws of the United States, and Treaties made, or which shall be made, under their Authority;—to all Cases affecting Ambassadors, other public Ministers and Consuls;—to all Cases of admiralty and maritime Jurisdiction;—to Controversies to which the United States shall be a party;—to Controversies between two or more States;—between a State and Citizens of another State;—between Citizens of different States;—between Citizens of the same State claiming Lands under Grants of different States, and between a State, or the Citizens thereof, and foreign States, Citizens or Subjects.

(2) In all Cases affecting Ambassadors, other public Ministers and Consuls, and those in which a State shall be Party, the supreme Court shall have original Jurisdiction. In all the other Cases before mentioned, the supreme Court shall have appellate Jurisdiction, both as to Law and Fact, with such Exceptions, and under such Regulations as the Congress shall make.

(3) The Trial of all Crimes, except in Cases of Impeachment, shall be by Jury; and such Trial shall be held in the State where the said Crimes shall have been committed; but when not committed within any State, the Trial shall be at such Place or Places as the Congress may by Law have directed.

Section 3. (1) Treason against the United States, shall consist only in levying War against them, or in adhering to their Enemies, giving them Aid and Comfort. No Person shall be convicted of Treason unless on the Testimony of two Witnesses to the same overt Act, or on Confession in open Court.

(2) The Congress shall have Power to declare the Punishment of Treason, but no Attainder of Treason shall work Corruption of Blood, or Forfeiture except during the Life of the Person attainted.

Article IV

Section 1. Full Faith and Credit shall be given in each State to the public Acts, Records, and judicial Proceedings of every other State. And the Congress may by general Laws prescribe the Manner in which such Acts, Records and Proceedings shall be proved, and the Effect thereof.

Section 2. (1) The Citizens of each State shall be entitled to all privileges and Immunities of Citizens in the several States.

(2) A Person charged in any State with Treason, Felony, or other Crime, who shall flee from Justice, and be found in another State, shall on Demand of the executive Authority of the State from which he fled, be delivered up, to be removed to the State having Jurisdiction of the Crime.

(3) No Person held to Service of Labour in one State, under the Laws thereof, escaping into another, shall, in Consequence of any Law or Regulation therein, be discharged from such Service or Labour, but shall be delivered up on Claim of the Party to whom such Service or Labour may be due.

Section 3. (1) New States may be admitted by the Congress into this Union; but no new State shall be formed or erected within the Jurisdiction of any other State; nor any State be formed by the Junction of two or more States, or Parts of States, without the Consent of the Legislatures of the States concerned as well as of the Congress.

(2) The Congress shall have power to dispose of and make all needful Rules and Regulations respecting the Territory or other Property belonging to the United States; and nothing in this Constitution shall be so construed as to Prejudice any Claims of the United States, or of any particular State.

Section 4. The United States shall guarantee to every State in this Union a Republican Form of Government, and shall protect each of them against Invasion; and on Application of the Legislature, or of the Executive (when the Legislature cannot be convened) against domestic Violence.

Article V

The Congress, whenever two thirds of both Houses shall deem it necessary, shall propose Amendments to this Constitution, or, on the Application of the Legislatures of two thirds of the several States, shall call a Convention for proposing Amendments, which, in either Case, shall be valid to all Intents and Purposes, as Part of this Constitution, when ratified by the Legislatures of three fourths of the several States, or by Conventions in three fourths thereof, as the one or the other Mode of Ratification may be proposed by the Congress; Provided that no Amendment which may be made prior to the Year One thousand eight hundred and eight shall in any Manner affect the first and fourth Clauses in the Ninth Section of the first Article; and that no State, without its Consent, shall be deprived of its equal Suffrage in the Senate.

Article VI

(1) All Debts contracted and Engagements entered into, before the Adoption of this Constitution, shall be as valid against the United States under this Constitution, as under the Confederation.

(2) This Constitution, and the Laws of the United States which shall be made in Pursuance thereof; and all Treaties made, or which shall be made, under the Authority of the United States, shall be the supreme Law of the Land; and the Judges in every State shall be bound thereby, any Thing in the Constitution or Laws of any State to the Contrary notwithstanding.

(3) The Senators and Representatives before mentioned, and the Members of the several State Legislatures, and all executive and judicial Officers, both of the United States and of the several States, shall be bound by Oath or Affirmation, to support this Constitution; but no religious Test shall ever be required as a Qualification to any Office or public Trust under the United States.

Article VII

The Ratification of the Conventions of nine States, shall be sufficient for the Establishment of this Constitution between the States so ratifying the Same.

ARTICLES IN ADDITION TO, AND AMENDMENT OF, THE CONSTITUTION OF THE UNITED STATES OF AMERICA, PROPOSED BY CONGRESS, AND RATIFIED BY THE SEVERAL STATES, PURSUANT TO THE FIFTH ARTICLE OF THE ORIGINAL CONSTITUTION

AMENDMENT I (1791)

Congress shall make no law respecting an establishment of religion, or prohibiting the free exercise thereof; or abridging the freedom of speech, or of the press; or the right of the people peaceably to assemble, and to petition the Government for a redress of grievances.

AMENDMENT II (1791)

A well regulated Militia, being necessary to the security of a free state, the right of the people to keep and bear Arms, shall not be infringed.

AMENDMENT III (1791)

No Soldier shall, in time of peace be quartered in any house, without the consent of the Owner, nor in time of war, but in a manner to be prescribed by law.

AMENDMENT IV (1791)

The right of the people to be secure in their persons, houses, papers, and effects, against unreasonable searches and seizures, shall not be violated, and no Warrants shall issue, but upon probable cause, supported by Oath or affirmation, and particularly describing the place to be searched, and the persons or things to be seized.

AMENDMENT V (1791)

No person shall be held to answer for a capital, or otherwise infamous crime, unless on a presentment or indictment of a Grand Jury, except in cases arising in the land or naval forces, or in the Militia, when in actual service in time of War or public danger; nor shall any person be subject for the same offence to be twice put in jeopardy of life or limb; nor shall be compelled in any criminal case to be a witness against himself, nor be deprived of life, liberty, or property, without due process of law; nor shall private property be taken for public use, without just compensation.

AMENDMENT VI (1791)

In all criminal prosecutions, the accused shall enjoy the right to a speedy and public trial, by an impartial jury of the State and district wherein the crime shall have been committed, which district shall have been previously ascertained by law, and to be informed of the nature and cause of the accusation; to be confronted with the witnesses against him; to have compulsory process for obtaining witnesses in his favor, and to have the Assistance of Counsel for his defence.

AMENDMENT VII (1791)

In Suits at common law, where the value in controversy shall exceed twenty dollars, the right of trial by jury shall be preserved, and no fact tried by a jury, shall be otherwise re-examined in any Court of the United States, than according to the rules of the common law.

AMENDMENT VIII (1791)

Excessive bail shall not be required, nor excessive fines imposed, nor cruel and unusual punishments inflicted.

AMENDMENT IX (1791)

The enumeration in the Constitution, of certain rights, shall not be construed to deny or disparage others retained by the people.

AMENDMENT X (1791)

The powers not delegated to the United States by the Constitution, nor prohibited by it to the States, are reserved to the States respectively, or to the people.

AMENDMENT XI (1798)

The Judicial power of the United States shall not be construed to extend to any suit in law or equity, commenced or prosecuted against one of the United States by Citizens of another State, or by Citizens or Subjects of any Foreign State.

AMENDMENT XII (1804)

The Electors shall meet in their respective states and vote by ballot for President and Vice-President, one of whom, at least, shall not be an inhabitant of the same state with themselves; they shall name in their ballots the person voted for as President, and in distinct ballots the person voted for as Vice-President, and they shall make distinct lists of all persons voted for as President, and of all persons voted for as Vice-President, and of the number of votes for each, which lists they shall sign and certify, and transmit sealed to the seat of the government of the United States, directed to the President of the Senate;—The President of the Senate shall, in the presence of the Senate and House of Representatives, open all the certificates and the votes shall then be counted;—The person having the greatest number of votes for President, shall be the President, if such number be a majority of the whole number of Electors appointed; and if no person have such majority, then from the persons having the highest numbers not exceeding three on the list of those voted for as President, the House of Representatives shall choose immediately, by ballot, the President. But in choosing the President, the votes shall be taken by states, the representation from each state having one vote; a quorum for this purpose shall consist of a member or members from two-thirds of the states, and a majority of all the states shall be necessary to a choice. And if the House of Representatives shall not choose a President whenever the right of choice shall devolve upon them, before the fourth day of March next following, then the Vice-President shall act as President, as in the case of the death or other constitutional disability of the President—The person having the greatest number of votes as Vice-President, shall be the Vice-President, if such number be a majority of the whole number of Electors appointed, and if no person have a majority, then from the two highest numbers on the list, the Senate shall choose the Vice-President; A quorum for the purpose shall consist of two-thirds of the whole number of Senators, and a majority of the whole number shall be necessary to a choice. But no person constitutionally ineligible to the office of President shall be eligible to that of Vice-President of the United States.

AMENDMENT XIII (1865)

Section 1. Neither slavery nor involuntary servitude, except as a punishment for crime whereof the party shall have been duly convicted, shall exist within the United States, or any place subject to their jurisdiction.

Section 2. Congress shall have power to enforce this article by appropriate legislation.

AMENDMENT XIV (1868)

Section 1. All persons born or naturalized in the United States and subject to the jurisdiction thereof, are citizens of the United States and of the State wherein they reside. No State shall make or enforce any law which shall abridge the privileges or immunities of citizens of the United States; nor shall any State deprive any person of life, liberty, or property, without due process of law; nor deny to any person within its jurisdiction the equal protection of the laws.

Section 2. Representatives shall be apportioned among the several States according to their respective numbers, counting the whole number of persons in each State, excluding Indians not taxed. But when the right to vote at any election for the choice of electors for President and Vice-President of the United States, Representatives in Congress, the Executive and Judicial officers of a State, or the members of the Legislature thereof, is denied to any of the male inhabitants of such State, being twenty-one years of age, and citizens of the United States, or in any way abridged, except for participation in rebellion, or other crime, the basis of representation therein shall be reduced in the proportion which the number of such male citizens shall bear to the whole number of male citizens twenty-one years of age in such State.

Section 3. No person shall be a Senator or Representative in Congress, or elector of President and Vice-President, or hold any office, civil or military, under the United States, or under any State, who, having previously taken an oath, as a member of Congress, or as an officer of the United States, or as a member of any State legislature, or as an executive or judicial officer of any State, to support the Constitution of the United States, shall have engaged in insurrection or rebellion against the same, or given aid or comfort to the enemies thereof. But Congress may by a vote of two-thirds of each House, remove such disability.

Section 4. The validity of the public debt of the United States, authorized by law, including debts incurred for payment of pensions and bounties for services in suppressing insurrection or rebellion, shall not be questioned. But neither the United States nor any State shall assume or pay any debt or obligation incurred in aid of insurrection or rebellion against the United States, or any claim for the loss or emancipation of any slave; but all such debts, obligations and claims shall be held illegal and void.

Section 5. The Congress shall have power to enforce, by appropriate legislation, the provisions of this article.

AMENDMENT XV (1870)

Section 1. The right of citizens of the United States to vote shall not be denied or abridged by the United States or by any State on account of race, color, or previous condition of servitude.

Section 2. The Congress shall have power to enforce this article by appropriate legislation.

AMENDMENT XVI (1913)

The Congress shall have power to lay and collect taxes on incomes, from whatever source derived, without apportionment among the several States, and without regard to any census or enumeration.

AMENDMENT XVII (1913)

The Senate of the United States shall be composed of two Senators from each State, elected by the people thereof, for six years; and each Senator shall have one vote. The electors in each State shall have the qualifications requisite for electors of the most numerous branch of the State legislatures.

When vacancies happen in the representation of any State in the Senate, the executive authority of such State shall issue writs of election to fill such vacancies: Provided, That the legislature of any State may empower the executive thereof to make temporary appointments until the people fill the vacancies by election as the legislature may direct.

This amendment shall not be so construed as to affect the election or term of any Senator chosen before it becomes valid as part of the Constitution.

AMENDMENT XVIII (1919)

Section 1. After one year from the ratification of this article the manufacture, sale, or transportation of intoxicating liquors within, the importation thereof into, or the exportation thereof from the United States and all territory subject to the jurisdiction thereof for beverage purposes is hereby prohibited.

Section 2. The Congress and the several States shall have concurrent power to enforce this article by appropriate legislation.

Section 3. This article shall be inoperative unless it shall have been ratified as an amendment to the Constitution by the legislatures of the several States, as provided in the Constitution, within seven years from the date of the submission hereof to the States by the Congress.

AMENDMENT XIX (1920)

The right of citizens of the United States to vote shall not be denied or abridged by the United States or by any State on account of sex.

Congress shall have power to enforce this article by appropriate legislation.

AMENDMENT XX (1933)

Section 1. The terms of the President and Vice President shall end at noon on the 20th day of January, and the terms of Senators and Representatives at noon on the 3d day of January, of the years in which such terms would have ended if this article had not been ratified; and the terms of their successors shall then begin.

Section 2. The Congress shall assemble at least once in every year, and such meeting shall begin at noon on the 3d day of January, unless they shall by law appoint a different day.

Section 3. If, at the time fixed for the beginning of the term of the President, the President elect shall have died, the Vice President elect shall become President. If a President shall not have been chosen before the time fixed for the beginning of his term, or if the President elect shall have failed to qualify, then the Vice President elect shall act as President until a President shall have qualified; and the Congress may by law provide for the case wherein neither a President elect nor a Vice President elect shall have qualified, declaring who shall then act as President, or the manner in which one who is to act shall be selected, and such person shall act accordingly until a President or Vice President shall have qualified.

Section 4. The Congress may by law provide for the case of the death of any of the persons from whom the House of Representatives may choose a President whenever the right of choice shall have devolved upon them, and for the case of the death of any of the persons from whom the Senate may choose a Vice President whenever the right of choice shall have devolved upon them.

Section 5. Sections 1 and 2 shall take effect on the 15th day of October following the ratification of this article.

Section 6. This article shall be inoperative unless it shall have been ratified as an amendment to the Constitution by the legislatures of three-fourths of the several States within seven years from the date of its submission.

AMENDMENT XXI (1933)

Section 1. The eighteenth article of amendment to the Constitution of the United States is hereby repealed.

Section 2. The transportation or importation into any State, Territory or possession of the United States for delivery or use therein of intoxicating liquors, in violation of the laws thereof, is hereby prohibited.

Section 3. This article shall be inoperative unless it shall have been ratified as an amendment to the Constitution by conventions in the several States, as provided in the Constitution, within seven years from the date of the submission hereof to the States by the Congress.

AMENDMENT XXII (1951)

Section 1. No person shall be elected to the office of the President more than twice, and no person who has held the office of President, or acted as President, for more than two years of a term to which some other person was elected President shall be elected to the office of the President more than once. But this Article shall not apply to any person holding the office of President when this Article was proposed by the Congress, and shall not prevent any person who may be holding the office of President, or acting as President, during the term within which this Article becomes operative from holding the office of President or acting as President during the remainder of such term.

Section 2. This Article shall be inoperative unless it shall have been ratified as an amendment to the Constitution by the legislatures of three-fourths of the several States within seven years from the date of its submission to the States by the Congress.

AMENDMENT XXIII (1961)

Section 1. The District constituting the seat of Government of the United States shall appoint in such manner as the Congress may direct:

A number of electors of President and Vice President equal to the whole number of Senators and Representatives in Congress to which the District would be entitled if it were a State, but in no event more than the least populous State; they shall be in addition to those appointed by the States, but they shall be considered, for the purposes of the election of President and Vice President, to be electors appointed by a State; and they shall meet in the District and perform such duties as provided by the twelfth article of amendment.

Section 2. The Congress shall have power to enforce this article by appropriate legislation.

AMENDMENT XXIV (1964)

Section 1. The right of citizens of the United States to vote in any primary or other election for President or Vice President, for electors for President or Vice President, or for Senator or Representative in Congress, shall not be denied or abridged by the United States or any State by reason of failure to pay any poll tax or other tax.

Section 2. The Congress shall have power to enforce this article by appropriate legislation.

AMENDMENT XXV (1967)

Section 1. In case of the removal of the President from office or of his death or resignation, the Vice President shall become President.

Section 2. Whenever there is a vacancy in the office of the Vice President, the President shall nominate a Vice President who shall take office upon confirmation by a majority vote of both Houses of Congress.

Section 3. Whenever the President transmits to the President pro tempore of the Senate and the Speaker of the House of Representatives his written declaration that he is unable to discharge the powers and duties of his office, and until he transmits to them a written declaration to the contrary, such powers and duties shall be discharged by the Vice President as Acting President.

Section 4. Whenever the Vice President and a majority of either the principal officers of the executive departments or of such other body as Congress may by law provide, transmit to the President pro tempore of the Senate and the Speaker of the House of Representatives their written declaration that the President is unable to discharge the powers and duties of his office, the Vice President shall immediately assume the powers and duties of the office as Acting President.

Thereafter, when the President transmits to the President pro tempore of the Senate and the Speaker of the House of Representatives his written declaration that no inability exists, he shall resume the powers and duties of his office unless the Vice President and a majority of either the principal officers of the executive department or of such other body as Congress may by law provide, transmit within four days to the President pro tempore of the Senate and the Speaker of the House of Representatives their written declaration that the President is unable to discharge the powers and duties of his office. Thereupon Congress shall decide the issue, assembling within forty-eight hours for that purpose if not in session. If the Congress, within twenty-one days after receipt of the latter written declaration, or, if Congress is not in session, within twenty-one days after Congress is required to assemble, determines by two-thirds vote of both Houses that the President is unable to discharge the powers and duties of his office, the Vice President shall continue to discharge the same as Acting President; otherwise, the President shall resume the powers and duties of his office.

AMENDMENT XXVI (1971)

Section 1. The right of citizens of the United States, who are eighteen years of age or older, to vote shall not be denied or abridged by the United States or by any State on account of age.

Section 2. The Congress shall have power to enforce this article by appropriate legislation.

AMENDMENT XXVII (1992)

No law, varying the compensation for the services of the Senators and Representatives, shall take effect, until an election of Representatives shall have intervened.

Results of Presidential Elections, 1789-2004

Year	Candidates		Electoral vote		Popular vote	
	(Federalist)					
1789	Washington		69 100%			
1792	Washington		132 98%			
	(Democratic Republican)	**(Federalist)**				
1796	Jefferson	Adams	68 49%	71 51%		
1800	Jefferson	Adams	73 53%	65 47%		
1804	Jefferson	Pinckney	162 92%	14 8%		
1808	Madison	Pinckney	122 69%	47 27%		
1812	Madison	Clinton	128 59%	89 41%		
1816	Monroe	King	183 83%	34 15%		
	(Democratic Republican)	**(Independent Democratic Republican)**	**(Democratic Republican)**	**(Independent Democratic Republican)**		
1820	Monroe	Adams	231 98%	1 0%		
1824	Jackson	Adams	99 38%	84 32%		
	(Democratic Republican)	**(National Republican)**	**(Democratic Republican)**	**(National Republican)**	**(Democratic Republican)**	**(National Republican)**
1828	Jackson	Adams	178 68%	83 32%	642,553 56.1%	500,897 43.6%
1832	Jackson	Clay	219 76%	49 17%	701,780 54.2%	484,205 37.4%

Year	Candidates		Electoral vote		Popular vote	
	(Democrat)	(Whig)	(Democrat)	(Whig)	(Democrat)	(Whig)
1836	Van Buren	Harrison	170 58%	73 25%	764,176 50.8%	550,816 36.6%
1840	Van Buren	Harrison	60 20%	234 80%	1,128,854 46.8%	1,275,390 52.9%
1844	Polk	Clay	170 62%	105 38%	1,339,494 49.5%	1,300,004 48.1%
1848	Cass	Taylor	127 44%	163 56%	1,223,460 42.5%	1,361,393 47.3%
1852	Pierce	Scott	254 86%	42 14%	1,607,510 50.8%	1,386,942 43.9%
	(Democrat)	(Republican)	(Democrat)	(Republican)	(Democrat)	(Republican)
1856	Buchanan	Fremont	174 59%	114 39%	1,836,072 45.3%	1,342,345 33.1%
1860	Douglas	Lincoln	12 4%	180 59%	1,380,202 29.5%	1,865,908 39.8%
1864	McClellan	Lincoln	21 9%	212 91%	1,812,807 45.0%	2,218,388 55.0%
1868	Seymour	Grant	80 27%	214 73%	2,708,744 47.30%	3,013,650 52.7%
1872	Greeley	Grant	— —	286 78%	2,834,761 43.8%	3,598,235 55.6%
1876	Tilden	Hayes	184 50%	185 50%	4,288,546 51.0%	4,034,311 47.9%
1880	Hancock	Garfield	155 42%	214 58%	4,444,260 48.2%	4,446,158 48.3%
1884	Cleveland	Blaine	219 55%	182 45%	4,874,621 48.5%	4,848,936 48.2%
1888	Cleveland	Harrison	168 42%	233 58%	5,534,488 48.6%	5,443,892 47.8%
1892	Cleveland	Harrison	277 62%	145 33%	5,551,883 46.1%	5,179,244 43%
1896	Bryan	McKinley	176 39%	271 61%	6,511,495 46.7%	7,108,480 51%
1900	Bryan	McKinley	155 35%	292 65%	6,358,345 45.5%	7,218,039 51.7%
1904	Parker	Roosevelt	140 29%	336 71%	5,028,898 37.6%	7,626,593 56.4%
1908	Bryan	Taft	162 34%	321 66%	6,406,801 43.0%	7,676,258 51.6%
1912	Wilson	Taft	435 82%	8 2%	6,293,152 41.8%	3,486,333 23.2%
1916	Wilson	Hughes	277 52%	254 48%	9,126,300 49.2%	8,546,789 46.1%
1920	Cox	Harding	127 24%	404 76%	9,140,884 34.2%	16,133,314 60.3%
1924	Davis	Coolidge	136 26%	382 72%	8,386,169 28.8%	15,717,553 54.1%
1928	Smith	Hoover	87 16%	444 84%	15,000,185 40.8%	21,411,991 58.2%

Year	Candidates		Electoral vote		Popular vote	
	(Democrat)	*(Republican)*	*(Democrat)*	*(Republican)*	*(Democrat)*	*(Republican)*
1932	Roosevelt	Hoover	472 89%	59 11%	22,825,016 57.4%	15,758,397 39.6%
1936	Roosevelt	Landon	523 90%	8 2%	27,747,636 60.8%	16,679,543 36.5%
1940	Roosevelt	Willkie	449 85%	82 15%	27,263,448 54.7%	22,336,260 44.8%
1944	Roosevelt	Dewey	432 81%	99 19%	25,611,936 53.4%	22,013,372 45.9%
1948	Truman	Dewey	303 57%	189 36%	24,105,587 49.5%	21,970,017 45.1%
1952	Stevenson	Eisenhower	89 17%	442 83%	27,314,649 44.4%	33,936,137 55.1%
1956	Stevenson	Eisenhower	73 14%	457 86%	26,030,172 42.0%	35,585,245 57.4%
1960	Kennedy	Nixon	303 56%	219 41%	34,221,344 49.7%	34,106,671 49.5%
1964	Johnson	Goldwater	486 90%	52 10%	43,126,584 61.1%	27,177,838 38.5%
1968	Humphrey	Nixon	191 36%	301 56%	31,274,503 42.7%	31,785,148 43.4%
1972	McGovern	Nixon	17 3%	520 97%	29,171,791 37.5%	47,170,179 60.7%
1976	Carter	Ford	297 55%	240 45%	40,830,763 50.1%	39,147,793 48.0%
1980	Carter	Reagan	49 9%	489 91%	35,483,883 41.0%	43,904,153 50.7%
1984	Mondale	Reagan	13 2%	525 98%	37,577,185 40.6%	54,455,075 58.8%
1988	Dukakis	Bush	111 21%	426 79%	41,809,074 45.6%	48,886,097 53.4%
1992	Clinton	Bush	370 69%	168 31%	44,909,326 43.0%	39,103,882 37.4%
1996	Clinton	Dole	379 70%	159 30%	47,401,054 49.2%	39,197,350 40.7%
2000	Gore	Bush	267 50%	271 50%	50,996,582 50.2%	50,546,062 49.8%
2004	Kerry	Bush	252 46.8%	286 53.2%	59,028,111 48.3%	62,040,610 50.7%

Supreme Court Justices By Appointing President, State Appointed from, and Political Party

President / Justices Appointed	State Appointed from	Political Party
Washington		
John Jay (1745–1829)*	N.Y.	Federalist
John Rutledge (1739–1800)	S.C.	Federalist
William Cushing (1732–1810)	Mass.	Federalist
James Wilson (1724–1798)	Pa.	Federalist
John Blair (1732–1800)	Va.	Federalist
James Iredell (1751–1799)	N.C.	Federalist
Thomas Johnson (1732–1819)	Md.	Federalist
William Paterson (1745–1806)	N.J.	Federalist
Samuel Chase (1741–1811)	Md.	Federalist
Oliver Ellsworth (1745–1807)	Conn.	Federalist
Adams, J.		
Bushrod Washington (1762–1829)	Va.	Federalist
Alfred Moore (1755–1810)	N.C.	Federalist
John Marshall (1755–1835)	Va.	Federalist
Jefferson		
William Johnson (1771–1834)	S.C.	Democratic Republican
Henry Livingston (1757–1823)	N.Y.	Democratic Republican
Thomas Todd (1765–1826)	Va.	Democratic Republican
Madison		
Gabriel Duvall (1752–1844)	Md.	Democratic Republican
Joseph Story (1779–1845)	Mass.	Democratic Republican
Monroe		
Smith Thompson (1768–1843)	N.Y.	Democratic Republican
Adams, J. Q.		
Robert Trimble (1776–1828)	Ky.	Democratic Republican

President / Justices Appointed	State Appointed from	Political Party
Jackson		
John McLean (1785–1861)	Ohio	Democrat
Henry Baldwin (1780–1844)	Penn.	Democrat
James M. Wayne (1790–1867)	Ga.	Democrat
Roger B. Taney (1777–1864)	Va.	Democrat
Philip P. Barbour (1783–1841)	Va.	Democrat
Van Buren		
John Catron (1778–1865)	Tenn.	Democrat
John McKinley (1780–1852)	Ala.	Democrat
Peter V. Daniel (1784–1860)	Va.	Democrat
Tyler		
Samuel Nelson (1792–1873)	N.Y.	Democrat
Polk		
Levi Woodbury (1789–1851)	N.H.	Democrat
Robert C. Grier (1794–1870)	Pa.	Democrat
Fillmore		
Benjamin R. Curtis (1809–1874)	Mass.	Whig
Pierce		
John A. Campbell (1811–1889)	Ala.	Democrat
Buchanan		
Nathan Clifford (1803–1881)	Maine	Democrat
Lincoln		
Noah H. Swayne (1804–1884)	Ohio	Republican
Samuel F. Miller (1816–1890)	Iowa	Republican
David Davis (1815–1886)	Ill.	Republican
Stephen J. Field (1816–1899)	Calif.	Democrat
Salmon P. Chase (1808–1873)	Ohio	Republican
Grant		
William Strong (1808–1895)	Pa.	Republican
Joseph P. Bradley (1813–1892)	N.J.	Republican
Ward Hunt (1810–1886)	N.Y.	Republican
Morrison Waite (1816–1888)	Ohio	Republican
Hayes		
John M. Harlan (1833–1911)	Ky.	Republican
William B. Woods (1824–1887)	Ga.	Republican
Garfield		
Stanley Matthews (1824–1889)	Ohio	Republican
Arthur		
Horace Gray (1828–1902)	Mass.	Republican
Samuel Blatchford (1820–1893)	N.Y.	Republican
Cleveland		
Lucius Q. C. Lamar (1825–1893)	Miss.	Democrat
Melville W. Fuller (1833–1910)	Ill.	Democrat
Harrison		
David J. Brewer (1837–1910)	Kans.	Republican
Henry B. Brown (1836–1913)	Mich.	Republican
George Shiras, Jr. (1832–1924)	Pa.	Republican
Howell E. Jackson (1832–1895)	Tenn.	Democrat
Cleveland		
Edward D. White (1845–1921)	La.	Democrat
Rufus W. Peckham (1838–1909)	N.Y.	Democrat

President / Justices Appointed	State Appointed from	Political Party
McKinley		
Joseph McKenna (1843–1926)	Calif.	Republican
Roosevelt, T.		
Oliver W. Holmes (1841–1935)	Mass.	Republican
William R. Day (1849–1923)	Ohio	Republican
William H. Moody (1853–1917)	Mass.	Republican
Taft		
Horace H. Lurton (1844–1914)	Tenn.	Democrat
Charles E. Hughes (1862–1948)	N.Y.	Republican
Willis Van Devanter (1859–1941)	Wyo.	Republican
Joseph R. Lamar (1857–1916)	Ga.	Democrat
Mahlon Pitney (1858–1924)	N.J.	Republican
Wilson		
James C. McReynolds (1862–1946)	Tenn.	Democrat
Louis D. Brandeis (1856–1941)	Mass.	Independent
John H. Clarke (1857–1945)	Ohio	Democrat
Harding		
William H. Taft (1857–1930)	Conn.	Republican
George Sutherland (1862–1942)	Utah	Republican
Pierce Butler (1866–1939)	Minn.	Democrat
Edward T. Sanford (1865–1930)	Tenn.	Republican
Coolidge		
Harlan F. Stone (1872–1946)	N.Y.	Republican
Hoover		
Owen J. Roberts (1875–1955)	Pa.	Republican
Benjamin N. Cardozo (1870–1938)	N.Y.	Democrat
Roosevelt, F. D.		
Hugo L. Black (1886–1971)	Ala.	Democrat
Stanley F. Reed (1884–1980)	Ky.	Democrat
Felix Frankfurter (1882–1965)	Mass.	Independent
William O. Douglas (1898–1980)	Conn.	Democrat
Frank Murphy (1890–1949)	Mich.	Democrat
James F. Byrnes (1879–1972)	S.C.	Democrat
Robert H. Jackson (1892–1954)	N.Y.	Democrat
Wiley B. Rutledge (1894–1949)	Iowa	Democrat
Truman		
Harold H. Burton (1888–1964)	Ohio	Republican
Fred M. Vinson (1890–1953)	Ky.	Democrat
Tom C. Clark (1899–1977)	Texas	Democrat
Sherman Minton (1890–1965)	Ind.	Democrat
Eisenhower		
Earl Warren (1891–1974)	Calif.	Republican
John M. Harlan (1899–1971)	N.Y.	Republican
William J. Brennan (b. 1906)	N.J.	Democrat
Charles E. Whittaker (1901–1973)	Mo.	Republican
Potter Stewart (1915–1986)	Ohio	Republican
Kennedy		
Byron R. White (b. 1917)	Colo.	Democrat
Arthur J. Goldberg (b. 1908)	Ill.	Democrat
Johnson, L. B.		
Abe Fortas (1910–1982)	Tenn.	Democrat
Thurgood Marshall (b. 1908)	N.Y.	Democrat

President / Justices Appointed	State Appointed from	Political Party
Nixon		
Warren E. Burger (b. 1907)	Minn.	Republican
Harry R. Blackmun (b. 1908)	Minn.	Republican
Lewis F. Powell, Jr. (b. 1907)	Va.	Democrat
William H. Rehnquist (1924–2005)	Ariz.	Republican
Ford		
John Paul Stevens (b. 1920)	Ill.	Republican
Reagan		
Sandra Day O'Connor (b. 1930)	Ariz.	Republican
Antonin Scalia (b. 1936)	N.J.	Republican
Anthony M. Kennedy (b. 1936)	Calif.	Republican
Bush, George H. W.		
David Souter (b. 1939)	N.H.	Republican
Clarence Thomas (b. 1948)	Va.	Republican
Clinton		
Ruth Bader Ginsburg (b. 1933)	Wash., D.C.	Democrat
Stephen G. Breyer (b. 1938)	Mass.	Democrat
Bush, George W.		
John G. Roberts, Jr. (b. 1955)	Maryland	Republican

Note: Dates in parentheses indicate birth and death dates.

Glossary

A

active and attentive class   Those persons who pay attention to politics and participate frequently in the political process.

actual malice   The deliberate intention to cause harm or injury.

adoption   The phase of the policy-making process when a decision is made to deal with a public problem; the most common form of adoption is a legislative enactment, although the other branches of government and the bureaucracy may also play a key role at this stage.

advice and consent   The constitutional power of the Senate to ratify treaties and confirm presidential appointments.

advisory opinions   Judicial opinions, not involving adverse parties in a "case or controversy," that is given at the request of the legislature or executive. The U.S. Supreme Court has a long-standing policy of not rendering advisory opinions.

affective response   A response to the political world that is based on feelings.

affirm   A higher court's decision to uphold the decision of a lower court.

affirmative action   A program under which women and/or persons of particular minority groups are granted special consideration in employment, government contracts, and/or admission to programs of higher education.

agency point of view   Attitude of bureaucrats that stresses the protection of their own agency's budget, powers, staff, and routines, often at the expense of what elected officials may want.

agenda setting   The stage of the policy-making process when different political actors attempt to get an issue in the public view so that government officials will take policy action.

amicus curiae **("friend of the court") briefs**   Legal documents filed on behalf of organized groups that have an interest in the outcome of a case.

amnesty   A blanket pardon given to a large group of lawbreakers.

anarchy   The absence of government; referred to as the "state of nature" by political theorists.

apartheid   A legal system that requires strict racial segregation in every aspect of life.

appropriations   Money allocated by Congress for the purpose of funding government programs.

aristocracy   A hereditary ruling class; government by such a class of rulers.

Articles of Confederation   The colonists' first attempt at a charter for the national government. Although the Articles were adopted by Congress in 1777, they were not ratified until 1781. In 1788, they were superseded by the U.S. Constitution.

at-large election   An election system in which representatives are chosen by voters in a vote from the whole community rather than from separate districts within the community.

at-large voting   A system of voting in which all voters in a given community choose a set of representatives for the entire community, as opposed to a system in which the community is divided into districts and voters in those districts choose representatives only for those districts.

attitudes   More or less enduring orientations toward an object or situation and predispositions to respond positively or negatively toward that object or situation; attitudes are built on both values and beliefs.

Australian ballot   The secret ballot; used today in American elections, it allows secrecy for the voter and a choice between individuals of each party for each office.

authoritarian regime   A political system in which power is concentrated in one or very few elites, which are not accountable to the masses except in the rare instances of revolutions.

authority   The right to enforce laws or issue commands.

authorization   Legislative approval of a program.

B

balanced response sets   Sets of possible answers to a survey question in which the number of possible answers to one side of a question equals the number of answers to the other side of the question.

beliefs   Ideas people hold about what is true or false.

bicameral legislatures   Two-house legislative bodies. Both houses in a bicameral legislature must agree in order to pass legislation.

bifurcated trial   A criminal trial with separate phases for determining guilt and punishment.

bill of attainder   A legislative act imposing punishment on a party without benefit of trial in a court of law.

Bill of Rights   The first ten amendments to the Constitution, enumerating rights that are protected from government infringement.

bipartisan consensus   Agreement between the two major political parties about the basic outline of American foreign policy.

Black Codes   Laws enacted by southern states following ratification of the Thirteenth Amendment that were aimed at perpetuating the secondary social and economic status of African Americans within their borders.

block grants   Federal monies provided to state and local governments that are to be spent in specified general areas, such as housing or law enforcement, but do not carry the restrictions and requirements of categorical grants.

blocs   Groups of decision makers in a collegial body who usually vote the same way. In judicial politics, the term refers to groups of judges or justices on appellate courts who usually vote together.

bloggers   Slang term for people who operate "web logs," websites on which they and others comment on current issues and events of interest to them.

board of commissioners An elected body empowered to govern a county.

Boston Tea Party An act of protest against the British tax on imported tea. It occurred in 1773, when about 150 American colonists disguised as Native Americans boarded three ships and dumped the tea they were carrying into Boston harbor.

boycott A collective decision by a large number of people who refuse to purchase a particular good or service to dramatize opposition to the actions of particular companies.

briefs Written documents containing legal arguments in support of a party's position.

budget authority The amount government agencies are allowed to spend in implementing their policy programs.

budget outlays The actual amount of money agencies are expected to spend in a given fiscal year.

budget receipts See **revenue**.

bureaucracy The collection of agencies a government creates to impose regulations, implement policies, and administer programs

business cycle The alternating periods of economic growth and recession that mark a capitalist economy.

busing The transportation of students to ensure racial balance in the public schools.

C

cabinet Advisers to the chief executive, who is responsible for implementing legislative acts. In a parliamentary system, the cabinet is chosen from the parliament.

candidate-centered campaigns Campaigns for office that stress the personal characteristics of the candidates rather than the party.

candidate image The emotional reaction that people have toward a political candidate.

capitalist economy Economic system characterized by private property, private enterprise, and limited governmental control.

career civil servants Members of the bureaucracy who occupy the middle-management, professional, technical, and clerical positions; career civil servants obtain their jobs on the basis of merit and are protected from being fired for political reasons.

case or controversy principle Article III of the U.S. Constitution extends the federal judicial power to actual cases or controversies, not to hypothetical cases or abstract questions of law.

casework The activities a legislator engages in to help constituents obtain government services.

categorical grant Federal monies provided to state and local governments for a narrowly defined purpose.

CATI system A computer-assisted telephone interviewing system.

caucus A meeting of party members to discuss policy and direction, including the selection of presidential candidates.

certiorari Literally, "to be informed." An order from a higher court to a lower court to send up the record in a particular case so that it may be reviewed.

chain ownership Growing trend in the United States whereby different elements of the mass media are owned and operated by one parent company.

charismatic leader A leader who arouses fervent and enthusiastic support among his or her followers.

checks and balances Fundamental principle underlying the American constitutional system whereby institutions of government can check one another in order to prevent one branch from becoming too powerful.

chief of staff The head of the White House staff; the person responsible for controlling the president's calendar and advising the president on all aspects of domestic and foreign policy.

citizen A person who is a member of a given political community.

city manager A professionally trained public administrator hired by a city council to oversee the day-to-day operations of the city government.

civil case A judicial proceeding, outside the criminal law, by which a party seeks to enforce rights or to obtain redress for wrongs, usually seeking monetary damages.

civil disobedience The intentional breaking of the law to make a political point; does not include actions that directly harm individuals.

civil liberties The freedoms protected by the Constitution and statutes—for example, freedom of speech, religion, and assembly.

civil rights Legal protections against unreasonable discrimination.

civil rights movement The social movement of the 1960s aimed at ending racial segregation and achieving voting rights and other civil rights for African Americans.

clear and present danger doctrine The doctrine that the First Amendment protects expression up to the point that it poses a clear and present danger of bringing about some substantive evil that government has a right to prevent.

closed primary A type of direct primary in which a person must be registered as a Democrat or Republican to participate in the election to choose that party's nominee.

coalition A loose collection of groups who join to accomplish some common goal.

coattails A presidential candidate's influence on the election of other members of the same party who are running for Congress.

cognitive dissonance The psychological discomfort a person feels in trying to process contradictory feelings or thoughts.

cognitive response A response to the political world that is based more on thought than on emotion.

cold war The hostile relationship between the United States and the former Soviet Union during the period between the end of World War II and the fall of the Soviet Union in the 1990s.

commander-in-chief The constitutional role of the president as supreme commander of the armed forces.

Committee of the Whole A device used by the House to expedite consideration of a bill.

common law The body of judge-made law inherited from England; also refers to the legal tradition that accepts judicial decisions as the source of law.

communitarians Those who believe that unbridled individualism is corrosive to a democratic political system. Their concern is that American citizens are losing their sense of community and their sense of the public interest.

compulsory self-incrimination The requirement that an individual give testimony leading to his own criminal conviction; forbidden by the Fifth Amendment to the Constitution.

concurring opinion An opinion written by a judge agreeing with the decision of the court, which may or may not agree with the rationale adopted in the majority opinion.

confederation A political system in which the right to rule is vested in a league of states and the central government exists at the will of the states.

conference committee Congressional committee that exists only temporarily when the two chambers need to reconcile differences between two versions of the same bill.

confidential source A source of information whose identity is known only to the reporter.

congressional caucus A meeting of all those members of a legislature from a particular political party.

conservatives Those persons on the right of the liberal-conservative continuum. Generally speaking, conservatives believe in maintaining traditional values and institutions.

Constitutional Convention   Meeting in Philadelphia during the summer of 1787; called originally for the purpose of revising the Articles of Confederation but ultimately framed a new constitution. A meeting of delegates for the purpose of creating or changing a constitution.

constitutional democracy   A governmental system in which a fundamental law is superior to the will of transient majorities and changeable only through extraordinary means requiring a firm national consensus. Characteristic of the U.S. system of governance.

constitutional theory   A theory of presidential power holding that the president cannot exercise any power unless it can be traced back to the Constitution.

consultants   Professionals who provide guidance to political candidates regarding such activities as polling, media relations, advertising, campaign strategies, and fundraising.

contempt of court   An action that embarrasses, hinders, or obstructs or is calculated to lessen the dignity of a judicial body.

continuing resolution   Legislative act that temporarily continues the current level of funding for a program until an annual budget can be passed.

cooperative federalism   Characterization of the American federal system that emphasizes the cooperation and joint arrangements among the three levels of government.

county manager   A professional administrator hired by a county commission to oversee the administration of the county government.

coup d'état   The overthrow of rulers by those who become the rulers.

Court-packing plan   Proposal by President Franklin D. Roosevelt in 1937 to expand the number of justices on the Supreme Court in order to create a Court majority likely to support his policies.

courts-martial   Military courts established to conduct trials of persons in military service alleged to have committed crimes.

courts of law   Governmental institutions established for the purpose of resolving disputes and interpreting the law.

cracking   A type of vote dilution that results from deliberate attempts to draw district lines in such a way that minority voters are dispersed among a number of districts.

criminal case   A judicial proceeding in which a party is accused of a crime.

cruel and unusual punishments   Torture and other barbaric punishments forbidden by the Eighth Amendment to the Constitution.

cutback   An initiative of the Reagan administration to reduce the fiscal role of the federal government in state and local affairs.

D

dealignment   The movement of voters away from identifying with a political party.

debt   An accumulation of all past years' deficits minus all surpluses.

Declaration of Independence   Document adopted July 4, 1776, that proclaimed and justified the independence of the American colonies from Great Britain.

de facto **segregation**   Racial segregation as a matter of fact.

defendant   A party charged with a crime or against whom a civil action is brought.

deficit   When spending exceeds revenues in a fiscal year.

defining events   Major events that shape and define one's response to the political world.

de jure **segregation**   Racial segregation required or maintained by law.

delegate style of representation   A style of representation in which a legislator votes in a manner consistent with constituents' preferences.

democracy   Literally, "rule by the people." As defined by Aristotle, the term refers to the rule of the many, as distinct from the rule of the few.

democratization   The process of making a political system more democratic.

depression   A severe decline in economic activity characterized by extremely high unemployment, a high rate of bankruptcies, and a general decline in the value of assets.

descriptive representation   One of the various roles of Congress in which the membership in the legislative body is expected to reflect the key demographic characteristics of the population.

détente   The relaxation of tensions between nation-states; the period in the late 1960s and 1970s when relations improved between the United States and the Soviet Union.

devolution   In general, this term means "going back to how things once were," but in politics, it refers specifically to the movement to restore authority and autonomy to state and local governments.

dictatorship   An extreme form of authoritarianism whereby power is concentrated in the hands of one individual.

direct democracy   A political system in which all citizens participate in the making of significant public policy decisions rather than elect representatives to make these decisions.

direct mail   A technique used by interest groups to solicit funds directly from individuals or organizations.

direct primary   An election held for the purpose of nominating a party's candidate for elective office.

discount rate   The rate of interest that Federal Reserve banks charge to lend money to the private banks that are members of the Federal Reserve System.

discrimination   The conscious or unconscious denial of equal treatment to a person based on her membership in some recognizable group.

dissenting opinion   An opinion by a judge or justice setting forth reasons for disagreeing with a particular decision of the court.

distributive articles   The first three articles of the Constitution, which define the legislative, executive, and judicial powers, respectively, of the national government.

divided-party government   A condition in which one political party controls Congress and the other party controls the presidency.

domino theory   The belief that if one country becomes Communist, neighboring countries will follow like falling dominoes.

double-barreled question   A survey question that presents two stimuli but allows only one response.

double jeopardy   The condition of being prosecuted or punished a second time for the same offense; prohibited by the Fifth Amendment to the U.S. Constitution.

dual federalism   Classical characterization of the American federal system that recognizes strictly limited federal involvement in matters of traditional state and local concern.

due process of law   Legal procedures designed to ensure that life, liberty, and property cannot be arbitrarily or capriciously taken by government.

E

electoral college   The constitutional body that formally selects the president and vice president.

electronic media   That part of the media that includes radio, television, and computers.

electronic voting   The process by which members of Congress cast recorded votes electronically.

elites   Those persons in a society who possess a disproportionate amount of wealth, power, or status. In a political system, elites are those persons who possess the authority to make decisions affecting the masses.

enabling legislation   Statutory provisions defining the function and powers of government agencies.

English Bill of Rights   Document adopted in 1689 after the Glorious Revolution; supplemented the Magna Carta by guaranteeing the supremacy of Parliament over royal authority and further strengthening the rights of English subjects.

enumerated powers   Those powers that are expressly granted to Congress by the Constitution.

equality   One of the core values of democracy—the idea that people should be equal before the law and equal before their government.

equality of opportunity   Condition in which members of society are afforded an equal chance to succeed.

equality of result   Condition in which wealth, power, and status are distributed equally among the members of a society.

equal protection of the laws   Principle established by the Fourteenth Amendment that restricts states from arbitrarily discriminating against persons.

evaluation   The stage of the policy-making process when the policy is assessed. If the assessment shows that the policy was ineffective, too costly, unconstitutional, or unpopular or that it has other problems, the process starts over at the problem-definition stage, and agenda-setting begins anew.

exclusionary rule   Judicially created rule barring the use of illegally obtained evidence in a criminal prosecution.

executive agencies   Institutions of government responsible for implementing the laws passed by the legislature.

executive agreements   Agreements between the United States and one or more foreign countries, entered into by the president without the necessity of ratification by the Senate.

executive privilege   The right of the president to withhold certain information from Congress or a court of law.

exit poll   A survey of voters exiting the voting place.

expectations game   The process in which political experts and the media establish who they think will win in a particular election.

ex post facto **law**   A legislative act that retroactively criminalizes some action that was not a crime when it was committed.

expressive conduct   See **symbolic speech.**

F

fairness doctrine   A requirement by the Federal Communications Commission that allowed for equal opportunities for expression on controversial issues or policies.

federalism   The constitutional distribution of sovereignty between the national government and the states.

federal system   A political system in which a division of authority and responsibility exists between a central government and a set of regional governments.

feedback   Information from the public that leads to the reassessment of a particular policy output.

fighting words   Direct personal insults that are inherently likely to provoke a violent reaction from the person or persons at whom they are directed; "fighting words" are not protected by the First Amendment.

First Continental Congress   Meeting of delegates in Philadelphia in 1774 to protest British treatment of the colonies.

fiscal federalism   A system under which the federal government uses money to induce state and local governments to enact certain policies.

fiscal policy   The government's taxing and spending policies.

fiscal year   The period in which the budget is implemented.

foreign aid   A policy of assisting other countries both economically and militarily.

foreign policy   The decisions that one country makes in its dealings with other countries.

formulation of alternatives   The stage of the policy-making process when political actors propose various policies to overcome the public problem.

franking privilege   The power of any member of Congress to sign or have a printer reproduce her signature on any piece of mail and have it delivered, without cost to the member.

freedom   One of the core values of democracy—the idea that citizens should be free from unwarranted governmental control.

freedom of association   Although it is not explicitly mentioned by the Constitution, the courts have recognized the right to associate with people of one's choosing.

free, fair, and open elections   Elections in which all citizens have a right to vote, but are not required to do so, and the results of the voting are reported accurately.

free riders   Persons who enjoy the benefits of an organization's activity without having to contribute.

G

gender gap   Differences in political attitudes and behavior between men and women.

general election   An election in which voters choose among the nominees of various parties to determine who will be elected to public office.

general revenue sharing   Federal monies that were provided to state and local governments to be spent as elected officials saw fit. These funds were abolished in 1986.

general strike   Action taken by a large segment of the population in which people refuse to work for a day to dramatize their opposition to the government; not seen in the United States.

gerrymandering   The process of drawing political district borders to advantage or disadvantage certain groups.

government   The institutions in a society that have authority to make rules that are binding on that society.

governmental institutions   Specific offices of government that have the authority to make rules that are binding on society.

grandfather clause   A legal provision limiting the right to vote to those persons whose ancestors held the right to vote before the passage of the Fifteenth Amendment in 1870.

grand jury   A group of twelve to twenty-three citizens convened to hear evidence in criminal cases to determine whether indictment is warranted.

grants-in-aid   Federal monies provided to state and/or local governments for particular projects, usually following an application and review process.

grassroots lobbying   A form of lobbying in which interest groups attempt to get a large number of citizens to contact their own legislators directly and express their opinions on an issue.

grassroots party politics   Activities that originate at the local level and work their way up through the party.

gridlock   The inability of government to make decisions that sometimes result from divided party control of the policy-making institutions.

gunboat diplomacy   The use of the threat of military force as a tool in international relations.

gun control   Legislative attempts to regulate the sale, possession, use, and distribution of firearms.

H

habeas corpus   A legal device by which an individual can go to court to challenge and, if successful, escape unlawful confinement.

home rule   A municipal charter that allows a city to make governmental decisions without the concurrence of the state legislature.

honeymoon period   The first one hundred days of a presidential administration in which Congress, the media, and the public give the president more leeway in pushing his policy agenda.

human rights   Basic political and religious freedoms in addition to the right to equal treatment under the law and the right to due process of law.

hyperpluralism   A condition in which the prevalence of group demands makes it impossible for government to plan, deal with long-term problems, and make policies that further the public interest.

I

ideology   A coherent system of political beliefs and values, such as conservatism or liberalism; those ideas, or system of ideas, that are in conflict in society.

imminent lawless action   The First Amendment doctrine under which advocacy of lawlessness is protected to the point that lawless action is imminent.

implementation   The stage of the policy-making process when an adopted policy is carried out.

implied powers, doctrine of   A basic doctrine of constitutional law derived from the Necessary and Proper Clause of Article I, Section 8 (*McCulloch v. Maryland*, 1819). Under this doctrine, Congress is not limited to exercising those powers specifically enumerated in Article I but rather may exercise powers reasonably related to the fulfillment of its broad constitutional powers and responsibilities.

impoundment   The refusal of the president to allow an expenditure of funds appropriated by Congress.

incumbency advantage   The various factors contributing to the high rates of electoral success and low rates of turnover for members of Congress.

independent agencies   Government agencies located outside the fifteen major executive departments. Examples include the Interstate Commerce Commission and the Federal Reserve Board.

indictment   A formal criminal charge handed down by a grand jury.

individualism   A concept used to refer to the American idea of self-reliance, especially as it applies to economic and social activities.

inflation   A decline in the purchasing power of money.

inherent power   The power existing in an agency, institution, or individual by definition of the office.

initiative and referendum   One process by which a state constitution may be amended. Initiative refers to the act of petitioning the state government to put an issue before the voters in a referendum, or election.

injunction   A judicial order requiring a person to do, or refrain from doing, a designated thing.

institution   An established pattern of behavior that transcends and outlives the individuals who occupy it.

institutional agenda   The set of issues being actively considered by some governmental authority.

intelligence   Information about activities in other countries that is used in making foreign-policy decisions.

interest   Something that someone wants to achieve from government; a goal.

interest aggregation   The process of bringing together various interests.

interest articulation   The process of speaking on behalf of issue positions.

interest group liberalism   A term coined by the political scientist Theodore Lowi to describe the philosophy underlying American pluralism.

interest groups   Private organizations formed to advance the shared interest of their members.

intermediary institutions   Institutions, such as political parties and interest groups, that mediate between government and the people.

interventionism   The practice of using American military power, or the threat of military action, to achieve American interests abroad.

involvement model   Conception of the policy-making process that stresses the importance of activist groups at every stage of the process.

Iowa caucus   The first major event of the presidential nomination process in which party members in Iowa meet to select delegates to the national party conventions.

iron curtain   Metaphor coined by Winston Churchill that became a symbol of the threat posed by the Soviet Union and its allies during the cold war.

iron triangle   A three-way relationship involving a legislative committee, an executive agency, and an interest group.

isolationism   The belief that U.S. foreign policy should be marked by political isolation and economic self-sufficiency; dominant foreign policy theme during the early days of the Union.

issue network   A small group of political actors involved in a particular policy area.

issue voting   Voting on the basis of the candidates' positions on the policy issues addressed in the campaign.

J

Jim Crow laws   Laws enacted by southern states following the ratification of the Fourteenth Amendment that were aimed at legally subordinating and segregating blacks from the white community. Laws passed in the late nineteenth century that required blacks and whites to be segregated.

joint committees   Congressional committees that have no legislative authority but instead exist for the purpose of carrying out administrative duties; committees made up of members from both chambers of Congress.

judicial activism   Judicial philosophy that embraces innovative constitutional doctrines and supports the expansion of the Court's jurisdiction and powers.

judicial federalism   Principle under which state courts are free to interpret their state laws in a way that provides additional rights beyond those secured by federal law.

judicial restraint   Judicial philosophy which holds that judges should exercise power cautiously and show deference to precedent and to the decisions of other branches of government.

judicial review   The authority of a court of law to strike down legislative and executive decisions if they are found to be unconstitutional.

jurisdiction   The authority of a court of law to hear and decide a case.

K

Keynesian theory   A theory which holds that the state of the economy is the result of the relationship between the demand for goods and the productive capacity of the economy.

L

laissez-faire   The principle that there should be minimal governmental interference with the free enterprise system.

lame duck   An elected official who cannot or will not return to office after her current term expires.

landslide   An overwhelming electoral victory.

leaks   The unauthorized release of information about a policy or appointment.

legislative agenda   The set of policy goals the president wants to pursue through congressional legislation.

legislative proposal   A means of amending a constitution whereby a legislative body proposes a constitutional amendment that must be ratified by some other authority.

legislative supremacy   A characteristic of parliamentary systems of government in which other agencies of government are subordinate to the legislature.

legislative veto   A device whereby Congress, one chamber of Congress, or even one congressional committee can veto agency decisions that are based on delegated authority.

legislature   A governmental institution that makes laws for the society.

legitimacy Acknowledgment by a society that government has the right to rule.

libel Defamation of character through published material.

liberal-conservative continuum The standard approach to describing the range of political ideologies in the United States.

liberals Those persons on the left of the liberal-conservative continuum. Generally speaking, liberals favor progress and reform and question traditional modes of thought and behavior.

libertarian A person who is liberal on social issues but conservative on economic issues.

limited government A government that is limited to certain powers and responsibilities and is prohibited from transgressing the rights of citizens.

line-item veto A reform measure aimed at curbing congressional spending that would allow the president to veto specific items within a piece of legislation without vetoing the entire bill.

literacy test A test of reading and/or writing skills given as a condition for voting.

lobbying Any effort by an individual or group to contact public officials for the purpose of influencing their policy decisions.

loyal opposition The minority party in government. Its major roles are to criticize the majority party, provide useful debate on legislation, and block the more extreme policies of the majority party.

M

Magna Carta The "Great Charter" of 1215 in which King John guaranteed the rights of English subjects.

majority/individual problem The possibility that government based squarely on majority rule will diminish the rights of individuals.

majority leader The leader of the dominant party in each chamber of Congress. The majority leader in the House is second in rank to the Speaker. In the Senate, the majority leader is more powerful in that he is responsible for scheduling bills for debate.

majority minority districts Electoral districts in which the majority of voters are members of a racial minority.

majority/minority problem The possibility that government based squarely on majority rule will oppress members of minority groups.

majority opinion An opinion joined by a majority of judges or justices on a collegial court.

majority party The party with which the majority of citizens expressing a party preference identify.

majority rule A basic tenet of democracy which holds that laws are subject to majority approval.

majority whip A member who ranks just below the majority leader. The whip's duties include monitoring how party members plan to vote and notifying members of important legislation.

malapportionment The condition in which legislative districts are unequal in population.

managed competition President Clinton's proposal for a health-care system in which many health-care providers compete with each other to sign up individuals and businesses under a set of rules and regulations set by the government.

mandate The idea that the voters, through a resounding electoral victory, are sending a clear signal that they want the president to enact his policy preferences after taking office.

manifest destiny The doctrine that the United States had the right to expand its territory and influence throughout North America.

marble cake federalism Characterization of the American federal system that emphasizes the shared responsibilities among levels of government in the policy process.

marginal tax rates Different tax rates that apply to different levels of income. That is, one pays a certain rate on income up to a certain point and a higher rate on income above that point. Our progressive income tax system is constructed in this way.

markup session Session of a congressional subcommittee in which members literally mark up bills by crossing out provisions they do not support.

Marshall Plan Economic effort by the United States aimed at rebuilding Europe after World War II.

masses The great numbers of people in a society.

mass media The technologies and organizations that disseminate information to the public.

Mayflower Compact The first written agreement for self-government in America, adopted in 1620 by Puritans coming to America on the Mayflower.

McGovern–Fraser Commission Part of the Democratic party reform movement of the 1970s that designed rules aimed at opening the party to wider participation by women, minorities, and young people. The rules also loosened the grip of traditional party bosses.

means test The requirement that a recipient who benefits from a program demonstrate financial need for the benefits.

Medicaid A joint program between the states and the federal government whereby the national government provides matching funding, but the states decide which indigent persons are eligible for medical care.

Medicare Congressional program approved in 1965 that provided for a payroll tax to be split between employers and employees to fund medical care for the elderly.

meritocracy A hiring system in which officials are recruited, selected, and retained on the basis of demonstrable skills.

Miller test A three-part test developed by the Supreme Court in *Miller v. California* (1973) to determine whether a particular work is obscene.

minority party A party that does not claim the allegiance of a majority of party identifiers.

Missouri Plan A plan for judicial selection and retention that originated in Missouri in 1940. The essential idea is that judges are selected and retained based on merit rather than on politics.

moderates Those persons who are in the middle of the liberal-conservative continuum; that is, neither liberal nor conservative. Also known as "centrists."

modern administrative state The highly bureaucratic nature of American government in the modern era, in which day-to-day functions of government are performed by bureaucratic agencies.

modern pluralist theory Academic theory developed in the twentieth century that views democratic politics as a competition among interest groups rather than as a process dominated by one elite group.

monetarists Economists who believe that proper management of the money supply is the principal factor influencing inflation, recession, and economic growth.

monetary policy Government policy aimed at controlling the supply of money and controlling interest rates.

Monroe doctrine President James Monroe's proclamation that North and South America were no longer open for colonization by European countries and that the United States would reject any European intervention in the Americas. It was never accepted as international law.

multiculturalism The belief that different cultures can and should coexist in the same society.

multiparty systems Political party systems in which several legitimate parties vie for control of the governmental system.

multiple referral system Technique employed by the House of Representatives in which more than one committee could consider a piece of legislation. This practice was abolished in 1995 in favor of a sequential referral system.

municipal charter   An act of a state legislature creating a city and authorizing the creation of a city government.

N

national agenda   A compilation of those issues that deserve national attention.

national conventions   Meetings of party delegates to nominate their candidate for president. The conventions are also important in that they draw up the party platform, establish the rules that will govern the party, and select the new national committee.

national defense   The policies and strategies that guide a nation's military forces.

national interest   The idea that the country has long-term foreign policy interests, such as protection against invasion or maintenance of energy supplies.

nation-centered federalism   A federal system in which the central government is the dominant actor.

natural law   Laws whose existence does not depend on recognition by government.

natural rights   Rights ordained by God or by nature, which cannot be infringed by government. In classical liberal thought, these rights include the right to life, liberty, and property.

Necessary and Proper Clause   The final paragraph of Article I, Section 8 of the Constitution that allows Congress to make laws that are necessary and proper to further its enumerated powers.

New Deal   Policy initiative of President Franklin D. Roosevelt consisting of unprecedented efforts by the federal government to regulate and manage the economy.

New Hampshire primary   The first primary in the presidential nomination process.

New Jersey Plan   Plan proposed at the Constitutional Convention to counter the Virginia Plan. The New Jersey Plan called for preserving Congress as it was under the Articles of Confederation.

nomination   The process by which a political party selects one candidate from a field of contenders to run against the nominees of other parties in a general election.

nonpartisan election   An election in which candidates are not formally affiliated with a political party.

nonresponse bias   A situation in which those who respond to a survey hold different opinions from those who do not respond.

North Atlantic Treaty Organization (NATO)   Anti-Soviet military alliance established in 1949 that guaranteed the collective security of its twelve member nations: Belgium, Canada, Denmark, France, Great Britain, Iceland, Italy, Luxembourg, the Netherlands, Norway, Portugal, and the United States.

nullification, doctrine of   Rooted in historical Southern culture, the belief that a state is sovereign and can decide for itself whether it will recognize, and ultimately abide by, a law passed by the national government.

O

ombudsman   An official who investigates and tries to resolve problems that people have with public agencies.

one person, one vote   Judicially recognized principle, derived from the Equal Protection Clause of the Constitution, that requires political districts to be made equal in population.

open-market operations   Measures used by the Federal Reserve to regulate the money supply in the economy.

open primary   A type of direct primary in which any voter can choose to participate in either primary (Republican or Democrat) merely by declaring her intention after entering the voting place.

opinion   A written statement accompanying a judicial decision, authored by one or more of the judges supporting or dissenting from the decision.

opinion of the Court   An opinion announcing both the decision of the court and its supporting rationale. The opinion can be either a majority opinion or a unanimous opinion.

opinions   People's preferences or judgments about public issues and candidates.

oral argument   A public hearing in which lawyers for both parties appear before an appellate court to make verbal presentations and answer questions from the bench.

ordinances   Laws enacted by a local governing body, such as a city council or county commission.

original jurisdiction   The authority of a court of law to hear a case for the first time, usually for the purpose of conducting a trial or holding a hearing.

oversight   Congressional supervision of the various executive departments and agencies.

P

packing   A type of vote dilution that occurs when all minority voters are placed in one district, thereby limiting the possibility of racial or ethnic residents from effectively contesting two or more seats.

pack journalism   When reporters decide on what questions to ask and what stories to cover based on what other members of the press corps are doing.

pardons   Acts of executive clemency by which persons who have committed crimes are absolved of their guilt.

parliament   Any legislative body in a parliamentary system of government. The legislative body in England.

parliamentary systems   Governmental systems in which the legislature is supreme and the executive exists only for the purpose of implementing the legislature's enactments.

participatory democracy   A system of government in which ordinary citizens are directly involved in the day-to-day decisions of government.

particularism   Situations in which a member of Congress considers legislation only in terms of whether it produces tangible benefits for her home district.

partisan realignment   A massive long-term shift in voter allegiance from one party to another.

party caucus   An organization that is composed of members of one party in each chamber of the Congress but is not formally part of the legislature. The caucus is used to determine how leaders will be chosen and how committee assignments will be made.

party identification   The sense of belonging to a particular political party.

party image   The reaction that people have toward a political party.

party in Congress   The partisan-based activities of representatives and senators.

party in government   The partisan-based activities of government officials.

party in the electorate   Voters who identify with a party label but do not participate in the party's day-to-day activities.

party machines   Local party organizations that dominate elections in an area over a long period through a variety of both legal and illegal means, including distributing government jobs and contracts to loyal voters.

party out of power   The party that does not control either the legislative or executive branch of government.

party platform   A statement of a political party's goals and policies.

perks   Tangible benefits received by members of Congress, such as subsidized medical care.

photo opportunity An event staged with the hope that it will be photographed or filmed by the news media.

plaintiff The party initiating legal action.

pluralism Democratic theory that conceives of politics as perpetual competition among interest groups.

pocket veto A means of vetoing legislation whereby the president refuses to sign a bill passed by Congress during the last ten days before it adjourns, thus preventing the bill from becoming law.

police power The power of the state to enact laws regulating economic activity for the purpose of promoting public health, safety, and welfare.

policy-making process The process by which public policy is produced.

policy of containment Dominant foreign policy theme following World War II in which the United States sought to prevent the Soviet Union from expanding its sphere of influence.

policy representation A style of representation in which the legislator makes policy decisions that are best for her constituents.

political action committees (PACs) Organizations established by interest groups to support political candidates who support their agendas.

political activists Those people who participate in depth in one political arena by contributing large amounts of time and money either to a single cause or across a variety of causes.

political alienation A feeling of distance from and deep-seated hostility toward the political process.

political apathy Lack of interest in the political process.

political appointees Those members of the bureaucracy who hold the highest executive positions and are appointed by the president.

political culture Values generally held in a society about what government should do and what issues should be addressed in the political arena.

political efficacy The feeling that one can make a difference in politics.

political elite A small group of citizens who wield greater influence over politics than do average citizens.

political entrepreneurs Individuals who invest their own resources to establish interest groups, think tanks, institutes, and the like.

political questions, doctrine of Legal principle which holds that cases may be dismissed if the issues they present are extremely "political" in nature and would be answered more appropriately by either the legislature or executive branch.

political resources The means by which an individual or group can affect the political process. Political resources include money, time, communication skills, and personal connections.

political socialization The transmission of political values and beliefs; the process by which people learn about their political world.

political values Basic sets of feelings about what ought to be and how people ought to behave.

politics The process by which societies are governed and conflicts are resolved.

pollsters Professionals who conduct surveys aimed at measuring public opinion.

poll tax A fee paid for the privilege of voting.

popular culture The elements of culture consumed by masses of people. They include movies, music, novels, and television programs.

population In survey research, the group of people about whom a survey is designed to generalize.

populist A person who is conservative on social issues but liberal on economic issues.

pork barrel A pejorative term for wasteful government spending that provides benefits to particular congressional districts.

precedent A judicial decision on a point of law giving direction to or authority for later cases presenting the same legal problem, although involving different parties.

presidential system A governmental system in which a clear division of powers exists between the legislative and executive branches of government.

press conference A media event in which a public official, candidate, or political activist holds a meeting with reporters to make announcements and answer questions.

primary election An election in which voters go to the polls to choose among the contenders for a party's nomination.

prime minister The executive head in a parliamentary system who is selected directly from the legislative body.

priming A subtle biasing of a respondent's answer to a survey question caused by where the question is placed in the survey.

print media That part of the media that includes newspapers, journals, tabloids, and magazines.

prior restraint An official act preventing the publication of a particular work.

private enterprise An element of capitalist economy that is closely linked to the doctrine of *laissez-faire*.

private property Claims by individuals and corporations involving the right to use and control real estate and other forms of property.

probable cause Knowledge of specific facts providing reasonable grounds for believing that criminal activity is afoot.

problem definition The initial phase of the policy-making process in which different political actors attempt to show that a problem is a concern that government can take some action to remedy.

professional associations Organizations of people who are employed, or self-employed, in a variety of professions, such as medicine, law, accounting, and engineering.

progressive movement A movement during the early 1900s aimed at reforming government by eliminating fraud, corruption, and inefficiency.

Prohibition The national policy in the 1920s barring the importation, production, or transportation of alcoholic beverages.

propaganda A government's promotion of its own policies or actions through the mass media.

proportional representation An electoral system in which the percentage of votes received by a given political party entitles that party to the same percentage of seats in the legislature.

prospective voting A method of choosing between candidates in which voters look forward and predict how the candidates will perform in the future.

protective tariffs Charges imposed on a product being brought into a state; the purpose is to protect those in the state who want to produce and sell that product.

public benefits Projects and programs that benefit society as a whole, such as schools, roads, dams, water and sewer systems, airports, and parks.

public defender An attorney appointed by a court or employed by a government agency whose work consists primarily of defending people who are unable to afford lawyers in criminal cases.

public interest A common interest shared by all members of the society.

public interest group Organization that seeks a collective good, the achievement of which will not materially benefit the members of the organization.

public opinion The aggregation of individual opinions on issues of concern to the public.

public policy Whatever government attempts to do about an issue or problem.

public regardedness A willingness to acknowledge public interests that are superior to one's immediate self-interest and, moreover, a willingness to sacrifice one's interests for the common good.

pundits Knowledgeable political commentators in the mass media.

Q

quorum The minimum number of members of a legislative body required in order to transact business.

R

racial profiling The use of a person's race or ethnicity as a factor in forming suspicion that he is involved in unlawful activity.

random-digit dialing A survey technique in which respondents are chosen on the basis of phone numbers randomly generated by a computer.

random sample A sample in which every member of the sampling frame has an equal chance of being selected.

realigning election An election in which large numbers of voters change their allegiance from one party to another.

reapportionment The process by which legislative boundaries are redrawn to reflect changes in population.

reasonable time, place, and manner regulations Reasonable government regulations concerning the time, place, and manner of expressive activities protected by the Constitution.

recession A mild slowdown of economic activity.

reckless disregard of the truth Careless indifference to whether a story is true or false.

reformed cities Cities that utilize a professional manager, nonpartisan elections, and at-large elections of a substantial proportion of the members of the city council.

regulatory state A characterization used to describe the increasing role of government in the economic affairs of American citizens subsequent to the industrial revolution.

reliability In survey research, a property of a question, meaning that it would produce the same response if immediately asked a second time of the same respondent.

representative government A political system in which most policy decisions emanate from legislatures that represent the people, even if indirectly.

representative institutions Governmental institutions whose members are chosen so as to reflect the interests of their constituencies.

republic A form of government in which power is exercised by representative institutions that are limited by the rule of law.

retrospective voting A method of choosing between candidates in which voters look back and evaluate how the incumbent has performed.

revenue The money the government expects to receive during the fiscal year.

revenue bills Legislative acts aimed at raising the money the government intends to spend.

reversal A higher court's decision to overturn the decision of a lower court.

rider An amendment to a bill that is not directly related to the policy issue in the original bill.

right of privacy The right of an individual to make intimate personal decisions without undue interference by the government.

right to keep and bear arms Right protected by the Second Amendment to own and use firearms subject to reasonable regulation.

right-to-work laws Laws that prevent labor agreements from requiring all workers to join a union.

rule of four The requirement that at least four justices of the Supreme Court agree before the Court will grant certiorari in a given case.

rule of law The idea that the power of government is based on legal principles rather than on the personal wishes of the rulers.

Rules Committee Powerful House committee that establishes when a bill will be placed on the legislative calendar, how much debate will be allowed, and whether amendments will be permitted.

S

safe seat A representative's district that is so one-sidedly partisan that it always elects a member of the same party to the House.

safety net A guaranteed level of support beneath which individuals will not be allowed to fall.

sample The group of people selected to be representative of a given population.

sampling frame The list of potential survey respondents from which the survey respondents are chosen.

sampling plan A method of choosing a sample to represent a given population.

school choice A policy whereby parents and students maintain the right to choose the school, public or private, that the children will attend.

search warrant A court order authorizing a search of a specified area or person for a specified purpose.

secession, doctrine of The doctrine that holds that a state can secede, or withdraw, from the Union.

Second Continental Congress Colonial body that drafted the Declaration of Independence and served as the government until the Articles of Confederation were ratified in 1781.

secret ballot See **Australian ballot**.

secular humanism A philosophy that elevates human interests, desires, and values over religious beliefs and precepts.

seed money Election funds used primarily to identify potential contributors to campaigns.

select committees Temporary panels that allow members to investigate a problem and make recommendations for legislation.

selective benefits Benefits that are limited to individuals who are members of a particular group or organization.

selective incentives Special inducements offered by organizations to their members.

selective incorporation Judicial doctrine under which most of the provisions of the Bill of Rights are deemed applicable to the states by way of the Fourteenth Amendment.

senatorial courtesy The tradition of allowing senators from the president's party to exercise significant influence in the selection of judges for the district courts located within their states.

seniority The number of years served continuously on a given committee; a key criterion in making committee assignments.

separate but equal The legal principle established in *Plessy v. Ferguson* (1896) stating that racial segregation could be maintained as long as the facilities provided to each race were equal.

separation of powers A system of government in which the three functions of government—legislative, executive, and judicial—are dispersed among three equal and separate branches.

sequential referral system System under which the Speaker of the House of Representatives can refer a bill to another committee after one committee has finished with it.

service representation A style of representation in which a legislator emphasizes providing services to his constituents.

sexual harassment Unwanted sexual attention of a threatening, insulting, demeaning, or bothersome character.

Shays' Rebellion An uprising in western Massachusetts in 1786. The rebellion helped demonstrate the weaknesses of the Articles of Confederation and served as a catalyst in the call for the Constitutional Convention.

shield laws Laws that protect journalists from legal action when they refuse to divulge their sources.

single-issue groups Organizations that focus their efforts on one particular policy area, such as gun control or abortion.

single-issue politics Activities centered around one particular policy area, such as gun control or abortion.

single-member districts Electoral system in which only one person represents a particular geographic area.

social contract A hypothetical agreement among rational individuals in a society who choose to be ruled by others in order to escape the chaos and insecurity of anarchy.

social desirability bias   The bias resulting from a question being phrased in such a way that it elicits an answer that a person feels is the socially desirable response.

socialism   An ideology stressing government control of the means of production for the purpose of equalizing the wealth in society.

socialist economy   An economic system in which government controls major industries and works to eradicate differences in wealth.

social movement   The purposeful, directed actions of a large number of people attempting to achieve some collective purpose, for example, the civil rights movement.

societal culture   All socially transmitted patterns of behavior as well as all the beliefs, customs, and institutions within the society.

societal institutions   Institutions that exist primarily by custom and are not primarily political in character.

soft money   The unlimited funds donated to political parties for the purpose of party-building activities, such as party bumper stickers, get-out-the-vote drives, and party mailings.

sound bite   A short media clip that provides a catchy phrase.

sovereign immunity   Legal concept established in the Eleventh Amendment that grants states immunity from being sued in federal court by their own citizens or citizens from another state.

sovereignty   The legitimate right to rule a society.

special committees   See **select committees**.

spectator activities   The simplest kinds of political activities that demand a minimal amount of effort and a correspondingly low amount of political resources, for example, voting or wearing a political button.

spin control   An attempt by political candidates and their consultants to control the messages that the media communicate to the voters.

spoils system   A system of staffing government in which supporters are rewarded with jobs and contracts.

stakeholders   The groups in the policy-making process that stand to win or lose as a result of a policy decision.

Stamp Act   Act of British Parliament that required American colonists to purchase stamps to be placed on envelopes, newspapers, wills, playing cards, college degrees, marriage licenses, land titles, and other documents.

standing   The legal requirement that a party must have suffered, or be about to suffer, an injury in order to bring suit. The injury need not be physical in nature; it may be economic or even aesthetic.

standing committees   Those congressional committees that possess the authority to consider legislation within a fixed policy domain; the most important committees in Congress.

stare decisis, doctrine of   Literally, "to stand by decided matters." The legal principle which holds that past decisions should stand as precedents for future decisions.

state-centered federalism   A federal system in which the states remain dominant over the central government.

state of nature   A condition of society, postulated by both John Locke and Thomas Hobbes, in which there is no government.

states' rights   The doctrine that certain powers and responsibilities belong exclusively to the states and should not be interfered with by the national government.

statutes   General laws enacted by a legislature.

stewardship theory   A theory of presidential power holding that the president is authorized to do whatever he believes to be necessary as long as it is not prohibited by the Constitution.

straw poll   A nonscientific survey in which respondents take the initiative in deciding whether to participate.

strike   A collective decision by a large number of people to refuse to work in order to dramatize a situation or force those who are adversely affected to make some concession.

strong mayor-council system   A form of local government in which the mayor is responsible for the day-to-day operation of the city. In many cities, the mayor has veto power over ordinances passed by the city council.

subcommittees   Smaller units of full committees that are responsible for considering smaller segments of the broad range of issues considered by the full committees.

subpoena   A court order requiring a person to appear in court in connection with a designated proceeding.

summit conference   A meeting between the highest officials of two or more governments.

sunshine laws   Laws that require most bureaucratic organizations to open their meetings to the public.

superdelegate   Key party member, usually an elected official, who is not required to commit to a nominee until the national convention.

Super Tuesday   The second Tuesday in March when most southern states hold their presidential primaries.

supply-side economics   A school of economic thought which holds that a reduction in government taxation will stimulate the economy so that government revenue will eventually increase, thus reducing the deficit.

Supremacy Clause   The second paragraph of Article VI of the Constitution, which asserts the superiority of federal laws and the U.S. Constitution over state laws and state constitutions when they are in conflict.

surplus   The amount that revenues exceed spending in a fiscal year.

symbolic representation   A style of representation in which a legislator employs various symbolic strategies to make people feel that they are playing a significant role in the political process.

symbolic speech   An activity that expresses a point of view or message symbolically rather than through pure speech.

systematic sample   A sampling plan in which every third, fourth, fifth, or nth member of the sampling frame is selected.

systemic agenda   The issues that are generally viewed as deserving of public attention and as legitimate concerns of government. Generally, the systemic agenda contains abstract ideas that merit discussion.

T

talk radio   Radio shows featuring discussion of public issues among a studio host, one or more invited guests in the studio, and the listening public.

tariff   A tax charged on products imported into a country.

Tet offensive   The defining event of the Vietnam War, when the Viet Cong attacked posts throughout South Vietnam, including the American embassy in Saigon.

think tanks   Groups that employ policy specialists, scientists, and lawyers to perform research on various topics and propose policy changes.

third-party candidate   A candidate who runs for political office under some political party label other than Democrat or Republican.

tort   A civil wrong remediable through a lawsuit seeking monetary damages.

tracking polls   Technique employed to gauge how well political candidates perform over time.

trade associations   Organizations that represent persons who possess common skills.

trade policy   The set of rules governing trade between the United States and other countries.

traditional democratic theory   Eighteenth- and nineteenth-century ideas regarding democratic citizenship, procedures, and institutions.

treaty   An agreement between two or more nations containing promises to behave in specified ways; U.S. treaties require ratification by a two-thirds vote of the Senate.

trial balloons   The release, without attribution, of proposed policies or appointments to the press for the purpose of gauging public reaction.

Truman doctrine   Foreign policy stance enunciated in 1947 by President Harry Truman, who asserted, "It must be the policy of the United States to support free peoples who are resisting attempted subjugation by armed minorities or outside pressures."

trustee style of representation   A style of representation in which a legislator makes policy decisions based on her own values rather than on the demands of constituents.

turnout   The number of people voting either as a percentage of those who are registered to vote or as a percentage of the voting-age population.

two-party system   A term used to describe the American political party system in which only two parties (Democrats and Republicans) have a realistic chance of controlling the government.

tyranny of the majority   Disregard of the rights of individuals or minority groups by the majority of the people in a society.

U

unanimous consent agreements   Agreements made in the Senate as a means of establishing a format for considering a bill.

unfunded mandates   Programs or policies that the federal government requires but does not fund.

unicameral legislature   A one-house legislative body.

union density   The proportion of the nonagricultural workforce belonging to unions.

unitary system   A system of government in which sovereignty is vested exclusively in one central government.

universal suffrage   A condition under which all adult citizens have the right to vote.

unreformed cities   Cities characterized by a strong mayor, partisan elections, and council members who represent districts within those cities.

V

validity   In survey research, a property of a question, meaning that it measures what it is designed to measure.

veto   The power of the chief executive to nullify acts of the legislature.

vetting   Unofficial airing of a candidacy of an individual before an official nomination.

Virginia Plan   Governmental plan conceived by James Madison and presented to the Constitutional Convention by Virginia governor Edmund Randolph, which called for a bicameral Congress, in which representation in both houses would be based on state population.

vote dilution   A situation in which the voting strength of racial or ethnic groups or both is significantly diminished.

voucher   A grant to the parents of school-age children to be used at any accredited school, public or private.

W

war chest   The funds a political candidate accumulates to use for a campaign.

Warsaw Pact   The former military alliance of Eastern European Communist regimes that was originally formed to counter the establishment of NATO.

weak mayor-council system   A form of city government in which the city council has the power to hire and fire administrators. In this system, the mayor's role is largely ceremonial.

welfare state   A characterization used to describe the increasing role of government in creating programs to ensure social welfare.

whistle blowers   Individuals working for either the government or a company under government contract who expose corruption, violations of the law, and environmental abuses within an organization.

White House press corps   Newspaper, radio, and television reporters assigned to cover the president on a day-to-day basis.

white primary   A primary election in which participation is limited to whites.

winner-take-all   An electoral system in which a party must capture the most votes in a district to obtain any representation in the government.

writ of mandamus   A court order requiring a governmental official to carry out her official duties.

writs   Court orders requiring or prohibiting the performance of some specific action.

Y

yellow journalism   Reporting that distorts or exaggerates facts to sensationalize the news.

Case Index

Note: Page numbers followed by *n* indicate material in endnotes.

Subject Index

Note: Page numbers in *italics* indicate figures or illustrations and their captions; page numbers followed by *t* indicate tables; page numbers followed by *n* indicate material in endnotes. Names of specific court cases may be found in the Index of Cases.